Larissa Mitiagova

D0824780

UNIX®

System Administrator's Edition

Robin Burk and David B. Horvath, CCP, et al.

SAMS
PUBLISHING

201 West 103rd Street
Indianapolis, IN 46290

UNLEASHED

To Stephen P. Kowalchuk, who provided an IS manager and practicing network administrator's point of view.

——Robin Burk

This edition is dedicated to my parents and grandparents. Education and doing one's best were always important to them.

——David B. Horvath

Copyright © 1997 by Sams Publishing

SECOND EDITION

All rights reserved. No part of this book shall be reproduced, stored in a retrieval system, or transmitted by any means, electronic, mechanical, photocopying, recording, or otherwise, without written permission from the publisher. No patent liability is assumed with respect to the use of the information contained herein. Although every precaution has been taken in the preparation of this book, the publisher and authors assume no responsibility for errors or omissions. Neither is any liability assumed for damages resulting from the use of the information contained herein. For information, address Sams Publishing, 201 W. 103rd St., Indianapolis, IN 46290.

International Standard Book Number: 0-672-30952-1

Library of Congress Catalog Card Number: 96-67964

2000   99   98   97   4   3   2

Interpretation of the printing code: the rightmost double-digit number is the year of the book's printing; the rightmost single-digit, the number of the book's printing. For example, a printing code of 97-1 shows that the first printing of the book occurred in 1997.

Composed in AGaramond and MCPdigital by Macmillan Computer Publishing

Printed in the United States of America

Trademarks

All terms mentioned in this book that are known to be trademarks or service marks have been appropriately capitalized. Sams Publishing cannot attest to the accuracy of this information. Use of a term in this book should not be regarded as affecting the validity of any trademark or service mark. UNIX is a registered trademark of The Open Group.

President	Richard K. Swadley
Publisher and Director of Acquisitions	Jordan Gold
Director of Product Development	Dean Miller
Managing Editor	Brice P. Gosnell
Indexing Manager	Johnna L. VanHoose
Director of Marketing	Kelli S. Spencer
Associate Product Marketing Manager	Jennifer Pock
Marketing Coordinator	Linda Beckwith

Acquisitions Editors
Cari Skaggs
Sunthar Visuvalingam

Development Editor
Sunthar Visuvalingam

Software Development Specialists
Patricia J. Brooks
Jordan Hubbard

Production Editor
Sandy Doell

Copy Editors
Fran Blauw
Mitzi Foster
Charles A. Hutchinson
Mary Inderstrodt

Indexer
Erika Millen

Technical Reviewers
Billy Barron
Raj Mangal
Lay Wah Ooi

Editorial Coordinators
Mandie Rowell
Katie Wise

Technical Edit Coordinator
Lynette Quinn

Resource Coordinators
Deborah Frisby
Charlotte Clapp

Editorial Assistants
Carol Ackerman
Andi Richter
Rhonda Tinch-Mize

Cover Designer
Jason Grisham

Book Designer
Alyssa Yesh

Copy Writer
David Reichwein

Production Team Supervisors
Brad Chinn
Andrew Stone

Production Team
Jenaffer Brandt, Jeanne Clark, Ayanna Lacey, Shawn Ring

Contents

Acknowledgments

Special thanks to Roger for support and grocery shopping. Also to the Laurelwood English Cockers, who intuitively understand how to negotiate a communications session (beg), allocate resources (if it's on the counter, it's ours!), and travel in encapsulated cells (show crates) over broadband highway networks.

——Robin Burk

As with all the other projects I get involved with, my wife and muse, Mary, has been tremendously supportive. Even when I spent my evenings and weekends at the keyboard. Of course, she filled her time by shopping (she said this, not me).

My parents, brothers, and the rest of the family, who always wondered about the time I spent with computers, are now seeing the concrete results of it all.

I've been involved with this project for close to a year now. The development staff were very helpful and have certainly kept it interesting. I want to thank them and the other authors (especially those that I talked into helping out). This certainly turned out to be a bigger project (and resulting book) than any of us expected. I hope and expect that people will be looking at these two volumes as *the* definitive reference!

After I take a short rest, I will be looking for the next project. Although these things are really tiring, especially with the effort this one entailed, I miss them when I'm not working on one.

—— David B. Horvath

About the Authors

Robin Burk has over 25 years' experience in advanced software, computer, and data communications technologies. She has provided technical and managerial leadership for the development of language tools, communications software, operating systems, and multimedia applications. A successful executive in entrepreneurial companies, she consults on software product development and the use of the Internet for business success. Robin's undergraduate degree is in physics and math. She also holds an MBA in finance and operations. Robin's other passion is breeding, training, and showing dogs. She moderates an e-mail list for English Cocker Spaniel fanciers and can be reached at robink@wizard.net.

David B. Horvath, CCP, is a Senior Consultant with CGI Systems, Inc., an IBM company, in the Philadelphia, Pennsylvania, area. He has been a consultant for over 12 years and is also a part-time Adjunct Professor at local colleges teaching topics that include C Programming, UNIX, and Database Techniques. He is currently pursuing an M.S. degree in Dynamics of Organization at the University of Pennsylvania. He has provided seminars and workshops to professional societies and corporations on an international basis. David is the author of "UNIX for the Mainframer" and numerous magazine articles.

When not at the keyboard, he can be found working in the garden or soaking in the hot tub. He has been married for over ten years and has several dogs and cats.

David can be reached at unx2@cobs.com for questions related to this book. No Spam, please!

Fred Trimble holds a master's degree in computer science from Villanova University. In his nine years with Unisys Corporation, he held many positions, including UNIX system administrator, C programmer, and Oracle database administrator. Currently, he is a senior consultant and instructor with Actium Corporation in Conshohocken, Pennsylvania, specializing in C++, Java, and the Brio data warehousing product line. He is currently pursuing a master's degree in software engineering from Drexel University.

Sanjiv Guha has 14 years of experience in managing and developing financial and other application systems. He specializes in C, UNIX, C++, Windows, and COBOL. Sanjiv holds a Master of Technology Degree from Indian Institute of Technology, New Delhi, India.

William A. Farra's computer career started in the summer of 1978, working in a time sharing shop on an IBM 365. It had 768 KB, 8 disk packs totaling 125 MB, and a cost of 10 million dollars. That fall, Mr. Farra went to the University of Delaware for electrical engineering and worked part-time at Radio Shack playing with the trash 80's. He continued to work for the Shack until he met a bright guy who was writing custom programs for the larger computers the Shack sold. Bill took a full-time job with him in September of 1983, working on Microsoft's first versions of UNIX (called Xenix at the time) and writing BASIC and C code.

In 1985, Bill went out on his own for six years, writing UNIX-based data processing systems for various clients in the Philadelphia area, including Dan Peter Kopple and Associates, the architects who renovated 30th Station. Since 1991, Bill has returned to employment, developing and/or enhancing various systems including "Fraud Detection Delivery System" for MBNA and Settlement systems for EPS "MAC card ATM processor." Recently he got away from the "Big Cities" and is living at the Jersey shore. He is a lead developer for National Freight Industries, working with various UNIX-based systems, including real-time tracking of vehicles using national transportation satellite and ground-based networks.

Richard E. Rummel, CDP, is the president of ASM Computing, Jacksonville, Florida, which specializes in UNIX software development and end-user training. He has been actively employed in the computer industry for over 20 years. Married for 25 years, he is the father of two children.

Sriranga Veeraraghavan is earning his B.E. from UC Berkeley in 1997. He is a GUI designer on UNIX, and uses Java for multiple Web-based applications. He is currently working at Cisco Systems. Sriranga amuses himself with Perl, Marathon, and MacsBugs.

Christopher Johnson is currently studying at Sheffield Hallam University in the U.K. for a degree in Electronic and Information Engineering. He is mostly self taught in the computer field, with experience being gained from helping other students, people on Usenet, and colleagues at work. He is part of a team that administers a Linux server on the university's network, and administers a Web server on it. When not working, his interests include cycling and music, and he enjoys traveling.

John Valley lives in Richmond, Virginia, with his wife, Terri, and his Labrador retriever, Brandon. Mr. Valley currently operates a small practice as an independent consultant for UNIX and Windows tools and applications. With more than 20 years of experience in the computer industry, his background ranges from COBOL business applications and mainframe operating system development to UNIX tools and Windows programming. He teaches courses in C/C++ programming and UNIX fundamentals.

Mr. Valley has published three books on UNIX topics and was a contributing author for the first edition of *UNIX Unleashed*.

Sydney S. Weinstein, CDP, CCP, is a consultant, columnist, lecturer, author, professor, and president of Myxa Corporation, an Open Systems technology company specializing in helping companies move to and work with Open Systems. He has 20 years experience with UNIX, dating all the way back to Version 6.

Sean Drew is a distributed object software developer, working primarily with UNIX, C++, and CORBA. Sean is married to his college sweetheart, Sheri, and together they have two children, Dylan Thomas and Terran Caitlin. At the time of this writing, a third child is on the way and, depending on the gender, will probably be named Erin Nichole, Brenna Nichole, or Ryan Patrick. When Sean is not busy with his family or church, he likes to brew beer. Anybody up for a nice imperial stout? Sean can be reached at `ninkasi@worldnet.att.net`.

Eric Goebelbecker has been working with market data and trading room systems in the New York City area for the past six years. He is currently the Director for Systems Development with MXNet, Inc., a subsidiary of the Sherwood Group in Jersey City, New Jersey, where he is responsible for developing new market data and transaction distribution systems.

Ron Rose is an international management consultant with over 20 years of data processing management experience. He has led large-scale data processing installations in Asia, Europe, and the United States, and he has managed several software product start-up efforts. He completed a master's degree in information systems from Georgia Institute of Technology after completing undergraduate work at Tulane University and the University of Aberdeen, Scotland.

Lance Cavener is co-founder of Senarius. His function is to provide support to employers in Eastern Canada. Tasks such as payroll, work force deployment, and more are part of his business. He is also the President and Senior Network Administrator of ASCIO Communications, a subsidiary of Senarius. He provides the public and businesses with Internet-related services. Lance has been actively involved in UNIX since 1990 as an administrator for corporate networks at various companies in Eastern Canada. His work includes working with BIND/DNS, Sendmail, Usenet setup, Web servers, and UNIX security. He has also written various programs for SunOS, MS-DOS, MS Windows, and VMS.

David Gumkowski currently is a senior systems analyst for Digital Systems Group, Inc., Warminster, PA. Nineteen years ago, he emerged from his computing womb at Purdue University and cut his system administration teeth using Control Data and Texas Instruments machines. For the last 11 years, he developed his UNIX skills prodding Sun, Hewlett-Packard, Digital Equipment, and Silicon Graphics machines to behave for approximately 3,000 users. He would publicly like to thank his wife and children for their support when trying new things, such as writing chapters for this book.

John Semencar is a senior software analyst for Thomas Jefferson University, Philadelphia, PA. Beginning system administration on Control Data legacy systems 10 years ago, and with a background that also includes DEC and SGI, he presently surrounds himself with Hewlett-Packard 9000 servers running HP-UX v10.x. He would like to thank his wife, Georgia, and little Buster for their support.

Steve Shah is a systems administrator for the Center of Environmental Research and Technology at the University of California, Riverside. He received his B.S. in Computer Science with a minor in Creative Writing from UCR and is currently working on his M.S. there as well. In his copious spare time, he enjoys writing fiction, DJing, and spending time with his friends, family, and sweet, Heidi.

Daniel Wilson currently performs UNIX Systems Administration and Database Administration work for the Defense Finance and Accounting Services Financial Systems Organization, which is a financial organization within the Department of Defense.

William D. Wood currently works at Software Artistry, Inc., as a support specialist on UNIX systems. He supports the Expert Advisor software it runs on SUN OS, HP-UX, and IBM AIX. He has specialized in multi-systems and remote systems support since 1985, when he started work at the Pentagon. He has solely supported infrastructures that span the world and just the U.S. He has also supported up to 80 UNIX machines at one time.

William G. Pierce currently performs UNIX Systems Administration and is the Technical Lead for the MidTier Management Operation at the Defense Finance and Accounting Services Financial Systems Organization, Indianapolis, Indiana.

Salim M. Douba (`Salim_Douba@ott.usconnect.com`) is a senior computer network consultant mainly specializing in UNIX, NetWare, and mainframe connectivity. He also designs and implements TCP/IP-based networks and enterprise network management solutions. Salim holds a master's degree in electrical engineering from the American University of Beirut. His experience and main career interests have primarily been in internetworking, multiplatform integration, and network analysis and management.

Chris Byers is a systems administrator for a financial securities firm in Philadelphia. As a former consultant and disaster recovery specialist, he has many years of experience in the UNIX world with its many different variants. He lives in South Jersey with his wife, his son, and his cat. He can be reached at `southst@voicenet.com`.

Jeff Smith is a psychology major who took a wrong turn and ended up working with computers. Jeff has worked with UNIX systems since 1982 as a programmer and systems administrator. He has administered mail, news, security, and the domain name system on several varieties of UNIX, including 2.9 BSD, 4.3 BSD, Dynix, SunOS, and AIX.

James C. Armstrong, Jr., is a software engineer with more than ten years of industry experience with UNIX and C.

James Edwards (`jamedwards@deloitte.ca`) is an IT professional experienced in data communications, network integration, and systems design in both North America and Europe. He holds an M.S. in information technology from the University of London and a B.A. (Hons) from Middlesex University, both in the United Kingdom. James currently resides in Toronto, Canada, where he is employed as a manager with the Deloitte & Touche Consulting Group. His spare time is taken up with his girls, Denise, Lauren, and Poppy.

Tell Us What You Think!

As a reader, you are the most important critic and commentator of our books. We value your opinion and want to know what we're doing right, what we could do better, what areas you'd like to see us publish in, and any other words of wisdom you're willing to pass our way. You can help us make strong books that meet your needs and give you the computer guidance you require.

Do you have access to the World Wide Web? Then check out our site at `http://www.mcp.com`.

> **NOTE**
>
> If you have a technical question about this book, call the technical support line at 317-581-3833 or send e-mail to support@mcp.com.

As the team leader of the group that created this book, I welcome your comments. You can fax, e-mail, or write me directly to let me know what you did or didn't like about this book—as well as what we can do to make our books stronger. Here's the information:

Fax:	317-581-4669
E-mail:	opsys_mgr@sams.mcp.com
Mail:	Dean Miller
	Comments Department
	Sams Publishing
	201 W. 103rd Street
	Indianapolis, IN 46290

Introduction

by Robin Burk and David B. Horvath, CCP

Welcome to *UNIX Unleashed, System Administrator's Edition*.

Who Should Read This Book

Our highly popular first edition brought comprehensive, up-to-date information on UNIX to a wide audience. That original edition was already 1,600 pages. The new topics covered in this edition have obliged us to split the second edition into two volumes, namely, the *System Administrator's Edition* and the *Internet Edition*, which we'll refer to jointly as "the new" or the second edition. Though each volume can stand alone and may be read independently of the other, they form a complementary set with frequent cross-references.

This new edition is written for:

- People new to UNIX
- Anyone using UNIX who wants to learn more about the system and its utilities
- Programmers looking for a tutorial and reference guide to C, C++, Perl, awk, and the UNIX shells
- System administrators concerned about security and performance on their machines
- Webmasters and Internet server administrators
- Programmers who want to write Web pages and implement gateways to server databases
- Anyone who wants to bring his or her UNIX skills and knowledge base up-to-date

A lot has happened in the UNIX world since the first edition of *UNIX Unleashed* was released in 1994. Perhaps the most important change is the tremendous growth of the Internet and the World Wide Web. Much of the public Internet depends on UNIX-based servers. In addition, many corporations of all sizes have turned to UNIX as the environment for network and data servers. As UNIX fans have long known, the original open operating system is ideal for connecting heterogeneous computers and networks into a seamless whole.

What's New in *UNIX Unleashed*

This edition of *UNIX Unleashed* includes a substantial amount of new information describing Internet and World Wide Web technologies in UNIX. New topics include:

- Programming Web pages with HTML
- Object-oriented programming in C++

- Programming Common Gateway Interfaces (CGI) using Perl, C/C++, HTML, and the UNIX shells
- MIME, the Multipurpose Internet Mail Extension
- HTTP, the Hypertext Transfer Protocol
- Web servers and server performance

As UNIX becomes the platform of choice for critical network and data applications, UNIX vendors have placed increased emphasis on system maturity, ease-of-use, and security capabilities. Even with the growth of Microsoft Windows NT, UNIX still has a place in the industry. It is more mature, more stable, more scalable, and has a wider array of applications than NT. Many people claim that NT is the open operating system of the future; that may be true (I have my own *personal* opinion), but for now, UNIX holds that place.

We've also updated this edition of *UNIX Unleashed* to bring you current information regarding:

- Frequently Asked Questions (FAQs) about the most popular variants of UNIX
- Security issues and the technologies you can use to protect your system and its information against intruders and malicious users
- The most popular Graphical User Interfaces (GUIs)

As with the original edition, we set out to bring users the most comprehensive, useful, and up-to-date UNIX guide. To meet this goal, we've added nearly two dozen new chapters and have revised much of the original material in the book. The resulting book is so large that it is now divided into two volumes. The *System Administrator's Edition* introduces UNIX and contains much of the information required for basic users and for systems administrators. The *Internet Edition* includes advanced information for programmers, Internet/Web developers, and those who need detailed information regarding specific UNIX flavors.

Coverage of Popular UNIX Variants

Based on input from some of the experts, application developers, consultants, and system administrators working in the industry, we have provided information about a number of the UNIX variants. We split the variants into two categories: major and minor. This is not a comment on the quality or capabilities of the variant, but on the penetration in the marketplace (popularity).

We consider AIX, HP-UX, Solaris, and SVR4 to be major and BSD, IRIX, Linux, and SunOS to be minor players in the marketplace. There are other variants; the next edition may cover them as they become more popular.

You can identify where something specific to a variant is discussed by the icon next to it:

AIX	major	IBM's version that runs on the RS/6000 series of RISC systems and mainframes. Over 500,000 RS/6000 systems have been sold!	

BSD/OS	BSD	minor	This version has a lesser presence in the marketplace. Although many variants can trace their heritage to BSD, it is not that popular as a product.
HP-UX	HP-UX	major	Hewlett-Packard's (HP) version with a strong hardware presence in the marketplace and a strong future growth path.
IRIX	IRIX	minor	While the Silicon Graphics (SGI) machines are wonderful for graphics, they have not found wide acceptance in business environments.
LINUX	Linux	minor	Although this is a very nice and free variant, it has little commercial presence in the marketplace (probably because corporations do not want to run their mission-critical applications without a vendor they can sue when there is a problem). See the SAMS Linux Unleashed series books (Red Hat and Slackware) for detailed information.
Solaris	Solaris	major	Sun Microsystems' version with a strong hardware presence in the marketplace and a strong future growth path.
SUN/OS	SunOs	minor	Largely being superseded by Solaris installations. A good variant, but it is difficult for a company to support two versions of UNIX at a time.
SVR4	SVR4	major	This version has a strong presence in the marketplace. In addition, many variants can trace their heritage to System V Release 4.

CD-ROM Contents

We've also enhanced our CD-ROM with a C compiler, the most popular Web server software, and megabytes of other useful tools and information. The CD-ROM packaged with each volume contains exactly the same software and materials. Here are some of the noteworthy inclusions:

- The entire text of both volumes in HTML format
- Listings and code examples from various chapters in the volume
- FreeBSD 2.2.5, full binary release
- Linux Red Hat 4.2, full binary release [x86 platform only]
- BASH, sources and documentation
- sendmail version 8.7

- RFCs 821, 822, 1425, 1123, 976, 977, 1036
- latest version of INN source code
- GNU findutils 4.1
- GNU fileutils 3.16
- xv-3.10a
- disktool (v2.0)
- tcl/tk
- screen
- xarchie
- xrn
- SATAN
- Crack (or equivalent)
- Perl 5.x
- LaTeX
- Lynx
- elm and pine
- pico
- UNIX sort utility
- GNU awk, gawk
- APACHE Web server
- GNU C compiler
- emacs editor
- gtar
- gzip
- gcc
- gmake
- NCSA Web server
- asWedit
- missinglink
- Weblint
- Isearch and Isearch-cgi
- @cgi.pm
- LessTif 0.80 sources, Linux & FreeBSD bins
- fvwm window manager

- Enlightenment window manager
- libg 2.7.2 (useful companion to C compiler)
- acroread, Adobe Acrobat PDF reader (for Linux and FreeBSD)

More information about the CD-ROM contents is available on the final page, "What's on the CD-ROM."

 To make use of the CD-ROM easier, whenever a reference in print is made to the CD-ROM, you will see an icon. You can also scan through the text to find the CD-ROM icons to find more information about the disk contents.

Enjoy!

How These Volumes Are Organized

The books are divided into parts (detailed information about each volume is in the next sections). Each volume also contains a glossary of terms and an index.

Whenever there is special information you should pay attention to, it will be placed in a block to grab your attention. There are three types of special blocks: note, tip, and caution.

> **NOTE**
>
> A note is used to provide you with information that you may want to pay attention to but is not critical. The information can be critical but should not cause too much trouble.

> **TIP**
>
> A tip is used to make your life easier. It provides you with information so you do not have to go digging to solve a problem. These are based on real-life exposure to problems (and how they were solved).

> **CAUTION**
>
> A caution is used to grab your attention to prevent you from doing something that would cause problems. Pay close attention to cautions!

The icons shown in the "CD-ROM Contents" and "Coverage of Popular UNIX Variants" sections, earlier in this introduction, also provide a quick means of referencing information.

How *UNIX Unleashed* Is Organized

The first volume, *UNIX Unleashed, System Administrator's Edition*, consists of three major sections or parts. The general focus is on getting you started using UNIX, working with the shells, and then administering the system.

Part I, Introduction to UNIX, is designed to get you started using UNIX. It provides you with the general information on the organization of the UNIX operating system, how and where to find files, and the commands a general user would want to use. Information is also provided on how to get around the network and communicating with other users on the system.

Part II, UNIX Shells, provides you the information on how to choose which shell to use and how to use that shell. The most popular shells: Bourne, Bourne Again (BASH), Korn, and C, are covered, as well as a comparison between them. Under UNIX, the shell is what provides the user interface to the operating system.

Part III, System Administration, gets you started and keeps you going with the tasks required to administer a UNIX system. From installation through performance and tuning, the important topics are covered. The general duties of the system administrator are described (so you can build a job description to give to your boss). In case you are working on a brand-new UNIX system, the basics of UNIX installation are covered. Other topics covered in this section include: starting and stopping UNIX, user administration, file system and disk administration, configuring the kernel (core of the operating system), networking UNIX systems, accounting for system usage, device (add-on hardware) administration, mail administration, news (known as netnews or Usenet) administration, UUCP (UNIX to UNIX Copy Program, an early networking method still in wide use today) administration, FTP (File Transfer Protocol) administration, and finally, backing up and restoring files.

The second volume, *UNIX Unleashed, Internet Edition*, consists of seven major parts. The general focus is programming (GUI, application languages, and the Internet), text formatting (which involves embedding commands in your text and then processing it), security considerations (advanced system administration), developing for the Internet, "programming," source code control and configuration management, and Frequently Asked Questions (FAQ) for the different variants of UNIX.

Part I, Graphical User Interfaces, provides you with information about using and writing GUI applications. When the operating system is UNIX, the GUI is the X-windowing system.

Part II, Programming, introduces the most popular program development tools in the UNIX environment. The most important part is how to enter your program (editing with vi and emacs)! The awk, Perl, C, and C++ programming languages are covered. Awk and Perl are interpreted languages designed for quick program development. C is the compiled language developed by Kernighan and Ritchie—UNIX is written in this language. C++ is an enhancement to the C language that supports object-oriented programming. The final chapter in this section discusses the make utility, which provides a rule-based method to control program compilation.

Part III, Text Formatting and Printing, covers the tools that support the development, formatting, and printing of documents in the UNIX environment. These tools were much of the original justification for hardware that was used to develop UNIX. The formatting programs, nroff and troff, the standard macro packages, and many of the other document preparation tools are covered. In addition, developing your own text formatting macros is discussed.

Part IV, Security, is an advanced area of systems administration. One of the criticisms of UNIX is that it is not secure. It was developed in an environment where the individuals were trusted and sharing information was important. UNIX is capable of being very secure; you just have to know how to set it up. This section provides that information. The risks, available tools, and helpful organizations are covered.

Part V, UNIX and the Internet, introduces the tools used with the World Wide Web and the transmission of binary files via e-mail (MIME). The Web page definition language, HTML, is introduced, along with the methods of developing CGI (Common Gateway Interface programs that run on the Web server processing data from Web pages) programs in shell scripting languages, Perl, and C/C++. Administrative information is provided in chapters on HTTP (Hypertext Transfer Protocol) and monitoring server activity.

Part VI, Source Control, covers the tools that UNIX provides to maintain control of your source code as different versions (and revisions) are created. The three major tools are RCS, CVS, and SCCS.

Part VII, Frequently Asked Questions, provides answers, as the name implies, to the most frequently asked questions about the various variants of UNIX. AIX, BSD, HP-UX, Linux, Solaris, SVR4, and IRIX are covered in individual chapters.

Conventions Used in This Volume

This book uses the following typographical conventions:

- Menu names are separated from the individual menu options with a vertical bar (|). For example, "File|Save" means "Select the File menu and then choose the Save option."
- New terms appear in *italic*.
- All code appears in monospace. This includes pseudocode that is used to show a general format rather than a specific example.
- Words that you are instructed to type appear in **monospace bold**.
- Placeholders (words that stand for what you actually type) appear in *italic monospace*.

■ Lines of code that are too long to fit on only one line of this book are broken at a convenient place and continued on the next line. A code continuation character (➥) precedes the new line. Any code that contains this character should be entered as one long line without a line break.

■ An ellipsis (…) in code indicates that some code has been omitted for the sake of brevity.

IN THIS PART

I

PART

Introduction to UNIX

The UNIX Operating System

by Rachel and Robert Sartin,
and Robin Burk

IN THIS CHAPTER

CHAPTER 1

Welcome to the world of UNIX. Once the domain of wizards and gurus, today UNIX has spread beyond the university and laboratory to find a home in global corporations and small Internet servers alike. This ability to scale up or down, to accommodate small installations or complex corporate networks with little or no modification, is only one of the characteristics that have won UNIX its popularity and widespread use.

As we'll see through the course of this book, UNIX is a rich and complex system, built upon simple, powerful elements. Although many more recent operating systems have borrowed concepts and mechanisms from UNIX, those who are most familiar with legacy mainframe environments, or whose experience is mostly limited to single-user personal computers, may find UNIX to be a bit intimidating at first. The best advice I can give is to take it slowly, but don't give up. As you read through these chapters and begin to use some of the features and utilities described in this book, you'll find that once-foreign ideas have taken clear and concrete shape in your mind.

NOTE

One distinctive characteristic of UNIX compared to other operating systems is the fact that there are several flavors, or variants, of the operating system. Because the source code of the early versions was made available to a variety of computer manufacturers and third parties, many slightly different forms of UNIX co-exist. Some are specific to a given hardware manufacturer; others differ in the utilities, configuration methods, or user interfaces they offer. In this book, we will call your attention to the differences among the most commonly used UNIX variants, including:

- HP-UX (Hewlett-Packard)
- Solaris (SunSoft)
- SVR4 (AT&T)
- AIX (IBM)

Other UNIX variants we will examine in these two volumes include:

- BSD (Berkeley Software)
- Linux
- SunOS (predecessor to Solaris)
- IRIX

TIP

In this book, you will find specific details regarding how to accomplish tasks in each of the most popular versions of UNIX. In addition, this book's companion volume, *UNIX Unleashed, Internet Edition*, contains answers to Frequently Asked Questions for each major UNIX flavor.

At its base, UNIX is both simple and elegant, with a consistent architecture that, in turn, underlies and guides the design of its many application programs and languages. If you are new to UNIX, I want you to know that I'm a bit jealous of the fun you'll have as you begin to explore this fascinating environment for the first time. If you are a more experienced UNIX user, administrator, or programmer, this revised edition of *UNIX Unleashed* contains a wealth of information that can help you extend your UNIX use to Internet and World Wide Web applications, guard against hackers and other unauthorized intruders, and fine-tune your system management skills.

What Is UNIX?

UNIX is

- A trademark of Novell Corporation
- A multitasking, multiuser operating system
- The name given to a whole family of related operating systems and their most common application, utility, and compiler programs
- A rich, extensible, and open computing environment

Let's take these one at a time. To begin with, UNIX is a trademark, which means that there is intellectual property associated with UNIX that is not in the public domain. Some versions of UNIX require a paid license for their use.

The term *UNIX* also refers to a powerful multitasking, multiuser operating system.

Once upon a time, not so long ago, everyone knew what an operating system (OS) was. It was the complex software sold by the maker of your computer system, without which no other programs could function on that computer. It spun the disks, lit the terminals, and generally kept track of what the hardware was doing and why. Application (user) programs asked the operating system to perform various functions; users seldom talked to the OS directly.

Today those boundaries are not quite so clear. The rise of graphical user interfaces, macro and scripting languages, suites of applications that can exchange information seamlessly, and the increased popularity of networks and distributed data—all of these factors have blurred the traditional distinctions. Today's computing environments consist of layers of hardware and software that interact together to form a nearly organic whole.

At its core (or, as we say in UNIX, in the kernel), however, UNIX does indeed perform the classic role of an operating system. Like the mainframe and minicomputer systems that came before, UNIX enables multiple people to access a computer simultaneously and multiple programs and activities to proceed in parallel with one another.

Unlike most proprietary operating systems, however, UNIX has given birth to a whole family of related, or variant, systems. Some differ in functionality or origin; others are developed by computer vendors and are specific to a given line of machines; still others were developed specifically as shareware or even freeware. Although these various flavors of UNIX differ from one another to some degree, they are fundamentally the same environment. All offer their own versions of the most common utilities, application programs, and languages. Those who use awk, grep, the Bourne shell, or make in one version of UNIX will find their old favorites available on other UNIX machines as well.

Those who do not care much for these programs, however, will find themselves free to substitute their own approach for getting various computing jobs done. A salient characteristic of UNIX is that it is extensible and open. By extensible, I mean that UNIX allows the easy definition of new commands, which can then be invoked or used by other programs and terminal users. This is practical in the UNIX environment, because the architecture of the UNIX kernel specifically defines interfaces, or ways that programs can communicate with one another without having been designed specifically to work together.

Understanding Operating Systems

An operating system is an important part of a computer system. You can view a computer system as being built from three general components: the hardware, the operating system, and the applications. (See Figure 1.1.) The hardware includes pieces such as a central processing unit (CPU), a keyboard, a hard drive, and a printer. You can think of these as the parts you are able to touch physically. Applications are why you use computers; they use the rest of the system to perform the desired task (for example, play a game, edit a memo, send electronic mail). The operating system is the component that on one side manages and controls the hardware and on the other manages the applications.

FIGURE 1.1.

*Computer system
components.*

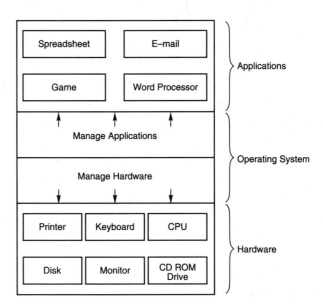

When you purchase a computer system, you must have at least hardware and an operating system. The hardware you purchase is able to use (or run) one or more different operating systems. You can purchase a bundled computer package, which includes the hardware, the operating system, and possibly one or more applications. The operating system is necessary in order to manage the hardware and the applications.

When you turn on your computer, the operating system performs a series of tasks, presented in chronological order in the next few sections.

Hardware Management, Part 1

One of the first things you do, after successfully plugging together a plethora of cables and components, is turn on your computer. The operating system takes care of all the starting functions that must occur to get your computer to a usable state. Various pieces of hardware need to be initialized. After the start-up procedure is complete, the operating system awaits further instructions. If you shut down the computer, the operating system also has a procedure that makes sure all the hardware is shut down correctly. Before turning your computer off again, you might want to do something useful, which means that one or more applications are executed. Most boot ROMs do some hardware initialization but not much. Initialization of I/O (input/output) devices is part of the UNIX kernel.

Process Management

After the operating system completes hardware initialization, you can execute an application. This executing application is called a process. It is the operating system's job to manage execution of the application. When you execute a program, the operating system creates a new process. Many processes can exist simultaneously, but only one process can actually be executing on a CPU at one time. The operating system switches between your processes so quickly that it can appear that the processes are executing simultaneously. This concept is referred to as time-sharing or multitasking.

When you exit your program (or it finishes executing), the process terminates, and the operating system manages the termination by reclaiming any resources that were being used.

Most applications perform some tasks between the time the process is created and the time it terminates. To perform these tasks, the program makes requests to the operating system, and the operating system responds to the requests and allocates necessary resources to the program. When an executing process needs to use some hardware, the operating system provides access for the process.

Hardware Management, Part 2

To perform its task, a process may need to access hardware resources. The process may need to read or write to a file, send data to a network card (to communicate with another computer), or send data to a printer. The operating system provides such services for the process. This is referred to as resource allocation. A piece of hardware is a resource, and the operating system allocates available resources to the different processes that are running.

See Table 1.1 for a summary of different actions and what the operating system (OS) does to manage them.

Table 1.1. Operating system functions.

Action	OS Does This
You turn on the computer.	Hardware management
You execute an application.	Process management
Application reads a tape.	Hardware management
Application waits for data.	Process management
Process waits while other process runs.	Process management
Process displays data on screen.	Hardware management
Process writes data to tape.	Hardware management
You quit, the process terminates.	Process management
You turn off the computer.	Hardware management

From the time you turn on your computer until you turn it off, the operating system is coordinating the operations. As hardware is initialized, accessed, or shut down, the operating system manages those resources. As applications execute, request, and receive resources or terminate, the operating system takes care of these actions. Without an operating system, no application can run, and your computer is just an expensive paperweight.

The UNIX Operating System

The previous section looked at operating systems in general. This section looks at a specific operating system: UNIX. UNIX is an increasingly popular operating system. Traditionally used on minicomputers and workstations in the academic community, UNIX is now available on personal computers, and the business community has started to choose UNIX for its openness. Previous PC and mainframe users are now looking to UNIX as their operating system solution. This section looks at how UNIX fits into the operating system model.

UNIX, like other operating systems, is a layer between the hardware and the applications that run on the computer. It has functions that manage the hardware and functions that manage executing applications. So what's the difference between UNIX and any other operating system? Basically, two things: internal implementation and the interface that is seen and used by users. For the most part, this book ignores the internal implementation. If you want to know these details, many texts exist that cover them. The interface is what this book describes in detail.

The majority of UNIX users need to be familiar with the interface and need not understand the internal workings of UNIX.

The UNIX system is actually more than strictly an operating system. UNIX includes the traditional operating system components. In addition, a standard UNIX system includes a set of libraries and a set of applications. Figure 1.2 shows the components and layers of UNIX. Sitting above the hardware are two components: the file system and process control. Next is the set of libraries. On top are the applications. The user has access to the libraries and to the applications. These two components are what many users think of as UNIX, because together they constitute the UNIX interface.

FIGURE 1.2.
The layers of UNIX.

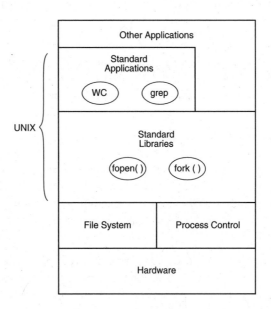

The part of UNIX that manages the hardware and the executing processes is called the kernel. In managing all hardware devices, the UNIX system views each device as a file (called a device file). This allows the same simple method of reading and writing files to be used to access each hardware device. The file system (explained in more detail in Chapter 4, "The UNIX File System") manages read and write access to user data and to devices, such as printers, attached to the system. It implements security controls to protect the safety and privacy of information. In executing processes (see Chapter 18, "File System and Disk Administration"), the UNIX system allocates resources (including use of the CPU) and mediates access to the hardware.

One important advantage that results from the UNIX standard interface is application portability. Application portability is the ability of a single application to be executed on various types of computer hardware without being modified. This can be achieved if the application uses the UNIX interface to manage its hardware needs. UNIX's layered design insulates the application from the different types of hardware. This allows the software developer to support the single application on multiple hardware types with minimal effort. The application writer has lower development costs and a larger potential customer base. Users not only have more applications available, but can rely on being able to use the same applications on different computer hardware.

UNIX goes beyond the traditional operating system by providing a standard set of libraries and applications that developers and users can use. This standard interface allows application portability and facilitates user familiarity with the interface.

The History of UNIX

How did a system such as UNIX ever come to exist? UNIX has a rather unusual history that has greatly affected its current form.

The Early Days

In the mid-1960s, AT&T Bell Laboratories (among others) was participating in an effort to develop a new operating system called Multics. Multics was intended to supply large-scale computing services as a utility, much like electrical power. Many people who worked on the Bell Labs contributions to Multics later worked on UNIX.

In 1969, Bell Labs pulled out of the Multics effort, and the members of the Computing Science Research Center were left with no computing environment. Ken Thompson, Dennis Ritchie, and others developed and simulated an initial design for a file system that later evolved into the UNIX file system. An early version of the system was developed to take advantage of a PDP-7 computer that was available to the group.

An early project that helped lead to the success of UNIX was its deployment to do text processing for the patent department at AT&T. This project moved UNIX to the PDP-11 and resulted in a system known for its small size. Shortly afterward, the now famous C programming language was developed on and for UNIX, and the UNIX operating system itself was rewritten into C. This then-radical implementation decision is one of the factors that enabled UNIX to become the open system it is today.

AT&T was not allowed to market computer systems, so it had no way to sell this creative work from Bell Labs. Nonetheless, the popularity of UNIX grew through internal use at AT&T and licensing to universities for educational use. By 1977, commercial licenses for UNIX were being granted, and the first UNIX vendor, Interactive Systems Corporation, began selling UNIX systems for office automation.

Later versions developed at AT&T (or its successor, UNIX System Laboratories, now owned by Novell) included System III and several releases of System V. The two most recent releases of System V, Release 3 (SVR3.2) and Release 4 (SVR4; the most recent version of SVR4 is SVR4.2) remain popular for computers, ranging from PCs to mainframes.

All versions of UNIX based on the AT&T work require a license from the current owner, UNIX System Laboratories.

Berkeley Software Distributions

In 1978, the research group turned over distribution of UNIX to the UNIX Support Group (USG), which had distributed an internal version called the Programmer's Workbench. In 1982, USG introduced System III, which incorporated ideas from several different internal versions of and modifications to UNIX, developed by various groups. In 1983, USG released the original UNIX System V, and thanks to the divestiture of AT&T, was able to market it aggressively. A series of later releases continued to introduce new features from other versions of UNIX, including the internal versions from the research group and the Berkeley Software Distribution.

While AT&T (through the research group and USG) developed UNIX, the universities that had acquired educational licenses were far from inactive. Most notably, the Computer Science Research Group at the University of California at Berkeley (UCB) developed a series of releases known as the Berkeley Software Distribution, or BSD. The original PDP-11 modifications were called 1BSD and 2BSD. Support for the Digital Equipment Corporation VAX computers was introduced in 3BSD. VAX development continued with 4.0BSD, 4.1BSD, 4.2BSD, and 4.3BSD, all of which (especially 4.2 and 4.3) had many features (and much source code) adopted into commercial products.

UNIX and Standards

Because of the multiple versions of UNIX and frequent cross-pollination between variants, many features have diverged in the different versions of UNIX. With the increasing popularity of UNIX in the commercial and government sector came the desire to standardize the features of UNIX so that a user or developer using UNIX could depend on those features.

The Institute of Electrical and Electronic Engineers (IEEE) created a series of standards committees to create standards for "An Industry-Recognized Operating Systems Interface Standard based on the UNIX Operating System." The results of two of the committees are important for the general user and developer. The POSIX.1 committee standardizes the C library interface used to write programs for UNIX. (See *UNIX Unleashed, Internet Edition*, Chapter 6, "The C and C++ Programming Languages.") The POSIX.2 committee standardizes the commands that are available for the general user.

In Europe, the X/Open Consortium brings together various UNIX-related standards, including the current attempt at a Common Open System Environment (COSE) specification. X/Open publishes a series of specifications called the X/Open Portability. The MOTIF user interface is one popular standard to emerge from this effort.

The United States government has specified a series of standards based on XPG and POSIX. Currently, FIPS 151-2 specifies the open systems requirements for federal purchases.

Various commercial consortia have attempted to negotiate UNIX standards as well. These have yet to converge on an accepted, stable result.

UNIX for Mainframes and Workstations

Many mainframe and workstation vendors make a version of UNIX for their machines. We will be discussing several of these variants (including Solaris from SunSoft, AIX from IBM, and HP-UX from Hewlett-Packard) throughout this book.

UNIX for Intel Platforms

Thanks to the great popularity of personal computers, there are many UNIX versions available for Intel platforms. Choosing from the versions and trying to find software for the version you have can be a tricky business, because the UNIX industry has not settled on a complete binary standard for the Intel platform. There are two basic categories of UNIX systems on Intel hardware: the SVR4-based systems and the older, more established SVR3.2 systems.

SVR4 vendors include NCR, IBM, Sequent, SunSoft (which sells Solaris for Intel), and Novell (which sells UnixWare). The Santa Cruz Operation (SCO) is the main vendor in the SVR3.2 camp.

Source Versions of "UNIX"

Several versions of UNIX and UNIX-like systems have been made that are free or extremely cheap and include source code. These versions have become particularly attractive to the modern-day hobbyist, who can now run a UNIX system at home for little investment and with great opportunity to experiment with the operating system or make changes to suit his or her needs.

An early UNIX-like system was MINIX, by Andrew Tanenbaum. His book *Operating Systems: Design and Implementations* describes MINIX and includes a source listing of the original version of MINIX. The latest version of MINIX is available from the publisher. MINIX is available in binary form for several machines (PC, Amiga, Atari, Macintosh, and SPARCStation).

The most popular source version of UNIX is Linux (pronounced "*lin nucks*"). Linux was designed from the ground up by Linus Torvalds to be a free replacement for UNIX, and it aims for POSIX compliance. Linux itself has spun off some variants, primarily versions that offer additional support or tools in exchange for license fees. Linux has emerged as the server platform of choice for small to mid-sized Internet Service Providers and Web servers.

Making Changes to UNIX

Many people considering making the transition to UNIX have a significant base of PC-based MS-DOS and Microsoft Windows applications. There have been a number of efforts to create programs or packages on UNIX that would ease the migration by allowing users to run their existing DOS and Windows applications on the same machine on which they run UNIX. This is a rapidly changing marketplace as Microsoft evolves its Windows and Windows NT operating systems.

Introduction to the UNIX Philosophy

As described in the section "The History of UNIX," UNIX has its roots in a system that was intended to be small and supply orthogonal common pieces. Although most UNIX systems have grown to be fairly large and monolithic applications are not uncommon, the original philosophy still lives in the core commands available on all UNIX systems. There are several common key items throughout UNIX:

- Simple, orthogonal commands
- Commands connected through pipes
- A (mostly) common option interface style
- No file types

For detailed information on commands and connecting them together, see the chapters on shells (Chapters 8–13) and on common commands (Chapters 5–7).

Simple, Orthogonal Commands

The original UNIX systems were very small, and the designers tried to take every advantage of those small machines by writing small commands. Each command attempted to do one thing well. The tools could then be combined (either with a shell script or a C program) to do more complicated tasks. One command, called wc, was written solely to count the lines, words, and characters in a file. To count all the words in all the files, you would type wc * and get output like that in Listing 1.1.

Listing 1.1. Using a simple command.

```
$ wc *
351    2514   17021 minix-faq
1011    5982   42139 minix-info
1362    8496   59160 total
$
```

Commands Connected Through Pipes

To turn the simple, orthogonal commands into a powerful toolset, UNIX enables the user to use the output of one command as the input to another. This connection is called a *pipe*, and a series of commands connected by pipes is called a *pipeline*. For example, to count the number of lines that reference MINIX in all the files, one would type grep MINIX * ¦ wc and get output like that in Listing 1.2.

Listing 1.2. Using a pipeline.

```
$ grep MINIX * ¦ wc
105    982   6895
$
```

A (Mostly) Common Option Interface Style

Each command has actions that can be controlled with options, which are specified by a hyphen followed by a single letter option (for instance, -1). Some options take option arguments, which are specified by a hyphen followed by a single letter, followed by the argument (for instance, -h Header). For example, to print on pages with 16 lines each all the lines in the file minix-info that mention Tanenbaum, you would enter wc minix-info ¦ pr -l 16 and get output like that in Listing 1.3.

Listing 1.3. Using options in a pipeline.

```
$ grep Tanenbaum minix-info ¦ pr -l 16


Feb 14 16:02 1994   Page 1


  [From Andy Tanenbaum <ast@cs.vu.nl> 28 August 1993]
The author of MINIX, Andrew S. Tanenbaum, has written a book describing
Author:    Andrew S. Tanenbaum
subjects.ast (list of Andy Tanenbaum's
Andy Tanenbaum since 1987 (on tape)
Version 1.0 is the version in Tanenbaum's book, "Operating Systems: Design




$
```

The bad news is that some UNIX commands have some quirks in the way they handle options. As more systems adopt the standards mentioned in the section "The History of UNIX," you will find fewer examples of commands with quirks.

No File Types

UNIX pays no attention to the contents of a file (except when you try to run a file as a command). It does not know the difference between a spreadsheet file and a word processor file. The meaning of the characters in a file is entirely supplied by the command(s) that uses the file. This concept is familiar to most PC users but was a significant difference between UNIX and other earlier operating systems. The power of this concept is that any program can be used to operate on any file. The downside is that only a program that understands the file format can fully decode the information in the file.

Summary

UNIX has a long history as an open development environment. More recently, it has become the system of choice for both commercial and some personal uses. UNIX performs the typical operating system tasks but also includes a standard set of commands and library interfaces. The building-block approach of UNIX makes it an ideal system for creating new applications.

Getting Started:
Basic Tutorial

by Rachel and Robert Sartin

IN THIS CHAPTER

CHAPTER 2

UNIX is a multiuser, multi-tasking environment. Unlike personal computers, UNIX systems are inherently designed to allow simultaneous access to multiple users.

Whether you are working with UNIX on a large, multiuser system or have a dedicated UNIX-based workstation on your desk, the multiuser, multi-tasking architecture of the operating system influences the way you will work with the system and the requirements it will place on you as a user and a system administrator.

The purpose of this chapter is to acquaint you with the basics of UNIX from the user's point of view. Not all UNIX boxes actually support multiple users with keyboards or terminals of their own. Some workstations are dedicated to a single person, and others function as servers that support multiple remote computers rather than end users. In all cases, however, UNIX operates as if it might be called upon to furnish a fully multiuser, multi-tasking capability. For the purpose of this tutorial, we'll assume that you have a dedicated UNIX workstation on your desk.

Logging In

Several people can be using a UNIX-based computer at the same time. In order for the system to know who you are and what resources you can use, you must identify yourself. In addition, since UNIX expects to communicate with you over a terminal (or a PC running terminal-emulation software), your terminal and the UNIX system must establish the ground rules that will govern the transfer of information. The process of establishing the communications session and identifying yourself is known as "logging in."

NOTE

UNIX actually distinguishes between a communications session and a login session, in that it is possible to log in as one user, log out, and log in again as another user without disrupting the communications session. Because an increasing number of people access UNIX systems from a PC, and for purposes of simplicity in this tutorial, we've treated the communications and login sessions as identical in this chapter. As you become more familiar with the UNIX environment and with utilities such as telnet, this distinction will become more important.

User Account Setup

After a UNIX system is booted, you cannot simply start using it as you do a PC. Before you can access the computer system, someone—usually the system administrator—must configure the computer for your use. If you are running UNIX on your PC at home, you will most likely need to do these things for yourself. If you are a UNIX novice trying to set up your home computer system, you can refer to Chapter 15, "UNIX Installation Basics." If you are using a computer system in your place of work, your employer may have a person or persons whose specific job it is to administer all the systems. If this is the case, you will have to coordinate with a staff member to set up your system account. The company may have an application form on which you can request such things as a certain user name, a temporary password, which shell you want to use (see Chapter 13, "Shell Comparison"), what your default group is, what groups you should belong to, and which mail aliases you should be added to. Many of these things will depend on what work you will be doing and whom you will be working with.

No matter who sets up your computer account, you must know two things before you can use the system: your user name and your password. If you don't know what these are, you must stop and find out what has been assigned to you. The user name is a unique name that identifies you to the system. It is often related to your real name, such as your first name, your last name, or a combination of first initial and last name (for example, "frank," "brimmer," or "fbrimmer," respectively). If you get to request a user name, try to choose something that makes others think of you alone, and is not vague or common enough to cause confusion with others. The system administrator will verify that no one else on your system has this name before allowing you to have it. The password that you request or that has been assigned to you is a temporary string that allows you to initially access the computer system. The initial password isn't of any real importance because you should change it to something of your choice the first time you log in to the system (see "Managing Your Password," later in this chapter).

The other items on the account application form are harder for a novice user to determine. Asking a peer who uses the same system for the values his or her account has might be a good place to start. The system administrator may be able to help you figure out what values you should have. But don't worry; these are all easily changed later if you wish.

Logging In to the System

Now that you know your user name (say it's "brimmer") and password (say it's "new_user"), you can access the system. When you sit down in front of a UNIX workstation, you are expected to log in to the system. The system prompts (asks) you for your user name by printing `login:`. You should then enter your user name. Next, UNIX prompts you for your password by printing `Password:`. Enter your password. As you type your password, don't be alarmed if the characters you type are not displayed on your screen. This is normal and is for your protection. No one else should know your password, and this way no one can look at your screen and see your password when you log in.

```
login: brimmer
Password:
Please wait...checking for disk quotas

Marine biology word of the day:
Cnidaria (n.) Nigh-DARE-ee-uh (L. a nettle)  - a phylum of basically
radially symmetrical marine invertebrates including corals, sea
anemones, jellyfish and hydroids. This phylum was formerly known
as Coelenterata.
$
```

> **TIP**
>
> Some keyboards have a key labeled "Return." Some have a key labeled "Enter." If your keyboard has both, "Return" is probably the correct key to use.

> **TIP**
>
> On some systems, Erase is # and Kill is @. On others, Erase is Backspace or Delete and Kill is Control+U or Control+X.

If you typed everything correctly and the system administrator has everything set up correctly, you are now logged in and may use the system. If you get a message saying `Login Incorrect`, you may have typed your user name or password incorrectly. If you make a mistake during your user name, the Backspace key and the Delete key may not undo this mistake for you. The easiest thing to do is to start over by pressing Enter twice to get to a new `login:` prompt.

Other error messages you might receive are `No Shell`, `No Directory`, or `Cannot Open Password File`. If you see any of these messages, or if multiple attempts at logging in always produce the `Login Incorrect` message, contact your system administrator for help.

> **TIP**
>
> The `No Shell` message means that UNIX is not able to start the command interpreter, which was configured when your account was set up. Depending on the UNIX system, your login may complete successfully and the default shell will be used. If this happens, you can use the chsh command, which will change the shell specified in your account. See Part II, "UNIX Shells," for more information about various shells. The `No Directory` message means that UNIX cannot access your home directory, which was specified when your account was set up. Again, depending on the system, your login may complete successfully, placing you in a default directory. You may need to then enlist the help of the system administrator to create your home directory or change the home directory value for your account. See Chapter 4, "The UNIX File System," regarding directories and, specifically, your home directory. The `Cannot Open Password File` message means that UNIX is having a problem accessing the system password file, which holds the account information (user name, password, user ID, shell, group, and so on) for each user. If there is a problem with this file, no user can log in to the system. Contact your system administrator if you see this message.

If your system is configured to use a graphical user interface (GUI), you probably have a login screen. This screen performs the same function as the command-line prompts but is presented as a graphical display. The display probably has two boxes for you to fill in, each with a label. One box is for your user name and the other is for your password.

After Login Succeeds

After a successful login, several messages appear on your screen. Some of these may be the date and time of your last login, the system's informative message (called the "Message of the Day"), and a message informing you whether you have (electronic) mail. The Message of the Day can be an important message to watch because it is one way that administrators communicate with the system users. The next scheduled down time (when no one can use the system) is an example of information that you might see here.

After all the messages scroll by, the system is ready and waiting for you to do something. This ready-and-waiting condition is signified by a prompt followed by a cursor. Typical prompts are $ or %. The dollar-sign prompt is commonly used by Bourne and Korn shells and the percent sign by C shells. The value of this prompt (your primary prompt) can be changed if you wish. The person who set up your account may have already configured a different prompt value. To change this prompt, you need to change the value of the environment variable PS1 (for Bourne and Korn) or prompt (for C shell). (See the section "Configuring Your Environment" in this chapter for details on environment variables.) The cursor (the spot on the screen where the next character you type is displayed) is commonly an underline (_) or a box, either of which can be blinking. The cursor you see may vary from system to system.

Different Privileges for Different Users

If you are administering your own personal system, it is still important for you to set up a personal account for yourself, even though your system will come configured with some type of administrative account. This account should be used to do system-wide administrative actions. It is important to be careful when using this account because it has special privileges. UNIX systems have built-in security features. Most users cannot set up a new user account or do other administrative procedures. The user "root" is a special user, sometimes called super-user, which can do anything at all on the system. This high degree of power is necessary to fully administer a UNIX system, but it also allows its user to make a mistake and cause system problems. For this reason, you should set up a personal account for yourself that does not have root privilege. Then, your normal, day-to-day activities will affect only your personal environment and you will be in no danger of causing system-wide problems. In a multiuser, nonpersonal environment, you will most likely have only user (and not super-user) privileges. This security is even more important when more than one person is involved because one mistake by the root can affect every user and the entire system.

UNIX also has security to help prevent different users from harming each other on a multiuser system. Each user "owns" his or her environment and can selectively let groups or all others have access to this work. If you are doing private work in one area that no one else should be allowed to see, then you should restrict access to the owner (you). If you and your team members are working on a group project, you can restrict access to the owner (you) and everyone in your group. If this work should be shared with many or all people on the system, then you should allow access to everyone.

Logging Out

When you are done using the system, you should log out. This will prevent other people from accidentally or intentionally getting access to your files. It will also make the system available for their use.

The normal way to log out from almost any shell is to type `exit`. This causes your shell to exit, or stop running. When you exit from your login shell, you log out. If you are using `csh`, you can also type `logout`; if you are in a login shell, then `csh` will log out. Some shells, depending on your configuration, will also log you out if you type the end-of-file character (typically Control+D; see "Working on the System," later in this chapter).

If you have a graphical user interface, your logout procedure may be different. Please consult your manuals or online help to learn about logging out of your GUI.

Using Commands

During the login process, described in the "Logging In" section, UNIX performs several actions that prepare you and the system for each other. These include performing system accounting, initializing your user environment, and starting a command interpreter (commonly called a shell). Commands are how you tell the system to do something. The command interpreter recognizes these commands and passes the information off to where it is needed. UNIX systems originally came with a command interpreter called the Bourne shell (usually referred to as sh, though some systems ship Korn or POSIX as sh—see the Note that follows). This shell is still available on most UNIX computer systems. A newer shell that is common to most UNIX systems is the C shell (referred to as csh). Another commonly used, but not as pervasive, shell is the Korn shell (referred to as ksh). Among different shells, there is some variation of the commands that are available. Refer to Part II for details on these UNIX shells.

NOTE: WHAT'S IN A NAME?

There are a number of different common shells on various UNIX operating systems. The most common are as follows:

sh   The Bourne shell is the most common of all the shells. (May be installed as bsh.)

ksh   The Korn shell is a derivative of the Bourne shell, which adds history and command-line editing. (Sometimes installed as sh.)

sh   The POSIX shell is much like the Korn shell. The POSIX standard requires it to be installed as sh. Some vendors install it as /bin/sh. Some put it in a special directory and call it sh, leaving the Bourne shell as /bin/sh.

csh   The C shell is based on the popular C language.

bash   The Born Again shell is less common.

tcsh   This is a version of the C shell with interactive command-line editing.

What Is a Command?

A UNIX command is a series of characters that you type. These characters consist of words that are separated by whitespace. Whitespace is the result of typing one or more Space or Tab keys. The first word is the name of the command. The rest of the words are called the command's arguments. The arguments give the command information that it might need, or specify varying behavior of the command. To invoke a command, simply type the command name, followed by arguments (if any). To indicate to the shell that you are done typing and are ready for the command to be executed, press Enter.

Try it out. Enter the date command. The command's name is "date" and it takes no arguments. Therefore, type date and press Enter and see what happens. You should see that the computer has printed the current date and time. If the date or time does not match reality, ask the system administrator to fix it. How about trying a command that has arguments? Try the echo command. The name of the command is "echo" and it takes a series of arguments. The echo command will then write, or echo, these arguments out to your screen. Try creating a command that will write your first and last name on the screen. Here is what these commands and output look like on our system:

```
$ date
Sat Aug  5 11:11:00 EST 1997
$ echo MyName
MyName
$
```

NOTE

Some commands such as echo are part of the particular shell you are using. These are called built-ins. In this case, the commands are not standard from one shell to another. Therefore, if you learn one shell and then later have to (or want to) switch to using a different shell, you may have to learn new commands (and unlearn others). Other commands are standard UNIX commands and do not depend on what shell you are using. These should be on every UNIX system. The remaining commands are nonstandard UNIX and may or may not be on a particular UNIX system.

UNIX commands use a special type of argument called an option. An option commonly takes the form of a dash (made by using the minus sign key) followed by one or more characters. The options provide information to the command. Most of the time, options are just a single character following a dash. Two of the other lesser-used forms are a plus sign rather than a minus sign, and a word following a dash rather than a single character. The following paragraph shows a common command with two of its common options. The ls command lists the files in your current directory.

First, try the ls command with no arguments. Then, try it with the -a option and note that the directory listing contains a few files that start with a period. These hidden files get listed by the ls command only if you use the -a option. Next, try the ls command with the -l option. This option changes the format of the directory listing so that each file is displayed along with some relevant details. Finally, try the ls command with both of these options, so that your command is as follows: ls -a -l.

```
$ ls
visible
$ ls -a
.            ..            .hidden   visible
$ ls -l
total 0
-rw-rw-rw-   1 sartin    uu              0 Mar   5 12:58 visible
$ ls -a -l
total 16
drwxrwxrwx   2 sartin    uu           1024 Mar   5 13:03 .
drwxr-xr-x  37 sartin    uu           3072 Mar   5 13:03 ..
-rw-rw-rw-   1 sartin    uu              0 Mar   5 12:58 .hidden
-rw-rw-rw-   1 sartin    uu              0 Mar   5 12:58 visible
$
```

A command developer often tries to choose option letters that are meaningful. Regarding the ls command, you might think of the -a as meaning that "all" files should be listed (including the special files starting with period). And you might think of the -l option as meaning a "long" directory listing because the format is changed so that each line contains one file along with its details. This makes for a longer listing.

Redirecting Input and Output

One very pervasive concept in UNIX is the redirection of commands' input and output. Before looking at redirection, though, it is a good idea to look at input and output without modification. UNIX uses the word standard in this subject to mean the default or normal mode. Thus, UNIX has the term *standard input*, which means input coming from the default setting, and the term *standard output*, which means output going to the normal place. When you first log in to the system, and your shell executes, your standard input is set to be what you type at the keyboard, and your standard output is set to be your display screen. With this in mind, follow along with the example.

The cat command takes any characters from standard input, and then echoes them to standard output. For example, type the cat command, with no arguments. Your cursor should be sitting on the next line without a prompt. At this point, the cat command is waiting for you to enter characters. You can enter as many as you like, and then you should specify that you are finished. Type a few words and then press Return. Now type the special character, Control+D (hold down the Control key while typing the D key). This is the "eof" control character. (See "Working on the System," later in this chapter, for a description of control characters.) The words you typed should be on your screen twice—once caused by you entering them from the keyboard, and next as the cat command outputs them to your screen. This first step used standard input (from you typing on the keyboard), and standard output (the command results being printed on the screen).

```
$ cat
s
A few words
<CTRL><D>
A few words
```

Although this simple case may not seem terribly useful yet, wait to see its use as you add redirection.

UNIX shells have special characters that signify redirection. Only the basics are covered here. Refer to Part II for details on each shell's redirection syntax. Output redirection is signified by the > character and input redirection is signified by the < character. Output is commonly redirected to and input is redirected from a file. Now, continue with the rest of the example.

Next, try the cat command using output redirection, leaving standard input alone. Enter cat > *filename*. The filename is a name of your choice. Once again, the cat command should be waiting for input (coming from standard input, which is your keyboard) at the beginning of the next line. Enter a few words, as you did before, press Return, and then, at the start of the next line, press Control+D. The words you typed didn't show up on your screen because you redirected the output of the cat command. The output was directed to go to the file *filename*. But how do you know it is there? In order to verify this, use the cat command with input redirection—which is the next order of business.

```
$ cat > scotty
Meow, whine
meow
<CTRL><D>
```

CAUTION

<Ctrl><D> must be specified as the first character of an input line for it to be seen as "eof."

To see the contents of the file *filename*, you would like the input of the cat command to come from that file, and the output to go to the screen so that you can see it. Therefore, you want to redirect standard input and leave the output alone. Enter cat < *filename*. This time, the cat command did not wait for you—because you were not supplying the input. The file supplied the input. The cat command printed the contents of the file to the screen.

```
$ cat < scotty
Meow, whine
meow
```

> **TIP**
>
> Note the subtle distinction between these two commands: cat > *filename* and cat < *filename*. You can remember the difference by verbalizing which way the sign points; does it point into the command or out of the command? Into the command is input redirection and out of the command is output redirection.

The cat command allows you to specify a filename to use as input. Try showing the contents of the file this (more common) way: enter cat *filename*. Many commands are designed similarly—they have an argument that is used to specify a file as the input. Because of this common command design, redirecting input in this way is not nearly as common as redirecting the output.

```
$ cat scotty
Meow, whine
meow
$
```

UNIX was developed with the philosophy of having simple commands that do well-defined, simple things. Then, by combining these simple commands, the user could do very powerful things. Pipes are one of the ways UNIX allows users to combine several commands. The pipe is signified by the vertical bar (¦) symbol. A pipe is a means of taking the output of one command and redirecting it as the input of another command.

Say that you want to know how many files you have in your current directory. Recall that the ls command will list all the files in your current directory. You could then count the number of files. But UNIX has a command that counts the number of characters, words, and lines of input and displays these statistics. Therefore, you can combine these two commands to give you the number of files in your directory.

One way you could do this is as follows: ls -l ¦ wc -l. Analyzing this command, you can see that the first part is something familiar. The ls -l command gives a directory listing in long format. In fact, it prints one file per line. The wc -l command gives the number of lines that are in the input. Combining the two commands via a pipe takes the output of the first command (the long directory listing) and gives it to the input of the second command. The output of the second command (which is not redirected—it goes to standard output) is displayed on your screen.

These basic forms of redirection allow you to be very versatile as you learn a few commands at a time. Try to learn a command and use it with various options and arguments, then add redirection of input and output. And finally, combine commands with pipes. This approach should help you to feel comfortable with the commands and their varied uses.

Configuring Your Environment

In order to make using the shell easier and more flexible, UNIX uses the concept of an environment. Your environment is a set of values. You can change these values, add new values, or remove existing ones. These values are called environment variables—environment because they describe or define your environment, and variables because they can change.

Viewing and Setting Environment Variables

Every user's environment looks a little different. Why don't you see what your environment looks like? Type the env command with no arguments. The output formatting and variable names depend on which shell you are using and how your system is configured. A typical environment might include some of the following:

```
$ env
HOME=/u/sartin
LOGNAME=sartin
MAIL=/usr/mail/sartin
MANPATH=/usr/man:/usr/contrib/man:/usr/local/man
PATH=/bin/posix:/bin:/usr/bin:/usr/contrib/bin:/usr/local/bin
SHELL=/bin/sh
TERM=vt100
TZ=CST6CDT
```

Sometimes the number of variables in your environment grows quite large, so much so that you don't want to see all of the values displayed when you are interested in just one. If this is the case, you can use the echo command to show an environment variable's current value. To specify that a word you type should be treated differently—as a value of an environment variable—you immediately precede the variable name with a dollar sign ($). Be careful not to type any whitespace between the $ and the word. One of the variables in the example is HOME. You probably have this variable in your environment, too. Try to display its value using echo.

```
$ echo $HOME
/u/sartin
$
```

NOTE

If you use csh, some environment variables are automatically copied to and from csh variables. These include HOME, TERM, and PATH, which csh keeps in home, term, and path.

You can create a new environment variable by simply giving it a value. If you give an existing variable a value, the old value is overwritten. One difficulty in setting environment variables is that the way you set them depends on the shell you are using. To see how to set environment variables, look at the details about the shell you are using in Part II.

In order for your screen to display the output correctly, the environment variable TERM needs to have a reasonable value. This variable name comes from the times when terminals were used as displays (before PCs and graphics displays were common). Different terminals supported varying output control. Therefore, UNIX systems have various terminal types that they support. These are not standard, so you need to find out which terminal type to use from your support personnel. If you are using a PC to connect to a UNIX system, your PC is running a terminal emulation tool. Most of these tools have the capability to emulate several types of terminal. The important point here is to make sure that your emulator and your TERM variable are the same (or compatible). Start by seeing what your TERM variable is set to by entering echo $TERM. Refer to your PC terminal emulation manual and ask your system administrator for help to make sure that this is set up correctly.

TIP

Many terminal emulators (including the Microsoft Windows "Terminal" program) support either "VT100" or ANSI standard terminal control sequences. Try setting TERM to vt100 or ansi for this type of terminal emulator.

Using Shell Startup Files

Where do all these environment variables come from? Well, the system sets up various ones for you. And each user commonly sets up others during the login process. Yes, you may be doing this without even knowing it. During the startup, which happens at login, a shell is started. This shell automatically looks in a special place or two for some startup information. One of these places is in your home directory. The startup information in your home directory is found in special files. The specific shell you are using will determine the name of the particular file. When the shell starts up, it examines this file and performs whatever actions are specified. One of the common actions is to give values to environment variables. This action is called initializing or setting the values.

One environment variable that is commonly set in a user's shell startup file is the PATH variable (or lowercase path for C-shell users). This variable's value is a list of places (directories) on the system where the shell should look to locate a command. Each command you type is physically located as a file somewhere on your file system. It is possible for the same command name to be located in different places (and to have either the same or different behavior when executed). Say that you have a program called my_program that is stored in your home directory, and your friend has a program called my_program, which is in her home directory. If you type my_program at the prompt, the shell needs to know where to look to find the storage location of my_program. The shell looks at the value of the PATH variable and uses the list of directories as an ordered directory search list. The first directory that has a my_program stops the search, and the shell executes that file. Because all files within a single directory must be unique, this gives a straightforward and sufficient method for finding executables (commands).

You probably want $HOME/bin to be toward the beginning of your PATH directory list, whereas you may want your friend's binary directory to be toward the end, or not listed at all. This way, when you type my_program, you will execute your my_program rather than hers. You can do all types of things in shell startup files in addition to setting environment variable values. If you want, you can add an echo command that prints out a greeting or reminds you to do something. One common item that is configured inside a shell startup file is the setup of your control characters. (See "Working on the System," later in this chapter.) These startup files are a powerful tool for you, the user of the shell, to configure the behavior of the shell automatically. Shell startup files are covered in more detail in Part II.

> **TIP**
>
> It is a good idea to create a bin directory in your HOME and store executables there. Include $HOME/bin in your path.

Configuring with rc files

The idea of having a file that is read on startup is not only used by the shells. In fact, many commands have special files containing configuration information that the user can modify. The general class of files is called rc files. This comes from the naming convention of these files. Most of these files end with the letters rc. Some of the more common files are .exrc, .mailrc, and .cshrc. These are all dot files; that is, they begin with a period (dot). The significance of starting a filename with a dot is that this file is not displayed during normal directory listing. If you want to see these files, use the -a option to the ls command. The .exrc file is used by the vi and ex editors (see *UNIX Unleashed, Internet Edition*, Chapter 3, "Text Editing with vi and emacs"). The .mailrc file is used by various electronic mail tools (see Chapter 7, "Communicating with Others"). The .cshrc file is the C-shell startup file just discussed. The rc files are normally found in your home directory; that is, the default location for most of these files. Look at which rc files you have in your home directory (use the ls -a command). Then examine the contents of one of the files (use the cat *filename* command).

Your environment has a great effect on the use of your system. It is initialized during login with a shell startup file, and it grows and changes as you create new variables and change existing ones. Your environment affects every command you execute. It is important to get your environment set up to make your common actions easy. Spend the time to do this now and you will be glad you did later.

Managing Your Password

During login, UNIX asked you to enter your password. If this is your first time on this computer, your password was configured by the system administrator. One of the very first things you should do after logging in is change your password so that no one, not even the system administrator, knows what it is. You can do this via the `passwd` command. But before you do this, you should put some thought into what you want your password to be. Here are some points to consider:

1. It should be easy for you to remember. If you forget what your password is, no one, not even the system administrator, can look it up for you. The only thing the system administrator can do is to reset your password to a value. This wastes the administrator's time as well as yours.

2. It shouldn't be easy for anyone to figure out. Do not make it anyone's name or birth date, or your user name, or any of these spelled backwards. It is also wise to avoid something that appears in a dictionary. A good idea would be to include at least one nonalphabetic character (for example, a period or a dollar sign).

3. Make it a reasonable length. Some systems impose a minimum number of characters for a password. At least five characters is adequate. There isn't usually a limit as to the maximum number of characters, but only the first eight are significant. The ninth character and after are ignored when checking to see whether you typed your password correctly.

4. Change your password once in a while. Some systems check the last time you changed your password. If a time limit has been reached, you will be notified that your password has expired as you log in. You will be prompted to change it immediately and won't be allowed to log in until you successfully get it changed. This time limit is system imposed. Changing your password every few months is reasonable.

5. Don't write it down or tell it to anyone. Don't write it on scraps of paper. Don't tell your mother. Don't write it in your calendar. Don't write it in your diary. Don't tell your priest. Don't put it in a dialup terminal configuration file. Nowhere. Nobody. Maybe in your safe deposit box.

After you have thought about what you want your password to be, you can change it with the `passwd` command. Try it now; you can change your password as often as you like. Enter `passwd`. First, a prompt asking you to enter your old password is displayed. Type your old password and press Return. Next, you are prompted for your new password. Type it in and press Enter. Finally, you are prompted to re-enter your new password. This confirmation helps avoid changing your password if you made a typing error. If you make a mistake entering your old password, or if the two new password entries are not identical, then no change is made. Your old password is still in effect. Unless you make the same mistake both times that you enter the new password, you are in no danger of erroneously changing your password.

Working on the System

Most keys on the keyboard are fairly obvious. If you type the S key, an s character appears on your screen. If you hold down the Shift key and type the S key, a capital s character (S) appears on your screen. In addition to the letters and digits, the symbols, some of which are above the digits, are familiar—such as the percent sign (%) and the comma (,). There are some UNIX and system-specific special characters in addition to these, which you should become familiar with. They will help you manage your work and typing more effectively. The general type of character is called a control character. The name comes from the way in which you type them. First, locate the Control key—there should be one or maybe two on your keyboard. It may be labeled Ctrl or some other abbreviation of the word Control. This key is used like the Shift key. You press it but don't release it. While the Control key is depressed, you type another key, often a letter of the alphabet. If you type the Q key while the Control key is held, this is called Control+Q, and is commonly written ^Q (the caret symbol, which is found above the digit 6, followed by the alphabetic character).

NOTE

When you see the notation ^Q, this does *not* mean to hold the Control and Shift down while pressing Q. All you do is to hold down the Control key while pressing Q.

UNIX uses these control keys for various common keyboard actions. They can come in very handy. But the hard part is that different systems have different default Control key settings for these actions. Therefore, first you should find out what your current settings are, and then you can change them if you wish. In order to look at what your current settings are, use the stty command. Enter stty -a at your command prompt and look at the results. Refer to the next example for an output of this command.

TIP

If you're typing and nothing is showing on your screen, a ^S (or stop control character) inadvertently may have been typed. Try typing ^Q (or start control character) and see whether your typed characters now appear.

```
$ stty -a
speed 28800 baud; line = 0; susp <undef>; dsusp <undef>
rows = 44; columns = 120
intr = ^C; quit = ^\; erase = ^H; kill = ^X; swtch <undef>
eof = ^D; eol = ^@; min = 4; time = 0; stop = ^S; start = ^Q
-parenb -parodd cs8 -cstopb hupcl cread -clocal -loblk -crts
-ignbrk -brkint -ignpar -parmrk -inpck -istrip -inlcr -igncr icrnl -iuclc
ixon -ixany -ixoff -rtsxoff -ctsxon -ienqak
isig icanon iexten -xcase echo echoe echok -echonl -noflsh
opost -olcuc onlcr -ocrnl -onocr -onlret -ofill -ofdel -tostop tab3
$
```

Referring to the preceding example of stty output, look for the section that has the words erase, kill, and eof. Associated with each word is a control character. Find the similar part of your stty output. Keep this handy as you read the next topics.

Erase

Look at the word `erase` in the `stty` output. Next to this word is `^H` (verbalized as Control+H). Therefore, on my system, Erase, which means to back up over the last character typed, is done by typing ^H. The Erase key is how you can fix your typing errors. Remember to look at your `stty -a` output because your system may be configured differently than this example. Try it out on your system. First, type a character you wish to erase, say, an A. Now type your Control, Backspace, or Delete key associated with your Erase. If everything goes right, your cursor should have backed up to be on top of your A and the next key you type will be where the A was. Try typing a correct series of keys, say `date<Return>`, to make sure that the control character actually worked. If you get a message similar to "A^H date not found," then Erase is not working. To make it work correctly, pick the key you want associated with Erase and input the following (assuming that you have picked the backspace key):

```
$ stty erase '^H'
$
```

Now, try entering the date command again and deleting the A in dAte and replacing it with a.

> **NOTE**
>
> Depending on your display, erasing characters may not actually make the character disappear. Instead, it may reposition the cursor so that the next keystroke overwrites the character.

The Erase key is one of the most-used control keys, because typing without mistakes is difficult to do. Therefore, most keyboards have one or more special keys that are suited to this job. Look for keys labeled "Delete" or "Backspace." One of these usually works as an erase key. Try typing some characters and seeing what happens when you then press Backspace or Delete. Normally the Backspace key is set up to be ^H, so, if your erase is configured to be ^H, Backspace most likely will work.

Kill

The Kill control character is similar to the Erase control character, in that it allows you to back up over typing mistakes. Whereas Erase backs up one character at a time, Kill backs up all the way to the prompt. Therefore, if you are typing a really long command and you realize, toward the end, that you forgot to do some other command first, you can start over by typing the control character associated with Kill. If you can't see what your Kill is set to, redo the `stty` command. In the `stty` output example, the system has Kill set to ^X. Again, remember that your system can be configured differently than this example. Now, try typing several characters followed by your Kill control character and see what happens. All the characters should be erased and your cursor should be after the prompt.

Stop and Start

Two other commonly used control characters are Stop and Start. Their normal values are ^S and ^Q, respectively. Stop allows you to temporarily pause what is happening on your screen, and Start allows you to resume activity following a stop. This is useful if text is scrolling on your screen too fast for you to read. The Stop control character will pause the scrolling indefinitely so that you can read at your leisure. You might try this during your next login while the Message of the Day is scrolling by (see the section earlier in this chapter called "Logging In"). But remember to be prepared and be swift, because that text can scroll by quite quickly. Try to stop the scrolling, and then don't forget to continue the scrolling by typing your Start control character.

2

GETTING STARTED:
BASIC TUTORIAL

> **NOTE**
>
> On modern GUIs and high-speed connections, Stop and Start give very poor control of output. This is because the output is so fast an entire screen may go by before you type the Stop character.

eof

The eof control character is used to signal the end of input. The letters eof come from end of file. The normal value of the eof control character is ^D, but be sure to verify this using the stty command. You can see how the eof character is used in the section called "Redirecting Input and Output," earlier in this chapter.

There are several other control characters that we will not look at here. You should refer to the stty command in your system documentation for information. Or better yet, keep reading because we will show you how to find information about commands via the UNIX online help facility.

The stty command is also used to set the value of control characters. You can simply enter stty erase '^H' to change your Erase character to Backspace. Do not enter a Control+H here; rather, enter '^H'. Some shells, including the original Bourne shell, treat the caret specially, so you may need the quotes. (Double quotation marks would also work in this example.) Try changing the value of your Erase control character and then use the stty -a command to make sure it happened.

> **TIP**
>
> Remember that typing the end-of-file character to your shell might log you out of the system!

Online Help

One of the most important things to know about UNIX or any computer system is how to get help when you don't know how to use a command. Many commands will give you a usage message if you incorrectly enter the command. This message shows you the correct syntax for the command. This can be a quick reminder of the arguments and their order. For many commands, you can get the usage message by using the option -?. The usage message often does not give you any semantic information.

The UNIX command man is a powerful tool that gives you complete online access to the UNIX manuals. In its simplest form, the man command takes one argument, the name of the command or manual entry on which you need information. Try using the man command now—perhaps you could use one of the previous commands you were interested in as the argument. Or, if you want to get a head start on this section, you might try entering man man to get information on the man help facility itself.

The manual entry is called a man page, even though it is often more than one page long. There are common sections to man pages. Depending on the command, some or all of the sections may be present. At the start of the man page is the Name. This is usually a one-liner that gives the command's name along with a phrase describing what it does. Next is the Synopsis, which gives the command's syntax including its arguments and options. In the Synopsis, if an argument is enclosed in square brackets ([ ]), then that argument is optional. If two elements of the syntax are separated with a vertical bar (¦), then either one or the other (but not both) of the items is allowed.

```
$ man page
```

Depending on the man page, there are several more sections that you may see. A few of the more common are Description, Files, and See Also. The Description section contains the details of the command's usage. It describes each option, argument, and the interrelations and accepted values of each. This will help you to learn exactly how the command should be used. The Files section contains a list of the UNIX files used by this command. You may want to look at the contents of these files to help you understand some of the command's behaviors. The See Also section can be very important when you either want to learn more on a similar topic or don't have quite the right man page. This section lists pointers to related or dependent commands.

The man command has a very useful option, especially for users who are unfamiliar with UNIX. This option is -k and is used to find all commands that have to do with a word you supply following the -k. For instance, if you would like to find out information on printing, you might enter the command man -k print. The man command then searches a special database, called the whatis database, for commands and descriptions that contain the word print. During the search, if print or any word that contains print (such as printing) is found, this command is displayed on your screen. Therefore, the final result is a list of all commands having to do with print. Then you can use the man command to find out the details about any or all of the commands on this list. On some systems, another way to do this search is via the command apropos, which is equivalent to man -k.

Although having the complete set of manual entries online is extremely useful, it also takes a fairly large amount of disk space. One option that some people use to help lower the amount of disk space needed is to have the manual entries stored on one machine that everyone can access via the network. Because of this, the manual entries may not be stored in the directories expected. In order to show the man command where the entries are stored, you can set the MANPATH variable (see the section "Viewing and Setting Environment Variables" that appeared earlier in this chapter).

Another potential problem you might see when trying to use man has to do with the -k option. Recall that the -k option searches the whatis database for a keyword you specify. This works only if the system administrator has created this database ahead of time. The system administrator does this via the catman command. If the database has not yet been created, you will see an error regarding the whatis database not being found whenever you use the -k option (or the apropos command). Ask your system administrator to fix this.

Summary

The start of this chapter helped you prepare for what needs to happen before and during login. The section "Configuring Your Environment" looked at your environment and how you can configure it. Look at the manual entry for the shell you're using to find out more about environments. Also read Part II, "UNIX Shells," for shell details. The section on "Managing Your Password" discussed how managing your password via the passwd command is important for security reasons. Look at the manual entry for passwd if you need more information. The "Working on the System" section helped make your typing easier through the use of control characters. The stty man page is a good place to look for more information on control characters. The section on online help is probably the most important section of this chapter; by describing the man command, it showed you how to access the UNIX manual online. Using this, you can look up anything you want or need. The commands that you saw in the "Using Commands" section are in the online manual. Use the man command and learn more about them. With this as a start, you should be comfortable with the basics.

Additional UNIX Resources

by Fred Trimble

IN THIS CHAPTER

CHAPTER 3

There is an abundance of information available to help you learn about all of the UNIX variants. In fact, the two volumes of *UNIX Unleashed, System Administrator's Edition* (this book) and *Internet Edition*, contain a wealth of information on many varieties of UNIX. Aside from these two books, one of the best ways to find information is to do a simple keyword search on the Internet using your favorite browser. Doing so usually yields a lot of hits, given the popularity of UNIX on the World Wide Web. Also, ask your system administrator if she knows of any good reference material. She can probably recommend a good publication or user group for your flavor of UNIX.

This chapter discusses several different resources to help you learn UNIX. The first source of information to be discussed is the documentation that comes with UNIX systems: the online manual pages. There is a lot more information to help you learn UNIX besides the "man" pages. Because the UNIX operating system has had a profound impact on the development of the Internet, many Internet and Web sites exist that provide information on many facets of UNIX. In addition to identifying some important Web sites, this chapter identifies some key newsgroups, user groups, and publications to help you become a UNIX guru!

UNIX Manual Pages

Each UNIX system comes with a set of printed documentation. Most UNIX system administrators configure their systems to make this information available to their users. This documentation is often referred to as "man pages," because it is accessed with the man command. The man command is discussed later in this section. If the manual pages are not available on your system, see your system administrator.

Manual Page Organization

The manual pages are divided into eight sections. They are organized as follows:

1. Commands   This section provides information about user-level commands, such as ps and ls.

2. UNIX System Calls   This section gives information about the library calls that interface with the UNIX operating system, such as open for opening a file, and exec for executing a program file. These are often accessed by C programmers.

3. Libraries   This section contains the library routines that come with the system. One library that comes with each system is the math library, containing such functions as fabs for absolute value. Like the system call section, this is relevant to programmers.

4. File Formats   This section contains information on the file formats of system files, such as init, group, and passwd. This is useful for system administrators.

5. File Formats   This section contains information on various system characteristics. For example, a manual page exists here to display the complete ASCII character set (ascii).

6. Games   This section usually contains directions for games that come with the system.

7. Device Drivers   This section contains information on UNIX device drivers, such `scsi` and `floppy`. These are usually pertinent to someone implementing a device driver, as well as the system administrator.

8. System Maintenance   This section contains information on commands that are useful for the system administrator, such as how to format a disk.

At first, knowing which section to search can seem bewildering. After a little practice, however, you should be able to identify the appropriate section. In fact, certain man page options allow you to span sections when conducting a search.

The Manual Page Command

The `man` command enables you to find information in the online manuals by specifying a keyword. You can use it to in the following ways:

■ List all entries whose one-line summary contains the keyword.

■ Display all one-line descriptions based on the specified keyword.

■ Display the complete manual page entry for the specified keyword.

■ Search only the specified section, as outlined above, for the specified keyword.

The simplest way to invoke the man command is to specify a keyword without any options. For example, if you want more information on the `finger` command, invoke the `man finger` command. On an HP system running the HP-UX version of UNIX, the output is displayed as shown in Figure 3.1.

Notice that the man page is divided into a number of sections, such as NAME, SYNOPSIS, and DESCRIPTION. Depending on the manual page, there are other sections, including DIAGNOSTICS, FILES, and SEE ALSO.

If you have a particular subject that you want to investigate in the online documentation but don't know where to start, try invoking the `man` command with the `-k` option. This searches all of the descriptions in all eight of the manual page sections, and returns all commands where there is a match. For example, suppose you want to find out information related to terminals, but you aren't sure which command you should specify. In this case, specify the command `man -k terminal`. The following is sent to your screen:

```
clear (1) - clear terminal screen
ctermid (3s) - generate file name for terminal
```

```
getty (8) - set terminal mode
gettytab (5) - terminal configuration database
lock (1) - reserve a terminal
lta (4) - Local Area Terminal (LAT) service driver
pty (4) - pseudo terminal driver
script (1) - make typescript of terminal session
```

FIGURE 3.1.

Output to `man finger` *command on an HP-UX machine.*

```
NAME
    finger-user information lookup program

SYNOPSIS
    finger [options] user_name...

DESCRIPTION
    By default, finger lists for each user_name on the system:

        +Login name,
        +Full given name,
        ...

OPTIONS
    finger recognizes the following options:

        -b          Suppress printing the user's home directory and shell.
        ...

WARNINGS
    Only the first line of the .project file is printed.

FILES
    /etc/utmp   who file

SEE ALSO   who(l)
```

You can then use the `man` command to find more information on a particular command.

Unfortunately, not all systems are configured to use this option. In order to use this feature, the command `/usr/lib/whatis` must be in place. If it is not in place, see your system administrator.

Finally, when you invoke the `man` command, the output is sent through what is known as a `pager`. This is a command that lets you view the text one page at a time. The default pager for most UNIX systems is the `more` command. You can, however, specify a different one by setting the `PAGER` environment variable. For example, setting it to `pg` allows you to use features of the `pg` command to go back to previous pages.

Web Sites

The World Wide Web has an abundance of sites with useful information on UNIX. This section presents a survey of some very helpful ones. This section provides their URL (Uniform Resource Locator) for access through a Web browser, along with a brief description of the kinds of information you'll find.

Book Lists

`http://www.amsoft.ru/unixbooks.html`

This site gives a bibliography of UNIX books. It also includes comments for some of the books. Most of the titles come from `misc.books.technical faq`.

`http://www.cis.upenn.edu/~lwl/unix_books.html`

This site provides a list of UNIX titles, along with a brief review of the book.

`http://wwwhost.cc.utexas.edu/cc/docs/unix20.html`

This site also contains a list of recommended UNIX titles, along with a discussion of the book contents. Its contents include books on introductory UNIX, text editing and processing, networking topics, advanced UNIX programming, and UNIX system administration.

Frequently Asked Questions (FAQ)

`http://www.cis.ohio-state.edu/hypertext/faq/usenet/unix-faq/faq/top.html`

This site contains the Usenet FAQ for questions in the `comp.unix.questions` and `comp.unix.shell` newsgroups. Due to its size, it is divided here into seven sections.

`gopher://manuel.brad.ac.uk/11/.faq/.unix`

This gopher site contains links to the FAQs for many UNIX-related topics, such as RCS, SCCS, shells, and UNIX variants.

Finally, many UNIX FAQs have been reproduced and appear at the end of the *Internet Edition*.

Tutorials

`http://www.tc.cornell.edu/Edu/Tutor`

This page contains a link called "UNIX Basics." It includes sections on basic UNIX concepts for beginners, as well as tutorials on `vi`, `emacs`, and `ftp`.

`http://www.cs.indiana.edu/eip/tutorial.html`

This site contains a tutorial for the `emacs` editor and the `elm` mail program, along with a brief overview of some UNIX commands.

`http://www.cco.caltech.edu/cco/refguide/unixtutorial.html`

This site contains an extensive tutorial on UNIX, including logging in, manual pages, file and directory structure, mail, and job control. It ends with a summary of useful UNIX file commands.

`http://www.eos.ncsu.edu/help/tutorials/brain_tutorials`

Here, you will find a wide variety of practical tutorials, covering vi, emacs, e-mail, ftp, tar, remote system access, network news reader, advanced UNIX commands, and more!

`http://www.cs.indiana.edu/usr/local/www`

From this page, check out the UNIX link. It contains links to scores of other UNIX-related Web pages. Here, you will find information on Usenet FAQs, UNIX shell FAQs, IBM AIX, HP-UX, UNIX for PCs, Sun Systems, X Window, Networking, Security, Linux, UNIX humor, and much more.

`http://www.physics.orst.edu/tutorial/unix`

This site provides an excellent interactive UNIX tutorial called "Coping With UNIX: An Interactive Survival Kit." It is sponsored by the Northwest Alliance for Computational Science and Engineering. The tutorial runs best on a Web browser that supports frames and is Java-enabled.

`http://www.towson.edu/~michele/GUIDES/dirstruc.html`

This page contains an overview of the UNIX directory structure.

`http://www.uwsg.indiana.edu/uhelp/tutorials/toc.html`

This page contains a list of UNIX tutorials that can be found on systems at Indiana University, and on outside systems as well. This page contains five links: beginning tutorials, intermediate tutorials, advanced topics and tutorials, quick references, and other references. Each link contains a number of UNIX references.

`gopher://hp.k12.ar.us/11/classes/unixbasics`

This gopher site contains five introductory UNIX lessons. Each lesson can be downloaded to your system.

`http://goophy.physics.orst.edu/~maestri/work/book.html`

This tutorial is named "Coping With UNIX, A Survival Guide." It covers UNIX basics with a sense of humor.

`http://wsspinfo.cern.ch/file/doc/unixguide/unixguide.html`

This UNIX tutorial is very extensive, containing information about many UNIX commands and utilities. It also contains information about the Internet and the World Wide Web.

`http://albrecht.ecn.purdue.edu/~taylor/4ltrwrd/html/unixman.html`

This tutorial, entitled "UNIX is a Four Letter Word, and vi is a Two Letter Abbreviation," contains a humorous look at some basic UNIX commands and the vi editor.

```
http://www.cs.curtin.edu.au/units/cg252-502/src/notes/html/contents.shtml
```

This tutorial contains an outline of X Window programming concepts.

```
http://www.uwsg.indiana.edu/usail/
```

This tutorial is entitled USAIL, which stands for UNIX System Administration Independent Learning. It is designed to be an independent study course for prospective UNIX system administrators. It contains information on typical system administrator tasks, including installation, network administration, maintaining mail, backup and restore, and system performance. It contains a self-evaluating quiz.

```
http://www.bsd.org/unixcmds.html
```

This page contains a summary of UNIX commands.

```
http://www.indiana.edu/~ucspubs/b017
```

This site also contains a summary of UNIX commands.

```
http://www.bsd.org
```

This site contains many interesting links, including FAQ lists for most popular UNIX vendors, a DOS-to-UNIX command information sheet, and a number of links to other interesting sites.

```
http://www.nda.com/~jblaine/vault
```

This site, named "Jeff's UNIXVault." contains a great number of links to interesting UNIX sites. Topics include "unices" (links to sites that focus on different flavors of UNIX), windowing systems on UNIX, shells, security, shell scripting, organizations, publications, UNIX and PCs, and UNIX newsgroups.

```
http://www.perl.com
```

As the name implies, this site contains a link to "The Perl Language Home Page." It gives information on how to download the latest version of Perl, as well as documentation, a Perl FAQ, and Perl bug reports. It also contains links to other Perl sites, Perl mailing lists, Perl security information, and "The Perl Journal," a newsletter dedicated to Perl.

```
http://wagner.princeton.edu/foldoc
```

While working with UNIX, you are likely to come across terms that you haven't seen before. This site provides a free online dictionary of computing that will help you discover the meaning of such terms. It even provides a search mechanism for ease of use.

```
http://rossi.astro.nwu.edu/lentz/misc/unix/home-unix.html
```

This site contains a number of links to other interesting sites. It contains links to sites that cover networking issues, UNIX organizations, and various UNIX utilities, such as Perl, Tcl/Tk, Python, elm, and pine.

```
http://alabanza.com/kabacoff/Inter-Links/guides.html
```

Here, you will find many links to Internet guides. The site also contains a couple of UNIX-specific links.

```
http://www.python.org
```

Python is a portable, interpreted, object-oriented language which runs on many UNIX systems. This site contains a wealth of information, including links to other relevant sites.

```
http://athos.rutgers.edu/~patra/unix.html
```

This site contains many links to a wide variety of sites, including UNIX FAQ, UNIX security, Perl, UNIX system administration, and C and C++ programming.

```
http://www.intersource.com/faqs/unix.html
```

Here, you will find a nice description of many UNIX and Internet commands.

FTP Sites

```
ftp://ftp.gnu.ai.mit.edu
```

This site contains all of the programs available from the GNU Software Foundation.

```
ftp://ftp.x.org
```

This site contains a great deal of X Window software.

```
ftp://src.doc.ic.ac.uk/computing/systems/unix
```

Here, you will find many UNIX utilities for programmers and system administrators alike.

Newsgroups

The UNIX operating system has played a major role in the development of the Internet and the World Wide Web. Consequently, there are a number of newsgroups dedicated to various aspects of UNIX. For more information on how to participate in a newsgroup on the Internet, see Chapter 7, "Communicating with Others." Here is a listing of various UNIX discussion groups, in alphabetical order:

`cern.security.unix`	This newsgroup holds discussions on UNIX security at CERN. CERN is the European Particle Physics Laboratory, and is where the World Wide Web originated.
`comp.lang.c`	Discussion about the C programming language.
`comp.lang.perl`	Discussion of the Perl programming language.
`comp.os.linux.advocacy`	These groups discuss the benefits of Linux, compared to other operating systems.
`comp.os.linux.answers`	This is a moderated discussion group that includes FAQs on Linux.

`comp.os.linux.hardware`	This group discusses hardware compatibility and Linux.
`comp.os.linux.misc`	General information about Linux that is not covered in the other group.
`comp.os.linux.setup`	Linux installation and system administration.
`comp.security.unix`	Discussion of UNIX security.
`comp.sources.unix`	This contains postings of complete UNIX-oriented source code (moderated).
`comp.std.unix`	Discussion for the P1003 UNIX committee (moderated).
`comp.unix.admin`	This newsgroup discusses any topic related to UNIX system administration.
`comp.unix.aix`	This group is dedicated to discussions of IBM's flavor of UNIX (AIX).
`comp.unix.amiga`	Discussion of UNIX on the Commodore Amiga.
`comp.unix.aux`	Discussion of UNIX on the Apple Macintosh II computer.
`comp.unix.internals`	Discussions on UNIX internals.
`comp.unix.large`	UNIX on mainframes and on large networks.
`comp.unix.misc`	UNIX topics that seem to fit other groups.
`comp.unix.programmer`	This is a question and answer forum for people who program in a UNIX environment.
`comp.unix.questions`	This group is appropriate for newcomers to UNIX, with general questions about UNIX commands and system administration. It is one of the most widely used newsgroups on the Internet.
`comp.unix.shell`	This group discusses using and programming shells, including the Bourne shell (sh), Bourne again shell (bash), C Shell (csh), Korn shell (ksh), and restricted shell (rsh).
`comp.unix.solaris`	Discussion of Sun's Solaris variant of UNIX.
`comp.unix.sys5.r4`	Discusses UNIX System V Release 4.
`comp.unix:ultrix`	This group is dedicated to discussions of DEC's flavor of UNIX (ultrix).
`comp.unix.unixware`	Discussion about Novell's UnixWare products.
`comp.unix.user-friendly`	Discussion of UNIX user-friendliness.
`comp.unix.xenix.misc`	This group discusses general questions about Xenix, not including SCO.

3

ADDITIONAL
UNIX RESOURCES

`comp.unix.xenix.sco`	This group discusses Xenix from SCO (Santa Cruz Operation).
`comp.unix.wizards`	This is a moderated discussion group for advanced UNIX topics.
`comp.windows.x`	This is a discussion group for the X Window system.
`info.unix-sw`	UNIX software that is available via anonymous ftp.

UNIX User Groups

Joining a UNIX user group can be a great way to learn about UNIX. Many groups sponsor meetings, which often include a guest speaker as well as a forum to share ideas and experiences. There are literally hundreds of UNIX user groups in existence worldwide, so to list them here would not be practical. However, an excellent listing of UNIX user groups can be found by visiting `http://www.sluug.org/~newton/othr_uug.html`.

Professional Associations

There are many professional associations that are dedicated to the discussion and advancement of UNIX and Open Systems. This section gives information about some of the larger groups.

The Electronic Frontier Foundation

The Electronic Frontier Foundation (EFF) is a nonprofit organization dedicated to privacy and free expression, including social responsibility, for online media. For anyone interested in encryption, the Internet, and legal issues, this site is a must.

For more information, including membership, contact them at `http://www.eff.org`, or at the following:

> The Electronic Frontier Foundation
> 1550 Bryant Street, Suite 725
> San Francisco CA 94103-4832 USA
> Phone: (415) 436-9333
> Fax: (415) 436-9993
> E-mail: `ask@eff.org`

The Open Group

The Open Group, consisting of X/Open and the OSF (Open Software Foundation), is an international consortium of vendors and end users from many disciplines, including industry, government, and academia. It is dedicated to the advancement of multivendor information systems. The group is actively involved in creating UNIX standards that incorporate widely accepted practices. For more information about The Open Group, including membership information, see their Web site at `http://www.osf.org`.

USENIX

USENIX is the advanced computing system's technical and professional association. Since 1975, USENIX has supported the presentation and discussion of advanced developments in all aspects of computing. Each year, the association sponsors a number of conferences, symposia, and workshops covering a wide variety of topics. Their conferences are usually well attended, and are aimed at the UNIX developer and researcher. USENIX also has a number of programs for colleges and universities, including student research grants, undergraduate software projects, scholarship programs, and student stipends so that students can attend USENIX events. They also provide a discount to the yearly dues for students.

USENIX also sponsors a technical group called SAGE (System Administrator's Guild). SAGE is an organization dedicated to the system administration profession. They publish a number of excellent booklets and pamphlets with practical information on system administration. They also publish a bi-monthly newsletter with useful tips for system administrators.

For more information, you can contact USENIX at `http://www.usenix.org`. In addition to membership information, you will find a number of useful articles from their publication, ";`login:`," as well as papers published at previous conferences.

You can also contact USENIX with the following information:

> The USENIX Association
> 2560 Ninth Street, Suite 215
> Berkeley, CA 94710 USA
> Phone: (510) 528-8649
> Fax: (510) 548-5738
> E-mail: `office@usenix.org`

UniForum

UniForum is a professional association aimed at promoting the benefits and practices of open systems. Its members come from a wide variety of backgrounds, including engineers, developers, system administrators, system integrators, MIS directors, and CIOs. One of their stated goals is to provide a vendor-neutral approach to the evaluation and development of open systems. Each year, they sponsor a number a high-quality conferences and seminars. They also provide a number of technical publications that help you to understand open systems technologies. For example, you can access their online newsletter, "UniNews Online," through their Web site (`http:/www.uniforum.org`). They have a number of excellent technical articles on their Web site as well. Perhaps their most popular publication is the Open Systems Products Directory. It contains a description of thousands of open systems products and services, and is free of charge to members.

For more information about UniForum, including how to become a member, contact them at `http://www.uniforum.com`, or at the following address or phone numbers:

> UniForum Association
> 10440 Shaker Drive, Suite 203
> Columbia, MD 21046
> (410) 715-9500
> (800) 255-5620 (U.S. Only)

The X Consortium

This group was recently incorporated into The Open Group. It is dedicated to the X Window desktop environment and its role in the UNIX environment. It is a nonprofit organization for developing user interface standards and graphics technology in an open systems environment. For more information, including membership, visit their Web site at `http://www.x.org`.

Publications

Several useful UNIX-related publications are available. Some are available free of charge for qualified individuals.

UNIX Review

UNIX Review is a monthly magazine that covers the latest in UNIX technologies. It contains useful information for both UNIX developers and administrators. The magazine covers many aspects of UNIX-based systems, including software, hardware, peripherals, and support services. You can subscribe to *UNIX Review* by filling out an online qualification form at their Web site (`http://www.unixreview.com`). In fact, you may qualify for a free subscription.

UNIX World

UNIX World is a subscription-free Web-based magazine. It provides practical tutorials on a wide variety of subjects. It contains a handy online search facility for searching for articles in their archives. You can find *UNIX World* at `http://www.unixworld.com/uworld`.

Sys Admin

Sys Admin magazine focuses on UNIX system administration. It provides in-depth coverage of multiple versions of UNIX on a variety of platforms. It covers a number of topics, including system monitoring, system security, backup and recovery, crash recovery, shell scripting, and X Window. You can subscribe to *Sys Admin* by filling out the subscription form on their Web page at `http://www.samag.com`.

Sun World

This is an online magazine with a focus on Sun products and services. Each month, it contains many practical articles for users and system administrators alike, such as the column "UNIX 101." It also provides a means to search for back issues by keyword. You can access the magazine at `http://www.sun.com/sunworldonline/index.html`.

SunExpert

This is another magazine dedicated to the Solaris flavor of UNIX. Monthly columns include "Ask Mr. Protocol," "UNIX Basics," and "System Administration." It recently merged with another UNIX publication entitled *RS/magazine*. It is free of charge to qualified readers. For subscription information, visit `http://www.netline.com/sunex/sunex.main.html`.

Summary

This section has presented a number of additional resources for learning UNIX. The manual pages are a good place to start; they usually contain a description of each command and service on the system. Given the popularity of UNIX, a number of other resources are available to help you become a UNIX expert. The Internet contains a great deal of information, including tutorials, newsgroups, UNIX FAQ lists, and online publications. There are also a number of user groups and organizations dedicated to the pursuit and sharing of knowledge.

3

ADDITIONAL UNIX RESOURCES

The UNIX File System

by Sanjiv Guha

IN THIS CHAPTER

CHAPTER 4

In the UNIX operating system, a file is a repository of raw or processed data stored as a stream of bytes (also known as characters). In UNIX, the data is encoded using ASCII, although systems such as IBM 3090 mainframe store a file's data in EBCDIC. The ASCII and EBCDIC codes are different from each other; that is, the same code means different things and the same character is denoted by different code in these two coding schemes. On different operating systems, the data is stored differently, which might cause problems if you are trying to process files created on a different operating system. You will need special programs to convert the data in the files created in one operating system to suit the needs of another.

Files contain different types of information. For example, a file can contain source code for a program in C or COBOL or C++, be a text document containing mail from a friend, or contain executable code for a program. These are some of the native file types supported by UNIX; that is, you can view or copy these types of files using UNIX commands. However, some files can't be processed by native UNIX commands. For example, a file containing data for a third-party database such as Oracle will need special programs to be processed, viewed, and so on.

A file can reside on different media. A file can also be a permanent file on disk, a temporary file in the memory, or a file displaying or accepting data from the terminal. If the file is a permanent file, you might be able to view it—but if the file is temporary, you might not know it exists.

The functions usually performed on a file are as follows:

- Opening a file for processing
- Reading data from a file for processing
- Writing data to a file after processing
- Closing a file after all the necessary processing has been done

Now that you have an idea about what a file is and what it contains, it's time to learn more about different types of files you will encounter.

File Types

This section discusses the various file types available in UNIX. You might be familiar with some of these types of files, such as text documents and source files.

Regular Files

Regular files are the ones with which you are probably most familiar. They are permanent in nature and contain data such as source code for a program, mail received from the boss, and a letter that you are writing to a friend. These files almost always contain text information. In these files, the data is organized into *records*. If, for example, this book were a file containing data about UNIX operating systems, each line in this book would be called a record.

How does UNIX know about these records? The answer is that there is a special character, called a *newline character*, which is used by UNIX to find out where one record ends and the next one starts. As you will see later, most of the UNIX commands support text processing. However, keep in mind that text files are not the only type of regular files. Some files have a stream of bytes without any newline characters. Although UNIX is built to process text documents, the data in these files cannot be processed by UNIX.

The following are examples of some of the regular files:

- `prog.c` is a file containing a C source program.
- `prog.cbl` is a file containing a COBOL source program.
- `prog.exe` is a file containing executable code for a program.
- `invite.doc` is a file containing an invitation to a party from a co-worker.

NOTE

The examples provided here follow the usual UNIX file naming conventions. However, these are just conventions, not rules. So, it is possible for someone to name a file `prog.c`, even though it contains a letter to her boss.

Here is an example of the list of attributes a file has. The file is called `testfile`, and the attributes are obtained by using the following command:

```
ls -al testfile
```

The result is

```
rwxr-xr-x   2 guhas    staff      1012 Oct 30 18:39 testfile
```

UNIX keeps track of the file attributes using a data-structure called *i-node*. Each i-node in the system is identified by a number called the *i-node number*. Each file in the system has an associated i-node that contains information such as the following:

- Ownership details of a file
- Permission details of a file
- Timestamps of a file (date and time of creation, data and time of modification, and so on)
- Type of the file

A number of timestamps are associated with a file. These times are

- Last access time
- Last modification time
- Last i-node modification time

4

THE UNIX FILE SYSTEM

The last access time changes whenever you perform any operation on a file. The last modification date changes when the contents of the file are modified. The last i-node modification time is when any of the information stored in the i-node changes.

> **NOTE**
>
> Some UNIX versions, for instance, AIX, do not modify the last access time when you execute them.

Directory Files

A *directory file* is a special file that contains information about the various files stored in the directory, such as file locations, file sizes, times of file creation, and file modifications. This special file can be read only by the UNIX operating system or programs expressly written to do directory processing. You may not view the content of the directory file, but you may use UNIX commands to inquire about these attributes of the directory. A file directory is like a telephone directory that contains address information about the files in it. When you ask UNIX to process a filename, UNIX looks up the specified directory to obtain information about the file. In each directory, you will always find two files:

1. . (single period)
2. .. (two consecutive periods)

The single period (.) refers to the current directory, and the two consecutive periods (..) refer to the directory one level up (sometimes referred to as parent directory).

An example of the directory attributes of a `testdir` are presented here:

```
drwxr-xr-x   2 guhas     writer      512 Oct 30 18:39 testdir
```

`rwxr-xr-x` defines the permissions of `testdir` created by a user called `guhas` belonging to a group called `writer`. The size of the directory entry `testdir` is 512 bytes. The directory was last modified on October 30 at 6:39 p.m.

A directory is treated as a file by UNIX, but it has some special characteristics. A directory has at least two names. For example, if the current directory were `/u/guhas` and you created a subdirectory called `testdir`, two links would be created:

- `/u/guhas/testdir`
- `/u/guhas/testdir/.`

The entry `/u/guhas/testdir` is created in the directory `/u/guhas`, and the entry `/u/guhas/testdir/.` is created in the directory `/u/guhas/testdir`.

First, the entry /u/guhas/testdir is created as an empty directory and then is linked to /u/guhas/testdir/. (single period). Both these links exist during the life of the directory and are deleted when you delete the directory.

Character and Block Device Files

The character special files are used for unbuffered I/O to and from a device, and the block special files are used when data is transferred in fixed-size packets. The character special files do I/O on one character at a time mode while the block special file use buffer chaching mechanism to increase the efficiency of data transfer by keeping in-memory copy of the data. Some examples of these files are

- Floppy disk device—character or block special file
- Tape device—character special file
- Terminal—character special file

UNIX treats the keyboard and the monitor (terminal) as files. The keyboard is considered an input file, also referred to as a *standard input file* (*stdin* in UNIX terminology). The terminal is considered an output file, also referred to as the *standard output file* (*stdout* in UNIX terminology).

An important corollary of the standard input and output is referred to as *I/O redirection*. In UNIX, using I/O redirection makes it possible to change the standard input file from keyboard to a regular file, and change the standard output file from terminal to a new or existing regular file.

All UNIX commands, by default, accept input from standard input, display output on standard output, and send error messages to standard error output. By using I/O redirection, it is possible to control the source and destination of the command input and output, respectively. It is possible to direct the output of a command to a different file than the standard output. Similarly, it is possible to accept the input from a file rather than standard input. It is also possible to direct error messages to a file rather than the standard output. This gives you the flexibility to run commands in background, where these special files, that is, standard input, standard output, and standard error output, are not available. You can use regular files to redirect these input, output, or error messages when you are running commands in the background.

Another interesting special file is the *bit bucket*. This is defined as the file /dev/null. If you redirect the output of a command to /dev/null, the output is not produced at all. Suppose you wanted to run a command and were interested only in finding out whether the command execution generated errors. You would redirect the standard output to /dev/null. When you do so, the output will not be produced for the command.

Sockets

A socket is an application programming interface (API), which is used to communicate between two host computers. In other words, the socket performs network I/O. The abstraction of socket has been designed similar to files, but a socket is not a real file. To use a socket in a program, create a socket and configure it with the required addresses of the local and remote hosts. After the socket is connected, the program can use the socket to communicate with the remote hosts. However, there are ways to communicate between hosts using connectionless sockets. A connected socket transfers data between two points between which connection has been established. In the case of a connectionless socket for each transfer the destination address has to be specified; that is, transfer is not limited between two points. A connectionless socket can be used to communicate between any two computers in a network.

A network program communication has typically two parts: a client and server. Client programs usually actively seek to connect to the server; server programs passively listen for incoming requests from clients. UNIX I/O does not have passive capabilities. So, the sockets, although similar to files, are not exactly identical to files. Sockets have extra system functions to handle capabilities needed by servers, such as passively listening and waiting for client requests.

The files with which most people are familiar reside on hard disks and have fixed addresses. Although an address may be modified by moving the file to a new location, this does not happen during operations on the file. This concept is suited for fixed-connection network communications. However, computers might need to communicate without fixed addresses, using connectionless communication. For connectionless communication, the UNIX concept of a file does not work because the point-to-point connection is not achieved. For this purpose, sockets have a number of special APIs.

Let us see how a connectionless communication is achieved. The program specifies the destination address to which the data has to be delivered. However, the program does not actually deliver this data; instead, it passes the data to the network to do the actual delivery.

The following is a list of socket API functions to transmit data:

- `send`: Transmits data through a connected socket
- `write`: Transmits data through a connected socket using a simple data buffer
- `writev`: Transmits data through a connected socket (using noncontiguous memory locations)
- `sendto`: Transmits data through an unconnected socket
- `sendmsg`: Transmits data through an unconnected socket using a special data structure

The following is a list of functions used for receiving data using a socket:

- `recv`: Reads data through a connected socket
- `read`: Reads data through a connected socket using simple buffer

- ■ `readv`: Reads data through a connected socket (using noncontiguous memory locations)
- ■ `recvfrom`: Reads data through an unconnected socket
- ■ `recvmsg`: Reads data through an unconnected socket using a special data structure

A socket has a number of arguments associated with it. These arguments must be specified during socket creation. The first argument is the communication protocol family to be used to communicate. A number of protocols are available, of which Internet's TCP/IP is the most popular. While working with the protocol families, you should also know about the address families. Each network has a different format for the address of computers attached to it. The second argument is the type of the communication to be used. This data can be sent as a stream of bytes, as in a connection-oriented communication or as a series of independent packets (called datagrams), as in a connectionless communication. The last argument is the actual protocol to be used, which is part of the protocol family specified as the first argument.

Named Pipes

A *named pipe* is a file created to do interprocess communication. That is, it serves as a go-between for data between two programs. The sending process writes data to the named pipe, and the receiving process reads data from the named pipe. It is a temporary file that lasts as long as the processes are communicating. The data is processed in a FIFO (first-in, first-out) basis from the named pipe.

Symbolic and Hard Links

Links create pointers to the actual files, without duplicating the contents of the files. That is, a link is a way of providing another name to the same file. There are two types of links to a file:

- ■ Hard link
- ■ Symbolic (or soft) link; also referred to as *symlink*

With hard links, the original filename and the linked filename point to the same physical address and are absolutely identical. There are two important limitations of a hard link. A directory cannot have a hard link, and it cannot cross a file system. (A *file system* is a physical space within which a file must reside; a single file cannot span more than one file system, but a file system can have more than one file in it.) It is possible to delete the original filename without deleting the linked filename. Under such circumstances, the file is not deleted, but the directory entry of the original file is deleted and the link count is decremented by 1. The data blocks of the file are deleted when the link count becomes zero.

With symbolic or soft links, there are two files: One is the original file, and the other is the linked filename containing the name of the original file. An important limitation of the symbolic link is that you may remove the original file and it will cause the linked filename to be there, but without any data. However, a symbolic linked filename can cross file systems.

You should be careful about symbolic links. If you are not, you will be left with files that do not point anywhere because the original file has been deleted or renamed.

An important feature of the symbolic link is that it can be used to link directories as well as files.

If we have a file called `origfile` in the directory /u/guhas, whose characteristics are

```
-rw-r--r--   2 guhas    writer        30 Nov  8 01:14 origfile
```

a file called `hlinkfile`, which has been hard linked to `origfile`, will have the following characteristics:

```
-rw-r--r--   2 guhas    writer        30 Nov  8 01:20 hlinkfile
```

The 2 before guhas signifies that there are two files linked to the same physical address (`origfile` and `hlinkfile`).

A file called `slinkfile`, which has been soft linked to `origfile`, will have the following characteristics:

```
lrwxrwxrwx   1 guhas    writer         8 Nov  8 01:18 slinkfile -> origfile
```

The link is evident in the filename. In this case, if you delete `origfile`, `slinkfile` will be rendered useless.

Naming Files and Directories

Each file is identified by a name, which is a sequence of characters. The older versions of UNIX had limitations on the numbers of characters that could be used in a filename. All the newer versions of UNIX have removed this limitation. You should be careful when naming the files, though. Although UNIX allows most characters to be used as part of the filename, some of the characters have special meaning in UNIX and can pose some problems.

For example, the character > is used as an output redirection operator in UNIX. If you wanted to create a file named x>y, you would use the `touch` command:

```
touch x>y
```

You would then get two files: one named x and one named y.

To circumvent this problem, use a special character (\) (in Korn and C shell) and use the `touch` command, as follows:

```
touch x\>y
```

CAUTION

Using special characters such as asterisks (*) and dollar signs ($) as part of the filename doesn't work because the shell interprets these characters differently. The presence of these characters can trigger the shell to interpret the filename as a command and execute it.

The following is a list of characters that may be used as part of the UNIX filenames:

- A through Z or a through z
- Numerals 0 through 9
- Underscore (_)
- Period (.)

The underscore can separate words in a filename, thus making the filename easier to read. For example, instead of naming a file `mytestfile`, you could name it `my_test_file`.

A period may be used to append an extension to a filename in a way similar to DOS filenames. For example, a C language source file containing a program called `prog` may be named `prog.c`. However, in UNIX you are not limited to one extension. You should keep in mind that a period (.), when used as the first character in a filename, has a special meaning. The period as the first character gives the file a hidden status. For example, if you had the files x and .x in your current directory, issuing an `ls` command will show you only the file x. To list both the files, use `ls -a`.

CAUTION

UNIX is case-sensitive. For example, a file named abc is different from a file named ABC.

Some of the system files which begin with a . (period), also called hidden files, will not be displayed until special flags are used. For example, the `.profile` file.

4

THE UNIX FILE SYSTEM

Table 4.1 provides a list of characters or combination characters that should be avoided because they have special meanings. This list is not exhaustive and depends on the UNIX shell you are running.

Table 4.1. Meaning of some special characters.

Character	Meaning
$	Indicates the beginning of a shell variable name. For example, $var will look for a shell variable named var.
¦	Pipes standard output to next command.

continues

Table 4.1. continued

Character	Meaning
#	Start a comment.
&	Executes a process in the background.
?	Matches one character.
*	Matches one or more characters.
$#	Number of arguments passed to a shell script.
$*	Arguments passed to a shell script.
$?	Returns code from the previous executed command.
$$	Process identification number.
>	Output redirection operator.
<	Input redirection operator.
` (backquote)	Command substitution.
>>	Output redirection operator (to append to a file).
[ ]	Lists a range of characters. [a-z] means all characters a through z. [a,z] means characters a or z.
. *filename*	Executes the file *filename*
:	Directory name separator in the path.

File System Organization

This chapter has discussed different types of files and filenames. You have also learned about special directory files. In this section, you will learn about the ways UNIX provides for organizing files so that you can easily locate and use them.

UNIX has provided the directory as a way of organizing files. The directory is a special file under which you can have files or more directories (also referred to as subdirectories). You can visualize the UNIX file structure as a bottom-up tree with the root at the top. Thus, the top-level directory is called the *root directory* and is denoted by a single / (forward slash). All the directories and files belong to the root directory. You can also visualize the UNIX file system as a file cabinet in which the file cabinet is the root directory, the individual cabinets are various directories under the root directory, the file folders are the subdirectories, and the files in the individual folders are the files under the directories or subdirectories. Figure 4.1 shows a typical directory tree structure.

Table 4.2 provides you with a list of standard directory names in the UNIX file system. This list is not exhaustive. A complete list would depend on the UNIX system you are working with.

FIGURE 4.1.

A directory tree.

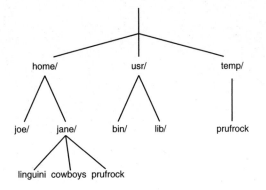

Table 4.2. List of standard UNIX directories.

Directory Name	Details About the Directory
/	Root directory. This is the parent of all the directories and files in the UNIX file system.
/bin	Command-line executable directory. This directory contains all the UNIX native command executables.
/dev	Device directory containing special files for character- and block-oriented devices such as printers and keyboards. A file called null existing in this directory is called the bit bucket and can be used to redirect output to nowhere.
/etc	System configuration files and executable directory. Most of the administrative, command-related files are stored here.
/lib	The library files for various programming languages such as C are stored in this directory.
/lost+found	This directory contains the in-process files if the system shuts down abnormally. The system uses this directory to recover these files. There is one lost+found directory in all disk partitions.
/u	Conventionally, all the user home directories are defined under this directory.
/usr	This directory has a number of subdirectories (such as adm, bin, etc, and include. For example, /usr/include has various header files for the C programming language.

Pathnames

In UNIX, the filename used by the operating system to uniquely identify the file has all the directory names start from the root directory as part of the filename. This allows you to use the same filename for different files present under a different directory. For example, if you kept mail received by month and day, you could create directories named january, february, march, and so on. Under each of these directories, you could create files such as day01, day02, and day03. The same holds true for directories. That is, you can have the same directory name under different directories.

This brings in the concept of current directory and relative pathnames. For example, if you were in the directory named january and you executed the command

```
ls -l day01
```

you would get the attributes of the file day01 under the january directory, which means that UNIX looked in the directory you were currently in to find out whether the file you specified was present or not. All the commands in UNIX use the current directory to resolve the filename if the filename does not have directory information. The relative pathname is always specified relative to the current directory you are in.

If you were in the directory january and wanted to get the attributes of file day01 in directory february, you would specify the absolute pathname of the file. That is, you would execute the command

```
ls -l /u/guhas/february/day01
```

UNIX uses the special characters .. (two consecutive periods) as a relative pathname to indicate the directory one level up or the parent directory. For example, if you were in the directory /u/guhas/january, .. (two consecutive periods) in the relative pathname would indicate the /u/guhas directory (which is the parent directory of /u/guhas/january) and ../.. in the relative pathname would indicate the /u directory.

Working with Directories

When working with UNIX, you will always be placed in a directory. The directory you are in will depend on what you are working on. The directory you are currently in is called the *current directory*. UNIX uses the current directory information to resolve the relative pathname of a file.

A forward slash (/) in the filename means that you are working with a file in another directory. If the filename starts with .. (two consecutive periods), you are using them (two consecutive periods) to get to a file using the relative pathname of the file. If there are no .. (two consecutive periods) in the filename, you are trying to get to a file using the absolute pathname of the file. An absolute pathname always starts with a forward slash (/).

When you log into a UNIX system, the directory you are placed in is known as the home directory. Each user in the system has his or her own home directory and, by convention, it is

/u/username. Korn shell and C shell use a special character tilde (~) as a shortcut to identify the home directory of a user. For example, if guhas is the user currently logged in, the following would hold true:

- ~ refers to the home directory of guhas.
- ~friend refers to the home directory of a user friend.

Listing Files and Directories with ls

You can use ls (with its various options) to list details about one or more files or directories on the system. Use ls to generate list of files and directories in different orders, such as order by name and order by time. It is possible to list only certain details about files and directories—for example, only the filename. You will learn more about the options of ls command in Chapter 5, "General Commands," but here are some examples that give insight into the details of a file or directory UNIX system stores. For example, executing the command in the current directory /u/guhas

```
ls -l
```

shows the following:

```
-rwxrwxrwx   1 guhas      staff        7161 May  8 15:35 example.c
drwxrwxrwx   3 guhas      staff        1536 Oct 19 00:54 exe
-rw-r--r--   2 guhas      staff          10 Nov  3 14:28 file1
-rw-r--r--   2 guhas      staff          10 Nov  3 14:28 file112
```

The details about a file include

- Permission attributes of the file
- Number of links
- User
- Group of the user who created the file
- Size of the file date and time when the file was last modified
- Name of the file

The previous example shows that the current directory has a directory called exe and three files—example.c, file1, and file2. For the directory exe, the number of links shown is three, which can be counted as one to the parent directory /u/guhas, one that is the directory entry exe itself, and one more that is to a sub-directory under exe. The number of links for the file example.c is one, because that file does not have any hard links. The number of links in files file1 and file2 are two, because they are linked using a hard link.

As mentioned, you should be careful about hidden files. You will not know they exist if you do not use the option -a for ls. In the previous example, if you use

```
ls -al
```

you will see two more entries, . (single period) and .. (two consecutive periods), which are the directory and the parent directory entries.

In the previous examples, the first character before the permissions (for example, d in drwxrwx ---) provides information about the type of the file. The file-type values are as follows:

- d: The entry is a directory.
- b: The entry is a block special file.
- c: The entry is a character special file.
- l: The entry is a symbolic link.
- p: The entry is a first-in, first-out (FIFO) special file.
- s: The entry is a local socket.
- -: The entry is an regular file.

Creating and Deleting Directories: `mkdir` and `rmdir`

When you are set up as a user in a UNIX operating system, you usually are set up with the directory /u/username as your home directory. You will need to organize your directory structure. As with the files, you can use relative or absolute pathnames to create a directory. If your current directory is /u/guhas,

```
mkdir temp
```

will create a sub-directory called temp under the directory temp whose absolute pathname is /u/ guhas/temp.

```
mkdir /u/guhas/temp
```

can also be used to have the same effect as the previous one.

```
mkdir ../temp
```

can be used to create the directory /u/temp. This example uses .. (two consecutive periods) as part of the relative pathname to indicate that the directory temp will be created under the directory one level up, which is /u. Using mkdir, it is possible to create more than one directory at a time. For example, from your current directory, issue the following command:

```
mkdir testdir1 /u/guhas/temp/testdir2
```

which will create testdir1 in the current directory and testdir2 under /u/guhas/temp (assuming it exists). In this example, testdir1 uses a relative pathname, and /u/guhas/temp/testdir2 uses an absolute pathname.

If the directory is already present, UNIX will display an error stating that the directory already exists.

To create a directory, you must have write permission to the parent directory in which you are creating the subdirectory, and the parent directory must exist. However, many UNIX systems provide an option -p with mkdir so that the parent directory is also created if it does not already exist.

After you are finished using a directory or you run out of space and want to remove a directory, you can use the command rmdir to remove the directory.

If your current directory is /u/guhas and directory temp is under it, to remove the directory temp, use the command

```
rmdir temp
```

When you execute this command, you might get an error message stating Directory temp is not empty, which means that you still have files and directories under temp directory. You can remove a directory only if it is empty (all the files and directories under it have been removed). As with mkdir, it is possible to specify multiple directory names as part of the rmdir command. You cannot delete files using the rmdir command. For deleting files you will need to use the rm command instead.

Using the find Command

If you are working on multiple projects at the same time, it might not be possible for you to remember all the details about the various files you work with. The find command comes to your rescue. The basic function of the find command is to find the filename or directory with specified characteristics in the directory tree specified.

The most basic form of the find command is

```
find . -print
```

There are a number of arguments you can specify with the find command for different attributes of files and directories. You will learn more about these arguments and their usage in Chapter 5, but here are some examples of these arguments:

- name: Finds files with certain naming conventions in the directory structure
- modify date: Finds files that have been modified during the specified duration
- access date: Locates files that have been accessed during the specified duration
- permission: Locates files with certain permission settings
- user: Locates files that have specified ownership
- group: Locates files that are owned by specified group
- size: Locates files with specified size
- type: Locates a certain type of file

4

THE UNIX FILE SYSTEM

Using the find command, it is possible to locate files and directories that match or do not match multiple conditions, for example:

- a to have multiple conditions ANDed
- o to have multiple conditions ORed
- ! to negate a condition
- expression to satisfy any complex condition

The find command has another group of arguments used for specifying the action to be taken on the files or directories that are found, for example:

- print prints the names of the files on standard output.
- exec command executes the specified command.

The most common reason for using the find command is to utilize its capability to recursively process the subdirectories.

> **NOTE**
>
> Always use the -print option of find command. If you do not, the find command will execute but will not generate any output. For example, to find all files that start with "t" in the current directory or sub-directories under that, you should use find . -name "t*" -print rather than find . -name "t*".

If you want to obtain a list of all files accessed in the last 24 hours, execute the following command:

```
find . -atime 0 -print
```

If the system administrator want a list of .profile (this file has special use while logging into UNIX system) used by all users, the following command should be executed:

```
find / -name .profile -print
```

You can also execute the find command with multiple conditions. If you wanted to find a list of files that have been modified in the last 24 hours and which has a permission of 777, you would execute the following command:

```
find . -perm 777  -a -mtime 0 -print
```

Reviewing Disk Utilization with du and df

Until now, this chapter has discussed files and directories but not the details of their physical locations and limitations. This section discusses the physical locations and limitations of the files and directories.

In UNIX, the files and directories reside on what are called *file systems*. File systems define the attributes of the physical devices on which the files reside. UNIX imposes restrictions on the file system size. A file cannot span across file systems; a file cannot exceed the size of a file system. A UNIX system will have multiple file systems, each of which have files and directories. To access files in a file system, a file system must be mounted. Another important concept is that of a network file system (NFS), which is used to access files on a physically different computer from the local computer. Similar to the local file system, NFS also must be mounted in order for you to access the files in it.

The command `df` is used to obtain the attributes of all or specified file systems in the system. Typically, the attributes displayed by the `df` command are as follows:

- `file system`: Name of the file system
- `kbytes`: Size of the file system in kilobytes
- `used`: Amount of storage used
- `avail`: Amount of storage still available
- `iused`: Number of i-nodes used
- `capacity`: Percentage of the total capacity used
- `%iused`: Percentage of the available i-nodes already used
- `mounted on`: The name of the top-level directory

If you are in your home directory and execute the following command

```
df .
```

which returns the following

```
File system    Total KB    free %used    iused %iused Mounted on
/dev/hd1        151552     41828   72%     5534    14% /u
```

it means that the your home directory is on a file system called `/dev/hd1` and the top-level directory in the file system is called `/u`. For this example, you will get the same result regardless of what your current directory is, as long as you are in a directory whose absolute pathname starts with `/u`.

You can execute the `df` command without any arguments to obtain a list of all the file systems in your system and their attributes. You can provide an absolute or a relative pathname for a directory to find out the file system attributes of the file system to which it belongs.

The `du` command displays the number of blocks for files and directories specified by the file and directory arguments and, recursively, for all directories within the specified directory argument.

You can execute the following command from your current directory:

```
du or du .
```

and obtain the following result

```
8       .
```

which means that the file system on which the current directory is present has only the current directory in it and it has taken up eight blocks. If there were more directories in that file system, all of them and their sizes would have been displayed.

Determining the Nature of a File's Contents with `file`

The command `file` can be used to determine the type of the file the specified file is. The `file` command actually reads through the file and performs a series of tests to determine the type of the file. The command then displays the output in standard output.

If a file appears to be ASCII, the `file` command examines the first 512 bytes and tries to determine the language. If a file does not appear to be ASCII, the `file` command further attempts to distinguish a binary data file from a text file that contains extended characters.

If the file argument specifies an executable or object module file and the version number is greater than 0, the `file` command displays the version stamp.

The `file` command uses the `/etc/magic` file to identify files that have some sort of a magic number—that is, any file containing a numeric or string constant that indicates type.

For example, if you have a file called `letter` in your current directory and it contains a letter to your friend, executing the command

```
file letter
```

will display the following result:

```
letter:  commands text
```

If you have a file called `prog` and it is a executable program (and you are working on IBM RISC 6000 AIX version 3.1), executing the command

```
file prog
```

displays the following result:

```
prog:       executable (RISC System/6000 V3.1)
```

If you are in the `/dev` directory, which contains all the special files, executing the command

```
file hd1
```

for a file called `hd1` (a disk on which a file system has been defined) will display the following result:

```
hd1:        block special
```

You will learn more about the options to be used with the file command in Chapter 5.

File and Directory Permissions

Earlier in this chapter, you saw that the `ls` command with the option `-al` displayed the permissions associated with a file or a directory. The permissions associated with a file or a directory tell who can or cannot access the file or directory, and what the user can or cannot do.

In UNIX, each user is identified with a unique *login ID*. Additionally, multiple users can be grouped and associated with a *group*. A user can belong to one or more of these groups. However, a user belongs to one *primary group*. All other groups to which a user belongs are called *secondary groups*. The user login id is defined in the `/etc/passwd` file, and the user group is defined in `/usr/group` file. The file and directory permissions in UNIX are based on the user and group.

All the permissions associated with a file or a directory have three types of permissions:

- Permissions for the owner: This identifies the operations the owner of the file or the directory can perform on the file or the directory

- Permissions for the group: This identifies the operations that can be performed by any user belonging to the same group as the owner of the file or the directory.

- Permissions for world: This identifies the operations everybody else (other than the owner and members of the group to which the owner belongs) can do.

Using the permission attributes of a file or directory, a user can selectively provide access to users belonging to a particular group and users not belonging to a particular group. UNIX checks on the permissions in the order of owner, group, and other (world)—and the first permission that is applicable to the current user is used.

Here is an example of a file called `testfile` in the current directory, created by a user called guhas belonging to a group called `staff`. The file is set up so that only the user guhas can read, modify, or delete the file; users belonging to the group can read it, but nobody outside the group can access it. Executing the following command from current directory

```
ls -al testfile
```

displays the permissions of the file `testfile`:

```
-rw-r-----   1 guhas     staff       2031  Nov 04 06:14 testfile
```

You should be careful when setting up permissions for a directory. If a directory has read permissions only, you might be able to obtain a list of the files in the directory, but you will be prevented from doing any operations on the files in that directory.

For example, if you have a directory called `testdir` in the current directory, which contains a file called `testfile`, and the group permissions for `testdir` is read-only, executing the following command

```
ls testdir
```

will display the result

```
testfile
```

However, if you want to see the content of the file `testfile` using the following command:

```
cat testdir/testfile
```

you will get the following error message:

```
cat: testdir/testfile permission denied
```

To perform any operation on `testfile` in `testdir`, you must have the execute permission for `testdir`.

If you want all the members in your group to know the names of the files in a particular directory but do not want to provide any access to those files, you should set up the directory using only read permission.

The owner of a file is determined by the user who creates the file. The group to which the file belongs is dependent on which UNIX system you are working on. In some cases, the group is determined by the current directory. In other cases, you might be able to change to one of your secondary groups (by using the `newgrp` command) and then create a file or directory belonging to that group.

Similarly, if you set up a directory with just execute permission for the group, all members of the group can access the directory. However, without read permission, the members of the group cannot obtain a list of directories or files in it. However, if someone knows the name of a particular file within the directory, he or she can access the file with the file's absolute pathname.

For example, let us assume that we have a sub-directory `testdir` under `/u/guhas` that has a file called `testfile`. Let us assume the sub-directory `testdir` has been set up with 710 permission (that is execute permission for the group). In such a case, if a member of the group executes the `ls` command on `testdir`, the following will be the result

```
ls -l testdir
```

```
testdir unreadable
```

```
total 0
```

while if someone is aware of the file `testfile` and executes the following command

```
ls -l testdir/testfile
```

```
-rw-r--r--   1 guhas     staff          23 Jul  8 01:48 testdir/testfile
```

then he or she will get all the information about the file `testfile`.

In UNIX, there is a special user who has blanket permission to read, write, and execute all files in the system regardless of the owner of the files and directories. This user is known as `root`.

The Permission Bits

You know that files and directories have owners and groups associated with them. The following are three set of permissions associated with a file or directory:

- Owner permission
- Group permission
- World (other) permission

For each of these three types for permissions there are three permission bits associated. The following is a list of these permission bits and their meanings for files:

- Read (r): The file can be read.
- Write (w): The file can be modified, deleted, and renamed.
- Execute (x): The file can be executed.

The following is a list of these permissions and their meanings for directories:

- Read (r): The directory can be read.
- Write (w): The directory can be updated, deleted, and renamed.
- Execute (x): Operations may be performed on the files in the directory. This bit is also called the *search bit,* because execute permission in a directory is not used to indicate whether a directory can be executed or not but to indicate whether you are permitted to search files under the directory.

Let us examine the directory permissions more closely. Suppose there is a sub-directory called testdir under the directory /u/guhas with the following permissions:

```
drwxrws---   3 guhas    staff     1536 Nov  4 06:00 testdir
```

Also a file called testfile is in the directory testdir with the following permission:

```
-rwxr-----   1 guhas    staff     2000 Nov  4 06:10 testfile
```

This means that the user guhas can read, modify, and rename the directory and files within the directory. Any member of the group staff also has access to the directory. The file testfile is set up with read permissions only for all members of group staff. However, because all members of staff have read, write, and execute permissions on testdir, anyone belonging to group staff may modify, delete, and rename the file testfile.

CAUTION

If a user has write permissions to a directory containing a file, the permissions of the files in that directory are overridden by permissions of the directory.

Permissions (for owners, groups, and others) are stored in the UNIX system in octal numbers. An octal number is stored in UNIX system using three bits so that each number can vary from 0 through 7. Following is how a octal number is stored:

- Bit 1, value 0 or 1 (defines read permission)
- Bit 2, value 0 or 1 (defines write permission)
- Bit 3, value 0 or 1 (defines execute permission)

The first bit (read) has a weight of 4, the second bit (write) has a weight of 2, and the third bit (execute) has a weight of 1. For example, a value of 101 will be 5. (The value of binary 101 is (4 * 1) + (0 * 1) + (1 * 1) = 5.)

Let us now examine how to use the octal number to define the permissions. For example, you might want to define the following permissions for the file testfile in the current directory:

- Owner read, write, and execute
- Group read and execute
- Others—no access at all

This can be defined as (using binary arithmetic):

- Owner 111 = 7
- Group 101 = 5
- Others 000 = 0

Thus, the permission of the file testfile is 750.

Some versions of UNIX provide an additional bit called the *sticky bit* as part of a directory permission. The purpose of the sticky bit is to allow only the owner of the directory, owner of the file, or the root user to delete and rename files.

The following is a convention for setting up permissions to directories and files. For private information, the permission should be set to 700. Only you will have read, write, and execute permissions on the directory or file.

If you want to make information public but you want to be the only one who can publish the information, set the permission to 755. Nobody else will have write access, and nobody else will be able to update the file or directory.

If you do not want the information to be accessed by anybody other than you or your group, set the permission for other 0. The permission may be 770 or 750.

The following is an example of where you can set up permissions to deny permissions to a particular group. Assume that there is a directory called testdir in the current directory owned by a group called outsider. If you execute the following command in the current directory, the group outsider will not be able to perform any function on the directory testdir:

```
chmod  705 testdir
```

Default Permissions: umask

When a user logs into a UNIX system, she is provided with a default permission. All the files and directories the user creates will have the permissions defined in umask.

You can find out what the default permissions you have by executing the following command:

```
umask
```

It might display the following result:

```
022
```

umask is stored and displayed as a number to be subtracted from 777. 022 means that the default permissions are

```
777 - 022 = 755
```

That is, the owner can read, write, and execute; the group can read and execute; and all others can also read and execute.

The default umask, usually set for all users by the system administrator, may be modified to suit your needs. You can do that by executing the umask command with an argument, which is the mask you want. For example, if you want the default permissions to be owner with read, write, and execute (7); group with read and write (5); and others with only execute (1), umask must be set to 777 - 751 = 026. You would execute the command as follows:

```
umask 026
```

Changing Permissions: chmod

You have just seen how the default permissions can be set for files and directories. There might be times when you will want to modify the existing permissions of a file or directory to suit your needs. The reason for changing permissions might be that you want to grant or deny access to one or more individuals. This can be done by using the chmod command.

With the chmod command, you specify the new permissions you want on the file or directory. The new permissions can be specified using one the following two ways:

- In a three-digit, numeric octal code
- In symbolic mode

You are already familiar with the octal mode. If you wanted the file testfile to allow the owner to read, write, and execute; the group to read; and others to execute, you would need to execute the following command:

```
chmod 741 testfile
```

4

When using symbolic mode, specify the following:

- ■ Whose (owner, group, or others) permissions you want to change
- ■ What (+ to add, - to subtract, = to equal) operation you want to perform on the permission
- ■ The permission (r, w, x)

Assuming that the current permission of testfile is 740 (the group has read-only permission), you can execute the following command to modify the permissions of testfile so that the group has write permissions also:

```
chmod g+w testfile
```

Another example of symbolic mode is when you want others to have the same permissions as the group for a file called testfile. You can execute the following command:

```
chmod o=g testfile
```

Another example of symbolic mode is when you want to modify the permissions of the group as well as the world. You can execute the following command to add write permission for the group and eliminate write permission for the world:

```
chmod  g+w, o-w testfile
```

Changing Owner and Group: chown and chgrp

If you wanted to change the owner of a file or directory, you could use the chown command.

CAUTION

On UNIX systems with disk quotas, only the root user may change the owner of a file or directory.

If the file testfile is owned by user guhas, to change the ownership of the file to a user friend, you would need to execute the following command:

```
chown friend testfile
```

If you wanted to change the group to which file belongs, you may use the chgrp command. The group must be one of the groups to which the owner belongs. That is, the group must be either the primary group or one of the secondary groups of the owner. Let us assume that user guhas owns the file testfile and the group of the file is staff. Also assume that guhas belongs to the groups staff and devt. To change the owner of testfile from staff to devt, execute the following command:

```
chgrp devt testfile
```

Setuid and Setgid

When you execute some programs, it becomes necessary to assume the identity of a different user or group. It is possible in UNIX to set the SET USER ID(setuid) bit of an executable so that when you execute it, you will assume the identity of the user who owns the executable. For example, if you are executing a file called testpgm, which is owned by specialuser, for the duration of the execution of the program you will assume the identity of specialuser. In a similar manner, if SET GROUP ID(setgid) of a executable file is set, executing that file will result in you assuming the identity of the group that owns the file during the duration of execution of the program.

Here is an example of how the SET USER ID bit is used. Suppose you wanted a backup of all the files in the system to be done by a nightshift operator. This usually is done by the root user. Create a copy of the backup program with the SET USER ID bit set. Then, the nightshift operator can execute this program and assume the identity of the root user during the duration of the backup.

Summary

This chapter discussed what files are, the various types of files, and how to organize the files in different directories. You learned how to define permissions on files and directories. You also saw some of the commands used on files, such as ls to list files and its details, chmod to change permissions on files and directories, chown to change the ownership of a file or directory, chgrp to change the group ownership of a file, umask to display and change default permission settings for the user, and du or df to find out about utilization of disk space. You will learn more about various UNIX commands in Chapter 5.

4

THE UNIX FILE
SYSTEM

General Commands

by Sanjiv Guha

IN THIS CHAPTER

CHAPTER 5

UNIX has commands that are native to UNIX, and commands that you (or someone at your installation) can write. Depending on the UNIX version you are running and the shell you are in, the commands differ. In this chapter, commands that are available in most UNIX versions are discussed. Each command can have several arguments and several flags associated with it. The general form of a command is

```
command [flags] [argument1] [argument2] ...
```

Flags are preceded by a hyphen. Several flags can be specified together with only one hyphen. For example, the following two commands are equivalent:

```
ls -a -l
```

```
ls -al
```

Depending on the command, the arguments can be optional or mandatory. All commands accept inputs from the standard input, display output on standard output and display error message on standard error. You can use UNIX redirection capabilities to redirect one or more of these. Standard input is where UNIX gets the input for a command, standard output is where UNIX displays output from a command, and standard error is where UNIX displays any errors as a result of the execution of a command.

All commands, when executed successfully, return a zero return code. However, if the commands are unsuccessful or partially successful, they return non-zero return codes. The return codes can be used as part of control logic in shell scripts.

> **CAUTION**
>
> Though the commands described here work on most of the UNIX systems in a general way, the behavior of the flags associated with each command can differ. You should use the man command on your system to learn about details of the command and its flags.

User-Related Commands

The commands related to logging in and out of the system are discussed in the following sections. User-related commands are those that are used to log in and out of your UNIX system. They might differ slightly from system to system, but the commands discussed here are common to most systems.

login

When you start working on a UNIX system, the first thing you need is a login ID. Each user in a UNIX system has a unique login ID that identifies the user and any characteristics associated with the user. When you first connect to a UNIX system, you get the login prompt. The login prompt usually asks for the following information:

```
login:
password:
```

You will be allowed into a system, if, and only if, you enter the login ID and password correctly. When the login is successful, you get information, such as last unsuccessful login, last successful login, whether you have any mail, messages from the system administrator, and more. Following is an example of a successful login:

```
******************************************************************************
*                                                                            *
* You are now logged on to the host1 computer                                *
*                                                                            *
******************************************************************************
Last unsuccessful login: Thu Nov  7 22:32:41 1996 on tty1
Last login: Fri Nov  8 01:17:04 1996 on tty1
/u/testuser:>>
```

While logging in, there are shell scripts that are executed. The script that gets executed depends on the shell you are running. For example, in Bourne shell, the `.profile` file in your home directory is executed, in Korn shell, the file pointed to by the environment variable ENV is executed.

You should put in as part of the startup file all the commands that you want to be executed before login. For example, you can set the search path, the terminal type, and various environment variables or run special programs, depending on your requirements. The following is an example of a Korn shell `.profile` file for user `testuser`. Here the PATH variable is being set to include directories that user `testuser` uses for daily work, and the mail is being checked.

```
PATH=$PATH:/u/testuser:/u/testuser/exe:/u/testuser/script
PATH=/usr2/cdirect/local:$PATH
export PATH
```

You can invoke the `login` command from the command line also. The user is optional. If `user` is not provided, the system prompts for `login id` followed by the password prompt, if needed. If `user` is provided, the system prompts for a password, if needed.

rlogin

UNIX provides you with the `rlogin` command to let you move between various computers in a network. The `rlogin` command is similar to the `telnet` command described in this section.

To be allowed access to a remote host, you must satisfy the following conditions:

- The local host is included in the `/etc/hosts.equiv` file of the remote host, the local user is not the `root` user and the `-l User` option is not specified.
- The local host and username are included in the `$HOME/.rhosts` file in the remote user account.

If the user on the remote host is set up without a password, `rlogin` will allow you to log in without using any password, provided the above defined conditions are satisfied. However, it is not advisable to set up users without passwords. When you exit from the remote host, you are back on the local host.

Examples

Here is an example of the `rlogin` command where the user ID has not been specified. Executing the following command will prompt you for a password (if one is required) and entering the correct password will let you into the remote host:

```
rlogin box2
```

In this case, the user ID for the remote host is assumed to be the same as that of the logged in user ID in the local host. For example, if `testuser` is logged in currently on `box1`, UNIX will assume that you are trying `rlogin` for `testuser` on `box2`.

If, however, your user ID is different on `box2` than on `box1`, you can use another option of the `rlogin` command:

```
rlogin box2 -l testusernew
```

In this option, you tell `rlogin` that the user ID to be used for the remote host is `testusernew`.

telnet

If you are in an environment where you work with multiple UNIX computers networked together, you will need to work on different machines from time to time. The `telnet` command provides you with a facility to login to other computers from your current system without logging out of your current environment. The `telnet` command is similar to the `rlogin` command described earlier in this section.

The hostname argument of `telnet` is optional. If you do not use the host computer name as part of the command, you will be placed at the `telnet` prompt, usually, `telnet>`. There are a number of sub-commands available to you when you are at the `telnet>` prompt. Some of these sub-commands are as follows:

- ■ `exit` to close the current connection and return to the `telnet>` prompt if sub-command `open` was used to connect to the remote host. If, however, `telnet` was issued with the `host-name` argument, the connection is closed and you are returned to where you invoked the `telnet` command.
- ■ `display` to display operating arguments.
- ■ `open` to open a connection to a host. The argument can be a host computer name or address. `telnet` will respond with an error message if you provide an incorrect name or address.
- ■ `quit` to exit Telnet.
- ■ `set` to set operating arguments.
- ■ `status` to print status information.
- ■ `toggle` to toggle operating arguments (`toggle ?` for more).
- ■ `?` to print help information.

Examples

Assume that you work with two networked computers, `box1` and `box2`. If you are currently logged in on `box1`, you can execute the following command to log in to `box2`:

```
telnet box2
```

As a response to this command, `box2` will respond with the login screen where you can enter your `userid` and password for `box2` to login. After completing your work on `box2`, you can come back to `box1`.

passwd

As you have seen, every time you try to log in to a computer system, you are asked for your user ID and password. Although users can be set up without passwords, most users will have a password, which they will must use when logging in to a computer system.

When you first get you user ID set up in a computer, the system or security administrator will assign you a temporary password using the `root` user ID. The first time you try to log in, the system will ask you to change your password; you will use the new password for all subsequent logins.

However, you can change you password if, for example, you think that somebody else has come to know it. As a security precaution, it is a good practice to modify your password frequently. You can use the `passwd` command to change your password.

When you issue the `passwd` command, you are first prompted for your current password, followed by two prompts to enter your new password. The new password must match on both entries. This is a precaution to ensure that you do not type in something you did not intend and are subsequently unable to log in. Your new password cannot be the same as you current password. When you are typing your password (both old and new), UNIX does not display them.

Whenever you change your password, the new password must follow the rules set up at your installation. Some of the rules that govern passwords are as follows:

- The minimum number of alphabetic characters.
- The maximum number of times a single character can be used in a password.
- The minimum number of weeks that must elapse before a password can be changed.
- The maximum number of weeks after which the password must be changed. The system will prompt you to modify the password when this happens.

Some UNIX systems have additional flags for the `passwd` command.

You should be careful about choosing passwords. If you choose passwords that other people can make an educated guess about, your login will not be secure. Following are some guidelines for choosing passwords:

- Avoid using proper nouns such as name of spouse, children, city, place of work, and so on.
- Avoid using strings of characters followed by numbers, such as `xyz01`.
- Use both uppercase and lowercase letters mixed with numbers.
- The length should be at least 7 characters.
- You should never write down your password.
- You should be able to type it quickly.

Examples

In Korn shell, you can execute the following command to get `finger` related information

```
passwd -f
```

which may result in the following display:

```
testuser's current gecos:
            "Sanjiv Guha, UNIX Programmer, X 9999"
Change (yes) or (no)? >
```

exit

When you log in to a UNIX system, you are always placed in a shell. The shell may be the Bourne shell, C shell, Korn shell, or other. As you have seen, you can log in to other systems with `rlogin` or `telnet` commands. The `exit` command allows you to exit the current shell.

You can also exit your current shell by typing CTRL-d. (Hold down the Ctrl key and the d key together.) If you are on the command line and press Ctrl-d, you will be logged off.

Locating Commands

When you try to execute a command, UNIX has to locate the command before it can execute it. UNIX uses the concept of *search path* to locate the commands you are trying to execute. The search path is a list of directories in the order to be searched for locating commands.

The default search paths set by the installation usually have the standard directories such as `/bin`, `/usr/bin`, and other installation specific directories. You can modify the search path for your environment as follows:

- Modify the `PATH` statement in the `.profile` file (Korn shell and Bourne shell).
- Modify the set `path=(....)` in the `.cshrc` or `.login` file (C shell).

Add the directory that contains your commands, or any commands you have modified, to the beginning of the path. They will be found first and executed first. Make sure you do not give your modified command a name that is the same as a UNIX native command.

which

This command can be used to find whether a particular command exists in you search path. If it does exist, which tells you which directory contains that command.

Examples

To find out where the which command resides, you can execute the following command:

```
which which
```

The system responds with the following message, meaning that the command which exists in the directory /usr/bin.

```
/usr/bin/which
```

whence

The whence command is a more verbose form of the which command in Korn shell. It has a flag -v associated with it to produce output in a verbose form. For a native command that has not been aliased, it generates output similar to which.

Examples

To get information about the which command, you can execute the following command:

```
whence which
/usr/bin/which
```

If you use the -v flag, you get the verbose form

```
which is /usr/bin/which
```

However, if you have aliased commands, then the output is different. For example, if you have aliased rm as rm -i (remove command with confirmation flag set), the command

```
which rm
```

generates the output

```
rm -i
```

while with the flag -v, it generates the output

```
rm is an alias for rm -i
```

where

The where command is used to obtain the full pathname of one or more files or directories. There are no flags associated with the where command. When the pathname is displayed, it is prefixed by the hostname, and if there are no arguments, the full pathname of the current directory is displayed.

Examples

If you want to find the pathname of the current directory, assuming that you are in the directory /u/testuser, the following command

```
where
```

will result in

```
box1:/u/testuser
```

Determining Command Usage

UNIX provides you with online help to learn about various commands and their options and flags. You may be familiar with the most often used commands and their various options, but to find out about less popular commands or command usage, you can use the online help provided by UNIX.

man

The man command is used to display the online UNIX manual pages, which include commands, files, sub-routines, and so on. You have to provide the man command with the name of the object you are looking for. If you do not know the full name, you can use the UNIX wildcard to specify the object name. You can even find out more about the man command itself by using the man command.

The following are some of the flags and arguments that can be used for the man command:

- ■ -k *keyword* for a list of summary information of manual sections in the keyword database for the specified keyword.
- ■ -f *command* for details associated with the command. The root user must set up the file /usr/man/whatis before you can use this option.
- ■ -M *path* to specify the search path for the man command.

You can specify a section name as part of the command. This will allow you to search for a title in the specified section. The following is a list of sections that can be specified:

- ■ 1—Commands
- ■ 2—System calls
- ■ 3—Subroutines
- ■ 4—File formats
- ■ 5—Miscellaneous
- ■ 7—Special files
- ■ 8—Maintenance

Examples

If you want to find out about the `find` command, execute the following command:

`man find`

To find out about filesystem-related keywords, execute the following command:

`man -k filesystem`

Administration

There are some functions that only the UNIX system administrator at you installation can perform. These include starting the system, shutting down the system, setting up new user accounts, monitoring and maintaining various filesystems, installing new software on the system, and more. In this section we will discuss the commands necessary to fulfill these duties.

install

The `install` command is used to install new versions of current software programs or brand new software programs. The basic function of the `install` command is to copy the binary executable and any associated files to the appropriate directories. In the case of new versions of existing software, the files are copied over the existing files and retain their permissions. The `install` command also prints a log of messages of what it has done. The system administrator can then modify the permissions and ownership defined for that installation.

> **NOTE**
>
> For new software, the default permissions are set to 755 with owner and group both set to bin. The default directories searched to find whether the command is present are `/usr/bin`, `/etc`, and `/usr/lib` in that order.

The following are some of the flags that can be used for the `install` command:

- `-c` *directory* to install the files in the specified directory, if, and only if, the command does not already exist. If it exists, the operation is aborted.

- `-f` *directory* to install the files in the specified directory, even if the command already exists in that directory. If the file is new, the default owner, group, and permissions are applied.

- `-G` *group* to set the group of installed files to the specified group instead of the default group `bin`.

- `-O` *owner* to set the ownership of the installed files to the specified user instead of the default owner `bin`.

■ -o to save the current version with the prefix OLD; that is, if the name of the file is sample, it is saved as OLDsample.

■ -i if you do not want to search the default directories but want to search the command line specified directories.

■ -n *directory* if you want to install the files in the specified directory if they are not found in the search directories.

Examples

You can execute the following command to install the file sample_program in the directory /usr/bin (default directory):

```
install sample_program
```

Assuming that sample_program already exists in the /u/testuser/exe directory, you can install the new version by executing the following command:

```
install -f /u/testuser/exe sample_program
```

To save a copy of the old version of the sample_program as OLDsample_program and install a new version in the directory /u/testuser/exe, you can execute the following command:

```
install -f /u/testuser/exe -o sample_program
```

shutdown

The system administrator may need to shut down the system at the end of the day or to do hardware maintenance on the UNIX machine. To shut down the machine in an orderly fashion, use the shutdown command. This command can be executed only with the root user authority. All users get a shutdown message when this command is executed, and they receive a final completion message. This process is not complete until all users receive the message. By default, this command brings down the system to a single user mode from a multi-user mode.

The following is a list of some of the flags that can be used with the shutdown command:

■ -h halts the operating system completely.

■ -i for interactive messages are displayed to guide the user through the shutdown.

■ -k to avoid shutting down the system. This only simulates a system shutdown.

■ -m brings the system down to maintenance (single user) mode so that the system administrator or hardware engineer can do system maintenance, which can include installing new hardware or software or scheduled maintenance of existing hardware or software.

It is possible also to specify the time when restart is to be done by specifying a future date or relative time. In that case, the system sends messages to the users periodically about the impending shutdown.

ulimit

The `ulimit` command is available in Korn shell and Bourne shell, and can be used to set limits on certain resources for each process. The corresponding command in C shell is `limit`. There are two types of limits:

- Hard limits are those defined on the resources on a system-wide basis and which can be modified only by `root` authority.
- Soft limits are the default limits applied to a newly created process. Soft limits can be increased to the system-wide hard limit.

Following are the flags that can be used with the `ulimit` command:

- `-a` to show the soft limits
- `-Ha` to show the hard limits
- `-c` *size* to set the `coredumpsize` in blocks
- `-t` *size* to set the CPU time in seconds
- `-f` *size* to set the maximum file size in blocks
- `-d` *size* to set the maximum size of the data block in kilobytes
- `-s` *size* to set the maximum size of the stack in kilobytes
- `-m` *size* to set the maximum size of the memory in kilobytes

Examples

To obtain the current setting of the hard limits, execute the following command:

```
ulimit -Ha
time(seconds)     unlimited
file(blocks)      4097151
data(kbytes)      unlimited
stack(kbytes)     unlimited
memory(kbytes)    unlimited
coredump(blocks)  unlimited
```

To obtain the current setting of the soft limits, execute the following command:

```
ulimit -a
time(seconds)     unlimited
file(blocks)      4097151
data(kbytes)      2048576
stack(kbytes)     82768
memory(kbytes)    909600
coredump(blocks)  102400
```

You should keep in mind that the soft limits set by the system administrator can be modified by you. For example, if you want to change the above setting of the CPU time limit to only 60 seconds for a process, you can execute the following command:

```
ulimit -t 60
```

5

GENERAL
COMMANDS

You should also be aware that these limits are imposed on a per process basis. Usually, most of the jobs have multiple processes; therefore, this limit does not impose real limits on the jobs.

umask

The umask command is used by the system administrator to set the default value to be assigned to each file created by a user. You, as a user, can modify this default setting.

Three groups of permissions are associated with a file or directory—owner, group, and world (sometimes referred to as others). The permissions for these three groups are assigned using octal numbers—one octal number for each group. The values for each group depend on the following three bits:

- read bit (0 or 1)
- write bit (0 or 1)
- execute bit (0 or 1)

Using binary arithmetic, the value can vary from 0 (all bits having a value of zero) to 7 (all bits having a value of 1).

You should be careful while interpreting the value associated with umask. The value associated with umask can be used to derive the value of the default permission by subtracting it from 777. That is, if the value of umask is 022, then the value of the permission is 777 – 022 = 755 (read, write, execute for owner; read, execute for group; and read, execute for the world).

Examples

To obtain the default value of the umask, execute the following command:

```
umask
```

To set the value of the permission to, say, 751, you should set umask to the value 026 (777 – 751). To achieve this, execute the following command:

```
umask 026
```

Process-Related Commands

In UNIX, a process is a program that has its own address space. Usually, a command or a script that you can execute consists of one or more processes. Simple commands like umask have only one process associated with them, while a string of commands connected by pipes has multiple processes associated.

The processes can be categorized into the following broad groups:

- Interactive processes, which are those executed at the terminal. The interactive processes can execute either in foreground or in background. In a foreground process, the input is accepted from standard input, output is displayed to standard output, and error messages to standard error. While executing a process in the background, the terminal is detached from the process so that it can be used for executing other commands. It is possible to move a process from foreground to background and vice versa.

■ Batch processes are not submitted from terminals. They are submitted to job queues to be executed sequentially.

■ Daemons are never-ending processes that wait to service requests from other processes.

In UNIX, each process has a number of attributes associated with it. The following is a list of some of these attributes:

■ Process ID is a unique identifier assigned to each process by UNIX. You can identify a process during its life cycle by using process ID.

■ Real User ID is the user ID of the user who initiated the process.

■ Effective User ID is the user ID associated with each process. It determines the process's access to system resources. Under normal circumstances, the Real User ID and Effective User ID are one and the same. But, it is possible for the effective user ID to be different from the real user ID by setting the Set User ID flag on the executable program. This can be done if you want a program to be executed with special privilege without actually granting the user special privilege.

■ Real Group ID is the group ID of the user who initiated the process.

■ Effective Group ID is the group ID that determines the access rights. The effective group ID is similar to the effective user ID.

■ Priority (Nice Number) is the priority associated with a process relative to the other processes executing in the system.

kill

The `kill` command is used to send signals to an executing process. The process must be a nonforeground process for you to be able to send a signal to it using this command.

The default action of the command is to terminate the process by sending it a signal. It is possible, however, that the process may have been programmed for receiving such a signal. In such a case, the process will handle the signal as programmed. You can kill only the processes initiated by you. However, the `root` user can kill any process in the system.

The flags associated with the `kill` commands are as follows:

■ `-l` to obtain a list of all the signal numbers and their names that are supported by the system.

■ `-signal` *number* is the signal number to be sent to the process. You can also use a signal name in place of the number. The strongest signal you can send to a process is `9` or `kill`.

The argument to `kill` command is the Process ID (PID). You can specify more than one PID as arguments to kill more than one process. The value of the PID can be one of the following:

- PID greater than zero to kill specified processes.
- PID equal to zero to kill all processes whose process group ID is the same as the process group ID of the user initiating the kill command.
- PID equal to -1 to kill all processes owned by the effective user ID of the user initiating the kill command.
- PID equal to a negative number but not −1 to kill processes whose PID is equal to the absolute value of the number specified.

Examples

If you are running a command in the background and think it has gone into a loop, you will want to terminate it. If the process number is, for example, 2060, execute the following command:

```
kill 2060
```

If, for some reason, this does not kill it, use the stronger version

```
kill -kill 2060 (same as kill -9 2060)
```

If you want to kill all the processes owned by you, execute the following command:

```
kill -kill 0
```

You should be aware, however, that this command also logs you off, because specifying 0 means that all processes, including your current login, will be killed.

nice

As you have seen, a relative priority is associated with each process. The relative priority governs the resources allocated to it by the operating system. The `nice` command lets you modify the priority of one or more processes so that you can assign them higher or lower priority. You can increase the priority only if you have `root` privileges though.

A negative number signifies a higher priority than a positive number. The value is usually in the range of −20 to 20.

If you do not specify an increment, the nice command takes a value equal to or higher than the current process, provided you have appropriate privileges. If you do not have sufficient privileges, the priority is not affected at all.

Usually, you should use the `nice` command to lower the priority of background or batch processes for which you do not need fast turn around.

Examples

If you want to find, at a lower priority in background, all the C source files in the current directory or its sub-directories, execute the following command:

```
nice find . -name *.c -print &
```

This will set the process to a default `nice` priority, which may be 10. To run the process at an even lower priority, execute the following command:

```
nice 16 find . -name *.c -print &
```

The following command can also be executed to achieve the same result:

```
nice -n 16 find . -name *.c -print &
```

ps

The `ps` command is used to find out which processes are currently running. Depending on the options, you can find all processes or only those initiated by your user ID. This command provides you with details about the various background and batch processes running in the system. It can provide information only about the active processes.

When the `ps` command is executed without any flags or arguments, it lists all processes (if any) initiated from the current terminal.

Following is a list of some of the flags that determine what processes are listed by the `ps` command:

- `-A` to list details of all processes running in the system
- `-e` to list details of all processes, except kernel processes
- `-k` to list all the UNIX kernel processes
- `-p` *list* to list details of all processes specified in the list
- `-t` *list* to list details of all processes initiated from the terminals specified in the list
- `-U` *list* (`-u` *list*) to list details of all processes initiated by the users specified in the list
- `a` to list details of all processes that have terminals associated wit them
- `g` to list details of all processes
- `x` to list details of all processes that do not have any terminal associated with them

The following is a list of some of the flags for the `ps` command that determine which details are displayed for each process listed:

- `-l` to generate the listing in a long form
- `-f` to generate a full listing
- `-F` *format* to generate a formatted output

> **NOTE**
>
> Some of the flags used in the ps command are not preceded by a hyphen (-).

The following details are displayed if formatting flags are not used:

- Process ID of the process.
- Terminal ID associated with the process. Hyphen (-), if no terminals are associated.
- CPU time consumed by the process.
- Command being executed as part of the process.

By using the formatting command, some of the details that can be obtained are as follows:

- User ID of the user who initiated the process.
- Process ID of the process.
- Parent Process ID of the process.
- CPU utilization of the process.
- Start time of the process. If the process has been started on the same day, it shows the time; otherwise, it shows only the date.
- Terminal ID associated with the process. It display a hyphen (-) if there are no terminals associated with the process.
- CPU time consumed by the process.
- Commands being processed as part of the process.

Examples

To display the processes initiated by the current user at the current terminal, execute the following command:

```
ps
```

The result is displayed as follows:

```
  PID    TTY  TIME CMD
66874      2  0:00 -ksh
71438      2  0:00 ps
```

The two processes displayed here are the login shell running (Korn shell) and the ps command itself.

If you want more details, execute the following command:

```
ps -f
```

This generates the following display:

```
 USER    PID   PPID   C     STIME    TTY   TIME CMD
testuser 66874      1   1 22:52:26     2   0:00 -ksh
testuser 480076 66874   6 00:21:33     2   0:00 ps -f
```

If you want to know all the processes executing at terminal tty2, execute the following command:

```
ps -f -t tty2
```

The result is

```
 USER    PID   PPID   C     STIME    TTY   TIME CMD
testuser 66874      1   1 22:52:26     2   0:00 -ksh
testuser 703277 66874   6 00:24:17     2   0:00 ps -f -t tty2
```

If there are no terminals associated with a process, a hyphen (-) is displayed. Therefore, you can use a hyphen as a terminal name to get a list of processes that are not associated with any terminals. For example, you can execute the following command:

```
ps -t -
```

To find out all the processes being executed by your friend with the user ID friend, execute the following command:

```
ps -f -ufriend
```

jobs

In UNIX, there is a subtle difference between processes and jobs. A job typically is one command line of commands, which can be a single command, a shell script, or a chain of piped commands. In a chain of piped commands, each command has a unique process ID, but all have the same job ID.

The C shell and some versions of the Korn and Bourne shell offer the jobs command. You can use the jobs command to find out the details about active jobs. Once you have the job ID, you can start using it to do primitive job controls.

You can use % (percent sign) in front of the job number to indicate that the number is a job number rather than a process ID.

Examples

If you want to bring job number 5 from background to foreground, execute the following command:

```
fg %5
```

If you had used 5 instead of %5, UNIX would have interpreted it as the process ID 5.

If you have one job called sample_job running in the background, execute

```
jobs
```

to get the details of the job. The display looks like

```
[1] +  Running                    nohup sample_job > sample_log &
```

If you use the `-l` option, the process number will also be displayed as follows:

```
[1] + 270384      Running                    nohup sample_job > sample_log &
```

You need not know the job number to take any action on it. You can use the name of the job preceded by a `%` (percent sign) to identify the job. You can use regular UNIX wildcards to achieve this.

In the preceding example, you can use the name `sample_job` to identify the job. UNIX also allows you to use `%\?` to identify the unique part of the job name. In this example, it may be `%\?job` (Please note that the character `\` has been used as `?` has special meaning in UNIX. Specifying a `\` in front of a character tells UNIX not to interpret the character as a control character.) To kill the job `sample_job`, use

```
kill %sample_job
```

or you cause the following, if `sample_job` is the only one you are currently executing. Otherwise, it will kill all jobs with job name ending in `job`:

```
kill %\?job
```

wait

You can use the `wait` command to wait for completion of jobs. This command takes one or more process IDs as arguments. This is useful while doing shell programming when you want a process to be finished before the next process is invoked. If you do not specify a process ID, UNIX will find out all the processes running for the current environment and wait for termination of all of them.

Examples

If you want to find out whether all the processes you have started have completed, execute the following command:

```
wait
```

If you want to find out whether the process ID `15060` has completed, execute the following command:

```
wait 15060
```

The return code from the `wait` command is zero if you invoked the `wait` command without any arguments. If you invoked the `wait` command with multiple process IDs, the return code depends on the return code from the last process ID specified.

nohup

When you are executing processes under UNIX, they can be running in foreground or background. In a foreground process, you are waiting at the terminal for the process to finish. Under such circumstances, you cannot use the terminal until the process is finished. You can put the foreground process into background as follows:

```
Ctrl-z
bg
```

The processes in UNIX will be terminated when you log out of the system or exit the current shell whether they are running in foreground or background. The only way to ensure that the process currently running is not terminated when you exit is to use the nohup command.

The nohup command has default redirection for the standard output. It redirects the messages to a file called nohup.out under the directory from which the command was executed. That is, if you want to execute a script called sample_script in background from the current directory, use the following command:

```
nohup sample_script &
```

The & (ampersand) tells UNIX to execute the command in the background. If you omit the &, the command is executed in the foreground. In this case, all the messages will be redirected to nohup.out under the current directory. If the nohup.out file already exists, the output will be appended to it. If the permissions of the nohup.out file is set up so that you cannot write to that file, UNIX will create or append to the nohup.out file in your home directory. There may be instances where neither of these files can be accessed. For example, you may have run out of disk space. In such circumstances, UNIX will not initiate the nohup command.

The nohup command allows you to redirect the output into any file you want instead of the default file nohup.out by using standard UNIX redirection capabilities.

When you initiate the nohup command in the background (by using & at the end of the command line), UNIX displays the process ID associated with it, which can later be used with commands such as ps to find out the status of the execution.

Examples

If you want to find the string sample_string in all the files in the current directory, and you know that the command will execute for quite a while, execute the following command:

```
nohup grep sample_string * &
```

UNIX responds with the following message:

```
[2]     160788
Sending output to nohup.out
```

The first line of the display is the process ID, and the second line is the informational message about the output being directed to the default nohup.out file. You can later go into the file nohup.out to find out the result of the grep command.

In the preceding example, if you would like to redirect the output to a file called `mygrep.out`, execute the following command:

```
nohup grep sample_string * > mygrep.out &
```

In this case, UNIX displays only the process ID as follows:

```
[2]     160788
```

You can also execute shell scripts, which can contain multiple commands, using the `nohup` command. For example, if you want to execute a script called `my_script` in the current directory and redirect the output to a file called `my_script.out`, execute the following command:

```
nohup my_script > my_script.out &
```

> **CAUTION**
>
> You should be careful not to redirect the output of a script you want to execute to the script itself.

sleep

If you want to wait for a certain period of time between execution of commands, use the `sleep` command. This can be used in cases where you want to check for, say, the presence of a file, every 15 minutes. The argument is specified in `seconds`.

Examples

If you want to wait for 5 minutes between commands, use

```
sleep 300
```

Here is part of a small shell script that reminds you twice to go home, with a 5-minute wait between reminders. (The script is incomplete.)

```
echo "Time to go home"
sleep 300
echo "Final call to go home ....."
```

Communication

UNIX has several commands that are used to communicate with host computers for purposes of connecting to another host, transferring files between host computers, and more. You may need these commands, for example, to transfer a file from another host to the local host you are working on (provided you have sufficient access to do so). These commands are different from the commands used to log in to other computers because these allow you to communicate with other hosts without logging in.

cu

The `cu` command allows you to connect to another host computer, either directly or indirectly. That is, if you are currently on host1 and you use `cu` to connect to host2, you can connect to host3 from host2, so that you are connected directly to host2 and indirectly to host3.

Following is a list of some of the flags that can be used with `cu` command:

- ■ `-d` to print diagnostic messages.
- ■ `-lLine` to specify the device to be used for communication. By default, UNIX uses the first available appropriate device. You can use this flag to override the default.
- ■ `-n` to confirm the telephone number. If this flag is used, `cu` prompts you for the telephone number rather than accepting it as part of the command line.
- ■ `-sSpeed` to specify the speed of the line to be used for communication between hosts. The line speed is specified is in bauds and can be 300, 1200, 2400, and so on. UNIX in most cases should be able to default to the right line speed.
- ■ `-Tseconds` to specify the time-out parameter. This is the time up to which UNIX will try to connect to the remote host.

The following arguments can be specified with the `cu` command:

- ■ `System Name` is the name of the system to which you want to connect. This name must be defined in the `/etc/uucp/Systems` file. Also defined in this file are parameters, such as telephone number, line speed, and more, which are used to connect to the remote host. If you are using `System Name`, you should not use the `-l` and `-s` option.
- ■ `Telephone Number` is the telephone number to be used to connect to the remote host. The number can be a local or long-distance.

After making the connection, `cu` runs as two processes: The transmit process reads data from the standard input and, except for lines beginning with ~ (tilde), passes the data to the remote system; the receive process accepts data from the remote system and, except for lines beginning with ~ (tilde), passes it to the standard output.

Once you are able to successfully log in to the remote host, you will be able to use several sub-commands provided by `cu`. These sub-commands allow you to operate on files, directories, and so on that are on the remote host.

The following is a list of some of these sub-commands (You should prefix the ~ with a \ so that UNIX does not apply special meaning to ~):

- ■ `~.` to disconnect from the remote host.
- ■ `~!` to activate an interactive shell on the local host. You can toggle between interactive shells of local and remote hosts using ~! and Ctrl-d. That is, ~! puts you into a shell at the local host, while Ctrl-d returns you to the remote host.

- ~!*Command* to execute *Command* at the local host.

- ~%cd *directory* to change the directory on the local host to the specified directory.

- ~%put *From* [*To*] to copy a file on the local system to a file on the remote system. If the *To* variable is not specified, the local file is copied to the remote system under the same filename. The progress of the file transfer is displayed as consecutive single digits for each block transferred between the hosts. Only files containing text (ASCII) files can be transferred using this sub-command.

- ~%take *From* [*To*] to copy a file from the remote system to a file on the local system. If the *To* variable is not specified, the remote file is copied to the local system under the same filename. The progress of the file transfer is displayed as consecutive single digits for each block transferred between the hosts. Only files containing text (ASCII) files can be transferred using this sub-command.

- ~$*Command* to run, on the local system, the command denoted by the *Command* variable, and send the command's output to the remote system for execution.

Examples

If you know the remote host name and the name is defined in the /etc/uucp/Systems file, you can use it to cu to the remote host. For example, if the remote host name is remote2, you can execute the following command:

```
cu remote2
```

If you want to connect to a specific device, tty1, on a remote host at a specified line speed, 2400, execute the following command:

```
cu -s 2400 -l tty1
```

Once you are in the remote host, you can execute any of the cu sub-commands.

If you want to change to the directory /u/testuser on the local host, execute

```
\~%cd /u/testuser
```

If you have a file called local_file from directory /u/testuser on the local host, to copy it to the current directory in the remote host with the same name, execute the following command:

```
\~%put /u/testuser/local_file
```

If you want to modify the name of the file to local_file in the directory /u/testuser while copying it to remote_file under the /u/testuser/testdir on the remote host, execute the following command:

```
\~%put /u/testuser/local_file /u/testuser/testdir/remote_file
```

You can do the opposite using the `take` sub-command. For example, if you want to copy a file `/u/testuser/remote_file` from the remote host to a file called `/u/testuser/local_file` on the local host, execute the following command:

```
\~%take /u/testuser/remote_file /u/testuser/local_file
```

To execute the `ls` command on the local system, execute the following command:

```
\~!ls
```

ftp

You can use the `ftp` command to transfer files between two host computers. This command allows you to move files from a remote host to a local host, or to move files from the local host to a remote host. The `ftp` command allows only simple forms of file transfer. That is, you will not be able to copy files from directories recursively using a single `ftp` command. Instead you must transfer each file or directory individually. You should also be aware that `ftp` can be used between different types of systems, which means that system-dependent file attributes might not be preserved when files are transferred.

While using the `ftp` command, you need to use a login and password to log in to the remote host. However, it is possible to log in to the remote host without a password if the home directory has a `.netrc` file and that file contains the macro necessary for login to the remote host.

If a login ID and password are needed, the `ftp` command prompts for that information. In such a case, you will not be able to proceed until you are able to successfully log in using the correct user ID and password.

Once you are able to log in successfully, the `ftp` command displays an `ftp>` prompt. In the `ftp>` prompt, you can use a number of sub-commands to perform file transfers.

You can specify the hostname as part of the `ftp` command or open a connection to a host in the `ftp>` prompt. If you specify the hostname as part of the command line, you are prompted for login and password before you are put into the `ftp>` prompt. For example, if you execute

```
ftp box2
```

you will be prompted for user ID and password.

Some of the flags that can be used with the `ftp` command are as follows:

- `-i` if you do not want to be prompted with filenames in case more than one file is being transferred using a single command.
- `-d` for debug information.
- `-n` to prevent automatic login in case a `.netrc` file is present.
- `-v` to display the messages from the remote host on the terminal.

Once you are at the `ftp>` prompt, you can use several sub-commands. These sub-commands are

- `!` to invoke the interactive shell on the local host. Optionally, you can invoke a command with arguments by specifying the command and arguments after the `!` sign.

- `?` to display a list of sub-commands available. Optionally, a sub-command can be specified after the `?` to get information specific to that sub-command.

- `type` to set the file transfer mode. Valid modes are: `ASCII` for text files, `binary` for files which may contain special files so that the data is transferred without any translation, and `EBCDIC` to transfer files in EBCDIC code.

- `cd` to change to the home directory on the remote host. If a directory is specified, the current directory is changed to the specified directory on the remote host.

- `pwd` to print the current working directory on the remote host.

- `ls` to print a list of the files on the remote host. If no directory is specified, files and directories in the specified directory are printed. You can direct the list of files to a file on the local host by specifying a local filename.

- `mkdir` *directory* to make a new directory under the current directory on the remote host.

- `dir` to generate a list of files. Similar to the `ls` command but produces a detailed list.

- `rmdir` *directory* to remove the specified directory on the remote host, provided the directory is empty.

- `rename` *oldname newname* to rename a file from *oldname* to *newname* on the remote host.

- `delete` *filename* to delete the specified file on the remote host.

- `get` *filename* to transfer a file from the remote host to the local host. The name of the file is not altered. Optionally, you can specify a `local` *filename* to which the file from the remote host will be copied.

- `mget` to transfer multiple files from the remote host to the local host. You can specify a filename using a wildcard, which is expanded by UNIX. If the prompt option is set, you will be prompted for each filename for confirmation. If a prompt option is not set, all files are copied without any confirmation.

- `put` *filename* to transfer a file from the local host to the remote host. The name of the file is not altered. Optionally, you can specify a `local` `filename` to which the file from the remote host will be copied.

- `mput` to transfer multiple files from the local host to the remote host. You can specify a filename using a wildcard, which is expanded by UNIX. If the `prompt` option is set, you will be prompted for each filename for confirmation. If the `prompt` option is not set, all files are copied without confirmation.

- `mdelete` to delete multiple files by specifying wildcard filenames.

- append *filename* to append a local file to the end of a file on the remote host. Option-ally, you can specify a filename on the remote host to append at the end of the specified file. If the remote filename is not specified, the local filename is used by default.

- open to open a connection to a remote host by specifying a remote hostname.

- close to close the existing connection to the remote host.

- bye or quit to quit the ftp session.

- lcd to change to the home directory on the local host. If a directory is specified, the current directory is changed to the specified directory on the local host.

Examples

To open an ftp session on a remote host named otherhost, execute the following command:

```
ftp otherhost
```

or

```
ftp
ftp> open otherhost
```

In both cases, you will be prompted with user ID and password prompts, if you are not set up in the .netrc file with the user ID and password. The prompts and messages will appear as follows:

```
Connected to otherhost.
220 otherhost FTP server (Version 4.14 Fri Oct 10 13:39:22 CDT 1994) ready.
Name (otherhost:testuser): testuser
331 Password required for testuser.
Password:
230 User testuser logged in.
```

Once you are at the ftp> prompt, you can execute the FTP sub-commands. If you want to find out which directory you are in on the remote host, execute the following sub-command:

```
ftp> pwd
257 "/home/testuser" is current directory.
```

To copy a file called testfile from otherhost to the local host, execute the get sub-command. Following is the sub-command and its response:

```
ftp> get testfile
200 PORT command successful.
150 Opening data connection for testfile (73 bytes).
226 Transfer complete.
80 bytes received in 0.02583 seconds (3.025 Kbytes/s)
```

Similarly, to copy a file called testfile from the local host to the remote host, otherhost, use the put sub-command. Following is the sub-command and its response:

```
ftp> put testfile
200 PORT command successful.
```

```
150 Opening data connection for testfile.
226 Transfer complete.
142 bytes sent in 0.02954 seconds (4.695 Kbytes/s)
```

Following is a series of commands and responses. Here, we are trying to copy a file called `testfile` in binary mode from the `/u/testuser` directory on the local host to a directory called `/u/testuser/testdir` on the remote host `otherhost`.

```
ftp otherhost
Connected to otherhost.
220 otherhost FTP server (Version 4.14 Fri Aug 5 13:39:22 CDT 1994) ready.
Name (otherhost:testuser): testuser
331 Password required for testuser.
Password:
230 User testuser logged in.
ftp> lcd /u/testuser
Local directory now /u/testuser
ftp> cd /u/testuser/testdir
250 CWD command successful.
ftp> binary
200 Type set to I.
ftp> put testfile
200 PORT command successful.
150 Opening data connection for testfile.
226 Transfer complete.
46197 bytes sent in 0.03237 seconds (1394 Kbytes/s)
ftp> quit
221 Goodbye.
```

Here are some more examples of transferring multiple files, listing files, and deleting multiple files:

```
ftp otherhost
Connected to otherhost.
220 otherhost FTP server (Version 4.14 Fri Aug 5 13:39:22 CDT 1994) ready.
Name (otherhost:testuser): testuser
331 Password required for testuser.
Password:
230 User testuser logged in.
ftp> mput file*
mput file1? y
200 PORT command successful.
150 Opening data connection for file1.
226 Transfer complete.
46197 bytes sent in 0.03323 seconds (1358 Kbytes/s)
mput file2? y
200 PORT command successful.
150 Opening data connection for file2.
226 Transfer complete.
44045 bytes sent in 0.01257 seconds (3422 Kbytes/s)
mput file3? y
200 PORT command successful.
150 Opening data connection for file3.
226 Transfer complete.
41817 bytes sent in 0.01172 seconds (3485 Kbytes/s)
ls -l
200 PORT command successful.
150 Opening data connection for /bin/ls.
```

```
total 176
-rw-r-----   1 testuser    author        1115 Dec 15 11:34 file1
-rw-r-----   1 testuser    author       43018 Dec 15 11:34 file2
-rw-r-----   1 testuser    author       40840 Dec 15 11:34 file3
226 Transfer complete.
mdel file*
mdel file1? y
250 DELE command successful.
mdel file2? y
250 DELE command successful.
mdel file3? y
250 DELE command successful.
```

mailx

In UNIX, you can send mail to other users in the system and receive mail from them by using the `mailx` commands. The `mailx` commands provide sub-commands to facilitate saving, deleting, and responding to messages. This command also provides facilities to compose and edit messages before finally sending it to one or more users.

The mail system on UNIX uses mailboxes to receive mail for a user. Each user has a system mailbox in which all mail for that user is received pending action by the user. The user can read, save, and delete the mail once the mail is received. Once the user has read mail, it can be moved to a secondary or personal mailbox. The default secondary mailbox is called the `mbox`. The `mbox` is usually present in the home directory of the user. However, the user can specify the name of a file as a secondary mailbox. All messages saved in the mailbox `mbox` are save indefinitely until moved to other secondary mailboxes, which are sometimes known as folders. You can use the folders to organize your mail. For example, you can organize folders by subject matter and save all mail pertaining to a subject in a particular mailbox.

You can send messages to one or more users using the `mailx` command. This command allows you to send mail to users on the same host or other hosts in the network to which the local host is connected. You will not get a positive acknowledgment if the mail delivery is successful, but if the mail cannot be delivered, you will get notification.

Following is a list of some of the flags that can be used with the mail command:

- `-d` to display debug information.
- `-f` to display a list of messages in the default mailbox `mbox`. Optionally, you can specify the name of a folder in which you have saved your mail previously.
- `-s` *subject* to associate a subject for the mail to be created.
- `-v` to display detailed information by the `mailx` command.

Each mail has information associated with it. The following is a list of this information:

- `status` indicates the status of a mail message. Following is a list of the various statuses of a mail item:
  - `M` indicates that the message will be stored in your personal mailbox.
  - `>` indicates the current message.

- N indicates that the message is a new message.
- P indicates that the message is to be preserved in the system mailbox.
- R indicates that you have read the message.
- U indicates an unread message. An unread message is one that was a new message at the last invocation of `mailx` but was not read.
- * to indicate that the message has been saved or written to a file or folder.
- A message without a status indicates that the message has been read but has not been deleted or saved.

- `number` indicates a numerical ID of the message by which it can be referred to.
- `sender` indicates the user who sent the message.
- `date` indicates when the mail was received in the mailbox.
- `size` indicates the size of the message in number of lines and number of bytes.
- `subject` indicates the subject matter of the mail if the sender has associated a subject with the mail. This may or may not be present depending on whether the mail has an associated subject.

Following is a list of sub-commands you can use while in `mail>` prompt:

- `q` to apply mailbox commands entered this session.
- `x` to quit.
- `!command` to start a shell, run a command, and return to mailbox.
- `cd` to place you in the home directory. Optionally, you can specify a directory name to place you in the specified directory.
- `t` to display current message. Optionally, you can specify a message list to display messages in that list.
- `n` to display the next message.
- `f` to display headings of the current message. Optionally, you can specify a message list and display all headings in that message list.
- `e` to edit the current message. Optionally, you can specify a message number to modify that message.
- `d` to delete messages the current message. Optionally, you can specify a message list to delete the message in the message list.
- `u` to restore deleted messages.
- `s` *file* to append the current message, including its heading, to a file. Optionally, you can specify a message list between s and *file* to append the specified messages to the file.
- `w` *file* to append the current message, excluding its heading, to a file. Optionally, you can specify a message list between w and *file* to append the specified messages to the file.

- ■ pre to keep messages in the system mailbox. Optionally, you can specify a list of messages to keep them in system mailbox.

- ■ m *addresslist* to create or send a new message to addresses in the address list.

- ■ r to send a reply to senders and recipients of messages. Optionally, you can specify a list of messages to send a reply to senders and recipients of all messages in the list

- ■ R to send a reply only to senders of messages for the current message. Optionally you can specify a list of messages to send a reply to senders of the messages.

- ■ a to display a list of aliases and their addresses.

Examples

You can invoke the mailx command by itself to put you into the mail> prompt where you can use the sub-commands. You will be able to get into the mail> prompt only if you have mail. Otherwise, you will get a message similar to "you have no mail". If you have mail, prompts similar to the following will be displayed:

```
mailx
Mail [5.2 UCB] Type ? for help.
"/usr/spool/mail/testuser": 1 message 1 new
>N  1 testuser    Sat Nov 16 22:49  285/9644
&
```

If you now quit the mailx command using the quit sub-command (can be abbreviated as q), the mail is saved in your personal mailbox (mbox file in your home directory).

Now to see the mail, use the mailx -f command, which results in the following dialog:

```
mailx -f
Mail [5.2 UCB] Type ? for help.
"/u/testuser/mbox": 1 message
>   1 testuser    Sat Nov 23 00:11  162/5175
&
```

To save mail in a folder while in the mailx command, execute the following sub-command:

```
& save 1 /u/testuser/folder1/file1
```

This will create file1 from the first message in the directory /u/testuser/folder1.

Now, if you invoke the mailx command to read the file /u/testuser/folder1, it results in the following dialog:

```
mailx -f /u/testuser/folder1
Mail [5.2 UCB] Type ? for help.
"/u/testuser/folder1": 1 message
>   1 testuser    Sat Nov 23 00:11  162/5175
&
```

Once you are in mailx, you can execute the sub-command m to create and send mail to other users as follows:

```
& m friend1
Subject: Testing mailx command
```

```
This is test of the mailx command
Here we are trying to send a mail to user friend1 with cc to friend2
Cc: friend2
&
```

The body of the mail is terminated by Ctrl-d. You can send mail to multiple users using the m sub-command.

talk

You can converse with another user in real time using the `talk` command if the other user is logged on. Using the `talk` command, you can converse with users on local host or remote host.

The `talk` command takes one mandatory argument—username or user- and hostname. You can optionally provide a second argument specifying the TTY onto which the user is logged.

The user on the remote host can be specified in one of the following formats:

- `username@host`
- `host!username`
- `host.username`
- `host:username`

When you execute the `talk` command, it opens two windows—one for sending messages and one for receiving messages, and it will wait for the other user to respond.

Examples

If you execute the following command to converse with the user `friend`,

```
talk friend
```

you will get the following screen

```
[Waiting for your party to respond]
```

- -

with the one half for sending message and other half for receiving messages. If the specified user is not logged on, you get a message similar to "`Your party is not logged on`".

Meanwhile the user `friend` will get the following message:

```
Message from Talk_Daemon@host1 at 0:46 ...
talk: connection requested by testuser@host1.
talk: respond with:  talk testuser@host1
[Waiting for your party to respond]
```

The user `friend` has to respond with the command

```
talk testuser@host1
```

to start the conversation.

To quit the talk session, use Ctrl-c.

vacation

If you want to notify a mail sender that you are on vacation, you can use the `vacation` command. The message sent can be a customized message if you create the message in a file called `.vacation.msg` in your home directory. If this file does not exist, a system default message is sent. By default, the system message is sent only once a week to a user who sends mail to you.

The `vacation` command can be used to forward messages you receive during vacation to other users by using the `.forward` file in your home directory. Include the user names of all the users to whom you want the messages to be forwarded. The entry in the `.forward` file is of the following format:

```
testuser, "¦/usr/bin/vacation testuser"
```

The `vacation` command also lets you store the names of users who sent messages to you while you were on vacation. These user names are stored in the `.vacation.dir` and `.vacation.pag` files in your home directory.

The `vacation` command has one option flag, which is used as follows:

- ■ `-i` to initialize the `.vacation.dir` and `.vacation.pag` files before the start of your vacation.

The presence of the `.forward` file in your home directory is used by the system to identify that you are on vacation. So, once you are back, you should delete or rename the `.forward` file.

Before you go on vacation, use the following command to initialize the `.vacation.dir` and `.vacation.pag` files in your home directory:

```
vacation -I
```

This should be followed by the creation of the `.forward` and `.vacation.msg` file.

write

The `write` command can be used to hold a conversation with another user in the local host or remote host just like the `talk` command. To hold a conversation with another user, the following must be true:

> The user must be logged on.

> The user must not have denied permission by using the `mesg` command.

A message consists of all the characters you have typed until you hit the Enter key. Both you and the other user can send messages this way. To end the conversation, use Ctrl-d.

The following is a list of some of the flags that can be used with the `write` command:

- `-h` *Handle*,*Reply* to reply to a message sent by a utility or shell script using `write` with the `reply` option. The handle is a number that is generated by the system. The reply can be `ok`, `cancel`, or `query`.

- `-n`*Host* to specify a remote host if you want to hold conversation with a user on a remote host. It is also possible to specify user at a remote host as *username@host*.

- `-q` to find out about messages awaiting replies from users on a host and display them with their handles.

Examples

If you want to hold a conversation with a user called `friend`, execute the following command:

```
write friend
```

If user `friend` is not logged on, you will get a message similar to the following:

```
friend is not logged on.
```

If the user `friend` has used the `mesg` command to turn the permission off for conversations, then you will get a message similar to the following:

```
write: permission denied
```

If, however, the `write` command succeeds, the user will get a message similar to the following:

```
Message from testuser on mainhost(pts/3) [Fri Nov 22 19:48:30 1996] ...
```

You can use the UNIX input redirection operator to send long messages from a file called, for example, `long_message`:

```
write friend < long_message
```

To start the conversation, the other user also has to use the `write` command the same way as follows:

```
write testuser
```

If you want to hold a conversation with user `friend` on the remote host `otherhost`, execute either of the following two commands:

```
write friend@otherhost
```

or

```
write -n otherhost friend
```

File Comparison

Here some of the commands that can be used for comparing the contents of the file are presented. These commands compare the contents and, depending on various options, generate outputs of what the differences are between the various files. There are also commands that can be used to compare the contents of directories.

cmp

The `cmp` command compares the contents of two files and generates output into standard output. It is possible to have one of the files be standard input but not both. You can use a - (hyphen) to indicate that the file is standard input, which is terminated using Ctrl-d. The `cmp` command should be used for nontext files to find out whether they are identical. For text files, use the `diff` command, discussed later.

The following are the outputs generated by the `cmp` command:

- No output if the files are exactly identical.
- Displays the byte number and line number of the first position where the files are different.

The flags that can be used with `cmp` command are

- `-l` to display, for each difference, the byte number in decimal and the differing bytes in octal.
- `-s` to return only an exit value without generating any output. The values of return code are: 0 for identical files, 1 if the files are different, or 2 if the `cmp` file is not successful in comparing the files.

Examples

If you want to compare the new version of an executable file with the old version of the executable file, execute the following command:

```
cmp new_prog1 old_prog1
```

If the files are identical, no output will be generated, but if they are different, output similar to the following will be generated:

```
new_prog1 old_prog1 differ: byte 6, line 1
```

You can use the `-s` flag, if you are using the `cmp` command in a shell script to determine whether two files are identical. Following is part of a shell script that uses the `-s` command:

```
ret_code=`cmp -s new_prog1 old_prog1`
if [[ $ret_code -eq 0 ]] then
   echo "Files are identical ..."
else
   echo "Files are different ..."
fi
```

5

GENERAL
COMMANDS

If the files are identical except that one file has extra bytes at the end, use of the -l flag will generate the following output:

```
cmp -l new_prog1 old_prog1
    18  12  63
cmp: EOF on new_prog1
```

comm

If you have files that are sorted and you want to compare them, use the comm command. The comm command can be used to either exclude or include the common lines between the two files. You can use a - (hyphen) to indicate that one of the files is to be accepted from standard input.

The default output is generated on the standard output in three columns, which are as follows:

- Lines that exist only in the first file.
- Lines that exist only in the second file.
- Lines that exist in both files.

The following is a list of flags that can be used with the comm command:

- -1 to suppress the display of the first column.
- -2 to suppress the display of the second column.
- -3 to suppress the display of third column.

Examples

Let us assume that the there are two files named file1 and file2. The content of the files has been displayed using the more command as follows:

```
more file1
line 1
line 2
line 3
line 5
line 6
line 7
line 8
line 9

more file2
line 1
line 2
line 3
line 4
line 5
line 6
line 7
line 9
```

If you compare the two files, `file1` and `file2`, you will get the following output:

```
comm file1 file2
                line 1
                line 2
                line 3
        line 4
                line 5
                line 6
                line 7
line 8
                line 9
```

The output shows that `file1` has one line that is not there in `file2` (in column 1); `file2` has one line that is not there in `file1` (in column 2); and there are seven lines that exist in both `file1` and `file2`.

If you are interested only in the differences, you can drop column 3 as follows:

```
comm -3 file1 file2
        line 4
line 8
```

If you are interested only in finding out which lines are identical in `file1` and `file2`, you can drop columns 1 and 2 as follows:

```
comm -12 file1 file2
line 1
line 2
line 3
line 5
line 6
line 7
line 9
```

diff

You can compare text files with the `diff` command but cannot compare nontext files. You can use `diff` to compare individual files or multiple files with identical names in different directories. For comparing individual files, use a - (hyphen) to indicate that one of the files is to be accepted from the standard input.

The group of output lines of the `diff` command is preceded by an information line containing the following information:

- Lines that are different in the first file. This may be a single line number or two line numbers separated by a comma, meaning the lines within that range.
- Action code, valid values of which are a (for lines added), c (for lines modified), and d (for lines deleted).
- Lines that are different in the second file. This may be a single line number or two line numbers separated by a comma, meaning the lines within that range.

The diff command generates ed commands. The ed commands can be applied to the first file, and doing so will make the second file identical to the first file.

Three forms of output are generated by the diff command. These are as follows:

- Number1aNumber2,Number3, which means that the lines Number2 through Number3 in the second file must be added to the first file after line Number1 to make them identical. This form is followed by the actual lines from the second file preceded by a > (greater than sign).

- Number1dNumber2, which means that the lines Number1 through Number2 must be deleted from the first file to make them identical. This form is followed by the actual lines from the first file preceded by a < (less than sign).

- Number1,Number2cNumber3,Number4, which means that the lines Number1 through Number2 in the first file must be modified by the lines Number3 through Number4 in the second file to make them identical. This form is followed by the actual lines from the first file, each preceded by < (less than sign), and then actual lines from the second file each preceded by > (greater than sign)

The following is a list of some of the flags that can be used with the diff command:

- -b to ensure that more than one space or tab character is considered as one. However, leading space or tab characters are processed as is.

- -c LINE to produce the output is a format different from the default format. The LINE parameter is optional. The output first identifies the files being compared along with their creation date and time. Each modified group of lines is separated by a line with an * (asterisk) followed by lines from the first file and lines from the second file. The lines removed from the first file are designated with a - (hyphen). The lines added to the second file are designated with a + (plus sign). Lines that exist in both files but differ are designated with an ! (exclamation point). Changes that lie within the specified context lines of each other are grouped together as output.

- -D String to create a merged version of the first and second files on the standard output. The C preprocessor controls are included so that a compilation of the results, without defining String, is equivalent to compiling the first file, while defining String compiles the second file.

- -e to generate output that can be input to ed to produce the second file from the first file.

- -f to create output that is the reverse of what is produced by the -e flag.

- -i to compare the two files ignoring case of letters.

- ■ -l to generate formatted output. It also generates a summary at the end.

- ■ -n to generate output in the reverse order of the -e flag. Additionally, it generates the count of lines added and deleted.

- ■ -r to execute the diff command on all identically named sub-directories of the specified directory.

- ■ -s to generate output to obtain a list of identical files along with differences between identically named files. This will also generate a list of files that are only in one of the directories.

- ■ -S *FILE* to ignore files. This option can be used while comparing directories to ignore filenames that collate less than that of the specified *FILE*.

- ■ -t to preserve the original indentation of the lines. The indentation of lines in the output can be modified by the use of > (greater than sign) or < (less than sign in the output).

- ■ -w to ignore all space and tab characters. That is, treat them identically for comparison purposes.

Examples

Let us assume that we have two files, file1 and file2. The contents of the files are shown using the more command:

```
more file1
This is the first line
This is the second line
This is the fourth line
This is the fifth line
This is the sixth line
This is the seventh            line
This is the eighth line
This is the NINTH line

more file2
This is the first line
This is the second line
This is the third line
This is the fourth line
This is the sixth line
This is the seventh line
This is the eighth            line
This is the ninth line
```

The plain vanilla diff command on file1 and file2 will generate output as follows:

```
diff file1 file2
2a3
> This is the third line
4d4
< This is the fifth line
6,8c6,8
```

```
< This is the seventh                    line
< This is the eighth line
< This is the NINTH line
---
> This is the seventh line
> This is the eighth              line
> This is the ninth line
```

This means add `This is the third line` to `file1`, delete `This is the fifth line` from `file1` and modify line 6 and 7 to `This is the seventh line` and `This is the eighth` line in `file1` to make `file1` identical to `file2`.

If you do not care about space and tab characters, use the `-b` flag in the following command:

```
diff -b file1 file2
2a3
> This is the third line
4d4
< This is the fifth line
8c8
< This is the NINTH line
---
> This is the ninth line
```

As you can see, lines 6 and 7 are not displayed because the only reason these lines are different is the existence of extra space and tab characters.

You can display the output in special format using the `-C` or `-c` flag in the following command:

```
diff -C 0 file1 file2
*** file1        Thu Nov 28 22:15:23 1996
--- file2        Thu Nov 28 18:05:59 1996
***************
*** 2 ****
--- 3 ----
+ This is the third line
***************
*** 4 ****
- This is the fifth line
--- 4 ----
***************
*** 6,8 ****
! This is the seventh                    line
! This is the eighth line
! This is the NINTH line
--- 6,8 ----
! This is the seventh line
! This is the eighth              line
! This is the ninth line
```

The output contains the filenames being compared and their creation date and time, and the output has a format different from the default `diff` format.

If you want to generate output in a format that can be input to `ed`, use the `-e` flag as in the following command:

```
diff -e file1 file2
6,8c
```

```
This is the seventh line
This is the eighth              line
This is the ninth line
.
4d
2a
This is the third line
.
```

This output can then be input to `ed` to be applied to `file1` to make it identical to `file2`. This can be used to maintain a base version and incremental changes so that any version can be created by applying the changes to the base version. Here is an example of how you can make `file1` identical to `file2` using the `-e` command.

Redirect the output of the `diff` command to a file called `diffout` as in the following command:

```
diff -e file1 file2 > diffout
```

If you execute the `more` command on `diffout`, you will get the following output:

```
more diffout
6,8c
This is the seventh line
This is the eighth              line
This is the ninth line
.
4d
2a
This is the third line
.
```

Now add an extra command line at the end of the file `diffout`. The command is `w`, which will ensure that when it is input to `ed`, the output is written back to the file on which it is applied. If you execute `more` on the file `diffout`, you can see the extra line at the end:

```
more diffout
6,8c
This is the seventh line
This is the eighth              line
This is the ninth line
.
4d
2a
This is the third line
.
w
```

To update `file1` and see the result, you now use the following command:

```
ed - file1 < diffout
more file11
This is the first line
This is the second line
This is the third line
This is the fourth line
This is the sixth line
```

```
This is the seventh line
This is the eighth              line
This is the ninth line
```

If you do not want to update the original file, use the command 1,$p instead of w. This generates the output to the standard output instead. You can also redirect the output to a file as follows:

```
ed - file1 < diffout > file1.new
```

To generate output in reverse order to that specified by -e, execute the following command with the -f flag:

```
a2
This is the third line
.
d4
c6 8
This is the seventh line
This is the eighth              line
This is the ninth line
.
```

If you do not care about whether the files have lowercase or uppercase letters, use the -i flag to execute case-insensitive diff as in the following command:

```
diff -i file1 file2
2a3
> This is the third line
4d4
<This is the fifth line
6,7c6,7
< This is the seventh              line
< This is the eighth line
- - -
> This is the seventh line
> This is the eighth
```

Notice that the lines This is the ninth line in file1 and This is the ninth line in file2 are evaluated to be equal due to use of the -i flag.

If you want to know the number of lines affected by each insertion or deletion, use the -n flag as in the following command:

```
diff -n file1 file2
a2 1
This is the third line
d4 1
d6 3
a8 3
This is the seventh line
This is the eighth              line
This is the ninth line
```

The information in the above lines is with respect to file1. It tells you that one line is to be inserted after line 2, followed by the lines to be inserted, one line is to be deleted at line 4, three lines are deleted at line 6, and 3 lines are to be inserted after line 8, followed by lines to be inserted.

To ignore all tab and space characters, use the -w flag. The difference between the -b and -w flags is that -b ignores all space and tab characters except leading ones, while -w ignores all. Following is an example of the -w flag:

```
diff  -w file1 file2
2a3
> This is the third line
4d4
< This is the fifth line
8c8
< This is the NINTH line
---
> This is the ninth line
```

So far, we have seen the actions of the diff command for comparing two files. Now let us see some examples of comparing two directories. Let us assume that the two following sub-directories exist under the current directory:

testdir1 and testdir2

Further, let us see what files exist under these directories:

```
ls -R test*

testdir1:
file1      file2      file3      file4      file5      file6      testdir3

testdir1/testdir3:
filea  fileb  filec  filed  filee

testdir2:
file2      file4      file5      file7      file8      testdir3

testdir2/testdir3:
fileb  filed  filee  filef  fileg
```

The simplest form of the diff command without any flags to compare two directories will result in the following output:

```
diff testdir1 testdir2
Only in testdir1: file1
Only in testdir1: file3
Only in testdir1: file6
Only in testdir2: file7
Only in testdir2: file8
Common subdirectories: testdir1/testdir3 and testdir2/testdir3
```

In the above example, the diff command does not go through the sub-directory testdir3 under the directory testdir1 and testdir2. If you want the diff command to traverse the sub-directory under the directories, use the -r flag as in the following command:

```
diff -r testdir1 testdir2
Only in testdir1: file1
Only in testdir1: file3
```

5

GENERAL
COMMANDS

```
Only in testdir1: file6
Only in testdir2: file7
Only in testdir2: file8
Only in testdir1/testdir3: filea
Only in testdir1/testdir3: filec
Only in testdir2/testdir3: filef
Only in testdir2/testdir3: fileg
```

If you want to know a list of all files in the directories that are identical, use the -s command as in the following command:

```
diff -rs testdir1 testdir2
Only in testdir1: file1
Files testdir1/file2 and testdir2/file2 are identical
Only in testdir1: file3
Files testdir1/file4 and testdir2/file4 are identical
Files testdir1/file5 and testdir2/file5 are identical
Only in testdir1: file6
Only in testdir2: file7
Only in testdir2: file8
Only in testdir1/testdir3: filea
Files testdir1/testdir3/fileb and testdir2/testdir3/fileb are identical
Only in testdir1/testdir3: filec
Files testdir1/testdir3/filed and testdir2/testdir3/filed are identical
Files testdir1/testdir3/filee and testdir2/testdir3/filee are identical
Only in testdir2/testdir3: filef
Only in testdir2/testdir3: fileg
```

If you do not want to process all files whose names collate before the specified filename (in this case file2), use the -S flag as in the following command:

```
diff -r -S file2  testdir1 testdir2
Only in testdir1: file3
Only in testdir1: file6
Only in testdir2: file7
Only in testdir2: file8
Only in testdir1/testdir3: filea
Only in testdir1/testdir3: filec
Only in testdir2/testdir3: filef
Only in testdir2/testdir3: fileg
```

diff3

The diff command compares two files. If you want to compare three files at the same time, use the diff3 command. The diff3 command writes output to the standard output that contains the following notations to identify the differences:

- ==== means all three files differ.
- ====1 means the first file differs.
- ====2 means the second file differs.
- ====3 means the third file differs.

The following is a list of flags that can be used with the `diff3` command:

- `-3` to produce an edit script that contains only lines containing the differences from the third file.

- `-E`, `-X` to produce an edit script where the overlapping lines from both files are inserted by the edit script, bracketed by `<<<<<<` and `>>>>>>` lines.

- `-e` to create an edit script that can be input to the `ed` command to update the first file with differences that exist between the second and third (that is, the changes that normally would be flagged `====` and `====3`).

- `-x` to produce an edit script to incorporate only changes flagged `====`.

The format of the generated output is as follows:

- `File Id:Number1` a means that lines are to be added after line `Number1` in the file `File Id`. The `File Id` can be 1, 2, or 3, depending on the file it is referring to. This is followed by the lines to be added.

- `File Id:Number1[,Number2]c` means that lines in the range `Number1` through `Number2` are to be modified. This is followed by the lines to be modified.

Examples

Let us assume that we have three files: `file1`, `file2`, and `file3`. The contents of these three files are shown below using the `more` command:

```
more file1
This is the first line in first file
This is the second line
This is the third line
This is the fourth line
This is the fifth line
This is the sixth line
This is the seventh line
This is the eighth line
This is the ninth line

more file2
This is the first line
This is the second line
This is the third line
This is the 3.5th line
This is the fourth line
This is the sixth line in second file
This is the seventh line
This is the eighth line
This is the ninth line

more file3
This is the first line
This is the second line
This is the third line
This is the fourth line
```

```
This is the sixth line in third file
This is the seventh line
This is the eighth line
This is the ninth line
This is the tenth line
This is the eleventh line
```

Now execute `diff3` on these three files without using any flag, as in the command below:

```
diff3 file1 file2 file3
====1
1:1c
  This is the first line in first file
2:1c
3:1c
  This is the first line
====2
1:3a
2:4c
  This is the 3.5th line
3:3a
====
1:5,6c
  This is the fifth line
  This is the sixth line
2:6c
  This is the sixth line in second file
3:5c
  This is the sixth line in third file
====3
1:9a
2:9a
3:9,10c
  This is the tenth line
  This is the eleventh line
```

The first group of lines starting with ====1 show that line 1 of file1 is different from the line 1 of file2 and file3. The lines starting with ====2 show that line 4 in file2 should be inserted after line 3 of file1 and file3 to make them identical. The lines starting with ==== show that line 5, 6 of file1, line 6 of file2, and line 5 of file3 are all different. The lines starting with ====3 show that line 9, 10 of file3 should be inserted after line 9 of file1 and file2 to make them identical.

If you are interested in only finding out the differences in file3, use the -3 flag as in the following command:

```
diff3 -3 file1 file2 file3
9a
This is the tenth line
This is the eleventh line
.
w
q
```

This tells that there are two lines lines 9 and 10 that are present in file3 but not in file1 or file2.

If you want to apply changes between `file2` and `file3` to `file1`, use the `-e` flag to create an edit script as in the following command:

```
diff3 -e file1 file2 file3
9a
This is the tenth line
This is the eleventh line
.
5,6c
This is the sixth line in third file
.
w
q
```

This output means that `file3` has two extra lines at `line 9` and `line 6` of `file2` has been replaced by `line 5` of `file3`. If, however, you are interested in changes, use the `-x` flag as in the following command:

```
diff3 -x file1 file3 file2
5,6c
This is the sixth line in second file
.
w
q
```

dircmp

If you want to compare the contents of two directories, use the `dircmp` command. This command compares the names of the files in each directory and generates a list of filenames that exist only in one of the directories followed by filenames that exist in both and whether they are identical or not.

The following is a list of flags that can be used with `dircmp` command:

- `-d` to generate a list of files that exist in either of the directories followed by a list of files that exist in both and whether they are identical or different. This is further followed by output of `diff` command on pairs of files that are different
- `-s` to generate a list of files that exist in either of the directories followed by list of files that are different

Examples

Let us assume that the there are two directories `testdir1` and `testdir2` in the current directory. The list of files in these directories are as follows:

```
ls testdir1
file1  file2  file3  file4  file5  file6

ls testdir2
file2  file3  file5  file6  file7  file8
```

If you want to do a plain vanilla `dircmp` between these two directories, execute the following command:

```
dircmp testdir1 testdir2

Fri Nov 29 22:51:34 1996 testdir1 only and testdir2 only Page 1


./file1          ./file7
./file4          ./file8

Fri Nov 29 22:51:34 1996 Comparison of testdir1 and testdir2 Page 1


directory        .
different        ./file2
same             ./file3
same             ./file5
same             ./file6
```

The first part of the above report shows the files present only in `testdir1` on the left and only in `testdir2` on the right. The second part shows a comparison of the directories and also shows which files are identical and which are different. If you want further information on what are the differences between the files `file2` in these directories, use the `-d` flag as in the following command:

```
testdir -d testdir1 testdir2

Fri Nov 29 22:56:01 1996 testdir1 only and testdir2 only Page 1


./file1          ./file7
./file4          ./file8

Fri Nov 29 22:56:01 1996 Comparison of testdir1 and testdir2 Page 1

directory        .
different        ./file2
same             ./file3
same             ./file5
same             ./file6

Fri Nov 29 22:56:01 1996 diff of ./file2 in testdir1 and testdir2 Page 1


1c1
< This file is in testdir1
---
> This file is in testdir2
```

If you want only a list of files that are unique to each directory and files that are different, use the `-s` flag as in the following command:

```
dircmp -s testdir1 testdir2

Fri Nov 29 23:39:59 1996 testdir1 only and testdir2 only Page 1
```

```
./file1        ./file7
./file4        ./file8

Fri Nov 29 23:39:59 1996 Comparison of testdir1 and testdir2 Page 1


different      ./file2
```

If you want to suppress the display of identical files, but you want list of the files that are different and the difference between these files, execute the `dircmp` command with both `-s` and `-d` flags.

sdiff

The command `sdiff` compares two files and displays output on the standard output in a side-by-side format. Following is the detail of the display format:

- If the two lines are identical, then each line of the two files is displayed with a series of spaces between them.
- If the line only exists in the first file, then a < (less than sign) is displayed at the end of the line.
- If the line only exists in the second file, then a > (greater than sign) is displayed at the beginning of the line.
- If the lines from the two files are different, then a | (vertical bar) is displayed between the lines.

The flags that can be used with `sdiff` command are as follows:

- `-s` if you do not want to display the identical lines
- `-w` *number* to set the width of the display to *number*
- `-1` to display only the line from the first file if the lines from the two files are identical
- `-o` *file* to create a merged file from the first and second file depending on a number of sub-commands you can specify

Examples

Let us assume that we have two files `file1` and `file2` whose contents are displayed below using the `more` command:

```
more file1
This is the first line in first file
This is the second line
This is the third line
This is the fourth line
This is the fifth line
This is the sixth line
This is the seventh line
This is the eighth line
This is the ninth line
```

```
more file2
This is the first line
This is the second line
This is the third line
This is the 3.5th line
This is the fourth line
This is the sixth line in second file
This is the seventh line
This is the eighth line
This is the ninth line
```

If you execute sdiff command on the two files file1 and file2, you get the following result:

```
sdiff file1 file2
This is the first line in first file                      | This is the f
irst line
This is the second line                                     This is the s
econd line
This is the third line                                      This is the t
hird line
                                                        >   This is the 3
.5th line
This is the fourth line                                     This is the f
ourth line
This is the fifth line                                    | This is the s
ixth line in second file
This is the sixth line                                  <
This is the seventh line                                    This is the s
eventh line
This is the eighth line                                     This is the e
ighth line
This is the ninth line                                      This is the n
inth line
```

If, however, you do not want to display the identical lines, use the -s flag as in the following command:

```
sdiff -s file1 file2
This is the first line in first file                      | This is the f
irst line
                                                        >   This is the 3
.5th line
This is the fifth line                                    | This is the s
ixth line in second file
This is the sixth line                                  <
```

You can use the -l to display only the line from the first file if the lines are identical so that the other lines stand out as in the following command:

```
sdiff -l  file1 file2
This is the first line in first file                      | This is the f
irst line
This is the second line
This is the third line
                                                        >   This is the 3
.5th line
This is the fourth line
This is the fifth line                                    | This is the s
ixth line in second file
```

```
This is the sixth line                                    <
This is the seventh line
This is the eighth line
This is the ninth line
```

File Manipulation Commands

Here we will discuss several commands that can be used to manipulate various attributes of one or more files, as well as to copy and move files from one location to another. The various attributes that can be manipulated include modification time, permission, and more.

touch

The `touch` command can be used for a number of purposes depending on whether a file already exists. If a file does not exist, the `touch` command will create it if you have write access to the directory. If a file is already present, the `touch` command modifies the last modification time of the file.

Examples

To create a file called `testfile` in the current directory, execute the following command:

```
touch testfile
```

To create `testfile` in the `/u/testuser/testdir`, execute the following command:

```
touch /u/testuser/testdir/testfile
```

chmod

You may need to modify the permission of a directory or files either to secure them or to make them accessible to others. You can use the `chmod` command to modify the permission or files and directories. The permission in UNIX is specified in octal number (0 thorough 7). Permission for a file or directory can be specified for the following:

- Owner   The user who created the file
- Group   The group to which the owner belongs
- World or others   Users other than the owner and users in the group to which the owner belongs

For each of these, one octal number is specified to designate the permission.

The permission for the owner, group, and world is derived on the basis of three bits associated with read, write, and execute authority for the file. That is, the bit for read will have a value of one if read permission is to be granted, the bit for write will have a value of one if write permission is to be granted, and the bit for execute will have a value of one if execute permission is to be granted.

You should be aware that the execute bit functions differently for directories. The execute permission for a directory is used to designate whether you are able to access that directory.

The combination of these three bits is expressed as an octal number and is used to designate the permission. The weight associated with the read bit is 4, the weight associated with write is 2, and the weight associated with execute is 1. The value of the permission is derived as follows:

```
(4 * value of read bit) + (2 * value of write bit) + (1 * value of execute bit)
```

The value of the permission can vary from 0 (no read, write, or execute permission) to 7 (read, write, and execute permission).

For example, if you want to provide read and write permission but no execute permission, then the value to be used will be

```
(4 * 1) + (2 * 1) + (1 * 0) = 6
```

You should be aware that execute permission on a directory means that the directory can be accessed. That is, operations can be performed on files residing in that directory. If you provide write permissions to a directory, the user will be able to read, write, delete, and execute all files in that directory, irrespective of the permissions of the individual files.

With the chmod command, you specify the new permissions you want on the file or directory. The new permission can be specified in one the following two ways:

- As a three-digit numeric octal code
- As symbolic mode

Examples

If you want testfile to have the permission: owner with read, write, execute; group with read only; and others with execute only, you must execute the following command:

```
chmod 741 testfile
```

While using the symbolic mode, the following will need to be specified:

- Whose (owner, group, or others) permission you want to change
- What operation (+ (add), – (subtract), or = (equals)) you want to perform on the permission
- The permission (r, w, x, and so on)

If you want to setup the permission for testfile owned by you in the current directory so that only you and users in your group can read and write the file, execute the following command using absolute permissions:

```
chmod 660 testfile
```

If you want to add write permission for the group for testfile in the current directory (assuming that currently testfile has 741 permission), execute the following command:

```
chmod g+w testfile
```

Similarly, if you want to revoke the read permission for others for `testfile` in the current directory, execute the following command:

```
chmod o-r testfile
```

If you want to grant the same permissions to the world (other) as the group for `testfile` in the current directory, execute the following command:

```
chmod o=g testfile
```

> **NOTE**
>
> Modifying the permissions will not have any effect on the root user. The `root` user has access to all files and directories irrespective of the permissions you may have granted.

chgrp

If you want to change the group to which the file belongs, use the `chgrp` command. The group must be one of the groups to which the owner belongs. That is, the group must be either the primary group or one of the secondary groups of the owner.

Examples

Assume user `testuser` owns the file `testfile`, and the group of the file is `staff`. Also assume that `testuser` belongs to the groups `staff` and `devt`. To change the owner of `testfile` from `staff` to `devt`, execute the following command:

```
chgrp devt testfile
```

chown

In case you want to change the owner of a file or directory, use the `chown` command.

> **CAUTION**
>
> On UNIX systems with disk quotas, only the `root` user can change the owner of a file or directory.

Examples

If the file `testfile` is owned by the user called `testuser`, to change ownership of the file to user `friend`, you must execute the following command:

```
chown friend testfile
```

rm

Once you are done using a file and you do not want to use it any more, then you would like to remove the file so as to regain the space utilized by the file. The rm command lets you do this by removing files permanently from the disk. If an entry is the last link to a file, the file is deleted. To remove a file from a directory, you do not need either read or write permission to the file, but you do need write permission to the directory containing the file. The rm command is usually used to remove files, but it provides a special flag -r to remove files in a directory recursively, including the directory and its sub-directories.

Following is a list of some of the flags that can be used with the rm command:

- -i to interactively remove the files.
- -f to remove the files without any messages. This will not generate any messages for cases where a file does not exist or you do not have permission to remove one or more files.
- -r to remove files within a directory and directories themselves recursively.

The native version of the rm command does not ask for confirmation while removing files. So you should be careful when using wildcards with the rm command.

Examples

If you want to remove all files starting with test in the current directory, execute the following command:

```
rm test*
```

However, if you make a typing mistake and type the following:

```
rm test *
```

you will remove all the files because of the asterisk (*).

> **CAUTION**
>
> Be careful when using wildcards with the rm command. Be sure before you remove a file, because once a file is removed, it cannot be recovered.

To avoid any such mistakes, use the -i flag to indicate that you want to execute the rm command in interactive mode. In this mode, the system will ask you for confirmation before removing the file. Only if you confirm it with a y will the system remove the file. Following is the dialog you can have with the system if you want to remove two files in the current directory: testfile1 and testfile2, using the -i flag with the rm command:

```
rm -i testfile*
Remove file testfile1? y
Remove file testfile2? y
```

You can use the flag -f with the rm command if you do not want to get any messages from the command. Usually rm will display a messages that a file is not present if you do not provide the correct name of the file. However, using the -f flag forces rm to not display any messages. If you execute the following command:

```
rm -f testfile
```

the file testfile will be deleted if present, and no action will be taken if testfile is not present. In either case, you will not get any message from the rm command. Also, the *rm -f* command always has a return code of 0 (zero).

You can use the -r flag to remove files in directories recursively including directories and sub-directories. If there is a directory called testdir under the current directory that, in turn, has the files testfile1 and testfile2, execute the following command to remove the files testfile1 and testfile2 as well as the directory testdir:

```
rm -r testdir
```

It is advisable that you should set up an alias for the rm command as *rm -i* in your environment so that you have to confirm before deleting the files.

The rm command processes the hard linked file in a different way. If you have a testfile1 in your current directory, execute the following command to create a file called testfile2 that is hard linked to the file testfile1:

```
ln testfile1 testfile2
```

This, in effect, creates two identical files: testfile1 and testfile2. If you now execute the following command,

```
ls -l testfile*
```

you will get the following result:

```
-rw-r--r--  2 testuser    staff         10 Nov  3 14:28 testfile1
-rw-r--r--  2 testuser    staff         10 Nov  3 14:28 testfile2
```

Here both testfile1 and testfile2 show the number of links as 2, because they are linked using hard link. Now if you remove the file testfile1 using the rm command

```
rm testfile1
```

there will be two actions—to remove the file testfile1 and to decrease the link count of the file testfile2 from 2 to 1. Now if you repeat the ls command, you will get the following display,

```
-rw-r--r--  1 testuser    staff         10 Nov  3 15:38 testfile2
```

where the number of links of testfile2 is now 1.

mv

If you are not satisfied with a filename, you may wish to name the file differently. The mv command will let you do that. In addition, it allows you to move files from one directory to another retaining the original filename, which is equivalent to copying the files from the source directory to the destination directory and then removing the file from the source directory. You may do that if you are reorganizing your files. While moving files or directories, the target file or directory gets the permission of the source file or directory, irrespective of whether the target file or directory already exists or not.

Following is a list of some of the flags that may be used with the mv command:

- ■ -i to move or rename files interactively.
- ■ -f to move or rename files without any messages. Use of this flag will suppress messages when you are trying to rename a nonexistent file or you do not have permission to rename a file.

The mv commands takes two arguments. The first argument is the source file or directory name, and the second argument is the destination file or directory. However, the behavior of the mv command depends on whether the destination file or directory name exists.

If you move files within the same filesystem, all links to other files are retained. But if you move the files across filesystems, the links are not retained.

Examples

To rename a file in the current directory, use the following command:

```
mv source_file dest_file
```

If the file dest_file does not exist, a new dest_file is created by copying source_file into it, and source_file is removed. If dest_file exists and you have write permission to it, source_file is copied to dest_file and removed. On the other hand, if you do not have permission, then mv does not take any action.

To move source_file from the current directory to the /u/testuser/target_dir directory, retaining the name, execute one of the following commands:

```
mv source_file /u/testuser/target_dir
```

```
mv source_file /u/testuser/target_dir/.
```

If the file already exists in /u/testuser/target_dir, the existing file is overwritten.

To move source_file from the current directory to the /u/testuser/target_dir directory with the name target_file, execute the following command:

```
mv source_file target_dir/target_file
```

If you are not sure whether the file target_file exists, use the -i flag as follows:

```
mv -i source_file target_dir/target_file
```

If the file `target_file` exists, the system will prompt you with a message to confirm whether you want to move the file.

The . (period) as the target filename indicates that the source filename is to be retained. This is especially useful if you want to move multiple files to another directory. If you want to move all files with names beginning with `test` to the `/u/testuser/target_dir` directory, execute the following command:

```
mv test* /u/testuser/target_dir/.
```

To rename a directory, `source_dir` to `/u/testuser/target_dir` directory, execute the following command:

```
mv /u/guahs/source_dir /u/testuser/dest_dir
```

If the directory `dest_dir` does not exist, the directory `/u/testuser/source_dir` is renamed to `/u/testuser/dest_dir`. If `/u/testuser/dest_dir` exists and you have write permissions to it, all the files and sub-directories under `/u/testuser/source_dir` are moved to `/u/testuser/dest_dir`.

cp

The `cp` command can be used to make a copy of the contents of one or more source files as specified target files. If the target file already exists, it is overwritten with the contents of the source file. The `cp` command behavior varies depending on whether the source and the target are files or directories.

The following is a list of some of the flags that can be used with the `cp` command:

- `-p` to retain the modification date and time as well as permission modes of the source file.
- `-i` to execute the `copy` command in an interactive mode so that it asks for confirmation if the target file exists.
- `-h` to follow the symbolic links.
- `-r` to copy files under the specified directories and their sub-directories. Treats special files, such as linked files, the same way as regular files.

Examples

In its simplest form, you can execute the following command to copy `source_file` to `target_file` under the current directory:

```
cp source_file target_file
```

If you want to copy `source_file` to the `/u/testuser/target_dir` directory retaining the filename, execute the following command:

```
cp source_file /u/testuser/target_dir/.
```

To copy all files in `/u/testuser/source_dir` to the `/u/testuser/target_dir` directory while retaining the filenames and the last modification time and permissions, execute the following command:

```
cp -p /u/testuser/source_dir/* /u/testuser/target/dir/.
```

This will not copy any sub-directories or any files under those sub-directories. To copy all the files in a directory as well as sub-directories and files in those sub-directories while retaining the last modification date and time and permissions for all files and sub-directories, use the following command:

```
cp -r /u/testuser/source_dir /u/testuser/target_dir/.
```

If you are not sure whether the target file already exists, use the `-i` flag. Following is a dialog for copying `testfile` from the current directory to the `/u/testuser/testdir` directory assuming that `testfile` already exists in the `/u/testuser/testdir` directory:

```
cp -i testfile /u/testuser/testdir/.
overwrite /u/testuser/testdir/testfile? y
```

cat

You have seen that the `cp` command allows you to copy one file into another file. It does not allow you, however, to copy multiple files into the same file. To concatenate multiple files into a single file, use the `cat` command. By default, the `cat` command generates outputs into the standard output and accepts input from standard input. The `cat` command takes in one or more filenames as its arguments. The files are concatenated in the order they appear in the argument list.

The following is a list of some of the flags that can be used with the `cat` command:

- `-b` to eliminate line numbers from blank lines when used with the `-n` flag.
- `-e` to display a $(dollar sign) at the end of each line, when specified with the `-v` flag.
- `-n` to display output lines preceded by line numbers, numbered sequentially from 1.
- `-q` to suppress message if the `cat` command cannot find one or more of the input files.
- `-v` to display nonprintable characters in the file as printable characters.

CAUTION

If you are using the output redirection operator (>) to redirect the standard output of the `cat` command, be careful not to use one of the input filenames as the output filename. If you do that, the input filename will be overwritten. Some UNIX versions may give you an error message when you try to do that but overwrite the file anyway.

While accepting input from the standard input, you should use Ctrl-d to indicate the end of the input.

Examples

In its most simple form, you can just type in the command `cat`, which should put you in the entry mode. In this mode you can enter multiple lines followed by Ctrl-d to signal the end. The `cat` command will display the lines you have just entered:

```
cat
This is test line 1
This is test line 1
This is test line 2
This is test line 2
Ctrl d
```

You should be aware that the `cat` command does not provide any prompt in the above case.

If you want display a file called `testfile` in the current directory on your terminal, execute the following command:

```
cat testfile
```

This will produce output as follows:

```
This is a test file
This does not contain anything meaningful
This is for demo only
```

You should be careful if the file is big. A large file will scroll by on your terminal, and you will see only the last few lines. You can get around this by piping the output to either the `more` or `pg` command as follows:

```
cat testfile ¦ more
```

To concatenate multiple files for display on the terminal, use the following command:

```
cat testfile1 testfile2 testfile3
```

If you want to concatenate these files into a file called `testfile`, use the redirection operator > as follows:

```
cat testfile1 testfile2 testfile2 > testfile
```

If the file `testfile` already exists, it is overwritten with the concatenated files `testfile1`, `testfile2`, and `testfile3`. If `testfile` already exists and you want to concatenate at the end of the existing file, instead of using the redirection operator >, you must use the >> (two consecutive greater than signs) operator as follows:

```
cat testfile1 testfile2 testfile2 >> testfile
```

If you try to concatenate a file or a number of files so that one or more files do not exist, `cat` will concatenate all the available files and, at the end, generate a message about the nonexistent files. If you want to concatenate two files, `testfile1` and `testfile2`, into the file `testfile` in the current directory and you mis-type `testfile2` as `testtile2` while executing the following command,

```
cat testfile1 testtile2 > testfile
```

you will get a message similar to the following, and `testfile` will only have the contents of `testfile1`:

```
cat: cannot open testtile2
```

If you use the `-q` flag, you will not get the error message.

If you have `testfile` in the current directory containing the following lines (note that the last line contains special characters), cat will show the following:

```
This is a test file

This file does not contain anything meaningful
This file is for demo only
^F^F^F^F^F
```

If you execute the `cat` command with the `-n` flag, cat will display lines with line numbers, but the last line with special characters will be displayed as a blank line:

```
cat -n testfile
    1  This is a test file
    2
    3  This file does not contain anything meaningful
    4  This is for demo only
    5
```

If you want to be sure that the blank lines displayed actually do not contain any characters other than nonprintable ones, use the `-v` flag with the `cat` command. This ensures that the nonprintable characters are displayed as printable characters as follows:

```
cat -v testfile
This is a test file

This file does not contain anything meaningful
This is for demo only
^F^F^F^F^F
```

rcp

So far we have seen a number of commands to move or copy files between directories within the local host. If you need to copy files from one host to another, the rcp command can be used to copy files between different or the same hosts. You can execute the rcp command on a local host to copy files between local host and a remote host or between two remote hosts.

The filename on the remote host is preceded by the remote host ID as `hostname:/dirname/filename`. The colon (:) is used as a delimiter between the hostname and the filename.

It is also possible to specify the username at the remote host as `username@hostname:/dirname/filename`. The at-sign (@) is used as a delimiter between the username and the hostname. The username, however, is optional. If not specified, username at the remote host is the same as username at the local host.

If neither the source nor the target file specifies the host name, the rcp command behaves the same way as the cp command.

If the filename on the remote host is not qualified fully, starting with the root directory, the filename or directory name is assumed to start with the home directory of the remote user.

If the files do not already exist on the remote host, they are created with the default permission of the remote user. If the files already exist on the remote host, the permissions of the target files are preserved.

Like the cp command, you can use the rcp command to copy directories and files within directories.

The following is a list of some of the flags that can be used with the rcp command:

- -p to create the target file with the modification date and time of the source file as well as permission of the source file.
- -r to copy files recursively while copying directories.

> **NOTE**
>
> For you to use the rcp command to transfer files from or to a remote host, you must have the local hostname defined in the /etc/hosts.equiv file at the remote host, or the local hostname and the username defined in the .rhosts file in the home directory of the user on the remote host.

Examples

If you want to copy testfile from the current directory to testfile in the directory testdir under the home directory on the remote host called otherhost, execute the following command:

```
rcp testfile otherhost:testdir/testfile
```

If the username on the local host is testuser, this command will assume that the username on the remote host is testuser. If the username testuser does not exist on the remote host and you must use the username newtestuser on the remote host, execute the following command:

```
rcp testfile newtestuser@otherhost:testdir/testfile
```

If you must transfer testfile from a remote host otherhost1 to another remote host otherhost2, and you want to preserve the modification date and time as well as the permission, execute the following command:

```
rcp -p testuser1@otherhost1:testfile testuser2@otherhost2:testfile
```

This copies testfile from the home directory of user testuser1 on the remote host otherhost1 to testfile in the home directory of testuser2 on remote host otherhost2.

If you want to copy all the files in the directory /u/testuser/testdir from the remote host otherhost to the current directory on the local host, execute the following command:

```
rcp testuser@otherhost:/u/testuser/testdir/* .
```

This will not copy any sub-directories you may have in `testdir` or any files in those sub-directories. To copy all the sub-directories and files in those sub-directories, use the following command:

```
rcp -r testuser@otherhost:/u/testuser/testdir/* .
```

ln

Sometimes you need to provide alternate names for the same file. This can be achieved by linking a filename to another using the `ln` command. It is possible to link a file to another name in the same directory or the same name in another directory.

When linking a filename to another filename, you can specify only two arguments: the source filename and the target filename. When linking a filename to a directory, you can specify multiple filenames to be linked to the same directory.

If you are linking using hard links, you cannot link to a file in another filesystem, but using soft links, you can link filenames across filesystems.

The flags that can be used with the `ln` command are as follows:

- `-s` to create a soft link to another file or directory. In a soft link, the linked file contains the name of the original file. When an operation on the linked filename is done, the name of the original file in the link is used to reference the original file.

- `-f` to ensure that the destination filename is replaced by the linked filename if the file already exists.

By default, the `ln` command creates a hard link.

Examples

If you want to link `testfile1` to `testfile2` in the current directory, execute the following command:

```
ln testfile1 testfile2
```

This creates a hard linked `testfile2` linking it to `tesftfile1`. In this case, if one of the files is removed, the other will remain unaltered.

If `testfile` is in the current directory and is to be linked to `testfile` in the directory `/u/testuser/testdir`, execute the following command:

```
ln testfile /u/testuser/testdir
```

To create a symbolic link of `testfile1` in the current directory, execute the following command:

```
ln -s testfile1 testfile2
```

This creates a linked `testfile2`, which will contain the name of `testfile1`. If you remove `testfile1`, you will be left with an orphan `testfile2`, which points to nowhere.

If you want to link all the files in the current directory to another directory, `/u/testuser/testdir`, execute the following command:

```
ln * /u/testuser/testdir/.
```

Directory Manipulation Commands

When you are set up as a user in a UNIX operating system, you usually are set up with the directory `/u/username` as your home directory. To organize your files, you must set up directories of your liking. Here we will present the commands to create and remove directories.

mkdir

To create a directory, use the `mkdir` command. The `mkdir` command accepts multiple directory names for creation at the same time. As you did with the files, use relative pathname or absolute pathname to create a directory. To create a directory, you must have write permission for its parent directory, and UNIX uses the current permission setting (refer to the `umask` command) to set the permission for the directory.

The following is a list of the flags that can be used with the `mkdir` command:

- `-p` to create all the directories in the part name of the specified directory if they do not exist.
- `-m` permission to specify permission for the directory to be created.

Examples

If your current directory is `/u/testuser`,

```
mkdir temp
```

will create a directory called `temp` under the directory `/u/testuser`, whose absolute pathname is `/u/testuser/temp`.

```
mkdir /u/testuser/temp
```

can also be used to have the same effect as the previous one.

```
mkdir ../temp
```

can be used to create the `/u/temp` directory. Here we have used `..` (two consecutive periods) as part of the relative pathname to indicate that the directory `temp` will be created under the directory one level up, that is, `/u`.

To create `testdir1` and `testdir2` in the current directory, use

```
mkdir testdir1 /u/testuser/temp/testdir2
```

which will create `testdir1` in the current directory and `testdir2` in `/u/testuser/temp` (assuming it exists). In this example, `testdir1` uses a relative pathname while `/u/testuser/temp/testdir2` uses an absolute pathname.

If the directory `testdir` is already present and if you try to create the directory again, you will get a message similar to the following:

```
mkdir: cannot create testfir.
testdir: File exists
```

If you want to create the directory `testdir` under the current directory and grant the access `770` to it, execute the following command:

```
mkdir -m 770 testdir
```

If you want to create the directory `testdir` under the current directory and subdirectory `temp` under `testdir`, create both of them using a single command as follows:

```
mkdir -p testdir/temp
```

rmdir

Once you are done with a directory or you run out of space and want to remove a directory, use the `rmdir` command. You can remove a directory only if it is empty, that is, all the files and directories in it have been removed. You can specify multiple directory names as arguments to `rmdir` command. To remove a directory, you must have write permission to the parent directory.

The following is a flag that can be used with `rmdir` command:

- ■   -p to remove all the directories in the specified pathname

Examples

If your current directory is `/u/testuser` and it contains the `temp` subdirectory, to remove `temp`, use the command:

```
rmdir temp
```

If the directory `temp` is not empty, you will get a message similar to the following:

```
rmdir: Directory temp is not empty.
```

Assume you are in the directory `/u/testuser` and it contains a sub-directory `testdir` and the sub-directory `testdir` contains a sub-directory `temp`. To remove the directory `testdir` in the current directory and the sub-directory `temp` under `testdir`, execute the following command (assuming that all the files and directories under them have been removed):

```
rmdir -p testdir/temp
```

File Information Commands

Each file and directory in UNIX has several attributes associated with it. UNIX provides several commands to inquire about and process these attributes.

ls

The `ls` command can be used to inquire about the various attributes of one or more files or directories. You must have read permission to a directory to be able to use the `ls` command on that directory and the files under that directory. The `ls` command generates the output to standard output, which can be redirected, using the UNIX redirection operator >, to a file.

You can provide the names of one or more filenames or directories to the `ls` command. The file and directory names are optional. If you do not provide them, UNIX processes the current directory.

Be default, the list of files within a directory is sorted by filename. You can modify the sort order by using some of the flags discussed later.

You should also be aware that the files starting with . (period) will not be processed unless you use the `-a` flag with the `ls` command. This means that the entries . (single period) and . . (two consecutive periods) will not be processed by default.

Following is a list of some of the flags that can be used with the `ls` command:

- `-A` to list all entries in a directory except . (single period) and . . (two consecutive periods).

- `-a` to list all entries in a directory including hidden files (filenames starting with . [period]).

- `-b` to display nonprintable characters. The characters are displayed in an octal (`\nnn`) notation.

- `-c` to use the time of last modification of the i-node. When used with the `-t` flag, the output is sorted by the time of last modification of the i-node. When used with the `-1` flag, the time displayed is the last modification time of the i-node. This flag must be used with the `-t` or `-1` flag.

- `-C` to sort output vertically in a multiple column format. This is the default method when output is to a terminal.

- `-d` to restrict the information displayed only to that of the directory specified. By default, the information of the files or sub-directories under a directory is also displayed.

- `-e` to display the following information for each specified file or directory:
    1. Permission associated with the files and directories
    2. Number of links
    3. Owner
    4. Group
    5. Size (in bytes)
    6. Time of last modification

7. Name of each file. If a special file, the size field contains the major and minor device numbers. If the file is a symbolic link, the path name of the linked-to file is printed preceded by a -> (minus sign followed by greater than sign). The attributes of the symbolic link are displayed.

■ -f to list the name in each slot for each directory specified in the directory parameter. This flag turns off the -1, -t, -s, and -r flags, and turns on the -a flag. The order of the listing is the order in which entries appear in the directory.

■ -F to put special characters before different file types as follows:

1. / (slash) after each directory
2. * (asterisk) if the file is executable
3. = (equal sign) if the file is a socket
4. ¦ (pipe sign) if the file is a FIFO
5. @ (at sign) for a symbolic link

■ -g displays the following information for files and directories:

1. Permission
2. Number of links
3. Group
4. Size (in bytes)
5. Time of last modification

■ -i to display the i-node number in the first column of the report for each file.

■ -1 to display the following information about specified files and directories:

1. Permission
2. Number of links
3. Owner
4. Group
5. Size (in bytes)
6. Time of last modification

■ -m to display the output in a comma-separated format.

■ -n to display the following information for specified files and directories:

1. Permission
2. Number of links
3. Owner ID
4. Group ID
5. Size (in bytes)
6. Time of last modification

■ -o to display the following information about specified files and directories:

   1. Permission

   2. Number of links

   3. Owner id

   4. Size (in bytes)

   5. Time of last modification

■ -p to put a slash (/) after each directory name.

■ -q to display nondisplayable characters in filenames as a ? (question mark).

■ -r to reverse the order of the sort. If the list is to be displayed in name order, it will be displayed in reverse name order. If the list is to be displayed in descending time order (using the -t flag), that is, latest one first, the list will be displayed in ascending time order, oldest one first.

■ -R to list all subdirectories recursively under the specified directory.

■ -s to provide the size of files and directories in kilobytes.

■ -t to sort the list of entries by time of last modification (latest first) instead of by name.

■ -u to use time of last access instead of time of last modification. If used with -l, time of last access is displayed instead of time of last modification. If used with -t, the output is sorted by time of last access instead of last modification. This flag must be used with the -l and -t flags.

■ -x to sort the output horizontally in a multiple column format.

■ -1 to display the output as one entry per line.

The permission details displayed by the ls command when certain flags, such as -l, are used consists of 10 characters, details of which are as follows:

■ Byte 1: d designates a directory, b designates a block special file, c designates a character special file, l designates a symbolic link, p designates a first-in, first-out (FIFO) special file, s designates a local socket, designates an ordinary file (for example, one which contains text).

■ Byte 2: r if read permission for owner has been granted, - (hyphen) if read permission for owner has not been granted.

■ Byte 3: w if write permission for owner has been granted, - (hyphen) if write permission for owner has not been granted.

■ Byte 4: x if execute permission for owner has been granted, - (hyphen) if execute permission for owner has not been granted, s if the file has set-user-ID mode.

■ Byte 5: r if read permission for group has been granted. - (hyphen) if read permission for group has not been granted.

- Byte 6: w if write permission for group has been granted, - (hyphen) if write permission for group has not been granted.

- Byte 7: x if execute permission for group has been granted, - (hyphen) if execute permission for group has not been granted, s if the file has set-group-ID mode.

- Byte 8: r if read permission for others has been granted, - (hyphen) if read permission for others has not been granted.

- Byte 9: w if write permission for others has been granted, - (hyphen) if write permission for others has not been granted.

- Byte 10: x if execute permission for others has been granted, - (hyphen) if execute permission for others has not been granted.

The execute permission for a file means that the file is an executable file. But the execute permission for a directory means that you can execute searches on the specified directory to locate one or more files.

Examples

Let us assume that the following files and directories are present in the current directory .dot1, test1, test2, test3, and test4. Also assume that test2 is a directory.

The simplest form of the ls command can be used to get the list of files and directories in the current directory as follows:

```
ls
test1  test2 test3  test4 test5
```

In this list the entry .dot1 is not displayed because the file .dot1 is a hidden file. To display all the entries including the hidden files, execute the following command:

```
ls -a
. .. .dot1 test1  test2 test3  test4 test5
```

From the above list, you cannot get details about the entry. To get a detailed list of all the files and directories, execute the following command with the -a flag:

```
ls -la
total 56
drwxrwx---    3 testuser    author     3072 Nov 24 17:35 .
drwxr-xr-x   36 root        system     2048 Nov 23 19:51 ..
-rw-r--r--    1 testuser    author        0 Nov 24 14:54 .dot1
-rw-r--r--    1 testuser    author       10 Nov 24 17:36 test1
drwxr-xr-x    2 testuser    author      512 Nov 24 17:32 test2
-rw-r--r--    1 testuser    author        0 Nov 24 14:58 test3
-rw-r--r--    1 testuser    author        0 Nov 24 17:33 test4
-rw-r--r--    1 testuser    author    11885 Nov 24 11:50 test5
```

Use of the -a flag displays the two special entries that are present in all directories: . (a single period) to identify the specified directory and .. (two consecutive periods) to identify the parent directory of the specified directory. In the above example, . (a single period) identifies current directory and .. (two consecutive periods) identifies the parent directory.

If you just want to have a list of directories, execute the following command with the -d flag:

```
ls -ald
drwxrwx---   3 testuser   author       3072 Nov 24 17:15 .
```

As you have seen in the above examples, the list of files and directories are ordered by name. If you want to get a list of the entries by time of last modification so that you know which you have worked on last, execute the following command with the -t flag:

```
ls -lat
total 56
drwxrwx---   3 testuser   author       3072 Nov 24 17:37 .
-rw-r--r--   1 testuser   author         10 Nov 24 17:36 test1
-rw-r--r--   1 testuser   author          0 Nov 24 17:33 test4
drwxr-xr-x   2 testuser   author        512 Nov 24 17:32 test2
-rw-r--r--   1 testuser   author          0 Nov 24 14:58 test3
-rw-r--r--   1 testuser   author          0 Nov 24 14:54 .dot1
-rw-r--r--   1 testuser   author      11885 Nov 24 11:50 test5
drwxr-xr-x  36 root       system       2048 Nov 23 19:51 ..
```

Until now, we have not specified any file or directory name in the ls command. If you want to search for all entries that start with test, specify test* as the entry name as follows:

```
ls -la test*
-rw-r--r--   1 testuser   author         10 Nov 24 17:36 test1
-rw-r--r--   1 testuser   author          0 Nov 24 14:58 test3
-rw-r--r--   1 testuser   author          0 Nov 24 17:33 test4
-rw-r--r--   1 testuser   author      11885 Nov 24 11:50 test5

test2:
total 16
drwxr-xr-x   2 testuser   author        512 Nov 24 17:32 .
drwxrwx---   3 testuser   author       3072 Nov 24 17:41 ..
-rw-r--r--   1 testuser   author          0 Nov 24 17:45 test21
-rw-r--r--   1 testuser   author          0 Nov 24 14:58 test22
```

Notice that the entries . (single period), .. (two consecutive periods) and .dot1 are not displayed above because the wildcard * (asterisk) does not match the . (period) character.

If you want to obtain a comma-separated list of file and directory names in the current directory, execute the following command with the -m flag:

```
ls -am
., .., .dot1, test1, test2, test3, test4, test5
```

If you want to obtain a list of entries while being able to identify the directories with / (slash), execute the following command with the -p flag:

```
ls -ap
./              test1           test4
../             test2/          test5
.dot1           test3
```

A similar output can be obtained using the -F flag, although -F is more versatile. That is, -F can also identify executable files, symbolic links, and so on.

If you want to get the list of entries in the reverse order of name, execute the following command with the -r flag:

```
ls -rla
total 56
-rw-r--r--   1 testuser    author    11885 Nov 24 11:50 test5
-rw-r--r--   1 testuser    author        0 Nov 24 17:33 test4
-rw-r--r--   1 testuser    author        0 Nov 24 14:58 test3
drwxr-xr-x   2 testuser    author      512 Nov 24 17:32 test2
-rw-r--r--   1 testuser    author       10 Nov 24 17:36 test1
-rw-r--r--   1 testuser    author        0 Nov 24 14:54 .dot1
drwxr-xr-x  36 root        system     2048 Nov 23 19:51 ..
drwxrwx---   3 testuser    author     3072 Nov 24 18:00 .
```

To obtain a list of all files in the current directory as well as all files under all the sub-directories, execute the following command with the -R flag:

```
ls -lR
total 40
-rw-r--r--   1 testuser    author       10 Nov 24 17:36 test1
drwxr-xr-x   2 testuser    author      512 Nov 24 17:32 test2
-rw-r--r--   1 testuser    author        0 Nov 24 14:58 test3
-rw-r--r--   1 testuser    author        0 Nov 24 17:33 test4
-rw-r--r--   1 testuser    author    11885 Nov 24 11:50 test5

./test2:
total 0
-rw-r--r--   1 testuser    author        0 Nov 24 17:45 test21
-rw-r--r--   1 testuser    author        0 Nov 24 14:58 test22
```

Following are examples of the ls command with and without the -u flag. The list without the -u flag displays the time of last modification while the one with the -u flag displays the time of last access:

```
ls -lu
total 40
-rw-r--r--   1 testuser    author       10 Nov 24 17:34 test1
drwxr-xr-x   2 testuser    author      512 Nov 24 18:19 test2
-rw-r--r--   1 testuser    author        0 Nov 24 14:58 test3
-rw-r--r--   1 testuser    author        0 Nov 24 17:33 test4
-rw-r--r--   1 testuser    author    11885 Nov 24 17:56 test5

ls -l
total 40
-rw-r--r--   1 testuser    author       10 Nov 24 17:36 test1
drwxr-xr-x   2 testuser    author      512 Nov 24 17:32 test2
-rw-r--r--   1 testuser    author        0 Nov 24 14:58 test3
-rw-r--r--   1 testuser    author        0 Nov 24 17:33 test4
-rw-r--r--   1 testuser    author    11885 Nov 24 11:50 test5
```

find

If you are not sure where a particular file exists, use the find command to search for the particular file. The find command gives you the flexibility to search for a file by various attributes, such as name, size, permission, and so on. Additionally, the find command allows you to execute commands on the files that are found as a result of the search.

The format of the `find` command is as follows:

`find *directory-name* search-expression`

The directory name can be a full pathname or a `.`(single period) for the current directory.

The following is a list of terms that can be used with the `find` command:

- `-name` *filename* to specify the name of the file (including wildcards) to be used for searching. You can also use range as part of the wildcards. If you want to use wildcard characters, you must specify them within quotes. For example, `"test*"` will find all files starting with `test`. If you specify, `"test[1-2]"`, you will find files that start with `test` and have `1` or `2` as the last characters such as `test1` and `test2`.

- `-size` *Number* to specify the size of the file to be used for searching. The file size specified is in blocks. To specify that you want to match size of files less than the specified size, use a - (minus sign) in front of the size and if you want to match size of files greater than the specified size use a + (plus sign) in front of the size. For example, `-size 5` will match files that have size of 5 blocks (the size of a file while matching is always rounded up to the next nearest block), `-size -5` will match files that have size of less than or equal to 5 blocks and `-size +5` will match files that have size of more than 5 blocks.

- `-size` *Numberc* to specify the size of the file to be used for searching. That is, specify a `c` at the end of the number. The file size is then taken to be specified in number of bytes. To specify that you want to match size of files less than the specified size, use a - (minus sign) in front of the size and if you want to match size of files greater than the specified size use a + (plus sign) in front of the size. For example, `-size 50c` will match files that have size of 50 bytes blocks, `-size -50c` will match files that have size of less than or equal to 50 bytes and `-size +50c` will match files that have size of more than 50 bytes.

- `-prune` to restrict the `find` command not to process directories recursively. By default `find` recursively processes all the directories and sub-directories under the specified directory.

- `-atime` *number* to search for files that have been accessed in the specified number of 24-hour periods. The number of 24-hour periods is computed by adding 1 to the number specified. 0 means the last 24 hours.

- `-mtime` *number* to search for files that have been modified in the specified number of 24-hour periods. The number of 24-hour periods is computed by adding 1 to the number specified. 0 means the last 24 hours.

- `-ctime` *number* to search for files whose i-node has been modified in the specified number of 24-hour periods. The number of 24-hour periods is computed by adding 1 to the number specified. 0 means the last 24 hours.

- **-type** *filetype* to search for a specific type of file. The following is a list of types that can be used:
  - b—Block special file
  - c—Character special file
  - d—Directory
  - f—Regular file
  - l—Symbolic link
  - p—FIFO (a named pipe)
  - s—Socket
- **-user** is the username to search for files whose owner matches the specified username.
- **-perm** *permission* to search for files with specified permission. The permission is specified as an octal number of up to 3 digits. If the permission is not preceded by a - (hyphen), an exact match of the permission specified is made with the file permissions. If permission is preceded by a - (hyphen), file permission is ANDed with the specified permission. For example, if you want to search for files with owner read permission, use -perm -400.
- **-newer** *filename* to search for files that has time of modification later than that of the specified filename.
- **-group** *groupname* to search for files that belong to the specified group.
- **-inum** *Number* to search for files whose i-node number matches the specified i-node number.
- **-links** *Number* to search for files with a specified number of links. To specify that you want to match number of links less than the specified number of links, use a – (minus sign) in front of the number of links, and if you want to match a number of links greater than the specified number of links use a + (plus sign) in front of number of links.
- **-ls** to print the current path name along with the following attributes:
  - i-node number
  - Size in kilobytes (1024 bytes)
  - Protection mode
  - Number of hard links
  - User
  - Group
  - Size in bytes
  - Modification time

- -exec *command* to execute the command. To execute the command on the list of the files found by the `find` command use {} followed by \; (backslash followed by semicolon).

- -ok *command* to execute the command. To execute the command on the list of the files found by the `find` command use {} followed by \; (backslash followed by semicolon). UNIX asks for confirmation before proceeding with executing the command.

- -print to print the output generated as a result of the search.

These operators can be specified in conjunction with each other to form complex criteria for searches. You can combine several operators as follows:

- *operator* -a *operator* to search for files that satisfy both the specified conditions.

- *operator* -o *operator* to search for files that satisfy either of the specified conditions.

- !*operator* to search for files that do not satisfy the specified condition.

Examples

Assume the following files exist in the current directory:

```
ls -al
total 64
drwxrwx---   3 testuser    author      3072 Nov 25 00:41 .
drwxr-xr-x  36 root        system      2048 Nov 23 19:51 ..
-rw-r--r--   1 testuser    author         0 Nov 24 14:54 .dot1
-rw-------   1 testuser    author        10 Nov 24 17:36 test1
drwxr-xr-x   2 testuser    author       512 Nov 24 17:32 test2
-r-x------   1 testuser    author         0 Nov 24 14:58 test3
-rw-r--r--   1 testuser    author         0 Nov 24 17:33 test4
-rw-r--r--   1 testuser    author     15647 Nov 24 18:32 test5
```

In its simplest form, you can execute the following command to get a list of all the files in the current directory and its sub-directories.

```
find . -print
.
./test5
./test1
./test3
./test4
./test2
./test2/test21
./test2/test22
./.dot1
```

If you want to search for all the files in the current directory that have been modified in the last 24 hours, use the -mtime operator as follows:

```
find . -mtime 0 -print
.
./test5
./test1
./test3
./test4
```

```
./test2
./test2/test21
./test2/test22
./ /.dot1
```

To search for a file whose permission is `600` (only owner has read and write permissions), execute the following command using the `-perm` operator:

```
find . -perm 600  -print
./test1
```

In this case, only the file that has permission of exactly `600` is displayed. However, if you want to search for a file with owner read and write permission, execute the following command using a `-`(hyphen) in front of `600`:

```
find . -perm -600  -print
.
./test5
./test1
./test4
./test2
./test2/test21
./test2/test22
./ /.dot1
```

If you are interested in searching for directories only, use the `-type` operator and execute the following command:

```
find . -type d -print
.
./test2
```

To get more information about the files that are found as a result of the search, use the `-ls` operator and execute the following command:

```
find . -ls
    2    4 drwxrwx---  3 settlea   eod          3072 Nov 25 01:11 .
   16   16 -rw-r--r--  1 testuser  author        647 Nov 24 18:32 ./test5
   18    4 -rw-------  1 testuser  author         10 Nov 24 17:36 ./test1
   19    0 -r-x------  1 testuser  author          0 Nov 24 14:58 ./test3
   20    0 -rw-r--r--  1 testuser  author          0 Nov 24 17:33 ./test4
67584    4 drwxr-xr-x  2 testuser  author        512 Nov 24 17:32 ./test2
67585    0 -rw-r--r--  1 testuser  author          0 Nov 24 17:45 ./test2/test21
67586    0 -rw-r--r--  1 testuser  author          0 Nov 24 14:58 ./test2/test22
   22    0 -rw-r--r--  1 testuser  author          0 Nov 24 14:54 ./ /.dot1
```

To search for all filenames that start with `test`, use the `-name` operator and execute the following command:

```
find . -name "test*" -print
./test5
./test1
./test3
./test4
./test2
./test2/test21
./test2/test22
```

As you can see, the `find` command traversed the sub-directory `test2` to obtain the filenames under that also. If you want to restrict the search only to the current directory and leave out the sub-directories, use the operator `-prune` and execute the following command:

```
find . -name "test*" -prune -print
./test5
./test1
./test3
./test4
./test2
```

To find a list of files in the current directory that are newer than the file `test1`, use the operator `-newer` and execute the following command:

```
find . -newer test1  -print
./test5
./test2/test21
```

On the other hand, if you want to find a list of files older than the file `test1`, use the negation operator `!` in conjunction with the operator `-newer` in the following command:

```
find . ! -newer test1  -print
.
./test3
./test4
./test2
./test2/test22
./.dot1
```

If you want a list of all files that are exactly 10 bytes in size, use the `-size` operator and execute the following command:

```
find . -size 10c  -print
./test1
```

If you want to create a list of all files that are less than 10 bytes in size, execute the following command (the command is exactly the same as preceding one except the hyphen in front of the 10):

```
find . -size -10c -print
./test3
./test4
./test2/test21
./test2/test22
./.dot1
```

If you want a list of all files that have zero size, execute the `find` command with the `-exec` parameter as follows:

```
find . -size 0c -exec ls -l {} \;
-r-x------  1 testuser     author        0 Nov 24 14:58 ./test3
-rw-r--r--  1 testuser     author        0 Nov 24 17:33 ./test4
-rw-r--r--  1 testuser     author        0 Nov 24 17:45 ./test2/test21
-rw-r--r--  1 testuser     author        0 Nov 24 14:58 ./test2/test22
-rw-r--r--  1 testuser     author        0 Nov 24 14:54 ./.dot1
```

If you want to remove all the files with zero size but want to confirm the delete before you actually removed them, execute the following command with the -ok operator:

```
find . -size 0c -ok rm {} \;
< rm ... ./test3 > (yes)?   y
< rm ... ./test4 > (yes)?   n
< rm ... ./test2/test21 > (yes)?   y
< rm ... ./test2/test22 > (yes)?   y
< rm ... ./.dot1 > (yes)?   y
```

Here you have decided not to remove the file test4.

All the examples we have seen so far use one operator at a time. It is possible to execute the find command with complex conditions with multiple operators combined with each other using or or and conditions. If you want to find out about all the files that start with test and have a size of zero, execute the following command:

```
find . -name 'test*' -size 0c -print
./test3
./test4
./test2/test21
./test2/test22
```

In this example we have combined two different operators. It is possible to use the same operator multiple times and combine it with and or or operators. If you want to search for all files in the current directory that have a size of more than zero bytes and less than 50 bytes and whose name starts with test, use the following command:

```
find . -size +0c -a -size -50c -name 'test*' -exec ls -l {} \;
-rw------- 1 testuser    author       10 Nov 24 17:36 ./test1
```

file

The command file can be used to determine the type of the specified file. The file command actually reads through the file and performs a series of tests to determine the type of the file. The command then displays the output as standard output.

If a file appears to be ASCII, the file command examines the first 512 bytes and tries to determine its language. If a file does not appear to be ASCII, the file command further attempts to distinguish a binary data file from a text file that contains extended characters.

If the File argument specifies an executable or object module file and the version number is greater than 0, the file command displays the version stamp.

The file command uses the /etc/magic file to identify files that have some sort of a magic number; that is, any file containing a numeric or string constant that indicates type.

Examples

If you have a file called letter in you current directory that contains a letter to your friend, then executing the command

```
file letter
```

will display the following result:

```
letter:  commands text
```

If you have a file called `prog` that is an executable program and you are working on IBM RISC 6000 AIX version 3.1, then executing the command

```
file prog
```

will display the following result (if you are on a RISC 6000 system):

```
prog:        executable (RISC System/6000 V3.1)
```

If you are in `/dev` directory, which contains all the special files, then executing the command

```
file hd1
```

for a file called `hd1` (which is a disk on which a filesystem has been defined) will display the following result:

```
hd1:         block special
```

File Content–Related Commands

Here we will discuss some of the commands that can be used to look at the contents of the file or parts of it. You can use these commands to look at the top or bottom of a file, search for strings in the file, and so on.

more

The `more` command can be used to display the contents of a file one screen at a time. By default, the `more` command displays one screen worth of data at a time. However, the number of lines displayed can be modified. The `more` command pauses at the end of display of each page. To continue, press a space bar so that the next page is displayed or press the Return or Enter key to display the next line. Mostly the `more` command is used where output from other commands are piped into the `more` command for display.

Following is a list of flags that can be used with the `more` command:

- ◼ `-d` for `more` to prompt to quit, continue, or get help.
- ◼ `-f` to count logical lines in the file.
- ◼ `-number` to set the size of the display window to `number`.
- ◼ `-p` to disable scrolling. This will result in the `more` command clearing the screen at the start of each page.
- ◼ `-s` to display only one blank line when multiple contiguous blank lines are present in the file.
- ◼ `-u` to display lines without special attributes if lines in the file have special attributes.

- ■ -v to prevent display of nondisplayable characters graphically.
- ■ -w to allow you to go back in a file after reaching end of file. Default for more is to exit when end of file is reached.
- ■ +*number* to start display at line *number* in the file.
- ■ +g to start at the end of the file and be able to go backwards.
- ■ +/*pattern* to start in the file at the line number where *pattern* occurs first.

As we have already stated the more command pauses at the end of each page of display. There are several sub-commands you can use, when more pauses, to control further behavior of the more command. These sub-commands are as follows:

- ■ *number*spacebar to page forward by *number* and by one screen if *number* is not specified.
- ■ *number*d to page forward by a default number of lines (usually 11) if *number* is not specified and by *number* of lines if *number* is specified.
- ■ *number*z to page forward by specified number of lines if *number* is specified; otherwise, by one screen page.
- ■ *number*s to skip specified number of lines and display one screen page. If *number* is not specified, the next line is displayed.
- ■ *number*f to skip forward the specified *number* of screens. If *number* is not specified, the next screen is displayed.
- ■ *number*b to skip backward the specified number of screens. If *number* is not specified, the previous screen is displayed.
- ■ *number*Ctrl-B or *number*Ctrl-b to skip backward the specified number of screens. If *number* is not specified, the previous screen is displayed.
- ■ q to quit more command.
- ■ v to invoke vi editor.
- ■ *number*/*expression* to search for the expression and its position the number of occurrences specified by *number*. If the file has less than the specified number of occurrences of the expression, the display remains unaltered.
- ■ *number*n to search forward for the specified occurrence of the last expression entered. If number is not specified, the next occurrence is searched for and the screen is displayed.
- ■ !command to start command with the filename as argument if command is specified. If command is not specified, you will be returned to the shell prompt. You can then use the exit command to get back to the more command.
- ■ *number*:n to skip to the specified file following the current file if you have invoked the more command with multiple files. If the specified relative file *number* is invalid, more skips to the last file.

- *number*:p to skip to the specified file previous to the current file if you have invoked the more command with multiple files. If the specified relative file number does not exist, more skips to the first file.
- :f (followed by return key) to display the filename of the current file being displayed and the current line number being displayed at the top of the screen.
- :q or :Q (followed by return key) to quit the more command.
- . (single period) to repeat the last command executed.

Examples

Let us assume that we have a file called file1 in the current directory. The content of the file is shown below:

```
This is the line 1
This is the line 2
This is the line 3
This is the line 4
This is the line 5
This is the line 6
This is the line 7
This is the line 8
This is the line 9
This is the line 10
This is the line 11
This is the line 13
This is the line 14
This is the line 15
This is the line 16
This is the line 17
This is the line 18
This is the line 19
This is the line 20
This is the line 21
This is the line 22
This is the line 23
This is the line 24
This is the line 25
```

If you want to display file1, use the following command:

```
more file1
This is the line 1
This is the line 2
This is the line 3
This is the line 4
This is the line 5
This is the line 6
This is the line 7
This is the line 8
This is the line 9
This is the line 10
This is the line 11
This is the line 13
This is the line 14
```

```
This is the line 15
This is the line 16
This is the line 17
This is the line 18
This is the line 19
This is the line 20
This is the line 21
This is the line 22
This is the line 23
--More--(91%)
```

This has a disadvantage because once the end of file is reached, the more command is exited. If do not want to exit from the more command even when the end of file is reached, use the -w flag. This is especially useful if you are looking at a file that is in the process of being created. The following command shows the use of -w flag:

```
more -w file1
```

If you want to start from the bottom of the file rather than the top of the file and go backwards, use the +g flag as in the following command:

```
more +g file1
This is the line 3
This is the line 4
This is the line 5
This is the line 6
This is the line 7
This is the line 8
This is the line 9
This is the line 10
This is the line 11
This is the line 12
This is the line 13
This is the line 14
This is the line 15
This is the line 16
This is the line 17
This is the line 18
This is the line 19
This is the line 20
This is the line 21
This is the line 22
This is the line 23
This is the line 24
This is the line 25
--More--(EOF)
```

If you want to start the display of the file at line number 20 of file1, use the following command:

```
more +20 file1
This is the line 20
This is the line 21
This is the line 22
This is the line 23
This is the line 24
This is the line 25
```

If you want to display the five files: `file1`, `file2`, `file3`, `file4`, and `file5`, execute the following command:

```
more file1 file2 file3 file4 file5
```

less

The `less` command is one more in the family of commands to view the contents of a file. This may not be available by default on all UNIX systems. It behaves similarly to the `more` command. The `less` command allows you to go backward as well as forward in the file by default.

The following is a list of sub-commands that can be used once you are in the `less` command:

- ■ `h` to display a list of the sub-commands that can be used.
- ■ `spacebar` or `Ctrl-v` or `Ctrl-f` or `f` to go forward in the file one screen. If preceded by a number, moves forward by the specified number of lines.
- ■ `return key` or `Ctrl-n` or `Ctrl-e` or `e` or `j` to move forward by 1 line. If preceded by a number, moves forward by the specified number of lines.
- ■ `Ctrl-b` or `b` to go backward in the file by one screen. If preceded by a number, moves backward by the specified *number* of lines.
- ■ `Ctrl-d` or `d` to go forward by half screen (default of 11 lines). If preceded by a number, moves forward by the specified number of lines. The new number is then registered as the new default for all subsequent `d` or `u` commands.
- ■ `g` to go the top of the file by default. If preceded by a number, the file is positioned at the line specified by the number.
- ■ `G` to go the bottom of the file by default. If preceded by a number, the file is positioned at the line specified by the number.
- ■ `p` or `%` to go to the top of the file by default. If preceded by a number between 0 and 100, positions to the percentage of file specified by the number.
- ■ `Ctrl-p` or `Ctrl-k` or `Ctrl-y` or `k` or `y` to go backward by 1 line. If preceded by a number, moves backward by the specified number of lines.
- ■ `Ctrl-u` or `u` to go backward by half a screen (default of 11 lines). If preceded by a number, moves backward by the specified number of lines. The new number is registered as the new default for all subsequent `d` or `u` commands.
- ■ `Ctrl-l` or `Ctrl-r` or `r` to redraw the current screen.
- ■ `mlowercaseletter` to mark the position with the *lowercaseletter* marker for use later.
- ■ `'lowercaseletter` to go to the position marked with *lowercaseletter* using the `m` sub-command. If `'` is followed by `^` (caret), `less` displays the top of the file. If `'` is followed by `$` (dollar sign), `less` displays the bottom of the file.
- ■ `number/pattern` to position the file in the specified occurrence of the *pattern* in the file. You can use the following special characters to indicate special actions:

- ! to search for lines that do not contain the specified `pattern`.
- * to search multiple files if invoked with multiple files.
- @ to start search at the top of the first file if invoked with multiple files.
- n to repeat the last search executed. If the sub-command is preceded by a number, the file is positioned to the specified occurrence of the *pattern* previously specified. You can use the N sub-command to search in the reverse direction.
- :e *filename* or :E *filename* to execute the `less` command for a specified *filename* and add it to the list of files for subsequent use.
- :n to execute the `less` command on the next file on the list of files. The list of files can be specified by invoking `less` with multiple files, or added to the list by using the :e sub-command. You can use the :p sub-command similarly for previous file in the list.
- :*number*x to execute `less` on the first file in the list if number is not specified. If a number is specified, the `less` command on the file in that position in the list is executed.
- = or :f to get information about the file and the current position in the file.
- q or Q to exit `less`.
- v to invoke `vi` with the current filename.
- !*command* to execute a shell *command*. If *command* is omitted, you will be put into a shell prompt. You can exit the shell by using the `exit` command to be back into the `less` command.

Examples

To invoke the `less` command for a file named `file1`, use the following command:

```
less file1
```

tail

You can use the `tail` command to display, on standard output, a file starting from a specified point from the start or bottom of the file. Whether it starts from the top of the file or end of the file depends on the parameter and flags used. One of the flags, -f, can be used to look at the bottom of a file continuously as it grows in size. By default, `tail` displays the last 10 lines of the file.

The following is a list of flags that can be used with the `tail` command:

- -c *number* to start from the specified character position number.
- -b *number* to start from the specified 512-byte block position number.
- -k *number* to start from the specified 1024-byte block position number.
- -n *number* to start display of the file in the specified line number.

■ `-r` *number* to display lines from the file in reverse order.

■ `-f` to display the end of the file continuously as it grows in size.

With all these flags, the number you can specify may be a number prefixed by a + (plus sign) or a – (minus sign). If you specify a + the `tail` command starts processing from the start of the file. If you specify a – or do not specify any sign, `tail` starts processing from the bottom of the file.

Examples

Let us assume that we have a file called `file1` that contains 30 lines. The contents of the file are displayed below:

```
This is the line 1
This is the line 2
This is the line 3
This is the line 4
This is the line 5
This is the line 6
This is the line 7
This is the line 8
This is the line 9
This is the line 10
This is the line 11
This is the line 12
This is the line 13
This is the line 14
This is the line 15
This is the line 16
This is the line 17
This is the line 18
This is the line 19
This is the line 20
This is the line 21
This is the line 22
This is the line 23
This is the line 24
This is the line 25
This is the line 26
This is the line 27
This is the line 28
This is the line 29
This is the line 30
```

If you want to see the last 10 lines of the file, execute the `tail` command without any flags as follows:

```
tail file1
This is the line 21
This is the line 22
This is the line 23
This is the line 24
This is the line 25
This is the line 26
This is the line 27
This is the line 28
This is the line 29
This is the line 30
```

In the preceding example, the last 10 lines of `file1` are displayed. If you want to skip 27 lines from the start of the file, execute the following command:

```
tail +27 file1
This is the line 28
This is the line 29
This is the line 30
```

In this example, the display starts at the 28th line from the top of the file. If you want to start from a specified byte position in the file instead of the line position, use the -c flag as follows:

```
tail -c +500 file1
the line 27
This is the line 28
This is the line 29
This is the line 30
```

In this example, the display start at the 500th byte from the top of the file. If you want to specify an absolute line number from which to display the file, use the -n flag as in the following command:

```
tail -n -5 file1
This is the line 26
This is the line 27
This is the line 28
This is the line 29
This is the line 30
```

In this example, the display starts at the 5th line from the bottom. If you want to display the lines of `file1` in reverse order, use -r flag as in the following command:

```
tail -r -n -5 file1
This is the line 30
This is the line 29
This is the line 28
This is the line 27
This is the line 26
```

In this example, the last 5 lines are displayed in reverse order with the last line first.

head

The head command displays a file on the standard output. The head command starts from the top of the file and displays the specified number of bytes or lines from the start of the file. By default, head displays 10 lines.

Following are the flags that can be used with the head command:

- ■ -c *number* to display the number of bytes from the top of the file.
- ■ -n *number* to display the number of lines from the top of the file.

The number can be specified without any sign or preceded by a –, both of which mean the same thing.

Examples

Let us assume that we have `file1` whose contents are the same as the one shown in the `tail` command.

If you want to display a specified number of lines from the top, use the `-n` flag as in the following command:

```
head -3 file1
This is the line 1
This is the line 2
This is the line 3
```

In this example, the first three lines of `file1` are displayed. If you want to display the first specified number of bytes from the top of the file, use the `-c` flag as in the following command:

```
head -c 29 file1
This is the line 1
This is th
```

In this example, the first 29 bytes of `file1` are displayed.

WC

The `wc` command counts the number of bytes, words, and lines in specified files. A word is a number of characters stringed together delimited by either a space or a newline character.

Following is a list of flags that can be used with the `wc` command:

- `-l` to count only the number of lines in the file.
- `-w` to count only the number of words in the file.
- `-c` to count only the number of bytes in the file.

You can use multiple filenames as argument to the `wc` command.

Examples

If you want to know the number of bytes, words, and lines in `file1`, execute the following command:

```
wc file1
    25     125     491 file1
```

This example shows that `file1` has 25 lines, 125 words, and 491 bytes. If you want to find only the number of words in `file1`, use the `-w` flag as in the following command:

```
wc -w file1
    125 file1
```

If you want to get the word count on `file1` and `file2`, execute the following command:

```
wc -w file1 file2
    125 file1
    463 file2
    588 total
```

5

GENERAL
COMMANDS

Notice that if you use multiple files, you will get an extra line in the output that has the total of all files.

read

The `read` command is used in shell scripts to read each field from a file and assign them to shell variables. A field is a string of bytes that are separated by a space or newline character. If the number of fields read is less than the number of variables specified, the rest of the fields are unassigned.

The following is a flag that can be used with `read` command:

- ■ `-r` to treat a \ (backslash) as part of the input record and not as a control character.

Examples

Following is a piece of shell script code that reads first name and last name from `namefile` and prints them:

```
while read -r lname fname
do
        echo $lname","$fname
done < namefile
```

od

The `od` command can be used to display the contents of a file in a specified format. Usually, this command is used to look at executable files or other files that are nontext, which most of the UNIX commands cannot process. You can also specify the offset from where you want the display of the file start.

Following is a list of flags that can be used with the `od` command:

- ■ `-d` to display the output as a signed decimal number.
- ■ `-i` to display the output as an unsigned decimal number.
- ■ `-f` to display the output as a floating number.
- ■ `-b` to display the output as an octal value.
- ■ `-h` to display the output as a hexadecimal value.
- ■ `-c` to display the output as ASCII characters.

You can specify the offset of the byte where you want to start the display after the filename. If the offset is preceded by `0x`, the offset is interpreted as a hexadecimal number. If the offset is preceded by `0`, the offset is interpreted as an octal number. The offset can be suffixed by `b` for bytes, `k` for kilobytes (1024 bytes) and `m` for megabytes (1024 × 1024 bytes).

Examples

To display the contents of `file1`, execute the following command:.

```
od file1 ¦ more
0000000   000737 000007 031147 104407 000000 000000 000000 000000
0000020   000110 010007 000413 000001 000002 024250 000001 056674
0000040   000012 030504 000001 052320 000000 001000 000000 000000
0000060   000001 055020 000004 000002 000004 000004 000007 000005
```

This displays `file1` in decimal format. If you want to display the file in hexadecimal format, use the `-h` flag as in the following command:

```
od -h file1 ¦ more
0000000   01df 0007 3267 8907 0000 0000 0000 0000
0000020   0048 1007 010b 0001 0002 28a8 0001 5dbc
0000040   000a 3144 0001 54d0 0000 0200 0000 0000
0000060   0001 5a10 0004 0002 0004 0004 0007 0005
```

If you want to start the display at byte position 40 and display in ASCII format, use the following command:

```
od -c file1 +40 ¦ more
0000040   \0  \n   1   D  \0 001   T 320  \0  \0 002  \0  \0  \0  \0  \0
0000060   \0 001   Z 020  \0 004  \0 002  \0 004  \0 004  \0 007  \0 005
```

It is possible to display the contents of `file1` in octal, ASCII, and hexadecimal format all at once, using the following command:

```
od -bch file1 ¦ more
0000000   001 337 000 007 062 147 211 007 000 000 000 000 000 000 000 000
          001 337  \0 007   2   g 211 007  \0  \0  \0  \0  \0  \0  \0  \0
            01df      0007      3267      8907      0000      0000      0000      0000
0000020   000 110 020 007 001 013 000 001 000 002 050 250 000 001 135 274
           \0   H 020 007 001 013  \0 001  \0 002   ( 250  \0 001   ] 274
            0048      1007      010b      0001      0002      28a8      0001      5dbc
0000040   000 012 061 104 000 001 124 320 000 000 002 000 000 000 000 000
           \0  \n   1   D  \0 001   T 320  \0  \0 002  \0  \0  \0  \0  \0
            000a      3144      0001      54d0      0000      0200      0000      0000
0000060   000 001 132 020 000 004 000 002 000 004 000 004 000 007 000 005
           \0 001   Z 020  \0 004  \0 002  \0 004  \0 004  \0 007  \0 005
            0001      5a10      0004      0002      0004      0004      0007      0005.
```

pg

The `pg` command can be used to display the contents of a file one page at a time, just like the `more` and `less` commands. The `pg` command pauses at the end of each screen display so that you can enter a number of sub-commands that can be used to search a string in the file, go backward or forward in the file, and so on.

Following is a list of flags that can be used with the `pg` command:

■ `-c` to clear the screen at the end of each page of display and start the display at the top of the screen.

■ -e continues to the next file at the end of one file, if the pg command is invoked with multiple files. Usually, pg pauses at the end of each file.

■ -f to truncate lines that are longer than the width of screen display.

■ -p *string* to display the *string* as the pg command prompt. The default prompt is : (colon). If the string specified is %d, the page number is displayed at the prompt.

■ -s to highlight all messages and prompts issued by the pg command.

■ +*number* to start the display at the specified line number in the file.

■ -*number* to set the size of the display screen to the specified number of lines.

■ +/*pattern*/ to search for the *pattern* in the file and start the display at that line.

A number of sub-commands can be used with the pg command when it pauses at the end of each screen of display. You must press the Return key after entering each sub-command. Following is a list of some of these sub-commands:

■ -*number* to go backward the number of pages specified by *number*.

■ +*number* to go forward the number of pages specified by *number*.

■ l to go forward in the file by one line.

■ *number*l to start the display in the file at the line specified by *number*.

■ +*number*l to go forward the number of lines specified by *number* in the file.

■ -*number*l to go backward the number of lines specified by *number* in the file.

■ d to go forward by half a screen.

■ -d to go backward by half a screen.

■ -n to indicate to pg that it should interpret and execute the sub-commands as they are entered without waiting for the newline character to be entered.

■ Ctrl-l to redraw the current screen.

■ $ to go to the last page of the file.

■ *number*/*pattern*/ to search forward for the *pattern* in the file starting at the beginning of the next page. If *number* is specified, then pg searches for the specified occurrence number of *pattern*. The search does not wrap around. If you want to search backward, use ? (question mark) instead of / (slash).

■ *number*p to start executing the pg command on the previous file if *number* is not specified. If *number* is specified, start at the file whose position in the list of files is *number* before the current file.

■ *number*n to start executing the pg command on the next file if *number* is not specified. If *number* is specified, start at the file whose position in the list of files is *number* after the current file.

■ s*filename* to save the current file being processed in the specified *filename*.

■ q or Q to quit the pg command.

Examples

Let us assume that we have `file1` whose content is the same as that shown in the `tail` command.

To change the number of lines to be displayed by the `pg` command, prefix the size by a – (minus sign) as in the following command:

```
pg -7 file1
This is the line 1
This is the line 2
This is the line 3
This is the line 4
This is the line 5
This is the line 6
This is the line 7
:
```

In this example, the number of lines displayed is modified to 7. On the other hand, if you want to start the display at the 7th line, prefix the number by a + (plus sign) as in the following command:

```
pg +7 file1
```

If you want to modify the default prompt of : (colon) with your personalized prompt, use the `-p` flag as in the following command:

```
pg -7 -s -p "Enter Sub-command -> " file1
This is the line 1
This is the line 2
This is the line 3
This is the line 4
This is the line 5
This is the line 6
This is the line 7
Enter Sub-command ->
```

In this example, the default prompt has been replaced by `Enter Sub-command ->` prompt. If you want to start the file with the line where the pattern `line 5` appears, execute the following command:

```
pg +/"line 5"/ file1
```

tee

If you want to execute a command and want its output redirected to multiple files in addition to the standard output, use the `tee` command. The `tee` command accepts input from the standard input, so it is possible to pipe another command to the `tee` command.

Following is an optional flag that can be used with the `tee` command:

■ `-a` to append to the end of the specified file. The default of the `tee` command is to overwrite the specified file.

Examples

If you want to use the cat command on file1 to display on the screen, but you want to make a copy of file2, use the tee command as follows:

```
cat file1 ¦ tee file2 ¦ more
```

If you want to append file1 to the end of an already existing file2, use the flag -a as in the following command:

```
cat file1 ¦ tee -a file2 ¦ more
```

vi

The vi command can be used to edit one or more files using full screen mode. If a filename is not provided, UNIX creates an empty work file without any name. If a filename is provided, the file does not exist, and an empty work file with the specified name is created. The vi command does not modify existing files until the changes are saved.

> **CAUTION**
>
> The vi command does not lock a file while editing it. So it is possible that more than one user can edit it at the same time. The version of the file saved last is the one that is retained.

Following is a list of some of the flags that can be used with the vi command:

- -c *sub-command* to execute the specified *sub-command* before placing the specified file in editing mode.
- -r *filename* to recover the specified *filename*.
- -R to place the specified file in editing mode with read-only option so that any modifications made cannot be saved.
- -y*number* to set the editing window to a size with *number* of lines.

The following is a list of modes the vi editor has:

- command mode is the default mode when you enter vi. In this mode, you can enter various sub-commands to manipulate the lines, such as deleting lines, pasting lines, moving to a different word, moving to a different line, and so on.
- text input mode is the mode in which you can modify the text in the lines or enter new lines. You can enter this mode by using sub-command a, i, or c from the command mode. To return to the command mode, press the Escape key.
- command entry mode is the mode in which you can enter certain sub-commands that require entering additional parameters. Some of these sub-commands are the w sub-command, which requires a filename, or the / sub-command, which requires entry of a pattern. You can use the Escape key to return to command mode.

Following is a quick reference of sub-commands that can be used in the command mode for moving within the same line:

- ◾ h to move the cursor left to the previous character in the same line.
- ◾ l to move the cursor right to the next character in the same line.
- ◾ j to move the cursor down to the next line in the same column.
- ◾ k to move the cursor up to the previous line in the same column.
- ◾ w to move the cursor to the start of next small word in the same line.
- ◾ W to move the cursor to the start of the next big word in the same line.
- ◾ b to move the cursor to the start of the previous small word in the same line.
- ◾ B to move the cursor to the start of the previous big word in the same line.
- ◾ e to move the cursor to the end of the next small word in the same line.
- ◾ E to move the cursor to the end of the previous big word in the same line.
- ◾ f*c* to move to the next character *c* in the same line.
- ◾ F*c* to move to the previous character *c* in the same line.
- ◾ t*c* to move the cursor to one column before the next character *c* in the same line.
- ◾ T*c* to move the cursor to one column after the previous character *c* in the same line.
- ◾ *number*¦ to move the cursor to the specified column *number*.

Following is a quick reference of sub-commands that can be used in the command mode for moving across the lines:

- ◾ + or Enter to move the cursor to the next line's first non-blank character.
- ◾ - to move the cursor to the previous line's first non-blank character.
- ◾ 0 to move the cursor to the first character of the current line.
- ◾ $ to move the cursor to the last character of the current line.
- ◾ H to move the cursor to the top line of the screen.
- ◾ L to move the cursor to the last line of the screen.
- ◾ M to move the cursor to the middle of the screen.

Following is a quick reference of sub-commands that can be used in the command mode for re-drawing screen:

- ◾ z- to make the current line as the last line of the screen and redraw the screen.
- ◾ z. to make the current line as the middle line of the screen and redraw the screen.
- ◾ Ctrl-l to redraw the screen.
- ◾ /*pattern*/z- to find the next occurrence of the *pattern* and make that the last line of the screen.

Following is a quick reference of sub-commands that can be used in the command mode for scrolling across pages:

- Ctrl-f to move forward by one screen.
- Ctrl-d to move forward by one-half screen.
- Ctrl-b to move backward by one screen.
- Ctrl-u to move backward by one-half screen.
- Ctrl-e to scroll window down by one line.
- Ctrl-y to scroll window up by one line.

Following is a quick reference of sub-commands that can be used in the command mode for searching patterns in the file:

- /pattern to search for the specified pattern in the forward direction. If end of file is reached, the search wraps around.
- ?pattern to search for the specified pattern in the backward direction. If top of the file is reached, the search wraps around.
- n to repeat the last search in the same direction as was specified in the last search.
- N to repeat the last search in the opposite direction of what was specified in the last search.
- /pattern/+number to position the cursor at the specified of number lines after the line in which the pattern has been found.
- /pattern/-number to position the cursor the specified number of lines before the line in which the pattern has been found.
- % to find the matching braces or parentheses.

Following is a quick reference of sub-commands that can be used to enter text in the text entry mode. (You can terminate the text entry at any time by pressing the Escape key.)

- a to start entering text after the cursor position.
- A to start entering text at the end of the line.
- i to start entering text before the cursor position.
- I to start entering text before the first non-blank character in the line.
- o to insert an empty line after the line in which the cursor is positioned.
- O to insert an empty line before the line in which cursor is positioned.

Following is a quick reference of sub-commands that can be used to modify text from the command mode. (You can terminate the text entry at any time by pressing the Escape key.)

- cc or S to change a complete line.
- C to change the contents of a line after the cursor position.
- cw to change the word where the cursor is positioned.

- dd to delete the current line.
- D to delete the rest of the line beyond where the cursor is positioned.
- dw to delete part of the word where the cursor is positioned.
- J to join the contents of the next line to the end of the current line.
- rc to replace the character at the cursor position with the character c.
- R to overwrite the contents of the current line.
- u to undo the last modification.
- x to delete the character at the cursor position.
- X to delete the character to the left of the cursor position.
- ~ (tilde) to change uppercase letter to lowercase or vice versa.
- . to repeat the last change.
- << to shift the current line to the left.
- >> to shift the current line to the right.

Following is a quick reference of sub-commands that can be used to move or copy text from one part of the file to another:

- p to paste contents of the undo buffer (as a result of deleting or yanking) after the cursor position.
- P to paste contents of the undo buffer (as a result of deleting or yanking) before the cursor position.
- "bd to delete text into the named buffer b.
- "bp to paste contents of the named buffer b.
- yy to yank the current line into the undo buffer.
- Y to yank the current line into the undo buffer.
- yw to yank the word from the current cursor position into the undo buffer.

Following is a quick reference of sub-commands that can be used to save a file:

- :w to save the changes to the original file.
- :w *filename* to save the changes to the specified *filename* if the file *filename* does not exist. If you try to save an already existing file using this sub-command, you will get an error.
- !w *filename* to save the changes to the specified *filename* if the file *filename* already exists.

Following is a quick reference of sub-commands that can be used to move between various files if you have invoked vi with multiple files:

- :n to start editing the next file in the list of files specified when vi was invoked.
- :n *filenames* to specify a new list of files to be edited.

Following is a quick reference of sub-commands that can be used to move between the current file and the alternate file:

- ▪ :e *filename* to invoke vi with *filename* becoming the alternate file.
- ▪ :e! to load the current file again. If there have been changes made to the current file, those changes are discarded.
- ▪ :e + *filename* to invoke vi with *filename* and start editing at the end of the file rather than at the start.
- ▪ :e + *number filename* to invoke vi with *filename* and start editing at the specified line number.
- ▪ :e # to start editing the alternate file.

Following is a quick reference of sub-commands that can be used to add lines to the current file from other sources:

- ▪ :r *filename* to read the complete *filename* and add it after the current line.
- ▪ :r !*command* to execute the specified *command* and add the output after the current line.

Following is a quick reference of some of the miscellaneous sub-commands:

- ▪ Ctrl-g to get information about the current file being edited.
- ▪ :sh to start shell so that commands can be executed. You can return by using the exit command or Ctrl-d.
- ▪ :!*command* to execute the specified *command*.
- ▪ !! to re-execute the last :!*command*.
- ▪ :q to quit vi. If you try to quit using this sub-command and you have made modifications to the file, UNIX will not allow you to quit.
- ▪ :q! to quit vi irrespective of any changes made to the file.
- ▪ ZZ or :wq to save changes to the original file and exit vi.

You can use a special file called .exrc in which you can specify special vi sub-commands. To use these sub-commands in a vi session, use a : (colon) in front of the command. Some of these sub-commands are as follows:

- ▪ Ab abb ph to abbreviate ph to abb.
- ▪ unab *abbreviation* to turn the *abbreviation* off.
- ▪ map m seq to map a sequence of vi commands to a character or key.

File Content Search Commands

We have seen that we can use the find command to search for filenames in a directory. For searching for a pattern in one or more files, use the grep series of commands. The grep commands search for a string in the specified files and display the output on standard output.

egrep

The egrep command is an extended version of grep command. This command searches for a specified pattern in one or more files and displays the output to standard output. The pattern can be a regular expression where you can specify special characters to have special meaning, some of which are as follows:

- . to match any single character.
- * to match one or more single characters that precede the asterisk.
- ^ to match the regular expression at the beginning of a line.
- \$ to match the regular expression at the end of a line.
- \+ to match one or more occurrences of a preceding regular expression.
- ? to match zero or more occurrences of a preceding regular expression.
- [ ] to match any of the characters specified within the brackets.

Following is a list of flags that can be used with the egrep command:

- -b to display the block number at the start of each line found.
- -c to display the count of lines in which the pattern was found without displaying the lines.
- -f *filename* to specify a *filename* that contains the patterns to be matched.
- -h to suppress the filenames as part of the display if more than one file is being searched.
- -i to search, ignoring the case of the letter.
- -l to list just the filenames in which the specified pattern has been found.
- -n to display the relative line number before each line in the output.
- -q to suppress all outputs.
- -s to display error message if an error occurs.
- -v to find lines not matching the specified pattern.
- -w to search for specified patterns as words.
- -x to match the patterns exactly to a line.

The egrep command has some special features for the patterns you can specify. The features are as follows:

- You can specify a + (plus sign) at the end of a pattern that matches one or more occurrences of the pattern.
- You can specify a ? (question mark) at the end of a pattern that matches zero or one occurrence of the pattern.

■ You can specify a ¦ (vertical bar or pipe) between two patterns to match either one or both (or operator).

■ You can specify a pattern within a left and a right parentheses to group the patterns.

Examples

Let us assume that we have a file called `file1` whose contents are shown below using the `more` command:

```
more file1
*****  This file is a dummy file *****
which has been created
to run a test for egrep
grep series of commands are used by the following types of people
    programmers
    end users
Believe it or not, grep series of commands are used by pros and novices alike
*****  THIS FILE IS A DUMMY FILE *****
```

If you want to find all occurrences of `dummy`, use the following command:

```
egrep dummy file1
*****  This file is a dummy file *****
```

If you want to find all occurrences of `dummy`, irrespective of the case, use the `-i` flag as in the following command:

```
egrep -i dummy file1
*****  This file is a dummy file *****
*****  THIS FILE IS A DUMMY FILE *****
```

If you want to display the relative line number of the line that contains the pattern being searched, use the `-n` flag as in the following command:

```
egrep -i -n dummy file1
1:*****  This file is a dummy file *****
8:*****  THIS FILE IS A DUMMY FILE *****
```

If you are just interested in finding the number of lines in which the specified pattern occurs, use the `-c` flag as in the following command:

```
egrep -i -c dummy file1
2
```

If you want to get a list of all lines that do not contain the specified pattern, use the `-v` flag as in the following command:

```
egrep -i -v dummy file1
which has been created
to run a test for egrep
grep series of commands are used by the following types of people
    programmers
    end users
Believe it or not, grep series of commands are used by pros and novices alike
```

If you are interested in searching for a pattern that you want to search as a word, use the -w flag as in the following command:

```
egrep -w grep file1
grep series of commands are used by the following types of people
Believe it or not, grep series of commands are used by pros and novices alike
```

Notice that the search did not result in finding the pattern egrep because it contains e before the pattern grep. The use of -w flag forced egrep to search for the pattern grep delimited by spaces or newline characters.

If you want to search for a pattern that is the only string in a line, use the -x command as in the following command:

```
egrep -x "   end users" file1
   end users
```

Now, let us examine some of the special features of egrep. If you want to find out where either of two specified patterns occur, use the following command where you can use the ¦ (vertical bar) to separate the two patterns:

```
egrep "(dummy¦pro)" file1
*****  This file is a dummy file *****
   programmers
Believe it or not, grep series of commands are used by pros and novices alike
```

In the above example, the lines that contain either the pattern dummy or pro occur are displayed. In case you are interested in searching for either pros or programmers, use the ? (question mark) at the end of the pattern as in the following command:

```
egrep "pro(grammer)?s" file1
   programmers
Believe it or not, grep series of commands are used by pros and novices alike
```

In the above example, the pattern matches both pros and programmers due to the fact that (grammer)? matches zero or one occurrence of grammer with the zero occurrence giving pros and one occurrence giving programmers.

To search for lines containing only capital letters C, D, E or F, use regular expressions as follows:

```
egrep [C-F] file1
*****  THIS FILE IS A DUMMY FILE *****
```

fgrep

Like egrep and grep, fgrep also searches one or more files for a specified string and displays output on standard output. The fgrep command is supposed to be the faster version of the grep command but in reality may not be. Please notice that the fgrep command is used to search for a specified string and not pattern (regular expression where special characters can be used to indicate special meaning).

Following is a list of flags that can be used with the fgrep command:

- -b to display the block number at the start of each line found.
- -c to display the count of lines in which the pattern was found without displaying the lines.
- -f *filename* to specify *filename* that contains the patterns to be matched.
- -h to suppress the filenames as part of the display if more than one file is being searched.
- -i to search ignoring the case of the letter.
- -l to list just the filenames in which the specified pattern has been found.
- -n to display the relative line number before each line in the output.
- -q to suppress all outputs.
- -s to display error message if an error occurs.
- -v to find lines not matching the specified pattern.
- -w to search for specified patterns as words.
- -x to match the patterns exactly with a line.

Examples

Let us assume that we have a file called file1 whose contents are shown below using the more command:

```
more file1
*****  This file is a dummy file *****
which has been created
to run a test for egrep
grep series of commands are used by the following types of people
    programmers
    end users
Believe it or not, grep series of commands are used by pros and novices alike
*****  THIS FILE IS A DUMMY FILE *****
```

If you want to find all occurrences of dummy, use the following command:

```
fgrep dummy file1
*****  This file is a dummy file *****
```

If you want to find all occurrences of dummy irrespective of the case, use the -i flag as in the following command:

```
fgrep -i dummy file1
*****  This file is a dummy file *****
*****  THIS FILE IS A DUMMY FILE *****
```

If you want to display the relative line number of the line that contains the pattern being searched, use the -n flag as in the following command:

```
fgrep -i -n dummy file1
1:*****  This file is a dummy file *****
8:*****  THIS FILE IS A DUMMY FILE *****
```

If you are just interested in finding the number of lines in which the specified pattern occurs, use the -c flag as in the following command:

```
fgrep -i -c dummy file1
2
```

If you want to get a list of all lines that do not contain the specified pattern, use the -v flag as in the following command:

```
fegrep -i -v dummy file1
which has been created
to run a test for egrep
grep series of commands are used by the following types of people
    programmers
    end users
Believe it or not, grep series of commands are used by pros and novices alike
```

If you are interested in searching for a pattern that you want to search as a word, use the -w flag as in the following command:

```
fgrep -w grep file1
grep series of commands are used by the following types of people
Believe it or not, grep series of commands are used by pros and novices alike
```

Notice that the search did not result in finding the pattern egrep because it contains e before the pattern grep. The use of -w flag forced egrep to search for grep delimited by spaces or newline characters.

If you want to search for a pattern that is the only string in a line, use the -x command as in the following command:

```
fgrep -x "   end users" file1
   end users
```

grep

The grep command can be used to search for a specified pattern in one or more files, and displays the matching output on standard output.

Following is a list of flags that can be used with grep command:

- ◼ -b to display the block number at the start of each line found.
- ◼ -c to display the count of lines in which the pattern was found without displaying the lines.
- ◼ -E to indicate that the grep command behaves as the egrep command.
- ◼ -F to indicate that the grep command behaves as the fgrep command.
- ◼ -f *filename* to specify *filename* that contains the patterns to be matched.
- ◼ -h to suppress the filenames as part of the display if more than one file is being searched.
- ◼ -i to search, ignoring the case of the letter.
- ◼ -l to list just the filenames in which the specified pattern has been found.

- ■ -n to display the relative line number before each line in the output.
- ■ -q to suppress all outputs.
- ■ -s to display error message if an error occurs.
- ■ -v to find lines not matching the specified pattern.
- ■ -w to search for specified patterns as words.
- ■ -x to match the patterns exactly with a line.

Examples

Let us assume that we have a file called file1 whose contents are shown below using the more command:

```
more file1
*****  This file is a dummy file *****
which has been created
to run a test for egrep
grep series of commands are used by the following types of people
    programmers
    end users
Believe it or not, grep series of commands are used by pros and novices alike
*****  THIS FILE IS A DUMMY FILE *****
```

If you want to find all occurrences of dummy, use the following command:

```
grep dummy file1
*****  This file is a dummy file *****
```

If you want to find all occurrences of dummy irrespective of the case, use the -i flag as in the following command:

```
grep -i dummy file1
*****  This file is a dummy file *****
*****  THIS FILE IS A DUMMY FILE *****
```

If you want to display the relative line number of the line that contains the pattern being searched, use the -n flag as in the following command:

```
grep -i -n dummy file1
1:*****  This file is a dummy file *****
8:*****  THIS FILE IS A DUMMY FILE *****
```

If you are just interested in finding the number of lines in which the specified pattern occurs, use the -c flag as in the following command:

```
grep -i -c dummy file1
2
```

If you want to get a list of all lines that do not contain the specified pattern, use the -v flag as in the following command:

```
grep -i -v dummy file1
which has been created
to run a test for egrep
```

```
grep series of commands are used by the following types of people
    programmers
    end users
Believe it or not, grep series of commands are used by pros and novices alike
```

If you are interested in searching for a pattern that you want to search as a word, use the -w flag as in the following command:

```
grep -w grep file1
grep series of commands are used by the following types of people
Believe it or not, grep series of commands are used by pros and novices alike
```

Notice that the search did not result in finding the pattern egrep because it contains e before the pattern grep. The use of -w flag forced egrep to search for the pattern grep delimited by spaces or newline characters.

If you want to search for a pattern that is the only string in a line, use the -x command as in the following command:

```
grep -x "   end users" file1
    end users
```

Now, let us examine some of the special features of grep. If you want to find out which lines start with capital letter A through C, use the following command:

```
grep "^[A-C]" file1
Believe it or not, grep series of commands are used by pros and novices alike
```

In this example, the ^ (caret) indicates that the following character is searched for at the beginning of each line. In case you are interested in searching for all lines that do not start with capital letters A through F, use the following command:

```
grep "^[^A-F]" file1
*** his fle is a dummy file *****
which has been created
to run a test for egrep
grep series of commands are used by the following types of people
    programmers
    end users
*****   THIS FILE IS A DUMMY FILE *****
```

In this example, the ^ (caret) outside the [ ] searches for the following character at the beginning of the line where the ^ (caret) inside the [ ] indicates the match should be made where it does not contain A through F, thus meaning that all lines that do not have A through F at the beginning of the line will be matched.

To search for lines containing only capital letters C, D, E or F, use regular expression as follows:

```
grep [C-F] file1
*****   THIS FILE IS A DUMMY FILE *****
```

strings

The `strings` command can be used to search for strings in executable files where a string consists of four or more printable characters terminated by a null or newline.

Following is a list of some of the flags that can be used with the `strings` command:

- -a or - to search the entire file, not just the data section.
- -o to list each string preceded by its offset in the file (in octal).
- *-Number* to specify minimum string length other than the default of 4.

Examples

If you want to find the strings that exist in the `strings` command executable file, execute the following command in a directory that contains the command:

```
strings strings
¦@(#)56
1.17  com/cmd/scan/strings.c, cmdscan, bos320, 9227320b 5/7/92 10:21:20
Standard input
strings.cat
/usr/mbin/strings
Usage: strings [ -a ] [ -o ] [ -# ] [ file ... ]
%7o
%7o
```

If you also want the offset of the strings in the executable file for the `strings` command, use the -o flag as follows:

```
strings -o strings
   6017 ¦@(#)56
   6027 1.17  com/cmd/scan/strings.c, cmdscan, bos320, 9227320b 5/7/92 10:21:20
   6140 Standard input
   6164 strings.cat
   6200 /usr/mbin/strings
   6224 Usage: strings [ -a ] [ -o ] [ -# ] [ file ... ]
   6314 %7o
   6330 %7o
```

If you want to limit you search to only, say, 15 characters or more in size in the `strings` command executable, execute the following command:

```
strings -o -15 strings
   6027 1.17  com/cmd/scan/strings.c, cmdscan, bos320, 9227320b 5/7/92 10:21:20
   6200 /usr/mbin/strings
   6224 Usage: strings [ -a ] [ -o ] [ -# ] [ file ... ]
```

Printing

You may have several documents that you want to print, and you may have several printers attached to your computer where you can print. Here we will discuss some of the commands that direct printing of specified documents to specified printers and find out the status of the printers. We also will discuss commands to cancel specified printing jobs.

In a UNIX system, you can have multiple printers but only one of the printers can be set up as the default printer to which all the print requests are sent if a printer name is not specified.

cancel

If you have earlier queued up requests to print one or more documents using the `lp` command and you wish to cancel these requests, use the `cancel` command. Using the `cancel` command, you can either cancel a specified job or all queued requests to a specified printer queue. If you are an ordinary user, cancel jobs that have your user ID only.

You can either specify one or more job ID, or a printer name with the `cancel` command.

Examples

To cancel a job with ID 734, use the following command:

```
cancel 734
```

To cancel all queued requests that you have queued up in the printer `our_printer`, use the following command:

```
cancel our_printer
```

lp

To print one or more files to a specified printer, use the `lp` command. By default, the `lp` command accepts input from the standard input. If more than one file is specified, the files are printed in order of their appearance in the command. The files you are printing should exist until they are printed because the `lp` command does not make copies of the file while printing (unless you use the -c flag).

Following is a list of a commands that can be used with the `lp` command:

- `-c` to make a copy of the file so that the file can be deleted or modified while the printing is still going on.
- `-dprintqueue` to specify the print queue where the print request is to be directed.
- `-m` to notify the requesting user upon successful completion of the print request by mail.
- `-ncopies` to specify the number of copies to be printed.
- `-ttitle` to print the specified title on the banner page.

Examples

To print the file `file1`, execute the following command:

```
lp file1
```

5

GENERAL COMMANDS

In this example, `file1` will be printed on the default line printer. If you want to print on `our_printer` that is next to you, use the `-d` flag in the following command:

```
lp -dour_printer file1
```

If `file1` is big and you want to get notification after the print job is successfully completed, use the `-m` flag in the following command:

```
lp -m -dmain_printer file1
```

If you want to print multiple copies of `file1` for distribution to your colleagues, use the `-n` flag in the following command:

```
lp -n15 -dour_printer file1
```

The above example will print 15 copies of `file1` on the printer called `our_printer`. If you want to print a title `urgent memo` in the banner page, use the `-t` flag as in the following command:

```
lp -n15 -t"urgent memo" -dour_printer file1
```

The above example will print 15 copies of `file1` on `our_printer` with the title `urgent memo` printed on the banner page.

pr

The `pr` command accepts input from the standard input and generates output on the standard output by default. This command formats the output into pages with name of file, date, time, and page numbers. If the line length is larger than the page width, it is truncated. As the `pr` command formats and paginates the output, you can pipe the output of the `pr` command to a print command such as `lp` to print the output.

Following is a list of some of the flags that can be used with the `pr` command:

- ◼ `-d` generates the output with double spacing.
- ◼ `-f` or `-F` to use a form-feed to a new page instead of a sequence of line-feed characters.
- ◼ `-h "heading"` to print *heading* instead of the filename as header on each page.
- ◼ `-l pagelength` to set the number of lines to be printed on each page to *pagelength* instead of the default of 66.
- ◼ `-n` to specify the width of the line number to be printed in front of each line. Optionally, you can specify a character to be printed between the line number and the contents of the line.
- ◼ `-oindent` to indent each line by *indent* columns.
- ◼ `-p` to pause after each page if the output is being directed to standard output. To continue, use the Enter key.
- ◼ `-r` to suppress diagnostics messages.
- ◼ `-t` to suppress printing of page header and page footers.

- ■ -w*width* to set the width of each page to *width* instead of the default of 72.
- ■ +page*number* to specify that the display should start at page number page*number* instead of 1.

Examples

Let us assume we have a file called `file1` in the current directory, the contents of which are shown below using the `more` command:

```
more file1
This is a test file for pr command
We will use it to show the usage of various flags of pr command
```

The plain vanilla use of the `pr` command is as follows:

```
pr file1
Wed Dec  4 00:40:14 1996 file1 Page 1


This is a test file for pr command
We will use it to show the usage of various flags of pr command
```

If you want to display the output in double spacing, use the `-d` flag in the following command:

```
pr -d file1
Wed Dec  4 00:40:14 1996 file1 Page 1


This is a test file for pr command

We will use it to show the usage of various flags of pr command
```

If you want to print a title other than the filename, use the `-h` flag in the following command:

```
pr -h "TEST FILE FOR pr COMMAND" file1
Wed Dec  4 00:40:14 1996 TEST FILE FOR pr COMMAND Page 1


This is a test file for pr command
We will use it to show the usage of various flags of pr command
```

If you do not want to print the headers, use the `-t` flag in the following command:

```
pr -t file1
This is a test file for pr command
We will use it to show the usag fvrious fags of pr command
```

If you want to print the line numbers in front of each line and you want to print a - (hyphen) between the line number and the line, use the `-n` flag in the following command:

```
pr -n-5 file1
Wed Dec  4 00:40:14 1996 file1 Page 1


    1-This is a test file for pr command
    2-We will use it to show the usage of various flags of pr command
```

lpstat

You can use the lpstat command to display the current status of all line printers. If the lpstat command is executed without any flags, it displays the status of each printer with the entries queued by the lp command.

Following is a list of some of the flags that can be used with the lpstat command:

- ■ -a*queue* or -c*queue* or -p*queue* to display status as well as information on jobs in the specified list of queue.
- ■ -d to display the default line printer information.
- ■ -o*queue* or -oj*obnumber* to display the status of the specified *queue* or to display the status of the specified j*obnumber*.
- ■ -r to display status and job information of all queues.
- ■ -s to display summary information on all queues.
- ■ -t to display detailed status information on all queues.
- ■ -u*username* to display status of print requests started by specified *username*.
- ■ -v*printername* to display a list of specified *printername*.

Examples

If you want to find out about all the printers in you system, use the lpstat command without any flags as in the following command:

```
lpstat ¦ more
Queue   Dev   Status   Job Files            User        PP %  Blks   Cp  Rnk
------- ----- -------- --- ----------------- ----------- ---- -- ------ --- ---
m_prt   lp0   READY
prt_01  bshde READY
prt_02  lp0   READY
```

If you want to get information about the default line printer, use the -d flag as in the following command:

```
lpstat -d
Queue   Dev   Status   Job Files            User        PP %  Blks   Cp  Rnk
------- ----- -------- --- ----------------- ----------- ---- -- ------ --- ---
m_prt   lp0   READY
```

If you are printing file1 on printer_01, to find out about the status of the printer and the job, use the -a flag as in the following command:

```
lpstat -aprinter_01
Queue   Dev   Status   Job Files            User        PP %  Blks   Cp  Rnk
------- ----- -------- --- ----------------- ----------- ---- -- ------ --- ---
systems lpprt READY
prt_01: prt_01 is ready and printing
prt_01: Rank   Owner    Job  Files                     Total Size
prt_01: active testuser      735  file1                   156486 bytes
```

Scheduling

UNIX gives you the ability to schedule scripts and commands for execution at a later point in time. You can specify the exact time when the command should be run. UNIX also provides a way of reporting on the scheduled jobs and removing them if you do not want to execute them.

at

The at command allows you to:

■ Schedule a command for execution at a specified time.

■ Display a list of scheduled jobs.

■ Remove jobs from the scheduled jobs list.

You can schedule jobs by specifying either the absolute time or a time relative to the current time.

Following is a list of some of the flags that can be used with the at command:

■ -l to display a list of jobs scheduled by you.

■ -m to mail a report of successful execution of the job.

■ -t *date* to schedule a job to be executed at the specified date and time.

■ -r *joblist* to remove the jobs specified in the job list from the queue.

You will be allowed to execute the at command provided at least one of the following is true:

■ The system has at.allow and your user name appears in the at.allow file.

■ The system has at.deny and your name does not appear in the at.deny file.

The exact location of the at.allow and at.deny files depends on the UNIX system you are working with.

The at commands accepts the time, day, and relative increments in a variety of formats. Some of the formats are as follows:

■ 1830 December 4

■ 6:30 pm December 4

■ 6:30 P December 4

■ now + 2 hours

■ tomorrow 1830

■ 1830 next week

■ 1830 Tuesday next week

Examples

If you want to schedule a job called `my_job` at 11:00 p.m. today, assuming that the current time is 9:30 p.m., execute any one of the following commands:

```
at 2300 my_job
```

```
at 23:00 my_job
```

```
at 11:00 pm my_job
```

```
at 11:00 P my_job
```

```
at 2300 today my_job
```

If the current time is 11:30 p.m., the jobs will be scheduled at 11:00 p.m. the next day.

To schedule `my_job` 6 hours from now, use the following command:

```
at now + 6 hours my_job
```

To schedule `my_job` at 6:30 p.m. next week, use the following command:

```
at 6:30 pm next week my_job
```

In the preceding example, if today is Thursday and the current time is 5:30 p.m., `my_job` will be scheduled for 5:30 p.m. next Thursday. If the current time is 7:30 p.m., `my_job` will be scheduled for 6:30 p.m. next Friday.

To list the jobs scheduled, use the `-l` flag as in the following command:

```
at -l
testuser.850519800.a        Fri Dec 13 18:30:00 1996
testuser.849858400.a        Fri Dec  6 02:46:40 1996
```

To remove a scheduled job, use the `-r` command as in the following command:

```
at -r testuser.850519800.a
at file: testuser.850519800.a deleted
```

atq

The `atq` command can be used to list the jobs scheduled at a later time. The jobs are displayed in the order of the time scheduled with earlier scheduled jobs displayed first.

Following is list of flags that can be used with the `atq` command:

- `-c` to display a list of jobs in order of time at which the at command was executed to schedule the jobs.
- `-n` to display the number of scheduled jobs.

Examples

To list all jobs scheduled using the at command, use the following command:

```
atq
testuser.849915000.a      Fri Dec  6 18:30:00 1996
testuser.850519800.a      Fri Dec 13 18:30:00 1996
```

If you want to list all jobs scheduled by the time the corresponding at command was run rather than when the scheduled jobs are supposed to run, use the -c flag as in the following command:

```
atq -c
testuser.850519800.a      Fri Dec 13 18:30:00 1996
testuser.849915000.a      Fri Dec  6 18:30:00 1996
```

If you want to find out the number of jobs scheduled currently, use the -n flag in the following command:

```
atq -n
2 files in the queue
```

crontab

UNIX systems have a daemon running all the time that can run jobs at regularly scheduled intervals. You can specify the jobs that the crontab command will execute in a file, and the cron daemon will check it when the cron daemon is initialized or when additions or modifications are made to the file.

The entries you can make in the crontab file consist of the following fields (separated by spaces or tab character):

- minute
- hour
- day (of the month)
- year
- day of the week
- command

Each of these fields can have more than one discrete value (separated by commas) or a range of values or an * (asterisk) meaning all values are to be matched.

Following is a list of flags that can be used with the crontab command:

- -l to list your crontab file.
- -e to edit or create the crontab file.
- -r to remove your crontab file.
- -v to list the status of the crontab jobs.

Examples

If you want to display the string Time to go for lunch at 12:30 pm every day, set up the following:

```
30 12 * * * echo "Time to go for lunch"
```

If you want to execute my_job on Friday at 4:00 p.m. every week, setup the following:

```
0 16 * * 5 my_job
```

Storage

In this section we will discuss a number of commands that can be used for file management, that is, to backup files to different media, to restore files from different media, to compress files to save disk space, to uncompress files to restore, and so on.

compress

You can use the compress command to reduce the size of a file. A file created by the compress command has a .Z appended to its name. The compressed file retains the permission and time attributes of the original file.

Following is a list of flags that can be used with the compress command:

- ■ -d to force the compress command to act as an uncompress command.
- ■ -c to compress the file to standard output (which can be redirected to another file) so that the original file is intact.
- ■ -f or -F to compress the file and overwrite the compressed file if it already exists.
- ■ -v to display the compression percentage.
- ■ -V to display the current version and compile options.

Examples

To compress file1, execute the following command:

```
compress file1
```

If you want the compression statistics, use the -v flag in the following command:

```
compress -v file1
file1: Compression: 50.85%  -- replaced with file1.Z
```

cpio

You can use the cpio command to copy files to archival medium from disk or to restore from archival medium to disk. There are three major forms of the cpio command:

- ■ cpio -o to read standard input for path names and copy them to standard output.
- ■ cpio -i to read from standard input archival files and create disk files.
- ■ cpio -p to read standard input for path name and copy to the specified directory.

Following is a list of some of the flags that can be used with the `cpio` command:

- a to modify the access time of copied files to the current file.
- B to indicate that `cpio` should do block I/O.
- d to create a directory if the specified directory does not exist.
- f to copy files that do not match the specified pattern.
- r to copy files interactively with the option of modifying the filename.
- t to create a list of files without actually copying a file.
- u to overwrite a file if it already exists.
- v to list the filenames being copied.

Examples

If you have a list of files that you want to copy to a floppy disk, execute the following command:

```
ls *.txt | cpio -ov > /dev/rfd0
file1.txt
file2.txt
55 blocks
```

The above example will copy all files that have an extension of `.txt` and will display filenames being copied.

Now if you want to list the files on the floppy disk, use the t and v flags as in the following command:

```
cpio -itv < /dev/rfd0
100644 testuser      13771 Dec 07 00:13:38 1996 file1.txt
100644 testuser      13947 Dec 07 00:13:30 1996 file2.txt
55 blocks
```

If you want to copy the files from the floppy disk and rename them while copying, use the r flag as in the following command:

```
cpio -ir "*.txt" < y
Rename <file1.txt>
file3.txt
Rename <file2.txt>
file4.txt
55 blocks
```

In the preceding example, `file1.txt` will be renamed to `file3.txt` and `file2.txt` will be renamed to `file4.txt`.

If you want to copy all files from the current directory as well as all the files under its sub-directories, use the `-p` flag. Additionally, you can use the d flag so that all the needed directories are created. You can execute the commands as follows:

```
find . -print | cpio -pd /u/testuser/cpiodir
```

dd

The `dd` command can be used to read data from standard input and copy it to the standard output after converting the data according to specified conversion parameters. Along with the data conversion, the physical attributes, such as block size, can also be modified by specifying appropriate parameters.

Following is a list of flags that can be used with the `dd` command:

- `bs=blocksize` to specify the block size of the input and output file. This overrides the `ibs` and `obs` flags.
- `if=filename` to specify the input filename to be copied.
- `ibs=blocksize` to specify the block size of the input file.
- `fskip=numberofeof` to specify number of End-Of-File markers to be skipped in the input file before starting copy.
- `files=numberoffiles` to specify the number of files to be copied such as from a tape containing multiple files.
- `count=numberofblocks` to copy specified number of blocks from the input file.
- `skip=numberofblocks` to skip the specified number of blocks in the input file before starting copy.
- `of=filename` to specify the output filename to be created.
- `obs=blocksize` to specify the block size of the output file.
- `seek=recordnumber` to specify the record number in the output file to start copying the input file to.
- `conv=conversionparameter` to specify the type of conversion to be used. Some of the values of this parameter can be `ASCII`, `EBCDIC`, `block`, `unblock`, `lcase`, `ucase`.

Examples

If you have a file from a system that stores data in EBCDIC and you want to convert the data to ASCII, use the following command:

```
dd if=file1 of=file2 conv=ascii
```

The above command will read `file1` and convert each character of this file to ASCII and copy them to `file2`.

If you want to copy `file1` on disk to a tape with a block size of 1024, use the following command:

```
dd if=file1 of=/dev/rmt0 bs=1024 conv=sync
```

If you want to copy the third file on a tape to a file called `file1`, use the following command:

```
dd if=/dev/rmt0 fskip=2 of=file1
```

If you want to print a memo in capital letters, use the following command to convert `file1` to `file2` and then print `file2`:

```
dd if=file1 of=file2 conv=ucase
lp -dmain_printer file2
```

pack

If you want to save space, use the `pack` command to compress a file in a way similar to the `compress` command. The `pack` command compresses a file and generates a new file with `.z` appended to the filename. The original file is removed. The amount of space saved depends on the contents of the file. Usually you can get about 30 percent to 50 percent compression for text files. By default, the `pack` command will not compress if it cannot reduce the size of the file.

Following is a list of flags that can be used with the `pack` command:

- ■ - to display statistics about compression.
- ■ -f to force packing.

Examples

If you have a file called `file1` that you want to compress, use the following command:

```
pack file1
pack: file1: 41.7% Compression
```

If you want more information about the compression, use the - (hyphen) flag in the following command:

```
pack - file1
pack: file1: 41.7% Compression
        from 28160 to 16404 bytes
        Huffman tree has 15 levels below root
        102 distinct bytes in input
        dictionary overhead = 124 bytes
        effective  entropy  = 4.66 bits/byte
        asymptotic entropy  = 4.62 bits/byte
```

In some cases, pack may not compress the file and will give you an error, as in the following command:

```
pack file1
pack: file1: no saving
        - file unchanged
```

In such a case, to force compression, use the -f flag, as in the following command:

```
pack -f  file1
pack: file1: 40.8% Compression
```

pcat

The `pcat` command can be used to uncompress a file to the standard output. This command does not have any flags.

Examples

If you want to uncompress a file called `file1.z` that you have earlier created using `pack` command on `file1`, use the following command:

```
pcat file1
```

You can also use

```
pcat file1.z
```

tar

The `tar` command is used to copy files from disk to an archival medium (usually tape) or vice versa. The `tar` command does not provide any recovery from tape errors.

Following is a list of some of the flags that can be used with the `tar` command:

- `-c` to create a new archive and write the file details at the beginning of the archive.
- `-t` to generate a list of files in the archive.
- `-x` to obtain one or more file from an archive. If you specify a directory name, all files in the directory are extracted. If no file or directory is specified, all files in the specified archive are extracted. If the one or more files extracted do not exist, they are created with the original user ID if you have `root` authority; otherwise, they are created with your user ID.
- `-m` to use the time of extraction from the archive as the modification time of the extracted file.
- `-p` to restore the files with their original permission ignoring the current setting of the `umask`.
- `-f` *archive* to use the specified *archive* as the archive name instead of the system default.
- `-v` to display the name of each file as it is processed.

Examples

If you want to extract all files in the `/u/testuser` directory from the archive file on the `/dev/rmt1` tape device, use the following command:

```
tar --xvf /dev/rmt1 /u/testuser
```

If you want to archive a file to an archive on the default tape drive, use the following command:

```
tar -c file1
```

uncompress

The uncompress command can be used to uncompress a file that has earlier been compressed using the compress command. By default, the uncompress command uncompresses a file in place; that is, the compressed file is deleted and the uncompressed file without the .z suffix is created in its place. The uncompressed file retains the permission and modification time attributes of the compressed file, but the user and the group of the file are changed to that of the user uncompressing the file.

Following is a list of some of the flags that can be used with the uncompress command:

- ■ -f or -F to force the uncompress even though a file by the name of the uncompressed file may already exist.
- ■ -c to uncompress the specified by file to the standard output retaining the original compressed file.
- ■ -v to display a message with the uncompressed filename.
- ■ -q to suppress display of compression statistics from the uncompress command.

Examples

If you want to uncompress file1.Z, use either of the two following commands:

```
uncompress file1
```

or

```
uncompress file1.Z
```

If you want to uncompress file1.Z to standard output retaining the original compressed file, use the -c flag in the following command:

```
uncompress -c file1
```

unpack

The unpack command can be used to uncompress files that have been compressed using the pack command and have the .z extension. The uncompressed file is created at the same place as the compressed file and the compressed file is removed. The uncompressed file retains attributes, such as the user, group, permission, access and modification time of the compressed file. The unpack command will not uncompress the file if a file by the name of the uncompressed file already exists.

If you want to uncompress file1.z, use either of the following two commands:

```
unpack file1
```

or

```
unpack file1.z
```

zcat

The zcat command can be used to uncompress a file (that has been compressed using the compress command) to the standard output, retaining the compressed file. You can redirect the standard output to another file to get an expanded version of the compressed file. This command works the same way as the uncompress command with the -c flag.

Examples

If you want to create a copy of the uncompressed version of a file without destroying the compressed file, use the following command:

```
zcat file1.Z > file2
```

The above example will create file2, which is the uncompressed version of file1.Z, at the same time retaining file1.Z.

Status Commands

In this section we will discuss several commands that display the status of various parts of the system. These commands can be used to monitor the system status at any point in time.

date

You can use the date command to display the current date and time in a specified format. If you are root user, use the date command to set the system date.

To display the date and time, you must specify a + (plus) sign followed by the format. The format can be as follows:

- ▪ %A to display date complete with weekday name.
- ▪ %b or %h to display abbreviated month name.
- ▪ %B to display complete month name.
- ▪ %c to display default date and time representation.
- ▪ %d to display the day of the month as a number from 1 through 31.
- ▪ %D to display the date in mm/dd/yy format.
- ▪ %H to display the hour as a number from 00 through 23.
- ▪ %I to display the hour as a number from 00 through 12.
- ▪ %j to display the day of year as a number from 1 through 366.
- ▪ %m to display the month as a number from 1 through 12.
- ▪ %M to display the minutes as a number from 0 through 59.
- ▪ %p to display AM or PM appropriately.
- ▪ %r to display 12-hour clock time (01–12) using the AM-PM notation.

- ■ %S to display the seconds as a number from 0 through 59.
- ■ %T to display the time in hh:mm:ss format for 24-hour clock.
- ■ %U to display the week number of the year as a number from 1 through 53 counting Sunday as first day of the week.
- ■ %w to display the day of the week as a number from 0 through 6, with Sunday counted as 0.
- ■ %W to display the week number of the year as a number from 1 through 53, counting Monday as first day of the week.
- ■ %x to display the default date format.
- ■ %X to display the time format.
- ■ %y to display the last two digits of the year from 00 through 99.
- ■ %Y to display the year with century as a decimal number.
- ■ %Z to display the time-zone name, if available.

Examples

If you want to display the date without formatting, use date without any formatting descriptor as follows:

```
date
Sat Dec  7 11:50:59 EST 1996
```

If you want to display only the date in mm/dd/yy format, use the following commands:

```
date +%m/%d/%y
12/07/96
```

If you want to format the date in yy/mm/dd format and time in hh:mm:ss format, use the following command:

```
date "+%y/%m/%d %H:%M:%S"
96/12/07 11:57:27
```

Following is another way of formatting the date:

```
date +%A","%B" "%d","%Y
Sunday,December 15,1996
```

If you want the Julian date, use the following command:

```
date +%j
350
```

If you want to find the week number for the current week, you have two options, the W and U, as shown in the following commands:

```
date +%W
49
date +%U
50
```

env

The `env` command can be used to display the current environment or change one or more of the environment variables and run a specified command. The changes are effective only during the execution of the command.

Following is an optional flag that you can use with the `env` command:

- ■ `-i` to indicate that only the variables setup as part of the `env` command are used for the specified command and all the current variable setups are ignored.

Examples

If you want to display the current environment, use the following command:

```
env
```

Let us assume that we have a script called `my_job` that displays the current setting of the variable called `LANG`.

If you execute the script `my_job` as part of the `env` command without modifying the `LANG` variable, you will get the following result:

```
env PATH=/u/testuser/jobs:$PATH my_job
LANG = C
```

If you modify the `LANG` variable as part of the `env` command, you will get the following result:

```
env LANG=C++ PATH=/u/testuser/jobs:$PATH my_job
LANG = C++
```

If you use the `-i` flag and do not modify `LANG` as part of the `env` command, that variable is not available to `my_job` and you will get the following result:

```
env -i PATH=/u/testuser/jobs:$PATH my_job
LANG =
```

iostat

The `iostat` command can be used to obtain statistics about CPU, disks, and TTY for a system. The first time you run `iostat` after the most recent booting of the system, the `iostat` provides the statistics since then. After that, `iostat` provides statistics since the last execution of the `iostat` command.

The `iostat` command displays the following details:

- ■ TTY and CPU header
- ■ TTY and CPU statistics detail
- ■ Physical volume header
- ■ One line for each physical volume

Following is a list of data items displayed for TTY and CPU statistics:

- `tin` displays the number of characters read by the system for all TTYs.
- `tout` displays the number of characters written by the system for all TTYs.
- `%user` displays the utilization percentage of the CPU at the application level.
- `%system` displays the utilization percentage of the CPU at the system level.
- `%idle` displays the utilization percentage of the CPU while it was idling (this represents the unused utilization of the CPU).
- `%iowait` displays the idling percentage of the CPU while waiting for the i/o request.

Following is a list of data items displayed as part of the physical volume utilization:

- `%tm_act` displays the active utilization percentage of the physical volume.
- `Kbps` displays the number of kilobytes transferred per second to or from the physical volume.
- `tps` displays the number of physical i/o requests to the physical volume.
- `msps` displays the average number of milliseconds required for each seek of the physical volume.
- `Kb_read` displays the number of kilobytes read from the physical volume.
- `Kb_wrtn` displays the number of kilobytes written to the physical volume.

Following is a list of flags that can be used with the `iostat` command:

- `-d` to display only physical volume utilization report. This cannot be used with `-t` flag.
- `-t` to display only TTY and CPU utilization report. This cannot be used with the `-d` flag.

Examples

If you want to display only the TTY and CPU utilization, use the `-t` flag as in the following command:

```
iostat -t

tty:    tin      tout     cpu:  % user   % sys    % idle    % iowait
        0.5      78.7           32.6     25.2     35.7      6.4
```

If you want only the utilization of physical volume of `disk1`, use the `-d` flag, as in the following command:

```
iostat -d disk1

Disks:      % tm_act    Kbps     tps    Kb_read    Kb_wrtn
disk1          6.7       4.3     5.0    2339721    4048758
```

sar

You can use the sar command to report on system information. The sar command allows you to save the information and report on it. By default, the sar command generates the CPU utilization reports, but you can use various flags to collect information about other system activities.

Following is a list of some of the flags that can be used with the sar command:

- ■ -A to report data on all system activities.
- ■ -a to report data on the usage of file system access routine.
- ■ -b to report buffer activities.
- ■ -c to report system calls such as forks, execs, and so on.
- ■ -e optionally followed by time in hh:mm:ss format to specify the time when the data accumulation should be terminated.
- ■ -f *file* to extract data from the specified file.
- ■ -i *seconds* to extract data from the file for time closest in seconds.
- ■ -k to report on kernel activity.
- ■ -m to report on semaphore and message activities.
- ■ -o *file* to save the activity data in the specified file.
- ■ -r to report on paging statistics.
- ■ -s optionally followed by time in hh:mm:ss format to specify the time to start the data accumulation.
- ■ -v to report on process and i-node activity.
- ■ -y to report on TTY activity.

uname

The uname command displays details about the operating system and computer system on the standard output. You can use certain flags to set the system name.

Following is a list of some of the flags that can be used with the uname command:

- ■ -m to display the machine ID.
- ■ -r to display the release number of the operating system.
- ■ -s to display system name.
- ■ -v to display operating system version.
- ■ -S *name* to modify the system name.
- ■ -a to display the machine ID, release number of operating system, and system name.

Examples

If you want to display details about the hardware and operating system, you can use the -a flag, as in the following command:

```
uname -a
AIX main_system 2 3 000010000526
```

In the above example, the information displayed is as follows:

- Operating system name   `AIX`
- Machine name   `main_system`
- Operating system release number   `2`
- Operating system version number   `3`
- Machine is   `000010000526`

uptime

The `uptime` command displays the following information:

- The current time
- The length of time the system has been up
- The number of users currently logged on
- The number of jobs executing in the system

vmstat

The `vmstat` command can be used to get information about the processes, virtual memory, physical volumes and CPU activity. The information includes the utilization of CPU, virtual memory, and physical volume, which can be used to monitor the load on the system.

The first invocation of `vmstat` displays the statistics since the system startup, and subsequent invocations display statistics since the last invocation. You can specify a count and an interval parameter to control the number of reports generated and interval between the reports.

The details displayed by `vmstat` are as follows:

- Processes
- Virtual memory
- Page
- Faults
- CPU

The details displayed for the processes are as follows:

- `r` displays the number of processes placed in the queue ready to execute.
- `b` displays the number of processes placed in the queue waiting for execution.

The details displayed for the memory are as follows:

- avm displays the number of pages being consumed (the pages are from the page space).
- fre displays the number of pages in the free list.

The details displayed for page are as follows:

- re displays the number of page reclaims per second observed in the specified interval.
- pi displays number of pages brought in from page space in the specified interval.
- po displays the number of pages swapped out to page space in the specified interval.
- fr displays the number of pages freed in the specified interval.
- sr displays the number of page examined, to determine whether they can be freed, in the specified interval.
- cy displays the number of clock revolutions per second.

The details displayed for faults are as follows:

- in displays the number of interrupts per second in the specified interval.
- sy displays the number of system calls per second in the specified interval.
- cs displays the number of context switches per second in the specified interval.

The details displayed for CPU are as follows:

- us displays the percentage utilization of CPU at the application during the specified interval.
- sy displays the percentage utilization of CPU at the system during the specified interval.
- id displays the percentage utilization of CPU idling during the specified interval without any I/O wait.
- wa displays the percentage utilization of CPU idling during the specified interval due to disk I/O requests.

You can specify up to four physical volume names to get the number of transfers that occurred in those disks in the specified interval.

Following is a flag that can be used with the vmstat command:

- -s to display the statistics since the system initialization.

Examples

If you want to display the statistics five times intervals of five seconds, execute the following command:

```
vmstat 5 5
procs     memory              page                faults        cpu
----- -------------- ------------------------ ------------ -----------
 r  b   avm   fre  re  pi  po  fr   sr   cy   in   sy   cs  us sy id wa
 1  0 44036  120   0   0   0  125  275   0   366 1458 391  33 25 36  6
 1  0 44036  120   0   0   0  542  938   0   446 4932 246  65 24  0 12
 1  0 44036  121   0   0   0  624 1116   0   453 5848 259  64 25  0 11
 1  0 44037  124   0   0   0  512 1010   0   434 4812 266  59 25  0 16
 0  0 44037  121   0   0   0  564 1109   0   426 4838 265  64 24  0 11
```

Text Processing

UNIX provides several commands to process the contents of a text file.

cut

You can use the cut command to extract data from each line of a text file. This command can be used from a file that contains data records so that each line consists of one or more fields separated by tab characters.

Following is a list of some of the flags that can be used with the cut command:

- ■ -c*characterlist* to specify a list of characters to be cut from each line.
- ■ -f*fieldlist* to specify a list of fields to be cut from each line. You can additionally specify a flag -d*character* to override the character to be interpreted as the field delimiter. You can also specify flag -s to suppress lines that do not have the specified delimiter character.

Examples

Let us assume that we have a file called file1 whose contents are as follows:

```
more file1
Misty      Ghosh
Saptarsi          Guha
Sanjiv  Guha
```

In this file, the fields are separated by tab characters.

If you want to extract the first field, use the following command:

```
cut -f1 file1
Misty
Saptarsi
Sanjiv
```

If you want to cut the characters 2 to 6, use the following command:

```
cut -c2-5 file1
isty
apta
anji
```

If you want to cut all characters in the first field up to the first s character, use the following command:

```
cut -d"s" -f1  file1
Mi
Saptar
Sanjiv  Guha
```

You will notice that the third line is cut completely. To suppress lines that do not contain the s character, use the `-s` flag as in the following command:

```
cut -d"s" -s -f1  file1
Mi
Saptar
```

ex

The `ex` command invokes the `ex` editor to edit one or more files.

Following is a list of some of the flags that can be used with the `ex` command:

- `-c` *sub-command* to perform the specified *sub-command* on the specified file before invoking the `ex` command.
- `-R` to disallow updating the file.
- `-w`*size* to set the window to number of lines equal to *size*.
- `-v` to invoke the `vi` editor.
- `-r` *file* to do the recovery on the specified file.

Once you are in the `ex` editor, you can use the following sub-commands to move around in the file and edit the file:

- `z` to invoke full screen mode.
- `u` to undo the last change made.
- `n` to move to the next file if you have invoked `ex` editor with multiple files.
- `/pattern/` to find a pattern in the file.
- `d` to delete one or more lines.
- `a` to append.

The `ex` operates in the following modes:

- `command mode`: When the `ex` editor starts, it is in command mode which is a : (colon) prompt where you can enter a sub-command.
- `text input mode`: In this mode, you can add or change text in the file. You can enter text using the a, i or c sub-commands. The use of these sub-commands will allow you to enter text in the buffer. You can return to the command mode by entering a . (a single period) as the first character of the text buffer.

fmt

The `fmt` command can be used to format files to a 72-character line by default. The `fmt` command preserves the blank lines in the input file as well as the spacing between words. You can modify the line length using the `-Width` flag.

Examples

Let us assume that we have `file1` whose contents are shown below:

```
more file1
This is a test file for fmt

The fmt command      formats a file
for mail command
```

Notice that we have a blank line in the file and the spacing between `command` and `formats` on the third line is more than one character. Let us now format `file1` using the `fmt` command to create `file2` as in the following command:

```
fmt file1 > file2
```

Now let us see the contents of `file2` using the `more` command as follows:

```
more file2
This is a test file for fmt

The fmt command      formats a file for mail command
```

In the above file, the blank line and inter-word spacing have been preserved.

fold

The `fold` command can be used to generate multiple lines from a single line by splitting the line at the specified position. By default, the line length is 80 bytes. A newline character is inserted at the end of the line.

Following is list of flags that can be used with the `fold` command:

- ■ `-b` to specify the position in bytes.
- ■ `-s` to split a line after the last space at a position that is less than or equal to the specified width.
- ■ `-w width` to specify the line width.

Examples

Let us assume that we have `file1` containing one line of 129 characters which is shown below:

```
more file1
The fold command can be used on files which have line lengths more than 80 bytes
, it breaks the line into multiple 80 byte lines
```

If you want to split the line at byte position 40, use the following command:

```
fold -w 40  file1 > file2; more file2
The fold command can be used on files wh
ich have line lengths more than 80 bytes
, it breaks the line into multiple 80 by
te lines
```

In the above example, the split happens in the middle of words. If you do not want to split words, use the -s flag, as in the following command:

```
fold -w 40 -s  file1 > file2; more file2
The fold command can be used on files
which have line lengths more than 80
bytes, it breaks the line into multiple
80 byte lines
```

join

The join command can be used to merge two files (one can be standard input) to create a third file (can be standard output). Each line in the file is merged on the basis of a field that has the same value in both input files to create one line in the output file. The fields in each file are separated by either a space or tab character.

Following is a list of flags that can be used with the join command:

- -1 *field* or -j1 *field* to specify that the join should be made on the basis of the *field* in the first file.
- -2 *field* or -j2 *field* to specify that the join should be made on the basis of the *field* in the second file.
- -e *string* to specify that blank fields in the output file be replaced by the specified *string*.
- -o *fileid.fieldnumber* to specify that the output should consist of the specified fields. You can specify multiple fields separating them by commas.
- -t *character* to modify the field separator character from the default value of space.
- -a *fileid* to generate output line for each line in the file specified by the *fileid* parameter for lines that cannot be matched to the lines in the other file using join field. The output lines are produced in addition to the default output.
- -v *fileid* to generate output line for each line in the file specified by the *fileid* parameter for lines that cannot be matched to the lines in the other file using join field. The default output is not produced.

Examples

Let us assume we have two files, file1 and file2, whose contents are shown as follows:

```
more file1
computer1 16MB 1.2GB 17inch CDROM
computer2 8MB 840MB 14inch
computer3 12MB 1.6GB 17inch
computer4 4MB 270MB 14inch
```

```
more file2
computer1 1stfloor office5
computer3 2ndfloor office9A
computer4 1stfloor office2
computer5 3rdfloor office1
```

If you want to join the two files and display only the matching lines, execute the following command:

```
join file1 file2
computer1 16MB 1.2GB 17inch CDROM 1stfloor office5
computer3 12MB 1.6GB 17inch 2ndfloor office9A
computer4 4MB 270MB 14inch CDROM 1stfloor office2
```

If you want to join the two files and display the matching lines as well as the nonmatching lines from the specified file, use the -a flag in the following command:

```
join -a1 file1 file2
computer1 16MB 1.2GB 17inch CDROM 1stfloor office5
computer2 8MB 840MB 14inch
computer3 12MB 1.6GB 17inch 2ndfloor office9A
computer4 4MB 270MB 14inch CDROM 1stfloor office2
```

The above example displays the line with computer2 from file1 because it does not have a matching line in file2. If you want to display only the lines that do not match lines from the specified file, use the -v flag in the following command:

```
join -v2 file1 file2
computer5 3rdfloor office1
```

The above example displays the line with computer5 from file2 because it does not have a matching line in file1.

If you want to display only certain fields from the input files to the output file, use the -o flag as in the following command:

```
join -o 1.1 2.2 2.3 1.5 file1 file2
computer1 1stfloor office5 CDROM
computer3 2ndfloor office9A
computer4 1stfloor office2 CDROM
```

In the above example, the line with computer3 is displayed with one field short because that field is not present in the input file. You can insert a fixed legend in the empty field in the output by using the -e flag in the following command:

```
join -o 1.1 2.2 2.3 1.5 -e"NO CDROM" file1 file2
computer1 1stfloor office5 CDROM
computer3 2ndfloor office9A NO CDROM
computer4 1stfloor office2 NO CDROM
```

paste

The paste command can be used to paste lines from one or more files (one of them can be a standard input) to the standard output, which can be redirected to a file. The paste command concatenates the line from each input file to the output file separating them by the tab character (default).

Following is a list of flags that can be used with the `paste` command:

- `-dlist` to specify characters that will be used to separate corresponding lines from the input files in the output file. You can specify multiple characters if you have multiple input files.

- `-s` to merge subsequent lines from input file for each input file, one at a time, separated by the specified delimiter character.

Examples

Let us assume that we have two files, `file1` and `file2`, whose contents are shown below:

```
more file1
computer1 16MB 1.2GB 17inch CDROM
computer2 8MB 840MB 14inch
computer3 12MB 1.6GB 17inch
computer4 4MB 270MB 14inch

more file2
computer1 1stfloor office5
computer3 2ndfloor office9A
computer4 1stfloor office2
computer5 3rdfloor office1
```

If you want to merge `file1` and `file2`, use the following command:

```
paste file1 file2
computer1 16MB 1.2GB 17inch CDROM        computer1 1stfloor office5
computer2 8MB 840MB 14inch        computer3 2ndfloor office9A
computer3 12MB 1.6GB 17inch        computer4 1stfloor office2
computer4 4MB 270MB 14inch        computer5 3rdfloor office1
```

The lines from `file1` and `file2` are separated by tab characters.

If you want to modify the default separator from the tab character to, say, / (slash), use the `-d` flag in the following command:

```
paste -d"/" file1 file2
computer1 16MB 1.2GB 17inch CDROM/computer1 1stfloor office5
computer2 8MB 840MB 14inch/computer3 2ndfloor office9A
computer3 12MB 1.6GB 17inch/computer4 1stfloor office2
computer4 4MB 270MB 14inch /computer5 3rdfloor office1
```

If you want to merge the lines from within each input file, use the `-s` flag in the following command:

```
paste -d"/" -s file1 file2
computer1 16MB 1.2GB 17inch CDROM/computer2 8MB 840MB 14inch/computer3 12MB 1.6G
B 17inch/computer4 4MB 270MB 14inch
computer1 1stfloor office5/computer3 2ndfloor office9A/computer4 1stfloor office
2/computer5 3rdfloor office1
```

sort

The sort command is used to sort one or more files in the specified order by the specified key. It also can be used to merge files that have already been sorted. When more than one file is used, the sort command concatenates these files before sorting according to specifications.

Following is a list of some of the flags that can be used with the sort command:

- ■ -kkey to specify the key on which to sort. The specification for the key includes the starting field and column position and end field and column position.
- ■ -A to specify that sorting be done according to ASCII collating sequence.
- ■ -c to check whether the specified files are sorted according to the specified key and order.
- ■ -d to sort according to dictionary order.
- ■ -f to change all letters to uppercase before the sort.
- ■ -i to ignore nondisplayable characters for comparison.
- ■ -m to merge pre-sorted input files.
- ■ -n to sort according to numeric value.
- ■ -ofile to redirect the output to the specified *file* instead of standard output.
- ■ -r to sort the output in the reverse order of the specified order.
- ■ -u to create only one line in the output for lines that sort identically.

Examples

Let us assume that we have a file called file1 whose contents are shown below:

```
more file1
disk drive
memory
video memory
monitor
[tape drive]
CD-ROM
3.5inch diskette
modem
monitor
sound blaster
```

If you want to sort file1, use the following command:

```
sort file1
3.5inch diskette
CD-ROM
[tape drive]
disk drive
memory
modem
monitor
monitor
sound blaster
video memory
```

If you want to sort in the reverse order, use the -r flag in the following command:

```
sort -r file1
video memory
sound blaster
monitor
monitor
modem
memory
disk drive
[tape drive]
CD-ROM
3.5inch diskette
```

If you want to sort according to alphabetic order, use the -d flag in the following command:

```
sort -d file1
3.5inch diskette
CD-ROM
disk drive
memory
modem
monitor
monitor
sound blaster
[tape drive]
video memory
```

In the above example, the line [tape drive] is sorted as tape drive because the [and] are ignored due to the -d flag.

If you want only one line to be retained in case more than one line are sorted equally, use the -u flag in the following command:

```
sort -u file1
3.5inch diskette
CD-ROM
[tape drive]
disk drive
memory
modem
monitor
sound blaster
video memory
```

In the above example, the line monitor appears only once, although there are two such entries in the file, due to use of the -d flag.

If you want to sort file1 according to the uppercase letter sort order, use the -f flag as in the following command:

```
sort -f file1
3.5inch diskette
CD-ROM
disk drive
memory
modem
```

```
monitor
monitor
sound blaster
video memory
[tape drive]
```

tr

You can use the `tr` command to translate or delete characters from standard input to generate standard output. Following is the detail of the main functions of the `tr` command:

- Translate characters specified input to a new specified character in the output.
- Delete specified characters input from the input to generate the output.
- Delete all but the first occurrence of the specified characters.

Following is a list of some of the flags that can be used with the `tr` command:

- `-c` to translate all but the specified characters by the specified new character.
- `-d` to delete the specified characters.
- `-s` to delete all but the first occurrence of the specified characters.

You can specify the input and output sequence of characters in certain special ways as follows:

- `[character1-character2]` to specify a range of characters including `character1` and `character2`.
- `[character*number]` to specify *number* occurrences of `character`.
- `[character*]` to specify the use of as many as are needed occurrences of `character` so that the input string of characters to be translated matches the output characters to be translated to.
- `[:characterlist:]` to specify a list of characters as input or output string. The `characterlist` can be `upper`, `lower`, `alpha`, `space`, `digit`, and so on.

Examples

Let us assume that we have `file1` whose contents are shown as follows:

```
more file1
"this        is a test file
for tr command"
"it has 4 lines
but should be 1 line"
```

If you want to change the double quotes to spaces use the following command:

```
tr '\"' ' ' < file1
 this        is a test file
for tr command
 it has 4 lines
but should be 1 line
```

If you want to change all lowercase letters to uppercase letters, use the following command:

```
tr [:lower:] [:upper:] < file1
"THIS      IS A TEST FILE
FOR TR COMMAND"
"IT HAS 4 LINES
BUT SHOULD BE 1 LINE"
```

If you want to delete all the newline characters from this file, use the -d flag in the following command:

```
tr -d '\n' < file1
"this       is a test file for tr command""it has 4 lines but should be 1 line"
```

If you want to delete all but the first occurrence of a space and replace the space by a - (hyphen), use the -s flag in the following command:

```
tr -s ' ' '-' < file1
"this-is-a-test-file-
for-tr-command"
"it-has-4-lines-
but-should-be-1-line"
```

uniq

The uniq command can be used to eliminate duplicate adjacent lines from a file or from standard input to generate standard output or another file. This is the default operation. However, it is possible to use only part of a line for comparison by using certain flags.

Following is a list of some of the flags that can be used with the uniq command:

- -c to precede each line with a number while displaying the output (the number specifies the number of occurrence of the line in the input file).
- -d to display only the lines that occur multiple times adjacent to each other in the input file.
- -u to display only the lines that appear only once in the input file.
- -s *numberofcharacters* or *+numberofcharacters* to specify the number of characters from the start of a line that will be ignored while comparing adjacent lines.
- *-numberoffields* or -f *numberoffields* to specify the number of fields from the start of a line that will be ignored while comparing adjacent lines.

Examples

Let us assume that we have file1 whose contents are displayed below:

```
more file1
This is line 1
This is line 1
This is line 2
This is line 3
THIS IS line 3
This is line 4
```

If you want to find out unique lines in `file1`, use the following command:

```
uniq file1
This is line 1
This is line 2
This is line 3
THIS IS line 3
This is line 4
```

In the above example, the first line has been dropped because it is identical to the second line. If you want to display only the duplicate lines use the `-d` flag in the following command:

```
uniq -d file1
This is line 1
```

If you want to display the lines that appear only once in `file1`, use the `-u` flag in the following command:

```
uniq -u file1
This is line 2
This is line 3
THIS IS line 3
This is line 4
```

In the above example, the first two lines have not been displayed because they are identical. If you want to skip the first two fields while comparing adjacent lines, use the `-f` flag in the following command:

```
uniq -f 2 file1
This is line 1
This is line 2
This is line 3
This is line 4
```

sed

You can use the `sed` command to edit a file using a script. In the script, you can specify commands to edit one or more lines according to rules specified as part of one or more commands.

Following is a list of some of the flags that can be used with the `sed` command:

- ■ `-e command` to use the specified `sed` *command* to edit the file.
- ■ `-f filename` to use the *filename* as the editing script to edit the file.
- ■ `-n` to suppress messages from `sed`.

The `sed` command uses two different areas while performing editing:

- ■ `pattern area` to hold selected lines for editing.
- ■ `hold area` to temporarily hold the lines.

The `sed` sub-commands can affect either all the lines or only the specified lines.

Following is a list of some of the sub-commands that can be used with the sed command:

- # to specify start of comments. Everything in a line following the # is treated as comments.

- :label to specify an addressable *label* that can be used in the script.

- [/pattern/]= to write to output the line number of each line that contains the specified *pattern*.

- [address]a\textstring to append *textstring* to each line specified by the *address*.

- [address1][,address2]c\textstring to replace the lines in the specified address range with the *textstring*.

- [address1][,address2]d to delete the lines in the specified address range.

- [address]i\textstring to insert *textstring* before each specified line.

- [address1][,address2]p to print the lines in the specified address range.

- [address1][,address2]n to specify that the current line be displayed and the next line be made the current line.

- [address1][,address]N to specify that the current line be appended to the contents of the pattern area separated by a newline character.

- [address]q to exit when the specified address is encountered.

- [address1][,address2]s/old pattern/new pattern/[flag] to specify that the *old pattern* be replaced by the *new pattern* in the specified range. The behavior of the replacement can be modified by specified flags.

- [address1][,address2]w file to write the contents of the specified range to the specified *file*.

- [address1][,address2]y/old character list/new character list/ to modify each character in the old character list by the corresponding character in the new character list.

The above sub-commands are the ones that affect the pattern area used by the sed command. Now let us look at some of the sub-commands that affect the hold area:

- [address1][,address2]g to copy the contents of the hold area to the pattern area which then become the new content of the pattern area.

- [address1][,address2]G to append the contents of the hold area to the pattern area following the specified address.

- [address1][,address2]h to copy the contents of the pattern area to the hold area which then become the new contents of the hold area.

- [address1][,address2]H to append the contents of the pattern area to the hold area following the specified address.

- [address1][,address2]x to exchange the contents of pattern and hold area.

Examples

Let us assume that we have file1 whose contents are displayed below:

```
more file1
This file is a test file for sed command
-----------------------------------------
The sed command is used for stream editing files
-------------------------------------------------
The sed command a number of sub-commands which may be used to do the
---------------------------------------------------------------------
editing in specified line
-------------------------
```

If you want to print the line numbers of the line in which a specified pattern is found, use the following command:

```
sed -e "/sed/=" file1
1
This file is a test file for sed command
-----------------------------------------
3
The sed command is used for stream editing files
-------------------------------------------------
5
The sed command a number of sub-commands which may be used to do the
---------------------------------------------------------------------
editing in specified line
-------------------------
```

In the above example, the line numbers are displayed for the lines containing the pattern sed. If you want to add a specified text after each specified line, use the following command:

```
sed -f sfile file1
This file is a test file for sed command
++++++++++++++++++++++++++++++++++
-----------------------------------------
The sed command is used for stream editing files
++++++++++++++++++++++++++++++++++
-------------------------------------------------
The sed command a number of sub-commands which may be used to do the
++++++++++++++++++++++++++++++++++
---------------------------------------------------------------------
editing in specified line
-------------------------
```

where the file sfile contains the following line:

```
/sed/a\
++++++++++++++++++++++++++++++++++
```

In the above example, a string of +s (plus signs) is printed after each line containing the string sed. If you want to delete lines containing a specified string, use

```
sed -f sfile file1
This file is a test file for sed command
The sed command is used for stream editing files
The sed command a number of sub-commands which may be used to do the
editing in specified line
```

where `sfile` contains the following:

```
/---/d
```

In the above example, all lines that contain the string --- will be deleted. If you want to change all occurrences of a particular string by another one, use

```
sed -f sfile file1
This file is a test file for sed command
++++++++++++++++++++++++++++++++++++++++++
The sed command is used for stream editing files
------------------------------------------------
The sed command a number of sub-commands which may be used to do the
--------------------------------------------------------------------
editing in specified line
-------------------------
```

where `sfile` contains the following:

```
1,3s/----/++++/g
```

In the above example, all occurrences of ---- are replaced by ++++ for lines 1 through 3. If you want to insert a specified string before each line containing a specified string, use

```
sed -f sfile file1
++++
This file is a test file for sed command
----------------------------------------
++++
The sed command is used for stream editing files
------------------------------------------------
++++
The sed command a number of sub-commands which may be used to do the
--------------------------------------------------------------------
editing in specified line
-------------------------
```

where `sfile` contains the following:

```
/sed/i\
++++
```

In the above example, a string ++++ is printed before each line in which the string sed appears. If you want to change each occurrence of a character by another, use

```
sed -f sfile file1
This file is A test file for sed commAnd
++++++++++++++++++++++++++++++++++++++++++
The sed commAnd is used for streAm editing files
------------------------------------------------
The sed command a number of sub-commands which may be used to do the
--------------------------------------------------------------------
editing in specified line
-------------------------
```

where `sfile` contains the following:

```
1,3s/-/+/g
```

In the above example, each occurrence of a - (hyphen) is modified to a + (plus) and each occurrence of a is modified to A between lines 1 through 3, both inclusive. If you want to delete all lines but the ones in which the specified pattern occurs, use

```
sed -f sfile file1
This file is a test file for sed command
The sed command is used for stream editing files
The sed command a number of sub-commands which may be used to do the
```

where sfile contains the following:

```
/sed/!d
```

In the above example, the ! (exclamation mark) is used to denote that all lines except those which contain the string sed are to be processed.

Miscellaneous Commands

In this section we will discuss some of the commands available to do miscellaneous operations in UNIX.

banner

You can use the banner command to print one or more characters in large size.

Example

If you want to print the word banner in large size on the standard output, use the following command:

```
banner banner

#####     ##    #     #  #     #  ######  #####
#    #   #  #   #     #  ##    ##  #       #    #
#####    #    #  # #   #  # #   #  #####   #    #
#    #  ######  #  # #   #  # #   #       #####
#    #  #    #  #   ##   #  ##   #       #    #
#####   #    #  #    #   #  ######  #    #
```

bc

If you want to perform simple arithmetic expression in UNIX, use the bc command. By default, all the numbers are assumed to be decimal numbers, but you can perform operations on octal or hexadecimal numbers. You can also scale the decimal numbers. The bc command accepts input first from the specified file followed by standard input. You can, however, use input redirection to accept input only from a file.

The arguments that can be used with the bc commands are as follows:

- Variable name (one letter)
- Variable array name (letter[expression])
- A literal such as scale

Some of the other operands that can be used are as follows:

- + for adding
- - for subtracting
- / for division
- * for multiplication
- % for percentage
- ++ for adding one to the preceding variable
- -- for subtracting one from the preceding variable
- = to assign a value
- sqrt for square root computation
- length for getting length of a number
- scale for specifying the number of digits after the decimal

You can also use C program-like statements, expressions, and functions. There are some special arithmetic functions you can use in bc. Some of these functions are:

- s(x) for sine of x
- c(x) for cosine of x
- l(x) for log of x

Following is a list of flags that can be used with the bc command:

- -c to compile the bc program parameters but not execute them
- -l to include the library of math functions

Examples

Let us assume that we have file1, which contains the following bc command parameters:

```
more file1
b=5
c=10
a=b+c
a
```

If you want to compile the contents of file1 without executing them, use the -c flag in the following command:

```
bc -c < file1
 5sb
 10sc
lblc+sa
laps.
q
```

If you want to execute the contents of file1, use the following command:

```
bc < file1
15
```

Let us assume that we have `file1` whose contents are displayed below:

```
a=0
j=50
for (i=1; i<=j; i++) a=i+a;
a
```

If we execute the `bc` command with this file as input, this will add all numbers from 1 through 50 and display the total as follows:

```
bc < file1
1275
```

cal

You can use the `cal` command to display the calendar for one or more months on standard output. If you do not specify any arguments, `cal` displays the calendar for the current month. You can specify the month and year for which you want to display the calendar. If you specify only one argument, `cal` will display a calendar for all 12 months of the specified year.

Examples

If you want to display the calendar of the current month, execute the following command:

```
cal
      December 1996
Sun Mon Tue Wed Thu Fri Sat
  1   2   3   4   5   6   7
  8   9  10  11  12  13  14
 15  16  17  18  19  20  21
 22  23  24  25  26  27  28
 29  30  31
```

If you want to display the calendar for January, 1995, use the following command:

```
cal 1 1995
      January 1995
Sun Mon Tue Wed Thu Fri Sat
  1   2   3   4   5   6   7
  8   9  10  11  12  13  14
 15  16  17  18  19  20  21
 22  23  24  25  26  27  28
 29  30  31
```

If you want to obtain calendars for all 12 months of 1997, use the following command:

```
cal 1997
                          1997

        January                     February
Sun Mon Tue Wed Thu Fri Sat   Sun Mon Tue Wed Thu Fri Sat
              1   2   3   4                             1
  5   6   7   8   9  10  11     2   3   4   5   6   7   8
 12  13  14  15  16  17  18     9  10  11  12  13  14  15
 19  20  21  22  23  24  25    16  17  18  19  20  21  22
 26  27  28  29  30  31        23  24  25  26  27  28
```

```
              March                           April
 Sun Mon Tue Wed Thu Fri Sat     Sun Mon Tue Wed Thu Fri Sat
                           1               1   2   3   4   5
   2   3   4   5   6   7   8       6   7   8   9  10  11  12
   9  10  11  12  13  14  15      13  14  15  16  17  18  19
  16  17  18  19  20  21  22      20  21  22  23  24  25  26
  23  24  25  26  27  28  29      27  28  29  30
  30  31
               May                            June
 Sun Mon Tue Wed Thu Fri Sat     Sun Mon Tue Wed Thu Fri Sat
                   1   2   3       1   2   3   4   5   6   7
   4   5   6   7   8   9  10       8   9  10  11  12  13  14
  11  12  13  14  15  16  17      15  16  17  18  19  20  21
  18  19  20  21  22  23  24      22  23  24  25  26  27  28
  25  26  27  28  29  30  31      29  30
               July                          August
 Sun Mon Tue Wed Thu Fri Sat     Sun Mon Tue Wed Thu Fri Sat
           1   2   3   4   5                           1   2
   6   7   8   9  10  11  12       3   4   5   6   7   8   9
  13  14  15  16  17  18  19      10  11  12  13  14  15  16
  20  21  22  23  24  25  26      17  18  19  20  21  22  23
  27  28  29  30  31              24  25  26  27  28  29  30
                                  31
            September                       October
 Sun Mon Tue Wed Thu Fri Sat     Sun Mon Tue Wed Thu Fri Sat
       1   2   3   4   5   6                   1   2   3   4
   7   8   9  10  11  12  13       5   6   7   8   9  10  11
  14  15  16  17  18  19  20      12  13  14  15  16  17  18
  21  22  23  24  25  26  27      19  20  21  22  23  24  25
  28  29  30                      26  27  28  29  30  31
            November                        December
 Sun Mon Tue Wed Thu Fri Sat     Sun Mon Tue Wed Thu Fri Sat
                           1           1   2   3   4   5   6
   2   3   4   5   6   7   8       7   8   9  10  11  12  13
   9  10  11  12  13  14  15      14  15  16  17  18  19  20
  16  17  18  19  20  21  22      21  22  23  24  25  26  27
  23  24  25  26  27  28  29      28  29  30  31
  30
```

calendar

You can use the calendar command to get reminders from messages stored in a special file named calendar in the current directory. The messages are stored as either

- date message
- message date

where date can be in a variety of formats such as:

- March 7
- Mar 7
- mar 7
- march 7th

- 3/7
- */7 (7th of each month)

On a Friday, the `calendar` command will display the messages for four days—Friday, Saturday, Sunday, and Monday.

clear

You can use the `clear` command to clear the screen of your workstation. This command checks the terminal type to determine how to clear the screen.

Examples

To clear the screen on your terminal, use the following command:

```
clear
```

time

You can use the `time` command to obtain the execution time of a script, command, or program. The execution time is displayed with the following times:

- real
- user
- system

Examples

If you want to find out the execution time of a script `sample`, use the following command:

```
time sample
real    0m6.49s
user    0m0.02s
sys     0m0.03s
```

xargs

You can use the `xargs` command to group multiple arguments and input them to a command. `xargs` passes as many arguments to the command as necessary to ensure that the maximum size limit for command line arguments is not exceeded.

Following is a list of some of the flags that can be used with the `xargs` command:

- `-eendoffilecharacter` to specify the character to be used to terminate the argument string. The default is _ (underline) character
- `-istring` to use each line as a single parameter in place of the `string` variable specified as part of the command line. The default `string` is {}.
- `-lnumber` to specify the number of non-empty lines to be used as arguments to the command for each invocation. The last invocation can use fewer than the specified `number`.

■ -n*number* to specify the number of arguments to be used in each invocation. The last invocation can use fewer than the *number* specified.

■ -p to ask for confirmation before executing the command.

■ -s*size* to set the maximum size of the argument list for each invocation.

■ -t to echo the constructed command to the standard error.

Examples

Let us assume that we have xfile whose contents are shown below:

```
more xfile
file1 file2 file3
file4 file5 file6
file7 file8 file9
```

If you want to pass only two arguments to the ls command at a time, use the -n flag in the following command:

```
xargs -n2 ls  < xfile
file1   file2
file3   file4
file5   file6
file7   file8
file9
```

If you want to pass two lines at a time to the ls command, use the -l flag in the following command:

```
xargs -l2 ls  < xfile
file1   file2   file3   file4   file5   file6
file7   file8   file9
```

If you want to confirm the command to be executed before executing the command, use the -p flag in the following command:

```
xargs -l2 -p ls  < xfile
sfile1file2 file3 file4 file5 file6 ?...y
file1   file2   file3   file4   file5   file6
ls file7 file8 file9 ?...y
file7   file8   file9
```

In the above example, you have to use the character y to confirm that the command should be executed. If you want to rename all the files that start with the name file (file1 through file9), use the -i flag in the following command:

```
ls file* ¦ xargs -t -i cp {} {}.old
cp file1 file1.old
cp file2 file2.old
cp file3 file3.old
cp file4 file4.old
cp file5 file5.old
cp file6 file6.old
cp file7 file7.old
cp file8 file8.old
cp file9 file9.old
```

In the above example, the `-t` flag forces the display of the constructed command to the standard error.

Regular Expression

A regular expression in UNIX is a string of one or more characters and meta-characters. The commands that accept regular expressions first have to expand it to get the specified pattern before matching it to the input. The matching is done character by character.

> **CAUTION**
>
> The regular expression looks like the file matching pattern used by some commands such as the `find` command. But the regular expression is not the same as the file matching pattern.

A regular expression contains the following:

- character set, which matches one or more characters at the specified position.
- count, which specifies the number of the previous character to be repeated. This is an * (asterisk) to specify that zero or more of the previous character should be repeated.
- position specifier, which is a set of special characters to indicate certain fixed positions such as start of a line, end of a line, and so on.
- meta characters to specify special meaning.

Character Set

A character set is a list of one or more specified characters. The character set can be specified as follows:

- range of characters, which can be specified as two characters separated by a hyphen enclosed within square brackets. This matches one occurrence of a character within the specified range. If you specify a ^ (caret) in front of the range, the matching is reversed—that is, all characters except those in the specified range will be matched.
- list of characters, which can be a list of individual characters enclosed within square brackets. This matches one occurrence of one of the characters in the list. You can specify a ^ (caret) in front of one or more characters to match all characters except those.

Position Specifier

UNIX allows use of a number of special characters to specify certain special positions in a line. Following is a list of these special characters:

- ^ at the start of a regular expression to specify beginning of a line.
- $ at the end of the regular expression to specify end of a line.

Meta Characters

A meta character is a character that, when used as part of a regular expression, has a special meaning. Following is a list of these meta characters:

- . to match all characters except newline.
- * to match zero or more of the preceding characters or regular expressions.
- ^ to match the regular expression following it at the beginning of the line (for this to work, you must specify ^ as the first character of the regular expression).
- $ to match the regular expression preceding it at the end of the line (for this to work, you must specify $ as the last character of the regular expression).
- [ ] to match exactly one of the enclosed characters. The characters enclosed can be a range or a list of individual characters.
- \{*n1*,*n2*\} to match a minimum of *n1* and a maximum of *n2* occurrences of the preceding character or regular expression.
- \ to interpret the following character as a regular character rather than a meta-character.
- \(\) to save the enclosed regular expression for later use. These can then be reused by using \1 through \9.
- \< to match the following regular expression at the beginning of a word.
- \> to match the preceding regular expression at the end of a word.
- ? to match zero or one instance of the preceding regular expression.
- + to match one or more instance of the preceding regular expression.

Examples

Let us assume that we have a file called `file1` whose contents are shown below:

```
more file1
This is a test
THIS IS A TEST
This is really a test
Believe it, this is really a test
This is a test, better believe it
```

In its simple form, you can specify a string of characters as a regular expression. If you want to find the string `really` in `file1` use the following command:

```
grep really file1
This is really a test
Believe it, this is really a test
```

If you want to find the string THIS at the beginning of a line, use ^(caret) at the beginning of a regular expression in the following command:

```
grep ^THIS file1
THIS IS A TEST
```

If you want to find the string it at the end of a line, use $ (dollar sign) at the end of a regular expression in the following command:

```
grep it$ file1
This is a test, better believe it
```

If you want to find both believe and Believe, use the following command:

```
grep [Bb]elieve file1
Believe it, this is really a test
This is a test, better believe it
```

In the above example, [Bb] matches the single characters B or b. If you want to find characters other than the specified one, use the following command:

```
grep [T][^h] file1
THIS IS A TEST
```

In the above example, the [^h] matches anything other than h, hence the [T][^h] matches anything that starts with T and followed by any character other than h. If you want to match any six-character string preceded and followed by a space, use the following command:

```
grep " ...... " file1
This is really a test
Believe it, this is really a test
This is a test, better believe it
```

In the above example, the " ......" will match a string such as really or better preceded and followed by a space. If you want to modify all strings that start with a t and have a t at the end and have any two characters in the middle, use the following command:

```
sed "s/\(t\)..\1/----/g" file1
This is a ----
THIS IS A TEST
This is really a ----
Believe i----his is really a ----
This is a ----, better believe it
```

In the above example, \(t\) saves the character t and \1 uses the t at the specified position. If you want to find one or more instances of a regular expression, use the following command:

```
egrep it+ file1
Believe it, this is really a test
This is a test, better believe it
```

In the above example, it+ tells egrep to find one or more instances of the string it. If you want to find whether a regular expression is repeated a specified number of times, use the following command:

```
egrep tt\{1,4\} file1
This is a test, better believe it
```

In the above example, at least one, and a maximum of four, repetitions of the expression it are matched. If you want to modify all characters other than letters, use the following command:

```
sed "s/[^a-zA-Z ]/:/g" file1
This is a test
THIS IS A TEST
```

```
This is really a test
Believe it: this is really a test
This is a test: better believe it
```

In the above example, all characters other than a through z, A through Z and spaces will be replaced by a : (colon).

Executing Commands

There are several ways to execute the commands you have learned so far. In this section, we will learn about some of the ways in which a command can be executed in isolation and in conjunction with other commands.

UNIX, by default, accepts input from standard input, which is the keyboard, and displays output on standard output, which is the terminal. You can, however, use the UNIX redirection facility to redirect the input from a file or output to a file.

You can execute a command in the foreground or in the background. When you invoke a command, by default it executes in the foreground. You can force a command in the background by using the & (ampersand) sign. You can start a command in the foreground, then force it into the background. To achieve this, you use Ctrl-z to suspend it and then use the bg command to put it in the background.

Because all UNIX commands accept input from standard input and generate output to standard output, there is a convenient way of passing output of one command to the next using the ¦ (pipe) character. You can have a string of commands, each connected to the next using a pipe.

Summary

In this chapter you have learned about various UNIX commands. Most of these commands should work on different UNIX systems as described, but you may find that some of the commands or flags behave differently. Following is a list of some of the activities you can do using various UNIX commands:

- Log in to related activities using commands such as login, rlogin, and passwd.
- Create, rename, delete, and copy files and directories using commands such as cp, rm, rmdir, and mkdir.
- Search for text in files using commands such as grep.
- Grant access to files and directories for users using commands such as chmod and chgrp.
- Modify contents of files using commands such as vi and sed.
- Display contents of files using commands such as more, tail, head, and pg.

Getting Around the Network

by Rachel and Robert Sartin

IN THIS CHAPTER

The "information superhighway" has received a lot of attention recently. Much of this "network of the future" is with us today. This chapter introduces you to the basic UNIX software that is used today to connect hundreds of thousands of machines together in the Internet and Usenet.

Connecting machines in a network gives you even more computing and information resources than you can get from simply having a computer at your desk or in your computing center. With a network of machines connected together, you will be able to share data files with co-workers, send electronic mail, play multiuser games with people from all over the world, read Usenet news articles, contribute to worldwide discussions, perform searches for software or information you need, and much more. In this chapter you will learn about the two most common ways to connect UNIX machines together in a network: UUCP and TCP/IP. On this simple base exists a worldwide network of machines and services that has the potential to greatly increase your productivity. By learning to use these services effectively, you will open the door to new possibilities using your computer. This chapter only begins to probe the extent of available software and resources. Please refer to the Sams Publishing book *Internet Unleashed* for even more information on this topic.

What Is a Network?

A *network* is a system of two or more computers connected to one another. In this chapter you will learn about some of the common ways to network UNIX machines together. At the simplest end of the scale, a network can be two UNIX machines connected to each other using a serial line (typically through a modem) and running *UUCP*, the UNIX-to-UNIX Copy Program. More complicated network configurations run *TCP/IP*, the Transfer Control Protocol/Internet Protocol, the common name for the protocol family used on the Internet, a collection of networks that allows you to connect your computer to hundreds of thousands of other computers.

UUCP—The Basic Networking Utilities

Early in the history of UNIX, it became apparent that it would be advantageous to connect UNIX machines so that they could share some resources. One of the attempts to connect machines together resulted in the UUCP protocol, which allows you to connect two UNIX machines to each other using a serial line (often with a modem attached). The primary focus of UUCP is to allow files to be copied between two UNIX machines, but there are services built on top of UUCP that allow execution of certain commands, such as news and mail commands, thus enabling more sophisticated processing. You can use UUCP to send electronic mail between two UNIX machines and to transmit and receive Usenet news articles. The most common release of UUCP available now is often called either *BNU*, the Basic Networking Utilities—the System V version of UUCP, or HoneyDanBer (HDB). There are other freely available and commercial implementations of UUCP. Although UUCP originated on UNIX and was designed specifically for copying between UNIX machines, there are now versions of UUCP that run on MS-DOS and other platforms.

TCP/IP—LAN, WAN, and the Internet

In the 1970s, the United States Department of Defense began a research program called DARPA, the Defense Advanced Research Projects Administration. One of the efforts of DARPA was to create an *Internet*, an interconnected set of networks, that would allow research labs across the country to interact. This network was called the ARPAnet and the protocol that ran the interconnections was and is called *IP*, or Internet Protocol. Since the original ARPAnet, internetworking has grown incredibly and there is now a huge and difficult-to-define thing called the Internet that allows interconnections between computers all over the world. The Internet includes hundreds of thousands of machines (because of the amorphous nature of the Internet, it is difficult even to get an accurate count) connected through a series of public and private networks.

The Internet Protocol allows the sending of packets between any two computers that are connected to the Internet. IP supplies only a primitive service and further levels of protocol exist that use IP to perform useful functions. Two very common protocols are *TCP/IP* and *UDP/IP*. TCP/IP connects two programs in much the same way a serial line connects two computers. UDP/IP, the User Datagram Protocol/IP, supplies a simple way of sending short messages between two programs. Most interesting user programs that use IP networking use TCP to create a connection, so *TCP/IP* is often used to refer to the interconnection protocol on the Internet.

Names and Addresses

To use machines and resources on the network, you need to locate them. Hostnames use a hierarchical naming space that allows each hostname to be unique, without forcing it to be obscure or unpronounceable. For example, `ftp.uu.net` is the name of one host on the Internet. IP itself uses *Internet addresses*, unique identifiers of Internet hosts, which are usually written in *dot notation*, four numbers (each between 0 and 255), separated by periods. For example, `192.48.96.9` is the address (as of this writing) of the host `ftp.uu.net`, which is covered in the section "Transferring Files—`rcp`, `ftp`, `uucp`."

What's in a Name?

Hostnames on the Internet are a series of "words" separated by periods, or *dots*. The dots separate different parts of the name. The naming system used is called the *domain naming system* (DNS) because it separates responsibility for unique names into administrative domains. The administrator of each domain is responsible for managing and assigning unique names within that domain. The management of the *top-level* or *root* domain, the extreme right word in a hostname, is responsible for the naming conventions. The best way to understand hostnames is to start out by reading them right to left, one word at a time. See Figure 6.1 for a sketch of the hierarchical name space used in these examples.

FIGURE 6.1.

A tree of hostnames.

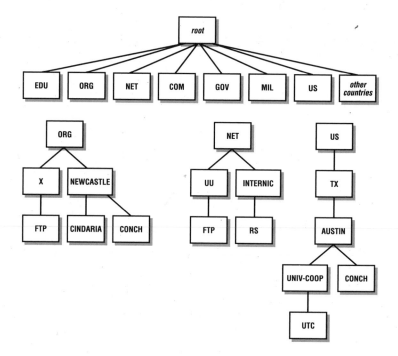

Look at the hostname `ftp.uu.net`. Reading right to left, the first word is `net`, which means that the hostname is a network service provider; see Table 6.1 for explanations of this and other top-level names. The next word is `uu`. Within `.net`, `uu` belongs to UUNET Communications, a company that supplies networking services. Elsewhere in the domain naming space, the name `uu` may mean something else.

Table 6.1. Top-level domains.

Domain	Meaning
EDU	Educational. Colleges and Universities.
ORG	Organizations. Nonprofit and not-for-profit.
NET	Networks. Networking services providers (some under COM).
COM	Commercial. Businesses.
GOV	Government. United States government offices.
MIL	Military. The U.S. Armed Forces.

Domain	Meaning
cc	Countries. *cc* is an ISO country code.
US	An example of a country code. The United States.

> **NOTE**
>
> Due in part to the history of the ARPAnet, most hosts in the United States (and some international organizations and businesses) are under EDU, ORG, NET, COM, GOV, or MIL. Many hosts in other countries are under a top-level domain that is the two-character ISO country code for the country. To further confuse things, the United States has a U.S. zone that includes local organizations, primary and secondary schools, and local governments.

Look at the hostnames conch.newcastle.org and conch.austin.tx.us. The org means that the name belongs to an organization. The newcastle means that Newcastle Associates is the owner. Finally, conch is a particular host in Newcastle's network. In the second name, us means the United States, tx means Texas, austin means the city Austin, and conch is a particular hostname. Note that the two machines are completely different machines with different owners. They happen to share one component of their name, but that is not a problem because of the hierarchical namespace presented by DNS.

In fact, there are many repetitions of names. There are many machines on the Internet that have ftp as the first part of their domain names, and many that have www as the first part of their names. The advantage of using the DNS is that these repetitions are not in conflict. It has been said about names that "all the good ones are taken," but the DNS allows you to reuse some of the good ones in a different context. Try using Figure 6.1 to figure out these hostnames:

```
ftp.x.org
ftp.uu.net
ftp.newcastle.org
rs.internic.net
utc.univ-coop.austin.tx.us
```

Notice that utc.univ-coop.austin.tx.us has a different number of components than some of the other names you looked at. The DNS can grow by creating a deeper tree. The owner of a domain may add new domains to make it easier to add more hosts.

> **NOTE**
>
> In addition to having an official name, some hosts have *aliases* as well. The alias is simply another name for the host. For example, ftp.x.org is actually an alias for the current machine being used for ftp by x.org.

Using Shorter Names

Usually, the DNS is configured to use a *search path* for hostnames that don't end in a dot. This lets you use shorter names for hosts in your search path. Typically, your DNS will be configured to search your domain and then search progressively up to the root domain. Check your system documentation to see if you can change the DNS search path. If you were on `cnidaria.newcastle.org` and used the name `newcstle.net`, it would try the following names, matching the first one that exists:

- `newcstle.net.newcastle.org`
- `newcstle.net.org`
- `newcstle.net`

> **TIP**
>
> Because of the search algorithm, you may see faster network access if you use full names ending in a dot for machines outside your local domain.

Decoding Addresses and Ports

Although DNS names are a reasonably convenient way for humans to refer to hosts, the Internet Protocol needs to use a 32-bit Internet address to find a host on the network. For example, as of this writing the host `ftp.uu.net` has the Internet Address `192.48.96.9`. Internet address are usually written using *dot names*, with four numbers between 0 and 255, separated by dots. Note that each of the four numbers is 8 bits, so you end up with a 32-bit Internet address.

It is not enough just to connect to the correct machine. You also need to connect to the correct program. TCP/IP and UDP/IP use *ports* to specify where a connection will go. In order to make a connection to a remote computer, there has to be some program listening on the correct port. If you think of IP addresses as being like phone numbers, a *port number* is like an extension. Once your IP message reaches the correct machine, the port number enables it to be delivered to the correct program.

When a new protocol is adopted as a standard, it is assigned a port number that will always be used for that protocol. For example, the login protocol used to implement `rlogin` is assigned port 513, and `telnet` is assigned port 23. You can examine the assignments of ports to protocols by looking at the file `/etc/services` on your machine. If you are running NIS (the Network Information System, formerly called the Yellow Pages), you can run the command `ypcat services` to look at the map.

Look at what happens when you run the command `rlogin remotehost`. If `remotehost` is willing to accept `rlogin` requests, there is a program waiting for connections on port 513 on `remotehost`; this program (called `inetd`) will handle all of the work on `remotehost` that needs to be performed to allow you to use `rlogin` (`inetd` does this by handing the incoming connection to a program called `rlogind`, which implements the protocol). The `rlogin` program on your host attempts to open a connection to port 513 on the *remotehost*. The program monitoring port 513 on *remotehost* will accept the connection and let your `rlogin` program perform the setup necessary to perform a login.

Converting Names to Addresses

You have seen what hostnames look like and what the low-level Internet address and port numbers are, but you still need to learn how names get converted to addresses.

Hostname conversion is usually handled by the domain naming system, which, in addition to specifying what hostnames look like, specifies a protocol for translating hostnames to addresses. First look at a hostname conversion of the name `ftp.x.org`. When your local host tries to convert the name `ftp.x.org` to an IP address, it contacts a *nameserver*, a machine that has DNS mappings loaded and is prepared to answer questions about them. Your nameserver is also configured with information about how to contact other nameservers so it can look up names that it doesn't already know.

A Brief Introduction to NIS

When implementing a network, one of the common problems that arises is management of `passwd` and group files. Some organizations wish to have a common user and group list for all or most hosts in a network. The Network Information Service, introduced by Sun, is one way to solve this problem. NIS allows sharing of `passwd`, group, and other information between hosts that share administrative control. Other (commercial and freely available) solutions to this problem exist, but none have yet become as widespread as NIS.

If you are running NIS, you should use the command `ypcat passwd` to examine the `passwd` information on your system. The actual `/etc/passwd` file will not list all of the users who can log in to a machine running NIS. If you are using NIS to manage `passwd` files, your password will be the same on any machine in your network that runs NIS. NIS may also be used to create an environment where you can share files transparently between systems. This is done using the network file system, NFS, which enables you to mount a file system from a mount computer and access it as if it were local. Some computing environments configure NIS so that your HOME is always the same directory, no matter what machine you use. This means that your files will be accessible no matter what machine in the network you are using. Check with your system administrators to find out whether NIS is running and whether it is being used to handle automounting of home (and other) directories.

I'm on the Wire—`rlogin`, `telnet`, `cu`

With the three services `rlogin`, `telnet`, and `cu`, you can connect to a remote computer over the network. `rlogin` uses the login service to connect using the TCP/IP protocol over the network, `telnet` uses the Telnet service to connect using the TCP/IP protocol over the network, and `cu` connects over a phone line.

Before Using `rlogin`, `rsh`, and `rcp`

Before you use `rlogin`, some user configuration may be needed. The same configuration is used for `rsh` and `rcp`. You should refer to these details when reading the next section as well. For reference, *loc-host* is used as the local machine name and *rem-host* is the name of the remote machine.

Two files on the remote machine affect your remote access ability: `/etc/hosts.equiv` and `.rhosts` in the remote user's home directory. The `hosts.equiv` file contains a list of hostnames. Each machine in this list is considered to be a trusted host. Any user who has an account on both *loc-host* and *rem-host* is allowed to access the remote machine from the local machine without question. The "without question" is important and means that the user does not have to supply a password for access.

> **TIP**
>
> System administrators should seriously consider disabling the `rlogin` and rexec protocols on machines that are directly connected to the Internet since the authentication used on these protocols is very weak. At the very least, be extremely careful about entries in `/etc/hosts.equiv` and any `.rhosts` files.

The `.rhosts` file in the remote user's home directory contains a list of trusted host and user pairs. This is similar to the trusted hosts of the `hosts.equiv` file, but gives a finer grain of control. Each entry grants trusted access to one particular user on a particular host rather than to all common users on a particular host. Lines in `.rhosts` that name only a machine will grant access to a user with the same login name. The user on *loc-host* can access *rem-host* without question (that is, without specifying a password). The user authentication is done by the protocol.

Usually only the system administrator can change the values in the `/etc/hosts.equiv` file. Since this file allows many users access, this is a system configuration file. But each user can set up his or her own `.rhosts` file. This file must live in the user's home directory and be owned by the user (or by `root`). The ownership restrictions are security measures preventing a user from gaining access to another user's account.

Listing 6.1 and Listing 6.2 show examples of the `hosts.equiv` and `.rhosts` files. These two files are located on the machine called `flounder`, and the `.rhosts` file is owned by user `rob` and is located in his home directory. The two hosts listed in the `/etc/hosts.equiv` file, `manatee` and `dolphin`, are trusted hosts to `flounder`. Any user with an account on `manatee` and `flounder` may remotely access `flounder` from `manatee` without specifying a password. Likewise, any user with an account on `dolphin` and `flounder` may remotely access `flounder` from `dolphin` without specifying a password.

Listing 6.1. `/etc/hosts.equiv` **and** `$HOME/.rhosts` **files.**

```
manatee
dolphin
```

Listing 6.2. `/users/rob/.rhosts` **on machine** `flounder`.

```
french-angel
rob yellowtail
rob dolphin
rob dolphin
root dolphin
diane stingray
rob stingray
root flying-gurnard
root
```

The `.rhosts` file of the user `rob` contains a list of users on a remote machine who may access `flounder` as user `rob` without specifying a password. That sentence packed several important points together that need expanding:

- ■ **The `.rhosts` file of user `rob`.**   This implies that the machine `flounder` has a user account, with `rob` as the username. The home directory of user `rob` (the example implies it is `/users/rob`) has a file named `.rhosts` that is owned by `rob`.

- ■ **Users on a remote machine who may access `flounder`.**   Each entry in the list is a pair of names—the machine name and the associated username. This pair of names describes one particular user who may access `flounder`. That user must be accessing `flounder` from the specified machine. It is not enough for the user to simply have an account on the machine; the remote access must be initiated from that machine (by that user).

- ■ **As user `rob`.**   This is probably the most subtle of all the points, so be careful here. Any of the users who are in the list may access `rob`'s account on `flounder`, as `rob`. He "becomes" `rob` on `flounder` even if he was a different user on the initiating machine. This is effectively the same as giving `rob`'s password on machine `flounder` to this user. Because of this, be extremely selective about entries in your `.rhosts` files!

- ■ **Without specifying a password.**   Some services (`rlogin`) allow for the possibility of a password prompt. If the user authentication was not successful via the equivalence files, the service is able to fall back on the prompt method of authentication. So the ability to access a remote host without specifying a password may not be needed. Other services (`rsh` and `rcp`) do not have a way to prompt for a password. In order to use these services, the access must be configured so that specifying a password is unnecessary.

Using Listing 6.2, for each of the following scenarios, decide if the user would be able to access flounder—as rob—without a password. Assume that each user has an account on the local machine in the question, as well as on flounder.

1. User root on machine stingray?
2. User root on machine manatee?
3. User root on machine french-angel?
4. User frank on machine dolphin?
5. User frank on machine stingray?
6. User frank on machine tarpon?
7. User diane on machine manatee?
8. User diane on machine dolphin?
9. User diane on machine flying-gurnard?
10. User rob on machine yellowtail?
11. User rob on machine dolphin?
12. User rob on machine manatee?
13. User rob on machine flying-gurnard?

Here are the answers:

1. Yes; rob's .rhosts file has an entry stingray root.
2. No; rob's .rhosts file does not have an entry manatee root. However, root from manatee could access flounder—as root—without a password, because manatee is listed in /etc/hosts.equiv.
3. No; rob's .rhosts file does not have an entry french-angel root.
4. No; rob's .rhosts file does not have an entry dolphin frank. However, frank from dolphin could access flounder—as frank—without a password, because dolphin is listed in /etc/hosts.equiv.
5. No; rob's .rhosts file does not have an entry stingray frank.
6. No; rob's .rhosts file does not have an entry tarpon frank.
7. No; rob's .rhosts file does not have an entry manatee diane. However, diane from manatee could access flounder—as diane—without a password, because manatee is listed in /etc/hosts.equiv.
8. Yes; rob's .rhosts file has an entry stingray diane.
9. No; rob's .rhosts file does not have an entry flying-gurnard diane.
10. Yes; rob's .rhosts file has an entry yellowtail rob.
11. Yes; the /etc/hosts.equiv file has an entry dolphin. Note that if the system administrator removed this entry, this answer would still be yes because of the dolphin rob entry in his .rhosts file.

12. Yes; the /etc/hosts.equiv file has an entry manatee rob.

13. No; the /etc/hosts.equiv file does not have an entry flying-gurnard nor does rob's .rhosts file have an entry flying-gurnard rob.

Using rlogin

If you need or wish to be logged in to a computer that is away from your current location, rlogin can help you. The rlogin application establishes a remote login session from your machine to another machine that is connected via the network. This machine could be next door, next to you on your desk, or even on a different continent. When you successfully execute an rlogin from your screen, whether it is a terminal, or one window of your graphical display, the shell that prompts you and the commands you enter are executing on the remote machine just as if you sat down in front of the machine and entered login.

Establishing an rlogin Connection

The rlogin command takes a mandatory argument that specifies the remote host. Both the local and remote host must have rlogin available for a connection to be established. If this is the case, the local rlogin will connect to the specified remote machine and start a login session.

During a nonremote login, the login process prompts you for two things: your user name and your password. Your user name identifies you to the computer and your password authenticates that the requester is really you. During an rlogin, the rlogin protocol takes care of some (or even all) of this identification/authorization procedure for you. The rlogin protocol initiates the login session on the remote host for a particular user. By default, this user is the same as the local user (that is, you). In this case, you never have to type in your user name. However, if you wish to log in to the remote host as a different user, you may override the default user name by using the -1 option to specify a user name.

The rlogin protocol may even take care of the authentication for you. If you (or your system administrator) have made the proper entry in the /etc/hosts.equiv or your $HOME/.rhosts file, no authentication is necessary (that is, you will not be prompted for your password). If these files do not have entries for your host and username, a password prompt will be printed just like in a local login attempt.

Let's look at a few examples. Assume that your user name is rachel and the local machine to which you're logged in is called moray-eel. To log in as yourself on machine flounder you would enter this:

```
$rlogin flounder
```

The connection to flounder would take place, and a login session would be initiated for user rachel (and fail if user rachel doesn't exist on flounder). Next, the rlogin protocol checks the special files to see if authentication is necessary. If moray-eel is listed in the file /etc/hosts.equiv or in ~rachel/.rhosts, no authentication is needed.

To log in to flounder as user arnie you would enter rlogin -1 arnie flounder.

Here the login session is initiated with the username `arnie`. If user `arnie` exists on `flounder`, the special files are checked for authentication. Since the username for the remote login is different than the local username, the `/etc/hosts.equiv` file does not provide authentication. If the file `~arnie/.rhosts` has an entry `moray-eel rachel`, no authentication is necessary (that is, login succeeds without password). If this entry does not exist, the password prompt will appear and you must enter the password associated with user `arnie`. This is not a prompt for your password.

Failed Connect

Several things may go wrong when you try to connect to a remote machine via `rlogin`. Some of these are problems that are out of your control. In these instances, you should contact a system administrator to help you solve the problem.

In cases where authentication is necessary, you might enter the password incorrectly. If this happens, the result is the same as in a local login attempt. The login process lets you try again by prompting first for your username and then your password. Note that this is the only situation in which you must supply your username if you're trying to `rlogin` as yourself.

For most other problems you will need your system administrator's help. See the section "Troubleshooting" for ways to identify the cause of the problem. Any details about the problem symptoms will help the person who is responsible for fixing the problem. Some of the problems you might see are the following:

- The user account does not exist on the remote.
- Your local host is not connected to the remote via the network.
- The remote host is down.
- The remote host does not support `rlogin`.
- The network between the local and remote hosts is having problems.

Using the Remote Login Session

After a successful remote login, the `rlogin` protocol initiates your session using some information from your local session. This saves you the trouble of having to initialize your environment totally from scratch. Your terminal type (the value of the TERM environment variable) is propagated. Other information, such as baud rate and your screen (window) size, may also be propagated, depending on what the local and remote hosts support.

Then the login process proceeds as if you were actually directly connected to this machine. All of the information and files are taken from the remote. The remote password file contains the user account information, including the login shell to be executed and the starting (HOME) directory. All shell start-up files (found on the remote) execute, which further initializes your environment. When the start-up completes, the shell prompt you see is the shell that is running on the remote host.

NOTE

In some LAN environments, the network is configured such that your HOME directory is on a remote file server that is mounted on each machine you access. In this case, you actually have just one physical HOME directory, and thus just one set of dot files (for example, .login). This results in the same login environment for you on each machine. However, this makes writing your dot files a little more complicated because you need to take into account all the different machines to accommodate.

TIP

Because the remote prompt and local prompt may look alike, you may wish to include *hostname* in your prompt variable (PS1). If you're ever in doubt about what host the shell prompt is coming from, use the *hostname* command.

When you see the remote prompt, you can enter any commands you would in a local environment. The `rlogin` protocol transfers input and output between the local and remote hosts. This transfer is transparent to you. Sometimes you may notice slow performance, depending on the network speed and load.

During your remote session, you may want to access your local machine. You could just exit your remote session, at which point you would be back at your local prompt. But if you aren't finished using the remote, using `exit` followed by another `rlogin`, possibly multiple times, is tedious. There is a better way—using the escape character.

Using the Escape Character

The `rlogin` protocol provides an escape character that, when typed as the first character on the command line, is treated specially. The default escape character is the tilde (~) character, but you may change this on the `rlogin` command line via the `-e` option. If the character immediately following the escape character is one that the local `rlogin` process recognizes, it performs the function associated with this character. Otherwise the escape character (and the remaining characters) are executed on the remote.

The ~. character sequence is the command to disconnect from remote. This is not a graceful disconnect, as in an `exit`. It immediately disconnects from the remote. This should only be used when, for some reason, you are unable to execute the `exit` command.

If the local `rlogin` was executed by a job-control shell (C shell or Korn shell), then you can suspend the `rlogin` by the escape sequence ~*susp*, where *susp* is your suspend control character, usually Ctrl+Z. This is very convenient. It saves the multiple `exit` followed by another `rlogin` sequence you would otherwise need for accessing the local machine. In a graphical user interface environment, having two windows—one for the `rlogin` and one locally—solves this problem as well.

It is possible to `rlogin` to one machine, then `rlogin` from there to another machine. You can use multiple escape characters to denote any one of the machines in this chain. As an example, say you are locally logged in to Host A. You are using a job-control shell with suspend set to Ctrl+Z. From Host A, you `rlogin` to Host B. From there you log in to Host C. And from there you `rlogin` to Host D. At this point, everything you enter is going all the way to D to execute. In order to reach any host in the chain, just associate one escape character with each host. You must start with your local host, and then go in the same order as the `rlogin`s. In this example, a single ~ refers to Host A, ~~ refers to Host B, ~~~ refers to Host C.

To suspend the `rlogin` from Host B to Host C you would type ~~^z. This will leave you in your original shell on Host B. In order to return to `rlogin` you would use the `fg` command as with any suspended process.

To disconnect the `rlogin` from Host C to Host D you would type ~~~..

One very common escape sequence, which is not supported on all platforms, is the shell escape, ~!. Typing this sequence causes the `rlogin` to give you a subshell on the machine that is referred to by ~. You can use multiple escape characters to denote any host within a chain of `rlogin`s. To return to the `rlogin`, simply `exit` the subshell.

NOTE

There is a difference between ~*susp* and ~!. The suspend command will put `rlogin` in the background and let you interact with your original shell (the one from which you ran `rlogin`). The shell escape will start a new shell as a child of `rlogin`. (See Figure 6.2.)

FIGURE 6.2.
Processes for suspend and shell escape.

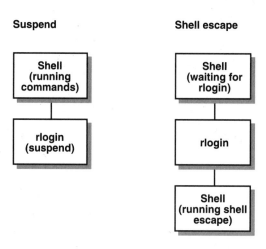

Using Telnet

The Telnet service is used to communicate with a remote host via the Telnet protocol. Invoking Telnet with the remote host as an argument causes Telnet to connect to that host. The remote Telnet server usually initiates a login just as you would get on a terminal connected to the machine. After your login name and password are entered and verified, you will see the shell prompt on the remote machine. All commands and input you enter go to the remote; all output you receive comes from the remote.

If you wish to enter Telnet command mode while you are connected to a remote, type the escape character. The default escape character is Ctrl+], but this can be changed via the `set` command. To return to the remote connection, simply execute a command. A `set` command will do this. If you have nothing you want to send or set, do a `send nop`. The `nop` argument stands for *no operation.*

If you enter `telnet` without any arguments, you will start up the Telnet service in command mode. You will see a special Telnet prompt (`telnet>`). You can enter any of the Telnet commands. Following is a list of some of the most common commands you might use. Refer to your system's manual for `telnet`, for a complete list.

`open`	Connects to specified host.
`close`	Disconnects from host and returns to command mode.
`quit`	Closes the connection (if one exists) and exits Telnet.
`set`	Changes the value for a given argument.
`send`	Sends a command to the remote and returns to remote connection.
`display`	Shows current setting of Telnet configuration.
`status`	Shows current status of Telnet connection.
`?`	Gives help.

The following sections look at some of these in a bit more detail.

open

The `open` command takes two parameters, host and port. The host, which is mandatory, can be a hostname or an IP address. This specifies the remote host to which a connection is to be established. This remote host must be reachable via the network and must support the Telnet service. The port, which is optional, specifies the port number to use in connecting to the remote host. By default, the port to which Telnet connects is the well-known Telnet port (23). When a connection on the remote comes in on the telnet port, the remote's telnet service handles the connection. The remote Telnet service assumes that the local connector wants to log in and invokes the login process on this connection. You can use this feature to do certain kinds of debugging and troubleshooting. For example, to connect to the mail server on a machine, you could enter `telnet` *hostname* `smtp` (or replace `smtp` with `25` if the first doesn't work). This will connect you directly to the Simple Mail Transfer Protocol on *hostname*, and you can use this connection to troubleshoot mail problems. Sometimes network services are offered by Telnet to a specific port number. For example, many gopher and WWW providers offer a special port for Telnet access to the service.

In this default mode, a Telnet open is somewhat like an rlogin. A remote login is initiated on the remote host. But the Telnet protocol, unlike rlogin, does not perform any conveniences for you. It does not propagate any of your local environment. It does not perform any part of the login procedure (user identification and authentication).

If the first thing you will use Telnet for is an open command, you do not need to enter Telnet command mode at all. On the Telnet command line, you can enter a host followed optionally by a port number. This causes Telnet to immediately do an open with the command-line arguments.

close

The close command terminates the open connection (if one exists). On some versions of Telnet, this does not exit Telnet command mode. So if you are connected to Host B but decide you really want to be connected to Host C, enter close and then enter an open B command.

quit

The quit command should be used when you are finished using Telnet. This will perform a close on the open connection (if one exists). Then it terminates the Telnet service, returning you to your local shell prompt.

set

Telnet has several internal variables used for configuration. You can use the set command to change these values. To see the current variable values, use the display command. The Telnet escape character can be changed via set.

> **TIP**
>
> You can set certain special characters (such as erase) with Telnet, but these settings may only work if you run Telnet in line mode. Line mode is often used for connecting to remote machines that have line-oriented user interfaces and allows you to compose an entire line of text input before sending it to the remote (when you press return). You should probably not use line mode when connecting to a UNIX machine since interactive commands (such as vi), job control, and some shell history (ksh interactive command editing) rely on receiving characters as they are typed.

?

The question mark (?) is a Telnet command that, without arguments, gives a list of all the Telnet commands. This is useful if you've forgotten the name of a command. To get help about a specific command, use ? with the command as an argument. The ? can also be used as an argument to the `set`, `send`, and `toggle` commands to list the valid arguments of the command.

Before Using cu

Before you can use `cu`, your system administrator will need to configure the appropriate devices and machines for UUCP access. Check your system's UUCP documentation for information on how to do this.

Using cu

The `cu` service calls up another system. This service is used only to connect two computers via phone lines. Your local host must have an outgoing modem and the remote host must have a modem that supports incoming calls.

Your system administrator may have configured the parameters necessary to call up certain systems. This configuration is kept in the file `/etc/uucp/Systems`.

> **NOTE**
>
> The actual file depends on which version of UUCP you have. This is correct for SVR4. Since the location may vary, consider this the "`systems`" file.

You can enter `cu` *system-name* to dial the remote host. If the remote host has not been configured in the `/etc/uucp/Systems` file, you can specify the necessary parameters on the command line. The `cu` *phone-number* command will call up the specified phone number. For example, `cu 9=14085551212` will call using the ad device and give it the phone number 914085551212. The equals sign specifies that a pause is desired before the next digit is dialed.

You can also call up using a local device by specifying it with the `-1` option. You can use the `-1` option to specify the device to use for making the connection. This is generally used only for hardwired connections: `cu -1` *dev* `dir` will connect directly to the line named `dev`.

Transferring Files—rcp, ftp, uucp

Files are the basis for everything you do in UNIX. When you execute a command (aside from Shell built-ins), the associated file contains the executing instructions. When you store or retrieve information, the data is kept in one or more files. The UNIX interface to hardware devices is through device files. Files are pervasive. Therefore, having the necessary files within your reach is extremely important.

Sometimes files you need are not stored on your local machine. Client-server environments are designed to provide a means of sharing files among many machines. When machines on a LAN are configured to share files (via the network), many more files become reachable to you. If you are using NFS, some directories on your system will be mounted from remote machines. These directories and files will be available as part of the normal UNIX file system, and you need no special techniques to access them.

Not all UNIX environments are configured this way. Even those that are may not share all file systems of all machines. Many files exist outside of a local LAN environment. In these cases, you may want to obtain a copy of a file from somewhere other than your local environment. You could use the tools in "I'm on the Wire—`rbgin`, `telnet`, `cu`" to remotely log in and access them. But if you need to execute the file locally, or wish to have your own copy of the file, you need to copy the remote file to your local system.

The next section presents several tools to do remote copies. Your local configuration, the remote configuration, the way the remote and local configurations are connected, as well as your personal preference will determine which tool you choose.

Using `rcp`

Before you read this subsection, you should review the section "Before Using `rlogin`, `rsh`, and `rcp`." For `rcp` to work, you must configure the remote machine(s) so that user authentication is not necessary. For each remote you access via `rcp`, an entry in one or both of `/etc/hosts.equiv` and `$HOME/.rhosts` is mandatory. This is because `rcp` does not have a mechanism for in-process authentication (unlike `rlogin`).

Once the configuration is complete, you can use `rcp` in much the same way you use the `cp` command. Each command basically says to "copy File A to Location B." The `rcp` command adds some syntax that enables you to specify remote machines and users.

Specifying a Remote File

You can specify a remote file in several different ways. In general, unless a hostname is specified, the file is considered local. If the character string has a colon (:) before any slashes (/), the string before the colon specifies the remote host and the string after the colon specifies the file path. Here are three forms of the complete remote file specification:

```
hostname:filepath
user@hostname:filepath
user@hostname.domain:filepath
```

The file path in each can be an absolute path, a relative path, or blank. If it is relative, is it relative to the remote user's HOME directory. The remote user is considered the same as the local user unless explicitly included in the remote specification. In the second and third forms above, the remote user is explicitly included.

If the file path is absolute, this is an absolute path on the remote system. If the file path is blank, the user's HOME directory is assumed.

6

The hostname can be a simple name or an alias of the remote machine, or it can be a host domain name as in the third form above.

If you wish to use a different user account on the remote machine, you can specify the remote file, including the username. The username must refer to an account on the remote machine, and the user's $HOME/.rhosts file must contain the proper entry for your local machine.

Understanding the `rcp` Command Line Syntax

The `rcp` command line is flexible; to support this flexibility, there are a few variations of the command line:

- **`rcp single-file dest`.**   In this variation, the first argument, `single-file`, is a single file. This file is copied to the destination `dest`. If `dest` is an existing directory, the file `dest/single-file` is created. If `dest` is an existing file, `dest` is overwritten with `single-file`. Otherwise the file `dest` is created by copying `single-file`.

- **`rcp sources dest`.**   In this variation, the first argument, `sources`, is one or more files and/or directories. `dest` must be a directory. Only the members of `sources` that are files are copied to the destination `dest`. If `dest` is an existing directory, the files are copied under directory `dest`. It is unwise to specify a `dest` directory that does not exist with this form of the `rcp` command. The results vary from system to system. See the next form for copying a single directory.

- **`rcp -r sources dest`.**   By adding the option `-r`, the files in `source` as well as the directories (and all their subdirectories) are copied to `dest`.

  If `sources` is a single directory, it is okay to specify a destination `dest` that doesn't exist. The directory will be created for you. This is probably what you want. Beware of this situation, because if `dest` *does* exist, the copied directory will be placed as a subdirectory of `dest`.

  If `sources` is multiple directories and/or files, `dest` must be an existing directory. If it doesn't exist, the results are not specified and differ from one UNIX system to another.

  Each version of the `rcp` command line supports an additional option, `-p`. This option causes `rcp` to preserve the modification times as well as the modes when the copy is made.

Using ftp

The ftp service is the interface to the file transfer protocol. This service provides a connection service to a remote computer along with file manipulation functions including sending and receiving files. It also provides user authentication, unlike `rcp`. It supports different file types.

To connect with a remote host, you can simply type `ftp` *hostname*. The *hostname* can either be a hostname or an Internet address. If you do not specify a remote host on the command line, you enter ftp command mode. Then you can use the `open` command to initiate a connection.

By default, when a connection is initiated via `ftp`, the remote ftp server starts up the login process. You must enter a valid username and password in order to access the remote system. Once you have been authenticated, you are connected to the remote ftp server and it awaits your commands.

The ftp service has a large number of commands. Several common commands are covered in Table 6.2. For complete details, refer to your system's manual for `ftp`.

Table 6.2. Common ftp service commands.

Connection-Related Commands	
`open`	Open a connection to specified host.
`close`	Close current open connection.
`quit`	Close current open connection and exit ftp.
File Transfer–Related Commands	
`binary`	Change the file representation type to `binary`.
`ascii`	Change the file representation type to `ascii`.
`put`	Transfer a single file from the local to the remote host.
`mput`	Transfer multiple files from the local to the remote host.
`get`	Transfer a single file from the remote to the local host.
`mget`	Transfer multiple files from the remote to the local host.
File- and Directory-Management Commands	
`cd`	Change remote's current working directory (UNIX `cd`).
`lcd`	Change the local's current working directory (UNIX `cd`).
`cdup`	Change remote's current working directory to be the parent directory (UNIX `cd ..`).
`dir`	List the remote's current working directory (UNIX `ls`).
`pwd`	Print the remote's current working directory (UNIX `pwd`).
`mkdir`	Make a new directory on the remote (UNIX `mkdir`).
`rmdir`	Delete a directory on the remote (UNIX `rmdir`).
`rename`	Change the name of a remote file or directory (UNIX `mv`).
`delete`	Delete a remote file (UNIX `rm`, with one file specified).
`mdelete`	Delete multiple remote files (UNIX `rm`, with multiple files).
Miscellaneous Commands	
`?`	Obtain help about ftp.
`!`	Escape shell.

Connection-Related Commands

The ftp connection-related commands are fairly straightforward. The open command tries to connect to the ftp server on the specified remote host. The close command terminates the open connection (if one exists) and then returns to command mode. This is usually used when you want to connect to a different host, so you will commonly follow it with an open. The quit command closes the connection and then exits ftp.

File Transfer–Related Commands

The ftp service defines several file representation types for transfer. The two most common are ascii and binary. By default, the type is set to ascii. Any file that is plain ASCII text can be transferred using ascii type. Binary files, like a compiled and linked executable file, must be transferred using binary type. Be sure to set the correct type before transferring any files.

TIP

Transferring ASCII text files between UNIX machines is slightly faster with binary type, but using binary type to transfer an ASCII text file between a UNIX and a non-UNIX machine may corrupt the file.

TIP

If you are having trouble decoding or executing a binary file you get elsewhere, check to make sure you used binary type transfer.

The get and mget commands transfer files from the remote to the local host. The put and mput commands transfer files from the local to the remote host. Both get and put transfer one file per command. On both of these commands you may specify the destination for the file copy. If the destination is not specified, the file is placed in the current working directory. Both mget and mput transfer multiple files per command. The files are placed in the current working directory.

File- and Directory-Management Commands

The file- and directory-management commands are analogous to UNIX file and directory commands. In Table 6.2, the UNIX command that is analogous to the ftp command is given in parentheses. Remember that all of these commands, except lcd, operate on the remote file system. If you need to perform more in-depth local file management, use the shell escape command (!) to escape to a local shell prompt.

Miscellaneous Commands

The ? command provides help about ftp commands. If you want help about a specific command, you can specify this command as the first argument to the ?. The shell escape command (!) is used to start a subshell on the local machine. This is very useful if you need to perform some operations on your local host while you are connected to a remote ftp server. After you are finished working on the local host, simply exit the (sub)shell and you will return to ftp.

Configuring with .netrc

The ftp command can automatically perform the login to remote ftp servers and initialize your connection. It does this by reading in the .netrc file in your home directory. You can configure the login, password, and account (some ftp servers allow or require an extra account specification at authentication time) to use for a particular machine. In the following example from the .netrc file, automatic login is included as anonymous for several popular servers:

```
machine dg-rtp.rtp.dg.com login anonymous password sartin@pencom.com
machine town.hall.org login anonymous password sartin@pencom.com
machine ftp.uu.net login anonymous password sartin@pencom.com
machine rtfm.mit.edu login anonymous password sartin@pencom.com
machine ftp.x.org login anonymous password sartin@pencom.com
machine prep.ai.mit.edu login anonymous password sartin@pencom.com
machine ftp.ncsa.uiuc.edu login anonymous password sartin@pencom.com
machine emx.cc.utexas.edu login anonymous password sartin@pencom.com
machine boombox.micro.umn.edu login anonymous password sartin@pencom.com
machine rs.internic.net login anonymous password guest
```

> **TIP**
>
> Most versions of ftp will use your .netrc for password information only if the file is readable by you only. For password security this file should be unreadable by others or, better yet, should contain no sensitive passwords.

Anonymous ftp

There is a special login for ftp that allows you to anonymously access files on part of a remote machine. Anonymous access is not entirely anonymous, since some machines will log the connection, the password used, and all files retrieved. To use anonymous ftp, you use the login anonymous (on some machines, the login ftp will work) and supply any non-empty string for the password.

> **TIP**
>
> Some machines do password validation on anonymous logins. Most require that you supply a valid e-mail address.

Once you have successfully logged in as anonymous you will be granted limited access to the anonymous ftp subtree on the remote machine. All of the commands described in this section can be used. Some sites have a directory called /incoming (or a directory named incoming somewhere in the ftp tree) where you will be able to put files. Many sites put the publicly accessible files under /pub.

Using uucp, uuto, and uupick

The file copying tools, uucp, uuto, uupick, are part of the Basic Networking Utilities software release. These may not be on your UNIX system. Even if they are, more recent networking services (for example, ftp and rcp) are preferred. If you are interested in using the uu tools, check your system documentation to see if they are supported.

Following, for the sake of completeness, is a brief summary of these tools. For details, check your system's manual entry for each command.

uucp

The UUCP service copies one or more files from one UNIX machine to another UNIX machine. Use the uuname command to see what remote machines you can reach via uucp. uucp uses an older host naming scheme in the form *hostname!filepath*. To copy a local file, *myfile*, to remote machine *rem-host* to directory /tmp, enter the command uucp *myfile rem-host!/tmp/*.

uuto and uupick

The uuto tool sends a file to a specific user on a remote UNIX host. The file is deposited in a special place on the specified remote host. In order for the remote user to receive this file, she or he must use the uupick tool. The remote host and user are specified by the syntax *rem-host!username*. To send the local file *myfile* to user arnie on machine sturgeon enter the command uuto *myfile* sturgeon!arnie

Then user arnie must use the uupick tool to receive the file.

When you are ready to receive files that were sent via uuto, simply enter the uuto command without any arguments. Each file that has been sent to you is displayed, one at a time. As each is displayed, you have the choice of skipping it, moving it, deleting it, or printing it.

Other Networking Services

This section gives a very abbreviated introduction to some other services that are currently available on the Internet. These services give you access to the wealth of information available on the Internet, including source code, current weather information, financial data, computer conferences on a wide variety of topics, and some more frivolous programs, including a computerized tarot reader.

CAUTION

These programs will only be useful to you if you are connected to the Internet and have a gateway that allows you to make outgoing connections. Check your local network configuration to be sure.

CAUTION

These programs can be addictive. Make sure you get enough sleep and social activity between your Net surfing excursions.

archie

The `archie` program offers access to a large list of files that are available via anonymous ftp. When you run an `archie` *string* search, the server will search for a name that is an exact match for *string* in its list of archives and will return the matches to you. You can modify the search behavior by specifying one of the following:

`-c`	Case-sensitive substring search.
`-r`	Regular expression search.
`-s`	Case-insensitive substring match.

For example, if you were looking for the source to xmosaic, you could enter `archie -s xmosaic`. The output lists a large number of sites that have xmosaic available via anonymous ftp. Here is part of the response from `archie -s xmosaic`:

```
Host ftp.engr.ucf.edu

    Location: /pub/linux-mirrors/tsx11/binaries/usr.bin.X11.nomirror
          FILE -rw-r--r--   497473  Dec 26 18:06  xmosaic-1.2.term.tar.z
```

For each host that had a match of the string there is a list of locations that had matches. The best way to use `archie` output is to look for a host "near" you (for example, your service provider, someone in the same city/state as your service provider, someone in the same country) and use ftp to retrieve the desired files.

gopher

The University of Minnesota has developed a program called `gopher`, that you can use to retrieve information over the Internet. They report (in the `00README` file available by anonymous ftp from `boombox.umn.edu` in `/pub/gopher/00README`):

```
The internet Gopher uses a simple client/server protocol that can be used to
publish and search for information held on a distributed network of hosts. Gopher
clients have a seamless view of the information in the gopher  world even though
```

```
the information is distributed over many  different hosts. Clients can either
navigate through a  hierarchy of directories and documents -or- ask an index server
to return a list of all documents that contain one  or more words. Since the index
server does full-text searches every word in every document is a keyword.

If you want to test a gopher client without setting up your own gopher server you
should configure the client to talk to "gopher.micro.umn.edu" at port 70. This will
allow you to explore the distributed network of gopher servers at the University of
Minnesota. You can try the Unix client by telneting to consultant.micro.umn.edu and
logging in as "gopher".
```

World Wide Web

In 1991, the European Laboratory for Particle Physics began a project that turned into the World Wide Web, also known as WWW or W3. WWW is fairly hard to pigeonhole, and the best way to become familiar with it is to explore it. WWW is a set of software, conventions, servers, and a protocol (HTTP) for organizing information in a hypertext structure. It allows linking of pictures (both still and moving), sounds, and text of various kinds into a web of knowledge. You can start at any place (a particularly good place to start is the default home page at NCSA or a copy of it, using `xmosaic`) and choose the links that interest you. Information is located using a *Uniform Resource Locator* (URL), which generally looks like this: `protocol://hostname/path`. The `protocol` tells how to access the data (and is often `http`, which indicates the HyperText transfer protocol). The `hostname` tells the name of the host to access. The `path` gives a host-specific location for the resource; paths often look like normal UNIX filenames. A big difference between a URL path and a filename is that a URL path often points to information that is generated on the fly (for example, a current weather report), and the actual data returned may depend on what features your WWW client supports. By exploring the Web, you will be able to find information ranging from your personal biorhythms to common questions about the PowerPC to an archive of SCUBA diving destination reports.

The National Center for Supercomputing Applications at the University of Illinois has developed World Wide Web interfaces called Mosaic. The UNIX version runs with Motif widgets using X11 and is called `xmosaic`.

Troubleshooting TCP/IP

Sometimes you may find that your attempts at making network connection are not working. Some of the common errors for each command were covered in the sections "I'm on the Wire—`rlogin`, `telnet`, `cu`" and "Transferring Files—`rcp`, `ftp`, `uucp`." This section covers some system-level troubleshooting you might want to try if you are having trouble making network connections using TCP/IP (`rlogin`, `telnet`, `rcp`, `ftp`, and the commands mentioned in the section "Other Services"). The suggestions here will help solve simple problems and will help classify problems. See Chapter 20, "Networking," for more information on troubleshooting network problems.

nslookup to Check Address Mapping

One common failure in trying to make network connections is either having the wrong hostname or encountering an error or delay in the name service. One way to check the validity of the hostname is to try using the nslookup command. The simplest way to run the nslookup command is nslookup *hostname*:

```
$ nslookup ftp.uu.net.
Name Server:  lazerus.pencom.com
Address:  198.3.201.57

Name:    ftp.uu.net
Address:  192.48.96.9

$ nslookup no.such.name.org
Name Server:  lazerus.pencom.com
Address:  198.3.201.57

*** lazerus.pencom.com can't find no.such.name.org: Non-existent domain
$
```

This will query the DNS for the name of *hostname* (ftp.uu.net in the first example, no.such.name.org in the second).

TIP

When a machine is newly added to the DNS, it may take a while before the nameservers learn about it. During that time, you may get "unknown host" errors. The person who adds a new host to the DNS should be able to give an estimate of how long to wait before a DNS failure should be considered an error.

Is There Anybody Out There? (ping)

If you can find the address of a host but your connections are failing, it may be because the host is unreachable or down. Sometimes you may get a "host unreachable" or "network unreachable" error. You will get these messages when the software that manages interconnections was able to determine that it could not send a packet to the remote host. The network routing software has internal tables that tell it how to reach other networks and hosts and these error messages indicate that there is no table entry that lets you reach the desired network or host.

When a host is simply down, you may get connection time-outs. You may want to try using the ping command to test if a host is running. The ping command sends a special kind of message called an *Internet control echo request message* or *ICMP echo request* (ICMP is the Internet control message protocol). This message asks the remote computer to send back an echo reply that duplicates the data of the echo request message. The low-level networking software of the remote computer will handle responding to an echo request, so a machine should be able to respond to a ping as long as the network software is running.

In the following example, we use ping to check the status of two hosts:

```
$ /etc/ping conch 100 10
PING conch.pencom.com: 100 byte packets
100 bytes from 198.3.200.86: icmp_seq=0. time=3. ms
100 bytes from 198.3.200.86: icmp_seq=1. time=4. ms
100 bytes from 198.3.200.86: icmp_seq=2. time=3. ms
100 bytes from 198.3.200.86: icmp_seq=3. time=5. ms
100 bytes from 198.3.200.86: icmp_seq=4. time=4. ms
100 bytes from 198.3.200.86: icmp_seq=5. time=8. ms
100 bytes from 198.3.200.86: icmp_seq=6. time=3. ms
100 bytes from 198.3.200.86: icmp_seq=7. time=3. ms
100 bytes from 198.3.200.86: icmp_seq=8. time=3. ms
100 bytes from 198.3.200.86: icmp_seq=9. time=3. ms

conch.pencom.com PING Statistics--
10 packets transmitted, 10 packets received, 0% packet loss
round-trip (ms)  min/avg/max = 3/3/8

$ /etc/ping brat 100 10
PING brat.pencom.com: 100 byte packets

--brat.pencom.com PING Statistics--
10 packets transmitted, 0 packets received, 100% packet loss
$
```

In the first example, the 100 says to use 100 bytes of data in each message and the 10 says to use 10 messages. All 10 message were returned. The second example shows what happens when you attempt to ping a host that is not up.

Once you determine that the remote host is not responding, you can either attempt to get the machine back up or wait until later to use it. If the machine is on your LAN, it should be fairly easy to go to it and start it running or talk to a local administrator. If the machine is somewhere remote, you may need to phone or e-mail someone to get assistance. If the machine is a resource on the Internet that is offered by some other school or company, you should probably just wait until it is running again unless your need is urgent (for both you and the remote administrator).

Summary

In this chapter, you have learned how UNIX machines are networked and how to take advantage of that networking. You have learned to log in to remote machines, copy files, begin to surf the Internet, and troubleshoot minor problems. By using these network services, you will be able to perform useful work on networked systems and explore the "information superhighway."

Communicating with Others

by Ron Dippold and Fred Trimble

IN THIS CHAPTER

CHAPTER 7

From its inception, the purpose of the Internet has been to facilitate communication among people. It was originally developed by the military to provide a vast distributed communications network capable of continued operation in case of a nuclear attack. Its designers wanted a distributed network to eliminate the possibility of a "vulnerable central node." They also wanted a communications protocol that would be independent of any particular physical media. Despite its military roots, it has become characterized by the general public as the "Infobahn," "Information Superhighway," and "Cyberspace." Today, some twenty years later, the benefits of the Internet are being realized by many groups of people, including secondary schools, home users, and private industry. The Internet infrastructure was originally designed to support applications such as electronic mail and file transfer. Although electronic mail is still the most popular application on the Internet, other networking hardware and protocols continue to evolve so that they can support other types of communication, including real-time audio and video.

Throughout the history of the Internet, UNIX has certainly played a major role. Most early UNIX systems provided built-in support for the Internet's main protocol: TCP/IP. Therefore, this chapter covers the following topics, with an emphasis on UNIX facilities where appropriate:

E-mail	Electronic mail allows you to exchange messages with other people all over the world. Many electronic mail programs have extended features, such as the ability to attach binary files.
Usenet	Usenet is the world's largest electronic discussion forum. One of the most popular features of the Internet, it allows people all over the world to discuss topics and exchange ideas on a wide variety of subjects.
Talk	The talk command allows two people to exchange text messages in real-time.
IRC	Internet Relay Chat extends the capabilities of the "talk" command. It provides a real-time multiple person discussion forum, much like a CB radio channel.
Multimedia	The Internet allows real-time audio and video to be transmitted.
The Future	This section provides a glimpse into the future of the Internet.

Electronic Mail (E-Mail)

Electronic mail is the most widely used application on the Internet. It is known as an asynchronous type of communication system, because after a mail message has been sent, it resides on the recipient's computer until the recipient logs on and retrieves the message. This section focuses on many facets of e-mail, including the structure of a mail message, sending binary data (such as a graphics file) with a mail message, e-mail addressing, how messages are sent over the Internet, and common end-user mail programs.

Components of a Mail Message

A mail message consists of two main sections: a message header and a message body. The header contains information such as who sent the message and when it was sent. The body contains the actual message text. Some people finish their messages with an optional third part known as a "signature." Each of these mail message sections is described in detail in the following sections.

Message Headers

The message header consists of several lines at the top, formatted as "keyword: value" pairs. Messages sent to a user who is located on the same local UNIX host using the `mail` or `mailx` program have a very simple structure. For example,

```
From smithj Thu Apr 24 00:42 EDT 1997
To: jonest
Subject: Code Review Meeting
Status: R

Please plan on attending the code review
meeting tomorrow at 10:00am.
```

The message header of a mail message that ends up going over the Internet, however, is much more complex. For example,

```
From nihil@eniac.seas.void.edu Thu Apr  24 08:15:01 1997
Flags: 000000000015
Received: from phones.com (phones.com [229.46.62.22]) by
happy.phones.com (8.6.5/QC-BSD-2.1) via ESMTP;
id IAA13973 Thu, 24 Apr 1997 08:14:59 -0800 for
<rdippold@happy.phones.com>
Received: from linc.cis.void.edu (root@LINC.CIS.VOID.EDU
[230.91.6.8]) by phones.com (8.6.5/QC-main-2.3) via ESMTP;
id IAA14773 Thu, 24 Apr 1997 08:14:56 -0800 for
<rdippold@phones.com>
Received: from eniac.seas.void.edu (nihil@ENIAC.SEAS.VOID.EDU
[230.91.4.1]) by linc.cis.void.edu (8.6.5/VOID 1.4) with
ESMTP id LAA17163 for <rdippold@phones.com>
Thu, 24 Apr 1997 11:14:45 -0500
Received: from localhost by eniac.seas.void.edu
id LAA24236; Thu, 24 Apr 1997 11:14:44 -0500
From: nihil@eniac.seas.void.edu [B Johnson]
Sender: nihil@ocean.void.edu
Reply-To: nihil@void.edu,nihil@freenet.com
Cc: group-stuff@uunet.UU.NET
Cc: james@foobar.com
Message-Id: <199302011614.LAA24236@eniac.seas.void.edu>
Subject: Re: Apple IIe/IIgs Software and books for SALE...
To: rdippold@phones.com (Ron Dippold)
Date: Thu, 24 Apr 97 11:14:44 EST
In-Reply-To:     <CMM.342342.rdippold@happy.phones.com>;
from "Ron Dippold" at Apr 24, 97 1:00 am
X-Mailer: ELM [version 2.3 PL11-void1.13]
Mime-Version: 1.0
```

```
Content-Type: text/plain; charset=US-ASCII
Content-Transfer-Encoding: 7bit
Content-Length: 10234
```

Message headers are constructed for you automatically by mail software known as "mail user agents" (MUA) and "mail transport agents" (MTA). In fact, the presence of certain items in the header, such as carbon copies and receipt notification, depend on the sophistication of the mail software itself. These components of an electronic mail system are discussed in detail in a later section. Some header information is intuitive. Other sections require some explanation.

Here's the first line from the previous example:

```
From nihil@eniac.seas.void.edu Thu Apr  24 08:15:01 1997
```

This line was added by the MTA on the local system (`sendmail`). It is used as a quick message summary, noting who sent the message and when. Because many mail systems store all of a user's mail messages in a single text file, such summary lines are also used to separate messages within the file. This provides a way to tell the end of one message from the start of the next. For most mail programs, this is the text `From` at the start of a line. This also means that if you try to place a `From` at the start of a line of text in your actual message, your mail program should place a > or some other character before it, so that it doesn't falsely indicate the start of a new message.

```
Flags: 000000000015
```

The `Flags` field, which is specific to Berkeley mail and mailx, was also added by the local mail program. Each message can have several different statuses, such as deleted, unread, and flagged for further attention. This varies with the sophistication of the mail program.

```
Received: from phones.com (phones.com [229.46.62.22]) by
happy.phones.com (8.6.5/QC-BSD-2.1) via ESMTP;
id IAA13973 Thu, 24 Apr 1997 08:14:59 -0800 for
<rdippold@happy.phones.com>
```

Each system that receives mail adds its own received header on top of the message. Because this is the first such header in the message, it must indicate the last mail transfer. The machine `happy.phones.com` (where my mail is located) received the message from `phones.com` (our company gateway) on April 24, 1997. The transfer was done using sendmail 8.6.5 (although you can't tell from this header that it was sendmail) and the protocol used was ESMTP. The intended recipient is listed last. This can change as the message goes through gateways, so it's helpful for tracking mail problems.

```
Received: from linc.cis.void.edu (root@LINC.CIS.VOID.EDU
[230.91.6.8]) by phones.com (8.6.5/QC-main-2.3) via ESMTP;
id IAA14773 Thu, 24 Apr 1997 08:14:56 -0800 for
<rdippold@phones.com>
```

Here's the mail transfer that got the message from `void.edu` to my site. It's a direct connection with no intermediate hops.

```
Received: from eniac.seas.void.edu (nihil@ENIAC.SEAS.VOID.EDU
[230.91.4.1]) by linc.cis.void.edu (8.6.5/VOID 1.4) with
ESMTP id LAA17163 for <rdippold@phones.com>
Thu, 24 Apr 1997 11:14:45 -0500
```

Here, the mail system (`linc.cis`) at `void.edu` received the mail from another system at `void.edu` (`eniac.seas`).

```
Received: from localhost by eniac.seas.void.edu
id LAA24236; Thu, 24 Apr 1997 11:14:44 -0500
```

Finally, here's the original sending of the message. One interesting piece of information that can be gleaned from this whole exchange is the amount of time that it took to transfer the message. The message was sent at `11:14:44` `-0500` and was received at `08:14:59` `-0800` on the same day. The `-0500` and `-0800` show the time zone differences. To get equivalent times for both messages, you add 5 hours to the time of the sending and 8 hours to the time of receipt, to get 16:14:44 and 16:14:59, respectively. The message arrived in 15 seconds!

```
From: nihil@eniac.seas.void.edu [B Johnson]
```

This is the sender of the message. The portion in brackets is a comment. It usually contains the person's name.

```
Sender: nihil@ocean.void.edu
```

`Sender` is the authenticated identity of the person who sent the message. This is where the sending computer tells you, as nearly as it can determine, the account that actually sent the message, regardless of what the From header says. This is useful if one person, such as a secretary, is authorized to send mail for another or if one member of a group is sending a message on behalf of the whole group. If the Sender header is the same as the From header, it doesn't need to be added. In this case, `Nihil` sent mail from a machine within his organization different from the one given in his address. If the From and Sender headers are radically different, however, the mail could be a forgery.

```
Reply-To: nihil@void.edu,nihil@freenet.com
```

The Reply-To header specifies who your reply should go to if you respond. Most mail software is smart enough to do this automatically. There are usually two reasons for using a Reply-To header. The first is if the address given in the From header is broken and you can't fix it. The second is if the specified primary address is somewhat unreliable. `Nihil` has another mail account at `freenet.com`—if for some reason `void.edu` goes offline, he can still get much of his mail at his freenet account.

```
Cc: group-stuff@zznet.ZZ.NET
Cc: james@foobar.com
```

The message was also sent to `group-stuff@zznet.ZZ.NET` and `james@foobar.com`. You can choose whether to include them in your reply. This also could have been done in a single header statement:

```
Cc: group-stuff@zznet.ZZ.NET,james@foobar.com
```

Either form is acceptable. Headers such as From or Sender, however, should appear only once in the entire header.

```
Message-Id: <199302011614.LAA24236@eniac.seas.void.edu>
```

Message identification is very helpful when trying to track a message for debugging purposes. It can also be used for message cancellation on Usenet. The method of generating this unique ID varies from site to site. There should never be another message with this specific ID generated by any machine anywhere on the network.

```
Subject: Re: Apple IIe/IIgs Software and books for SALE...
```

This is the subject of the message. My mail program shows me a one-line summary of each message, including the From, Date, and Subject headers.

```
To: rdippold@phones.com (Ron Dippold)
```

This is who the message was sent to. Sometimes your local computer will strip off the domain (@phones.com).

```
Date: Thu, 24 Apr 97 11:14:44 EST
```

This is the date the mail was originally sent. EST is Eastern Standard Time.

```
In-Reply-To:  <CMM.342342.rdippold@happy.phones.com>;
from "Ron Dippold" at Apr 24, 97 1:00 am
```

This message is a reply to a message that Ron sent with the message ID given above.

```
X-Mailer: ELM [version 2.3 PL11-void1.13]
```

The sender used the Elm Mail System to send this piece of mail. This information can also be useful in debugging.

```
Mime-Version: 1.0
Content-Type: text/plain; charset=US-ASCII
Content-Transfer-Encoding: 7bit
```

MIME message format is discussed later in the chapter. Briefly, this says that the message contains only 7-bit text.

```
Content-Length: 10234
```

The length of the body of the message (not shown here) is 10,234 characters.

There are some other header items that might be occasionally useful for you to know:

```
Bcc: recipient
```

Bcc is blind carbon copy. This is like the Cc header, except that those recipients listed in the To and Cc headers don't see that the message was sent to those specified in the Bcc header. Use this to send a copy of a message to someone without letting the others know you're sending it.

```
Encrypted: software keyhelp
```

This indicates that the message body is encrypted with encryption software, and the `keyhelp` option helps with selecting the key used to decode. Note that the header itself cannot be encrypted because it contains vital routing information.

Dates used in headers look like this:

```
Thu, 24 Apr 97 11:44 -500
```

The day of week (`Thu`) is optional. The time is given in 24-hour format (`00:00` — `23:59`) local time. The last field is the time zone in one of several formats.

```
UT or GMT       Universal/Greenwich Mean Time
EST or EDT      Eastern time zone
CST or CDT      Central time zone
MST or MDT      Mountain time zone
PST or PDT      Pacific time zone
-HHMM           HH hours and MM minutes earlier than UT
+HHMM           HH hours and MM minutes later than UT
```

RFC 822, which documents the standard format for Internet text messages, contains information about the header format.

> **NOTE**
>
> Throughout this chapter, reference will be made to RFCs. RFC stands for Request For Comments and is the means by which the research and development community has documented the standards that form the basis of the Internet. For example, RFC 821 documents the SMTP protocol for sending mail.

The Message Body

The message body is separated from the message header by a single blank line. The message body contains the actual text of the message. Here, you are free to type whatever you want to the recipient. However, there are a few recommended guidelines to follow.

Many mail systems can only handle lines of up to 65 characters. It is usually a good idea to keep the number of characters on a line less than that amount. Also, try to use a good mix of upper and lower case characters. IF YOU USE ALL UPPERCASE CHARACTERS, IT LOOKS LIKE YOU'RE SHOUTING! In addition to text, the message body sometimes contains a special character sequence known as an *emoticon*, such as : -). If you view this emoticon sideways, it looks like a smiley face.

NOTE

When conversing with others, our body language, facial expressions, and tone of voice provide a framework for how our words are understood. Because this is not possible in an e-mail message, special character sequences called emoticons are used to embellish the text to connote emotion. Here is a list of some emoticons you might see, along with their usual meaning:

:-)	humor, laughter, friendliness
:-(	sadness, anger, upset
:-O	shocked
:-$	put your money where your mouth is
:-y	said with a smile
:-T	keeping a straight face
:-¦	no expression
(:-D	has a big mouth

It is considered good practice not to overuse these symbols.

Signatures

Some e-mail messages conclude with an optional signature. A signature is a brief description of who sent the message, such as full name, telephone and fax numbers, and e-mail address. Some signatures try to embellish this information with a picture drawn with ASCII characters. It is considered good practice to limit your signature to five lines or less. Most modern mail programs can be configured to automatically append your signature to the end of your message.

Sending Binary Data

The protocol for sending e-mail over the Internet (SMTP) allows only for the transmission of ASCII text characters. Therefore, binary files, such as audio or video files, are not directly supported. The preferred method for sending binary data is to use a mail program that supports Multi-purpose Internet Mail Extensions (MIME). This is discussed in a later section. Before the advent of MIME, a technique used to circumvent this restriction is to encode such data as ASCII text before sending it with a mailer program, such as Elm or mailx. On UNIX systems, use the uuencode program to convert a binary file to ASCII text. On the receiving end, the uudecode program to convert the data back to binary. For example, the following command can be used to mail a graphics file to a remote user:

```
uuencode picture.tif picture.tif ¦ mailx -s "image file" gcobb@netx.com
```

The first argument to uuencode is the image file that will be encoded. The second argument is the name of the file that will be created on the remote user's system when the recipient runs the uudecode program. Since uuencode writes directly to standard output, it is piped to the mailx program. The mailx program will send a message to the remote user with a subject line of `image file`.

> **NOTE**
>
> The uuencoded file will be about 35 percent larger than the original file. About 33 percent of that comes from converting 8-bit bytes to 6-bit bytes; the other 2 percent comes from control information in the encoding.

On the remote system, the mail recipient first saves the message to a file, for instance, `mail.save`. The following command converts the ASCII characters back into binary format:

```
uudecode mail.save
```

In addition to the encrypted binary data, the file contains the mail header information put there by the mailx program. It is also possible that the sender added a commentary before the encrypted data. Upon examination of the encrypted file, there should appear a mail header and any commentary added by the sender. The encrypted data begins directly after the line containing the word `begin`, followed by UNIX file permissions and a filename. After the section with the encrypted data the word `end` appears on a line by itself. This information is used by the uudecode program for creating the file. In the preceding example, the following line appeared directly after the mail header:

```
begin 777 picture.tif
```

Therefore, after the uudecode program is run against the `mail.save` file, a file named `picture.tif` with file permissions 777 is created. Using the `begin` and `end` keywords, the uudecode program is usually able to distinguish between the mail text and the encrypted data. If uudecode cannot handle the file properly, you can edit the file and remove all text before the `begin` keyword and after the `end` keyword. The uudecode program should then work as expected.

> **TIP**
>
> The technique specified above works okay for relatively small files, but what if you want to send someone a 10 megabyte file? Add 35 percent more for encryption overhead, and you have a hefty message by any estimation. Although you usually won't run into the problem with normal messages, a few sites running really old MTAs have a limit on message size, usually around 64,000 bytes. If you send your file as one big chunk, only a fourth of it may get there. What you need to do is split it into smaller chunks.
>
> You can do this manually, but there's a nice UNIX utility that will do the job for you: `split`. Just tell `split` the number of lines you want in each piece, and it creates a file containing
>
> *continues*

continued

the specified number of lines. The number of lines doesn't tell you the size of each file exactly, but you can experiment. We find that using 800 lines per piece on average provides nice, safe 50,000-byte chunks. Here's how it works:

```
uuencode bigfile bigfile > bigfile.uue
split -800 bigfile.uue splits
mail -s "Bigfile.uue 1 of 3" mybuddy < splitsaa
mail -s "Bigfile.uue 2 of 3" mybuddy < splitsab
mail -s "Bigfile.uue 3 of 3" mybuddy < splitsac
rm bigfile.uue splits??
```

The split command takes as arguments the number of lines and the file to split, as well as a base name for the output files. In the above example, splits was used as the base name. It then names the resulting files splitsaa, splitsab, splitsac, and if necessary, all the way up to splitszz. This gives you 676 pieces. If that's not enough, you should probably use another method to transfer the file. The subjects with 1 of 3, 2 of 3, and 3 of 3 are just to let the receiver know the total number of pieces, and their proper sequence.

Now the receiver has to save all the messages into a big file, edit out everything except the uuencoded stuff, and run uudecode on the resulting file. It is a cumbersome process, but it works. If you do this type of transfer, consider writing a UNIX shell script to automate the uuencode splitting, mailing, and recombining of the files.

If you're on a UNIX system, uuencode, uudecode, and split should be standard. If you're using DOS or a Mac, you can obtain a copy via anonymous ftp.

If you're using DOS, point your Web browser to http://oak.oakland.edu/pub/simtelnet/msdos/decode.. From here, download the file uuexe655.zip. This is a very nice uuencode and uudecode for the PC that is actually superior to the standard UNIX version. For instance, it automatically reorders the pieces of the file if they're out of order.

If you're using a Mac, point your Web browser to http://tucows.idirect.com/mac/comp.html and download the file for UULite version 3.0. It's a very full-featured uuencoder for the Mac.

For any computer for which you have a C compiler available, you can get the source code for uuencode.c and uudecode.c by pointing your Web browser to http://oak.oakland.edu/pub/misc/unix. This is the portable C source for the standard uuencode and uudecode and should work on almost any computer. The portable C versions of uuencode and uudecode are simple but are always there.

Mail programs such as mailx are also discussed in more detail later in the chapter.

Addressing Remote Systems

To send a message over the Internet, you need to specify a specially formatted Internet address. It is composed of two major sections separated by an @ sign. The part of the address to the left of the @ sign is the Internet account that will receive the mail message. This is usually the login name of the mail recipient. The part of the address to the right of the @ sign is known as the domain name. It uniquely identifies a host on the Internet. All domain names on the Internet comprise the Domain Name System, which is a hierarchy that divides the Internet into logical groups (domains). The domain is read from right to left and specifies a series of progressively smaller logical domain names. Each part of the domain name is separated with a period. For example, note the following Internet address:

```
ccarter@minn.com
```

The rightmost portion of the domain, .com, indicates that this is a commercial site. The following list shows the most popular domains for the United States:

com	commercial
edu	education
gov	government
mil	military
net	network
org	organization

Outside of the United States, sites can be registered to .com, .net, and .org. In addition, the two-letter ISO country code can also be used. For example, "ca" for Canada, "uk" for the United Kingdom, and so on.

To the left of the highest level domain name (edu, org, and so on) can appear any number of logical subdomains. These are used to specify, in greater detail, the name of the host where the mail recipient can be found. By Internet convention, capitalization in the domain name is ignored. Therefore, the following Internet addresses are equivalent: `ccarter@Minn.com`, `ccarter@MINN.com`, and `ccarter@MINN.COM`. Most modern mail software ignores case in the username portion of the address for consistency. However, this is not a requirement. Therefore, it is considered good practice to preserve case for the username, just in case the recipient's system is using older mail software.

An older type of addressing scheme is known as a UUCP bang-path address (*bang* is computer jargon for an exclamation point). It is unlikely that you will see an address in this format, though, and is mentioned here for historical reasons. In this type of scheme, you must indicate each system you want the mail to pass through. For example, note the following address for user `katherine`:

```
comp01!comp02!comp03!katherine
```

This indicates that you want the mail to pass through systems named `comp01`, `comp02`, and `comp03`. Once the message has been delivered to `comp03`, it will be delivered to `katherine`.

7

COMMUNICATING
WITH OTHERS

How Messages Are Routed Over the Internet

Before an Internet address in *username@domain* format can be used for transmission, it must be converted into an IP address. An IP address consists of four numbers, separated by dots, which uniquely identify a host on the Internet. For example, "128.254.17.7" is an example of an IP address. Translating an Internet address to an IP address is the province of systems on the Internet known as name servers.

When a mail message is sent over the Internet, it is sent as a stream of packets, each containing a portion of the message. Each packet also contains the IP address of the destination. The packets are sent over the Internet using the IP protocol. Specialized networking systems on the Internet, known as routers, examine the IP address in each packet, and route it to the appropriate host. Many factors, such as network traffic volume, on various Internet backbones are taken into consideration in order to determine the best possible path. In fact, packets from the same mail message may take different routes. All packets are combined in the correct order on the receiving host using the TCP protocol.

Sending Mail to Other Networks

In addition to sending e-mail over the Internet, it is possible to send mail to other networks, such as online services.

Internet E-Mail Gateways

In theory, the Internet is a competitor with all the existing services such as AT&T Mail, CompuServe, and the rest. In practice, it's a neutral competitor. It's not some guided, malevolent entity that is trying to do away with any of the other services. Rather, it competes just by its existence; it offers more information and more connectivity than most of the services can ever hope to offer. Smart information services finally realized that this could be put to their advantage. Anyone who cares to can join the Internet, and a service that joins the Internet has advantages over its competitors.

One huge advantage is connectivity. As soon as a mail service adds a computer (known as a *gateway*) that can transfer from its system to the Internet and vice versa, its users can exchange mail with anyone on the service or with anyone on the Internet. That's a lot of people. So many services are now offering some sort of mail gateway. Even Prodigy, which was somewhat late to grasp the possibilities, has one now.

Instead of GEnie needing to install a special gateway to talk to Prodigy, and one to CompuServe, and one to SprintMail, and one to BubbaNet, it can set up and maintain just one gateway to the Internet, through which everything flows. Given the glacial speed with which most of the online services implement upgrades like this, requiring only a single gateway is a good thing.

So now anyone can send e-mail anywhere! Well, not exactly.

Addressing Issues

It turns out that the services that connect to the Internet keep their same old account names and horrible mail systems. CompuServe's octal account addresses are as much an anachronism as punch cards, but because of the company's current investment, it isn't going to change them. And you can't just send a mail message to a CompuServe account using an Internet-style address. A CompuServe ID looks something like this:

```
112233,44
```

In Internet addressing, a comma separates members of a list so you can't use the comma in the CompuServe address. There's a way around that (use a period instead of a comma) but you have to know that in advance. Someone trying to send mail to a system has to deal with those quirks. Hence this section, which details the translation that has to be done between the major networks.

Again, an Internet e-mail address looks something like this:

```
user@machine.site.domain
```

Any address to a mail gateway is going to be some variation (minor or major) on this theme.

X.400 Addressing

The Internet uses what is formally known as RFC-822 addressing. Many large commercial services specializing in electronic mail use something known as an X.400 gateway to talk to the Internet. Those addresses look something like this:

```
/A=value/B=value/C=value
```

This style is usable from the Internet, because RFC-822 allows slashes and equals signs. In fact, there's the opposite problem: RFC-822 allows many characters to be used in addressing that cause an X.400 gateway to go into convulsions, including the @ sign. Since this appears in all Internet-style mail addresses, there's an obvious problem.

Whenever the Internet address has a special character, you need to use the following translation table:

Internet	X.400
@	(a)
%	(p)
!	(b)
"	(q)
_	(u)
(	(l)
)	(r)

For any other special character, such as #, substitute (xxx), where *xxx* is the three-digit decimal ASCII code for the character. For #, you would use (035).

For example, to convert the Internet address

```
oldvax!Mutt#Jeff@cartoon.com
```

into something that can be sent from an X.400 service such as MCI Mail, you need to turn it into this:

```
oldvax(b)Mutt(035)Jeff(a)cartoon.com
```

> **NOTE**
>
> The ! is replaced with (b) because computer users like short names, and refer to an exclamation point as a *bang*.

Gateway Translation Specifics

Using the following instructions should be fairly easy. To send mail to CompuServe from an Internet mail account, see the translation instructions in the "CompuServe" section later in this chapter.

Parts of the address that you have to replace with appropriate information are given in italics. For instance, with

```
userid@aol.com
```

you need to replace *userid* with the recipient's account name or number. *domain* is the part of the Internet address after the @.

If you are sending mail from one service to another through the Internet, for example from WWIVNet to CompuServe, you will have to do two translations. First, check the "CompuServe" section and see how to translate the ID "From Internet." Then check the "WWIVNet" section and see how to translate that address "To Internet." If you do this from one strange network to another, the name may be a crawling horror, but at least it should be possible.

America Online

America Online (AOL) is a major commercial information system that recently joined the Internet (although it has had Internet e-mail for a while). Its Internet e-mail is seamless from an Internet point of view.

From Internet: America Online looks just like any other normal Internet site.

```
userid@aol.com
```

Example: `jjones@aol.com`

To Internet: There's no need to do anything special; just use the regular Internet format.

userid@domain

Example: `bsmith@wubba.edu`

To Others: America Online lets you use special abbreviated domains for mail to AppleLink, CompuServe, or GEnie. Send your mail to *userid*`@applelink`, *userid*`@cis`, or *userid*`@genie`, respectively.

Example: `11111.2222@cis`

AT&T Mail

From Internet: Use standard Internet addressing:

userid`@attmail.com`.

To Internet: Use the following. Note the backward order here—this is the old bang-path type addressing. Oh well.

Example: `internet!wubba.edu!bsmith`.

BIX

BIX is the Byte magazine Information eXchange, a commercial service oriented toward techies and/or Byte magazine readers. It's been bought by Delphi, but still operates as a separate source.

From Internet: Use standard Internet addressing:

userid`@bix.com`

Example: `jjones@bix.com`

To Internet: You'll need to use the Internet Services menu option from the main menu, then use standard Internet addressing:

userid@domain

CompuServe

CompuServe is a very large commercial system. It's so large that it hasn't yet felt the pressure to join the Internet except by offering a mail gateway.

From Internet: Use standard Internet addressing with one difference: CompuServe IDs are in the form *77777,7777*. Because Internet dislikes commas in addresses, you need to change the comma to a period:

77777.7777`@compuserve.com`

Example: `12345.677@compuserve.com`

To Internet: You need to add a prefix to the standard Internet addressing:

`>INTERNET:`*`userid@domain`*

Example: `>INTERNET:bsmith@wubba.edu`

Delphi

Delphi was the first of the large commercial services to really embrace Internet. It looks like any standard Internet site as far as Internet Mail is concerned:

From Internet: Use the following addressing:

`userid``@delphi.com`

Example: `jjones@delphi.com`

To Internet: There's no need to do anything special; just use the regular Internet format:

`userid@domain`

Example: `bsmith@wubba.edu`

EasyLink

This is a set of commercial Internet services from AT&T.

For more information on AT&T's EasyLink, you can contact them at `http://www.att.com/easycommerce/easylink/mail.html`.

Envoy-100

This is Telecom Canada's commercial service with X.400 gatewaying.

From Internet: Use the following addressing:

`uunet.uu.net!att!attmail!mhs!envoy!`*`userid`*

Remember that we told you the bang-path format is almost obsolete? That's not true here yet.

Example: `uunet.uu.net!att!attmail!mhs!envoy!12345`

To Internet: Brace yourself—you need to use the following addressing:

`[RFC-822="`*`userid`*`(a)`*`domain`*`"]INTERNET/TELEMAIL/US`

(a) replaces @ because X.400 doesn't like the @ character. For other special X.400 characters, see the "X.400 Addressing" section.

Example: `[RFC-822="bsmith(a)wubba"]INTERNET/TELEMAIL/US`

For more information on Envoy-100, contact `http://library.usask.ca/~scottp/envoy.html`.

FidoNet

FidoNet is a large international BBS network—sort of the Internet for the BBSing crowd. It's not as fast as the Internet, but access is usually very cheap, and chances are there's a FidoNet BBS in your area.

Because it's run over phone lines, the BBS operators will rack up long-distance charges for any mail transferred, so please don't send large messages to FidoNet sites. Many sites will even chop your messages to 8,000 or 16,000 bytes, so much of your message won't get through.

From Internet: First, you need to know the network address of the BBS your recipient is on. It will be in a form such as `Z:N/F.P`. Then send the mail to the following address:

`userid@pP.fF.nN.zZ.fidonet.org`

If the network address of the BBS doesn't have a `P` component, leave the `pP.` part out of the address. For the `userid` replace any non-alphanumeric characters (such as spaces) with periods (`.`).

Example: `Jim_Jones@p4.f3.n2.z1.fidonet.org`

To Internet: Use standard Internet addressing with a suffix:

`userid@userid ON gateway`

The `gateway` is a special FidoNet site that acts as a gateway to Internet. You can use `1:1/31` unless you find a better one.

Example: `bsmith@wubba.edu ON 1:1/31`

GEnie

GEnie is General Electric's commercial information service.

From Internet: Use standard Internet addressing:

`userid@genie.com`

Example: `jjones@genie.com`

To Internet: Use standard Internet addressing with a suffix:

`userid@domain@INET#`

Example: `bsmith@wubba.edu@INET#`

Gold 400

Gold 400 is British Telecom's commercial X.400 system.

From Internet: Use the following addressing:

`userid@org_unit.org.prmd.gold-400.gb`

You'll need to have the recipient tell you his or her `userid`, `org_unit` (organization unit), `org` (organization), and `prmd` (private mail domain).

Example: `jjones@foo.bar.baz.gold-400.gb`

To Internet: Again, see the section "X.400 Addressing" to see how to handle nonstandard characters in addresses, but here's the format:

`/DD.RFC-822=`*userid*`(a)`*domain*`%%/O=uknet/PRMD=uk.ac/ADMD=gold 400/C=GB`

Example: `/DD.RFC-822=bsmith(a)wubba.edu/O=uknet/PRMD=uk.ac/ADMD=gold 400/C=GB`

KeyLink

KeyLink is Telecom Australia's commercial X.400 mail service.

From Internet: Use the following addressing:

userid`@`*org_unit*`.`*org*`.telememo.au`

You'll need to have the recipient tell you his or her *userid*, *org_unit* (organization unit), and *org* (organization). The *org_unit* might not be used—in that case, just eliminate it and the period that follows it.

Example: `jjones@froboz.grue.telememo.au`

To Internet: Again, see the section "X.400 Addressing" to see how to handle nonstandard characters in addresses, but this is the general format:

`(C:au,A:telememo,P:oz.au,"RFC-822":"`*name*` - <`*userid*`(a)`*domain*`>")`

name isn't actually used for delivery, just as a comment.

Example: `(C:au,A:telememo,P:oz.au,"RFC-822":"Bubba Smith - <bsmith(a)wubba.edu>")`

MCI Mail

MCI Mail is MCI's commercial e-mail service.

From Internet: There are several options. Each MCI user has a name (`Jim Jones`) and a phone number (`123-4567`) associated with his or her account. The number is unique to that account, so you can always send mail to an address such as the following:

number`@mcimail.com`

Example: `1234567@mcimail.com`

If you know there is only one J Jones with an account at MCI Mail, you can send mail to

FLast`@mcimail.com`

where *F* is the first initial and *Last* is the last name. Or, if you know there is only one Jim Jones you can send mail to

First_Last`@mcimail.com`

where *First* is the first name and *Last* is the last name. Note the underscore between them.

Example: `Jim_Jones@mcimail.com`

To Internet: When MCI prompts you with `To:` enter

`$$name (EMS)`

`name` isn't actually used for mail delivery, but you can put the person's real name here. MCI then prompts you with `EMS:`. Respond with

`INTERNET`

Then MCI asks for `Mbx:` and here you can enter the real Internet address:

`userid@domain`

Prodigy

Prodigy is a large commercial service, Prodigy Information Services (jointly developed by Sears and IBM).

From Internet: Use standard Internet addressing:

`domain@prodigy.com`

Example: `jone45a@prodigy.com`

To Internet: When online, `Jump` to `ABOUT MAIL MANAGER` and proceed from there.

SprintMail

Hmm…AT&T and MCI have commercial mail services. Sprint has to have one, if only for the principle of the matter. Actually, to be fair, Sprint has always been one of the more network-oriented phone companies. You may have used their Telenet network.

From Internet: Use this addressing:

`/G=first/S=last/O=organization/ADMD=TELEMAIL/C=US/@sprint.com`

`first` and `last` are the recipient's first and last names, of course, and `organization` is the recipient's SprintMail organization name.

Example: `/G=Chris/S=Smith/O=FooInc/ADMD=TELEMAIL/C=US/@sprint.com`

To Internet: Use this addressing:

`C:USA,A:TELEMAIL,P:INTERNET,"RFC-822":<userid(a)domain>) DEL`

Again, see the section "X.400 Addressing" to see how to handle nonstandard characters in addresses.

Example: `C:USA,A:TELEMAIL,P:INTERNET,"RFC-822":<bsmith(a)wubba.edu>) DEL`

Other Gateways

There are other gateways around, and more are sure to appear. Most services offering this type of gateway should have at least some clue of how the address translation needs to be done—ask the service if you need to know.

Finding Addresses

There are many places on the World Wide Web that keep track of people's names and their corresponding e-mail addresses. There also exist many sites that provide a nice "front end" to these databases, allowing you to search for someone's e-mail address.

One such site is `http://www.four11.com`. It allows you to narrow your search based on geographic regions, such as country and state. It also has a handy "smart name" feature, that will expand a search for certain variations in a name (for instance, Robert = Bob). It currently contains over 6.5 million listings. Other worthwhile sites include `http://www.iaf.net` and `http:// www.bigfoot.com`. Finally, be sure to check out `http://www.starthere.com/index.html`. It has links and descriptions of many sites which, in turn, do the actual e-mail address searches on the Web.

To find someone in the communications field, try RPI's address server. Send mail to Internet address `comserve@vm.its.rpi.edu` with `help` as the body of the message.

UNINNETT of Norway maintains an X.500 address registry service. Send mail to Internet address `directory@uninett.no` with `help` as the body of the message.

PSI runs an X.500 service at Internet address `whitepages@wp.psi.com` with `help` as the message body.

Usenet Address Server

MIT keeps track of every person who has ever posted an article to Usenet since the late 1980s (many Usenet readers would be shocked to know this). This includes those from other networks who use a news gateway. If the person you are looking for has posted an article to Usenet since then, he or she might be in this database.

Send mail to the Internet address `mail-server@rtfm.mit.edu`. In the body of the message, put this:

```
send usenet-addresses/key1 key2 key...
```

The keys should include all the words you think might appear in the address, usually parts of the person's name. In many cases you will use only *key1*. The keys are case insensitive.

You can try the following:

```
send usenet-addresses/dippold
```

to return several entries. The server will return only 40 matches, so if your keys are overly general (Smith) you will need to give more keys, such as a first name, to narrow the search.

You can do several searches at once by placing several `send usenet-addresses/keys` lines in the message.

Your Address and Business Card

The business card of the 1990s includes your Internet address. E-mail is almost always cheaper, faster, and more convenient than a fax or snail mail. Putting your e-mail address on your business cards is one of the best ways to encourage people to use it.

How do you give your address on your business card? We've heard people recommend E-mail Address, E-mail, Internet, and other variations. My suggested solution is simple and elegant: just give your address without giving it any kind of label at all. The @ should give it away.

For best results, give the address in Internet format, even if your account is on another service. If you're on CompuServe as ID `11111,2222`, give your address as `11111.2222@compuserve.com` rather than as `CompuServe ID: 11111,2222`. With the first format anyone who can send Internet mail can reach you, and CompuServe users will be smart enough to realize that the first part is your CompuServe ID. The second format requires that someone know how to do the `11111,2222` to `11111.2222@compuserve.com` conversion, and they haven't all read this book. Of course, this assumes that you want non-CompuServe people sending you mail.

Mail Programs

There are three main components involved in sending mail. First there's the *link level transport layer*. Directly above the transport layer is the mail transport agent (MTA). This layer is responsible for the movement and delivery of mail messages. An MTA has several components, including routing mechanisms, a local delivery agent, and a remote delivery agent. The MTA for most UNIX systems is the sendmail program. An MTA that takes liberties in modifying the contents of a message is known as a hostile MTA. Finally, there's the mail user agent (MUA) that provides the user interface. It allows you to read, send, and otherwise manipulate mail messages. This is what people usually mean when they talk about a *mail program*.

There are many mail programs from which to choose. The next section covers the elements that are common to them all.

Your Mail Files

Normally, you have a mail account on whatever computer handles your mail. Often, you can do other things with your account besides access your mail, but that's not important for now. All your new mail, known as incoming mail, is kept in what is usually called a mail spool file. It's quite common for your computer to occasionally look at the spool file and notify you if you have new mail. This is your clue to run your mail program.

Your mail program then grabs all the incoming mail and displays it for your edification. If you don't delete the mail, it is placed in your mailbox file. This is not the same as your incoming mail file—the mailbox file holds all your old mail. Many users eventually outgrow the single mailbox and have several for different subjects, but there is almost always a default mailbox used whenever you run your mail program, and this is what is referred to as your mailbox.

If you send mail to someone else, it is sent directly to your site's mail computer, which can do what it pleases with the mail—it either sends it on immediately or saves the mail to send in batches.

Using Mail Programs

As mentioned earlier, there are many mail programs, each with their own quirks. But they try to accomplish the same task and tend to present the messages in a similar format. Learning about one mail program will give you the concepts needed to use almost any program in existence.

Message Summaries

Almost every mail program summarizes your messages like this:

```
FA     1) 14-Feb bfarve           Re: Congratulations! (2457 chars)
F      2) 15-Feb broth            requirements.doc (1/1) (17464 chars)
F      4) 18-Feb dgreen           Re: Sign Chester (2576 chars)
F D    5) 18-Feb clinton@whiteho  Re: Overnight Stay (13786 chars)
FA     6) 19-Feb Dwayne Rudd      Re: thank  you (1451 chars)
U      7) 21-Feb Eddie Lepman     noise (2653 chars)
```

There's one line per message. Again, the information for each message won't always be presented in exactly the same format, but the contents should be similar. From left to right for this mail program (named `mm90`), the lines give the following information:

■ **Message flags.** Each message has several state variables associated with it. In this case, the flags are whether the message is unread (U), whether I have answered the message (A), whether the message is deleted (D), and whether I have flagged the message for further attention (F). Some programs let you give each message one of several priority levels.

■ **Message number.** It helps to be able to refer to a message by a unique identifier for printing, reading, or deleting. Usually, the mail program just calls the first message in your mailbox 1 and counts up from there.

■ **Date.** This tells when the message was sent, from the Date header of the message.

■ **Name.** This is the name of the person who sent the mail, from the From header. If no name is given, the Internet address of the person is used.

■ **Subject.** When the sender entered the message, his or her mail program asked for a message subject. It's shown here. If there's not enough room, the subject is truncated.

■ **Length.** This shows how large the message is. Here it's given in characters—other programs give it in number of lines.

Reading New Messages

All mail programs have a read new mail command. Usually, you use just r or press Enter for character-based interfaces, or "point and click" for graphical user interfaces. This shows you your new messages one at a time. When you're reading each message you have several options available, such as replying or deleting the message.

Operating on Old Messages

The same functions that are available when you're reading a message are usually available when you're not reading any particular message, and can apply to a single old message or to a group of them. As an example, when you're reading a message, you can tell the mail program to delete the message. When you're not reading any messages you should be able to tell the mail program, "Delete messages 3, 6, 8, and 10 through 12."

Messages are usually given by number, but if you're using a mail program that uses a mouse, you may be able to select messages by clicking on them.

Common Mail Functions

Here's the standard list of mail functions you should learn to use in your program:

- **Read message(s).** Obviously, if you can't do this, not much else matters.

- **Delete message(s).** Mailboxes can become very cluttered with old mail, and you can even lose important mail because it's so buried in junk. You need to be able to get rid of mail you don't care about.

- **Flag message(s).** You should be able to flag messages as being important. The mail program should then make them stand out in some way so you remember to deal with them later.

- **Send message.** You should be able to send mail to other people.

- **Reply to message.** You should be able to easily send a response to the person who sent you a piece of mail, and include a portion of the sender's message text for reference.

- **Save message(s) to file.** You'll probably get mail that contains important information you want to use in another program. You should be able to save the body of a message to file, which you can then manipulate at will.

- **Switch to other mailbox.** If you start getting enough mail, you may find it handy to create other mailboxes. Perhaps one for the Bulgarian cooking mailing list of which you're a member. Your mail program should be able to handle several mailboxes.

- **Move message(s) to other mailbox.** If you have multiple mailboxes, it should be possible to move mail from one to another.

Mail Configuration File

Since how you handle your mail involves a lot of personal preference, almost all mail programs have many options that can be set. So that you don't have to set these every time you run your mail program, most mail programs have some sort of configuration file that is read every time the program starts.

You should definitely look into how to set this up for your mail program—while doing so, you will often find many options you didn't even know about. For instance, many programs will let you set aliases; for example, you can use just `bill` instead of `wblowhard@longname .deep.stuff.edu`. The mail program turns the alias into the full name.

7

COMMUNICATING
WITH OTHERS

Common UNIX Mail Programs

There are dozens of mail programs available for UNIX systems. This chapter covers the most popular ones, including mail, mailx, Elm, and PINE.

mail (Berkeley Mail)

The mail program is a simple mail user agent that has its roots in the BSD (Berkeley Software Distribution) version of UNIX. It is sometimes referred to as Berkeley Mail. This program is minimal in both functionality and presentation, and is still in use at a few sites.

To send a message, type **mail**, followed by one or more user addresses (local or remote). For example, the following command will send mail to two different users:

```
mail ccarter jrandle
```

On the next line, start typing in the message. When you have finished, type a . or control-d on a line by itself to indicate that you are finished typing. The mail transport agent then delivers the message(s). For convenience, you can put the message text in a file and send it with the following one-line command:

```
mail ccarter jrandle < file
```

To read incoming mail, simply type in the command **mail**. Each mail message will be printed (last-in first-out order), followed by a question mark command prompt. To save the message, including the header, type **s *filename***. To save the message without the header, type **w *filename***. Use the d command to delete the message. Following is a summary of all the commands recognized:

```
q               quit
x               exit without changing mail
p               print
s [file]        save (default mbox)
w [file]        save without header
-               print previous
d               delete
+               next (no delete)
m user          mail to user
! cmd           execute cmd
```

See the manual page for mail(1) for more details.

TIP

Every time you log in to your UNIX system, you can customize your environment to inform you that you have mail waiting to be read. Both the mail and mailx programs can be invoked with the -e option. It returns a 0 if there is mail waiting to be read. It returns a 1 if there is no mail. Bourne and Korn shell users can put the following code in their .profile file:

continues

continued

```
if [ -f /bin/mail ]
then
    if mail -e  # notify if mail.
    then
        echo "You have mail."
    fi
fi
```

A similar statement can be put in the .login file for C shell users. The C shell also allows you to be notified when new mail arrives while you are logged on. For example, the following statement in the .cshrc file checks for new mail every 60 seconds and prints the message "You have new mail." when it arrives. A utility called notify exists for some UNIX platforms that provides similar functionality, if you are not using the C shell.

mailx

The mailx command is an extended version of the Berkeley mail command. To send a mail message, type **mailx** followed by a list of local and/or remote users. For example:

```
mailx ccarter jrandle
```

Before typing the text for the message, you are prompted for a subject. You can type a one-line description for the subject, or simply type a carriage return to continue. After that, type in the text for the message, just like the mail command. You can also send mail by redirecting standard input from a file, as in the previous example for mail.

The mailx command provides some extended features for entering text into the message. For example, type ~v on a line by itself, and it will bring up the vi editor. When you are done composing the message within vi, type **ESC** and **ZZ** to get out of the editor, and you will go right back to the mailx command. This feature is available on Berkeley Mail.

Another useful feature is to import the contents of a file into the message body. Type **~r** *filename*, and a line appears showing the filename, along with the number of lines and characters in the file. The following example shows how to use this option to import the results of a command (uuencode) into a mail message. This feature is available on Berkeley Mail as well.

```
$ mailx trimblef
Subject: tif file

Here is the tif file that I promised you.

~r !uuencode picture.tif picture.tif
"uuencode picture.tif picture.tif" 368/22606
.
EOT
$
```

The following set of commands shows how the mail recipient can save and uudecode the contents of the file:

```
$ mailx
mailx Revision: 70.7    Date: 92/04/16 15:39:44    Type ? for help.
"/usr/mail/trimblef": 1 message 1 new
>N  1 trimblef          Sun Apr 27 14:36  376/22723 tif file
? s file.tif
"file.tif" [New file] 376/22723
? q
$ uudecode file.tif
$ ls -l
total 260
-rw-rw-rw-   1 trimblef users       22733 Apr 27 14:38 file.tif
-rwxrwxrwx   1 trimblef users       16384 Apr 27 14:40 picture.tif
$
```

At the question mark prompt, the command s `file.tif` was used to save the contents of the message, which is the uuencoded tif file. After running the uudecode program, the `picture.tif` file is created.

The preceding example also illustrates how to read mail. Simply type `mailx`, and the message header is displayed for each message in your mail box. The first field indicates the status of the message (`N` for new messages and `U` for unread messages). The second field is the message number in the queue. The third field is the address of the sender. The next field is the date the message was received. Finally, the last field indicates the number of lines/characters in the message. At the question mark prompt, you can type `p` to print the next message, s *filename* to save the contents to a file, or `n` to read the next message. If you want to respond to the sender from within the mailx program, type `r`.

NOTE

On Ultrix, HP-UX, and AIX systems, the r command is used to reply to everyone in the "To:" and "CC:" sections of the header, and R is used to reply to the sender only. However, on SunOS, the reverse occurs. Read the manual page to clarify the behavior on your system.

For a complete list of commands, see the manual page for `mailx`.

The mailx environment can also be customized. When the `mailx` command is invoked, it first executes commands in a global configuration file named `/usr/lib/mailx/mailx.rc`. Here are the contents of a typical `mailx.rc` file:

```
set asksub
set dot
set crt=23
set PAGER=more
```

The `asksub` option tells the mailx program to prompt the user for a subject line if the `-s` option is not specified when sending mail. The `dot` option allows a user to type a `.` on a line by itself to end a message, just like the `mail` command. The `crt` option specifies the number of lines to display from a message to pipe to the program specified in the PAGER setting. In the above example, 23 lines of output at a time will be sent to the more command. After reading the global configuration file, the mailx command reads the user's local configuration file in $HOME/.mailrc. The most common types of entries in a local configuration file are display options and defining user aliases. The complete set of configuration options is documented in the manual page for mailx.

TIP

Some UNIX systems have a very useful program called vacation that allows you to respond to e-mail automatically with a pre-defined message. This is useful when you do not intend to respond to e-mail for an extended period of time, hence the program name. The program sends mail to each person you specify in the vacation command. The vacation command was intended to be put in the $HOME/.forward file. Another good use of the vacation program is to forward all of your mail to another e-mail address, while sending a message back to the sender indicating your new e-mail address. The following commands can be used to set up the vacation command to respond to your e-mail:

```
$ cd $HOME
$ rm .forward
$ vacation -I
$ vi .forward

\username, "¦ vacation username"

$ vi .vacation.msg

I'll be out of the office until 5/20/97 ...

$
```

When you are able to respond to e-mail and want to disable forwarding, simply remove the .forward file. It is a good idea to test this command to make sure it is in proper working order. See the manual page for the vacation(1) command for details.

Elm

In contrast to the mail and mailx programs, Elm provides a full-screen and menu-driven interface. It was created as an easy-to-use UNIX mail program but actually has a fair amount of configurability and power. The support programs that come with it might be worth getting on their own. If you like printed manuals, it comes with over a hundred pages of documentation in PostScript format.

The Elm program is probably not standard on your system, so you'll have to get it yourself. Fortunately, it is available via anonymous ftp it from ftp://ftp.uu.net under /networking/mail/elm, or from ftp://wuarchive.wustl.edu under /packages/mail/elm. The packed source code is about a megabyte. In order to install the package, you'll have to compile it and answer a few system configuration questions.

The menu displayed by `Elm` appears as follows:

```
Mailbox is '/usr/mail/trimblef' with 3 message(s) [Elm revision: 70.85]


      1   Apr 27 trimblef        (9)     Project status
   N  2   Apr 27 trimblef        (10)    Flyers tickets
   N  3   Apr 27 trimblef        (10)    Going away party


   You can use any of the following commands by pressing the first character;
 D)elete or U)ndelete mail,  M)ail a message,  R)eply or F)orward mail,  Q)uit
    To read a message, press <return>.  j = move down, k = move up, ? = help

Command:
```

Messages are displayed in a format similar to `mailx`. In order to access help, press ? at any time.

TIP

`Elm` tip 1: Press o from the main menu to get the options screen. Press > and Elm creates a file named `.Elm/Elmrc`—this is a special options file that you can edit with `vi` or emacs (or whatever you use). Most of these options aren't easily set from inside Elm. Be sure to read the `Ref.guide` file for more information on these options.

TIP

`Elm` tip 2: Elm can act as a command-line mailer just as Berkeley mail does—it even uses the same syntax:

```
Elm -s "subject" recipient < messagefile
```

TIP

`Elm` tip 3: Don't ignore the support programs that come with Elm. A few of the most useful ones are the following:

`autoreply` answers all your incoming e-mail with an automatic reply. This is good if your mailbox is backlogged, or if you go on vacation or otherwise want to let people know that you're behind on reading your mail.

`filter` saves your incoming e-mail to different incoming mailboxes, deletes it, forwards it, and so on, based on the content of the e-mail message or its headers. This is useful if you subscribe to a mailing list or get lots of mail on a particular subject.

`frm` lists From and Subject headers for each message, one line per message. This is useful for quickly checking your incoming e-mail.

messages gives a quick count of the messages in your mailbox.

newmail and wnewmail are programs that immediately inform you when new e-mail has arrived. wnewmail runs in a window.

readmsg takes selected messages from a mailbox and sends them to standard output. This is good for quickly extracting and processing mail messages in bizarre ways.

There's even a Usenet group for Elm: comp.mail.Elm.

PINE

Another mail program available for UNIX systems is PINE. PINE stands for **P**rogram for **I**nternet **N**ews and **E**-mail. (Early in its history, some referred to PINE as **P**ine **I**s **N**ot **E**lm, since the original source code for Elm was used as a starting point!) It was developed at the University of Washington with naive users in mind. These users could navigate the program without fear of making mistakes. Along with a forgiving user interface, it contains a number of options for sophisticated users too.

PINE's's user interface is very similar to Elm's. However, the number of features is less over-whElming, and there's a concerted effort to keep the same keys performing the same functions from screen to screen. PINE even comes with its own text editor, Pico, which can be used as a general text editor. For the faint of heart, it's certainly an improvement over emacs or vi.

Pre-compiled versions of PINE are available for certain UNIX platforms. You can anonymous ftp to ftp://ftp.cac.washington.edu and look in the /mail directory. Pre-compiled versions for AIX3.2, HP/UX 9.01, Linux, NeXTstep, Solaris 2.2 (SPARC), and SunOS 4.1.3 (SPARC) are available in the unix-bin subdirectory under the pine directory. If not, you'll need to compile your own version. The source code is available in the pine.tar.z file.

To customize PINE's behavior, edit the file .pinerc in your home directory. The configuration items are explained well. There's not a lot to do here, but make sure you set personal-name, smtp-server (if you're using SMTP), and inbox-path (usually /usr/spool/mail/yourid).

Remote Mail Clients

The "Common UNIX Mail Programs" section has generally assumed that you will run your mail program on the computer that contains your Internet mail. In many cases, however, you will wish to do all your mail reading on your personal computer, both because you may be charged for all the time you are logged onto your mail account, and because the programs on Macs and PCs are much friendlier than those on many UNIX systems.

What you want is a program that will call the system that receives your mail (or that will connect to it by whatever means necessary), grab all your new mail, and disconnect. Then you can read your mail at your leisure and enter new messages. If there are any new messages, the program should call your mail system and give it the new messages for delivery. As you have probably guessed, these programs exist and are known as mail clients.

The big difference between this approach and the "read your mail on your Internet computer" approach is that your mailbox is kept on your personal computer instead of on the Internet computer.

Obviously, there has to be a way for your mail client to talk to your Internet computer and transfer messages. There are several standards for this.

SMTP–Simple Mail Transfer Protocol

Simple Mail Transfer Protocol (SMTP), or some variation of it (such as Extended SMTP) is used by computers on the Internet that handle mail to transfer messages from one machine to another. It's a one-way protocol—the SMTP client contacts the SMTP server and gives it a mail message.

Most mail client programs support SMTP for sending outgoing mail, simply because it's very easy to implement. Few mail clients support SMTP for incoming mail, because normally your mail computer can't contact your personal computer at will to give it mail. It's possible if your personal computer happens to be permanently networked to the mail computer via EtherNet, for instance, or if your mail computer knows how to use a modem to call your personal computer, but in most cases this isn't done.

POP3 (Post Office Protocol 3)

The standard protocol used by most mail clients to retrieve mail from a remote system is the post office protocol POP3. This protocol enables your mail client to grab new messages, delete messages, and do other things necessary for reading your incoming mail. POP only requires a rather "stupid" mail server in the sense that your mail client needs to have most of the intelligence needed for managing mail. It's a very simple protocol, and is offered by most mail clients.

POP3 is somewhat insecure in that your mail client needs to send your account name and password every time it calls. The more you do this, the greater the chance that someone with a network snooper might get both. (We're not trying to scare you, but it's possible.) An extension known as APOP uses a secure algorithm known as MD5 to encrypt your password for each session.

Finally, note that standard POP3 has no way to send mail back to the mail server. There is an optional extension to POP3 known as XTND XMIT that allows this, but both the client and the server have to support it. Generally, a mail client uses SMTP to send messages and POP3 to retrieve them.

Desirable Features in Mail Clients

Here are some useful features to look for when shopping for a mail client:

- **Delete on retrieve.** The client should have the option to automatically delete mail on the server after it has been downloaded. If you only read mail using your client, you don't want a huge mail file building up on the server. On the other hand, if you only occasionally use your mail client you might want to leave your mail messages on the host so you can access them with your UNIX mail program.

- **Header only retrieve.** You can tell quite a bit about a message just by looking at the message header. If reconnecting to your server is easy, you might want to have your mail program download only the header. Then, if you want to see the actual text of the message, the program will download that. This can be very useful if someone mails you a large file—you can be spared the time it takes to download the whole thing to your computer.

- **Name server support.** A machine name such as `mailserv.bozo.edu` is actually just a logical name for a computer that is truly identified by its IP number, something that looks like 130.029.13.12. Obviously, the machine name is easier to remember, and if anything happens to `mailserv` that requires the machine to move to a new IP address (such as a hardware upgrade), the administrators can map the name to the new IP address and you won't even notice. Those who are accessing the machine by number will have to find the new number and enter it. To turn the name into an IP number, though, your client needs to be smart enough to use a domain name server, which keeps track of what numbers go to what names.

- **POP3.** This is the standard way for a mail client to retrieve mail from the mail server. If your client doesn't support this, it darn well better have some way to retrieve mail that your mail server understands (for example, IMAP).

- **Retrieve on start-up.** The client should enable you to immediately contact your mail server and retrieve all unread mail whenever you start it, because this will probably be your most common operation.

- **Separate SMTP server.** In some cases you will need to use a different machine to send mail (using SMTP) than you use to retrieve mail (using POP3). A good mail client should let you specify a different server for each.

- **SMTP.** This is the standard way for a mail client to give mail to the mail server. If your mail client doesn't understand SMTP, it should have some special protocol that your mail server understands to do the same thing (unless you don't want to send mail, of course). Some mail clients support SMTP connections as a way to receive messages, which can be useful if you expect your computer to be hooked up to the network all the time.

- **TCP/IP, SLIP, or PPP.** Your client should be able to access whatever network your mail host is on. Otherwise you'll just be talking to yourself. TCP/IP is the most common network protocol mail programs are likely to need, and PPP is becoming more popular. SLIP, on the other hand, is becoming less popular. If you have a SLIP or PPP driver that looks like TCP/IP to your mail program, all it needs is TCP/IP support.

- **Timed retrieval.** The client should be able to automatically connect to your mail server and check for new mail every so often, and beep if it finds new mail. If you're calling in using a modem, you might want to make this every few hours, or even once a day, but if you're directly networked with the server (perhaps via EtherNet), you might want to check every five minutes.

■ **Other mail items.** A good mail client makes reading your mail as easy as possible. You shouldn't have to give up any of the features you enjoy under a UNIX mail program. These include a good text editor, header field filtering, an address book (aliases), and multiple mailboxes.

A Few Mail Clients

Again, there are dozens of mail clients available. If your organization has standardized on one of the big ones, such as cc:Mail, Microsoft Mail, Lotus Notes, or BeyondMail, you're already familiar with one. These clients are a bit more "homegrown" on the Internet and have at least a demo version you can try first, before you buy the real (and expensive) program.

Eudora

Eudora is a full-featured mail client for Macs or PCs running Windows. It comes in two sub-flavors: Version 1 of Eudora is free, and Version 2 and above are commercial. Obviously, Version 2 has nifty features not available in 1, but 1 is pretty powerful by itself.

Eudora is fully windows-, menu-, and icon-driven, so you are bound to like this program. Eudora pretty much has it all—features galore. The only thing we could ask for is a native OS/2 version...

You can download a copy of Eudora Lite software for Macintosh and Windows platforms by pointing your Web browser at `http://www.eudora.com/freeware`. To use Eudora Lite, you must have a mail account on a POP server to receive mail, and access to an SMTP server to send mail.

Eudora Pro Mail is sold in a variety of pricing plans, starting at $89.00 for a single user license. Check out the QualComm website at `http://www.qualcomm.com` for more information, or call 1-800-2-Eudora.

Pegasus Mail

Pegasus Mail runs on Novell and supports MHS and SMTP. It has DOS, Windows, and Macintosh versions, which gives you a wide range of platforms with a single program. There are a number of utilities available for use with it, such as Mercury, which is an SMTP gateway for Novell. It's fairly flexible in allowing you to set up user-defined mail gateways and has a large features list.

It's got its own text editor, which is integrated with the rest of the program, although if you're attached to your text editor (Ron couldn't give up QEdit), you can define your own external editor.

To find all the versions and add-on utilities, you can access the Web site `http://risc.ua.edu/pub/network/pegasus`. The software is free! However, there is a charge for printed documentation. Please see the Web site `http://risc.ua.edu/pub/network/pegasus/FAQs/manuals.faq` for more information. You can contact David Harris by fax in New Zealand at (+64) 3 453-6612.

This is a DOS version of the UNIX PINE mail program. You can have the same mail interface on your UNIX and DOS platforms. PINE's big limitation is that it doesn't support POP3—it only supports IMAP and SMTP. For more information on PINE, see the "Common UNIX Mail Programs" section where the UNIX version is discussed.

To get it, anonymous ftp to `ftp://ftp.cac.washington.edu` and look in the `/mail/pine/pcpine` directory. Grab the file that's appropriate for your networking software: 32-bit Windows and NT (`pcp_32.zip`), 16-bit Windows version 3.x (`pcp_w16.zip`), FTP Inc's PC-TCP (`pcp_pct.zip`), Novell's LAN Workplace for DOS (`pcp_lwp.zip`), Sun's PC-NFS (`pcp_pcn.zip`),and the WATTCP/Packet Driver (`pcp_wat.zip`). It should be noted that the Winsock versions are not complete Windows application, with a detailed graphical user interface (GUI). The interface is similar to the UNIX and DOS interfaces with a modest GUI.

Simeon

Simeon, formerly known as ECSMail, is impressive for its wide range of support. It includes not only a mail client, but a mail transport and handling service known as Simeon MessageStore, so you can build a complete mail system. It includes a number of features, including sharing of user documents, address books, and folders, as well as cross-platform compatibility and Kerberos and PGP security options. The server currently runs in Solaris, AIX, IRIX, HP/UX, Digital UNIX, SunOS, and Linux environments. The client is available on Windows, Macintosh, and UNIX environents. We're talking enterprise-wide solution here, if you're into that level of standardization.

For more information, visit ESYS Corporation at `http://www.esys.com`.

Other Mail Programs/Clients

This isn't all that's available for mail, by a long shot. Read the Usenet group `comp.mail.misc` for more information.

Mailing Lists

With e-mail you can carry on a conversation with another person. But why not with three others? Easy enough—just use the Cc header or specify multiple recipients on the To header. What about hundreds? Well, that might be tough. But what if there were enough interest in something (such as the band REM) that someone agreed to serve as a central dispatch point? All mail to that account would be sent to all other people in the discussion. This is known as a mailing list, and they are quite popular. The REM list mentioned has over 800 subscribers.

Clutter

The first thing you have to realize is that when you join (subscribe to) a mailing list, all of a sudden you're going to have a lot of messages in your mailbox. Can you handle the extra time it's going to take to read these new messages? Are you paying for mail? Many people don't comprehend exactly what they're getting into when they sign up for a mailing list. Remember to save the instructions on how to un-subscribe from the group, so you don't send your un-subscribe request to all the members of the group and feel like a fool.

Finding Lists

First you need to find some lists. Every month several informative postings are made to the Usenet group news.answers, describing hundreds of mailing lists and how to subscribe to them. For example, Stephanie da Silva posts "Publicly Accessible Mailing Lists." If you have Usenet access, news.answers is your best bet. Perhaps some of the people you correspond with know of some lists.

If neither approach works, you can use the uga.cc.uga.edu mailserver described in the following section.

LISTSERV Sites

LISTSERVers are nifty automatic programs that handle much of the drudgery involved in maintaining a mailing list. There are several such LISTSERVs, but you need only one to get started. We suggest you use listserv@uga.cc.uga.edu.

Others include listserv@mizzou1.missouri.edu, listserv@jhuvm.bitnet, listserv@vm1.nodak.edu, listserv@ucsd.edu, listserv@unl.edu, LISTSERV@PSUVM.PSU.EDU, and LISTSERV@SJSUVM1.SJSU.EDU.

Commands to these sites are simple. You can give a new instruction on each line of the body if you like, although generally most of your requests will consist of a single line. To start with, try sending mail to listserv@uga.cc.uga.edu with only the text help in the body of the message (the subject doesn't matter). You should get back a list of valid commands. Probably the most interesting for you will be listserv refcard, which returns a reference card and lists global, which returns a big list of all known mailing lists on many LISTSERVers—it's over 300,000 bytes. You're in mailing list heaven! If that's too big, try just lists.

Joining and Dropping

If your mailing list is managed by a LISTSERVer, joining a list is easy. Send mail to listserv@domain, with the following message line:

SUB *LISTNAME Firstname Lastname*

LISTNAME is the name of the list, such as HUMOR. *Firstname* and *Lastname* are your first and last names.

To sign off the list, use this:

SIGNOFF *LISTNAME*

Do not send your un-subscribe request to the mailing list itself. You'll just irritate people and they'll laugh at you.

If you would rather get one mailing a day—consisting of all the posts to the mailing list in one big chunk—rather than receiving dozens of little messages during the day, use this:

SET *LISTNAME* DIGEST

To get each piece as it is sent, use this:

```
SET LISTNAME MAIL
```

There are other commands—the `help` command should get them for you.

If the mailing list isn't being handled by a LISTSERVer, you're at the mercy of the mailing list maintainer as to how subscriptions are handled.

Generally, the address to send messages to for a mailing list is this:

```
listname@domain
```

The address to send messages to for subscribing and un-subscribing is this:

```
listname-request@domain
```

However, you can't always count on these. Sigh. In this case you have to rely on the instructions for the specific list, which you need to get from the maintainer or a friend.

Automatic Mail Sorting

We're not going to go into too much detail about mail sorting because it's a rather complex subject, but sometimes you get to the point where you can't treat your incoming mail file as a single entity.

We get literally hundreds of messages a day, and we would go insane if we didn't use a program known as a mail filter. These look at your incoming mail, and based on criteria you set regarding the contents of header items or message text, they sort the mail into several mailboxes before you even see them.

For instance, Ron subscribes to several mailing lists. He routes messages from each of these into a separate mailbox for reading at his leisure. He has Usenet voting ballots arriving all the time—these go into a special voting file for processing by the voting software. Everything that's left goes into my general mailbox for normal reading.

Actually, mail filters can often do more than this. You can use them to selectively forward mail to other users, or to send automatic responses to certain messages. You can even have them send only a single informational message to anyone who mails you while you're on vacation, no matter how many messages they send you during that time.

The drawback to a filter program is that they can be tough to set up, unless you're using a mail client with the capability built in (for example, Eudora). You need to carefully check your configuration files to make sure you aren't accidentally dropping messages on the floor!

procmail

`procmail` is probably the most popular of the mail filters. You have quite a bit of control over your messages, and can even pass them through other programs, such as a formatter, before they are saved. It can execute other programs on demand, and can be used to run simple mailing lists or mail servers. It's been extensively tested, it is stable, and it is fast. Be careful, though, that you don't accidentally tell it to send some of your mail into a black hole.

You can get the latest version by anonymous ftp to `ftp://ftp.informatik.rwth-aachen.de` as `/pub/packages/procmail`.

deliver

Although `procmail` is the king of the hill for mail filter programs, we personally like `deliver`. You write shell scripts to handle all incoming messages. This requires more work on your part, usually, than would `procmail`, but it's very clean, almost infinitely flexible, and limits what you can do with your e-mail only to how well you can program scripts. The speed shouldn't be too much of a concern on that fast machine of yours.

We found `deliver` by anonymous ftp at `sunsite.unc.edu` as `ftp://sunsite.unc.edu/pub/Linux/distributions/slackware/contrib/deliver.tgz`.

mailagent

`mailagent` is another well-known e-mail filter. This one is written in the Perl language, which again means that you can do anything with your e-mail by extending mailagent yourself (if you know Perl). It comes with quite a few built-in features. We would suggest this if you know Perl. Anonymous ftp to `ftp://ftp.foretune.co.jp` and get `/pub/network/mail/mailagent`.

Elm

`Elm` comes with a support program named `filter`, which does mail filtering.

Usenet

As described in the introduction, Usenet is the world's largest electronic discussion forum. One of the most popular features of the Internet, it allows people all over the world to discuss topics and exchange ideas on a wide variety of subjects.

One way to describe Usenet is in terms of e-mail. Think of your mailbox, with all its new and old messages. Imagine what it might be like if everyone on Internet could read that mailbox, enter new messages, and leave replies. Now imagine having 20,000 mailboxes. This is analogous to how Usenet works.

Usenet is a huge public messaging system. It is divided into thousands of discussions of different subjects—each separate piece is known as a newsgroup, or group. When someone enters a message while "in" a group, that message goes to all other Usenet sites in the world, and people reading that same group can read the message and reply to it if they care to. Generally, there are dozens of different conversations (also known as "threads") going on in any particular group—each is distinguished by a subject name, much like the Subject in a mail message. There are thousands of new messages posted each day.

Usenet is commonly thought of as being the same thing as the Internet, but they're not the same thing. The Internet is an international network of computers tied together via dedicated lines. Usenet is just one of the services that uses the Internet. If you're familiar with bulletin board systems (BBSes), you might think of the Internet as the BBS hardware, and Usenet as the message bases.

Not all computers on the Internet have Usenet (it can take a lot of space!). Not all computers carrying Usenet groups are on the Internet—like e-mail, some systems call Internet systems to exchange Usenet messages.

UseNet Is Usenet Is NetNews

Frankly, capitalization standards on Internet are quite relaxed. You can call it Usenet; you can call it UseNet. People will know what you mean. If you call it UsEnEt, people will start edging nervously for the exits. You can even refer to it by the ancient moniker Netnews (or NetNews). People will understand what you mean.

You can call the subject groupings into which Usenet is divided groups or newsgroups. Please don't call them BBoards, as, for some reason, this upsets some inhabitants.

Usenet Is Too Big

Usenet comprises gigabytes of new posts a day and thousands of groups. Your goal is to find as much possible useful information on subjects that interest you in the time you allot for yourself each day.

Usenet Is an Information Bonanza

If you're interested in something, it's probably talked about in some group on Usenet, and the amount of information is staggering. It can quickly become your prime information source for several of your interest areas.

Usenet Is a Noise Overload

That information is buried among lots of noise—things you aren't interested in or posts that are of no use to anybody and may even be designed to confuse. Your goal is to separate the wheat from the chaff with maximum efficiency—hopefully keeping the wheat.

Usenet Is a Controlled Anarchy

Usenet isn't an anarchy in the popular sense of being total chaos. But while anarchy excludes outside control, it doesn't preclude self-control, and Usenet is a Web of written and unwritten agreements on the proper rules of behavior. Your goal is to avoid violating these codes of behavior until you know enough about them to decide when they can be broken.

Usenet Messages

Usenet messages are much like the Internet mail messages described earlier in this chapter—they consist of a header, which has information about the message, and the body, which has the actual message. They even use the same format as mail messages, and most of the same headers are valid. There are a few new ones, which are covered in the following sections.

The Usenet Distribution Model

Every computer that gets Usenet keeps a database of Usenet messages. When a new message is entered, it is sent to neighboring Usenet sites using NNTP (Network News Transfer Protocol). These distribute the post to other sites, until it is on every machine on Usenet. There are various mechanisms to prevent a message from showing up on the same machine more than once, which we don't need to get into here. Only occasionally does a broken machine (usually a FidoNet gateway) regurgitate old articles back onto the Net.

Because posts can take different paths to reach different machines, there's no guarantee that you'll see a specific post before you see the reply to the post. For example, someone posts a message from Machine A, which sends the post through slow Machine B to get to your machine. It also sends the post to another machine, C, which gets it immediately. Someone there replies to it quickly, and C sends out the post to its neighbors, including Machine D. Machine D sends the reply on to you, where you see it immediately. In the meantime, the original post still hasn't gotten past Machine B to your computer. This is fairly common, although the scenario is usually more complicated. Don't be alarmed.

We said that all machines get all posts. Well, sort of—because Usenet is so huge, many sites only carry a subset of all the available groups. A site won't get posts for groups it doesn't care about, or if it does, it won't keep them. In addition, there's something called a Distribution header that you can put in your message to try to restrict its distribution to a geographical area, such as San Diego. This is useful for messages that affect only San Diego.

Newsgroup Names

Newsgroups are named like this:

```
comp.sys.ibm.pc.games.action
```

This is a hierarchy reading down from left to right. Reading the group name, you have a computer group for computer systems from IBM, the PCs to be exact. You're talking about games for those systems, more specifically action games.

Here's another one:

```
talk.politics.guns
```

You have a group for talk about politics, more specifically gun control. We'll talk more about these hierarchies later.

The newsgroup with which your post is associated is given in the header of the message, in the Newsgroups item. It looks like this:

```
Newsgroups: news.announce.newgroups
```

Unlike traditional bulletin board systems, each post can go in multiple groups! If we do this:

```
Newsgroups: alt.usenet.future,news.groups
```

my post will appear in both groups. This is known as crossposting. While you should know it is possible, you shouldn't actually do this until you've looked around a while, because frivolous crossposting is frowned on.

In fact, there's another header that can be used to send any replies back to a specific group. For instance, you might make a wide informational post to several groups, but specify that the discussion (if any) should be only in a single group. This is the `Followup-To` header. Together, the headers look like this:

```
Newsgroups: rec.arts.comics.misc,rec.arts.comics.strips,
rec.arts.comics.animation
Followup-To: rec.arts.comics.animation
```

Remember from the e-mail header discussion that one header can spread over several lines, as long as succeeding lines are indented. That's what you did to split `Newsgroups` over two lines. All replies to the post will go to `rec.arts.comics.animation`, unless the person replying overrides that.

Crossposting can be abused, but more on that later.

Threads

An original post and all the replies to it are considered to be a single "thread" of conversation. This can actually look more like a Christmas tree than a straight line, as there are replies to replies, and replies to those replies, which branch off until each sub-branch dies of finality or boredom.

Each Usenet message has a Subject associated with it that is supposed to summarize the contents of the message (although this is often not the case). One way to track a thread is to note the message subjects, which those who reply to the post are supposed to preserve until the discussion wanders too far from the original subject. The only way to fully keep track of threads is to use a threaded newsreader, which is discussed in the next section.

Newsreaders

The first item of business is which program you will use to read Usenet. Your choice of these programs (known as newsreaders) can hugely impact how you read the Net, how much information you get out of it, and how much garbage you have to sludge through.

rn (readnews)

rn is free, so there's a good chance the system you use to read mail has it, and a good chance that it will be offered to you as your default newsreader. Avoid using it if you can!

Back when rn was first written, one person could read every single message posted to Usenet and still have time for a life. It reflects those simpler times—its default is to dive in and show you all the messages in the group, one at a time.

This sounds reasonable, but it's a fact that the majority of the posts on most newsgroups you will read are of no interest to you. There will come a time when you no longer wish to slog through every post on the group and become choosy about which posts you read. rn does not let you do this easily. Since popular groups can get over 100 messages a day, rn's preference for showing you every single message really wastes your time.

Message Overview and Threading

Just how much of your time rn wastes is evident the first time you run another news program that first gives you an overview of the group. It provides you with a summary line for each post, just as a mail program does—it gives you the poster's name, the subject, and possibly the message size. Scroll through the pages of summaries and choose which posts look interesting. When you're done choosing, read the posts you've selected.

This is already a major shift in concept—instead of having to read everything to decide what you don't want to read, you are choosing which few posts look interesting.

Now we'll add another concept to that—the newsreader should keep track of which posts are related to each other and group them, so you can select or ignore whole groups of posts at once. It can do this by noticing the threads and subject names mentioned before.

These two changes account for an almost unbelievable difference in speed between a good threaded newsreader and something like rn. Now that we've gotten good at determining which threads look promising and which don't, we can read Usenet literally 100 times faster than I could before. We'll recommend some right after this…

Kill Files

What if you knew a particular subject were of no interest to you, and that you would never read a post by that name again? It's a waste of time for the newsreader to even offer it to you. This goes doubly for certain people who do nothing but generate noise on Usenet. It'd be nice never to see any of their posts.

This is the purpose of a kill file. In its most primitive form, you give it a subject or poster whom you never wish to hear from again. Usually you'll be allowed a little bit of fine-tuning—you may wish to kill that subject only in one particular newsgroup.

In a group where over half the discussion is about something you don't care about (for instance, a particular author on a fantasy group), having the newsreader kill all articles relating to that author can save you time and make you less likely to lose valuable articles in the crush.

There's also the opposite of a kill file. If you know you will want to read every posting on a particular subject or from a particular person, a selection file lets you have the newsreader automatically mark them for reading. This isn't quite as common as the kill file.

Which Newsreader?

This is one of those religious preference questions, similar to "What's the best editor?" We would say that any newsreader that has the following features is a contender:

- Offers a message overview that lets you select messages to read before actually reading any.

- Enables you to group posts together by common subject and/or thread.

- Lets you specify authors or subjects that will be automatically killed by the newsreader so you never see them. You should be able to do this for one group or for all groups.

- Lets you do the opposite—automatically select certain authors or subjects.

The rest is just gravy, although we're tempted to add "Is very configurable" to the list.

Unfortunately, compiling and configuring a new newsreader can be a very hairy business, especially if you're new to Usenet. For now, you might have to use whatever your system has available—if there's nothing but rn, pester your administrator.

NN (No News)

NN is fast, flexible, very configurable, has very nice kill and selection options, sorts messages in several ways, and offers several ways to manage the old messages. It even has its own group, `news.software.nn`. This is definitely worth a look.

Other UNIX Readers

Other UNIX readers that are worth looking at (if your site offers them) are TRN, STRN, and TIN. TIN happens to have the largest number of UNIX readers at this time. They meet or exceed the criteria given. You can also read the Usenet group `news.software.readers` for the latest information.

Netscape

The Netscape Web browser provides facilities for tracking, replying to, and initiating user group postings. To access a particular news group, invoke the "File" and "Open Location" menu items, and enter the URL for the news group. The URL for a news group consists of the word news, followed by a colon (:) and the name of the group. For example, to access the Oracle database news group, you would enter `news:comp.databases.oracle`. You can even use an asterisk (*) to display all items at a particular level in the hierarchy. For example, the URL `news:comp.databases.*` would list all database discussion groups.

When you have opened a particular group, a set of command buttons appear that perform some common Usenet functions. For example, buttons are available to subscribe/unsubscribe to groups, as well as initiate and receive postings.

When you subscribe to a newsgroup, the entry is maintained for future use by the Netscape software. The list of all of your newsgroups can be accessed by selecting the "Directory" and "Go To Newsgroups" menu options.

Other Readers

For other systems, you should be reading the Usenet groups `comp.os.msdos.mail-news` and `news.software.readers`. There are, most likely, programs out there for your system. For instance, there's Trumpet for DOS and WinTrumpet for Windows. If you have a complete TCP/IP package, you might want to see if it includes a mail reader (other than `rn`).

Offline Readers

Just as you can use a mail client to do your mail processing off-line, you can use an off-line reader to do your Usenet processing off-line. This is useful if you're paying by the minute for your connect time. See the group `alt.usenet.offline-reader` for help with these.

Finding Your Groups

There are literally thousands of newsgroups in which you can participate. This section helps you find the groups in which you are interested.

The Hierarchies

As mentioned earlier, group names are arranged in hierarchies from left to right. The left item is known as the top-level of the hierarchy. In the case of a group such as this:

```
alt.tv.animaniacs
```

it is said that the group is "in the `alt` hierarchy" (or "`alt.` hierarchy"). The Net is organized into eight major hierarchies, one anarchic hierarchy, and a bunch of smaller, less important hierarchies.

The Big Eight Hierarchies

The big eight hierarchies are the following:

`comp.`	**Computer topics.** This ranges from programming to hardware to peripherals to folklore. Most popular computer systems and operating systems have their own set of groups here.
`misc.`	**Miscellaneous.** When nobody can figure out where to put a new group, it often ends up under `misc.`. For example, the `misc.jobs` groups don't clearly belong in any of the other six hierarchies, so they go under `misc.`.
`news.`	**The business of Usenet.** This is where people talk about Usenet administration, propose new groups, and argue about when Usenet is going to die of its own excesses.

`rec.`	**Recreational topics.** This is where most of the hobbyist stuff, such as `rec.crafts.jewelry`, goes. It also contains artistic and music discussions, crafts, and more in that vein.
`sci.`	**Science.** This is where the math and physics types hang out. Medical, too, such as `sci.med.radiology`.
`soc.`	**Social topics.** This is a grab bag of many cultural groups for different regions, such as `soc.culture.chile`, social research groups, religious discussion groups, and alternative lifestyle groups. It's something of a milder version of the talk hierarchy.
`talk.`	**Heated debate.** Incredibly vicious personal attacks by people (most of whom seemingly haven't even heard of the concept of "critical thinking") that go on interminably about all the things you would expect—politics and religion. See `talk.politics.mideast`, for example. No debate here is ever really ended.
`humanities.`	**Literature and fine arts.** This hierarchy contains a wealth of discussion regarding music, philosophy, and fine art. For example, see `humanities.lit.author.shakespeare`.

These hierarchies are sometimes known as Usenet proper and are considered by many news administrators to be the only "real" hierarchies. For a new group to be created in any of these eight hierarchies, it has to go through a group interest polling procedure that discourages overly frivolous group creation. More on this later.

The Sewer of alt.

Actually, some of my favorite groups are in the `alt.` hierarchy, but it has a mixed reputation. Unlike the big eight hierarchies, anyone who cares to send a group creation message for a new group can make an `.alt` group. This is often followed by someone else sending out a group removal message if they consider the group outrageous, but still it's a lot looser than the big eight groups. For instance, one group in the `alt.` hierarchy is `alt.elvis.sightings`. The `alt.` hierarchy is also controversial because groups such as `alt.sex.stories` reside here, and because of the `alt.binaries.pictures` groups, which involve huge amounts of message space chewed up by pictures. Because of all the hassles involved with `alt.`, many sites don't carry any of the groups.

We consider that a shame, because `alt.` is also a haven for groups that can't find a home in the big eight hierarchies. For instance, discussions of TV shows are generally considered transitory, since interest in the show will probably eventually die out. For this reason, people are unwilling to vote to place a group for a show such as "Twin Peaks" in the big eight hierarchies, so they end up in the fertile `alt.tv` section of the `alt.` hierarchy, where they are the source of years of enjoyment to many (we feel like a commercial).

`alt.` is also nice because groups can be quickly created, unlike in the big eight, where it takes two months. So a group such as `alt.current-events.la-quake` can be created overnight in response to special situations.

`alt.` has become somewhat more organized in recent years. Anyone can create a new group, but anyone can also send out a removal message, and there are several `alt.` volunteer police who will summarily do so if the group hasn't been proposed on `alt.config` or if it's clearly a joke group. This has cut down on the number of "triple-word" joke groups, such as `alt.french.captain.borg.borg.borg`, which were first made popular by the group `alt.swedish.chef.bork.bork.bork`. But it isn't the big eight by a long shot, and we'd hate to see the day when it is.

The Other Hierarchies

Anybody can create a hierarchy for a specialized reason (all you have to do is persuade other sites to carry the groups), and there are often good reasons for doing so. Especially useful are hierarchies for regional groups. For instance, there are many `ca.` groups for discussion of California topics (for example, `ca.politics`). This keeps local stuff where the rest of the Net doesn't have to read it. Cities that have active Net communities often have their own hierarchies, such as `sdnet.` for San Diego. The same goes for universities (`ucsd.`) and companies.

There are other hierarchies that are intended to be more widely spread, but are limited for other reasons. Many of the BITNET mailing lists are echoed on Usenet in the `bit.` groups. Much child education discussion goes on in the `k12.` groups.

A few hierarchies have made a bid for the big eight but have failed. `trial.` and `us.` both failed from lack of interest, although at this time people are trying to resurrect the `us.` hierarchy.

Where Do I Go?

Back to your original question—how do you know where to go for a particular subject? There are several ways.

First, your newsreader may be smart enough to find part of a group name. If I tell NN to go to group `beer`, for instance, it asks me if I mean `alt.beer` or `rec.food.drink.beer`. In this way I just found two groups, and if I look for brewing I'll find more.

Dave Lawrence posts "List of Active Newsgroups" and "Alternative Newsgroup Hierarchies" to `news.groups` and `news.answers`. This is the mother lode—all "official" groups (although with `alt.` "official" doesn't mean much), each with a short description. Get it if you can.

Your newsreader probably has a way to show you a list of all groups. This might take some digging to find. (It's `:show groups all` in NN.)

Next, you can look through a file your newsreader leaves in your home directory, named `.newsrc` or something similar. This is just a list of group names, but they might give you some hints.

You can always ask for help on the group `news.groups.questions`, which is just for this sort of question.

Netiquette

This is perhaps the most important piece of this Usenet section. You can muddle through the rest, but your use of netiquette (Net etiquette—more geek hilarity) determines how you are perceived by others on the Net—and a reputation can be a very hard thing lose. You may be shocked to engage in a debate and find someone dredging up a post that you submitted six months ago.

Newbie

If you're reading this, you're probably a newbie. That's Usenet slang for "new person." It's not a bad thing to be a newbie, nor is it a hanging offense (or even something most people will look down at you for). People just treat newbies with a bit more caution, because they know that people who haven't grasped the local customs are more likely to commit a *faux pas*.

Even if you've been posting on your local BBS or FidoNet for 10 years, you're still a newbie. The customs are unique. Welcome to the Jungle; please obey our laws.

Newbie No More

The best way to learn the customs of Usenet is just to read it without posting for six weeks. You also get the feel of each group—each one has its own special ambiance.

The length of time you should read before posting varies according to what you feel comfortable with. Most people on Usenet are actually full-time "lurkers"—they just read and don't post. Sometimes this is by choice, sometimes it's due to software or administrative limitations. But it's estimated that there are more than 100 readers of a group for every person who posts to it.

Signature Files

Most newsreaders enable you to attach a signature to every post you make. It takes the contents of the file .signature in your home directory and attaches it to the end of the post. This is intended to be used for identification purposes—perhaps your name and place of work if it's not obvious from the header. Or sometimes it's used for disclaimers.

By far, the most common use is as a small personality statement—this usually involves your name, Internet address, a favorite quote, and maybe a small picture drawn with text characters. We often identify people by their signatures, rather than by looking at the header, since they're immediately recognizable by general look.

Excessive Quoting

Because of the nature of the Net, it's easy to lose track of where you were in a conversation or debate. If someone just replies, "That's the stupidest thing I ever heard!" you may have a hard time determining just who they were talking about or which side they're taking. Comments need a bit of context.

For that reason, most news software "quotes" the entire previous message into your editor for you. It does this by putting a quote character, usually a >, to the left of each line of text. You are supposed to trim this message down to the bare essentials necessary for context to be established for your following comments.

A lot of people seem to be incapable of grasping this concept. In the most heinous cases, they quote pages and pages of a previous message, including the person's signature, only to add a single line comment such as "This is stupid." Please trim your quotes. It means less space spent storing redundant data, it means people can read your message quicker, which makes them happier, and it makes your comments much more understandable.

It's up to your personal preference, but we've generally found that we never need more than about four lines of text from the previous message for any point we wish to make. In responding to a complex message it's quite acceptable to quote some text, reply to it, quote some more text, reply to it, and so on. You can even quote the entire message doing this in a few cases, but since you're doing it to establish context for each of your quotes, it's considered acceptable.

Also, watch how deep the quotes go. Someone quoting your message will also quote text you quoted—that text then has a >> in front of it. Too many levels of this gets confusing and makes it more likely that someone will be mis-attributed.

One final caution—while your quoting doesn't have to preserve the full context of the person's message, using "selective quoting" to make it appear that someone argued a point they did not make is also frowned upon.

Pyramid Schemes

Occasionally, you'll see something about "Make Money Fast," or some other type of get rich scheme. Don't Do It!

This chain letter never goes away, and since the people who post it tend to be very obnoxious about where they post it (some even post it to every single group on Usenet—think about that), people are not tolerant of this at all. You'll get a few thousand upset e-mail messages that will probably shut down your machine and make your administrator less than amiable. Also, it may be illegal.

Excessive Crossposting

Earlier, we showed how to make a post go to several groups at once, which is known as crossposting. Crossposting is hardly ever necessary, and only once in a blue moon is it necessary to crosspost to more than four groups at once except for special informational Usenet postings.

Newbies usually mess up on crossposting a plea for help—they're not sure where to ask for it, so they crosspost to any group that looks like it might have something to do with it. They always manage to hit a few inappropriate groups, and between the complaints about the crossposting and the alienation of those who might have helped due to the crossposting, the newbie doesn't get the question answered.

Take the time to look at a few messages in each group to see if it looks appropriate. If you find one that looks right, post to that one group asking your question. You can note that you're not 100 percent sure if you're in the right place and ask for better directions. People are usually very friendly to this type of posting. And, of course, you can ask on the group `news.groups.questions` where you should direct your questions.

Read the FAQ!

One day, the people of Usenet noted that new users all tended to ask the same few questions. They decided to create a Frequently Asked Questions List (FAQ—the L just didn't sound good), which would present the answers to these questions, just preventing them from being asked over and over and over and over and over and over and, well…

That worked pretty well, and now many groups have FAQs. This means that if you pop up on a group and ask a question that is in the FAQ, you're going to get some very negative responses ("Read the FAQing FAQ!") If you enter a new group for the purpose of asking a question, make sure you look for a post with "FAQ" in the title. If you find any, read them first. Your answers (and answers to questions you hadn't even thought of yet) may be in there.

If you're looking for information in general, most FAQs are posted to `news.answers`. You can go there and browse all the beautiful FAQs.

Keep the Flaming to a Minimum

In Net parlance, a flame is a heated attack on someone or something. An extended series of exchanged flames (flames are catching, it seems) is a *flamewar*.

An occasional flame is usually warranted and cleans out your system, but be careful of letting it get away with you. Some people have a reputation of being much too quick to flame—even an honest mistake might earn you a litany of your mother's dating habits from this kind of person. Others have the reputation of enjoying flaming just for the sake of doing it. Actually, there's a whole group for these people (`alt.flame`).

If you ever want to acquire a reputation as being a cool-headed, capable debater, however, watch yourself. We find it useful to let the message sit for five minutes, then come back to it. You may find, as we do, that a non-antagonistic-appearing message is actually more damaging to the other person's case. And if you watch carefully, you can see what the Net pros have learned: how to flame with a precise acetylene torch, deftly vaporizing someone's ill-thought post with facts, style, and wit. This is much more devastating than the standard "Oh, yeah? Moron!" type of argument.

Don't Bluff

Trying to pretend you know something you don't is bound for failure on the Net much more often than you might think. There are a large number of well-informed people on the Net (some seem to be virtual information sinks on certain subjects), and chances are good that someone who knows more than you do is going to call your bluff.

This extends to less drastic claims as well—if you're going to make a claim, you had better be prepared to back it up. It's not known as the Net of a Million Lies for nothing, and most users who have been there awhile tend to be a bit skeptical. And then there are the people who actively oppose your position and have the facts to argue their side…

It's somewhat sad to see someone backing down from an ill-advised position, so be careful. And if you should ever be caught in an out-and-out falsehood, you might as well start humming a funeral march.

Whew!

Looking back on that list of "Don't do this," "Beware of that" is a bit exhausting. Again, we don't want you to be afraid of Usenet—the worst that will probably happen if you do screw up royally is that someone writes you a nasty letter. Remember, you can absorb all this without risk just by reading newsgroups for a period of time before you post to them.

Usenet Miscellany

Wait, we're not done with you yet—we have so much more to give! This section contains some random bits of advice and frequently asked questions.

Creating a New Group

This one comes up often. "Hey, there's no group for discussing indigo feebles! How do I start one?"

In this case, we doubly recommend reading both `news.announce.newgroups` and `news.groups` for a three-month period before you try to create your own group. This seems extreme, but it's a whole new level of politics, written and unwritten rules, and various subtleties.

To help, you should grab "How to Create a Usenet Newsgroup" and the "Usenet Newsgroup Creation Companion" from `http://www.uvv.org`. The first is the official guidelines, the second is a helper written by Ron.

Basically, creating a new group boils down to this: You issue a Request for Discussion (RFD), crossposted to `news.announce.newgroups`, `news.groups`, and any interested groups. For more information on RFDs, see `http://www.uvv.org/rfd-info.html`. It should give the proposed name of your group, its charter, and why it should be created. Follow-up discussion will take place in `news.groups`. To facilitate this process, fill out the questionaire at `http://www.uvv.org/cfv-questions.html`. If you need any assistance, contact the Usenet group mentor program at `http://www.uvv.org/uvv/group-mentors.html`.

If the discussion yields any major changes to the name or charter, you'll need to issue a second RFD explaining the changes. This repeats until a consensus is reached.

The Call for Votes (CFV) can be held 30 days after the first RFD. You should contact the Usenet Volunteer Votetakers (UVV) at `contact@uvv.org` to have your vote run by an experienced group of neutral votetakers. The UVV will take care of the voting, which runs 22 days.

At the end of this time, the votes are tallied. If your proposed group has at least 100 more YES votes regarding its creation than it has NO votes, and if there are twice as many YES votes as NO votes, then the group passes and will be created by the `news.announce.newgroups` moderator after five days or so.

All this is a massive oversimplification, but it gives you some idea of the work involved, and the time period (two months). You might consider whether you want an `alt.` hierarchy group instead (read `alt.config`) or if you want to start a mailing list.

How Can I Get That Person Off the Net?

Uh oh…someone called you some nasty names or said something you consider offensive. Now what? Well, now you deal with it by yourself. Among the advantages of the Net is that someone with an unpopular viewpoint can't be kicked off just because their philosophy isn't in line with what the Acceptable Opinions Squad has decided are the required ways of thinking this year. This is somewhat of a disadvantage in that some people use it as just an excuse to be rude. You're an adult—you can presumably figure out some way to deal with it, such as just ignoring the person. If you go complaining to someone's administrator just because they called you a name, you're probably going to be disappointed, not to mention mocked.

There are a few situations in which it is considered okay to contact someone's administrator: if you receive an actual threat of violence and think it's serious, or if you are clearly defrauded by said person in a transaction that was arranged on the Net. You can probably see the trend here—if there was actual (or threatened) damage that occurred in the real world, you certainly might be justified.

Recommend Some Newsgroups!

We showed you earlier how to retrieve the posting of all the newsgroups and their short descriptions. We could really send our page count through the roof by just including that here, but we'll settle for recommending a few varied ones that might interest you:

`alt.binaries.*`	This is where all the pictures and other data are posted. You can get pictures, sounds, and music files among these groups.
`alt.comic.dilbert`	Discussion group for the comic strip popular in the data processing community.
`alt.fan.dave_barry`	Discussion group for humorist and syndicated columnist Dave Barry.
`alt.folklore.computers`	This is anything you wanted to know (or didn't) about the history of computers. Some of it is even true.
`alt.folklore.urban`	Randy Beaman knew this kid who drank Pop Rocks and soda at the same time, and his head exploded! Okay, bye. Folk tales…

`alt.internet.services`	This shows what's where on the Internet.
`alt.quotations`	This is just what it looks like—lots of quotations.
`alt.support.stop_smoking`	Online assistance to help you kick the habit.
`comp.lang.java`	This group discusses programming in Java, the popular programming language for the Internet.
`comp.risks`	This is the RISKS digest—examining the risks involved with technology.
`comp.sys.*`	Do you have a computer? It's probably got its own groups under `comp.sys`. Even the redoubtable HP 48 calculator has its own.
`control`	This is where newsgroup creation and removal actually takes place. It's interesting to watch if you read `alt.config` or `news.groups`.
`news.answers`	All the FAQs get posted here. It's information central.
`news.future`	Shows the future of the Net—a bit whiny, but sometimes interesting.
`news.groups`	This is for the discussion of Usenet group creation and is the focus of a lot of Usenet politics.
`news.newusers.questions`	This is just what it looks like. Ask away! Or at least read this for a while.
`news.software.readers`	Is your newsreader up to snuff?
`rec.arts.movies`	There's lots of information here about, like, movies.
`rec.humor.oracle`	This is the Usenet oracle. It's definitely something different.
`soc.genealogy`	If you are interested in tracing your roots, this group can be a big help.
`talk.politics.misc`	Newbies seem to like to talk politics, but be careful! This is one of the most cutthroat groups on the Net.

Watch Out for Pranks

You may take Usenet utterly seriously, or you may treat is as a playground for pranks. Most people fall somewhere in between, but there are a lot of people who lean towards the latter.

If you see something that seems too strange to be true, it probably is. Check the Newsgroups header line and look at the crossposts—if it's posted to a bizarre group, chances are someone's being funny. If you post a heated response, you'll just end up looking silly.

Look carefully at the Followup-To header—a favorite of those soft in the head is to send your reply to `misc.test`, `alt.dev.null`, or some totally inappropriate group. Whenever you reply to a message, you should always get in the habit of noticing which Newsgroups your message is being sent to so you don't get caught by something like this.

This baiting of the gullible is known as "trolling" and is quite a pastime on some groups, such as `alt.folklore.urban`. Basically, there are subjects that have come up so often that they're beyond Frequently Asked Questions and into "Good Grief!" status. After the subject has been dormant for awhile, someone who's been on the group awhile will make a post that ostensibly asks for information or makes a claim related to the subject. It'll be a post of the type that will make all newbies immediately want to write "Geesh, what are you? Stupid?" The group oldies will, of course, obtain great entertainment value from these posts. The more insulting, the better. You've been reeled in. How do you tell a troll from someone actually saying something stupid? Often, you can't unless you've been reading the group for awhile.

Talk

Talk is a program that allows two users to communicate in real-time using a split screen interface. A user "talks" to another user by typing text in one area of the split screen, and "listens" as the other user's text appears in another area of the screen. It can be used for users on the same system, or over a TCP/IP network.

Before initiating a talk session, you will need the other person's address. If the user is connected to the same local machine as you, the login name will suffice.

Next, you need to make sure that the other user is logged in. You can find out with the `finger` command. For example:

```
$ finger userid
leibniz 24: finger trimblef
Login name: trimblef                    In real life: Frederick Trimble
Directory: /users/leibniz/INFO780-543/trimblef  Shell: /bin/csh
On since Apr 28 00:21:37 on pty/ttys0 from ts2.noc.drexel.e

No Plan.
$
```

In the above example, the finger command indicates that user trimblef is logged on to the system on pseudo-terminal pty/ttys0. The `finger` command can also determine whether a remote user is logged in by specifying a remote address. For example:

```
finger userid@domain
```

After you verify that the user with whom you wish to speak is logged on, he must agree to talk with you. To initiate a talk session, first issue the `talk` command:

```
talk userid@domain
```

On the talk initiator's screen, the screen will clear, and the talk header will appear at the top of the screen:

```
[Waiting for connection...]
```

On the other screen, the following text will appear:

```
talk: connection requested by username@host
talk: respond with: ntalk username@host
```

After the user responds with the appropriate message, the connection is established. Everything that is typed at this point will appear on the other terminal, until the connection is terminated. The talk session is terminated when one of the users types Control-c.

In certain situations, receiving a talk connect request can be disrupting. You can use the following command to disable any such request from a remote user:

```
mesg n
```

To enable such requests, use the mesg command with the y option:

```
mesg y
```

To see the current status of your talk request mode, use the mesg command with no options.

The talk command is based on a set of protocols that allows communication to take place. There are two protocols for the talk command: One is based on version 4.2 BSD UNIX, and the other on version 4.3 BSD UNIX. Unfortunately, these versions are not compatible. Therefore, you cannot establish a talk session between UNIX systems whose talk command is based on different versions of the protocol.

Another variation of the talk command is the ytalk command. The most interesting feature of ytalk is that it allows more than two users to partake in a conversation. In addition, it supports both versions of talk protocols. Therefore, the ytalk command can establish a connection with either version of the talk command.

To establish a ytalk session with multiple users, type the address of each user on the command line. For example,

```
ytalk mary@gwyned.edu fred@drexel.edu katherine@nova.edu
```

The ytalk command then splits the screen into several panes. Each screen is labeled with the corresponding user, so you always know who is typing.

If you need assistance with any ytalk options, simply hit the Escape key. A small menu of ytalk commands appears as follows:

```
################################################
# a) add a new user to session                 #
# b) delete a user from session                #
# c) output a user to a file                   #
# Your choice:                                  #
################################################
```

TIP

Since typing is slow compared to real conversation, it can be annoying watching the other party backspacing over misspelled words. If you feel the other party should be able to figure out the intention of the misspelled word, it is considered acceptable to continue typing after a spelling mistake.

Also, it is not uncommon for more experienced users to abbreviate commonly used phrases. Here is a list of abbreviations that you may encounter:

BCNU	Be seeing you
BRB	Be right back
BTW	By the way
BYE	Good-bye
CU	See you
CUL	See you later
FYI	For your information
FWIW	For what it's worth
GA	Go ahead and type
IMHO	In my humble opinion
IMO	In my opinion
JAM	Just a minute
O	Over
OO	Over and out
OBTW	Oh, by the way
ROTFL	Rolling on the floor laughing
R U THERE	Are you there
SEC...	Wait a second
WRT	With respect to

Internet Relay Chat (IRC)

Each day, thousands of people worldwide hold "keyboard conversations" using Internet Relay Chat (IRC). Like the `ytalk` facility, it allows multiple people to converse at the same time. When it is your turn to type, the characters appear on all other workstations that are logged in to the same channel.

> **NOTE**
>
> During the attempted Communist coup in Russia in 1993, an IRC channel was set up in order to relay eyewitness accounts of the event. IRC channels have also been set up during other natural disasters, such as earthquakes and hurricanes.

Basic IRC Structure

IRC uses a client/server model. The IRC "universe" consists of hundreds of channels with names such as `#initgame`. Users join (using their client software) in a channel that interests them and are then in conversation with everyone else who is on that same channel. You can talk with everyone or direct your comments to certain individuals. This is a flexible format that allows something as freeform as a general babble to many pairs of private conversations to a game of IRC Jeopardy, which plays much like the TV show. Some channels are private.

In addition, IRC users have their own nicknames and become quite attached to them (since your reputation goes with your nickname, this is quite understandable).

Getting IRC Clients

Before you can do anything, you'll need an IRC client. You'll need to grab the source code appropriate for your machine and compile it.

You can get the UNIX IRC client by pointing your Web browser to `ftp://cs-ftp.bu.edu`. The software is located in the `irc/clients` directory. Look to see which file the symbolic link `CURRENT` points to—it will be linked to the latest UNIX source code for `ircII`.

A PC client running under MS-DOS, OS/2, or Windows can anonymous ftp to `ftp://cs-ftp.bu.edu` and look under `/irc/clients/pc`. You'll have your choice of several for each operating system. MIRC is now the most popular client for the Windows environment.

A Mac client can also anonymous ftp to `ftp://cs-ftp.bu.edu` and look under `/irc/clients/macintosh`. Grab the latest version of `Homer` you find there.

Connecting to a Server

Once you have your client, you need to figure out which IRC server you will be talking to. Anonymous ftp to `cs.bu.edu` and look under `/irc/support`. There should be a file named `servers.950301` (the last number is the date, so that part will change). Grab this and look for a server that's close to you.

Then tell your client to connect to this server. With luck, it'll talk back to you and you'll be in the world of IRC.

Choosing Channels

Once you get on an IRC server, all commands start with a /.

/help gives you a list of commands. To get the new user help, do /help intro then /help newuser.

/list shows all the current IRC channels. It looks something like this, except that there will be a heck of a lot more channels:

```
*** Channel    Users  Topic
*** #wubba     3      Wherefore the wubba?
*** #hoffa     5      i know where the body is
*** #litldog   2      where oh where has he gone
```

/names might be more interesting. It shows who's logged on each channel and whether it's a private or public channel:

```
Pub: #wubba       @wubba jblow jdoe
Prv: *     marla donald ivana bill hillary
Pub: #litldog   @yakko dot
```

Then use /join *channel* to participate on *channel*. Here you might do a /join #wubba.

/nick *nickname* enables you to change to a new nickname in case your old one is too stodgy.

/msg *nickname message* enables you to send a private *message* to *nickname*. Use the /query *nickname* to enter a private conversation with *nickname*. Use /query to exit it.

If you get ambitious and create a channel (using /join on a nonexistent channel creates it), be sure to look at the /mode command, which lets you determine the behavior of the channel.

Need Help?

/join #Twilight_zone is where IRC operators often hang out, and some are willing to help. Just ask your question—don't announce that you need to ask a question first.

Bad Moves

Don't use someone else's nickname if you can help it—people are very protective about them.

Never type anything that someone asks you to type if you aren't sure what it does. You might find that you've just given someone else control of your client!

Don't abuse the Telnet server. If you're going to IRC a lot, get your own client.

Further Info

More information on IRC can be found via anonymous ftp on ftp://cs-ftp.bu.edu in the /irc/support directory. IRC also has several alt. groups dedicated to it: alt.irc.corruption, alt.irc.ircii, alt.irc.lamers, alt.irc.opers, alt.irc.questions, alt.irc.recovery, and alt.irc.undernet.

Multimedia

Multimedia is defined as the presentation of information in which more than one medium is used at a time. Using animation and sound in addition to ordinary text is such an example. By using more than one medium, multimedia enhances our ability to communicate and understand one another. The advent of powerful desktop computers equipped with high-resolution color monitors and stereo sound has increased the demand.

Internet Infrastructure

Delivering multimedia to the desktop over the Internet presents several obstacles. First, the Internet and its supporting protocols were designed to transmit 7-bit ASCII text in order to support e-mail and file transfer. Second, the original NSFnet was made up of 56K data communication lines. (The Internet backbone has been upgraded in recent years with higher network speeds.) Although this was sufficient for its original purpose of supporting e-mail and file transfer, it is not adequate for supporting the growing demand for multimedia.

Files containing multimedia data require large amounts of disk space. When such files are transferred across a network, they require large amounts of network bandwidth. When a router handles a packet of data, it has no knowledge of data flow. It only sees individual packets and handles them separately. When transferred across a network using a connectionless-oriented protocol like IP, individual packets of data may arrive out of order. The TCP protocol is responsible for reassembling the packets before they are made available to an application. There is also no priority information specified in the IP packet, so that real-time data could take precedence over other types of data with a lower priority. This type of protocol was fine for supporting applications such as e-mail and text-based chat sessions. It is not acceptable, however, for packets of data that are sensitive to time delay, such as real-time audio and video. Thus, in order to support large-scale multimedia, fundamental changes in the Internet infrastructure are necessary, including the data communication lines, routers, and protocols.

MIME

Remember the technique used for sending binary data, such as graphics or sound files, over the Internet? Before it was sent over the Internet, it was converted to ASCII characters using uuencode. Although this technique works much of the time, there are instances where it can fail. For example, mail gateways that convert between EBCDIC and ASCII character formats have been known to modify some of the characters in uuencode format. While most versions of uuencode are interoperable, there is no one clear standard. As previously mentioned, e-mail headers undergo modification by MUAs and MTAs during the transport process. Occasionally, this header modification can corrupt what has been uuencoded. The MIME specification is more robust in that it is better able to survive header modification.

A specification known as MIME (Multi-purpose Internet Mail Extensions) was developed to enhance the multimedia capabilities of e-mail. MIME effectively extends e-mail capabilities, including:

■ Multiple objects within a mail message

■ Text with unlimited line lengths

■ Character sets other than 7-bit ASCII

■ Multi-font messages

■ Image, audio, and video data

■ Binary files

Mime handles encryption using a technique known as base64. This encoding scheme is designed to represent arbitrary sequences of octets in a 65-character subset of ASCII characters, including A–Z, a–z, 0-9, +, /, and =.

Most mail programs, including Eudora, Elm, and mh, are MIME-aware. Most mail programs that support MIME perform encryption and decryption for you. If you receive a message in MIME format but don't have a MIME-aware mail program, you can decode it with the munpack utility. If you want to send a message to someone who has a MIME-aware mail program, you can encode it with the mpack utility. Both of these utilities are available for many platforms over the Internet free of charge. They can be retrieved via anonymous ftp from ftp://ftp.andrew.cmu.edu under the directory /pub/mpack. Please note that if you must resort to unpacking the MIME data yourself, you are still responsible for extracting the appropriate portion of the mail, say, with a text editor.

For more information, consult the Usenet group comp.mail.mime. The FAQ list is an excellent starting point. The detailed specification for MIME is described in RFC 1521.

NOTE

Although MIME is able to preserve the integrity of data during transport, it was never meant to translate data for compatibility between platforms. For example, the non-standard ASCII character for a bullet item with a word processor document is different on an Amiga than on a Macintosh. It is important to be aware of the target system to which you send data.

Delivering Multimedia Over the Internet

As mentioned previously, the current Internet infrastructure is not adequate for supporting multimedia. This section examines two attempts at updating the infrastructure in order to deliver large scale multimedia.

RTP/RSVP

The connectionless nature of the IP protocol does not lend itself to the time-sensitive nature of data packets carrying real-time audio and video. The Real-Time Transport Protocol (RTP) and the ReSerVation Setup Protocol (RSVP) protocols are currently being developed by the

IETF (Internet Engineering Task Force) to make such multimedia support a reality. One of the major challenges of this effort is to minimize the amount of change in the existing Internet infrastructure to support them.

The initial specification of RSVP defines four levels of Quality of Service (QoS) without requiring wholesale changes to the Internet:

- Guaranteed delay
- Controlled delay
- Predictive service
- Controlled load

While these QoS specifications vary in the priority in which they are handled, each adds a higher degree of determinism to the time in which packets will be routed. RSVP/RTP advocates claim that this is sufficient for meeting the needs of multimedia applications.

The fundamental idea behind RSVP is to create a reservation with each router through which the data packets will pass. This reservation consists of a flow identifier, in order to identify the data stream, and a flow specification, which identifies the QoS that must be provided to the data flow. In essence, the reservation defines a contract for service between the network and the requesting application.

Multimedia applications will be able to access these protocols by using a Winsock version 2-compliant application programming interface (API). The interface calls will even allow specification of the QoS. Changing the API to support new features, while minimizing the amount of changes that need to be made to existing software will not be easy.

Another issue that will need to be resolved is payment for additional services. How will users be billed for specifying a higher level of service?

Multicast Backbone

As previously mentioned, the backbone of the Internet consists of high speed data comunication lines. Many experiments are being conducted to find ways of upgrading the physical hardware to support the transmission of real-time audio and video. One such experiment is known as the Multicast Backbone (MBONE). MBONE is not separate from the Internet. Rather, it is a set of Internet sites with powerful hosts and high-speed connections between them.

Unfortunately, MBONE is able to handle the display of only three to five frames per second. Full-motion video, on the other hand, requires the display of thirty frames per second. While its potential does not approach broadcast quality, it is sufficient for a number of useful applications, such as teleconferencing. For more information, you can visit the `http://www.mbone.com` Web site.

> **NOTE**
>
> On July 20th, 1996, the National Science Foundation and NASA sponsored a live broadcast over the MBONE. The presentation, given to commemorate the 20th anniversary of the Mars Viking Landings, discussed the Mars Pathfinder and Mars Global Surveyor missions.

Audio Over the Internet

At this moment in time, there are two methods for handling audio data over the Internet. The first technique requires that an audio data file be transferred to a workstation, which is then handled by the appropriate audio player. The second technique does not require the complete file to be transferred before the file can begin to be played.

Audio File Transfer

There are many sound files on the Internet in a variety of formats. Each format has a unique file extension associated with it, such as .wav or .au. The following list shows file extensions that you are likely to see, along with their associated platform:

File Extension	*Platform*
AU	UNIX
SND	Macintosh
WAV	PC
AIF, AIFF	Macintosh
RA (RealAudio)	Macintosh, PC, UNIX

Each file type requires a special "player" utility. In most cases, these utilities can be configured to work with your favorite Web browser, so that they can be played automatically when referenced within the browser. These are known as "helper" applications in Web terminology.

The major disadvantage of this technique, however, is the amount of time it takes to transfer the files. Even though the files are usually compressed, they are still quite large.

Streaming Audio

A technique known as *streaming audio* was developed to improve the performance of the plain file transfer method. This method allows the file to be played at the same time that the file is being transferred. To utilize this technique, you must use audio files and a player application capable of supporting streaming audio. The most popular audio streaming technology today is RealAudio.

While the audio file is being played, the audio server and audio player exchange information about the connection. If it is a low-speed connection, a smaller version of the file is sent. If it is a high-speed connection, a larger, higher quality version of the file will be used.

In order to reduce the amount of time necessary to transfer the data over the Internet, the file is compressed. The User Datagram Protocol (UDP) is used in conjunction with the IP protocol to transfer the data packets. Unlike TCP, UDP will not resend packets if problems in the transmission occur. If this were the case, the sound player would not be able to play the file due to frequent interruptions.

Phone Calls Over the Internet

Another form of audio over the Internet is making phone calls. Technically speaking, you can call anyone who has an e-mail address. All that is needed are a speaker and microphone for your desktop computer, along with software to interpret the digitized packets of data. There are a number of competing companies that make phone products for the Internet, including "WebTalk" by Quarterdeck, "NetPhone" by Electric Magic, and "Internet Phone" from VocalTec.

The main benefit of making phone calls over the Internet is the price. The only charge incurred is the cost of an Internet connection. The main disadvantages are voice quality and compatibility between Internet phone products. Other users must have the same exact software as you in order to have a phone conversation.

Video Over the Internet

Just like audio, there are two primary methods for handling video data over the Internet. The first technique requires that a video data file be transferred to a workstation, which is then handled by the appropriate video player. The second technique does not require the complete file to be transferred before the file is processed.

Video File Transfer

There are many video files on the Internet in a variety of formats. Each format has a unique file extension associated with it. The following list shows file extensions for video files that you are likely to see, along with their associated platform:

File Extension	*Platform*
QT (QuickTime)	Macintosh, PC
AVI	PC
MPG, MPEG	Macintosh, PC, UNIX
MOV	Macintosh, PC

Just like audio files, there are corresponding "player" applications for each file type. Even when compressed, they suffer from the same problem as audio files: They are simply too large.

Streaming Video

Conceptually, streaming video works in the same way as streaming audio. That is, compressed files are transferred over the Internet using the UDP/IP protocol. The user actually sees the file being played before the file transfer is complete. This can deliver reasonable performance when sent over a high-speed network, such as the MBONE.

The first attempt at implementing streaming video over the Internet is a product called VDOLive. Just like RealAudio, it tries to adjust the quality of the video based on speed of the connection. VDOLive is able to deliver 10 to 15 frames per second on a two-inch section of the screen over a 28.8 Kbps line. Over an ISDN line, 30 frames per second are possible. Before video data is transmitted, it must be compressed. Therefore, it does not lend itself to live broadcasts. Despite these limitations, VDOLive has a lot of potential.

Two newer products are RealPlayer and Streamworks. They are able to combine both audio and video.

Video Conferencing

An application that uses both audio and video over the Internet is video conferencing. In addition to a specially equipped workstation, including a microphone and a video camera, special software is needed as well.

The most popular video conferencing software in use to date is a product called CU-SeeMe. This technology works much like streaming audio and video. When someone wants to participate in a video conference, she or he first must log into a special system on the Internet known as a reflector. A reflector hosts many video conferences that you can join. After you log in, voice and video data are digitized and compressed before transport over the Internet. For efficiency reasons, the UDP protocol is used instead of TCP. Any missing packets are ignored by the application.

CU-SeeMe also tries to reduce the amount of network bandwidth needed by only sending relevant portions of the images. For example, if someone is speaking, but rarely makes any motion in the field of the camera, only the changes from previous video frames need to be sent.

It is also possible to have a video conference without a reflector site. If you know the other person's IP address, you can contact them directly and have a two-way conference.

NOTE

NASA has quite a few reflector sites from which live videos can be seen using CU-SeeMe. They also have an excellent collection of audio and video clips that are available for downloading. See http://www.nasa.gov for details.

Future Directions

The Internet, also known as the Information Superhighway, is still evolving. It was built to support applications such as e-mail and file transfer. In order for it to support multimedia, such as audio and video, the infrastructure will need to be upgraded. Researchers are busy at work trying to figure out how to upgrade the infrastructure without requiring a major overhaul. Efforts such as RSVP/RTP are promising, but are still on the horizon.

A more compelling problem is the data communications structure in place that connects to our homes and schools. In order to support multimedia, more bandwidth will be needed at this juncture. This is known as the "last mile" problem.

It spite of these physical limitations, technology is still growing by leaps and bounds. Once these bottlenecks are removed, a whole new world of possibilities for communicating with others will be at our fingertips.

UNIX Shells

II PART

What Is a Shell?

by William A. Farra

IN THIS CHAPTER

CHAPTER 8

Nearly every human-usable invention has an interface point with which you interact. Whether you are in the front seat of a horse and buggy, in the cockpit of a plane, or at the keyboard of a piano, this position is where you manipulate and manage the various aspects of the invention to achieve a desired outcome. The human interface point for UNIX is the *shell,* which is a program layer that provides you with an environment in which to enter commands and parameters to produce a given result. As with any invention, the more knowledge and experience you have with it, the greater the accomplishment you make with it.

To meet varying needs, UNIX has provided different shells. Discussed in Chapters 9 through 13 are Bourne, Bourne Again, Korn, and C shells. Each of these offers features and ways to interact with UNIX. Topics discussed in this chapter are the following:

- How shells works with you and UNIX
- The features of a shell
- Manipulating the shell environment

How the Kernel and the Shell Interact

When a UNIX system is brought online, the program `unix` (the Kernel) is loaded into the computer's main memory, where it remains until the computer is shut down. During the bootup process, the program `init` runs as a background task and remains running until shutdown. This program scans the file `/etc/inittab`, which lists what ports have terminals and their characteristics. When an active, open terminal is found, `init` calls the program `getty`, which issues a `login:` prompt to the terminal's monitor. With these processes in place and running, the user is ready to start interacting with the system.

UNIX Calls the Shell at Login

Figure 8.1 shows the process flow from the kernel through the login process. At this point the user is in an active shell, ready to give commands to the system.

During login, when you type your user name, `getty` issues a `password:` prompt to the monitor. After you type your password, `getty` calls `login`, which scans for a matching entry in the file `/etc/passwd`. If a match is made, `login` proceeds to take you to your home directory and then passes control to a session startup program; both the user name and password are specified by the entry in `/etc/passwd`. Although this might be a specific application program, such as a menu program, normally the session startup program is a shell program such as `/bin/sh`, the Bourne shell.

From here, the shell program reads the files `/etc/profile` and `.profile`, which set up the system-wide and user-specific environment criteria. At this point, the shell issues a command prompt such as $.

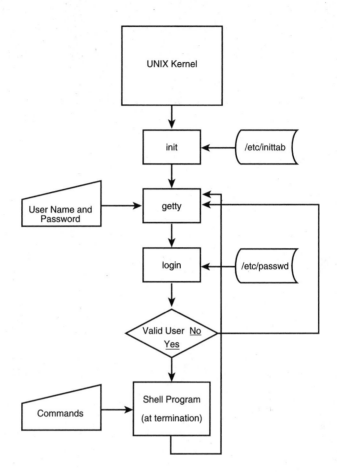

FIGURE 8.1.
*How a shell is started
from login.*

When the shell is terminated, the kernel returns control to the init program, which restarts the login process. Termination can happen in one of two ways: with the `exit` command or when the kernel issues a kill command to the shell process. At termination, the kernel recovers all resources used by the user and the shell program.

The Shell and Child Processes

In the Unix system, there are many layers of programs starting from the kernel through a given application program or command. The relationship of these layers is represented in Figure 8.2.

After you finish logging on, the shell program layer is in direct contact with the kernel, as shown in Figure 8.2. As you type a command such as `$ ls`, the shell locates the actual program file, `/bin/ls`, and passes it to the kernel to execute. The kernel creates a new child process area, loads the program, and executes the instructions in `/bin/ls`. After program completion, the kernel recovers the process area and returns control to the parent shell program. To see an example of this, type the following command:

`$ps`

FIGURE 8.2.

UNIX system layers.

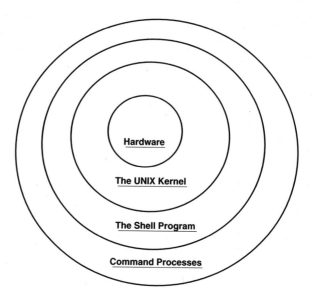

This lists the processes you are currently running. You will see the shell program and the ps program. Now type the following:

```
$sleep 10 &
$ps
```

The first command creates a sleep child process to run in background, which you see listed with the ps command. Whenever you enter a command, a child process is created and independently executes from the parent process or shell. This leaves the parent intact to continue other work.

Auto-Execution of the Shell

Some UNIX resources, such as cron, can execute a shell program without human interaction. When using this feature, the user needs to specify which shell to run in the first line of the shell program, like this:

```
#! /bin/sh
```

This specifies the Bourne shell.

You should also redirect any output, because no terminal is associated with auto-execution. This is described in the "File Handling: Input/Output Redirection and Pipes" section later in this chapter.

The Functions and Features of a Shell

It doesn't matter which of the standard shells you choose, because they all have the same purpose: to provide a user interface to UNIX. To provide this interface, all the shells offer the same basic characteristics:

- Command-line interpretation
- Reserved words
- Shell meta-characters (wild cards)
- Access to and handling of program commands
- File handling: input/output redirection and pipes
- Maintenance of variables
- Environment control
- Shell programming

Command-Line Interpretation

When you log in, starting a special version of a shell called an *interactive shell,* you see a shell prompt, usually in the form of a dollar sign ($), a percent sign (%), or a pound sign (#). When you type a line of input at a shell prompt, the shell tries to interpret it. Input to a shell prompt is sometimes called a *command line.* The basic format of a command line is

```
command arguments
```

command is an executable UNIX command, program, utility, or shell program. *arguments* are passed to the executable. Most UNIX utility programs expect *arguments* to take the following form:

```
options filenames
```

For example, in the command line

```
$ ls -l file1 file2
```

there are three arguments to `ls`; the first is an option, and the last two are filenames.

One of the things the shell does for the kernel is to eliminate unnecessary information. For a computer, one type of unnecessary information is whitespace; therefore, it is important to know what the shell does when it sees whitespace. Whitespace consists of space characters, horizontal tabs, and newline characters. Consider this example:

```
$ echo part A     part B     part C
part A part B part C
```

Here, the shell has interpreted the command line as the echo command with six arguments and has removed the whitespace between the arguments. For example, if you were printing headings for a report and wanted to keep the whitespace, you would have to enclose the data in quotation marks, as in

```
$ echo 'part A     part B      part C'
part A      part B      part C
```

The single quotation mark prevents the shell from looking inside the quotes. Now the shell interprets this line as the echo command with a single argument, which happens to be a string of characters including whitespace.

Reserved Words

All shell versions have words that have special meaning. In shell programming, words such as do, done, for, and while provide loop control—and if, then, else, and fi provide conditional control. Each shell version has different reserved word pertaining to its specific features.

Shell Meta-Character (Wild Cards)

All shell versions have meta-characters, which allow the user to specify filenames. The following are wild cards:

Wild Card	Description
*	Matches any portion
?	Matches any single character
[]	Matches a range or list of characters

Wild cards can be useful when processing a number of specific files. The following are some examples:

```
$ls t*
```

This lists all files starting with t.

```
$ls test?5.dat
```

This lists all files starting with test, any single character and ends with 5.dat.

```
$ls [a-c]*
```

This lists all files starting with a through c.

```
$ls [e,m,t]*
```

This lists all files starting with e, m, or t.

Program Commands

When a command is typed, the shell reads the environment variable $path, which contains a list of directories containing program files. The shell looks through this set of directories to find the program file for the command. The shell then passes the true filename to the kernel.

File Handling: Input/Output Redirection and Pipes

In previous chapters, you learned about standard input and output. Unless otherwise specified with arguments, most UNIX commands take input from the terminal keyboard and send output to the terminal monitor. To redirect output to a file, use the > symbol. For example,

```
$ls > myfiles
```

lists the files in your current directory and places them in a file called myfiles. Likewise, you can redirect input with the < symbol. For example,

```
$wc -l < myfiles
```

feeds the command wc with input from the file myfiles. Although you could obtain the same output by having the filename as an argument, the need for input redirection becomes more apparent in shell programming.

To string the output from one command to the input of the next command, you can use the ¦ (pipe) symbol. For example,

```
$ls -s ¦ sort -nr ¦ pg
```

lists the files in the current directory with blocksize and then pipes the output to the sort, which sorts the files in numeric descending order and pipes that output to the paging command pg for final display on the terminal's monitor. The pipe command is one of the most useful tools when creating command constructs.

Command Substitution

Command substitution is similar to redirection except that it is used to provide arguments to a command from the output of another. For example,

```
$grep `wc -l myfiles` *
```

takes the number of lines in the file myfiles from the wc command and places the number as an argument to the grep command to search all files in the current directory for that number.

Maintenance of Variables

The shell is capable of maintaining variables. *Variables* are places you can store data for later use. You assign a value to a variable with an equal (=) sign:

```
$ LOOKUP=/usr/mydir
```

Here, the shell establishes LOOKUP as a variable and assigns it the value /usr/mydir. Later, you can use the value stored in LOOKUP in a command line by prefacing the variable name with a dollar sign ($). Consider these examples:

```
$ echo $LOOKUP
/usr/mydir

$ echo LOOKUP
LOOKUP
```

To make a variable available to child processes, you can use the export command—for example:

```
$ LOOKUP=/usr/mydir
$export LOOKUP
```

> **NOTE**
>
> Assigning values to variables in the C shell differs from doing so in the Bourne and Korn shells. To assign a variable in the C shell, use the set command:
>
> ```
> % set LOOKUP = /usr/mydir
> ```
>
> Notice that spaces precede and follow the equal sign.

Like filename substitution, variable name substitution happens before the program call is made. The second example omits the dollar sign ($). Therefore, the shell simply passes the string to echo as an argument. In variable name substitution, the value of the variable replaces the variable name.

For example, in

```
$ ls $LOOKUP/filename
```

the ls program is called with the single argument /usr/mydir/filename.

Shell Startup—Environment Control

When a user begins a session with UNIX and the shell is executed, the shell creates a specified environment for the user. The following sections describe these processes.

Shell Environment Variables

When the login program invokes your shell, it sets up your environment variables, which are read from the shell initialization files /etc/profile and .profile. These files normally set the type of terminal in the variable $TERM and the default path that is searched for executable files in the variable $PATH. Try these examples:

```
$ echo $TERM
$ echo $PATH
```

You can easily change the variables the same way you assign values to any shell variable.

NOTE

C shell assigns values to environment variables using the setenv command:

```
% setenvM TERM vt100
```

Shell Startup Files

The file .profile is the local startup file for the Bourne shell. The Korn shell uses .kshrc, and the C shell uses .cshrc. You can edit these files to manipulate your startup environment. You can add additional variables as the need arises. You also can add shell programming to have conditional environment settings, if necessary.

Shell Startup Options

When invoking the shell either from /etc/passwd or the command line, you can set several options as arguments to the shell program. For example, the Bourne shell has a -x option that displays commands and their arguments before they are executed. This is useful for debugging a shell program. These options are described in detail in the following chapters.

Shell Programming

You've seen that the shell is used to interpret command lines, maintain variables, and execute programs. The shell is also a programming language. You can store a set of shell commands in a file. This is known as a *shell script* or *shell programming*. By combining commands and variable assignments with flow control and decision making, you have a powerful programming tool. Using the shell as a programming language, you can automate recurring tasks, write reports, and build and manipulate your own data files. The remaining chapters in Part II, "UNIX Shells," discuss shell programming in more detail.

Summary

The shell provides an interface between the user and the heart of UNIX—the kernel. The shell interprets command lines as input, makes filename and variable substitution, redirects input and output, locates the executable file, and initiates and interfaces programs. The shell creates child processes and can manage their execution. The shell maintains each user's environment variables. The shell is also a powerful programming language.

While this chapter gives an overview of the UNIX shell, Chapters 9 through 13 describe in detail the various shells, their features, and language specifics. Also described are the fundamentals of shell programming and execution. Continued reading is highly recommended.

The Bourne Shell

written by Richard E. Rummel
revised by William A. Farra

IN THIS CHAPTER

CHAPTER 9

Presented in this chapter are the fundamentals and many useful specifics of the Bourne shell, currently the most popular of the UNIX shells for execution of application programs. Also described are the steps to organize and script shell commands to produce a program that you can run by name at the shell prompt, or other UNIX methods of program initiation.

The following topics are discussed in this chapter:

- Shells Basics
    - Invocation
    - Environment
    - Options
    - Special Characters
- Shell Variables
    - User Defined Variables
    - Environment Variables
    - Positional Variables or Shell Arguments
- Shell Script Programming
    - Conditional Testing
    - Repetition and Loop Control
- Customizing the Shell

Shell Basics

Stephen Bourne wrote the Bourne shell at Bell Laboratories, the development focal point of UNIX. At the time, Bell Laboratories was a subsidiary of AT&T. Since then, many system corporations have produced hardware specific versions of UNIX but have remarkably kept Bourne shell basics consistent.

> **NOTE**
>
> $man sh or $man bsh on most UNIX systems will list the generalities of the Bourne shell, as well as detail the specifics to that version of UNIX. It is recommended that the reader familiarize herself with the version she is using before and after reading this chapter.

The Shell Invocation and Environment

The first level of invocation occurs when a user logs on to a UNIX system and is specified by his entry into /etc/passwd file. For example,

```
farrawa:!:411:102:William Farra, Systems Development,x385:/home/farrawa:/bin/bsh
```

This entry (which is : delimited) has the login ID, encrypted password (denoted by !), user ID #, default group ID #, comment field, home directory, and startup shell program. In this case, it is the Bourne shell. As the shell executes, it will read the system profile /etc/profile. This may set up various environment variables, such as PATH, which the shell uses to search for executables, and TERM, the terminal type being used. Then the shell continues to place the user into the associated home directory and reads the local .profile. Finally, the shell displays the default prompt $.

NOTE

On UNIX systems, the super-user, also referred to as root, is without restriction. When the super-user logs in, she sees the pound sign (#) as a default prompt. It is a reminder that as super-user some of the built-in protections are not available and that extra care is necessary in this mode. Since the super-user can write to any directory and can remove any file, file permissions do not apply. Normally, the root login is used only for system administration and adding or deleting users. It is strongly recommended that only well-experienced UNIX users be given access to root.

Shell Invocation Options

When invoking or executing the shell, you can use any of the several options available to the Bourne shell. To test a shell script for syntax, you can use the -n option, which reads the script but does not execute it. If you are debugging a script, the -x option will set the trace mode, displaying each command as it is executed.

The following is a list of Bourne shell options available on most versions of UNIX.

-a	Tag all variables for export.
-c "string"	Commands are read from string.
-e	Non-interactive mode.
-f	Disable shell filename generation.
-h	Locate and remember functions as defined.
-i	Interactive mode.
-k	Put arguments in the environment for a command.
-n	Read commands but do not execute them.
-r	Restricted mode.
-s	Commands are read from the standard input.
-t	A single command is executed, and the shell exits.
-u	Unset variables are an error during substitution.
-v	Verbose mode, displays shell input lines.
-x	Trace mode, displays commands as they are executed.

There are many combinations of these options that will work together. Some obviously will not, such as -e, which sets noninteractive mode, and -i, which sets interactive mode. However, experience with options gives the user a multitude of alternatives in creating or modifying his shell environment.

The Restricted Shell

`bsh -r or /bin/rsh or /usr/bin/rsh.`

Depending on the version of UNIX, this will invoke the Bourne shell in the restricted mode. With this option set, the user cannot change directories (cd), change the PATH variable, specify a full pathname to a command, or redirect output. This ensures an extra measure of control and security to the UNIX system. It is typically used for application users, who never see a shell prompt, and dialup accounts, where security is a must. Normally, a restricted user is placed, from login, into a directory in which she has no write permission. Not having write permission in this directory does not mean that the user has no write permission anywhere. It does mean she cannot change directories or specify pathnames in commands. Also, she cannot write a shell script and later access it in her working directory.

> **NOTE**
>
> If the restricted shell calls an unrestricted shell to carry out the commands, the restrictions can be bypassed. This is also true if the user can call an unrestricted shell directly. Remember that programs like vi and more allow users to execute commands. If the command is sh, again it is possible to bypass the restrictions.

Changing Shell Options with set

Once the user is at the command prompt $, she can modify her shell environment by setting or unsetting shell options with the set command. To turn on an option, use a - (hyphen) and option letter. To turn off an option, use a + (plus sign) and option letter. Most UNIX systems allow the options a, e, f, h, k, n, u, v, and x to be turned off and on. Look at the following examples:

`$set -xv`

This enables the trace mode in the shell so that all commands and substitutions are printed. It also displays the line input to shell.

`$set +u`

This disables error checking on unset variables when substitution occurs. To display which shell options have been set, type the following:

`$echo $-`

`is`

This indicates that the shell is in interactive mode and taking commands from standard input. Turning options on and off is very useful when debugging a shell script program or testing a specific shell environment.

The User's Shell Startup File: `.profile`

Under each Bourne shell user's home directory is a file named `.profile`. This is where a system administrator or user (if given write permission) can make permanent modifications to his shell environment. To add a directory to the existing execution path, just add the following line into `.profile`.

```
PATH=$PATH:/sql/bin ; export PATH
```

With this line in `.profile`, from the time the user logs in, the directory `/sql/bin` is searched for commands and executable programs. To create a variable that contains environment data for an applications program, follow the same procedure.

Shell Environment Variables

Once at the command prompt, there are several environment variables that have values. The following is a list of variables found on most UNIX systems.

CDPATH	Contains search path(s) for the `cd` command.
HOME	Contains the user's home directory.
IFS	Internal field separators, normally space, tab, and newline.
MAIL	Path to a special file (mail box), used by UNIX e-mail.
PATH	Contains search path(s) for commands and executables.
PS1	Primary prompt string, by default $.
PS2	Secondary prompt string, by default >.
TERM	Terminal type being used.

If the restricted mode is not set, these variables can be modified to accommodate the user's various needs. For instance, to change your prompt, type the following:

```
$PS1="your wish:" ; export PS1
```

Now instead of a $ for a prompt, `your wish:` appears. To change it back, type the following:

```
$PS1="\$" ; export PS1
```

To display the value(s) in any given variable, type the **echo** command, space, and a **$**, followed by the variable name.

```
$echo $MAIL
```

```
/usr/spool/mail/(user id)
```

Care should be used when modifying environment variables. Incorrect modifications to shell environment variables may cause commands either not to function or not to function properly. If this happens, it is recommended that the user log out and log back in. Experience with these variables will give you even more control over your shell environment. Also, there is a set of environment variables that are identified by special characters. These are detailed in the next section of the chapter.

Special Characters and Their Meanings

The Bourne shell uses many of the non-alphanumeric characters to define specific shell features. Most of these features fall into four basic categories: special variable names, filename generation, data/program control, and quoting/escape character control. While this notation may seem cryptic at first, this gives the shell environment the ability to accomplish complex functions with a minimal amount of coding.

Special Characters for Shell Variable Names

There are special characters that denote special shell variables, automatically set by the shell. As with all variables, they are preceded by a $. The following is a list of these variables.

$#	The number of arguments supplied to the command shell.
$-	Flags supplied to the shell on invocation or with set.
$?	The status value returned by the last command.
$$	The process number of the current shell.
$!	The process number of the last child process.
$@	All arguments, individually double quoted.
$*	All arguments, double quoted.
$n	Positional argument values, where *n* is the position.
$0	The name of the current shell.

To display the number of arguments supplied to the shell, type the following:

```
$echo $#

0
```

This indicates that no arguments were supplied to the shell on invocation. These variables are particularly useful when writing a shell script, which is described later in this chapter in the section "Positional Variables or Shell Arguments."

Special Characters for Filename Generation

The Bourne shell uses special characters or meta-characters to indicate pattern matches with existing filenames. These are those characters:

*	Matches any string or portion of string
?	Matches any single character
[-,!]	Range, list, or not matched

To match files beginning with f, type the following:

$ls f*

To match files with a prefix of invoice, any middle character, and a suffix of dat, type the following:

$ls invoice?dat

To match files starting with the letter a through e, type the following:

$ls [a-e]*

To match file starting with a, c, and e, type the following:

$ls [a,c,e]*

To exclude a match with the letter m, type the following:

$ls [!m]*

NOTE

To use the logical not symbol, !, it must be the first character after the left bracket, [.

Special Characters for Data/Program Control

The Bourne shell uses special characters for data flow and execution control. With these characters, the user can send normal screen output to a file or device or as input to another command. These characters also allow the user to run multiple commands sequentially or independently from the command line. The following is a list of those characters.

>(file)	Redirect output to a file.
>>(file)	Redirect and append output to the end of a file.
<(file)	Redirect standard input from a file.
;	Separate commands.
¦	Pipe standard output to standard input.
&	Place at end of command to execute in background.
` `	Command substitution, redirect output as arguments.

There are many ways to use these controls; those are described in more detail later in this chapter in the section "Entering Simple Commands."

Special Characters for Quoting and Escape

The Bourne shell uses the single quotes, ' ', and double quotes, " ", to encapsulate special characters or space delineated words to produce a single data string. The major difference between single and double quotes is that, in using double quotes, variable and command substitution are active, as well as the escape character.

```
$echo "$HOME $PATH"

$/u/farrawa /bin:/etc:/usr/bin:
```

This example combines the values of $HOME and $PATH to produce a single string.

```
$echo '$HOME $PATH'

$$HOME $PATH
```

This example simply prints the string data enclosed. The shell escape character is a backslash, \, which is used to negate the special meaning or shell function of the following character.

```
$echo \$HOME $PATH

$$HOME /bin:/etc:/usr/bin:
```

In this example, only the $ of $HOME is seen as text, and the variable meaning the shell is negated, $PATH, is still interpreted as a variable.

How the Shell Interprets Commands

The first exposure most people have to the Bourne shell is as an interactive shell. After logging onto the system and seeing any messages from the system administrator, the user sees a shell prompt. For users other than the super-user, the default prompt for the interactive Bourne shell is a dollar sign ($). When you see the dollar sign ($), the interactive shell is ready to accept a line of input, which it interprets.

The shell sees a line of input as a string of characters terminated with a newline character, which is usually the result of pressing Enter on your keyboard. The length of the input line has nothing to do with the width of your computer display. When the shell sees the newline character, it begins to interpret the line.

Entering Simple Commands

The most common form of input to the shell is the simple command, in which a command name is followed by any number of arguments. In the example

```
$ ls file1 file2 file3
```

ls is the command and *file1*, *file2*, and *file3* are the arguments. The command is any UNIX executable. It is the responsibility of the command, not the shell, to interpret the arguments. Many UNIX commands, but certainly not all, take the following form:

```
$ command -options filenames
```

Although the shell does not interpret the arguments of the command, the shell does make some interpretation of the input line before passing the arguments to the command. Special characters, when you enter them on a command line, cause the shell to redirect input and output, start a different command, search the directories for filename patterns, substitute variable data, and substitute the output of other commands.

Substitution of Variable Data

Many of the previous examples in this chapter have used variables in the command line. Whenever the shell sees (not quoted or escaped) a dollar sign ($), it interprets the following qualified text as a variable name. Whether the variable is environmental or user-defined, the data stored in the variable is substituted on the command line. For example, the command

```
$ ls $HOME
```

lists the contents of the user's home directory, regardless of what the current working directory is. HOME is an environment variable. Variables are discussed in more detail in the next major section of this chapter. As in filename substitution, the ls command sees only the result of the substitution, not the variable name.

You can substitute variable names anywhere in the command line, including for the command name itself. For example,

```
$ dir=ls
$ $dir f*
file1
file1a
form
```

This example points out that the shell makes its substitutions before determining what commands to execute.

Redirection of Input and Output

When the shell sees the input (<) or output (>) redirection character, the argument following the redirection symbol is sent to the subshell that controls the execution of the command. When the command opens the input or output file that has been redirected, the input or output is redirected to the file.

```
$ ls -l >dirfile
```

In this example, the only argument passed on to ls is the option -l. The filename dirfile is sent to the subshell that controls the execution of ls. To append output to an existing file, use (>>).

```
$ ls –l /tmp >> dirfile
```

This example takes the file listing from the /tmp directory and appends it to the end of the local file dirfile.

Entering Multiple Commands on One Line

Ordinarily, the shell interprets the first word of command input as the command name and the rest of the input as arguments to that command. The shell special character—the semicolon (;)—indicates to the shell that the preceding command text is ended and the following is a new command. For example, the command line

```
$ who -H; df -v; ps -e
```

is the equivalent of

```
$ who -H
$ df -v
$ ps -e
```

In the second case, however, the results of each command appear between the command input lines. When you use the semicolon to separate commands on a line, the commands are executed in sequence. The shell waits until one command is complete before executing the next. Also, if there is an error, the shell will stop executing the command line at the position the error occurred.

Linking Multiple Commands with Pipes

One of the most powerful features of the Bourne shell is its ability to take standard output from one command and used it as standard input to another. This is accomplished with the pipe symbol, ¦. When the shell sees a pipe, it executes the preceding command and then creates a link to the standard input of the following command in the order the commands are on the command line. For example,

```
$who ¦ grep fred
```

This takes the list of users logged in from the who command and searches the list for the string fred using the grep. This creates output only if user fred is logged in.

```
$ls -ls ¦ sort -nr ¦ pg
```

This creates a list of files in the current directory with the block size as the first data item of each line. It hen sorts the list in reverse numeric order and finally pages the output on the screen. This results in paged listing of all files by size with the largest on top. This is useful when trying to determine where disk space is being consumed. Any UNIX command that takes input from standard input and sends output to standard output can be linked using the pipe.

Entering Commands to Process in Background

To take advantage of the UNIX ability to multitask, the shell allows commands to be processed in background. This is accomplished by placing the ampersand symbol, &, at the end of a command. For example,

```
$find / -name "ledger" -print > find.results 2>/dev/null &
```

This command line searches the entire file system for files named `ledger`, sends its output to a local file named `find.results`, eliminates unwanted errors, and processes this command independent of the current shell (in background).

```
$wc -l < chapter5.txt > chapter5.wcl 2> chapter5.err &
```

In this example, the command `wc` takes its input from the file `chapter5.txt`, sends its output (a line count) to the file `chapter5.wcl`, sends errors to the file `chapter5.err`, and executes in background.

> **NOTE**
>
> If a user has processes running in the background and she logs off, most UNIX systems will terminate the processes owned by that login. Also when you enter a command to process in background, the shell will return and display the process ID number.

Substituting the Results of Commands in a Command Line

Sometimes it is useful to pass the output or results of one command as arguments to another command. You do so by using the shell special character, the back quotation mark (`` ` ``). You use the back quotation marks in pairs. When the shell sees a pair of back quotation marks, it executes the command inside the quotation marks and substitutes the output of that command in the original command line. You most commonly use this method to store the results of command executions in variables. To store the five-digit Julian date in a variable, for example, you use the following command:

```
$ julian=`date '+%y%j'`
```

The back quotation marks cause the `date` command to be executed before the variable assignment is made. Back quotation marks can be extremely useful when you're performing arithmetic on shell variables; see "Shell Programming" later in this chapter.

Shell Variables

In algebra, variables are symbols that stand for some value. In computer terminology, variables are symbolic names that stand for some value. Earlier in this chapter, you saw how the variable HOME stood for the name of a user's home directory. If you enter the change directory command, `cd`, without an argument, `cd` takes you to your home directory. Does a generic program like `cd` know the location of every user's home directory? Of course not, it merely knows to look for a variable, in this case HOME, which stands for the home directory.

Variables are useful in any computer language because they allow you to define what to do with a piece of information without knowing specifically what the data is. A program to add two and two is not very useful, but a program that adds two variables can be, especially if the value of the variables can be supplied at execution time by the user of the program. The Bourne shell has four types of variables: user-defined variables, positional variables or shell arguments, predefined or special variables, and environment variables.

Storing Data or User-Defined Variables

As the name implies, user-defined variables are whatever you want them to be. Variable names are comprised of alphanumeric characters and the underscore character, with the provision that variable names do not begin with one of the digits 0 through 9. Like all UNIX names, variables are case sensitive. Variable names take on values when they appear in a command line to the left of an equal sign (=). For example, in the following command lines, COUNT takes on the value of 1, and NAME takes on the value of Stephanie:

```
$ COUNT=1
$ NAME=Stephanie
```

> **TIP**
>
> Because most UNIX commands are lowercase words, shell programs have traditionally used all capital letters in variable names. It is certainly not mandatory to use all capital letters, but using them enables you to identify variables easily within a program.

To recall the value of a variable, precede the variable name by a dollar sign ($):

```
$ NAME=John
$ echo Hello $NAME
Hello John
```

You also can assign variables to other variables, as follows:

```
$ JOHN=John
$ NAME=$JOHN
$ echo Goodbye $NAME
Goodbye John
```

Sometimes it is useful to combine variable data with other characters to form new words, as in the following example:

```
$ SUN=Sun
$ MON=Mon
$ TUE=Tues
$ WED=Wednes
$ THU=Thurs
$ FRI=Fri
$ SAT=Satur
$ WEEK=$SAT
$ echo Today is $WEEKday
Today is
$
```

What happened here? Remember that when the shell's interpreter sees a dollar sign ($), it interprets all the characters until the next white space as the name of a variable, in this case WEEKday.

You can escape the effect of this interpretation by enclosing the variable name in curly braces ({ }) like this:

```
$ echo Today is ${WEEK}day
Today is Saturday
$
```

You can assign more than one variable in a single line by separating the assignments with white space, as follows:

```
$ X=x Y=y
```

The variable assignment is performed from right to left:

```
$ X=$Y Y=y
$ echo $X
y
$ Z=z Y=$Z
$ echo $Y

$
```

You may notice that when a variable that has not been defined is referenced, the shell does not give you an error but instead gives you a null value.

You can remove the value of a variable using the unset command, as follows:

```
$ Z=hello
$ echo $Z
hello
$ unset Z
$ echo $Z

$
```

Conditional Variable Substitution

The most common way to retrieve the value of a variable is to precede the variable name with a dollar sign ($), causing the value of the variable to be substituted at that point. With the Bourne shell, you can cause variable substitution to take place only if certain conditions are met. This is called conditional variable substitution. You always enclose conditional variable substitutions in curly braces ({ }).

Substituting Default Values for Variables

As you learned earlier, when variables that have not been previously set are referenced, a null value is substituted. The Bourne shell enables you to establish default values for variable substitution using the form

```
${variable:-value}
```

where *variable* is the name of the variable and *value* is the default substitution. For example,

```
$ echo Hello $UNAME
Hello
```

```
$ echo Hello ${UNAME:-there}
Hello there
$ echo $UNAME
$
$ UNAME=John
$ echo Hello ${UNAME:-there}
Hello John
$
```

As you can see in the preceding example, when you use this type of variable substitution, the default value is substituted in the command line, but the value of the variable is not changed. Another substitution construct not only substitutes the default value but also assigns the default value to the variable as well. This substitution has the form

```
${variable:=value}
```

which causes *variable* to be assigned *value* after the substitution has been made. For example,

```
$ echo Hello $UNAME
Hello
$ echo Hello ${UNAME:=there}
Hello there
$ echo $UNAME
there
$ UNAME=John
$ echo Hello ${UNAME:-there}
Hello John
$
```

The substitution value need not be literal; it can be a command in back quotation marks:

```
USERDIR={$MYDIR:-`pwd`}
```

A third type of variable substitution substitutes the specified value if the variable has been set, as follows:

```
${variable:+value}
```

If *variable* is set, then *value* is substituted; if *variable* is not set, then nothing is substituted. For example,

```
$ ERROPT=A
$ echo ${ERROPT:+"Error Tracking is Active"}
Error Tracking is Active
$ ERROPT=
$ echo ${ERROPT:+"Error Tracking is Active"}

$
```

Conditional Variable Substitution with Error Checking

Another variable substitution method allows for error checking during variable substitution:

```
${variable:?message}
```

If *variable* is set, its value is substituted; if it is not set, *message* is written to the standard error file. If the substitution is made in a shell program, the program immediately terminates. For example,

```
$ UNAME=
$ echo ${ UNAME:?"UNAME has not been set"}
UNAME has not been set
$ UNAME=Stephanie
$ echo ${UNAME:?"UNAME has not been set"}
Stephanie
$
```

If no message is specified, the shell displays a default message, as in the following example:

```
$ UNAME=
$ echo ${UNAME:?}
sh: UNAME: parameter null or not set
$
```

Positional Variables or Shell Arguments

You may recall that when the shell's command-line interpreter processes a line of input, the first word of the command line is considered to be an executable file, and the remainder of the line is passed as arguments to the executable. If the executable is a shell program, the arguments are passed to the program as positional variables. The first argument passed to the program is assigned to the variable $1, the second argument is $2, and so on up to $9. Notice that the names of the variables are actually the digits 1 through 9; the dollar sign, as always, is the special character that causes variable substitution to occur.

The positional variable $0 always contains the name of the executable. Positional variables are discussed later in this chapter in the section "Shell Programming."

Preventing Variables from Being Changed

If a variable has a value assigned, and you want to make sure that its value is not subsequently changed, you may designate a variable as a read-only variable with the following command:

```
readonly variable
```

From this point on, *variable* cannot be reassigned. This ensures that a variable won't be accidentally changed.

Making Variables Available to Subshells with export

When a shell executes a program, it sets up a new environment for the program to execute in. This is called a subshell. In the Bourne shell, variables are considered to be local variables; in other words, they are not recognized outside the shell in which they were assigned a value. You can make a variable available to any subshells you execute by exporting it using the export command. Your variables can never be made available to other users.

Now suppose you start a new shell.

```
Enter Command: sh
$ exit
Enter Command:
```

When you started a new shell, the default shell prompt appeared. This is because the variable assignment to PS1 was made only in the current shell. To make the new shell prompt active in subshells, you must export it as in the following example.

```
$ PS1="Enter Command: "
Enter Command: export PS1
Enter Command: sh
Enter Command:
```

Now the variable PS1 is global; it is available to all subshells. When a variable has been made global in this way, it remains available until you log out of the parent shell. You can make an assignment permanent by including it in your .profile, see the section "Customizing the Shell."

Shell Script Programming

In this major section, you learn how to put commands together in such a way that the sum is greater than the parts. You learn some UNIX commands that are useful mainly in the context of shell programs. You also learn how to make your program perform functions conditionally based on logical tests that you define, and you learn how to have parts of a program repeat until its function is completed. In short, you learn how to use the common tools supplied with UNIX to create more powerful tools specific to the tasks you need to perform.

What Is a Program?

A wide assortment of definitions exist for what is a computer program, but for this discussion, a computer program is an ordered set of instructions causing a computer to perform some useful function. When you cause a computer to perform some tasks in a specific order so that the result is greater than the individual tasks, you have programmed the computer. When you enter a formula into a spreadsheet, for example, you are programming. When you write a macro in a word processor, you are programming. When you enter a complex command such as

```
$ ls -R / ¦ grep myname ¦ pg
```

in a UNIX shell, you are programming the shell; you are causing the computer to execute a series of utilities in a specific order, which gives a result that is more useful than the result of any of the utilities taken by itself.

A Simple Program

Suppose that you back up your data files daily with the following command:

```
$ cd /usr/home/myname; ls * ¦ cpio -o >/dev/rmt0
```

As you learned earlier, when you enter a complex command like this, you are programming the shell. A useful thing about programs, though, is that they can be placed in a program library and used over and over, without having to do the programming each time. Shell programs are no exception. Rather than enter the lengthy backup command each time, you can store the program in a file named `backup`:

```
$ cat >backup
cd /usr/home/myname
ls * ¦ cpio -o >/dev/rmt0
Ctrl+d
```

You could, of course, use your favorite editor (see *UNIX Unleashed, Internet Edition*, Chapter 3, "Text Editing with vi and emacs"), and in fact with larger shell programs, you almost certainly will want to. You can enter the command in a single line, as you did when typing it into the command line, but because the commands in a shell program (sometimes called a shell script) are executed in sequence, putting each command on a line by itself makes the program easier to read. Creating easy-to-read programs becomes more important as the size of the programs increase.

Now to back up your data files, you need to call up another copy of the shell program (known as a subshell) and give it the commands found in the file `backup`. To do so, use the following command:

```
$ sh backup
```

The program `sh` is the same Bourne shell that was started when you logged in, but when a filename is passed as an argument, instead of becoming an interactive shell, it takes its commands from the file.

An alternative method for executing the commands in the file `backup` is to make the file itself an executable. To do so, use the following command:

```
$ chmod +x backup
```

Now you can back up your data files by entering the newly created command:

```
$ backup
```

If you want to execute the commands in this manner, the file `backup` must reside in one of the directories specified in the environment variable `$PATH`.

The Shell as a Language

If all you could do in a shell program was to string together a series of UNIX commands into a single command, you would have an important tool, but shell programming is much more. Like traditional programming languages, the shell offers features that enable you to make your shell programs more useful, such as: data variables, argument passing, decision making, flow control, data input and output, subroutines, and handling interrupts.

By using these features, you can automate many repetitive functions, which is, of course, the purpose of any computer language.

Using Data Variables in Shell Programs

You usually use variables within programs as place holders for data that will be available when the program is run and that may change from execution to execution. Consider the `backup` program:

```
cd /usr/home/myname
ls ¦ cpio -o >/dev/rmt0
```

In this case, the directory to be backed up is contained in the program as a literal, or constant, value. This program is useful only to back up that one directory. The use of a variable makes the program more generic:

```
cd $WORKDIR
ls * ¦ cpio -o >/dev/rmt0
```

With this simple change, any user can use the program to back up the directory that has been named in the variable `$WORKDIR`, provided that the variable has been exported to subshells. See "Making Variables Available to Subshells with `export`" earlier in this chapter.

Entering Comments in Shell Programs

Quite often when you're writing programs, program code that seemed logical six months ago may be fairly obscure today. Good programmers annotate their programs with comments. You enter comments into shell programs by inserting the pound sign (#) special character. When the shell interpreter sees the pound sign, it considers all text to the end of the line as a comment.

Doing Arithmetic on Shell Variables

In most higher-level programming languages, variables are typed, meaning that they are restricted to certain kinds of data, such as numbers or characters. Shell variables are always stored as characters. To do arithmetic on shell variables, you must use the `expr` command.

The `expr` command evaluates its arguments as mathematical expressions. The general form of the command is as follows:

```
expr integer operator integer
```

Because the shell stores its variables as characters, it is your responsibility as a shell programmer to make sure that the integer arguments to `expr` are in fact integers. Following are the valid arithmetic operators:

+	Adds the two integers.
-	Subtracts the second integer from the first.
*	Multiplies the two integers.
/	Divides the first integer by the second.
%	Gives the modulus (remainder) of the division.

```
$ expr 2 + 1
3
$ expr 5 - 3
2
```

If the argument to expr is a variable, the value of the variable is substituted before the expression is evaluated, as in the following example:

```
$ $int=3
$ expr $int + 4
7
```

You should avoid using the asterisk operator (*) alone for multiplication. If you enter

```
$ expr 4 * 5
```

you get an error because the shell sees the asterisk and performs filename substitution before sending the arguments on to expr. The proper form of the multiplication expression is

```
$ expr 4 \* 5
20
```

You also can combine arithmetic expressions, as in the following:

```
$ expr 5 + 7 / 3
7
```

The results of the preceding expression may seem odd. The first thing to remember is that division and multiplication are of a higher precedence than addition and subtraction, so the first operation performed is 7 divided by 3. Because expr deals only in integers, the result of the division is 2, which is then added to 5, giving the final result 7. Parentheses are not recognized by expr, so to override the precedence, you must do that manually. You can use back quotation marks to change the precedence, as follows:

```
$ int='expr 5 + 7'
$ expr $int / 3
4
```

Or you can use the more direct route:

```
$ expr 'expr 5 + 7' / 3
4
```

Passing Arguments to Shell Programs

A program can get data in two ways: either it is passed to the program when it is executed as arguments, or the program gets data interactively. An editor such as vi is usually used in an interactive mode, whereas commands such as ls and expr get their data as arguments. Shell programs are no exception. In the section "Reading Data into a Program Interactively," you see how a shell program can get its data interactively.

Passing arguments to a shell program on a command line can greatly enhance the program's versatility. Consider the inverse of the backup program presented earlier:

```
$ cat >restoreall
cd $WORKDIR
cpio -i </dev/rmt0
Ctrl+d
```

As written, the program `restoreall` reloads the entire tape made by `backup`. But what if you want to restore only a single file from the tape? You can do so by passing the name of the file as an argument. The enhanced `restore1` program is now:

```
# restore1 - program to restore a single file
cd $WORKDIR
cpio -i $1 </dev/rmt0
```

Now you can pass a parameter representing the name of the file to be restored to the `restore1` program:

```
$ restore1 file1
```

Here, the filename `file1` is passed to `restore1` as the first positional parameter. The limitation to `restore1` is that if you want to restore two files, you must run `restore1` twice.

As a final enhancement, you can use the `$*` variable to pass any number of arguments to the program:

```
# restoreany - program to restore any number of files
cd $WORKDIR
cpio -i $* </dev/rmt0
```

```
$ restoreany file1 file2 file3
```

Because shell variables that have not been assigned a value always return null, or empty, if the `restore1` or `restoreany` programs are run with no command-line parameters, a null value is placed in the `cpio` command, which causes the entire archive to be restored.

Consider the program in Listing 9.1; it calculates the length of time to travel a certain distance.

Listing 9.1. Program example with two parameters.

```
# traveltime - a program to calculate how long it will
# take to travel a fixed distance
# syntax: traveltime miles mph
X60=`expr $1 \* 60`
TOTMINUTES=`expr $X60 / $2`
HOURS=`expr $TOTMINUTES / 60`
MINUTES=`expr $TOTMINUTES % 60`
echo "The trip will take $HOURS hours and $MINUTES minutes"
```

The program in Listing 9.1 takes two positional parameters: the distance in miles and the rate of travel in miles per hour. The mileage is passed to the program as $1 and the rate of travel as $2. Note that the first command in the program multiplies the mileage by 60. Because the `expr` command works only with integers, it is useful to calculate the travel time in minutes. The user-defined variable X60 holds an interim calculation that, when divided by the mileage rate, gives the total travel time in minutes. Then, using both integer division and modulus division, the number of hours and number of minutes of travel time is found.

Now execute the `traveltime` for a 90-mile trip at 40 mph with the following command line:

```
$ traveltime 90 40
The trip will take 2 hours and 15 minutes
```

Decision Making in Shell Programs

One of the things that gives computer programming languages much of their strength is their capability to make decisions. Of course, computers don't think, so the decisions that computer programs make are only in response to conditions that you have anticipated in your program. The decision making done by computer programs is in the form of conditional execution: if a condition exists, then execute a certain set of commands. In most computer languages, this setup is called an `if-then` construct.

The `if-then` Statement

The Bourne shell also has an `if-then` construct. The syntax of the construct is as follows:

```
if command_1
then
  command_2
  command_3
fi
command_4
```

You may recall that every program or command concludes by returning an exit status. The exit status is available in the shell variable `$?`. The `if` statement checks the exit status of its command. If that command is successful, then all the commands between the `then` statement and the `fi` statement are executed. In this program sequence, *command_1* is always executed, *command_2* and *command_3* are executed only if *command_1* is successful, and *command_4* is always executed.

Consider a variation of the `backup` program, except that after copying all the files to the backup media, you want to remove them from your disk. Call the program `unload` and allow the user to specify the directory to be unloaded on the command line, as in the following example:

```
# unload - program to backup and remove files
# syntax - unload directory
cd $1
ls -a ¦ cpio -o >/dev/rmt0
rm *
```

At first glance, it appears that this program will do exactly what you want. But what if something goes wrong during the `cpio` command? In this case, the backup media is a tape device. What if the operator forgets to insert a blank tape in the tape drive? The `rm` command would go ahead and execute, wiping out the directory before it has been backed up! The `if-then` construct prevents this catastrophe from happening. A revised `unload` program is shown in Listing 9.2.

Listing 9.2. Shell program with error checking.

```
# unload - program to backup and remove files
# syntax - unload directory
cd $1
if ls -a ¦ cpio -o >/dev/rmt0
then
    rm *
fi
```

In the program in Listing 9.2, the rm command is executed only if the cpio command is successful. Note that the if statement looks at the exit status of the last command in a pipeline.

Data Output from Shell Programs

The standard output and error output of any commands within a shell program are passed on the standard output of the user who invokes the program unless that output is redirected within the program. In the example in Listing 9.2, any error messages from cpio would have been seen by the user of the program. Sometimes you may write programs that need to communicate with the user of the program. In Bourne shell programs, you usually do so by using the echo command. As the name indicates, echo simply sends its arguments to the standard output and appends a newline character at the end, as in the following example:

```
$ echo "Mary had a little lamb"
Mary had a little lamb
```

The echo command recognizes several special escape characters that assist in formatting output. They are as follows:

\b	Backspace
\c	Prints line without newline character
\f	Form Feed: advances page on a hard copy printer; advances to new screen on a display terminal
\n	Newline
\r	Carriage return
\t	Tab
\v	Vertical Tab
\\	Backslash
\0nnn	A one-, two-, or three-digit octal integer representing one of the ASCII characters

If you want to display a prompt to the user to enter the data, and you want the user response to appear on the same line as the prompt, you use the \c character, as follows:

```
$ echo "Enter response:\c"
Enter response$
```

The `if-then-else` Statement

A common desire in programming is to perform one set of commands if a condition is true and a different set of commands if the condition is false. In the Bourne shell, you can achieve this effect by using the `if-then-else` construct:

```
if command_1
then
    command_2
    command_3
else
    command_4
    command_5
fi
```

In this construct, *command_1* is always executed. If *command_1* succeeds, the *command_2* and *command_3* are executed; if it fails, *command_4* and *command_5* are executed.

You can now enhance the `unload` program to be more user friendly. For example,

```
# unload - program to backup and remove files
# syntax - unload directory
cd $1
if ls -a ¦ cpio -o >/dev/rmt0
then
    rm *
else
    echo "A problem has occurred in creating the backup."
    echo "The directory will not be erased."
    echo "Please check the backup device and try again."
fi
```

TIP

Because the shell ignores extra white space in a command line, good programmers use this fact to enhance the readability of their programs. When commands are executed within a then or else clause, indent all the commands in the clause the same distance.

Testing Conditions with `test`

You've seen how the `if` statement tests the exit status of its command to control the order in which commands are executed, but what if you want to test other conditions? A command that is used a great deal in shell programs is the `test` command. The `test` command examines some condition and returns a zero exit status if the condition is true and a nonzero exit status if the condition is false. This capability gives the `if` statement in the Bourne shell the same power as other languages with some enhancements that are helpful in shell programming.

The general form of the command is as follows:

```
test condition
```

The conditions that can be tested fall into four categories: 1) String operators that test the condition or relationship of character strings; 2) Integer relationships that test the numerical relationship of two integers; 3) File operators that test for the existence or state of a file; 4) Logical operators that allow for *and/or* combinations of the other conditions.

Testing Character Data

You learned earlier that the Bourne shell does not type cast data elements. Each word of an input line and each variable can be taken as a string of characters. Some commands, such as expr and test, have the capability to perform numeric operations on strings that can be translated to integer values, but any data element can be operated on as a character string.

You can compare two strings to see whether they are equivalent or not equivalent. You also can test a single string to see whether it has a value or not. The string operators are as follows:

str1 = str2   True if str1 is the same length and contains the same characters as str2

str1 != str2   True if str1 is not the same as str2

-n str1   True if the length of str1 is greater than 0 (is not null)

-z str1   True if str1 is null (has a length of 0)

str1   True if *str1* is not null

Even though you most often use test with a shell program as a decision maker, test is a program that can stand on its own as in the following:

```
$ str1=abcd
$ test $str1 = abcd
$ echo $?
0
$
```

Notice that unlike the variable assignment statement in the first line in the preceding example, the test command must have the equal sign surrounded by white space. In this example, the shell sends three arguments to test. Strings must be equivalent in both length and characters by character.

```
$ str1="abcd "
$ test "$str1" = abcd
$ echo $?
1
$
```

In the preceding example, str1 contains five characters, the last of which is a space. The second string in the test command contains only four characters. The nonequivalency operator returns a true value everywhere that the equivalency operator returns false.

```
$ str1=abcd
$ test $str1 != abcd
$ echo $?
1
$
```

Two of the string operations, testing of a string with no operator and testing with the -n operator, seem almost identical, as the following example shows:

```
$ str1=abcd
$ test $str1
$ echo $?
0
$ test -n $str1
$ echo $?
0
$
```

The difference between the two commands in the preceding example is a subtle one, but it points out a potential problem in using the test command, as shown in the following example of two different tests:

```
$ str1="        "
$ test $str1
$ echo $?
1
$ test "$str1"
$ echo $?
0
$ test -n $str1
test: argument expected
$ test -n "$str1"
$ echo $?
0
```

In the preceding example, the first test is false. Why? Remember that the shell interpreter makes variable substitutions before it processes the command line, and when it processes the command line, it removes excess white space. Where $str1 does not have double quotation marks, the blanks are passed to the command line and stripped; when the double quotation marks are used, the blanks are passed on to test. What happens in the third test? When the interpreter removes the white space, test is passed only the -n option, which requires an argument.

Testing Numeric Data

The test command, like expr, has the capability to convert strings to integers and perform numeric operations. Whereas expr performs arithmetic on integers, test performs logical comparisons. The available numerical comparisons are as follows:

int1 -eq *int2*	True if *int1* is numerically equal to *int2*
int1 -ne *int2*	True if *int1* is not equal to *int2*
int1 -gt *int2*	True if *int1* is greater than *int2*
int1 -ge *int2*	True if *int1* is greater than or equal to *int2*
int1 -lt *int2*	True if *int1* is less than *int2*
int1 -le *int2*	True if int1 is less than or equal to int2

This difference between numeric equivalency and string equivalency is shown in the following example, which defines two strings and then compares them using numeric equivalency first and then string equivalency.

```
$ str1=1234
$ str2=01234
$ test $str1 = $str2
$ echo $?
1
$ test $str1 -eq $str2
$ echo $?
0
$
```

In the second case here, the strings were converted to integers and found to be numerically equivalent, whereas the original strings were not.

Testing for Files

The third type of condition that `test` can examine is the state of files. Using the `test` command in your program, you can determine whether a file exists, whether it can be written to, and several other conditions. All the file test options return true, only if the file exists. The file test options are

`-r filenm`	True if the user has read permission
`-w filenm`	True if the user has write permission
`-x filenm`	True if the user has execute permission
`-f filenm`	True if `filenm` is a regular file
`-d filenm`	True if `filenm` is a directory
`-c filenm`	True if `filenm` is a character special file
`-b filenm`	True if `filenm` is a block special file
`-s filenm`	True if the size of `filenm` is not zero
`-t fnumb`	True if the device associated with the file descriptor `fnumb` (1 by default) is a terminal device

Combining and Negating test Conditions

The expressions that have been discussed thus far are called primary expressions because each tests only one condition. The characters following the hyphen are the operators, and the terms to the right and left of the operators are the arguments. Some of the operators, like the numeric comparison operators, are binary because they always have two arguments, one on the right and one on the left. Some of the operators, like the file test options, are unary because the operator takes only one argument, which is always placed on the right.

Sometimes you may not be interested in what is true, but in what is not true. To find out what is not true, you can use the unary negation operator, the exclamation (!), in front of any primary. Create an empty file and try some of the file operators shown in the following example:

```
$ cat >empty
Ctrl+d
$ test -r empty
$ echo $?
0
$ test -s empty
$ echo $?
1
$ test ! -s empty
$ echo $?
0
$
```

The primary expressions in a test command can be combined with a logical and operator, -a, or with a logical or operator, -o. When you use the -a operator, the combined expression is true if and only if both of the primary expressions are true. When you use the -o operator, the combined expression is true if either of the primary expressions is true. Using the empty file from above, test to see whether the file is readable and contains data:

```
$ test -r empty -a -s empty
$ echo $?
1
$
```

The combined expression is false. The first expression is true because the file is readable, but the second expression fails because the file has a size of 0.

A Shorthand Method of Doing Tests

Because the test command is such an important part of shell programming, and to make shell programs look more like programs in other languages, the Bourne shell has an alternative method for using test: you enclose the entire expression in square brackets ([ ]).

```
$ int1=4
$ [ $int1 -gt 2 ]
$ echo $?
0
$
```

Remember that even though it looks different, the preceding example is still the test command, and the same rules apply.

Using test, you can make the unload program from Listing 9.2 more user friendly, as well as more bullet proof, by making sure that a valid directory name is entered on the command line. The revised program is shown in Listing 9.3.

Listing 9.3. Program using test for error checking.

```
# unload - program to backup and remove files
# syntax - unload directory
# check arguments
if [ $# -ne 1 ]
then
```

continues

9

THE BOURNE
SHELL

Listing 9.3. continued

```
    echo "usage: unload directory"
    exit 1
fi
# check for valid directory name
if [! -d "$1" ]
then
    echo "$1 is not a directory"
    exit 2
fi
cd $1
ls -a ¦ cpio -o >/dev/rmt0
if [ $? -eq 0 ]
then
    rm *
else
    echo "A problem has occurred in creating the backup."
    echo "The directory will not be erased."
    echo "Please check the backup device and try again."

    exit 3
fi
```

There are several items of interest in the revised program in Listing 9.3. One is the introduction of the exit statement. The exit statement has two purposes: to stop any further commands in the program from being executed and to set the exit status of the program. By setting a nonzero exit status, subsequent programs can check the $? variable to see whether unload is successful. Notice that in the test to see whether the argument is a valid directory, the variable substitution is made within double quotation marks. Using double quotation marks prevents the test command from failing if the program were called with an argument containing only blanks; the test still fails, but the user does not see the error message from test. One other change to the program is to remove the actual backup command from the if statement and place it on a line by itself and then use test on the exit status to make the decision. Although using if to check the exit status of the backup is legitimate and probably more efficient, the meaning may be unclear to the casual observer.

Consider the traveltime program shown in Listing 9.1. Suppose you execute the program with the following command line:

```
$ traveltime 61 60
The trip will take 1 hours and 1 minutes
```

Although this answer is correct, it may make your English teacher cringe. You can use numeric testing and if-then-else statements to make the output more palatable. The revised program is shown in Listing 9.4.

Listing 9.4. Revised traveltime program.

```
# traveltime - a program to calculate how long it will
# take to travel a fixed distance
# syntax: traveltime miles mph
```

```
X60=`expr $1 \* 60`
TOTMINUTES=`expr $X60 / $2`
HOURS=`expr $TOTMINUTES / 60`
MINUTES=`expr $TOTMINUTES % 60`
if [ $HOURS -gt 1 ]
then
    DISPHRS=hours
else
    DISPHRS=hour
fi
if [ $MINUTES -gt 1 ]
then
    DISPMIN=minutes
else
    DISPMIN=minute
fi
echo "The trip will take $HOURS $DISPHRS \c"
if [ $MINUTES -gt 0 ]
then
    echo "and $MINUTES $DISPMIN"
else
    echo
fi
```

Now traveltime supplies the appropriate singular or plural noun depending on the amount of time:

```
$ traveltime 50 40
The trip will take 1 hour and 15 minutes
$ traveltime 121 60
The trip will take 2 hours and 1 minute
$ traveltime 120 60
The trip will take 2 hours
$
```

The Null Command

You have now enhanced the unload program to accept the name of a directory from the command line, to check for a valid directory name, and to give the user of the program more information on any errors that may occur. The only real difference between the unload function and the backup function is that unload removes the files from the directory after it has been archived. It would seem that a simple modification to unload—taking out the rm statement— would transform unload to an enhanced version of backup. The only problem is that the rm command is the only command following a then statement, and at least one command must follow every then statement. The Bourne shell provides a solution with the null command. The null command, represented by a colon (:), is a place holder whose purpose is to fulfill a requirement where a command must appear. To change unload to backup, you replace the rm command with the null command and change some of the messages.

```
# backup - program to backup all files in a directory
# syntax - backup directory
# check arguments
if [ $# -ne 1 ]
```

```
then
    echo "usage: backup directory"
    exit 1
fi
# check for valid directory name
if [ ! -d "$1" ]
then
    echo "$1 is not a directory"
    exit 2
fi
cd $1
ls -a ¦ cpio -o >/dev/rmt0
if [ $? -eq 0 ]
then
    :
else
    echo "A problem has occurred in creating the backup."
    echo "Please check the backup device and try again."
```

Displaying the Program Name

In the previous two examples, a helpful message was displayed for the user who failed to enter any command-line arguments.

In this message, the name of the program is displayed as part of a literal string. However, if you renamed this program, this message would no longer be valid. In the Bourne shell, the variable $0 always contains the name of the program, as entered on the command line. You can now make the program more general, as in the following example:

```
if [ $# -ne 1 ]
then
    echo "usage: $0 directory"
    exit 1
fi
```

Nested if Statements and the elif Construct

Often you may want your program to do the following:

1. Check for a primary condition, and

   A. If the primary condition is true, perform an operation.

   B. If the primary condition is false, check a secondary condition.

      (1) If the secondary condition is true, perform another operation, but

      (2) If the secondary condition is false, check a third condition.

          (a) If the third condition is true, perform another operation.

You can do so by nesting if-else statements, as in the following syntax:

```
if command
then
    command
else
    if command
    then
```

```
        command
   else
      if command
      then
         command
      fi
   fi
fi
```

Nesting can be useful but can also be confusing, especially knowing where to place the `fi` statements. Because this kind of programming occurs frequently, the Bourne shell provides a special construct called `elif`, which stands for `else-if` and indicates a continuation of the main `if` statement. You could restate the sequence described above with `elif` statements, as follows:

```
if command
then
    command
elif command
then
    command
elif command
then
    command
fi
```

Either method produces the same results. You should use the one that makes the most sense to you.

Reading Data into a Program Interactively

Up to this point, all the input to your programs has been supplied by users in the form of command-line arguments. You can also obtain input for a program by using the `read` statement. The general syntax of the `read` statement is as follows:

```
read var1 var2 ... varn
```

When the Bourne shell encounters a `read` statement, the standard input file is read until the shell reads a newline character. When the shell interprets the line of input, it does not make filename and variable substitutions, but it does remove excess white space. After it removes white space, the shell puts the value of the first word into the first variable, and the second word into the second variable, and so on until either the list of variables or the input line is exhausted. If there are more words in the input line than in the variable list, the last variable in the list is assigned the remaining words in the input line. If there are more variables in the list than words in the line, the leftover variables are null. A word is a group of alphanumeric characters surrounded by white space.

In the following example, the `read` statement is looking for three variables. Since the line of input contains three words, each word is assigned to a variable.

```
$ read var1 var2 var3
Hello       my              friend
$ echo $var1 $var2 $var3
Hello my friend
```

9

```
$ echo $var1
Hello
$ echo $var2
my
$ echo $var3
friend
$
```

In the next example, the read statement is looking for three variables, but the input line consists of four words. In this case, the last two words are assigned to the third variable.

```
$ read var1 var2 var3
Hello my dear friend
$ echo $var1
Hello
$ echo $var2
my
$ echo $var3
dear friend
$
```

Finally, in this example, the input line contains fewer words than the number of variables in the read statement, so the last variable remains null.

```
$ read var1 var2 var3
Hello friend
$ echo $var1
Hello
$ echo $var2
friend
$ echo $var3

$
```

Suppose that you want to give the user of the unload program in Listing 9.3 the option to abort. You might insert these lines of code:

```
...
echo "The following files will be unloaded"
ls -x $1
echo "Do you want to continue: Y or N \c"
read ANSWER
if [ $ANSWER = N -o $ANSWER = n ]
then
    exit 0
fi
...
```

In the preceding example, you use the \c character in the user prompt so that the user's response appears on the same line as the prompt. The read statement will cause the program to pause until the operator responds with a line of input. The operator's response will be stored in the variable ANSWER. When you're testing the user's response, you use the -o operator so that the appropriate action is taken, regardless of whether the user's response is in upper- or lowercase.

The case Statement

Earlier in this section, you saw that the Bourne shell provided a special construct for a common occurrence by providing the `elif` statement to be used in place of nested `if-then-else` constructs. Another fairly common occurrence is a series of `elif` statements where the same variable is tested for many possible conditions, as in the following:

```
if [ variable1 = value1 ]
then
    command
    command
elif [ variable1 = value2 ]
then
    command
    command
elif [ variable1 = value3 ]
then
    command
    command
fi
```

The Bourne shell provides a cleaner and more powerful method of handling this situation with the `case` statement. The `case` statement is cleaner because it does away with the `elifs` and the `thens`. It is more powerful because it allows pattern matching, much as the command-line interpreter does. The `case` statement allows a value to be named, which is almost always a variable, and a series of patterns to be used to match against the value, and a series of commands to be executed if the value matches the pattern. The general syntax of `case` is as follows:

```
case value in
    pattern1)
        command
        command;;
    pattern2)
        command
        command;;
    ...
    patternn)
        command;
esac
```

The `case` statement executes only one set of commands. If the value matches more than one of the patterns, only the first set of commands specified is executed. The double semicolons (;;) after a command act as the delimiter of the commands to be executed for a particular pattern match.

In the program in Listing 9.5, the `case` statement combines the three sample programs—`backup`, `restore`, and `unload`—into a single interactive program, enabling the user to select the function from a menu.

Listing 9.5. An interactive archive program.

```
# Interactive program to restore, backup, or unload
# a directory
```

continues

Listing 9.5. continued

```
echo "Welcome to the menu driven Archive program"
echo _
# Read and validate the name of the directory
echo "What directory do you want? \c"
read WORKDIR
if [ ! -d $WORKDIR ]
then
    echo "Sorry, $WORKDIR is not a directory"
    exit 1
fi
# Make the directory the current working directory
cd $WORKDIR
# Display a Menu
echo "Make a Choice from the Menu below"
echo _
echo "1  Restore Archive to $WORKDIR"
echo "2  Backup $WORKDIR "
echo "3  Unload $WORKDIR"
echo
# Read and execute the user's selection
echo "Enter Choice: \c"
read CHOICE
case "$CHOICE" in
    1) echo "Restoring..."
       cpio -i </dev/rmt0;;
    2) echo "Archiving..."
       ls ¦ cpio -o >/dev/rmt0;;
    3) echo "Unloading..."
       ls ¦ cpio -o >/dev/rmt0;;
    *) echo "Sorry, $CHOICE is not a valid choice"
       exit 1
esac
#Check for cpio errors
if [ $? -ne 0 ]
then
    echo "A problem has occurred during the process"
    if [ $CHOICE = 3 ]
    then
        echo "The directory will not be erased"
    fi
    echo "Please check the device and try again"
    exit 2
else
    if [ $CHOICE = 3 ]
    then
        rm *
    fi
fi
```

In the program in Listing 9.5, notice the use of the asterisk (*) to define a default action if all the other patterns in the case statement fail to match. Also notice that the check for errors in the archive process occurs only once in the program. This check can be done in this program because the exit status of the case statement is always the exit status of the last command executed. Because all three cases end with the execution of cpio, and the default case ends with an exit statement, the exit status variable at this point in this program is always the exit status of `cpio`.

Another powerful capability of the `case` statement is to allow multiple patterns to be related to the same set of commands. You use a vertical bar (¦) as an or symbol in the following form:

```
pattern1 ¦ pattern2 ) command
                    command;;
```

You can further modify the interactive archive program to allow the user to make a choice by entering either the menu number or the first letter of the function, by changing the `case` statement:

```
read CHOICE
case "$CHOICE" in
   1 ¦ R ) echo "Restoring..."
           cpio -i </dev/rmt0;;
   2 ¦ B ) echo "Archiving..."
           ls ¦ cpio -o >/dev/rmt0;;
   3 ¦ U ) echo "Unloading..."
           ls ¦ cpio -o >/dev/rmt0;;
   *) echo "Sorry, $CHOICE is not a valid choice"
      exit 1
esac
```

Building Repetitions into a Program

Up to now, the programs you have looked at have had a top-to-bottom, linear progression. The program statements are executed from top to bottom. One of the most beneficial things about computer programs is their capability to process data in volume. For this to occur, the programming language must have some construct to cause portions of the program to be repetitive. In computer terminology, this construct is often called looping.

For example, suppose you had a computer file containing records with mailing addresses and ZIP codes and you wanted to print only records matching a specific ZIP code. You would want to write a program that reads a record, performs a matching test on the ZIP code, prints those that match, and then repeat the process until the data is exhausted. You could do this within a loop.

The Bourne shell has three different looping constructs built into the language. One of the key concepts in program looping is the termination of the loop. Many hours of computer time are wasted by programs that inadvertently go into infinite loops. The main difference between the shell's three looping constructs is the method by which the loop is terminated. The three types of loops are the `while` loop, the `until` loop, and the `for` loop; each is discussed separately in the following sections.

Repeating Within a `while` Loop

The `while` construct enables you to specify commands that will be executed while some condition is true.

The general format of the while construct is as follows:

```
while command
do
    command
    command
    ...
    command
done
```

Consider the following example in a program called squares in Listing 9.6.

Listing 9.6. Example of a while loop.

```
# squares - prints the square of integers in succession
int=1
while [ $int -lt 5 ]
do
    sq=`expr $int \* $int`
    echo $sq
    int=`expr $int + 1`
done
echo "Job Complete"

$ squares
1
4
9
16
Job Complete
$
```

In the program in Listing 9.6, as long as the value of int is less than five, the commands inside the loop are executed. On the fifth repetition, the test condition associated with the while statement returns a nonzero value, and the command following the done statement is executed.

In the interactive archive program in Listing 9.5, the user is allowed to make a single request and the program terminates. Using while, you can change the program to allow the user to enter multiple requests. The revised program is shown in Listing 9.7.

Listing 9.7. Revised interactive archive program.

```
# Interactive program to restore, backup, or unload
# a directory
echo "Welcome to the menu driven Archive program"
ANSWER=Y
while [ $ANSWER = Y -o $ANSWER = y ]
do
    echo _
# Read and validate the name of the directory
    echo "What directory do you want? \c"
    read WORKDIR
    if [ ! -d $WORKDIR ]
    then
```

```
        echo "Sorry, $WORKDIR is not a directory"
        exit 1
    fi
# Make the directory the current working directory
    cd $WORKDIR
# Display a Menu
    echo "Make a Choice from the Menu below"
    echo _
    echo "1  Restore Archive to $WORKDIR"
    echo "2  Backup $WORKDIR "
    echo "3  Unload $WORKDIR"
    echo
# Read and execute the user's selection
    echo "Enter Choice: \c"
    read CHOICE
    case "$CHOICE" in
        1) echo "Restoring..."
           cpio -i </dev/rmt0;;
        2) echo "Archiving..."
           ls ¦ cpio -o >/dev/rmt0;;
        3) echo "Unloading..."
           ls ¦ cpio -o >/dev/rmt0;;
        *) echo "Sorry, $CHOICE is not a valid choice"
    esac
#Check for cpio errors
    if [ $? -ne 0 ]
    then
        echo "A problem has occurred during the process"
        if [ $CHOICE = 3 ]
        then
            echo "The directory will not be erased"
        fi
        echo "Please check the device and try again"
        exit 2
    else
        if [ $CHOICE = 3 ]
        then
            rm *
        fi
    fi
    echo "Do you want to make another choice? \c"
    read ANSWER
done
```

By initializing the ANSWER variable to Y, enclosing the main part of the program within a while loop, and getting a new ANSWER at the end of the loop in the program in Listing 9.7, the user is able to stay in this program until he or she answers N to the question.

Repeating Within an until Loop

The while construct causes the program to loop as long as some condition is true. The until construct is the complement to while; it causes the program to loop until a condition is true. These two constructs are so similar, you can usually use either one. Use the one that makes the most sense in the context of the program you are writing.

The general format of the `until` construct is as follows:

```
until command
do
    command
    command
    ...
    command
done
```

You could have made the modification to the interactive archive program just as easily with an `until` loop by replacing the `while` with `until`:

```
until [ $ANSWER = N -o $ANSWER = n ]
```

Processing an Arbitrary Number of Parameters with `shift`

Before considering the `for` loop, it would be helpful to look at the `shift` command, since the `for` loop is really a shorthand use of `shift`.

In the examples presented so far, the number of positional parameters, or command-line arguments, is either presumed to be solitary or is passed on to a command as a whole using the `$*` variable. If a program needs to process each of the command-line arguments individually, and the number of arguments is not known, you can process the arguments one by one by using the `shift` command in your program. The `shift` command shifts the position of positional parameters by one; `$2` becomes `$1`, `$3` becomes `$2`, and so on. The parameter that was `$1` before the `shift` command is not available after `shift`. The following simple program illustrates this concept:

```
# shifter
until [ $# -eq 0 ]
do
    echo "Argument is $1 and `expr $# - 1` argument(s) remain"
    shift
done

$ shifter 1 2 3 4
Argument is 1 and 3 argument(s) remain
Argument is 2 and 2 argument(s) remain
Argument is 3 and 1 argument(s) remain
Argument is 4 and 0 argument(s) remain
$
```

You may have noticed that the `$#` variable decremented each time the `shift` command was executed in the preceding example. Using this knowledge, you can use an `until` loop to process all the variables. Consider the example in Listing 9.8, a program to sum an integer list supplied as command-line arguments.

Listing 9.8. An integer summing program.

```
# sumints - a program to sum a series of integers
#
if [ $# -eq 0 ]
```

```
then
    echo "Usage: sumints integer list"
    exit 1
fi
sum=0
until [ $# -eq 0 ]
do
    sum=`expr $sum + $1`
    shift
done
echo $sum
```

Following is the execution of `sumints`:

```
$ sumints 12 18 6 21
57
$
```

You also can use the `shift` command for another purpose. The Bourne shell predefines nine positional parameters, `$1` through `$9`. This does not mean that only nine positional parameters can be entered on the command line, but to access positional parameters beyond the first nine, you must use the `shift` command.

The `shift` command can take an integer argument that causes it to shift more than one position at a time. If you know that you have processed the first three positional parameters, for example, and you want to begin a loop to process the remaining arguments, you can make `$4` shift to `$1` with the following command:

```
shift 3.
```

Repeating Within a for Loop

The third type of looping construct in the Bourne shell is the `for` loop. The `for` loop differs from the other constructs in that it is not based on a condition being true or false. Instead the `for` loop executes one time for each word in the argument list it has been supplied. For each iteration of the loop, a variable name supplied on the `for` command line assumes the value of the next word in the argument list. The general syntax of the `for` loop is as follows:

```
for variable in arg1 arg2  ... argn
do
    command
    ...
    command
done
```

The following simple example illustrates the construct:

```
$ for LETTER in a b c d; do echo $LETTER; done
a
b
c
d
$
```

9

THE BOURNE
SHELL

Because the argument list contained four words, the loop is executed exactly four times. The argument list in the `for` command does not have to be a literal constant; it can be from a variable substitution.

You can also write the `sumints` program in Listing 9.8 using a `for` loop, by passing the command-line arguments to the `for` loop. The modified program appears in Listing 9.9.

Listing 9.9. Modified integer summing program.

```
# sumints - a program to sum a series of integers
#
if [ $# -eq 0 ]
then
    echo "Usage: sumints integer list"
    exit 1
fi
sum=0
for INT in $*
do
    sum=`expr $sum + $INT`
done
echo $sum
```

Getting Out of a Loop from the Middle

Normally, a looping construct executes all the commands between the `do` statement and the `done` statement. Two commands enable you to get around this limitation: the `break` command causes the program to exit the loop immediately, and the `continue` command causes the program to skip the remaining commands in the loop but remain in the loop.

A technique that is sometimes used in shell programming is to start an `infinite loop`, that is, a loop that will not end until either a `break` or `continue` command is executed. An infinite loop is usually started with either a `true` or `false` command. The `true` command always returns an exit status of zero, whereas the `false` command always returns a nonzero exit status. The loop

```
while true
do
    command
    ...
    command
done
```

executes until either your program does a `break` or the user initiates an interrupt. You can also write an infinite loop as follows:

```
until false
do
    command
    ...
    command
done
```

We could use this technique to make the interactive archive program of Listing 9.7 a little easier to use. The revised program is shown in Listing 9.10.

Listing 9.10. Another version of the interactive archiver.

```
# Interactive program to restore, backup, or unload
# a directory
echo "Welcome to the menu driven Archive program"
while true
do
# Display a Menu
   echo
   echo "Make a Choice from the Menu below"
   echo _
   echo "1  Restore Archive"
   echo "2  Backup directory"
   echo "3  Unload directory"
   echo "4  Quit"
   echo
# Read the user's selection
   echo "Enter Choice: \c"
   read CHOICE
   case $CHOICE in
      [1-3] ) echo _
               # Read and validate the name of the directory
               echo "What directory do you want? \c"
               read WORKDIR
               if [ ! -d "$WORKDIR" ]
               then
                  echo "Sorry, $WORKDIR is not a directory"
               continue
               fi
               # Make the directory the current working directory
               cd $WORKDIR;;
        4) :;;
        *) echo "Sorry, $CHOICE is not a valid choice"
               continue _
   esac
   case "$CHOICE" in
      1) echo "Restoring..."
         cpio -i </dev/rmt0;;
      2) echo "Archiving..."
         ls ¦ cpio -o >/dev/rmt0;;
      3) echo "Unloading..."
         ls ¦ cpio -o >/dev/rmt0;;
      4) echo "Quitting"
         break;;
   esac
#Check for cpio errors
   if [ $? -ne 0 ]
   then
      echo "A problem has occurred during the process"
      if [ $CHOICE = 3 ]
      then
         echo "The directory will not be erased"
      fi
      echo "Please check the device and try again"
```

continues

Listing 9.10. continued

```
      continue
   else
      if [ $CHOICE = 3 ]
      then
         rm *
      fi
   fi
done
```

In the program in Listing 9.1, the loop continues as long as `true` returns a zero exit status, which is always, or until the user makes selection four, which executes the `break` command and terminates the loop. Notice also, that if the user makes an error in choosing the selection or in entering the directory name, the `continue` statement is executed rather than the `exit` statement. This way, the user can stay in the program even if he or she makes a mistake in entering data, but the mistaken data cannot be acted on.

Notice also the use of two `case` statements. The first `case` statement requests that the operator enter a directory name only if option 1, 2, or 3 is selected. This example illustrates how pattern matching in a `case` statement is similar to that on a command line. In the first `case` statement, if the user selects option 4, the null command (`:`) is executed. Because the first `case` statement checks for invalid selections and executes a `continue` if an invalid selection is made, the second `case` statement need not check for any but valid selections.

Structured Shell Programming Using Functions

A common feature among higher-level programming languages is the capability to group computer instructions together into functions that can be called from anywhere within the program. These functions are sometimes called subroutines. The Bourne shell also provides you with this capability.

The general syntax of a function definition is as follows:

```
funcname ()
{
   command
   ...
   command;
}
```

Once it is defined, a function can be called from anywhere within the shell by using *funcname* as a command. There are two reasons you might want to group commands into a function. One good reason is to break a complex program into more manageable segments, creating a structured program. A structured program might take the following form:

```
# start program
setup ()
{  command list ; }

do_data ()
{  command list ; }
```

```
cleanup ()
{  command list ; }_

errors ()
{  command list ; }_

setup
do_data
cleanup
# end program
```

In the above example, setup, do_data, and cleanup are functions. When you look at a well-structured program, the names of the functions give you a fair idea of what the functions might do. If you were trying to analyze this, you might assume what the setup and cleanup functions do and concentrate on the do_data section.

TIP

Always give variables and functions meaningful names. It may seem at the time you are writing a program that you will remember what the variables and functions are used for, but experience has proven that after the passage of time things are not always so clear. You should also remember that there will probably come a time when someone else will look at your programs, and that person will appreciate descriptive names.

Another legitimate reason for grouping commands into functions is that you may want to execute the same sequence of commands from several points within a program. At several points in the interactive archive program in Listing 9.10, a non-fatal error occurs and the continue command is executed. You can give the user the option of continuing at each of these points with an interactive continue function named icontinue.

```
icontinue ()
{
while true
do
    echo "Continue? (y/n) \c"
    read ANSWER
    case $ANSWER in
      [Yy] ) return 0;;
      [Nn] ) return 1;;
      * ) echo "Answer y or n";;
    esac
done
}
```

Now you can replace the continue statements in the program with the icontinue function.

```
if icontinue then continue else break fi
```

All of the prompting, reading, and error checking are carried out by the icontinue function, instead of repeating these commands at every continue point. This example also illustrates the function's capability to return an exit status with `return`. If no `return` command is available within the function, the exit status of the function is the exit status of the last command in the function.

Shell functions are very much like shell programs—with one very important difference. Shell programs are executed by subshells, whereas shell functions are executed as part of the current shell. Therefore, functions can change variables that are seen in the current shell. Functions can be defined in any shell, including the interactive shell.

```
$ dir () { ls -l; }_
$ dir
-rw-rw-r--  1 marsha   adept      1024 Jan 20 14:14 LINES.dat
-rw-rw-r--  1 marsha   adept      3072 Jan 20 14:14 LINES.idx
-rw-rw-r--  1 marsha   adept       256 Jan 20 14:14 PAGES.dat
-rw-rw-r--  1 marsha   adept      3072 Jan 20 14:14 PAGES.idx
-rw-rw-r--  1 marsha   acct        240 May  5  1992 acct.pds
$
```

You have now defined `dir` as a function within your interactive shell. It remains defined until you log off or `unset` the function, as follows:

```
$ unset dir
```

Functions can also receive positional parameters, as in the following example:

```
$ dir () {_
> echo "Permission  Ln Owner   Group    File Sz Last Access"
> echo "----------  -- -----    -----    ------- -----------"
> ls -l $*;
>}
$ dir L*
Permission  Ln Owner   Group    File Sz Last Access
----------  -- -----    -----    ------- -----------
-rw-rw-r--   1 marsha   adept      1024 Jan 20 14:14 LINES.dat
-rw-rw-r--   1 marsha   adept      3072 Jan 20 14:14 LINES.idx
```

In this example, the argument `L*` was passed to the `dir` function and replaced in the `ls` command for `$*`.

Normally, a shell script is executed in a subshell. Any changes made to variables in the subshell are not made in the parent shell. The dot (.) command causes the shell to read and execute a shell script within the current shell. You make any function definitions or variable assignments in the current shell. A common use of the dot command is to reinitialize login values by re-reading the `.profile` file. For information about `.profile`, see "Customizing the Shell" later in this chapter.

```
$ . .profile
```

Handling the Unexpected with `trap`

When you're writing programs, you should keep in mind that programs do not run in a vacuum. Many things can happen during a program that are not under the control of the program. The user of the program may press the interrupt key or send a `kill` command to the process, or the controlling terminal may become disconnected from the system. In UNIX, any of these events can cause a signal to be sent to the process. The default action when a process receives a signal is to terminate.

Sometimes, however, you may want to take some special action when a signal is received. If a program is creating temporary data files, and it is terminated by a signal, the temporary data files remain. In the Bourne shell, you can change the default action of your program when a signal is received by using the `trap` command.

The general format of the `trap` command is as follows:

```
trap command_string signals
```

On most systems, you can trap 15 signals. The default action for most is to terminate the program, but this action can vary, so check your system documentation to see what signals can occur on your system. Any signal except 9 (known as the sure kill signal) can be trapped, but usually you are concerned only with the signals that can occur because of the user's actions. Following are the three most common signals you'll want to trap:

Signal	Description
1	Hangup
2	Operator Interrupt
15	Software Termination (kill signal)

If the command string contains more than one command, which it most certainly should, you must enclose the string in either single or double quotation marks. The type of quotation marks you use determines when variable substitution is made.

Suppose you have a program that creates some temporary files. When the program ends normally, the temporary files are removed, but receiving a signal causes the program to terminate immediately, which may leave the temporary files on the disk. By using the `trap` command in the following example, you can cause the temporary files to be removed even if the program does not terminate normally due to receiving a hangup, interrupt, or kill signal:

```
trap "rm $TEMPDIR/*$$; exit" 1 2 15
```

When the `trap` command is executed, the command string is stored as an entry in a table. From that point on, unless the trap is reset or changed, if the signal is detected, the command string is interpreted and executed. If the signal occurs in the program before the `trap` command is executed, the default action occurs. Remember that the shell reads the command string twice— once when the `trap` is set and again when the signal is detected. This determines the distinction between the single and double quotation marks. In the preceding example, when the `trap` command line is read by the interpreter, variable substitution takes place for `$TEMPDIR` and `$$`.

9

THE BOURNE
SHELL

After the substitution, the resultant command string is stored in the trap table. If the `trap` command is changed to use single quotation marks

```
trap 'rm $TEMPDIR/*$$; exit' 1 2 15
```

when `trap` is executed, no variable substitution takes place, and the command string

```
rm $TEMPDIR/*$$; exit
```

is placed in the trap table. When the signal is detected, the command string in the table is interpreted, and then the variable substitution takes place. In the first instance, `$TEMPDIR` and `$$` have the value that they had at the time the trap was executed. In the second instance, `$TEMPDIR` and `$$` assume the value that they have at the time the signal is detected. Make sure that you know which you want.

The command string for the `trap` command almost always contains an `exit` statement. If you don't include an `exit` statement, then the `rm` command is executed when the signal is detected, and the program picks right up where it left off when the signal occurred. Sometimes you might want the program to pick up where it left off instead of exiting. For example, if you don't want your program to stop when the terminal is disconnected, you can trap the hangup signal, specifying the `null` command, as shown in the following example:

```
trap : 1
```

You can set a trap back to the default by executing the `trap` command with no command string, like this:

```
trap 1
```

The following command has the effect of making the user press the interrupt key twice to terminate a program:

```
trap 'trap 2' 2
```

Conditional Command Execution with the And/Or Constructs

As you have already seen, often you can write a shell program more than one way without changing the results of the program. The `until` statement, for example, is simply a reverse way of using a `while` statement. You can cause commands to be conditionally executed using the `if-then-else` construct, but you also can accomplish conditional execution using the `&&` and `||` operators. In the C programming language, these symbols represent the logical *and* and the logical *or* operations respectively. In the Bourne shell, the `&&` connects two commands in such a way that the second command is executed only if the first command is successful.

The general format of `&&` is as follows:

```
command && command
```

For example, in the statement

```
rm $TEMPDIR/* && echo "Files successfully removed"
```

the echo command is executed only if the rm command is successful. You also can do this programming in an if-then statement like this one:

```
if rm $TEMPDIR/*
then
    echo "Files successfully removed"
fi
```

Conversely, the ¦¦ connects to commands in such a way that the second command is executed only if the first command is not successful, as in this command:

```
rm $TEMPDIR/* ¦¦ echo "Files were not removed"
```

The preceding line is the programming equivalent of

```
if rm $TEMPDIR/*
then
    :
else
    echo "Files were not removed"
fi
```

You also can concatenate these operators. In the following command line, *command3* is executed only if both *command1* and *command2* are successful:

```
command1 && command2 && command3
```

You can also concatenate operators of different types. In the following command line, *command3* is executed only if *command1* is successful and *command2* is unsuccessful:

```
command1 && command2 ¦¦ command3
```

The && and ¦¦ are simple forms of conditional command execution and are usually used only in cases where single commands are to be executed. Although the commands can be compound, if too many commands appear in this format, the program can be difficult to read. Generally, if-then constructs seem to be more clear if you use more than one or two commands.

Reading UNIX-Style Options

One of the nicer things about UNIX is that most of the standard commands have a similar command-line format:

```
command -options parameters
```

If you are writing shell programs for use by other people, it is nice if you use the same conventions. To help you do so, a special command is available in the Bourne shell for reading and processing options in this format: the getopts command, which has the following form:

```
getopts option_string variable
```

where *option_string* contains the valid single-character options. If getopts sees the hyphen (-) in the command input stream, it compares the character following the hyphen with the characters in *option_string*. If a match occurs, getopts sets *variable* to the option; if the character following the hyphen does not match one of the characters in `option_string`, `variable` is set to a question mark (?). If `getopts` sees no more characters following a hyphen, it returns a nonzero exit status. This capability enables you to use `getopts` in a loop.

The program in Listing 9.11 illustrates how you use `getups` to handle options for the `date` command. The program creates a version of `date`, which conforms to standard UNIX style, and it adds some options.

Listing 9.11. A standardized date function `newdate`.

```
#newdate
if [ $# -lt 1 ]
then
   date
else
   while getopts mdyDHMSTjJwahr OPTION
   do
      case $OPTION
      in
         m) date '+%m ';;   # Month of Year
         d) date '+%d ';;   # Day of Month
         y) date '+%y ';;   # Year
         D) date '+%D ';;   # MM/DD/YY
         H) date '+%H ';;   # Hour
         M) date '+%M ';;   # Minute
         S) date '+%S ';;   # Second
         T) date '+%T ';;   # HH:MM:SS
         j) date '+%j ';;   # day of year
         J) date '+%y%j ';;# 5 digit Julian date
         w) date '+%w ';;   # Day of the Week
         a) date '+%a ';;   # Day abbreviation
         h) date '+%h ';;   # Month abbreviation
         r) date '+%r ';;   # AM-PM time
         \?) echo "Invalid option $OPTION";;
      esac
   done
fi
```

In the program in Listing 9.11, each option is processed in turn. When `getopts` has processed all the options, it returns a nonzero exit status, and the `while` loop terminates. Notice that `getopts` allows options to be stacked behind a single hyphen, which is also a common UNIX form.

The following examples illustrate how `newdate` works:

```
$ newdate -J
94031
$ newdate -a -h -d
Mon
Jan
31
$ newdate -ahd
Mon
Jan
31
$
```

Sometimes an option requires an argument, which getopts also parses if you follow the option letter in *option_string* with a colon. When getopts sees the colon, it looks for a value following a space following the option flag. If the value is present, getopts stores the value in a special variable OPTARG. If it can find no value where one is expected, getopts stores a question mark in OPTARG and writes a message to standard error.

The program in Listing 9.12 makes copies of a file and gives the copies a new name. The -c option takes an argument specifying the number of copies to make, and the -v option instructs the program to be verbose, that is to display the names of the new files as they are created.

Listing 9.12. duplicate program.

```
# Syntax: duplicate [-c integer] [-v] filename
#    where integer is the number of duplicate copies
#    and -v is the verbose option
COPIES=1
VERBOSE=N

while getopts vc: OPTION
do
    case $OPTION
    in
        c) COPIES=$OPTARG;;
        v) VERBOSE=Y;;
        \?) echo "Illegal Option"
            exit 1;;
    esac
done

if [ $OPTIND -gt $# ]
then
    echo "No file name specified"
    exit 2
fi

shift `expr $OPTIND -1`

FILE=$1
COPY=0

while [ $COPIES -gt $COPY ]
do
    COPY=`expr $COPY + 1`
    cp $FILE ${FILE}${COPY}
    if [ VERBOSE = Y ]
    then
        echo ${FILE}${COPY}
    fi
done
```

9

In the program in Listing 9.12, allowing the user to enter options presents a unique problem; when you write the program, you don't know which of the positional parameters will contain the name of the file that is to be copied. The getopts command helps by storing the number of the next positional parameter in the variable OPTIND. In the duplicate program, after getopts has located all the options, OPTIND is checked to make sure that a filename is specified and then the shift command makes the filename the first positional parameter.

```
$ duplicate -v fileA
fileA1
$ duplicate -c 3 -v fileB
fileB1
fileB2
fileB3
```

Customizing the Shell

The shell performs some very specific tasks and expects its input to follow some specific guide-lines—command names first, for instance. But the Bourne shell does allow the user some con-trol over his or her own environment. You can change the look of your shell and even add your own commands.

Customizing the Shell with Environment Variables

In the section "Variables" earlier in this chapter, you learned that one type of variable is called an environment variable. The shell refers to these variables when processing information. Chang-ing the value of an environment variable changes how the shell operates. You can change your command-line prompt, get mail forwarded to you, and even change the way the shell looks at your input.

Adding Command-Line Separators with IFS

When a command line is entered in an interactive shell, each word on the command line is interpreted by the shell to see what action needs to be taken. By default, words are separated by spaces, tabs, and newline characters. You can add your own separators by changing the IFS environment variable, as in the following example:

```
$ IFS=':'
$ echo:Hello:My:Friend
Hello My Friend
$
```

Setting additional field separators does not void the default field separators; space, tab, and newline are always seen as field separators.

Checking Multiple Mailboxes with MAILPATH

Most users have only one mailbox for their electronic mail. Some users, however, may require multiple mailboxes (see Chapter 7, "Communicating with Others" for a discussion of elec-tronic mail). For example, Dave wants to read mail addressed to him personally (which arrives to his personal user account), mail addressed to sysadm (which arrives to his system administra-tor account), and mail addressed to root (which arrives to his main account), but Dave can be logged in as only one of these accounts at any one time. Dave therefore can cause his current shell to check all three mailboxes by setting the environment variable `MAILPATH`, as follows:

```
$ MAILPATH="/usr/spool/mail/Dave:/usr/spool/mail/sysadm\
:/usr/spool/mail/root"
```

Now when mail is sent to any of these names, Dave receives the following message:

```
you have mail.
```

The only problem is that Dave does not know which mailbox to check when he receives this message. You can help solve Dave's problem by changing the mail message associated with each mailbox. You terminate the mailbox name in `MAILPATH` with a percent sign (`%`) and supply a message like this:

```
$ MAILPATH="/usr/spool/mail/Dave%Dave has mail\
:/usr/spool/mail/sysadm%sysadm has mail\
:/usr/spool/mail/root%root has mail
```

Adding Your Own Commands and Functions

This chapter has shown how you can group UNIX commands together in files and create your own programs or shell scripts. Sometimes though, you don't achieve the desired results. The program in Listing 9.13 changes the working directory, and at the same time changes the environment variable `PS1`, which contains the command-line prompt.

Listing 9.13. Change directory program `chdir`.

```
# Directory and Prompt Change Program
# Syntax: chdir directory

if [ ! -d "$1" ]
then
  echo "$1 is not a directory"
  exit 1
fi

cd $1
PS1="`pwd`> "
export PS1
```

When you execute the following `chdir` command from Listing 9.13, nothing happens.

```
$ chdir /usr/home/teresa
$
```

There is no error message, yet the command-line prompt is not changed. The problem is that `chdir` is executed in a subshell, and the variable `PS1` that was exported is made available only to lower shells. To make `chdir` work like you want, it must be executed within the current shell. The best way to do that is to make it a function. You can write the function in your `.profile` file, but there is a better solution. Group your personal functions into a single file and load them into your current shell using the transfer command (.). Rewrite `chdir` as a function, changing the `exit` to `return`. The function definition file `persfuncs` is shown in Listing 9.14.

Listing 9.14. Personal function file with `chdir` written as a function.

```
#Personal function file persfuncs
chdir ()
{
# Directory and Prompt Change Program
# Syntax: chdir directory

if [ ! -d "$1" ]
then
  echo "$1 is not a directory"
  return
fi

cd $1
PS1="`pwd`> "
export PS1;
}
$ . persfuncs
$ chdir /usr/home/teresa
/usr/home/teresa> chdir /usr/home/john
/usr/home/john> _
```

Keeping personal functions in a separate file makes them easier to maintain and debug than keeping them in your `.profile`.

You can make your personal functions a permanent part of your environment by putting the command

```
.persfuncs
```

in your `.profile`.

Specialized Topics

There are many topics from a programming standpoint that pertain to the shell. Of particular importance are debugging, command grouping, and program layering. These topics are discussed in the following sections.

Debugging Shell Programs

When you begin to write shell programs, you will realize something that computer users have known for years: programmers make mistakes! Sometimes what seems to be a perfectly reasonable use of computer language produces results that are unexpected. At those times, it is helpful to have some method of tracking down your errors.

The Bourne shell contains a trace option, which causes each command to be printed as it is executed, along with the actual value of the parameters it receives. You initiate the trace option by using set to turn on the -x option or execute a shell with the -x option. The sumints program is reproduced in Listing 9.15.

Listing 9.15. An integer summing program.

```
# sumints - a program to sum a series of integers
#
if [ $# -eq 0 ]
then
    echo "Usage: sumints integer list"
    exit 1
fi
sum=0
until [ $# -eq 0 ]
do
    sum='expr $sum + $1'
    shift
done
echo $sum
```

Running sumints with the trace option looks like this:

```
$ sh -x sumints 2 3 4
+ [ 3 -eq 0 ]
+ sum=0
+ [ 3 -eq 0 ]
+ expr 0 + 2
+ sum= 2
+ shift
+ [ 2 -eq 0 ]
+ expr 2 + 3
+ sum= 5
+ shift
+ [ 1 -eq 0 ]
+ expr 5 + 4
+ sum= 9
+ [ 0 -eq 0 ]
+ echo 9
9
$
```

The trace shows you each command that executes and the value of any substitutions that were made before the command was executed. Notice that the control words if, then, and until were not printed.

Grouping Commands

Commands to a shell can be grouped to be executed as a unit. If you enclose the commands in parentheses, the commands are run in a subshell; if you group them in curly braces ({}), they are run in the current shell. The difference in the two has to do with the effect on shell variables. Commands run in a subshell do not affect the variables in the current shell, but if commands are grouped and run in the current shell, any changes made to variables in the group are made to variables in the current shell.

```
$ NUMBER=2
$ (A=2; B=2; NUMBER='expr $A + $B'; echo $NUMBER)
4
$ echo $NUMBER
2
```

In the previous example, note that the variable NUMBER had a value of 2 before the command group was executed. When the command group was run inside of parentheses, NUMBER was assigned a value of 4, but after execution of the command group was complete, NUMBER had returned to its original value. In this next example, when the commands are grouped inside of curly braces, NUMBER will keep the value it was assigned during execution of the command group.

```
$ {A=2; B=2; NUMBER='expr $A + $B'; echo $NUMBER}
4
$ echo $NUMBER
4
$
```

Note that the second example looks somewhat like a function definition. A function is a named group of commands, which executes in the current shell.

Using the Shell Layer Manager `shl`

UNIX is a multi-programming operating system. Some UNIX systems take advantage of this feature, allowing the user to open several shells at one time, which they can accomplish using the shell layer manager shl. Only the active layer can get terminal input, but output from all layers is displayed on the terminal, no matter which layer is active, unless layer output is blocked.

A layer is created and named with shl. While the user is working in a layer, he or she can activate the shell manager by using a special character (Ctrl+Z on some systems). The shell layer manager has a special command-line prompt (>>>) to distinguish it from the layers. While in the shell layer manager, the user can create, activate, and remove layers. Following are the shl commands:

create name	Creates a layer called *name*.
delete name	Removes the layer called *name*.
block name	Blocks output from *name*.
unblock name	Removes the output block for *name*
resume name	Makes *name* the active layer.
toggle	Resumes the most recent layer.
name	Makes *name* the active layer.
layers [-l] name ...	For each *name* in the list, displays the process ID. The -l option produces more detail.
help	Displays help on the shl commands.
quit	Exits shl and all active layers.

Summary

In this chapter you have learned the fundamental aspects of the Bourne shell, using shell variables, and the basics of shell scripting. What you have learned here will be useful in the other shell chapters, such as Chapter 11, "The Korn Shell," and Chapter 12, "The C Shell," as well as other scripting languages. Most operating systems have a variety of available languages and some sort of system command scripting capability. However, few have the system command script language capabilities of the UNIX shell. Writing shell programs can save countless hours of coding using tradition languages like C, COBOL, BASIC, and so on. Becoming experienced with UNIX shell scripts is a valuable asset for any systems administrator or programmer. Pursuing additional learning and experience in shell scripting is highly recommended.

9

THE BOURNE
SHELL

The Bourne Again Shell

by Sriranga Veeraraghavan

IN THIS CHAPTER

CHAPTER 10

Bash stands for GNU Bourne Again Shell and is the GNU project's shell. It will be the default shell on the GNU operating system. As its name implies, Bash is based on the Bourne shell, `sh`, originally written by Stephen Bourne.

Bash includes c shell (`csh`), tc shell (`tcsh`) and Korn shell (`ksh`) features while only differing slightly from the Bourne shell, `sh`. Thus most `sh` scripts can be run in bash with no modification. The differences between bash and `sh` are because bash is an implementation of the IEEE POSIX 1003.2/ISO 9945.2 Shell and Tools specification.

Bash was written by Brian Fox (`bfox@gnu.ai.mit.edu`) of the Free Software Foundation and is currently maintained by Chet Ramey (`chet@ins.cwru.edu`) of Case Western Reserve University.

Bash is distributed for free, which means that anyone is free to use it and redistribute it under certain conditions, but it is not public domain. It is distributed under the GNU General Public License, a copy of which comes with the distribution. As stated in the license, bash does not come with a warranty, so the author and maintainer should not be considered sources of technical support.

The most recent release version of bash as of this writing is 2.0.0, which was released on December 31, 1996, but version 2.0.1 is currently being beta tested. The next release version of bash will, according to the FAQ, "appear sometime in 1997. Never make predictions." The predecessor to version 2.0.x was version 1.14.7, which was released on August 28, 1996.

This chapter concentrates on version 2.0.0 because it implements several new features, including one-dimensional arrays and the built-in `shopt`. Unless noted, all examples will also run under version 1.14.7.

Bash is available via anonymous ftp from any of the GNU archive sites, including the main GNU archive site, `ftp://prep.ai.mit.edu/pub/gnu/bash-2.0.tar.gz`. It is also available from the maintainer's machine, `ftp://slc2.ins.cwru.edu/pub/dist/bash-2.0.tar.gz`.

Bash is extremely portable and can be built on most UNIX systems because many of the environment dependent variables are determined at build time. Bash has been ported as a shell for several non-UNIX platforms like QNX, Minix, OS/2, Windows 95 and Windows NT. It is the default shell for BeOS.

The bash FAQ is available at `ftp://slc2.ins.cwru.edu/pub/bash/FAQ`.

Additional bash help can be obtained from Usenet newsgroups such as `gnu.bash.bug` and `comp.unix.shell`.

Features

Bash incorporates several features that make it an excellent shell for novices and experts alike. Many of the features are similar to `csh`, `tcsh` and `ksh`, which eases the difficulty encountered in switching among them.

- Bash has command line editing similar to tcsh and ksh. The cursor can be moved to any position in the command line allowing commands to be edited. The editing controls can be set to vi, emacs, or user-defined modes.

- Bash also features history recall and editing. Recalled commands can be edited and executed. Bash can save the history from one session for use in other sessions, including multi-line commands, such as loops or functions. Bash also features several variables that can customize the behavior of history saving and recall.

- Bash has the ability to complete partially typed words. Completion is available for variable names, user names, hostnames, commands, and filenames.

- The bash built-in cd command can correct simple misspellings in pathnames.

- Bash features functions and aliases. Aliases are useful for simple tasks like creating an alternate name for a command. Functions have more extended capabilities and are useful for more complex tasks.

- Bash allows users to suspend and restart processes, along with moving between foreground and background jobs. Bash also implements a disown command that allows background jobs to continue running even if the parent exits.

- Bash 2.0 supports arrays of unlimited size.

- Bash allows arithmetic from base two to base sixty-four and supports most C arithmetic operators. Bash has built-in numeric expression evaluation and substitution on the command line and allows arithmetic expressions to be given as a commands.

- Bash provides special character sequences that customize the prompts. Bash allows for other shell constructs to be used in the prompt.

Definitions

The following terms are defined in the BASH(1) manual page and are used in the same context in this chapter:

blank	A space or tab.
word	A sequence of characters considered as a single unit by the shell. Also known as a *token*.
name	A word consisting only of alphanumeric characters and underscores, and beginning with an alphabetic character or an underscore. Also referred to as an identifier.
metacharacter	A character that, when unquoted, separates words. One of the following: ¦ & ; ( ) < > space tab
control operator	A token that performs a control function. It is one of the following symbols: ¦ & && ; ;; ( ) ¦ <newline>

Installing Bash

Bash is available on many systems, but if you must install bash, the following section covers the procedure.

Requirements

The following applications are required to build and install bash:

- gunzip: to unzip the archive
- tar: to untar the archive
- ar: to build a library that bash uses
- gcc or cc: to build bash
- make: to control the compilation process

To make sure these programs are available, use the whereis command.

Procedure

Once the file bash-2.0.tar.gz has been obtained, use the following procedure to build bash:

1. cd into the directory containing the g-zipped tar file, bash-2.0.tar.gz.

2. Unzip the file:

   gunzip bash-2.0.tar.gz

   The file bash-2.0.tar.gz will be replaced by the file bash-2.0.tar. To see what gunzip does, give it the -v option.

3. Extract the source files from bash-2.0.tar:

   tar -xvf bash-2.0.tar

   This creates the directory bash-2.0, and puts the source files in that directory.

4. cd into the directory with the source files:

   cd bash-2.0

5. Configure the source tree for your machine:

   ./configure

   The shell script configure attempts to guess correct values for system-dependent variables used during compilation and then creates appropriate makefiles along with the following files:

   config.h, the file containing system-dependent definitions

   config.status, a shell script that re-creates the current configuration

   config.cache, the file that saves the test results to speed up reconfiguring

   config.log, the file containing the compiler output

The configuration can be customized, but the default configuration is usually good enough for most installs. Configure has a help option that details the other configuration options:

```
./configure --help
```

One useful configuration option specifies which directory bash should be installed in instead of the default location, /usr/local:

```
./configure --prefix=[directory]
```

On some older versions of System V, if configure is executed from csh, csh may try to execute configure as a csh script. To avoid this use:

```
sh ./configure
```

The configuration process can take some time, about 15 minutes on a Sun Sparc10 and about 10 minutes on a Sun Ultra1.

6. Build bash:

```
make
```

By default, make will use gcc, even if cc is installed and works. To use cc:

```
make CC="cc"
```

The make also takes a long time, about 20 to 25 minutes on a Sun Sparc10 and 15 to 20 minutes on a Sun Ultra1.

7. Test the build (optional but recommended):

```
make tests
```

This will make and run the tests that come with the source code to confirm that bash works properly. If any problems are detected, bash should probably be rebuilt. After the tests are completed, it is probably a good idea to invoke the newly built version and execute some commands to make to confirm that it works.

8. Strip the executable to remove debugging symbols (optional but recommended):

```
strip bash
```

To see the effect of strip on the size of the bash executable:

```
ls -l bash ; strip bash ; ls -l bash
```

This reduces the size of the bash executable by about 1 MB on a Sun Sparc. The actual size reduction varies, depending on the compiler used, the options supplied to the compiler, the hardware platform, and so on.

9. Install bash and its documentation:

```
make install
```

This places bash in the default location, /usr/local. To see what the default install will do without actually installing bash:

```
make -n install
```

10

THE BOURNE
AGAIN SHELL

To install bash in another location other than the configured one:

```
make install prefix=[directory]
```

Invocation

Bash can be invoked in several different modes. The two major modes are interactive and non-interactive.

Interactive Shells

An interactive shell is a shell whose standard input and standard output are connected to a terminal. The three major types of interactive shells are login, non-login, and restricted.

Bash determines whether a shell is interactive by using the `isatty` library call. In initialization files and scripts, interactive shells can be determined by using `tty -s` or `test -t`, which return 0 (true) if the standard input is a `tty`. Interactive shells set $PS1, so testing for its existence is another common method of identifying interactive shells.

When bash is invoked as a login shell, bash attempts to read several initialization files and reports any errors it encounters. If initialization files do not exist, then a default environment is used. First, bash reads and executes commands in `/etc/profile`. Then it reads and executes commands from the first one of the files `~/.bash_profile`, `~/.bash_login`, and `~/.profile` that exists and is readable. Bash can be given the `--noprofile` option to prevent it from reading any initialization files. When a login shell exits, if `~/.bash_logout` exists, bash will read and execute commands from it. Only login shells will read the `~/.bash_logout` when exiting.

When a non-login interactive bash is started, bash reads and executes commands from `~/.bashrc` file. A non-login interactive bash can be forced to read a different initialization file by using the `--rcfile file` option. It can be prevented from reading any initialization files by giving the `--norc` option.

Bash can also be started in posix mode if it is given the `--posix` option. In posix mode, bash first checks to see if $ENV is defined. If it is, bash expands $ENV to a filename and then reads and executes commands from that file. Bash will not read any other startup files when invoked in posix mode. Under posix mode, the behavior of bash changes slightly to conform with the POSIX standard.

On some systems where bash is named `sh` (for instance, Linux), bash will start up like `sh` and then enter posix mode. A login bash invoked as `sh` will try to read and execute commands in `/etc/profile` followed by `~/.profile`. The `--noprofile` option will prevent the reading of these initialization files. If a non-login bash is invoked as `sh`, its startup behavior is the same as in posix mode.

The final interactive mode of interest is restricted mode. Bash can be started in restricted mode by using the `-r` option or invoking it as `rbash`. In restricted mode, bash behaves normally, except that it does not allow certain operations, such as changing directories, modifying $SHELL or $PATH, running exec, running commands containing /, and using redirection. The restricted mode is not available in bash 1.x.

Non-Interactive Shells

Non-interactive bash shells are mostly used to run shell scripts. A non-interactive shell also runs when bash is invoked with the -c option. When a non-interactive bash is started, bash looks at $BASH_ENV. If it exists, bash tries to read and execute commands from the file named by the variable. The behavior is as if the command

```
if [ -n "$BASH_ENV" ] ; then . "$BASH_ENV"; fi
```

were executed. The filename that $BASH_ENV specifies is not searched against $PATH.

Invocation Options

As noted above, bash can be invoked with several single character and multicharacter options. Following is a summary of these options along with a brief description of the function they serve:

-c string	This option causes commands to be read from string. If string contains more than one word, the first word is assigned to $0, the command name, and the other words are assigned to the positional parameters; that is, $1, $2, and so on. An example would be: bash -c ls /tmp.
-i	This option forces bash to run in interactive mode.
-r	These options force bash to run in restricted mode.
--restricted	These options are not available in bash 1.x.
--login	This option forces bash to behave as if it were the login shell.
--posix	This option forces bash to conform to the POSIX standard. This option is implied if bash is invoked with the name sh.
--verbose	This option forces bash to echo all input lines after they are read.
--help	This option causes bash to print a usage message.
--version	This option causes bash to print out version information. In version 2.0 or newer, bash will exit successfully after printing out the version information. In versions 1.14.x and earlier, bash must be exited manually.
--noprofile	This option causes an interactive login bash to skip reading initialization files.

10

THE BOURNE
AGAIN SHELL

`--norc`	This option causes an interactive non-login bash to skip reading the `~/.bashrc`.
`--rcfile file`	This option causes an interactive non-login bash to read initialization commands from `file` instead of `~/.bashrc`.

Using Bash as the Login Shell

The most common way to change the login shell is to use the change shell command, `chsh`. On some systems where `chsh` is not available, `passwd -s` or `passwd -e` can be used to change the shell. On still other systems, `ypchsh` must be used to change the shell. On many systems (for instance, SunOS 5.5.x), the full pathname to the bash executable has to be included in `/etc/shells` before bash can be specified as a valid login shell.

If the default login shell cannot be changed, bash can still run as the login shell by modifying the initialization files for the default shell. If the default login shell is `csh` or `tcsh` and bash is in `/usr/local/bin/bash`, adding the following line to `~/.login` will allow bash to be executed as the login shell:

```
if ( -f /usr/local/bin/bash ) exec /usr/local/bin/bash --login
```

It is better to invoke bash in the `~/.login` file because it is read only at login time, unlike the `~/.cshrc` file, which is read every time a `csh` is started. Executing bash in the `~/.cshrc` could lead to problems when `csh` scripts try to run. The best way to invoke bash in the `~/.cshrc` file is to run bash only if the `csh` is interactive:

```
if ( $?prompt ) exec /usr/local/bin/bash --login
```

If the login shell is `sh` or `ksh`, two things must be done. First, in `~/.profile`, a line similar to the following must be added:

```
[ -f /usr/local/bin/bash ] && exec /usr/local/bin/bash --login
```

Second, an empty file, `~/.bash_profile`, must be created to prevent the executed bash from attempting to read `~/.profile`, and re-executing itself. Alternatively the following could be added to `~/.profile`:

```
case "$0" in
    *bash)
        : "Bash already running"
        ;;
    *)
        [ -f /usr/local/bin/bash ] && exec /usr/local/bin/bash --login
        ;;
esac
```

If you use a case statement in the `~/.profile`, an empty `~/.bash_profile` does not need to be created.

Syntax

Bash supports a syntax similar to sh and ksh.

Variables

Bash 2.0 supports both scalar and array variables. To set variables in bash, a standard sh assignment statement is used:

```
name=value
```

Array variables can be set in two ways. The first form sets a single element:

```
name[index]=value
```

The second form can be used to set multiple elements (not the entire array):

```
name=(value1 ... valuen)
```

In this form, consecutive array indices beginning at 0 are used. For example,

```
myarray=(derri terry mike gene)
```

is equivalent to

```
myarray[0]=derri
myarray[1]=terry
myarray[2]=mike
myarray[3]=gene
```

When setting multiple array elements, an array index can be placed before the value, so a third way to do the preceding assignments is:

```
myarray=([0]=derri [3]=gene [2]=mike [1]=terry)
```

There is no maximum limit on array indices nor is there any requirement that all consecutive indices be used.

Bash also supports two built-in commands, declare and typeset, that allow the modification of variable attributes. These two commands are synonymous and allow for variables to be designated as arrays, integers, and read only along with marking variables for export. The declare command should be used since the typeset command is now obsolete.

A variable marked as an integer behaves similarly to the int type in the C programming language when it is used in an arithmetic expression. Read only variables, once assigned, cannot be reassigned. The commands declare and typeset accept the following options:

-a	Sets/unsets the array attribute for a variable
	`declare -a foo # foo is now an array`
[-/+] i	Sets/unsets the integer attribute for a variable
	`declare -i foo # foo will be treated as an integer`
	`declare +i bar # bar will be treated normally`

`[-/+] r`	Sets the read only attribute for a variable.

```
declare -r foo # foo's value cannot be changed
declare +r foo # generates an error, if foo is readonly
```

`[-/+] x`	Sets/unsets the export attribute for a variable

```
declare -x foo # foo is marked for export
declare +r bar # bar will not be exported
```

`-p variable`	Shows a variables attributes. If a variable is not given, displays all variables and their values. This option is not available in bash 1.x.

Exporting variables for use in the environment is the same as in `sh`. For `csh` and `tcsh` users, it is similar to creating environment variables with `setenv`. Marking a variable for export means that it is available for use in the environment of a shell's child processes. Exporting can be done in two ways:

```
export name
```

```
export name=value
```

The first form marks the named variable for export. The second form assigns the given value to the named variable and then marks that variable for export. More than one *name* or *name=value* pair may be given. Variables can be unexported if the `-n` option is given. If export is invoked by itself or if it is invoked with a `-p` option, it will print a list of the currently exported variables. Both of the following examples are valid methods of exporting the variable PATH:

```
PATH=/bin:/sbin:/usr/bin:/usr/local/bin:/usr/ucb
export PATH
```

```
export PATH=/bin:/sbin:/usr/bin:/usr/local/bin:/usr/ucb
```

In addition to these attributes, bash allows for variables to be marked as local, using the `local` built-in command. Local means that a separate instance of the variable is created for the function in which `local` is used (`local` can only be used in functions). There are two forms:

```
local name
```

```
local name=value
```

The first form creates a variable of the given name and marks it as local. The second creates a variable of the given name with the given value . If local is invoked without *name* or *name=value*, it will print out a list of the current local variables.

Bash automatically sets several variables at startup time, and several of these have special properties as long as they are not unset. The following is a partial list of these shell variables:

`$PWD`	The current working directory as set by the `cd` command.
`$UID`	Expands to the numeric user ID of the current user, initialized at shell startup.

$BASH	Expands to the full pathname used to invoke this instance of bash.
$BASH_VERSION	Expands to a string describing the version of this instance of bash.
$BASH_VERSINFO	An array variable whose members hold version information for this instance of bash.
$SHLVL	Incremented by one each time an instance of bash is started. This variable is useful for determining if the built-in exit command will end the current session.
$REPLY	Expands to the last input line read by the read built-in command when it is given no arguments.
$RANDOM	This parameter generates a random integer between 0 and 32,767 each time it is referenced. The sequence of random numbers can be initialized by assigning a value to $RANDOM. If $RANDOM is unset, it loses its special properties, even if it is subsequently reset.
$SECONDS	Each time this parameter is referenced, the number of seconds since shell invocation is returned. If a value is assigned to $SECONDS, the value returned upon subsequent references is the number of seconds since the assignment plus the value assigned. If $SECONDS is unset, it loses its special properties, even if it is subsequently reset.
$HISTCMD	The history number, or index in the history list, of the current command. If $HISTCMD is unset, it loses its special properties, even if it is subsequently reset.
$IFS	The Internal Field Separator that is used by the parser for word splitting after expansion. $IFS is also used to split lines into words with the built-in read command. The default value is

```
<space><tab><newline>
```

The following variables are used by bash, but are initially set by other programs:

$PATH	The search path for commands. It is a colon-separated list of directories in which the shell looks for commands. A common value is

```
PATH=/bin:/sbin:/usr/bin:/usr/local/bin:/usr/ucb
```

$HOME	The home directory of the current user; the default argument for the cd built-in command.

10

THE BOURNE AGAIN SHELL

In addition to these types of variables, bash also supports two additional types of parameters: positional and special. Both of these parameters have their values assigned by bash, but only the positional parameter's values can be changed.

Positional parameters are denoted by one or more digits starting at 1, and can be accessed individually by giving the argument number as the variable name. If the argument number consists of multiple digits, brackets must be used. For example the first argument can be accessed as $1 but the eleventh argument must be accessed as ${11}.

There are several special parameters associated with positional parameters:

$*	This expands to a single word containing the list of all positional parameters separated by the first character of $IFS (normally a space).
$@	This positional parameter is replaced with a series of words rather than a single word as with $*.
$#	This expands to the number of positional parameters.

The positional parameters are the arguments that a function or shell script is invoked with. This means that the value of $1 is different inside and outside a function.

The other special parameters relate to command execution and are covered in the "History Variables" section.

Both variables and arrays can be unset with the unset command:

```
unset name
unset -v name
```

The -v option in the second form is used to indicate to unset that name is a shell variable. It is not required.

Expansion

When bash encounters an assignment statement of the form:

```
name=value
```

the value is assigned to name after tilde, variable, and string expansions are performed. Bash will also do command substitution, arithmetic evaluation, and quote removal on the value before it is assigned.

Tilde expansion is performed when a ~ (tilde) is the first character of a word. When appropriate, bash treats the characters following the tilde as a login name and tries to substitute the home directory associated with characters after the tilde. If the tilde appears by itself or is followed by a slash (/) and $HOME is set, bash replaces the tilde with the value of $HOME. Otherwise, it replaces the tilde with the home directory of the current user. If ~+ is given, bash replaces it with the value of $PWD, the current directory. If ~- is given, it is replaced with the value of $OLDPWD, the previous working directory. If none of the tilde expansions work, bash leaves the tilde as is.

Bash performs variable expansion when a `$` is encountered. The simplest forms are

```
foo=$bar
```

```
foo=${bar}
```

Here the value of the variable `$bar` is substituted and assigned to the variable `$foo`. In the second form, the brackets are present to explicitly indicate to the parser where the variable's name ends. For example,

```
foo=24
echo $footh
```

prints the value of the variable `$footh`, whereas

```
foo=24
echo ${foo}th
```

prints `24th`, which is the value of `foo` with a "th" appended:

Variables can also be substituted in several more advanced ways:

- If `$bar` is unset or null and an error needs to be produced:

  ```
  ${bar:?"Error, no bar"}
  ```

- If `$bar` is unset or null, but it needs to have a default value:

  ```
  ${bar:="foose"}
  ```

- If `$bar` is unset or null but `$foo` needs to have a value:

  ```
  foo=${bar:-"foose"}
  ```

- If `$foo` needs to have a value when `$bar` is not unset or null:

  ```
  foo=${bar:+"foose"}
  ```

Bash also supports substring variable expansions, which can be used to assign parts of one variable value to another:

```
foo=${bar:offset:length}
```

The `offset` is the starting position in `$bar`, and `length` is the number of characters to get. If the length is not specified, all characters after the offset are returned.

Command substitution is performed when a command is given as

```
$(command)
`command`
```

Both forms are replaced with the output of the command. Unless given in a double-quoted context, each output line from the command becomes a separate word. In a double-quoted context, the output is treated as a single word with embedded newlines.

Arithmetic evaluation is performed when the following form is encountered:

```
$((expression))
```

The expression will be evaluated according to the C programming language rules, and the result will be substituted. For example,

```
foo=$(( ((5 + 3*2) - 4) / 2 ))
```

will set the value of foo to 3 (not 3.5, because this is integer arithmetic, or 6, due to operator precedence).

Quote removal is performed after all the other expansions have taken place, and it removes all the remaining unquoted occurrences of the characters: \ (backslash), ' (single quote), and " (double quote).

Bash performs two other types of expansion. These are brace and pathname expansions. These are primarily used for commands that are issued on the command line. Brace expansion is primarily used to create several strings that have common elements. The general form is

```
stringx{string1, string2, ... , stringn}stringy
```

Bash expands this into [] strings, each containing one of the strings listed in the brackets, and preceded by stringx and suffixed by stringy. The preceding string or the trailing string can be omitted, but the minimum number of strings within the braces, { }, is one, and items within the brackets must be separated by commas. Brace expansion can be used in situations like:

```
mkdir /home/ranga/docs/{school,work,personal}/mail
mkdir -p /usr/local/{bin,lib,man/man{1,2,3},etc}
```

These are equivalent to

```
mkdir /home/ranga/docs/school/mail/home/ranga/docs/work/mail/home/ranga/docs/
➥personal/mail
mkdir -p /usr/local/bin/usr/local/lib/usr/local/man/man1/usr/local/man/man2/usr/
➥local/man/man3/usr/local/etc
```

Brace expansion can be used in conjunction with pathname expansion, which allows for certain special characters to be given in pathnames. If these characters are given, the word in which they are present is regarded as a pattern and is replaced with a sorted list of filenames matching the pattern. The special characters are

*	Matches any string, including the null string.
?	Matches any single character.
[...]	Matches any one of the enclosed characters. A pair of characters separated by a minus sign denotes a range and any character between those two characters is matched. For example, [A-Z] matches all uppercase letters, and [a-zA-Z] matches all letters.

Quoting

Quoting is used to disable the meaning of certain characters that the shell treats in a special way. Quoting can be used to make strings, by surrounding a set of characters with single quotes (') or double quotes ("). For example, the following are strings formed by quoting:

```
"Hello, I am a string"
'So am I'
```

Single characters can also be quoted if the character is preceded by a backslash (\). Some of the characters whose meanings are disabled by quoting are

```
` ~ ! # $ % ^ & * ( ) - + = \ ¦ ; ' " , . < > ?
```

The basic quoting rules are a combination of sh and csh quoting rules. Strings enclosed in single quotes, 'string', have all the special characters in them disabled. Strings enclosed in double quotes, "string", have all the special characters except !, $, `, \, and { disabled. Characters preceded by a backslash (\) will have their special meaning disabled.

In addition to quoting, bash recognizes several standard escape sequences familiar to C language programmers, such as \t for tab and \n for newline.

Simple Commands

Simple commands in bash are either variable assignments, single command names, or single command names whose output is redirected. Bash treats the first word on the command line as the command to be executed and the rest of the words as arguments to the command, unless the command is preceded by variable assignments. A simple command will return its exit status, or 128+SIG if it is terminated by a signal of number SIG.

Pipelines

Several simple commands can be connected using pipes, forming a *pipeline.*

```
command1 ¦ command2 ¦ ...
```

The pipe character, ¦, connects the standard output of command1 to the standard input of command2, and so on. Each command is executed as a separate process. The exit status of the pipeline is the exit status of the last command. Examples of pipeline commands are

```
tail -f /var/adm/messages ¦ more

ps -ael ¦ grep "$UID" ¦ more

tar -cf - ./foo ¦ { cd /tmp; tar -xf - }
```

In the first example the standard output of the `tail` command is piped into the standard input of the `more` command, which allows the output to be viewed one screen at a time. In the second example the standard output of `ps` is connected to the standard input of `grep`, and the standard output of grep is connected to the standard input of more, so that the output of grep can be viewed one screen at a time. The third example is an obscure but somewhat useful way for root to copy files without changing their ownership.

Lists

In addition to pipelines, commands can be executed in lists, where several pipelines are joined using the operators ;, &, &&, or ¦¦. List can be used to execute commands and pipelines in sequence:

```
command1; command2; command3 ...
command1 ¦ command2; command3 ¦ command4 ...
```

Lists are commonly used for tasks such as

```
lpr foo; lpq;
ps -ael ¦ head -1; ps -ael ¦ grep "$UID"
```

which cannot be executed in a single command.

Lists can also be used to execute commands based on the exit status of previous commands if the logical AND or logical OR operators are given:

```
command1 && command2
command1 ¦¦ command2
```

If the logical AND operator is used, as in the first case, command2 will only be executed if command1 returns an exit status of 0. If the logical OR operator is used, as in the second case, command2 will only be executed if command1 returns with a nonzero exit status. The logical operators are often used instead of if statements; this form will seem intuitive to those familiar with the C programming language and its "lazy" logical operators.

A common use of the && operator is in situations like

```
mkdir foo && cd foo
```

where a directory change is appropriate only if the directory was successfully created.

An example using the ¦¦ operator is

```
grep root /etc/passwd ¦¦ echo "Help! No one in charge!"
```

Any list can be executed either in the current shell environment or in a subshell. Enclosing a list in braces

```
{ list ; }
```

causes the list to be executed in the current shell, whereas enclosing a list in parentheses

```
( list ; )
```

causes the list to be executed in a subshell. For example

```
{ ps -ael ¦ head -1; ps -ael ¦ grep " $UID " ; } ¦ more
```

runs the list, ps -ael ¦ head -1; ps -ael ¦ grep "$UID", in the current shell and then pipes the output to more. The same list could be run in a subshell:

```
( ps -ael ¦ head -1; ps -ael ¦ grep " $UID " ; ) ¦ more
```

but this is probably not a good idea, since each subshell that runs takes up more system resources. It would be more efficient to run all the programs in the current shell. Running lists in subshells is useful because a subshell effectively makes all variables local and because subshells have their own working directories. This is illustrated by the following example:

```
pwd; ( cd /tmp ; pwd ) ; pwd;
```

The current working directory is only changed for the subshell.

Redirection

Lists can also include redirection of input and output using the < and > operators. By default < redirects the standard input and > redirects the standard output, but the redirection operators can also be used to open and close files. In general, output redirection is either

```
command > file
```

```
list > file
```

The first form redirects the output of command to file, while the second redirects the output of list to file. For example,

```
date > now
```

redirects the output of the date into the file now. The output of lists can also be redirected.

```
{ date; uptime; who ; } > mylog
```

will redirect the output of all of the commands date, uptime, and who into the file mylog. In addition to this output redirection, which overwrites the output file, there is appended output redirection. Output will be appended to a file, or a file will be created if it doesn't exist if the >> operator is used. In general, appended output redirection is

```
command >> file
list >> file
```

If the file mylog (above) shouldn't be erased each time data is added, the following could be used:

```
{ date; uptime; who ; } >> mylog
```

Bash also allows for the standard output and error to be redirected together. In general, this is done by

```
&> file
>& file
> file 2>&1
```

The manual page states that the first form is preferred, but all three forms are equivalent. The third form works by using the file descriptors for standard output (file descriptor 1) and standard error (file descriptor 2); it effectively does the same thing as the dup2() C library function. A common situation where it is necessary to redirect both the standard output and the standard error is

```
if type emacs &> /dev/null ; then
    EDITOR=emacs
else
    EDITOR=vi
fi
```

Here, only the return value of the type built-in command is of interest, its output or any error message it prints out are not, so they are redirected to /dev/null.

The input can also be redirected in a similar fashion. In general, input redirection is

```
command < file
```

Here the contents of file will become the input to command. For example, the following is a common use of redirection:

```
Mail ranga@soda.berkeley.edu < Final_Exam_Answers
```

where the input to Mail, which becomes the body of the mail message, will be the file Final_Exam_Answers.

An additional use of input redirection is in the creation of Here documents. The general form for a Here document is

```
command << delimiter
document
delimiter
```

The shell will interpret the << operator as an instruction to read input until a line containing the specified delimiter is found. All the input lines up to the line containing the delimiter are fed into the standard input of the command. Bash does not perform any kind of expansion on the given delimiter, but bash does perform expansion on the lines in the Here document. For example, to print out a quick list of URLs, the following Here document could be used:

```
lpr << MYURLS
http://www.csua.berkeley.edu/~ranga/
http://www.macintouch.com/
http://www.marathon.org/story/
http://www.gnu.org/
MYURLS
```

This provides a handy alternative to creating temporary files. In order to strip the tabs in this example, the << operator can be given a - option.

Flow Control

Bash provides two powerful flow control mechanics, the `if`-`fi` block and the `case`-`esac` block. The `if` statement is normally used for the conditional execution of commands, whereas `case` statements allow any of a number of command sequences to be executed depending on which one of several patterns matches a variable first. It is often easier to write `if` statements as `case` statements if they involve matching a variable to a pattern.

The basic `if` syntax is `if list ; then list; [elif list; then list; ] ... [else list;] fi`, which is usually written as:

```
if list1 ; then
list2
elif list3 ; then
list4
else
list5
fi
```

Both the `elif` and the `else` statements are optional. An `if` statement can be written with any number of `elif` statements and `if` statements can contain just the `if` and `elif` statements. The lists in `if` statements can be lists of the form discussed in the previous section.

In the general `if` statement, shown above, `list1` first is evaluated. If the exit code of `list1` is 0, indicating a true condition, `list2` is evaluated and the `if` statement exits. Otherwise, `list3` is executed and then its exit code is checked. If `list3` returns a 0, then `list4` is executed and the `if` statement exits. If `list3` does not return a 0, `list5` is executed. A simple use of the `if` statement is

```
if uuencode koala.gif koala.gif > koala.uu ; then
echo "Encoded koala.gif to koala.uu"
else
echo "Error encoding koala.gif"
fi
```

"`Encoded koala.gif to koala.uu`" will be echoed if the uuencode command's exit code indicates success. Otherwise, the error will be reported.

Most often the `list` given to an `if` statement will be one or more `test` commands, which can be invoked either by calling `test` as `test expression` or `[ expression ]`. The `test` command returns either a 0 (true) or a 1 (false) after evaluating an expression. The following is a list of the more commonly used options that `test` can be run with:

-d file	True if file exists and is a directory.
-e file	True if file exists.
-f file	True if file exists and is a regular file.
-k file	True if file exists and has its "sticky" bit set.
-L file	True if file exists and is a symbolic link.

`-r file`	True if `file` exists and is readable.
`-s file`	True if `file` exists and has a size greater than zero.
`-t fd`	True if `fd` is opened on a terminal.
`-w file`	True if `file` exists and is writable.
`-x file`	True if `file` exists and is executable.
`-O file`	True if `file` exists and is owned by the effective user ID.
`file1 -nt file2`	True if `file1` is newer (according to modification date) than `file2`.
`file1 -ot file2`	True if `file1` is older than `file2`.
`-z string`	True if the length of `string` is zero.
`-n string`	True if the length of `string` is non-zero.
`string1 = string2`	True if the strings are equal.
`string1 == string2`	True if the strings are equal.
`string1 != string2`	True if the strings are not equal.
`! expr`	True if expr is false. The expr can be any of the test given above.
`expr1 -a expr2`	True if both `expr1` AND `expr2` are true.
`expr1 -o expr2`	True if either `expr1` OR `expr2` is true.
`arg1 OP arg2`	OP is one of `-eq`, `-ne`, `-lt`, `-le`, `-gt`, or `-ge`. These arithmetic binary operators return true if `arg1` is equal to, not equal to, less than, less than or equal to, greater than, or greater than or equal to `arg2`, respectively. `Arg1` and `arg2` may be positive or negative integers.

Examples of common uses of a simple `if` statement in conjunction with test are

```
if [ -d $HOME/bin ] ; then PATH="$PATH:$HOME/bin" ; fi

if [ -s $HOME/.bash_aliai ] ; then . $HOME/.bash_aliai ; fi
```

In the first example, test is used to determine whether a directory exists and then some action is taken. In the second example, test is used to determine whether a file exists and has non-zero size before any action is taken.

Here are two more equivalent examples that demonstrate how to combine tests:

```
if [ -z "$DTHOME" ] && [ -d /usr/dt ] ; then DTHOME=/usr/dt ; fi

if [ -z "$DTHOME" -a -d /usr/dt ] ; then DTHOME=/usr/dt ; fi
```

Some users prefer the first form because it is obvious what tests are being done and what the evaluation criteria are. Other users prefer the second form because it only invokes the `[` command once and may be marginally more efficient.

The other form of flow control is the `case-esac` block. The basic syntax is `case word in [ pattern [ ¦ pattern ] ... ) list ;; ] ... esac`, but it is usually written as

```
case word in
pattern)
list
;;
pattern2)
list2
;;
esac
```

In this form, `word` is either a string or a variable, whose value is compared against each `pattern` until a match is found. The `list` following the matching `pattern` is executed. Once a list is executed, program flow jumps to the end of the entire `case` statement. If no matches are found, bash will exit the `case` statement. Some default actions can be performed by giving the `*` pattern, which matches anything. The number of patterns does not matter, but there must be at least one. The patterns can use the same special characters as patterns for pathname expansion, along with the OR operator, `¦`. The `;;` signifies to bash that the list has concluded and is similar to a `break` in the C programming language. An example of a simple `case` statement is

```
case "$TERM" in
*term)
TERM=xterm
;;
network¦dialup¦unknown¦vt[0-9]*)
TERM=vt100
;;
esac
```

Loops

Bash supports three types of loops: the `for`, `while`, and `select` loops. A `for` loop is used when a set of commands needs to simply be executed repeatedly. A `while` loop is used when a set of commands needs to be executed while a certain condition is true. A common use for a `select` loop is to provide a convenient selection interface.

The basic `for` loop syntax is `for name [ in list1; ] do list2 ; done`, but is usually written as

```
for name in list1
do
list2
done
```

In the `for` loop, the variable `name` is set to each element in `list1`, and `list2` is executed for each element of `list1`. If `in list1` is not given, bash will iterate over the positional parameters. If `list1` is given as a word, expansions will be performed on it. A simple `for` loop example is

```
for i in 1 2 3 4 5 6 7 8 9 10
do
echo $i
done
```

A more common use of the `for` loop is

```
for files in ~/.bash_*
do
echo "<HTML>" > ${files}.html
echo "<HEAD><TITLE>$files</TITLE></HEAD>" >> ${files}.html
echo "<BODY><PRE>" >> ${files}.html
cat $files >> ${files}.html
echo "</PRE></BODY>" >> ${files}.html
echo "</HTML>" >> ${files}.html
chmod guo+r ${files}.html
done
```

The basic `while` loop syntax is `while list1 ; do list2 ; done`. This is usually written as

```
while list1
do
    list2
done
```

In the `while` loop, `list1` is evaluated each time, and as long as it is true, `list2` is executed. This allows for infinite loops to be written with `/bin/true` as `list1`. A simple `while` loop example is

```
x=1
while [ $x -lt 10 ]
do
    echo $x
    x=$(($x+1))
done
```

This `while` loop copies its input to its output, like the `cat` program:

```
while read
do
    echo $REPLY;
done
```

If input redirection is used, this loop will write the contents of the input file to the standard output, similar to `cat`.

A variation on the `while` loop is the `until` loop:

```
until list1
do
    list2
done
```

In the `until` loop, `list2` is executed until `list1` is true. The `until` loop is the same as a `while` loop where `! list1` is given. The following `while` and `until` loops are equivalent:

```
x=1; while ! [ $x -ge 10 ]
do
 echo $x
 x=$(($x+1))
done
x=1; until [ $x -ge 10 ]
do
 echo $x
 x=$(($x+1))
done
```

The `select` loop is an easy way to create a numbered menu from which users can select options. The basic select syntax is `select name [ in list1; ] do list2 ; done`, and is usually written as

```
select name in list1
do
    list2
done
```

In the `select` loop, the items in `list1` are printed onto the standard error preceded by a number. A prompt is then displayed and a line is read in. If `$REPLY`, the variable containing the value of the line that is read, contains a number of a displayed item, then `list2` is executed. Otherwise, the list of items in `list1` is displayed again. The `select` loop ends if an `EOF` (end of file) is read.

The following `select` loop displays a number list of the files in the directory `/tmp` and runs an `ls -1` on files that exist:

```
select file in /tmp/* QUIT
do
    if [ -e $file ] ; then
        ls -1 $file
    else
        break
    fi
done
```

The output will be similar to

```
1) /tmp/.            6) /tmp/job.control.ms
2) /tmp/..           7) /tmp/job.control.ps
3) /tmp/.X11-unix    8) /tmp/ps_data
4) /tmp/intro7.html  9) /tmp/sunpro.c.1.157.3.00
5) /tmp/java        10) QUIT
#?
```

where `#?` is the prompt at which a number is typed by the user.

All loops in bash can be exited immediately by using the built-in `break` command. This command also accepts as an argument an integer, greater or equal to 1, that indicates the number of levels to break out of. This feature is useful when nested loops are being used.

Comments

Bash comments start with the `#` character. Every character between the `#` and the newline is considered part of the comment and is ignored by bash. By default, this is true for both interactive shells and non-interactive shells. Interactive shells can change this behavior by using the `shopt` built-in function.

10

THE BOURNE AGAIN SHELL

Initialization Files

An interactive login bash reads the files ~/.bash_profile, ~/.bash_login, and ~/.profile, while a non-login interactive bash will read the file ~/.bashrc. The number of initialization files that bash tries to read is a source of confusion for many users.

Initialization File Considerations

One of the main problems confronting someone who is new to bash is which initialization files to create and what to put in them. The easiest solution, employed by many bash users, is to create one initialization file and have the other initialization files be symbolic links to that file.

Most users create the ~/.bash_profile and have the ~/.bashrc file be a link to the ~/.bash_profile, which insures that both login and non-login interactive bash shells have the same environment. The ~/.bash_profile is a better file to use as the initialization file than the ~/.bash_login, since bash tries to read the ~/.bash_profile first.

Some bash users, who use sh and ksh along with bash, use only the ~/.profile, and include a special section for bash, by using a test like

```
if [ -n "$BASH" ] ; then ... (Bash specific code here) ... ; fi
```

In this case the ~/.bashrc will be a symbolic link to the ~/.profile. If bash is the only sh-like shell that will be used, it is probably best to create a ~/.bash_profile, because compatibility issues arising from the use of the ~/.profile can be avoided.

The most basic initialization files should set the file creation mask and $PATH, the search path for commands, since these are used by both interactive and non-interactive shells. Most initialization files will include much more, usually setting many variables and options for interactive shells only. Some common things that are done in initialization files for interactive shells are

- Ensure the terminal is set up properly
- Set $MANPATH, the manual page search path
- Set $LD_LIBRARY_PATH, the library search path
- Set $PS1 and $PS2, the primary and secondary prompts

Some users also define aliases and functions inside their initialization files, but many choose to define these in another file called .bash_aliases or .bash_aliai. One of the reasons this is done is to avoid modifying a working initialization file every time an alias or function needs to be added. Since it is easy to source the file containing the aliases, using another file does not add complexity to the initialization file.

Shell Variables

The following section contains a list of some variables that bash uses and are often set in initialization files. Most of these variables are set in the sample initialization file given in a following section.

These variables are colon (:)-separated lists of directory names that are used when searching for files:

$PATH	The searchpath for commands, usually something like `PATH=/bin:/usr/bin:/usr/local/bin:/usr/ucb/`
$MANPATH	The manpage searchpath, usually something like `/usr/man:/usr/local/man`
$LD_LIBRARY_PATH	The library searchpath, usually something like `/lib:/usr/lib:/usr/local/lib:/usr/ucbinclude:/usr/ucblib`
$CD_PATH	The cd commands searchpath for directories, usually something like `.:~:~/docs`

Theses variables pertain to the default editor and are usually the name of the editor command, including options, to be run:

$EDITOR	The name of the default line editor (ed)
$VISUAL	The name of the default visual editor (vi)
$FCEDIT	The name of the editor for use with the `fc` built-in command

Bash uses these variables when checking for mail:

$MAIL	The file where the users mail is stored, and the file that bash will check for mail. It is usually preset to a value like `/usr/spool/mail/ranga`.
$MAILCHECK	This variable's value is the time in seconds between mail checks. The default is 60. Bash will not check for mail if this variable is unset.
$MAIL_PATH	A colon (:)-separated list of files in which to check for mail.

These variables control how and where bash places commands in the history.

$HISTSIZE	This variable's value is the number of commands to remember in the history. Its default value is 500.
$HISTFILE	This variable contains the name of the file in which the history is saved. By default it is `~/.bash_history`.

$HISTFILESIZE	This variable's value is the maximum number of lines to include in the history file. The default is 500.
$HISTCONTROL	This variable can be set to three special values, ignorespace, ignoredups, and ignoreboth. Other values have no effect. If it is set to ignorespace, commands starting with a space are not remembered by the history. If it is set to ignoredups, identical consecutive commands are not remembered in the history. Setting the variable to ignoreboth combines the other two options.

Bash also uses the following variables:

$TERM	The terminal's type (for example, xterm, vt100).
$PAGER	The name of the default page by page viewer (for example, less, more).
$PRINTER	The name of the default printer.
$IGNOREEOF	This variable's value is the number of EOF characters that can be received as sole input, before bash exits. The default value is 10.
$TMOUT	If set, this variable's value is the number of seconds to wait for input before terminating.
$FIGNORE	This variable is a list of suffixes to ignore when completing a filename. It usually has a value like .o:'~'.

Bash also has several prompt variables, which control how the prompt is displayed. They are covered in the "Prompting" section.

Prompting

The prompt is the string displayed by bash when it is running interactively and is ready to read or complete a command. Bash supports four different prompts, $PS1, $PS2, $PS3, and $PS4. Of these, usually only the variables $PS1 and $PS2 are of interest in interactive shells. The primary prompt's string is the value of $PS1 and is displayed when bash is ready to read a command. The secondary prompt, $PS2, is displayed when bash needs more input to finish a command it has already started reading. The variable $PS3 contains the prompt issued when a select statement is issued. The variable $PS4 is displayed only during execution traces. Most users do not use $PS3 or $PS4 very often and thus they are not commonly set in initialization files. All the prompts are equally customizable and understand the following special character sequences:

\d	The date in "Weekday Month Date" format ("Tue May 26")
\h	The hostname up to the first dot (.)
\H	The complete hostname

\s	The name of the shell
\t	The current time in 24-hour HH:MM:SS format
\T	The current time in 12-hour HH:MM:SS format
\@	The current time in 12-hour am/pm format
\u	The username of the current user
\v	The version of bash (for example, 2.00)
\V	The release of bash, version + patchlevel (for example, 2.00.0)
\w	The current working directory
\W	The basename of the current working directory
\!	The history number of this command (this is the number of the current command as stored in the history file)
\#	The command number of this command (this is the number of the current command since the shell was invoked, and is usually different than the history number)
\$	If the effective UID is 0, a #, otherwise a $

A few examples of common values of $PS1 and corresponding sample prompts are

```
PS1="\s-\v\$ "     bash-2.00$

PS1="\h \#\$ "     soda 2$

PS1="\h:\w [\#]\$ "     soda:~ [3]$

PS1="\t \H \#\$ "     19:10:21 soda.berkeley.edu 16$
```

In addition to these special character sequences, variables and commands can be included in the prompts, which are expanded in the manner discussed in the expansion section.

Bash also recognizes the variable $PROMPT_COMMAND, which can be set to the name of a command to be executed before a primary prompt is set. Some users like to have this set to display the load averages of the machine they are working on:

```
PROMPT_COMMAND="uptime ¦ cut -d: -f4"
```

The value of $PROMPT_COMMAND can be set to any shell command, ranging from frivolous, PROMPT_COMMAND="fortune", to dangerous, PROMPT_COMMAND="/bin/rm -rf *".

set and shopt

The set and shopt built-in commands can be used to customize the behavior of bash. This customization is usually done in the initialization file. The set built-in is available in bash 1.x as well as in 2.0.x, whereas the shopt built-in is available only in bash 2.0.x.

The basic syntax of a set command is set [+/-][options]. For example

```
set -a
set -o allexport
```

sets the allexport option while

```
set +a
set +o allexport
```

unsets the allexport option.

The set command can be used interactively from the command line to change shell behavior, or it can be run in initialization files and shell scripts. The following is a list of useful options that are understood by the set command (equivalent options are given together):

-a -o allexport	These options force bash to automatically mark all variables for export when they are created or modified.
-b -o notify	These options force bash to report the status of terminated background jobs immediately, rather that waiting till the next primary prompt is issued.
-e -o errexit	If these options are given bash will exit as soon as a simple command exits with non-zero status. The shell will not exit if the command is part of a loop, in a conditional list or if the return value of the command is being inverted with the ! operator.
-f -o noglob	These options disable pathname expansion.
-h -o hash all	These options force bash to remember the location of commands that are looked up for execution. These options are enabled by default.
-n -o noexec	These options force non-interactive bash shells to read commands without executing them, and are frequently used to check shell script syntax.
-v -o verbose	These options force bash to echo input lines after they are read. These options have an effect similar to the --verbose invocation option.

`-B`		
`-o braceexpand`		These options allow bash to perform brace expansion. These options are enabled by default.
`-C`		
`-o noclobber`		If these options are set, bash will not overwrite an existing file when redirection is performed. This can be overridden by using the `>!` operator.
`-H`		
`-o histexpand`		These options enable history substitution, and by default, are enabled for interactive shells.
`-o emacs`		This option causes bash to use command line editing commands similar to those used in emacs. By default, this option is enabled for all interactive shells, except those invoked with the `--noediting` option.
`-o history`		This option enables command history, and is enabled by default for interactive shells.
`-o ignoreeof`		This option sets the value of `$IGNOREEOF` to 10.
`-o posix`		This option forces bash into posix mode. This option has an effect similar to the `--posix` invocation option.
`-o vi`		This option causes bash to use command line editing commands similar to those used in vi.

If `set -o` is given without any other arguments, a list of all the currently set options is listed. If `set` is given without any arguments, all currently set variables are listed.

The built-in `shopt` command in bash 2.0.x allows for several other shell options to be set that affect bash's behavior. In general, a shell option is set by giving the `shopt -s` command, and a shell option is unset by giving the `shopt -u` command. For example

```
shopt +s cdable_vars
```

enables the shell option `cdable_vars` while

```
shopt +u cable_vars
```

disables it. Some of the shell options that can be set are

`cdable_vars`	Setting this shell option allows the `cd` command to assume that a given argument, which is not a directory, is the name of a variable whose value is the name of the directory to change to.
`cdspell`	If this shell option is set, `cd` will correct minor errors in the spelling of a pathname and echo the correct pathname before changing directories.

10

checkhash	If this shell option is set, bash will check to see whether commands found in the hash table exist before trying to execute them. Commands that no longer exist are searched for in $PATH.
checkwinsize	Setting this shell option forces bash to check the window size after each command is executed and, if necessary, update the values of LINES and COLUMNS.
cmdhist	Setting this shell option allows bash to save all the lines of multiline commands in the same history entry.
lithist	If this shell option and the shell option, cmdhist are set, multiline commands are saved in the history with the newlines.
histappend	If this shell option is set, the history list is appended to the history file rather than overwriting it.
histverify	Setting this option forces bash to reload a line for further editing after history substitutions have occurred.
dotglob	If this shell option is set, bash includes filenames beginning with dots (.) in the results of pathname expansion.
hostcomplete	If this shell option is set, bash will attempt to perform hostname completion when a word beginning with an @ is encountered. This shell option is enabled by default.
Interactive_comments	Setting this shell option allows for comments to be entered in an interactive shell. This shell option is enabled by default.
mailwarn	If this shell option is set, bash checks for new mail.
promptvars	If this shell option is set, prompt strings undergo standard expansion. This option is enabled by default.
expand_aliases	This shell option, if set, allows bash to expand aliases.

shopt also understands the option, -p, which lists all the shell options that are set, and -q, which suppresses output.

Aliases

Aliases are an easy way to shorten long commands in interactive shells, to perform several commands by giving a single word, or to make sure that certain programs are always called with some handy options. In bash, aliases are created (set) by using the alias command and destroyed (unset) by using the unalias command. The basic syntax is similar to sh:

```
alias name=value
```

When bash encounters a command, it checks to see whether the command contains known aliases. If it is does, those words are replaced by the corresponding alias text. The resulting text is checked for aliases also, but recursive substitution is not performed. Thus, if an alias such as

```
alias rm="rm -i"
```

is declared, and rm is given as a command name, once `rm -i` is inserted, the `rm` in the resulting text is not expanded.

The simplest types of aliases are those that are used to slightly change how a command works. For example, the following aliases simply executes the given command, with some default options each time:

```
alias m="more"

alias mv="mv -i"    # ask before overwriting a file when moving files

alias cp="cp -i""    # ask before overwriting a file when copying files

alias ls="ls -aFc""    # list all files and their file types in columns
```

Simple aliases are also handy for correcting common misspellings in command names:

```
alias chomd="chmod"

alias more="mroe"
```

Bash also supports more complex aliases like

```
alias mq="/usr/lib/sendmail -bp" # print out the current mail queue

alias psme="{ ps -ael ¦ head -1 ; ps -ael ¦ grep \" ${UID} \" ; } ¦ more"
```

Aliases can be overridden by preceding the alias name with a backslash (\), using the built-in command command, or giving the full pathname to the executable. If rm is aliased to `rm -i`, each of the following will override that alias:

```
\rm

command rm

/bin/rm
```

Two features that bash aliases do not support are arguments and assignments. If an alias needs to use these, a shell function should be implemented.

Functions

Functions serve a similar purpose as aliases, but are much more powerful and are akin to shell scripts. The basic syntax for defining a function is `function name () { list; }`. The keyword `function` is not required, and functions are frequently written as

```
name () {
    list ;
}
```

When a function's *name* is given (without the parentheses), the associated list of commands is executed. The parentheses after the function's *name*, are used by the shell to identify functions and do not signify a null argument list.

The simplest functions are similar to aliases. For example, the following alias and function are equivalent:

```
alias mq="/usr/lib/sendmail -bp"

mq () { /usr/lib/sendmail -bp ; }
```

Functions are also used where small changes need to be made to the environment. For example, the following function changes the value of $IFS so that each directory in the path is printed on a separate line:

```
printpath ()
{
( IFS=:;
for i in $PATH;
do
echo $i;
done )
}
```

Functions are mostly used for more complex tasks where arguments are required. The simplest example of this is a function that only uses its first argument, $1:

```
mkcd ()
{
if [ -n "$1" ] && mkdir "$1"; then
cd "$1";
echo "Created" `pwd`;
fi
}
```

The following are examples of functions that process all the arguments given to them:

```
myuuencode ()
{
if [ -n "$1" ]; then
( for i in "$@";
do
if [ -e "$i" ] && uuencode $i $i >${i}.uu; then
echo "uuencoded $i to ${i}.uu";
else
echo "unable to uuencode $i";
fi;
done )
fi
}

murder ()
{
( for pattern in "$@";
do
```

```
ps -ef ¦ grep "$pattern" ¦ while read user pid junk; do
kill -HUP "$pid";
done;
done )
}
```

The first function is a handy way to uuencode files without having to type large commands, and the second function is a quick way of killing off processes that match certain patterns.

One important aspect of functions is that they can be called recursively. Since there is no limit on the amount of recursive calls that can be made, simply replacing an alias with a function like

```
cp () { cp -i ; }
```

is not advised.

Sample Initialization File

This section contains a sample initialization file, .bash_profile.

```
# .bash_profile
# For versions 1.14.7 or higher
# set the user file creation mask
umask 022

# set PATH, the search path for commands
export PATH=/bin:/usr/bin:/usr/sbin:/usr/etc:/usr/ucb:/usr/local/bin

# Execute commands for interactive shells. Alternate test: if tty -s ; then
if [ -t ] ; then

    # set some terminal specific stuff
    stty -decctlq >& /dev/null
    stty erase '^H' kill '^U' intr '^C'

    # set TERM, the terminal type to vt100 if TERM is not "valid"
    case "$TERM" in
*term)
    TERM=xterm
    ;;
    network¦dialup¦unknown)
        TERM=vt100
        ;;
    esac
    export TERM

    # set MANPATH, the manual page search path
    MANPATH="/usr/man:/usr/local/man"

    if [ -d "$HOME/man" ] ; then
    MANPATH="$MANPATH:$HOME/man"
    fi

    export MANPATH
```

```
# set  LD_LIBRARY_PATH, the library search path
export LD_LIBRARY_PATH=/usr/lib:/usr/local/lib:/lib

# set uid, required by some csh scripts (e.g.. which)
export uid="$UID"

# set CDPATH, the search path for cd
export CDPATH=.:~:~/docs

# set editing related variables
if type emacs >/dev/null 2>&1; then
EDITOR=emacs
else
EDITOR=vi
fi
FCEDIT="$EDITOR"
VISUAL="$EDITOR"
export EDITOR VISUAL FCEDIT

# set PAGER, for viewing files, manpages etc...
if type less >/dev/null 2>&1; then
PAGER="less -s"
else
PAGER="more -s"
fi
export PAGER


# set MAILCHECK, the delay between checking for mail
export MAILCHECK=$((60*10))

# set PS1 and PS2, the primary and secondary prompt strings
PS1="\h \#\$ "
PS2="\#> "
export PS1 PS2

# set history related variables
export HISTCONTROL=ignoredups

# set FIGNORE, suffixes for filename completion to ignore
export FIGNORE=.out:.o:'~'

# set options
set -o notify ignoreeof noclobber

# set/unset optional shell behavior
# available in v2.00.0 or newer
if type shopt > /dev/null 2>&1 ; then
shopt -s checkhash checkwinsize cmdhist lithist dotglob
shopt -s histappend histreedit histverify

if [ -n "$MAILCHECK" ] ; then
    shopt -s mailwarn
fi

fi

fi
```

Command Line and History

The following sections cover interacting with the command line. The key sequences discussed in this section assume that the default emacs keyboard setup is being used.

The Command Line

In interactive shells, commands are issued at the prompt. Bash accepts a line for execution when the accept-line characters, newline (\n) or return, are typed. For example when a command such as date is typed at the prompt in an interactive shell, bash splits it into simple commands with arguments. If the full pathname for a command is given, bash tries to run it; otherwise, bash first tries to find a shell function that matches the command, then a built-in shell, and, finally, a command located somewhere in the searchpath given by $PATH.

Command Line Editing

Often when commands are issued, typing mistakes occur. Bash provides a friendly interface to fix these mistakes, which is similar to ksh and tcsh. Using these key commands, users can move the cursor to any position on the command line and edit the text at that position.

In the following command descriptions, C- is used to indicate the control key (prefix) and M- is used to indicate the meta key (prefix); all other keystrokes are literal. If two key commands are given, both must be used. For example, a keystroke written C-f means press the key marked f while holding down the control key, and a keystroke written C-q C-v means press the key q while holding down the control key and then press the key v while holding down the control key.

The following is a list of commands for moving around on the command line:

C-a	Moves the cursor to the beginning of the command
C-e	Moves the cursor to the end of the command
C-f	Moves the cursor forward a character. On terminals/keyboards that support the arrow keys, the right arrow can be used to move the cursor forward one character.
C-b	Moves the cursor back a character. On terminal/keyboards that support the arrow keys, the left arrow can be used to move the cursor forward one character.
M-f	Moves the cursor forward one word.
M-b	Moves the cursor back one word.
C-l	Clears the screen and puts the current line at the top of the screen. This is equivalent to the clear command.

Bash allows for substantial editing of commands by deleting, killing, and yanking text. Kill and yank are similar to the cut and paste features in most word processors. These commands are

10

`delete`	Deletes the character behind the cursor.
`C-d`	Deletes the character under the cursor. If there is no character under the cursor, an EOF character is printed
`C-k`	Kills all the text from the cursor's position to the end of the line.
`C-x delete`	Kills all the text on the line.
`C-u`	Kills all the text between the cursor and the beginning of the line.
`C-y`	Yanks killed text.

Bash also supports the following editing-related commands:

`M-u`	Changes the current word to uppercase.
`M-l`	Changes the current word to lowercase.
`C-q, C-v`	Adds the next character that is typed verbatim.
`C-g`	Aborts editing.
`C-_`	Undo.
`C-x C-u`	Undo.
`M-r`	Undoes all changes made to the current line.
`C-]`	Reads a character and moves the cursor to the next occurrence of that character.
`M-C-]`	Reads a character and moves the cursor to the previous occurrence of that character.

In some instances, editing multiline commands for one, the command line editing tools are not sufficient. For these cases, bash provides the fix command built-in, `fc`. The `fc` command invokes an editor for command editing and runs the edited command once the editor exits. By default, `fc` invokes the editor and inserts the last command that was executed into the editor's buffer, but `fc` can be told which command number needs to be fixed along with the editor that should be used. For example,

```
fc 10
```

will invoke an editor on the tenth command executed since the shell began, while

```
fc -10
```

will invoke an editor on a command that was executed 10 commands ago. The editor invoked can be specified by giving the `-e` option followed by the name of an `editor`. For example,

```
fc -e emacs
```

will invoke emacs, and place the last command in the buffer for editing. If the `-e` option is not given, the value of `$FCEDIT`, if it exists, is used as the name of the editor; otherwise, the value of `$EDITOR` is used as the name of the editor. If neither `$FCEDIT` or `$EDITOR` are set, vi is used as the editor.

Completion

In addition to editing commands, bash also completes text before the cursor. Bash has the ability to complete variable names, usernames, hostnames, commands, and filenames. For words beginning with a `$`, variable completion is attempted. For words beginning with a `~`, bash username completion is attempted. For words beginning with an `@`, hostname completion is attempted. For other words, command completion is first attempted, followed by filename completion. The general completion command is given every time the `tab` key is pressed. Some of the other completion commands are

`M-?`	Lists all possible completions.
`M-*`	Inserts a string containing all possible completions at the cursor.
`M-/`	Forces bash to attempt filename completion.
`M-~`	Forces bash to attempt username completion.
`M-$`	Forces bash to attempt variable completion.
`M-@`	Forces bash to attempt hostname completion.
`M-!`	Forces bash to attempt command completion. Bash will attempt to find completions that are aliases, reserved words, shell functions, built-ins, and executables.

History Recall

The history is the list of commands that have been previously executed. By default, bash stores up to 500 commands in its history, starting at command 1 and incrementing by 1 each time a command is accepted. Once a command has been accepted (for instance, a `return` was typed) it is appended to the history file, `~/.bash_history`. There are several variables, discussed in the section on shell variables, that can be used to customize this behavior. In addition to storing commands in the history, bash recognizes the following commands for recalling previously executed commands:

`C-p`	Recalls the previous command in the history. On keyboards/terminals that support arrow keys, the up-arrow key can be used to recall the previous command.
`C-n`	Recalls the next command in the history. On keyboards/terminals that support arrow keys, the down-arrow key can be used to recall the next command.

M-<	Moves to the first command in the history.
M->	Moves to the last command in the history.
C-r	Searches through the history starting at the current line and moving backwards (looks through previous commands). This can be slow if the history is large.
C-s	Searches through the history starting at the current line and moving forward.

History Variables

Bash maintains several read-only special parameters that relate to commands that have been executed. These are

$?	This parameter's value is the exit value of the most recently executed pipeline.
$$	This parameter's value is the process number of the current shell.
$!	This parameter's value is the process number of the most recently executed background process.
$0	This is the name of the current shell or its reference in a shell script; it is the name with which the script was invoked.

History Substitution

On many occasions, recalling and editing commands may not be easy. For such instances, bash provides for history manipulation (substitution) using operators similar to csh. History substitution begins when bash encounters the ! operator, and it is not followed by a blank, =, or (. If the ! operator is followed by these characters, bash performs negation rather than history substitution.

A simple history substitution is the ! operator followed by the command number of the command that needs to be reexecuted. For example,

!213

will execute the command stored in the history with the command number of 213. In general, this history substitution is referred to as !n, where *n* is the command number. If *n* is negative, the command issued *n* commands before the current command is recalled and executed. For example, the following:

!-10

will execute the command that was given 10 commands ago, and the last command executed can be recalled with

!-1

Since recalling the previous command is a common task, bash provides the `!!` shorthand for it. In addition, a command can be recalled from the history by giving part of a string that it starts with or contains. For example, the last `mail` command can be recalled by

```
!mail
```

The general syntax for recalling commands that start with a particular string is `!string`. In the case of the previous example, this history substitution will not recall commands that contain the string mail in them, like `sendmail` or `rmail`, but it will recall the command `mailtool`, if it appears before the command `mail` in the history. Bash can recall commands that contain particular strings if the history substitution is of the form `!?string?`. For example,

```
!?host?
```

can be used to recall the commands `hostname`, `gethostname`, `ypcat hosts`, and echo `$host`.

Sometimes simply recalling commands is not enough, so bash supports several partial recall and replace history substitutions. The simplest of these is the `^string1^string2^` replacement, which replaces `string1` in the previous command with `string2`. If the command

```
xv koala.gif
```

is executed, and then the picture `kangaroo.gif` needs to be viewed, the following quick substitution can be employed:

```
^koala^kangaroo^
```

The more advanced replacement operations can recall arguments given to previous commands. The simplest of these is the `!:0`, which recalls the previous command name. For example, if the command

```
cpwd () { if [ -n "$1" ] ; then cd "$1"; fi ; pwd }
```

is given, and the formatted version needs to be viewed with the `type` command, the following command will produce the desired result:

```
type !:0
```

Once the formatted function is in view, it may need to be used, so the following command:

```
!:^ /bin
```

will recall the name of the function, which was given as the first argument to `type`, since `!:^` substitution recalls the first argument given to a command. Sometimes the last argument given to a command will need to be recalled, so the `!$` or the `!:$` substitution can be used. These operators are a shorthand for the more general `!:n` substitution, which recalls the *n*th argument given to a command. If the third argument from a command were required, the `!:3` substitution would be used.

Often it is not enough to just recall one argument to a command. For example, if the command

```
xman -background white -geometry 135x55
```

is executed, and a parameter of the same background color and geometry were desired, the substitution

```
perfmeter !*
```

would produce the desired results, since the !* and the !:* substitutions are used to recall the entire list of arguments given to a command. These substitutions are special forms of the !:x-y history substitutions, which recall all the arguments between x and y that are given to a command. For example, if the following command is given:

```
javac -d . -O rectPanel.java
```

and the second and third arguments (the compiler flags) are required for a subsequent compile, the substitution

```
javac !:1-3 javaStarDate.java
```

will produce the desired result.

As a general rule, history substitutions can be intermixed, and can be written as !string:option, where option is the previously discussed options, 0, n, ^, $, x-y, and *. For example, if the following finger command is run:

```
finger ranga@soda.berkeley.edu sriranga@ocf.berkeley.edu
```

and, after several other commands have been executed, mail needs to be sent to those users, the following history substitution

```
mail !finger:*
```

will produce the proper result.

Summary

Bash is a powerful shell, popular with both beginning and advanced users, since it provides many user-oriented features, such as command line editing and filename completion. Its power and popularity are also due to its integration of features found in the Bourne shell, the Korn shell, and the C shell. Bash is also available on many non-UNIX systems, so learning and using Bash is a valuable skill for everyone.

References

The following sources were used:

Manual Page BASH(1), Free Software Foundation, 1996

BASH FAQ version 2.1, 1996

The Korn Shell

by John Valley and Chris Johnson

IN THIS CHAPTER

CHAPTER 11

Chapter 8, "What Is a Shell?," introduced the basics of UNIX shells, and Chapter 9, "The Bourne Shell," discussed the Bourne shell in particular. This chapter expands on the subject of shells by introducing the Korn shell—the second of the three main shell languages available to you. The third major shell language is discussed in Chapter 12, "The C Shell."

The Korn shell is named after its author, David G. Korn of AT&T's Bell Laboratories, who wrote the first version of the program in 1986. Therefore, the Korn shell is a direct descendent of the Bourne shell. It is almost perfectly compatible with the Bourne shell; with a few minor exceptions, any shell script written to be executed by the Bourne shell can be executed correctly by the Korn shell. As a general rule, though, Korn shell scripts cannot be processed correctly by the Bourne shell.

This upward compatibility provides a number of advantages—not the least of which is that it enables you to capitalize on your knowledge of the Bourne shell immediately. It also drastically reduces the amount of material you need to learn to begin using the Korn shell.

Because the Korn shell is intended as a replacement for and an improvement on the Bourne shell, it is best discussed as a series of features added to the basic functionality of the Bourne shell. Many aspects of the shell's operation presented in Chapter 9 are not repeated here. Instead, this chapter summarizes the differences between the Bourne shell and the Korn shell.

The list of Korn shell enhancements is extensive, ranging from the profound to the trivial. The most dramatic enhancements are those intended to facilitate keyboard interaction with the shell, but you also should be aware of many important extensions to shell syntax and shell programming techniques. The categories of enhancements follow:

- **Command aliases.** Aliases enable you to abbreviate frequently used commands without resorting to shell programming, thus improving your overall keyboard productivity.

- **Command history.** You can use command history alone or with command editing to modify and reuse previously typed commands. You also can use command history as a log of keyboard actions.

- **Command editing.** The Korn shell provides two styles of command editing that enable you to revise and correct commands as you type them. Command editing can greatly reduce the amount of time you spend retyping commands.

- **Directory management.** The Korn shell provides extensions to the cd command, new pathname syntax, and new shell variables to facilitate switching between directories and to abbreviate long pathnames.

- **Arithmetic expressions.** The Bourne shell offers minimal arithmetic capabilities. The Korn shell offers much greater power for handling numbers, even though a handheld calculator is still a better tool for calculations.

- **Syntax improvements.** The Korn shell offers improvements in the syntax of the `if` statement, the built-in `test` command, and the command substitution expression, which can improve the power and readability of your shell scripts.

- **Wildcard expressions.** The Korn shell provides more wildcard formats to reduce your typing workload.

- **Coprocessing.** The conventional pipe of the Bourne shell is expanded to permit more flexible, programmed interaction between your shell script and the commands you invoke.

- **Job processing.** The Korn shell includes batch job monitoring features to simplify running processes in the background and to enable you to perform more tasks simultaneously.

- **Privileged mode switching.** The Bourne shell provides no special features to capitalize on the Set User ID capability of UNIX. The privileged mode of the Korn shell, on the other hand, enables you to switch the Set User ID mode on and off and to develop procedures as shell scripts that previously required C language programming.

Although you haven't been introduced to the C shell yet, you'll find that many of the Korn shell features duplicate those of the C shell, but with a different syntax. This is intentional. Although the C shell offers many desirable features, its general syntax is incompatible with the Bourne shell, making it somewhat of a square peg in a round hole in the UNIX world. The Korn shell solves this long-standing quandary in the UNIX world by offering the keyboard and shell programming features that people want, but in a form that is compatible with the old, well-established Bourne shell standard.

Shell Basics

As I mentioned earlier, the Korn shell is essentially a foundation, equivalent to the Bourne shell, with a new layer of goodies added on top. You can use the Korn shell as a one-for-one replacement of the Bourne shell, with no special knowledge of Korn shell features. Korn shell extensions do not come into play until you explicitly invoke them.

In particular, the Korn shell is identical to the Bourne shell in the following areas:

- **Redirecting input and output.** The Bourne shell redirection operators <, <<, >, and >> and the here document facility (<<*label*) all have identical syntax and work the same way. A here document is a way of inserting a block of text into a script that you can redirect into another process or to a file. For example,

```
$ cat <<-!
    This is a demonstration of a here document. As you can see, the
    document uses the operator << to tell the shell that all the text on the
    ➥line
    next to the label, in this case !, is all to be read in and
    ➥redirected to
    the cat command. This - tells the shell to remove leading tabs at the
```

```
start of the line.
!
```

would display on screen as:

```
This is a demonstration of a here document. As you can see, the
document uses the operator << to tell the shell that all the text on the next
line to the label, in this case is !, is all to be read in and redirected to
the cat command. This - tells the shell to remove leading tabs at the start
```

■ **Entering multiple commands on one line.** The semicolon (;) marks the end of a shell statement. To enter multiple commands on one line, simply end each command except the last with a semicolon.

■ **Supporting filename substitutions.** The Korn shell supports the familiar substitution characters (also known as wildcards) `*`, `?`, and `[...]`; when used in a word, these characters cause the word to be replaced with all matching filenames. The Korn shell also supports additional filename matching patterns that have the general form `*(expression)` and the tilde (~) abbreviation, but you don't need to use these extensions. For example, if you had three files, say `time.x`, `time.y` and `tame.x`, then `time.?` will match `time.x` and `time.y`. `t*` will match all three files, and `t[ai]me.x` will match `time.x` and `tame.x`. The `*(expression)` wildcard is similar in principle to `[...]`; however, unlike `[...]`, the new wildcard `*(expression)` can specify longer patterns. Also, wildcards can be embedded in it, so you could end up with a wildcard expression that looked like: `file*([123].*(doc¦txt)¦0?.doc)`, which would match the following names: `file1.doc`, `file1.txt`, `file2.doc`, `file2.txt`, `file03.doc`, `file0d.doc`.... The complete list would be too long to display here, but you can see the power of the new wildcard.

■ **Substituting variables.** The Korn shell supports the variable substitution form `$name`, as well as all the special variable references `$*`, `$@`, `$$`, `$-`, `$?` and the parameters `$0` through `$9`. The `${name}` special form and the `${name[op]text}` form are supported with their usual meanings. In addition, the Korn shell supports `${name[index]}` array variables, `$(...)` special command substitutions, and others. The extensions do not conflict with Bourne shell syntax, and you do not need to use them.

■ **Substituting commands.** The Bourne shell command substitution form, `'command'`, is fully supported in the Korn shell, with the same syntax and behavior as the Bourne shell format. The Korn shell also supports the variant syntax, `$(...)`, to simplify the use of command substitutions.

■ **Recognizing escaping and quoting.** The Korn shell recognizes quoted strings of the form, `"..."` and `'...'`, with the same meaning and effect. A single special character can be deprived of its meaning with the backslash (\); the backslash is removed from the generated command line, except when it appears within single quotes. There are no extensions to the standard escaping and quoting techniques.

■ **Extending a command over multiple lines.** To extend a command over multiple lines, end the line with a backslash (\). The backslash must be the last character of the line. The combination of the backslash, followed immediately by a newline character, is recognized and simply deleted from the command input. This is the same behavior as the Bourne shell.

The general philosophy of the Korn shell is to invoke extensions and special features with syntax that is not legal for the Bourne shell. As a result, any commands and shell scripts that are syntactically correct for the Bourne shell will be interpreted identically by the Korn shell. All Korn shell extensions use syntactic forms that do not appear in the Bourne shell language.

Features that are not invoked directly by commands, such as command history and command editing, are controlled instead by shell options. To use command editing, you first must issue the command set -o vi or set -o emacs. If you don't, the Korn shell command line works the same as the Bourne shell. Also note that the set command follows the general philosophy: set -o is not valid in the Bourne shell and generates a syntax error.

The compatibility between the Bourne shell and the Korn shell is nearly perfect; one of the design objectives of the Korn shell was that it be able to execute system-provided shell scripts written for the Bourne shell without the need to revise those scripts or to invoke the Bourne shell to run them. This objective meant that even minor idiosyncrasies of Bourne shell behavior could not be overlooked; the Korn shell design had to implement them all.

The upshot of all this is that everything in Chapter 9 applies equally well, without restriction or caveat, to the Korn shell.

Wildcard Expressions

The Bourne shell supports a number of syntactic forms for abbreviating a command-line reference to filenames. These forms are based on the idea of embedding one or more special pattern-matching characters in a word. The word then becomes a template for filenames and is replaced by all the filenames that match the template. The pattern-matching characters supported by the Bourne shell are *, ?, and the bracketed expression [. . .].

These pattern-matching characters are supported by the Korn shell, as well as a tilde expansion that uses the ~ character to shorten pathnames and the extended pattern-matching expressions, *(), ?(), +(), @(), and !(). The syntax of pattern-matching expressions is based on the recognition of unquoted parentheses—()—in a word. Parentheses are special to the shell in both the Bourne and Korn shells; they must be quoted to avoid their special meaning. The Bourne shell attaches no special significance to a word such as here+(by¦with), but it would complain about the parentheses. Thus, words containing embedded parentheses do not occur in the Bourne shell. The Korn shell therefore uses this syntax to extend wildcard pattern-matching without impairing Bourne shell compatibility.

Tilde Expansion

A word beginning with ~ (the tilde) is treated specially by the Korn shell. To avoid its special meaning, you must quote the tilde. Note that words containing a tilde in any position except the first are treated normally. The tilde has a special meaning only when it appears as the first character of a word.

Table 11.1 lists the four styles of tilde expansion.

Table 11.1. Tilde expansion styles.

Style	Description	Example
~	When used by itself or followed by a slash (/), the tilde is replaced by the pathname of your home directory. It is the same as writing $HOME or $HOME/....	`$ echo ~` `/usr/home/fran` `$ echo ~/bin` `/usr/home/fran/bin`
~string	A tilde followed by an alphanumeric string is replaced by the home directory of the named user. It is an error if no entry exists in the /etc/passwd file for string.	`$ echo ~bill` `/usr/home/bill`
~+	A tilde followed by a plus sign is replaced by the full pathname of the current directory. It is the same as writing $PWD or $PWD/....	`$ pwd` `/usr/lib` `$ echo ~+/bin` `/usr/lib/bin`
~-	A tilde followed by a minus sign is replaced by the full pathname of the previous directory. It is the same as writing $OLDPWD or $OLDPWD/....	`$ pwd` `/usr/lib` `$ cd ~/lib` `/usr/home/fran/lib` `$ echo ~-/bin` `/usr/lib/bin`

As you can see, the tilde shorthand is a great time saver.

Pattern Expressions

A *pattern expression* is any word consisting of ordinary characters and one or more shell pattern-matching characters. The pattern-matching characters are the familiar *, ?, and [...] from the Bourne shell, as well as any of the extended pattern-matching expressions shown in Table 11.2.

Table 11.2. Extended pattern-matching expressions.

Expression	Description
`*(pattern[¦pattern]...)`	Matches zero or more occurrences of the specified patterns. For example, `time*(.x¦.y)` matches the filenames `time`, `time.x`, `time.y`, `time.x.x`, `time.y.y`, `time.x.y`, and `time.y.x`, but it doesn't match the filename `time.z`.
`+(pattern[¦pattern]...)`	Matches one or more occurrences of the specified patterns. For example, `time+(.x¦.y)` matches `time.x`, `time.x.x`, `time.y`, `time.x.y`, and so on, but it doesn't match `time`.
`?(pattern[¦pattern]...)`	Matches any one of the patterns. It won't concatenate or repeat patterns to match files, unlike `*(pattern)`. For example, `time?(.x¦.y)` only matches `time`, `time.x`, and `time.y`, but it doesn't match `time.x.x`.
`@(pattern[¦pattern]...)`	Matches exactly one occurrence of the pattern. For example, `time@(.x¦.y)` matches `time.x` or `time.y`, but it doesn't match `time`, `time.x.x`, or `time.x.y`.
`!(pattern[¦pattern]...)`	Same as *, except that strings that would match the specified patterns are not considered matches. For example, `time!(.x¦.y)` matches `time`, `time.x.y`, `time.0`, and everything beginning with `time` except for `time.x` and `time.y`.

CAUTION

You'll notice that the expressions `*(pattern[¦pattern]...)` and `+(pattern[¦pattern]...)` will match any combination of the specified pattern. This can be both useful and dangerous. If in doubt, use echo to find out what files the patterns will match. You won't be popular if you end up removing the system configuration by mistake!

Note that the definition of pattern expressions is recursive. Each form contains one or more pattern strings. This means that nested pattern expressions are legal. Consider, for example, `time*(.[cho]¦.sh)`. It contains the pattern `[cho]` inside the pattern expression, which causes it to match `time.sh`, `time.c`, `time.h`, `time.o`, `time.sh.c`, `time.c.o`, and so on. The pattern `time*(.*(sh¦obj))` matches the filename `time.sh` or `time.obj`.

The main value of these extended pattern-matching expressions is in enabling you to select a subset of files without having to list each filename explicitly on the command line. Pattern expressions also are legal in other contexts where the shell does pattern matching, such as in the expression of the `case` statement.

Command Substitution

Another noteworthy enhancement provided by the Korn shell is a more convenient syntax for command substitutions. Remember from Chapter 10, "The Bourne Again Shell," that a string quoted with backquotes (`` `command` ``) is replaced with the standard output of `command`. The backquote notation isn't easy to use, though. The Korn shell supports the following alternative form in addition to the standard Bourne shell backquote notation:

`$(command-list)`

where `command-list` is any valid list of commands. In its simplest form, a command list is a list of commands separated by semicolons. Not only does the parenthesized form avoid the problem of recognizing backquotes on printed listings, but it also acts as a form of quoting or bracketing. You can use all the standard quoting forms inside the parentheses without having to use backslashes to escape quotes. Furthermore, the parenthesized form nests; you can use `$()` expressions inside `$()` expressions without difficulty.

For example `` `ls` `` can be replaced with `$(ls)`. Similarly, `` `ls;who` `` can be replaced with `$(ls;who)`.

An Improved cd Command

For directory movement, the Korn shell supports two new forms of the `cd` command:

`cd -`

`cd oldname newname`

The command `cd -` is especially helpful. It switches back to the directory you were in before your last `cd` command. This command makes it easy for you to switch to another directory temporarily and then move back to your working directory by typing **cd -**. The PWD and OLDPWD variables are maintained to carry the full pathnames of your current and previous directory, respectively. You can use these variables for writing commands to reference files in a directory without typing the full pathname.

You can use the `cd oldname newname` command to change a component of the pathname of your current directory. This makes lateral moves in a directory structure somewhat easier.

Suppose that your current directory is `/usr/prod/bin` and you want to switch to the directory `/usr/test/bin`. Just type the command **cd prod test**. Similarly, the command `cd usr jjv` switches from `/usr/prod/bin` to `/jjv/prod/bin`, assuming that the latter directory exists.

Aliases

The command-aliasing feature of the Korn shell is certainly one of its most attractive and flexible enhancements over the Bourne shell. It's an enhancement you'll start using right away.

When you define a command alias, you specify a shorthand term to represent a command string. When you type the shorthand term, it is replaced during command execution with the string it represents. The command string can be more than just a command name; it can define options and arguments for the command as well.

You might have one or more preferred ways of listing your directory contents, for example. I like to use the `-FC` options on my `ls` command when I just want to see what's in the directory. Typing the command `ls -FC ...` repeatedly all day long, though, would not be one of my favorite things to do. The command-alias feature makes it easy to set up a shorthand for the `ls` command. You do it like this:

```
$ alias lx=`ls -FC`
```

Now, whenever you enter `lx` on the command line, the command `ls -FC` is executed.

Defining Aliases

The `alias` command is a *built-in shell*, meaning that it is available to you only when running the Korn shell. It is not part of the UNIX operating system at large. You use the `alias` command to define new aliases and to list the command aliases currently in effect.

The general syntax of the `alias` command follows:

```
alias [ -tx ] [ name[=value] ... ]
```

The arguments of `alias` are one or more specifications, each beginning with an alias name. The alias name is the shorthand command you enter at the terminal. After the equal sign (=), you enter the text with which you want the shell to replace your shorthand. You should enclose the alias value string in single quotes to hide embedded blanks and special characters from immediate interpretation by the shell. The `-t` and `-x` arguments enable you to manipulate the alias command in different ways. Specifying `-t` enables you to see all the tracked aliases, and using `-x` enables you to define an alias as exportable—much in the same way variables are exportable if you use the `export` command. For more details on these options, see "Using Tracked Aliases" and "Using Exported Aliases," later in this chapter.

The Korn shell stores alias names and their definitions in an internal table kept in memory. Because the table is not stored in a disk file, you lose your alias definitions whenever you log out or exit the Korn shell. To keep an alias from session to session, you need to define the alias in your *logon profile*—a file in your home directory named .profile. There's nothing tricky about it. The same command you enter at the keyboard to define an alias works just as well when issued from a logon profile script. Thus, for aliases you want to use over and over, simply type the alias command in your logon profile; you only have to do it once. (For more information about using the logon profile, see "Customizing the Korn Shell," later in this chapter.)

The syntax of the alias command enables you to define more than one alias on a command. The general syntax follows:

```
alias name=value [name=value]...
```

You don't usually write multiple definitions on one alias command, because you usually think them up one at a time. In your logon profile, it's a good idea to write only one alias definition per alias command. This makes it easier to add and delete alias definitions later.

After you define an alias, you might want to list the aliases in effect to see your new definition. Simply enter the alias command with no arguments, as in this example:

```
$ alias
true=let
false=let
lx=ls -FC
```

In all likelihood, there are a good many more alias definitions in effect than you defined. The Korn shell automatically defines a number of aliases when it starts up, such as when you log on, to provide convenient abbreviations for some Korn shell commands. The true and false definitions fall into this category. The UNIX operating system provides true and false commands, but, as programs, they must be searched for and loaded into memory to execute. As aliases, the shell can execute these commands much more quickly, so these two particular aliases are provided as an easy performance enhancement for the many shell scripts you execute, usually unknowingly, throughout the day.

To use the lx command alias shown in the last example, use it as a new command name, as in this example:

```
$ lx
```

This, by itself, lists all the files in the current directory in a neat, columnar format sorted for easy inspection. To list a directory other than the current directory, use this command:

```
$ lx /usr/bin
```

After alias substitution, the shell sees the command ls -FC /usr/bin.

The capability to prespecify command options in an alias is a great help. Even better, you usually can augment or alter prespecified command options when you use the alias. Suppose that you want to add the command option -a when listing /usr/bin so that you can see all dot files in the directory. You might think that you have to type the full ls command, because the lx alias doesn't include an `-a` option letter. This is not so. The following command works quite well:

```
$ lx -a /usr/bin
```

When the shell executes this command, it immediately replaces `lx` with the alias value string, obtaining the following internal form:

```
$ ls -FC -a /usr/bin
```

The `ls` command, like most other UNIX commands, is comfortable with command options specified in multiple words. In effect, the `-a` option has been added to the `-FC` options provided automatically by the alias.

Removing an Alias

To remove an alias that you or the Korn shell defined previously, use the `unalias` command:

```
$ unalias name [ name ... ]
```

Notice that, just as you can define multiple aliases on one command line, you also can remove multiple aliases with one `unalias` command.

Writing an Alias Definition

One of my favorite aliases is the following one for the `pg` command:

```
$ alias pg=`/usr/bin/pg -cns -p"Page %d:"`
```

The `pg` alias is instructive in a number of ways. Take a look at it in detail.

First, note that the alias name is `pg`. This is the same as the `pg` command itself, so, in effect, the alias hides the `pg` command. You can invoke the real UNIX `pg` command by using an explicit pathname—calling `/usr/bin/pg`—but not by the short command `pg`, which invokes the alias instead.

Choosing the same name for an alias as a real command name is unusual. It implies that you never want to execute the real command directly and that you always want to dress it up with the options specified in the alias.

Because of the way I work, the options `-c`, `-n`, `-s`, and `-p` should have been built into the `pg` command; I always want to use them. The `-c` option causes `pg` to clear the screen when it displays a new page. On a video terminal, this is more natural and faster than scrolling the lines. The `-n` option causes `pg` to execute a command key immediately without waiting for the Enter key to be pressed. All `pg` commands consist of only one letter. The only reason not to use the `-n` option is to avoid the slack in performance that results from generating a terminal interrupt for each keypress, which the `-n` option requires. Single-user workstations and modern high-performance computers don't notice the extra workload, however. Therefore, unless you're working on an old PDP-11, go ahead and specify the `-n` option for the convenience it adds.

The -s option displays messages, such as the current page number, in highlighted mode and usually in inverse video, which makes the non-text part of the display easier to notice or ignore.

The -p option causes the pg command to display the page number at the bottom of each screen. I like page numbering because it gives me a rough idea of where I am in the displayed document. By default, the page number is displayed as a bare number, run on with the rest of the command line. The pg command, however, enables you supply a format for the page number. I specified -p"Page %d:". It identifies the page number with the word Page and provides a colon (:) to separate the page number from the input command line.

Because the page number format string contains characters special to the shell (specifically, an embedded blank), it must be enclosed in quotes. The alias command also requires that the entire alias definition be enclosed in quotes. Therefore, I need a quote within a quote.

If you understood the discussion of quotes in Chapter 9, you also should realize that there are at least three ways to write the pg alias command:

```
$ alias pg=`/usr/bin/ls -cns -p"Page %d:"`
$ alias pg="/usr/bin/ls -cns -p'Page %d'"
$ alias pg="/usr/bin/ls -cns -p\"Page %d\""
```

The first form is the form I chose for the example. The second form embeds a single quoted string inside a double quoted string; it works just as well. The third form uses an escape character to embed a double quote inside a double quoted string. In this case, the shell strips off the backslashes before it stores the alias value. I avoid this form because I don't like to use escape sequences unless I have to. An escape sequence is a two-character sequence, the first character of which is a backslash (\). The second character is the one that is being escaped, which means that the shell will not try and interpret the character in any way and just treat it as it is.

The point here is that alias definitions usually must be enclosed in quotes unless the alias value is a single word. Thus, you must occasionally embed quoted strings inside a quoted string. You should recognize that this need can arise. Be prepared to handle it by making sure that you understand how the shell-quoting mechanism works.

> **CAUTION**
>
> If you do get a handle on how the shell-quoting syntax works, it incites many otherwise nice people to brand you as a UNIX guru. So be careful.

Using Exported Aliases

The alias command supports a number of options, including -x (export) and -t (tracking).

An exported alias is much the same concept as an exported variable. Its value is passed into shell scripts that you invoke.

Exporting a command alias can be both helpful and harmful. Exporting the `pg` alias shown earlier would be helpful, for example, because it would cause `pg` commands issued by a shell script—many UNIX commands are implemented as shell scripts—to work as I prefer. On the other hand, if you define an alias for the `rm` command that always prompts the user before deleting a file, you might be inundated with requests from system-supplied shell scripts to delete temporary files that you've never heard of.

Use the command `alias -x` to display only those command aliases that are exported. When used in the form `alias -x name`, the alias `name` is redefined as an exported alias; it should have been defined previously. To define a new exported alias, use the full form

```
alias -x name=value
```

Using Tracked Aliases

By default, the Korn shell automatically creates a tracked alias entry for many of the commands you invoke from the keyboard. This feature helps to improve performance. When an alias is tracked, the Korn shell remembers the directory where the command is found. Therefore, subsequent invocations don't have to search your PATH list for the command file. Essentially, the alias for the command simply is set to the full pathname of the command.

You can display the commands for which a tracked alias exists by using the command `alias -t`.

To request explicit tracking for a command you use frequently, use the form

```
alias -t name
```

If no alias exists with the given name, the Korn shell performs a path search and stores the full pathname of the command `name` as the alias value. Otherwise, the shell simply marks the alias as tracked for future reference.

Note that you generally don't set the tracked attribute for command aliases that you write— that is, when the alias name differs from the alias value. The values for tracked aliases usually should be set by the Korn shell. You can achieve the effect of a tracked alias by supplying the full pathname of the command in the alias value; this eliminates path searches. The `lx` alias shown earlier, for example, would be better written as

```
alias lx='/usr/bin/ls -FC'
```

This would achieve the same effect as tracking.

As a final example, suppose that the `vi` command is not in the list when you issue the command `alias -t`, but that you know you will be using the command fairly frequently. To request tracking for the `vi` command, simply issue the command `alias -t vi`.

One of the major reasons for name tracking is that the Korn shell takes account of the possibility that your *search path*—the value of the PATH shell variable—may include the directory . (dot), which is a reference to your current directory. If you switch to another directory, commands that were available might become unavailable, or they might need to be accessed by a different pathname. Alias tracking interacts with the `cd` command to keep the full pathnames of tracked aliases current. In other words, alias tracking keeps track of the proper full pathname for commands as you switch from directory to directory and create, remove, or relocate executable files. You can use the `set` command to toggle alias tracking on and off. Typing

```
set -o trackall
```

forces the shell to track every command you use, whereas

```
set +o trackall
```

switches the tracking off.

Shell Options

Because the Korn shell is a rather sophisticated program, it deals with many human-interface issues that might be resolved in two or more ways. To help you use the shell in ways most convenient to you, the shell enables you to choose how it behaves by setting options.

You can set Korn shell options in two ways: with the `ksh` command when you invoke the shell and with the `set` command from within the shell after you've started it. Options that you don't set explicitly take on a default value. Thus, you never need to bother with option settings unless you want to.

The `ksh` command generally is issued on your behalf by the UNIX logon processor, using a template stored in the `/etc/passwd` file for your logon name. Generally, the system administrator constructs the password entry for you, but unless he's very busy or very mean-spirited, he'll be happy to adjust your password entry to invoke the shell with your preferred settings. Of course, you can replace your logon shell with the Korn shell at any time by using this command:

```
$ exec ksh options ...
```

The `exec` statement you encountered in your study of the Bourne shell does the same thing under the Korn shell. It replaces the current shell with the command named as its first argument—usually also a shell, but perhaps of a different type or with different options and arguments.

The syntax of the `ksh` command follow:

```
ksh [ ±aefhkmnpstuvx- ] [-cirs] [±o option] ... [±A name] [arg ...]
```

The `-c`, `-i`, `-r`, and `-s` options can be specified only on the `ksh` command line. All the other options can be specified on the `set` command as well.

Table 11.3 lists the options specifiable only on the `ksh` command line.

Table 11.3. Options specifiable only on the `ksh` command line.

Option	Specifies	Description
-c	Command	The first (and only) arg is a command. The -c option prevents the shell from attempting to read commands from any other source. It merely executes the command given as arg and then exits. This option is not used often from the keyboard or from within shell scripts. It most often is used internally by programs written in the C language.
-i	Interactive shell	Forces the shell to behave as though its input and output are a terminal. Usually, you don't need to specify the -i option explicitly. Its main purpose is to prevent the abnormal termination of commands invoked by the shell from terminating the shell itself.
-r	Restricted shell	The Korn shell runs as a restricted shell and prevents the user from using the cd command, modifying the PATH variable, redirecting output, and invoking a command by its full pathname. This option generally is of interest only to the system administrator for setting up specialized user accounts. The Korn shell also starts off as a restricted shell if the first character of its name when invoked is an r. Copying (or linking) ksh to rksh, for example, and then running rksh gives the same result as ksh -r. The reason for using the rksh form is that ksh -r isn't always guaranteed to run a restricted shell if it is defined as a logon shell in the password database /etc/passwd.
-s	Standard input	The Korn shell doesn't activate the protections against abnormal termination given by option -i. The shell reads commands from standard input until the end-of-file character and then exits normally. This is a handy option, because it enables you to pipe a stream of commands to the shell for execution.

Table 11.4 lists additional options you can specify on the ksh command or the set command. You can specify options with a letter in the usual way (for example, -a) or by name (for example, -o allexport). An option that has been set explicitly or by default can be turned off with the + flag, as in +a or +o allexport.

Table 11.4. Other options you can specify with the ksh command or the set command.

Option	Description
-a	The equivalent option name is allexport. All variables are treated implicitly as exported variables. You don't need to invoke the typeset -x command or export alias to export the variable. A variable becomes eligible for export when it is defined, whether by the typeset statement or by an assignment statement. The typeset -x command and export alias are permitted, but they have no additional effect.
-e	The equivalent option name is errexit. Any command returning a non-zero exit code causes immediate termination of the shell. When this option is set within a shell script, only the shell script is terminated.
-f	The equivalent option name is noglob. Filename expansion is disabled. Wildcard expressions are treated literally and, with the -f option in force, have no special meaning or effect. You might use set -f and set +f to disable wildcard expansion for a short range of statements.
-h	The equivalent option name is trackall. Every command issued is defined automatically as a tracked alias, just as though you executed alias -t *xxx* in front of each command. The -h option is set to on by default for non-interactive shells. Commands that specify a full pathname or that use names not valid as command alias names are not tracked.
-k	The equivalent option name is keyword. When -k is set, command arguments with the form *name=value* are stripped from the command line and are executed as assignment statements before the command is executed. The assignment is exported temporarily for the duration of the one command. The effect is equivalent to adding keyword arguments to the shell language and to UNIX commands and shell scripts that support this kind of argument. Most UNIX commands and shell scripts, however, do not support keyword arguments. Therefore, the -k option has little real application.

Option	*Description*
-m	The equivalent option name is `monitor`. `-m` runs commands that you launch in the background—using the `&` shell operator—in a separate process group, automatically reports the termination of such background jobs, and enables use of the `jobs` command for managing background jobs. If `-m` is not set, commands launched with the `&` operator execute in the same manner as with the Bourne shell, and job control is not in effect. The default is to enable this option automatically for interactive shells.
-n	The equivalent option name is `noexec`. `-n` causes the shell to read and process commands but not execute them. You can use this option in the form `ksh -n shell-script-filename` to check the syntax of a shell script. You probably won't want to use this option with your logon shell.
-p	The equivalent option name is `privileged`. The `-p` option is useful for script writers. A shell script file that has the Set User ID bit, the Set Group ID bit, or both will, when invoked by the Korn shell, have the effective User ID and effective Group ID set according to the file permissions, the Owner ID, and the Group ID; also, the `-p` option will be on. In this mode, the shell script enjoys the permissions of the effective User ID and Group ID—not those of the real user. Setting the `-p` option off—for example, with `set +p`—causes the Korn shell to set the effective User ID and Group ID to those of the real user, effectively switching to the user's rather than the file's permissions. You subsequently can use the `set -p` command to revert to Privileged mode. Not all versions of the Korn shell support this definition of the `-p` option; only the more recent UNIX operating system releases include this facility.
-s	When used on the set command, `-s` sorts the `arg` command arguments into alphabetical sequence before storing. When used with the `ksh` command, the `-s` option reads commands from the standard input (refer to Table 11.3).
-t	The Korn shell, when invoked with the `-t` option, reads and executes one command and then exits. You should set the `-t` option with the `ksh` command instead of with the `set` command.

continues

Table 11.4. continued

Option	Description
-u	The equivalent option name is nounset. -u causes the shell to generate an error message for a reference to an unset variable—for example, referring to $house when no value has been assigned to house. The default behavior is to replace the variable reference with the null string. This option is useful to script writers for debugging shell scripts.
-v	The equivalent option name is verbose. Each command is printed before scanning, substitution, and execution occur. This is useful for testing shell scripts when used in the form ksh -v shell-script-filename or with set -v and set +v from within a shell script to force the display of a range of commands as they are being executed.
-x	The equivalent option name is xtrace. -x causes the Korn shell to display each command after scanning and substitution but before execution. Each line is prefixed with the expanded value of the PS4 variable. Using this option enables you to see the effects of variable and command substitution on the command line. When used in the form ksh -x shell-script-filename, the -x option is a handy debugging tool for script writers.
—	Used with the ksh or set command, this option forces interpretation of the remaining words of the command line as arguments rather than options—even for words beginning with - or +. The — option often is used with the set command for setting new values for the positional parameters, because it ensures that no substituted values are construed as set statement options.

> **CAUTION**
>
> Use caution when writing scripts that will use the privileged option. A badly written script may give potential attackers doors they need to access a more privileged user.

In addition to the letter options listed in Table 11.4, the -o keyletter supports the additional named options listed in Table 11.5.

Table 11.5. Options supported by the -o keyletter.

Option	Description
bgnice	Requests that the shell automatically reduce the priority of background jobs initiated with the & shell operator as though the nice command had been used.
emacs	Invokes the EMACS Edit mode. EMACS editing remains switched on until set +o emacs or set -o vi is entered.
gmacs	Invokes the GMACS (*Gosling EMACS*) Edit mode with the alternative definition of the Ctrl+T transpose function.
ignoreeof	Requests that the shell ignore an end-of-file character entered at the beginning of the command line. Ordinarily, an EOF character entered in this position causes the shell to terminate. You can set this option to avoid accidentally terminating the shell. You must use the exit command to terminate the shell and log out.
markdirs	Causes wildcard expansion to append a slash (/) to any generated pathnames that are the pathnames of directories.
noclobber	Modifies the behavior of the > redirection operator to inhibit the overwriting of existing files. If you name an existing file after >, the shell writes an error message and doesn't open the output file. Use >¦ to redirect output to an existing file when noclobber is set.
nolog	Inhibits the storing of functions in your command-history file.
vi	Enables the vi Edit mode with line input. Line input provides only a subset of the features of vi command editing, but it provides better performance than the viraw option. You can switch off vi Edit mode with set +o vi or set -o emacs.
viraw	Enables vi Edit mode with character input. Character input provides all the features of vi Edit mode but with more overhead than the vi option.

The -A option can be used on the ksh command line or the set command to define an array variable with initial values. When you specify -A, the next argument must be the name of the array variable to be initialized. Subsequent arguments are stored as consecutive elements of the array, beginning with element 0. The -A option resets any previous value of the array variable before it assigns new values. Thus, the ending value of the array consists of only those arguments specified as arg.

The +A option assigns the arg values successively, starting with element 0, but it doesn't reset any previous values of the array. Thus, if the array variable previously had 12 values and only six values were provided with +A, after execution, the first six elements of the array would be the arg values and the last six elements would be left over from the previous value of the array.

The significance of the arg values depends on the options specified. If option -A is specified, the values are taken as initial array element values. If option -s or -i is specified, or if option -i defaults because the shell input is a terminal, the arg values are used to initialize the positional parameters $1, $2, and so on. If option -c is specified, the first arg is taken as a command string to be executed. If none of the options -A, -c, -i, or -s is specified, the first arg is taken as the name of a file of shell commands to be executed, and subsequent arg values are set temporarily as the positional parameters $1, $2, and so on during the file's execution.

Command History

Command history and command editing are somewhat interrelated features. To fully use all the benefits of command editing, however, you need an understanding of how command history works.

Command history is simply the automatic recording of commands that you enter in a numbered list. The list is kept in a special disk file in your home directory to preserve it from logon session to session. Therefore, when you log on, the command-history list from your previous session is available for reference and use. New commands you enter are added to the end of the list. To keep the list from growing too large, the oldest commands at the beginning of the list are deleted when the list grows to a certain fixed size.

You don't need to do anything to activate the command-history feature, and you don't need to specify its maximum size. Its operation is completely automatic. Your only mission, should you decide to accept it, is to use the list to make your life easier.

You can use the command-history list in one of three ways:

- **View the commands in the history list by using the history command.** Use the history command when you can't remember whether you've already performed an action or if you want to refer to the syntax or operands of a previous command.

- **Resubmit a command from the list by using the r command.** Except for very short commands, it's faster to resubmit a command you typed before with the r command than it is to type the command again. The r command provides several alternate ways for you to identify which command in the history list you want to reexecute. You can also modify a command in the history list and then execute the modified command.

- **Modify a command in the list using the fc command.** You can use any text editor you want to edit the chosen command. By default, the Korn shell invokes the crusty old ed command for you, but you can change the default to any text editor you want by changing the value in the FCEDIT variable. The modified command will execute immediately after you leave the editor.

NOTE

Performing command editing with the `fc` command, although a convenient and useful feature of command history, is not the same as the command-editing feature discussed later, in the "Command Editing" section.

Now take a closer look at these commands for viewing and manipulating command history.

Displaying the Command-History List

The command `history` command displays the commands in the command-history list. Each command is listed with a line number preceding it. The line number uniquely identifies each command in the history list, and it is one way you can refer to a specific line in the history list—for example,

```
$ history
[122] cd /usr/home/jim/src/payapp/pay001
[123] vi main.c
[124] cc -I../include -o main main.c
[125] fgrep include *.c ¦ grep '^#'
[126] vi checkwrite.c checkfile.c checkedit.c
[127] lint -I../include checkfile.c >errs; vi errs
[128] vi checkfile.c
[129] cc -I../include -o checks check*.c
[130] cp checks /usr/home/jim/bin
```

NOTE

The `history` command is actually an alias for the `fc` command—specifically, for `fc -l`.

The complete syntax for the history command follows:

```
history [first] [last]
```

For *first*, specify the first line to be displayed. You can designate a specific line directly by its line number—for example, `history 35`—or as a number of lines back from the current line—for example, `history -10`. You also can give the command name of the line from which the display should begin—for example, `history vi`. The Korn shell looks backward from the current line until it finds a command beginning with `vi` and then displays lines from that point forward.

For *last*, specify the last line to be displayed. If you omit *last*, history lines are displayed from *first* up to the current, most recently entered line in the command history. You can use an actual line number, a relative line number, or a command name to designate the last line to be displayed.

If you omit both *first* and *last*, the Korn shell lists the last 16 lines of history.

> **TIP**
>
> You won't know what line numbers to use until you first list some history. Most people begin a search of command history without any operands. If you want to see more lines before line number 160, you might want to try `history 140`.

Reexecuting a Command from the History

The `r` command enables you to reexecute a command from the command-history list. The `r` command itself isn't added to the history, but the command you reuse is added.

> **NOTE**
>
> The `r` command is actually a preset alias for the `fc` command—specifically, `fc -e -`.

The general syntax for `r` follows:

```
r [ old=new ] [ line ]
```

If you omit *line*, the most recently entered command is reexecuted.

Specify a line number (25), a relative line number (-8), or a command name (vi) for *line* to designate the command you want to reuse. As with the `history` command, if you specify a command name, the most recently entered command with that name is reused.

You can modify a word or phrase of the reused command by using the syntax *old=new*. Suppose that the command history contains the following line:

```
135 find /usr -type f -name payroll -print
```

You could reuse the `find` command, changing only the filename `payroll` to `vendors`, like this:

```
$ r payroll=vendors find
```

The `r` command echoes the line that will be executed, showing any changes that might have been made. For example, the `r` command here yields the following output:

```
$ r payroll=vendors find
find /usr -type f -name vendors -print
```

Accessing the History List: `fc`

The `fc` (fix command) command is a built-in Korn shell command. It provides access to the command-history list. Forms of the `fc` command enable you to display, edit, and reuse commands you previously entered. The Korn shell automatically defines the alias names `history` and `r` for you to reduce the amount of typing needed to perform simple history functions.

The syntax of the `fc` command follows:

```
fc [ -e editor ] [ -nlr ] [ first ] [ last ]
```

When invoked with no options, the `fc` command selects a line from the command history using the values of *first* and *last*, invokes the default command editor, and waits for you to edit the command or commands selected. When you exit the editor by filing the altered command text or by quitting the editor, the commands are executed.

The `fc` command actually copies the selected commands to a temporary file and passes the file to the text editor. The contents of the file after editing become the command or commands to be executed.

For example, if you enter the command

```
$ fc vi
```

where `vi` represents the value of *first*, the Korn shell copies the most recent `vi` command to a temporary file. The temporary file has an unrecognizable name, such as `/usr/tmp/fc13159`, and is located in a directory designated for temporary files. The file you actually edit is `/usr/tmp/fc13159`. Regardless of whether you change the text in file `/msr/tmp/fc13159`, the Korn shell executes its contents immediately after you exit the editor.

You can specify the command or commands to be processed in the following manner:

- To process the command you most recently entered—other than `fc`, of course—omit both *first* and *last*.

- To select and process only one command, specify the command as the value of *first* and omit *last*.

- To select a range of commands, specify the first command in the range with *first* and specify the last command in the range with *last*.

- To designate a command by its line-number position in the history list, use a plain number—for example, 219.

- To designate a command preceding the most recent command in the history list, use a negative number. In this command-history list, for example, the command `fc -2` selects the `vi` command:

  ```
  135 mkdir paywork
  136 mv paymast/newemps paywork
  137 cd paywork
  138 vi newemps
  139 payedit newemps
  ```

- To select a command by its name instead of by its position in the history list, use a command name or any prefix of a command name. The most recent command line that begins with the string you specify will be selected. In this command-history example, you also could select the `vi` command by entering **fc vi**.

The *first* and *last* command-line selectors don't have to use the same formats. You could select line 145 of the history list through the fifth-to-last line by entering **fc 145 -5**, for example.

By default, the fc command invokes a text editor on the selected lines and reexecutes them after editing. You can modify this default behavior with the options shown in Table 11.6.

Table 11.6. Options to modify the behavior of the fc command.

Option	Stands For	Description
-e	Editor	Use the -e option to override the Korn shell's default editor. To use the vi editor to modify and reuse commands, for example, type **fc -e vi ....** Use **fc -e vi ...** to override the default editor.
		The special format -e - suppresses the use of an editor. The selected lines are executed immediately with no opportunity to change them. This form of the fc command—as in fc -e - 135—is equivalent to the r command. When you use this form, the second dash must be a word by itself. The command fc -e - 135 immediately reexecutes line 135 of the command history, whereas the command fc -e -135 attempts to edit the most recent command in the history list with an editor named -135, which probably doesn't exist. Alternatively, the command fc -e- 135 generates another kind of error, because -e- isn't a valid option of the fc command.
-l	List	The selected lines are listed. No editor is invoked, and the lines are not reexecuted. The command fc -l is equivalent to the alias history.
-n	Numbers	Use the -n option to suppress the printing of line numbers in front of the command history. The -n option is meaningful only in combination with the -l option—for example, fc -nl.
-r	Reverse	The -r option causes the command history to be printed in reverse order. The most recently entered command is shown first, and successive lines show progressively older commands. Use the -r option with the -l option—for example, fc -lr.

Command Editing

Command editing is arguably the most important extension of the Bourne shell included in the Korn shell. It is a great timesaver, and it makes the shell much easier to use for UNIX beginners.

The basic idea of command editing is to enable you to use common keys on most terminal keyboards to correct keying errors as you enter commands.

To bring this basic idea to reality, the Korn shell must have some support from the terminal you're using. If you're going to backspace and retype a character, for example, it would be helpful if the terminal is capable of backspacing, erasing a character already displayed, and typing a new character in its place. For this reason, command editing is most useful with video-display terminals. Hard-copy terminals such as teletypes are inappropriate for use with the command-editing feature of the Korn shell.

The Korn shell supports two distinct styles of command editing: vi Edit mode—named after the vi text editor—and EMACS Edit mode—named after EMACS. If you're familiar with either of these editors, you can begin to use command editing immediately.

Activating Command-Edit Mode

Before you can use command editing, you first must activate it. Until you do so, the Korn shell command line works much the same as the Bourne shell: Everything you type goes into the command line indiscriminately as text, including control and function keys. This is a compatibility feature you'll want to disable as soon as possible—typically, by activating command editing in your logon profile.

To enable vi Edit mode, enter the following command line or place it in your profile (see "Customizing the Korn Shell," later in this chapter):

```
set -o vi
```

To enable EMACS Edit mode, enter the following command line or place it in your profile:

```
set -o emacs
```

If you're not familiar with the vi or EMACS text editor, but you want to use command editing, read through the following sections and choose the editing interface you find most natural.

vi Edit Mode

vi Edit mode uses the editing commands and methods of the vi text editor, although with some minor differences due to the fact that you're editing only one line of text and not an entire file.

You can activate vi Edit mode by entering this command:

```
set -o vi
```

If you prefer to always use the vi Edit mode, add the command to your profile. Note that you can't have the vi and EMACS Edit modes both active at once, though. You can switch between them or shut them both off.

Just like the vi editor, vi command-editing uses two modes: Command and Input. Normally, your keyboard is in Input mode, and every character you type is entered into the command line. To enter Command mode, press ESC. In Command mode, the upper- and lowercase letters of the keyboard represent editing commands, and pressing a key causes an editing action. If no command corresponds to a given key, pressing it in Command mode causes the terminal to beep; you cannot enter text in Command mode. This error is the most common mistake beginners make with vi-style editing. It is a stumbling block responsible for the vi editor's miserable reputation as a text editor.

Pressing the Enter key always returns you to Input mode. After you make any editing changes to the line, you can press Enter no matter where your cursor is in the line to enter and execute the command.

CAUTION

Keystrokes you type while in Command mode are not displayed. You can see only the effect of an edit command—not the command itself. This can be unsettling if you're inexperienced with the vi style of editing or if you're entering a command of more than a few keystrokes.

TIP

If you forget whether you're in Command or Edit mode, the invisible nature of Command mode can make your keyboard appear to go wild and not respond to your input in any recognizable fashion. If this happens to you, the best thing to do is to try to cancel the current line completely with the kill function—normally, by pressing the @ or Ctrl+U keys. If all else fails, press the Enter key. Pressing the Enter key might give you an error message when it attempts to execute a garbled command, but at least it is guaranteed to return you to Input mode.

Table 11.7 summarizes the vi Edit mode commands. As you'll notice if you're already familiar with vi, nearly all the vi commands are supported—even those that cause movement upward and downward in a file. Commands that move from one line to another actually cause movement in the history file. This enables you to browse through the command history, select a command, modify it if necessary, and reenter it—all with a few simple keystrokes.

Some commands can be prefixed by a count—a non-zero number. A *count* causes the command to be repeated that number of times. For example, B moves backward one word, but 12B moves backward 12 words. If you don't specify a count, it defaults to 1.

A few commands—notably c (change), d (delete), and y (yank)—must be followed by a cursor-motion command. Such commands are marked with the right-arrow symbol (→). Using cursor-motion commands is discussed after Table 11.7.

Table 11.7. vi command editing: Command-mode commands.

Command	Action
a	Inserts text after the cursor.
A	Inserts text at the end of the line.
[n]b	Moves backward one word.
[n]B	Moves backward one blank-delimited word.
[n]c→	Changes text.
C	Changes to end of line.
[n]d→	Deletes text.
dd	Discards the entire current line.
[n]D	Deletes to end of line.
[n]e	Moves to end of current word.
[n]E	Moves to end of blank-delimited word.
[n]fc	Moves cursor to next c in current line.
[n]Fc	Moves cursor to previous c in current line.
[n]G	Moves to the last—least recent—line in the command history. If nG is entered, it selects line n from the command history.
[n]h	Moves the cursor one position to the left.
i	Inserts text before cursor.
I	Inserts text in front of the first nonblank character of the line.
[n]j	Moves down one line—that is, to a more recent history line. This command discards whatever you have typed on the current line.
[n]k	Moves up one line—that is, to a less recent history line. This command discards whatever you have typed on the current line.
[n]l	Moves cursor one position to the right.
n	Repeats the previous / or ? command.

continues

Table 11.7. continued

Command	Action
N	Repeats the previous / or ? command but in the reverse direction. It causes a / command to be repeated as the equivalent of ?, and ? to be repeated as the equivalent of /.
[n]p	Inserts text into the edit buffer after the current cursor position.
[n]P	Inserts text into the edit buffer before the current cursor position.
[n]rc	Replaces the current character with c. A repeat factor replaces n consecutive characters with c.
R	Replaces characters in the current line—Replace mode. This command differs from c in that it does not discard characters following the cursor; only as many characters as you type are replaced. You end Replace mode by pressing Enter or ESC.
s	Deletes entire line and enters Input mode.
tc	Moves cursor to the next c in the line.
Tc	Moves cursor to the previous c in the line.
u	Undoes the last text change. You can undo the previous u command. Successive u commands alternate between the original and the changed form of text.
U	Undoes all changes to the current line.
[n]v	Edits the current command—or line n of the history file—with the vi editor. When you exit vi, the edit file is executed as commands, one per line.
[n]w	Moves cursor to next word.
[n]W	Moves cursor to next blank-delimited word.
[n]x	Deletes characters after the cursor.
[n]X	Deletes characters before the cursor.
[n]y→	Yanks text into the edit buffer.
yy	Yanks (copies) the entire current line.
Y	Yanks (copies) text to the end of the line.
^	Moves cursor to the first character of the line that is not a space or tab.
0	Moves cursor to the first position of the line.
$	Moves cursor to the last character of the line.
[n]-	Moves to the preceding line in the command history.

Command	Action
[*n*]+ $	Moves to the next line in the command history. Use + only if you have used - or k to move backward in the history file. Use G to skip back to the earliest line in the history file.
[*n*]¦ $	Moves to the *n*th character of the line—that is, to column *n*.
[*n*]_ $	(underscore) Inserts the last (*n*th) word of the previous command.
/string$	Selects the most recent line in command history that contains string. string cannot be a regular expression.
/^string$	Same as / except that it selects only a line that begins with string. That is, / selects a line that contains string anywhere in the line, but /^ looks only for lines that begin with string in column 1.
?string$	Searches forward in the history file—that is, toward more recent lines—until it finds a line that contains string. The selected line replaces the current line. string cannot be a regular expression.
?^string	Same as ? except that it selects only a line that begins with string. That is, ? selects a line that contains string anywhere in the line, but ?^ looks only for lines that begin with string in column 1.
; $	Repeats the previous f, F, t, or T command.
,	Repeats the previous f, F, t, or T command but reverses the search through the command.
~	Inverts the capitalization of the current character.
.	Repeats the previous text-modifying command.
#	Inserts a pound sign (#) at the beginning of the line. If you then press Enter, the shell treats the line as a comment, and the line is added to the command history.
=	Lists filenames in the current directory that begin with the same characters as the current word. The listed filenames are not inserted into the current line, and the current line is not changed. You can use the displayed information to select a file, though, and finish typing a complete filename.
\	Appends characters to the word containing the cursor so that the word forms a valid pathname. The shell searches the current directory—or the directory specified by the incomplete word—for filenames that begin with the same characters as the word.

continues

Table 11.7. continued

Command	Action
	Then it appends characters from the matching filenames until a full filename is formed, or, in the case of multiple matches, the filenames differ. This command is a handy way to abbreviate a filename or to enter a filename when you can remember only a few leading characters of the name.
*	Replaces the word with the list of filenames in the current directory—or in the directory specified by the word—that all begin with the same characters as the replaced word. This has the same effect as the wildcard expression string* if entered directly, except that the filenames are entered into the command line now instead of during shell processing.
Space	Moves cursor to the right. It doesn't change characters spaced over.
Backspace	Moves cursor to the left. It doesn't change characters backspaced over.
Enter	Executes the current command line.
Ctrl+L	Redraws the current line. This command is useful if the screen becomes garbled. It redraws only the display line used for command input—not the entire screen.

NOTE

Although many vi editors support cursor keys for cursor control, the vi Edit mode does not recognize these keys, so you must use h, j, k, and l to control the cursor.

The vi command-editing feature also supports a few control operations you can use while in Input mode, which are described in Table 11.8. Using one of these operations doesn't require you to switch to Command mode first, and it doesn't switch you to Command mode.

Table 11.8. vi Command editing: Input mode commands.

Control	Action
Enter	Executes the command line. You can press Enter while in Command mode or Input mode, regardless of the current cursor position. If the cursor is somewhere in the middle of the line, pressing Enter doesn't truncate the remainder of the line; instead, it executes the whole line.

Control	Action
Erase	Normally the # or Backspace key. This is the `erase` function, defined with the `stty` command. The cursor is backspaced, and the character at that position is erased.
Kill	Normally the @ or `^u` (Ctrl+U) character. This is the `kill` function defined with the `stty` command. The current line is discarded; the input line is erased and the cursor returns to the start of the line. Notice that this differs from the normal shell action when command editing is not in effect. Normally, the `kill` function scrolls the discarded line up and starts a new line below it.
Ctrl+v	Escapes the next character. It enables you to enter the Erase, Kill, or \ character as data, avoiding the normal control function.
Ctrl+w	Deletes the previous word. It is similar to Backspace, but it backspaces over the preceding *word* instead of the preceding *character.*
\	Escapes the next Erase or Kill character. It is similar to Ctrl+v, but it doesn't escape other commands.

Most vi commands can be preceded with a repeat factor, shown in the box as [n]. If you omit the repeat factor, the command executes its normal function one time. A repeat factor larger than 1 causes the command to repeat its action the specified number of times. Thus, 2W causes the cursor to skip forward not one but two words, and 7r. replaces seven characters, starting at the cursor position, with seven periods.

Commands shown with the symbol → require a cursor motion command following the main command letter. The c, d, and y commands must be followed by a cursor motion command to define the amount of text to be changed, deleted, or yanked (copied). The cursor motion command can be any command that, if by itself, would move the cursor beyond the desired text. For example, dw deletes the current word. cte changes text up to, but not including, the next e in the line. y0 yanks the characters from the beginning of the line up to, but not including, the character at the cursor position.

Framing cursor-motion commands to meet your text-editing objectives is your responsibility. No prespecified limitations exist on the method for selecting a range of text; you are free to choose whatever comes naturally to you. Until you are comfortable with the use of cursor-motion commands, however, stick to simple combinations, such as cw or cW, to change a word.

The capitalized cursor-movement commands B, E, and W differ from their lowercase counterparts in their choice of delimiters. The lowercase b, e, and w commands consider a word to end at the next nonalphanumeric punctuation character, which can be a blank or tab but also includes apostrophes, commas, and so on. The B, E, and W commands consider a word to be delimited strictly by blanks or tabs. They skip over, or select, punctuation characters as well as alphanumerics.

Most of the commands leave you in Command mode. A few—a, A, c, C, i, I, R, and S—switch to Input mode to enable you to enter text. If, after entering the text, you are ready to execute the command, simply press Enter. If you want to edit the line some more, however, you must switch back to Command mode. In that case, press ESC after entering the desired text.

Not all commands supported by the vi editor are shown in Table 11.8. Commands not shown are not supported by the built-in vi Edit mode of the Korn shell. Noteworthy omissions include the o and O (open) commands, the m (mark) command, and scrolling commands such as z, H, and M. These omissions are due to the difference between a command editor and a file editor. In a command-editing context, they have no useful purpose.

> **NOTE**
>
> For a fuller discussion of the vi text-editing commands, refer to Chapter 3 in *UNIX Unleashed, Internet Edtion*, "Text Editing with vi and emacs."

EMACS Edit Mode

The EMACS Edit mode is designed to parallel the editing interface offered by the EMACS editor. The EMACS editor is not as widely available as the vi editor, but many people feel that its modeless, full-screen editing style is more natural than vi. Be that as it may, a modal editing style is well suited to command editing. Even if you're already an EMACS devotee, you might want to try your hand at the vi Edit mode before discarding it out of hand.

The EMACS Edit mode is activated when you enter this command:

```
set -o emacs
```

If you prefer to always use the EMACS Edit mode, you can add the command to your .profile file. Note, however, that you can't have the EMACS and vi Edit modes both active at once. You can switch between them or shut off both of them.

Because the EMACS editing interface is modeless, you always can enter text into the current line. To perform an editing operation, you generally enter a command prefixed by the ESC key. Therefore, commands generally require at least two keystrokes. Because ESC isn't conveniently located on most keyboards, entering a series of editing commands is quite a feat of gymnastics.

The EMACS keyboard commands are described in Table 11.9. Notes specific to the commands discussed in the table immediately follow Table 11.9. The commands are listed in alphabetical order by the command letter, with special characters (*, =, and so on) listed first. All commands are one letter, preceded by Ctrl or ESC. As usual, you hold down the Ctrl key while pressing the command letter, but you press and release ESC before pressing the command-letter key. Several notes explaining the table entries are located after this table.

Many commands enable you to specify a repeat count in the form ESC *n* before the command. The repeat count repeats the action of the command that number of times or specifies a column relative to which the command should operate. The value of *n* starts at 1. `Esc 1` executes the command once; it is the same as omitting ESC *n*, or column 1 of the current line.

CAUTION

The EMACS Edit mode edits lines—not commands. Command history might contain multiline commands, such as `if` or `while`, if you use such commands at the keyboard. The vi Edit mode processes such commands as a single entity, but in EMACS Edit mode, you might need to use the Ctrl+O (operate) command to step through multiline commands when you retrieve them from the command history.

The EMACS command-editing interface is an example of a user interface designed for an alien species, because it obviously requires the use of three hands to perform well. If you are a beginner or a casual user of command editing, you might nevertheless find EMACS Edit mode preferable to vi mode, because, with EMACS, there's no confusion between Command mode versus Input mode. As your proficiency and keyboard speed increase, however, the vi Edit mode becomes a more attractive interface.

Table 11.9. EMACS Edit mode commands.

ESC n	*Key Sequence*	*Action*
	Enter	Executes the current line. On some terminals, it is labeled `Return`.
	Erase	The `stty` erase character. It deletes the character preceding the cursor.
ESC *n*	Erase	Backspaces *n* characters.
	Kill	Deletes the entire line. When entered twice in quick succession, it causes subsequent Kill characters to print blank lines.
	\	Escapes the next character, enabling the Erase, Kill, EOF, and ESC characters and Ctrl+x characters to be entered into the current line. The \ itself is discarded. Type \\ to enter a single backslash.

continues

Table 11.9. continued

ESC n	Key Sequence	Action
	ESC ESC	Appends characters to the current word to complete the pathname.
	ESC Space	Sets a mark at the cursor position.
	ESC *	Performs a pathname expansion on the current word as though an * were appended and replaces the word with the list of pathnames that match, if any.
	ESC =	Lists pathnames that match the current word, as though * were appended to the word. The current line is not changed.
	ESC <	Fetches the least recent line from command history.
	ESC >	Fetches the most recent line from command history.
	ESC .	Inserts the last word of your preceding command at the current cursor position.
ESC n	ESC .	Inserts the *n*th word of your previous command at the cursor position.
	ESC _	Same as ESC ..
	ESC Ctrl+?	Same as ESC Ctrl+H. (see Note)
ESC n	ESC Ctrl+?	Same as ESC Ctrl+H. (see Note)
	ESC letter	Invokes the macro defined as an alias named _letter. (see Note)
	Ctrl+] c	Moves cursor to next occurrence of character c in this line.
	Ctrl+A	Moves cursor to start of line.
	Ctrl+B	Moves cursor left one character. (see Note)
ESC n	Ctrl+B	Moves cursor left *n* characters.
	ESC b	Moves cursor to beginning of word.
ESC n	ESC b	Moves back *n*-1 words.
	Ctrl+C	Makes the current character uppercase.
ESC n	Ctrl+C	Makes *n* characters uppercase.
	ESC c	Makes everything to end of current word uppercase. (see Note)

ESC n	Key Sequence	Action
ESC n	ESC c	Uppercases n words from cursor position. (see Note)
	Ctrl+D	Deletes one character. (see Note)
ESC n	Ctrl+D	Deletes n characters. (see Note)
	ESC d	Deletes to the end of the current word.
ESC n	ESC d	Deletes to end of nth word right.
	Ctrl+E	Moves cursor to end of line.
	Ctrl+F	Moves cursor right one character. (see Note)
ESC n	Ctrl+F	Moves cursor right n characters.
	ESC f	Moves cursor right one word.
ESC n	ESC f	Moves cursor right n words.
	ESC h	Same as ESC Ctrl+H.
ESC n	ESC h	Same as ESC n ESC Ctrl+H.
	ESC Ctrl+H	Deletes backward to beginning of current word. (see Note)
ESC n	ESC Ctrl+H	Deletes backward to beginning of nth previous word. (see Note)
	Ctrl+J	Same as Enter.
	Ctrl+K	Deletes to end of line.
ESC n	Ctrl+K	Deletes characters back to or up to column n.
	Ctrl+L	Redisplays the entire current line.
	ESC l	Makes all characters to end of current word lowercase. (see Note)
ESC n	ESC l	Makes n words from cursor position lowercase. (see Note)
	Ctrl+M	Same as Enter.
	Ctrl+N	Fetches the next line from the command-history file. Successive presses retrieve more recent lines in progression. (see Note)
ESC n	Ctrl+N	Fetches the nth line forward from your present position in the command-history file.

continues

Table 11.9. continued

ESC n	Key Sequence	Action
	Ctrl+O	Executes the current line and then fetches the next line from the command history. (see Note)
	Ctrl+P	Replaces the current line with the last line of the command history. Successive presses retrieve consecutively older lines from the command history. (see Note)
ESC *n*	Ctrl+P	Fetches the *n*th line back from the command history.
	ESC p	Copies text from cursor to the mark into an internal buffer. To set a mark use ESC Space. This will mark the current position internally as a reference point.
	Ctrl+R string Enter	Searches command history for the most recent line containing string. To repeat the preceding search, omit string.
ESC 0	Ctrl+R string Enter	Searches the command history starting at the oldest line forward for the first occurrence of string. To repeat the preceding search, omit string.
	Ctrl+R ^string Enter	Same as Ctrl-R string, except that it matches string only at the beginning of a line.
ESC 0	Ctrl+R ^string Enter	Same as ESC 0 Ctrl-R string, except that it matches string only at the beginning of a line.
	Ctrl+T	Transposes the current and next characters. (see Note)
	Ctrl+U	Multiplies count of next command by 4. Thus, Ctrl+U Ctrl+F moves the cursor right four positions.
	Ctrl+V	Displays the current version of the Korn shell. To redisplay the current line, press any key.
	Ctrl+W	Deletes characters from cursor to mark. Marks are set using ESC+Space.

ESC n	*Key Sequence*	*Action*
	Ctrl+X Ctrl+X	Moves cursor to the mark position, setting a new mark at the old cursor position. This is called *swap cursor and mark.*
	Ctrl+Y	Inserts most recently deleted text at the current cursor position.

NOTE

The sequence Ctrl+? is not to be taken literally. It represents the ASCII Del (127) character. Most terminals generate the Del character in response to the Delete key, in which case ESC Delete is a synonym for ESC Backspace.

NOTE

A macro is defined with the `alias` shell built-in command. Its name must begin with an underscore (_) and must be followed by one letter. The value of the alias is processed as if you typed the characters of the value at the time of invoking the macro. Thus, sequences such as Ctrl+f in the alias value move the cursor to its current position. The letter used in the macro name should not be b, c, d, f, h, l, or p; these letters already are assigned to EMACS commands.

NOTE

In addition to using the control-key sequences to move the cursor, you can use the cursor-control keys to navigate the history list and move the cursor. The capability to do this depends on how your terminal is set up, though.

NOTE

Changing character case also moves the cursor to the right, spacing over the changed character(s).

> **NOTE**
>
> If the Ctrl+d key is assigned to the EOF function with the `stty` command, it is interpreted as your EOF key when typed at the beginning of the line. Otherwise, it performs the Delete function.

> **NOTE**
>
> Most terminals generate Ctrl+h for the Backspace key. Some terminals generate the ASCII Del character (0177), though. Therefore, the shorthand ESC Backspace might not work for your terminal.

> **NOTE**
>
> To use the `operate` (Ctrl+o) command, you must have previously established a position in the command-history file by using Ctrl+p, Ctrl+n, or another history command. Successive presses of Ctrl+o step through lines of command history in the forward—older to newer—direction, executing one line at a time. You have the opportunity to change each line before pressing Ctrl+o to execute it.

> **NOTE**
>
> If `set -o gmacs` is used instead of `set -o emacs`, Ctrl-t transposes the current and preceding character, not the current and next. This is the only difference between EMACS and GMACS Edit modes.

Variables

You were introduced to the concept of shell variables in Chapter 9. Everything you learned there remains true for the Korn shell. The Korn shell provides some significant extensions to shell variable support, though. Among these is a greatly expanded set of variables that has special meaning to the shell. These variables often are called *predefined variables*, because the shell provides an initial default value for them when you log on. The Korn shell also supports array variables and enhanced arithmetic on shell variables, both of which are a great boon to shell-script writers. Naturally, the syntax of shell variable references is expanded to support these capabilities.

Predefined Variables

Variables that have special meaning to the shell fall into two main groups: those you can set to affect the behavior of the shell, and those the shell sets for you to provide information.

Variables whose values are set by the shell include the familiar $@, $*, $#, $-, $?, and $$, as well as the new $!. The new variable $! provides the Process ID of the last command you invoked. It differs from $$ in that the value of $$—your current Process ID—generally is that of the shell itself and doesn't change, whereas the value of $! changes each time you invoke a command. The values of the other shell variables have the same meanings as they do in the Bourne shell.

Table 11.10 lists the named variables set by the Korn shell.

Table 11.10. Named variables set by the Korn shell.

Variable	Description
_	Starts as the full pathname of the last command you invoked. It then becomes the last argument of the preceding command, though, so if you type after the command ls -1, the value of $_ is -1. This variable also is used by the shell to hold the name of the MAIL file when checking for mail. This variable is not really of any use and is used internally by the shell.
ERRNO	The nonzero exit code of the last command that failed. This variable is similar to $?, but it differs because its value changes only when a command fails. Successfully executed commands don't change the value of $ERRNO. This variable is primarily a diagnostic aid for use at the keyboard; it is of little use to shell scripts.
LINENO	This variable is meaningful only within a shell script. Its value is the line number of the line in the script currently being executed. You can assign a value to LINENO, but it will be changed by the next shell script you invoke. Or, if it is inside a shell script, it will be changed by the next line executed.
OLDPWD	The value of this variable is always the full pathname of the directory that was current immediately before the last cd command. In other words, repeated executions of cd $OLDPWD switch you back and forth between your current and preceding directories. An important use of the $OLDPWD variable is to facilitate cp and mv commands. cd someplace followed by cp filelist $OLDPWD copies files to your original directory without you having

continues

Table 11.10. continued

Variable	Description
	to type the full directory pathname. Then use cd $OLDPWD to switch back to your original directory. (In the Korn shell, the shorthand cd - means the same thing as cd $OLDPWD.)
OPTARG	This value is set by the getopts command—a new built-in command provided by the Korn shell. (For more information, see "Shell Programming," later in this chapter.)
OPTIND	This value is set by the getopts command. (For more information, see "Shell Programming," later in this chapter.)
PPID	This value is your current parent Process ID. That is, if $$ is the current Process ID, $PPID is the Process ID of the parent process of $$. This variable is useful especially to shell script writers. It has little use at the keyboard.
PWD	Specifies the full pathname of your current directory. Because of symbolic links, the value of $PWD isn't necessarily the same as the value printed by the pwd command. Suppose that a directory /usr/bin exists and that a symbolic link to /usr/bin exists named /bin. After cd /bin, the pwd command prints /usr/bin—the real pathname of the directory—but the statement print $PWD prints /bin—the pathname by which you reached the directory. (Links are explained in Chapter 4, "The UNIX File System.")
RANDOM	This value is an integer in the range of 0 to 32,767. The value is different in a random way every time you examine it. This variable is not much use at the keyboard; however, in shell scripts, it is useful for generating temporary filenames.
REPLY	The select statement, which is new with the Korn shell, sets the value of $REPLY to the user's input text. The read built-in command stores the user's typed input in $REPLY if you supply no variable names on the read command. (For more information, see "Using the select Statement," later in this chapter.)
SECONDS	The integer number of seconds since you invoked the Korn shell—usually, since you logged on, unless you explicitly invoked the Korn shell with the ksh command. This variable simply records the wall-clock time the Korn shell has been running at your terminal.

The shell variables set by the Korn shell listed in Table 11.10 don't require your attention. If you have a use for one of them, refer to this table while at your keyboard or in a shell script.

You don't need to assign values to them, though. In some cases, you aren't even allowed to assign a value.

Some variables require attention from you, however. In most cases, the Korn shell assigns a default value to these variables when it starts. You can override this default value in your *logon profile*—a file named `.profile` in your home directory—or at any later time by using an assignment statement from the keyboard. The values of these variables affect the way the Korn shell works. Proper setup of these variables can enhance your effectiveness and productivity.

Table 11.11 lists the variables used by the Korn shell.

Table 11.11. Variables used by the Korn shell.

Variable	Description
CDPATH	The value of $CDPATH is a list of colon-separated directory pathnames. The value is referenced only by the `cd` command. Use the CDPATH variable to name a list of directories to be searched when you issue `cd` with a directory's simple filename. The benefit of CDPATH is that it enables you to switch to a directory by giving only its filename instead of the full pathname. There is no default value for CDPATH.

> **NOTE**
>
> I always put the following definition in my logon profile:
>
> `CDPATH=.:..:$HOME`
>
> The command `cd src` first looks for a directory named src as a subdirectory in the current directory. Failing that, the `cd` command looks for src in the parent directory. If no directory named src is found in either place, it tries to change to src in my home directory. I find that proper use of the CDPATH variable saves a lot of typing.

Variable	Description
COLUMNS	The value of $COLUMNS defines the display width used by the Korn shell Command-Edit mode—either vi or EMACS—as a view window for long lines and as the screen width for printing the `select` list. The default value is 80.
EDITOR	The value of $EDITOR is used primarily by programs other than the Korn shell. If you set the value of EDITOR (in your profile or at the keyboard), however, the Korn shell inspects the value for a pathname ending in vi or emacs. If either value is found, the Korn shell sets the corresponding vi, emacs, or gmacs option,

continues

Table 11.11. continued

Variable	Description
	enabling command editing. This is only a convenience. You still can toggle the Command-Edit mode by using the set -o command. There is no default value for EDITOR.
ENV	The value of $ENV is the pathname of a shell script containing commands to be executed when the Korn shell is invoked. Note that the Korn shell is implicitly invoked every time you invoke a command written as a Korn shell script. You also can invoke the Korn shell from within other UNIX commands such as vi and pg. By placing alias, export, and set commands in a file and supplying the file's pathname as the value of $ENV, you can ensure that you have the same shell environment whenever you invoke the Korn shell. Keep the file pointed to by $ENV small, because its execution is added to the execution of every shell script you execute. (For more information, see "Customizing the Korn Shell," later in this chapter.) There is no default value for ENV.
FCEDIT	The value of $FCEDIT is the pathname of the text editor to be invoked by the fc command. You can override the value of FCEDIT by using the -e option with the fc command. The default value of FCEDIT is /bin/ed.
FPATH	The value of $FPATH is a colon-separated list of directories—the same format as for CDPATH and PATH. The directory list is searched for autoload function definitions. (See "Shell Programming," later in this chapter, for a discussion of autoload functions.) There is no default value for FPATH.
HISTFILE	HISTFILE is the filename of the Korn shell history file. If you want to specify an explicit filename for your history file, supply a value for HISTFILE in your logon profile. The default value of HISTFILE is $HOME/.sh_history.
HISTSIZE	The value of HISTSIZE is an integer number specifying the maximum number of commands—not lines—to be retained in the history file. The shell may retain more than HISTSIZE commands in memory while you are working, but it will not accumulate more than HISTSIZE commands in the history file on disk. Note that a value you set for HISTSIZE is treated somewhat like a suggestion; depending on the specific version of the Korn shell you are using, it may act as a fixed upper limit to the number of commands remembered or as an at-least value. The default value of HISTSIZE is 128.

Variable	Description
HOME	HOME with the Korn shell works the same as it does with the Bourne shell. The value of HOME is the pathname of your home directory. The value of HOME is used primarily by the cd command as the default directory when you specify no argument. It also is used by a great many commands and shell scripts. The variable is initialized by the UNIX logon procedure before any shell is invoked. It is almost never proper for you to change the value of HOME. The default value of HOME is the sixth part of the /etc/passwd file entry for your logon name.
IFS	IFS with the Korn shell works the same as it does with the Bourne shell. The value of IFS is zero or more characters to be treated by the shell as delimiters when parsing a command line into words or using the read command. The first character of IFS is used by the shell to separate arguments for the $* variable. Rarely manipulated at the keyboard, the IFS variable can be altered in a shell script to parse a string into substrings using arbitrary delimiters. Improper alteration of the IFS variable can cause bizarre problems, so you always should manipulate it with care and always restore it to its original value. The default value of IFS consists of the three characters Blank, Tab, and Newline in succession.
LINES	The value of LINES is an integer number representing the number of lines displayed by your terminal. The Korn shell uses the value of LINES, if set, to limit the printing of select lists (see "Using the select Statement," later in this chapter). If no value is set, select lists can be arbitrarily long, and some lines may scroll off the display. There is no default value for LINES.
LOGNAME	The logon name of the user as mentioned in the user database /etc/passwd. Modification of this variable can upset some programs, so exercise caution when using it, and restore it to its original value after using it.
MAIL	MAIL with the Korn shell works the same as it does with the Bourne shell. The value is the pathname of a file to be monitored by the shell for a change in its date of last modification. If a change is noted, the shell issues the message You have mail at the next opportunity. There is no default value for MAIL. You should set MAIL to the name of your mail file in your logon profile.

continues

Table 11.11. continued

Variable	Description
MAILCHECK	The value of MAILCHECK is an integer number of seconds that specifies how often the shell should check for a change to the MAIL file. If MAILCHECK is not set or is zero, the shell checks at each command-line prompt for a change in the mail file. The default value of MAILCHECK is 600.
MAILPATH	The value of MAILPATH is a colon-separated list of pathnames, each of which identifies a file to be monitored for a change in the date of last modification. A pathname can be suffixed with a question mark and message to customize the You have mail message—for example, you can use MAILPATH=/var/spool/mail/jjv?New mail in /var/spool:/usr/mail/jjv?New mail in /usr/mail. Generally, you should set the MAIL or the MAILPATH variable but not both. There is no default value for MAILPATH.
PATH	PATH with the Korn shell works the same as it does with the Bourne shell. The default value is system dependent. This variable cannot be changed if the shell was started as a restricted shell.
PS1	PS1 is the primary prompt string. The Korn shell performs a full substitution on the value of $PS1 before displaying it at the beginning of each command-input line. You therefore can customize your prompt in the Korn shell environment to a much greater degree than when using the Bourne shell. Specify PS1='$PWD: ', for example, to make your prompt your current directory. (The quotes are important to prevent substitution of the value of PWD as part of the assignment; this enables the substitution to occur later when the value of $PS1 is printed.) You also can use an exclamation point (!) in the prompt that is replaced by the command number (see "Command History," earlier in this chapter). The default value is "$ ".
PS2	PS2 is the secondary prompt string. It is the same as with the Bourne shell. The default value is ">".
PS3	PS3 is the select prompt string. The value of $PS3 is printed as the selection prompt by the select command. (See "Using the select Statement," later in this chapter.)
PS4	PS4 is the debug prompt string. The value of $PS4 is scanned for variable substitution and is printed in front of each line displayed by the trace or -x option.

Variable	*Description*
SHELL	SHELL is the pathname of the shell. The Korn shell sets a default value for $SHELL only if it is not set when ksh begins. The value isn't used directly by the Korn shell, but many other commands (such as vi and pg) use the value of $SHELL as the pathname of the shell to be called when invoking a subshell. If the $SHELL variable is defined when ksh begins and starts with an r, the Korn shell behaves as a *restricted shell*. That is, the user cannot invoke commands with a full pathname, cannot use the cd command, and cannot modify the PATH variable.
TERM	The value of TERM is a symbolic alphanumeric string that identifies the type of your terminal. Not used by the Korn shell directly, the variable name TERM is reserved for general system use. The proper setting of $TERM is important to the proper and reasonable operation of your terminal and should be initialized appropriately when you log on. For the allowable values at your installation, consult your system administrator. There is no default value for TERM.
TMOUT	The value of TMOUT is an integer specifying the number of seconds after which no terminal activity should cause the Korn shell to automatically log out. A value of zero disables the automatic logout function.
VISUAL	The value of $VISUAL is used primarily by programs other than the Korn shell. If you set the value of VISUAL (in your profile or at the keyboard), however, the Korn shell will inspect the value for a pathname ending in vi, emacs, or gmacs. If one of these values is found, the Korn shell sets the corresponding vi, emacs, or gmacs option, enabling command editing. This is only a convenience. You still can toggle the Command-Edit mode by using the set -o command. There is no default value for VISUAL.

As with the Bourne shell, variable names in the Korn shell begin with a letter or an underscore, and they contain an arbitrary number of letters, underscores, and digits. The variable name is a symbolic representation for the variable's value, which can be changed by an assignment statement; by the set, read, or select statement; as a by-product of the execution of a built-in shell or other commands; or by the Korn shell itself. There is no arbitrary upper limit to the number of variables you can define and use, but the amount of memory available to the shell sets a practical (usually large) upper limit.

You can explicitly assign a value to a variable name by using an assignment in the format *name=value*. Note that you don't include a dollar sign ($) in front of *name* when you write the assignment. The dollar sign is appropriate only when referring to the value of the variable.

The value of a variable is a *string*—a sequence of alphanumeric and special characters—of arbitrary length. The Korn shell provides a number of extensions that enable the value of a variable to be manipulated by arithmetic methods. The variable's value still is stored as a string, however.

A variable retains its value from the time it is set—whether explicitly by you or implicitly by the Korn shell—until the value is changed or the shell exits. Note that the value isn't passed to commands and shell scripts that you invoke unless the variable is marked for exportation. You mark a variable for exporting with the typeset built-in shell command or the export alias. Alternatively, if the allexport option is switched on (by typing set -o allexport, for example), all variables created are exported automatically. Exported variables become part of the environment of all invoked commands.

Because the values of variables are retained internally in a memory table by the shell, all variables that the shell didn't inherit are lost when the shell exits. For this reason, you cannot assign a value to a shell variable inside a shell script—one invocation of the shell—and expect the value to be retained after the shell script exits; the shell returns to a higher level shell. In other words, you can assign values to variables and export the variables to pass values downward to subshells of your current shell, but you cannot pass values upward to higher level shells or shell scripts.

This limitation on the use of shell variables isn't normally visible to you at the keyboard. It generally arises in issues related to shell programming. However, if you invoke the shell directly (by entering the sh, ksh, or csh command) or indirectly (by entering the shell environment from within another UNIX command, such as vi or pg), you should realize that any changes to the shell environment, including variable settings and aliases, are lost when you return to your original shell level by exiting the subshell.

Referencing Variables

The Korn shell replaces strings that begin with $ and are followed by a reference expression appearing in command lines with the value of the reference expression. Any number of reference expressions may appear in the same command line. Adjacent references, when replaced, don't introduce new word boundaries into the command line. That is, a single word—a command name, option, or argument—isn't split into two or more words by replacement even if the replaced value contains blanks, tabs, or other delimiter characters. You can use the eval built-in shell command when you want delimiters in the replacement text to cause further word splitting.

Valid reference expressions for the Korn shell follow:

name	*{name#pattern}*
{name}	*{name##pattern}*
{name[n]}	*{name%pattern}*
{name[*]}	*{name%%pattern}*
{name[@]}	*{#@}*
{name:word }	*{#*}*
{name-word }	*{#name}*
{name=word }	*{#name[*]}*
{name?word }	*{#name[@]}*
{name+word }	

name

The expression $*name* is replaced by the current value of the shell variable *name*. If no value for the variable has been defined, the dollar sign and the variable name are replaced with the null string. For example,

```
$ today="January 13"
$ print Today is:$today.
Today is:January 13.
$ print Today is $tomorrow.
Today is:.
```

{name}

The expression $*{name}* is replaced by the current value of the shell variable *name*. The braces help to separate the variable reference from surrounding text; they are discarded after substitution. You must use braces to reference a shell parameter greater than $9—for example, ${10} or ${12}—or to reference an array variable. For example,

```
$ Person1=John
$ Person2=Mike
$ print $Person1 and $Person2
John and Mike
$ print $Person1and$Person2
Person1and: not defined
$ print ${Person1}and$Person2
JohnandMike
```

{name[n]}

The value of the expression is the value of the *n*th element of the array variable *name*; it is null if the *n*th element isn't set. The first element of an array variable is $*{name[0]}*. For example,

```
$ set -A words hello goodbye
$ echo $words[1]
```

```
hello[1]
$ echo ${words[1]}
goodbye
$ echo $words
hello
```

{name[*]}

The value of the expression is the value of all the elements of the array variable name that are set, separated by blanks. Substitution occurs in the same way as for the special expression $* with regard to embedded blanks and word splitting. For example,

```
$ set -A planets Mercury Venus Earth Mars
$ planet[9]=Pluto
$ print ${planets[*]}
Mercury Venus Earth Mars Pluto
```

{name[@]}

The value of the expression is the value of all the elements of the array variable name that are set, separated by blanks. If elements of the array contain strings with embedded blanks and if the expression ${name[@]} is contained inside quotes, the number of words in the substituted expression is equal to the number of non-null array elements. Otherwise, embedded blanks cause word splitting to occur, and the number of substituted words will be greater than the number of non-null array elements. For example,

```
$ set -A committee "B Jones" "M Hartly" "C Rogers"
$ for word in ${committee[@]}
> do
> print $word
> done
B
Jones
M
Hartly
C
Rogers
$ for word in "${committee[@]}"
> do
> print $word
> done
B Jones
M Hartly
C Rogers}
```

{name:-word}

The expression is replaced by the value of variable *name*, if the variable has a value and the value consists of at least one character. Otherwise, the expression is replaced by *word*. Note that *word* should not contain embedded blanks or tabs, although it may contain quoted strings.

Combine : with -, =, ?, or + to treat a variable with a null value (that is, a zero-length string) the same as an unset variable. Without :, the variable is tested only for whether it is set. For example,

```
$ month=January
$ print This month is ${month:-unknown}
This month is January
$ print This year is ${year:-unknown}
This year is unknown
```

{name-word}

The expression is replaced by the value of *name*, if the variable has a value. Otherwise, it is replaced by *word*. You can use ${*name*:-*word*} to ignore a value that is not set or is null. For example,

```
$unset month
$ month=January
$ print This month is ${month-unknown}
This month is January
$ print This year is ${year-unknown}
This year is unknown
```

This may look similar to the previous expression, {*name*:-*word*}, so to clarify, look at this example:

```
$ unset month
$ month=""
$ echo ${month-unknown}

$echo ${month:-unknown}
unknown
```

{name=word}

The expression is replaced by the value of *name*, if the variable has a value. Otherwise, *word* is assigned as the value of *name*, and the expression is replaced by *word*. You can use ${*name*:=*word*} to assign *word* to *name* if the variable is not set or is null. For example,

```
$ print This month is $month.
This month is .
$ print This month is ${month=January}.
This month is January.
$ print This month is $month.
This month is January.
```

{name?word}

The expression is replaced by the value of *name*, if the variable has a value. Otherwise, the string *word* is printed as an error message. An unset variable is recognized as an error and halts processing of the current command line. If the error is recognized inside a shell script, execution of the shell script is terminated. Use ${*name*:?*word*} to recognize an unset or null value as an error. *word* can be omitted from the expression; if it is, a standard error message is displayed. For example,

```
$ month=January
$ print This month is ${month?unknown}
This month is January
$ print This year is ${year?unknown}
ksh: year: unknown
$ print This year is ${year?}
ksh: year: parameter null or not set
```

{name+word}

The expression is replaced by the value of *word* if the variable *name* has a value. If the variable is not set, the expression is replaced by the null string. That is, if *name* has a value, it temporarily treats the value as though it were *word*. If *name* doesn't have a value, the expression has no value either. Use ${*name*:+*word*} to treat a null value the same as an unset value. For example,

```
$ month=January
$ print This month is ${month+unknown}
This month is unknown.
$ print This year is ${year+unknown}
This year is .
```

{name#pattern}

The value of the expression is the value of *name* with the leftmost occurrence of *pattern* deleted. The shortest match for *pattern* is recognized. For *pattern*, specify a string that contains any character sequence, variable and command substitutions, and wildcard expressions. Only the first occurrence of *pattern* is deleted. For example,

```
$ print $PWD
/usr/home/valley
$ print ${PWD#*/}
usr/home/valley
```

{name##pattern}

The value of the expression is *name*, with anything to the left of the longest match of *pattern* removed. For example,

```
$ print $PWD
/usr/home/valley
$ print ${PWD##*/}
valley
```

{name%pattern}

The value of the expression is the value of *name*, with the shortest rightmost string matching *pattern* deleted. For example,

```
$ print $FNAME
s.myfile.c
$ print ${FNAME%.*}
s.myfile
```

{name%%pattern}

The value of the expression is the value of name, with the longest rightmost string matching pattern deleted. For example,

```
$ print $FNAME
s.myfile.c
$ print ${FNAME%%.*}
s
```

{#@}

The value of the expression is the integer number of arguments that would be returned by $@.

{#*}

The value of the expression is the integer number of arguments that would be returned by $*. It is the same as $#.

{#name}

The value of the expression is the length of the string value of variable name. For example,

```
$ print $FNAME
s.myfile.c
$ print ${#FNAME}
10
```

{#name[*]}

The value of the expression is the number of elements of the array variable name that are set. For example,

```
$ set -A planets Mercury Venus Earth Mars
$ print ${#planets[*]}
4
```

{#name[@]}

{#name[@]} is the same as {#name[*]}.

Array Variables

An *array variable* is a variable with more than one value. Array variables are helpful for managing lists of strings, because you can reference an individual element in the list without resorting to string-splitting techniques.

You can assign values to an array one at a time by using the assignment statement. For example,

```
$ planets[1]=Mercury
$ planets[2]=Venus
$ planets[3]=Earth
$ print ${planets[2]}
Venus
```

The general syntax *name*[*subscript*] is supported by the Korn shell for referring to elements of an array. For *subscript*, supply an integer number in the range of 0 through 511, or write a variable expression with the value of the desired element number. Element numbers begin at zero. Thus, the first element in an array is ${*name*[0]}.

You can use the -A option of the set command to set many array elements with one statement. For example, the preceding code could be rewritten as this:

```
$ set -A planets Mercury Venus Earth
$ print ${planets[2]}
Venus
```

You also can substitute all the elements of an array by using the special notation ${*name*[*]} or ${*name*[@]}. For example,

```
$ set -A planets Mercury Venus Earth
$ planets[9]=Pluto
$ planets[7]=Uranus
$ print The known planets are: ${planets[*]}
The known planets are: Mercury Venus Earth Uranus Pluto
```

You should remember a few points when using array variables:

- If you reference the array variable without a subscript, the value of the reference is the first element of the array:

  ```
  $ print $planets
  Mercury
  ```

- Array variables cannot be exported.

- The special expression ${#*name*[*]} or ${#*name*[@]} can be used to get the number of non-null elements in an array. For example,

  ```
  $ print There are ${#planets[*]} planets: ${planets[*]}
  There are 5 planets: Mercury Venus Earth Uranus Pluto
  ```

- You must use the brace-enclosed expression syntax to refer to elements of an array. Without the braces, the Korn shell interprets the expression in the same way the Bourne shell would. For example,

  ```
  $ print The known planets are $planets[*]
  The known planets are Mercury[*]
  $ print The second planet from the Sun is $planets[2]
  The second planet from the sun is Mercury[2]
  ```

Variable Arithmetic

An exciting new addition to the capabilities of the old Bourne shell offered by the Korn shell is the capability to do arithmetic. The Bourne shell provides no built-in calculating capability, so even the simplest arithmetic requires command substitutions that resort to calling other UNIX programs such as expr. The Korn shell adds some built-in capabilities to do basic arithmetic.

The two major tools you'll use when doing arithmetic inside the Korn shell are the typeset command and the let command. The typeset command provides number-formatting capability and the capability to declare—or set aside—some variables for the special purpose of doing arithmetic. The `let` command is where all this magic really happens.

Using typeset

The Korn shell is still a very slow tool for performing repetitive calculations, even with the `typeset` statement. Floating-point—real numbers with decimal points, fractions, and so on—calculations aren't supported. Therefore, all your calculations must use integer values, and they will yield integer results. The shell arithmetic is sufficient to support programming concepts such as loop control with counters, however.

The `typeset` statement is an extension provided by the Korn shell to permit some amount of control over the format and use of shell variables. When `typeset` is used for managing variables, its syntax is as follows:

```
typeset [ ±HLRZilrtux [n] ] [ name[=value] ] ...
```

The particular set of options you use with the command determines the required format for the syntax of the command. Not all combinations of option letters are legal. Only the options listed in Table 11.12 should be specified.

Table 11.12. typeset options.

Option	Description
-H	The -H option is supported only by versions of the Korn shell that execute on non-UNIX operating systems. When -H is specified, each of the *name* variables is presumed to be used to hold a filename or pathname. Assignment of a value to the variable causes mapping of the name to filename formats compatible with the host operating system. You then can use the variable as a filename argument on subsequent commands. You must specify one or more *name* arguments with this option. The -H option is ignored on UNIX operating systems.
-i	Declares the variable to be of type `integer`. Use the optional *n* to specify the number base to which the value should be converted on substitution. The number always is carried in base 10, and only base-10 decimal values should be assigned to the variable. On substitution, however, the value is converted to the equivalent octal digit string. You also can specify the -L, -LZ, -R, or -RZ option for the named variable(s).
-l	The value of the named variable(s) should be converted to all lowercase letters when it is substituted. Don't specify this option

continues

Table 11.12. continued

Option	Description
	with -u. You must specify at least one *name* argument, and you can provide an optional initial value for some or all of the named variables.
-L	The value of the named variable(s) should be left-justified and padded with blanks on the right to a length of *n* when it is substituted. Obviously, you must specify a field length *n*. For example, -L4 expands the variable value to four characters on substitution. You must specify at least one *name* argument, and you can provide an optional initial value for some or all of the named variables.
-LZ	Similar to -L, but it strips any leading zeroes from the variable value before substitution.
-r	The named variable(s) is treated as read-only, meaning that subsequent assignments of a value to the named variables are inhibited. If the variable is to have a non-null value, you should supply a *value* for the listed variable names. You must name at least one variable to have the read-only attribute. You can use the -r option with any of the other options.
-R	The value of the named variable(s) should be right-justified and padded with blanks on the left to a length of *n* when it is substituted. You must specify a field length *n*. For example, -R4 expands the variable value to four characters on substitution. You must specify at least one *name* argument, and you can provide an optional initial value for some or all of the named variables. Don't specify the -L or -LZ options with -R.
-RZ	Similar to -R, but it pads the value with zeroes on the left. If the value of the named variable contains only digits, the result is a numeric field of length *n*.
-u	The value of the named variable(s) should be converted to all uppercase letters when it is substituted. Don't specify this option with -1. You must specify at least one *name* argument, and you can provide an optional initial value for some or all of the named variables.
-x	The named variables should be exported—made available—to shell scripts and subshells. Note that typeset -x is the only command provided by the Korn shell for establishing exported variables. A command alias is provided at start-up by the shell

Option	*Description*
	named export, which is equivalent to the command typeset -x. Unlike the Bourne shell export statement, which permits only variable names, the Korn shell (using command aliases) supports statements of the form export *name=value* ..., providing an initial value for each exported variable. If the variable already exists when the typeset -x command is given, the shell adds the export attribute to the variable. If a you define a new variable but specify no *value*, the variable is initialized to the null string and is marked as exportable.
-Z	Same as -RZ.

Apart from exporting variables, usually by way of the export alias, the typeset command is used mainly for two purposes:

- Setting up variables that you plan to use for calculation as integer variables
- Defining special formatting options for variables

Although the Korn shell doesn't require that a variable be declared as an integer to do arithmetic with it, doing so provides some advantages. Calculations are more efficient when you use arithmetic variables in the let statement, because the shell can maintain the numeric value of the variable in an internal binary format, which is more suitable to the computer's math instructions. Similarly, there are contexts in which the shell recognizes arithmetic operators in an expression if the expression contains integer variables, but it won't if the expression uses standard variables.

The general procedure for using typeset to define integer variables is straightforward. Before using variables for calculation, simply issue a typeset command to declare the variables as integers. For example,

```
typeset -i x y sum
read x y
let sum=x+y
print $sum
```

The Korn shell automatically defines an alias named integer that is equivalent to typeset -i:

```
alias integer="typeset -i"
```

You can use the alias to make your integer definitions more readable, as in this revision:

```
integer x y sum
read x y
let sum=x+y
print $sum
```

The second use of typeset—to set up output formatting options for variables—is of interest primarily to shell-script writers who want to generate nicely formatted output. The formatting options -L, -R, -LZ, and -RZ are also of some use in generating filenames. Suppose that you want to create a series of files that all end with a four-digit number. By writing the typedef statement

```
typeset -Z4 suffix
```

you easily can generate the required filenames by using code such as this:

```
typeset -Z4 suffix=0
while ...
do
    let suffix=suffix+1
    print sampfile.$suffix
done
```

The Korn shell automatically right-justifies the value of $suffix in a four-character field and fills the number out to four digits with leading zeros. Thus, it generates the series of filenames sampfile.0001, sampfile.0002, and so on.

Using let

Use let to perform an arithmetic calculation. The syntax for the let statement, the second major element in the shell's support for arithmetic, is simple:

```
let expr
```

For expr, write an expression that consists of terms and operators. A *term* is a variable or a literal integer number—for example, 3 or 512. A *literal integer number* is assumed to be written in base 10. You can specify another base by using the format radix#number, where radix is the number base and number is the value of the number. For a radix greater than 10, digits consist of the characters 0 through 9 and A through Z. In radix 16 (hexadecimal), for example, the digits are 0 through 9 and A through F.

Table 11.13 shows the arithmetic operators supported by the Korn shell for use in arithmetic expressions.

Table 11.13. Arithmetic operators in the Korn shell.

Operator	Expression	Value of Expression
–	-exp	Unary minus—the negative of exp
!	!exp	0 when exp is non-zero; otherwise, 1
~	~exp	Complement of exp
*	exp1 * exp2	Product of exp1 and exp2
/	exp1 / exp2	Quotient of dividing exp1 by exp2
%	exp1 % exp2	Remainder of dividing exp1 by exp2

Operator	Expression	Value of Expression
+	exp1 + exp2	Sum of exp1 and exp2
–	exp1 – exp2	Difference of exp2 from exp1
<<	exp1 << exp2	exp1 is shifted left exp2 bits
>>	exp1 >> exp2	exp1 is shifted right exp2 bits
<=	exp1 <= exp2	1 if exp1 is less than or equal to exp2; otherwise, 0
>=	exp1 >= exp2	1 if exp1 is greater than or equal to exp2; otherwise, 0
<	exp1 < exp2	1 if exp1 is less than exp2; otherwise, 0
>	exp1 > exp2	1 if exp1 is greater than exp2; otherwise, 0
==	exp1 == exp2	1 if exp1 is equal to exp2; otherwise, 0
!=	exp1 != exp2	1 if exp1 is not equal to exp2; otherwise, 0
&	exp1 & exp2	Bitwise AND of exp1 and exp2
^	exp1 ^ exp2	Exclusive OR of exp1 and exp2
¦	exp1 ¦ exp2	Bitwise OR of exp1 and exp2
&&	exp1 && exp2	1 if exp1 is non-zero and exp2 is non-zero; otherwise, 0
¦¦	exp1 ¦¦ exp2	1 if exp1 is non-zero or exp2 is non-zero; otherwise, 0
=	var = exp	Assigns the value of exp to Variable ID
+=	var += exp	Adds exp to Variable ID
–=	var –= exp	Subtracts exp from Variable ID
*=	var *= exp	Multiplies var by exp
/=	var /= exp	Divides var by exp
%=	var %= exp	Assigns the remainder of var divided by exp to var
<<=	var <<= exp	Shifts var left exp bits
>>=	var >>= exp	Shifts var right exp bits
&=	var &= exp	Assigns the bitwise AND of var and exp to var
¦=	var ¦= exp	Assigns the bitwise OR of var and exp to var
^=	var ^= exp	Assigns the exclusive OR of var and exp to var

The Korn shell also supports expression grouping using parentheses. An expression in parentheses is evaluated as a unit before any terms outside the expression are evaluated. Parentheses are used to override the normal precedence of operators.

The operators in Table 11.13 are listed in decreasing order of precedence. The Korn shell uses the normal precedence for arithmetic operators, which you know from the C programming language or from the use of an ordinary calculator. Because of these precedence rules, the expression a+b*y is computed by first multiplying b*y and then adding the product to a, just as though the expression had been written a+(b*y). With parentheses, you can change the order of calculation. For example, (a+b)*y would be computed by first adding a and b and then multiplying the sum by y.

The let command is a built-in shell command. Like any command, it sets an exit value. The exit value of the let command is 0 if the value of the last or only expression computed is non-zero. If the last or only expression evaluates to 0, the exit value of the let command is 1. This strange inversion is an adaptation of the if statement, where a command setting a zero exit value is true—that is, it causes execution of the then clause—and a command setting a non-zero exit value is false—that is, it causes execution of the else clause.

Because of the let command's inverted exit value, for example, the statement if let "a == b", when a and b are equal, is considered true. The logical result of the equality comparison would be 1, which is equivalent to if let 1. The last expression has a value of 1. Therefore, the exit value from let is 0, and the if statement is considered true, thus invoking the then clause as expected.

Notice that you need to quote operators used in a let expression that are special to the shell. The command let prod=x¦y would give very strange results if it were written without quotes. The shell would see a pipe between the two commands let prod=x and y. Acceptable quoting is any of the following forms:

- let "prod=x¦y"
- let prod="x¦y"
- let prod=x\¦y

Many Korn shell users employ the convention of always quoting an expression in its entirety, so they avoid the problem of shell metacharacters entirely.

Take another look at the syntax of the let command. Notice that each of its terms is an arbitrary expression. A command such as let x+y is valid, but it is ordinarily of little use. This is because the sum of variables x and y is computed, but the result is thrown away. You should use an assignment expression—for example, let sum=x+y—to retain the result of the calculation in a variable named sum for later reference. The only time it makes sense to evaluate an expression without assigning the result to a new variable is when the purpose of the let command is to set a command exit value—namely, for use in statements such as if and while. In these cases, however, you can use a more convenient form of the let statement: the (( )) expression.

A statement such as

```
if (( x+y < 25 ))
then ...
fi
```

is more clearly readable than this equivalent:

```
if let "x+y < 25"
```

An additional advantage is that using quotes to hide operators is unnecessary inside an (( )) expression. The ((and)) operators are in effect special kinds of parentheses. They notify the Korn shell that the text they enclose is intended to be an arithmetic expression; this turns off the normal interpretation of metacharacters such as < and ¦, and it permits the unambiguous interpretation of these symbols as operators. Compatibility with the Bourne shell isn't compromised, because the ((and)) operators don't occur in shell scripts written for the Bourne shell.

You can use the (( )) expression form wherever the `let` command itself would be valid, as well as in a number of other places. Unlike the `let` command, however, the (( )) syntax permits only one expression between the doubled parentheses.

There is also a version of (( )) that returns the string representation of the calculation; this is `$(( ))`. In this form, the result is returned to the shell. For example,

```
$ echo "(( 4+5 ))"
(( 4+5 ))
$ echo "$(( 4+5 ))"
9
```

You can use arithmetic expressions in any of these contexts:

- As an array subscript
- As arguments of the `let` command
- Inside doubled parentheses (( ))
- As the shift count in `shift`
- As operands of the `-eq`, `-ne`, `-gt`, `-lt`, `-ge`, and `-le` operators in `test`, `[`, and `[[` commands
- As resource limits in `ulimit`
- As the right-hand side of an assignment statement, but only when the variable name being assigned was defined as an integer variable with the `typeset` or `integer` statement

Practical Examples of Arithmetic

Now that you have reviewed all the basics of arithmetic in the Korn shell, you should take a look at some specific examples. This is an example of how *not* to use arithmetic expressions, for example:

```
$ x=4 y=5
$ print x+y
x+y
```

The first command line assigns numeric values to the non-integer variables x and y. The print line attempts to print their sum, but the `print` command isn't one of the places where arithmetic expressions are supported. The result is fully compatible with the Bourne shell. The `print` statement simply echoes its arguments.

Now look at a first attempt to fix the problem:

```
$ let x=4 y=5
$ print $x+$y
4+5
```

The assignment statements have been changed to a `let` command, which has no significant effect on anything. The dollar signs ($) on the `print` statement help the shell recognize that x and y are variables. The variable references are substituted with their respective values, but the Korn shell still fails to recognize the presence of an expression on the `print` command argument. There is, in fact, no way to get the shell to recognize an expression and to evaluate it on a `print` command.

Here is a working solution:

```
$ integer x=4 y=5
$ let sum=x+y
$ print $sum
9
```

The key element of the solution is the use of the `let` statement to calculate the sum. It stores the calculated result in a new variable called `sum`, which can be referenced later.

You might think that using a hand calculator would be an easier way to perform a simple arithmetic problem at the keyboard, and I would tend to agree with you. At the keyboard, a more effective approach is simply to use the `expr` command. For example,

```
$ expr 4 +
9
```

`expr` achieves the same result at the keyboard, but it is of little use inside shell scripts, where the result of the `expr` calculation—written to standard output—isn't readily available for use.

Now consider this example of a counter-controlled loop:

```
integer i=0
while (( i<5 ))
do
    i=i+1
    print $i
done
```

This little program simply prints the numbers 1 through 5. Notice the use of an assignment statement instead of a `let` command to increment i. This works only because the variable i was declared previously as an integer. The example works fine typed in at the keyboard. Try it.

For a more practical example, consider the following:

```
$ typeset -i16 hex
$ hex=125
$ print $hex
16#7d
```

Here, the variable hex is declared to be an integer and to be represented in base 16. The second line assigns a normal integer numeric value to the hex variable, and the third line prints it.

Magically, though, the effect of the 16 from the typeset command becomes clear: The value of hex is shown in hexadecimal (base-16) notation. Going the other way—converting from hexadecimal to decimal—is just as easy:

```
$ integer n
$ n=16#7d
$ print $((n))
125
```

At the keyboard, after you declare the hex and n variables, they remain in effect indefinitely. You can use them repeatedly to convert between hexadecimal and decimal. For example,

```
$ hex=4096; print $hex
16#1000
$ n=16#1000; print $((n))
4096
```

Shell Programming

Although the main thrust of the Korn shell's features is to enhance productivity at the keyboard, the Korn shell also provides a number of boons for writing shell scripts, which makes the Korn shell an attractive environment for program development. This section reviews the Korn shell enhancements that apply to shell-script writing. Of course, all the programming constructs of the Bourne shell are available, so the material in Chapter 9 pertains equally to the Korn shell and isn't repeated here.

The Korn shell extensions useful for writing shell scripts are conditional expressions, which enhance the flexibility of the following:

- if, while, and until statements
- Array variables, integer variables, extended variable reference expressions, and arithmetic expressions
- A new select statement for constructing a menu of prompts from which the user can select a choice
- Extended support for functions, including autoload functions
- An enhanced form of the command expression $(...), which is simpler to use than the backquoted form ` ... `
- Extended support for process communication withcoprocessing using the operator—¦&

If you are going to be writing shell scripts that will be used by many people, it is wise to place this on the first line of the script:

```
#!/bin/ksh
```

This tells the user's shell under which shell the script actually should run. Running a Korn shell script under the C shell, for example, just won't work no matter how hard you try!

The section "Variables," earlier in this chapter, discussed the Korn shell's extended variable support, including array variables, integer variables, variable reference expressions, and arithmetic expressions. The other new features are explained in the following sections.

Conditional Expressions

The `if`, `while`, and `until` statements support two new kinds of expressions. The `(( ))` doubled parentheses operator, which evaluates an arithmetic expression, enables you to perform complex arithmetic tests. A zero result is considered true, and a non-zero result is considered false. You also can write an extended conditional test expression as the argument of `if`, `while`, or `until`. A conditional test expression has this general form:

```
[[ conditional-exp ]]
```

where `conditional-exp` is any of the forms shown in Table 11.14.

Notice that the conditional-expression forms are similar to those of the `test` and `[ ]` expressions. The Korn shell supports the `test` and `[ ]` expressions identically with how the Bourne shell does. The `[[ ]]` expression provides extended capabilities without compromising compatibility with the Bourne shell.

Table 11.14. Conditional expressions.

Expression	Bourne Shell	Condition When True
`-r file`	Yes	File exists.
`-w file`	Yes	File exists and has Write permission enabled. The file might not be writable even if Write permission is set or if it is within a file system that is mounted as read-only.
`-x file`	Yes	File exists and has Execute permission set. The file might not actually be executable. Directories usually have the Execute permission flag set.
`-f file`	Yes	File exists and is a regular file.
`-d file`	Yes	File exists and is a directory.
`-c file`	Yes	File exists and is a character-special file.
`-b file`	Yes	File exists and is a block-special file.
`-p file`	Yes	File exists and is a named pipe.
`-u file`	Yes	The Set User ID permission flag is set for `file`.
`-g file`	Yes	The Set Group ID permission flag is set for `file`.
`-k file`	Yes	The Sticky permission flag is set for `file`.

Expression	Bourne Shell	Condition When True
-s `file`	Yes	File has a size greater than zero.
-L `file`	No	File is a symbolic link.
-O `file`	No	File has an Owner ID equal to the effective User ID of the current process.
-G `file`	No	File has a Group ID equal to the effective Group ID of the current process.
-S `file`	No	File is a socket.
-t [`fildes`]	Yes	The file descriptor `fildes`—whose default is 1—is a terminal.
-o `option`	No	The named `option` is set.
-z `string`	Yes	`string` is a zero-length string.
-n `string`	Yes	`string` is not a zero-length string.
`string`	Yes	`string` is not a zero-length or null string.
`string` = `pat`	Yes	`string` matches the pattern `pat`.
`string` != `pat`	Yes	`string` does not match the pattern `pat`.
s1 < s2	No	String s1 is less than string s2. That is, `pat` collates before s2.
s1 > s2	No	String s1 is greater than string s2. That is, `pat` collates after s2.
`file1` -nt `file2`	No	File `file1` is newer than file `file2`.
`file1` -ot `file2`	No	File `file1` is older than file `file2`.
`file1` -ef `file2`	No	File `file1` is the same file as file `file2`.
e1 -eq e2	No	Expressions e1 and e2 are equal.
e1 -ne e2	No	Expressions e1 and e2 are not equal.
e1 -gt e2	No	Expression e1 is greater than e2.
e1 -ge e2	No	Expression e1 is greater than or equal to e2.
e1 -lt e2	No	Expression e1 is less than e2.
e1 -le e2	No	Expression e1 is less than or equal to e2.

Functions

The Korn shell fully supports Bourne shell functions. It also provides some extensions.

Defining Functions

In addition to the Bourne shell syntax, the Korn shell supports the following alternate syntax for defining a function:

```
function identifier
{
    command-list
}
```

Using Variables in Functions

The Korn shell allows a function to have local variables. A *local variable* exists only during the execution of the function and is destroyed when the function returns. A local variable can have the same name as a variable in the calling environment. During execution of the function, the local variable hides the outer variable. You define a local variable with the typeset command. For example,

```
function square
{
    typeset product
    let "product=$1*$1"
    print $product
    return
}
```

Using Traps in Functions

In the Bourne shell, traps set with the trap command remain in force after the function's return. In the Korn shell, traps set in the calling environment are saved and restored.

You can use the typeset command with the -f option to manage functions. The -f option has four forms, which are listed in Table 11.15.

Table 11.15. -f option forms.

Form	Description
typeset -f	Lists the functions currently defined and their definitions. The predefined alias functions does the same thing.
typeset -ft *name* ...	Activates the xtrace option whenever the function name is invoked. Tracing reverts to its former state when the function returns.
typeset -fx *name* ...	Defines functions as exported. Exported functions are inherited by shell scripts. A function cannot be exported to another instance of ksh, however. There is no method for passing function definitions through the command environment, as there is for variables.

Form	Description
typeset -fu *name* ...	Defines functions for autoload. A call to an autoload function before its definition is recognized as a function call when the function has been declared with typeset. The Korn shell searches the directories named in the FPATH variable for a file that has the same name as the function. If the Korn shell finds such a file, the function is loaded and executed, and the definition is retained as though an inline definition of the function had been read at that point.

Using Autoload Functions

Autoload functions provide superior performance versus conventional shell scripts, because they are retained in memory for fast execution on repeated calls; however, unreferenced functions incur no overhead other than processing of the typeset -fu command. You create autoload functions in much the same manner as shell scripts, except that the definition file should be in the form of a function; it should begin with the statement function *name*. To use autoload functions, you must set the FPATH environment variable to the directory or directories to be searched (in the same manner as you set the PATH environment variable), and you must declare the functions in advance with the typeset -fu command.

Any function definition is eligible for use as an autoload function, although frequently used functions are preferred. Remember that after an autoload function is read, its definition is retained in the shell's available memory. Large programs should be written as conventional shell scripts instead of as autoload functions unless the program is used heavily.

Undefining Functions

To undefine a function, use the unset command:

```
unset -f name ...
```

The named functions are purged from memory, and any typeset -fu declaration for the named function is deleted. The unset -f command is not used often, but it is useful particularly when debugging a function. Using unset -f is the only way to force the shell to reread an autoload function definition file.

When to Use Functions

Functions are a handy way of creating new keyboard commands. Because a function executes as part of the current shell environment, a directory change made with the cd command remains in force after the function exits. This isn't true for ordinary commands and shell scripts. Because I almost always like to take a quick peek at a directory's contents after changing to it, I created the following short function definition and added it to my logon profile:

```
function go
{
    cd $1
    /usr/bin/ls -FC
}
```

The go function, used in the form go *dirname*, not only changes to the directory but also prints a sorted listing so that I can see immediately what's in the directory.

Adding the go function to my logon profile means that it's always present in the shell memory. Because go is a small function, this does no harm, considering how often I use it. For larger functions, it is better to store the function definition in a separate file and to replace the function definition in the profile with a typeset -fu declaration, thus making the function an autoload function.

Scanning Arguments with getopts

The Bourne shell provides negligible assistance with the processing of command-line options. As a result, many user-written shell scripts process options clumsily at best, and they often don't support the generalized UNIX command format for options. The getopt command, long a standard part of the UNIX command set, helps a little. The Korn shell, however, goes one step further by adding a built-in command called getopts, which provides the same power and flexibility to script writers that C programmers have long enjoyed.

The syntax of the getopts built-in command is straightforward:

getopts *options var* [*arg* ...]

For *options*, provide a string that defines the letters that can legally appear as command-line options. If an option letter can be followed by a value string, indicate this in the *options* string by following the letter with :. For example, I: represents the option syntax -I*string*.

If *options* begins with :, the Korn shell provides user error handling. The invalid option letter is placed in OPTARG, and *var* is set to ?. Without :, the getopts command issues an error message on an invalid letter and sets *var* to ? so that you can recognize that an error occurred and skip the invalid option, but it doesn't identify the invalid letter.

For *var*, write the name of a variable to receive the option letter. The shell stores the letter in *var* when it identifies the letter as an option in the command line.

For *arg*, write the argument list from the command line that is to be scanned for options. The *arg* list usually is written in the form $* or "$@".

For reasons of practicality, the getopts command cannot scan, identify, and process all option letters in a command on one invocation. Instead, each time you call getopts, you get the next option on the command line. Of course, getopts can't look at the real command line that invoked your shell script. It examines the *arg* list that you provide with getopts, stepping once through the list on each call.

When you call getopts, it starts by determining its current position in the *arg* list. If its current position is within a word and the word starts with -, the next character in the word is taken as an option letter. If this is your first call to getopts, or the last invocation finished scanning a word, getopts examines the next *arg* for a leading hyphen.

In any case, when getopts identifies an option, it stores the letter in *var*. If the option takes a value string (indicated in the *option* string by being followed by :), the option value is scanned and stored in a predefined variable named OPTARG. If getopts has started a new *arg* variable, it increments the predefined variable OPTIND to indicate which argument it is working on—1, 2, and so on. It then updates its position in the argument list and exits.

After calling getopts, you inspect the *var* variable to find out which option has been identified. If the option takes a value, you'll find its value string in the predefined variable OPTARG. The return value from getopts is zero if it finds an option or non-zero if it can find no more options in the command-line argument list.

The code for using getopts is almost a set piece that you need to memorize. Listing 11.1 is a shell program for scanning command-line options like those you might find in a script file. Here, the example merely prints the options it recognizes.

Listing 11.1. Scanning options with getopts.

```
# A routine to scan options
# ... allowable options are -a, -c, -R, -Aname, or -Iname.

while getopts :acRA:I: KEY $*
do
    case $KEY in
    a)    print Found option -a;;
    c)    print Found option -c ;;
    R)    print Found option -R ;;
    A)    print Found option -A, value is "'$OPTARG'" ;;
    I)    print Found option -I, value is "'$OPTARG'" ;;
    *)    print -u2 Illegal option: -$OPTARG
    esac
done
# Strip option arguments, leaving positional args
shift OPTIND-1
print ARGS: $*
```

The code in Listing 11.1 is executable. Enter the statements into a file and mark the file executable with chmod +x *filename*. Then invoke the file's name with a sample set of option letters and arguments. You'll see the shell script's idea of the options and positional arguments that you entered.

You should note two special points about Listing 11.1. First, the *option* string for the getopts command begins with a colon (:). When the *option* string begins with a colon, the getopts command provides user error handling; an unrecognized option letter is put into the OPTARG variable, and the *var* keyletter variable is set to ?. You can test explicitly for ? as the letter value, or you simply can provide your own error message for any unrecognized option letter.

If the *option* string doesn't begin with :, getopts provides its own error handling. After finding an unrecognized option letter, getopts prints an error message and sets *var* to ?, but it doesn't set the option letter in OPTARG. Therefore, although you can tell that an invalid option has been found, you don't know what the invalid letter is. Of course, an invalid option letter is simply any letter that doesn't appear in the *option* string.

Second, note the use of the shift statement to identify the remaining position arguments from the original command line. By itself, the getopts command doesn't strip words containing options from the *arg* list. After identifying options with getopts, however, you don't want to see them again when you examine the remaining positional arguments. You must throw away the option words yourself. The shift statement, inherited from the Bourne shell, does the job eminently well, assisted by the arithmetic expression-handling syntax of the Korn shell. The expression OPTIND-1 computes the number of positional arguments remaining on the command line. Notice that, because OPTIND-1 occurs in the shift command line in the position of an expression, OPTIND is recognized as a variable reference; you don't need to include a dollar sign in front of it.

Using the select Statement

If you've ever written a shell script that enables the user to specify values on the command line or to be prompted for them, you know what an elaborate piece of drudgery such a user-interface nicety can be. The Korn shell helps you out, though, with a new built-in command that automates the entire process—from printing a selection menu to prompting for the user's choice to reading it.

In fact, because the user might choose an illegal option (requiring you to repeat the menu-selection process) or in case you want to display the menu repeatedly until the user decides to quit, the select statement is actually an iterative statement, much like while or until. You must use the break statement to terminate execution of select.

The syntax of the select statement follows:

```
select identifier [ in word ... ]
do command-list
done
```

The select statement first displays the word list (*word* ...) in one or more columns. If the LINES variable is set and specifies an integer number, it is taken as the maximum number of lines available for displaying the word list. If there are more items to display than this maximum, the list is broken into a multicolumn display. Each *word* is prefixed by a number, starting at 1. *word* may be a single word or a quoted string. It is scanned for variable and command substitutions prior to display.

In effect, the list of strings that you specify for *word* ... becomes a series of menu items that are automatically numbered and displayed for the user.

The `select` statement next displays the value of variable PS3 as a menu prompt. By default, the value of PS3 is #?, suggesting that the user should enter a number. If you want a different prompt, assign a value to PS3 before you execute the `select` statement.

The `select` statement next reads a reply from the user. The entire line entered by the user is saved in the special shell variable REPLY. If the user enters a null line (that is, presses Enter or Return without typing anything), `select` redisplays the list and issues the prompt again without invoking *command-list*. Otherwise, if the user entered a number, the variable named *identifier* is set to the *word* corresponding to that number. That is, entering 1 sets *identifier* to the first *word*, entering 2 sets *identifier* to the second *word*, and so on. If the number is greater than the number of words, or if the user input isn't a number, `select` sets *identifier* to null. In any case, the `select` statement then executes *command-list*.

Consider the following example, in which the user is given a choice of colors from which to select. The `select` statement continues to execute until the user chooses one of the allowable color names.

```
PS3="Select color by number (e.g., 3):"
select color in Blue Green Yellow Red White Black Burnt-umber "Natural Wool"
do case $color in\
    Blue ¦ Green ¦ Yellow ¦ Red ¦ White ¦ Black ¦
    Burnt-umber ¦ "Natural Wool") break ;;
    *) print "Please enter a number from 1-8. Try again." ;;
    esac
done
print "Your color choice is: $color"
```

Notice the use of quotes to specify Natural Wool as one of the menu choices. If the words were not quoted, the `select` statement would view them as two separate menu items, and the user would be able to select either Natural (item 8) or Wool (item 9).

Also note that the example does nothing to execute the menu choice procedure repetitively until the user enters a valid selection. Iteration of `select` is automatic. It lists the valid choices that must do something special to break out of the `select` loop—in this case, by executing the break statement.

Nothing prevents you from implementing a primitive, menu-driven system with `select`. Listing 11.2 uses the `select` statement to offer the user a choice of application actions. The example continues to execute until the user chooses the Exit item. Then the `select` statement and any shell script in which it is contained is terminated with the `exit` built-in shell command.

Listing 11.2. Implementing a menu system with `select`.

```
PS3=Choice?
select choice in "Enter Transactions" \
       "Print trial balance" \
       "Print invoices" \
       "Exit"
```

continues

Listing 11.2. continued

```
do case "$choice" in
    "Enter Transactions")  . daily-trans ;;
    "Print trial balance") . trial-balance ;;
    "Print invoices")      . invoices ;;
    "Exit")                    print "That's all, folks!"; exit ;;
    *)  print -u2 "Wrong choice. Enter a number (1-4)."
   esac
done
```

Using Coprocesses

The Bourne shell supports a minimal amount of communication between processes—typically, by way of the pipe operator. You can invoke the ed line editor from a shell script to make a specific text change by using a command such as the one shown in Listing 11.3.

Listing 11.3. Basic process communication.

```
 (echo "/^Payroll
+1
i"
cat newlist
echo "."
echo "w"
echo "q"
) ¦ ed - paylist
```

This form of intertask communication is sufficient if you just need to pass some data to another command or to read its output. Suppose that in Listing 11.3, though, you want to provide for the case that the file paylist doesn't contain a line beginning with Payroll by skipping the insert, write, and quit editor commands. With the Bourne shell, you couldn't do this. With the Korn shell, you can maintain an interactive session with the ed command, with your program providing the instructions to ed and responding to its output.

To use *coprocessing* (a fancy term for the simultaneous execution of two procedures that read each other's output), you first must launch the program with which you want to communicate as a background process by using the special operator ¦&. The ¦& operator is intended to suggest a combination of & (background execution) and ¦ (the pipe operator). When the background command is started, its standard and standard output are assigned to pipes connected to your own process—one for writing to the command and one for reading the command's output.

The simplest way of sending a line to the coprocess is to use the print -p command. The -p option tells print to write to the coprocess's input pipe. To read output from the coprocess, use read -p. Once again, -p tells read to read from the coprocess pipe.

Using these facilities, you could rewrite the preceding procedure as the one shown in Listing 11.4.

Listing 11.4. Process communication using coprocessing.

```
ed paylist ¦&
exec 3>&p
exec 4<&p
read -u4               # discard initial message line
print -u3 P            # Turn on prompting
print -u3 "/^Payroll"  # search for the insert location
read -u3               # read prompt indicating success or failure
case "$REPLY" in
    '*'*) # search must have been successful
          print -u3 i
          cat text >&3 # file containing data to be inserted
          print -u3 .
          read -u4 # read the ending prompt
          print -u3 w; read -u4
          print -u3 q
          ;;
    *)    # not found
          print -u3 q
          echo "invalid paylist file"
          exit
          ;;
    esac
done
```

You should note the following in this example:

- The exec command (exec 3>&p) is used to move the coprocess input pipe from its default location to a numbered file descriptor.

- The exec command (exec 4<&p) is used again to move the coprocess output pipe to number file descriptor 4.

- Subsequent read and print commands specify the file descriptor as the source or destination of the operation, using the -u option.

- Ordinary UNIX commands can write to the coprocess by redirecting to file descriptor 3 (cat filename >&3).

NOTE

Use read -p or print -p to read from or write to the coprocess until you have moved the coprocess input or output to a number file descriptor. Then read or write to that file descriptor: read -u4 or print -u3.

Admittedly, Listing 11.4, which uses coprocessing, is more complicated than Listing 11.3, but it is also safer. The Bourne shell version would have added new lines after the first line if the search for Payroll failed. The Korn shell version fails gracefully without damaging the paylist file.

Notice that the Korn shell example of coprocessing in Listing 11.4 contains an incomplete `cat` command. This is because you need a special syntax to transcribe a file into the coprocess pipe. The standard Bourne shell syntax—`>filename` and `>&fildes`—is inadequate. This is because `>filename` and `>&fildes` do not give you a way to reference the coprocess input and output pipes.

Actually, by using a Korn shell feature designed especially to support coprocessing, you can use I/O redirection to send output to or read input from the background process with any UNIX command. The technique required is to switch the default input and output pipes created by the `¦&` operator to explicit file descriptors. You use the `exec` command to do this:

```
exec 3>&p
```

When used with the `exec` command, this special form of output redirection operator causes the pipe for writing to the coprocess to be assigned to file descriptor 3. (The lack of a command on the `exec` statement, of course, tips off the Korn shell that you want to modify the current environment instead of execute another program.)

Similarly, the following code reassigns the pipe for reading from the coprocess:

```
exec 4<&p
```

If you place these two lines at the front of the `ed` example, the `cat` command can be written in the familiar fashion—by using I/O redirection to an open file descriptor. For example,

```
cat newlist >&3
```

Of course, the new syntax for the `exec` statement is a terrible kludge, amounting to a form of syntactic code that is difficult to remember. However, the basic outlines of coprocessing, including the `¦&` operator and the `-p` options for `print` and `read`, are straightforward enough, as is the underlying concept. Coprocessing is a powerful capability, making it possible to do things in a shell script that previously required the C programming language. So sharpen up your coding pencils and try your hand at coprocessing.

Cautionary Tales

The Korn shell is a very powerful shell to script with; however, it has its problems. One of the more obscure problems involves piping. Consider this script:

```
person=noone
echo At start: $person
who ¦ while read person tty junk
do
      echo $person is logged on at terminal $tty
done
echo At end: $person
```

What will be the value of person after you run this script? The answer is you don't know—you can't know. This script gave me two different results on two different implementations of the Korn shell. On one system, person was an empty (null) string. On the other system, it contained noone.

The reason for this unpredictability is that you're piping the output into another command. When you use a pipe, you effectively start another shell to manage the output. Different implementations may carry out the piping in a different way, though, because `while` and `read` are internal to the shell, so there is no need to start a second shell to manage them.

Don't write a scripts that work under one implementation of a shell perfectly. Little bugs like this can creep in and render your script unusable. Create safeguards against this by saving variables and restoring them. One day, your script actually might be needed on a different system, and the last thing you want is lots of people asking you why it won't work.

Customizing the Korn Shell

It almost might be said that the term *shell* refers to what you have before you customize it—an empty shell. Of course, that's a gross exaggeration. The shell is more feature-laden than most programs you'll get an opportunity to shake a stick at. Still, the Korn shell permits so much customization that it's no exaggeration to say that you might find another user's logon environment so foreign as to be almost unusable by you. Indeed, some places try to place a limit on user customization.

You can adapt the Korn shell to your preferred way of working in many ways. Of course, keep in mind that if you're a beginning UNIX user, you might not have many preferences. As your familiarity with UNIX and the Korn shell increases, you'll find many conveniences, shorthand methods, and customary uses that seem comfortable to you. The Korn shell helps you along by enabling you to encapsulate favorite behaviors into your logon profile script and elsewhere.

Customizing the Korn shell begins with your logon profile script, which is named `.profile` and resides in your home directory. The file `$HOME/.profile` is of special importance, because the Korn shell executes it every time you log on—or, more precisely, every time you launch an interactive shell.

Often, the system administrator will place a starter `.profile` script in your home directory when he creates your logon. Don't let yourself be cowed into thinking that there is anything sacrosanct in the hand-me-down `.profile` given to you. The contents of your `.profile` script affect only you. Your script is specific to your logon name and home directory. Altering it conceivably could affect only those people who have your password and can log on with your logon name. Almost always, that is only you. Therefore, you should feel free to add to, change, or delete anything in the `.profile` script, including deleting the whole file. It doesn't matter to the shell. The `.profile` is supported only for your convenience; it isn't needed for Korn shell operation.

Your `.profile` script is, in fact, a shell script. Any shell-programming techniques valid in a shell script are valid in the `.profile` script. If you're not a shell programmer, don't be daunted. Useful logon profiles can be made up that contain nothing more than straightforward UNIX and shell commands, without an `if` or `while` statement in sight. If you know how to use shell conditional and iterative statements, so much the better. Don't think that mastery of them is essential to writing good profile scripts, though. It isn't.

Your .profile script is an ideal place to put your favorite things. You might want to do the following things with your .profile file. You also should observe the order in which these items are listed. Placing similar things together helps simplify the job of maintaining your .profile.

- Set control keys with the stty command.
- Set environment variables.
- Set local variables for shell control.
- Define aliases you like to use.
- Define functions you like to use, including autoload functions.
- Set your favorite shell options.
- Execute commands you want to run each time you log on.

Setting Control Keys with stty

Use the stty command to establish the control keys that you prefer to use. The default Erase key is #, and the default Kill key is @. Both are bad choices, because their use as terminal control characters conflicts with their use as ordinary text characters. You should redefine these keys with a statement similar to this:

```
stty erase '^H' kill '^U' intr '^C'
```

This example uses the caret (^) in front of an upper- or lowercase letter to designate a control-key combination. Thus, erase '^H' specifies the Ctrl+h key combination as your Backspace key. Of course, you would prefer to specify the actual characters generated by your Backspace key as the value for the erase character—if you can figure out what it is. The presence of a caret forces the use of quote marks. The caret is special to the shell; a lack of quotes causes improper interpretation of the stty command. (For details about the stty command, see your UNIX User's Reference Manual.)

Controlling Resources with ulimit

Using ulimit to control resources can be a handy feature, especially if you are a system administrator. Although UNIX comes with a ulimit command, the Korn shell offers its own alternative. The syntax for ulimit follows:

```
ulimit [-HSacdfnstv] [limit]
```

The H and S flags tell ulimit that you are defining a hard or soft limit. A *hard limit* cannot be increased after it is set. A *soft limit* can be modified up to the value of the hard limit. If both H and S are omitted, the specified limit is applied to both the hard and soft limits.

If limit is omitted, the current value of the specified limit is displayed. If ulimit is invoked with no options, it returns the number of blocks that can be written by a process (the same as typing ulimit -f). Table 11.16 lists the ulimit parameters.

Table 11.16. The `ulimit` parameters.

Parameter	Function
-a	Lists all resource limits
-c	Specifies the number of blocks for a core file
-d	Specifies the number of kilobytes for the data area
-f	Specifies the number of blocks that may be written to a file
-n	Specifies one more than the number of files that may be open at once
-s	Specifies the number of kilobytes for the stack area
-t	Specifies the number of seconds that may be used by each process
-v	Specifies the number of kilobytes for virtual memory

> **TIP**
>
> Unless you are going to be doing a lot of programming, it is useful to place `ulimit -c 0` in your profile. This prevents any program that crashes from creating a core file, so it also saves disk space. Many core files can be megabytes in size, so any way of reducing them is often a welcome method!

Setting Environment Variables

At the very least, you'll want to make sure that the variables PATH and MAIL have values. Usually, you'll want to set a great many more variables. If you use Bourne shell syntax, your variable settings will look like this:

```
PATH=/usr/bin:/usr/ucb:/usr/local/bin:$HOME/bin:
MAIL=/var/spool/mail/$LOGNAME
MAILCHECK=60
FCEDIT=/usr/bin/vi
VISUAL=/usr/bin/vi
export PATH MAIL MAILCHECK FCEDIT VISUAL
```

Alternatively, you can use the Korn shell `export` alias to avoid the need to remember to add each variable that you set to the `export` variable list; it does little good to set a variable if you don't export it. Using the `export` alias, the preceding code would look like this:

```
export PATH=/usr/bin:/usr/ucb:/usr/local/bin:$HOME/bin:
export MAIL=/var/spool/mail/$LOGNAME
export MAILCHECK=60
export FCEDIT=/usr/bin/vi
export VISUAL=/usr/bin/vi
```

When you write your environment variable settings, keep in mind that some are set by the UNIX logon processor. Your system administrator also can provide a logon script to set values before your .profile script runs. The PATH and MAIL variables usually have initial values already set when your script starts, for example. Overriding the default PATH variable is usually a good idea; you should have full control over your program search path, starting with its initial value. Overriding the default MAIL or MAILPATH variable is risky unless you know which mail subsystems are in use.

Setting Local Variables for Shell Control

Local variables are variables the shell uses but aren't exported. They include FCEDIT, which designates the text editor to be used by the fc command, and the PS1 variable, which is your primary prompt string. You also might want to define a few local variables to hold the names of directories that you commonly access, which enables you to use cd $dir instead of the longer full pathname.

Defining Aliases

Define the aliases you like to use. You must invent your own aliases; each user tends to have a different set. Most users make up some aliases for the ls command. You even can redefine the default behavior of the ls command by defining an alias named ls. Here are some typical aliases I like to use:

```
alias lx='/usr/bin/ls -FC'
alias l='/usr/bin/ls -l'
alias pg='/usr/bin/pg -cns -p"Page %d:"'
alias mail='/usr/bin/mailx'
alias -t vi
```

Notice that, in most cases, I tend to use the full pathname for commands in the alias definition. I do this because it eliminates directory searches for the command, and it provides much the same effect as the Korn shell's alias-tracking mechanism. Note also the explicit use of the alias -t command to request the shell to track the vi command. The shell looks up the full pathname of the vi command and defines an alias named vi for me so that the plain command vi has all the performance but none of the typing overhead of /usr/bin/vi.

Defining Functions

Define any functions you like to use, including autoload functions. I use some function definitions as keyboard shorthand, because a function can do things an alias can't. You might want to use the go function described earlier in this chapter, for example, for switching directories.

Setting Shell Options

If you find yourself frequently setting the same shell options at the command line, you can set them in your .profile instead. To set the preferred shell options, use the set command. If you prefer to use vi mode for command history and editing, and you want full job control support, you might add these two lines to your `.profile`:

```
set -o vi
set -o monitor
```

Executing Commands Every Time You Log On

Execute commands you like to run every time you log on. You might want to run the who command to find out who's currently logged on, for example. Similarly, df, which isn't present on all UNIX systems, displays the amount of free disk space available on mounted file systems.

Executing Your `.profile` After Changing It

Whenever you change your `.profile` script, you should execute it before you log out. If you make an error in your script, you might have difficulty logging back on. To test your `.profile` script, you can run it with the . (dot) command:

```
$ . ./.profile
```

Be sure to leave a space after the first period: it's the command name, and `./.profile` is the command argument. (Although `.profile` usually is adequate by itself, you might need to use `./.profile` if your current directory is not in the search path.) The dot command not only executes the script but also leaves any environment changes in effect after the script terminates.

Alternatively, you can run the script with ksh -v to have the shell execute the script and print each statement as it is executed:

```
$ ksh -v ./.profile
```

Using the -n option would cause the Korn shell to read your `.profile` and check it for syntax errors but not execute the commands it contains.

Creating an ENV File

After you have your `.profile` set up the way you want, you're ready to tackle the environment file. The *environment file* is any file that contains shell scripts you designate by assigning its pathname to the ENV variable. The shell executes the ENV file whenever you start a new invocation of the shell and when it executes a command. If you've ever shelled out from commands like pg and vi, you know that when you call the shell again, some environment settings, such as aliases, aren't carried over from your logon shell. By placing aliases, function definitions, and even global variable settings in a separate file and setting ENV to its pathname in your `.profile` script, you can ensure that you have a consistent Korn shell environment at all times.

Don't get carried away, though. In some cases, the file designated by the pathname value of ENV is executed in front of shell commands that you call. Because many UNIX commands are implemented as shell scripts, this means that a large environment file can add surprising overhead to some unexpected places.

NOTE

As a rule, the environment file is executed as a preliminary step to invoking a shell script only when the shell script requires a new invocation of the Korn shell. This usually isn't the case when you invoke a shell script by its name.

To use an environment file, create a file that contains the aliases, functions, and exported variable settings you prefer. Then add the statement `export ENV=`*pathname*, where *pathname* is the full pathname of your environment file, to your `.profile`. The environment file becomes effective the next time you log on. It becomes effective immediately if you test your `.profile` with the following `.` command:

```
. .profile
```

Commands you want to put in your ENV file include alias definitions and shell options. You may prefer them in here instead of `.profile` to be sure of always getting a shell that looks and acts the same way each time.

TIP

A very useful `if` statement to put in your ENV file follows:
```
if [[ -o interactive ]]
then
     ....
     insert your ENV lines in here.
     ....
fi
```
Any lines placed inside the `if` statement are executed only if the shell is to be interactive—that is, it gives you a prompt at which you can type commands. This can cut down on the overhead of processing a new shell many times if the shell is being called with a command line that will run a command—for example,

```
ksh -c ls -l
```

If you have a lot of aliases and/or functions, it might be a good idea to place these in a separate file again and call this file from ENV to set them up. In my ENV file, I have these two lines:

```
. .ksh_alias
. .ksh_funcs
```

In `.ksh_alias`, I've placed all my alias definitions, and in `.ksh_funcs`, I've placed all my function definitions. This shortens my ENV file substantially and makes everything look a lot neater.

Adding Settings for Other Programs to Your `.profile`

Customizing your environment doesn't stop with using the logon profile and environment file to establish shell options and settings you want; it's also a handy place to put settings used by other programs. One way to customize your vi editing environment is by defining a variable EXINIT that contains the commands vi will run every time you start it. You could place the EXINIT variable setting in your logon profile to establish your preferred vi settings. Many UNIX commands respond to environment variables, which enables you to customize these commands in your logon profile.

Controlling Jobs

The idea of a job might be somewhat foreign to UNIX users, because in UNIX, most of the action is interactive. Nevertheless, even the Bourne shell provides basic tools for running background jobs, and UNIX the operating system always has provided such tools. The more recent releases of UNIX have even enhanced background job management.

The basic idea of a *background job* is simple. It's a program that can run without prompts or other manual interaction and can run in parallel with other active processes. With the Bourne shell, you launch a background job with the & operator. The command `cc myprog.c &`, for example, compiles the source program `myprog.c` without tying up the terminal. You can do other work—even edit files with a full-screen editor—while the `cc` command works behind the scenes.

Enhancements to the `stty` command and the terminal driver in recent UNIX releases have added a new control key to your terminal: Suspend. Suspend is usually Ctrl+Z. This new tool enables you to take an interactive program you're currently running, such as a vi editing session, and to put it temporarily into the background. If the program wants to talk to your terminal, the system suspends the program. Otherwise, it continues running.

The Korn shell adds some tools that help you manage the family of processes you can accumulate. These tools consist of the `jobs`, `kill`, `wait`, `bg`, and `fg` commands.

To use the Korn shell's job-control tools, you must have the `monitor` option enabled. Normally, the `monitor` option is enabled for you automatically; it's the default for interactive shells. If your operating system doesn't support job management, the default for the `monitor` option is off. Even without operating system support—the Suspend key and `stty` function are an operating system service, not a Korn shell service—you still can use some of the Korn shell's job-control tools, but you must set the `monitor` option on yourself. You do that with the command `set -o monitor`.

The `jobs` command, which takes no arguments, simply lists the jobs that you currently have active. The output of `jobs` looks like this:

```
$ jobs
[1] + Running              xlogo&
[2] + Running              xclock -bg LightGreen&
[3] + Stopped              vi myprog.c
```

You use the `kill`, `bg`, and `fg` commands to manage jobs. When referring to a job, you use the job number shown in brackets in the output of `jobs`, preceded by a percent (%) sign. For example, `kill %1` would terminate the xlogo program you currently have running. The `wait`, `kill`, `bg`, and `fg` commands also can refer to background jobs by their Process ID, which you generally can obtain from the output of the `ps` command. The use of Korn shell job numbers is preferred, however, because they are simpler and safer to use than Process IDs.

You create jobs in one of three ways:

■ By explicitly designating a command for background execution with the & operator

■ By switching a job into the background with the Korn shell `bg` command

■ By pressing the Suspend key—usually Ctrl+Z—while a foreground program is running

By convention, a job started or switched into the background continues to run until it tries to read from your terminal. Then it is suspended by the operating system until you intervene. When it is in this state, the `jobs` command shows that the command is `Stopped`.

A job that has been stopped usually needs to talk to you before it can continue. In the previous `jobs` example, the `vi` command is shown to be stopped. The command won't continue until you reconnect it to your terminal. You do this with the `fg` command—for example, `fg %3` or `fg %vi`. The `vi` command then becomes the foreground process, and it resumes normal interactive execution with you.

NOTE

A full-screen program such as vi probably won't recognize that the screen no longer matches your last edit screen. You probably will need to press Ctrl+L to redraw the screen before you resume your edit session. Other programs that merely need your response to a prompt don't require any special action when you resume them with fg.

Table 11.17 shows the full syntax of the % argument accepted by the `wait`, `kill`, `fg`, and `bg` commands.

Table 11.17. Job reference argument syntax.

Syntax	References
%number	The job number
%string	The job whose command begins with *string*
%?string	The job whose command contains *string*
%%	The current job

Syntax	References
%+	The current job (also %%)
%-	The preceding job

The syntax of the Korn shell job-control commands is summarized in the following sections.

Displaying Background Jobs and Their Status

Use the `jobs` command to display background jobs and their status. For example,

```
jobs [ -lp ] [ job ... ]
```

The `-l` option causes the `jobs` command to list the Process ID for each job in addition to its job number. The `-p` option causes the `jobs` command to list only the Process ID for each job instead of its job number.

If you omit the `job` arguments, `jobs` displays information about all background jobs, as in this example:

```
$ jobs
[1] + Running            xlogo&
[2] + Running            xclock -bg LightGreen&
[3] + Stopped            vi myprog.c
```

If you include `job` arguments, they display information only for the specified jobs. For `job`, specify a Process ID or a job reference beginning with `%`. To find out whether job 2 from the preceding example is still running, you would enter this command:

```
$ jobs %2
[2] + Running            xclock -bg LightGreen&
```

Sending Signals to a Job

Use the `kill` command to send a signal to the specified jobs. Some signals cause a job to terminate. The TERM signal—also called signal 15 or interrupt—usually causes a job to terminate gracefully, whereas signal 9 always terminates a job but may leave files unclosed or wreak other havoc on the job that was in progress. You should use `kill -9` only when you cannot terminate the job any other way.

The `kill` command generally is a UNIX system command, but the Korn shell provides `kill` as a built-in command with enhanced capabilities. The Korn shell supports the basic functionality of the UNIX `kill` command transparently. Its syntax follows:

```
kill [ -signal ] job ...
```

For *signal*, specify a signal number or a signal name. Signal numbers 1 through 15 are always valid. A signal name is one of a predefined list of mnemonic symbols that correspond to the valid signal numbers. Use `kill -l` to obtain a list of the valid signal names. The names TERM (terminate) and HUP (hang-up) are always valid. (See your UNIX User's Reference Manual for more information about the `kill` and `signal` commands.)

> **NOTE**
>
> The reason for the vagueness about signal names is that they vary from one version of
> UNIX to another. You'll have to use `kill -1` to find out which names pertain specifically to
> your system.

For *job*, provide one or more Process ID numbers or job references. Job references begin with
`%`. You must provide at least one *job* argument with the `kill` command.

Suppose that you have started an `xclock` process, displaying a clock on your X terminal screen:

```
$ xclock -bg LightGreen&
[4] + Running    xclock -bg LightGreen&
```

You can cancel the `xclock` window (a background job) with either of the following commands:

```
$ kill %4
```

or

```
$ kill %xclock
```

Suspending the Shell Until a Job Finishes

Use `wait` to suspend the shell until the specified job, if any, finishes. The visible effect of `wait`
is simply to cause the shell not to issue another prompt to you. To get the prompt back if you
decide not to wait, simply press Enter. This causes the shell to issue a prompt, and it terminates the `wait` command. The syntax of the `wait` command follows:

```
wait [ job ... ]
```

For *job*, specify one or more Process ID numbers or job references that designate the job or
jobs for which you want to wait. If you specify no jobs, the shell waits until any job finishes. If
you specify two or more jobs, the shell waits until all the specified jobs finish.

You won't use the `wait` command too often, but it is convenient when you have done all the
interactive work you have and need the results of one or more background jobs before you
continue. Without the `wait` command, you would have to execute the `jobs` command repeatedly until the job or jobs you want were marked `Done`.

One situation in which the `wait` command is useful is when developing some formatted text
files. You might want to run `nroff` or `troff` as background jobs, capturing the output to a disk
file for review. While the `nroff` or `troff` job is running, you can edit other text files. When you
have no other editing work to do, you'll need to wait for `nroff` or `troff` to finish, because you
have nothing else to do but review your previous work. A hypothetical console session might
look like Listing 11.5.

Listing 11.5. A console session.

```
$ vi chap1.nr
$ nroff -me chap1.nr >chap1.nrf &
[4] + Running     nroff -me chap1.nr
$ vi chap2.nr
$ nroff -me chap2.nr > chap2.nrf &
[5]   Running     nroff -me chap2.nr
$ jobs
[4]   Running     nroff -me chap1.nr
[5]   Running     nroff -me chap2.nr
$ wait
```

In this listing, you overlapped the editing of chap2.nr with the formatted printing of chap1.nr. After finishing the edit of chap2.nr, you see by running the jobs command that both nroff jobs still are running. Because you have no more editing tasks to perform, you can use the wait command to wait until one of the two background jobs finishes. The shell will not issue another prompt until one of the two jobs is done. Then you'll receive a Done message:

```
$ wait
[5]   Done        nroff -me chap2.nr
$
```

Another useful application of wait is managing X sessions. When you log on and use X, one of two files is processed: .xinitrc or .xsession. The file processed depends on the method you used to run X. When I connect, my .xsession file gets processed. When .xsession terminates, my X session is finished and I get logged out. An extract from my .xsession looks like this:

```
ctwm &
WINM=$!
xv -quit -root etc/pics/space.gif &
xterm -sb -sl 2000 -ls -title "Xterm 1" -geometry 80x24+0+86 &
xterm -sb -sl 2000 -ls -title "Xterm 2" -geometry 80x24+523+430 &
wait $WINM
```

This code uses two features of the Korn shell. First, I use $! to get the Process ID of the Window Manager I run, ctwm, and assign it to the variable WINM. I then start two xterms and set the desktop background by using xv. Then I issue a wait command that waits for the process $WINM to finish. In this case, WINM is the Process ID of the Window Manager, so, in other words, after my Window Manager shuts down, my .xsession is terminated and I get logged out.

Moving Background Jobs into the Foreground

Use fg to move background jobs into the foreground. Foreground execution implies interactive processing with the terminal. Therefore, using fg to bring more than one job into the foreground establishes a race condition; the first job to get your terminal wins, and the others revert to Stopped status in the background. The syntax for fg follows:

```
fg [ job ... ]
```

For *job*, specify one or more Process ID numbers or job references. If you omit *job*, the current background process is brought into the foreground. The *current job* is the job you most recently stopped or started.

The need to use the fg command often arises as a result of actions you take yourself. Suppose that you are editing a text file with vi and, when trying to save the file and quit, you discover that you do not have Write permission for the file. You can't save the file until you correct the condition, but you're currently stuck inside the editor. What do you do?

First, stop the vi editor session by pressing Ctrl+Z. You'll immediately get the following console output:

```
[1]    Stopped      vi chap2.nr
$
```

Now, determine the cause of the problem and correct it. For the sake of brevity, assume that the problem is nothing more than that you've tried to edit a file you've write-protected:

```
$ ls -l chap2.nr
-r-r-r-   1 barbara    user     21506 May 5 10:52
$ chmod u+w chap2.nr
$ ls -l chap2.nr
-rw-r-r-  1 barbara    user     21506 May 5 10:52
```

Finally, use the fg command to bring the vi edit session, currently stopped in the background, back into execution:

```
$ fg %vi
```

You might need to type Ctrl+L (a vi editor command) to redraw the screen.

Moving Foreground Jobs into the Background

Use the bg command to place jobs currently in the Stopped status (as indicated by the jobs command) into the background and to resume execution. Note that a job immediately switches back to the Stopped state if it requires terminal input. The syntax for bg follows:

```
bg [ job ... ]
```

For *job*, specify one or more Process ID numbers or job references. A job reference begins with %. If you omit *job*, the command refers to the current job, which is the job you most recently started or stopped.

In actual practice, you don't use the bg command to move a foreground job into the background, because there's no way to do so; the shell is not listening to your terminal while a foreground job is running. To get the shell's attention while a foreground command is running, you need to use Ctrl+Z to stop (suspend) the foreground job.

After you stop the job and have a shell prompt, you need to decide what to do with the job you stopped. You can perform other tasks and restart the stopped job with the fg command when finished, as described earlier. But if the job you stopped is not interactive (if it can run without constant input from you), you can tell the shell to restart the job but leave it in the background.

Suppose that you start a long-running format of a text file using the `troff` command:

```
$ troff -me chap1.nr > chap1.trf
```

If, after waiting a few minutes for the job to finish, you find that you want to do something else instead of just sitting there, you can use the following sequence to switch the `troff` command to background execution:

```
[ctrl-z]
$ bg
$
```

By default, the shell assumes that you mean the job you last stopped. Now that the `troff` command is running in the background, you can do other work.

The net result of these actions is the same as if you had started the `troff` job in the background to begin with:

```
$ troff -me chap1.nr > chap1.trf &
```

Summary

This chapter presented the features of the Korn shell. Because the Korn shell has many features in common with the Bourne shell, only the features special to the Korn shell were discussed here.

The Korn shell is one of several shells available to you on most contemporary versions of the UNIX operating system. It is a newer, enhanced version of the original Bourne shell, with command history, command editing, command aliases, and job control to improve your keyboard productivity. The Korn shell also offers a number of improvements for the shell-script writer, including arithmetic variables and arithmetic expressions, array variables, a `select` statement for prompting the user with menus, and a coprocess mechanism for interactively executing other UNIX commands from within a shell script.

The initial impetus for construction of the Korn shell was to bring many of the enhancements in `csh` to users in a format consistent with the Bourne shell syntax and behavior. The C shell (`csh`) was implemented by the Berkeley group and initially was offered only in the BSD variant of UNIX. The Korn shell ported its extensions, with many additional improvements, into the System V environment. Many people feel that the Korn shell is a successor to both the Bourne and C shells. It is now the shell of choice for use at the keyboard and for writing shell scripts.

The command-history feature enables you to capture in a disk file each command as you execute it. The file is preserved across logons so that you have some of the context of your previous session when you next log on. You can use the command-history file for reference or for reexecuting commands. When you reexecute a command, you can use it as it was written originally, or you can modify it before execution. The `fc` command and the `history` and `r` aliases provide the user interface to the command-history file.

The command-editing feature provides two text editor styles for editing commands as you write them. You must explicitly enable command editing to use it. By default, the Korn shell manages the command line in the same way as the Bourne shell. The vi Edit mode implements most of the vi input and command modes, and it enables you to access and reuse commands stored in the command-history file. The EMACS Edit mode is compatible with the EMACS editor commands. Most users find the vi or EMACS Command-Edit mode to be more natural than the equivalent bang (!) notation of the C shell.

The command alias feature enables you to define new command names that stand for a leading portion of the command line of existing commands. The definition of an alias can replace not only the name of an existing command but also initial options and arguments of the command line. This feature greatly reduces the amount of typing needed for frequently executed commands. It also replaces the command-tracking feature of the Bourne shell.

Extensions to wildcard file-naming patterns provide more complex expressions that you can use to narrow in on the specific files you want to reference.

Features added for the benefit of the script writer are numerous and powerful. They eliminate some of the kludges you used to have to deal with when writing new commands.

The typeset command provides a host of new features surrounding the use of shell variables. Array variables with the form ${name[n]} permit the convenient processing of lists. Integer variables defined with typeset, the let command, and the (( )) expression notation enable you to perform basic numeric calculations without having to leave the shell environment. You no longer have to resort to command substitution for the expr or bc command.

An improved syntax for command substitution makes even this chore more palatable. The syntax $(...) for command replacement reduces the need for quoting substrings inside backquoted expressions. You even can nest them, which permits expressions such as $(...$(...)...) on the command line.

Coprocessing, a new feature of the shell, enables you to read and write from background commands, using them in an interactive fashion. You can respond to error messages produced by the invoked command, and you can provide a programmed response. You launch a coprocess with the |& operator, using it in place of the & symbol. Once launched, a coprocess runs in parallel with your shell's process. To write to the command, use print -p. To read its output, use read -p. You can reassign the input and output pipes by using the exec *fd*>&p and exec *fd*<&p special commands. Now the script writer can do things previously possible only in the C programming language.

Another boon is the Privileged shell mode. You can set the Set User ID and Set Group ID flags on your shell scripts. You can use the set -o privileged or set -p option to toggle between the user's real User ID and the effective User ID. Use this feature to write special system services—for example, a tape library management system, a device-allocation facility, or a file-sharing system. Remember to exercise caution, though: Badly written scripts can give a potential attacker a door to a more privileged user.

Last but not least, the Korn shell provides a way of getting around the problem of not being able to export aliases and functions. By using the ENV exported variable, you can define a miniprofile to be executed at each invocation of the shell. You no longer have to switch to the shell from vi, pg, or sdb only to find a bare-bones environment without your favorite aliases and functions.

All in all, the Korn shell seems to be just about the final word in command-line environments. Now your main concern will be whether compatibility constraints enable you to use the Korn shell for script writing. Although the Korn shell can execute Bourne shell scripts, the Bourne shell can't execute Korn shell scripts, and only the C shell can execute C shell scripts. At least you're free to use the Korn shell for your keyboard environment, which is a step up for sure!

The C Shell

by John Valley and Sean Drew

IN THIS CHAPTER

CHAPTER 12

As a UNIX user, you have a wide variety of shells available to you: the Bourne shell, Bourne Again shell, POSIX shell, C shell, TC shell, Z shell, and Korn shell. Although this is not an all encompassing list of available shells, it does cover the more commonly used shells. Most UNIX systems come pre-installed with some subset of the shells mentioned. If you wish to use a shell that was not pre-installed on your system, you will more than likely find the one you want on the Internet. The C shell—the subject of this chapter—is one of the more popular and widely available shells in UNIX. It was developed after the Bourne shell but before the Korn shell. The C shell incorporates many features of the Bourne shell and adds many new ones that make your UNIX sessions more efficient and convenient.

Each shell has certain advantages and disadvantages. You might want to review Chapter 13, "Shell Comparison," to help you decide which one to use.

The C shell, written by Bill Joy (also the author of the vi text editor), was not patterned after the Bourne shell. Bill chose the C programming language as a syntax model. The C shell commands—especially if, while, and the other structured programming statements—are somewhat similar in syntax to the equivalent statements in C. A shell is quite a different animal from a compiler, though, so the C programming language served only as a model; many forms and structures in the C shell have nothing to do with the C programming language.

Because the C shell is not just an extension of the Bourne shell syntax, this chapter will cover all aspects of C shell operation. You therefore can read it independently of Chapter 9, "The Bourne Shell," Chapter 10, "The Bourne Again Shell," and Chapter 11, "The Korn Shell."

Invoking the C Shell

Each time you log on to UNIX, you're placed in an interactive shell referred to as your *logon shell*. If your logon shell is using the default prompts, you can tell if your logon shell is the C shell by its command-line prompt: the percent sign (%). The default C shell prompt differs from the default dollar-sign prompt ($) of the Bourne shell to remind you that you're using the C shell. You can customize your command-line prompt when using the C shell; for more information, see the definition of *prompt* in "Variables," later in this chapter.

The most foolproof way to determine your logon shell is to query the passwd file. The seventh field contains the path to your logon shell. The command

```
grep `whoami` /etc/passwd |cut -f7 -d:
```

will print the path of your logon shell. If you are using Network Information Service (NIS) to manage user information, the /etc/passwd file is not accessible, so the command

```
ypcat passwd |grep `whoami` |cut -f7 -d:
```

will do the trick.

If your logon shell is not the C shell, and the C shell is available on your system, you can invoke it as an interactive shell from the command-line. Even when you're already running the

C shell, there will be times when you want to launch the C shell again—for example, to run a shell script or to temporarily change the shell's options. To invoke the C shell interactively, use this command:

```
$ csh
%
```

> **NOTE**
>
> The `csh` command usually is located in the `/bin` or `/usr/bin` directory. Because both directories are usually in your search path, you shouldn't have any trouble finding the `csh` command if your system has it. If you don't find it right away, you might look in the directory `/usr/ucb` (the standard home for BSD components in a UNIX System V system) or in `/usr/local/bin`. `/usr/local/bin` is a home for programs your site has acquired that were not provided with the original system software. Remember that, for many years, the C shell was available only to those sites using the BSD variant of UNIX; unlike the Bourne shell, there is no guarantee that you will have the `csh` command on your system.

The `csh` command also supports a number of options and arguments (described later in this chapter in "Shell Options"), but most options are not relevant to running an interactive shell.

Whenever csh is invoked, whether as the logon shell or as a subshell, it loads and executes a profile script named `.cshrc`. If it is a logon shell, the C shell also executes a profile script on startup named `.login` and another on exit named `.logout`. Note that the `.login` script is executed after `.cshrc`—not before. For additional information about C shell profile scripts, see "Customizing Your Shell Environment," later in this chapter.

Most versions of the C shell import environment variables such as *PATH* into local array variables at startup. The C shell does not refer to the public environment variables (including *PATH*) for its own operation. This means that you'll usually want to maintain the *path* variable for directory searches—not *PATH*. Some versions of the C shell do not properly import environment variables, which can give you confusing results. If it appears that you have no search path set, but the *PATH* variable is set and accurate (as shown by echo $*PATH*), check that the variable *path* has a matching value. If not, you'll need to import critical environment variables into local variables yourself.

> **NOTE**
>
> If you are familiar with the Bourne shell, you won't notice much difference when working with the C shell unless you use advanced shell features such as variables, command replacement, and so on.
>
> *continues*

continued

Important differences do exist, however. Among these are the set of punctuation characters that have a special meaning to the shell (often called *metacharacters*). The C shell is sensitive to all the special characters of the Bourne shell, as well as the tilde (~), the commercial at sign (@), and the exclamation point (!). Don't forget to quote or escape these characters when writing commands unless you intend to use their special shell meaning. (See "Quoting or Escaping from Special Characters," later in this chapter, for a discussion of the details.)

Shell Basics

When you enter commands at the shell prompt, you are providing input to the shell. The shell sees a line of input as a string of characters terminated with a newline character; the newline is usually the result of pressing Enter on your keyboard. Input to the C shell can be anything from a single, simple command to multiple commands joined with command operators. Each command line you enter is actually a shell statement. In addition to providing input to the shell manually by entering shell statements on the command line, you can provide input to the shell by putting shell statements into a file and executing the file. Files of shell statements commonly are known as *shell scripts*.

This section covers the basics of interacting with the shell by entering shell statements on the command line. (Of course, anything you can enter on the command line also can be put into a file for later, "canned" execution.) The subsection "Shell Statements: A Closer Look" provides a more detailed, technical look at the components of shell statements. If you plan to write shell scripts, you'll definitely want to read this section.

When you finish this section, you will feel like you know a good deal about the C shell, but this is really just the beginning. In addition to the C shell's basic service of providing a means to instruct the computer, the C shell also provides a number of tools you can use to expedite your work flow. These tools or features of the shell are described in subsequent sections of this chapter.

Executing Commands: The Basics

The C shell accepts several types of commands as input: UNIX commands, built-in shell commands, user-written commands, and command aliases. This section describes the types of commands you can execute and the ways you can execute them.

Command Names as Shell Input

A command is executed by entering the command's name on the command-line. The C shell supports any of the following as command names:

- **Built-in C shell command.** The shell provides a number of commands implemented within the shell program. When you invoke a built-in command, it therefore executes very quickly because no program files need to be loaded. A built-in command is always invoked by a simple name—never by a pathname (for example, never by /usr/ bin/command).

    Because the shell first checks a command name for built-in commands before searching for a file of the same name, you cannot redefine a built-in command with a shell script. You can use aliases, however, to redirect a built-in command to a shell script. The next subsection, "Built-In Shell Commands," briefly describes each built-in command. Detailed descriptions of built-in commands with examples are presented in the task-oriented sections of this chapter.

- **Filename.** You can specify the filename (% *filename*), a relative pathname (% ../ *filename*), or an absolute pathname (% /**bin**/*filename*) of a file as a command. The file must be marked as executable and must be a binary load file or a shell script in the C shell language. Additionally, if pathnames are not used, the file must exist in one of the directories listed in your path shell variable. The C shell cannot process shell scripts written for the other shells unless your UNIX variant supports the #! notation for specifying the correct command processor. (See "Shell Programming," later in this chapter, for notes about using shell scripts with the C shell.)

    All UNIX commands are provided as executable files in the /bin or /usr/bin directory. A UNIX command generally is invoked by entering its filename or full pathname.

- **Command alias.** A command alias is a name you define by using the alias built-in shell command.

    An alias can have the same name as a built-in shell command or an executable file. You always can invoke an executable file that has the same name as an alias by using the file's full pathname. An alias that has the same name as a built-in command effectively hides the built-in command, however. Aliases are described in detail in "Aliases," later in this chapter.

Built-In Shell Commands

C shell provides a number of commands implemented within the shell program. Built-in commands execute very quickly, because no external program file needs to be loaded. Table 12.1 lists the built-in C shell commands. The remainder of this chapter groups these commands into subsections dedicated to particular tasks you'll perform in the shell and describes how to use each command.

Table 12.1. Built-in C shell commands.

Command	Description
alias	Defines or lists a command alias
bg	Switches a job to background execution
break	Breaks out of a loop
breaksw	Exits from a `switch` statement
case	Begins a case in `switch`
cd	Changes directory
chdir	Changes directory
continue	Begins the next loop iteration immediately
default	Specifies the default case in `switch`
dirs	Lists the directory stack
echo	Echoes arguments to standard output
eval	Rescans a line for substitutions
exec	Replaces the current process with a new process
exit	Exits from the current shell
fg	Switches a job to foreground execution
foreach	Specifies a looping control statement
glob	Echoes arguments to standard output
goto	Alters the order of command execution
hashstat	Prints hash table statistics
history	Lists the command history
if	Specifies conditional execution
jobs	Lists active jobs
kill	Signals a process
limit	Respecifies maximum resource limits
login	Invokes the system logon procedure
logout	Exits from a logon shell
newgrp	Changes your Group ID
nice	Controls background process dispatch priority
nohup	Prevents termination on logout
notify	Requests notification of background job status changes
onintr	Processes an interrupt within a shell script
popd	Returns to a previous directory

Command	Description
pushd	Changes directory with pushdown stack
rehash	Rehashes the directory search path
repeat	Executes a command repeatedly
set	Displays or changes a shell variable
setenv	Sets environment variable
shift	Shifts parameters
source	Interprets a script in the current shell
stop	Stops a background job
suspend	Stops the current shell
switch	Specifies conditional execution
time	Times a command
umask	Displays or sets the process file-creation mask
unalias	Deletes a command alias
unhash	Disables use of the hash table
unlimit	Cancels a previous `limit` command
unset	Deletes shell variables
unsetenv	Deletes environment variables
wait	Waits for background jobs to finish
while	Specifies a looping control
%job	Specifies foreground execution
@	Specifies expression evaluation

Executing Simple Commands

The most common form of input to the shell is the *simple command,* where a command name is followed by any number of arguments. In the following command line, for example, `ftp` is the command and *hostname* is the argument:

```
% ftp hostname
```

It is the responsibility of the command, not the shell, to interpret the arguments. Many commands, but certainly not all, take this form:

```
% command -options filenames
```

Although the shell does not interpret the arguments of the command, the shell does interpret some of the input line before passing the arguments to the command. Special characters entered on a command line tell the shell to redirect input and output, start a different command, search the directories for filename patterns, substitute variable data, and substitute the output of other commands.

Entering Multiple Commands on One Line

Ordinarily, the shell interprets the first word of command input as the command name and the rest of the input as arguments to that command. The semicolon (;) directs the shell to interpret the word following the symbol as a new command, with the rest of the input as arguments to the new command. For example, the command line

```
% echo "<h1>" ; getTitle; echo "</h1>"
```

is the equivalent of

```
% echo "<h1>"
% getTitle
% echo "</h1>"
```

except that, in the second case, the results of each command appear between the command input lines. When the semicolon is used to separate commands on a line, the commands are executed in sequence. The shell waits until one command is complete before executing the next command. You also can execute commands simultaneously (see "Executing Commands in the Background," later in this chapter) or execute them conditionally, which means that the shell executes the next command if the command's return status matches the condition (see "Executing Commands Conditionally," later in this chapter).

Entering Commands Too Long for One Line

Command lines can get quite lengthy. Editing and printing scripts is easier if command lines are less than 80 characters, the standard terminal width. Entering commands that span multiple lines is accomplished by escaping the newline character, as in the following command, which translates some common HTML sequences back to a readable format:

```
% sed -e "s/%3A/:/" -e "s@%2F@/@g" -e "s@%3C@<@g" \
-e 's/%5C/\\/g' -e "s/%23/#/g" -e "s/%28/(/g" \
-e "s/%29/)/g" -e "s/%27/'/g" -e 's/%22/\"/g' infile > outfile
```

The shell sees a line of input as a statement terminated with a newline character; however, the newline character also is considered to be a whitespace character. If you end a line with a backslash (\), the next character—the newline character—is treated literally, which means that the shell does not interpret the newline character as the end of the line of input.

Executing Commands in the Background

Normally, when you execute commands, they are executed in the foreground. This means that the C shell will not process any other commands, and you cannot do anything else until the command finishes executing. If waiting for long commands to complete is not in your top 10 list of things to do, you can have your current shell handle more commands without waiting for a command to finish. You can execute the command in the background by putting an ampersand (&) at the end of the command:

```
% find . -name "*.c" -print &
[2] 13802
%
```

You also can run multiple commands in the background simultaneously:

```
% xterm & xclock & xload &
```

A command executing in the background is referred to as a *job*, and each job is assigned a job number—the bracketed number in the previous example. The C shell provides you with several commands for managing background jobs; see "Job Control," later in this chapter, for more information.

Repeatedly Executing a Command: repeat

You can use the repeat command to execute some other command a specified number of times. Although the repeat command isn't used frequently, it can be quite handy on occasion. If you are writing a shell script to print a document, for example, you might use the command

```
repeat 5 echo ###############################
```

to mark its first page clearly as the start of the document.

The syntax of the repeat command follows:

```
repeat count command
```

For *count*, specify a decimal integer number. A *count* of zero is valid and suppresses execution of the command.

For *command*, specify a simple command that is subject to the same restrictions as the first format of the if statement. The *command* is scanned for variable, command, and history substitutions; filename patterns; and quoting. It can't be a compound command (foo;bar), a pipeline (foo¦bar), a statement group (using {}), or a parenthesized command list ((foo;bar¦bas)).

Any I/O redirections are performed only once, regardless of the value of *count*. For example,

```
repeat 10 echo Hello >hello.list
```

results in 10 lines of Hello in a file named hello.list.

Executing Commands in a Subshell: ( )

A command (or a list of commands separated by semicolons) enclosed in parentheses groups the command or commands for execution in a subshell. A *subshell* is a secondary invocation of the shell, so any change to shell variables, the current directory, or other such process information lasts only while executing the commands in the subshell. This is a handy way, for example, to switch to another directory, execute a command or two, and then switch back without having to restore your current directory:

```
% (cd /usr/local/etc/httpd/htdocs; cp *.html /users/dylan/docs)
```

Without the parentheses, you would have to write this:

```
% cd /usr/local/etc/httpd/htdocs
% cp *.html /users/dylan/docs
% cd /previous/directory
```

The syntax for grouping commands follows:

```
( commands )
```

Enclosing a list of commands in parentheses is a way to override the default precedence rules for the &&, ¦¦, and ¦ operators, at the expense of invoking a subshell and losing any environmental effects of the commands' execution. For example, (grep ¦¦ echo) ¦ pr pipes the output of the grep command, and possibly that of echo if grep sets a nonzero exit code, to the pr command.

I/O redirections can be appended to the subshell just as for a simple command; the redirections are in effect for all the commands within the subshell. For example,

```
(cat; echo; date) > out
```

writes the output of the cat, echo, and date commands to a file named out without any breaks. If you look at the file afterward, first you'll see the lines written by cat, followed by the lines written by echo, and finally the lines written by date. Similarly, input redirections apply to all commands in the subshell, so that each command in turn reads lines from the redirected file, starting with the line following those read by any previously executed commands in the subshell.

Executing Commands Conditionally

Compound commands are actually two or more commands combined so that the shell executes all of them before prompting for (or, in the case of shell scripts, reading) more input.

Compound commands are not often needed for interactive work. Compound commands form a very useful extension to the C shell's syntax, however, especially in shell scripts. Some compound command formats, such as & (background job) and ¦ (the pipe operator) are essential to work effectively with UNIX.

Conditional Execution on Success: && (And)

You use the double ampersand operator (read *and*) to join two commands: command1 && command2. It causes the shell to execute command2 only if command1 is successful (that is, command1 has an exit code of zero).

For command1 or command2, you can write a simple command or a compound command. The && operator has higher precedence than ¦¦ but lower precedence than ¦. For example,

```
grep mailto *.html ¦ pr && echo OK
```

echoes OK only if the pipeline grep ¦ pr sets a zero exit code. (For pipelines, the exit code is the exit code of the last command in the pipeline.)

The compound command

```
tar cvf docs.tar docs && rm -rf docs
```

shows one possible benefit of using &&: The rm command deletes the docs directory only if it first is backed up successfully in a tar file.

Conditional Execution on Failure: ¦¦ (Or)

You use the or operator to join two commands: *command1* ¦¦ *command2*. It causes the shell to execute *command2* only if *command1* failed (that is, returned a nonzero exit code).

For *command1* or *command2*, you can write a simple command or a compound command. The ¦¦ operator has lower precedence than both the && and ¦ operators. For example, in the following command

```
grep mailto *.html ¦¦ echo No mailto found ¦ pr
```

either grep succeeds and its output is placed to standard output, or the words No mailto found are piped to the pr command.

Use the ¦¦ operator to provide an alternative action. In the following case, if the mkdir command fails, the exit command prevents further execution of the shell script:

```
mkdir $tmpfile ¦¦ exit
```

Shell Statements: A Closer Look

A *command* is a basic command or a basic command embellished with one or more I/O redirections.

A *basic command* is a series of words, each subject to replacements by the C shell, which, when fully resolved, specifies an action to be executed and provides zero or more options and arguments to modify or control the action taken. The first word of a basic command, sometimes called the *command name*, must specify the required action.

In plainer terms, a *statement* is the smallest executable unit. When the shell is operating in interactive mode, it displays its prompt when it requires a statement. You must continue to enter shell statement components, using multiple lines if necessary, until you complete a full statement. If the statement is not completed on one line, the shell continues to prompt you, without executing the line or lines you have entered, until it receives a full statement.

Shell statements are formed from a number of tokens. A *token* is a basic syntactic element and can be any of the following:

- **Comments.** A comment begins with any word having a pound sign (#) as its first character and extends to the end of the line. This interpretation can be avoided by enclosing the pound sign (or the entire word) in quotes. (See "Quoting or Escaping from Special Characters," later in this chapter.) The # is considered a comment for non-interactive C shell sessions only.

■ **White space.** White space consists of blanks and tabs and sometimes the newline character. White space is used to separate other tokens which, if run together, would lose their separate identity. Units of text separated by white space are generically called *words.*

■ **Statement delimiters.** Statement delimiters include the semicolon (;) and the newline character (generated when you press Return). You can use the semicolon to place commands together on the same line. The shell treats the commands as if they had been entered on separate lines.

Normally, every command or shell statement ends at the end of the line. The Return (or Enter) key you press to end the line generates a character distinct from printable characters, blanks, and tabs, which the shell sees as a newline character. Some statements require more than one line of input, such as the `if` and `while` commands. The syntax description for these commands shows how they should be split over lines; the line boundaries must be observed, and you must end each line at the indicated place, or you will get a syntax error.

■ **Operators.** An operator is a special character, or a combination of special characters, to which the shell attaches special syntactic significance. Operators shown as a combination of special characters must be written without white space between them, or they will be seen as two single operators instead of a two-character operator. For example, the increment operator ++ cannot be written as + +.

Punctuation characters that have special significance to the shell must be enclosed in quotes to avoid their special interpretation. For example, the command `grep '(' *.cc` uses quotes to hide the right parenthesis from the shell so that the right parenthesis can be passed to `grep` as an argument. See "Quoting or Escaping from Special Characters," later in this chapter, for details about using quotes.

■ **Words.** A word is any consecutive sequence of characters occurring between white space, statement delimiters, or operators. A word can be a single group of ordinary characters, a quoted string, a variable reference, a command substitution, a history substitution, or a filename pattern; it also can be any combination of these elements. The final form of the word is the result of all substitutions and replacements, together with all ordinary characters, run together to form a single string. The string then is used as the command name or command argument during command execution.

Filename Substitutions (Globbing)

Filename generation using patterns is an important facility of the Bourne shell. The C shell supports the filename patterns of the Bourne shell and adds the use of {} (braces) to allow greater flexibility. *Globbing* also is known as *wildcarding.*

Several shell commands and contexts allow the use of pattern-matching strings, such as the `case` statement of `switch` and the `=~` and `!~` expression operators. In these cases, pattern strings are formed using the same rules as for filename generation, except that the patterns are matched to another string.

When any of the pattern expressions described in Table 12.2 are used as arguments of a command, the entire pattern string is replaced with the filenames or pathnames that match the pattern. By default, the shell searches the current directory for matching filenames, but if the pattern string contains slashes (/), it searches the specified directory or directories instead. Note that several directories can be searched for matching files in a single pattern string; a pattern of the form `dir/*/*.cc` searches all the directories contained in `dir` for files ending with `.cc`.

Table 12.2. Pattern expressions.

Expression	Definition
*	The asterisk, also known as a *star* or *splat*, matches any string of characters, including a null string (the asterisk matches zero or more characters). When the asterisk is used by itself, it matches all filenames. When the asterisk is used at the beginning of a pattern string, leading prefixes of the filename pattern are ignored: `*.cc` matches any filename ending with `.cc`. When the asterisk is used at the end of a pattern string, trailing suffixes of the filename pattern are ignored: `foo*` matches `foo.cc`, `foobar.html`, and any filename beginning with `foo`. An asterisk in the middle of a pattern means that matching filenames must begin and end as shown but can contain any character sequences in the middle: `pay*.cc` matches filenames beginning with `pay` and ending with `.cc`, such as `payroll.cc`, `paymast.cc`, and `paycheck.cc`. Multiple asterisks can be used in a pattern: `*s*` matches any filename containing an s, such as `sean.txt` or `apps.hh`.
?	The question mark matches any one character. For example, `?` as a complete word matches all filenames one character long in the current directory. The pattern `pay?.cc` matches `pay1.cc` and `pay2.cc` but not `payroll.cc`. Multiple question marks can be used to indicate a specific number of don't-care positions in the filename: `pay.??` matches filenames beginning with `pay.` and ending in any two characters, such as `pay.cc` and `pay.hh`, but does not match `pay.o`.
[]	The square brackets enclose a list of characters. Matching filenames contain one of the indicated characters in the corresponding position of the filename. For example, `[abc]*` matches any filename beginning with the letter a, b, or c. Because of the asterisk, the first character can be followed by any sequence of characters.

continues

Table 12.2. continued

Expression	Definition
-	Use a hyphen (-) to indicate a range of characters. For example, pay[1-3].cc matches filenames pay1.cc, pay2.cc, and pay3.cc, but not pay4.cc or pay11.cc. Multiple ranges can be used in a single bracketed list. For example, [A-Za-z0-9]* matches any filename beginning with a letter or a digit. To match a hyphen, list the hyphen at the beginning or end of the character list: [-abc] or [abc-] matches an a, b, c, or hyphen.
~	The tilde (~) can be used at the beginning of a word to invoke directory substitution of your home directory. The (~) is substituted with the full pathname of your home directory. Also used in the form ~/*path* to refer to a file or directory under your home directory. If the tilde does not appear by itself as a word and is not followed by a letter or a slash, or it appears in any position other than the first, it is not replaced with the user's home directory. Thus, /usr/rothse/file.cc~ is a reference to the file file.cc~ in the directory /usr/rothse.
~*name*	Substituted with the full pathname of user *name*'s home directory. For example, ~ken/bin refers to /usr/ken/bin if the home directory for user Ken is /usr/ken. The password file /etc/passwd is searched for *name* to determine the directory pathname; if *name* is not found, the shell generates an error message and stops.
{}	Braces enclose a list of patterns separated by commas. The brace expression matches filenames having any one of the listed patterns in the corresponding position of the name. For example, the pattern /usr/home/{kookla,fran,ollie}/.cshrc expands to the path list /usr/home/kookla/.cshrc /usr/home/fran/.cshrc /usr/ home/ollie/.cshrc Unlike *, ?, and [], brace-enclosed lists are not matched against existing filenames; they simply are expanded into words subject to further substitution, regardless of whether the corresponding files exist. Brace-enclosed lists can be nested—for example, /usr/{bin,lib,home/{john,bill}} refers to any of the directories /usr/bin, /usr/lib, /usr/home/john, and /usr/home/bill.

It is important to realize that filename generation using pattern strings can cause a replacement of one word with many. A filename pattern must be a single word. The ordinary characters and pattern-matching characters in the word describe a rule for choosing filenames from the current or specified directory. The word is replaced with each filename or pathname found that matches the pattern. If you had three files in your current directory (ch1.txt, ch2.txt, and chlast.txt), then the pattern *.txt would expand to match those three files:

```
% echo Files: *.txt
Files: ch1.txt ch2.txt chlast.txt
```

You can use pattern expansion in many ways; for example, the expansion below is used to set a shell variable to be an array of three items. The array is then queried for its length and second element. See "Using Array Variables," later in this chapter, for more information about C shell arrays.

```
% set files=(*.txt)
% echo Found $#files files
Found 3 files
% echo $files[2]
ch2.txt
```

TIP

Another powerful C shell feature for determining files in a directory is the command/ filename viewing feature that uses control D (Ctrl-D). This feature enables you to determine the files available for a command without aborting the command. For example, if you type cp ~sdrew/docs/ind and want to see which files match the specification, pressing Ctrl-D displays a list of matching files in a multicolumn format. Certain files have a character appended to indicate the file type (this behavior is similar to the output of ls -F): Executables are marked with an asterisk (*), directories are marked with a slash (/), and links are marked with an at sign (@). After the column-sorted list is displayed, the command is redisplayed so that you can continue typing. The files listed will be those that match the pattern ~sdrew/docs/ind*. Note that ~(Ctrl-D) prints a list of all users who have accounts on the system.

Commands can be completed in a similar manner if the C shell is expecting a command as part of your current input. The current command pattern is sought in each directory specified in the *PATH* environment variable. Note that aliases are not expanded by Ctrl-D. If my *PATH* is set to /bin:~/bin:/usr/bin and I complete the command pri using Ctrl-D, the output is roughly the same as ls /bin/pri* ~/bin/pri* /usr/bin/pri*.

In addition to getting lists of commands and filenames, the Escape (ESC) key can be used to complete partially typed commands and filenames. The automatic completions are known as command completion and filename completion, depending on whether you are completing a filename or a command. The pattern matching is done as in the Ctrl-D viewing utility. If the partial name is unique, the name is completed; otherwise, the terminal

continues

continued

bell is sounded. If ambiguities are encountered (that is, more than one file matches), the name is completed to the ambiguity, and the terminal bell is sounded. Suppose you had two files in a directory named `veryLongName.txt` and `veryLong_Name.txt` and you wanted to edit the file `veryLong_Name.txt`. You can save yourself a great deal of typing by using filename completion. You can type `vi ve(Esc)`, which completes to `vi veryLong` and rings the bell. Then, if you type `_(Esc)`, the name completes to `vi veryLong_Name.txt`, at which point you can press Enter and begin your `vi` session.

Redirecting Input and Output

The C shell provides several commands for redirecting the input and output of commands. You might be familiar with the input (<) or output (>) redirection characters from earlier chapters. The C shell provides you with these and more.

An *I/O redirection* is an instruction to the shell you append to a command. It causes one of the standard file descriptors to be assigned to a specific file. You might have encountered standard files in the discussion of the Bourne shell in Chapter 9. The UNIX operating system defines three standard file descriptors: *standard input* (stdin), *standard output* (stdout), and *standard error* (stderr).

NOTE

The UNIX operating system actually provides at least 25 file descriptors for use by a command. It is only by convention that the first three are set aside for reading input, writing output, and printing error messages. Unless you instruct otherwise, the shell always opens these three file descriptors before executing a command and assigns them all to your terminal.

A *file descriptor* is not the file itself; it is a channel, much like the audio jack on the back of your stereo—you can connect it to any audio source you want. Similarly, a file descriptor such as standard input must be connected to a file—your terminal by default, or the disk file or readable device of your choice.

You can change the location where a command reads data, writes output, and prints error messages by using one or more of the I/O redirection operators. Table 12.3 lists the operators.

Table 12.3. I/O redirection operators.

Format	Effect
	Input Redirection
`< filename`	Uses the contents of `filename` as input to a command.
`<< word`	Provides shell input lines as command input. Lines of the shell input that follow the line containing this redirection operator are read and saved by the shell in a temporary file. Reading stops when the shell finds a line beginning with *word*. The saved lines then become the input to the command. The lines read and saved are effectively deleted from the shell input and are not executed as commands; they are "eaten" by the << operator. Shell execution continues with the line following the line beginning with *word*. If you use the << operator on a command you type at the terminal, be careful: Lines you type afterward are gobbled up by the shell—not executed—until you enter a line beginning with whatever you specified as *word*. The << operator most often is used in shell scripts. This technique is known as providing a *here document*.
	Output Redirection
`> filename`	Writes command output to `filename`.
`>! filename`	Writes command output to `filename` and ignores the `noclobber` option. The `noclobber` option is fully explained in "Using Predefined Variables," later in this chapter. Briefly, `noclobber` causes the shell to disallow the `> filename` redirection when `filename` already exists; *noclobber* is therefore a safety you can use to prevent accidentally destroying an existing file. Sometimes, you will want to redirect output to a file even though it already exists. In such a case, you must use the `>!` operator to tell the shell you really want to proceed with the redirection. If you don't set the *noclobber* option, you don't need to use the `>!` operator.
`>& filename`	Writes both the command output and error messages to `filename`.
`>&! filename`	Writes both the command output and error messages to `filename` and ignores the *noclobber* option.
`>> filename`	Writes command output at the end of `filename` (Append mode).

continues

Table 12.3. continued

Format	Effect
`>>!` *filename*	Writes command output at the end of *filename* (Append mode) and ignores the *noclobber* option.
`>>&` *filename*	Writes command output and error messages at the end of *filename* (Append mode).
`>>&!` *filename*	Writes command output and error messages at the end of the *filename* (Append mode) and ignores the *noclobber* option.

In Table 12.3, *filename* represents any ordinary filename or pathname, or any filename or pathname resulting after variable substitution, command substitution, or filename generation.

I/O redirection operators are appended to a command; for example, `date >curdate` writes the current date to the file `curdate` instead of to your terminal. You also can use more than one redirection per command: Simply list them one after another at the end of the command. The order doesn't matter: for example, both `cat <infile >outfile` and `cat >outfile <infile` have the same effect.

Input Redirection

Some commands make no special use of the standard input file, such as the `date` and the `ls` system commands; others require an input file to function properly, such as the `cat` and `awk` commands. You can use the `<` redirection operator in the form *command < filename* to designate a file as the source of input for commands such as `cat` and `awk`; if you do not, these commands read data from your keyboard—sometimes useful, but usually not. If you provide an input redirection, but the command does not read data (such as `ls`), the I/O redirection still is performed by the shell; it is just ignored by the command. Note that it is an error to redirect standard input to a file that doesn't exist.

The redirection `<< word` is a special form of the input-redirection operator. Instead of taking input from a file, input to the command comes from the current shell input stream—your keyboard, if you append `<<` to a command you type in, or your shell script if you use `<<` on a command in a shell script.

For *word*, you choose an arbitrary string to delimit the lines of input. Then write the lines to be provided to the command as input immediately following the command line, and follow the last line of desired input with a line beginning with *word*. The shell reads the lines up to *word*, stores the lines in a temporary file, and sets up the temporary file as standard input for the command.

The `<< word` form of input redirection is called a *here document*, because it is located here, in line with your shell commands. Here documents are useful when you want to provide predefined data to a command, and they save you from having to create a file to hold the data.

Unlike the `filename` part of other I/O redirection operators, *word* for the here document is not scanned for variable references, command substitutions, or filename patterns; it is used as is. All the following shell input lines are checked for the presence of *word* as the only word on the line before any substitutions or replacements are performed on the line.

Normally, lines of the here document are checked for variable references and command replacements; this enables you to encode variable information in the here document. If you quote any part of *word*, however, the lines are read and passed to the command without modification. The redirection << STOP reads lines up to STOP and performs substitutions on the lines it reads, for example. The redirection << "STOP" reads lines up to the line beginning with STOP and passes the lines directly to the command, as they are, without substitutions or replacements of any kind.

The line beginning with *word* is discarded; it is not passed to the command in the here document or executed by the shell.

The following example shows the use of a here document to create an HTML form:

```
cat <<HERE
 <FORM method=post action=http://host.com/cgi-bin/addTime.sh>
 <select NAME=username>
 `./doUserQuery;./parseList.sh users_$$.txt "$userName"`
 </select>
 <input type=submit value=Submit>
 </form>
HERE
```

The line containing the word HERE will not appear in the output; it is simply a mark to let the shell know where the redirected lines end.

Output Redirection

Output redirections have the general form > *filename* and >> *filename*. The first operator creates a new file of the specified *filename*. The file is opened before command execution begins, so even if the command fails or cannot be found, or if the shell finds an error on the command line and stops, the output file still is created.

> **NOTE**
>
> For purposes of understanding shell syntax, you should note that appending an I/O redirection to a simple command yields a simple command. Except where specifically prohibited, a command with redirections appended can be used wherever a simple command is allowed, such as on the single-line `if` statement.

If you've set the `noclobber` option (with set `noclobber`), the shell refuses to create the named output file if it already exists; doing so would destroy the file's current contents. If you want to perform the output redirection even if the file `filename` already exists, use the redirection operator >! instead; it overrides the `noclobber` option.

The >> command arranges for command output to be added to the end of the named file. For this redirection operator, the *noclobber* option requires that the named file already exist. If you use the alternative form >>! or if you use >> and the *noclobber* option is not set, the shell creates the named file if necessary.

The >& and >>& operators redirect both the standard output and standard error files to *filename*. The Bourne shell enables you to redirect the standard output and standard error files separately; the C shell does not.

TIP

Although the C shell offers no direct means for redirecting standard error and standard output at the same time, you can achieve the net result at the expense of a subshell. In the subshell, redirect standard output via the > operator to the desired location for non-error messages and then redirect standard error and standard output from the subshell via the >& operator to the desired location for error messages. Because the standard output was redirected in the subshell, the standard output and standard error redirection from the subshell will contain only the standard error.

Suppose that you want to run a script, buildSystem, that builds a large software class library and generates nearly 1MB of output, of which a few messages might be errors. The following command places standard output in a file named build.log and error messages from standard error in buildErr.log:

```
% (buildSystem -version 5.1 > build.log) >& buildErr.log
```

Quoting or Escaping from Special Characters

As you saw in previous sections, certain characters have special meanings for the shell. When the shell encounters a special character, the shell performs the action defined by the special character. The following punctuation characters available on the standard keyboard are special to the shell and disrupt the scanning of ordinary words:

```
~  '  !  @  #  $  %  ^  &  *  (  )  \  ¦  {  }  [  ]  ;  '  "  <  >  ?
```

In some contexts, particularly within the switch statement, the colon (:) is also a special character. The colon is recognized as a special character only when expected, in a case or default statement, and as a statement label. It does not need to be quoted except to avoid these specific interpretations.

To use one of these characters as a part of a word without its special significance, you can escape the character by placing a backslash (\) immediately in front of the character. Note that a backslash intended as an ordinary character must be written as two backslashes in succession: \\. To escape a two-character operator such as >>, you must insert a backslash in front of each character: \>\>. The $ character can be escaped if followed by white space:

```
% echo escaped $ sign
escaped $ sign
```

Alternatively, you can enclose the special character or any portion of a word containing the special character in quotes. The C shell recognizes three kinds of quotes: the apostrophe ('), the quote ("), and the backquote (`). The C shell does not consider the enclosing quotes as part of the input passed to commands. The output for

```
% echo "Enter name>"
Enter name>
```

does not contain quotes. Use two apostrophes (also called *single quotes, foreticks,* or just simply *ticks*) to enclose a character sequence and avoid all interpretation by the shell. I often call a string enclosed in apostrophes a *hard-quoted string,* because the shell performs absolutely no substitution, replacement, or special interpretation of characters that appear between the apostrophes (except for history substitutions). Even the backslash character is treated as an ordinary character, so there are no escapes (except for \ newline and \!) within an apostrophe-enclosed string. As a result, you cannot embed an apostrophe in such a string. That is, the string 'who's there' causes a shell error; the C shell interprets the string as who concatenated with an s, followed by a white-space delimiter, followed by there, and then the starting apostrophe of another string. When the shell does not find the matching apostrophe, an error is generated:

```
Unmatched '.
```

One of the uses of quoted strings is to specify a single word containing blanks, tabs, and newline characters. The following code, for example, shows the use of a single echo command to print two lines of output:

```
% echo -n 'Hello.\
Please enter your name: '
Hello.
Please enter your name:
```

The double apostrophe or quote (") also provides a special bracket for character strings. The quote hides most special characters from the shell's observation. Quoted strings are subject to two kinds of scan and replacement: variable references and command substitutions.

Any of the reference forms for shell variables ($1, $name, ${name}, $name[index], $*, and others) are recognized inside quoted strings and are replaced with the corresponding string value. The replacement occurs inside the quoted string, leaving its unity as a single word intact (even if the substituted value includes blanks, tabs, or newline characters).

Command substitution occurs for strings enclosed in backquotes (`). The entire string enclosed between matching backquotes (also known as *backticks*) is extracted and executed by the current shell as if it were an independent command. The command can be two or more commands separated by semicolons, a pipeline, or any form of compound statement. Any data written to standard output by the command is captured by the shell and becomes the string value of the backquoted command. The string value is parsed into words, and the series of words replaces the entire backquoted string. Using backquotes to perform command substitution can be thought of as an I/O redirection to the command line.

> ## TIP
>
> Although command substitution is a powerful feature of the C shell, it does have limitations. Some commands generate more output than a command line can hold, for example. (Command-line length is determined by the LINE_MAX and ARG_MAX system parameters; consult your *limits* man page or look over /usr/include/limits.h.) Additionally, at times, you will need to process each item of output individually, in which case command substitution is not of much use.
>
> Suppose that you want to find all your C++ source files (*.{hh,cc}), starting from your home directory down your entire directory tree, and search the files found for the use of a certain class (RWString). The command
>
> ```
> % grep RWString `find $home -name "*.[ch][ch]" -print -follow`
> ```
>
> generates the message /bin/grep: Arg list too long on my system. The UNIX command xargs was tailor-made to solve this problem. The general use of xargs follows:
>
> ```
> xargs [options] [command]
> ```
>
> xargs reads from the standard input and places that input on the command line of *command*. As many arguments as possible are passed to *command* on its command line. As a result, the *command* executed by xargs may be called multiple times in order to use up all the input read from standard input. Transforming the preceding command to use xargs results in this command:
>
> ```
> % find $home -name "*.[ch][ch]" -print -follow ¦ xargs grep RWString
> ```
>
> This command produces the desired results. (Note that xargs is more efficient than the -exec option of find, because *command* is executed as few times as possible with as many arguments as possible. xargs -i is equivalent to the -exec option.) xargs also can be set to process each line of input individually by using the -i option, which is useful for commands that take only one argument, such as basename. When using the -i option, a replacement string—{} is the default replacement string—must be added to the *command* supplied for xargs to execute. The following command finds all directories that contain C++ source files:
>
> ```
> % find $home -name "*.[ch][ch]" -print -follow ¦ xargs -i dirname {} ¦ sort -u
> ```
>
> The xargs command has a few other nifty options and is worth a perusal of your friendly local man page.

All forms of shell substitution occur inside backquoted command strings, including variable replacement, nested command executions, history substitutions, and filename patterns.

A backquoted command string (or any number of them) can appear inside a quoted string and will have its normal effect; this is the second form of substitution performed on "-quoted strings. A quoted command substitution (echo "xxx`commands`xxx") generates new words only at the end of each line, except at the end of the last line. If the executed command prints only one line of text, the text replaces the backquoted expression without introducing any word breaks.

Both quoting forms '...' and "..." suppress filename generation. For example, note the difference in the following echo commands:

```
% echo *.cc
main.cc io.cc parse.cc math.cc
% echo "*.cc"
*.cc
```

Apostrophes can appear inside a double-quoted string. The apostrophe has no special significance when appearing inside a double-quoted string and does not need to be backslashed. The following example shows quotes inside quoted strings:

```
% echo '<input type=submit value="Return to Tracking Screen">'
<input type=submit value="Return to Tracking Screen">
% echo "Your shell: '$SHELL'"
Your shell: '/bin/csh'
```

A backslash that appears inside an apostrophe-quoted string is retained and appears in the string's value, because no substitutions occur inside an apostrophe-quoted string, as in the example below.

```
% echo 'Single \' quote
Single \ quote
```

Inside a double-quoted string or a command substitution using `, or in a normal unquoted word, a backslash has the effect of suppressing shell interpretation of the character that follows it. The backslash then is removed from the string. The following examples show the effect of a backslash removing shell interpretation of quoting characters:

```
% echo Double \" quote
Double " quote
% echo Single \' quote
Single ' quote
```

TIP

For some particularly complicated shell commands, it is necessary to get many instances of quotes and apostrophes and still have desired variable and command substitution. Simple awk commands are loaded with special shell characters, for example, and must be hard quoted:

```
ls -l | awk '{printf("\t%s\t\t%s\n", $9, $5)}')
```

If you want to turn this command into an alias, the combination of quotes seems impossible, because there are only two types of quotes and three levels of nesting. The following alias command yields incorrect results (note that the first command sets the alias, and the second command displays the alias):

```
% alias myls "ls -l | awk '{printf("\t%s\t\t%s\n", $9, $5)}'"
% alias myls
ls -l | awk '{printf(t%stt%sn, , )}'
```

continues

continued

The solution is to alternate quoting methods as needed to get the desired results. The following command alternates between using double quotes and single quotes (the portion of the command enclosed in double quotes is shown in bold, and the portion enclosed in single quotes is italicized):

```
alias myls "ls -l ¦ awk '"'{printf("\t%s\t\t%s\n", $9, $5)}'"'"
ls -l ¦ awk '{printf("\t%s\t\t%s\n", $9, $5)}'
```

Working with Directories and the Directory Stack

The C shell provides you with several built-in commands for working with directories. The cd, chdir, pushd, and popd commands all change the current working directory.

The pushd and popd commands provide a pushdown stack mechanism for changing directories, and the dirs command displays the contents of the stack. If you switch to another directory by using pushd instead of cd, the pathname of your previous directory is "saved" in the directory stack. A subsequent popd then returns you to the previous directory. Be aware that the cd command does not maintain the directory stack; you cannot use popd to return to a directory that you left using cd.

Changing Directories: cd and chdir

In the C shell, you can choose from two commands for changing your current working directory: cd and chdir. The chdir command is equivalent to cd in every way. The syntax for these commands follows:

```
cd [ pathname ]
```

```
chdir [ pathname ]
```

If you omit the *pathname* argument, the command attempts to change to the directory whose pathname is given by the value of the C shell variable home. See "Using Predefined Variables," later in this chapter, for more information about home.

If you specify a name, the cd or chdir command uses a search hierarchy to attempt to locate the referenced directory. It follows this process:

1. If *pathname* has a /, ./, or ../ as the first character, the command attempts to switch to the named directory; failure terminates the command immediately. In other words, if you use a relative or absolute pathname, the specified directory must exist and must be accessible to you; otherwise, the command fails.

2. The command searches your current directory. A partial *pathname* of the form *name1/ name2/namen* implies searching your current directory for the entire subtree.

3. If `pathname` cannot be found in your current directory, the command checks to see whether the shell variable `cdpath` exists and has a value. If it does, each of the directories named in `cdpath` is checked to see whether it contains `pathname`. If successful, the command changes to the `pathname` in that directory and prints the full pathname of the new current directory.

4. If no variable `cdpath` exists, or if `pathname` cannot be found in any of the directories listed in `cdpath`, the command checks to see whether `pathname` is a variable name and has a value with / as the first character. If so, the command changes to that directory.

5. If the name still cannot be found, the command fails.

For more information about the `cdpath` variable, see "Using Predefined Variables," later in this chapter.

The `cd` and `chdir` commands as implemented by the C shell provide a great deal of flexibility in generating shortcuts for directory names. There is nothing more painful than having to repeatedly supply long directory names to the `cd` command. The purpose of the `cd` command's search hierarchy is to provide some mechanisms you can use for shortening a reference to a directory name. The `cdpath` variable is your principal tool. If you set it to a list of directories you often reference, you can switch to one of those directories just by giving the base directory name. If `cdpath` is not sufficiently flexible to suit your needs, you can define a shell variable as an alias for a directory's full pathname, and `cd varname` switches you to that directory for the price of a few keystrokes.

NOTE

When using a shell variable as a pseudonym for a directory path, you do not need to include $ in front of the variable name. Doing so is permitted and also works because of the shell's variable substitution mechanism but is not required. Only shell variables (use the set command) work as a directory alias—not environment variables (the setenv command).

Listing the Directory Stack: `dirs`

The *directory stack* is a mechanism you can use to store and recall directories to which you have changed by using the special change-directory commands `pushd` and `popd`, which are discussed in the next two sections. The `dirs` command lists the directories in the directory stack:

```
% dirs
/usr/local/bin ~/html/manuals /users/wadams/bin
```

Three directories are on the directory stack in this example. The first directory listed is the current directory (the one you see if you enter the `pwd` command). Directories to the right are previous directories, and the farthest to the right are the least recent. In this example, the directory `/users/wadams/bin` was the first directory to be changed to—that is, "pushed" onto the pushdown directory stack; `~/html/manuals` was the next directory, and `/usr/local/bin` was the directory most recently changed to (the current directory).

Changing to a Directory by Using the Directory Stack: pushd

To save the pathname of a directory on the directory stack, you can use the pushd command to change to another directory. Using pushd saves the pathname of your previous directory on the directory stack so that you can return to it quickly and easily by using the popd command. Use dirs to display the directories currently saved on the pushdown stack.

Three forms of the pushd command exist:

pushd

pushd *name*

pushd *+n*

Used in the form pushd, the command exchanges the top two directory-stack elements, making your previous directory the current and your current directory the previous. Successive pushd commands used without an argument switch you back and forth between the top two directories.

Used in the form pushd *name*, the command changes to directory *name* in the same way as cd would have; pushd uses the *cdpath* directory list to resolve *name* and succeeds or fails in the same cases as cd. The pathname of the current directory is saved in a directory stack prior to the change. The directory stack is an implicit array variable maintained by the shell (which you cannot access directly), and each pushd adds the current directory to the left and pushes all existing entries to the right. The top (or first) element is always your current directory, and subsequent entries are the pathnames of your previous directories in reverse order. The popd command discards the top stack entry and changes to the new top entry, reducing the total number of items on the stack by one.

Use the form pushd *+n* to perform a circular shift of the directory stack by *n* positions, changing to the new top directory. A *circular shift* treats the list of elements as if they were in a ring, with the first preceded by the last and the last followed by the first. The shift changes your position in the ring without deleting any of the elements. Consider the following example:

```
% dirs
/home/john /home/mary /home/doggie /home/witherspoon
% pushd +2
/home/doggie
% dirs
/home/doggie /home/witherspoon /home/john /home/mary
```

Note that both before and after the pushd, /home/john precedes /home/mary, and /home/doggie precedes /home/witherspoon. The example also shows that, for the purpose of the pushd *+n* command form, /home/witherspoon (the last entry) is effectively followed by /home/john (the first entry).

Returning to a Previous Directory by Using the Directory Stack: popd

After you have saved directories on the directory stack with pushd, you can use popd to return to a previous directory. The syntax for the popd command follows:

popd [*+n*]

Used in the form `popd +n`, the command deletes the *n*th entry in the stack. Stack entries are numbered from 0, which is your current directory. The following example shows the use of `pushd`, `dirs`, and `popd` together:

```
% pwd
/usr/home/john
% pushd /usr/spool
% pushd uucppublic
% pushd receive
% dirs
/usr/spool/uucppublic/receive /usr/spool/uucppublic /usr/spool
_/usr/home/john
% popd
/usr/spool/uucppublic
% dirs
/usr/spool/uucppublic /usr/spool /usr/home/john
% popd +1
/usr/spool/uucppublic /usr/home/john
% popd
/usr/home/john
% dirs
/usr/home/john
```

Changing the Active Shell

The C shell provides a number of commands for changing the active shell. Although your logon shell may be the C shell, you are not limited to it; you can change your shell to the Bourne shell or the Korn shell at any time by using the `exec` command. The `exit` and `logout` commands also change the active shell by returning you to the shell that was active before your current shell. When you issue these commands from your logon shell, they return you to the logon screen, which is itself a kind of shell (of somewhat limited functionality).

Other commands, such as `umask` and `nohup`, change the manner in which UNIX treats the shell.

Invoking a New Process: exec

The `exec` command transfers control to the specified command, replacing the current shell. The command you specify becomes your new current shell. The syntax of the `exec` command follows:

`exec command`

Control cannot be returned to the invoking environment, because it is replaced by the new environment. Shell variables exported with the `setenv` command are passed to the new shell in the usual manner; all other command contexts, including local variables and aliases, are lost.

The `exec` command is used mainly in C shell scripts. The normal C shell behavior for executing commands that are C shell scripts uses two child processes: one process is a new C shell to interpret the script, and the other process is command(s) being executed. The `exec` command causes the C shell to eliminate one of the processes by having the C shell process replaced by the command process. exec most often is used if a script is used to set up an execution environment for a command (to set environment variables and check arguments, for example) and then run the command.

The exec command is equivalent to the Bourne shell exec.

Exiting from the Current Shell: exit

The exit command causes the current shell invocation to be exited. Its syntax follows:

```
exit [ (exitExpression) ]
```

If the exit command is issued from within a shell script, the shell script is terminated, and control returns to the invoking shell. If exit is issued from your logon shell, the .logout script in your home directory is executed before the shell exits. Normally, the UNIX operating system redisplays a logon screen after an exit from the logon shell.

If you provide the optional exitExpression argument (which must be enclosed in parentheses), the argument is evaluated as an arithmetic expression, and the resulting value is used as the shell's exit code; otherwise, the current value of the status variable is taken as the shell's exit code. The status variable is described in "Using Predefined Variables," later in this chapter.

Invoking the System Logon Procedure: login

You can use the login command to log out from your current shell and to immediately log on under the same or a different User ID. Its syntax follows:

```
login name [ arg ... ]
```

Using this built-in shell command is not quite equivalent to logging out in the normal manner and then logging on. If you use the login command from a remote terminal, the line connection is not dropped, whereas logging out in the normal manner drops the line and requires you to reestablish the connection before you can log on again.

You cannot execute the login built-in command from a subshell; it is legal only for your logon shell.

For name, specify the user name with which you want to log on. Any arguments you specify after name are passed to the /bin/login command and are defined by /bin/login—not by the shell.

Exiting from a Logon Shell: logout

You can use the logout command to log out from your logon shell:

```
logout
```

You also can terminate the logon shell (or any subshell) with the exit command. If you have the ignoreeof option set, you cannot use the EOF key (usually, Ctrl-D) to exit from the shell; in such a case, use logout or exit. See "Using Predefined Variables," later in this chapter, for a definition of the ignoreeof option.

Preventing a Command from Terminating Execution After Logout: nohup

You can use the nohup command to run a command that is insensitive to the hang-up signal:

```
nohup [ command ]
```

The UNIX operating system always sends a hang-up signal (signal 1) to a process when its process group leader logs out. The net effect is that, generally, any command you are running when you log out is terminated. (Although you can't ordinarily issue the logout or exit command or enter an EOF character while you are running a command, you always can force a logout by turning off your terminal; or, if you are using a remote terminal connection, you can hang up the line.)

When you invoke command with nohup, the shell effectively disables the hang-up signal so that command cannot receive it, which enables command to continue to execute after you log out. Use nohup command to run command with the hang-up signal disabled.

You can disable the hang-up signal for your interactive shell or from within a shell script by using the trap built-in command. Programs written in the C or C++ language also can disable or ignore the hang-up signal. Not all commands are able to ignore a hang-up signal, however. If you use nohup to invoke the command, you are assured that the hang-up signal will be ignored, regardless of whether the command disables the signal.

Use nohup with no arguments from within a shell script to disable the hang-up signal for the duration of the script. A job placed in the background (see "Executing Jobs in the Background: &," later in this chapter) using the & operator has nohup automatically applied to it.

Displaying and Setting the File-Creation Mask: umask

The *file-creation mask* (commonly called the *umask*) is an attribute of the shell process, just like the current directory is an attribute. The file-creation mask specifies the default permissions assigned to new files you create. When redirecting the output of a command to a file with the > operator, for example, it would be extremely inconvenient if the system prompted you for file permissions every time it created a file. Prompting would be especially annoying because, most of the time, you would assign the same permissions to all new files.

If you're not familiar with file permissions, you might want to review Chapter 4, "The UNIX File System." Briefly, file permissions indicate who may read, write, or execute the file.

The file-creation mask is a device you use to indicate what permissions UNIX is to assign to a new file by default. If you want some other access permissions for a file, the usual approach is to first create the file and then change the file's permissions with the chmod command.

The file-creation mask itself is a binary value consisting of nine bits; each bit corresponds to the permission bits for a file. As a matter of convention, the nine bits are represented by three octal digits; each digit represents three bits. Using octal number representation for the file-creation mask is a matter of convention, not necessity, yet the umask command does not enable you to use any other number form for displaying or setting the file-creation mask. You must use octal to set the mask, and you must interpret octal values to understand the mask when displayed.

As for the mask itself, each of the bits in the mask indicates whether the corresponding bit of the file permission should be set to off (set to zero). By default, virtually all UNIX commands attempt to set reasonable permission bits to 1 when creating a file. A command that creates a data file (such as a text file) tries to create the file with permissions of 666. In octal, this grants read and write permissions to you (the file's owner), to other members of your UNIX group, and to all other system users; however, it leaves the Execute permission unset. Commands that create executable files (such as cc and ld) attempt to set the file's permissions to 777, which, in octal, sets the Read, Write, and Execute bits for all users.

Because of this default action by UNIX commands, it is the function of the file-creation mask to specify permissions you don't want set. When you set a bit in the file-creation mask, it causes the corresponding bit of the file's permissions to be forced to 0. Bits not set in the file-creation mask are interpreted as *don't care*: the file-permission bit remains unchanged.

The bits of the file permissions are written as rwxrwxrwx. The first three bits represent Read, Write, and Execute permissions for the file's owner; the second set of three bits represents Read, Write, and Execute permissions for the file's group; and the third set of three bits specifies the permissions for other users. To grant Read and Write permissions to the file's owner but only Read access to other users, the appropriate file-permission setting is the bits 110100100. Writing this in octal, you arrive at the familiar permissions value of 644, which you already may have seen in the output of the ls command.

Remember that UNIX commands try to create files with all reasonable permissions set. For a data file, these bits are 110110110, corresponding to rw-rw-rw-. To get the permissions switched to rw-r--r--, you need to set off the fifth and eighth bits. A file-creation mask of 000010010 (in octal 022) would do the trick. When the file is created, UNIX lines up the bits in the file permissions requested by the command and your file-creation mask like this:

```
1 1 0 1 1 0 1 1 0      attempted file permissions
0 0 0 0 1 0 0 1 0      file creation mask
----------------
1 1 0 1 0 0 1 0 0      actual file permissions
```

What you have to do when using the umask command, therefore, is to first decide what file permissions you want to assign to your new files by default and then write a bit mask as an octal number that sets the appropriate file-permission bits to 0.

As it happens, most UNIX users want to reserve Write permission for their files to themselves, but they are willing to let other people look at the files. The appropriate file-creation mask for this is 022 in octal. In many cases, the system administrator sets up the system so that the umask 022 command is executed for you when you log on. If the administrator has not set up a default or you want to use another file-creation mask, you can set a new mask in your logon profile.

The actual syntax of the umask command is straightforward. To display the current process file-creation mask, use the umask command like this:

```
% umask
022
```

You also can use umask to set the process file-creation mask by specifying the octal argument:

```
% umask octal
```

The process file-creation mask is set to the bit pattern corresponding to the low-order three bits of each digit in the octal number *octal*.

Echoing Arguments to Standard Output

C shell provides two commands for echoing arguments to standard output: echo and glob. The only difference between them is the delimiter used to separate words in the output line.

The echo command, although most often used when writing shell scripts, also comes in handy in a number of keyboard situations—for example, when constructing a pipe to a non-interactive command (echo arg1 ¦ command). One of the best examples of the echo command is using it to display the value of a shell variable:

```
% echo $path
/usr/bin /bin /usr/local/bin /users/chen/bin
```

In this case, the variable substitution expression $path does the real work; the echo command provides only the step of printing the value on the terminal. Nonetheless, without the echo command, it would be cumbersome to check the value of a variable. The set command not only prints a single variable, but set can be used to print all variables. Using set to print all shell variables can produce a lengthy list that takes time to search through for the entry you want.

The glob command, on the other hand, rarely is used in any context. Originally, it was intended to be called from a C program (not a shell script) to get the shell to expand a filename wildcard expression. Most C programmers don't use this technique, though, because it relies on the existence of the C shell.

Using the echo Command

The echo command prints a line containing its arguments to standard output. The syntax for the command follows:

```
echo [ -n ] wordlist
```

The arguments are printed with one intervening blank between them and a newline character after the last one. The echo command does not modify the words in *wordlist* in any way, but the arguments as seen by echo might differ from those on the original command because of variable, command, and history replacement and filename globbing. For example, the command

```
echo Directory $cwd contains these files: *.cc
```

might generate the following line to standard output:

```
Directory /usr/lib1 contains these files: myprog.cc bigprog.cc
```

Specify option `-n` to suppress printing a newline character; this enables the next input or output to occur on the same line as the output of the `echo` command.

Using the `glob` Command

The `glob` command also prints a line containing its arguments to standard output. The syntax for the command follows:

```
glob [ wordlist ]
```

Use `glob` to print the words in *wordlist* to standard output. The words are printed with a null character between each (not white space, as with `echo`). The last word in *wordlist* is not followed by a newline character.

The words in *wordlist* are subject to variable, command, and history substitution and filename expansion in the usual manner. After scanning for substitutions, the resulting strings are redivided into words, which then are written using the null character delimiter.

The `glob` command is similar to `echo` and differs only in the delimiter used to separate words in the output line. Because most terminals cannot print a null character, `glob` generally is not used to generate terminal output. It is intended to be called from a C language program, in the form

```
system("/bin/csh -c 'glob *.doc'");
```

to invoke the shell substitution and filename-expansion mechanisms.

TIP

The C shell provides no direct means of logging messages to standard error. The lack of direct support from the C shell to log specifically to standard error can be very problematic when writing scripts—especially scripts intended to be part of a pipeline (for example, `command1 ¦ yourScript ¦ command2`) or otherwise have the script's output redirected in some fashion (for example, `yourScript > outputFile`). Error messages not placed on the standard error will be redirected, while error messages placed on the standard error will be seen unless the user specifically redirects the standard error. In short, placing a message on standard error ensures that the user will see the message. The following code shows an alias named `stderr` that places a message on the standard error. It is a bit cumbersome because it requires three extra processes to accomplish the task, but this should not be an issue, because logging to standard error is infrequent and occurs only in error situations.

```
% alias stderr 'echo \!*¦sh -c '"'"'cat 1>&2'"'"'"
% stderr Unable to locate file $file in directory $cwd.
Unable to locate file main.cc in directory /users/ziya
```

```
% stderr 'multi line output \
line two'
multi line output
line two
%
```

The alias saves a process over using a script file but suffers from two drawbacks. It does not accept input from standard input (cat errFile ¦ stderr), and the alias does not permit redirection on the same command line (stderr message > errFile). The following script file, at the expense of an extra process, provides command-line redirection and handles input from standard input or command-line arguments:

```
#!/bin/csh
# echo to standard error
alias say 'echo "$*"'; if ($#argv == 0) alias say cat
say ¦ sh -c 'cat 1>&2'
```

Rescanning a Line for Substitutions: eval

```
eval  [arg ... ]
```

You can use eval to rescan the arguments *arg* for variable, command, and history substitutions, filename expansion, and quote removal, and then execute the resulting words as a command. For example, if eval were passed the argument 'ls foo*' and the files foo.txt and foo.doc matched the pattern foo*, eval would expand the foo* expression and then execute the following command:

```
ls foo.txt foo.doc
```

With eval, you essentially can write shell script lines with a shell script and execute the resulting generated commands. Remember that to embed variable symbols in a string, however, you must hide the leading dollar sign from earlier shell substitutions.

eval is useful when used with commands that generate commands, such as resize or tset. For example, resize generates a series of setenv commands. Without eval, using resize is a three-step task:

```
resize > /tmp/out; source /tmp/out; rm /tmp/out
```

With eval, using resize is considerably simpler:

```
eval `resize`
```

The eval command implemented by the C shell is equivalent to the Bourne shell eval command.

Changing Your Group ID: newgrp

The newgrp command is the same as the UNIX newgrp command:

```
newgrp groupname
```

Although issued from your logon shell (not to be confused with a logon shell script—the logon shell is simply the shell started up for you when you log on), `newgrp` causes the current shell to be replaced by a new shell with the real and effective Group IDs both changed to the specified group *groupname*. Because the shell is replaced, all context, including exported variables and aliases, is lost.

Use the `newgrp` command when you have been authorized by the system administrator for membership in two or more user groups, and you want to change your Group ID from your current or logon group to another group. Your Group ID is used by the system when determining whether to grant you access to files.

Timing the Execution of a Command: `time`

You can use `time` with no argument to display the amount of CPU time in seconds used by the current shell and all commands and subshells invoked since its start. This form of the command is usually of interest only to folks who are being billed for the amount of machine time they use, as might be the case if you are renting time on a commercial machine. By occasionally entering the command with no arguments, you can monitor how much machine time you have used and limit your online time accordingly.

```
time [ command ]
```

Only for your logon shell will this be the amount of machine time used since you logged on. Also, note that the time reported is not elapsed wall-clock time—it is only the machine (or CPU) time used.

Use the form `time command` to execute *command* and report the amount of CPU time used by the command's execution. The *command* must be a simple command—not a compound command, statement group, or parenthesized statement—and cannot be a pipeline.

You might be interested in timing the execution of a command if you are a production operations manager and you want to find out how much time a new application is adding to your daily workload. A development programmer would use the `time` command to determine whether a new program has a performance problem. The average interactive user, however, would have infrequent occasion to use the `time` command.

Aliases

One of the handier features of the C shell is the alias feature. An *alias* is a shorthand method of referring to a command or part of a command. If you have several favorite options that you always supply to the `ls` command, for example, instead of having to type the whole command every time, you can create a two-character alias. Then you can type the two-character alias, and the shell executes the alias definition. In addition to providing shortcuts, aliases are a convenient way of handling common typos. I often type **mroe** for `more` or **jbos** for `jobs`, for example. Setting up aliases for `mroe` and `jbos` therefore saves me time, because I don't have to retype those commands.

An alias can represent not only a command name, but also leading options and arguments of the command line. Any words you type following the alias name are considered to follow options and arguments included in the alias definition, enabling you to customize the command with key options and arguments.

You can achieve more complex processing by using shell scripts, where the function performed by the shell script file's name used as a command can be arbitrarily complex. The command alias feature was provided only for use as a keyboard shortcut, and anything that can be achieved by using an alias can be done with shell scripts.

You should add command aliases you use often to your `.login` file, so that the alias is defined every time you log on. It is often handy, however, to define command aliases at the keyboard for special commands you'll be using during your current session. If you don't incorporate the alias into your `.login` file, it is lost when you log out.

Defining, Listing, and Changing Command Aliases: `alias`

The `alias` command enables you to list currently defined aliases, to define a new command alias, or to change an existing alias. The command format follows:

```
alias [ name [ definition ... ]]
```

For *name*, choose a word consisting of upper- and lowercase letters and digits. For *definition*, write any sequence of words that defines the command string for which you want *name* to stand. The following defines two aliases for the `rlogin` command, each providing a different host. It's shorter to type the alias name for the destination host than it is to type the `rlogin` command and options.

```
alias druid rlogin druid -l root
alias ducati rlogin ducati.moto.com
```

If you want to change the definition of an alias, just define the alias again.

After you define aliases, you can display a list of their names and definitions by entering the `alias` command without arguments, as in this example:

```
% alias
druid    (rlogin druid -l root)
ducati   (rlogin ducati.moto.com)
```

You also can display the definition of a specific alias by specifying its name as an argument:

```
% alias druid
rlogin druid -l root
```

Alias substitution occurs early in the shell's processing cycle for commands, thereby enabling you to use globbing (filename replacement), variable substitution, command substitution, and command-history substitution in the wordlist. You therefore often will need to quote at least one of the words of definition and perhaps the entire alias definition. Some people always enclose the alias definition in quotes to avoid surprises. Consider the following alias:

```
alias lc ls *.{cc,hh}
```

For a C++ language programmer, the alias would be rather natural: Simply by typing `lc`, you get a listing of all source program files in the current directory, devoid of any other file clutter.

> **NOTE**
>
> Note that substitutions occur when the `alias` command is processed unless you quote all or part of the wordlist.

The preceding alias definition does not work as expected, however. The filename pattern `*.{cc,hh}` is substituted on the `alias` command itself, and the actual alias stored (depending on the actual directory contents when you enter the `alias` command) follows:

```
% alias lc
ls CIM_EnvImp.cc CIM_Util.hh EventManager.cc LogInstances.cc
```

Because the filename pattern is replaced before the alias definition is stored by the shell, the `lc` alias doesn't list all files ending in `.cc` or `.hh`. It attempts to list the files `CIM_EnvImp.cc`, `CIM_Util.hh`, `EventManager.cc`, and `LogInstances.cc`, whether or not they exist in the current directory.

The alias should have been defined as this:

```
% alias lc ls '*.{cc,hh}'
```

An alias definition also can use command aliases. During alias substitution, the alias definition is scanned repeatedly until no further substitutions can be made. An alias definition for *name*, however, cannot invoke the name alias within itself; a reference to *name* in the *definition* is taken as a reference to the built-in shell command or executable file *name*, not as a reference to the alias. This enables you to use an alias to redefine a system command or a built-in shell command. For example,

```
% alias pg pg -cns -p"Page %d:"
```

You can refer to arguments of the original command line—before any substitutions are made—by using the command-history substitution syntax (see "Command History," later in this chapter). For example, the command

```
alias print 'pr \!* ¦ lp'
```

defines an alias named `print` that executes the `pr` command using all the arguments of the original command line (`\!*`) and then pipes the output to `lp` for printing.

To properly understand and use the `alias` command, you must be clear about the way an alias is used. When you define an alias by entering the `alias` command, the only thing that happens at that time is that the system stores the alias in computer memory. Later, when you enter a command with the same name as the alias, the C shell does a little magic. The command you typed is not executed in the form in which you typed it. Instead, the command name (which is an alias name) is replaced by the *value* of the alias. The result is a new command text—the first part is the alias definition, and the rest consists of any other arguments you typed.

Suppose that you define an alias for the `ls` command as this:

```
% alias lax ls -ax
```

If you later enter the command

```
% lax big*.txt
```

the command actually executed is

```
ls -ax big*.txt
```

The command alias (`lax`) is replaced by its definition (`ls -ax`). Remaining arguments on the command line (`big*.txt`) simply are tacked on after the alias substitution to yield the command the computer actually executes.

Using history substitutions (for example, `!*`, `!^`, `!:2 ...`) in an alias provides additional flexibility by enabling the executed command to use arguments in a different order or a different form than entered; this requires a little extra work from the shell. Consider the following alias definition:

```
alias lsp 'ls \!* | lp'
```

Entering the command `lsp *.cc *.csh` results in alias substitution for `lsp`. The symbol `!*` causes the arguments you entered on the line `*.cc *.csh` to be inserted into the alias definition instead of being tacked on after the alias definition. In other words, if an alias definition contains a history substitution, the shell suspends its normal action of tacking on command arguments after the alias value. The command actually executed is `ls *.cc *.csh | lp`. Without this special mechanism, the executed command would have been `ls | lp *.cc *.csh`, with the final `*.cc *.csh` tacked on in the usual manner. This would lead to an undesirable result: Instead of printing a directory listing, the `lp` command would print the full contents of the files.

When writing an alias, you therefore need to visualize what will happen when the alias is substituted in later commands.

Deleting a Command Alias: `unalias`

You can use `unalias` to delete one or more aliases. You can delete a specific alias by specifying its name as an argument, or you can delete multiple aliases by using pattern-matching:

```
unalias name
unalias pattern
```

If you specify a specific alias *name*, only that alias definition is deleted. If you specify a *pattern*, all those currently defined aliases whose names match the pattern are deleted. *pattern* can contain the pattern-matching characters *, ?, and [...]. In the following example, the first line deletes the `lx` alias, and the second line deletes all currently defined aliases:

```
unalias lx
unalias *
```

Shell Options

The C shell command-line options provide a convenient way of modifying the behavior of a C shell script to suit your needs. Options can be specified on a command line, such as this:

```
% csh -f
```

Or, if your UNIX version supports the #! notation, you can specify an alias on the first line of a script, such as this:

```
#!/bin/csh -f
echo *
```

If an option is needed temporarily, the command line is the best place to supply the option. If the option is needed permanently, place it on the #! line.

Unless one of the -c, -i, -s, or -t options is set, the C shell assumes that the first argument on the command line is the command to be executed and that each additional argument is intended for the command being executed. For example, the command

```
% csh command arg1 arg2 arg3
```

causes the C shell to execute *command* with three arguments (*arg1, arg2, arg3*), which will be assigned to the argv array variable. When the -i, -s, or -t option is set, the shell assigns all arguments, including the first, to the argv array variable. The -c option allows only one command-line argument and takes it as a list of commands to be executed; after execution of the argument string, csh exits.

Command-line options are used by the C shell itself—not by the command to be executed. Command-line options are indicated with a dash (-) followed by this option: csh -v. If multiple options are needed, the options may be preceded by only one dash (csh -fv) or by using one dash per option (csh -f -v). Mixing option-specification methods is allowed (csh -f -vx). The following command shows the mixing of command-line options with normal command execution:

```
% csh -fv command arg1 arg2 arg3
```

Table 12.4 provides a summary of C shell command-line options.

Table 12.4. C shell command-line options.

Option	Name	Description
-b	Break	Delimits a break in command-line option processing between arguments intended for the C shell and arguments intended for a C shell script. All command options before -b are interpreted as C shell arguments, and all

Option	Name	Description
		command options after `-b` are passed on to the C shell script. Note: The `-b` option is not available on all UNIX platforms.
`-c commandString`	Commands	Executes commands from the `commandString` parameter that immediately follows the `-c` option. The commands in `commandString` may be delimited by newlines or semicolons. All command-line arguments after `-c` are placed in the `argv` variable. The `-c` option is used when calling the C shell from a C or C++ program. `-c` is the only option that requires a parameter.
`-e`	Exit	Exits the current shell if any command returns a nonzero exit status or otherwise terminates abnormally. Setting this option is easier than checking the return status of each command executed.
`-f`	Fast	Uses fast-start execution. The C shell does not execute the `.cshrc` or `.login` file, which speeds up the execution of a C shell script. This is a good optimization if a C shell script does not need any of the variables or aliases set up in the initialization files.
`-i`	Interactive	Forces interactive-mode processing. If shell input does not appear to be from a terminal, command-line prompts are not issued.
`-n`	Not	Parses shell syntax but does *not* execute commands. The `-n` option is useful for debugging shell syntax without actually having to execute resultant commands after all shell substitutions are made (for example, aliases, variables, and so on).
`-s`	Standard	Reads command input from standard input. All command-line arguments after `-s` are placed in the `argv` variable. Using `-s` can prevent unnecessary temporary files by piping output of commands directly into the shell (`genCshCmds ¦ csh -s`).

continues

12

THE C SHELL

Table 12.4. continued

Option	Name	Description
-t	execuTe	Reads and executes a single line of input. You can use the backslash (\) to escape the newline to continue the input on the next line.
-v	Verbose	Sets the predefined verbose variable. When verbose is set, all commands are echoed to standard output after history substitutions are made but before other substitutions are made. -v is useful for debugging C shell scripts.
-V	Very	Sets the predefined verbose variable before the .cshrc is executed.
-x	eXecution	Sets the predefined echo variable. Commands are echoed to standard output right before execution but after all substitutions are made.
-X	eXtra	Performs extra command echoes. The -X option sets the predefined echo variable before .cshrc is executed.

The shell supports additional options that you can switch on or off during shell operation. These options are controlled by variables; if the variable is set, the corresponding option is activated; if it is not, the option is off. These options are described in "Using Predefined Variables," later in this chapter. Their names are *echo*, *ignoreeof*, *noclobber*, *noglob*, *nonomatch*, *notify*, and *verbose*.

Additionally, the shell variables *cdpath*, *history*, *mail*, *path*, *prompt*, and *shell*, although not options as such, enable you to control certain shell behaviors such as searching for commands and checking for mail. See "Using Predefined Variables," later in this chapter, for further information.

Command History

The C shell's command-history service maintains a list of previously executed commands. You can use the command history for two purposes:

- As a reference to determine what you've already done
- With history substitution, as a shorthand method to reuse all or part of a previous command to enter a new command

Displaying the Command History

The history command enables you to print all or selected lines of the current command history:

```
history [ -r ] [-h] [ n ]
```

To display all the lines currently held in the history list, simply enter the history command (it takes no arguments):

```
% history
1  cd src
2  ls
3  vi foo.cc
4  cc foo.cc
5  grep '#include' foo.cc
```

The C shell displays each line, preceded with a line number. You can use the line number to refer to commands with the history-substitution mechanism. Line numbers start with 1 at the beginning of your session, assuming that no previous saved history exists. (See "Using Predefined Variables," later in this chapter, for more information on the shell variable *savehist*.)

The amount of history a shell maintains depends on the amount of memory available to the shell. History is not saved in an external disk file until after the session exits if *savehist* is set, so capacity is somewhat limited. You can set the history variable to a value indicating the number of lines of history you want the shell to maintain; it keeps that number of lines and more if possible, but your specification is only advisory. The value of history must be a simple number to be effective. For example, set *history*=25 retains at least 25 lines of history.

> **CAUTION**
>
> The history service retains command lines—not commands. As the history area becomes full, the shell discards old lines. This might result in some lines containing incomplete, partial commands. You need to use caution with the history-substitution facility to avoid calling for the execution of an incomplete command.

To limit the number of lines displayed, specify a positive integer for *n* to limit the number of lines displayed to the last *n* lines of history.

Specify the -r option to print history lines in reverse order, from the most recent to the oldest.

The -h option lists the history buffer without the line numbers. This can be useful for creating scripts based on past input (history -h > script.csh) or for cutting and pasting a series of commands by using your mouse.

Using History Substitutions to Execute Commands

History substitutions are introduced into a command with the ! (exclamation point, usually called the *bang operator*). You append one or more characters to ! to define the particular kind of history substitution you want. If followed by a blank, tab, newline, equal sign (=), or open parenthesis (, the exclamation point is treated as an ordinary character.

> **NOTE**
>
> The exclamation point is an ordinary character to other shells, but it is special to the C shell. You must precede it with \ (backslash) to avoid its special meaning, even inside hard-quoted strings (for example, echo '!!' does not echo !! but the previous command). The shell attempts a history substitution wherever it finds an exclamation point in the command line, without regard to any quoting; only the backslash can avoid interpretation of ! as a history-substitution mark.

You can write a history substitution anywhere in the current shell input line, as part or all of the command. When you enter a command containing one or more history substitutions, the shell echoes the command after performing the substitutions so that you can see the command that actually will be executed. (You do not have an opportunity to correct the command; it is executed immediately after being displayed.)

The simplest forms of history substitution are !! and !*number*. The !! symbol is replaced with the entire previous command line. The expression !*number* is replaced with a line number from the command-history list.

Suppose that the command history currently contains the following lines:

```
1  cd src
2  ls
3  vi foo.cc
4  cc foo.cc
5  grep '#include' foo.cc
```

If you now enter the command !!, the shell repeats the grep command in its entirety. Press Return to execute the grep command, or type additional words to add to the end of the grep command:

```
% !! sna.hh
grep '#include' foo.cc sna.hh
```

Now suppose that, after running grep, you want to edit the foo.cc file again. You could type the vi command as usual, but it already appears in the command history as line 3. A history substitution provides a handy shortcut:

```
% !3
vi foo.cc
```

That's almost all there is to basic history substitution. Actually, the shell supports any of the forms listed in Table 12.5 for referring to command-history lines.

Table 12.5. Forms for referring to command-history lines.

Form	Replaced With
!!	The preceding command line (the last line of command history).
!number	The line number of the command history.
!-number	The history line *number* lines back; !-1 is equivalent to !!.
!string	The most recent history line that has a command beginning with *string*. For example, use !v to refer to a previous vi command.
!?string?	The most recent history line containing *string* anywhere in the line. For example, use !?foo? to repeat a previous vi foo.cc command. Most C shell versions support not supplying the trailing question mark, so !?foo would execute the same vi command.

You can do more with history substitutions than merely reuse a previous command. The shell also provides extensions to the history operator that enable you to select individual words or a group of words from a history line, inserting the selected word or words into the current command. These extensions are in the form of a suffix beginning with a colon (:). For example, !vi:1 is replaced not with the most recent vi command, but with its first argument word. Similarly, !3:3-4 is replaced with arguments 3 and 4 of history line 3. You can use any of the expressions listed in Table 12.6 as word selectors by appending the expression to a line reference preceded by a colon.

Table 12.6. Using command history word selectors.

Expression	Specifies
0	First word of the command (usually, the command name).
n	*n*th argument of the command. Arguments are numbered from 1. Note that 0 refers to the command name, which is actually the first word of the line, whereas 1 refers to the second word of the line.
^	Same as :1, the first argument.
$	Last argument word of the command.

continues

Table 12.6. continued

Expression	Specifies
%	For the !?*string*? format, the word matched by *string*. Use this word selector only with the !?*string*? history reference. Its value is the entire word-matching string, even though *string* might have matched only a part of the word.
m-n	Multiple word substitution. Replaced with words *m* through *n* of the history line. For *m* and *n*, specify an integer number or one of these special symbols: ^, $, or %.
m-	Substitution of words beginning with the *m*th word and extending up to but not including the last word.
-n	Same as 0-*n*; substitutes words beginning with the first word of the history line (the command name) through the *n*th word.
m*	Same as *m*-$; substitutes words beginning with the *m*th word and extending through the last word of the line.
*	Same as ^-$; substitutes all argument words of the line.

If the word selector expression you want to write begins with ^, $, *, -, or %, you can omit the colon between the line selector and the word selector. For example, !vi* refers to all the arguments of the previous vi command and is the same as !vi:* or !vi:^-$.

> **NOTE**
>
> Some versions of the C shell require the : between the ! operator and the selector if you are not using a line number. The command !3^ would give the first argument of command 3, but !vi^ would return an error.

You can use any number of word selectors in the same command line. By combining multiple word selectors, you can reuse arguments of a previous command in a different order (cp foo.cc ~/project/src/new; chmod -w !$/!^) and use arguments that originally appear on different commands. For example, the command rm !115^ !117^ removes files that were named on two earlier commands.

When counting words of a previous command line, the shell takes quoting into consideration but uses the line as it appears in the history list. Words generated by variable or command substitution or filename generation are not accessible. The following example demonstrates the effects of quoting and command substitution:

```
% echo "one two three" four
one two three four
% echo !^
```

```
echo "one two three"
one two three
% echo `ls *.cc`
bar.cc foo.cc
% echo !^
echo `ls *.cc`
bar.cc foo.cc
```

You can append modifiers to a word selector to alter the form of the word before insertion in the new command. A modifier is written in the form :*x*, where *x* is a letter specifying how the word should be modified. For example, !vi^:t substitutes the tail of the first argument of the vi command: for the argument /usr/X/lib/samples/xclock.c, the value of :t is xclock.c.

Table 12.7 lists the modifiers that can be appended to a word selector to alter the selected word before substitution.

Table 12.7. History substitution modifiers.

Modifier	Function
:e	Removes all but the filename suffix. For the argument foo.sh, :e returns .sh.
:h	Removes a trailing path component. Successive :h modifiers remove path components one at a time, right to left. Thus, for the argument /usr/local/etc/httpd/htdocs/index.html :h returns /usr/local/etc/httpd/htdocs whereas :h:h returns /usr/local/etc/httpd
:p	When used in any history-substitution expression on the command line, causes the shell to print the command after substitutions but not to execute it. Use :p to try the effect of a history substitution before executing it.
:q	Encloses the substituted word or words in quotes to prevent further substitutions.
:r	Removes a filename suffix of the form .*string*. For example, for the argument foo.cc, :r returns foo. Successive :r operators remove one suffix at a time. For example, :r:r applied to arch.tar.Z returns arch.
:s/*x*/*y*/	Replaces the string *x* in the selected word with the string *y*. String *x* cannot be a regular expression. The symbol & appearing in *y* is replaced with the search string *x*—for example, :s/bill/&et/ substitutes billet for bill. Any character can be

continues

Table 12.7. continued

Modifier	Function
	used in place of the slash—for example, `:s?/usr?/user?`. The final `/` can be omitted if followed by a newline. You can use the delimiter (`/` or your delimiter) or `&` as a text character by escaping it with a backslash (`\`)—for example, `:s/\/usr/\/user/`. The search string *x* can be omitted, in which case the search string of the previous `:s` on the same line is used. Or, if no previous `:s` occurred, the string of `!?string?` is used.
`:t`	Removes all leading components of a path, returning just the filename part. For the word `/usr/bin/ls`, the value of `:t` is `ls`.
`:x`	Breaks the selected word or words at blanks, tabs, and newlines.
`:&`	Reuses the previous string-substitution modifier. For example, if `:s` appears in the same command line, `!grep:2:s/bill/marty/ !:3:&` is the same as `!grep:2:s/bill/marty/ !3:s/bill/marty/`

Normally, a modifier affects only the first selected word. When selecting multiple words, such as with `!12:2*`, you can apply a modifier to all the selected words by inserting a `g` in front of the modifier letter. For example, `!12:2*:gh` applies the `:h` modifier to all the words. The `g` is not valid with the `:p`, `:q`, and `:x` modifiers.

You can omit the command identifier from a history substitution when using two or more `!` expressions in the same line; successive history references then refer to the same command as the first. For example,

```
% vi %grep^:t %:3:t %:4:t
```

all refer to the same `grep` command but select the first, third, and fourth arguments.

The history mechanism supports the special abbreviation `^`, which is useful for correcting a keying error in the preceding line. The general form of the abbreviation is `^x^y`, where *x* and *y* are strings. The preceding command line is selected and searched for string *x*; if found, it is replaced with *y* and then executed. After the command `cd /usr/ban`, for example, enter the line `^ban^bin` (or `^a^i`) to execute the command as `cd /usr/bin`. The caret (`^`) must be the first nonblank character of the line to be recognized as a line-editing substitution. This abbreviation is available only for the immediately preceding command line; you must use the full history expression `!line:s/x/y/` to edit any line other than the last.

One final, important provision of the history-substitution mechanism is that you can enclose any history reference in braces {} to isolate it from characters following it. Thus, !{vi^:h}.cc forms a word beginning with the selected history reference and ending in .cc.

TIP

Use the history substitution !* to prevent unintentional file removal. When creating a file expression to delete files, use the ls command to see the results. After you are satisfied that only the intended files are being removed, issue the rm command with the !* substitution. In the following example, the user is trying to delete all publish-related C++ source files and a Makefile.

```
% ls pub* Makefile
Makefile pubList.txt  publish.cc    publish.hh
% ls publ* Makefile
Makefile publish.cc   publish.hh
% rm !*
```

Variables

You can use shell variables to hold temporary values, and shell scripts can use variables to manage changeable information. The shell itself also has variables of its own that you can use to customize features of the C shell and your C shell environment.

A *variable* is actually an area of the shell's memory set aside to hold a string of characters. The string value is dereferenced by using a variable name. You assign the name of a variable when you define it with the built-in set command. You can change the value of a variable in several ways.

The shell provides a complex syntax set for referring to the value of a variable. Any variable reference, when scanned in a command line, is replaced by the corresponding value of the reference before the command is executed. In its simplest form, a variable reference simply replaces the name of a variable with its string value.

This section looks at the kinds of variables the C shell supports and the rules for naming variables and referring to variable values.

Variable Names

The C shell imposes no set limit on the size of variable names. People commonly use variable names of six to eight characters, and names consisting of up to 16 characters are not unusual.

A variable name can consist of only letters (uppercase and lowercase), underscores (_), and digits. A variable name cannot begin with a digit, because names beginning with a digit are reserved for use by the C shell. Generally, all capital letters are used for the names of environment variables, and all lowercase letters are used for local variables, although the C shell imposes no such restriction.

You assign a value to a variable by using the set or setenv built-in commands, depending on the type of variable you are setting.

> **NOTE**
>
> The C shell does not support the assignment statement *name=value*, which might be familiar to you from the Bourne and Korn shells.

Creating Shell Variables

You can use the set statement to create new local variables and, optionally, to assign a value to them. Local variables are known only to the current shell and are not passed to shell scripts or invoked commands.

Use the setenv statement to create new environment variables. Environment variables are passed to shell scripts and invoked commands, which can reference the variables without first defining them (no setenv statement is required or should be used in a shell script for passed environment variables you want to access). See the section, "Displaying and Setting Global Environment Variables: setenv," for more about environment variables.

A shell variable can contain any characters, including unprintable characters, as part of its value. A shell variable also can have a null value (a zero-length string containing no characters). A variable with a null value differs from an unset variable. A reference to the null value merely deletes the variable reference, because it is replaced with a zero-length string. A reference to an unset variable is an error; it generates an error message and causes the shell interpretation of commands to stop.

Displaying and Setting Local Shell Variables: set

You can use the set command to display or set local variables:

```
set
set name=word
set name=(wordlist)
set name[index]=word
```

You can use set with no arguments to list the currently defined variables and their respective values. The listing includes exported variables as well as local variables, although many versions of the C shell print only nonexported variables.

Any of the operand formats can be combined with a single set statement. Each statement assigns a value to a single shell variable or element of an array variable (for example, set *var1=(foo bar bas) var2=value2 var1[1]=phou*). Note that no white space can separate the variable name, equal sign, or value when writing an assignment; any white space appearing in *word* or *wordlist* must be hidden with quotes.

You can use set *name* to define a variable name and to initialize it with a null string. You can use this form to set a number of shell options (such as set `ignoreeof`). A variable with a null value is not the same as an unset variable. A variable with a null value exists but has no value, whereas an unset variable does not exist. A reference to an unset variable results in a shell error message; a reference to a null variable results in substitution of the null string.

You can use set *name=word* to assign the string *word* as the current value of variable *name*. The string replaces the current value of *name* if the variable already is defined; otherwise, a new variable called *name* is created. If *word* contains characters special to the shell (including blanks or tabs), it must be enclosed in single or double quotes.

You can use the form set *name=(wordlist)* to assign each word in *wordlist* to successive elements of the array variable *name*. After the assignment, the expression $*name*[1] refers to the first word in *wordlist*, $*name*[2] refers to the second word, and so on. Any word in *wordlist* must be quoted if it contains characters special to the shell (including blanks or tabs).

You can use the form set *name[i]=word* to assign the string *word* as the current value of the *i*th element of the array variable *name*. For *i*, specify a positive integer number not less than 1. You do not have to assign a value to every element of an array. The number of elements in an array is effectively the highest-numbered element to which a value has been assigned. Elements to which no values have been assigned have effective values of the null (zero-length) string. Also note that you cannot assign a (*wordlist*) to an array element; an array variable can have multiple values, but each element can represent only one string value.

> **NOTE**
>
> Many versions of the C shell do not support sparse arrays. A sparse array is an array that does not have a value for every index. An array element cannot be addressed unless the array already has an element in that position. A
>
> `set: Subscript out of range`
>
> message is generated when the assignment
>
> `set name[4]=foo`
>
> or reference
>
> `echo $name[4]`
>
> is attempted on a three-element array.

Deleting Local Shell Variables: unset

You can use the unset command to delete one or more shell variables from the shell's memory:

`unset pattern`

The unset command is effective for variables defined with the set command only; use the unsetenv command to delete variables defined with setenv.

For *pattern*, specify a string that might optionally contain one or more occurrences of the pattern-matching characters *, ?, or [. . .]. All local variables known to the shell whose names match the specified *pattern* are deleted. You receive no warning message if nothing matches *pattern* and no confirmation that the variables were deleted.

Displaying and Setting Global Environment Variables: `setenv`

You can use the `setenv` statement to create new environment variables. Environment variables are passed to shell scripts and invoked commands, which can reference the variables without first defining them (no `setenv` statement is required or should be used in a shell script for passed environment variables you want to access). See "Customizing Your Shell Environment," later in this chapter, for more about environment variables.

The format of the `setenv` command follows:

```
setenv [name value]
```

When issued without arguments, the `setenv` command lists all global environment variables currently in effect and their values. When used in the form `setenv name value` , the shell creates a new global variable with the specified name and assigns the string *value* as its initial value. If the value contains characters such as a space or tab, be sure to enclose the value string in quotes. See "Quoting or Escaping from Special Characters," earlier in this chapter, for information about C shell special characters and using quoting techniques.

UNIX also provides a command (`env`) for displaying the current list of environment variables and their values. The `env` command supports a number of options and arguments for modifying the current environment.

The section "Using Predefined Variables," later in this chapter, provides a list of all variables (local and environment) that are defined by the C shell. Environment variables defined by other UNIX components are defined in the documentation for those components. Unfortunately, no comprehensive list of environment variables exists, because some variables are defined by non-shell programs. The `mailx` command, for example, defines some variables, and the `vi` command looks for some variables of its own. Altogether, the environment-variable pool is optional, anyway: If you don't know of a variable a UNIX command uses, the command still works without it. At any rate, be aware that the C shell is not responsible for defining all environment variables; the shell merely provides a means for manipulating and accessing variables.

Deleting Global Environment Variables: `unsetenv`

To delete global environment variables, you use the `unsetenv` command:

```
unsetenv variablename
unsetenv pattern
```

Use the `unsetenv` command to delete one or more environment variables from the shell's memory. The `unsetenv` command is effective only for variables defined with the `setenv` command; use the `unset` command to delete variables defined with `set`.

To delete a particular variable definition, specify its name as *variablename*. To delete multiple variable definitions, use *pattern* to specify a string that might optionally contain one or more occurrences of the pattern-matching characters *, ?, or [...]. All environment variables known to the shell whose names match the specified *pattern* are deleted. You receive no warning message if nothing matches *pattern* and no confirmation that the variables were deleted.

Obtaining Variable Values with Reference Expressions

You obtain the value of a shell variable by writing a variable reference on the command line. A *variable reference* results in the replacement of the entire reference expression—including the $ that introduces the reference, the variable's name, and any other characters that might adorn the reference—with a string value of the reference.

A variable reference does not itself define the start or end of a word; the reference can be a complete word or part of a word. If the reference is part of a word, the substituted string is combined with other characters in the word to yield the substituted word. If the reference value substitutes one or more blanks or tabs into the word, though, the word is split into two or more words unless it is quoted. If the value of shell variable *var* is "two words," for example, the reference expression $var appears as two words after substitution, but the quoted string "$var" appears as the one token "two words" afterward.

A variable reference can result in the substitution of the value of a local or a global variable. A local variable is used if it exists; otherwise, the value of an environment variable is taken. If a shell variable and an environment variable have the same name, the shell variable effectively hides the value of the environment variable. If the value of the environment variable is needed, the shell variable must be unset.

You can use any of the variable reference forms shown in Table 12.8 in a word.

Table 12.8. Shell variable references.

Syntax	Meaning
${*name*} $*name*	Replaced with the value of *name*. It is an error if the $*name* variable name is not defined.
${*name*[*n*]} $*name*[*n*]	Replaced with the value of elements of array variable *name*. For *n*, use an element number or a range of element numbers in the form *m-n*. Use -*n* to substitute elements 1-*n*, and use *m*- to substitute elements *m* through the end of the array.
${#*name*} $#*name*	Replaced with the number of elements in array variable *name*.
${?*name*} $?*name*	Replaced with 1 if the variable *name* is set; otherwise, replaced with 0.

Variable names are terminated by the first illegal variable name character—in other words, any character that is not a digit, letter or underscore (_). As a result, variable references can be used without braces when the next character is not a legal variable name character. If the shell variable *var* is set to foo, the variable references $*var*.cc, $*var*$*var*, and $*var*"bar" resolve to foo.cc, foofoo, and foobar, respectively.

The reference forms using braces (for example, ${*name*} and ${#*name*}) are useful when the variable *name* would run onto the remainder of the current word, yielding an undefined variable name. If the variable *dir*, for example, contains the path prefix /usr/bin/, the word ${*dir*}name.cc forms the full pathname /usr/bin/name.cc upon expansion. The simpler form $*dirname*.cc, however, is taken as a reference to variable *dirname*, which is not at all what was intended. The net effect of the braces is to set off the variable reference from the remainder of the word.

A reference to an unset variable generates a shell error message and, if the reference occurs inside a shell script, causes reading of the shell script to terminate. You can use the $?*name* or ${?*name*} forms to handle the case where a variable might not be set. For example,

```
if ($?nfiles) echo "File count is $nfiles"
```

Using Array Variables

Unless you provide otherwise, a variable can have only one value. An *array variable*, on the other hand, can have any number of values (as long as the shell has sufficient memory available to store the values). The path variable, for example, which is used by the shell as a list of directories to search for commands, is an array variable in which each element is a directory path.

You can assign values to an array variable in one of two ways: all at once or one at a time. Not all C shell versions allow the one-member-at-a-time method of assignment, though. To assign many values at once, use a wordlist argument to the set command. A *wordlist* is a parenthesized list of words. For example, the following array contains four values:

```
set path=(/bin /usr/bin ~/bin .)
```

Each of the words in a wordlist is assigned to the next available element of the array variable. Assigning a wordlist to a variable automatically defines the variable as an array.

To assign values individually to elements of an array, you must use array subscript notation. Written in the form *name*[*index*], the *index* must be a number designating an array element; elements are numbered starting with 1, so $*name*[1] is a reference to the first element of an array. The following example assigns three values to the array *planets* and then prints one of them using an array reference:

```
% set planets[1]=Mercury
% set planets[2]=Venus
% set planets[3]=Earth
% echo Planet 3 is $planet[3]
Planet 3 is Earth
```

If you reference the array variable name without an index, the shell replaces the reference with a wordlist:

```
% echo The planets are $planets
The planets are (Mercury Venus Earth)
```

Many versions of the C shell will not put the parenthesis in the output. If your C shell adds the parenthesis, you can also use the reference $name[*] to obtain all the words of the array without the surrounding parentheses:

```
% echo The planets are: $planets[*]
The planets are: Mercury Venus Earth
```

You can reference a specific range of elements by using the notation $name[m-n], where m and n are the beginning and ending index numbers of the elements you want. For example, the following lists only the Earth-like planets:

```
% set planets=(Mercury Venus Earth Mars Jupiter Saturn Uranus Neptune Pluto)
% echo The terraform planets are: $planets[2-4]
The terraform planets are: Venus Earth Mars
```

The special form $name[-n] refers to elements of the array, beginning with the first and extending through n:

```
% echo The inner planets are: $planets[-4]
The inner planets are: Mercury Venus Earth Mars
```

The special form $name[n-] refers to the elements of the array, beginning with n and extending through the last:

```
% echo The outer planets are: $planets[5-]
The outer planets are: Jupiter Saturn Uranus Neptune Pluto
```

One of the primary reasons for using array variables is to permit looping through the array, inspecting and manipulating each array element in turn. This programming technique, often used in shell scripts, can be used at the keyboard as well:

```
% set files=(main io math dbase)
% foreach file ($files)
? cp $file.cc $file.cc.bak
? end
```

This example first assigns the root names of a number of files to an array variable and then uses the foreach shell statement to process each of the files in turn by copying the file to a backup file and changing its filename in the process. In the preceding example, the question mark (?) is the shell's prompt when it requires additional lines to complete an outstanding statement; it signals that you haven't finished the command yet.

Arrays can be used as a more efficient way of parsing output from commands. Using cut or awk requires an extra process, and the shell script more than likely will be harder to read. If different fields are needed, multiple calls to cut and awk can be avoided, which provides even more efficiency. Suppose that you need to repeatedly refer to the month and year in a shell script.

The script snippet that follows shows the use of cut and awk to do this. (The use of both cut and awk is for illustrative purposes. Normally, only cut or awk would be used.)

```
set month=`date | cut -f2 -d" "`
set year=`date | awk '{print $6}'`
```

This snippet requires two calls to date and two calls to parse the output: one for awk and one for cut. That means that four processes are run to extract the needed date information. You can reduce the number of processes down to two with some awk trickery:

```
eval `date | awk '{print "set month=" $2, "year=" $6}'`
```

Although the command is elegantly done on one line, it is not very readable and therefore not very maintainable. Using a C shell array to parse the output improves efficiency by using only one process—that of the date program. The use of an array also increases readability:

```
set current_date=(`date`)
set month=$current_date[2] year=$current_date[6]
```

The array parsing is similar to the default parsing done by awk, because all white space is ignored; cut, however, treats each white space character as a field delimiter. Parsing output that has a variable amount of white space between fields, such as output from ls or date, is not a good candidate for cut, but it is a good candidate for awk or a C shell array. If non-white space field delimiters are needed or the parsing is part of a pipeline, awk or cut must be used.

TIP

A good rule to follow when programming is the *Once and Only Once* rule. This rule states that script elements such as commands and values should appear at most once in any given script. Variables and aliases provide a powerful and convenient way to accomplish the goal of "oneness." Consider this script snippet:

```
echo Jim and I, the twins > /tmp/foo.$$
ls > /tmp/foo.$$
```

Here, the filename /tmp/foo.$$ appears twice. If that filename needs to be changed, multiple locations must be changed. If the filename is stored in the variable

```
set filename=/tmp/foo.$$
```

only one place must be updated. Using a variable for the filename helps prevent errors. If you accidentally forget to type the dot (.) and enter the filename /tmp/foo$$, an extra temporary file is created. If the variable name is mistyped, the shell reports an error.

An extension of the Once and Only Once rule is that command-line arguments should be dereferenced at most once by using the $n or $argv[n] syntax. Always create a new variable if the command-line argument must be looked at multiple times. The script

```
if (-e $1 && -d $2) then
  mv $1 $2
  echo $1 moved to $2
endif
```

is not only hard to read because $1 has little semantic meaning, it also is hard to maintain if the argument use changes (new arguments are introduced, arguments are removed, or arguments are reordered). Transform the script by referencing the command-line arguments directly only once:

```
#argument checking omitted for brevity
set srcFile="$1" targetDir="$2"
if (-e $srcFile && -d $targetDir) then
  mv $srcFile $targetDir
  echo $srcFile moved to $targetDir
endif
```

Using Special Read-Only Variables

In addition to ordinary variables you define with the set and setenv commands, a number of variables are defined by the shell and have preset values. Often, the value of a special variable changes as the result of a command action. You can use these variables to acquire specific information that isn't available in any other way. You cannot use set or setenv to define these variables, however, and you can't assign new values to them.

The special variables can be referenced by using the notations shown in Table 12.9.

Table 12.9. Shell special variables.

Variable	Meaning
$0	Replaced with the name of the current shell input file, if known. If unknown, this variable is unset, and a reference to it is an error. $0 is shorthand for $argv[0]. $0 can be used with other variable reference operators. For example, $?0 returns 1 if the current filename of the shell is known and 0 if the filename is not known. (Note that argv is the only shell array where referencing the zeroth element returns a value other than the null string.)
$1, $2, ... $9	Replaced with the value of the shell command's first (second, third, ...) argument. If used within a shell script invoked by name, these symbols refer to the command-line arguments. Up to nine arguments can be referenced this way. To reference arguments beyond nine, you must use the reference notation $argv[n] or the built-in command shift.
$*	Equivalent to $argv[*]. Replaced with all the arguments passed to the shell.

continues

Table 12.9. continued

Variable	Meaning
$$	Replaced with the process number of the current shell. When a subshell is invoked, $$ returns the process ID of the parent shell.
$<	Replaced with a line of text read from the standard input file.

The variables $1, $2, ... $9 have special significance when used inside a shell script, because they refer to the arguments of the command line that invoked the shell script. The same command arguments are accessible via the array variable *argv*. By using the *argv* variable, you can refer to all command-line arguments, not just the first nine. For example, $argv[10] references the tenth argument, and $argv[$n] references whichever argument is designated by another variable $n.

The shift built-in command can be used to manipulate command arguments. See "Shell Programming," later in this chapter, for details about the shift command.

Using Predefined Variables

The C shell also recognizes a number of conventionally named variables as having special meaning. Some are initialized automatically when the shell starts; you set others via the set command or by using command-line options when the C shell program csh is invoked. You can assign a value to most of these variables, but some variables are set automatically by the shell when a corresponding event occurs.

> **NOTE**
>
> Note that all predefined shell variables have lowercase names. This is to avoid conflicts with environment variables, which usually have uppercase names.

To set any predefined variable, use the set command. You need to specify a value only if the variable requires one; otherwise, you can omit the value string. For example, use set *noclobber* to enable the *noclobber* option, but use set *prompt*='$cwd: ' to assign a new command-line prompt string. See "Displaying and Setting Local Shell Variables: set," earlier in this chapter, for more information about set.

You can use the unset built-in command to destroy the variable and any associated value, but be aware that an unset variable does not revert to its initial or default value and is not the same as a variable having a null value; an unset variable simply doesn't exist. See the unset built-in command in "Deleting Local Shell Variables: unset," earlier in this chapter, for more information about unset.

Table 12.10 describes the variables to which the shell is sensitive and indicates any initialization or assignment restrictions.

Table 12.10. Predefined shell variables.

Variable	Description
argv	An array variable containing the current shell parameters. A reference to argv[1] is equivalent to $1, argv[2] to $2, and so on, up to $9. The value of argv is set by the shell at startup and just prior to the execution of each command.
cdpath	An array variable specifying a list of directories to be searched by the cd command. The C shell does not provide an initial value for cdpath. If you do not provide a value, the cd command searches only the current directory to resolve unanchored pathnames (pathnames starting with . or / are considered to be anchored).
cwd	Contains the full pathname of the current directory. On startup, the shell initializes cwd to the pathname of your home directory. Each cd command you execute changes the value of cwd. Note that $cwd may return a different value than the UNIX command pwd if a link was used to go to the current directory.
echo	If set, the shell prints each command before execution. The echo variable is initialized to the null string if the -x or -X option is present on the csh command line; otherwise, the variable is left unset. You can activate command tracing at any time by executing the command set echo; to turn it off, use unset echo. Command tracing is effective only for the current shell invocation; it is not propagated into called shell scripts. For built-in commands, the echo occurs after all expansions are performed except command and filename substitution. Commands that are not built in are echoed immediately before execution.
history	Specifies the number of commands to be maintained in the history list. The shell retains at least this many lines of command history if sufficient memory is available. The history variable is not initialized automatically and does not need to be assigned a value. If unset, the shell maintains an optimum amount of command history for the size of available memory. You can set the value of history at any time.

continues

Table 12.10. continued

Variable	Description
home	Initialized to the value of the *home* environment variable at shell startup. The value of *home* is used as the default directory for cd and as the value substituted for ~. It is almost always improper for you to change the value of *home*, but you are not prevented from doing so.
ignoreeof	If set, the shell ignores an end-of-file (EOF) character typed at the beginning of a line. If not set, an EOF character typed at the beginning of the line signals the shell to exit, which, for your logon shell, also logs you out. The specific key corresponding to the EOF character can be displayed and changed by using the UNIX stty command. Many C shell versions still log you out if a large number of consecutive EOF characters are received.
mail	An array variable listing the files to be monitored for change. If the first value is numeric, it specifies the frequency in seconds that the shell should check for new mail. The default frequency varies between C shell versions but is commonly 5 or 10 minutes. If the last modification date of any one of the files is observed to change, the file issues the message New mail in *name*, where *name* is the name of the file that changed. (If *mail* lists only one file to be monitored, the notification message is You have new mail.) The following command monitors two mail files and specifies a 10-second interval for mail checking: set *mail*=(10 /usr/mail/taylort /usr/spool/mail/taylort).
noclobber	If set, the shell does not replace an existing file for the I/O redirection >. For >>, it requires that the target file already exist. You can activate the option with the command set *noclobber* and turn it off with unset *noclobber*. When *noclobber* is set, you can use >! and >>! to perform the redirection anyway. The *noclobber* variable is unset initially.
noglob	If set, filename expansion using the pattern characters *, ?, and [...] is disabled. The *noglob* variable is unset initially.
nonomatch	If set, a filename pattern that matches no files is passed through unchanged to the command. By default, the shell issues an error message and ignores a command if no

Variable	Description
	matching files can be found for a filename pattern argument. (Note that *nonomatch* is the default behavior of the Bourne shell.) Use set *nonomatch* to accept unmatched pattern arguments and unset *nonomatch* to force a shell error message. The *nonomatch* variable is unset initially.
notify	If set, the shell writes a message to your terminal at once if the status of a background job changes. By default, the shell does not notify you of status changes until just before issuing the next command-line prompt. Be aware that setting *notify* can cause messages to appear on your screen at inopportune times, such as when using a full-screen editor. The initial value of *notify* is unset.
path	An array variable listing the directories to be searched for commands. If the *path* variable is not set, you must use full, explicit pathnames to execute non–built-in commands— even those in your current directory (. /mycmd, for example). The initial value of *path* is the same as the *PATH* environment variable.
	The shell maintains a hash table of all the executable files in your search path. The hash table is initialized at startup time and is rebuilt whenever you change the value of *path* or *PATH*. Note that if a new command is added to one of the files in your search path (including your current directory), however, the shell might not necessarily be aware of the addition and might fail to find the command even though it exists. Similarly, removing an executable file from a directory early in your search path might not allow the execution of a like-named command in some other directory. In either of these cases, use the rehash built-in command to force rebuilding of the shell hash table.
	Other than the cases mentioned earlier, the shell hash table is invisible to you. It exists to speed up the search for commands by skipping directories where a command is known not to exist.
prompt	Your prompt string. The value of *prompt* is printed at the start of each line when the shell is ready to read the next command. The value of *prompt* is scanned for variable and

continues

Table 12.10. continued

Variable	*Description*
	command substitutions before printing; history substitutions are allowed in the *prompt* string and refer to the command you last entered. The initial value of *prompt* is the string "`% `" (a percent sign followed by a blank). Or, if you are the superuser, the value is "`# `" (a pound sign followed by a blank).
`savehist`	Specifies the number of history lines to save to `~/.history` when you exit your logon shell. When you log on the next time, the C shell executes the equivalent of `source -h ~/.history`. Not all versions of the C shell support the `savehist` variable.
`shell`	Because the C shell is capable of executing only shell scripts written in the C shell language, a mechanism is needed so that shell scripts written for the Bourne shell can be detected and passed to the proper program for execution. Any shell script in which the first line begins with a nonexecutable command is considered to be a Bourne shell. To support this convention, Bourne shell scripts usually specify the `:` built-in command on the first line; there is no `:` command in the C shell. Similarly, scripts intended for the C shell usually begin with a command line and have the pound sign (#) in the first position. (Note that, for versions of UNIX that support the `#!commandInterpreter` notation, the first line for a C shell script is `#!/bin/csh` or, for the Bourne shell, `#!/bin/sh`. The `#!` notation helps eliminate the need for the `shell` variable.
	When the shell recognizes that a shell script has been invoked but is not a valid C shell script, the value of *shell* is used as the initial part of a command to execute the script. The value of *shell* is initialized to the full pathname of the C shell by using a system-dependent directory prefix (usually `/bin/csh`). Any number of options and arguments can be specified along with the shell pathname, however; the filename of the shell script is appended to the value of *shell*.
	You should change the value of *shell* if you intend to execute Bourne shell scripts. (Note that many commands supplied with UNIX are implemented as Bourne shell scripts.)

Variable	Description
status	Contains the exit code of the last command executed as a decimal number. The value of status is changed after the execution of each command, so it generally is useless for you to assign a value to status.
time	If set, the value of time should specify a number of seconds. Any command you execute that exceeds this time limit causes the shell to print a warning line giving the amount of time that the command used and the current CPU-utilization level as a percentage. The initial value of time is unset.
verbose	If set, causes each command to be printed after history substitutions but before other substitutions. The verbose option generally is used within a shell script to echo the commands that follow. The initial value of verbose is unset. The verbose variable can be set automatically by the -v and -V options.

Shell Programming

Although the C shell provides a number of useful extensions to the keyboard interface (such as the command-history mechanism, job control, and additional filename wildcards), its most significant departure from the traditional Bourne shell probably is its syntax for programming constructs—array variables; variable reference forms in general; arithmetic expressions; and the if, while, foreach, and switch statements.

Array variables were discussed in "Using Array Variables," earlier in this chapter. The syntax of variable references was discussed in "Obtaining Variable Values with Reference Expressions." The section "Using Expressions and Operators in Shell Statements," later in this chapter, discusses arithmetic expressions and the special @ command used for calculations. This section looks at the shell statements for flow control: the conditional statements if and switch and the loop control statements while and foreach.

What Is a Shell Script?

A *shell script* is simply a text file containing shell commands. What makes shell scripts especially handy is the capability to execute the commands in the file simply by typing the file's name as if it were a command. To put it another way, shell scripts provide a fairly painless way to add new commands to your UNIX system. A shell script can be as simple or as complicated to write as you choose. It can be designed to be used by yourself alone or by many people as a general-purpose command.

Generally, you'll want to write a shell script when you recognize either of two situations:

■ You find yourself repeating a lengthy series of commands over and over to accomplish one general task. Any time you need to accomplish a task on a fairly frequent basis (daily, weekly, or maybe several times a day) and the task requires more than one UNIX command, the task is a good candidate for packaging in a shell script.

■ A repeatable procedure needs to be established for a formal activity. Printing a weekly customer invoicing report, for example, might require a complex procedure—extracting billing information from a master file, computing the invoice data, setting up the printer, and actually generating the print file.

As a general rule, shell scripts written for the first purpose tend to be straightforward to write, whereas the more formal procedures demand generalized shell scripts of greater complexity.

Writing Shell Scripts: An Overview

Writing a shell script is much like entering commands at the keyboard, with a few important differences:

■ You might want to give arguments to your command. The shell automatically puts any words entered on the command line following your script's name into a set of parameters held by the shell variable argv. You don't need to take any special action to get arguments from the command line; they're already available in the parameter array argv when your script begins its execution. See "Using Predefined Variables," earlier in this chapter, for information on accessing argv.

■ You might want to support one or more options with your new command. The shell passes options to your script the same as other command-line arguments. Options, however, can have a complicated structure, especially if you intend to support the standard UNIX convention for options. See the description of the UNIX getopt command for help with processing command-line option strings.

■ Keyboard commands usually are entered with all information customized to the command's use (ls -l foo.html bar.gif), whereas commands inside shell scripts often are parameterized (ls $opt $1 $file) and can be executed conditionally. You parameterize a command by providing variable references and filename substitutions as the command's arguments instead of literal text. To write alternative sets of commands to handle different situations, you need to use the shell's if, switch, while, and foreach commands. These commands rarely are used at the keyboard but occur heavily in shell scripts.

You use the same general procedure for writing shell scripts, regardless of their purpose:

1. Create a text file containing the required commands.

2. Mark the text file as executable by using the chmod command:

```
chmod +x filename
```

3. Test the shell script.

4. Install the script in its permanent location.

5. Use your script.

You probably already know how to prepare text files by using a text editor. If not, see Chapter 3 of *UNIX Unleashed, Internet Edition,* "Text Editing with vi and emacs." You can use any text editor you want, because the shell is interested only in the file's contents, not in how you created it. The text file cannot contain the formatting characters generated by some word processors, however; the shell script must contain lines identical in format and content to those you would enter at the keyboard. For this reason, you'll probably use a general text editor, such as vi, to prepare shell script files.

A text file must be marked as executable in order to be invoked as a command by entering its filename. You can execute a file as a command even if it is not marked as executable by naming it as the first argument of a csh command. For example, csh payroll causes the shell to search for a file named payroll using the standard search path (defined by the path variable), to open the file for reading, and to proceed to execute the commands in the file. But if you mark the payroll file as executable, you don't have to type **csh** first: payroll becomes a new command.

The shell uses the same search path for locating script files as it does for locating the standard UNIX commands. To invoke a shell script by name, you must store it in a directory listed in your search path. Alternatively, you can add the directory in which the shell script resides to your search path. Naming too many directories in the search path can down slow the shell, though, so shell scripts commonly are gathered into a few common directories.

You'll find that if you do any shell script writing at all, having a directory named bin under your home directory is very handy. Place all the shell scripts you write for your personal use in ~/bin, and include the directory ~/bin in your search path. Then, to add a new command to your personal environment, simply write a command script file, mark it as executable, and store it in the ~/bin directory: It's ready for use. Because it generally is not a good idea to place your ~/bin ahead of the standard bin directories, /bin and /usr/bin, use aliases to reference customized common UNIX commands so you will not have to prepend the customized command with ~/bin/. For example, if you create a script that replaces/enhances the UNIX rm command, you should set up the following alias:

```
alias rm ~/bin/rm
```

Now you can use your new rm without typing **~/bin/rm** and without compromising your search path efficiency.

Shell scripts intended for use by a community of users generally are installed in a general directory not owned by any specific user, such as /usr/bin or /usr/local/bin. Most system administrators prefer to store locally written script files in a separate directory from the standard UNIX commands; this makes system maintenance easier. If your installation practices this procedure, you probably already have the path of the local commands directory in your search path. You'll need the help of the system administrator to store a shell script file in the public directory, though, because you probably won't have write access to the directory (unless you're the administrator).

There is nothing magical about testing shell scripts. As a rule, you'll develop a new shell script in a directory you set aside for that purpose. The directory might contain data files you use to test the shell script, and possibly several versions of the script. You won't want to make the script file accessible to others until you finish testing it.

If you find the behavior of a shell script confusing or otherwise unexplainable, you might find it helpful to see the commands the shell actually executes when you run the script. Simply invoke the script with the -x option (for example, csh -x payroll), or embed the command set echo in the script file or modify the #! directive to be #!/bin/csh -x while you are testing the script. With the echo variable set, the shell prints each command just before executing it. You'll see variable substitutions, filename expansions, and other substitutions all expanded, so that you'll know exactly what the shell is doing while running your script. With this trace to look at, you probably will have no difficulty finding errors in your script file.

If the -x output is especially voluminous, you can cut down the range of commands displayed by the shell by bracketing the commands you want to trace. Put the command set echo in front of the range of commands to be traced and the command unset echo at the end. The shell prints just the commands between set and unset while running your script file. Don't forget to remove the set and unset commands after you finish testing and before putting the shell script into production use.

A Simple Shell Script

Shell scripts can be very easy to write. The following lines, if entered into a file named lld, implement a new command that lists all the directories and subdirectories (often called the *directory tree*) contained in a directory:

```
# lld - long listing of directories only
if ($#argv < 1) set argv=(.)
find $argv[*] -type d -exec /bin/ls -ld \{\} \;
```

The lld script contains only three commands. The first, a line containing only a shell comment, serves as a heading and description of the file for anyone displaying it. Many shell script writers place one or more comment lines at the beginning of their script files to provide some documentation for others, in case anyone ever needs to read, change, or enhance the script. Actually, a well-written script file contains many comment lines to help explain the script's operation. Scripts you write for your own use don't need to contain as many comments as scripts written for more public consumption.

The operative statements in the lld script do two things:

■ Provide a default command-line argument if the user didn't provide any. In this case, if the user specifies no directory names, the lld command lists the current directory.

■ Execute the UNIX `find` command to locate just the directory and subdirectory files contained in the named directory. The `-exec` option invokes the `ls` command for each subdirectory located.

Even though the `lld` shell script is short, it serves the useful purpose of hiding the relatively complicated `find` command from its users. Even for users very familiar with the `find` command, it is much quicker to type `lld` than to type the complete `find` command.

> **TIP**
>
> Most UNIX commands are very spartan in their output. The undecorated output is used to help ease processing when passed to another program. When the output of a command is to the user, however, more adorned output (status messages, debug messages, and header lines, for example) often is desired. As a result, shell scripts should have an option for more or less verbosity. The alias vprint (short for *verbose print*) provides a mechanism to control verbosity. Use the vprint alias whenever output should be based on a verbosity level:
>
> ```
> alias vprint 'if ($?bewordy || $?BEWORDY) echo \!*'
> ```
>
> The shell and environment variable provide flexibility. If a verbose option is given to a C shell script, the bewordy variable should be set. The environment variable provides a mechanism to control the verbosity of scripts called by scripts. The following example shows a simple script for replacing the token date in files with the system date; the script takes advantage of the verbosity alias:
>
> ```
> #!/bin/csh
> if ("x$1" == "x-v") then
>   set bewordy;   shift
> endif
> set DATE="`date`"
> foreach F(*.html)
>   vprint Processing file $F
>   sed "s/DATE/$DATE/" $F > $F.$$
>   mv -f $F.$$ $F
> end
> ```

Using Expressions and Operators in Shell Statements

In a number of contexts, the shell requires you to write an expression. An *expression* is a combination of terms and operators which, when evaluated, yields an arithmetic or logical result. An arithmetic result always is represented as a string of decimal digits. A logical value is true or false. In the C shell, a true condition is indicated by 1, and a false condition is indicated by 0. An arithmetic value can be used where a logical value is expected. Any nonzero value is construed as true, and a zero value is construed as false.

> **NOTE**
>
> The logical values of true and false used by expressions are different from the values of true and false used by the conditional execution operators && and ¦¦. In fact, the values are reversed: true is zero and false is any nonzero value. This can be demonstrated by using the UNIX commands true and false:
>
> ```
> % true
> % echo $status
> 0
> % false
> % !ec
> echo $status
> 1
> ```
>
> The reason for this reversal is that only a zero return code indicates successful execution of a command; any other return code indicates that a command failed. So true indicates successful completion, and false indicates failure, as demonstrated in the following example with the C shell && and ¦¦ operators:
>
> ```
> % true && echo command OK
> command OK
> % false ¦¦ echo command Failed
> command Failed
> ```

A digit string beginning with 0 (for example, 0177) is considered an octal number. The shell generates decimal numbers in all cases, but wherever a number is permitted, you can provide a decimal or an octal value.

Expressions can be used in the @ (arithmetic evaluation), exit, if, and while commands. For these commands, most operators do not need to be quoted; only the < (less than), > (greater than), and ¦ (bitwise or) operators must be hidden from the shell. It is sufficient to enclose an expression or subexpression in parentheses to hide operators from the shell's normal interpretation. Note that the if and while command syntax requires the expression to be enclosed in parentheses.

When writing an expression, each term and operator in the expression must be a separate word. You usually accomplish this by inserting white space between terms and operators. Observe the shell's response to the following two commands, for example. (The @ built-in command is described later in this chapter; it tells the shell to evaluate the expression appearing as its arguments. Note that a space is required between the @ operator and its first argument.)

```
% set x=2 y=3 sum
% @ sum=$x*$y
2*3: no match
% @sum = 1 + 2
@sum: Command not found.
% @ sum=$x * $y
% echo $sum
6
```

In the first @ command, after substitution, the shell sees the statement @ *sum*=2*3. Because 2*3 is a single word, the shell tries to interpret it as a number or an operator. It is neither, so the shell complains because the word starts with a digit but contains non-digit characters.

Most operators have the normal interpretation you might be familiar with from the C programming language. Both unary and binary operators are supported. A complete list of the expression operators supported by the C shell appears in Table 12.11.

Operators combine terms to yield a result. A term can be any of the following:

- A literal number—for example, 125 (decimal) or 0177 (octal).

- An expression enclosed in parentheses—for example, (*exp*). Using a parenthesized expression hides the <, >, and ¦ operators from the shell's normal interpretation. The parenthesized expression is evaluated as a unit to yield a single numeric result, which then is used as the value of the expression. Parentheses override the normal operator precedence.

- Any variable, command, or history substitution (or combination of these) that, when evaluated, yields a decimal or octal digit string. The usual shell replacement mechanisms are used when scanning an expression. The only requirement you must observe is that, after all substitutions, the resulting words must form decimal or octal digit strings or expressions.

Arithmetic and Logical Operators

You can use the operators shown in Table 12.11 to combine numeric terms. Arithmetic operators yield a word consisting of decimal digits. Logical operators yield the string "1" or "0". Remember that operators containing the < (less than), > (greater than), and ¦ (bitwise or) operators must be hidden from the shell by using parentheses—for example, @ x = ($val << 2).

Table 12.11. Arithmetic and logical shell operators.

Operator	Syntax	Operation
~	~a	Bitwise 1's complement. The bits of the digit string a are inverted so that 1 yields 0 and 0 yields 1. The lower bit value for 5 is 0101; applying the ~ operator yields 1010 or 10 in decimal.
!	!a	Logical negation. If the value of digit string a is 0, the value of the expression is 1; if the value of digit string a is nonzero, the value of the expression is 0.
*	a*b	Multiplication. The value of the expression is the arithmetic product of a times b.
/	a/b	Division. The value of the expression is the integer quotient of a divided by b.

continues

Table 12.11. continued

Operator	Syntax	Operation
%	a%b	Remainder (also known as *modulo*). The value of the expression is the remainder from the integer division of a by b. The expression 12 % 5 yields 2, for example. Modulo often is used to test for odd or even numbers—for example, if n % 2 yields 0, the number is even.
+	a+b	Addition. Yields the sum of a and b.
–	a-b	Subtraction. Yields the product of a minus b.
<<	a << b	Left shift. Shifts the bit representation of a left the number of bits specified by b. Equivalent to a * 2b. The lower bit value for 5 is 0101; applying the << operator with a value of 2 (5 << 2) yields 010100 or 20 in decimal.
>>	a >> b	Right shift. Shifts a right the number of bits specified by b. Equivalent to a / 2b. The lower bit value for 20 is 010100; applying the << operator with a value of 2 (20 << 2) yields 0101 or 5 in decimal.
<	a < b	Less than. Yields 1 if a is less than b; otherwise, the expression evaluates to 0.
>	a > b	Greater than. Yields 1 if a is greater than b; otherwise, the expression evaluates to 0.
<=	a <= b	Less than or equal to. Yields 1 if a is not greater than b; otherwise, yields 0.
>=	a >= b	Greater than or equal to. Yields 1 if a is not less than b; otherwise, yields 0.
=~	a =~ b	Pattern matching. Yields 1 if string a matches pattern b.
!~	a !~ b	Pattern matching. Yields 1 if string a does not match pattern b.
==	a == b	String equivalency. Yields 1 if a is identical to b when a and b are compared as strings.
!=	a != b	String non-equivalency. Yields 1 if string a is not identical to string b.
¦	a ¦ b	Bitwise or. Yields the inclusive or of a and b. 1010 and 1100 are the low order bit patterns for 10 and 12, respectively. Applying the ¦ operator (10 ¦ 12) yields a pattern of 1110 or decimal 14.

Operator	Syntax	Operation
^	a ^ b	Bitwise exclusive or. Yields the exclusive or of *a* and *b*. 1010 and 1100 are the low order bit patterns for 10 and 12, respectively. Applying the ^ operator (10 ^ 12) yields a pattern of 0110 or decimal 6.
&	a & b	Bitwise and. Yields the and of corresponding bits of *a* and *b*. 1010 and 1100 are the low order bit patterns for 10 and 12, respectively. Applying the & operator (10 & 12) yields a pattern of 1000 or decimal 8.
&&	a && b	Logical and. Yields 1 if *a* is not 0 and *b* is not 0; otherwise, the expression evaluates to 0 if *a* or *b* is 0.
¦¦	a ¦¦ b	Logical or. Yields 1 if *a* is not 0 or *b* is not 0 (one or both are true); otherwise, the expression evaluates to 0.

Assignment Operators: Evaluating Expressions and Assigning the Results to Variables

You can use the @ command to evaluate an expression and assign the result to a variable or to an element of an array variable. The special characters <, >, and ¦ must be quoted or enclosed in parentheses if they are part of the expression; other expression operators can be used without quoting. For example,

```
@
@ name=expr
@ name[i]=expr
```

The assignment operators +=, -=, *=, /=, %=, <<=, >>=, ¦=, ^=, and &= also are supported. The format *name operator= expr* is equivalent to writing *name = name operator expr*; for example, @ x=x+y can be written as @ x += y.

The C operators ++ and – are supported in both postfix and prefix forms within *expr*. This usage is allowed for the @ command, but not for *expr* generally.

Use the form @ *name[i]=* to assign the result to the *i*th element of the array variable name.

The variable name (or array element *name[i]*) must exist prior to execution of the @ command; the @ command does not create it. A variable or array element is considered to exist even if it has a null value.

Operator Precedence for Arithmetic and Logical Operators

The C shell uses precedence rules to resolve ambiguous expressions. *Ambiguous expressions* are expressions containing two or more operators, as in a+b*c. This expression could be interpreted as (a+b)*c or as a+(b*c). In fact, the latter interpretation applies. Using the values a=3, b=5, and c=7, the expression a+b*c evaluates to 38—not 56.

> **NOTE**
>
> To make life easier for everyone, the shell's rules are identical to those of the C language and a superset of the same precedence rules used by the common hand-held calculator.

In Table 12.11, operators appear in decreasing order of precedence. Operators fall into eight precedence groups:

■ **Unary operators !, ~, and -.** These operators have the highest priority. In succession, they associate right to left, so `!~a` is equivalent to the parenthesized expression `!(~a)`.

■ **Multiplicative operators *, /, and %.**

■ **Additive operators + and -.**

■ **Shift operators << and >>.** The second argument (b) is used as a count and specifies the number of bits by which the first argument should be shifted left or right. Bits shifted out are discarded—for example, `5 >> 1` yields `2`.

■ **Relational operators <, <=, >, and >=.** These operators compare their operands as numbers and yield 1 (true) if the relation is true or 0 (false) if it is not.

■ **Equality operators ==, !=, =~, and !~.** Note that, unlike other operators, these operators treat their arguments as strings. This requires caution, because the strings `" 10"`, `"10 "`, and `" 10 "` all appear unequal even though they are equivalent numerically. To compare strings numerically, use an expression such as `$val == ($x + 0)`.

■ **Bitwise operators |, ^, and &.** These operators combine the internal binary form of their operands, applying an *inclusive or, exclusive or,* or an *and* function to corresponding bits. Definitions of these operations follow:

> **Inclusive or:** Generates a 1 if either of the argument's bits is 1—thus (in binary), `0110 | 1010` yields `1110`.
>
> **Exclusive or:** Generates a 1 if corresponding bits are different—thus (in binary), `0110 ^ 1010` yields 1100.
>
> **And:** Generates a 1 if both source bits are 1—thus, `0110 & 1010` yields `0010`.

■ **Logical operators && and ||.** These operators accept numeric values and yield 1 or 0.

Operators for Command Execution and File Testing

The shell also supports an additional, unconventional set of operators for command execution and file testing in expressions.

Within an expression, you can write a command enclosed in braces ({}). The value of a command execution is 1 if the command executes successfully; otherwise, the value is 0. In other words, a 0 exit code yields a value of 1 (logical true) for the command expression `{ command }`; a nonzero exit code yields a value of 0. Many versions of the C shell require a space between the braces—for example, `@ x = { true }` sets x to 1, whereas `@ x = {true}` yields a syntax error.

Operators for file testing enable you to determine whether a file exists and what its characteristics are. These operators have the form `-f filename` and are treated in expressions as complete subexpressions. For `filename`, specify the name or path of a file, optionally using pattern characters. The argument is subject to all forms of shell substitution, including filename expansion before testing.

Table 12.12 summarizes the file-testing operations supported within expressions.

Table 12.12. File-testing expressions.

Expression	Condition When True
`-r filename`	True if file exists and is readable
`-w filename`	True if file exists and is writable
`-x filename`	True if file exists and is executable
`-e filename`	True if file exists
`-o filename`	True if file exists and is owned by the current real User ID
`-z filename`	True if file exists and is zero length
`-f filename`	True if file exists and is a regular file
`-d filename`	True if file exists and is a directory

The following are examples of an expression that mixes file test operators with other operators. In the first case, the expression tests whether the file is readable and not a directory. The second case is somewhat contrived, but it shows how these operators can be part of an equation if necessary.

```
if (-r $thisfile && ! -d $thisfile) echo Good file

@ x = -f ~/.cshrc + { grep -q foo ¬/.cshrc }
```

> **TIP**
>
> Checking for the value of parameters passed into a shell script is a common task. This task is complicated by the fact that your shell script may take option flags in the form of `-option`, where `option` is a single character. Suppose that you want to test for the presence of a `-d` option, which places your script into a verbose debug mode. The `if` statement
>
> ```
> if ($1 == -d) then set debug
> ```
>
> works as long as the user does not pass in the `-d`, at which point the shell responds with a message like this:
>
> ```
> if: Missing file name
> ```
>
> *continues*

continued

Reversing the order of comparison—if (-d == $1)—only worsens the problem, because now the shell reports the error every time the script runs. The problem is that the -d argument is interpreted as the -d *directory* existence operator, whose syntax requires a filename to be present. You can use a technique known as *double aliasing* to overcome the undesired behavior. Simply place a lowercase x in front of both arguments to the operator ==. The if statement then is transformed to

```
if (x$1 == x-d) then set debug
```

Now the test for the -d option works. Unfortunately, all is not well yet; some perverse, pesky user will do something subversive that can break this syntax (and because I am the only one who uses most of my scripts, I know of what I am speaking). Suppose that you pass a quoted argument that is two words—for example,

```
x.csh "two words" more args
```

The C shell complains with a message like this:

```
if: Expression syntax
```

This last hurdle can be cleared by enclosing the test in quotes:

```
if ("x$1" == "x-d") then set debug
```

The test now is as bulletproof as possible.

Entering Comments in Shell Programs

Quite often, when writing programs, program code that was quite logical six months ago might seem fairly obscure today. Good programmers annotate their programs with comments. Comments are entered into shell programs by inserting the pound sign (#) special character. When the shell interpreter sees the pound sign, it considers all text to the end of the line as a comment.

The comment character is considered a comment only if the current shell is *not* considered interactive. If the command

```
% echo a pint is a # the world round
a pint is a # the world round
```

is entered interactively, the results include the # symbol. If the line is executed from a shell script, the words after the # symbol are not displayed, as in this example:

```
% cat pound.csh
echo a pint is a # the world round
% ./pound.csh
a pint is a
```

A special form of the comment can be used to specify the command processor of a script file. The #! comment tells the current shell what program will run the script. If you are writing C shell scripts, your first line should always be

```
#!/bin/csh
```

This ensures that your script always is run by the C shell. Not all versions of UNIX support this, but most do. Even if a version does not support the `#!` notation, the `#` is interpreted as a comment, so no harm comes by using the `#!` comment. If a Bourne shell user wants to run your script, he will not have to enter `"csh script"`—simply `"script"` suffices.

Conditional Statements

A *conditional statement* provides a way to describe a choice between alternative actions to the shell. The choice actually is made by the shell while executing commands, based on decision criteria you specify. You write a conditional statement when you want your shell script to react properly to alternative real-world situations—for example, to complain when the user omits required command-line arguments or to create a directory when it is missing.

The shell supports two (well, three) commands for conditional execution: `if`, which evaluates an expression to decide which commands should be executed next; and `switch`, which chooses commands based on matching a string. The `if` statement is more appropriate for deciding whether to execute a command or to choose between two commands. The `switch` statement poses a multiple-choice question; it is designed to handle a situation in which many different actions can be taken, depending on the particular value of a string.

The `goto` command, although not strictly a conditional statement because it makes no decision, is nonetheless generally used with a conditional statement to move around to arbitrary places in a shell script. The `goto` command, although valuable in some limited contexts, generally leads to poorly structured shell scripts that are difficult to test and maintain. Experience with the Bourne and Korn shells, which have no `goto` command, shows that `goto` is never necessary. You should try to avoid using the `goto` statement whenever possible.

The following subsections look at the `if` and `switch` statements in more detail.

Using the `if` Statement

There are really two different forms of the `if` statement: a single-line command and a multiline command.

The single-line command has the general syntax

```
if (expr) command
```

Use this form when you need to conditionally execute only one command. This form of the `if` statement provides the basic type of conditional execution: either you execute the command or you don't. *expr* can be any valid expression, as described in "Using Expressions and Operators in Shell Statements," earlier in this chapter. If the expression evaluates to a nonzero value at runtime, the expression is considered to be true, and the shell executes command. But if the value of the expression after evaluation is 0, the shell simply skips *command*, doing nothing. In either case, the shell continues to the next consecutive line of the script file.

> **CAUTION**
>
> Some implementations of the C shell perform an I/O redirection on *command* even if *expr* evaluates to false. Unless you have confirmed that your version of csh works otherwise, you should use redirections on the single-line if statement with this presumption in mind.

The multiline command has a more complex syntax:

```
if (expr) then
commands
else if (expr) then
commands
else
commands
endif
```

In this case, the if statement consists of all lines beginning with if, up to and including the endif line. The multiline form provides a way to tell the shell "either do this or do that." More precisely, the shell executes a multiline if statement as the following: Evaluate the *expr* expression. If the evaluated expression yields a nonzero result, execute the command group (*commands*) following then up to the next else or endif. If the evaluated expression yields a 0 result, skip the command group following then. For else, skip the commands following it up to the next else or endif when the evaluated expression is true, and execute the commands following else when the evaluated expression is false. For endif, simply resume normal command execution. The endif clause performs no action itself; it merely marks the end of the if statement.

Notice that, in its basic form, if...then...else, the multiline form of the if statement provides for choosing between two mutually exclusive actions based on a test. The *expr* expression provides the basis for the choice. The special words then and else introduce command groups associated with the true and false outcomes, respectively.

Because both the single-line and multiline forms of the if statement form complete commands, and you can (indeed, you must) embed commands within an if statement, you can nest if statements by writing one inside the other. Programmers refer to this construct as a *nested if* statement. Nested if statements are legal but can be confusing if the nesting is carried too far. Generally, one level of nesting (an if inside an if) is considered fair and reasonable; two levels deep (an if inside an if inside an if) is treading on thin ice, and three or more levels of nesting implies that you, as the writer, will forever be called on to make any necessary changes to the script file (the flypaper theory of programmer management). Of course, you are helpless to a certain extent; the amount of nesting you use depends on the job you are trying to do, and not very much on your sense of aesthetics.

In case you don't have a clear idea of how if statements work, here's an example of a single-line statement:

```
if (-d ~/bin) mv newfile ~/bin
```

This simple `if` statement provides an expression that is true only if a file named `bin` exists in your home directory (`~/bin`) and is a directory. If the directory exists, the shell proceeds to execute the `mv` command in the normal fashion. If the directory `~/bin` doesn't exist, the entire expression (`-d ~/bin`) is false, and the shell goes on to the next line in the script file without executing the `mv` command; the `mv` command is skipped. The entire statement can be interpreted as the directive *move the file* `newfile` *to the directory* `~/bin` *if (and only if) the directory* `~/bin` *exists; otherwise, do nothing.*

Here's a more complex example using the multiline `if` statement. In this example, the shell is directed to move the file `newfile` into the directory `~/bin` if it exists, and otherwise to write an error message to the user's terminal and abandon execution of the shell script:

```
if (-d ~/bin) then
mv newfile ~/bin
else
echo ~/bin: directory not found
exit 1
endif
```

The longer, multiline `if` statement is the more appropriate of the two examples for many situations, because it provides the user with some feedback when the script can't perform an expected action. Here, the user is given a helpful hint when the `if` statement fails to move the file as expected: Either create the missing directory or stop asking to move files there.

Even the dreaded nested `if` statement can arise from natural situations. For example, the following nests a single-line `if` statement inside a multiline `if` statement:

```
if (-f newfile) then
    if (! -d ~/bin) mkdir ~/bin
    mv newfile ~/bin
else
    echo newfile: file not found
    exit
endif
```

This last example uses a slightly different approach than the previous two; it begins by dealing with the basic choice between the case where the file to be moved exists or doesn't. If `newfile` doesn't exist, you can reasonably conclude that the user doesn't know what he's talking about—he should never have invoked the shell script containing these lines, so describe the problem to him and abandon the shell script (the error message is a good candidate to be printed on the standard error using the `stderr` alias described in "Echoing Arguments to Standard Output," earlier in this chapter). All the error work is done by the lines following `else`. If the file `newfile` exists, however, the script moves the file as expected, creating the directory `~/bin` on-the-fly if it doesn't already exist.

As the previous examples show, the `if` statement often is used in shell scripts as a safety mechanism; it tests whether the expected environment actually exists and warns the user of problems. At the keyboard, you simply would enter the `mv` command by itself and analyze any error message it reports. When used inside a shell script, the script must decide how to proceed when the mv statement fails, because the user didn't enter the mv command himself—in fact, he might not even realize that invoking the shell script implies executing an mv command. The responsible shell script writer takes into account command failures and provides proper handling for all outcomes, producing scripts that behave in a predictable fashion and appear reliable to their users.

Using the `switch` Statement

The switch statement is like if but provides for many alternative actions to be taken. The general form of the statement follows:

```
switch (string)
case pattern:
   commands
default:
   commands
endsw
```

Literally, the shell searches among the patterns of the following case statements for a match with string. In actual use, string generally is the outcome of variable and command substitution, filename generation, and possibly other forms of shell substitution. Each case statement between switch and endsw begins a different command group. The shell skips over command groups following case statements up to the first case statement that matches string. It then resumes normal command execution, ignoring any further case and default statements it encounters. The default: statement introduces a statement group that should be executed if no preceding case statement matched the string. The required endsw statement provides an ending boundary to the switch statement in case the shell still is skipping over commands when it reaches that point; the shell then reverts to normal command execution.

In practice, you'll usually place a breaksw statement after each commands group to prevent the shell from executing the commands in case groups after the one that matched. On rare occasions, you'll have two cases where one case requires some additional preliminary processing before the other case. You then can arrange the two case groups so that the shell can continue from the first case commands group into the second case commands group, by omitting a breaksw. Being able to arrange case groups to allow fall-through is rare, however.

Suppose that you want your shell script to prompt the user for a choice. The user should respond by typing **y** (for yes) to proceed or **n** (for no). The switch statement provides a natural implementation because of its string pattern-matching capability:

```
echo -n "Do you want to proceed?"
set reply=$<
switch ($reply)
case [Yy]*:
   mv newfile ~/bin
   breaksw
default:
   echo newfile not moved
endsw
```

The echo statement writes a prompt message to the terminal. The -n option causes the cursor to remain poised after the message so that the user can type a reply on the same line. The set statement uses the shell special variable $< to read a line from the terminal, which then is stored as the value of the reply variable. The switch statement tests the value of reply. Although the syntax of switch calls for a simple string between parentheses, variable substitution is performed before analysis of the switch statement, so by the time the shell executes switch, it sees the user's typed response as a string instead of a variable reference. In other words, if the user types **yes**, after substitution, the shell switch sees the switch statement as if it had been written switch ("yes").

There is only one case in the switch—a default case. If the user types any line beginning with the letter y or Y, the value of $reply matches the pattern string for the first case; the shell then executes the lines that follow the case statement. When it reaches breaksw, the shell skips forward to the next endsw statement.

If the user's typed reply does not begin with the letter y or Y, it won't match any of the case-statement patterns (there is only one). This causes the shell to reach the default: case while still in skipping mode. The effect of default: is to start executing statements if the shell is in Skipping mode (which means that the default: case must be last in the list of cases), so the effect is to provide a case where the user doesn't type y or Y. The shell script prints a little message to the terminal confirming that nothing was done. Normal execution then continues to and beyond the endsw.

Here's a slightly more advanced example, where the first command-line argument of the shell script could be an option beginning with - (dash). If the argument is an option, the script saves an indication of the option it found for later reference and discards the option. If it finds an unexpected option, it complains with an error message to the user and abandons execution.

```
if ($#argv >= 1) then
    switch ($argv[1])
        case -all:
            set flagall
            breaksw
        case -first:
            set flagfirst
            breaksw
        case -last:
            set flaglast
            breaksw
        default:
            echo Invalid option: "$1"
            exit 1
    endsw
    shift
else
    echo $0:t:  "Usage: [ -first ¦ -last ¦ -all ] filename ..."
    exit 1
endif
```

This example nests a switch statement inside a multiline if statement. If the user provides no command-line arguments, the script skips all the way down to the else statement, prints a brief description of the command's expected argument format, and exits the script. (Note the use of the :t command applied to $0 in order to strip off the path information when displaying the shell script name to the user in the usage message.) If the user provides at least one argument, a switch statement analyzes the first argument to see which option it is. If the argument matches any of the three strings -first, -last, or -all, the shell script discards the argument after setting an indicator variable. If the argument doesn't match any of the strings, the default: case types the error message Invalid option and terminates the script.

Beginning a Case in switch: case

For *label*, specify a pattern-matching expression to be compared to the control expression of the enclosing switch command:

case *label*:

If, for a given execution of the switch command, the control expression of switch matches the pattern label, statements following case are executed. Otherwise, the case statement and statements up to the next case, default, or endsw statement are skipped.

The pattern-matching expression label can consist of ordinary characters as well as the wildcard symbols *, ?, and [...]. The pattern is matched against the argument of switch in the same manner as filenames are matched, except that the search here is for a case statement label that matches the switch argument.

For additional information about switch, see "Conditional Statements," earlier in this chapter.

The case statement is intended primarily for use in shell scripts.

Using the Default Case in switch: default

Use default to designate a group of statements in the range of a switch statement that should be executed if no other case label matches the switch argument.

For consistent results, you should place the default statement group after the last case statement group in the switch.

For more information about the default statement, see "Conditional Statements," earlier in this chapter.

The default command is intended primarily for use in shell scripts.

Exiting from a switch Statement: breaksw

You can use the breaksw command to exit from the immediately enclosing switch statement. The breaksw command transfers control to the statement following the endsw statement. Note that breaksw can exit only from the immediately enclosing switch; any outer switch statements remain active.

For more information on breaksw, see "Conditional Statements," earlier in this chapter.

The breaksw command is intended primarily for use in shell scripts.

Iterative Statements

You use iterative statements to repeatedly execute a group of commands. The iterative statements are while and foreach.

Using the while Loop

You use the while statement to repeatedly execute a group of statements until a specified condition occurs. The while command is very generalized. It executes a group of commands repeatedly as long as a calculated expression yields a true result.

> **CAUTION**
>
> Some care is needed when writing a while loop, because an improper design could cause the commands to be repeated forever in an unending loop or never to be executed at all.

The general syntax of the while command follows:

```
while (expr)
commands...
end
```

For *expr*, write a shell expression (see "Using Expressions and Operators in Shell Statements," earlier in this chapter). For *commands*, write one or more commands to be executed on each iteration of the while loop. Simple and compound commands, pipelines, and parenthesized command lists are all valid.

It is customary when writing shell scripts to indent commands included in the scope of the while or foreach statement. The indentation helps to clarify the commands' subordination to the while or foreach statement and graphically highlights their inclusion in the loop.

The shell evaluates *expr* before the first iteration of the loop and before each subsequent iteration. If the value of *expr* is nonzero (in other words, true), *commands* is interpreted and executed. Any substitutions contained in *commands* are performed each time the command is encountered, allowing a different value to be substituted on each iteration.

When first encountered, the shell processes a while statement much like an if. It evaluates the expression *expr*, and, if it is true (nonzero), the shell proceeds with the next statement. Similarly, if *expr* is false when the shell first encounters the while statement, it skips forward to the end statement, effectively bypassing all the commands between while and end. When you write a while statement, you need to write the test expression *expr* carefully, realizing that the shell might entirely skip the while statement for certain cases of the expression.

Here is a simple example of a `while` statement:

```
while ($#argv > 0)
    if (! -f $1) echo $1: missing
    shift
end
```

The `while` statement evaluates the expression `$#argv > 0` on each repetition—that is, it tests to see whether there are any command-line arguments. As long as the answer is yes, it executes the following `if` and `shift` commands. It stops when the number of command-line arguments has gone to 0, which, after enough repetitions of `shift`, it will eventually do. For each repetition, the `if` command simply tests whether a file exists with the same name as the command-line argument—if not, it writes a warning message. The `while` statement, when invoked with a list of filenames, lists the arguments to standard out where the corresponding file is missing. You could obtain a similar effect simply by entering the command `ls` *name name name…*. The difference is that you would have to pick out the filenames generating a `not found` message from among the normal `ls` output, whereas the `while` example simply lists the files that don't exist.

The `end` statement must be used to mark the end of the range of the `while` loop. It is a valid statement only within the range of the `foreach` and `while` statements. Elsewhere, it generates a shell error message, and the C shell halts processing.

Using the `foreach` Loop

The `foreach` command is intended for processing lists. It executes a command group once for each word given as an argument to the `foreach` command. The shell sets a variable to indicate which argument word the iteration is for; you can use the variable in the repeated commands to take the same general action for each word in the list—hence the name of the command.

The general syntax of the `foreach` statement follows:

```
foreach name (wordlist)
commands
end
```

For *name*, specify the name of a shell variable to which the words of *wordlist* will be assigned in succession. The named variable does not need to be a new one; it can be an existing variable. Any current value of the variable will be lost, though. On exit from the loop, *name* contains the value of the last word in *wordlist*.

For *wordlist*, specify one or more words enclosed in parentheses. The words can be quoted strings (`"foo bar"` `'bas'`), strings of ordinary characters (`one two three`), variable references (`$var $array $arr[1]`), command-substitution strings quoted with backquotes (`` `cat /tmp/x.$$` ``), filename patterns (`*.{cc,hh}`), or history substitutions introduced with ! (`!$`). All the words are scanned and substitutions are performed, and the resulting strings are redivided into words (except where prevented by quoting) before the first loop iteration. You can omit the parenthesized *wordlist*, in which case the shell uses the command-line arguments as the list of words.

For `commands`, specify one or more complete commands using the normal shell syntax. `commands` can be a simple or compound command and can be any of the legal command types, including aliases and built-in shell commands.

The last command in `commands` must be followed with `end` as a separate command. It can appear on the same line as the last command, separated from it with the semicolon statement delimiter (;), or on a line by itself. Note that the `end` command is a valid shell command only when used with a `foreach` or `while` statement. In other contexts, it is considered an illegal command and causes a shell error.

The loop is executed once for each word in `wordlist`. The variable name is set to the current word before each iteration of the loop, in effect stepping through the `wordlist` word by word from left to right. It stops when the loop has been executed once for each word. In `commands`, you can use the value of `$name` to identify which word the repetition is for, or you can ignore its value. You even can change the value of `$name`—the shell won't complain. It simply sets `name` to each word in turn, stopping when it runs out of words.

The `foreach` statement is a very handy tool, because it enables you to repeat an action for each item in a list. It is as useful at the keyboard as inside shell scripts. In the following example, it is used to change the suffix of a series of files, renaming them from `.c` to `.cc`:

```
foreach file (*.c)
  mv $file $file:r.cc
end
```

Altering Loop Execution: `continue` and `break`

You can use two additional special shell commands in the command list within the scope of `foreach` or `while`: the `continue` and `break` commands.

The `continue` command, which takes no arguments, can be used as part of a conditional statement to terminate execution of the current loop iteration, skip the remaining statements in the command list, and immediately begin the next loop iteration. The `continue` command is provided as a convenience so that you don't have to use complex `if` statements to thread a path through the `foreach` loop. After you execute all the commands you want to for the current loop iteration, simply invoke `continue` to skip the remaining commands and start the next iteration of the loop with the first command following `foreach` or `while`.

The `break` command terminates the current and all subsequent iterations of the `foreach` or `while` loop. After `break`, the next statement executed is the one following the `end` statement. Like `continue`, `break` skips all intervening commands between itself and the `end` statement. Unlike `continue`, `break` also halts iteration of the loop.

You can nest `foreach` and `while` loop-control statements within each other, constructing nested loops. If you do so, you usually will want to use a different control-variable name on each inner `foreach` statement, although the shell doesn't enforce such a restriction. Keep in mind, however, that after execution of an inner `foreach` loop, the control variable will be changed. Changing the value of the control variable in one of the command statements does not affect the behavior of the `foreach` statement; on the next iteration, it is assigned the next word in `wordlist` in the usual manner.

When using `break` and `continue`, you must remember that they affect only the `foreach` statement on the same level. You cannot use `break` or `continue` to abandon an iteration of any outer loop. To break out of a `foreach` loop nested two or more levels deep, you need to use conditional statements (such as `if`) to test some condition and execute another `break` or `continue` statement. (Note that this is one of the few programming situations in which a well-documented `goto` actually can improve the quality of the code.)

Altering the Order of Command Execution: `goto`

You can use `goto` to change the order of command execution:

```
goto word
```

Ordinarily, commands are executed one after another in succession. The looping statements `foreach` and `while` enable you to repeat a group of statements a fixed or variable number of times, and the `if` and `switch` conditional statements enable you to choose between two or more alternative statement groups. Other than this, the general flow of control in statement execution is from the first to the last statement in a shell script or input command sequence. The `goto` command makes it possible to change the flow of control in an arbitrary way.

For *word*, specify an ordinary symbol (a string of characters not enclosed in quotes, not containing blanks or tabs, and not containing any punctuation characters having special meaning to the shell). *word* is subject to filename and command substitution. Assuming that a file named `index` exists in the current directory, all the following `goto` commands will jump to the label `index`: `"goto index"`, `"goto `echo index`"`, and `"goto ind*"`.

The shell searches the command-input stream for a line beginning with *word* followed immediately by a colon (*word*:); this forms a statement label. If the statement label is found, execution resumes with the first command following the label. If the statement label cannot be found, the shell writes an error message and stops.

The `goto` command generally is used inside a shell script, in which case the range of statements searched for the label is restricted to the contents of the script file. In any other context, the shell backspaces the input medium as far as possible and then searches forward to the statement label. Backspacing is not supported for the terminal, so the `goto` statement is limited to the current available command-history lines when `goto` is issued from the keyboard.

CAUTION

Using goto from the keyboard probably will put your session in an infinite loop, if there is actually a label to which to jump. Consider the history buffer

```
1 ls /usr/bin
2 jumpHere:
3 echo Infinite loop
```

with the label jumpHere:. If you type **goto jumpHere**, the C shell inserts the goto command into your history as command 4 and repeats forever commands 3 and 4 on your history list.

Specifying the Response to a Signal: onintr

Use onintr to specify the action to be taken when the shell receives a signal. For example,

```
onintr
onintr -
onintr label
```

The onintr command is roughly equivalent to the Bourne shell trap command but differs in syntax and usage.

When specified without arguments, the onintr command sets the default signal action for all signals. When used within a shell script, this causes most signals to result in termination of the shell script. When used from the keyboard, this resets any special signal-handling you established with previous onintr commands.

You can use onintr - to disable and ignore all signals. This form is handy when used within a shell script to protect a sensitive series of commands, which, if interrupted (abandoned because of shell script termination on receipt of a signal), might leave unwanted files or generate invalid results. You can use onintr without arguments to restore the normal default signal actions.

You can use onintr label to cause the shell to perform an implicit goto to the statement label label on receipt of a signal. The shell provides no indication of which signal was received. Because most signals represent a request for termination, though, this form of onintr can be used to perform orderly cleanup before exiting from a shell script. You might use onintr label in a shell script, for example, to provide a cleanup routine if the user presses the INTR key (interrupt key, often configured to be Ctrl-C; use stty -a to query your terminal settings), signaling his desire to cancel the shell script's execution. After performing any desired actions, exit the shell script with the exit command.

For more information about statement labels, see the goto command description in this section.

TIP

One of the basic tenets of programming is based on this old joke: I went to the doctor and told her, "It hurts when I do this." The doctor replies, "Then don't do that." Believe it or not, this is great programming wisdom. Keeping track of temporary files, which includes remembering to delete temporary files regardless of whether an interrupt was passed in,

continues

continued

can be problematic. Applying the preceding pearl of wisdom, if it hurts to create temporary files, do not create temporary files if it is at all avoidable. By judiciously using command substitution, pipelining, `eval`, shell variables, and `xargs`, you can greatly reduce the need for temporary files. (See "Quoting or Escaping from Special Characters," earlier in this chapter, for a discussion on the use of `xargs`.)

If you must create a temporary file, following a few simple guidelines can save a great deal of pain. Always use the $$ notation when naming a temporary file, and always place the file in `/tmp`. Using $$ ensures uniqueness, and, on most UNIX systems, the location `/tmp` regularly deletes unaccessed files. The following command creates a temporary filename for use in a script:

```
set tmpfile=/tmp/foo$$
```

Processing an Arbitrary Number of Parameters: `shift`

You can use `shift` to shift the shell parameters ($1, $2, $n) to the left:

```
shift
shift name
```

After execution, the value of $2 moves to $1, the value of $3 moves to $2, and so on. The original value of $1 is discarded, and the total number of shell parameters (as indicated by $argv#) is reduced by 1.

You can use `shift` *name* to perform the same type of action on the named array variable.

Interpreting a Script in the Current Shell: `source`

You can use `source` to read and interpret a script of shell commands within the current shell environment:

```
source [-h] name
```

No subshell is invoked, and any changes to the environment resulting from commands in the script remain in effect afterward. Possible changes that can result from execution of a script file with `source` include changing the current directory, creating or altering local and environment variables, and defining command aliases.

An `exit` statement encountered in a script interpreted with `source` results in an exit from the current shell level; if this is your logon shell, you are logged out.

For *name*, provide the filename or pathname of a file containing shell commands and statements. Some C shell versions search the current directory path (*path* variable) for the file if you do not specify a name beginning with /, ./, or ../.

The `-h` option enables the file to be sourced into the history buffer without the commands being executed.

Customizing Your Shell Environment

The C shell provides for two initialization scripts—the .cshrc and .login files—and one shut-down procedure—the .logout file.

The C shell always looks for a file in your home directory named .cshrc whenever it is in-voked, whether as a logon shell, as a command, implicitly by entering the filename of a shell script as a command, or by a subshell expression enclosed in parentheses.

The .cshrc script should perform only those initializations you require for any C shell envi-ronment, including shells you invoke from other commands such as vi and pg.

When invoked as a logon shell, the .login script is executed to perform any one-time-only initializations you require. These can include issuing the stty command to define your pre-ferred Erase, Kill, and INTR keys; setting your *cdpath*, *path*, and *mail* variables; and printing the news of the day.

When you exit a logon shell by typing the EOF key (end-of-file key, often configured to be Ctrl-D; use stty -a to query your terminal settings) at the start of a line or by entering the exit or logout command, the shell searches for a file named .logout in your home directory. If found, the shell executes it and then terminates. You could use the .login and .logout scripts to maintain a time-sheet log recording your starting and ending times for terminal sessions, for example.

What to Put in Your .cshrc Initialization File

You should define command aliases, variable settings, and shell options in your ~/.cshrc file. This file always is executed before the .login script, and by placing such definitions in .cshrc, you ensure that the definitions are available in subshells.

Typical items you will want to have in your .cshrc file include the following:

- `alias lx /usr/bin/ls -FC`

  You probably will want one or more aliases for the ls command. After developing some experience with UNIX, you'll find that you prefer certain options when listing directory contents. On some occasions, you'll want the long listing given by the -l option, but, more often, a multicolumn listing of some form will provide the quick overview of directory contents that helps orient you. You can have as many aliases for the ls command as you want, but only one named ls. If you define an alias for ls, remember that it affects your use of the command in pipelines.

- `set ignoreeof`

  The *ignoreeof* option prevents you from logging out by accidentally typing the EOF character (usually, Ctrl-D). When this option is set, you must explicitly invoke the exit or logout command to exit from the shell.

■ set *noclobber*

Some users prefer to use the *noclobber* option, and some don't. If this option is set, you can't accidentally destroy an existing file by redirecting a command's output to it with > *filename*. If you develop a feeling of frustration after destroying useful files too often with the > operator, by all means, try *noclobber*. Note that it provides no protection from accidentally deleting the wrong files with rm, though.

■ set *path=(dirname dirname ...)*

You might want to define your search path in .cshrc instead of .login. By defining your path in .cshrc, you ensure that you always have the same search path available for all invocations of the shell. However, you also prevent inheriting an environment. Most people find that it is sufficient to define the search path in the .login script.

You might want to place portions of your initialization into separate files and have the .cshrc source the separate files. For example, place all your aliases in a separate file, ~/.cshrc.alias, and set your path in ~/.cshrc.path. A separate alias and pathfile enable you to run most of your scripts using the -f option, and the script can source the portion of the initialization it needs. (See "Shell Options," earlier in this chapter, for a description of -f.)

For further information about variables and how to set them, see "Variables," earlier in this chapter.

What to Put in Your .login Initialization File

The .login script is an excellent place to do the following things:

■ Identify the kind of terminal you are using—perhaps by prompting the user to enter a code.

■ Set the TERM environment variable to match the terminal type. TERM is used by the vi command to send the correct terminal-control codes for full-screen operation; it can't work correctly with an incorrect TERM.

■ You can issue the stty command to set your preferred control keys:

```
stty erase '^H' kill '^U' intr '^C'
```

■ You can set global environment variables:

```
setenv TERM vt100
setenv EDITOR /usr/bin/vi
setenv PAGER /usr/bin/pg
```

■ You can set local variables:

```
set path=(/usr/bin /usr/ucb /usr/X/bin $home/bin .)
set cdpath=(. .. $home)
set mail=(60 /usr/spool/mail/$logname)
```

■ And, you can execute any system commands you find interesting:

```
news
df
```

For further information about variables and how to set them, see "Variables," earlier in this chapter.

What to Put in Your .logout File

There is no standard use for the .logout file. If you don't have a use for the .logout file, you can omit it without incurring any shell error messages.

Job Control

When you type a command on the command line and press Return, the command executes in the foreground, which means that it has your shell's undivided attention and ties up your shell until the job finishes executing. This means that you must wait until that command executes before you can do any other work in that shell. For commands or programs that finish quickly, this isn't usually a problem. It is a problem for commands or programs that take minutes or hours to finish. Most graphical applications, such as xterm, are made background jobs. By executing commands or programs in the background, you can free up your shell immediately to do other tasks.

The C shell provides you with a job-control mechanism for executing and managing background jobs.

> **NOTE**
>
> When csh was implemented years ago, its job-control mechanism was quite an advancement. In fact, when the Korn shell was implemented to provide C shell features in a Bourne shell style, the csh job-control interface was carried virtually intact and without change. The description of job control for the Korn shell in Chapter 11 is essentially accurate for the C shell as well.

Table 12.13 lists the C shell commands provided for managing background processes started with & (called *jobs*).

Table 12.13. C shell commands to manage background processes starting with &.

Command	Function
&	Executes a command in the background
bg	Resumes execution of stopped jobs in the background
fg	Switches background jobs to foreground execution
jobs	Lists active background jobs
kill	Sends a signal to specified jobs
wait	Waits for all jobs to finish

Executing Jobs in the Background: &

You can use & to execute a command in the background. A background process has no associated terminal:

```
command &
```

If the process attempts to read from your terminal, its execution is suspended until you bring the process into the foreground (with the `fg` command) or cancel it. A command executed in the background is called a *job* by the C shell.

For *command*, write a simple command or a compound command. The & operator must appear at the end of the *command*. The & operator also serves as a statement delimiter; any commands following & on the same line are treated as if they were written on the following line:

```
xterm & xclock & xload &
```

The & operator also has lower precedence than any other compound operators. In the following example, all the commands are executed in the background as a single job:

```
grep '#include' *.cc ¦ pr && echo Ok &
```

When you execute a command in the background by appending an &, the shell writes a notification message to your terminal identifying the job number assigned to the job. Use this job number, in the form %*number*, as the operand of `kill`, `fg`, `bg`, or `wait`, to manipulate the job.

Listing Active Background Jobs: jobs

The `jobs` command simply lists the process group leaders you have active in background execution. The *process group leader* is the process that owns itself and any additional subprocesses. A simple command appended with & launches one process and one process group leader (one job with one process). A pipe of three commands all executed in the background (for example, `ls ¦ sed ¦ xargs &`) launches three processes but is still one job.

You can use the `jobs` statement to list the current set of background jobs:

```
jobs [ -l ]
```

The output of `jobs` has the following general format:

```
% jobs
[1] + Stopped     vi prog.cc
[2]   Done        cc myprog.cc
```

A plus sign (+) marks the shell's current job; a minus sign (-), if shown, marks the preceding job. Various messages, including `Stopped` and `Done`, can be shown to indicate the job's current status.

Use option `-l` to print the process identifier of each job beside its job number:

```
% jobs -l
[1] + 2147 Stopped    vi prog.cc
[2]   1251 Done       cc myprog.cc
```

Referring to Job Numbers: fg and bg

Both the `bg` and `fg` commands require you to specify a job number. A job number can be any of those listed in Table 12.14.

Table 12.14. Job numbers.

Job Number	Description

%n	A reference to job number *n*. When you start a job using the & operator, the shell prints a job number you can use to refer to the job later. For example,
	
	 `% du ¦ sort -nr &`
	 `[1] 27442`
	
	 The number in brackets is the job number *n*. The other number is the process identifier of the job.

%string	A reference to the most recent background command you executed beginning with *string*. For *string*, you can specify only the first command name of the line, but you don't need to specify the entire command name: Any unique prefix of the command name will be accepted. Thus, you can use %da to mean the date command, but you can't safely use %pr to refer to a print command if you also have used the pr command in the same logon session.
%?string	A reference to the most recent background command containing *string* anywhere in the line. For example, %?myprog is a valid reference to the job cc myprog.cc.
%+	A reference to the current job—the job you last started, stopped, or referenced with the bg or fg command. In the listing produced by the jobs command, the current job is marked with + and can be referenced with the shorthand notation %+.
%%	Same as %+.
%	Same as %+.
%-	A reference to the preceding job. In the listing produced by the jobs command, the preceding job is marked with - and can be referenced by the shorthand notation %-.

Moving Foreground Jobs into the Background: bg

You can use the bg command to switch the specified jobs (or the current job, if no job arguments are given) to background execution. If any of the jobs currently are stopped, their execution resumes. bg is used most often after placing a job into the background by using the SUSP key (suspend key, often configured to be Ctrl-Z, use stty -a to query your terminal settings). For example,

```
bg [ job ... ]
```

A job running in the background is stopped automatically if it tries to read from your terminal. The terminal input is not executed unless the job is switched to foreground execution. If you use the bg command to resume a job that has been stopped for terminal input, the job immediately stops again when it repeats the pending terminal read request, making the bg command appear to have been ineffective. In such a case, you must terminate the job (by using the kill command) or switch the job to foreground execution and respond to its input request (see the fg command).

You must use the job number when referring to the job—for example, fg %3 or fg %cc. The C shell also supports an abbreviation for the fg command: %10 in itself switches job 10 to foreground execution, acting as an implied fg command. (The Korn shell doesn't exactly support this, although you can set up an alias to achieve the same effect.)

Pausing and Resuming Background Jobs

The Ctrl-Z mechanism provides a handy way to stop doing one thing and temporarily do another and then switch back. Although some interactive commands such as vi enable you to escape to the shell, not all do. Whether or not the command does, simply press Ctrl-Z to temporarily stop the command; you'll immediately see a shell prompt. Now you can do whatever you want. To resume the interrupted command, enter fg %vi (or %vi, or just %). When you have several outstanding jobs, the jobs command provides a quick summary to remind you of what commands you currently have stacked up.

Moving Background Jobs into the Foreground: fg

You can use fg to switch the specified jobs into foreground execution and restart any that were stopped. For example,

```
fg [ job ... ]
```

If you specify no job arguments, the current job is assumed. The current job is the last job you started, stopped, or referenced with the bg or fg command and is identified with a + in the listing produced by the jobs command.

For job, specify any percent expression, as described in "Referring to Job Numbers: fg and bg," earlier in this chapter. Note that %5 or %vi (or any of the allowable percent expressions), entered as a command, is equivalent to issuing the fg command with that argument. Thus, %5 restarts job 5 in the foreground, and `%vi` restarts the most recent `vi` command if it is one of your active jobs. (See also the `bg-`, `wait-`, and `jobs`-related commands.)

Stopping a Background Job: `stop`

You can pause a job that is executing in the background with `stop`. For example,

```
stop [ %job ]
```

This command sends a stop signal (`SIGSTOP`) to the named job, as if the SUSP key were pressed (usually Ctrl-Z). The job is stopped.

You can use the `bg` command to resume execution of the stopped job or `fg` to bring the job to the foreground and resume its execution.

To terminate the execution of a background job, use the `kill` command. See "Signaling a Process: `kill`," later in this chapter, for details.

Stopping the Current Shell: `suspend`

The `suspend` command suspends execution of, or stops, the current shell. Its effect is the same as pressing the SUSP key (ordinarily, Ctrl-Z). For example,

```
suspend
```

Waiting for Background Jobs to Finish: `wait`

You can use the `wait` command to wait for all background jobs to finish. For example,

```
wait
```

The shell simply stops prompting for command input until it receives notification of the termination of all background jobs.

To stop waiting, simply press the Return (or Enter) key. The shell prints a summary of all background jobs and then resumes prompting for commands in the normal fashion.

Requesting Notification of Background Job Status Changes: `notify`

You can use the `notify` command to request that the shell always report any change in the status of a background job immediately. For example,

```
notify [ %job ]
```

By default, the shell reports the completion, termination, stoppage, or other status change by writing a message to your terminal just before the command prompt.

You can use `notify` with no arguments to request immediate notification of background job status changes. Be aware that a notification message might be written to your terminal at inopportune times, however, such as when it is formatted for full-screen operation; the message could garble a formatted screen.

You can use `notify %job` to request a notification of status change for only the specified job. This form is handy when you run a background command and later decide you need its results before continuing. Instead of repeatedly executing `jobs` to find out when the background job is done, just issue `notify %job` to ask the shell to tell you when the job is done.

For `%job`, specify any of the job-reference formats, as described for the `bg` command.

Controlling Background Process Dispatch Priority: `nice`

You can use the `nice` command to change the default dispatch priority assigned to batch jobs. For example,

```
nice [ +number ] [ command ]
```

The idea underlying the `nice` facility (and its unusual name) is that background jobs should demand less attention from the system than interactive processes (interactive graphical user interface jobs are the exception). Background jobs execute without a terminal attached and usually are run in the background for two reasons:

- The job is expected to take a relatively long time to finish.
- The job's results are not needed immediately.

Interactive processes, however, usually are shells where the speed of execution is critical because it directly affects the system's apparent response time. It therefore would be nice for everyone (others, as well as yourself) to let interactive processes have priority over background work.

UNIX provides a `nice` command you can use to launch a background job and at the same time assign it a reduced execution priority. The `nice` built-in command replaces the UNIX command and adds automation. Whereas the UNIX `nice` command must be used explicitly to launch a reduced-priority background job, the shell always assigns a reduced execution priority to background jobs. You use the `nice` command to change the priority the shell assigns.

When invoked with no arguments, the `nice` built-in command sets the current `nice` value (execution priority) to 4. A logon shell always assumes a `nice` value of 0 (the same priority as interactive processes). You must execute `nice` or `nice +value` to change the `nice` value (until then, you aren't being nice; all your background jobs compete with interactive processes at the same priority).

Use `nice +number` to change the default execution priority for background jobs to a positive or zero value. A zero value (`nice +0`) is the same as interactive priority. Positive values correspond to reduced priority, so that `nice +5` is a lower priority than `nice +4`, `nice +6` is a lower priority than `nice +5`, and so on.

If you specify *command*, the `nice` command launches the command using the default or specified execution priority but doesn't change the default execution priority. For example, `nice cc myprog.c` launches the compilation using the default priority, whereas `nice +7 cc myprog.c` launches the compilation with an explicit priority of 7.

Note that you do not need to append `&` to the `nice` command to run a command as a background job; when you specify `command`, the background operator is assumed.

Signaling a Process: `kill`

You can use the `kill` built-in command to send a signal to one or more jobs or processes. For example,

```
kill [ -signal ] [%job ...] [pid ...]
kill -l
```

The built-in command hides the UNIX `kill` command. To invoke the UNIX `kill` command directory, use its full pathname (probably `/bin/kill` or `/usr/bin/kill`). The built-in command provides additional features that are not supported by `/bin/kill` and can be used in the same manner.

For *signal*, specify a number or a symbolic signal name. All UNIX implementations support signals 1 through 15; some implementations can support more. By convention, the signals listed in Table 12.15 are always defined.

Table 12.15. Signals.

Signal	Name	Meaning	Effect
1	HUP	Hang up	Sent to all processes in a process group when the terminal is disconnected by logout or, for a remote terminal, when the terminal connection is dropped.
2	INT	Interrupt	Sent after the user presses the INTR key (defined by the `stty` command; usually, Ctrl-C; sometimes, BREAK).
3	QUIT	Quit	Sent after the user presses the QUIT key (defined by the `stty` command; there is no default).
9	KILL	Kill	Sent only by the `kill` command; it forces immediate termination of the designated process and cannot be ignored or trapped.

continues

Table 12.15. continued

Signal	Name	Meaning	Effect
10	BUS	Bus error	Usually caused by a programming error, a bus error can be caused only by a hardware fault or a binary program file.
11	SEGV	Segment violation	Caused by a program reference to an invalid memory location; can be caused only by a binary program file.
13	PIPE	Pipe	Caused by writing to a pipe when no process is available to read the pipe; usually a user error.
15	TERM	Termination	Caused by the kill command or system function. This signal is a gentle request to a process to terminate in an orderly fashion; the process can ignore the signal.

If you omit *signal*, the TERM signal is sent by default (unless the -1 option is specified, in which case no signal is sent at all).

For *job*, specify one or more jobs or process identifiers. A job reference can be any one of the following:

■ Any of the valid % operators presented in "Referring to Job Numbers: fg and bg," earlier in this chapter.

■ A Process ID number.

The % operator and Process IDs may both be on the command line—for example, kill %2 1660 543 %3.

There is no default for *job*. You must specify at least one job or process to which the signal will be sent.

You can use the command kill -1 to list the valid symbolic signal names. Always use the kill -1 command to identify the exact signal names provided when using a new or unfamiliar version of csh.

Also see the bg, fg, wait, and jobs commands for more information about job control using the C shell.

Using the Shell's Hash Table

The C shell's hash table is used to expedite command searches by identifying the directory or directories where a command might be located. The hash table is created based on the directories specified in your *path* C shell variable. The order in which the directories are specified determines the search order as well as the efficiency of locating commands you execute.

For each directory in the search path or hash table, the shell invokes the exec UNIX operating system function to search for the command to be executed. If unsuccessful, the search continues with other possible locations for the command. However, the exec operating system function entails considerable operating system overhead; its use increases system load levels and degrades system performance. Consequently, the effectiveness of the shell's hash table is a matter of concern. C shell provides you with three commands for working with the hash table: hashstat, rehash, and unhash.

Determining the Effectiveness of the Hash Table: hashstat

You can use the hashstat command to determine the effectiveness of the shell's hash table mechanism. For example,

```
$ hashstat
```

The statistics printed by hashstat indicate the number of trials needed on average to locate commands, and hence the number of exec function calls per shell command issued. Ideally, every command would be found with one trial. If the hit rate is too low, many directory searches (exec invocations) are occurring for each command executed. You need to reorder the directories in your search path and, if possible, eliminate directories from your path that don't contain any commands you use. Poor hash table performance is caused by an improperly structured search path, as defined by the *path* C shell variable. The commands you use most frequently should be located in the directory named first in the path, and successive directories should be referenced less and less frequently. If you list directories in your path that don't contain any commands you use, the shell will waste time searching those directories for commands you do use.

Rebuilding the Hash Table: rehash

You can use the rehash command to rebuild the shell's hash table. The hash table is used to expedite command execution by reducing the set of directories that needs to be searched to locate a particular command. For example,

```
rehash
```

The hash table is updated automatically when you change the value of the *path* variable, but no automatic update is possible when you change the name of an executable file or you move executable files in or out of directories in your search path. Changes made by the system administrator to directories containing system commands also go unnoticed. In such cases, use rehash to resynchronize the shell's hash table with the real world.

You need to execute the rehash command only when an attempt to execute a command that you know exists in your search path results in a not found message.

Disabling the Use of the Hash Table: unhash

You can use the unhash command to discontinue the shell's use of a hash table to expedite directory searches for commands. The shell continues to search directories using the *path* variable for programs in the usual fashion, although with reduced efficiency. See the rehash command to resume usage of the hash table. For example,

unhash

You might want to issue the unhash command while developing a new shell script, when restructuring the contents of directories listed in your *path* variable, or if you have NFS mounts in your path and the NFS server goes awry.

Managing Resource Limits: limit and unlimit

UNIX imposes a number of limitations on the amount of resources any system user can commit. For each type of resource, there is a system-defined maximum. The system administrator can increase or reduce the size of a limitation by using the limit command or restore the limitation to its normal value with unlimit. Normal users also can employ the limit and unlimit commands, but only to further restrict resource usage—not to increase it.

The specific types of resources you can control with the limit and unlimit commands follow.

Unless you are the system administrator, changing a resource limit affects only the current process. It doesn't affect any other commands you are running as background jobs at the same time, and it doesn't affect any other users.

Manipulating resource limits is not something you do very often. It is of interest mainly to programmers and system administrators involved in problem determination. You should be aware of the kinds of limits that exist and what their values are, though, because a resource limit can cause a command to fail for spurious or misleading reasons. One of the resource limits sets an upper bound on the size of a disk file, for example. If a command you execute tries to write a file bigger than the file size limit, the command may fail, reporting that it is out of disk space. This may lead you to ask the system administrator to give you more disk space. Getting more disk space won't solve the problem, however, because the file size limit won't allow your command to use the space even if it's available. The proper resolution is to ask the system administrator to change the system's built-in file size limit or to stop trying to write such large files.

Displaying or Setting Maximum Resource Limits: `limit`

You can use the `limit` command to display or change system maximums that apply to the current invocation of the shell and all commands and jobs you launch from the shell. For example,

```
limit [ resource [ maximum ] ]
```

UNIX provides a `limit` command you can use to change the maximum file size you can write with any command. The `limit` built-in shell command can be used for the same purpose, as well as to change a number of other limits.

If you specify no arguments, the `limit` command lists all settable limits currently in effect.

For *resource*, specify one of the options shown in Table 12.16. (Note: The resource types you can specify depend on the particular implementation of `csh` and UNIX you are using.)

Table 12.16. `resource` options.

Option	Description
`coredumpsize`	The maximum size of a coredump file that can be written. The system defines a maximum size for core files. You can reduce the limit or increase the limit up to the system-defined limit.
`cputime`	The maximum number of CPU seconds any process can run. A process that exceeds this limit is terminated.
`datasize`	The maximum amount of memory that can be allocated to a program's data and stack area. The system defines a default upper limit for the amount of memory a program can use. You can reduce the limit or, if you previously reduced it, you can increase it back up to the system-defined limit.
`filesize`	The maximum number of bytes a file can contain. An attempt to create a new file or to append bytes to a file that would exceed this size causes the operating system to signal an end-of-medium condition to the program. The UNIX system specifies an upper limit for file size that you cannot change. You can use the `limit` command to display the limit or to reduce it; you cannot increase it, however, unless you have previously reduced the limit, in which case you can increase it up to the system-defined limit.
`stacksize`	The maximum amount of memory the system should allow for a program's stack area. The system defines a maximum size to which any program's stack area can grow. You can reduce the limit or, if you previously reduced it, you can increase it back up to the system-defined limit.

If you specify *resource* but omit *maximum*, the `limit` command displays the current limit value for the specified resource. Otherwise, specify a number of seconds (for *cputime*) or a number of kilobytes for any other resource (`limit` *filesize* `32` sets the maximum file size to 32 KB or 32,768 bytes). You can append `m` to the number to specify megabytes instead of kilobytes: `limit` `datasize` `2m` sets the maximum program data area to 2,097,152 bytes (2,048 KB).

Canceling a Previous `limit` Command: `unlimit`

You can use `unlimit` to cancel the effect of a previous `limit` restriction. For example,

```
unlimit [ resource ]
```

Because the `limit` command can be used only to reduce system-defined constraints even further (for other than the superuser), the `unlimit` command restores the named limit (or all limits) to their system-defined maximums. See "Displaying or Setting Maximum Resource Limits: `limit`" for a description of the allowable values for *resource*.

Summary

When compared to the Bourne shell, facilities provided by the C shell include extensions for both the keyboard environment and the shell programming environment. Besides more filename wildcards, command history, history substitution, and job control, the C shell also provides array variables, arithmetic expressions, a somewhat more convenient `if` statement, and briefer forms of `while` and `foreach` (dropping the useless `do` of the Bourne shell).

Virtually all the features of the C shell also are supported by the Korn shell in a form more consistent with the syntax and use of the Bourne shell. Because of its many extensions for both the keyboard user and shell script writer, the C shell is well worth your investigation; you might find that you like it.

This chapter provided a quick overview of the C shell syntax and features. You can find a more detailed, although turgid, presentation in the reference manuals for your particular version of UNIX; you should consult these for the last word on details of its operation. The C shell, being descended from BSD roots, has never been subjected to the same degree of standardization as the System V side of the UNIX family.

Shell Comparison

by John Valley and Sean Drew

IN THIS CHAPTER

CHAPTER 13

Most contemporary versions of UNIX provide three shells—the Bourne and/or POSIX shell, the C shell, and the Korn shell—as standard equipment. However, there are many other shells available for use, including, but not limited to: Z shell, TC shell, RC shell, and the Bourne Again shell. Choosing the right shell to use is an important decision because you will spend considerable time and effort learning to use a shell, and even more time actually using the shell. The right choice will allow you to benefit from the many powerful features of UNIX with minimal effort. This chapter is intended to assist you in choosing a shell by drawing your attention to the specific features of each shell.

Of course, no one shell is best for all purposes. If you have a choice of shells, then you need to learn how to choose the right shell for the job.

The shell has three main uses:

1. As a keyboard interface to the operating system

2. As a vehicle for writing scripts for your own personal use

3. As a programming language to develop new commands for others

Each of these three uses places different demands on you and on the shell you choose. Furthermore, each of the shells provides a different level of support for each use. This chapter describes the advantages and disadvantages of some of the more commonly used shells with respect to the three kinds of tasks you can perform with a shell.

Interactive Usage

The first point to keep in mind when choosing a shell for interactive use is that your decision affects no one but yourself. This gives you a great deal of freedom: You can choose any shell without consideration for the needs and wishes of others. Only your own needs and preferences matter.

The principal factors that affect your choice of an interactive shell are as follows:

- **Prior experience.** Prior experience can be either a plus or a minus when choosing a shell. For example, familiarity with the Bourne shell is an advantage when working with a Bourne shell variant, such as the Korn shell, but something of a disadvantage when working with the C shell or one of its variants. Don't let prior experience dissuade you from exploring the benefits of an unfamiliar shell. There are basically two main syntax styles for shells: Bourne and C. The main members of the Bourne family are Bourne, Bourne Again, POSIX, Korn, and Z. The main members of the C shell family are C and TC. Shells such as Z and Bourne Again have varying degrees of C shell syntax support built in.

- **Learning.** A lamentable fact of life is that as the power and flexibility of a tool increase, the tool becomes progressively more difficult to learn how to use. The much-maligned VCR, with its proliferation of convenience features, often sits with its clock unset as silent testimony. So, too, it is with UNIX shells. There is a progression of complexity from the Bourne shell, to the C shell, to the Korn shell, and on to other shells, with each shell adding features and shortcuts to the previous one. The cost of becoming a master of the extra features is extra time spent learning and practicing. You'll have to judge whether you'll really use those extra features enough to justify the learning time. Keep in mind that all shells are remarkably similar and relatively easy to learn at the most basic level. The Bourne shell family has a much richer (although more cryptic) programming language than the C shell family. While the C shell's Spartan programming interface is easier to learn, it can be quite a hindrance for most programming tasks, save for the simplest of scripts.

■ **Command editing**. All shells offer features to assist with redisplaying and reusing previous commands, the Bourne shell being the notable exception. The extra time savings you can realize from command editing features depends greatly on how much you use the shell. Generations of UNIX users lived and worked before shells such as the C shell and Korn shell were invented, demonstrating that the Bourne shell is eminently usable, just not as convenient for the experienced, well-practiced user of a shell with some form of command reuse.

■ **Wildcards and shortcuts**. Once again, your personal productivity (and general peace of mind) will be enhanced by a shell that provides you with fast ways to do common things. Wildcards, command aliases, and completion can save you a great deal of typing if you enter many UNIX commands in the course of a day.

■ **Portability**. If you sit in front of the same terminal every day, use the same UNIX software and applications for all your work, and rarely, if ever, deal with an unfamiliar system, then, by all means, choose the best tools that your system has available. If you need to work with many different computers running different versions of UNIX, as system and network administrators often must, you may need to build a repertoire of tools (shell, editor, and so on) that are available on most or all of the systems you use. Don't forget that being an expert with a powerful shell won't buy you much if that shell isn't available. For some UNIX professionals, knowing a shell language that's supported on all UNIX systems is more important than any other consideration.

Table 13.1 rates seven commonly available shells using the preceding criteria, assigning a rating of 1 for best choice, 2 for acceptable alternative, and 3 for poor choice.

Table 13.1. Ranking of shells for interactive use.

Shell	Experience	Editing	Shortcuts	Portability	Learning
Bourne	3	3	3	1	1
POSIX	2	1	2	1	2
C	2	2	2	3	2
Korn	1	1	2	2	2

continues

Table 13.1. continued

Shell	Experience	Editing	Shortcuts	Portability	Learning
TC	2	1	1	3	3
Bourne Again	2	1	1	2	3
Z	2	1	1	3	3

Bourne Shell

I rated the Bourne shell as your best choice for learning because it is the simplest of the three to use, with the fewest features to distract you and the fewest syntax nuances to confuse you. If you won't be spending a lot of time using a command shell with UNIX, then, by all means, develop some proficiency with the Bourne shell. You'll be able to do all you need to do, and the productivity benefits of the other shells aren't important for a casual user. Even if you expect to use a UNIX command shell frequently, you might need to limit your study to the Bourne shell if you need to become effective quickly.

I rated the Bourne shell as lowest in the productivity categories because it has no command editor and only minimal shortcut facilities. If you have the time and expertise to invest in developing your own shell scripts, you can compensate for many of the Bourne shell deficiencies, as many shell power users did in the years before other shells were invented. Even so, the lack of command editing and command history facilities means you'll spend a lot of time retyping and repairing commands. For intensive keyboard use, the Bourne shell is the worst choice. If you have any other shell, you'll prefer it over the Bourne shell.

Shells like the C shell and the Korn shell were invented precisely because of the Bourne shell's low productivity rating. The new shells were targeted specifically to creating a keyboard environment that would be friendlier and easier to use than the Bourne shell, and they are here today only because most people agree that they're better.

Portability concerns, however, might steer you toward the Bourne shell, despite its poor productivity rating. Being the oldest of the three shells (it was written for the very earliest versions of UNIX), the Bourne shell is available virtually everywhere. If you can get your job done using the Bourne shell, you can do it at the terminal of virtually any machine anywhere. This is not the case for shells such as the C and Korn shells, which are available only with particular vendors' systems or with current UNIX releases.

I gave the Bourne shell a rating of 3 for prior experience because prior experience using the Bourne shell is no reason to continue using it. You can immediately use any of Bourne shell variants, such as the Korn or Bourne Again shell, with no additional study and no surprises, and you can gradually enhance your keyboard skills as you pick up the new shell extensions. If you know the Bourne shell and have access to a Bourne shell variant, you have no reason not to use a variant.

The Bourne shell is provided by your UNIX vendor, although it is being phased out in favor of the POSIX shell. For example, on HP-UX 10.X systems, the Bourne shell now resides in `/usr/old/bin`, and the POSIX shell is now in the traditional `/usr/bin`.

POSIX Shell

If you graft some interactive productivity enhancements onto the Bourne shell, the result is the POSIX (Portable Operating System Interface) shell. The POSIX shell is very similar to the Korn shell in terms of the interactive features provided, right down to the keystroke in most cases. The Korn shell is not standardized, so there are annoying differences between various vendors' versions; the POSIX shell attempts to raise the bar for a universally available shell.

The current POSIX shells are based on POSIX.2 of the IEEE POSIX Shell and Tools Specification (IEEE Working Group 1003.2). The POSIX shell is a superset of the Bourne shell.

I rated the POSIX shell as a 2 for learning because it has many more interactive features than the Bourne shell, but fewer features than the Bourne Again or Z shells. The POSIX shell rates a 1 in the area of command editing, providing both `vi` and `emacs` command support. The command-line editing feature set supported by the POSIX shell is not as rich as TC, Bourne Again, or Z shell, but is more than adequate for most tasks.

The POSIX shell offers many shortcuts, such as aliases, `cd` path searches, filename completion and job control. The shortcut features rated a 2, because the POSIX shell has much more than the Bourne shell, but less than the TC, Bourne Again, and Z shells. The POSIX shell receives high marks for portability, as it should soon be available on most common UNIX versions.

The POSIX shell rated a 2 in the experience category, because if you know the POSIX shell and are satisfied with its feature set, there aren't a lot of compelling reasons to switch to another shell. The Bourne Again and Z shells offer more features and support most of the POSIX features, so if default availability is not an issue and you need the extra features, switching should be a fairly painless task.

The POSIX shell should be provided by your UNIX vendor as part of the default set of shells.

C Shell

The C shell rates a 2 for learning difficulty, based simply on the total amount of material available to learn. The C shell falls on the low end of the shell spectrum in terms of the number and complexity of its facilities. Make no mistake—the C shell can be tricky to use, and some of its features are rather poorly documented. Becoming comfortable and proficient with the C shell takes time, practice, and a certain amount of inventive experimentation. When compared to the Bourne shell only on the basis of common features, the C shell is no more complex, just different.

The C shell rates a passing nod for command editing because it doesn't really have a command editing feature. The C shell's history substitution mechanism is somewhat complicated to learn and can be clumsy to use at times, but it is much better than nothing at all. Just having a command history and history substitution mechanism is an improvement over the Bourne shell. But the C Shell is a poor comparison to the simple and easy (if your know vi or emacs) command editing of the Korn, POSIX, Bourne Again, TC, or Z shells.

For example, with the Korn shell, you can reuse a previously entered command, even modify it, just by recalling it (Esc-k if you're using the vi option) and overtyping the part you want to modify. With the C shell, you can also reuse a previous command, but you have five different forms for specifying the command name (!!, !11, !-5, !vi, and !?vi), additional forms for selecting the command's arguments (:0, :^, :3-5, :-4, :*, to name a few), and additional modifiers for changing the selected argument (:h, :s/old/new/, and so forth). Even remembering the syntax of command substitution is difficult, not to mention using it. The history substitution mechanism also provides no access to multiline commands such as foreach. The lack of access to multiline commands can be frustrating; you have to retype all the enclosed commands. History substitutions, once you have learned the syntax, can be much faster than editing in many cases, because fewer keystrokes are required. However, there is no substitute for a good command-line editor. The TC, Bourne Again, and Z shells support all the C shell history substitutions *and* provide command-line editing.

On the other hand, if you like to use wildcards, you'll find that the C shell wildcard extensions for filenames are easier to use—they require less typing and have a simpler syntax—than the Korn shell wildcard extensions. In addition to wildcards, csh provides command and filename completion with a single keystroke. Also, its cd command is a little more flexible. The pushd, popd, and dirs commands are not directly supported by some shells, such as the Korn and POSIX shells (although they can be implemented in those shells by the use of aliases and command functions). Altogether, the C shell rates well in terms of keyboard shortcuts available, perhaps in compensation for its only moderately successful command editing. Depending on your personal mental bent, you might find the C shell very productive. We have seen that those already familiar with the C shell have in the past not been driven away in droves by the Korn and other shells.

For portability considerations, the C shell ranks at the bottom, simply because it's a unique shell language. If you know only the C shell, and the particular system you're using doesn't have it, you're out of luck. A C shell user almost always feels all thumbs when forced to work with the Bourne shell, unless she is bilingual and knows the vagaries and peculiarities of both.

The C shell gets a 2 for prior experience. If you already know the C shell, the TC shell is a good candidate for a switch. The TC shell provides a command-line editor and other nifty shortcuts and is probably compatible with your current C shell version. On the other hand, staying with a C shell variant can be limiting because there are many more shells in the Bourne family tree. Unless you feel quite comfortable with the C shell's history substitution feature and use it extensively to repair and reuse commands, you might find another shell's command editing capability well worth the time and effort to make a switch. Anyone accustomed to using the shell's command editing capability feels unfairly treated when deprived of it—it's that good a feature. If you haven't already experimented with the Korn, TC, Bourne Again, or Z shell and you have the chance, I would strongly recommend spending a modest amount of time gaining enough familiarity with one of these shells to make an informed choice. You might be surprised and choose a different shell.

Altogether, the C shell is a creditable interactive environment with many advantages over its predecessor, the Bourne shell. Personal preference has to play a role in your choice here. However, if you're new to UNIX, the C shell is probably not the best place for you to start.

The C shell should be provided by your UNIX vendor as part of the default set of shells.

Korn Shell

In terms of time and effort required to master it, the Korn shell falls in the middle of the shell spectrum. That's not because it's poorly designed or poorly documented, but merely because it has more complex features than the Bourne and C shells. Of course, you don't have to learn everything before you can begin using the Korn shell.

The Korn shell's command editor interface enables the quick, effortless correction of typing errors, plus easy recall and reuse of command history. The reuse of multiline commands is still a bit on the awkward side, as all lines are concatenated together on a line, with control characters representing newlines.

On the down side, the Korn shell provides equivalents for the C shell's wildcard extensions, but with a complicated syntax that makes the extensions hard to remember and hard to use. You can have the `pushd`, `popd` directory interface, but only if you or someone you know supplies the command aliases and functions to implement them. The ability to use a variable name as an argument to `cd` would have been nice. The Korn shell's command aliasing and job control facilities are nearly identical to those of the C shell. The Korn shell does not provide command completion but does provide filename completion. Unlike most shells, two keystrokes are required to complete filenames. From the point of view of keyboard use, the Korn shell stands out over the C shell mainly because of its command editing feature. In other respects, its main advantage is that it provides many of the C shell extensions in a shell environment compatible with the Bourne shell; if Bourne shell compatibility doesn't matter to you, then the Korn shell might not matter either.

Speaking of Bourne shell compatibility, the Korn shell rates a close second to the Bourne and POSIX shells for portability. If you know the Korn shell language, you already know the Bourne shell, because `ksh` is really a superset of `sh` syntax. If you're familiar with the Korn shell, you can work reasonably effectively with any system having either the Bourne or Korn shell, which amounts to virtually one hundred percent of the existing UNIX computing environments.

Finally, in terms of the impact of prior experience, the Korn shell gets a rating of 2. If you know the Bourne shell, you'll probably want to beef up your knowledge by adding the extensions of the Korn shell and switching your login shell to `ksh`. If you already know `ksh`, you'll probably stick with it, unless you are tempted by some of the extra features of `bash` or `zsh`. If you know `csh`, the advantages of `ksh` may not be enough to compel you to switch.

If you're a first-time UNIX user, the Korn shell is a good shell for you to start with. The complexities of the command editing feature will probably not slow you down much; you'll probably use the feature so heavily that the command editing syntax will become second nature to you before very long.

The Korn shell should be provided by your UNIX vendor as part of the default set of shells.

TC Shell

The TC shell can be thought of as the next generation C shell. The TC shell supports all the C shell syntax and adds powerful command-line editing, including: spell checking for filenames and user IDs, additional completions (hostnames, variable names, aliases, and so on), and expansions (variable names, filenames). There are many other features too numerous to mention here.

The TC shell rates a 3 in the learning category because of the wealth of features to learn as well as the complexity of using/configuring some of the features. For example, the TC shell offers programmable completion, which is convenient to use but difficult to program. Fortunately, the TC shell provides several pre-programmed completions straight out of the box.

The TC shell provides an `emacs` or `vi` command-line editor. Unlike the Korn and POSIX shell, the `emacs` style of incremental searching is available. These features give the TC a 1 in the editing arena. However, room for improvement exists for multiline commands, such as `foreach`, which still do not have the loop contents available in the history editor as do the POSIX, Korn, Bash and Z shell command-line editors.

The TC shell is chock full of shortcuts and rates a 1; only the Z shell has more shortcuts available. The TC rates low in portability because it is not available on all systems and is not generally a shell shipped by vendors. Because there is only one source for the TC shell, however, it is the same on all systems, aside from release differences.

As far as prior experience is concerned, if you know the C shell, the TC shell is fairly simple to pick up. In fact, it will read your `.cshrc` file without modifications. You can incrementally pick up the advanced features as needed. So `tcsh` is a good shell to switch to if you are a C shell user. The TC shell does not rate a 1 in the experience category because it is not Bourne-compatible, so learning the TC shell would be hard for users of most other shells.

The TC shell is not generally provided as a standard shell; however, many systems have the TC shell installed. If your system does not have `tcsh` installed, check `http://www.primate.wisc.edu/software/csh-tcsh-book` for information on source and precompiled binaries. The previous URL also presents a wealth of information about the TC shell, including man pages, books, and supporting software. Should that URL fail, try your favorite WWW search engine for the keyword *tcsh*.

Bourne Again Shell

The Bourne Again shell is the GNU project's shell and is POSIX-compatible. The Bourne Again (bash) shell can be thought of as the next generation Korn shell, as bash is basically a superset of the 1988 version Korn shell, with many of the Korn shell 1993 features. The Bourne Again shell also offers good support for many C shell features, in order to help us C shell junkies feel at home, including: history substitutions using the ! operator, >& output redirection, {} wildcards, and the source command.

The Bourne Again shell has a great deal to offer; in fact, the current man page is 55 pages long. The large number of features does not make for an easy time to become a bash master, so a rating of 3 in the learning arena was awarded. However, don't be misled into thinking that the Bourne Again shell is overly difficult to learn, and if you choose not to learn all the features, you can still be quite productive.

The command-line editing of multiline commands is better than POSIX, Korn, and TC shell. Each line shows up as a separate entry in the command history, and as a result, it is a little easier to reuse portions of a command, but the separate entries make it difficult to easily reuse the entire command. However, bash offers a shell variable, command_oriented_history, which, when set, places the commands on one history line separated by semi-colons (;).

Bourne Again rates well with regard to shortcuts and received the coveted 1 rating. bash offers a directory stack with more features than the C shell, such as the ability to display individual members of the directory stack. The Bourne Again shell offers more completions and expansions on the command-line than the C, POSIX, and Korn shells.

bash is something of a conundrum when it comes to portability. I gave it the benefit of the doubt and assigned it a 1, because you can have the Bourne Again shell emulate the POSIX shell. In this mode, what you do can easily be replicated in the POSIX shell. On the other hand, bash is not universally available, and you need to be careful what features you rely on if portability is of concern to you.

The experience rating for bash is also a 1. If you use a shell from the Bourne family, switching to bash will be easy and likely provide you with more features than your current shell. If you are accustomed to a C shell derivative, the Bourne Again shell has enough C shell syntax to make the transition relatively painless. To even further reduce the pain, the Bourne Again shell provides a handy script for translating your C shell aliases to the Bourne Again syntax, as well as making semantic substitutions (for instance, $PWD for $cwd). The bash FAQ (Frequently Asked Questions) even has tips on how to emulate common C shell features, such as :r replacements.

 The Bourne Again shell is not generally provided as a standard shell from most UNIX vendors. However, many systems have bash installed. In fact, it is the standard shell for Linux systems. The CD-ROM included with this book has a version of bash on it. If you wish to locate additional information about source and binary locations, look in the bash FAQ , which can be found at the URL ftp://slc2.ins.cwru.edu/pub/bash/FAQ. Failing that, try your favorite WWW search engine for the keywords *Bourne Again* or *bash FAQ.*

13

SHELL COMPARISON

Z Shell

The Z shell is the ultimate shell for feature-hungry users. If you can think of something that a shell ought to do, the Z shell probably does it. All that power comes at a price: For example, on HP-UX 10.01, the zsh executable is nearly four times larger than the ksh (Korn shell) executable and almost three time larger than the sh executable (Bourne shell).

I don't think anyone knows all the features of the Z shell, not even the original author, Paul Falstad. Learning even half of the features would be quite an accomplishment, so a rating of 3 was given. However, this does not imply that the Z shell is poorly implemented, designed, or documented; this is strictly a bulk-of-features issue.

When it comes to command-line editing, Z shell stands head and shoulders over any shell reviewed in this chapter. Z shell handles multiline commands the best of all the shells, in my opinion. Each command is an editable buffer unto itself, which makes for easy editing of the command and easy reuse of the entire command, and it retains the original visual look of the command. Z shell has the most completions and expansions. Access to expansion is also the most intuitive. For example, the first press of the Tab key while typing a variable name will complete the variable name, the next Tab will expand the variable's value into the command-line (assuming no ambiguities in the completion). Both bash and tcsh require a separate editor command to expand the variables values (in bash emacs mode, Esc-$ will expand the variable). Z shell supports programmable completions that can even further help with command-line editing. For example, you can program the cd command to use only directories for completions or expansions. Z shell offers spelling correction for pathnames and user IDs. All these features make for a rating of 1 in the editing category.

Z shell receives a 1 and is number 1 when it comes to shortcuts. For example, suppose you have two developers working on a set of files for a project and you want to determine what files will need merging. In order to do that, you need to see which files the two developers have in common in their work directories. Let us further assume you wish to place that list of common files into a file for editing with vi. The edited list contains the candidates for merging. Suppose you are using the C shell (you have to pick a worst-case scenario for illustration). You could use a foreach loop with an if (-e *filename*) to test for file existence and echo the filename, but the C shell does not allow redirection from the looping constructs. Creating a temporary script is a pain, so it's best to use the UNIX comm command (comm selects or rejects lines common to two sorted files). The following is a sample C shell session, using #'s for comments.

```
% (cd ~harryman/cxxsource/proj1;ls *.{cc,hh}) > /tmp/davesFiles  #darn, need to name
a temp file
% (cd ~robic/dominic/proj1;ls *.{cc,hh}) > /tmp/mattsFiles        #darn, need to name
another temp file
% comm -12 /tmp/davesFiles  /tmp/mattsFiles  > needMerge          #show what is in
both files
% rm /tmp/davesFiles  /tmp/mattsFiles                            #kill those pesky
temporary files
% vi needMerge                                                    #vi at last!
```

Enter the Z shell and the process substitution syntax of `=()`. Process substitution removes the headache of temporary files, as can be seen from the following Z shell session, which accomplishes the same task as above.

```
% vi =(comm -12 =(cd ~harryman/cxxsource/proj1;ls *.{cc,hh}) =(cd ~robic/dominic/
proj1;ls *.{cc,hh}))
```

Process substitution automatically creates a temporary file for you, places the input in the temporary file, and then passes the name of the temporary file to the command that needs to process it.

Other nifty Z shell shortcuts include:

- Recursive directory searches (`ls **/file`).
- Easy teeing via multiple redirects (`ls >file1 >file2`).
- `autocd` option that enables directory changes without using `cd`, so `cd dirname` and `dirname` are equivalent commands.
- Null command shorthands. `< file` is equivalent to `more <file`, `> file` is the same as `cat >file`, and `>> file` is identical to `cat >>file`.
- Shell variable editing with the `vared` built-in command.
- Others too numerous to mention.

Portability is the Z shell's only Achilles' heel. The Z shell is not found on as many systems as most other shells. To ease this, the Z shell can emulate the Korn, C, or POSIX shell. A rating of 3 was given for portability.

Z shell also shines in the experience category. No matter what shell you know, switching to Z shell is not too tough. Even if you are a C shell junkie, and I am, then the various `CSH_JUNKIE` options can help you out until you have been properly weaned. The Z shell has support for the most C shell features of any non-C-shell shell, including: `^^` quick substitution, `foreach`, and `pushd`/`popd`. With the various shell emulation switches, Bourne, Korn, and POSIX users can also feel right at home. Save for the portability issue, it is very hard not to really like the Z shell. As the name implies, Z shell is the last shell you will ever need.

The Z shell is not provided as a standard shell by UNIX vendors, and zsh is not as ubiquitous as some of the other shells. If your system does not have zsh installed, check `http://www.mal.com/zsh/FAQ/toc.html` or `http://www.mal.com/zsh/zsh_home.shtml` for information on source and precompiled binaries. The previous URLs also provide other information about the Z shell, including man pages. Should the URLs fail you, try your favorite WWW search engine for the keyword *zsh*.

Interactive Shell Feature Comparison

Table 13.2 describes some of the interactive shell features that are not available in all shells for comparison purposes. The features that all shells have in common are not listed (for instance, use of * as a wildcard, search path variable for executables, ability to get and set environment variables, and so on). Many of these features could actually be used in scripts, but because the features listed are used primarily in interactive sessions, they are listed in Table 13.2.

Some of the features mention expansion or completion. In Table 13.2, expansion refers to the substitution of the value represented by a token on the command line. For example, the command-line token *.star could be *expanded* to dark.star dwarf.star ura.star (assuming that the previous three files were all that matched the wildcard expression *.star). If the variable $LOGNAME were expanded on my command line, the variable would be replaced with the token sdrew. Completion refers to the feature of partially typing a name and having the shell complete the rest of the name on your behalf. For example if you had typed $DIS on the command-line, using completion, the shell might have typed in PLAY for you, thus *completing* the variable name for you with an end result of $DISPLAY on your command line.

Table 13.2. Nonportable shell features—*Interactive*.

Feature	sh	csh	ksh	tcsh	bash	zsh
Aliases	POSIX	X	X	X	X	X
Alias completion	-	-	-	X	X	X
Aliases take arguments	-	X	-	X	-	-
Automatically list choices for ambiguous completions	-	-	-	X	X	X
cd path searches	POSIX	X	X	X	X	X
Command aliases	POSIX	X	X	X	X	X
Command editing (emacs)	POSIX	-	X	X	X	X
Command editing (vi)	POSIX	-	X	X	X	X
Command completion	-	X	-	X	X	X
Built-in command completion	-	-	-	X	X	X
Command documentation lookup while command is being typed	-	-	-	X	-	-
Command history	POSIX	X	X	X	X	X
Command history appending	POSIX	-	X	-	X	-
Co-process support	POSIX	-	X	-	-	X
History substitution	-	X	-	X	X	X
History expansion	-	-	-	X	X	X
Filename completion	POSIX	X	X	X	X	X
Filename expansion	POSIX	-	X	X	-	X

Feature	sh	csh	ksh	tcsh	bash	zsh
Function completion	-	-	-	-	X	X
Hostname completion	-	-	-	-	X	X
Incremental history searching	-	-	-	X	X	X
Job control (bg, fg, ...)	POSIX	X	X	X	X	X
Log in/out watching	-	-	-	X	-	X
Multiprompt commands in history buffer	POSIX	-	X	-	X	X
notify shell built in	POSIX	X	-	X	X	-
One key completion	-	X	-	X	X	X
Programmable completion	-	-	-	X	-	X
pushd, popd commands and/or other directory stack commands	-	X	-	X	X	X
Recursive command-line scans	POSIX	X	-	X	X	-
Spelling correction for user IDs, commands, and filenames	-	-	-	X	-	X
Substring selectors :x	-	X	-	X	X	X
Variable completion	-	-	-	X	X	X
Variable expansion	-	-	-	X	X	X
Variable editing	-	-	-	-	-	X
*(...) wildcards	POSIX	-	X	-	-	X
$(...) command expression	POSIX	-	X	-	X	X
{...} wildcards	-	X	-	X	X	X

Note: The sh column represents both the Bourne and POSIX shells. If a feature is specific only to one shell, then that shell's name will appear in the column, as opposed to an X. In short, - means neither shell, *X* means both shells, *Bourne* means just the Bourne shell, and *POSIX* means just the POSIX shell.

Shell Scripts for Personal Use

If you develop any shell scripts for your personal use, you'll probably want to write them in the same shell language you use for interactive commands. As is the case for interactive use, the language you use for personal scripts is largely a matter of personal choice.

Whether you use a C shell variant or a Bourne shell variant at the keyboard, you might want to consider using the Bourne shell language for shell scripts, for a couple of reasons. First, personal shell scripts don't always stay personal; they have a way of evolving over time and gradually floating from one user to another until the good ones become de facto installation standards. As you'll learn in the section titled "Shell Scripts for Public Consumption," writing shell scripts in any language but the Bourne shell is somewhat risky, because you limit the machine environments and users who can use your script.

Second, the C shell variants, while chock full of excellent interactive features, are sadly lacking in programming features. The chief drawback of C shell variants is the lack of shell functions (perhaps it is time for the C++ shell). The lack of shell functions greatly inhibits structured programming. Any function must either be a separate file or an alias. Aliases can be difficult or impossible to write for more complex tasks. The C shell variants also do not have parameter substitution nor nearly as many variable and file tests. Take it from someone who learned the hard way, when it comes to C shell programming, *just say no*. Of course, for truly trivial scripts containing just a few commands that you use principally as an extended command abbreviation, portability concerns are not an issue.

Writing short, simple shell scripts to automate common tasks is a good habit and a good UNIX skill. To get the full benefit of the UNIX shells, you almost have to develop some scriptwriting capability. This will happen most naturally if you write personal scripts in the same language that you use at the keyboard.

For purposes of comparison, Table 13.3 describes shell features used for programming that are not available in all shells. While the features listed here tend to be used mostly in scripts, as opposed to interactive sessions, there is nothing preventing these features from being used interactively.

Table 13.3. Nonportable shell features—*Programming.*

Feature	sh	csh	ksh	tcsh	bash	zsh
Arithmetic expressions	POSIX	X	X	X	X	X
Array variables	POSIX	X	X	X	X	X
Assignment id=string	X	-	X	-	X	X
case statement	X	-	X	-	X	X
clobber option	POSIX	X	X	X	X	X
echo -n option	-	X	-	X	X	X
for statement	X	-	X	-	X	X
export command	X	-	X	-	X	X
foreach statement	-	X	-	X	-	X

Feature	*sh*	*csh*	*ksh*	*tcsh*	*bash*	*zsh*
getopts built-in command	POSIX	-	X	-	X	X
glob command	-	X	-	X	-	-
Hash table problems, rehash and unhash commands	-	X	-	X	-	-
let command	POSIX	-	X	-	X	X
limit, unlimit commands	-	X	-	X	-	X
nice shell built-in	-	X	-	X	-	-
nohup shell built-in	-	X	-	X	-	-
onintr command	-	X	-	X	-	-
print command	POSIX	-	X	-	X	X
Redirection from iterative statements	X	-	X	-	X	X
RANDOM shell variable	POSIX	-	X	-	X	X
repeat shell built-in	-	X	-	X	-	X
select statement	POSIX	-	X	-	X	X
setenv, unsetenv commands	-	X	-	X	-	-
SHELL variable specifies command to execute scripts	-	X	-	X	-	-
switch statement	-	X	-	X	-	-
until statement	X	-	X	-	X	X
set -x	X	-	X	-	X	X
set *optionname*	-	X	-	X	X	X
Shell functions	X	-	X	-	X	X
trap command	X	-	X	-	X	X
typeset command	POSIX	-	X	-	X	X
ulimit command	X	-	X	-	X	X
Undefined variable is an error	-	X	-	X	-	-
! special character	-	X	-	X	X	X
@ command	-	X	-	X	-	-
>& redirection	-	X	-	X	X	X

13

SHELL COMPARISON

Shell Scripts for Public Consumption

Shell scripts developed for public consumption should be designed for enduring portability. Shell scripts developed for public use are almost always written in the Bourne shell language. Although there is a tendency today to write such scripts in the Korn shell language, people who do so realize they're taking a risk, albeit a modest one.

Some versions of UNIX allow you to specify the shell interpreter to use for a given script file by embedding a special command as the first line of the script: #! /bin/sh as the first line of a script would, on most modern UNIX systems, force the use of the Bourne shell to execute the script file. This is a handy device to allow you to develop scripts in the shell language of your choice, while also allowing users to avail themselves of the script regardless of their choice of an interactive shell. However, the #! device is not available on all versions of UNIX.

Shell scripts written in something other than the Bourne or POSIX shell require the operating system to include the corresponding shell. For example, the C shell and the Korn shell require that either csh or ksh be installed. Not all systems meet this requirement, and if portability among several platforms or between current and future platforms is a consideration (that is, if you're writing a script to be used by anyone anywhere, both now and years from now), common sense and reasonable prudence dictate that you avoid non-Bourne shell syntax constructs in your script. If you write scripts in the POSIX shell and avoid any of the new built-in commands, such as select, your scripts should be very portable. The main incompatibility between the Bourne and POSIX shells, assuming that only Bourne syntax is used, is the result of an old Bourne shell feature. The command-line arguments are corrupted once a function is called from a script in the Bourne shell; not so with the POSIX shell. Always follow the practice of saving off needed command-line arguments ($1, $2...). Saving command-line variables in other variables will make your scripts more readable, as well as more portable.

True portability also limits your use of UNIX commands and command options inside your shell script. Some versions of UNIX, especially the implementation by IBM, offer many new command options on many commands, leading the unwary into developing shell scripts that can run only under the IBM implementation of UNIX. Other versions of UNIX, such as ULTRIX and XENIX, support only the old-fashioned command library, along with some local peculiarities. If you're truly interested in developing portable programs and shell scripts, you should make use of the POSIX and X/Open compatibility guidelines, which describe only commands and command options that are generally available on most UNIX operating system implementations.

Even the dialect of the Bourne shell you use can be a portability consideration. For example, on ULTRIX systems, the command sh supplies only UNIX version 7 functionality; you have to invoke the command sh5 to run a System V–compatible Bourne shell. With the advent of POSIX and vendors wishing to be POSIX-compliant, these issues should lessen over time. The POSIX.2 standard requires a POSIX-compliant system to run the POSIX shell when the UNIX command sh is specified.

Because perfect portability is, like Scotty's transporter, simply not obtainable in the twentieth century, a further application of common sense dictates that the level of effort you invest in portable programming be suitable to the job at hand. You might want to adopt guidelines something like the following:

- For really important projects, choose any shell language (or other tool) you want—your choice simply becomes another requirement for installation and use of the system. (Don't forget to tell your user community of such requirements.)

- If your shell script might enter the public domain, restrict yourself to the Bourne shell language, and assume a System V Release 1 environment. This provides you with a great many tools but also suits your application to the vast majority of contemporary UNIX installations.

- If your shell script is targeted for use at your local installation, choose either the Bourne, POSIX, or Korn shell language. Use the Korn shell if you feel you need its features, but do not use it gratuitously or casually. The odds are heavily in your favor that any future operating system releases or vendor changes will still support your shell script.

- If your project must meet certain stated compatibility goals (for example, you must support the HP-UX and SunOS machines running at three offices in two different countries), then by all means adjust your project to meet those goals. There will still be aspects of your project where no stated goals apply. In those cases, choose the level of generality and portability that you (or your project timetable) can afford.

- In all other cases, choose the tools and languages that you feel permit the most effective, trouble-free, user-friendly implementation you can devise, and don't forget to maximize your own productivity and effectiveness.

Summary

Selecting a shell for use at the keyboard as an interactive command-line processor is a relatively straightforward task once you realize that your choice does not affect others. If you are new to UNIX, you should consider using the POSIX shell because its built-in command editing feature can significantly increase productivity. Users accustomed to the C shell are also advised to investigate the POSIX shell, for the same reason.

Familiarity with the Bourne and POSIX shells and their capabilities and restrictions is essential for individuals who must work with a variety of UNIX systems or with the general UNIX public. Bourne is the only shell that is universally available under all implementations of the UNIX operating system, and the POSIX shell is becoming nearly as ubiquitous.

For daily keyboard use, any shell but the Bourne shell is a good choice. The Bourne shell is not a good choice when other shells are available. The Bourne shell has a decided lack of interactive features, with command history and command editing being especially productivity degrading.

Choosing a shell for writing scripts is, however, a different matter entirely.

The newer shells offer tools to the scriptwriter that are hard to do without, such as simplified syntax for command substitutions, array variables, variable arithmetic and expressions, and better structured commands such as `select`. Because these tools are so helpful, they should be used for any work intended only for personal consumption. They should also be preferred for location-specific projects, where the environment can be predicted reasonably accurately. However, for shell scripts claiming a wider audience, the Bourne shell still serves as the *lingua franca* of the UNIX world and will for some time to come.

The script writer who cannot anticipate the hardware and software environment must consider the choice of commands and command options used in the script as well as the shell language. A few environments offer a wider variety of commands and command options than most, and some UNIX versions omit some of the conventional UNIX runtime features. For most purposes, an implementation compatible with UNIX System V Release 1 can be considered as a minimum portability base. In situations where portability is especially important, the POSIX and X/Open standards should be consulted as guides to available operating system features and capabilities, rather than the vendor's manuals.

Shell programming can be as simple or as complex as you wish it to be. Shells are sufficiently sophisticated programming tools and can permit the implementation of efficient, production quality software. In fact, shell scripts can be used instead of a more traditional third generation language, such as the C or C++ programming languages. In fact, I once replaced a 500-line C++ program with a 4-line shell script. The use of shell scripts has also become popular as a prototyping and rapid development method.

It would seem that, while one shell can be chosen for customary use at the keyboard, the choice of a shell environment for writing shell scripts needs to be reconsidered for each project.

IN THIS PART

III

PART

System Administration

What Is System Administration?

by Eric Goebelbecker

IN THIS CHAPTER

CHAPTER 14

System Administration is planning, installing, and maintaining computer systems. If that seems like a very generalized answer, it's because "What Is System Administration?" is a broad question.

In this chapter we'll describe what is expected from a System Administrator, and how she might approach her responsibilities.

HELP WANTED

Administer Sun and IBM UNIX systems and control Internet access. Assist with some database administration (Oracle). Administer Sun server and network: system configuration, user ID/creation/maintenance, security administration, system backup, and ensuring all applications are running on the system properly. Administer Internet access and services: internal/external security, user identification creation and maintenance, and Web server maintenance.

This is a typical "Help Wanted" advertisement for a UNIX System Administration position. From this description you might guess that a System Administrator has to install and configure the operating system, add new users, back up the system(s), keep the systems secure, and make sure they stay running. Setting up Internet access and keeping it running is part of the job, too.

Unfortunately, you'd only be considering about half of the job. Being an expert on installing, running, and maintaining all of the major UNIX variants isn't enough to be a truly good system administrator. There is a significant nontechnical component to being a system administrator, especially in terms of planning, organizational, and people skills.

As computers become more and more pervasive in business, system administration becomes a mission critical position in more and more organizations. The administrator has to understand the systems that he is responsible for, the people who use them, and the nature of the business that they are used for. A key skill in administration is planning, because at the rate that systems are being created, overhauled, and expanded, trying to improvise and design a network "on the fly" just doesn't work.

Companies are moving more and more processes not just to computers, but to point-of-sale systems, such as Web commerce and sophisticated in-store systems, such as electronic catalogs and cash registers that are directly connected to both inventory and credit systems. Companies that may have moved their inventory control to computers five years ago are scrambling to get order entry computerized and on the Web, while companies that haven't automated their inventory and ordering systems yet are scrambling to do so in order to remain competitive. E-mail is now regarded as just as important as faxes and telephones, while every part of customer service that can be manned by a computer and fax retrieval system already is. These companies are almost completely dependent on their computers, and their system administrators need to understand a lot more than how to partition a disk drive, add memory, and install Adobe Photoshop.

This chapter introduces some of the basic technical and organizational concepts that a system administrator needs to know in order to perform his job well. It also covers a few key system administration tools that are already found with most UNIX variants or are included on the *UNIX Unleashed* CD-ROM that accompanies this book.

The chapter is divided into the following sections:

- Technical Concepts for System Administrators—in this section we introduce some of UNIX's important characteristics and how they differ from operating systems like Windows and Macintosh.

- UNIX Is Heterogeneous—this section describes UNIX's diverse and sometimes self-contradictory user interfaces and how those interfaces ended up that way.

- System Administration Tasks—this part of the chapter is where basic administration tasks and responsibilities are introduced.

- Administration Resources—both the operating system itself and the Internet provide a wide variety of information for administrators. This section provides a few pointers to these resources.

- Tools of the Trade—UNIX provides users and administrators with an amazing set of tools. We briefly cover a few of them in the end of this chapter.

TIP

No one, regardless of how long they've "been in the business," can remember all of the configuration options, command-line switches, oddities, and outright bugs in the UNIX tool chest. Experienced users soon learn the value of UNIX's online documentation, the *manual pages*. Before you use any tool, read the man page(s) for it; many of them include useful examples. If you install a utility from the CD-ROM, be sure you read the installation instructions that accompany it and install the man page, too. Later in this chapter we'll cover some advanced features found in the manual page system.

Technical Concepts for New System Administrators

UNIX differs from Windows and Macintosh at a fundamental level. UNIX was originally intended for multiple users running multiple simultaneous programs. (At least it was by the time it was distributed outside of Bell Labs.) The phenomenon of a user having a low cost personal workstation, running Linux or any other variant of UNIX is actually a recent development in terms of the operating system's history. The fact that UNIX is designed for use by more than a single user is reflected throughout the operating system's file systems, security features, and programming model.

Networking is not an afterthought or a recent development for UNIX, the way it seems to be for Windows and Macintosh. Support for sharing files, moving from workstation to workstation, and running applications on remote computers that are controlled and viewed on a local workstation is not only intuitive and natural on UNIX, but was more powerful and stable on past versions of UNIX than the latest versions of Windows and Windows NT.

Multiple Users and Multiple Accounts

The DOS/Windows and Macintosh environments are "computer-centric" in terms of security and customization. The ownership of files and *processes* (programs that are currently running) is more or less governed by the computer where they are located as opposed to the notion of a user ID or session. If a person can physically get to a computer, he has access to all of the files and programs on it. If a truly malicious person wants access to the contents of a PC, even a password-protected screen saver can be overcome by restarting the system, because the files and programs belong to the PC, not a user, and the computer will boot ready for use. (Even the login prompt on Windows 95 can be bypassed with the Cancel button, bringing the user interface up with no network resources connected.)

Add-ons are available for DOS and Macintosh systems that enable users to identify themselves and save files in protected areas. But these are applications, not a part of the operating system, and come with their own set of problems, limitations, and rules. The fact is, as anyone who has ever had to share a computer with a family member or coworker will agree, personal computer operating systems are single user and geared toward supporting one user and one set of configuration options.

UNIX systems are multi-user. Users must log in to the system. Each has his own areas for saving files, the *home directory,* and files have properties that determine who can or cannot access them, their *mode.* All running programs are associated with a user, and, similar to the way files have access control, programs can only be started or stopped by certain users. Unless a user can log in as the *super-user,* she cannot access another user's files unless the owner gives her permission through one of several direct or indirect means. Only the super-user can reboot the computer (without the power switch) or stop another user's processes. Even if a system is rebooted, all of the security features will remain in effect, so restarting is not a valid means of subverting security.

Network Centricity

Networking has become an integral part of UNIX. The ability to share files, support network logins, share network configuration information, and run applications across a network is included in all of the major UNIX distributions, and more importantly is a natural extension of the base operating system, not an application that was designed by an individual vendor, with their idea of networking and administration, and that has to be purchased separately.

When configured to allow it, anything that can be done at the *console* (main keyboard and monitor) of a UNIX system can be done at another system via a network connection. (We'll refer to these other systems as *remote nodes* or *remote systems*.) Actually many server systems, such as Web servers and file servers, have consoles with very limited capabilities (such as a text-only terminal), and are deliberately designed with the idea of doing as much administration as possible from remote nodes outside the data center.

Two of the mechanisms that provide these capabilities are *remote* (or *pseudo*) terminals and *remote shells*. Remote terminals emulate an actual terminal session, just as if the user were logged into a terminal connected to the system via a serial line, where the network is the line and the application (usually *Telnet*) is the terminal. (Remote terminals are usually referred to as Telnet sessions, since Telnet is by far the most common application.) This is similar, in theory at least, to dialing into a system and using an application like Procomm.

Remote shells (or remote logins) are sessions on remote computers that are centered around the execution of a shell (or shell command) instead of a terminal on a remote system. A remote shell executes a command on a remote host, while a remote login runs a shell; both usually appear to be running on the local system. Remote shells are frequently used by administrators in shell scripts, allowing them to execute commands on several systems and consolidate the results in one place, such as collecting disk utilization statistics or automating backups.

The differences between a remote shell and a Telnet session are very important. Telnet sessions use terminal emulation and are run as separate applications. So the results cannot be shared with other applications unless a mechanism such as cut and paste is used, while remote shells allow the results of commands to be interspersed with local commands.

So a directory on one workstation could be backed up to a tape drive on another via a simple shell command:

```
tar cvfb  - tgt_dir ¦ rsh -n bilbo dd of=/dev/rmt/0
```

The `tar` command creates an archive of `tgt_dir` and sends it to *standard output*. This stream of data is redirected to the `rsh` command. `rsh` connects to the host `bilbo`, executes `dd`, and passes the output of `tar` to it. The `dd` command just happens to know how to save the archive to the tape drive on `/dev/rmt/0`. (This may seem complicated. By the end of this chapter, it will make perfect sense.) So two programs on two different computers are linked as one, without any special configuration requirements or extra software.

With remote logins and shells being so powerful, why would anyone use telnet? One reason is that telnet is much more robust over slow links, such as Internet and WAN connections between different sites than remote logins. The other is security. We'll cover some of the risks posed by remote shells later.

X Window is another example of UNIX's networking prowess. The X environment is a graphical user interface, much like the Windows or Macintosh environments. A key difference is that it is segmented into a client (the application) and a server (the display). The server is a process that manages the keyboard, mouse, and screen, and accepts connections from applications over a socket (a network connection). Because a network connection is the method of communication between the two programs, the application can be running on a different workstation than the display that is controlling it. (When applications are running on the same workstation as the server, the network connection is frequently bypassed in favor of faster methods. These enhancements are proprietary extensions and differ widely from vendor to vendor.)

The remote functionality of X Window is a very powerful advantage, especially when considered in terms of large database, Web, or file servers that tend to be installed in data centers or equipment rooms, but have graphical management and configuration applications. Another possibility is installing slower, less expensive workstations on desktops while still being able to run more demanding applications on shared, more powerful computers.

File sharing is another extension that has become a natural and integral part of UNIX computing. All of the major UNIX variants support *NFS* (Network File System) and can share files seamlessly between themselves and other UNIX versions.

Because NFS file systems are treated like any other type of disk, the same way SCSI, IDE, and floppy disks are implemented, network drives fully support user accounts, file permissions, and all of the mechanisms UNIX already uses for adding, removing, and managing other types of files and file systems, even when shared between different UNIX variants.

This means that two UNIX systems, regardless of what version of UNIX or on what type of computer they happen to be, can share files, maybe even from a common file server running on a third system type. Only the user IDs have to be coordinated in order for the files to be securely shared. No additional software or special modifications are required.

Any UNIX system can *export* or *share* file systems. This is one of the ways that the difference between servers and clients is blurred with UNIX systems; any system can provide or consume file system resources. When file systems are shared, the workstation can specify which systems can and cannot use it, and also whether or not users may write to it.

Clients specify where the file system will be mounted in their directory tree. For example, a system can mount the `/export/applications` directory from another system to the `/mnt/apps` directory.

UNIX Networking: Sharing Files and Information

Consider the following practical applications to illustrate how UNIX networking works, and how some common tools and planning can make administration very easy.

A system that is frequently used to administer NFS is the *automounter*. This program (or set of programs) allows administrators to specify file systems to be *mounted* (attached) and *unmounted* (detached) as needed, based on when clients refer to them. This process happens completely in the background, without any intervention after the automount program(s) are configured properly.

LINUX

Linux systems use a publicly available application called amd instead of automount. Although the configuration files differ slightly, the functionality amd provides Linux is the same. amd is provided with all of the major Linux distributions. As always, see the manual page for specifics.

automount is configured with *maps* (a fancy term used for referring to configuration files), where each map specifies a top-level directory. So, if the automount system is to create five directories, the *master* map, which is contained in the file /etc/auto_master might look like this:

```
/share      auto_share
/home       auto_home
/gnu        auto_gnu
/apps       auto_apps
/opt        auto_opt
```

This file provides the automount with the names of the directories it will create and the files that contain what the directories will contain.

For example, let's look at an organization that decided that all user directories belong under the directory /home. (Therefore, the user dan would find his files in /home/dan.) The first thirty home directories were located on the file server gandalf in the /export/home directory.

When the next user comes along, the administrator realizes that gandalf does not have enough drive space for a new user, and, as a matter of fact, moving a couple of users over to the other file server, balrog, which has been used for applications until now, would probably be a good idea.

automount simplifies this distribution by allowing us to create a virtual /home directory on every workstation that runs the automount daemon. An excerpt from the home directory map, /etc/auto_home, as named in /etc/auto_master above, would look like this:

```
eric   gandalf:/export/home/eric
dan    gandalf:/export/home/dan
mike   balrog:/export/home/michael
```

In this map, eric, dan, and mike are referred to as directory *keys*. The directories are called *values*. When a program refers to /home/eric for the first time, the system recognizes the key eric and arranges for /export/home/eric on gandalf to be mounted at /home/eric. Because automount does a simple key/value replacement, Eric and Dan's directories can be on gandalf while Mike's is on balrog. Also note that the directory names in balrog and the automounter *virtual* directory do not have to agree. After a period of inactivity, automount unmounts the directory.

automount alleviates the tedious task of mounting all of the directories that a user or group of users will need in advance. Permanently mounting all of those file systems leads to unnecessary system overhead and requires excessive human intervention. This system also makes it easier

14

WHAT IS SYSTEM ADMINISTRATION?

for users to travel from workstation to workstation, since they can always expect to find important application and data files in the same place.

Sun Microsystems defined *autofs* as a new file system type in Solaris 2.x, and created a multi-threaded automounter system. This makes automounted file systems perform extraordinarily well under Solaris, since the kernel is now aware that automounted file systems exist and can prevent bottlenecks in the automount program through the use of threads.

Hewlett-Packard's HP-UX and IBM's AIX provide a version of automount. Since automount uses NFS, it is compatible across different UNIX variants.

Newer versions of automount (and amd) also enable us to specify more than one file server for a directory, in order to provide a backup for when one file server is unavailable or overloaded. This system, with a little planning and thought, can simplify a distributed network and even make it a little more reliable.

The maps, however, still must be kept up to date and distributed to each workstation. This could be done using ftp, or even nfs, but on a large network this can become tedious. There are two very elegant solutions that are examples of how experienced system administrators tend to solve these problems.

The first is a tool called rdist. It is a tool for maintaining identical copies of software between remote hosts. It can accept filenames from the command line or use a configuration file (usually referred to as a distfile) that lists what files to copy to which hosts.

In order to distribute a set of automounter maps we might use a distfile like this simple example:

```
HOSTS = (bilbo frodo thorin snowball)
FILES = /etc/auto_master /etc/auto_home /etc/auto_apps
${FILES}->${HOSTS}
        install;
```

The distfile is a very powerful mechanism. In this example, we take advantage of the ability to create variables. By specifying the hosts to be updated and the files to send in lists, we can easily add to them. After we define $FILES and $HOSTS, we indicate that the lists of files should be kept up to date on the hosts that are listed. install (the one-line command after the dependency line) is one of many rdist commands; it indicates the rdist should keep the files up to date with the local copies. See the man page for more information on the numerous directives and distfile options.

To use this we could add the distfile to the /etc directory on the host where the master set of automounter maps are created. Whenever we make a change, we would execute

```
rdist -f /etc/auto_distfile
```

rdist can be used for much more complicated tasks, such as synchronizing user directories between redundant file servers or distributing new versions of software packages where nfs is not being used.

The disadvantage behind `rdist` is that it has the same security requirement as any other remote shell command. The user executing the `rdist` command must be able to attach to the remote host and execute commands without a password. (Refer to the following "Network Security Issues" section.)

If the security issues associated with `rdist` are unacceptable, how could we conveniently distribute these maps?

Sun Microsystems's *Network Information Service* (NIS) (also frequently called "yp" or yellow pages) may be an acceptable alternative. NIS provides common configuration information, such as IP addresses, service port numbers, and automount maps to hosts on a network from a server or set of servers.

The NIS server(s) have master copies of the files that are made available. Instead of copying the files to the clients, they are distributed as needed across the network. So the clients retrieve the information from the server instead of reading files.

NIS is used for `hosts`, `services`, `passwd`, `automount` and a few other configuration files. Configuring a network for NIS is beyond the scope of this chapter, and is not the same for each UNIX variant, since many vendors made their own "improvements" on Sun's system. Thoroughly consult the documentation for the platform(s) that you are using before you try to implement it, and make sure you understand any changes that the vendors have made. NIS does have some advantages and drawbacks that we can cover.

The main advantage to NIS is convenience. Changes can be made to a map and made available to clients almost instantly, usually by executing a single command after the file is edited. Being able to keep all of this information in one place (or a few places if secondary servers are used) is obviously convenient, especially since synchronizing user IDs, IP addresses, and service ports is crucial to keeping a network working well.

There are however, some significant disadvantages.

A workstation that uses NIS to resolve IP addresses cannot use DNS for Internet addresses without some important modifications. Sun's NIS+ solves this problem, but is not yet widely supported by other versions of UNIX and is considered to be a proprietary and very hard-to-use system (which is why it is not covered here).

If the `passwd` file is distributed by NIS, the encrypted password field can be read by anyone who connects to NIS. This can be used to subvert security by many hackers, because cracking the encrypted password field is susceptible to a brute force attack with publicly available software.

NIS has no mechanism for controlling who connects to the server and reads the maps. This adds to the security issues, and is one of the reasons you won't find any NIS servers on the Internet. (NIS+ also addresses this issue with a complex authentication system.)

If a client cannot contact a server to handle a request, the request tends to wait until a server is found instead of trying to find a way to continue.

Obviously, NIS comes with its own set of issues and is a system that requires considerable examination before being selected as an administration tool.

Network Security Issues

We've already mentioned a few security issues regarding UNIX and networking. These issues are very serious for administrators, and frequently have a huge impact on how a network is configured.

Earlier I mentioned that Telnet is still used extensively in favor of remote shells. Remote shells allow noninteractive logins, such as the preceding examples using `tar`, `dd`, and `rdist`. While this is a very convenient feature, it's also a very dangerous one when not carefully administered.

The automatic login feature is implemented with a pair of text files. One of them, `/etc/hosts.equiv`, controls users on the system level. The other, `.rhosts`, controls access for individual users. Each file lists the systems by name that a user can log in from without supplying a password if the user ID exists on the target host. All of the major UNIX variants treat these files the same way.

`hosts.equiv` provides this access for an entire workstation, except for the root account. Obviously this file should be very carefully used, if at all. The `.rhosts` file provides access for individual users, and is located in the user's home directory. It is consulted instead of `hosts.equiv`. If the `root` account has one of these files, then the `root` account from the listed hosts may enter the workstation without any authentication at all, since the `.rhosts` effectively supercedes the `hosts.equiv` file.

So the convenience of the remote logins and commands comes with a high price. If a set of workstations were configured to allow `root` to travel back and forth without authentication, then a malicious or, maybe even worse, ill-informed user only needs to compromise one of the workstations in order to wreak havoc on them all.

Some possible precautions are

- Use root as little as possible. Root should never be used for remote operations is a simple enough general rule.
- Avoid using `rlogin` where `telnet` will do.
- If you must use `rlogin`, try to get by without using `.rhosts` or `hosts.equiv`.
- If you need to use noninteractive logins for operations such as backups or information collection, create a special account for it that only has access to the files and devices necessary for the job.
- Remote logins are just about out of the question on any systems that are directly connected to the Internet. (Please note that a home system that is dialing into the Internet through an ISP is not truly directly connected.)

A little bit of explanation regarding the first rule is in order. The root account should be used as little as possible in day-to-day operations. Many UNIX neophytes feel that root access is necessary to accomplish anything worthwhile, when that's not true at all. There is no reason for common operations, such as performing backups, scanning logs, or running network services, to be done as root (other than the services that use ports numbered less than 1024. For historical reasons UNIX only allows processes run as root to monitor these ports). The more situations where root is used, the more likely it is that something unexpected and quite possibly disastrous will occur.

Even beyond remote logins, UNIX offers a lot of network services. File sharing, e-mail, X Window, and information services, such as DNS and NIS, comprise only part of the flexibility and extensibility offered by networking. However many of these services represent risks that are not always necessary and sometimes are unacceptable.

The right way to handle these services is to evaluate which ones are needed and enable only them. Many network services are managed by inetd. This daemon process listens for requests for network services and executes the right program in order to service them.

For example, the ftp service is administered by inetd. When a request for the ftp service (service port number 21) is received, inetd consults its configuration information and executes ftpd. Its input and output streams are connected to the requester.

Network services are identified by ports. Common services such as ftp and telnet have *well-known ports*, numbers that all potential clients need to know. inetd *binds* and *listens* to these ports based on its configuration data, contained in the file inetd.conf.

A typical configuration file looks like this:

```
# Configuration file for inetd(1M).  See inetd.conf(4).
#
# To re-configure the running inetd process, edit this file, then
# send the inetd process a SIGHUP.
#
# Syntax for socket-based Internet services:
#   <service_name> <socket_type> <proto> <flags> <user> <server_pathname> <args>
#
ftp       stream  tcp    nowait  root    /usr/sbin/in.ftpd      in.ftpd
telnet    stream  tcp    nowait  root    /usr/sbin/in.telnetd   in.telnetd
#
# Tnamed serves the obsolete IEN-116 name server protocol.
#
name      dgram   udp    wait    root    /usr/sbin/in.tnamed    in.tnamed
#
# Shell, login, exec, comsat and talk are BSD protocols.
#
shell     stream  tcp    nowait  root    /usr/sbin/in.rshd      in.rshd
login     stream  tcp    nowait  root    /usr/sbin/in.rlogind   in.rlogind
exec      stream  tcp    nowait  root    /usr/sbin/in.rexecd    in.rexecd
comsat    dgram   udp    wait    root    /usr/sbin/in.comsat    in.comsat
talk      dgram   udp    wait    root    /usr/sbin/in.talkd     in.talkd
```

As the comment states, information for inetd is available on two different manual pages.

Each configuration entry states the name of the service port, which is resolved by using the /etc/services file (or NIS map), some more information about the connection, the user name that the program should be run as, and, finally, the program to run. The two most important aspects of this file, from a security standpoint, are what user the services are run as and what services are run at all. (Details on network connection types are covered in Chapter 20, "Networking.")

Each service name corresponds to a number. Ports that are numbered less than 1024, which ftp, telnet, and login all use, can only be attached to as root, so inetd itself does have to be run as root, but it gives us the option of running the individual programs as other users. The reason for this is simple: If a program that is running as root is somehow compromised, the attacker will have root privileges. For example, if a network service that is running as root has a "back door" facility that allows users to modify files, an attacker could theoretically use the program to read, copy, or modify any file on the host under attack.

Some of the most serious and effective Internet security attacks exploited undocumented features and bugs in network services that were running as root. Therefore the best protection against the next attack is to avoid the service completely, or at least provide attackers with as little power as possible when they do find a weakness to take advantage of.

Most UNIX variants come from the vendor running unneeded and, in some cases, undesirable services, such as rexecd, which is used for the remote execution of programs, frequently with no authentication. As discussed, this service came from the vendor configured as root. Many organizations configure key systems to deny all network services except the one service that they are built to provide, such as Internet Web and ftp servers.

Well-written network software also takes these issues into consideration. For example, the Apache Web Server is usually configured to listen to the http port, which is number 80 and therefore can only be bound to by root. Instead of handling client requests as root and posing a significant security risk, Apache accepts network connections as root, but only handles actual requests as nobody, a user with virtually no rights except to read Web pages. It does this by running multiple copies of itself as nobody and utilizing interprocess communication to dispatch user requests to the crippled processes.

Sharing files on the network poses another set of security issues. Files should be shared carefully, with close attention to not only who can write to them, but who can read them, because e-mail and other forms of electronic communication have become more and more common and can contain important business information.

See Chapters 20, "Networking," and 21, "System Accounting," for more detailed information and instructions on how to properly secure your systems.

UNIX Is Heterogeneous

UNIX is frequently criticized for a lack of consistency between versions, vendors, and even applications. UNIX is not the product of any single corporation or group, and this does have a significant impact on its personality. Linux is probably the ultimate expression of UNIX's collective identity. After Linus Torvalds created the Linux kernel and announced it to the Internet, people from all over the world began to contribute to what has become called the Linux operating system. While there is a core group of a few developers who were key in its development, they do not all work for the same company or even live in the same country. Obviously, Linux reflects a few different views on how computers should work. UNIX does, too.

Administration Tools

UNIX vendors all offer their own GUI administrative tools that are generally useful, provided that you do not have to do something that the vendor did not anticipate. These tools vary widely in how they work and how they are implemented.

IBM's UNIX operating system, AIX, comes with a sophisticated tool called SMIT. Administrators can use SMIT to configure the system, add and remove users, and upgrade software. SMIT is widely considered to be the best and most mature of the system administration systems, because it can be customized and run in either X Window or a terminal session. It also allows the user to view the command line equivalent of each task before it is performed. The downside (in at least some system administrator's opinions) is that use of SMIT is just about mandatory for some basic administration tasks.

Hewlett-Packard's HP/UX has a similar tool called SAM, which provides much of the functionality offered by SMIT but is not quite as powerful or sophisticated. Its use is not required to administer the system, however.

Sun's Solaris does not come with a tool comparable to SMIT or SAM. However, Sun's individual tools for upgrading and installing software and administering NIS+ are functional and intuitive. Unfortunately, the tool supplied with Solaris for administering users, printers, and NIS/NIS+ requires X Window. It is not, however required to administer the system at all.

Linux distributions vary widely when it comes to administrative tools. RedHat offers a powerful desktop environment for adding software, administering users, configuring printers, and other everyday administrative tasks. Unlike the commercial tools, it's based on scripts, not binary code, and therefore can be examined and customized by administrators. The Slackware distribution comes with management tools for upgrading and adding software also.

14

WHAT IS SYSTEM ADMINISTRATION?

In addition to the different administrative tools and environments provided by the different UNIX vendors, each vendor has felt obligated to provide its own improvements to UNIX over the years. Fortunately, the threat of Windows NT and its homogeneous look and feel has made the UNIX vendors sensitive to these differences, and the tide has turned toward standardization.

UNIX has historically been divided into two major variants, AT&T's UNIX System V and The University of California's BSD UNIX. Most of the major vendors are now moving toward a System V system, but many BSD extensions will always remain.

Regardless of what the vendors do (and claim to do), UNIX's heterogeneous nature is a fact of life, and is probably one of its most important strengths, since that nature is what's responsible for giving us some of the Internet's most important tools, such as Perl, e-mail, the Web, and Usenet news. It also provides us with a lot of choices on how to administer our systems. Few problems in UNIX have only one answer.

Graphical Interfaces

Macintosh and Microsoft Windows benefit from a user interface that is designed and implemented by a single vendor. For the most part, a set of applications running on one of these computers shares not only a common look and feel but the same keyboard shortcuts, menus, and mouse movements. X Window does not have this advantage.

X Window is a collection of applications, not an integral part of the operating system. Because it is structured this way, it differs greatly from the windowing systems on a Macintosh or Microsoft Windows. As a result, the relationship between X applications and the operating system tends to be a bit more loose than on those platforms.

One of the things that gives an X desktop its "personality" is the *window manager*. This is the application that provides each window with a border and allows them to be moved and overlapped. However, it is just an application, not part of the X Window system. This separation enables users to select the manager they want, just like a shell. Individual users on the same system can also use different window managers. The differences between window managers are significant, having a significant impact on the look of the desktop, the way the mouse acts, and sometimes, what applications can be run.

The OpenLook window manager, which is distributed by Sun and also accompanies many Linux distributions, has many proprietary extensions and is very lightweight and fast. It bears little resemblance, however, to Macintosh or Microsoft Windows in look or feel. (For one thing, it makes heavy use of the right mouse button, which Microsoft Windows only recently started to do and does not even exist on a Macintosh.) The Sun OpenWindows package comes with OpenLook and a set of tools for reading mail, managing files, and a few other common tasks.

Motif, which has many similarities with Microsoft Windows, has become more popular in the past few years, with most of the major vendors having agreed to standardize on the *Common Desktop Environment (CDE)*, which is based largely on Motif. The CDE also has additional features, such as a graphical file manager, a toolbar, and support for virtual screens. The CDE also comes with a set of user applications.

Window managers also come with programming libraries for creating menus and other programming tasks. As a result, it is possible to create an application that runs poorly under some window managers or requires libraries that a UNIX version does not have. This is a common problem for Motif applications on Linux, because the libraries are not free. For this reason, many applications are available in a non-Motif version or with the libraries *statically linked,* which means they are built into the application. (This is generally considered undesirable because it makes the application larger and requires more memory and more disk space.)

Windows 3.*x* has the `win.ini` and `.ini` file scheme; Windows 95 and Windows NT have the system registry. Both serve as central repositories for application configuration information. X Window has its own standard interface for configuration information, called *X resources.* X resources are more flexible in many ways than the Windows mechanisms.

X resources support wildcards with parameters, which allows administrators (and users) to standardize behavior between diverse applications. Most X Window application developers recognize this ability and tend to use standard naming schemes for configuration parameters, which makes the use of wildcards even more convenient.

Users are able to customize applications to reflect their personal preferences without affecting others by maintaining personal resource files, unlike single user systems that maintain one set of parameters for an entire system. However, administrators still have the ability to set default parameters, so users who do not wish to customize an application still have minimal functionality.

Command Line Interfaces

The command line is where UNIX's long history and diversity really show. One would think that every utility was written by a different person for a different purpose, and one might be right.

There is little cohesion between command line tools as far as the interface goes. The directory list command `ls` covers just about the whole alphabet when it comes to command line options. The `find` command, however, uses abbreviations for options instead of letters and almost looks like a new language. Most commands require a "-" to delineate different arguments; others do not. Several commands use subtly different dialects of regular expressions (wildcards).

There are also frequently two versions of the same command: one from the System V world and one from the BSD world. My favorite example of this is the `mail` command. The `mail` command is a simple, text-based, virtually feature-free mail reading and sending tool. There are two versions of this command though, so there must have been something worth disagreeing about when it came time to create the most basic of mail readers.

Both `mail` commands can be used to send e-mail from the command line and are invaluable for unattended scripting jobs since they can alert administrators of problems via e-mail. The BSD version allows you to specify a subject on the command line, like this:

```
mail -s "Backup Results" {hyperlink mailto:eric@niftydomain.com } < backup.txt
```

where the -s is an option for the mail subject. The System V version of `mail` (which is the default for Solaris) quietly ignores the -s option. This has led to my actually troubleshooting why my mail had no subject on at least three different occasions.

Another endearing difference between the two major variants is the `ps` command. Both commands provide the same information about running programs. The command line arguments are completely different.

The best way to avoid problems with these pointless and gratuitous differences is to take full advantage of the wealth of information contained in the man pages. (In the "Administration Resources" portion of this chapter, we cover a few ways to get more information from them.) And keep these tips in mind:

- UNIX has been around for more than 25 years. What are the chances that you have a problem that hasn't been solved by someone yet? Before you spend a lot of time and effort solving a problem, spend some time reading man pages about the problem and the tools you are using.

- Many of the tools on a UNIX system have been around for those 25+ years. Software that lasts that long must have something going for it.

- Experiment with the tools and try to solve the same problem using different methods every once in awhile. Sometimes you can pick up new tricks that will save you hours of time in the future.

System Administration Tasks

System administration can generally be divided into two broad categories: supporting users and supporting systems.

Supporting Users

Users are your customers. Without them the network would be a single computer, probably running a frivolous application like DOOM and generating no business or creating no new sales. (Sounds awful, doesn't it?) We support users by creating their logins and providing them with the information they need to use their computers to get something done, without forcing them to become computer experts or addicts. (Like us.)

Creating User Accounts

The most fundamental thing that an administrator can do for a user is create her account. UNIX accounts are contained in the `/etc/passwd` file with the actual encrypted password being contained in either the `passwd` file or the `/etc/shadow` file if the system implements shadow passwords.

When a user is created, the account obviously has to be added to the `passwd` file. (The specifics behind user accounts are covered in Chapter 17, "User Administration.") This is a very easy task that can be performed in less than a minute with any text editor. However, if the UNIX version you are using has a tool for adding users, it may not be a bad idea to just take advantage of it.

These tools will frequently

- Add the user to the `passwd` file (and shadow file if it is used). Since all users require a unique user ID, letting the computer assign the number when you are administering a large number of users can be very convenient.
- Create a home directory for the user with the proper file permissions and ownership.
- Copy generic *skeleton files* to the account, which give the user a basic environment to work with. These files can be created by the administrator, so the paths to shared applications and necessary environment variables can be distributed to users as they are created.
- Register the new account with network systems, such as NIS and NFS, if the home directory needs to be accessed on other hosts.

So these tools can prevent common errors and save a bit of time. Most UNIX variants also provide a command line tool named `useradd` that will perform all or most of these steps. If using the GUI tool is uncomfortable or unworkable, `useradd` can be incorporated into a shell or Perl script.

Providing Support

Providing users with documentation and support is another key system administration task and potential headache. The best system administrator is both invisible and never missed. She also realizes that expecting users to get as excited about learning how to use a computer as she is is asking too much.

A famous proverb talks about teaching a man to fish instead of buying him a McFish sandwich. (Or something like that.) The idea behind this expression can be applied to users with amazing results. However, few users will go out of their way to learn how to use their systems. How can an administrator teach his users how to help themselves without fighting a never ending battle?

All user populations are different, and there is no universal solution to user training, but here are a couple of ideas that may help.

Try to provide and gently enforce a formal method for requesting changes to systems and getting help. If users get accustomed to instant answers to questions, they will become angry when you can't drop what you're doing to help them. Try to set up an e-mail or Web-based help system. It may seem bureaucratic to force users to use these systems, but it helps prevent your day from becoming "interrupt-driven" and also provides you with a log of requests. (Have you ever forgotten to take care of a request because you were too overloaded? Give yourself an automatic to do list.)

Provide as much documentation as you can through easy-to-use interfaces, such as Web browsers. The time you spend developing this information in user-friendly formats will be paid back in phone calls and conversations that never happen, and may help you learn some more about your systems as you do it.

If you have Internet access now, I'm sure your users spend hours glued to their browsers; take advantage of that. You may also find that a lot of the information your users need is already out there, so you may be able to link your users to some of the information they need, without generating it yourself. (We'll go over some of these resources later in the "Administration Resources" portion of this chapter.)

Supporting Systems

The other half of the job is supporting your systems. Systems have to be built, backed up, upgraded, and, of course, fixed.

Adding Nodes

A frequent system administration task is adding new nodes to the network. It's also one of the parts of the job that can truly benefit from some planning and insight.

Not all systems are created equal, and not all of them are used for the same thing. Spending some time understanding what your network is really used for and then applying that to systems is key in network planning. Workstations should have well-defined roles and should be configured in accordance with those roles.

When systems are designed and evaluated, some of the questions an administrator can ask are:

- Will users be able to access all or some of the systems? Do users need to access more than one system? Are there systems that users should never access?

- What network file systems will each workstation need to access? Are there enough that automount would help?

- What network services, such as telnet, remote logins, sharing file systems, and e-mail, do workstations need to provide? Can each service be justified?

- What networks will workstations need to access? Are there networks that should be inaccessible from others?

These questions should help us develop a profile for each workstation. Following a profile makes workstations easier to build, maintain, and troubleshoot, not to mention making them more reliable since they tend to be less complex.

Backups

Files get corrupted, lost, accidentally overwritten, or deleted. Our only protection against these situations is backups, since UNIX does not have an undelete command.

UNIX provides several backup tools, and deciding which tool(s) to use can be a difficult.

Earlier in the chapter we had an example of backing up a directory, using `tar` and `dd`, to a remote tape drive. In that example, `dd` was just be used as a way to copy a stream of data to a tape, while `tar` was the command actually performing the backup.

`tar` (**t**ape **ar**chive) is a commonly used backup tool.

```
tar -c -f /dev/rmt/0 /home/eric
```

The above command would back up the contents of the `/home/eric` directory to the first tape drive installed on a Solaris system. `tar` automatically traverses the directory, so all files in `/home/eric` and its subdirectories are archived.

The device name for tape drives on systems differs from variant to variant. BSD derivatives tend to refer to them as `/dev/rst1` where 0 is the first, 1 is the second, and so on. (Linux, HP-UX, and SunOS 4.1.*x* use this nomenclature.) System V derivatives usually use `/dev/rmt1` the same way. (AIX uses this model.) However, Solaris 2.*x*, which is System V based, adds a directory to the path, so it is `/dev/rmt/1`.

The `-f` option tells `tar` which tape drive to use, while the `-c` option is telling it to create a new archive instead of modifying an existing one. One of `tar`'s idiosyncrasies is that when a path is given to it as the backup specification, it is added to the archive, so when it is time to restore `/home/eric`, that is where it will be restored to. A more flexible way to back up the directory is to do this:

```
cd /home/eric
tar -cf /dev/rmt/0 .
```

`tar` recognizes `.` as meaning back up the current directory. When the archive is extracted, it will be placed in the current directory, regardless of where that is.

`cpio` is another standard UNIX tool for backups. Its interface is a little more difficult than `tar`'s, but has several advantages.

`cpio` is usually used with `ls` or `find` to create archives.

```
find . -print | cpio -o > /dev/rst0
```

The `find` command prints the full path of all of the files in its current directory to standard out. `cpio` accepts these filenames and archives them to standard output. This is redirected to the tape, where it is archived. This command is an excellent example of the UNIX way of combining commands to create a new tool.

`find` is a tool for finding files. They can be located by name, size, creation date, modification date, and a whole universe of other criteria too extensive to cover here. (As always, see the man page!) This example takes this tool for locating files and makes it the user interface to our backup system.

`cpio` is the file copying and archiving "Swiss Army Knife." In addition to streaming files in a format suitable for tape, it can

- Back up special files, such as device drive *stubs* like `/dev/rst0`.
- Place data on tapes more efficiently than `tar` or `dd`.
- Skip over bad areas on tapes or floppies when restoring, when `tar` would simply die. With `cpio`, you can at least restore part of a damaged archive.
- Perform backups to floppies, including spread a single archive over more than one disk. `tar` can only put a single archive on one disk.
- Swap bytes during the archive or extraction in order to aid in transferring files from one architecture to another.

This example also illustrates how we can redirect standard output to a device name and expect the device driver to place it on the device.

Our example could also be stretched into a full-featured backup system. Since `find` allows us to pick files based on creation and modification dates, we could perform a full backup to tape once a week by telling find to name all files, and perform incremental backups to floppy every other day. The UNIX command line is a very powerful tool, especially since programs have been designed for it steadily during the past three decades.

There are other backup tools, most notably `dump` or `ufsdump` as it is named on Solaris 2.*x*. These tools are oriented toward backing up entire disk partitions, instead of files. They are covered in Chapter 28, "Backing Up and Restoring Your System."

Larger sites with more comprehensive backup requirements may need a commercial package. Legato's *NetWorker* provides an advanced backup and restore system that supports the automated and unattended backup of UNIX systems, Windows and NT workstations, Macintoshes, PCs, and even database servers. The process of scheduling backups, selecting file for backup and confirming the integrity of archives is all done automatically. Restoring files and file systems is also very simple due to the GUI.

Sun bundles NetWorker with the Solaris 2.*x* server edition.

Just as important as picking a backup tool is designing a backup strategy.

Backing up the entire system daily is not acceptable, since it would take too long and would be too ponderous to restore if only one file is needed.

Here is another area where it pays to know your users and understand their business. It's also important to design the network with backup and recovery in mind.

- Do the users have important files that they modify daily?
- Are the users clustered into one of two directories on one system, or will systems have to be backed up across the network?

- If only a single file has to be restored, will it have to be done quickly? Will our current backup system allow us to find one file?

- How often and for how long are users not using the system? (It is better to back up directories when they are not in use.)

Depending on the requirements, a commercial backup tool may be a good investment. The commercial tools, such as NetWorker, do excel in allowing you to locate and restore one specific file quickly, which may be necessary in your situation.

System Load and Performance

The task of monitoring system load and system performance falls on the shoulders of the system administrator. This is yet another area where planning and anticipation are superior to waiting for something to happen and reacting to it.

Daily monitoring of usage statistics is a good idea, especially on mission-critical systems and systems that users interact with regularly, such as Web servers and X displays. These statistics can be gathered with automated scripts.

Some of the things to monitor are disk usage, CPU utilization, swap, and memory. The tools used for getting this information, such as `du` and `df` for disk information and `top` and `vmstat` for the rest, are covered in the next few chapters in Part III.

Administration Resources

A system administrator needs every shred of information and help he can get, and as much as UNIX vendors would hate to admit, the accompanying documentation that is sometimes lacking. Fortunately, it's a big world out there.

The Manual Pages

The famous rejoinder RTFM (Read The Fine Manual) refers to the manual pages installed on (hopefully) every UNIX system. The man pages, as they are frequently called, contain documentation and instructions on just about every UNIX command, C function call, and data file on your system.

The `man` command searches for documentation based on a command or topic name. So the command

```
man ls
```

provides us with documentation on the `ls` command, which happens to be in section one.

As simple as they may appear, the man pages actually have a sophisticated structure. The pages are divided into sections, with some of the sections being further divided into subsections.

14

WHAT IS SYSTEM
ADMINISTRATION?

The section layout resembles this:

- User commands—commands like `ls`, `tar`, and `cpio`.
- System calls—C programming functions that are considered system calls, like opening and closing files.
- C library functions—C programming functions that are not considered system calls, like printing text.
- File formats—descriptions of file layouts, such as `hosts.equiv` and `inetd.conf`.
- Headers, Tables, and Macros—miscellaneous documentation, such as character sets and header files, not already covered.
- Games and Demos—games and demo software. (Even DOOM for UNIX has a man page!)

This is a generalized table of contents. BSD and System V started out with slightly different section schemes, and vendors tend to add their own sections and make their own "improvements." (How could it be any other way?)

In order to view information about each section, we can view the intro page for it. In order to see information about section one, we would execute the following command:

```
man -s 1 intro
```

The `-s` option selects which section of the man pages to search with the System V version of the man command. BSD versions accept the section number as the first argument with no switch, while the Linux version will select the section from an environment variable or from a `-s` option.

All of the versions accept the `-a` option, which will force the man command to search all of the sections and display all pages that match. Since there are different pages with the same name, understanding the different sections and what belongs in each of them is helpful. However, there are additional tools, and it is not necessary to memorize the section layout for each system.

Man pages can be indexed and pre-formatted with a tool called `catman`. The pre-formatting part make the pages display faster and is less important than the indexing, which allows us to use more powerful information retrieval tools, namely `whatis` and `apropos`.

`apropos` displays the section number, name and short description of any page that contains the specified keyword. `whatis` gives us the man page name and section number.

For example, let's try the `apropos` command for the keyword `nfs`:

```
apropos nfs
```

A portion of the response would be this:

```
automount (8)            Automatically mount NFS file systems
exportfs (8)             Export and unexport directories to NFS clients
exports, xtab (5)        Directories to export to NFS clients
```

```
nfs, NFS (4P)                    Network file system
nfsd, biod (8)                   NFS daemons
```

(The output was edited, because the actual request returned 12 responses.)

Now let's try `whatis`:

```
whatis nfs
    nfs, NFS (4P)                Network file system
```

With `whatis` we only see the name of the actual `nfs` manual page and its section number.

In addition to the manual pages, Sun supplies *Answerbook* with Solaris. It's a GUI-based online help system that supports full text search and just about completely removes the need for hard copy documentation.

IBM supplies *Infoviewer*, which is also a GUI-based online help system. As a matter of fact, the default AIX installation program installs Infoviewer instead of the manual pages, which can be quite an inconvenience for users who do not use X Window.

Internet Information Resources

The Internet provides administrators with a wealth of resources, too.

1. Usenet news—While not as useful as it was in the past (due to overcrowding and a plummeting signal to noise ratio), Usenet news offers discussion groups about all of the UNIX variants and covers various aspects of them. Some examples are `comp.sys.sun.admin`, `comp.os.linux.setup`, and `comp.unix.admin`. Because of the high traffic on Usenet news, some sites do not carry it. If you cannot get access, try using a search service such as `http://www.dejanews.com` to find what you need. Sometimes searching for articles that interest you instead of browsing is a faster way to get what you need anyway. Deja News offers searching and browsing.

2. FAQ Lists—Frequently Asked Question Lists hold a wealth of information. Most of the computer-related Usenet groups have their own FAQ lists. They can be found posted periodically in the groups and at the `rtfm.mit.edu` ftp server. Many of the FAQs are also available in HTML format.

3. The Web—Documentation is available from the UNIX vendors and from people and groups involved with Linux. Many users and developers also post a wealth of information just to be helpful. Use the search services to get your research going. UNIX was one of the first operating systems to colonize the Internet, and, as a result, there is a huge number of UNIX users on it.

There is a large amount of documentation and help available free on the Internet, and there is a lot more to be learned from seeking out an answer than simply paying a consultant to tell you or leaning on someone else to do what has to be done for you.

Tools of the Trade

A successful administrator takes full advantage of the tools provided with a UNIX system. To the uninitiated, UNIX seems difficult and unwieldy, but once you get the idea you'll never want to use another system.

The Shell

Earlier, I demonstrated how `cpio` uses the output of the `find` command to learn what files to archive. This was a demonstration of shell pipes, which redirect the output of one command to another. We also used this to back up files to a tape drive that is located on another host.

I demonstrated mailing a file to a user on the command line using redirection, which opens a file and passes it to a command as if it were provided in the command line or typed in as a program requested it.

UNIX shells also support sophisticated programming constructs, such as loops, and provide comparison operators, such as equality, greater than, and less than.

Shell programming is essential to system administration, especially as networks grow larger and, as a result, more time consuming to maintain. File backups, adding users and nodes, collecting usage statistics, and a whole host of other administrative tasks are candidates for unattended scripts.

Perl and Other Automation Tools

Perl has become more and more popular over the past few years, and not without good reason. Many tasks that would have required the use of C in the past can now be done by a novice programmer in Perl. System administrators can benefit greatly from a little working knowledge of this language, since it can be used for tasks such as

- Analyzing log files and alerting the administrator of trouble via e-mail or pager.
- Automatically converting systems statistics into Web pages.
- Automating the process of creating user accounts, adding and distributing automounter maps, backing up systems, and creating HTML content.
- Creating and communicating over network connections.

These are only a few examples of what this language can do. Chapter 5, "Perl," in *UNIX Unleashed, Internet Edition* has in-depth coverage of Perl.

Some other tools worth noting are TCL/TK, which most of the RedHat administrative tools are written in and awk, which is covered extensively in Chapter 4, "Awk," in *UNIX Unleashed, Internet Edition*.

Intranet Tools

As mentioned earlier, consider using intranet tools like Web servers and e-mail to communicate with your users.

There are many Web discussion and guest book applications, all written in Perl, that could be modified and used to allow customers to enter requests for support. An internal home page could be used to announce scheduled outages and system enhancements. The Web also allows you to link clients to vendor-provided support resources and documentation.

Summary

What is system administration? This chapter kind of meandered along and tried to give you an idea of what administrators do and what they need to know.

A literal attempt at answering the question may say that administrators are responsible for

- Understanding how the systems for which they are responsible interact over the office or organizational LAN/WAN.
- Supporting users by creating their accounts, protecting their data and making their sometimes bewildering systems easier to use.
- Supporting systems by keeping them secure, up to date, and well tuned.
- Planning the efforts behind support and growth.
- Anticipating and resolving problems.

But it may be better to generalize and say that system administration is the process and effort behind supporting a system or systems so that a company or group can attain its goals.

The rest of this section delves much more deeply into the details of system support. Chapters 15 and 16 describe how to install a UNIX system and start it up and shut it down.

In Chapter 17, I cover supporting users much more in-depth than was covered here. Chapter 18 covers file systems and disk configuration, while 19 provides coverage on kernel configuration.

Chapter 20 is where the complete coverage on UNIX networking is located. In Chapter 21, I cover system accounting, which is key for administrators who are concerned with supporting large groups of users or who need to come up with a comprehensive system for charging users for access.

For information on system performance and how to improve it, see Chapter 22. In addition, Chapter 23 provides information on how to add and maintain new system components, such as tape drives and modems.

Managing mail, Usenet news, and other network services are covered in Chapters 23 through 27. The last chapter in this section, 28, covers system backup and restore.

UNIX Installation Basics

by Syd Weinstein and Lance Cavener

IN THIS CHAPTER

Installing UNIX on a machine requires more thought and planning than installing DOS or Microsoft Windows. You need to decide if this system will be stand-alone, or dependent on a server on your network. You also have to pay careful attention to system resources (such as hard drive space, processor speed, memory, and so on) and which packages are required to tailor this UNIX installation to your needs, and perhaps the needs of users in the future.

Why? DOS is a system that takes less than 10 MB of disk space. Windows takes a bit more, but it's still a rather small amount. UNIX is a large system depending on your configuration. The complete installation of just the operating system and all that comes with it for Sun's Solaris 2.3 release, for example, is about 300 MB. With that much disk space in use, it's often wise to share it across several systems. In addition, there are few options in installing DOS or Windows that can be made by the setup program. UNIX splits the install into many different sections, called packages. Each package consists of files that provide a specific set of features. These features range from networking tools, necessary system utilities, or applications. Many packages can be installed locally, remotely on a server, or not at all, depending on your needs.

You must also take into consideration the various flavors of UNIX that are available, and how much you have to spend. Linux, for example, is free and is publicly available to anyone over the Internet or on CD-ROM. FreeBSD and NetBSD are examples of free BSD-based operating systems; they are generally preferred for larger, more mission-critical sites; they are also free. If you have never used any flavor of UNIX before, you should experiment with as many as you can. You have to decide which one best suits your needs and expectations.

> **TIP**
>
> Linux and FreeBSD are both available on CD-ROM from Walnut Creek. Their Internet address is ref HYPERLINK http://www.cdrom.com. FreeBSD has a Web page at ref HYPERLINK http://www.freebsd.com. NetBSD is at ref HYPERLINK http://www.netbsd.org. Linux has a Web page at ref HYPERLINK http://www.linux.org.

On another note, you have commercial operating systems such as BSDI, SCO, UnixWare, NeXT, Solaris, and many others. These are generally expensive, although you get over-the-phone technical support and printed documentation. These are things to look for if you run a mission- critical site and might need a shoulder to lean on in the future should anything catastrophic happen to your server.

What Are the Differences Between the Different Distributions?

While I can't possibly go through every available distribution, I will give a brief description of some of the major UNIX operating systems.

■ Unixware is based on Svr4, and was originally developed by AT&T. Novell had control of it for a while, and now SCO is developing for it. Unixware runs primarily on x86 (Intel or 100 percent compatible) based machines.

■ BSDI's BSDI Internet Server is a commercial distribution of BSD/OS originally designed and programmed by Berkeley University. BSDI took BSD/OS and added many new utilities, programs, and features that make this distribution a very stable and productive addition to any corporate intranet or Internet gateway. Its main focus is on Internet Service Providers (ISPs) because of its perfect networking capabilities. BSDI runs on all x86 (Intel or 100 percent compatible) machines.

■ FreeBSD and NetBSD are free alternatives to BSDI Internet Server. They contain many of the great features that make BSD/OS very popular, but lack the professional technical support of any commercial distribution. If you don't need the over-the-phone technical support and want the stability and reliability you look for in an Internet/intranet-focused OS, these are for you. Did I mention they are both free? FreeBSD will run on the x86 platform, while NetBSD will run on the following: Dec Alpha, Amiga, Acorn RiscPC, Atari, HP 9000/300 series, x86, m86k Macintosh, PowerPC, Sun SPARC series, Sun 3, Dec VAX and many others. NetBSD is by far the most portable operating system available, although FreeBSD seems to be a more popular choice among x86 users.

■ SCO's SCO OpenServer is another variation of UNIX that is based on XENIX, an OS developed by Microsoft. It is very popular among corporate internets/intranets and has been for many years. It earns a respectable place on corporate servers, although it lacks the versatility of BSD. Its technical support cannot be matched, which is why many corporations choose this commercial OS as their server OS of choice. SCO also has a whole host of applications available—even Microsoft products such as Word and Excel.

■ Linux (RedHat, Slackware, Debian, and so on) was originally developed from the Minix source. It began as a hobby and grew to a frequently updated, used, and supported operating system. Linux is largely based on the POSIX standards, and SysV. Linux has a very wide range of applications available (more so than SCO) and is also free. There are commercial distributions available that usually contain commercial software (for instance, Applixware for RedHat). Linux is very popular among first-time UNIX users, and is easily installed. Linux is very frequently updated with new kernels and is not always as stable as some would like. While Linux is very popular for workstations, it is usually not given the task of a mission-critical server as it lacks the technical support, stability, and functionality of a high-quality professionally developed operating system such as BSDI Internet Server.

What Do I Need to Know from the Start?

The first thing you need to do is decide what you are going to install on this system. You decide this by looking, not only at this system, but at all the systems on this segment of the network.

> **NOTE**
>
> A network segment is a group of machines all plugged into the same Ethernet, a type of LAN which uses a bus topology. Because the Ethernet uses a bus topology, each of the machines sees all the traffic on the network. Each is local to each other and is immediately accessible via the network. Since the Ethernet LAN is only able to handle a finite amount of traffic, the network is broken into segments connected by routers or bridges. Traffic to systems within the segment is not repeated, or retransmitted, into the other segments. Only traffic that is for systems outside the segment is repeated. With proper planning, almost all of the traffic will be internal to the segment, and more systems can be placed on the overall network before everyone bogs down from trying to put more bytes out over the LAN than it can handle.

You base your decision about what to install on the intended usage of the system, what systems it can be served by, and for which systems it must provide services.

Space Requirements

DOS and Windows are not designed to easily share large sections of the installation. UNIX (especially because of its disk needs) almost expects that some sharing will occur. The degree of disk space sharing leads to the definition of stand-alone, server, and diskless machines.

A stand-alone system means that this particular machine can function on its own—it doesn't require any assistance from any other machine on the LAN.

A server is a machine that is connected to the LAN that runs daemons (programs that run like httpd or smtpd) to give remote clients some functions such as mail or news. Technically, a server can be a stand-alone machine, but because of its tasks, it never is.

If the client system has no disk drive at all, it is considered diskless. It depends on its server for booting, for the entire operating system, and for swap space. Many people use such machines as dumb terminals, or machines that just provide an interface to a remote machine.

Dataless machines contain only the necessary files to boot, although they are not used often because of the high load they put on the network (like diskless machines). To avoid network congestion, many people run stand-alone machines to avoid the added cost of faster network equipment.

In addition to sharing the operating system, UNIX systems can share other disks, such as drives containing databases or user files. Sharing these disks does not make a system a server in the "install" sense. The server name is reserved for serving the operating system or its utilities. A system might be an NFS server (sharing user files via Network File System (NFS)) and still be considered a stand-alone system for the installation of the UNIX operating system.

A diskless system does not require that any of these files be installed, because it uses them from the server. A dataless system requires that the core system files be installed. A stand-alone system could be set up with either end-user packages or with developer packages, whereas a server needs the entire distribution.

You are going to have different storage necessities for different installations. Developer installs usually require more disk space, while a dataless system only requires core files. Depending on the size of these files, you will configure the partition differently. Partitions that will contain Usenet articles should be configured to contain smaller *inodes*. This, in turn, increases the number of inodes available for storage of the small Usenet articles. Running out of inodes is like running out of disk space, even though you still have disk space left.

TIP

An *inode* is basically a unit where data is stored. If you have ten 512-byte inodes, and ten 3-byte files, you fill up those ten inodes even though you have not used up the space contained in them. As you can see, this is why decreasing the size of the inodes will produce more available inodes for storage of these small files.

So far this chapter just touches on the disk installation. There is still much to be discussed. You must plan for users, the network and its traffic, applications, printers, remote access, backups, security, and much more.

Thus, planning for a UNIX installation requires planning not only for this one system, but for all the systems in this segment of the network.

Who Is Going to Use This System?

Users who typically use their machine for word processing and other general office applications will not require an extremely large amount of disk space or system resources. However, a power user or application developer needs much more to be installed, perhaps including compilers and development libraries. To decide what to install on this segment of the LAN, let alone on this system, you need to determine which types of users are going to be using this system.

15

UNIX INSTALLATION BASICS

> **TIP**
>
> Not only will the type of user dictate what gets installed, it will also dictate how many systems can be put on this segment of the LAN, the server capacity, and swap space requirements.

Which Type of Users

UNIX users generally fall into one or more of several categories:

- **Application users.** These users run commercial or locally developed applications. They rarely interact with the shell directly and do not write their own applications. These users might be running a database application, a word processor or desktop publishing system, a spreadsheet, or some in-house-developed set of applications. They spend most of their time in think mode, where they are deciding what to do with the results the application has presented them, or in data entry mode, typing responses or data into the system. Their need for large amounts of local disk access is minimal, and they do not change applications frequently, nor are they running many applications simultaneously. (They might have them open, but they are generally interacting with only a couple of them at a time—the rest are waiting for the user to provide input.) Although application users might put a large load on their database servers, they do not normally put large disk loads on their own systems.

- **Power users.** These users run applications, just like the application users, but they also run shell scripts and interact more closely with the system. They are likely to be running multiple applications at once, with all these applications processing in parallel. These users keep several applications busy and access the disk more frequently and use more CPU resources than do the normal application users.

- **Developers.** Developers not only run applications, they also run compilers, access different applications than users, require access to the development libraries, and generally use more components of the operating system than do users. Furthermore, they tend to use debugging tools that require more swap space and access to more disk resources than the application user generally needs. The UNIX operating system has packages that are only needed by developers, and if a developer is on this segment of the LAN, these files must be installed and accessible to the systems used by the developers. Compiling takes up a great amount of processor power; therefore, you must plan to accommodate this need with the right type of system. Ten programmers compiling 10,000 lines of code in parallel can easily bog down a Pentium Pro 200 MHz.

> **TIP**
>
> You must not only consider who will use the system right away, but because you only install UNIX once, consider who might use the system over the next six months to a year. Remember, depending on what type of system you are going to set up, you will be adding users to your machine. If the programs these users need are not available, you will be forced to reinstall the whole system, or install the appropriate packages, depending on the OS. Because of the low cost of hardware these days, you are better off to invest in the added hardware and install all the packages that might be of use to you or anyone else in the future.

For What Purpose?

UNIX systems that are being used as shared development machines or are going be placed in a common user area, need a lot of swap space, a large section of the disk for temporary files. They also need more of the packages from the operating system than systems that are just being used on a single user's desk. In addition, if the system is going to be used as a computation or database server, it needs increased swap space and processor power.

What Other Systems Are Located on This Segment of the LAN?

As stated in the "What Do I Need to Know from the Start?" section, you must consider all of the systems on this segment of the LAN. You are looking for systems that provide access to sections of the operating system, provide access to application disk areas, have sufficient disk and memory resources to handle your diskless clients, and make suitable servers for the other systems on the segment.

If you have an office or a lab full of identical machines, all running the same applications with no need for any major customizations, then having a centralized installation is much easier to maintain. But since we now have hardware, such as CD-ROMs, capable of 16× speed, which can do upwards of 700 kbps, and Ethernet which can do anywhere from 10Mbps to 100Mbps (Ethernet and Fast Ethernet, respectively), it is usually easy to install over the network. It's also just as easy to upgrade machines, providing your operating system supports upgrades; it all depends on what the function of the machines on the segment are.

Determining Suitable Servers

It's usually easier to determine suitable servers than suitable clients, so start there. To make a good server system, you need the following:

Plenty of RAM—Servers must have plenty of RAM available for their use. Your server must be capable of handling many clients, each running different processes at the same time. In order for this to be done efficiently, you don't want much swapping happening. Your best bet is to put as much RAM as possible into the server; this will allow room for upgrades (and higher loads). Generally, 64 to 128 MB is sufficient for many installations. There are some exceptions, such as INN where it uses a lot of RAM, and for a full news feed, 64 MB will not last very long.

Fast Disks—The client sees the delay to read a disk block as the time to ask the server for the block, the time the server takes to read the block, and the time to transmit the block over the network back to the client. If the server has a fast disk, this time might be no longer, and is often shorter, than reading the same number of blocks locally.

Since a server is handling multiple clients, including itself, it is more likely that a disk block is already in the server's disk cache. This is especially true for program files and the operating system utilities, because they are used often. Access is then very fast, as the disk read time is not needed at all. This helps make servers as responsive as if they were reading the disk block locally on the client server.

Don't sacrifice quality for price. You pay for what you get; go for the highest possible (and fastest) hard drives and controllers available. Ultra-Wide SCSI controllers with high-quality UW-SCSI drives handle the task perfectly.

Sufficient disk space—A server will hold not only its own files and a copy of the UNIX operating system, but also the swap and temporary space for its diskless clients. A suitable server should have some spare disk space for adding not only the current clients, but some extra to account for growth. Here is a breakdown of some of the more frequently used packages and their sizes for BSDI (`http://www.bsdi.com`):

> 0.4 MB—Core (`/var`)
>
> 4.0 MB—Core root (`/`)
>
> 23.6 MB—Core usr (`/usr`)
>
> 9.9 MB—Additional user (`/usr`)
>
> 12.3 MB—Networking (`/usr`)
>
> 17.0 MB—Development (`/usr`)
>
> 17.3 MB—Manual pages (`/usr/share/man` & `/usr/contrib/man`)
>
> 92.7 MB—X11 XFree servers, development, man pages (`/usr/X11R6`)
>
> 26.3 MB—Emacs (`/usr/contrib`)
>
> 39.7 MB—TeX & LaTeX

As you can see, BSDI takes up a lot of space. There are still additional packages such as Hylafax, the kernel sources, ghostscript, MH, and many other tools that you may or may not want installed.

Spare CPU resources—A server needs to have enough CPU cycles to serve its local users and still provide disk and network access services to its clients. But that does not mean to make the fastest system the server. Often you should do just the opposite.

It does not take much CPU power to be a server. File access in UNIX is very efficient, as is network traffic. A system that is heavily loaded delays the response of disk block requests for its clients. To keep response time up for the clients, leave your power users on the faster systems and use a system with sufficient other resources and a light user load for the server, even if this system has a slower CPU.

Managing Network Traffic

Before you can decide how to install the new system, you need to check on the amount of traffic on the network. Sources of this traffic include the following:

- Traffic from the systems in Department A to its local server for the following:

  Remote file systems, including accessing shared UNIX OS partitions and user files.

  Access to client/server applications hosted on the Department A server.

  Diskless client access to swap, temporary, and spool partitions.

- Traffic between the systems in Department A, including the following:

  Client/server application traffic.

  Remote display updates (a window on one system showing output from a process on a different system).

  Sharing of local file systems that are not on the server.

- Traffic between the systems in Department A and the backbone server, including the following:

  Remote file access to company-wide files.

  Access to client/server applications running on the backbone, such as a master database.

- Traffic between the systems in Department A and those in Department B, including the following:

  Access to files located locally at Department B.

  Access to client/server applications running on the systems in Department B.

  Remote file access to local disks on Department B systems.

The additional traffic generated by the installation of this new system must be compared to the existing traffic on the network. Adding a diskless client on a network segment running at 80 percent utilization is asking for trouble.

You don't need sophisticated tools to monitor network traffic. Just take one of the workstations and use the tools provided by your vendor to count the packets it sees on the network. A simple approach is to use a tool such as `etherfind` or `snoop` to place the Ethernet interface into promiscuous mode, where it listens to all the packets on the network, not just those addressed to itself. Count the number of packets received by the system over a period of time and their respective length. Most UNIX systems can drive an Ethernet segment up to about 800 kbps in

15

UNIX INSTALLATION BASICS

bursts and over 500 kbps sustained. If the traffic is anything close to this, consider splitting the segment into two segments to reduce the traffic.

When splitting the network into segments, if you can place a server and its systems into each of the split segments, often you can use a less expensive bridge to reduce the traffic on each segment rather than using a router.

Summarizing What You Need to Know Before Starting

In summary, before starting to plan for the actual installation of the new system, you need to determine who is going to use the system. You need to determine how much disk access they will be performing and how much they will contribute to the overall network traffic; whether this system is going to be a client or a server; and whether the network can tolerate another system on this segment before the segment has to be split because of overloading.

Planning for the Installation

You now must determine on which segment to install this new system, decide what type of user it's for, and decide where to place it. What more do you need to plan for other than where to plug in the power cord and network connection?

This section guides you through a short pre-installation checklist to make the installation process go smoothly. It will have you answer the following questions:

- From where am I going to install?
- Is this to be a stand-alone, server, or diskless system?
- What is its hostname?
- What is its IP address?
- Which packages should be installed?
- How should the disk be partitioned?

These are some of the questions the system will ask as you install UNIX. Most of the rest have obvious answers, such as what time zone you are in.

From Where Am I Going to Install?

Traditionally, one installed a system by placing the medium in a drive and booting from that medium, such as floppy, tape, or CD-ROM. With the advent of networking, things are no longer so simple, but they can be a lot more convenient.

You have two choices for installing: local or remote. A local installation is the traditional case, where the media is inserted into some drive attached to the computer being installed, and the software is copied onto the system. A remote installation further falls into two types.

You might use the remote systems's CD-ROM or tape drive to read the media because the system you are installing does not have one. But if there is a large number of systems to install you would access an install server, which already has all of the installable files and boot images on its local disks. Because the local disks are faster than CD-ROM or tape, this is faster. It's only worthwhile to set up the install server, however, when you have a lot of systems to install.

Media Distribution Type

With upwards of 350 MB of software to install, floppies are no longer practical. UNIX software vendors have switched from floppies to either CD-ROM or tape as the install media. Regarding tapes, different UNIX vendors use different tape formats, some offering more than one. You need to make sure you know which format your vendor is supplying and that you will have access to a drive capable of reading the data.

If you have a choice, choose the CD-ROM media. It has several advantages over tape. CD-ROMs are much faster than tape, and they are also random access. This makes the installation much quicker and efficient.

Another advantage is that the media is read-only. It is impossible to overwrite it by mistake or by hardware malfunction. In addition, a CD-ROM is much less expensive to produce and holds more than the tape or floppies it replaces. With a CD-ROM, there is usually no need to change media partway through the installation.

If your computer is unable to boot off the CD-ROM or tape, the vendor also supplies a boot disk (or in the case of some distributions of Linux, a "root and boot" disk, which essentially contains the information needed to boot with your hardware: the installation program and the software that it requires). This is a minimal RAM-based system that is loaded off the floppy and is used to read the CD-ROM or tape. It basically contains the necessary drivers to access your CD-ROM or tape.

CAUTION

If you need boot floppies, be sure you order the proper boot floppies for your system. Many vendors of System V Releases 3 and 4 provide different boot floppies for systems that use SCSI-based tape drives than for those that use dedicated controllers for the tape drive. Also some provide different floppies for CD-ROM than for tape and for different versions of disk controllers. Some Linux distributions have many different boot disks to choose from, while some commercial UNIXes such as BSD/OS have only one generic boot disk.

15

UNIX INSTALLATION BASICS

CAUTION

Read the release notes carefully. Most PC-based UNIX systems support only a limited set of hardware. Be sure your display adapter card, network card, and disk controller are supported. Check to see if any special device drivers are required and that you have those drivers for your version of the operating system.

If not, before you start the installation, be sure to acquire current drivers for those cards from the manufacturer of the cards or from your UNIX vendor. Be sure the driver is specific to the version of UNIX you will be installing.

If the installation procedure does not ask you to install these drivers, be sure to install them before rebooting from the mini-root used to install the system to the operating system just installed. Otherwise, the system will not boot.

Using a Local Device or a Remote Device for Installation

Since most UNIX vendors have decided to switch to CD-ROM as the distribution media of choice, most likely you will have a CD-ROM drive somewhere in the network. At this time you have two choices:

- Unplug the drive from where it is currently and add it to the new system to perform the install. Then you have a local CD-ROM drive and can follow the instructions in the installation notes for using a local CD-ROM drive.

- If your version of UNIX has remote installation abilities, access the drive remotely from the system on which it currently resides.

Since the network is usually much faster than the CD-ROM drive, either choice will work. You just have to be sure that the drive remains available to you for the entire installation process. If someone else is going to need the CD-ROM drive, you will not be able to relinquish it to them until the entire install procedure is complete.

CAUTION

If the system must boot off the CD-ROM drive, it is not always possible to plug any CD-ROM drive into the system. Many UNIX workstation vendors have placed special roms in their CD-ROM drives to modify their behavior to look more like a disk drive during the boot process. When in doubt, it is best to have available a model of that workstation vendor's CD-ROM drive for the installation.

Diskless or Stand-Alone Server System?

Now is the time to decide whether this system is going to be a diskless client of some server, a dataless system, or a stand-alone system or server. You need to make this decision to make sure that the system ends up in the same domain as its server and in the same segment of the network if it's diskless.

In addition you need to decide how to partition the disk.

In general, price determines whether a system is totally diskless. If you can afford a disk drive, you should purchase one and make the system a dataless system. Reserve your use of diskless clients' times when it is impractical to place a disk locally with the system because of environmental or power concerns; or where access to the system to upgrade the local disk is going to be difficult or impossible. Then it will be necessary to perform all the administration and upgrades on the server system.

You should see the release notes of your system for specifics, but use the following disk space requirements as a guideline:

Diskless—Because there is no local disk, all disk space resides on the server. Each diskless client must mount its root, swap, temp, and spool partitions from the server. Expect to allocate the following from the server:

> root: 10–20 MB
>
> swap: Varies by memory size, but 16–256 MB is the normal range.
>
> spool: 10–20 MB
>
> tmp: 10–40 MB

Dataless—Dataless clients use the local disk for each of the partitions listed above for the diskless client.

Stand-alone—If the system is for an application user, the same sizes as those for the dataless clients are appropriate.

In addition, a /usr partition will be needed with an additional 100 MB to hold the remainder of the operating system. If the X Window system is also to be stored locally, it can require up to an additional 70 MB, depending on the number of tools and fonts that are installed. A minimal X installation requires about 30 MB.

If the user is a developer, the /usr partition will need to be about 150–200 MB to hold the compilers, libraries, additional tools, and local tools the user will need.

Server—Server systems generally need the entire operating system installed. Here is a guideline for overall sizes:

> root: 20 MB
>
> swap: varies by memory size, but 64–512 MB is normal range.

15

UNIX INSTALLATION BASICS

spool: 40–100 MB

tmp: 20–80 MB

usr: 250 MB

x: 75 MB

Per diskless client: 50–200 MB (more if large swap areas are needed for the client)

In addition, a server may have more than one network interface installed. This is so it can serve multiple segments.

Naming the System

Each UNIX system is given a set of names:

- Host name—a short name it is known by locally.
- UUCP name—usually the same as the host name. Used for modem-based communications between UNIX systems.
- Domain name—a name that identifies which set of systems this system is a part of for electronic mail and routing.
- NIS domain—a name that identifies which set of systems this system is grouped with for systems administration purposes. The set of systems shares a common password and other systems administration files.

This chapter deals with the systems host and domain names. Using a UUCP name that is different from the host name is covered in Chapter 26, "UUCP Administration."

Host Name

A host name is typed often, so it should be relatively short. While it can be up to 256 characters long in System V Release 4 systems, no one wants to type a name that long all the time. A short word usually is desired. If this name is to be shared as the UUCP name as well, it should be no longer than 8 characters.

TIP

At any organization, people generally come and go, and when they go, the system they were using gets reassigned. Hardware also gets replaced. It's not a good idea to name a system for its current user or for its current hardware.

These are some poor name choices:

- sun1051—Today it might be a Sun Sparc 10/51. Tomorrow it might be a Dec Alpha or something else. Choose a name that will retain its meaning regardless of the changes in hardware.

- `jerry`—It was Jerry's system, but who has it now? The name should help identify the system for the user and the administrators. You will be referring to the system by this name in many contexts.

- `mis1`—Systems migrate, even from department to department. When this system ends up in engineering, calling it `mis` anything could be confusing.

Instead, consider using some name that allows for a selection of one of a group of names.

These are some popular choices:

- The names of the seven dwarves—This gives the systems some personality, and at least allows for seven. You could expand to use the names of other characters in stories besides Snow White when more names are needed.

- Street names—Be careful, though. If you name the aisles of your cubicle system for streets, don't use the same street names for your systems. Moving them around could get confusing.

Don't take this tip too literally. If functional names, such as `mis1` or `database` make sense, use them. It isn't that difficult to retire the old name and change the system's name to a new one in the future.

Domain Name (DNS/Mail)

If you want to uniquely address every UNIX system by name and you try to use short names for local convenience, you quickly run into the problem bemoaned often on the Internet: "All the good ones are taken." One way around this problem is the same way people resolve it with their own names. You can give systems first, middle, and last names.

One of the results of UNIX and the Internet growing up together is the domain name system. This allows every machine to be uniquely addressed by giving its fully qualified domain name, which is comprised of its host name and its domain name, separated by dots, as in the following:

```
hostname.localdomain.masterdomain.topdomain
```

As an example, the mail gateway at my company, Ascio Communications, uses this fully qualified domain name:

```
mars.ascio.net
```

You read this name from right to left as follows:

`net`: This is the top-level or root domain in the United States and in Canada for network providers; `com:`, for commercial organizations. Other choices include `edu`, for educational institutions; `gov`, for governmental bodies; `org`, for charitable organizations; and `us`, used mostly for individuals. Outside of the United States and Canada, the International Standards Organization (ISO) country code is the top-level domain.

`ascio`: This is the chosen domain name for the entire organization. Because the company is connected to the Internet, `ascio.net` had to be unique before it could be assigned.

`mars`: This is the actual host name of this system.

The system is then referred to as `mars` within the local office, and `mars.ascio.net` from outside the company.

If this is an installation of a system into an existing network, you should already have an existing domain name to use. Then you have to choose only a host name. If this is the first system to install in a local group of systems, consider choosing a local domain name as well.

TIP

Why use a local domain name? In networked systems, a central administration group is responsible for assigning and maintaining all host names and their corresponding addresses. When the number of systems gets large, there is too much burden on this one group. It can cause delays while you wait for the administration group to get around to adding your new information to their master files. If they delegate this responsibility for a set of systems to a local group, they only need to add the local domain to their files and then you can add systems and make changes as needed.

Only if this is the first system in the organization will you have to choose the remaining levels of the domain name. They should be the same for all systems within the organization.

Choosing Which Packages to Install Locally

When you made the choice of being a server, stand-alone system, dataless client, or diskless client, you made the base choice of what portions of the operating system to install. You can fine-tune this choice if you need to conserve disk space. Linux, BSD/OS, Solaris, and many other operating systems give you a large choice of packages to install. Some of those packages are specific to hardware you may not have installed. You can choose to omit those packages now, and if you change the configuration later, you can always add them to the existing installation.

Once you have chosen the packages you intend to install, sum their sizes as specified in the release notes for that version and you will be ready to lay out the partitions.

Laying Out the Partitions

Rather than use an entire disk drive for one file system, which leads to inefficiencies and other problems, UNIX systems have the ability to split a single drive into sections. These sections are called partitions (FreeBSD calls them *slices*), because each is a partition of the disk's capacity.

Generally, a disk can be split into eight partitions, each of which the operating system treats independently as a logical disk drive.

Why Multiple File Systems?

Damage control—If the system were to crash due to software error, hardware failure, or power problems, some of the disk blocks might still be in the file system cache and not have been written to disk yet. This causes damage to the file system structure. While the methods used try to reduce this damage, and the `fsck` UNIX utility can repair most damage, spreading the files across multiple file systems reduces the possibility of damage, especially to critical files needed to boot the system. When you split the files across disk slices, these critical files end up on slices that rarely change or are mounted read-only and never change. Their chances of being damaged and preventing you from recovering the remainder of the system are greatly reduced.

Access control—Only a complete slice can be marked as read-only or read-write. If you desire to mount the shared operating system sections as read-only to prevent changes, they have to be on their own slice.

Space management—Files are allocated from a pool of free space on a per-file system basis. If a user allocated a large amount of space, depleting the free space, and the entire system were a single file system, there would be no free space left for critical system files. The entire system would freeze when it ran out of space.

Using separate file systems, especially for user files, allows only that single user, or group of users, to be delayed when a file system becomes full. The system will continue to operate, allowing you to handle the problem.

Performance—The larger the file system, within limits, the larger its tables that have to be managed. As the disk fragments and space become scarce, the further apart the fragments of a file might be placed on the disk. Using multiple smaller partitions reduces the absolute distance and keeps the sizes of the tables manageable. Although the UFS file system does not suffer from table size and fragmentation problems as much as System V file systems, this is still a concern.

Backups—Many of the backup utilities work on a complete file system basis. If the file system is very big, it could take more time than you want to allocate to back up. Multiple smaller backups are easier to handle and recover from.

> **NOTE**
>
> Just because you are doing multiple backups does not necessarily mean you need multiple tapes. UNIX can place more than one backup on a single tape, provided there is space on the tape to hold them.

The following partitions are required on all UNIX installations: `root` and `swap`.

It is recommended that you create partitions to hold `usr`, `var`, `home`, and `tmp`.

15

UNIX
INSTALLATION
BASICS

As you read the sections on each partition, make a map of your disk space and allocate each partition on the map. You will use this map when you enter the disk partitioning information as you install the system.

The root Partition

The root partition is mounted at the top of the file system hierarchy. It is mounted automatically as the system boots, and it cannot be unmounted. All other file systems are mounted below the root.

The root needs to be large enough to hold the following:

■ The boot information and the bootable UNIX kernel, and a backup copy of the kernel in case the main one gets damaged

■ Any local system configuration files, which are typically in the /etc directory

■ Any stand-alone programs, such as diagnostics, that might be run instead of the OS

This partition typically runs on between 10 and 20 MB. It is also usually placed on the first slice of the disk, often called slice 0 or the a slice.

The swap Partition

The note in the "For What Purpose" section describes how UNIX uses the swap partition. The default rule is that there's twice as much swap space as there is RAM installed on the system. If you have 16 MB of RAM, the swap space needs to be a minimum of 32 MB. If you have 256 MB of RAM, the recommended swap is 512 MB.

This is just a starting point. If the users of this system run big applications that use large amounts of data, such as desktop publishing or CAD, this might not be enough swap. If you are unsure as to the swap needs of your users, start with the rule of twice RAM. Monitor the amount of swap space used via the pstat or swap commands. If you did not allocate enough, most UNIX systems support adding additional swap at runtime via the swapon or swap commands.

The usr Partition

The usr slice holds the remainder of the UNIX operating system and utilities. It needs to be large enough to hold all the packages you chose to install when you made the list earlier.

If you intend to install local applications or third-party applications in this partition, it needs to be large enough to hold them as well.

The var Partition

The var partition holds the spool directories used to queue printer files and electronic mail, as well as log files unique to this system. It also holds the /var/tmp directory, which is used for larger temporary files. Every system, even a diskless client, needs its own var file system. It cannot be shared with other systems.

NOTE

Although the var file system cannot be shared, subdirectories under it can (for example, /var/news).

These would be mounted on top of the var file system after it is already mounted.

If you do not print very large files, accept the size the release notes suggest for this partition. If you do print a large number of files or large files, or if your site will be performing a large volume of UUCP traffic, consider increasing the size of this partition to accommodate your needs.

TIP

For print files, a good starting point is adding 10 times the size of the largest print file to the size recommended. Add more if there are a large number of users or multiple printers attached to this system.

For UUCP files, have enough space to hold at least a day's worth of traffic for every site.

The home Partition

This is where the user's login directories are placed. Making home its own slice prevents users from hurting anything else on the system if they run this file system out of space.

A good starting point for this slice is 5 MB per application user plus 10 MB per power user and 20 MB per developer you intend to support on this system.

TIP

Don't worry too much about getting it exactly right. If you need more space for a particular user, just move that user's directory to a different file system that does have room and create a symbolic link in /home to point to its new location. The user may never know you moved the directory.

The tmp Partition

Large temporary files are placed in /var/tmp but sufficient temporary files are placed in /tmp that you don't want it to run your root file system out of space. If your users are mostly application users, 5 to 10 MB is sufficient for this slice. If they are power users or developers, 10 to 20 MB is better. If there are more than 10 users on the system at once, consider doubling the size of this slice.

TIP

The files in the /tmp directory are very short-lived. Use the file system type TMPFS (Tmp file system, a RAM-based file system) for /tmp if your version of UNIX offers it. It can improve performance by placing this file system in RAM instead of on the disk. Losing the files on each reboot is not a concern, because UNIX clears the /tmp directory on each reboot anyway.

Assigning Partitions to Disk Drives

If you have more than one disk drive, a second decision you have is on which drive to place the partitions. The goal is to balance the disk accesses between all of the drives. If you have two drives, consider the following partitioning scheme:

Drive 1	Drive 2
root	usr
swap	home
var	

The remaining partitions split over the drives as space allows.

Assigning IP (Network) Addresses

If the system has a network connection, it must be assigned an IP address. IP addresses are explained in Chapter 20. An IP address is a set of four numbers separated by dots, called a dotted quad. Each network connection has its own IP address. Within a LAN segment, usually the first three octets of the dotted quad are the same. The fourth must be unique for each interface. The addresses 0 and 255 (all zeros and all ones) are reserved for broadcast addresses. The remaining 254 addresses may be assigned to any system.

NOTE

The IP address is not the Ethernet address. An Ethernet address is a hardware-level address assigned by the manufacturer. It is six octets long (48 bits). The first three represent the manufacturer of the network interface board. The remaining three octets are unique to the system. This is commonly called the MAC address. An IP address is a software level address. Part of the IP protocol, also called ARP or Address Resolution Protocol, is used to match the software IP address with the physical Ethernet address.

If this is your first system, you must decide on the first three octets as well. See Chapter 20 for applying for a network number. The number should be unique within the world and is obtainable at no cost.

If this is not the first system, then any unused value for the fourth octet can be used for this system.

Do You Have the Needed Network Connections?

Now is the time to check that you have a network connection for each network interface. Now is the time to check that you have the proper cables, transceivers (if needed), and connectors.

Ethernet comes in three varieties: thick (10Base5), thin (10Base2), and twisted pair (10BaseT). UNIX Systems come with some combination of three types of Ethernet connections: AUI, BNC, or RJ45. If your system has multiple connector types, they are all for the same network interface, unless you purchased an add-on interface that uses a connector type different from that of the main system. Using the matrix below, you can see which parts you need:

Connector Type	*Network Type*		
	10Base5	10Base2	10BaseT
AUI	AUI cable transceiver	AUI to BNC transceiver	AUI to RJ45 transceiver
BNC	10Base2 Hub	BNC Tee	10Base2 Hub
RJ45	10BaseT Hub with AUI port and RJ45 Cable	10BaseT Hub with BNC port and RJ45 Cable	RJ45 Cable and free slot on BaseT Hub

Using NIS/NIS+

Administering a UNIX system requires dealing with many files, such as the password, group, network, and Ethernet address control files. Having to maintain each one of these files on multiple systems can be time-consuming. Discrepancies in the files can lead to problems logging in to systems or to security issues.

One solution to this problem is the Network Information Service, or NIS. NIS is a network-wide set of databases for the common administrative files. This allows for centralized administration, even by using multiple servers with a redundant system in case the master server is down.

When installing a system in an NIS environment, you have to answer the install questions with the name of the NIS domain for this system.

The NIS domain does not unnecessarily match the mail domain entered earlier. Generally, it is for security reasons or to further subdivide the administrative responsibilities when they do not match.

Performing the Installation

By now, if you've been following along, you should have an installation checklist. It should contain the following:

■ The name of the system holding the drive for the installation, and its device name

TIP

Check your release notes—you might have to enter the name of the new system into the root user's .rhost file temporarily during the installation, or load the CD-ROM and mount the partition prior to running the remote installation.

■ Diskless, dataless, stand-alone, or server system

The name of the server for the new client, if it's a dataless or diskless system, should be on your sheet along with its IP address.

■ The name of the host and domain

■ The IP address

■ The packages to install

■ How to partition the disk (This is the map of the disk drive or drives you made earlier.)

■ Whether to use a network database (This is the name of the NIS domain, if you intend to run NIS.)

Now you should be all set.

CAUTION

You are about to do things that will change the information on the disks. If this is not a brand-new system, be sure you have readable backups in case something goes wrong.

Booting the Installation Media

The first step in installing a UNIX system is to load the mini-root into RAM (the mini-root is basically a scaled-down kernel that will give you the ability to run the UNIX installation programs). UNIX uses the UNIX operating system to perform its installation. It needs a version of UNIX it can run, and to do this the install loader uses RAM to hold a small version of the UNIX file system. When you boot the installation media, it builds a root file system and copies the files it needs to control the installation to this RAM-based file system. This is the reason it takes a while to boot the media.

Booting from Floppies

Take the first boot floppy and place it in what DOS would call drive A. Boot the system in the normal manner, by pressing the Ctrl+Alt+Del keys at the same time or by power-cycling the machine.

The system will load the boot loader off the first floppy and then use that to create the RAM-based file systems and load the UNIX image into RAM. It will ask for additional floppies as needed and then ask for the install media. Answer CD-ROM or tape, as appropriate, and the system will then load the remainder of the mini-root from the installation media.

Installing the Master System

Once the mini-root is loaded, you are presented with the install options. Some systems leave you at a shell prompt. If this happens, enter install to start the installation procedure. Your distribution may be different, or it may be automatic. Follow the installation procedure located in your manual.

UNIX contains a set of install procedures that walk you through the installation. They are almost identical to one another in concept, but they are slightly different in implementation. Given the information on the checklist produced as you followed this chapter, answer the questions as presented by the installation screens.

TIP

On Sun systems, to install a system with custom disk layouts, or to install any server, requires selecting the Custom Install menu option on the opening installation screen. This will walk you through all the questions, setting everything up for you automatically.

Expect it to take under an hour to read all the information off the install media to the local disks if you are installing more than just a dataless client. Most systems gives you a progress meter to show you how much it has done and how much further it has to proceed.

CAUTION

If you are installing from a nonstandard disk controller, be sure to select the option to add the custom driver for this controller and provide the floppy with the driver when requested. If you exit install and attempt to reboot without providing this driver, you will be unable to boot the system, and you will have to start the installation from the beginning.

Provided you plan ahead and fill out an installation checklist, installing a UNIX system is a simple and automatic process.

15
UNIX
INSTALLATION
BASICS

Installing Optional or Additional Packages

Once the system is installed and rebooted, you are running UNIX. Congratulations. Of course, you will still need to perform installations from time to time to add packages and applications. All UNIX packages and most standard applications for System V Release 4 use the pkgadd format. Installation of these packages and applications is automatic using the pkgadd utility. RedHat Linux uses rpm, and BSD uses pkgadd via installsw (to make life easier). There are a few different packaging formats used among distributions of Linux/UNIX, and they use their own installation format or tar format. Follow the release notes for these applications.

Using pkgadd and pkgrm

Packages are added to System V Release 4 systems, such as Solaris 2 and UnixWare, by using the pkgadd command. This command automatically installs the software from the release media and updates a database of what is currently installed on the system. Packages are deleted just as easily with the pkgrm command.

CAUTION

Many packages must be deleted before being reinstalled. If pkgadd is asked to install a package that is already installed, it will attempt to overwrite the existing package. Some packages work with this overwrite and some do not. If the installation is an upgrade to a newer version of a package, it is safer to first remove the old copy with the pkgrm program and then install the new one.

TIP

To determine which packages are currently installed, UNIX provides the pkginfo command. This command has two forms. The first form, when run with no pathname as an argument, lists which packages are currently installed. When run as pkginfo -1, it will also list when the package was installed, the version currently installed, whether any patches installed affect this version, and how much disk space it is currently consuming.

When run with a pathname, pkginfo tells you which packages reside on the installation media. Note that the -1 argument also works in this mode and can tell you how much space each package will take to install.

To run pkgadd on the install media, place the media in the drive and enter the command

```
pkgadd -d path-name-to-device pkg_name
```

pkgadd will then prompt you for which packages to install and give you progress messages as it installs the package. Different packages may also ask you questions prior to installation. These questions usually relate to where to install the package and any other installation options.

> **NOTE**
>
> pkgadd also checks to make sure that other packages this new package requires are already installed. It will warn you or not let you install a package if the prerequisites are not already installed.

Using swmtool

Sun's Solaris system provides an X application to guide you through running pkgadd. It displays the contents of the CD-ROM and provides point-and-click installation and removal of the entire media or selected packages.

To install new packages using swmtool, click on the Properties button to pop up the menu for where the packages are located.

Select the local or remote CD-ROM drive if the installation media is not already mounted. If it is already mounted, select Mounted File System, and then type the pathname of the directory containing the packages.

swmtool then displays the contents of the disk. It can provide details on sizes required and versions on the media. To start the installation, select each of the packages to install and press the Begin Installation button. swmtool runs pkgadd for you. You will still have to answer pkgadd's questions just as if you had run pkgadd by hand.

To remove software with swmtool, just select the Remove button from the top of the screen. Select the packages to remove and press the Begin Removal button. swmtool will run pkgrm for you.

Using rpm

RedHat Linux uses a packaging format called rpm. To manipulate these packages, you use the rpm program. It's very simple to use, and has a few simple command line arguments. As with other package formats, you cannot install a package if the same package (newer or older) is installed. You can use rpm's uninstall feature to uninstall the old package and then use it to install the newer one. You can also use rpm to query packages (see if they are installed) and verify them. The man page for rpm is very descriptive.

RedHat also comes with an X package tool which lets you select which packages you wish to install (along with the programs contained in them). Installing and uninstalling is very simple and efficient with this program. This program is called glint and is available through RedHat's control panel under package management.

Using `installsw`

Most BSD implementations use the `pkgadd` format, but come with a simple-to-use program called `installsw`. This program provides the administrator with an interface where the different packages can be selected and installed, or uninstalled. It's a much welcomed front end, and avoids the unfriendly command lines of `pkgadd`.

Adding a Diskless Client to a Server

You take two steps to add a diskless client to a server: Add the common files to support any client. Add the specific files for this client. The first needs to be done only if this is the first client of this type and revision of the operating system to be installed.

Installing the Diskless Client Operating System Support Files

Traditionally, diskless client support files are installed in the `/export` file system on the server. With System V Release 4, the common executable files are placed under the `/export/exec` directory. Each architecture will have its own subdirectory under `/export/exec`.

Each UNIX vendor that supports diskless clients has an install procedure for loading support files from the installation media for each supported architecture. In Solaris 2, the `swmtool edit` menu contains the pull-down item `Add client software....` This configures the server to support clients of each of the available architecture types.

Adding the Diskless Client

Once client support is available on the server, the client must be added to the server. Since the client has no disk, all installation occurs on the server. A shell script or window command is run to add the `/export/root/hostname` directory tree and the `/export/swap/hostname` swap file.

Under Solaris 2, this is performed under `admintool`'s host manager. Select the host manager icon from the `admintool` and then select Add Host from the Edit pull-down menu. Select diskless from the Client Type pull-down menu, and enter the host name, IP address, and Ethernet address onto the menu and select the time zone from the pull-down menu. The remainder of the parameters should be correct except for the swap size. Adjust that to the proper swap size for this client and click on the Add button.

Other UNIX systems provide shell scripts or administrative pull-down menus for adding diskless clients.

Summary

The key to a trouble-free installation of your UNIX system is advance planning, and using the guidelines in this chapter and the release notes that came with your software. These are the things you should plan:

- The type of system you are installing: server, stand-alone, dataless, or diskless
- Who will act as server for this system, if necessary

- What size and on what disk each slice will be located

    `root`, `usr`, `var`, `home`, and `tmp` file systems

    `swap` partition

- The name and address for this system: host name, domain name, IP address, and NIS domain name, if applicable

- Which packages you are going to install

- From where you are going to install

With these things planned, you can answer the UNIX install procedures questions. From there the installation is automatic.

Starting Up and Shutting Down

by David Gumkowski and John Semencar

IN THIS CHAPTER

Starting up and shutting down UNIX are unlike most system administration tasks in that after deciding when either occurs, the administrator is more a passive observer than a proactive participant. Vigilance and informed understanding are required more than anticipation of problems and needs. Outputting to the system console, startup generates a wealth of information about what is transpiring. Most importantly, it shows what devices appear or are interrupting and shows what tasks are beginning. Also, most boot problems reflect some kind of message to the system console. This chapter discusses what some common console messages mean during startup and shutdown, identifies what commands are involved in either process, and describes daemons normally spawned as a result of restarting the system.

Startup

In the most basic sense, starting up a UNIX-based operating system, booting, is an orderly method to accomplish a predefined set of tasks. Those tasks would normally include

- Running a limited self-test of basic machine parts
- Locating a boot device
- Reading the kernel from the boot device
- Having the kernel find and initialize peripherals
- Starting basic system tasks
- Running scripts that generate programs to provide services
- Beginning other applications

An abbreviated sample startup from a Hewlett-Packard HP-UX Release 10.x machine is found in Listing 16.1. Note that most startup messages are written to the system console device as well as the system log file. Please refer to your system's manual page for `syslogd` to find where your syslog configuration file is located. The configuration file will indicate to you in the last column where the system log files are located.

Listing 16.1. Sample startup from a Hewlett-Packard HP-UX Release 10.x machine.

```
**************************************************
HP-UX Start-up in progress
Thu May 01 06:00:00 EST 1997
**************************************************
Mount file systems
Output from "/sbin/rc1.d/S100hfsmount start":
-----------------------------
Setting hostname
Output from "/sbin/rc1.d/S320hostname start":
-----------------------------
Save system core image if needed
Output from "/sbin/rc1.d/S440savecore start":
-----------------------------
EXIT CODE: 2 -  savecore found no core dump to save
"/sbin/rc1.d/S440savecore start" SKIPPED
-----------------------------
```

```
Recover editor crash files
Output from "/sbin/rc2.d/S200clean_ex start":
- - - - - - - - - - - - - - - - - - - - - - - - - -
preserving editor files (if any)
List and/or clear temporary files
Output from "/sbin/rc2.d/S204clean_tmps start":
- - - - - - - - - - - - - - - - - - - - - - - - - -
Starting the ptydaemon
Start network tracing and logging daemon
Output from "/sbin/rc2.d/S300nettl start":
- - - - - - - - - - - - - - - - - - - - - - - - - -
Initializing Network Tracing and Logging...
Done.
Configure HP Ethernet interfaces
Output from "/sbin/rc2.d/S320hpether start":
- - - - - - - - - - - - - - - - - - - - - - - - - -
Start NFS server subsystem
Output from "/sbin/rc3.d/S100nfs.server start":
- - - - - - - - - - - - - - - - - - - - - - - - - -
starting NFS SERVER networking
Starting OpenView
Output from "/sbin/rc3.d/S940ov500 start":
- - - - - - - - - - - - - - - - - - - - - - - - - -
```

Initialization Process

Specifically, the kernel, commonly named /vmunix or /unix, whether it is located on the root partition directly or some subdirectory such as /stand on HP systems, will execute and give rise to a system father task, init. This father task will propagate children processes commonly needed for operation. Common operations normally completed during boot include such things as setting the machine's name, checking and mounting disks and file systems, starting system logs, configuring network interfaces and beginning network and mail services, commencing line printer services, enabling accounting and quotas, clearing temporary partitions, and saving core dumps. To understand how those functions come into being is to grasp how the father process operates. Though blurred by what constitutes BSD versus SYS V UNIX flavors today, the two flavors generate the identically named init, but their respective calling modes differ significantly.

Configuration File

Systems such as HP-UX, IRIX, Linux, and Solaris all use a very flexible init process that creates jobs directed from a file named /etc/inittab. Init's general arguments are shown here:

■ 0   Shut down the machine into a halted state. The machine enters a PROM monitor mode or a powered off condition.

■ 1   Put the machine into a system administration mode. All file systems continue to be accessible. Only a superuser console can access the system.

■ 2   Place the system into the normal multiuser mode of operation.

- 3   Place the system into the normal multiuser mode of operation. Also enable remote file sharing. Begin extra daemons to allow remote file sharing, mount remote resources, and advertise the remote resources (such as NFS).

- 4   Place the system into a user-defined multiuser environment. For HP-UX, the HP VUE (Visual User Environment), a powerful graphical environment and set of applications utilizing X Window, is activated.

- 5   Much like run level 0, except the system will not try to power itself off.

- 6   Shut down the machine and then restart it to run level 2 or 3.

- a,b,c   Not a true state because they do not change the run level. Basically, run a given set of programs.

- S/s   Begin single-user mode. This mode of operation is always selected if the `inittab` file is missing or corrupt.

- Q/q   Don't change run levels. Use the current one and re-examine the `inittab` file. This is a method to institute changes without actually having to reboot the system.

Listing 16.2 shows an abbreviated sample `inittab` file.

Listing 16.2. Abbreviated sample `inittab` file.

```
strt:2:initdefault:
        lev0:06s:wait:/etc/rc0 > /dev/console 2>&1 < /dev/console
        lev2:23:wait:/etc/rc2 > /dev/console 2>&1 < /dev/console
        lev3:3:wait:/etc/rc3 > /dev/console 2> &1 < /dev/console
        rebt:6:wait:/etc/init.d/announce restart
        ioin::sysinit:/sbin/ioinitrc > /dev/console 2>&1
        brcl::bootwait:/sbin/bcheckrc < /dev/console 2>&1
        cons:123456:respawn:/usr/sbin/getty console console
        powf::powerwait:/sbin/powerfail > /dev/console 2>&1
```

The general form of an entry in this file is as follows:

```
identifier:run-level:action-keyword: process
```

`identifier` is a text string of up to four characters in length and is used to uniquely identify an entry. Two character identifiers should be used with care because it is possible for PTY identities to conflict with an identifier. Ultimately, this would lead to corruption of the utmp file which keeps a record of all users currently logged in.

The run level is one or more of the `init` arguments described previously or blank to indicate all run levels. A default run level of 2 or 3 is common, depending on your system. run level 1 is usually reserved for special tasks such as system installation. When `init` changes run levels, all processes not belonging to the requested run level will be killed eventually. The exception to that rule are a,b,c started commands.

16

> **NOTE**
>
> HP system administrators can use SAM to shut down a system and change the current run level. SAM is HP's System Administration Manager tool that can be invoked in its graphical or character-based configuration.

The `action keyword` defines the course of action executed by `init`. Values and their meaning are found in Table 16.1.

Table 16.1. Action keyword table.

Action Keyword	Action	Wait	Restart
boot	Executed only during a system boot.	No	No
bootwait	Executed when going from single user to multiuser after the system is started.	Yes	No
initdefault	Start with this upon boot. The process field is ignored. If level is blank, default to run level 6.	N/A	N/A
off	Kill processes when in a given level. Ignore if the process doesn't exist.	N/A	N/A
once	Run the process once.	No	No
ondemand	Synonym for respawn for a,b,c types.	No	No
powerfail	Run processes when a powerdown is requested.	No	No
powerwait	Run processes when a powerdown is requested.	Yes	No
respawn	If the process doesn't exist, start it. If the process does exist, do nothing.	No	Yes
sysinit	Run processes before the login prompt is sent to the system console.	Yes	No
wait	Start processes once.	Yes	No
ctrlaltdel	(Linux only.) The sequence was pressed on the keyboard. Shutdown.	No	No
kbrequest	(Linux only.) Keyboard spawned request. This is ill-defined.		
powerokwait	(Linux only.) Power has come back on.	Yes	No

The *process* is any daemon, executable script, or program. This process can invoke other scripts or binaries.

In the example of an `inittab` file given previously, a system powerup would default to run level 2. Run levels `0` (shutdown), `6` (reboot), and `s` (single user) would all execute the script `/etc/rc0`, which in turn could call subscripts. Run levels `2` or `3` (multiuser/expanded multiuser) would execute the `/etc/rc2` script. Additionally, run level `3` (expanded multiuser) would also execute the `/etc/rc3` script. Run level `6` (reboot) would announce what is happening by executing the `/etc/init.d/announce` script given the `restart` argument. For any run level, before the console receives the login prompt, run `/sbin/ioinitrc` to check the consistency between the kernel data and I/O configuration file. For any run level going from single to multiuser, run a file system consistency check by executing `/sbin/bcheckrc`. For run levels 1-6, if `getty` doesn't exist for the console, begin it. For any run level in which powering down is requested, run the `/sbin/powerfail` script.

BSD type systems use an `init` process that is somewhat less flexible in usage. It runs a basic reboot sequence and depending on how it is invoked, begins a multiuser or single-user system. `init` changes states via *signals*. The signal is invoked using the UNIX `kill` command. For example, to drop back to single-user mode from multiuser mode, the superuser would `kill - TERM 1`. Table 16.2 lists the signals.

Table 16.2. Signals used with `kill` command.

Signal	*Mnemonic*	*Action*	*Value*
Hang-up	HUP.	Reread the `ttys` file	(01)
Software terminate	TERM	Begin single-user mode.	(15)
Interrupt	INT	Terminate all processes and reboot the machine.	(02)
Tty stop signal	TSTP	Slowly kill the system by not issuing any more getty processes.	(24)

RC Scripts

Each system type begins similarly by initializing an operating condition through calls to scripts or directories containing scripts generally of the type `/etc/rc*`. BSD systems normally would call `/etc/rc`, `/etc/rc.local`, or `/etc/rc.boot`. Because of the flexibility of the `inittab` version, it is best to look in that file for the location of the startup scripts. A methodology that is now favored by vendors supporting `inittab`, such as HP-UX and IRIX, creates directories such as `/sbin/rc[run-level].d` or `/etc/rc[run-level].d`. These directories contain files such as `S##name` (startup) or `K##name` (kill/shutdown) that are links to scripts in `/sbin/init.d` or `/etc/init.d`. The `##`s are ordered in the manner in which they are called by a superscript. A sample startup sequence is found in Listing 16.3. Listing 16.4 shows a sample shutdown sequence.

16

Listing 16.3. A sample startup sequence from an HP-UX system.

```
lrwxr-xr-x  1 root     sys              16 Apr  9
➥1997 S008net.sd -> /sbin/init.d/net
lrwxr-xr-x  1 root     sys
➥21 Apr  9  1997 S100swagentd -> /sbin/init.d/swagentd
lrwxr-xr-x  1 root     sys              21 Apr  9  1997 S120swconfig -> /sbin/init.d/
➥swconfig
lrwxr-xr-x  1 root     sys              21 Apr  9  1997 S200clean_ex -> /sbin/init.d/
➥clean_ex
lrwxr-xr-x  1 root     sys              23 Apr  9  1997 S202clean_uucp->/sbin/init.d/
➥clean_uucp
lrwxr-xr-x  1 root     sys              23 Apr  9  1997 S204clean_tmps->/sbin/init.d/
➥clean_tmps
lrwxr-xr-x  1 root     sys              22 Apr  9  1997 S206clean_adm -> /sbin/
➥init.d/clean_adm
lrwxr-xr-x  1 root     sys              20 Apr  9  1997 S220syslogd -> /sbin/init.d/
➥syslogd
lrwxr-xr-x  1 root     sys              22 Apr  9  1997 S230ptydaemon-> /sbin/init.d/
➥ptydaemon
                         .                              .
➥.                       .                              .
                         .                              .
➥.                       .                              .
                         .                              .
➥.                       .                              .
lrwxr-xr-x  1 root     sys              22 Apr  9  1997 S880swcluster -> /sbin/
➥init.d/swcluster
lrwxr-xr-x  1 root     sys              18 Apr  9  1997 S900hpnpd -> /sbin/init.d/
➥hpnpd
lrwxr-xr-x  1 root     sys              20 Apr  9  1997 S900laserrx -> /sbin/init.d/
➥laserrx
```

Listing 16.4. A sample shutdown sequence from an IRIX system.

```
lrwxr-xr-x  1  root   sys      14  Mar 18 1997   K02midi -> ../init.d/midi
lrwxr-xr-x  1  root   sys      16  Mar 18 1997   K02videod -> ../init.d/
➥videod
lrwxr-xr-x  1  root   sys      13  Mar 18 1997   K02xdm -> ../init.d/xdm
lrwxr-xr-x  1  root   sys      18  Mar 18 1997   K03announce -> ../init.d/
➥announce
lrwxr-xr-x  1  root   sys      16  Mar 18 1997   K04dbshut -> ../init.d/
➥dbshut
lrwxr-xr-x  1  root   sys      18  Mar 18 1997   K05availmon -> ../init.d/
➥availmon
lrwxr-xr-x  1  root   sys      14  Mar 18 1997   K06raid -> ../init.d/raid
lrwxr-xr-x  1  root   sys      16  Mar 18 1997   K09mediad -> ../init.d/
➥mediad
lrwxr-xr-x  1  root   sys      16  Mar 18 1997   K10cadmin -> ../init.d/
➥cadmin
            .                        .
➥.          .                        .
            .                        .
➥.          .                        .
            .                        .
➥.          .                        .
```

continues

Listing 16.4. continued

```
lrwxr-xr-x  1   root     sys      21  Mar 18 1997   K84filesystems -> ../
➥init.d/filesystems
lrwxr-xr-x  1   root     sys      13  Mar 18 1997   K98usr -> ../init.d/usr
lrwxr-xr-x  1   root     sys      20  Mar 18 1997   K99disk_patch -> ../
➥init.d/disk_patch
```

In the last example, K02midi would be executed followed by (in order), K02videod, K02xdm, K03announce, and so on, until K99disk_patch was executed. On this system, the ~/init.d/* files are used for startup and shutdown, depending whether they are invoked with a start (S types) or stop (K types) parameter. Some systems have a template superscript called ~/init.d/ template that should be used to initiate the daemon, program or, moreover, script. If a configuration file is needed by the superscript, it should be placed in /etc/rc.config.d.

Listing 16.5 is a partial example of a script utilizing the template to initiate the startup or shutdown of a relational database management, in this case Oracle 7 Server. Links are required for the execution of the superscript. Referring to the example, the following commands can be used to create the links:

```
ln -s  ~/init.d/oracle ~/rc2.d/S900oracle
ln -s  ~/init.d/oracle ~/rc1.d/K100oracle
```

In this case, Oracle will be stopped whenever the system is shut down from a run level higher than 1. It will be started when entering run level 2. The numbering of the start and kill scripts may be different than the ones used.

Listing 16.5. Example of an init startup/shutdown script.

```
case $1 in
'start_msg')
    echo "Starting ORACLE"
    ;;
'stop_msg')
    echo "Stopping ORACLE"
    ;;
'start')
    # source the system configuration variables
    if [ -f /etc/rc.config.d/oracle ] ; then
        . /etc/rc.config.d/oracle
    else
        echo "ERROR: /etc/rc.config.d/oracle file MISSING"
    fi
    # Check to see if this script is allowed to run...
    if [ $ORACLE_START != 1 ]; then
        rval=2
    else
            #Starting Oracle
            su - oracle -c /u99/home/dba/oracle/product/7.2.3/bin/dbstart
    fi
    ;;
'stop')
    # source the system configuration variables
```

```
    if [ -f /etc/rc.config.d/oracle ] ; then
        . /etc/rc.config.d/oracle
    else
        echo "ERROR: /etc/rc.config.d/oracle file MISSING"
    fi
    # Check to see if this script is allowed to run...
    if [ $ORACLE_START != 1 ]; then
        rval=2
    else
            #Stopping Oracle
            su - oracle -c /u99/home/dba/oracle/product/7.2.3/bin/dbshut
    fi
    ;;
*)
    echo "usage: $0 {start|stop|start_msg|stop_msg}"
    rval=1
    ;;
esac
```

Startup Daemons and Programs

When the system is operational, after you log in, run `ps -ef` (SYS V type) or `ps ax` (BSD type) from a shell prompt. This will list the processes currently running. An idle system with no users will most likely include at least a subset of the following tasks:

`init`	As described, this is the parent process for any user job and most system tasks. The process ID is always 1.
`inetd`	This is the Internet super server. It listens for connections on Internet sockets and calls appropriate servers to handle incoming information. This connects servers for things such as FTP, Telnet, finger, http, talk, and rsh.
`getty`	This is the programs that sets terminal type, speed, line discipline, and mode.
`syslogd`	This is the daemon to log system messages.
`cron`	This program is the clock daemon to execute programs at specified dates and times.
`named`	This is the domain-naming server software yielding name resolution for your system.
`routed/gated`	Either of these programs keeps routing tables so that your system knows what path to take when sending packets.
`nfsd/biod`	Network file system daemons allowing file system sharing via the network.
`lpsched/lpd`	SYS V/BSD line-printing schedulers.
`telnetd`	The Telnet protocol server that allows interactive connections via the network.

`ftpd`	The file transfer protocol (FTP) server that allows file transfers via the network.
`httpd`	The Hypertext Transfer Protocol daemon that coordinates World Wide Web serving.
`rpc.*`	The remote procedure call daemons that allow procedure calls to other machines connected via the network. Common entries of this type are `rpc.mountd`, `rpc.statd`, `rpc.locks`, `rpc.pcnfsd`, and `rcpbind`. Usually associated with these utilities is a program named portmap that converts RPC numbers to TCP or UDP protocol port numbers.

One last note about the start up process: If the file `/etc/nologin` exists, only the superuser may log in. Other users attempting to log in would see the textual contents of `/etc/nologin`.

Shutdown

As they say, "what goes up must come down. This is as true for computers as it is for other things in life. A normal shutdown is an attempt to terminate processes in an orderly fashion so that when the system comes back up, there will be little error. A graceful shutdown will kill running tasks as smoothly as it can. It will then synchronize the disks with any outstanding buffers in memory and dismount them. When this needs to be done, first and foremost, make sure a shutdown really needs to occur. Your decision to do this will have a lot to do with your site culture and how many users you impact. Also, many times, a little research will lead you to try killing and restarting a daemon or living with a non-volatile problem until a patch can be applied later, during the night. If the system must come down, however, depending on the current circumstances, there is a variety of ways to bring down a running system. Among the methods are the commands `shutdown`, `reboot`, `sync`, `init`, and `halt`—and by removing power from the machine. Generally, as you would expect, removing power or not having synchronized (all disk writes completed) quiescent disks, will almost ensure that some file system corruption will occur that will need correction during the next boot. More than likely, the file system consistency check program, fsck, will be able to autocorrect the problems—but, given a choice, use a safer method of bringing your system down. fsck is automatically invoked during system startup unless specifically turned off (`fastboot`). Its function is to check the consistency of inodes, free space, links, directory entries, pathnames, and superblocks. It does not perform a surface scan or remap bad blocks. Here, in more detail, is a summary of the possible commands for various operating environments. Note that these commands do not necessarily include all of the possible options for the command. See your local manual page for a complete list of options.

HP-UX

■ To reboot an HP-UX system, use the following command:

```
reboot [-t time] [-m message]
```

`time`: +Number of minutes (such as +5 for 5 minutes from now), an absolute time of `hh:mm`, or "now" until the reboot message: Message to display to users about the upcoming reboot.

■ To halt an HP-UX system, use the following command:

`reboot -h [-t time] [-m message]`

The parameters are the same as for reboot.

■ To synchronize the disks and invoke a new run level, use the following command:

`sync; init [run-level]`

Run-level: One of the choices described earlier in the chapter.

■ To perform a graceful shutdown, use the following command:

`shutdown [-h¦-r] [-y] [grace]`

Note that HP has a security feature tied to shutdowns. `/etc/shutdown.allow` can restrict who may or may not shut down the system. Most other variants allow only the superuser to bring the system down.

`-h`: Halt the system.

`-r`: Reboot the system.

Neither `-h` nor `-r`: Place system in single-user mode.

`-y`: Default answers to any interactive question.

grace: Integer seconds defining how long users have to log off.

The default value for *grace* is 60 seconds.

IRIX

■ To reboot an IRIX system, use the following command:

`reboot`

There are no parameters for this command.

■ To halt an IRIX system, use the following command:

`halt [-p]`

`-p`: Remove power from the machine, if possible.

■ To synchronize the disks and invoke a new run level, use the following command:

`sync; init [run-level]`

run-level: One of the choices described earlier in the chapter.

■ To perform a graceful shutdown, use the following command:

`shutdown [-y] [-ggrace] [-irun-level] [-p]`

Note that IRIX does not have a messaging facility attached to its `shutdown` command. It would behoove you to precede this command with a `wall` (write to all users) command to let the users know what is going to happen and why.

-y: Default answers to any interactive question.

grace: Integer seconds defining how long users have to log off.

The default value for grace is 60 seconds.

run-level: A subset of the choices described earlier in the chapter (such as 0, 1, 6, s, and S). The default is 0.

-p: Remove power from the machine, if possible.

Solaris

■ To reboot a Solaris system, use the following command:

```
reboot [-d]
```

-d: Dump system core before rebooting to allow for future debugging.

■ To halt a Solaris system, use the following command:

```
halt
```

halt should not be usually called with any parameters.

■ To synchronize the disks and invoke a new run level, use the following command:

```
sync; init [run-level]
```

run-level: One of the choices described earlier in the chapter.

■ To perform a graceful shutdown, use the following command:

```
shutdown [-y] [-ggrace] [-irun-level]
```

-y: Default answers to any interactive question.

grace: Integer seconds defining how long users have to log off.

The default value for grace is 60 seconds.

run-level: A subset of the choices described earlier in the chapter. The default is 0.

Linux

■ To reboot a Linux system, use the following command:

```
reboot [-f]
```

-f: If not in run levels 0 or 6, do not call shutdown.

■ To halt a Linux system, use the following command:

```
halt [-f]
```

Same parameter description as reboot.

■ To synchronize the disks and invoke a new run level, use the following command:

```
sync; init [run-level]
```

run-level: One of the choices described earlier in the chapter.

■ To perform a graceful shutdown, use the following command:

`shutdown [-t sec] [-fhrk] time [message]`

Normally, in Linux systems, an entry will be present in `inittab` for `ctrlaltdel` that calls `shutdown`.

`-t sec`: *sec* is the number of seconds to wait between sending the warning and kill signals to processes.

`-h`: Halt the system.

`-r`: Reboot the system.

`-f`: Do not run file system consistency check upon reboot.

`-k`: Do not actually shut down the system; just make it look like it is going to happen.

time: +Number of minutes (such as +5 for 5 minutes from now) or an absolute time of `hh:mm` (or "now") until shutdown.

message: Message to display to users about the upcoming shutdown.

In every given example, the most graceful way to shut down was purposely identified as such because `shutdown` is always the preferred way for an uncomplicated shutdown of the system.

Listing 16.6 shows a sample shutdown from an IRIX system.

Listing 16.6. Sample shutdown from an IRIX system.

```
Shutdown started.     Wed Apr 16 01:46:29 EDT 1997
        Broadcast Message from root (ttyq0) on indy Wed Apr 16 01:46:29 1997

        THE SYSTEM IS BEING SHUT DOWN! Log off now.

On the system console, once shutdown began, the following appeared:

        The system is shutting down.
        Please wait.
        unexported /usr1
        unexported /usr2
        Removing swap areas.
        Unmounting file systems:
```

As with starting up the system, shutting down the system will reflect parts of what is happening to the system console and system log file.

Summary

To recap, during system startup and shutdown, as the console spews information out, be an educated observer; unless problems occur, keep the rest of your system administration skills ready but in the background. This will probably be the easiest task of the day. Have a cup of coffee; you'll probably need it later in the day.

User Administration

*by David Gumkowski and
John Semencar*

IN THIS CHAPTER

CHAPTER 17

While performing user administration you will call upon all your skills in virtually every area of system management. Whether it is keeping disks as empty as possible, finding system bottle-necks, answering questions, or adding new users, your job revolves almost totally around the machine's users. Those users are much like the fans of a baseball game responding to your rendition of the umpire: You have done a good job if you are unnoticed. Though easy to forget in a harried environment, learning and interacting with system esoterica only can happen because the users are at least indirectly paying the freight.

This chapter deals with operations strictly limited to the administration of user IDs. It will refer to adding, removing, modifying, moving, keeping track of, checking, and limiting users. This section describes special IDs and user ID environments.

Adding New Users

Logically enough, user administration begins when adding users to a new machine. Function-ally, there are a variety of ways to accomplish this task. Each of the methods involves adding information to the password file, /etc/passwd. The /etc/group file is another file that requires attention as are miscellaneous files such as system shell startup files and the system mail alias file.

Password File

The format of /etc/passwd is consistent among most flavors of UNIX. This file contains the following colon-separated entries:

```
username:pswd:uid:gid:uid comments:directory:shell
```

BSD/OS

On some BSD type systems, the file contains slightly different colon-separated entries:

```
username:pswd:uid:gid:user class:pswd change:acct expiration:uid
➥comments:directory:shell
```

The *username* is what the user types in at the Unix login: prompt. Usually, the field's makeup is eight or fewer alphanumeric characters with the alphabetic characters in lowercase. It should be unique. This field should not contain colons because the colon is used as the field delimiter. For best compatibility, this field should not contain dots and should not begin with a hyphen or a plus sign.

The *pswd* field is a password entry and can have many different forms. The entry can be blank, indicating that there is no password required for login. The position can contain up to 13 characters that are the encrypted version of the password for the user. The location can contain a character not in the following set { . / 0–9 A–Z a–z } denoting that the username is valid but cannot be logged into. For example an "*" is not in this set. If it is used, the username is a valid account but cannot be logged into.

Additionally, under IRIX and HP-UX, the password entry can contain a comma followed by one or two characters.

The characters (in order) are: *. / 0–9 A–Z a–z.* The "." character is equal to the number zero and "z" is equal to 63. References made to characters using their numeric value are common. The characters indicate the number of weeks the password is valid and the number of weeks that must expire before a change is allowed to the password, respectively. If the former is zero (dot), the user must change the password at the next login attempt. Though generally frowned upon by security-conscious individuals, if the latter is greater than the former, only the superuser can change the password.

> **TIP**
>
> If the system has no built-in check for user base password selections, Alec Muffett's Crack utility can assist you in that endeavor.

The *uid* or user ID is simply a unique numerical user value for the username. Normally, this value is a positive number up to 65535, although some systems can handle nonrecommended double precision user ID numbers. If this is nonunique, all usernames with the same user ID look like a single (usually the first) username with this user ID. Some user IDs are reserved or special. They include:

0:	The superuser
1-10:	Daemons and pseudo users
11-99:	System, reserved and "famous" users
100+:	Normal users
60001:	"nobody" (occasionally 32000 or 65534)
60002:	"noaccess" (occasionally 32001)

The *gid* or group ID is a numerical default group ID for the username. This number corresponds to an entry in the `/etc/group` file. This file will be described later.

The *uid* comments field is historically known as GECOS, or GCOS, information for the operating system it originated from. For a generic `finger` command to accurately display this information, it should contain the user's real name, company or office number, office phone number, and home telephone number separated by commas. Not all entries need to be specified, although placeholders must be kept if trying to keep the general GECOS syntax. For example, `Homer User,,,800-IAM-HOME` would show entries for the user's real name and the user's home telephone number. The real username is also displayed by the mail system as part of the outgoing mail headers.

The *directory* field is commonly known as a username's home directory or initial working directory. Basically, it is the directory the user is placed in after being logged in by the system but before the user's personal startup files are executed.

The *shell* field is the command interpreter or program that the username is placed in after logging in. Among the many shells are: sh (Bourne), ksh (Korn), csh (C), tcsh (TENEX/TOPS-20 type C), BASH (Bourne Again Shell). If not specified, the default shell is the Bourne shell. Note that this entry does not have to be a shell; it can be a program that locks the username into a captive application. For this field to be valid, some systems require this entry to be present in a shell validation file.

The *class* field is unused but is for specifying a class of user attributes for the username.

The *pswd change* field indicates how soon a password must be changed. It is the number of seconds since the epoch (Jan 1 1970 @ 00:00). If omitted, no forced change of the password occurs.

The *acct expiration* field is the number of seconds since the epoch until the account will expire. If left blank, account expiration is not enforced for the username.

Additionally, if Network Information Service (NIS) / Yellow Pages (YP) is installed and running, the password file can include other types of entries. The additional username field entries include

+	all YP entries should be included
+*username*	include the explicit username from YP
-*username*	exclude the explicit username from YP
+@*netgroup*	include all usernames from YP from the desired group
-@*netgroup*	exclude all usernames from YP from the desired group

Generally, within such entries, if the uid, gid, uid comments, directory, or shell fields are specified, they supplant the value that YP sends for that field. Also, be aware that these entries are taken in order, so the first occurrence, not the last occurrence, dictates what is going to happen. For example,

```
root:x:0:0:Superuser:/:
daemon:*:1:5::/:/sbin/sh
bin:*:2:2::/usr/bin:/sbin/sh
sys:*:3:3::/:
adm:*:4:4::/var/adm:/sbin/sh
uucp:*:5:3::/var/spool/uucppublic:/usr/lbin/uucp/uucico
lp:*:9:7::/var/spool/lp:/sbin/sh
nuucp:*:11:11::/var/spool/uucppublic:/usr/lbin/uucp/uucico
hpdb:*:27:1:ALLBASE:/:/sbin/sh
nobody:*:-2:60001::/:
dave:x:100:10:Dave G,13,x3911,unlisted:/usr1/dave:/bin/tcsh
charlene:x:101:10:Charlene G,14,x1800,unlisted:/usr1/charlene:/bin/tcsh
john:x:102:60:John S,2,555-1234,x1400:/usr2/john:/bin/ksh
```

```
georgia:x:103:60:Georgia S,11,x143,x143:/usr2/georgia:/bin/csh
-steve::::::
+@friends:::20:::
+wayne::102::::/usr3/wayne:/bin/sh
```

Username steve is always excluded, even if it occurs within the netgroup friends. All friends are included—with the noted exception. Every friends included is placed into the 20 group by default. YP wayne is included. All of his fields, except the group ID and user ID comment fields, are overridden with the specified information. Notice in our sample that the letter x in the pswd field was substituted for the actual encrypted password for this publication. The character * in the pswd field is shown as found for these nonlogin pseudo users. For a further description of pseudo users, go to the end of the "Adding New Users" section.

Shadow Password File

Since /etc/passwd is usually globally readable, security-conscious sites normally use a shadow password scheme that is available under most UNIX operating systems. Ultimately, this redirects the encrypted passwords to another restricted read file that may or may not contain other information. This scheme is employed because average machines today can crack user passwords readily if the user's choice is bad. Bad choices include any dictionary word, the login name, no password, or any information included in the user ID comment field. The schemes used for shadow password files vary considerably among the various UNIX variants.

For example, IRIX and Solaris systems have a file named /etc/shadow that is generated by running the command pwconv that includes the following:

```
username:pswd:lastchg:min:max:warn:inactive:expire:flag
```

The *username* is a copy of the username from the /etc/passwd file.

The *pswd* field contains either the 13-character encrypted password;) null, indicating that no password is needed for login; or a string containing a character not from the following set—{./0–9A–Za–z}. If the password contains a character not from the encryption set, the username cannot be logged into. Normally, system administrators would use * or *LK* for the entry.

The *lastchg* field is the number of days from the epoch that the password was last changed.

The *min* field is the minimum number of days to elapse between a successful password change and another change.

The *max* field is the maximum number of days that the password will be valid.

The *warn* field contains the number of days before password expiration that the user will begin to get warnings that the password is about to expire.

The *inactive* field is the number of days that the username can remain inactive before not being allowed to log in.

The *expire* field is an absolute number of days specification. When used, this specifies when a username will no longer be considered valid to log into.

17

USER ADMINISTRATION

The `flag` field is currently unused.

HP-UX has adopted another scheme for shadowing the password file on a trusted system. Each username has a file named `/tcb/files/auth/first letter/username` where *first letter* is the beginning letter of the username, and *username* is the login name for the user. For example, `/tcb/files/auth/b/buster` would exist for the username `buster`. This file contains information that is `termcap` in appearance and at last count, there were 32 possible options contained within this file that deal with user security. A list of field names and their possible values can be found in the man page for `prpwd(4)`. In general, the file holds:

> The username and user ID mirrored from the password file.
>
> The encrypted password for the username, if any.
>
> The names of:
>> The owner of the account.
>> The last account to change the password on this account if it was not the account itself.
>> The last successful and unsuccessful login attempt terminal name or host name.
>
> The times indicating:
>> The number of seconds allowed between successful password changes.
>> When the password expires (next login will require the user change the password).
>> When the lifetime of the password expires (only the sysadmin can reallow login).
>> The last time a successful and unsuccessful password change or attempt was made.
>> When the account expires (an absolute-lifetime offsets from a password change).
>> The maximum time allowed between logins.
>> How long before password expiration that a user should be notified.
>> The time of day logins for the account are valid.
>> The last time a successful and unsuccessful login entry or attempt was made.
>
> Flags showing:
>> If the username is allowed to boot the system.
>> If audits occur for the username.
>> If the user can select the account's password or must use a system generated one.
>> If the user can have the system generate a password for the account.
>> Whether a chosen password undergoes a check for being too easily guessed.
>> If the account can have no (null) password.
>> If the user can generate "random" characters and letters for a password.
>> If the account is administratively locked.
>
> Numbers specifying:
>> An audit ID for the account.
>> The maximum length a password can be.
>> An additional random number an account must specify to a password if the system administrator reset the password.

The count of unsuccessful logins until the next successful one.
The maximum consecutive unsuccessful login attempts allowed before the account is locked.

Berkeley-type systems have yet another type of shadowing system that uses the files `/etc/master.passwd` or `/etc/spwd.db`.

Group File

Another file, referred to previously, that comes into play is `/etc/group`. It is part of the general protection scheme employed by UNIX: user, group, and other permissions on files. The colon-separated template for the file appears as:

```
group_name:password:group_id:list
```

The *group_name* field contains the textual name of the group.

The *password* field is a placeholder for an encrypted password for the group. If null, no password is required.

The *group_id* field contains a unique numerical value for the group.

The *list* field contains a comma-separated list of users who belong to this group. Users need not be listed in groups that are specified for their username in `/etc/passwd`. A sample `/etc/group` file follows.

```
root::0:root
other::1:root,hpdb
bin::2:root,bin
sys::3:root,uucp
adm::4:root,adm
daemon::5:root,daemon
mail::6:root
lp::7:root,lp
tty::10:
nuucp::11:nuucp
users::20:root,dave,charlene,john,georgia,operator,steve,judy,wayne,jamie
nogroup:*:-2:
systech::110:dave,disdb,diskf,disjs,dispm,diskj
dba::201:oracle,john,kathy,pete
psdev::202:ps001,ps002,ps101
hrdev::203:hrprw,hrpps,hrpsl,hrpla,consult1,consult3
fsdev::209:glpmk,glpsf,consult2
fsftp::222:glpmk,glpsf,glpjh
```

If Network Information Service/Yellow Pages is enabled, this file, like `/etc/passwd`, can contain entries beginning with a minus or plus sign to exclude or include (respectively) group information from NIS/YP.

Miscellaneous Files

A third file that user administration deals with is the system mail alias file. Depending on the UNIX version you are running, this can be located at: /etc/aliases, /usr/sbin/aliases, or /etc/mail/aliases. Users who want a mail address longer than an eight-character username can be satisfied here by creating an alias for themselves. For example, fred-flinstone: flinston would redirect any mail addressed to fred-flinstone on the host machine to the username flinston. Also a group of users occasionally request global mailing lists created for them and this is where you would satisfy their need. After you modify this file, remember to run newaliases for the changes to take effect.

You should be aware of a couple of other files that affect user login administration. These system shell startup up files are invoked before control is turned over to the username's personal startup (dot) files. You customize an operating environment for users by editing /etc/profile (SYSV sh/ksh users) or by editing /etc/csh.login, /etc/login, or /etc/stdlogin (SYS V csh/tcsh users). In these files, you can customize the default file permissions employed by users when creating files. By setting a umask for them, you can add elements to the default path to include local utilities in /usr/local, or you can add helpful alias or environment variables. Generally, it is a good idea to keep things uncluttered in these files because knowledgeable users customize their own environments. Most systems give a template, or model, to be placed in the user's home directory. HP-UX administrators can find them in the /etc/skel directory. An example of a ksh user's .profile follows:

```
# Set up the terminal:
        if [ "$TERM" = "" ]
        then
                eval ' tset -s -Q -m ':?hp' '
        else
                eval ' tset -s -Q '
        fi
        stty erase "^H" kill "^U" intr "^C" eof "^D"
        stty hupcl ixon ixoff
        tabs

        # Set up the search paths:
        PATH=$PATH:/usr/local/bin:$HOME/scripts.d/local:.

        # Set up the shell environment:
        set -u
        trap "echo 'logout'" 0

        # Set up the shell variables:
        export VISUAL=vi

        # Save PATH:
        ENVPATH=$PATH

        export ENVPATH
        ORACLE_TERM=vt100
        export ORACLE_TERM
```

```
# Set ENV:
ENV=/usr/contrib/bin/oracle_fun
export ENV

# Set user aliases:
alias rm="rm -i"                    # -- commonly practiced
```

Berkeley mail users' mail options can be customized globally in the mail start up file: `/usr/lib/Mail.rc`, `/usr/share/lib/mailx.rc`, `/etc/mail.rc`, `/etc/mail/mail.rc`, or `/etc/mail/Mail.rc`, depending on your UNIX variant. For example, you could force paging of mail longer than a page by inserting `set crt` in the mail start up file. Or if you wanted all mail to have a certain type of header line clipped, you could `ignore Message-Id`. Again, though, it is best to keep this simple and let users customize their own mail environment in their `.mailrc` file.

As seen in the description of the shadow password systems, security among UNIX operating systems is not very standard, so to fully understand what other files can be tweaked dealing with user logins, the chapter one login manual page should be read. For example, on HP-UX you can restrict from what terminal a root login can occur by editing `/etc/securetty`. On IRIX, `/etc/default/login` has multiple changeable options such as whether null passwords are acceptible, how many unsuccessful login attempts can be made before disconnecting the line, and if all logins should be logged or if just login failures should be recorded. It is in this file that root logins can be restricted.

Pseudo Users

Every flavor of UNIX contains password file entries for several pseudo users. Their entries are not to be edited. These nonlogin users are required to satisfy any ownership issues by their corresponding processes. The following list displays the most common:

daemon	Used by system server processes
bin	Owns executable user command files
sys	Owns system files
adm	Owns accounting files
uucp	Used by UUCP
lp	Used by lp or lpd subsystems
nobody	Used by NFS

There are more standard pseudo users such as `audit`, `cron`, `mail`, `new`, and `usenet`. They all are required by their associated processes and own their related files.

User Maintenance Commands

To generate, modify, and delete entries in the password and group files is very dependent upon which operating system you use. The basic ways include editing the password file directly, using a command-line instruction, or using a graphical tool to insert the entry for you. With benefits such as templates and point-and-click features, graphical tools used for user adminis-tration are well in use. In the IRIX Toolchest you can find User Manager, a graphical tool that is valued by those who use it.

The HP-UX system administration tool of choice is SAM, in its graphical or character-based mode.

Some command-line and graphical tools for selected operating systems are:

HP-UX   `useradd`, `userdel`, and `usermod`, `vipw`, or `SAM`

Solaris   `useradd`, `userdel`, and `usermod` or `admintool`

FreeBSD   `adduser` and `rmuser` or `vipw`

OpenBSD   `adduser` or `vipw`

IRIX   User Manager (`cpeople`)

Linux   `vipw`

The command-line instruction constructs are:

```
useradd [-c uid comment] [-d dir] [-e expire] [-f inactive] [-g gid] [-G
➥gid[,gid...]]
[-m [ -k skel_dir]] [-s shell] [-u uid [-o]] username
```

Also, `useradd` can set default values for: `base dir`, `expire`, `inactive`, `gid`, `skel_dir`, and `shell`.

```
adduser [-batch username [gid,[gid...]] [uid comment] [password]] OR adduser
```

The `adduser` command with no parameters runs interactively. This command also can set other defaults that will: 1. cause users to have login or profile information copied into their home directory, 2. set new users into a default group, 3. define home partitions for new users, 4. issue a welcoming message to new users, 5. set a default shell for new users, and 6. choose new user IDs from a select group of numbers.

```
userdel [-r] username
```

```
rmuser username
```

```
usermod [-c uid comment] [-d dir [-m]] [-e expire] [-f inactive] [-g gid] [-G
➥gid[,gid]]
```

```
[-l new username] [-s shell] [-u uid [-o]] username
```

In each of the preceding commands

username is the user's login name. This is the only nonoptional parameter in any command.

`uid comment` is what will be stored in the user ID comment (GECOS) field.

`dir` is the user initial or home directory.

`expire` is an absolute date when the username ceases valid logins.

inactive is the number of inactive continuous days before the username is locked.

gid is a group ID or group name that the username belongs to.

new_username is a replacement name for an existing username.

shell is the username's initial shell.

skel_dir is a directory containing files to copy to the newly created home directory.

uid is the unique user identifier for the username.

-m indicates create the home directory (add) or move current home directory files to the new home directory (mod).

-o allows the user ID to be nonunique and still have the command succeed.

-g selects the primary group for the username.

-G selects secondary groups for the username.

-r commands that the username's home directory be removed.

If the home directory of a username is altered, the previous initial directory files must be moved to the new directory. To move a user directory, issue the command:

```
cd /old_dir; tar -cf - . ¦ (cd /new_dir; tar -xpf -)
```

Verify the result and then remove old_dir. If the user base is not entirely knowledgeable, look for old_dir in existing files and change them to new_dir for the user. The system can locate any entries by

```
find /new_dir -exec grep -l old_dir {} \;
```

For any entries that find locates, change the entry to new_dir or, when appropriate, change the absolute path name to the more generic $HOME variable. Pay particular attention to the startup (dot) files contained within a user's home directory because errors in that class of file will surely get the attention of a user quickly.

Common dot files include

.login	Csh- and tcsh-executed during login after the system login processing occurs.
.cshrc	Csh-executed when spawning new subshells.
.tcshrc	Tcsh-executed when spawning new subshells.
.profile	Sh- or ksh-executed during login after the system login processing occurs.
.kshrc	Ksh-executed when forking new subshells.
.bashrc	Bash-executed when forking new subshells.
.history	Contains the last set of shell instructions executed.

`.rhosts`	Remote host/username lists that are trusted. Rlogin, rexec, rsh/remsh,...use this file to allow login, file access, and command processing without need of password.
`.netrc`	Used by the FTP auto-login process.
`.forward`	Allows the mailer to redirect mail to other addresses, files, or program processors.
`.mailrc`	A start-up file for mail that allows setting mailer options or aliases.
`.exrc`	A start-up file for ex or vi that allows setting specific editor options.
`.xinitrc`	A start-up file for X windowing.
`.xsession`	Another start-up file for X windowing.
`.xdefault`	Yet another start-up file for X windowing.

When removing usernames from the password file you must locate all of the user's files to delete them. Find once again can do this chore for you.

```
find / -user username
```

searches out all of the files belonging to *username*. To be safe, you might want to back the files up before you delete them. To ferret out and delete within a single command is to carry out the subsequent command:

```
find / -user username -exec rm {} \;
```

After purging the username's files, the group file and system mail alias file(s) should be modified by removing the username from them. Newaliases should be run to update the alias database.

User Monitor Commands

Occasionally, user administration functions as a detective because, among other things, the machine becomes overtaxed, security is breached, or statistical information is requested. In cases such as these, UNIX provides tools to gather information about users in general or one user in particular.

The first class of instructions tells you what is happening now. These commands give an indication if anyone is gathering more than her fair share of resources. In addition, they should be used to avoid potential performance problems by justifying the need for more CPU, memory, or disk resources to accommodate the growing needs of your user community.

uptime shows the current time, the number of days the machine has been up, the number of users logged into the system, and the system load average during the past 1, 5, and 15 minutes.

It is a somewhat nebulous description of what actually goes into the load average, but it is useful for making comparisons with previous attempts and gives indications if any user is monopolizing the machine's resources.

w gives the uptime information and indicates who is on now, what terminal port he is using, the name of the host the username logged in from, when the username logged in, how long they have been idle, the aggregate CPU time of all processes on that terminal port (JCPU), the CPU time of the active process listed in the next field (PCPU), and what command they are currently running. The idle time gives a good indication of who may be good candidates for being logged out.

ps -ef (SYS V) or ps -ax (Berkeley) gives a lot of information about all running system processes. Pay attention to the *time* column because this is the cumulative process execution time for the listed process. Any large number is suspect for running amok especially if the parent process ID is 1. Possibly you may use kill -9 out_of_control_process_id to tax the system less. If the procedure should not be killed, then possibly you might use the renice command to settle things a bit. renice +10 offending_process_id improves other user process responses. The second parameter (+10) corresponds to a sliding scale from -20 to +20 where -20 would get the most time slices and +20 would get the least.

top gives a ps-like output that is updated constantly. In particular, the *% cpu* and *time* columns can identify users who are exploiting the system a bit too much. The size parameter, indicating the process size in pages, can identify users who may be causing memory-to-disk swapping to occur too often. Possibly this information shows that the system needs more memory.

fuser can indicate who is tying up a file resource. Running fuser -u *filename* lists all the usernames and processes that currently use the specified filename. Either the user can be asked to stop tying up the resource, or the offending process can be killed. If a file system is the resource being tied up rather than a file, fuser -cku *filesystem_name* kills each task controlling a file residing on the file system. Once the command completes, the file system could be umounted.

[B]df in concert with du gives insight into disk overuse. [B]df gives a summary of how full each disk is. For overly full file systems, du -s */filesystem/** displays a grand total of used blocks for each component directory on the file system. You can continue chaining down the largest identified directories until finding something that can be moved, archived, or eliminated. Using find with its size parameter could automate the same result.

GlancePlus is a graphical realtime performance diagnostic tool offered by Hewlett-Packard for its HP-UX systems. It may be invoked in its graphical mode via the gpm command. Glance, the character-based component, may be invoked by the command glance. Combining the features of many of the conventional UNIX tools described above, system administrators are able to analyze system resources and isolate performance bottlenecks.

When first initiated, GlancePlus displays the Global or Process Summary screens. If you find the memory utilization graph consistently peaking, then press the F2, F3, or F4 keys to drill down and call up detail screens to identify the processes and users in question. Detail screens are available to monitor many system resources such as CPU, memory, swap, disk I/O, nfs, lan, and more. Further information is obtained from the Individual Process screens.

Detail is plentiful, and the ease of use is much appreciated. GlancePlus and its component Glance are valuable tools for system troubleshooting and should be utilized by anyone responsible for such troubleshooting.

The next set of utilities and procedures describe a user usage history. First, many network utilities can be placed into verbose modes. For example, `fingerd`, `ftpd`, `tftpd`, and `rshd` accept a `-l` or `-L` option that causes them to relate connection information to a system log file. Normally, adding these options is handled by modifying the program call statements in the `inetd` configuration file that usually resides at `/etc/inetd.conf` and then restarting `inetd` with the following command: `killall -HUP inetd`. The file can further be modified in conjunction with an add-on package known as `tcp_wrappers` created by Wietse Venema. The package is a port monitor and possibly a proactive limiting daemon depending on how it is configured. In any case, you are better able to determine and restrict your user base network usage.

Small changes to the `syslogd` configuration file (usually located at `/etc/syslog.conf`) can cause expression of more information. For example, if the line doesn't already exist, you can add

```
mail.debug /some_legal_directory/syslog
```

as the last line of the configuration file. Then have `syslogd` reread this modified file by executing:

```
kill -HUP syslogd_process_id
```

This directs `mail to`, `from`, and `deferred` messages to be placed in a mail queue log file, `/some_legal_directory/syslog`. This allows better understanding and manipulation of mail so your user's needs can be met.

Another historical tool is the `last` utility that shows which users are logging on from where and for how long. This tool usually is used in conjunction with `acctcom` or `lastcomm`. `Acctcom` and `lastcomm` identify system usage by username and tty port. They give administrators insight into what the system is being used for and how much CPU time and memory is being spent on which user tasks. The output indicates when your system is busiest and why it is busy. For these utilities to function, system accounting needs to be turned on and adequate space open for raw accounting files to appear and grow. To better understand how accounting functions work and what needs to be turned on or run, refer to the manual pages for `accton` and `sa` for Berkeley systems, and `acct` and `runacct` for SYS V systems. Nightly, these data files can be manipulated into human readable logs showing disk usage, cpu usage, memory usage, line printer usage, connection statistics, and command statistics. Again, this permits easier understanding of who is using the system's resources. The process also lets the powers-that-be charge the users for their resource usage.

Monitoring also extends into the realm of protecting the users from themselves. Correcting system vulnerabilities in general and fixing user's self-made problems in particular are user administration duties. The `find` utility is particularly helpful in this effort. In most instances, users should not have globally writable directories and probably should not have globablly readable ones either if you are to maintain some semblance of security.

```
find /user_directory_home /( -perm -o=w -o -perm -o=r /) -type d
```

locates any globally readable or writable directory. If the command locates many of these directories, you should check the default `umask` that users receive when logging in. Possibly a `umask` of `077` is in order. User's `.rhosts` and `.netrc` files should not be readable or writable either as they may aid attackers.

```
find /user_directory_home /( -name .rhosts -o -name .netrc \) \( -perm -o=r -o -
➥perm -g=r \)
```

finds all globally readable `.rhosts` and `.netrc` files. Especially in user directories, there should be very few unknown set uid (`SUID`) programs on the system, which would ultimately compromise every user and file and the system.

```
find / -perm -u=s
```

generates a list of all `SUID` programs on the system. Adding the `-user root` parameter on the command lists all root privileged `SUID` files, so you can verify that all such files are where they are expected to be. Dan Farmer's COPS add-on package can be ftp'd from the network and configured to make checks such as the previous as well as more intense security queries.

The best way to protect users from themselves is to back up their files nightly. Depending on how much information needs to be backed up, a good strategy is to do an incremental dump nightly and full dump weekly.

Another strategy is to give the users another `rm` command that doesn't remove files (at least not right away). The command would `move` the file to a temporary holding area that is flushed of files older than a predetermined age.

User Limiting Commands

Using disk quotas can protect the system from being overwhelmed by a few users. You can begin restricting disk usage by running `quotaon /user_filesystem`. That command allows users residing on *user_filesystem* to be reined in. Defining how much space each user can accumulate results by executing the `edquota` command. The general form of this command is:

```
edquota [-p previously_defined_quota_username] username
```

For example, `edquota charlene` brings up an edit session that allows (re)setting hard and soft values for total disk space in kilobytes and total number of inodes used. The difference between hard and soft is that hard can never be exceeded. Exceeding the soft limit begins a timer. If the user goes below the soft limit, the timer resets. If the timer alarms, the condition is treated the same as exceeding the hard limit. `Edquota -p charlene georgia` does not bring up an editor but instead duplicates username charlene quota information for username georgia.

To check on a username, you run `quota -v` *username* ... or `repquota /user_filesystem`. Quota reports a specified username's disk usage and limits. If the `-v` is left off, only the specified usernames exceeding their limits are output. `repquota` gives a summary of all users in the password file for the specified file system. Again, disk usage and limits are expressed. An example of the quota command and its output follows.

```
quota -v jamie
    Disk quotas for jamie (uid 315):
    Filesystem  usage   quota  limit  timeleft  files  quota  limit   timeleft
    /usr1       26015   25600  30720  5.1 days  488    500    750
```

Username `jamie` has exceeded the total kilobyte usage allowed and has 5.1 days left to reduce her usage. That username could create 12 more files before signaling an inode overage (assuming enough space exists).

`repquota` is a bit different because it lists all users under quota restrictions when run. An example is

```
Disk limits                File limits
User              used   soft    hard   timeleft   used   soft   hard   timeleft
alyssa      --    00417  25600   30720             0043   200    250
james       --    12871  25600   30720             0149   200    250
wayne       -+    04635  25600   30720             1072   500    750    EXPIRED
rayna       --    00002  25600   30720             0003   200    250
steve       --    11786  25600   30720             0155   200    250
judy        --    00015  25600   30720             0013   200    250
jamie       +-    26015  25600   30720  5.1 days   0488   500    750
holly       -+    11872  25600   30720             0200   200    250    6.0 days
kenny       --    02737  25600   30720             0134   200    250
irene       --    02704  25600   30720             0070   200    250
bert        --    03070  25600   30720             0173   200    250
al          --    00613  25600   30720             0021   200    250
connie      --    00558  25600   30720             0025   200    250
charlene    --    00539  25600   30720             0016   200    250
dave        +-    50226  50000   60000  EXPIRED    0430   500    750
mike        --    03853  25600   30720             0020   200    250
ann         --    05308  25600   30720             0162   200    250
kirstin     --    20672  25600   30720             0191   300    350
matthew     --    00444  25600   30720             0012   200    250
john        --    01303  25600   30720             0067   200    250
```

In the example, `wayne` and `dave` have faults that disallow use. Users `jamie` and `holly` need to lower their use in the specified time period or will have use disallowed. Alternately, the values for their use could be increased.

Though a subset of total disk usage, incoming mail file usage should be monitored specifically since all users generally share a common incoming mail directory space. One "pig" can disrupt the entire system. For example,

```
ls -l /var/mail ¦ awk '{if ($5 > 500000) printf"%-8.8s - %ld\n", $3, $5}'
```

will list all usernames with mail files greater than _ million characters. Either the user can be asked politely to reduce the number of messages or you can lessen the file space by saving and compressing or by archiving and deleting it.

Anonymous FTP

Lastly, user administration discussion would not be complete unless it included a description of how to enable a very special, if not insecure, user ID. This last section deals with setting up an anonymous ftp account.

First, create a user ID for the account in the `passwd` file. The entry should have a unique user ID, the group ID matching the user ID and an invalid password and shell. A sample entry could be

```
ftp:*:500:ftp:Anonymous ftp
        user:/usr_ftp_home_directory/ftp:/bin/false
```

Second, create the home directory.

```
    mkdir /usr_ftp_home_directory/ftp
    cd /usr_ftp_home_directory/ftp
    mkdir bin etc [lib] [dev] pub
    mkdir pub/incoming
    chown -R root .
    chgrp ftp . pub
    chmod ugo+rx .  pub [lib]
    chmod ugo+x bin etc [dev]
    chmod u+rwx,o+wx,+t pub/incoming
```

Third, fill the directories with appropriate information.

```
cp /bin or /sbin/ls bin
    chmod ugo+x bin/ls
    [ cp /usr/lib/libdl.so.* lib ]
    [ chmod ugo+rx lib/libdl.so.* ]
    [ ls -l /dev/zero ]
    [ mknod dev/zero c major# minor# ] -- major/minor numbers are the comma
➡seperated entries directly left of the date in the ouput of the "ls" command.
    [ chmod ugo+r dev/zero ]
    [ create an etc/passwd file that includes root, daemon, and ftp  whose
➡passwords are "*" ]
    [ create an etc/group file that includes the root default group and the ftp
➡group ]
```

You should now be in the anonymous ftp business. To make sure that things are set up correctly, look at the anonymous ftp directory. No file or directory should be owned by ftp because Trojan horse versions of the files could be inserted. Connect as anonymous ftp, and try to create a file in the current working directory. If you can, anonymous ftp is insecure.

Summary

Although it seems a thankless task, user administration is best when it is unnoticed. You should be available to answer questions, but otherwise be invisible to your users. Use the many inherent UNIX user administration tools in concert with the select add-on packages to oversee, monitor, and limit your user base. Satisfied users free you from the more mundane tasks of user administration and give you the free time to sift through other areas of the system, devoting your time to being productive rather than solving problems.

File System and Disk Administration

by Steve Shah

IN THIS CHAPTER

This chapter discusses the trials and tribulations of creating, maintaining, and repairing file systems. While these tasks may appear simple from a user's standpoint, they are, in fact, intricate and contain more than a handful of nuances. In the course of this chapter, we'll step through many of these nuances and, hopefully, come to a strong understanding of the hows and whys of file systems.

Before we really jump into the topic, you should have a good understanding of UNIX directories, files, permissions, and paths. These are the key building blocks in understanding how to administer your file systems, and I assume you already have a mastery of them. If the statement "Be sure to have `/usr/bin` before `/usr/local/bin` in your `$PATH`" confuses you in any way, you should be reading something more fundamental first. Refer to Part I, "Introduction to UNIX," for some basic instructions in UNIX.

This chapter goes about the explanation of file systems a bit differently from other books. We first discuss the maintenance and repair of file systems, then discuss their creation. This was done because it is more likely that you already have existing file systems you need to maintain and fix. Understanding how to maintain them also helps you better understand why file systems are created the way they are.

The techniques we cover here are applicable to most UNIX systems currently in use. The only exceptions are when we actually create the file systems. This is where the most deviation from any standard (if there ever was one) occurs. We cover the creation of file systems under the SunOS, Solaris, Linux, and IRIX implementations of UNIX. If you are not using one of these operating systems, you should check the documentation that came with your operating system for details on the creation of file systems.

> ## CAUTION
>
> Working with file systems is inherently dangerous. You may be surprised at how quickly and easily you can damage a file system beyond repair. In some instances, it is even possible to damage the disk drive as well. BE CAREFUL. When performing the actions explained in this chapter, be sure you have typed the commands in correctly and you understand the resulting function fully before executing it. When in doubt, consult the documentation that came from the manufacturer. Most importantly, the documentation that comes from the manufacturer is always more authoritative than any book.

> ## NOTE
>
> You should read the entire chapter before actually performing any of the tasks below. This will give you a better understanding of how all the components work together, thereby giving you more solid ground when performing potentially dangerous activities.

What Is a File System?

The file system is the primary means of file storage in UNIX. Each file system houses directories, which, as a group, can be placed almost anywhere in the UNIX directory tree. The topmost level of the directory tree, the root directory, begins at /. Subdirectories nested below the root directory may traverse as deep as you like so long as the longest absolute path is less than 1,024 characters.

With the proliferation of vendor-enhanced versions of UNIX, you will find a number of "enhanced" file systems. From the standpoint of the administrator, you shouldn't have to worry about the differences too much. The two instances where you will need to worry about vendor-specific details are in the creation of file systems and when performing backups. We will cover the specifics of

- SunOS 4.1.x, which uses 4.2
- Solaris, which uses ufs
- Linux, which uses ext2
- IRIX, which uses efs and xfs

Note that the ufs and 4.2 file systems are actually the same.

A file system, however, is only a part of the grand scheme of how UNIX keeps its data on disk. At the top level, you'll find the disks themselves. These disks are then broken into partitions, each varying in size depending on the needs of the administrator. It is on each partition that the actual file system is laid out. Within the file system, you'll find directories, subdirectories, and, finally, the individual files.

Although you rarely will have to deal with the file system at a level lower than the individual files stored on it, it is critical that you understand two key concepts: *inodes* and the *superblock*. Once you understand these, you will find that the behavior and characteristics of files make more sense.

inodes

An inode maintains information about each file. Depending on the type of file system, the inode can contain upwards of 40+ pieces of information. Most of it, however, is useful only to the kernel and doesn't concern us. The fields that do concern us are

mode	The permission mask and type of file
link count	The number of directories that contain an entry with this inode number
user ID	The ID of the file's owner
group ID	The ID of the file's group
size	Number of bytes in this file

access time	The time at which the file was last accessed
mod time	The time at which the file was last modified
inode time	The time at which this inode structure was last modified
block list	A list of disk block numbers which contain the first segment of the file
indirect list	A list of other block lists

The mode, link count, user ID, group ID, size, and access time are used when generating file listings. Note that the inode does not contain the file's name. That information is held in the directory file (see below for details).

Superblocks

This is the most vital information stored on the disk. It contains information on the disk's geometry (number of heads, cylinders, and so on), the head of the inode list, and free block list. Because of its importance, the system automatically keeps mirrors of this data scattered around the disk for redundancy. You only have to deal with superblocks if your file system becomes heavily corrupted.

Types of Files

Files come in eight flavors:

- Normal files
- Directories
- Hard links
- Symbolic links
- Sockets
- Named pipes
- Character devices
- Block devices

Normal Files

These are the files you use the most. They can be either text or binary files; however, their internal structure is irrelevant from a system administrator standpoint. A file's characteristics are specified by the inode in the file system that describes it. An `ls -l` on a normal file will look something like this:

```
-rw-------   1 sshah    admin        42 May 12 13:09 hello
```

Directories

These are a special kind of file that contains a list of other files. Although there is a one-to-one mapping of inode to disk blocks, there can be a many-to-one mapping from directory entry to inode. When viewing a directory listing using the ls -l command, you can identify directories by their permissions starting with the d character. An ls -l on a directory looks something like this:

```
drwx------    2 sshah    admin        512 May 12 13:08 public_html
```

Hard Links

A hard link is actually a normal directory entry except instead of pointing to a unique file, it points to an already existing file. This gives the illusion that there are two identical files when you do a directory listing. Because the system sees this as just another file, it treats it as such. This is most apparent during backups because hard-linked files get backed up as many times as there are hard links to them. Because a hard link shares an inode, it cannot exist across file systems. Hard links are created with the ln command. For example, given this directory listing using ls -l, we see

```
-rw-------    1 sshah    admin         42 May 12 13:04 hello
```

When you type ln hello goodbye and then perform another directory listing using ls -l, you see

```
-rw-------    2 sshah    admin         42 May 12 13:04 goodbye
-rw-------    2 sshah    admin         42 May 12 13:04 hello
```

Notice how this appears to be two separate files that just happen to have the same file lengths. Also note that the link count (second column) has increased from one to two. How can you tell they actually are the same file? Use ls -il. Observe

```
13180 -rw-------    2 sshah    admin         42 May 12 13:04 goodbye
13180 -rw-------    2 sshah    admin         42 May 12 13:04 hello
```

You can see that both point to the same inode, 13180.

> **WARNING**
>
> Be careful when creating hardlinks, especially when hardlinking to a directory. It is possible to corrupt a file system by doing so since the hardlink does not contain the fact that the inode being pointed to needs to be treated as a directory.

Symbolic Links

A symbolic link (sometimes referred to as a *symlink*) differs from a hard link because it doesn't point to another inode but to another filename. This allows symbolic links to exist across file systems as well as be recognized as a special file to the operating system. You will find symbolic links to be crucial to the administration of your file systems, especially when trying to give the appearance of a seamless system when there isn't one. Symbolic links are created using the `ln -s` command. A common thing people do is create a symbolic link to a directory that has moved. For example, if you are accustomed to accessing the directory for your home page in the subdirectory www but at the new site you work at, home pages are kept in the `public_html` directory, you can create a symbolic link from www to `public_html` using the command `ln -s public_html www`. Performing an `ls -l` on the result shows the link.

```
drwx------   2 sshah    admin        512 May 12 13:08 public_html
lrwx------   1 sshah    admin         11 May 12 13:08 www -> public_html
```

Sockets

Sockets are the means for UNIX to network with other machines. Typically, this is done using network ports; however, the file system has a provision to allow for interprocess communication through socket files. (A popular program that uses this technique is the X Window system.) You rarely have to deal with this kind of file and should never have to create it yourself (unless you're writing the program). If you need to remove a socket file, use the `rm` command. Socket files are identified by their permission settings beginning with an `s` character. An `ls -l` on a socket file looks something like this:

```
srwxrwxrwx   1 root     admin          0 May 10 14:38 X0
```

Named Pipes

Similar to sockets, named pipes enable programs to communicate with one another through the file system. You can use the `mknod` command to create a named pipe. Named pipes are recognizable by their permissions settings beginning with the `p` character. An `ls -l` on a named pipe looks something like this:

```
prw-------   1 sshah    admin          0 May 12 22:02 mypipe
```

Character Devices

These special files are typically found in the `/dev` directory and provide a mechanism for communicating with system device drivers through the file system one character at a time. They are easily noticed by their permission bits starting with the `c` character. Each character file contains two special numbers, the major and minor. These two numbers identify which device driver that file communicates with. An `ls -l` on a character device looks something like this:

```
crw-rw-rw-   1 root     wheel        21,   4 May 12 13:40 ptyp4
```

Block Devices

Block devices also share many characteristics with character devices in that they exist in the /dev directory, are used to communicate with device drivers, and have major and minor numbers. The key difference is that block devices typically transfer large blocks of data at a time versus one character at a time. (A hard disk is a block device, whereas a terminal is a character device.) Block devices are identified by their permission bits starting with the b character. An ls -l on a block device looks something like this:

```
brw-------   2 root     staff    16,  2 Jul 29  1992 fd0c
```

Managing File Systems

Managing file systems is relatively easy. That is, once you can commit to memory the location of all the key files in the directory tree on each major variation of UNIX as well as your own layout of file systems across the network…

In other words, it can be a royal pain.

From a technical standpoint, there isn't much to deal with. Once the file systems have been put in their correct places and the boot time configuration files have been edited so that your file systems automatically come online at every startup, there isn't much to do besides watch your disk space.

From a management standpoint, it's much more involved. Often you'll need to deal with existing configurations, which may not have been done "the right way," or you're dealing with site politics such as, "I won't let *that* department share *my* disks." Then you'll need to deal with users who don't understand why they need to periodically clean up their home directories. Don't forget the ever-exciting vendor-specific nuisances and their idea of how the system "should be" organized.

This section covers the tools you need to manage the technical issues. Unfortunately, managerial issues are something that can't be covered in a book. Each site has different needs as well as different resources, resulting in different policies. If your site lacks any written policy, take the initiative to write one yourself.

Mounting and Unmounting File Systems

As I mentioned earlier in this chapter, part of the power in UNIX stems from its flexibility in placing file systems anywhere in the directory tree. This feat is accomplished by mounting file systems.

Before you can mount a file system, you need to select a mount point. A mount point is the directory entry in the file system where the root directory of a different file system will overlay it. UNIX keeps track of mount points, and accesses the correct file system, depending on which directory the user is currently in. A mount point may exist anywhere in the directory tree.

NOTE

While it is technically true that you can mount a file system anywhere in the directory tree, there is one place you will NOT want to mount it: the root directory. Remember that once a file system is mounted at a directory, that directory is overshadowed by the contents of the mounted file system. Hence, by being mounted on the root directory, the system will no longer be able to see its own kernel or local configuration files. How long your system goes on before crashing depends on your vendor.

There is an exception to the rule. Some installation packages will mount a network file system to the root directory. This is done to give the installation software access to many packages that may not be able to fit on your boot disk. Unless you fully understand how to do this yourself, don't.

Mounting and Unmounting File Systems Manually

To mount a file system, use the `mount` command

```
mount /dev/device /directory/to/mount
```

where `/dev/device` is the device name you want to mount and `/directory/to/mount` is the directory you want to overlay in your local file system. For example, if you wanted to mount `/dev/hda4` to the `/usr` directory, you would type

```
mount /dev/hda4 /usr
```

Remember that the directory must exist in your local file system before anything can be mounted there.

There are options that can be passed to the `mount` command. The most important characteristics are specified in the `-o` option. These characteristics are

rw	read/write
ro	read only
bg	background mount (if the mount fails, place the process into the background and keep trying until success.)
intr	interruptible mount (if a process is pending I/O on a mounted partition, it will allow the process to be interrupted and the I/O call dropped)

An example of these parameters being used is

```
mount -o rw,bg,intr /dev/hda4 /usr
```

See the man page on your system for vendor-specific additions.

To unmount a file system, use the `umount` command. For example,

```
umount /usr
```

This unmounts the `/usr` file system from the current directory tree, unveiling the original directory underneath it.

There is, of course, a caveat. If users are using files on a mounted file system, you cannot unmount it. All files must be closed before this can happen, which on a large system can be tricky, to say the least. There are three ways to handle this:

- Use the `lsof` program (available at `ftp://vic.cc.purdue.edu/pub/tools/unix/lsof`) to list the users and their open files on a given file system. Then either wait until they are done, beg them to leave, or kill off their processes. Then unmount the file system. Often, this isn't very desirable.

- Use the `-f` option with `umount` command to force the unmount. This is often a bad idea because it leaves the programs (and users) accessing the partition confused. Files which are in memory that have not been committed to disk may be lost.

- Bring the system to single-user mode, then unmount the file system. While the largest inconvenience, it is the safest way because no one loses any work.

Mounting File Systems Automatically

At boot time, the system automatically mounts the root file system with read-only privileges. This enables it to load the kernel and read critical startup files. However, once it has bootstrapped itself, it needs guidance. Although it is possible for you to mount all the file systems by hand, it isn't realistic because you would then have to finish bootstrapping the machine yourself, and worse, the system could not come back online by itself (unless, of course, you enjoy coming into work at 2 a.m. to bring a system back up).

To get around this, UNIX uses a special file called `/etc/fstab` (`/etc/vfstab` under Solaris). This file lists all the partitions that need to be mounted at boot time and the directory where they need to be mounted. Along with that information you can pass parameters to the `mount` command.

Each file system to be mounted is listed in the `fstab` file in the following format:

```
/dev/device    /dir/to/mount       ftype parameters fs_freq fs_passno
```

where:

`/dev/device`	Is the device to be mounted, for instance, `/dev/hda4`.
`/dir/to/mount`	Is the location at which the file system should be mounted on your directory tree.

ftype	Is the file system type. This should be 4.2 under SunOS, ufs under Solaris, ext2 under Linux, efs or xfs in IRIX (depending on your version), nfs for NFS mounted file systems, swap for swap partitions, and proc for the /proc file system. Some operating systems, such as Linux, support additional filesystem types, although they are not as likely to be used.
parameters	Are the parameters we passed to mount using the -o option. They follow the same comma-delineated format. A sample entry would look like rw,intr,bg.
fs_freq	Is used by dump to determine whether a file system needs to be dumped.
fs_passno	Is used by the fsck program to determine the order in which to check disks at boot time.

Any lines in the fstab file that start with the pound symbol (#) are considered comments.

If you need to mount a new file system while the machine is live, you must perform the mount by hand. If you wish to have this mount automatically active the next time the system is rebooted, you should be sure to add the appropriate entry to your fstab file.

There are two notable partitions that don't follow the same set of rules as normal partitions. They are the swap partition and /proc. (Note that SunOS does not use the /proc file system.)

Mounting the swap partition is not done using the mount command. It is instead managed by the swap command under Solaris and IRIX, and by the swapon command under SunOS and Linux. In order for a swap partition to be mounted, it must be listed in the appropriate fstab file. Once it's there, use the appropriate command (swap or swapon) with the -a parameter followed by the partition on which you've allocated swap space.

The /proc file system is even stranger because it really isn't a file system. It is an interface to the kernel abstracted into a file system–style format. This should be listed in your fstab file with file system type proc.

TIP

If you need to remount a file system that already has an entry in the fstab file, you don't need to type in the mount command with all the parameters. Instead, simply pass the directory to mount as a parameter like this:

```
mount /dir/to/mount
```

mount automatically looks to the fstab file for all the details, such as which partition to mount and which options to use.

If you need to remount a large number of file systems that are already listed in the .fstab file (in other words, you need to remount directories from a system that has gone down), you can use the -a option in the mount command to try and remount all the entries in the fstab file like this:

```
mount -a
```

If mount finds that a file system is already mounted, no action is performed on that file system. If, on the other hand, mount finds that an entry is not mounted, it automatically mounts it with the appropriate parameters.

Here is a complete fstab file from a SunOS system:

```
#
# Sample /etc/fstab file for a SunOS machine
#

# Local mounts

/dev/sd0a          /        4.2    rw        1 1
/dev/sd0g          /usr     4.2    rw        1 2
/dev/sd0b          swap     swap   rw        0 0
/dev/sd0d          /var     4.2    rw        0 0

# Remote mounts

server1:/export/home        /home           nfs    rw,bg,intr   0 0
server1:/export/usr/local   /usr/local      nfs    rw,bg,intr   0 0
server2:/export/var/spool/mail   /var/spool/mail   nfs    rw,bg,intr   0 0
```

Common Commands for File System Management

In taking care of your system, you'll quickly find that you can use these commands and many of their parameters without having to look them up. This is because you're going to be using them *all the time*. I highly suggest you learn to love them.

NOTE

In reading this book you may have noticed the terms *program* and *command* are used interchangeably. This is because there are no "built-in" commands to the system; each one is invoked as an individual program. However, you will quickly find that both the people who use UNIX, as well as UNIX-related texts (such as this one), use both terms to mean the same thing. Confusing? A bit. But it's tough to change 25+ years of history.

NOTE

At the end of each command description, I mention the GNU equivalent. Linux users shouldn't worry about getting them, because Linux ships with all GNU tools. If you are using another platform and aren't sure whether you're using the GNU version, try running the command with the `--version` option. If it is GNU, it will display its title and version number. If it isn't GNU, it'll most likely reject the parameter and give an error.

---

df

The `df` command summarizes the free disk space by file system. Running it without any parameters displays all the information about normally mounted and NFS mounted file systems. The output varies from vendor to vendor (under Solaris, use `df -t`) but should closely resemble this:

```
Filesystem           1024-blocks  Used  Available Capacity Mounted on
/dev/hda3               247871   212909     22161    91%   /
/dev/hda6                50717    15507     32591    32%   /var
/dev/hda7               481998       15    457087     0%   /local
server1:/var/spool/mail
                        489702   222422    218310    50%   /var/spool/mail
```

The columns reported show

`Filesystem`	Which file system is being shown. File systems mounted using NFS are shown as *hostname:/dir/that/is/mounted*.
`1024-blocks`	The number of 1 KB blocks the file system consists of (its total size).
`Used`	The number of blocks used.
`Available`	The number of blocks available for use.
`Capacity`	Percentage of partition currently used.
`Mounted on`	The location in the directory tree this partition has been mounted on.

Common parameters to this command are

directory	Show information only for the partition on which the specified directory exists.
`-a`	Show all partitions including swap and `/proc`.
`-i`	Show inode usage instead of block usage.

The GNU `df` program, which is part of the `fileutils` distribution, has some additional print-formatting features you may find useful. You can download the latest `fileutils` package at `ftp://ftp.cdrom.com/pub/gnu`.

du

The du command summarizes disk usage by directory. It recurses through all subdirectories and shows disk usage by each subdirectory with a final total at the end. Running it without any parameters shows the usage like so:

```
409      ./doc
945      ./lib
68       ./man
60       ./m4
391      ./src
141      ./intl
873      ./po
3402     .
```

The first column shows the blocks of disk used by the subdirectory, and the second column shows the subdirectory being evaluated. To see how many kilobytes each subdirectory consumes, use the -k option. Some common parameters to this command are

directory	Show usage for the specified directory. The default is the current directory.
-a	Show usage for all files, not just directories.
-s	Show only the total disk usage.

Like the df program, this program is available as part of the GNU fileutils distribution. The GNU version has expanded on many of the parameters which you may find useful. The fileutils package can be downloaded from ftp://ftp.cdrom.com/pub/gnu.

ln

The ln program is used to generate links between files. This is very useful for creating the illusion of a perfect file system in which everything is in the "right" place when, in reality, it isn't. This is done by making a link from the desired location to the actual location.

The usage of this program is

```
ln file_being_linked_to link_name
```

where *file_being_linked_to* is the file that already exists, and you wish to have another file point to it called *link_name*. The command generates a hard link, meaning that the file *link_name* will be indistinguishable from the original file. Both files must exist on the same file system.

A popular parameter to ln is the -s option, which generates symbolic links instead of hard links. The format of the command remains the same:

```
ln -s file_being_linked_to link_name
```

The difference is that the *link_name* file is marked as a symbolic link in the file system. Symbolic links may span file systems and are given a special tag in the directory entry.

18

FILE SYSTEM AND DISK ADMINISTRATION

> **TIP**
>
> Unless there is an explicit reason not to, you should always use symbolic links by specifying the -s option to 1n. This makes your links stand out and makes it easy to move them from one file system to another.

tar

The tar program is an immensely useful archiving utility. It can combine an entire directory tree into one large file suitable for transferring or compression.

The command line format of this program is

```
tar parameters filelist
```

Common parameters are

- c   Create an archive
- x   Extract the archive
- v   Be verbose
- f   Specify a tar file to work on
- p   Retain file permissions and ownerships
- t   View the contents of an archive

Unlike most other UNIX commands, the parameters do not need to have a dash before them.

To create the tarfile myCode.tar, I could use tar in the following manners.

```
tar cf myCode.tar myCode
```

is where myCode is a subdirectory relative to the current directory where the files I wish to archive are located.

```
tar cvf myCode.tar myCode
```

is the same as the previous tar invocation, although this time it lists all the files added to the archive on the screen.

```
tar cf myCode.tar myCode/*.c
```

archives all the files in the myCode directory that are suffixed by .c.

```
tar cf myCode.tar myCode/*.c myCode/*.h
```

archives all the files in the myCode directory that are suffixed by .c or .h.

To view the contents of the myCode.tar file, use

```
tar tf myCode.tar
```

To extract the files in the `myCode.tar` file, use

```
tar xf myCode.tar
```

If the `myCode` directory doesn't exist, tar creates it. If the `myCode` directory does exist, any files in that directory are overwritten by the ones being untarred.

```
tar xvf myCode.tar
```

is the same as the previous invocation of `tar`, but this lists the files as they are being extracted.

```
tar xpf myCode.tar
```

is the same as the previous invocation of `tar`, but this attempts to set the permissions of the unarchived files to the values they had before archiving (very useful if you're untarring files as root).

TIP

The greatest use of `tar` for system administrators is to move directory trees around. This can be done using the following set of commands:

```
(cd /src;tar cf - *) ¦ (cd /dest;tar xpf -)
```

where /src is the source directory and /dest is the destination directory.

This is better than using a recursive copy because symbolic links and file permissions are kept. Use this and amaze your friends.

While the stock tar that comes with your system works fine for most uses, you may find that the GNU version of `tar` has some nicer features. You can find the latest version of GNU `tar` at `ftp://ftp.cdrom.com/pub/gnu`.

find

Of the commands that I've mentioned so far, you're likely to use `find` the most. Its purpose is to find files or patterns of files. The parameters for this tool are

```
find dir parameters
```

where *dir* is the directory where the search begins, and *parameters* define what is being searched for. The most common parameters you will use are

-name	Specifies the filename or wildcards to look for. If you use any wildcards, be sure to place them within quotes so that the shell doesn't parse them before `find` does.
-print	Typically turned on by default, it tells `find` to display the resulting file list.
-exec	Executes the specified command on files found matching the `-name` criteria.

`-atime n`	File was last accessed *n* days ago.
`-mtime n`	File's data was last modified *n* days ago.
`-size n[bckw]`	File uses *n* units of space where the units are specified by either b,c,k, or w. b is for 512-byte blocks, c is bytes, k is for kilobytes, and w is for two-byte words.
`-xdev`	Do not traverse down nonlocal file systems.
`-o`	Logical or the options.
`-a`	Logical and the options.

Some examples of the `find` command are

```
find / -name core -mtime +7 -print -exec /bin/rm {} \;
```

This starts its search from the root directory and finds all files named `core` that have not been modified in seven days.

```
find / -xdev -atime +60 -a -mtime +60 -print
```

This searches all files, from the root directory down, on the local file system, which have not been accessed for at least 60 days *and* have not been modified for at least 60 days, and prints the list. This is useful for finding those files that people claim they need but, in reality, never use.

```
find /home -size +500k -print
```

This searches all files from `/home` down and lists them if they are greater than 500 KB in size—a handy way of finding large files in the system.

The GNU version of `find`, which comes with the `findutils` package, offers many additional features you will find useful. You can download the latest version from `ftp://ftp.cdrom.com/pub/gnu`.

Repairing File Systems with `fsck`

Sooner or later, it happens: Someone turns off the power switch. The power outage lasts longer than your UPS's batteries and you didn't shut down the system. Someone presses the reset button. Someone overwrites part of your disk. A critical sector on the disk develops a flaw. If you run UNIX long enough, eventually a halt occurs where the system did not write the remaining cached information (sync'ed) to the disks.

When this happens, you need to verify the integrity of each of the file systems. This is necessary because if the structure is not correct, using the file systems could quickly damage them beyond repair. Over the years, UNIX has developed a very sophisticated file system integrity check that can usually recover the problem. It's called `fsck`.

The `fsck` Utility

The `fsck` utility takes its understanding of the internals of the various UNIX file systems and attempts to verify that all the links and blocks are correctly tied together. It runs in five passes, each of which checks a different part of the linkage and each of which builds on the verifications and corrections of the prior passes.

`fsck` walks the file system, starting with the superblock. It then deals with the allocated disk blocks, pathnames, directory connectivity, link reference counts, and the free list of blocks and inodes.

> **NOTE**
>
> The xfs filesystem now shipped with all IRIX-based machines no longer needs the `fsck` command.

The Superblock

Every change to the file system affects the superblock; that's why it is cached in RAM. Periodically, at the sync interval, it is written to disk. If it is corrupted, `fsck` checks and corrects it. If it is so badly corrupted that `fsck` cannot do its work, find the paper you saved when you built the file system and use the `-b` option with `fsck` to give it an alternate superblock to use. The superblock is the head of each of the lists that make up the file system, and it maintains counts of free blocks and inodes.

Inodes

`fsck` validates each of the inodes. It makes sure that each block in the block allocation list is not on the block allocation list in any other inode, that the size is correct, and that the link count is correct. If the inodes are correct, then the data is accessible. All that's left is to verify the pathnames.

What Is a Clean (Stable) File System?

Sometimes `fsck` responds

```
/opt: stable                    (ufs file systems)
```

This means that the superblock is marked clean and that no changes have been made to the file system since it was marked clean. First, the system marks the superblock as dirty; then it starts modifying the rest of the file system. When the buffer cache is empty and all pending writes are complete, it goes back and marks the superblock as clean. If the superblock is marked clean, there is normally no reason to run `fsck`, so unless `fsck` is told to ignore the `clean` flag, it just prints this notice and skips over this file system.

Where Is `fsck`?

When you run `fsck`, you are running an executable in either the `/usr/sbin` or `/bin` directory called `fsck`, but this is not the real `fsck`. It is just a dispatcher that invokes a file system type-specific `fsck` utility.

When Should I Run `fsck`?

Normally, you do not have to run `fsck`. The system runs it automatically when you try to mount a file system at boot time that is dirty. However, problems can creep up on you. Software and hardware glitches do occur from time to time. It wouldn't hurt to run `fsck` just after performing the monthly backups.

> **CAUTION**
>
> It is better to run `fsck` after the backups rather than before. If `fsck` finds major problems, it could leave the file system in worse shape than it was in prior to running. Then you can just build an empty file system and reread your backup, which also cleans up the file system. If you did it in the other order, you would be left with no backup and no file system.

How Do I Run `fsck`?

Because the system normally runs it for you, running `fsck` is not an everyday occurrence for you to remember. However, it is quite simple and mostly automatic.

First, to run `fsck`, the file system you intend to check must not be mounted. This is a bit hard to do if you are in multiuser mode most of the time, so to run a full system `fsck` you should bring the system down to single-user mode.

In single-user mode you need to invoke `fsck`, giving it the options to force a check of all file systems, even if they are already stable.

```
fsck -f              (SunOS)
fsck -o f            (Solaris)
fsck                 (Linux and IRIX)
```

If you wish to check a single specific file system, type its character device name. (If you aren't sure what the device name is, see the section on adding a disk to the system for details on how to determine this information.) For example,

```
fsck /dev/hda1
```

Stepping Through an Actual `fsck`

`fsck` occurs in five to seven steps, depending on your operating system and what errors are found, if any. `fsck` can automatically correct most of these errors and does so if invoked at boot time to automatically check a dirty file system.

The `fsck` we are about to step through was done on a `ufs` file system. While there are some differences between the numbering of the phases for different file systems, the errors are mostly the same, requiring the same solutions. Apply common sense liberally to any invocation of `fsck` and you should be okay.

Checking `ufs` File Systems

For `ufs` file systems, `fsck` is a five-phase process. `fsck` can automatically correct most of these errors and does so if invoked at boot time to automatically check a dirty file system. However, when you run `fsck` manually, you are asked to answer the questions that the system would automatically answer.

> **CAUTION**
>
> Serious errors reported by the ufs `fsck` at the very beginning, especially before reporting the start of phase 1, indicate an invalid superblock. `fsck` should be terminated and restarted with the `-b` option specifying one of the alternate superblocks. Block 32 is always an alternate and can be tried first, but if the front of the file system was overwritten, it too may be damaged. Use the hard copy you saved from the `mkfs` to find an alternate later in the file system.

Phase 1: Check Blocks and Sizes

This phase checks the inode list, looking for invalid inode entries. Errors requiring answers include

```
UNKNOWN FILE TYPE I=inode number (CLEAR)
```

The file-type bits are invalid in the inode. Options are to leave the problem and attempt to recover the data by hand later or to erase the entry and its data by clearing the inode.

```
PARTIALLY TRUNCATED INODE I=inode number (SALVAGE)
```

The inode appears to point to less data than the file does. This is safely salvaged, because it indicates a crash while truncating the file to shorten it.

```
block BAD I=inode number
block DUP I=inode number
```

The disk block pointed to by the inode is either out of range for this inode or already in use by another file. This is an informational message. If a duplicate block is found, phase 1b is run to report the inode number of the file that originally used this block.

Phase 2: Check Pathnames

This phase removes directory entries from bad inodes found in phase 1 and 1b and checks for directories with inode pointers that are out of range or pointing to bad inodes. You may have to handle

```
ROOT INODE NOT DIRECTORY (FIX?)
```

You can convert inode 2, the root directory, back into a directory, but this usually means there is major damage to the inode table.

```
I=OUT OF RANGE I=inode number NAME=file name (REMOVE?)
UNALLOCATED I=inode number OWNER=O MODE=M SIZE=S MTIME=T TYPE=F
(REMOVE?)
BAD/DUP I=inode number OWNER=O MODE=M SIZE=S MTIME=T TYPE=F (REMOVE?)
```

A bad inode number was found, an unallocated inode was used in a directory, or an inode that had a bad or duplicate block number in it was referenced. You are given the choice between removing the file, losing the data, or leaving the error. If you leave the error, the file system is still damaged, but you have the chance to try to dump the file first and salvage part of the data before rerunning fsck to remove the entry.

fsck may return one of a variety of errors indicating an invalid directory length. You will be given the chance to have fsck fix or remove the directory as appropriate. These errors are all correctable with little chance of subsequent damage.

Phase 3: Check Connectivity

This phase detects errors in unreferenced directories. It creates or expands the lost+found directory if needed and connects the misplaced directory entries into the lost+found directory. fsck prints status messages for all directories placed in lost+found.

Phase 4: Check Reference Counts

This phase uses the information from phases 2 and 3 to check for unreferenced files and incorrect link counts on files, directories, or special files.

```
UNREF FILE I=inode number OWNER=O MODE=M SIZE=S MTIME=T (RECONNECT?)
```

The filename is not known (it is an unreferenced file), so it is reconnected into the lost+found directory with the inode number as its name. If you clear the file, its contents are lost. Unreferenced files that are empty are cleared automatically.

```
LINK COUNT FILE I=inode number OWNER=O MODE=M SIZE=S MTIME=T COUNT=X
(ADJUST?)

LINK COUNT DIR I=inode number OWNER=O MODE=M SIZE=S MTIME=T COUNT=X
(ADJUST?)
```

In both cases, an entry was found with a different number of references than what was listed in the inode. You should let fsck adjust the count.

```
BAD/DUP FILE I=inode number OWNER=O MODE=M SIZE=S MTIME=T (CLEAR)
```

A file or directory has a bad or duplicate block in it. If you clear it now, the data is lost. You can leave the error and attempt to recover the data, and rerun fsck later to clear the file.

Phase 5: Check Cylinder Groups

This phase checks the free block and unused inode maps. It automatically corrects the free lists if necessary, although in manual mode it asks permission first.

What Do I Do After `fsck` Finishes?

First, relax, because `fsck` rarely finds anything seriously wrong, except in cases of hardware failure where the disk drive is failing or where you copied something on top of the file system. UNIX file systems are very robust.

However, if `fsck` finds major problems or makes a large number of corrections, rerun it to be sure the disk isn't undergoing hardware failure. It shouldn't find more errors in a second run. Then, recover any files that it may have deleted. If you keep a log of the inodes it clears, you can go to a backup tape and dump the list of inodes on the tape. Recover just those inodes to restore the files.

Back up the system again, because there is no reason to have to do this all over again.

Dealing with What Is in `lost+found`

If `fsck` reconnects unreferenced entries, it places them in the `lost+found` directory. They are safe there, and the system should be backed up in case you lose them while trying to move them back to where they belong. Items in `lost+found` can be of any type: files, directories, special files (devices), and so on. If it is a named pipe or socket, you may as well delete it. The process which opened it is long since gone and will open a new one when it is run again.

For files, use the owner name to contact the user and have him look at the contents and see if the file is worth keeping. Often, it is a file that was deleted and is no longer needed, but the system crashed before it could be fully removed.

For directories, the files in the directory should help you and the owner determine where they belong. You can look on the backup tape lists for a directory with those contents if necessary. Then just remake the directory and move the files back. Then remove the directory entry in `lost+found`. This re-creation and move has the added benefit of cleaning up the directory.

Creating File Systems

Now that you understand the nuances of maintaining a file system, it's time to understand how they are created. This section walks you through the three steps of

- Picking the right kind of disk for your system
- Creating partitions
- Creating the file system

Disk Types

Although there are many different kinds of disks, UNIX systems have come to standardize on SCSI for workstations. Many PCs also sport SCSI interfaces, but because of the lower cost and abundance, you'll find a lot of IDE drives on UNIX PCs as well.

SCSI itself comes in a few different flavors now. There are regular SCSI, SCSI-2, SCSI-Wide, SCSI-Fast and Wide, and now SCSI-3. Although it is possible to mix and match these devices with converter cables, you may find it easier on both your sanity and your performance if you stick to one format. As of this writing, SCSI-2 is the most common interface.

When attaching your SCSI drive, there are many important points to remember:

- Terminate your SCSI chain. Forgetting to do this causes all sorts of non-deterministic behavior (a pain to track down). SCSI-2 requires active termination, which is usually indicated by terminators with LEDs on them.

  If a device claims to be self-terminating, you can take your chances, but you'll be less likely to encounter an error if you put a terminator on anyway.

- There is a limit of eight devices on a SCSI chain with the SCSI card counting as a device. Some systems may have internal SCSI devices, so be sure to check for those.

- Be sure all your devices have unique SCSI IDs. A common symptom of having two devices with the same ID is their tendency to frequently reset the SCSI chain. Of course, many devices simply won't work under those conditions.

- When adding or removing a SCSI disk, be sure to power the system down first. There is power running through the SCSI cables, and failing to shut them down first may lead to problems in the future.

Although SCSI is king of the workstation, PCs have another choice: IDE. IDE tends to be cheaper and more available than SCSI devices with many motherboards offering direct IDE support. The advantage of using this kind of interface is its availability as well as lower cost. It is also simpler and requires less configuration on your part.

The down side to IDEs is that their simplicity comes at the cost of configurability and expandability. The IDE chain can hold only two devices, and not all motherboards come with more than one IDE chain. If your CD-ROM is IDE, you have space for only one disk. This is probably okay with a single-person workstation, but as you can imagine, it's not going to fly well in a server environment. Another consideration is speed. SCSI was designed with the ability to perform I/O without the aid of the main CPU, which is one of the reasons it costs more. IDE, on the other hand, was designed with cost in mind. This resulted in a simplified controller; hence, the CPU takes the burden for working the drive.

While IDE did manage to simplify the PC arena, it did come with the limitation of being unable to handle disks greater than 540 MB. Various tricks were devised to circumvent this; however, the clean solution is now predominantly available. Known as EIDE (Enhanced IDE), it is capable of supporting disks up to 8 GB and can support up to four devices on one chain.

In weighing the pros and cons of EIDE versus SCSI in the PC environment, don't forget to think about the cost-to-benefit ratio. Having a high speed SCSI controller in a single-person workstation may not be as necessary as the user is convinced it is. Plus, with disks being released in 2+ gigabyte configurations, there is ample room on the typical IDE disk.

Once you have decided on the disk subsystem to install, read the documentation that came with the machine for instructions on physically attaching the disk to the system.

What Are Partitions and Why Do I Need Them?

Partitions are UNIX's way of dividing the disk into usable pieces. UNIX requires that there be at least one partition; however, you'll find that creating multiple partitions, each with a specific function, is often necessary.

The most visible reason for creating separate partitions is to protect the system from the users. The one required partition mentioned earlier is called the root partition. It is here that critical system software and configuration files (the kernel and mount tables) must reside. This partition must be carefully watched so that it never fills up. If it fills up, your system may not be able to come back up in the event of a system crash. Because the root partition is not meant to hold the users' data, you must create separate partitions for the users' home directories, temporarily files, and so forth. This enables their files to grow without the worry of crowding out the key system files.

Dual boot configurations are becoming another common reason to partition, especially with the ever-growing popularity of Linux. You may find your users wanting to be able to boot to either Windows or Linux; therefore, you need to keep at least two partitions to enable them to do this.

The last, but certainly not least, reason to partition your disks is the issue of backups. Backup software often works by dumping entire partitions onto tape. By keeping the different types of data on separate partitions, you can be explicit about what gets backed up and what doesn't. For example, daily backup of the system software isn't necessary, but backups of home directories are. By keeping the two on separate partitions, you can be more concise in your selection of what gets backed up and what doesn't.

Another example relates more to company politics. It may be possible that one group does not want their data to be backed up to the same tape as another group's. (Note: Common sense doesn't always apply to intergroup politics...) By keeping the two groups on separate partitions, you can exclude one from your normal backups and exclude the others during your special backups.

Which Partitions To Create

As I mentioned earlier, the purpose of creating partitions is to separate the users from the system areas. So, how many different partitions need to be created? While there is no right answer for every installation, here are some guidelines to take into account.

You always need a root partition. In this partition, you'll have your `/bin`, `/etc`, and `/sbin` directories at the very least. Depending on your version of UNIX, this could require anywhere from 30 to 100 megabytes.

/tmp

The /tmp directory is where your users, as well as programs, store temporarily files. The usage of this directory can quickly get out of hand, especially if you run a quota-based site. By keeping it a separate partition, you do not need to worry about its abuse interfering with the rest of the system. Many operating systems automatically clear the contents of /tmp on boot. Size /tmp to fit your site's needs. If you use quotas, you will want to make it a little larger, whereas sites without quotas may not need as much space.

Under Solaris, you have another option when setting up /tmp. Using the tmpfs file system, you can have your swap space and /tmp partition share the same physical location on disk. While it appears to be an interesting idea, you'll quickly find that it isn't a very good solution, especially on a busy system. This is because as more users do their work, more of /tmp will be used. Of course, if there are more users, there is a greater memory requirement to hold them all. The competition for free space can become very problematic.

/var

The /var directory is where the system places its spool files (print spool, incoming/outgoing mail queue, and so on) as well as system log files. Because of this, these files constantly grow and shrink with no warning—especially the mail spool. Another possibility to keep in mind is the creation of a separate partition just for mail. This enables you to export the mail spool to all of your machines without having to worry about your print spools being exported as well. If you use a backup package that requires its own spool space, you may wish to keep this a separate partition as well.

/home

The /home directory is where you place your users' account directories. You may need to use multiple partitions to keep your home directories (possibly broken down by department) and have each partition mount to /home/*dept* where *dept* is the name of the respective department.

/usr The /usr directory holds noncritical system software, such as editors and lesser-used utilities. Many sites hold locally compiled software in the /usr/local directory where they either export it to other machines, or mount other machines' /usr/local to their own. This makes it easy for a site to maintain one /usr/local directory and share it amongst all of its machines. Keeping this a separate partition is a good idea since local software inevitably grows.

TIP

Several new versions of UNIX are now placing locally compiled software in the /opt directory. Like /usr/local, this should be made a separate partition as well. If your system does not use /opt by default, you should make a symbolic link from there to /usr/local. The vice versa is true as well: If your system uses /opt, you should create a symbolic link from /usr/local to /opt.

To add to the confusion, the Red Hat Distribution of Linux has brought the practice of installing precompiled software (RPMs) in the /usr/bin directory. If you are using Red Hat, you may want to make your /usr directory larger since locally installed packages will consume that partition.

swap This isn't a partition you actually keep files on, but it is key to your system's performance. The swap partition should be allocated and swapped to instead of using swap files on your normal file system. This enables you to contain all of your swap space in one area that is out of your way. A good guideline for determining how much swap space to use is to double the amount of RAM installed on your system.

The Device Entry

Most implementations of UNIX automatically create the correct device entry when you boot it with the new drive attached. Once this entry has been created, you should check it for permissions. Only root should be given read/write access to it. If your backups run as a nonroot user, you may need to give group read access to the backup group. Be sure that no one else is in the backup group. Allowing world read/write access to the disk is the easiest way to have your system hacked, destroyed, or both.

Device Entries under Linux

IDE disks under Linux use the following scheme to name the hard disks:

```
/dev/hd[drive][partition]
```

Each IDE drive is lettered starting from a. So, the primary disk on the first chain is a; the slave on the first chain is b; the primary on the secondary chain is c; and so on. Each disk's partition is referenced by number. For example, the third partition of the slave drive on the first chain is /dev/hdb3.

SCSI disks use the same scheme except instead of using /dev/hd as the prefix, /dev/sd is used. So to refer to the second partition of the first disk on the SCSI chain, you would use /dev/sda2.

To refer to the entire disk, specify all the information except the partition. For example, to refer to the entire primary disk on the first IDE chain, you would use /dev/hda.

Device Entries under IRIX

SCSI disks under IRIX are referenced in either the /dev/dsk or /dev/rdsk directories. The following is the format

```
/dev/[r]dsk/dksCdSP
```

where C is the controller number, S is the SCSI address, and P is the partition, s0,s1,s2, and so on. The partition name can also be vh for the volume header or vol to refer to the entire disk.

Device Entries under Solaris

The SCSI disks under Solaris are referenced in either the /dev/dsk or /dev/rdsk directories. The following is the format

```
/dev/[r]dsk/cCtSd0sP
```

where C is the controller number, S is the SCSI address, and P is the partition number. Partition 2 always refers to the entire disk and label information. Partition 1 is typically used for swap.

Device Entries under SunOS

Disks under SunOS are referenced in the /dev directory. The following is the format

```
/dev/sdTP
```

where T is the target number and P is the partition. Typically, the root partition is a, the swap partition is b, and the entire disk is referred to as partition c. You can have partitions from a through f.

An important aspect to note is an oddity with the SCSI target and unit numbering: Devices that are target three need to be called target zero, and devices that are target zero need to be called target three.

A Note About Formatting Disks

"Back in the old days," disks needed to be formatted and checked for bad blocks. The procedure of formatting entailed writing the head, track, and sector numbers in a sector preamble and a checksum in the postamble to every sector on the disk. At the same time, any sectors that were unusable due to flaws in the disk surface were marked and, depending on the type of disk, an alternate sector mapped into its place.

Thankfully, we have moved on.

Both SCSI and IDE disks now come pre-formatted from the factory. Even better, they transparently handle bad blocks on the disk and remap them without any assistance from the operating system.

> **WARNING**
>
> You should NEVER attempt to low-level-format an IDE disk.
>
> Doing so will make your day very bad as you watch the drive quietly kill itself. Be prepared to throw the disk away should you feel the need to low-level-format it.

Partitioning Disks and Creating File Systems

In this section, we will cover the step-by-step procedure for partitioning disks under Linux, IRIX, SunOS, and Solaris. Since the principles are similar across all platforms, each platform will also cover another method of determining how a disk should be partitioned up depending on its intended usage.

Linux

To demonstrate how partitions are created under Linux, we will setup a disk with a single user workstation in mind. It will need not only space for system software, but for application software and the user's home directories.

Creating Partitions

For this example, we'll create the partitions on a 1.6 GB IDE disk located on /dev/hda. This disk will become the boot device for a single user workstation. We will create the boot /usr, /var, /tmp, /home, and swap partitions.

During the actual partitioning, we don't name the partitions. Where the partitions are mounted is specified with the /etc/fstab file. Should we choose to mount them in different locations later on, we could very well do that. However, by keeping the function of each partition in mind, we have a better idea of how to size them.

A key thing to remember with the Linux fdisk command is that it does not commit any changes made to the partition table to disk until you explicitly do so with the w command.

18

FILE SYSTEM AND DISK ADMINISTRATION

LINUX

With the drive installed, we begin by running the `fdisk` command:

```
# fdisk /dev/hda
```

This brings us to the `fdisk` command prompt. We start by using the `p` command to print what partitions are currently on the disk.

```
Command (m for help): p

Disk /dev/hda: 64 heads, 63 sectors, 786 cylinders
Units = cylinders of 4032 * 512 bytes

   Device Boot  Begin   Start     End  Blocks   Id  System

Command (m for help):
```

We see that there are no partitions on the disk. With 1.6 GB of space, we can be very liberal with allocating space to each partition. Keeping this policy in mind, we begin creating our partitions with the `n` command:

```
Command (m for help): n
   e   extended
   p   primary partition (1-4)
p
Partition number (1-4): 1
First cylinder (1-786): 1
Last cylinder or +size or +sizeM or +sizeK ([1]-786): +50M
Command (m for help):
```

The 50 MB partition we just created becomes our root partition. Because it is the first partition, it is referred to as `/dev/hda1`. Using the `p` command, we see our new partition:

```
Command (m for help): p

Disk /dev/hda: 64 heads, 63 sectors, 786 cylinders
Units = cylinders of 4032 * 512 bytes

   Device Boot  Begin   Start     End  Blocks   Id  System
/dev/hda1           1       1      26   52384+  83  Linux native  ·

Command (m for help):
```

With the root partition out of the way, we will create the swap partition. Our sample machine has 32 MB of RAM and will be running X Window along with a host of development tools. It is unlikely that the machine will get a memory upgrade for a while, so we'll allocate 64 MB to swap.

```
Command (m for help): n
Command action
   e   extended
   p   primary partition (1-4)
p
Partition number (1-4): 2
First cylinder (27-786): 27
Last cylinder or +size or +sizeM or +sizeK ([27]-786): +64M

Command (m for help):
```

Because this partition is going to be tagged as swap, we need to change its file system type to swap using the t command.

```
Command (m for help): t
Partition number (1-4): 2
Hex code (type L to list codes): 82
Changed system type of partition 2 to 82 (Linux swap)

Command (m for help):
```

Because of the natt™µ of the user, we know that there will be a lot of local software installed on this machine. With that in mind, we'll create /usr with 500 MB of space.

```
Command (m for help): n
Command action
   e   extended
   p   primary partition (1-4)
p
Partition number (1-4): 3
First cylinder (60-786): 60
Last cylinder or +size or +sizeM or +sizeK ([60]-786): +500M
```

If you've been keeping your eyes open, you've noticed that we can have only one more primary partition to use, but we want to have /home, /var, and /tmp to be in separate partitions. How do we do this?

Create extended partitions.

The remainder of the disk is created as an extended partition. Within this partition, we can create more partitions for use. Let's create this extended partition:

```
Command (m for help): n
Command action
   e   extended
   p   primary partition (1-4)
e
Partition number (1-4): 4
First cylinder (314-786): 314
Last cylinder or +size or +sizeM or +sizeK ([314]-786): 786

Command (m for help):
```

We can now create /home inside the extended partition. Our user is going to need a lot of space, so we'll create a 500 MB partition. Notice that we are no longer asked whether we want a primary or extended partition.

```
Command (m for help): n
First cylinder (314-786): 314
Last cylinder or +size or +sizeM or +sizeK ([314]-786): +500M

Command (m for help):
```

Using the same pattern, we create a 250 MB /tmp and a 180 MB /var partition.

```
Command (m for help): n
First cylinder (568-786): 568
Last cylinder or +size or +sizeM or +sizeK ([568]-786): +250M
```

```
Command (m for help): n
First cylinder (695-786): 695
Last cylinder or +size or +sizeM or +sizeK ([695]-786): 786

Command (m for help):
```

Notice on the last partition we created that I did not specify a size, but instead specified the last track. This is to ensure that all of the disk is used.

Using the p command, we look at our final work:

```
Command (m for help): p

Disk /dev/hda: 64 heads, 63 sectors, 786 cylinders
Units = cylinders of 4032 * 512 bytes

   Device Boot   Begin   Start    End  Blocks   Id  System
/dev/hda1            1       1     26   52384+   83  Linux native
/dev/hda2           27      27     59   66528    82  Linux swap
/dev/hda3           60      60    313  512064    83  Linux native
/dev/hda4          314     314    786  953568     5  Extended
/dev/hda5          314     314    567  512032+   83  Linux native
/dev/hda6          568     568    694  256000+   83  Linux native
/dev/hda7          695     695    786  185440+   83  Linux native

Command (m for help):
```

Everything looks good. To commit this configuration to disk, we use the w command:

```
Command (m for help): w
The partition table has been altered!

Calling ioctl() to re-read partition table.
(Reboot to ensure the partition table has been updated.)
Syncing disks.
```

Reboot the machine to ensure that the partition has been updated, and you're done creating the partitions.

Creating File Systems in Linux

Creating a partition alone isn't very useful. In order to make it useful, we need to make a file system on top of it. Under Linux, this is done using the mke2fs command and the mkswap command.

To create the file system on the root partition, we use the following commands:

```
mke2fs /dev/hda1
```

The program takes only a few seconds to run and generates output similar to this:

```
mke2fs 0.5b, 14-Feb-95 for EXT2 FS 0.5a, 95/03/19
128016 inodes, 512032 blocks
25601 blocks (5.00%) reserved for the super user
First data block=1
```

```
Block size=1024 (log=0)
Fragment size=1024 (log=0)
63 block groups
8192 blocks per group, 8192 fragments per group
2032 inodes per group
Superblock backups stored on blocks:
        8193,16385,24577,32769,40961,49153,57345,65537,73729,
        81921,90113,98305,106497,114689,122881,131073,139265,147457,
        155649,163841,172033,180225,188417,196609,204801,212993,221185,
        229377,237569,245761,253953,262145,270337,278529,286721,294913,
        303105,311297,319489,327681,335873,344065,352257,360449,368641,
        376833,385025,393217,401409,409601,417793,425985,434177,442369,
        450561,458753,466945,475137,483329,491521,499713,507905
```

```
    Writing inode tables: done
Writing superblocks and file system accounting information: done
```

You should make a note of these superblock backups and keep them in a safe place. Should the time come that you need to use fsck to fix a superblock gone bad, you will want to know where the backups are.

Simply do this for all of the partitions, except for the swap partition.

To create the swap file system, you need to use the mkswap command like this:

```
mkswap /dev/hda2
```

Replace /dev/hda2 with the partition you chose to make your swap space.

The result of the command will be similar to

```
Setting up swapspace, size = 35090432 bytes
```

Now the swap space is ready.

To make the root file system bootable, you need to install the lilo boot manager. This is part of all the standard Linux distributions, so you shouldn't need to hunt for it on the Internet.

Simply modify the /etc/lilo.conf file so that /dev/hda1 is set to be the boot disk and run

```
lilo
```

The resulting output should look something like

```
Added linux *
```

where linux is the name of the kernel to boot, as specified by the name= field in /etc/lilo.conf.

SunOS

In this example, we will be preparing a Seagate ST32550N as an auxiliary disk to an existing system. The disk will be divided into three partitions: one for use as a mail spool, one for use as a /usr/local, and the third as an additional swap partition.

Creating the Partitions

> **CAUTION**
>
> The procedure for formatting disks is not the same for SunOS and Solaris. Read each section to note the differences.

Once a disk has been attached to the machine, you should verify its connection and SCSI address by running the `probe-scsi` command from the PROM monitor if the disk is attached to the internal chain, or the `probe-scsi-all` command to see all the SCSI devices on the system. When you are sure the drive is properly attached and verified to be functioning, you're ready to start accessing the drive from the OS.

After the machine has booted, run the `dmesg` command to collect the system diagnostic messages. You may want to pipe the output to `grep` so that you can easily find the information on disks. For example,

```
dmesg ¦ grep sd
```

On our system, this generated the following output:

```
sd0: <SUN0207 cyl 1254 alt 2 hd 9 sec 36>
sd1 at esp0 target 1 lun 0
sd1:    corrupt label - wrong magic number
sd1: Vendor 'SEAGATE', product 'ST32550N', 4194058 512 byte blocks
root on sd0a fstype 4.2
swap on sd0b fstype spec size 32724K
dump on sd0b fstype spec size 32712K
```

This result tells us that we have an installed disk on `sd0` that the system is aware of and using. The information from the `sd1` device is telling us that it found a disk, but it isn't usable because of a corrupt label. Don't worry about the error. Until we partition the disk and create file systems on it, the system doesn't know what to do with it, hence the error.

If you are using SCSI address 0 or 3, remember the oddity we mentioned earlier where device 0 needs to be referenced as 3 and device 3 needs to be referenced as 0.

Even though we do not have to actually format the disk, we do need to use the format program that come with SunOS because it also creates the partitions and writes the label to the disk.

To invoke the format program, simply run

```
format sd1
```

where `sd1` is the name of the disk you are going to partition.

The format program displays the following menu:

```
FORMAT MENU:
        disk        - select a disk
        type        - select (define) a disk type
```

```
       partition  - select (define) a partition table
       current    - describe the current disk
       format     - format and analyze the disk
       repair     - repair a defective sector
       show       - translate a disk address
       label      - write label to the disk
       analyze    - surface analysis
       defect     - defect list management
       backup     - search for backup labels
       quit
format>
```

We need to enter **type** at the `format>` prompt so that we can tell SunOS the kind of disk we have. The resulting menu looks something like this:

```
AVAILABLE DRIVE TYPES:
        0. Quantum ProDrive 80S
        1. Quantum ProDrive 105S
        2. CDC Wren IV 94171-344
        3. SUN0104
    ...
   13. other
Specify disk type (enter its number):
```

Because we are adding a disk this machine has not seen before, we need to select option 13, `other`. This begins a series of prompts requesting the disk's geometry. Be sure to have this information from the manufacturer before starting this procedure.

The first question, `Enter number of data cylinders:` is actually a three-part question. After you enter the number of data cylinders, the program asks for the number of alternative cylinders and then the number of physical cylinders. The number of physical cylinders is the number your manufacturer provided you. Subtract two from there to get the number of data cylinders, and then just use the default value of 2 for the number of alternate cylinders. For our Seagate disk, we answered the questions as follows:

```
Enter number of data cylinders: 3508
        Enter number of alternate cylinders [2]: 2
        Enter number of physical cylinders [3510]: 3510
        Enter number of heads: 11
        Enter number of data sectors/track: 108
        Enter rpm of drive [3600]:
        Enter disk type name (remember quotes): "SEAGATE ST32550N"
        selecting sd1: <SEAGATE ST32550N>
        [disk formatted, no defect list found]
        No defined partition tables.
```

Note that even though our sample drive actually rotates at 7200 rpm, we stick with the default of 3600 rpm because the software will not accept entering a higher speed. Thankfully, this doesn't matter because the operating system doesn't use the information.

Even though `format` reported that the disk was formatted, it really wasn't. It acquired only information needed to later write the label.

Now we are ready to begin preparations to partition the disk.

These preparations entail computing the amount each cylinder holds and then approximating the number of cylinders we want in each partition.

With our sample disk, we know that each cylinder is composed of 108 sectors on a track, with 11 tracks composing the cylinder.

From the information we saw in `dmesg`, we know that each block is 512 bytes long. Hence, if we want our mail partition to be 1 GB in size, we perform the following math to compute the necessary blocks:

```
1 gigabyte = 1048576 kilobytes
   One cylinder = 108 sectors * 11 heads = 1188 blocks
   1188 blocks = 594 kilobytes
   1048576 / 594 = 1765 cylinders
   1765 * 1188 = 2096820 blocks
```

Obviously, there will be some rounding errors because the exact one GB mark occurs in the middle of a cylinder and we need to keep each partition on a cylinder boundary. 1,765 cylinders is more than close enough. The 1,765 cylinders translate to 2,096,820 blocks.

The new swap partition we want to make needs to be 64 MB in size. Using the same math as before, we find that our swap needs to be 130,680 blocks long. The last partition on the disk needs to fill the remainder of the disk. Knowing that we have a 2 GB disk, a 1 GB mail spool, and a 64 MB swap partition, this should leave us with about 960 MB for /usr/local.

Armed with this information, we are ready to tackle the partitioning. From the `format>` prompt, type **partition** to start the partitioning menu. The resulting screen looks something like this:

```
format> partition


PARTITION MENU:
        a      - change 'a' partition
        b      - change 'b' partition
        c      - change 'c' partition
        d      - change 'd' partition
        e      - change 'e' partition
        f      - change 'f' partition
        g      - change 'g' partition
        h      - change 'h' partition
        select - select a predefined table
        name   - name the current table
        print  - display the current table
        label  - write partition map and label to the disk
        quit
partition>
```

To create our `mail` partition, we begin by changing partition a. At the `partition>` prompt, type **a**.

```
partition> a
```

This brings up a prompt for entering the starting cylinder and the number of blocks to allocate. Because this is going to be the first partition on the disk, we start at cylinder 0. Based on the math we did earlier, we know that we need 2,096,820 blocks.

```
    partition a - starting cyl     0, # blocks      0 (0/0/0)

Enter new starting cyl [0]: 0
Enter new # blocks [0, 0/0/0]: 2096820
partition>
```

Now we want to create the b partition, which is traditionally used for swap space. We know how many blocks to use based on our calculations, but we don't know which cylinder to start from.

To solve this, we simply display the current partition information for the entire disk using the p command:

```
partition> p
Current partition table (unnamed):
        partition a - starting cyl     0, # blocks   2096820 (1765/0/0)
        partition b - starting cyl     0, # blocks         0 (0/0/0)
        partition c - starting cyl     0, # blocks         0 (0/0/0)
        partition d - starting cyl     0, # blocks         0 (0/0/0)
        partition e - starting cyl     0, # blocks         0 (0/0/0)
        partition f - starting cyl     0, # blocks         0 (0/0/0)
        partition g - starting cyl     0, # blocks         0 (0/0/0)
        partition h - starting cyl     0, # blocks         0 (0/0/0)

partition>
```

We can see that partition a is allocated with 2,096,820 blocks and is 1,765 cylinders long. Because we don't want to waste space on the disk, we start the swap partition on cylinder 1765.

(Remember to count from zero!)

```
partition> b

    partition b - starting cyl     0, # blocks      0 (0/0/0)

Enter new starting cyl [0]: 1765
Enter new # blocks [0, 0/0/0]: 130680
partition>
```

Before we create our last partition, we need to take care of some tradition first, namely partition c. This is usually the partition that spans the entire disk. Before creating this partition, we need to do a little math.

108 cylinders × 11 heads × 3508 data cylinders = 4167504 blocks

Notice that the number of blocks we computed here does not match the number actually on the disk. This number was computed based on the information we entered when giving the disk type information.

It is important that we remain consistent.

18

FILE SYSTEM
AND DISK
ADMINISTRATION

Because the c partition spans the entire disk, we specify the starting cylinder as 0. Creating this partition should look something like this:

```
partition> c

        partition c - starting cyl     0, # blocks      0 (0/0/0)

Enter new starting cyl [0]: 0
Enter new # blocks [0, 0/0/0]: 4167504
partition>
```

We have only one partition left to create: /usr/local. Because we want to fill the remainder of the disk, we need to do one last bit of math to compute how many blocks are still free.

This is done by taking the size of partition c (the total disk) and subtracting the sizes of the existing partitions. For our example, this works out to be

```
4167504 - 2096820 - 130680 = 1940004 remaining blocks
```

Now we need to find out which cylinder to start from.

To do so, we run the p command again:

```
partition> p
Current partition table (unnamed):
        partition a - starting cyl     0, # blocks 2096820 (1765/0/0)
        partition b - starting cyl  1765, # blocks  130680 (110/0/0)
        partition c - starting cyl     0, # blocks 4167504 (3508/0/0)
        partition d - starting cyl     0, # blocks       0 (0/0/0)
        partition e - starting cyl     0, # blocks       0 (0/0/0)
        partition f - starting cyl     0, # blocks       0 (0/0/0)
        partition g - starting cyl     0, # blocks       0 (0/0/0)
        partition h - starting cyl     0, # blocks       0 (0/0/0)

partition>
```

To figure out which cylinder to start from, we add the number of cylinders used so far. Remember not to add the cylinders from partition c since it encompasses the entire disk.

```
1765 + 110 = 1875
```

Now that we know which cylinder to start from and how many blocks to make it, we create our last partition:

```
partition> d

        partition d - starting cyl     0, # blocks      0 (0/0/0)

Enter new starting cyl [0]: 1875
Enter new # blocks [0, 0/0/0]: 1940004
partition>
```

Congratulations! You've made it through the ugly part. Before we can truly claim victory, we need to commit these changes to disk using the label command. When given the prompt, Ready to label disk, continue? simply answer y.

```
partition> label
Ready to label disk, continue? y

partition>
```

To leave the format program, type **quit** at the partition> prompt, and then **quit** again at the format> prompt.

Creating File Systems

Now comes the easy part. Simply run the newfs command on all the partitions we created except for the swap partition (b) and the entire disk partition (c). Your output should look similar to this:

```
# newfs sd1a
/dev/rsd1a:    2096820 sectors in 1765 cylinders of 11 tracks, 108 sectors
        1073.6MB in 111 cyl groups (16 c/g, 9.73MB/g, 4480 i/g)
superblock backups (for fsck -b #) at:
 32, 19152, 38272, 57392, 76512, 95632, 114752, 133872, 152992,
 172112, 191232, 210352, 229472, 248592, 267712, 286832, 304160, 323280,
 342400, 361520, 380640, 399760, 418880, 438000, 457120, 476240, 495360,
 514480, 533600, 552720, 571840, 590960, 608288, 627408, 646528, 665648,
 684768, 703888, 723008, 742128, 761248, 780368, 799488, 818608, 837728,
 856848, 875968, 895088, 912416, 931536, 950656, 969776, 988896, 1008016,
 1027136, 1046256, 1065376, 1084496, 1103616, 1122736, 1141856, 1160976, 1180096,
 1199216, 1216544, 1235664, 1254784, 1273904, 1293024, 1312144, 1331264, 1350384,
 1369504, 1388624, 1407744, 1426864, 1445984, 1465104, 1484224, 1503344, 1520672,
 1539792, 1558912, 1578032, 1597152, 1616272, 1635392, 1654512, 1673632, 1692752,
 1711872, 1730992, 1750112, 1769232, 1788352, 1807472, 1824800, 1843920, 1863040,
 1882160, 1901280, 1920400, 1939520, 1958640, 1977760, 1996880, 2016000, 2035120,
 2054240, 2073360, 2092480,
```

Be sure to note the superblock backups. This is critical information when fsck discovers heavy corruption in your file system. Remember to add your new entries into /etc/fstab if you want them to automatically mount on boot.

If you created the first partition with the intention of making it bootable, you have a few more steps to go. First, mount the new file system to /mnt:

```
# mount /dev/sd1a /mnt
```

Once the file system is mounted, you need to clone your existing boot partition using the dump command like this:

```
# cd /mnt
# dump 0f - / ¦ restore -rf -
```

With the root partition cloned, use the installboot command to make it bootable:

```
# /usr/kvm/mdec/installboot /mnt/boot /usr/kvm/mdec/bootsd /dev/rsd1a
```

Be sure to test your work by rebooting and making sure everything mounts correctly. If you created a bootable partition, be sure you can boot from it now. Don't wait for a disaster to find out whether or not you did it right.

18

FILE SYSTEM AND DISK ADMINISTRATION

Solaris

For this example, we are partitioning a disk that is destined to be a web server for an intranet. We need a minimal root partition, adequate swap, tmp, var, and usr space, and a really large partition, which we'll call /web. Because the web logs will remain on the /web partition, and there will be little or no user activity on the machine, /var and /tmp will be set to smaller values. /usr will be a little larger because it may be destined to house web development tools.

Creating Partitions

> **TIP**
>
> In another effort on its part to be just a little different, Sun has decided to call partitions "slices." With the number of documents regarding the file system so vast, you'll find that not all of them have been updated to use this new term, so don't be confused by the mix of "slices" with "partitions"—they are the same.

Once a disk has been attached to the machine, you should verify its connection and SCSI address by running the probe-scsi command from the PROM monitor if the disk is attached to the internal SCSI chain, probe-scsi-all to list all the SCSI devices on the system. Once this shows that the drive is properly attached and verified to be functioning, you're ready to start accessing the drive from the OS. Boot the machine and login as root.

In order to find the device name we are going to use for this, we again use the dmesg command:

```
# dmesg ¦ grep sd
  ...
  sd1 at esp0: target 1 lun 0
  sd1 is /sbus@1,f8000000/esp@0,800000/sd@1,0
  WARNING: /sbus@1,f8000000/esp@0,800000/sd@1,0 (sd1):
    corrupt label - wrong magic number
    Vendor 'SEAGATE', product 'ST32550N', 4194058 512 byte blocks
  ...
```

From this message, we see that our new disk is device /dev/[r]dsk/c0t1d0s2. The disk hasn't been set up for use on a Solaris machine before, which is why we received the corrupt label error.

If you recall the layout of Solaris device names, you'll remember that the last digit on the device name is the partition number. Noting that, we see that Solaris refers to the entire disk in partition 2, much the same way SunOS refers to the entire disk as partition c.

Before we can actually label and partition the disk, we need to create the device files. This is done with the drvconfig and disks commands. They should be invoked with no parameters:

```
# drvconfig ; disks
```

Now that the kernel is aware of the disk, we are ready to run the `format` command to partition the disk:

```
# format /dev/rdsk/c0t1d0s2
```

This brings up the format menu as follows:

```
FORMAT MENU:
        disk       - select a disk
        type       - select (define) a disk type
        partition  - select (define) a partition table
        current    - describe the current disk
        format     - format and analyze the disk
        repair     - repair a defective sector
        label      - write label to the disk
        analyze    - surface analysis
        defect     - defect list management
        backup     - search for backup labels
        verify     - read and display labels
        save       - save new disk/partition definitions
        inquiry    - show vendor, product and revision
        volname    - set 8-character volume name
        quit
format>
```

To help the `format` command with partitioning, we need to tell it the disk's geometry by invoking the `type` command at the `format>` prompt. We will then be asked to select what kind of disk we have. Because this is the first time this system is seeing this disk, we need to select `other`. This should look something like this:

```
format> type

AVAILABLE DRIVE TYPES:
        0. Auto configure
        1. Quantum ProDrive 80S
        2. Quantum ProDrive 105S
        3. CDC Wren IV 94171-344
        . . .
       16. other
Specify disk type (enter its number): 16
```

The system now prompts for the number of data cylinders. This is two less than the number of cylinders the vendor specifies because Solaris needs two cylinders for bad-block mapping.

```
Enter number of data cylinders: 3508
Enter number of alternate cylinders[2]: 2
Enter number of physical cylinders[3510]: 3510
```

The next question can be answered from the vendor specs as well:

```
Enter number of heads: 14
```

The followup question about drive heads can be left as default:

```
Enter physical number of heads[default]:
```

The next question you must answer can be pulled from the vendor specs as well:

```
Enter number of data sectors/track: 72
```

The remaining questions should be left as default.

```
Enter number of physical sectors/track[default]:
Enter rpm of drive[3600]:
Enter format time[default]:
Enter cylinder skew[default]:
Enter track skew[default]:
Enter tracks per zone[default]:
Enter alternate tracks[default]:
Enter alternate sectors[default]:
Enter cache control[default]:
Enter prefetch threshold[default]:
Enter minimum prefetch[default]:
Enter maximum prefetch[default]:
```

The last question you must answer about the disk is its label information. Enter the vendor name and model number in double quotes for this question. For our sample disk, this would be

```
Enter disk type name (remember quotes): "SEAGATE ST32550N"
```

With this information, Solaris makes creating partitions easy. Dare I say, fun?

After the last question from the `type` command, you will be placed at the `format>` prompt. Enter **partition** to start the partition menu:

```
format>  partition

PARTITION MENU:
        0       - change '0' partition
        1       - change '1' partition
        2       - change '2' partition
        3       - change '3' partition
        4       - change '4' partition
        5       - change '5' partition
        6       - change '6' partition
        7       - change '7' partition
        select - select a predefined table
        modify - modify a predefined partition table
        name   - name the current table
        print  - display the current table
        label  - write partition map and label to the disk
        quit
partition>
```

At the `partition>` prompt, enter **modify** to begin creating the new partitions. This brings up a question about what template to use for partitioning. We want the `All Free Hog` method.

```
partition> modify
Select partitioning base:
     0. Current partition table (unnamed)
     1. All Free Hog
Choose base (enter number)[0]? 1
```

The `All Free Hog` method enables you to select one partition to receive the remainder of the disk once you have allocated a specific amount of space for the other partitions. For our example, the disk hog would be the `/web` partition because you want it to be as large as possible.

As soon as you select option 1, you should see the following screen:

```
Part    Tag      Flag    Cylinders    Size     Blocks
 0    root       wm      0            0      (0/0/0)
 1    swap       wu      0            0      (0/0/0)
 2    backup     wu      0 - 3507   1.99GB   (3508/0/0)
 3    unassigned wm      0            0      (0/0/0)
 4    unassigned wm      0            0      (0/0/0)
 5    unassigned wm      0            0      (0/0/0)
 6    usr        wm      0            0      (0/0/0)
 7    unassigned wm      0            0      (0/0/0)
Do you wish to continue creating a new partition
table based on above table [yes]? yes
```

Because the partition table appears reasonable, agree to use it as a base for your scheme. You will now be asked which partition should be the `Free Hog Partition`, the one that receives whatever is left of the disk when everything else has been allocated.

For our scheme, we'll make that partition number 5:

```
Free Hog Partition[6]? 5
```

Answering this question starts the list of questions asking how large to make the other partitions. For our web server, we need a root partition to be about 200 MB for the system software, a swap partition to be 64 MB, a `/tmp` partition to be 200 MB, a `/var` partition to be 200 MB, and a `/usr` partition to be 400 MB. Keeping in mind that partition 2 has already been tagged as the "entire disk" and that partition 5 will receive the remainder of the disk, you will be prompted as follows:

```
Enter size of partition '0' [0b, 0c, 0.00mb]: 200mb
Enter size of partition '1' [0b, 0c, 0.00mb]: 64mb
Enter size of partition '3' [0b, 0c, 0.00mb]: 200mb
Enter size of partition '4' [0b, 0c, 0.00mb]: 200mb
Enter size of partition '6' [0b, 0c, 0.00mb]: 400mb
Enter size of partition '7' [0b, 0c, 0.00mb]: 0
```

As soon as you finish answering these questions, the final view of all the partitions appears looking something like

```
Part    Tag      Flag    Cylinders     Size       Blocks
 0    root       wm      0 - 344     200.13mb   (345/0/0)
 1    swap       wu      345 - 455   64.39mb    (111/0/0)
 2    backup     wu      0 - 3507    1.99GB     (3508/0/0)
 3    unassigned wm      456 - 800   200.13mb   (345/0/0)
 4    unassigned wm      801 - 1145  200.13mb   (345/0/0)
 5    unassigned wm      1146 - 2817 969.89mb   (1672/0/0)
 6    unassigned wm      2818 - 3507 400.25mb   (690/0/0)
 7    unassigned wm      0            0         (0/0/0)
```

This is followed by the question

```
Okay to make this the correct partition table [yes]? yes
```

Answer **yes** since the table appears reasonable. This brings up the question

```
Enter table name (remember quotes): "SEAGATE ST32550N"
```

Answer with a description of the disk you are using for this example. Remember to include the quote symbols when answering. Given all of this information, the system is ready to commit this to disk. As one last check, you will be asked

```
Ready to label disk, continue? y
```

As you might imagine, we answer yes to the question and let it commit the changes to disk. You have now created partitions and can quit the program by entering **quit** at the `partition>` prompt and again at the `format>` prompt.

Creating File Systems

To create a file system, simply run

```
# newfs /dev/c0t1d0s0
```

where `/dev/c0t1d0s0` is the partition on which to create the file system. Be sure to create a file system on all the partitions except for partitions 2 and 3, the swap, and entire disk, respectively. Be sure to note the backup superblocks that were created. This information is very useful when `fsck` is attempting to repair a heavily damaged file system.

After you create the file systems, be sure to enter them into the `/etc/vfstab` file so that they are mounted the next time you reboot.

If you need to make the root partition bootable, you still have two more steps. The first is to clone the root partition from your existing system to the new root partition using

```
# mount /dev/dsk/c0t1d0s0 /mnt
# ufsdump 0uf - / ¦ ufsrestore -rf -
```

Once the file root partition is cloned, you can run the `installboot` program like this:

```
# /usr/sbin/installboot /usr/lib/fs/ufs/bootblk /dev/rdsk/c0t1d0s0
```

Be sure to test your new file systems before you need to rely on them in a disaster situation.

IRIX

For this example, we are creating a large scratch partition for a user who does modeling and simulations. Although IRIX has many GUI-based tools to perform these tasks, it is always a good idea to learn the command-line versions just in case you need to do any kind of remote administration.

Creating Partitions

Once the drive is attached, run a program called `hinv` to take a "hardware inventory." On the sample system, you saw the following output:

```
...
Integral SCSI controller 1: Version WD33C93B, revision D
  Disk drive: unit 6 on SCSI controller 1
Integral SCSI controller 0: Version WD33C93B, revision D
  Disk drive: unit 1 on SCSI controller 0
...
```

Our new disk is external to the system, so we know it is residing on controller 1. Unit 6 is the only disk on that chain, so we know that it is the disk we just added to the system.

To partition the disk, run the `fx` command without any parameters. It prompts us for the device name, controller, and drive number. Choose the default device name and enter the appropriate information for the other two questions.

On our sample system, this would look like:

```
# fx
fx version 6.2, Mar  9, 1996
fx: "device-name" = (dksc)
fx: ctlr# = (0) 1
fx: drive# = (1) 6
fx: lun# = (0)
...opening dksc(1,6,0)
...controller test...OK
Scsi drive type == SEAGATE ST32550N        0022

----- please choose one (? for help, .. to quit this menu)-----
[exi]t              [d]ebug/            [l]abel/
[b]adblock/         [exe]rcise/         [r]epartition/
fx>
```

We see that `fx` found our Seagate and is ready to work with it. From the menu we select **r** to repartition the disk. `fx` displays what it knows about the disk and then presents another menu specifically for partitioning the disk.

```
fx> r
----- partitions-----
part  type      cyls          blocks           Megabytes   (base+size)
  7:  xfs       3 + 3521      3570 + 4189990    2 + 2046
  8:  volhdr    0 + 3         0 + 3570          0 + 2
 10:  volume    0 + 3524      0 + 4193560       0 + 2048

capacity is 4194058 blocks

----- please choose one (? for help, .. to quit this menu)-----
[ro]otdrive         [u]srrootdrive      [o]ptiondrive      [re]size
fx/repartition>
```

Looking at the result, we see that this disk has never been partitioned in IRIX before. Part 7 represents the amount of partitionable space, part 8 the volume header, and part 10 the entire disk.

Because this disk is going to be used as a large scratch partition, we want to select the `optiondrive` option from the menu. After you select that, you are asked what kind of file system you want to use. IRIX 6 and above defaults to `xfs`, while IRIX 5 defaults to `efs`. Use the one appropriate for your version of IRIX.

Our sample system is running IRIX 6.3, so we accept the default of `xfs`:

```
fx/repartition> o

fx/repartition/optiondrive: type of data partition = (xfs)
```

Next we are asked whether we want to create a /usr log partition. Because our primary system already has a /usr partition, we don't need one here. Type **no**.

```
fx/repartition/optiondrive: create usr log partition? = (yes) no
```

The system is ready to partition the drive. Before it does, it gives one last warning allowing you to stop the partitioning before it completes the job. `Warning: you must reinstall all soft-ware and restore user data from backups after changing the partition layout. Changing partitions causes all data on the drive to be lost. Be sure you have the drive backed up if it contains any user data. Continue?` **y** Because you know you are partitioning the correct disk, you can give it "the go-ahead."

The system takes a few seconds to create the new partitions on the disk. Once it is done, it reports what the current partition list looks like:

```
----- partitions-----
part  type        cyls          blocks            Megabytes    (base+size)
  7: xfs        3 + 3521     3570 + 4189990       2 + 2046
  8: volhdr     0 + 3           0 + 3570          0 + 2
 10: volume     0 + 3524        0 + 4193560       0 + 2048

capacity is 4194058 blocks

----- please choose one (? for help, .. to quit this menu)-----
[ro]otdrive        [u]srrootdrive     [o]ptiondrive       [re]size
fx/repartition>
```

Looks good. We can exit `fx` now by typing `..` at the `fx/repartition>` prompt and **exit** at the `fx>` prompt.

Our one large scratch partition is now called `/dev/dsk/dks1d6s7`.

Creating the File System

To create the file system, we use the `mkfs` command like this:

```
# mkfs /dev/rdsk/dks1d6s7
```

This generates the following output:

```
meta-data=/dev/dsk/dks1d6s7    isize=256    agcount=8, agsize=65469 blks
data     =                     bsize=4096   blocks=523748, imaxpct=25
log      =internal log         bsize=4096   blocks=1000
realtime =none                 bsize=65536  blocks=0, rtextents=0
```

Remember to add this entry into the `/etc/fstab` file so that the system automatically mounts the next time you reboot.

Summary

As you've seen in this chapter, creating, maintaining, and repairing filesystems are not trivial tasks. They are, however, tasks which should be well understood. An unmaintained file system can quickly lead to trouble and without its stability, the remainder of the system is useless.

Let's make a quick rundown of the topics we covered:

- Disks are broken into partitions (sometimes called slices).
- Each partition has a file system.
- A file system is the primary means of file storage in UNIX.
- File systems are made of inodes and superblocks.
- Some partitions are used for raw data such as swap.
- The `/proc` file system really isn't a file system, but an abstraction to kernel data.
- An inode maintains critical file information.
- Superblocks track disk information as well as the location of the heads of various inode lists.
- In order for you to use a file system, it must be mounted.
- No one must be accessing a file system in order for it to be unmounted.
- File systems can be mounted anywhere in the directory tree.
- `/etc/fstab` (`vfstab` in Solaris) is used to by the system to automatically mount file systems on boot.
- The root file system should be kept away from users.
- The root file system should never get filled.
- Be sure to watch how much space is being used.
- `fsck` is the tool to use to repair file systems.
- Don't forget to terminate your SCSI chain!

In short, file systems administration is not a trivial task and should not be taken lightly. Good maintenance techniques not only help maintain your uptime, but your sanity as well.

Kernel Configuration

by Dan Wilson, Bill Pierce, and Bill Wood

IN THIS CHAPTER

You're probably asking yourself, "Why would I want to know about this thing called the UNIX kernel?" I can add users, run jobs, print files, perform backups and restores, and even start up and shut down the machine when it needs it. Why do I need to know about, and, more specifically, even change my system's configuration to do my job as a systems administrator?" The simple answer is, you don't need to know much about the UNIX kernel if you know you'll *never* have to add any hardware or change or tune your system to perform better. In all of our collective years of experience as systems administrators, we have rarely, if ever, experienced a situation where it was possible or desirable to operate an *Original Equipment Manufacturer* (OEM)-configured UNIX system. There are just too many different uses for this type of operating system for it to remain unchanged throughout its lifetime. So, assuming you are one of the fortunate individuals who has the title of system administrator, we'll try to provide you with some useful and general information about this all-powerful UNIX process called the kernel. After that, we'll take you through some sample configurations for the following UNIX operating systems:

> HP-UX 10.x
>
> Solaris 2.5
>
> System V Release 4 (SVR4)
>
> AIX
>
> Linux

What Is a Kernel?

Let's start by providing a definition for the term *kernel*. The UNIX kernel is the software that manages the user program's access to the systems hardware and software resources. These resources range from being granted CPU time, accessing memory, reading and writing to the disk drives, connecting to the network, and interacting with the terminal or GUI interface. The kernel makes this all possible by controlling and providing access to memory, processor, input/output devices, disk files, and special services to user programs.

Kernel Services

The basic UNIX kernel can be broken into four main subsystems:

> Process Management
>
> Memory Management
>
> I/O Management
>
> File Management

These subsystems should be viewed as separate entities that work in concert to provide services to a program that enable it to do meaningful work. These management subsystems make it possible for a user to access a database via a Web interface, print a report, or do something as complex as managing a 911 emergency system. At any moment in the system, numerous programs may request services from these subsystems. It is the kernel's responsibility to schedule work and, if the process is authorized, grant access to utilize these subsystems. In short, programs interact with the subsystems via software libraries and the systems call interface. Refer to your UNIX reference manuals for descriptions of the systems calls and libraries supported by your system. Because each of the subsystems is key to enabling a process to perform a useful function, we will cover the basics of each subsystem. We'll start by looking at how the UNIX kernel comes to life by way of the system initialization process.

System Initialization

System initialization (booting) is the first step toward bringing your system into an operational state. A number of machine-dependent and machine-independent steps are gone through before your system is ready to begin servicing users. At system startup, there is nothing running on the Central Processing Unit (CPU). The kernel is a complex program that must have its binary image loaded at a specific address from some type of storage device, usually a disk drive. The boot disk maintains a small restricted area called the boot sector that contains a boot program that loads and initializes the kernel. You'll find that this is a vendor-specific procedure that reflects the architectural hardware differences between the various UNIX vendor platforms. When this step is completed, the CPU must jump to a specific memory address and start executing the code at that location. Once the kernel is loaded, it goes through its own hardware and software initialization.

Kernel Mode

The operating system, or kernel, runs in a privileged manner known as *kernel mode.* This mode of operation allows the kernel to run without being interfered with by other programs currently in the system. The microprocessor enforces this line of demarcation between user and kernel level mode. With the kernel operating in its own protected address space, it is guaranteed to maintain the integrity of its own data structures and that of other processes. (That's not to say that a privileged process could not inadvertently cause corruption within the kernel.) These data structures are used by the kernel to manage and control itself and any other programs that may be running in the system. If any of these data structures were allowed to be accidentally or intentionally altered, the system could quickly crash. Now that we have learned what a UNIX kernel is and how it is loaded into the system, we are ready to take a look at the four UNIX subsystems Process Management, Memory Management, Filesystem Management and I/O Management.

Process Management

The Process Management subsystem controls the creation, termination, accounting, and scheduling of processes. It oversees process state transitions and the switching between privileged and nonprivileged modes of execution. The Process Management subsystem facilitates and manages the complex task of the creation of child processes.

A simple definition of a process is that it is an executing program. It is an entity that requires system resources, and it has a finite lifetime. It has the capability to create other processes via the system call interface. In short, it is an electronic representation of a user's or programmer's desire to accomplish some useful piece of work. A process may appear to the user as if it is the only job running in the machine. This "sleight of hand" is only an illusion. At any one time a processor is only executing a single process.

Process Structure

A process has a definite structure (see Figure 19.1). The kernel views this string of bits as the process image. This binary image consists of both a user and system address space, as well as registers that store the process's data during its execution. The user address space is also known as the user image. This is the code that is written by a programmer and compiled into an ".o" object file. An object file is a file that contains machine language code/data and is in a format that the linker program can use to then create an executable program.

The user address space consists of five separate areas: Text, Data, Bss, stack, and user area.

Text Segment

The first area of a process is its text segment. This area contains the executable program code for the process. This area is shared by other processes that execute the program. It is therefore fixed and unchangeable and is usually swapped out to disk by the system when memory gets too tight.

Data Area

The data area contains both the global and static variables used by the program. For example, a programmer may know in advance that a certain data variable needs to be set to a certain value. In the C programming language, it would look like:

```
int x = 15;
```

If you were to look at the data segment when the program was loaded, you would see that the variable *x* was an integer type with an initial value of 15.

Bss Area

The bss area, like the data area, holds information for the programs variables. The difference is that the bss area maintains variables that will have their data values assigned to them during the program's execution. For example, a programmer may know that she needs variables to hold certain data that will be input by a user during the execution of the program.

```
int a,b,c;      // a,b and c are variables that hold integer values.
char *ptr;      // ptr is an unitialized character pointer.
```

The program code can also make calls to library routines like malloc to obtain a chunk of memory and assign it to a variable like the one declared above.

FIGURE 19.1.
Diagram of process areas.

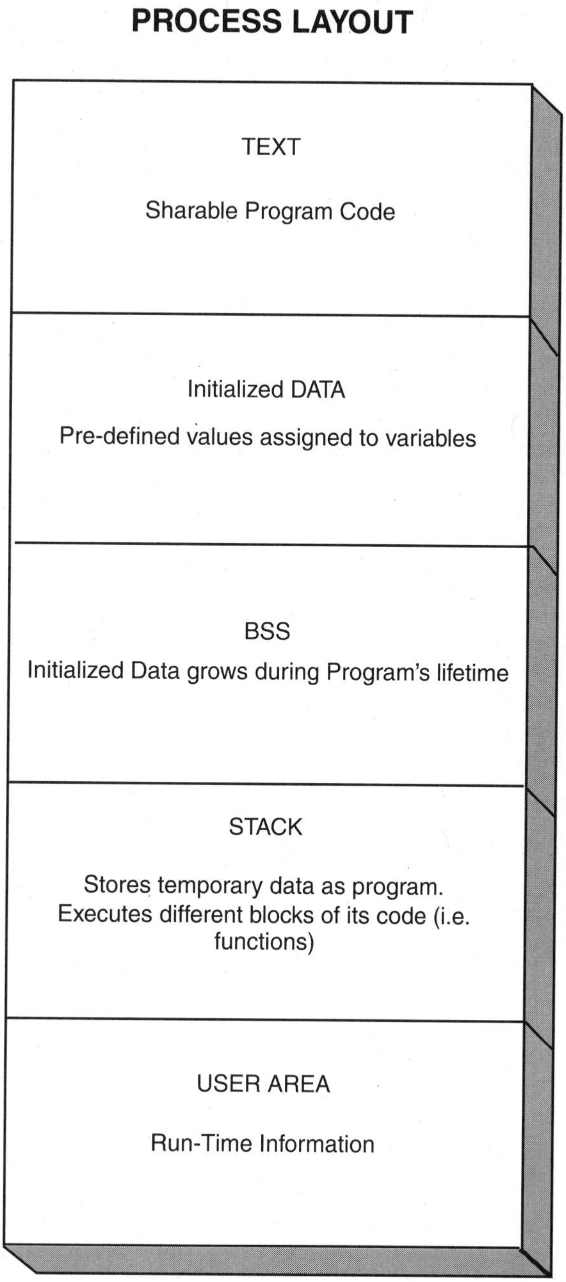

PROCESS LAYOUT

TEXT

Sharable Program Code

Initialized DATA

Pre-defined values assigned to variables

BSS

Initialized Data grows during Program's lifetime

STACK

Stores temporary data as program.
Executes different blocks of its code (i.e. functions)

USER AREA

Run-Time Information

19

KERNEL CONFIGURATION

Stack Area

The stack area maintains the process's local variables, parameters used in functions, and values returned by functions. For example, a program may contain code that calls another block of code (possibly written by someone else). The calling block of code passes data to the receiving block of code by way of the stack. The called block of code then process's the data and returns data back to the calling code. The stack plays an important role in allowing a process to work with temporary data.

User Area

The user area maintains data that is used by the kernel while the process is running. The user area contains the real and effective user identifiers, real and effective group identifiers, current directory, and a list of open files. Sizes of the text, data, and stack areas, as well as pointers to process data structures, are maintained. Other areas that can be considered part of the process's address space are the heap, private shared libraries data, shared libraries, and shared memory. During initial startup and execution of the program, the kernel allocates the memory and creates the necessary structures to maintain these areas.

The user area is used by the kernel to manage the process. This area maintains the majority of the accounting information for a process. It is part of the process address space and is only used by the kernel while the process is executing (see Figure 19.2). When the process is not executing, its user area may be swapped out to disk by the Memory Manager. In most versions of UNIX, the user area is mapped to a fixed virtual memory address. Under HP-UX 10.x, this virtual address is 0x7FFE6000. When the kernel performs a context switch (starts executing a different process) to a new process, it will always map the process's physical address to this virtual address. Since the kernel already has a pointer fixed to this location in memory, it is a simple matter of referencing the current u pointer to be able to begin managing the newly switched-in process. The file /usr/include/sys/user.h contains the user area's structure definition for your version of UNIX.

Process Table

The process table is another important structure used by the kernel to manage the processes in the system. The process table is an array of process structures that the kernel uses to manage the execution of programs. Each table entry defines a process that the kernel has created. The process table is always resident in the computer's memory. This is because the kernel is repeatedly querying and updating this table as it switches processes in and out of the CPU. For those processes that are not currently executing, their process table structures are being updated by the kernel for scheduling purposes. The process structures for your system are defined in /usr/include/sys/proc.h.

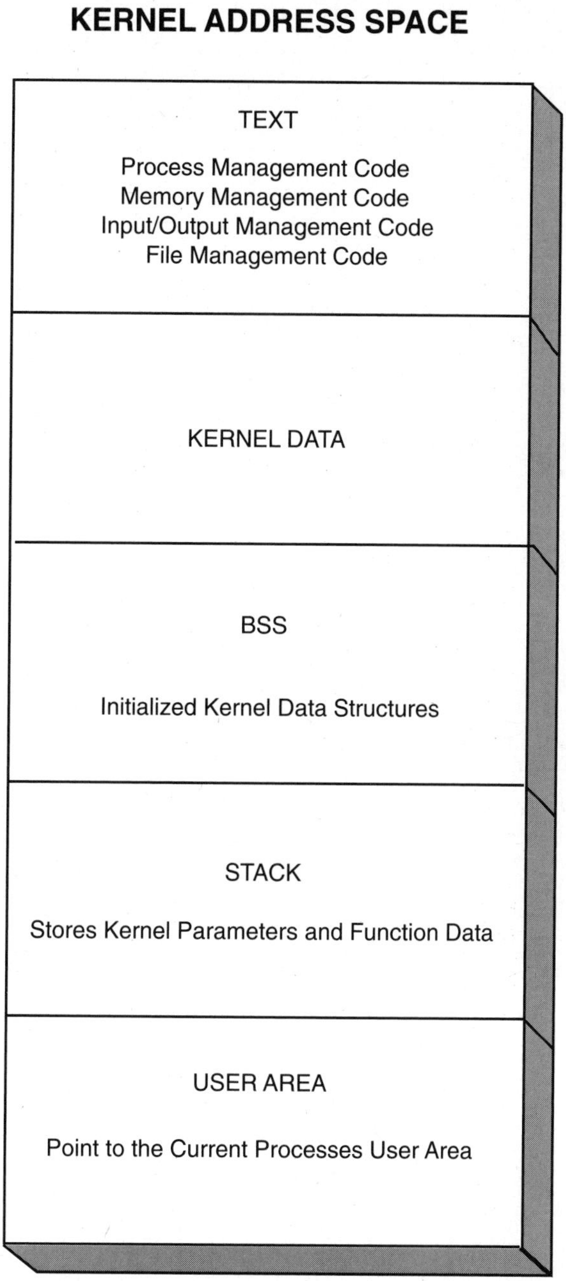

FIGURE 19.2.

*Diagram of kernel
address space.*

KERNEL ADDRESS SPACE

TEXT

Process Management Code
Memory Management Code
Input/Output Management Code
File Management Code

KERNEL DATA

BSS

Initialized Kernel Data Structures

STACK

Stores Kernel Parameters and Function Data

USER AREA

Point to the Current Processes User Area

19

KERNEL
CONFIGURATION

Fork Process

The kernel provides each process with the tools to duplicate itself for the purpose of creating a new process. This new entity is termed a *child process*. The fork() system call is invoked by an existing process (termed the *parent process*) and creates a replica of the parent process. While a process will have one parent, it can spawn many children. The new child process inherits certain attributes from its parent. The fork() system call documentation for HP-UX 10.0 (fork(2) in HP-UX Reference Release 10.0 Volume 3 (of 4) HP 9000 Series Computers) lists the following as being inherited by the child:

Real, effective, and saved user IDs

Real, effective, and saved group IDs

Supplementary group IDs

Process group ID

Environment

File descriptors

Close-on-exec flags

Signal handling settings

Signal mask

Profiling on/off status

Command name in the accounting record

Nice value

All attached shared memory segments

Current working directory

Root directory

File mode creation mask

File size limit

Real-time priority

It is important to note how the child process differs from the parent process in order to see how one tells the difference between the parent and the child. When the kernel creates a child process on behalf of the parent, it gives the child a new process identifier. This unique process ID is returned to the parent by the kernel to be used by the parent's code (of which the child also has a copy at this point) to determine the next step the parent process should follow: either continue on with additional work, wait for the child to finish, or terminate. The kernel will return the user ID of 0 (zero) to the child. Since the child is still executing the parent's copy of the program at this point, the code simply checks for a return status of 0 (zero) and continues executing that branch of the code. The following short pseudocode segment should help clarify this concept.

```
start
print     " I am a process "
print     " I will now make a copy of myself "
if fork() is greater than 0
    print    " I am the parent"
    exit    () or wait    ()
else if fork() = 0
    print     " I am the new child "
    print     " I am now ready  to start  a new program "
    exec("new_program")
else fork() failed
```

The child process can also make another system call that will replace the child's process image with that of a new one. The system call that will completely overlay the child's text, data, and BSS areas with that of a new program one is called exec(). This is how the system is able to execute multiple programs. By using both the fork() and the exec() systems calls in conjunction with one another, a single process is able to execute numerous programs that perform any number of tasks that the programmer needs to have done. Except for a few system-level processes started at boot time, this is how the kernel goes about executing the numerous jobs your system is required to run to support your organization.

To see how all this looks running on your system, you can use the ps command to view the fact that the system has created all these new child processes. The ps -ef command will show you that the child's parent process ID column (PPID) will match that of the parent's process ID column (PID). The simplest way to test this is to log on and, at the shell prompt, issue a UNIX command. By doing this you are telling the shell to spawn off a child process that will execute the command (program) you just gave it and to return control to you once the command has finished executing. Another way to experiment with this is to start a program in what is termed the *background*. This is done by simply appending an ampersand (&) to the end of your command line statement. This has the effect of telling the system to start this new program, but not to wait for it to finish before giving control back to your current shell process. This way you can use the ps -ef command to view your current shell and background processes.

```
Sample ps -ef output from a system running AIX 4.2
    UID   PID  PPID   C   STIME   TTY  TIME CMD
   root     1     0   0   Apr 24   -   2:55 /etc/init
   root  2060 17606   0 10:38:30   -   0:02 dtwm
   root  2486     1   0   Apr 24   -   0:00 /usr/dt/bin/dtlogin -daemon
   root  2750  2486   0   Apr 24   -   3:12 /usr/lpp/X11/bin/X -x xv -D /usr/
➥lib/X11//rgb -T -force :0 -auth /var/dt/A:0-yjc2ya
   root  2910     1   0   Apr 24   -   0:00 /usr/sbin/srcmstr
   root  3176  2486   0   Apr 25   -   0:00 dtlogin <:0>        -daemon
   root  3794     1   0   Apr 25   -   0:00 /usr/ns-home/admserv/ns-admin -d /
➥usr/ns-home/admserv .
   root  3854  2910   0   Apr 24   -   0:00 /usr/lpp/info/bin/infod
   root  4192  6550   0   Apr 24   -   0:00 rpc.ttdbserver 100083 1
   root  4364     1   0   Apr 24   -   2:59 /usr/sbin/syncd 60
   root  4628     1   0   Apr 24   -   0:00 /usr/lib/errdemon
   root  5066     1   0   Apr 24   -   0:03 /usr/sbin/cron
   root  5236  2910   0   Apr 24   -   0:00 /usr/sbin/syslogd
   root  5526  2910   0   Apr 24   -   0:00 /usr/sbin/biod 6
```

```
     root   6014   2910    0   Apr 24        -  0:00 sendmail: accepting connections
     root   6284   2910    0   Apr 24        -  0:00 /usr/sbin/portmap
     root   6550   2910    0   Apr 24        -  0:00 /usr/sbin/inetd
     root   6814   2910    0   Apr 24        -  9:04 /usr/sbin/snmpd
     root   7080   2910    0   Apr 24        -  0:00 /usr/sbin/dpid2
     root   7390      1    0   Apr 24        -  0:00 /usr/sbin/uprintfd
     root   7626      1    0   Apr 24        -  0:00 /usr/OV/bin/ntl_reader 0 1 1 1 1000
➥/usr/OV/log/nettl
     root   8140   7626    0   Apr 24        -  0:00 netfmt -CF
     root   8410   8662    0   Apr 24        -  0:00 nvsecd -O
     root   8662      1    0   Apr 24        -  0:15 ovspmd
     root   8926   8662    0   Apr 24        -  0:19 ovwdb -O -n5000 -t
     root   9184   8662    0   Apr 24        -  0:04 pmd -Au -At -Mu -Mt -m
     root   9442   8662    0   Apr 24        -  0:32 trapgend -f
     root   9700   8662    0   Apr 24        -  0:01 mgragentd -f
     root   9958   8662    0   Apr 24        -  0:00 nvpagerd
     root  10216   8662    0   Apr 24        -  0:00 nvlockd
     root  10478   8662    0   Apr 24        -  0:05 trapd
     root  10736   8662    0   Apr 24        -  0:04 orsd
     root  11004   8662    0   Apr 24        -  0:31 ovtopmd -O -t
     root  11254   8662    0   Apr 24        -  0:00 nvcold -O
     root  11518   8662    0   Apr 24        -  0:03 ovactiond
     root  11520   8662    0   Apr 24        -  0:05 nvcorrd
     root  11780   8662    0   Apr 24        -  0:00 actionsvr
     root  12038   8662    0   Apr 24        -  0:00 nvserverd
     root  12310   8662    0   Apr 24        -  0:04 ovelmd
     root  12558   8662    0   Apr 24        -  4:28 netmon -P
     root  12816   8662    0   Apr 24        -  0:04 ovesmd
     root  13074   8662    0   Apr 24        -  0:00 snmpCollect
     root  13442   2910    0   Apr 24        -  0:00 /usr/lib/netsvc/yp/ypbind
     root  13738   5526    0   Apr 24        -  0:00 /usr/sbin/biod 6
     root  13992   5526    0   Apr 24        -  0:00 /usr/sbin/biod 6
     root  14252   5526    0   Apr 24        -  0:00 /usr/sbin/biod 6
     root  14510   5526    0   Apr 24        -  0:00 /usr/sbin/biod 6
     root  14768   5526    0   Apr 24        -  0:00 /usr/sbin/biod 6
     root  15028   2910    0   Apr 24        -  0:00 /usr/sbin/rpc.statd
     root  15210   6550    0   Apr 24        -  0:00 rpc.ttdbserver 100083 1
     root  15580   2910    0   Apr 24        -  0:00 /usr/sbin/writesrv
     root  15816   2910    0   Apr 24        -  0:00 /usr/sbin/rpc.lockd
     root  16338   2910    0   Apr 24        -  0:00 /usr/sbin/qdaemon
     root  16520   2060    0 13:44:46        -  0:00 /usr/dt/bin/dtexec -open 0 -ttprocid
➥2.pOtBq 01 17916 1342177279 1 0 0 10.19.12.115 3_101_1 /usr/dt/bin/dtterm
     root  16640      1    0   Apr 24     lft0  0:00 /usr/sbin/getty /dev/console
     root  17378      1    0   Apr 24        -  0:13 /usr/bin/pmd
     root  17606   3176    0 10:38:27        -  0:00 /usr/dt/bin/dtsession
     root  17916      1    0 10:38:28        -  0:00 /usr/dt/bin/ttsession -s
     root  18168      1    0   Apr 24        -  0:00 /usr/lpp/diagnostics/bin/diagd
   nobody  18562  19324    0   Apr 25        -  0:32 ./ns-httpd -d /usr/ns-home/httpd-
➥supp_aix/config
     root  18828  22410    0 13:44:47    pts/2  0:00 /bin/ksh
     root  19100  21146    0 13:45:38    pts/3  0:00 vi hp.c
   nobody  19324      1    0   Apr 25        -  0:00 ./ns-httpd -d /usr/ns-home/httpd-
➥supp_aix/config
     root  19576   6550    0 13:43:38        -  0:00 telnetd
   nobody  19840  19324    0   Apr 25        -  0:33 ./ns-httpd -d /usr/ns-home/httpd-
➥supp_aix/config
     root  19982  17606    0 10:38:32        -  0:03 dtfile
   nobody  20356  19324    0   Apr 25        -  0:33 ./ns-httpd -d /usr/ns-home/httpd-
```

```
➡supp_aix/config
    root 20694 20948   0   Apr 25       -   0:00 /usr/ns-home/admserv/ns-admin -d /
➡usr/ns-home/admserv .
    root 20948  3794   0   Apr 25       -   0:01 /usr/ns-home/admserv/ns-admin -d /
➡usr/ns-home/admserv ./
    root 21146 23192   0 13:45:32 pts/3  0:00 /bin/ksh
  nobody 21374 19324   0   Apr 25       -   0:00 ./ns-httpd -d /usr/ns-home/httpd-
➡supp_aix/config
    root 21654  2060   0 13:45:31       -   0:00 /usr/dt/bin/dtexec -open 0 -ttprocid
➡2.pOtBq 01 17916 1342177279 1 0 0 10.19.12.115 3_102_1 /usr/dt/bin/dtterm
    root 21882 19576   0 13:43:39 pts/0  0:00 -ksh
    root 22038 19982   0 10:38:37       -   0:04 dtfile
    root 22410 16520   0 13:44:47       -   0:00 /usr/dt/bin/dtterm
    root 22950 21882   8 13:46:06 pts/0  0:00 ps -ef
    root 23192 21654   0 13:45:31       -   0:00 /usr/dt/bin/dtterm
    root 23438 18828   0 13:45:03 pts/2  0:00 vi aix.c
```

Process Run States

A process moves between several states during its lifetime, although a process can only be in one state at any one time. Certain events, such as system interrupts, blocking of resources, or software traps will cause a process to change its run state. The kernel maintains queues in memory that it uses to assign a process to, based upon that process's state. It keeps track of the process by its user ID.

UNIX version System V Release 4 (SVR4) recognizes the following process run states:

```
- SIDLE            This is the state right after a process has issued a fork()
➡system call. A process image has yet to be copied into memory.
      - SRUN            The process is ready to run and is waiting to be
➡executed by  the CPU.
      - SONPROC    The process is currently being executed by the CPU.
      - SSLEEP          The process is blocking on an event or resource.
      - SZOMB           The process has terminated and is waiting on either its
➡parent or the init process to allow it to completely exit.
      - SXBRK           The process is has been switched out so that another
➡process can be executed.
      - SSTOP           The process is stopped.
```

When a process first starts, the kernel allocates it a slot in the process table and places the process in the SIDL state. Once the process has the resources it needs to run, the kernel places it onto the run queue. The process is now in the SRUN state awaiting its turn in the CPU. Once its turn comes for the process to be switched into the CPU, the kernel will tag it as being in the SONPROC state. In this state, the process will execute in either user or kernel mode. User mode is where the process is executing nonprivileged code from the user's compiled program. Kernel mode is where kernel code is being executed from the kernel's privileged address space via a system call.

At some point, the process is switched out of the CPU because it has either been signaled to do so (for instance, the user issues a stop signal—SSTOP state), or the process has exceeded its quota of allowable CPU time and the kernel needs the CPU to do some work for another process. The act of switching the focus of the CPU from one process to another is called a *context switch*.

When this occurs, the process enters what is known as the SXBRK state. If the process still needs to run and is waiting for another system resource, such as disk services, it will enter the SSLEEP state until the resource is available and the kernel wakes the process up and places it on the SRUN queue. When the process has finally completed its work and is ready to terminate, it enters the SZOMB state. We have seen the fundamentals of what states a process can exist in and how it moves through them. Let's now learn how a kernel schedules a process to run.

Process Scheduler

Most modern versions of UNIX (for instance, SVR4 and Solaris 2.*x*) are classified as preemptive operating systems. They are capable of interrupting an executing a process and "freezing" it so that the CPU can service a different process. This obviously has the advantage of fairly allocating the system's resources to all the processes in the system. This is one goal of the many systems architects and programmers who design and write schedulers. The disadvantages are that not all processes are equal and that complex algorithms must be designed and implemented as kernel code in order to maintain the illusion that each user process is running as if it was the only job in the system. The kernel maintains this balance by placing processes in the various priority queues or run queues and apportioning its CPU time-slice based on its priority class (Real-Time versus Timeshare).

Universities and UNIX system vendors have conducted extensive studies on how best to design and build an optimal scheduler. Each vendor's flavor of UNIX—4.4BSD, SVR4, HP-UX, Solaris, and AIX, to name a few—attempts to implement this research to provide a scheduler that best balances its customers' needs. The systems administrator must realize that there are limits to the scheduler's ability to service batch, real-time, and interactive users in the same environment. Once the system becomes overloaded, it will become necessary for some jobs to suffer at the expense of others. This is an extremely important issue to both users and systems administrators alike. The reader should refer to Chapter 22, "Performance and Tuning," to gain a better understanding of what he can do to balance and tune his system.

Memory Management

Random access memory (RAM) is a very critical component in any computer system. It's the one component that always seems to be in short supply on most systems. Unfortunately, most organizations' budgets don't allow for the purchase of all the memory that their technical staff feels is necessary to support all their projects. Luckily, UNIX allows us to execute all sorts of programs without, what appears at first glance to be, enough physical memory. This comes in very handy when the system is required to support a user community that needs to execute an organization's custom and commercial software to gain access to its data.

Memory chips are high-speed electronic devices that plug directly into your computer. Main memory is also called *core memory* by some technicians. Ever heard of a core dump? (Writing out main memory to a storage device for post-dump analysis.) Usually it is caused by a program or system crash or failure. An important aspect of memory chips is that they can store data at specific locations called addresses. This makes it quite convenient for another hardware device called the central processing unit (CPU) to access these locations to run your programs. The kernel uses a paging and segmentation arrangement to organize process memory. This is where the memory management subsystem plays a significant role. Memory management can be defined as the efficient managing and sharing of the system's memory resources by the kernel and user processes.

Memory management follows certain rules that manage both physical and virtual memory. Since we already have an idea of what a physical memory chip or card is, we will provide a definition of virtual memory. *Virtual memory* is where the addressable memory locations that a process can be mapped into are independent of the physical address space of the CPU. Generally speaking, a process can exceed the physical address space/size of main memory and still load and execute.

The systems administrator should be aware that just because she has a fixed amount of physical memory, she should not expect it all to be available to execute user programs. The kernel is always resident in main memory and depending upon the kernel's configuration (tunable-like kernel tables, daemons, device drivers loaded, and so on), the amount left over can be classified as available memory. It is important for the systems administrator to know how much available memory the system has to work with when supporting his environment. Most systems display memory statistics during boot time. If your kernel is larger than it needs to be to support your environment, consider reconfiguring a smaller kernel to free up resources.

We learned before that a process has a well-defined structure and has certain specific control data structures that the kernel uses to manage the process during its system lifetime. One of the more important data structures the kernel uses is the virtual address space (`vas` in HP-UX and `as` in SVR4. For a more detailed description of the layout of these structures, look at the `vas.h` or `as.h` header files under `/usr/include` on your system.).

A virtual address space exists for each process and is used by the process to keep track of process logical segments or regions that point to specific segments of the process's `text` (code), `data`, `u_area`, `user`, and `kernel` stacks; shared memory; shared library; and memory mapped file segments. Per-process regions protect and maintain the number of pages mapped into the segments. Each segment has a virtual address space segment as well. Multiple programs can share the process's text segment. The data segment holds the process's initialized and uninitialized (BSS) data. These areas can change size as the program executes.

The `u_area` and `kernel` stack contain information used by the kernel, and are a fixed size. The user stack is contained in the `u_area`; however, its size will fluctuate during its execution. Memory mapped files allow programmers to bring files into memory and work with them while in memory. Obviously, there is a limit to the size of the file you can load into memory (check your system documentation). Shared memory segments are usually set up and used by a process to share data with other processes. For example, a programmer may want to be able to pass messages to other programs by writing to a shared memory segment and having the receiving programs attach to that specific shared memory segment and read the message. Shared libraries allow programs to link to commonly used code at runtime. Shared libraries reduce the amount of memory needed by executing programs because only one copy of the code is required to be in memory. Each program will access the code at that memory location when necessary.

When a programmer writes and compiles a program, the compiler generates the object file from the source code. The linker program (ld) links the object file with the appropriate libraries and, if necessary, other object files to generate the executable program. The executable program contains virtual addresses that are converted into physical memory addresses when the program is run. This address translation must occur prior to the program being loaded into memory so that the CPU can reference the actual code.

When the program starts to run, the kernel sets up its data structures (proc, virtual address space, per-process region) and begins to execute the process in user mode. Eventually, the process will access a page that's not in main memory (for instance, the pages in its working set are not in main memory). This is called a *page fault*. When this occurs, the kernel puts the process to sleep, switches from user mode to kernel mode, and attempts to load the page that the process was requesting to be loaded. The kernel searches for the page by locating the per-process region where the virtual address is located. It then goes to the segments (text, data, or other) per-process region to find the actual region that contains the information necessary to read in the page.

The kernel must now find a free page in which to load the process's requested page. If there are no free pages, the kernel must either page or swap out pages to make room for the new page request. Once there is some free space, the kernel pages in a block of pages from disk. This block contains the requested page plus additional pages that may be used by the process. Finally the kernel establishes the permissions and sets the protections for the newly loaded pages. The kernel wakes the process and switches back to user mode so the process can begin executing using the requested page. Pages are not brought into memory until the process requests them for execution. This is why the system is referred to as a *demand paging* system.

> **NOTE**
>
> The verb *page* means to move individual blocks of memory for a process between system memory and disk swap area. The *pagesize* is defined in the /usr/include/limits.h header file. For a definition of paging see RAM I/O.

The memory management unit is a hardware component that handles the translation of virtual address spaces to physical memory addresses. The memory management unit also prevents a process from accessing another process's address space unless it is permitted to do so (protection fault). Memory is thus protected at the page level. The *Translation Lookaside Buffer* (TLB) is a hardware cache that maintains the most recently used virtual address space to physical address translations. It is controlled by the memory management unit to reduce the number of address translations that occur on the system.

Input and Output Management

The simplest definition of *input/output* is the control of data between hardware devices and software. A systems administrator is concerned with I/O at two separate levels. The first level is concerned with I/O between user address space and kernel address space; the second level is concerned with I/O between kernel address space and physical hardware devices. When data is written to disk, the first level of the I/O subsystem copies the data from user space to kernel space. Data is then passed from the kernel address space to the second level of the I/O subsystem. This is when the physical hardware device activates its own I/O subsystems, which determine the best location for the data on the available disks.

The OEM (*Original Equipment Manufacture*) UNIX configuration is satisfactory for many work environments, but does not take into consideration the network traffic or the behavior of specific applications on your system. Systems administrators find that they need to reconfigure the systems I/O to meet the expectations of the users and the demands of their applications. You should use the default configuration as a starting point and, as experience is gained with the demands on the system resources, tune the system to achieve peak I/O performance.

UNIX comes with a wide variety of tools that monitor system performance. Learning to use these tools will help you determine whether a performance problem is hardware or software related. Using these tools will help you determine whether a problem is poor user training, application tuning, system maintenance, or system configuration. `sar`, `iostat`, and `monitor` are some of your best basic I/O performance monitoring tools.

> `sar`   The sar command writes to standard output the contents of selected cumulative activity counters in the operating system. The following list is a breakdown of those activity counters that `sar` accumulates.

- File access
- Buffer usage
- System call activity
- Disk and tape input/output activity
- Free memory and swap space
- Kernel Memory Allocation (KMA)
- Interprocess communication
- Paging
- Queue Activity
- Central Processing Unit (CPU)
- Kernel tables
- Switching
- Terminal device activity

`iostat`   Reports CPU statistics and input/output statistics for TTY devices, disks, and CD-ROMs.

`monitor`   Like the `sar` command, but with a visual representation of the computer state.

RAM I/O

The memory subsystem comes into effect when the programs start requesting access to more physical RAM memory than is installed on your system. Once this point is reached, UNIX will start I/O processes called *paging* and *swapping*. This is when kernel procedures start moving pages of stored memory out to the paging or swap areas defined on your hard drives. (This procedure reflects how swap files work in Windows by Microsoft for a PC.) All UNIX systems use these procedures to free physical memory for reuse by other programs. The drawback to this is that once paging and swapping have started, system performance decreases rapidly. The system will continue using these techniques until demands for physical RAM drop to the amount that is installed on your system. There are only two physical states for memory performance on your system: Either you have enough RAM or you don't, and performance drops through the floor.

Memory performance problems are simple to diagnose: Either you have enough memory or your system is *thrashing*. Computer systems start thrashing when more resources are dedicated to moving memory (paging and swapping) from RAM to the hard drives. Performance decreases as the CPUs and all subsystems become dedicated to trying to free physical RAM for themselves and other processes.

This summary doesn't do justice, however, to the complexity of memory management nor does it help you to deal with problems as they arise. To provide the background to understand these problems, we need to discuss virtual memory activity in more detail.

We have been discussing two memory processes: paging and swapping. These two processes help UNIX fulfill memory requirements for all processes. UNIX systems employ both paging and swapping to reduce I/O traffic and execute better control over the system's total aggregate memory. Keep in mind that paging and swapping are temporary measures; they cannot fix the underlying problem of low physical RAM memory.

Swapping moves entire idle processes to disk for reclamation of memory, and is a normal procedure for the UNIX operating system. When the idle process is called by the system again, it will copy the memory image from the disk swap area back into RAM.

On systems performing paging and swapping, swapping occurs in two separate situations. Swapping is often a part of normal housekeeping. Jobs that sleep for more that 20 seconds are considered idle and may be swapped out at any time. Swapping is also an emergency technique used to combat extreme memory shortages. Remember our definition of thrashing; this is when a system is in trouble. Some system administrators sum this up very well by calling it "desperation swapping."

Paging, on the other hand, moves individual pages (or pieces) of processes to disk and reclaims the freed memory, with most of the process remaining loaded in memory. Paging employs an algorithm to monitor usage of the pages, to leave recently accessed pages in physical memory, and to move idle pages into disk storage. This allows for optimum performance of I/O and reduces the amount of I/O traffic that swapping would normally require.

> **NOTE**
>
> Monitoring what the system is doing is easy with the ps command. ps is a "process status" command on all UNIX systems and typically shows many idle and swapped-out jobs. This command has a rich amount of options to show you what the computer is doing—too many to show you here.

I/O performance management, like all administrative tasks, is a continual process. Generating performance statistics on a routine basis will assist in identifying and correcting potential problems before they have an impact on your system or, worst case, your users. UNIX offers basic system usage statistics packages that will assist you in automatically collecting and examining usage statistics.

You will find the load on the system will increase rapidly as new jobs are submitted and resources are not freed quickly enough. Performance drops as the disks become I/O bound trying to satisfy paging and swapping calls. Memory overload quickly forces a system to become I/O and CPU bound. However, once you identify the problem to be memory, you will find adding RAM to be cheaper than adding another CPU to your system.

Hard Drive I/O

Some simple configuration considerations will help you obtain better I/O performance regardless of your system's usage patterns. The factors to consider are the arrangement of your disks and disk controllers and the speed of the hard drives.

The best policy is to spread the disk workload as evenly as possible across all controllers. If you have a large system with multiple I/O back planes, split your disk drives evenly among the two buses. Most disk controllers allow you to daisy chain several disk drives from the same controller channel. For the absolute best performance, spread the disk drives evenly over all controllers. This is particularly important if your system has many users who all need to make large sequential transfers.

Small Computer System Interface (SCSI) devices are those that adhere to the American National Standards Institute (ANSI) standards for connecting intelligent interface peripherals to computers. The SCSI bus is a daisy-chained arrangement originating at a SCSI adapter card that interconnects several SCSI controllers. Each adapter interfaces the device to the bus and has a different SCSI address that is set on the controller. This address determines the priority that the SCSI device is given, with the highest address having the highest priority. When you load balance a system, always place more frequently accessed data on the hard drives with the highest SCSI address. Data at the top of the channel takes less access time, and load balancing increases the availability of that data to the system.

After deciding the best placement of the controllers and hard drives on your system, you have one last item for increasing system performance. When adding new disks, remember that the seek time of the disk is the single most important indicator of its performance. Different processes will be accessing the disk at the same time as they are accessing different files and reading from different areas at one time.

The seek time of a disk is the measure of time required to move the disk drive's heads from one track to another. Seek time is affected by how far the heads have to move from one track to another. Moving the heads from track to track takes less time that shifting those same drive heads across the entire disk. You will find that seek time is actually a nonlinear measurement, taking into account that the heads have to accelerate, decelerate, and then stabilize in their new position. This is why all disks will typically specify a minimum, average, and maximum seek time. The ratio of time spent seeking between tracks to time spent transferring data is usually at least 10 to 1. The lower the aggregate seek time, the greater your performance gain or improvement.

One problem with allowing for paging and swap files to be added to the hard disks is that some system administrators try to use this feature to add more RAM to a system. *It does not work that way.* The most you could hope for is to temporarily avert the underlying cause, low physical memory. There is one thing that a systems administrator can do to increase performance, and that is to accurately balance the disk drives.

Don't overlook the obvious upgrade path for I/O performance—tuning. If you understand how your system is configured and how you intend to use it, you will be much less likely to buy equipment you don't need or that won't solve your problem.

Filesystem Management Subsystem

In discussing "Kernel Basics and Configuration" a very important topic, filesystems, must be considered. This discussion shall deal with the basic structural method of long-term storage of system and user data. Filesystems and the parameters that are used to create them have a direct impact on performance, system resource utilization, and kernel efficiency dealing with Input/Output (I/O).

Filesystem Types

There are several important filesystem types that are supported by different operating systems (OS), many of which are not used for implementation at this time. The reasons they are not used vary from being inefficient to just being outdated. However, many operating systems still support their filesystem structure so that compatibility doesn't become an issue for portability.

This support of other filesystem structures plays a large role in allowing companies to move between OS and computer types with little impact to their applications.

The following is a list of filesystem types that are supported by specific operating systems. The list will only cover local, network, and CD-ROM filesystems.

	Local Filesystem	*NFS**	*CD-ROM*
Solaris	ufs	yes	bsfs
SunOS	4.2	yes	bsfs
SCO	EAFS	yes	HS
IRIX	efs	yes	iso9660
Digital	ufs	yes	cdfs
HP-UX	bfs	yes	cdfs
AIX	jfs	yes	cdrfs
Linux	ext2	yes	iso9660

Hardware Architecture

Since filesystems are stored on disk, the systems administrator should look at basic disk hardware architecture before proceeding with specifics of filesystems. A disk is physically divided into tracks, sectors, and blocks. A good representation of a sector would be a piece of pie removed from the pie pan. Therefore, as with a pie, a disk is composed of several sectors (see Figure 19.3). Tracks are concentric rings going from the outside perimeter to the center of the disk, with each track becoming smaller as it approaches the center of the disk. Tracks on a disk are concentric; therefore, they *never* touch each other. The area of the track that lies between the edges of the sector is termed a block, and the block is the area where data is stored. Disk devices typically use a block-mode-accessing scheme when transferring data between the file management subsystem and the I/O subsystem. The block size is usually 512- or 1024-byte fixed-length blocks, depending upon the scheme used by the operating system. A programmer may access files using either block or character device files.

You now have a basic understanding of the terms tracks, sectors, and blocks as they apply to a single platter disk drive. But most disk today are composed of several platters with each platter having its own read/write head. With this in mind, we have a new term: *cylinder* (see Figure 19.4). Let's make the assumption that we have a disk drive that has six platters so, logically, it must have six read/write heads. When read/write head 1 is on track 10 of platter 1, then heads 2 through 6 are on track 10 of their respective platters. You now have a cylinder. A cylinder is collectively the same track on each platter of a multi-platter disk.

---

*Note: NFS stands for Networked FileSystem

FIGURE 19.3.

Diagram of a single platter from a hard drive showing disk geometry.

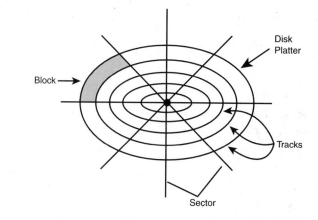

FIGURE 19.4.

Diagram showing multiple platters of a single disk drive.

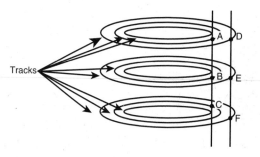

Filesystem Concepts and Format

The term filesystem has two connotations. The first is the complete hierarchical filesystem tree. The second is the collection place on disk device(s) for files. Visualize the filesystem as consisting of a single node at the highest level (ROOT) and all other nodes descending from the root node in a tree-like fashion (see Figure 19.5) . The second meaning will be used for this discussion, and Hewlett-Packard's High-performance Filesystem will be used for technical reference purposes.

The superblock is the key to maintaining the filesystem. It's an 8 KB block of disk space that maintains the current status of the filesystem. Because of its importance, a copy is maintained in memory and at each cylinder group within the filesystem. The copy in main memory is updated as events transpire. The update daemon is the actual process that calls on the kernel to flush the cached superblocks, modified inodes, and cached data blocks to disk. The superblock maintains the following static and dynamic information about the filesystem. An asterisk will denote dynamically maintained information.

Filesystem size

Number of inodes

Location of free space

Number of cylinder groups

Fragment size and number

Block size and number

Location of superblocks, cylinder groups, inodes, and data blocks

Total number of free data blocks

Total number of free inodes

Filesystem status flag (clean flag)

Figure 19.5.

Diagram of a UNIX hierarchical filesystem.

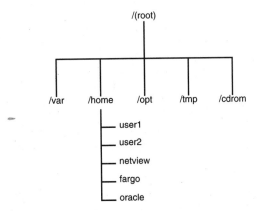

As you can see from the listed information, the superblock maintains the integrity of the filesystem and all associated pertinent information. To prevent catastrophic events, the OS stores copies of the superblock in cylinder groups. The locations of these alternate superblocks may be found in `/etc/sbtab`. When system administrators are using `fsck -b` to recover from an alternate superblock, they will be required to give the location of that alternate block. Again, the only place to find that information is in `/etc/sbtab`. As a qualification to that statement, there is always an alternate superblock at block 16.

Cylinder groups are adjacent groups of cylinders, 16 cylinders by default, that have their own set of inodes and free space mapping. This is done to improve performance and reduce disk latency. Disk latency is the time between when the disk is read and the I/O subsystem can transfer the data. Some factors that affect disk latency are rotational speed, seek time, and the interleave factor. This concept also associates the inodes and data blocks in closer proximity.

19

KERNEL CONFIGURATION

NOTE

The *interleave factor* is the value that determines the order in which sectors on a disk drive are accessed.

The layout of the cylinder group is:

Boot block

Primary superblock

Redundant superblock

Cylinder group information

Inode table

Data blocks

The boot block and the primary superblock will only be there if this is the first cylinder group; otherwise, it may be filled with data.

Inodes are fixed-length entries that vary in their length according to the OS implemented. SVR4 implementation is 128 bytes for a UFS inode and 64 bytes for an S5 inode. The inode maintains all of the pertinent information about the file except for the filename and the data. See Table 19.1. The information maintained by the inode is as follows:

File permissions or mode

Type of file

Number of hard links

Current owner

Group associated to the file

Actual file size in bytes

Time Stamps

Time/Date file last changed

Time/Date file last accessed

Time/Date last inode modification

Single indirect block pointer

Double indirect block pointer

Triple indirect block pointer

There are 15 slots in the inode structure for disk address or pointers (see Figure 19.6). Twelve of the slots are for direct block addressing. A direct address can either point to a complete block or to a fragment of that block. The block and fragment sizes we are discussing are configurable parameters that are set at filesystem creation. They cannot be altered unless the filesystem is removed and re-created with the new parameters.

FIGURE 19.6.

Diagram of an inode Structure of a UNIX filesystem

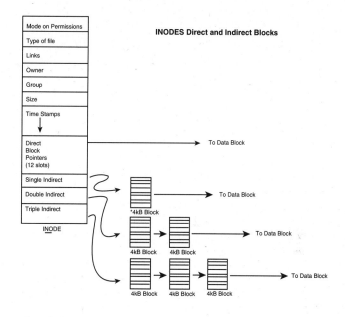

Table 19.1. List of a typical AIX Root directory using `ls -ali`, to indicate the inode numbers for each file entry in the directory.

inode	Permissions	ln	Owner	Group	Size	Access Date	Filename
2	drwxr-xr-x	23	bin	bin	1024	Apr 27 15:53	. (dot)
2	drwxr-xr-x	23	bin	bin	1024	Apr 27 15:53	.. (dot, dot)
765	-rw-r--r--	1	root	system	259	Apr 08 08:34	Guidefaults
1257	-rw-------	1	root	system	156	Apr 27 11:01	.Xauthority
2061	drwxr-xr-x	11	root	system	512	Apr 27 11:01	.dt
591	-rwxr-xr-x	1	root	system	3970	Apr 08 08:38	.dtprofile
6151	drwx------	3	root	system	512	Apr 17 13:42	.netscape
593	-rw-------	1	root	system	1904	Apr 11 08:12	.old_sh_history
1011	-rwxr-----	1	7	system	254	Apr 10 11:15	.profile
1007	-rw-------	1	root	system	3444	Apr 27 15:53	.sh_history
1009	-rw-r--r--	1	root	system	30	Apr 14 10:35	.showcase
2069	drwxr-xr-x	2	root	system	512	Apr 08 08:54	TT_DB

continues

19

KERNEL CONFIGURATION

Table 19.1. continued

inode	Permissions	ln	Owner	Group	Size	Access Date	Filename
2058	drwxr-xr-x	3	root	system	512	Apr 11 11:21	admin
109	lrwxrwxrwx	1	bin	bin	8	Apr 01 05:27	bin ->/usr/bin
23	drwxrwxr-x	4	root	system	2048	Apr 27 14:37	dev
24	drwxr-xr-x	12	root	system	6144	Apr 27 11:29	etc
2	drwxr-xr-x	5	bin	bin	512	Apr 02 01:52	home
8195	drwxr-xr-x	2	root	system	512	Apr 25 13:08	httpd
586	lrwxrwxrwx	1	bin	bin	20	Apr 02 01:57	launch_demo -> /welcome/ launch_demo
22	lrwxrwxrwx	1	bin	bin	8	Apr 01 05:27	lib ->/usr/lib
16	drwx------	2	root	system	512	Apr 01 05:27	lost+found
100	drwxr-xr-x	26	bin	bin	1024	Apr 11 15:23	lpp
101	drwxr-xr-x	2	bin	bin	512	Apr 01 05:27	mnt
4096	drwxr-xr-x	2	root	system	512	Apr 11 14:57	mnt10032
4097	drwxr-xr-x	2	root	system	512	Apr 14 10:31	mnt10086
1251	-rw-rw-rw-	1	root	system	3192	Apr 15 14:12	nv6000.log
102	drwxr-xr-x	2	root	system	512	Apr 02 01:54	opt
103	drwxr-xr-x	3	bin	bin	512	Apr 11 15:23	sbin
1252	-rw-r--r--	1	root	system	39265	Apr 27 13:29	smit.log
1253	-rw-r--r--	1	root	system	5578	Apr 27 13:24	smit.script
271	drwxrwxr-x	2	root	system	512	Apr 01 05:37	tftpboot
2	drwxrwxrwt	9	bin	bin	1536	Apr 27 15:47	tmp
99	lrwxrwxrwx	1	bin	bin	5	Apr 01 05:27	u ->/home
192	lrwxrwxrwx	1	root	system	21	Apr 01 05:30	unix -> /usr/lib/boot/ unix_up
2	drwxr-xr-x	26	bin	bin	512	Apr 25 13:19	usr
2	drwxr-xr-x	14	bin	bin	512	Apr 01 06:03	var
764	-rw-rw-rw-	1	root	system	3074	Apr 08 08:33	vim.log
2	drwxr-xr-x	12	bin	bin	2048	Apr 08 08:21	welcome

Single indirect addressing (slot 13) points to a block of four-byte pointers that point to data blocks. If the block that is pointed to by the single indirect method is 4 KB in size, it would contain 1024 four-byte pointers, and if it were 8 KB in size, it would contain 2048 four-byte pointers to data blocks. The double indirect block pointer is located in slot 14, and slot 15 maintains the triple indirect block pointer.

In the "Filesystem Concepts and Format" section, the initial discussion covered basic concepts of superblocks, alternate superblocks, cylinder groups, inodes, and direct and indirect addressing of data blocks. Further reading into these subjects is a must for all systems administrators, especially the new and inexperienced.

Kernel Configuration Process

Kernel configuration is a detailed process in which the systems administrator is altering the behavior of the computer. The systems administrator must remember that a change of a single parameter may affect other kernel subsystems, thus exposing the administrator to the "law of unintended consequences."

When Do You Rebuild the Kernel?

Kernel components are generally broken into four major groups, and if changes are made to any of these groups, a kernel reconfiguration is required.

> Subsystems—These are components that are required for special functionality (ISO9660).

> Dump Devices—System memory dumps are placed here when a panic condition exists. Core dumps are usually placed at the end of the swap area.

> Configurable Parameters—These are tuning parameters and data structures. There are a significant number, and they may have inter-dependencies, so it is important that you are aware of the impact of each change.

> Device Drivers—These handle interfaces to peripherals like modems, printers, disks, tape drives, kernel memory, and other physical devices.

HP-UX 10.X

There are two ways to rebuild the kernel:

A. Use the System Activity Monitor (SAM)

Step 1—Run SAM and select "Kernel Configuration."

You will now see the following four identified components:

> Subsystem
> Configurable Parameters
> Dump Devices
> Device Drivers

19

KERNEL CONFIGURATION

Step 2—Select the desired component and make the appropriate change(s).

Step 3—Now answer the prompts, and the kernel will be rebuilt.

Step 4—It will also prompt you for whether you want to reboot the kernel now or later.

Consider the importance of the changes and the availability of the system to answer this prompt. If you answer "YES" to reboot the system now, it cannot be reversed. The point is to know what you are going to do prior to getting to that prompt.

B. Manual Method

Step 1—Go to the build area of the kernel by typing the command line below.

```
# cd /stand/build
```

Step 2—The first step is to create a system file from the current system configuration by typing the command line below.

```
# /usr/lbin/sysadm/system_prep -s system
```

This command places the current system configuration in the filesystem. There is no standard that you call it system; it could be any name you desire.

Step 3—Now you must modify the existing parameters and insert unlisted configuration parameters, new subsystems, and device drivers, or alter the dump device. The reason you may not have one of the listed configurable parameters in this file: The previous kernel took the default value.

Step 4—The next step is to create the conf.c file, and we are using the modified *system* file to create it. Remember, if you did not use system for the existing configuration file, insert your name where I show *system*. The conf.c file has constants for the tunable parameters. Type the command below to execute the config program.

```
# /usr/sbin/config -s system
```

Step 5—Now rebuild the kernel by linking the driver objects to the basic kernel.

```
# make -f config.mk
```

Step 6—Save the old system configuration file.

```
# mv /stand/system /stand/system.prev
```

Step 7—Save the old kernel.

```
# mv /stand/vmunix /stand/vmunix.prev
```

Step 8—Move the new system configuration file into place.

```
# mv ./system /stand/system
```

Step 9—Move the new kernel into place.

```
# mv ./vmunix_test /stand/vmunix
```

Step 10—You are ready to boot the system to load the new kernel.

```
# shutdown -r -y 60
```

Solaris 2.5

Suppose we were going to run Oracle on our Sun system under Solaris 2.5, and you wanted to change max_nprocs to 1000 and set up the following Interprocess Communications configuration for your shared memory and semaphore parameters:

SHMMAX	2097152 (2 × the default 1048576)
SHMMIN	1
SHMNI	100
SHMSEG	32
SEMMNI	64
SEMMNS	1600
SEMMNU	1250
SEMMSL	25

Step 1—As root, enter the commands below:

```
# cd /etc
# cp system system.old - create a backup
```

Step 2

```
# vi system
```

Add or change the following:

```
set max_nprocs=1000
set shmsys:shminfo_shmmax=2097152
set shmsys:shminfo_shmmin=1
set shmsys:shminfo_shmmni=100
set shmsys:shminfo_shmseg=32
set msgsys:seminfo_semmni=64
set msgsys:seminfo_semmns=1600
set msgsys:seminfo_semmnu=1250
set msgsys:seminfo_semmsl=25
```

Save and close the file.

Step 3—Reboot your system by entering the following command:

```
# shutdown -r now
```

The above kernel parameter and kernel module variables are now set for your system.

19

KERNEL
CONFIGURATION

SVR4

In this example we will set the tunable NPROC to 500 and then rebuild the kernel to reflect this new value.

Step 1—Log into the system as root and make a backup of /stand/unix to another area.

```
# cp /stand/unix /old/unix
```

Step 2

```
#cd /etc/conf/cf.d
```

Edit the init.base file to include any changes that you made in the /etc/inittab file that you want to make permanent. A new /etc/inittab file is created when a new kernel is built and put into place.

Step 3—In this step you edit the configuration files in the /etc/conf directory. We will only change /etc/conf/cf.d/stune (although you can change /etc/conf/cf.d/mtune). The stune and mtune files contain the tunable parameters the system uses for its kernel configuration. stune is the system file that you should use when you alter the tunable values for the system. It overrides the values listed in mtune. mtune is the master parameter specification file for the system. It contains the tunable parameters' default, minimum, and maximum values.

The following command line is an example of how you make stune reflect a parameter change.

```
# /etc/conf/bin/idtune NPROC 500
```

You can look at stune to see the changes. (stune can be altered by using the vi editor.)

Step 4—Build the new kernel.

```
# /etc/conf/bin/idbuild
```

It will take several minutes to complete.

Step 5—Reboot the computer system to enable the new kernel to take effect.

```
# shutdown -I6 -g0 -y
```

To see your changes, log back into your system and execute the sysdef command. The system parameters will then be displayed.

AIX 4.2

Unlike the preceding examples, the AIX operating system requires a special tool to reconfigure the kernel. This tool is the System Management Interface Tool (SMIT), developed by IBM for the AIX operating system. The AIX kernel is modular in the sense that portions of the kernel's subsystems are resident only when required.

The following shows a SMIT session to change the MAX USERS PROCESSES on an AIX 4.2 system. This is demonstrated to the reader by screen prints of an actual kernel configuration session. While using SMIT you can see the commands sequences being generated by SMIT by pressing the F6 key. SMIT also makes two interaction logs that are handy for post configuration review. SMIT.LOG is an ASCII file that shows all menu selections, commands, and output of a session. SMIT.SCRIPT shows just the actual command line codes used during the session.

Step 1—At root, start SMIT with the following command. This will bring up the IBM SMIT GUI interface screen, as shown in Figure 19.7.

```
# smit
```

FIGURE 19.7.

Systems management interface tool.

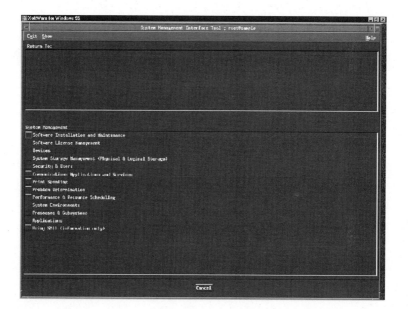

Step 2—Select "System Environments" from the System Management menu with your mouse. See Figure 19.8.

Step 3—Select "Change/Show Characteristics of Operating System" from the System Environment menu with your mouse. See Figure 19.9.

Step 4—Change "Maximum number of PROCESSES allowed per user" to "50" in the "Change/Show Characteristics of Operating System" menu. Do this by selecting the field for "Maximum number of PROCESSES" with your mouse. Then change the current value in the field to "50." See Figure 19.10.

19

KERNEL CONFIGURATION

FIGURE 19.8.

SMIT—System environments.

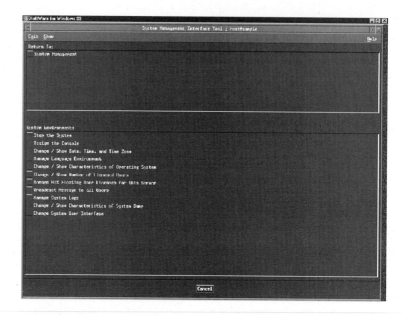

FIGURE 19.9.

SMIT—Change/Show Characteristics of Operating System.

Step 5—After making your change, select the "OK" button to make the new kernel parameters take effect.

Step 6—The System Management Interface Tool will respond with a "Command Status" screen. Verify that there are no errors in it. If there are none, you are done. See Figures 19.11 and 19.12.

FIGURE 19.10.

Maximum number of processes changed to 50.

FIGURE 19.11.

SMIT—Command Status screen.

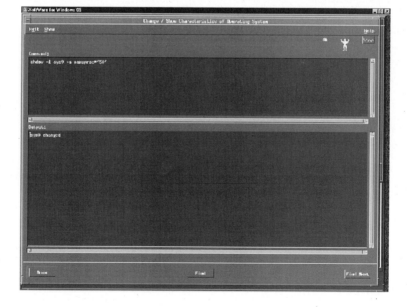

If an error is returned it would look like the screen print in Figure 19.12.

FIGURE 19.12.
SMIT—Possible Error Screen example.

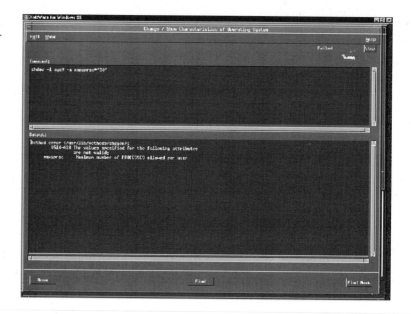

Linux

The point-to-point protocol (PPP) allows you to dial-in over a telephone line and run Transmission Control Protocol/Internet Protocol (TCP/IP). This allows you to run your GUI applications that use IP from a system that is not directly connected to a network. Let's look at how to configure PPP into the Linux kernel.

Step 1—Linux source code is usually found in the /usr/rc/linux directory. Let's start by changing to this directory by typing the following command.

```
# cd /usr/src/linux
```

Step 2—Type the following:

```
# make config
```

You will be presented with a series of questions asking if you would like to include or enable specific modules, drivers, and other kernel options in your kernel. For our build, we are concerned that we have a modem and the required networking device driver information configured into our kernel. Make sure you have answered [y] to

> Networking Support (CONFIG_NET)
>
> Network device support (CONFIG_NETDEVICES)
>
> TCP/IP networking (CONFIG_INET)
>
> PPP (point-to-point) support (CONFIG_PPP)

For the most part, you can accept the defaults of most of the questions. It's probably a good idea to go through this step once without changing anything to get a feel for the questions you will need to answer. That way you can set your configuration once and move on to the next step.

After you respond to all the questions, you will see a message telling you that the kernel is configured (it still needs to be built and loaded).

Step 3—The next two commands will set all of the source dependencies so that you can compile the kernel and clean up files that the old version leaves behind.

```
# make dep
# make clean
```

Step 4—To compile the new kernel, issue the `make` command.

```
# make
```

Don't be surprised if this takes several minutes.

Step 5—To see the new kernel, do a long listing of the directory.

```
# ls -al
```

You should see `vmlinux` in the current directory.

Step 6—You now need to make a bootable kernel.

```
# make boot
```

To see the compressed bootable kernel image, do a long listing on `arch/i386/boot`. You will see a file named `zImage`.

Step 7—The last step is to install the new kernel to the boot drive.

```
# make zlilo
```

This command will make the previous kernel (`/vmlinuz`) become `/vmlinuz.old`. Your new kernel image `zImage` is now `/vmlinuz`. You can now reboot to check your new kernel configuration. During the boot process, you should see messages about the newly configured PPP device driver scroll across as the system loads.

Once everything checks out and you are satisfied with your new Linux kernel, you can continue on with setting up the PPP software.

Summary

We began our discussion by defining the UNIX kernel and the four basic subsystems that comprise the Operating System. We described how Process Management creates and manages the process and how Memory Management handles multiple process in the system. We discussed how the I/O subsystem takes advantage of swapping and paging to balance the system's load and the interaction of the I/O subsystem with the file management subsystem.

19

KERNEL CONFIGURATION

Next, we covered the steps involved in altering the kernel configuration. We demonstrated in detail the steps involved in configuring:

HP-UX 10.X

Solaris 2.5

System V Release 4 (SVR4)

AIX

Linux

In the author's opinion, the systems administrator should become familiar with the concepts presented in this chapter. Further in-depth study of the kernel and its four subsystems will make the systems administrator more knowledgeable and effective at systems management.

Networking

by Salim Douba

IN THIS CHAPTER

Over the past few years, computer networks have become an increasingly integral part of most major production environments. Besides basic file and print services that users can transparently share, networks allowed them to use an ever-expanding suite of other productivity tools such as electronic mail, calendering, imaging, and voice/video conferencing applications. Another factor for the increased popularity of networks in production environments is the Internet. For many organizations, the Internet provided them with yet another business vehicle that they can use to promote their productivity and market reach—let alone the added capability of connecting remote branch offices to the headquarters via the Internet.

For the above reasons, implementing and maintaining networks that can meet the user demands on networked resources and productivity tools are becoming increasingly challenging tasks. UNIX networks are no less challenging than others. If anything, the task of installing and configuring UNIX networks is more complex than others. The complexity stems from the nature of protocols that underlie UNIX networks, namely the TCP/IP (Transmission Control Protocol/Internet Protocol) suite.

This chapter covers the necessary concepts and skills that the UNIX system administrator needs to possess in order to install, configure, and maintain UNIX connectivity. The first part is an overview of the basic concepts that govern TCP/IP communications, and second part provides a detailed treatment of the necessary UNIX tools and skill sets for achieving the objective of maintaining UNIX connectivity.

Basics of TCP/IP Communications

In 1969, the Defense Advanced Research Project Agency (DARPA) was given the mandate of looking at developing an experimental packet-switch network. The objective was to connect all government computing resources to a single global network without regard to the hardware or operating system platforms supporting these resources. Consequently, an experimental network, called ARPANET, was built for use in the development and testing of communications protocols that fulfill the assigned mandate. The TCP/IP communication protocol suite is a direct product of this effort. Using TCP/IP, large networks connecting hybrid platforms (not just UNIX platforms) can be built. Anything from mainframes to desktop computers can be made to belong to, and communicate across, the same TCP/IP network—there is no better manifestation of this capability than the Internet itself, which connects over 10 million computers from vendors the world over.

REQUEST FOR COMMENTS (RFCs)

Throughout this chapter, as well as some others in this book, references will be made to standard documents that contain the description and formal specification of the TCP/IP protocols being discussed in the form of RFC *XXXX*, where *XXXX* refers to the number of the document. For example, RFC 959 is the standards document specifying the File Transfer Protocol. Inquisitive readers might find reading some of the RFCs useful in order to better understand the issues at hand, or even sort problems encountered on their networks. Obtaining copies of the RFCs is a simple matter provided you have access to the Internet. One way of doing it is to send an e-mail to `rfc-info@ISI.EDU`, using the following format:

```
To: rfc@ISI.EDU
Subject: getting rfcs

help: ways_to_get_rfcs
```

In response to this message, you get an e-mail detailing ways by which you can gain access to the RFCs. Methods include FTP, WWW sites, and e-mail.

TCP/IP Protocol Architecture

The TCP/IP communications suite was designed with modularity in mind. This means that instead of developing a solution that integrates all aspects of communications in one single piece of code, the designers wisely chose to break the puzzle into its constituent components and deal with them individually while recognizing the interdependence tying the pieces together. Thus, TCP/IP evolved into a *suite* of protocols specifying interdependent solutions to the different pieces of the communications puzzle. This approach to problem solving is normally referred to as the *layering* approach. Consequently, hereafter, reference will be made to the TCP/IP suite as a layered suite of communications.

Figure 20.1 shows the four-layer model of the TCP/IP communications architecture. As shown in the diagram, the model is based on an understanding of data communications that involves four sets of interdependent processes: application representative processes, host representative processes, network representative processes, and media access and delivery representative process. Each set of processes takes care of the needs of entities it represents whenever an application engages in the exchange of data with its counterpart on the network. These process sets are grouped into the following four layers: application layer, host-to-host (also known as transport) layer, internet layer, and network access layer. Each of these layers may be implemented in separate, yet interdependent, pieces of software code.

Application Layer

Application representative processes take care of reconciling differences in the data syntax between the platforms on which the communicating applications are running. Communicating with an IBM mainframe, for example, might involve character translation between the EBCDIC and ASCII character sets. While performing the translation task, the application layer (for instance, application representative process) need not have (and shouldn't care to have) any understanding of how the underlying protocols (for instance, at the host-to-host layer) handle the transmission of translated characters between hosts. Examples of protocols supported at the application layer include FTP, Telnet, NFS, and DNS.

20

NETWORKING

FIGURE 20.1.
TCP/IP layered communications architecture.

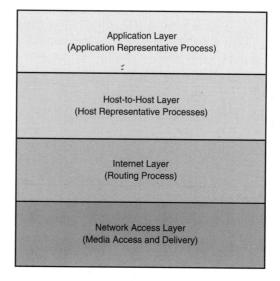

Host-to-Host Transport Layer

Host representative processes (for example, the host-to-host, or transport, layer) take care of communicating data reliably between applications running on hosts across the network. It is the responsibility of the host representative process to guarantee the reliability and integrity of the data being exchanged, without confusing the identities of the communication applications. For this reason the host-to-host layer is provided with the mechanism necessary to allow it to make the distinction between the applications on whose behalf it is making data deliveries. In other words, assume that two hosts, `tenor` and `alto`, are connected to the same network, as shown in Figure 20.2. Furthermore, assume that a user on host `alto` is logged in to FTP on host `tenor`. Also, while using FTP to transfer files, the user is utilizing Telnet to log in to host `tenor` to edit a document.

In this scenario, data exchanged between both hosts could be due to Telnet, FTP, or both. It is the responsibility of the host-to-host layer, hereafter called the transport layer, to make sure that data is sent and delivered to its intended party. What originates from FTP at one end of the connection should be delivered to FTP at the other end. Telnet-generated traffic should be delivered to Telnet at the other end, not to FTP. To achieve this, as will be discussed later, the transport layer at both ends of the connection must cooperate in clearly marking data packets so that the nature of the communicating applications is easily identifiable. Protocols operating at the transport layer include both UDP (User Datagram Protocol) and TCP (Transmission Control Protocol). Later sections will cover the characteristics of both protocols.

FIGURE 20.2.

Host-to-host (transport layer) is responsible for connecting applications and for delivering data to its destined process.

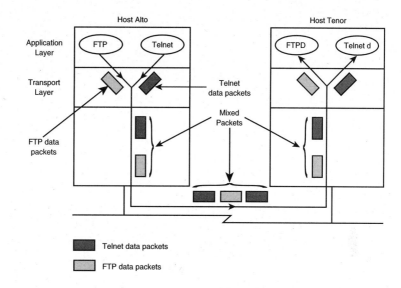

Internet Layer

The internet layer is responsible for determining the best route that data packets should follow to reach their destination. If the destination host is attached to the same network, data is delivered directly to that host by the network access layer; otherwise, if the host belongs to some other network, the internet layer employs a routing process for discovering the route to that host. Once the route is discovered, data is delivered through intermediate devices, called routers, to its destination. Routers are special devices with connections to two or more networks. Every router contains an implementation of TCP/IP up to and including the internet layer.

As shown in Figure 20.3, hosts alto and tenor belong to different networks. The intervening networks are connected via devices called routers. For host alto to deliver data to host tenor, it has to send its data to router R1 first. Router R1 delivers to R2 and so on until the data packet makes it to host tenor. The "passing-the-buck" process is known as routing and is responsible for delivering data to its ultimate destination. Each of the involved routers is responsible for assisting in the delivery process, including identifying the next router to deliver to in the direction of the desired destination. The protocols that operate at the internet layer include IP (Internet Protocol), and RIP (Route Information Protocol) among others.

Network Access Layer

The network access layer is where media access and transmission mechanisms take place. At this layer, both the hardware and the software drivers are implemented. The protocols at this layer provide the means for the system to deliver data to other devices on a *directly* attached network. This is the only layer that is aware of the physical characteristics of the underlying network, including rules of access, data frame (name of a unit of data at this layer) structure, and addressing.

20

NETWORKING

FIGURE 20.3.

Routers cooperate in the delivery of data packets to their destinations.

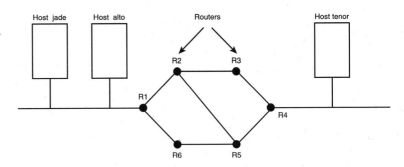

While the network access layer is equipped with the means for delivering data to devices on a directly attached network, it does so based on directions from IP at the internet layer. To understand the implications of this statement, look at the internetwork of Figure 20.3. Hosts jade and alto are said to belong to the same network since they are directly attached to the same physical wire. In contrast, host tenor belongs to a different network.

When a requirement arises to deliver data out of host alto, the internet layer (in particular the IP protocol) has to determine whether the destined host is directly attached to the same network. If so, IP passes the data packet to the network access layer and instructs it to deliver the data to the designated host. So, should, for example, the packet be destined to host jade, IP instructs the network access layer to take the necessary steps to deliver it to that host.

However, if IP on host alto is required to deliver the data packet to a host on a different network (for instance, host tenor), IP has to determine to which network the host belongs and how to get the packet there. As can be seen from the diagram, to deliver packets to host tenor, IP in host alto has to send the packet first to router R1, then R1 in turn has to forward it to R2 (or R3), and so on, as explained in the previous subsection. Consequently, IP passes the packet on to the network access layer and instructs it to deliver the packet to router R1. Notice how in both cases, the case of a host directly attached to same network (host jade) and the case of a host on different network (host tenor), the network access layer followed the addressing instructions imposed by IP at the internet layer. In other words, the network access layer relies on IP at the layer above it to know where to send the data.

TCP/IP Data Encapsulation

As data is passed down the layers, the protocol handling it at that layer adds its own control information before passing the data down to the layer below it. This control information is called the protocol header (simply because it's prepended to the data to be transmitted) and is meant to assist in the delivery of user data. Each layer is oblivious to the headers added to the user data by the layers above it. The process of adding headers to the user data is called data encapsulation.

Using headers, TCP/IP protocols engage in peer talk with their counterparts across the network. As shown in Figure 20.4, when data reaches its ultimate destination, each layer strips off its header information before passing the data on to the layer above. Subsequently, each header is interpreted and used in the handling of the user data.

FIGURE 20.4.

Data encapsulation under TCP/IP. All headers but the network access layer's remain the same. The network access layer's header is a function of the underlying physical network.

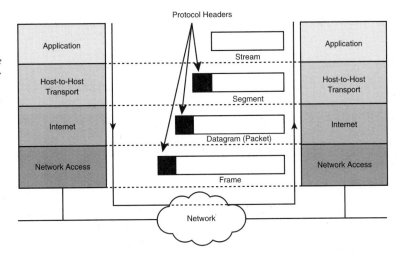

Following are examples of what each header can contain:

- At the transport layer, the header contents include destination and source port numbers. These are treated as process identification numbers, which help in the exchange of encapsulated data between designated processes, without confusing these processes with others that might be running simultaneously on the same involved hosts. The data and header at this layer form a data unit referred to as a *data segment*.

- At the internet layer, the header also contains the IP addresses identifying the ultimate communicating end systems. The data and header information at this layer are referred to as an *IP datagram*.

- At the network access layer, the header includes the media access control (MAC) addresses of source and destination devices on the *same* physical network. The data unit formed at this layer is referred to as a *data frame*.

The Network Access Layer

The network access layer is responsible for the delivery of data to devices connected to the same physical network. It is the only layer that is aware of the details of the underlying network. In other words, the network access layer is aware of details such as the media type (unshielded twisted pair, fiber, coax, and so on), electronic encoding of data, and media access method. Given that TCP/IP formalizes the exchange of data across protocol boundaries in the same host, you can see how a new network access technology can be implemented without affecting the rest of the protocol hierarchy. Ethernet and token ring are examples of underlying technologies that the network access layer relies on to receive data from, or deliver data to, the network.

The network access layer implementation includes the network interface card (that is, the communications hardware) that complies with the communications media, and the protocols that handle all the action (see Figure 20.5). An example of protocols implemented at this level is the Address Resolution Protocol (ARP, discussed in the "Address Resolution Protocol" section), which takes care of mapping the IP symbolic address to the corresponding hardware (MAC) address. It is worth noting from the diagram, that not all data that the network interface card (NIC) receives from the network is passed up the layer hierarchy. Some data might have to be passed by the MAC driver to adjacent protocols coexisting with the driver at the network access layer (for example, Reverse Address Resolution Protocol, discussed later in the chapter). This feature is commonly known as data multiplexing.

FIGURE 20.5.

The network access layer is aware of the details of the underlying physical network. It includes protocols implemented in software as well as the network interface card.

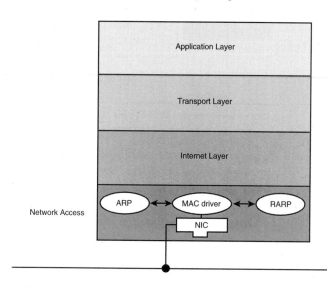

Among other functions, the network access layer encapsulates data that is passed to it by the internet layer into frames for subsequent delivery to the network. Keep in mind, however, that the frame format is a function of the media access technology in use, whereas the data format of upper layer protocols never changes.

The Internet Layer

Two protocols are implemented at this level: the Internet Control Message Protocol (ICMP, RFC792) and the Internet Protocol (RFC791). The purpose of the Internet Protocol (IP) is to handle routing of data around the internetwork (known as the *internet*), while that of ICMP is to handle routing error detection and recovery. IP is the cornerstone of the TCP/IP suite of protocols. All TCP/IP protocols communicate with their peers on the network by riding IP datagrams. Figure 20.6 shows the data structure of the IP datagram (including both the IP header and data passed on from the layer above). IP's header fields are presented in the following discussion of its functions. But first, take a look at its two main characteristics.

FIGURE 20.6.

IP datagram structure. The shaded part is IP's header. IP is oblivious to the contents of the data field passed on by the protocol in the layer above.

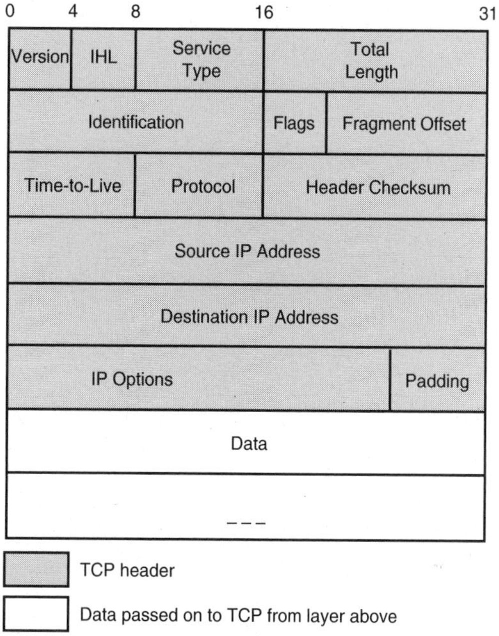

Main Characteristics of IP

IP is a *connectionless* protocol. This means that IP does not attempt to establish a connection with its peer prior to sending data to it. A *connection-oriented* protocol undergoes a sort of handshake with its peer in the remote system. The purpose of the handshake is twofold: It verifies the readiness of the remote peer to receive data before it is sent, and during the handshake both ends of the connection try to reach a mutual agreement on some of the parameters that should govern the data exchange process. An example of a negotiated parameter is the maximum size of the data unit that can be exchanged during the connection.

In addition to being connectionless, IP delivers an *unreliable* service. The unreliability stems from the fact that IP does not provide error detection and recovery. All that IP cares about is the delivery of data to its designated destination. What happens to the datagram during shipment is a concern that is delegated, by design, to IP service users (higher layer protocols). This is very much similar to the postal service, which delivers mail on a best effort basis, while not caring about the quality of what is being shipped or received.

Functions of IP

IP functions include:

Data encapsulation and header formatting

Data routing across the internetwork

Passing data to other protocols

Fragmentation and reassembly

Data Encapsulation

Data encapsulation involves accepting data from the transport layer, and adding to it IP's header control information. As shown in Figure 20.6, the IP header is five or six 32-bit words in length; this is because the sixth word is optional, justifying the IHL field (the Internet Header Length). The first field refers to the version of IP in use, with the current one being number 4. The third field is the type-of-service field (TOS). TOS can be set to specify a desired class of service, as requested by applications. Examples of class of service supported by IP are minimum delay, which is requested by application protocols such as RLOGIN and Telnet, and maximum throughput, which is requested by applications such as FTP and SMTP.

The total length field minus the IHL field indicates to IP the length of the data field. Both the identification and fragmentation fields will be discussed in the section "Fragmentation and Reassembly." The time to live (TTL) field is initialized by IP to the upper limit on the number of routers that a datagram can cross before it ultimately reaches its destination. Assuming that TTL was set to 32, it is decremented by one by each router it crosses. As soon as TTL reaches zero, the datagram is removed by the next router to detect the anomaly. The underlying idea is that with TTL, a lost datagram can be stopped from endless looping around the network. The protocol number field will be discussed later in this section.

Although IP is an unreliable protocol, in the sense that it does not perform error detection and recovery, it still cares about the integrity of its own control information header. With the help of the *header checksum,* IP verifies the integrity of data in the header fields. If the integrity check fails, IP simply discards the datagram. IP does not communicate a notification of the failure, also called *negative acknowledgment,* to the sending host.

The source and destination addresses are 32 bits in length. IP address classes and structure will be dealt with in more detail in the next subsection, "Data Routing." Addresses included in the address fields describe the identities of the ultimate communicating hosts. For example, whenever host alto (in Figure 20.3) is sending data to host tenor, the source and destination address fields will contain the 32-bit IP addresses of these hosts, respectively.

Finally, the options field, which may include other control information, is populated on an as-needed basis, rendering it variable in size. An example of optional information is the route record, which includes the address of every router the datagram traversed during its trip on the network.

Data Routing

Routing is perhaps the most important function that the internet layer performs. IP distinguishes between *hosts* and *gateways*. A gateway (see the following note) in TCP/IP is actually a router that connects two or more networks for the purpose of providing forwarding services between them. Figure 20.7 shows a gateway forwarding a datagram between two networks.

A host is the end system where user applications run. By default, routing on hosts is limited to the delivery of the datagram directly to the remote system, if both hosts are attached to the same network. If not, IP delivers the datagram to a *default gateway* (that is, router). The default gateway is defined on the host during TCP/IP configuration, and is a router attached to the same network, which the host should trust for assistance in deliveries made to other hosts on remote networks.

Figure 20.8 illustrates the concept of default routers. Host X in the diagram is configured to gateway A as its default router. Accordingly, whenever X wants to send data to Y, it delivers the datagram to gateway A (its default router), *not* B. Upon examining the destination IP address, gateway A realizes that the address belongs to host Y, which is on a network to which gateway B is connected. Consequently, gateway A forwards the datagram to gateway B for the subsequent handling and delivery to host Y.

ROUTERS AND GATEWAYS

Currently, the networking industry makes a distinction between a router and a gateway. Routers are said to provide routing services between networks supporting same network protocol stacks. Gateways, on the other hand, connect networks of dissimilar architectures (for example, TCP/IP and Novell's IPX/SPX). Historically, however, the TCP/IP community used the term *gateway* to refer to routing devices. Throughout this chapter, both terms are used interchangeably to refer to routing.

FIGURE 20.7.

A gateway providing routing services between two networks.

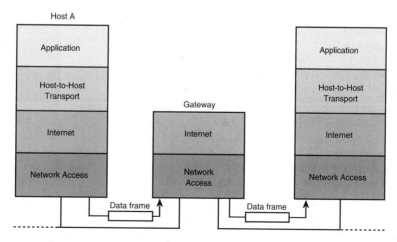

20

NETWORKING

FIGURE 20.8.

A host on an IP network forwards all deliveries pertaining to remote networks to its default router.

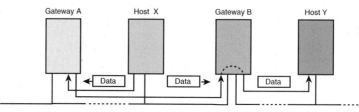

UNIX allows a host to attach to more than one network using multiple interface cards, each attaching to a different network. Such a host is commonly referred to as a *multihomed host.* Furthermore, a UNIX multihomed host can optionally be configured to route data between networks to which it is attached. In other words, it can be made to partly behave as a router. Otherwise, it behaves in exactly the same fashion as other hosts with a single interface card, the difference being that all hosts on networks to which it is attached can engage in the exchange of data with applications it supports.

Passing Data to Other Protocols

It was mentioned earlier in the chapter that all TCP/IP protocols send their data in IP datagrams. Hence, to assist IP in submitting a datagram it receives from the wire to the intended protocol, a *protocol field* is included in IP's header. By TCP/IP standards, each protocol that uses IP routing services is assigned a protocol identification number. Setting the protocol field to 6, for example, designates the TCP protocol, whereas 1 designates the ICMP protocol. A protocol number of 0, however, designates the IP protocol, in which case encapsulated data is processed by IP itself. Figure 20.9 illustrates how the protocol field is used to sort datagrams for subsequent delivery to their destined protocols.

FIGURE 20.9.

When IP receives a datagram from the wire, it internally routes the datagram to one of the shown protocols based on identification information contained in IP's header protocol field.

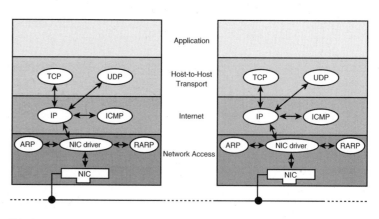

NIC: Network Interface Card

Fragmentation and Reassembly

As shown in Figure 20.6, the total length field in the IP header is 16 bits wide, which means that the largest datagram IP is allowed to handle is 64 kilobytes (65535 bytes) in size.

However, some underlying networks (media access technologies) do not tolerate as much data in a single frame. An Ethernet frame, for example, cannot exceed 1514 bytes. In cases like these, IP resorts to what is known as data *fragmentation*. Fragmentation takes place whenever data in sizes exceeding the frame capacity is passed to IP by another protocol, for subsequent handling on the network.

Although all data fragments are normally delivered using the same route, there is a possibility that a few of them traverse alternate routes. This may happen due to rising congestion on paths followed by earlier fragments, or to link failure. Whatever the case may be, fragments following different routes stand the chance of reaching their destination out of the order in which they were sent. To allow for the recovery from such an eventuality, IP makes use of the *fragmentation offset* field in its header. The fragmentation offset field includes sequencing information, which the remote IP peer uses to reorder data fragments it receives from the network, and to detect missing packets. Data isn't passed to the protocol described in the protocol field unless all related fragments are duly received and reordered. This process of fragment recovery and resequencing is known as *data reassembly*.

How does IP deal with situations in which it is required to fragment two or more large datagrams at the same time? What if all data is being sent to the same remote host? How can the receiving host distinguish between fragments belonging to different datagrams? Well, the answer to these questions lies in the *identification* field. Fragments belonging to the same datagram are uniquely associated by including the same value in the identification field. The receiving end makes use of this value in order to recover the IP fragments to their respective datagrams.

Finally, you may be asking yourself these questions: How can a receiving IP tell whether data is fragmented? How does it know when all fragments are being sent? Answers to both questions lie in the header *flags* field. Among other bits, the flags field includes a *more fragments* bit, which is set "on" in all fragments belonging to a datagram, except for the final fragment.

The Internet Control Message Protocol

The Internet Control Message Protocol (ICMP) forms an integral part of the IP protocol. It is the "messenger" that couriers messages between hosts. ICMP messages carry control, informational, and error recovery data. Below is a description of some of those messages:

- **Source quench:** This is a flow control message, which a receiving host sends to the source, requesting that it stop sending data. This normally happens as the receiving host's communications buffers are close to full.

- **Route redirect:** This is an informational message that a gateway sends to the host seeking its routing services. A gateway sends this message to inform the sending host about another gateway on the network, which it trusts to be closer to the destination.

- **Host unreachable:** A gateway, or a system encountering a problem in the delivery of a datagram (such as link failure, link congestion, or failing host), sends a host unreachable error message. Normally, the ICMP packet includes information describing the reason for unreachability.

■ `Echo request`/`echo reply`: UNIX users commonly use the `ping` command (more on this later) to test for host reachability. When entered, `ping` invokes both ICMP messages: echo request and echo reply. Echo request is sent from the host on which `ping` (covered in the "`ping`: Test for Reachability" section and throughout the chapter) was invoked to the remote system described on the command line. If the remote system is up and operational, it responds with an `echo reply`, which should be interpreted as proof of reachability.

You can invoke ICMP by using the UNIX `ping` command to check on the reachability of a remote host as shown here:

```
# ping 123.5.9.16
123.5.9.16 is alive
```

`ping` invokes an ICMP `echo request` message that is sent to the designated host. If, upon receiving the `echo request`, the host responds with an ICMP `echo response` message, it is reported as being alive (as shown in the example), and hence, reachable. Otherwise, the host is deemed not reachable.

IP Address Structure

In TCP/IP, every device on the network derives its unique *complete network address* by virtue of an address assignment to which the device is configured (more on configuration later in the chapter). The reason the address is termed *complete* is because it is pretty much all that is needed to locate it on the network regardless of its size (similar to the postal address, which completely describes your home address—thus helping others to unambiguously locate you).

The assigned address is known as a *symbolic IP address*, and is made up of two parts: 1) the network address, which is common to all hosts and devices on the same physical network, and 2) the node address, which is unique to the host on that network. As you will see, neither part has anything to do with the actual hardwired MAC address on the network address card. As a matter of fact, a network administrator has the freedom to change the node part of the address (with some restrictions), and to a lesser degree the network address, irrespective of the MAC address. For this reason, the address is described as symbolic.

Confusing as it may initially sound, the IP protocol uses these symbolic addresses to route data on the network. In other words, when a user requests that a Telnet session be established with another host, TCP/IP uses the administrator assigned 32-bit IP addresses in order to connect and establish the Telnet session between both the requesting and the target hosts. The details of this are going to be tackled later in the chapter (refer to the "Address Resolution Protocol" section). First, have a look at how IP addresses are made, and the classes to which they belong.

The IP address is 32 bits (or four bytes) long, including both the network and the node addresses, and it occupies the IP source and destination address fields of the IP header. How many bits of the address belong to the network part, versus the number of bits that belong to the node part is dependent on the IP address class into which the address falls. IP defines three main classes: A, B, and C. There is a Class D, which is lesser in significance than the other ones and will be touched on very briefly.

Figure 20.10 shows the different address formats corresponding to each of the three main classes that IP supports. Each IP address class is distinguishable by the very first few bits of the network portion. The following is a listing of the different IP classes and the rules by which they are governed:

FIGURE 20.10.

IP address classes, and their corresponding structures.

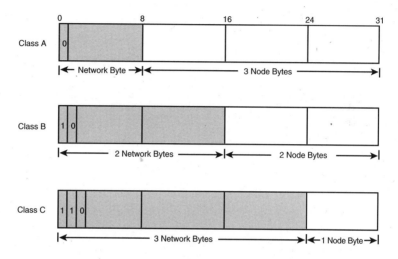

Class A address: The first bit is fixed to 0, and the first byte is called the network ID and identifies the network. The remaining three bytes are used to identify the host on the network, and comprise the host ID. It can be calculated that there is a maximum of 127 Class A networks, with each capable of accommodating millions of hosts.

Class B address: The first two bits are fixed to 10, the first and second byte are used to identify the network, and the last two bytes are used to identify the host. There can be 65,535 hosts on Class B networks, capable of accommodating thousands of hosts.

Class C address: The first three bits are fixed to 110, the first, second, and third bytes are used to identify the network, and the last byte is used to identify the host. Class C networks are the smallest of all classes, as each can accommodate a maximum of 254 hosts (not 256, because 0x0 and 0xFF are reserved for other purposes). With three bytes reserved to identify the network, millions of Class C networks can be defined.

Class D address: The first four bits are fixed to 1110. A Class D address is a multicast address, identifying a group of computers that may be running a distributed application on the network. As such, Class D does not describe a network of hosts on the wire.

20

NETWORKING

To make address administration a relatively easy task, TCP/IP network administrators can configure hosts and routers with addresses by using what is commonly known as dotted decimal notation. Dotted decimal notation treats the 32-bit address as four separate, yet contiguous, bytes. Each byte is represented by its decimal equivalent, which lies between 0 and 255 (the decimal range equivalent to an 8-bit binary pattern). Figure 20.11 shows an example of a class A address in both binary and dotted decimal (69.18.11.135) notation.

Figure 20.11.

IP address in binary and the equivalent dotted decimal notation.

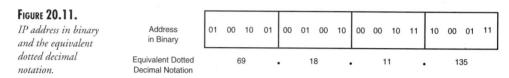

Given that an 8-bit binary pattern can assume any decimal equivalent in the range of 0 to 255 and given the initial bits of a certain class, you should be able to tell from the first byte the class of the network. Table 20.1 depicts the range of values for the first byte of each of the IP address that classes can assume.

Table 20.1. IP address classes and the range of values their respective first byte can assume.

Address Class	Decimal Range
A	0–127
B	128–191
C	192–223

Consider the address 148.29.4.121. By applying the rules learned above, it can be determined that this is a Class B address, because the first byte lies in the 128 to 191 range of values. And because a Class B address has the first two bytes for a network address, it can be derived that the network address is 148.29 while the host address is 4.121 on that network. To generalize, given an IP address, its class can be recognized by interpreting the first byte. Consequently, the network portion of the address can be derived from the remaining bytes.

Figure 20.12 shows an example of a Class B network. Notice how all the hosts have the 148.29 network address in common. A host misconfigured (for example, host X in Figure 20.12b) to any other network address will not be able to talk to other hosts on the network, be it on same physical network or other router connected networks. When a host or any other network device is assigned an IP address, IP derives its network class and network address from that assignment (148.29). Later, when it is required to deliver a datagram to a host, it compares the network address of the destination address submitted by the transport protocol (TCP or UDP) to that of its own. If the addresses match, IP refrains from routing the datagram (as explained earlier, the datagram won't be sent to a router for assistance in delivery). Instead, IP assumes that the host is on the same network and, therefore, attempts a direct delivery to the designated node address.

FIGURE 20.12.

(a) A properly configured network has all of the hosts belonging to it assigned the same network address. (b) Host X is configured to a network address that is inconsistent with the other hosts, resulting in routing conflicts.

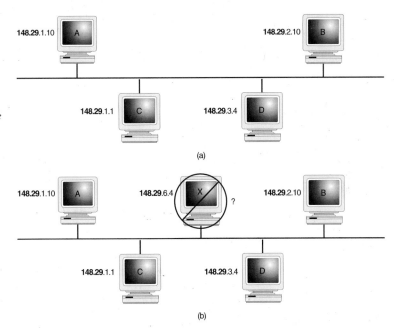

Assuming that you are on host X and want to establish a file transfer session with host A on the network, you can enter the command:

```
ftp 148.29.1.10
```

See the "Domain Name System" section later in this chapter to learn how to specify a host using a name instead of the IP address.

TCP picks up the address and passes it to IP, at the internet layer, along with a TCP segment (which in turn contains the user request for FTP connection) that it wants delivered to host A. IP, on host X, compares its own network address (147.29) with that of host A (148.29). Since they are not the same, IP concludes that host A must belong to a remote network, and therefore direct delivery is not possible. For simplicity, assume that the network in Figure 20.12b is the only one in its environment, in which case there can be no routers on the wire. IP won't be able to forward the packet any further and will report a failure to deliver to the upper layer or application.

In Figure 20.13 you are shown two networks, a Class B Ethernet network and a Class A token ring network. A router is also shown connecting the two networks. An important observation to make is that the router is configured to two addresses: 148.29.15.1 and 198.53.2.8. The question that normally arises is, "Which of the two is *the* address?" Well, as a matter of fact an

20

NETWORKING

address that you assign to the host is assigned to, or associated with, the network interface card that attaches the host to the network. Hence, in the case of a router and multihomed host, an address is required for every NIC card supported. Depending on which network the NIC attaches the host to, it must be assigned an IP address with a network part consistent with the network address assigned to the rest of the hosts community. Hosts on the token ring network use 198.53.2.8 to address the router, whereas those on Ethernet use 148.29.15.1.

FIGURE 20.13.

Routers are assigned as many addresses as network interface cards support.

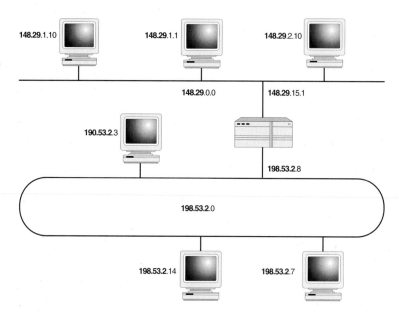

You saw earlier that all *0*s and all *1*s (0x0 and 0xff, respectively) are reserved for special purposes, and therefore cannot be used to designate a node on the network. This is because an all *0*s node address refers to all nodes on the network. For example, in the routing table of the router in Figure 20.13, a destination address of 198.53.2.0 refers to all hosts on the token ring network. While an all-*1*s node address is normally used to broadcast a message to all hosts on that network. Therefore, a host transmitting a broadcast message to 198.53.2.255 will have the message picked up by all active hosts on the token ring network only. Similarly, a broadcast to 148.29.255.255 will be picked up by all hosts on the Ethernet.

In addition to the reservations made on the node addresses described above, there are two class A network addresses that bear a special significance and cannot be used to designate a network. They are network addresses 0 and 127. Network 0 is used to designate the *default route*, whereas 127 is used to designate *this host* or the *loopback address*. As explained previously (refer to the "Data Routing" section) in this chapter, the default route refers to a router configuration that makes the routing of packets to destinations that are unknown to the router possible. The loopback address is used to designate the local host and is used to send to the interface an IP datagram in exactly the same way other interfaces on the network are addressed.

Conventionally, 127.0.0.1 is the address which is used to designate the local host. You can, however, use any other Class A 127 address for the same purpose. For example 127.45.20.89 is valid for designating the local host as is the 127.0.0.1. This is because a datagram sent to the loopback interface must not, in any case, be transmitted on the wire.

Subnet Mask

Class B networks accommodate approximately 65,000 hosts each, whereas Class A networks accommodate thousands of nodes. In practice, however, it is not feasible to put all on the same network. Here are two considerations:

- **Limitations imposed by the underlying physical network:** Depending on the type of physical network, there is an upper limit on the number of hosts that can be connected to the same network. Ethernet 10BASE-T, for example, imposes a limit of 1,024 nodes per physical network.

- **Network traffic:** Sometimes it might not be feasible even to reach the maximum allowable limit of nodes on the underlying physical network. Depending on the amount of traffic applications generate on the network you might have to resort to breaking the network into smaller subnetworks to alleviate prevailing network congestion conditions.

- **Geographic proximity:** Organizations with branch offices across the nation or around the globe connect their computing resources over wide area network (WAN) links. This requires treating the branch office local area networks (LANs) as a network of interconnected networks—commonly referred to as an internetwork (also as intranetwork).

In recognition of the eventual requirement that organizations might need to break their networks into smaller subnetworks, the TCP/IP protocol stack supports the use of same network address to achieve this objective. The use of same network address to implement a router-connected subnetworks is achieved by modifying the IP address structure, to extend the network ID portion beyond its default boundary. The mechanism for doing so is called subnet masking.

Because 148.29.0.0 is a Class B address, its default network ID consists of the two leftmost bytes (148.29), and the two lowest bytes are the node address (0.0). A network designer may choose to extend the network ID to include all of the second significant byte in order to break the network into smaller ones. Thus the only byte left for the node ID becomes the rightmost byte. Figure 20.14 illustrates the situation. As shown, each of the networks is now identified using the three left-most bytes (as though dealing with Class C networks). In other words, all hosts on the token ring network must have the 148.29.3 portion common to their addresses. Similarly, on the Ethernet networks, the 148.29.1 must be common to all addresses of hosts on the segment Ethernet 1, and 148.29.2 in common for all hosts on segment Ethernet 2.

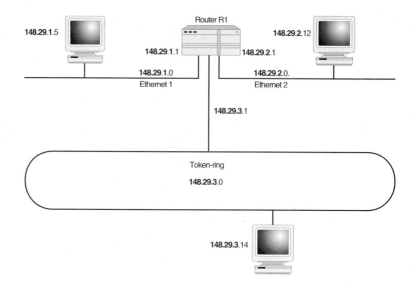

FIGURE 20.14.

A Class B address (148.29.0.0) being used on a subnetted network.

How does TCP/IP on a host or router know how to split the network address between the network ID and the host ID? Unless specified, TCP/IP assumes the default (16 bits for the network ID and 16 bits for the host ID for Class B addresses). To specify a different split, TCP/IP software supports a configuration parameter that is referred to as a *subnet mask*. Using a subnet mask, you can tell TCP/IP (in particular, IP protocol) which bytes constitute the network ID as opposed to the node ID.

A subnet mask is a 32-bit number that is applied to an IP address to identify the network and node address of a host or router interface. As a rule, you are required to assign a binary 1 to those bits in the mask that correspond in position to the bits that you want IP to treat as part of the network ID. Similar to the IP address when specified, the subnet mask is normally using the dotted decimal notation. As such, the default subnet masks corresponding to Classes A, B, and C networks are 255.0.0.0, 255.255.0.0, and 255.255.255.0, respectively (see Figure 20.15). In order to extend the network ID to include the third byte in a Class B address, its subnet mask then becomes 255.255.255.0 (same as Class C's).

IP Routing Dynamics

Now that we have enough of the needed background information, let's proceed to detailing the dynamics that govern the routing of data around the network. The depiction includes illustrations about some of the commonly useful and related UNIX commands.

As explained earlier, routers take part in the delivery of data only if the data is being exchanged between hosts that are connected to two different networks. Data being exchanged between hosts on the same network is never routed. For example, should host trumpet need to send data to host horn, it sends it directly to host horn without asking for the intervention of any of the routers (R1 and R2). Consequently, the data packets being exchanged between both hosts never shows on other networks—they remain local to the network that both hosts belong to.

Figure 20.15.

Default subnet masks. Bits set to 1 in the mask correspond to the bits in the IP address that should be treated as part of the network ID.

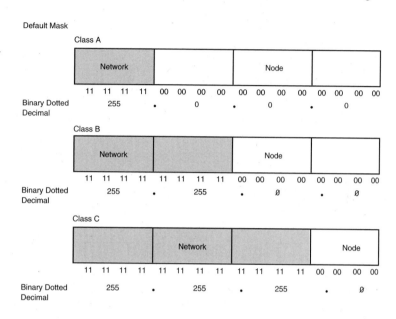

The IP protocol decides whether the destined host belongs to the same network by comparing the network ID portion of that host with its host's. Whenever the network IDs of both the originating and destination hosts mismatch, the IP protocol tries to seek the help of a router on the same network. As a network may have more than one router connecting it to other networks, IP chooses the router it *trusts* to be closer to the designated destination. If one is found, the data packet is forwarded to that router. As will be explained in the next subsection, IP knows which of the routers to forward the data to by looking up a routing database called route information table (RIT).

In Figure 20.16, whenever host trumpet wants to deliver to host trombone, the following happens:

1. Host trumpet compares its network ID of 100 with that of host trombone's of 148.67 (being Class B). Since they are different, the next step is to seek a router's help.

2. IP in host trumpet searches its RIT for a router it trusts that is closer to the destination network (148.67). If the routing table is properly maintained, host trumpet identifies router R3 as being the desired router. Consequently, the data packet is forwarded to that router.

3. Router R3 receives the data packet and compares the destination address encapsulated in the destination address field of the IP packet to the ID of the networks to which it is connected. The outcome of the comparison allows router R3 to decide whether the

designated host belongs to any of these networks. If so, the packet is sent directly to the host. Otherwise, router R3 goes through step 2 above. In our case, since host trombone belongs to network 148.67.0.0 (to which router R3 is directly attached), the comparison is favorable to sending the packet directly to that host.

FIGURE 20.16.

IP data routing.

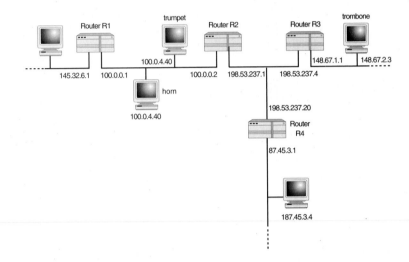

Route Information Table (RIT)

As mentioned in the previous section, IP protocol performs its routing function by consulting a database that contains information about routes (networks) that it recognizes. This database is called the route information table, and it is built and maintained by yet another protocol called the Route Information Protocol (RIP). RIP handles route discovery—that is, it is a process whose main purpose is to identify all the networks on the internetwork and the routers that are closest to each network. RIP is a protocol that runs on all hosts on routers. Hence, every RIP constructs and maintains the database (road map) from the perspective of the workstation or router in which it is running. The RIP includes the following information on each destination it recognizes on the internetwork:

- Distance: Serves as an indication of how far the destination is from the host or router. Normally, it is equal to the number of intervening routers the datagram has to go through to reach its destination. Distance is also referred to as the *metric*, or number of hops.

- Next Router: Includes the IP address of the router that is trusted to be closer to the destination, and therefore the datagram should be forwarded to in the delivery.

- Output Port: Specifies which of the network interfaces in the host (if multihomed) or router is attached to the same network as the next router.

For example, host `trumpet`'s routing table (see Figure 20.16) would include an entry saying that it is 2 hops (the distance or metric) or routers away from network 148.67.0.0, and that the next router to deliver to is at address 100.0.0.2. Router R2's routing table entry would say that it is one router away from the same destination network (148.67.0.0), and that the next router to send the data to is R3.

The UNIX command to display the contents of the routing information table is `netstat -rn` as shown here:

```
# netstat -rn
Routing tables
Destination      Gateway            Flags    Refs      Use   Interface
127.0.0.1        127.0.0.1           UH               1        0     lo0
87.45.3.4        198.53.237.20  UGH         0        0    e3B0
100                  100.0.0.2            U                    4       51    wdn0
221.78.39       198.53.237.20  UG          0        0    e3B0
default            198.53.237.5    UG            0        0    e3B0
198.53.237     198.53.237.1    U              3      624   e3B0
```

Here is how to interpret each of the preceding columns:

- The `Destination` column includes to the address of the network or host. When a host IP address is specified (as in the first and second entries), the destination is referred to as the *specific* route.

- The `Gateway` column refers to the next router.

- The `Flags` column provides status information about that route. Each of the characters in the `Flags` column describes a specific state. The interpretation of flag characters is

    U: The route is up. This implies that the destination is reachable.

    H: The route is specific, or leads, to a certain host (as shown in the first and second entries in the above example).

    G: The route is indirectly accessible via other routers. If the G flag is not set it means that the router (or host) is directly connected to that route.

    D: The route is *created* by the ICMP protocol's route redirect message.

    M: The route is *modified* by the ICMP protocol's route redirect message.

- The `Refs` column shows the number of active connections over that route. Active connections can be due to ongoing FTP or Telnet sessions among others. Any service or application that utilizes TCP as the underlying transport protocol increments this column by one upon invocation.

- The `Use` column keeps track of the number of packets that traversed this route since TCP/IP was started.

- The `Interface` column includes the name of the local interface from which the datagram should be forwarded to the next router. Upon configuring a network interface card, UNIX assigns it a label. For example, under SCO UNIX, e3B0 is the

20

NETWORKING

label assigned to the first 3c503 card in the host, whereas wdn0 refers to WD8003E interface card.

Route Table Maintenance

TCP/IP supports both static and dynamic means of maintaining the routing table. Static means of maintaining the routing table mainly involve the use of the two UNIX commands: `ifconfig` and `route add`. Using `ifconfig`, a network interface card can be configured to an IP address and the applicable subnet mask as shown in the following example:

```
# ifconfig e3B0 100.0.0.2 255.0.0.0
```

Aside from configuring the interface (e3B0) to the specified address and subnet mask, the `ifconfig` command has the effect of updating the route information table with static route information pertaining to the directly attached network (that is, `100.0.0.0`) as shown in the previous listing of the output of `netstat -rn` command.

Using the `route add` command a static route can be entered to the routing table of a UNIX host. The syntax of the route command is

```
route add destination_address next_router metric
```

in which

> *destination_address* is the route you want to add to the routing table.
>
> *next_router* is the address of the next router to forward the datagrams to.
>
> *metric* is a measure of distance to the destination, normally expressed in number of intervening routers.

The following example shows how `route add` can be used to add a new destination to the routing table:

```
# route add 87.45.3.4  198.53.237.20 1
```

The following example shows how to use `route add` to configure a host for the default route entry:

```
# route add 0.0.0.0 198.53.237.5 1
```

By virtue of the preceding entry, the host in question is being configured to recognize the router at address 198.53.237.5 as being its default gateway.

Dynamic route maintenance involves the automatic addition of new discovered routes to the route table. It also involves deletions of routes that are no longer valid by virtue of network reconfiguration or due to failures. There are several protocols that might be employed for the task of dynamic route maintenance. Among the currently common ones are Route Information Protocol (RIP), Open Shortest Path First (OSPF), and Internet Control Messaging Protocol (ICMP). Of the three, only ICMP was discussed earlier in the chapter. For detailed treatment of all routing information protocols the reader is referred to the section "Networking."

Address Resolution Protocol (ARP)

Every network interface card has a unique 48-bit address hardwired to the card itself. This address is commonly referred to as Medium Access Layer (MAC) address. The IP address you assign to a host is independent of the MAC address that is hardwired on the network interface card in that host. As such, every host ends up maintaining two addresses: the IP address which is significant to TCP/IP protocols only, and the MAC address that is significant to the network access layer only. Data frames exchanged on the wire, however, rely on the latter address, which indicates that there must be some sort of binding relation between these two forms of addresses. This section unravels this relationship. In particular, you will be shown how, given the IP address of a target host, the network access layer finds the corresponding MAC address, used later by the MAC protocol (for example, Ethernet) to communicate data frames.

Figure 20.17 includes a depiction of the events which take place between two hosts when they try to talk to each other. In the diagram, both the IP address and the MAC layer addresses are shown for both hosts. It is assumed that a user on host jade wanted to establish a Telnet session with host orbit. The following is what happens:

FIGURE 20.17.

IP address to physical MAC address resolution using ARP protocol.

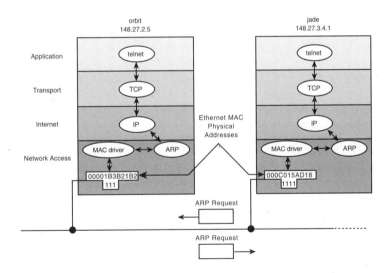

1. As a result of the user entering the command telnet jade, the application (Telnet, in this case) resolves the name jade to its corresponding IP address. See the note below for an introductory description of name resolution under TCP/IP (more details are provided later in the chapter). By the end of this stage, Telnet will have determined that host jade's address is 148.27.34.1.

2. Next, Telnet passes the address (148.27.34.1) to TCP/IP and requests connection to the target host. Subsequently, TCP packages the request in a TCP header and passes it along with the address to the IP protocol, requesting delivery to the corresponding host.

20

NETWORKING

3. At this point, IP compares jade's address with other destination addresses included in its routing database. Because both the source and target host have the same network ID (148.27.0.0), IP decides to make a direct delivery to jade. Subsequently, IP encapsulates the request passed to it by TCP in an IP datagram, including the destination and source IP addresses (148.27.34.1 and 148.27.2.5). Then it submits the datagram, along with jade's IP address to the network access layer for delivery on the physical network.

4. This is where ARP comes in to handle the resolution of the IP address, which is useless from Ethernet's point of view (assuming Ethernet at the MAC layer) to a MAC address which Ethernet understands. Put differently, ARP translates the symbolic IP address, assigned by the administrator, to the corresponding physical address which the host uses to identify itself at the physical and data link levels.

   ARP handles address resolution by sending out of the MAC interface (Ethernet) a broadcast message known as an *ARP request*, which simply says, "I, host 148.27.2.5, physically addressable at 0x00001b3b21b2, want to know the physical address of host 147.27.34.1." Of all of the hosts which receive the broadcast, only jade responds using a directed ARP response packet which says, "I am 147.27.34.1, and my physical address is 0x0000c015ad18."

5. At this point, both hosts become aware of the other's physical identity. The network access layer (on host orbit) then proceeds to the actual phase of data exchange by encapsulating the IP datagram, which it kept on hold until the ARP query was favorably answered, in a data frame and sending it to host jade.

NOTE

TCP/IP protocol suites define what is known as name services. Name services relieve users from the tedious and inconvenient task of entering target host IP addresses, simply by allowing them to specify a name designating that host. The simplest method of mapping the host name to its actual IP address involves the use of a hosts file which is normally maintained in the /etc directory of every host. The hosts file is an ASCII file with two columns: the IP address column and the host names column, similar to the one below

```
#IP address    host name
...    ...
148.27.34.1    jade
148.27.2.5     orbit
...    ...
```

When a user enters telnet jade, one way for telnet to find the corresponding IP address is by consulting the /etc/hosts database.

ARP Cache

When an IP address is resolved to its equivalent MAC address, ARP maintains the mapping in its own special ARP cache memory, improving transmission efficiency and the response time to user requests. Another benefit of ARP caching is the bandwidth saving realized by not requiring that a host sends an ARP request broadcast every time it has data to send to the same target host.

The ARP cache can be checked using the arp command as shown in the following:

```
$ arp -a
jade <100.0.0.10> at 0:0:1b:3b:21:b2
```

How long ARP maintains an entry in its cache table is a function of how often the host communicates with a specific host, and vendor implementation.

Proxy ARP

Proxy ARP is an implementation of ARP at the router which is designed to handle ARP queries on behalf of hosts on remote networks. Looking at Figure 20.10, with proxy ARP on the router, then whenever jade sends out an ARP query requesting the MAC address corresponding to IP address 129.34.2.6, the following events take place:

FIGURE 20.18.

Proxy ARP on the router handles ARP queries on behalf of remote hosts on the network.

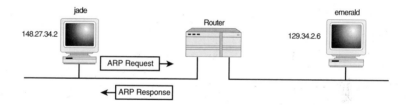

1. The ARP request broadcast is picked up by the router.

2. If the router recognizes the address as one belonging to a network which it can reach, it responds to the "ARPing" host with its own MAC address. Otherwise it discards the request silently.

3. From here, data destined to host emerald is delivered directly to the router, which in turn routes the data to emerald (how? Remember that routers route data based on the IP address embedded in the IP header, which in this case will be emerald's).

The Host-to-Host Transport Layer

The host-to-host layer is mainly supported by two protocols: User Datagram Protocol (UDP) and Transmission Control Protocol (TCP). Whereas the former is a connectionless and unreliable protocol, the latter is a connection-oriented and fully reliable protocol. Figure 20.19 shows the data structures of both protocol headers. Rather than delving deeply into the meaning of each field, this section focuses on the general features of both protocols and the use of the source and destination port numbers in both headers. The reader interested in a rigorous treatment of both protocols is referred to the book *Networking UNIX* by Sams Publishing (ISBN 0-672-30584-4).

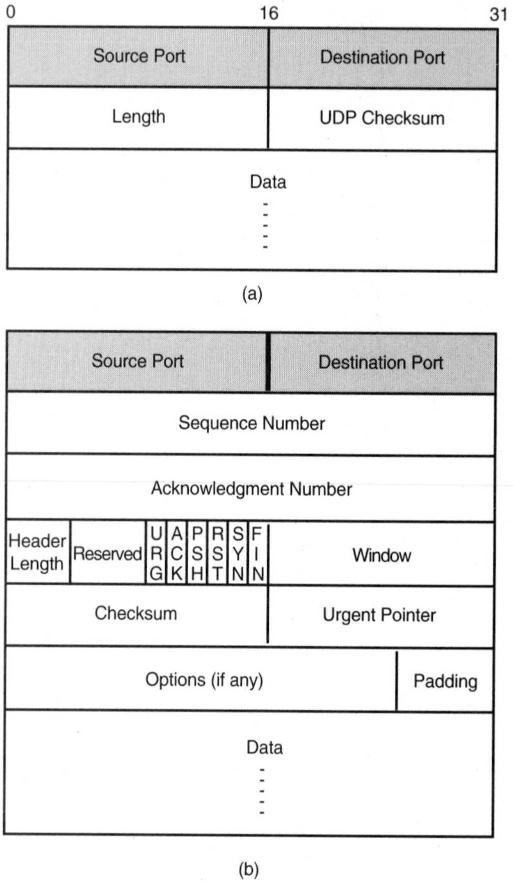

Figure 20.19.

a) Header of UDP, and b) Header of TCP transport protocol. Both protocols include source and destination port numbers identifying the applications on whose behalf they are exchanging data.

(a)

(b)

At the transport layer, application layer protocols are assigned *port numbers*. Port numbers are used in the source and destination port fields included in the transport protocol header. Transport layer protocols use them in much the same way as IP uses the protocol field. IP uses the protocol field to identify the protocol to deliver the contents of the data field to (refer to earlier discussion of IP header). Port numbers are used to distinguish which applications are using the services of the transport layer protocol.

Figure 20.20 illustrates this concept. In the figure, you are shown application protocols (SMTP, FTP, DNS, and SNMP), which are engaged in the exchange of data with their respective counterparts on remote host B. Unless the transport protocol at both ends uses port numbers, it will be confusing, if not impossible, for it to deliver the data to the appropriate application protocol. As shown in the diagram, at the Internet layer, IP decides where to submit the contents of data (whether to ICMP, TCP, UDP, or other) based on the protocol identifier. Assuming IP delivers the contents of the data field (which at this point consists of the user data as well as the transport header) to TCP, the latter has to identify the application (FTP, Telnet, SMTP, and so on) to submit the user data to.

FIGURE 20.20.

While IP relies on the protocol field in its header to internally route data to one of either TCP, UDP, or ICMP, the transport layer protocol (UDP or TCP) relies on port numbers when routing data to the higher user protocols.

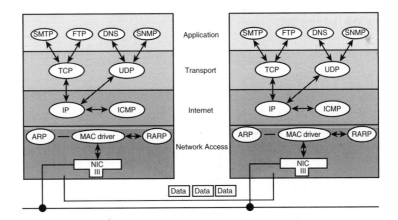

If you want to know how the port numbers are assigned, you need only to check out the contents of the file /etc/services. The details of this file are presented in the "/etc/services" section.

UDP Versus TCP

UDP is a connectionless, unreliable transport protocol. This means that UDP is not sophisticated enough (as reflected in the structure of its header, refer to Figure 4.19) to care about the datagrams it sends down the network. Being connectionless, UDP does not negotiate a connection with its peer for the sake of establishing a control mechanism that guaranties the reliable delivery of data. Once it delivers data to IP for subsequent transmission, UDP simply forgets about it and proceeds to other business.

TCP's behavior is quite opposite to UDP's. Its sophistication allows it to deliver data reliably. TCP's sophistication stems from its capability to establish a connection with its peer on behalf of the applications engaging in the exchange of data. This allows it to successfully track the progress of the data delivery process until the process is successfully concluded. Data lost or damaged on the wire, can be easily recovered by the TCP protocol by virtue of communicating the need for retransmitting the affected data segment to its sending peer across the network.

Why use UDP then, when TCP is the more reliable of the two? To applications that are designed to handle error detection and recovery, using UDP poses no serious threat. Rather, the choice of UDP becomes the reasonable one. Equally qualifying to the use of UDP is the size and nature of data being exchanged. Transactional services involving small amounts of data behave more efficiently using UPD services than TCP. This is especially applicable to transactions in which all the data can be accommodated in one datagram. Should a datagram be lost or deformed, retransmitting that datagram incurs less overhead than is involved in establishing a TCP connection and releasing it later.

Later (see the "Network Troubleshooting Using UNIX Tools" section) you will be shown how to use UNIX commands such as `netstat` to track transport protocol level activities.

Name Services

One way a user can establish a session with a remote host is by entering the IP address of that host as a command-line parameter to the application being invoked. For example, to invoke a remote login session with a host of IP address 100.0.0.2, the following command can be entered:

```
# rlogin 100.0.0.2
```

Rather than requiring users to enter the IP address of the desired host, TCP/IP provides the means of assigning and administering names to hosts and the accompanying mechanisms responsible for resolving user-specified names to machine-usable IP addresses.

Host names are normally assigned upon system installation. To find the name assigned to your host, use the uname command with the `-a` option as shown here:

```
# uname -a
SunOS tenor 5.5.1Generic i86pc i386 i86pc
```

According to this output, the host name is `tenor` (second field from the left). To change the name of a host you can use the `-S` option along with the new name. To change the host name to `violin`, enter the following:

```
# uname -S violin
```

Beware that host name changes are not implemented in the `/etc/hosts` file. Consequently, whenever the name is changed using the uname command, you ought to implement the change in the `/etc/hosts` to ensure proper name resolution.

Host Name and the `/etc/hosts` Table

The simplest method of resolving host names to IP addresses involves the maintenance of a host table on every UNIX system. This table is normally maintained in the `/etc/hosts` file. It is composed of a simple flat database in which each entry describes the IP address of a host and its associated (or assigned) name. Shown here are the contents of a sample hosts file:

```
#       @(#)hosts    1.2 Lachman System V STREAMS TCP   source
#       SCCS IDENTIFICATION
#       IP address    Hostname         aliases
127.0.0.1      localhost
100.0.0.2      jade.harmonics.com jade
198.53.237.1    pixel
100.0.0.1      alto
100.0.0.5      flyer
100.0.0.3      tenor
```

As shown, each entry consists of an IP address, the host name associated with the IP address, and, optionally, an alias—where an alias is another name for the same host in question. For example, jade and jade.harmonics.com refer to the same host (that of IP address 100.0.0.2). For a user to establish a Telnet session with jade, he has the choice now of entering

```
$ telnet jade
```

or

```
$ telnet jade.harmonics.com
```

All TCP/IP applications, such as Telnet and FTP, have a built-in name resolution mechanism that looks at the host's table and returns the corresponding IP address to the invoked application. The application then proceeds to contact the corresponding host across the network. Failure to resolve the name to an IP address normally results in the error message "Unknown host".

Domain Name System

The host's table-based approach to name resolution is convenient for reasonably small networks with few entries to include in the /etc/hosts file, provided that these networks are not connected to the Internet and have no need to run DNS services. Even if the network is not connected to the Internet, the idea of maintaining identical /etc/hosts files on all UNIX hosts is a time-demanding idea as it requires that changes made to one must be consistently implemented in all others. An approach that can easily become nightmarish as the size of the network increases.

Domain Name System (DNS, RFC 1035) is an alternative way to performing name resolution. Using DNS to resolve host names to IP addresses involves the use of a global, hierarchical, and distributed database containing information (including IP addresses) about all hosts on the network as well as those on the Internet. The hierarchy allows for the subdivision of the name space into independently manageable partitions called *domains* (or *subdomains*). The distributed nature allows for the relocation of partitions (subdomains) of the database onto name servers belonging to sites around the network or the Internet. Consequently, sites hosting name services can be delegated the responsibility for managing their subdomains.

A name server is a host maintaining a partition of the DNS database and running a server process (on UNIX it is called *named daemon*) that handles name-to-IP address resolution in addition to providing some other pertinent host information.

TCP/IP applications have the DNS client component, known as the *name resolver*, built into them. In other words, no special UNIX daemon is required to support name queries on behalf of applications. Figure 20.21 shows how a name query is handled as a user enters ftp jade.harmonics.com to start a file transfer session. Host name jade.harmonics.com is the fully qualified domain name (FQDN) by DNS naming rules, which will be discussed shortly. According to the diagram, resolver routines, included in the FTP client, package the name in a

DNS query and send it to a DNS server that the host is configured to recognize. The DNS server looks up the requested information (in this case, the IP address) and sends a reply to the requesting host.

FIGURE 20.21.

DNS name resolution and name servers.

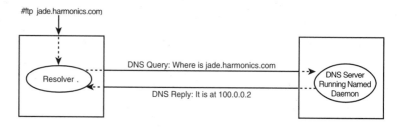

Logical Organization of DNS

When setting up DNS, you ought to follow certain rules in organizing your domain. Understanding those rules is as important to the proper implementation of DNS as understanding the rules which govern file system organization for the effective administration of you UNIX system.

The Internet's DNS organization will be used throughout the chapter to illustrate DNS concepts. Also, a fictitious subdomain (`harmonics.com`) will be introduced to illustrate some of the associated concepts at this level. It is important that you keep in mind that your situation may dictate a different organization from the Internet's. The rules and concepts, however, are still the same.

DNS is a hierarchical database of host information. Its structure resembles, to a great extent, that of computer file systems. Figure 20.22 draws an analogy between the organization of DNS and that of the UNIX file system. In both cases, the organization follows that of an inverted tree with the root at the top of the structure. Where the root of the file system is written as a slash "/", that of DNS is written as a dot "." representing the null "" character. Below the root level, the upper most domain is defined and may be subdivided into domains, which can then be further divided into subdomains—similar to dividing the UNIX file system into subdivisions called directories and subdirectories. Each subdomain is assigned a name (or a label), which can be up to 63 characters long, and can be divided further into subdomains. DNS allows nesting of up to 127 domains in one tree.

Each domain (or subdomain) represents a partition of the database, which may contain information about hosts in that domain, and/or information about lower domains (using the file system analogy, a directory or subdirectory represents a partition of the file system where information about both files and lower subdirectories is kept).

A directory, or file, under the UNIX file system, can be referred to using relative paths or an absolute path specified relative to the root. The `lib` directory in Figure 20.22b can be referenced relative to its parent `share` directory, or relative to the root "/", to become `/usr/share/lib`. In a similar fashion, a domain under DNS can be referred to relative to its parent domain using its name only, or relative to the root domain.

Figure 20.22.

Analogy between DNS domain and UNIX file system organization.

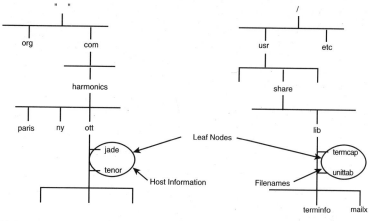

(a) Domain Name Space Organization   (b) UNIX Name Space Organization

A domain name specification relative to the root is known as the *fully qualified domain name* (FQDN). As Figure 20.23 illustrates, an absolute file or directory name is written as a sequence of relative names from the root to the target directory, or filename. Under DNS, a fully qualified domain name is written as a sequence of labels, starting with the target domain name and ending at to the root domain. For example, `ott.harmonics.com` is the fully qualified domain name of the subdomain `ott`.

Figure 20.23.

Absolute domain naming conventions compared with UNIX file system naming conventions.

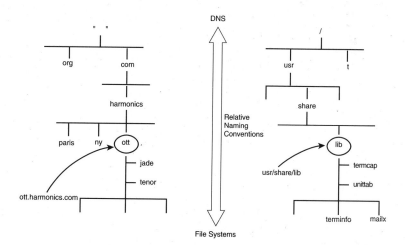

To translate these into real terms, you are presented with a partial portrait of the organization of the top level of the Internet's domain. The Internet authorities have divided the root level domain into top level domains, of which only the `org` and `com` domains are shown in the diagrams. While the root level domain is served by a group of root servers, top level domains are served in their turn by their own servers with each maintaining a partition of the global database.

20

NETWORKING

The harmonics domain, created under the com domain, represents further subdivision of the database. This implies that Harmonics (a fictitious institute of music, with branches in Ottawa, New York, and Paris) undertook the responsibility of maintaining and administering its own name space by setting up its own *authoritative server* for its domain.

As shown in Figure 20.22, files represent the leaf nodes of the file system, below which no further subdivision of the name space is possible. Hosts (jade and tenor) represent the leaf nodes in the domain system, and therefore the actual resource. The type of information that the leaf node might represent is quite general. For example, a leaf node may represent the IP address of the associated host, a *mail exchanger* (that is, mail router) or some domain structural information.

How does a DNS server know which type of information is being queried? Each *resource record* stored in the database is assigned a *type*. When a client sends a query to a name server it must specify which type of information is requested. To be capable to telnet a host for example, the client must request that the name be resolved into an IP address of a host. However, a mail application may request that the name be resolved into the IP address of a mail exchanger.

One last rule to point out: The hierarchical structure of DNS allows two or more hosts to have the same name as long as they do not belong to the same subdomain. Similarly two files may have the same filename as long as they belong to different subdirectories.

Delegation of Administrative Authority

Rather than centralizing the administration of the DNS service in the hands of a single administrative authority on the Internet, DNS's hierarchical organization allows for the breakup of this responsibility into smaller manageable parts, pertaining to the administration of smaller domains of the name space. Consequently, each of the member organizations of the Internet is delegated the authority for managing its own domain. In practical terms, this requires that each of the organizations set up its own name server(s). The name server would then maintain all the host information, and respond to name queries, pertaining to that organization.

When an organization joins the Internet, it is normally delegated the responsibility of administering its own domain name space. In Figure 20.24, the responsibility of the harmonics.com domain is delegated to Harmonics (the organization).

Once delegated the administration of its own domain, an organization can in turn break up its own domain into yet smaller subdomains and delegate the responsibility of administering them to other departments. Referring to the harmonics.com domain, Harmonics set up lower-level domains reflecting their geographical organization. Instead of centralizing the administration of the entire domain in the headquarters at Ottawa, the MIS department might choose to delegate the responsibility for each subdomain to local authorities at each site.

As mentioned earlier, the delegation of parts of a subdomain to member organizations or departments in practical terms translates the relocation of parts of the DNS database pertaining to those subdomains to other name servers. Hence, instead of maintaining all the information about subdomains that are delegated to other departments, the name server(s) of a the parent domain maintains pointers to subdomain servers only. This way, when queried for information about hosts in the delegated subdomains, a domain server knows where to send the query for an answer.

FIGURE 20.24.

Domain name space delegation.

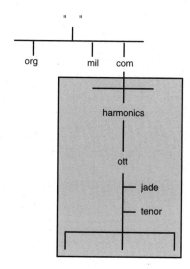

Delegation of administrative authority for subdomains has the following advantages:

- Distribution of workload: Relocating parts of the global DNS database to servers belonging to member organizations considerably reduces the burden of responding to name queries on upper- and top-level DNS servers.

- Improved response time: The sharing of the query load results in improved response time.

- Improved bandwidth utilization: Distribution of the database places servers closer to the local authority. This prevents traffic due to queries pertaining to local resources from needlessly consuming Internet bandwidth.

The Internet Top-Level Domains

Many readers may have already encountered domain labels in the form of rs.internic.net, or e-mail addresses in the form of NADEEM@harmonics.com. This section attempts to familiarize you with the organization of the Internet from which those labels are derived—a kind of familiarity which is particularly important if your network is currently connected to the Internet, or if you are planning on this connection some time in the future.

The Internet DNS name space is hierarchical in organization, and follows the same rules depicted earlier. Figure 20.25 shows this hierarchical organization.

As depicted in the diagram, upper levels of the Internet domain adhere to certain traditions. At the top level, the Internet started by introducing domain labels which designate organization associations. Table 20.2 provides a list of those domains and the associated affiliations.

20

NETWORKING

FIGURE 20.25.

Hierarchical organization of the Internet DNS domain name space.

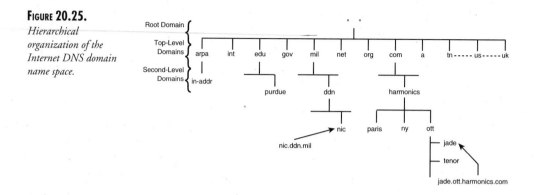

Table 20.2. Traditional top-level domains.

Top-Level Domain	Associated Affiliation
com	Commercial organizations
edu	Educational organizations
gov	U.S. government organizations
mil	Military organizations
net	Networking organizations
org	Non-commercial organizations
int	International organizations
arpa	Special domain, for reverse resolution

An example of an educational organization is Purdue University, which on the Internet is known as purdue.edu, whereas ibm.com represents IBM's commercial domain.

Most of the organizations joining the top-level domains are located in the U.S. This is due to the fact that the Internet started as an experiment led by a U.S. agency (ARPA), in which only U.S. organizations participated. As the Internet's success and popularity crossed national boundaries to become an international data highway, the top-level domains were reorganized to include domain labels corresponding to individual countries. Country domain labels followed the existing ISO 3166 standard which establishes an official, two-letter code for every country in the world. In Figure 20.25, labels such as ca and tn designate Canada and Tunisia. The U.S. also has its country domain label (us) to which organizations may choose to belong instead of belonging to any of the more traditional domains.

The arpa domain (refer to Table 20.2) is a very special domain used by DNS name servers to reverse resolve IP addresses into their corresponding domain names.

Domains and Zones

You learned earlier that once the authority for a subdomain is delegated to an organization, that organization may subdivide its domain into lower-level subdomains. Subdividing a domain should not necessarily lead to delegating every subdomain's autonomy to other member departments in the organization. So although a domain is partitioned into many lower-level domains, authority over the domain can be aligned along *zone* boundaries, in which case a zone may contain a subset of the domains that the parent domain contains.

Figure 20.26 illustrates the difference between a domain and a zone. As shown in the figure, the harmonics domain contains the ott, ny, and paris subdomains. Yet, only two zones of authority are established: the harmonics zone which includes both ott and paris subdomains, and the ny zone including to the ny domain. When setting up name servers, you will be assigning zones of authority—you will be configuring them to maintain complete information about the zone for which they are said to have authority. You can, if you wish, make a name server authoritative for more than one zone.

FIGURE 20.26.

Domains and zones. Authority for the harmonics *domain is reduced to two zones: the* harmonics *zone, which contains information about both* ott *and* paris *subdomains, and the* ny *zone, which contains information about the* ny *domain only.*

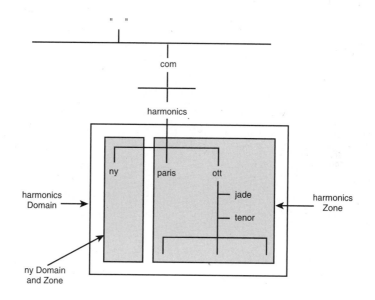

Name Servers

Setting up DNS services to support the domain or zone for which an organization is delegated authority involves creating a set of authoritative servers for that zone. At a minimum, two servers a primary and secondary should be setup.

The primary name server is where the database files are being maintained and is the most time consuming to setup. Changes made to the DNS—whether to the layout or structure of the domain being delegated or simple updates to the database—must be administered and reflected

20

NETWORKING

on the primary name server. For example, to add a new host to the network, you have to assign it both a name and an IP address, and you must enter those assignments in the DNS database contained on the primary server.

The secondary name server is easier to set up than the primary. It is different from the primary in that it derives its database from the primary's by virtue of replicating it through a process known as *zonal transfer*. Once set up, the secondary requires very little maintenance.

Every time the secondary server is rebooted, it undergoes the zonal transfer process by contacting the primary server for the zone for which they both are responsible, and requesting all the information pertaining to that zone. Thereafter, the secondary server routinely polls the primary server for any *updates* that might have been made to the database. As will be shown under the section "Domain Name Service Implementation," a secondary server can be easily configured to backup the zone data after transfer to disk files. This option allows the secondary server to reload its data using the backup files instead of undergoing zonal transfer every time the server is restarted—resulting in reduction in bandwidth consumption due to zonal transfers, and the better availability of data in case the secondary fails to hear from the primary when the transfer is initiated.

It is not absolutely necessary to install any server other than the primary server in order to bring up the DNS service. Including a secondary server has, however, the following advantages:

- *Redundancy*: There is no difference between a primary and secondary server except for the source of information that each relies on in responding to name queries. Both servers are equally capable of responding to such queries. Consequently, with the presence of a secondary server, should one of them accidentally stop responding to user queries, one will be capable of taking over, provided that user workstations are set up to contact both servers for queries.

- *Distribution of workload*: Because both servers are equally capable of responding to all types of queries, the environment can be set up so that the workload on these servers is fairly shared. The added benefit of sharing the workload is improved response time.

- *Physical proximity:* By having more than one server, you will be able to strategically locate each one of them so they are where they're needed most, thus cutting on response time.

Name Service Resolution Process

Whenever a name server is queried by a client, it is mandatory that the server responds with a valid answer regardless of whether the query pertains to the domain for which the server is authoritative or not. Queries pertaining to other domains, on the local network, or around the Internet should be forwarded to other servers for a response. To query name servers on behalf of the client, every name server must maintain pointers (that is, entries including the IP addresses) to the root servers. Root servers in turn must maintain data about all top-level domains, and so on. The process of querying other servers on behalf of a client is commonly known as the *resolution referral process*.

Figure 20.27 illustrates the resolution referral process. In the diagram, a DNS server (somewhere in the Internet universe) receives a name query from a client. The query requests the IP address of host `oboe.ny.harmonics.com`. Assuming that the server does not know the answer, rather than responding to the client with a negative response, it sends the query to a `root` server. The `root` server determines from the host name that it falls under the `com` domain. Consequently, it responds to the originating server with the address list of the `com` domain servers. The local server treats the response as a referral to the `com` servers, at which point it redirects the query to one of these servers. In its turn, the `com` server determines that the queried object falls under the `harmonics` subdomain's authority and therefore refers the local server to contact the subdomain's server, which in turn finally refers it to the server of `ny.harmonics.com` for answer.

FIGURE 20.27.

Name resolution referral process.

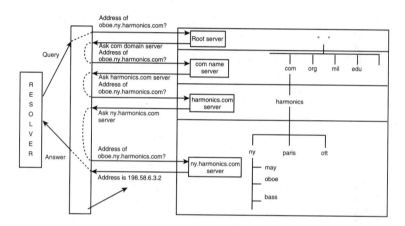

Caching

In order to save bandwidth and improve the response time it takes to answer a query, DNS defines a caching mechanism that allows name servers (of all types) to cache response data for future reference. In the example of Figure 20.27, the local name server caches the IP address-to-host name association of `oboe.ny.harmonics.com` after responding successfully to the client's query. This way, if queried for the same host (`oboe.ny.harmonics.com`), the server will be capable to respond directly from its cache instead of undergoing the time-consuming resolution referral process all over.

Name servers do not just cache data pertaining to the query in effect. Rather, they cache all the data they discover in the process of responding to that query. For example, the local server in Figure 20.27 would cache all the referral data that led to the response to the query pertaining to host `oboe.ny.harmonics.com`. The referral data includes names and IP addresses of the servers that are authoritative for the root-level, `com`, and `harmonic` domains. Caching referral data cuts the time that the referral process takes. In the event, for example, the name server is queried for host `fake.somewhere.com`, it does not have to start the referral process from the root level if it already has in its cache the necessary information to go directly to a `com` domain server for referral; thus cutting the number of referral steps by one in this case.

To avoid having a name server continue using cached data after it has expired (due to changes made to that data on authoritative name servers), DNS defines a time-to-live (TTL) configuration parameter for that data. After expiration of the specified TTL time, the server must discard the data in its cache and request an update from an authoritative name server.

Reverse Resolution of Pointer Queries

Figure 20.28 shows a partial portrait of the organization of the Internet's global DNS service. Of particular interest is the `in-addr.arpa` *reverse resolution domain*—called as such because it is used to reverse resolve an IP address to its fully qualified domain name.

Reverse resolution is particularly useful for security. Some of the remote access services, such as `rlogin` and remote copy (`rcp`), are accessible only if the hosts from which users are attempting access are privileged to do so. A host supporting such services normally maintains the names (*not* the IP addresses) of the other hosts allowed access in special files (such as `$HOME/.rhosts` and `/etc/hosts.equiv`). Upon receiving a request for remote access service, a secure server issues a query to the name server requesting the reverse resolving of the address to its domain name for subsequent verification for eligibility to the service.

The `in-addr.arpa` domain is designed to provide an efficient mechanism for responding to queries requesting reverse resolution. As shown in Figure 20.28, `in-addr.arpa` is simply another domain that uses IP addresses for subdomain names. The `in-addr.arpa` domain itself is organized into 256 domains, one corresponding to each possible value of the first byte of the IP address. Similarly, below each of those domains, there can be up to 256 subdomains corresponding to the second byte of the IP address, and so on, until the entire address space is represented in the `in-addr.arpa` domain.

FIGURE 20.28.

Organization of the
`in-addr.arp` *domain.*

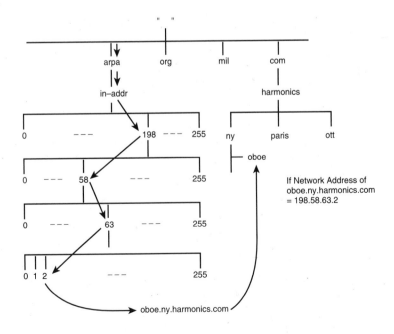

If Network Address of
oboe.ny.harmonics.com
= 198.58.63.2

Whenever an organization joins the Internet, it is delegated the responsibility to administer two or more domains. These are the official domains that it registered under. For example, in the case of Harmonics, Inc. it is the `harmonics.com` domain and the `in-addr.arpa` domain that correspond to the address range that it has been assigned by the appropriate Internet authority. If, for example, Harmonics Inc. was assigned the Class C pool of addresses 198.58.63.0, then it is delegated the authority for managing the `63.58.198.in-addr.arpa` domain. Notice how the IP address portion of the reverse domain is spelled backwards. This is in compliance with the DNS naming rules that were discussed earlier. For example, if the IP address of `oboe.ny.harmonics.com` is 198.58.63.2, its `in-addr.arpa` domain label becomes `2.63.58.198.in-addr.arpa`, again in conformance with the way fully qualified domain names should be referenced.

Assuming that a host receives a remote login request from host address 198.58.63.2, the receiving host authenticates the request by sending out a query for reverse resolution (officially known as a pointer query type) to its local name server. The local name server then must find the domain names corresponding to the specified host IP address by undergoing the same resolution referral process, which was outlined earlier, starting at the `198.in-addr.arpa` level and moving downward through the tree until it successfully reaches the domain label `2.63.58.in-addr.arpa`, which is then fetched for the corresponding host domain label (`oboe.ny.harmonics.com`). The name is then returned to the remote access server for use in verifying access privileges.

Configuring UNIX for TCP/IP

This section is devoted to detailing the setup process from the preparation phase to the actual implementation phase. Throughout, the discussion mainly addresses the "how to" process on UNIX SVR4 hosts. Whenever necessary, differences with other variants of UNIX will be highlighted.

Preparing to Set Up and Configure TCP/IP

Setting up and configuring TCP/IP on UNIX hosts is a fairly simple and straightforward matter provided that you have done a little bit of up-front preparation. Most of the preparation has to do with defining the parameters that are critical to the successful completion of the task of setting up the host for connection to the common network. Following are the points to consider when undertaking such a task:

- *Number of network interfaces.* A host might be required to have more than one network interface card in order to attach to more than one network. This is typically desired when the host is set up to route traffic between those networks or to behave as a security firewall.

- *Network interface labels.* UNIX vendors refer to network interfaces using labels. Each make is labeled uniquely from others. For example, on a Solaris 2.x system, a 3Com Etherlink III (3C5x9) interface is referred to, or labeled, as elx. The first interface of its kind is labeled elx0, the second as elx1, and so on. Before proceeding to configure the interfaces using the applicable parameters (such as IP address, netmask,...) make sure you know what the interface label(s) are.

■ *Host name*: Each host must be assigned a host name. Typically, the host name is the name set during system installation. Finding out what the host name is, is a simple matter of entering the uname -n command as shown here:

```
# uname -n
tenor
```

Bear in mind however, that the name assigned to the host during installation may not be suitable to use on the network. One obvious cause would be name collision—that is, the possibility of two computers having the same name. Another reason is the potential conflict with official host naming rules that are in force in your environment. Should the requirement arise for changing the name, use the uname command with the -S option as shown here:

```
# uname -S newname
```

where *newname* is the new host's name.

In the case of configuring the host for supporting more than one network interface, you ought to assign it one name per interface. You cannot have the same name associated with all supported interfaces. Consequently, have all the names ready for the time of implementation.

■ *Domain name*: If you have domain name service installed on your network, you must decide where in the domain hierarchy does the host belong and note the corresponding complete domain name of that host. For example, if host tenor is said to belong to ny.harmonics.com, its full domain name becomes tenor.ny.harmonics.com.

■ *IP addresses assigned to the network interfaces*: Each of the network interfaces must be assigned a unique IP address. Have the addresses ready in dotted decimal notation.

■ *Subnet masks*: Determine and note the applicable subnet mask if the default is not acceptable. The mask can be entered, when required in the setup process, using dotted decimal or hexadecimal notation.

■ *IP addresses of domain name servers*: If domain name service is installed on the network, you ought to have the addresses of at least the primary and one secondary name servers. These addresses will be required in the process of setting up the DNS resolver on the UNIX host.

■ *IP address of the default gateway (that is, default router)*: On a routed network (a network connected to other networks) every host must be configured to recognize a default router—hence the need for the IP address of the router.

The above completes the list of the *minimal* requirements for the graceful implementation of TCP/IP on UNIX hosts. There are situations where configuring hosts may require additional information. Additional information can, however, always be implemented after all the above parameters are taken care of and the network setup is verified to work satisfactorily.

TCP/IP Setup Files

Installing and configuring TCP/IP involves several files that you are required to be aware of. Each of the files depicted below takes care of a certain aspect of the TCP/IP services rendered by the UNIX host.

/etc/hosts

The /etc/hosts file is where the host names to IP address associations are maintained. The following is an example of an /etc/hosts file as it is on host jade (see Figure 20.29):

```
#
# Internet host table
#
# IP address    hostname    aliases
#
127.0.0.1    localhost
100.0.0.2    jade
198.53.237.1    jade1                # jade's second interface
100.0.0.3    tenor                nfsserver # is my nfs server
100.0.0.5    alto        # my gateway to the internet
```

FIGURE 20.29.

Host jade *connects to and routes data between two networks: 100.0.0.0 and 198.53.237.0.*

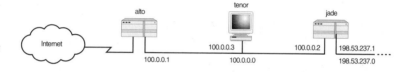

Text following the # character is ignored, and is meant to include comments and documentation. As shown above, every file entry consists of an IP address, the corresponding host name, and optional aliases. Three entries in this file pertaining to host jade are of particular interest:

- An entry which maps the 127.0.0.1 to localhost. This entry corresponds to the loopback interface. It is absolutely necessary that each system has an identical entry in its /etc/hosts file. The loopback address allows for the local testing of the various components of TCP/IP without introducing traffic (due to these tests) on the wire. For example, you can establish a local FTP session by entering the following command:

  ```
  # ftp localhost
  ```

  In this particular situation, the sanity of FTP service can be tested and established without needing another to establish a session with the host in question.

- An entry which maps 100.0.0.2 to the host's network node name jade.

- An entry which maps IP address 198.53.237.1 to jade1, a host name assigned to another network interface card supported by TCP/IP in this host. As shown in Figure 20.29, jade connects to two networks 100.0.0.0 and 198.53.237.0.

20

NETWORKING

Notice how tenor is also assigned an *alias*, nfsserver. An alias is just another name which you can use to refer to the same host or interface. Because tenor supports NFS services for the rest of the network, it was conveniently aliased as nfsserver. Consequently, the network administrator and users will be able to reference the host either by its name or its alias.

/etc/hosts also includes IP address to name mappings pertaining to other hosts (for example, alto). If you do not have DNS installed on your network, the /etc/hosts file may have be updated whenever a new host is set up on the network, or an existing one is reconfigured to a different IP address.

/etc/networks

The /etc/networks file is similar to the /etc/hosts file in function. Instead of host names, /etc/networks contains network names to network IP address associations. Optionally, aliases can be included. Names included in this file normally pertain to known networks which comprise the Internet. Following is a sample /etc/networks file:

```
# Name          Network Number

att                    12
xerox-net            13
hp-internet      15
dec-internet     16
milnet                 26
ucdla-net             31
nextdoor-net     198.53.237
loopback-net     127
```

The /etc/networks file allows you to refer to networks, local or on the Internet, by name when, for example, configuring the routing table on the host as shown here:

```
# route add nextdoor-net 100.0.0.1 1
add net nextdoor-net: gateway 100.0.0.1
```

/etc/services

As discussed earlier, each of the TCP/IP application layer services, such as FTP, Telnet, and rlogin, are assigned port numbers at the transport layer. The /etc/services database contains the information which maps every recognized service protocol to a static port number, also known as a *well-known port number*. An application uses a uniquely assigned port number to identify itself to the transport provider (at the host-to-host layer) and to remote peers across the network.

Following is a partial list of well-recognized services as documented in RFC 1060. Every entry in this list consists of the service name and its associated port number/transport protocol provider. Some services run over both TCP and UDP (for example, daytime service). In such a case the service is listed twice, once for TCP and once for UDP.

RFC 1060

In addition to assigned port numbers, RFC 1060 contains a complete listing of other categories of assigned numbers including (but not limited to) protocol numbers, UNIX assigned ports, and Ethernet assigned address blocks. It might prove useful to downloading and maintaining a copy of this RFC. This RFC, as well as all others referenced in the book, are available from the `ds.internic.net` Internet site.

`/etc/services` database file is created during TCP/IP installation. The only time you have to worry about it is when installing a new application/service. In this case you will have to edit the file to include an entry as directed by the application vendor. You may find the file a useful reference when troubleshooting the network.

```
#
#       assigned numbers from rfc1060
#

#service       port/transport
tcpmux     1/tcp
echo         7/tcp
echo         7/udp
discard      9/tcp         sink null
discard      9/udp         sink null
systat        11/tcp          users
systat        11/udp       users
daytime     13/tcp
daytime     13/udp
netstat        15/tcp
netstat        15/udp
qotd         17/tcp          quote
qotd         17/udp       quote
ftp-data     20/tcp
ftp          21/tcp
telnet         23/tcp
smtp         25/tcp          mail
time         37/tcp          timserver
time         37/udp       timserver
name         42/tcp          nameserver
name         42/udp       nameserver
whois        43/tcp          nicname        # usually to sri-nic
whois        43/udp       nicname     # usually to sri-nic
nameserver    53/udp      domain
nameserver    53/tcp          domain
apts         57/tcp                     #any private terminal service
apfs         59/tcp                     #any private file service
bootps         67/udp      bootp
bootpc         68/udp
tftp         69/udp
rje          77/tcp          netrjs         #any private rje
finger         79/tcp
link         87/tcp          ttylink
supdup       95/tcp
```

```
hostnames      101/tcp    hostname        # usually to sri-nic
sunrpc         111/udp    rpcbind
sunrpc         111/tcp    rpcbind
auth           113/tcp    authentication
sftp           115/tcp
uucp-path      117/tcp
nntp           119/tcp    usenet readnews untp # Network News Transfer
eprc           121/udp
ntp            123/tcp                    # Network Time Protocol
ntp            123/udp                    # Network Time Protocol
NeWS           144/tcp    news               # Window System
iso-tp0          146/tcp
iso-ip           147/tcp
bftp           152/tcp
snmp           161/udp
snmp-trap      162/udp
cmip-manage      163/tcp
cmip-agent       164/tcp
print-srv      170/tcp
#
# UNIX specific services
#
# these are NOT officially assigned
#
exec           512/tcp
login          513/tcp
shell          514/tcp    cmd             # no passwords used
printer          515/tcp    spooler         # line printer spooler
timed          525/udp    timeserver
courier        530/tcp    rpc             # experimental
```

/etc/protocols

Recall that the IP header (refer to Figure 20.6) includes a PROTOCOL field. This field contains a number which uniquely identifies the IP protocol service user. Similar in functionality to transport port numbers, protocol numbers help IP with internally routing data to their respective user protocols. /etc/protocols is created in your system during TCP/IP installation and should require no change. A sample file listing follows:

```
#
# Internet (IP) protocols
#
ip      0    IP    # internet protocol, pseudo protocol number
icmp    1    ICMP    # internet control message protocol
ggp     3    GGP    # gateway-gateway protocol
tcp     6    TCP    # transmission control protocol
egp     8    EGP    # exterior gateway protocol
pup     12   PUP    # PARC universal packet protocol
udp     17   UDP    # user datagram protocol
hmp     20   HMP    # host monitoring protocol
xns-idp   22    XNS-IDP    # Xerox NS IDP
rdp       27    RDP    # "reliable datagram" protocol
```

The /etc/protocols file is created and initialized during system installation. As an administrator, you will hardly have to change or update its contents. However, you shouldn't attempt to delete this file or tamper with its contents as it is referenced by TCP/IP daemons every time the system is brought up.

/etc/ethers

Unlike the files discussed above, /etc/ethers is not created by the system during TCP/IP installation. If you are planning on providing RARP or BOOTPD services, you need to create this file. RARP uses this file to map Ethernet addresses to IP addresses. An example of an /etc/ethers file follows:

```
#
# MAC to hostname mappings
#
# ether_mac_addr.    hostname    comments
#
00:00:c0:9e:41:26    violin         #strings dep't
02:60:8c:15:ad:18    bass
```

Rather than include IP addresses, the /etc/ethers file contains host names. On cross-referencing this file with /etc/hosts any MAC address can be easily mapped to its IP address. This means that unless both /etc/hosts and /etc/ethers are consistently maintained some users may end up having difficulties acquiring an IP address, and consequently connecting to the network at boot time.

/etc/netmasks

The /etc/netmasks file associates network IP addresses with network addresses. You need to create and maintain this file if you are planning on subnetting your network. Here is a sample netmasks file:

```
#
#Network subnet masks
#
#Unless your network is subnetted, do not bother to maintain this file
#
#Network        subnet mask
134.54.0.0        255.255.255.0
167.12.0.0        255.255.192.0
138.52.0.0         255.255.255.0
```

For each network that is subnetted, a single line should exist in this file with the network number and the network mask to use on that network. Network numbers and masks may be specified in the conventional dotted decimal notation. For example,

```
138.52.0.0     255.255.255.0
```

specifies that the Class B network 128.32.0.0 should have eight bits of subnet field and eight bits of host field, in addition to the standard sixteen bits in the network field.

/etc/hosts.equiv

/etc/hosts.equiv contains the names of *trusted hosts*. Users logging in to the system from a trusted host using any of the r-utilities are not required to supply a password, provided that they already have a valid login ID in the /etc/passwd file on the target host. The following listing provides an example of /etc/hosts.equiv:

```
#
# Trusted hosts
#
jade
tenor
alto
soprano
```

Users on `jade`, `tenor`, `alto`, and `soprano` can log in to the system on which the listed file is maintained, without supplying a password, provided they are in the `/etc/passwd` database of that system.

~/.rhosts

`.rhosts` must be created in the user's remote home directory. It allows or denies access to that specific user. In its simplest form, the `~/.rhosts` file looks like the following one:

```
#
#$HOME/.rhosts file
#
jade
tenor
```

The above entries mean that the user, in whose remote home directory `.rhosts` is created, can log in from `jade` and `tenor` without supplying a password.

/etc/inet Directory

In this directory the configuration file `inetd.conf` is maintained. This file dictates the behavior of the superserver `inetd` daemon. The superserver daemon's responsibility is to invoke and control application protocol daemons whenever the need arises. Examples of application daemons that are supervised and controlled the `inetd` daemon are the `ftpd` and `telnetd` (that is the FTP and Telnet server daemons).

Some SVR4 systems maintain the `hosts`, `protocols`, and `services` databases, discussed earlier, in `/etc/init` and maintain symbolic links to `/etc/hosts`, `/etc/protocols`, and `/etc/services`.

/etc/inet/inetd.conf

Rather than allowing every service daemon to listen to requests on its own port, UNIX developers chose to delegate the responsibility of listening to requests on behalf of all service daemons to one server (also known as the superserver) called `inetd`. In doing so, the demand on system resources is significantly reduced. Only when the superserver detects a service request will it invoke the daemon to which the service pertains. The `/etc/inet/inetd.conf` configuration file allows `inetd` to determine, upon startup, the daemons on whose behalf to listen to service requests. Unless a service daemon is enabled through the `inetd.conf` file, service requests pertaining to that daemon will be discarded by the `inetd` daemon. More details on `inetd` and `inetd.conf` are provided later in the chapter.

Startup of TCP/IP

Different variants of UNIX have different implementations of the TCP/IP startup process and associated scripts. In particular, three implementations are presented in this section; these are

- TCP/IP Startup on SVR4
- TCP/IP Startup on Solaris 2.x
- TCP/IP Startup on BSD

TCP/IP Startup on SVR4

TCP/IP is started at boot time when run level 2 (multiuser run level) is entered by the `/etc/init.d/inetinit` script. This script sets out by configuring, linking, and loading various STREAMS modules and drivers that are required for the STREAMS TCP/IP protocol stack. If STREAMS is loaded successfully, `inetinit` executes the `/etc/confnet.d/inet/config.boot.sh` to configure all of the supported network interfaces as defined in the `/etc/confnet.d/inet/interface` file (see the following note for a sample listing of its contents). Following is a listing of the contents of `inetinit` script:

```
#       @(#)inetinit    1.4 STREAMWare TCP/IP SVR4.2  source
#       SCCS IDENTIFICATION
#ident    "@(#)cmd-inet:common/cmd/cmd-inet/etc/init.d/inetinit    1.9.7.7"

#       inet startup

LOG=/tmp/inet.start
PermLog=/var/adm/log/inet.start
export LOG PermLog
exitcode=0

SLINK=/usr/sbin/slink
IFCONFIG=/usr/sbin/ifconfig
STRCF=/etc/inet/strcf
MSG1="\nTCP/IP startup was not entirely successful. Error messages in $LOG"
DATADIR=/etc/confnet.d/inet
DATASCRIPT=$DATADIR/config.boot.sh
DATABASE=$DATADIR/interface
NUstrcf=$DATADIR/strcf.custom
UPSAVE=$DATADIR/up.save      # ifconfig commands built for "up" operation
KLUDGE=kludge

export DATADIR DATASCRIPT DATABASE NUstrcf
#
# construct the commands to set-up and take-down the protocol stack.
#
UP="$SLINK -v -c $NUstrcf $KLUDGE"
DOWN="$SLINK -u -c $NUstrcf $KLUDGE"

case "$1" in
start)
    #the LOOP=up or LOOP=down portion of code is to determine
    #if we are running this 'start)' code following running
```

```
#the 'stop)' code.  Once we've run an ifconfig lo0 {address},
#ifconfig lo0 will not have a non-zero return code, even after
#unlinking the transport stack.
#So use the loopback transport UP|DOWN as a flag for the
#boot code.
ifout="`ifconfig lo0 2>/dev/null`"
ifret=$?
case X"$ifout" in
    Xlo0*flags=*\<UP,*)
        LOOP=up ;;
    *)    LOOP=down ;;
esac

if [ $ifret != 0 -o $LOOP != up ]
then
    #
    # the network stack is not yet up (at least there is
    # no loopback), "make" the strcf and ifconfig commands
    # (ie, iff any dependency changed).
    #
    cmd="$DATASCRIPT up"
    echo "The following commands ran from /etc/init.d/inetinit"
    echo \
"The following commands were run by the boot time configuration
script, $DATASCRIPT, by running
$cmd
"

        eval "$cmd"
        if [ $? -ne 0 ]
        then
            exitcode=1
        fi

        echo "$UP"
        if    $UP
        then
            if [ -f "$UPSAVE" ]
            then
                #
                # issue all the ifconfig commands
                #
                echo "Commands from $UPSAVE:"
                cat $UPSAVE
                echo
                . $UPSAVE
            fi
        else
            #
            # failed to build the stream stack so try to
            # unbuild it.
            #
            $DOWN >/dev/null 2>&1
            echo "$MSG1" >&2
            exit 1
```

```
        fi
        if [ -x /usr/eac/bin/initsock ]
        then
             /usr/eac/bin/initsock
        fi
    fi > $LOG 2>&1

    rm -f $LOG $PermLog

    # run startup script
    /bin/sh /etc/inet/rc.inet start
    if [ $? -ne 0 ]
    then
        exitcode=1
    fi
    exit $exitcode

    ;;

stop)
    #
    # rc0 and rc1 take care of killing when going down to states 0,1,5,6
    #
    set `who -r`
    if [ "$3" = "2" -o "$3" = "3" ]
    then
        #
        # kill the various standalone daemons
        #
        kill -9 `/usr/bin/ps -e \
        ¦ /usr/bin/awk '/in\.routed/ ¦¦ /in\.gated/ ¦¦ /in\.xntpd/ \
        ¦¦ /in\.timed/ ¦¦ /in\.named/ ¦¦ /in\.pppd/ ¦¦ /in\.snmpd/ \
        { print $1}'` 2>/dev/null

    fi
    #
    # bring down the protocol stack
    # use the strcf script compiled on the way up even if there
    # were changes made.  Those changes will go into effect
    # the next time it comes up.
    #
    $IFCONFIG -a down >/dev/null 2>&1
    if [ -f $NUstrcf ]
    then
        $DOWN >/dev/null 2>&1
    fi
    exit 0
    #the LOOP=up or LOOP=down portion of the 'start)' code is
    #checking to see if it is following the above 'stop)' code.
    #Once we've run an ifconfig lo0 {address},
    #ifconfig lo0 will not have a non-zero return code, even after
    #unlinking the transport stack.
    ;;

*)
    exit 1
esac
```

> **NOTE**
>
> The following is an example of the contents of the `/etc/confnet.d/inet/interface`:
>
> ```
> lo:0:localhost:/dev/loop::add_loop:
> ne2k:0::/dev/ne2k_0:-trailers::
> el3:0:orbit:/dev/el3_0:-trailers::
> ```
>
> According to this listing, two network interfaces are supported. These are `ne2k` and `el3` corresponding to the NE2000 and 3C509 network cards. The first entry (`lo`) pertains to the loopback interface. Each entry is made of colon-delimited fields. Entries in the interface file have the following format:
>
> `prefix:unit#:addr:device:ifconfig_opts:slink_opts:`
>
> where,
>
> `prefix` is used by the `ifconfig` or `netstat` commands to configure the interface, or to gather its statistics.
>
> `unit` # refers to the unit number (instance number) of that interface.
>
> `addr` should contain either the IP address assigned to the interface, or an existing host name in the `/etc/hosts` file. If null string is included instead, as in the second entry, then null will be expanded to `` `/usr/bin/uname -n` `` and the interface will be configured to the IP address of the corresponding network node name of the system.
>
> `device` refers to the node name of the transport provider. This field is used by `slink` (that is, STREAMS link) command for the configuration and installation of the protocol stack onto the STREAM head.
>
> `ifconfig_opts` is normally made to contain options that are supported by the `ifconfig` command. One common option is the `-trailers` (discussed later in the chapter) option.
>
> `slink_opts` is used by slink to initialize the device into the TCP/IP protocol stack. A null field allows for customization.

Once control is transferred to `config.boot.sh` (not listed due to its length), it loops through all of the interfaces specified in the `/etc/confnet.d/inet/interface` file, including the loopback interface, configuring each using `ifconfig` to the proper IP address, netmask, and broadcast address. It also uses `slink` command to configure and load the protocol stack onto the STREAMS head for each interface device.

If the network interfaces are successfully configured and brought up, `/etc/init.d/inetinit` runs the `/etc/inet/rc.inet` script.

> **NOTE**
>
> A final remark on the `inetinit` script is that it is used for both starting as well as stopping TCP/IP services. It starts TCP/IP when the system is brought to the multi-user level and stops

TCP/IP when the system is shutdown or brought down to single-user level. This is normally accomplished by linking `/etc/init.d/inetinit` to `/etc/rc2.d/S69inet`, which is run along with all the other scripts that begin with S in that directory.

/etc/inet/rc.inet

The contents of the `rc.inet` script are listed below. As can be seen from the listing, `rc.inet` starts TCP/IP daemons which have been verified as properly configured. Taking `in.named`, the domain name service daemon, as an example, `rc.inet` checks in the `/etc/inet` directory for the corresponding boot configuration file (`named.boot`). If `named.boot` is found, the daemon is invoked.

```
#       @(#)rc.inet    1.5 STREAMWare TCP/IP SVR4.2   source
#       SCCS IDENTIFICATION
#ident    "@(#)cmd-inet:common/cmd/cmd-inet/etc/inet/rc.inet     1.3.8.7"

# Inet startup script run from /etc/init.d/inetinit
LOG=/tmp/inet.start
PermLog=/var/adm/log/inet.start
export LOG PermLog
exitcode=0

# Label the error log
echo "The following commands were run from /etc/inet/rc.inet" > $LOG
#
# Add lines here to set up routes to gateways, start other daemons, etc.
#
#
# Run the ppp daemon if /etc/inet/ppphosts is present
#
if [ -f /etc/inet/ppphosts -a -x /usr/sbin/in.pppd ]
then
    /usr/sbin/in.pppd
fi
# This runs in.gated if its configuration file (/etc/inet/gated.conf) is
# present.  Otherwise, in.routed is run.
#
if [ -f /etc/inet/gated.conf -a -x /usr/sbin/in.gated ]
then
    /usr/sbin/in.gated
else
    #
    # if running, kill the route demon
    #
    kill `ps -ef¦grep in[.]routed¦awk '{print $2}'` 2>/dev/null
    /usr/sbin/in.routed -q
fi
#
# /usr/sbin/route add default your_nearest_gateway hops_to_gateway
# if [ $? -ne 0 ]
# then
#     exitcode=1
# fi
```

```
#
#  Run the DNS server if a configuration file is present
#
if [ -f /etc/inet/named.boot -a -x /usr/sbin/in.named ]
then
     /usr/sbin/in.named
fi


#
#  Run the NTP server if a configuration file is present
#
if [ -f /etc/inet/ntp.conf -a -x /usr/sbin/in.xntpd ]
then
     /usr/sbin/in.xntpd
fi
#
# return status to /etc/init.d/inetinit
```

There are situations in which you have to make changes to this file. For example, to install static routes at boot time, you need to edit the rc.init file to include as many route add commands as may be required to support those routes including support for the default gateway. Also, you may need to change the file path specifications of configuration files pertaining to some daemons such as in.named.

The startup process completes with the invocation of the superserver daemon inetd. As shown in a later section, inetd is responsible for invoking (on demand) and controlling many of the TCP/IP application service daemons such as ftpd and telnetd.

TCP/IP Startup on Solaris 2.x

Although Solaris 2.x is a UNIX SVR4 operating system, it does not follow the startup procedures depicted above. Solaris 2.x relies on three scripts for bringing up TCP/IP services. These are

- /etc/init.d/rootusr
- /etc/init.d/inetinit
- /etc/init.d/inetsrv

/etc/init.d/rootusr

Considering that some workstations rely on remote file systems resources (in particular /usr) to function properly, this script's primary function is to configure enough TCP/IP interfaces and services as necessary to mount (using Network File System—that is, NFS) these resources. Here is the code listing for this script:

```
#!/sbin/sh
# Make sure that the libraries essential
# to this stage of booting can be found.
LD_LIBRARY_PATH=/etc/lib; export LD_LIBRARY_PATH

#
#
# Configure the software loopback driver. The network initialization is
# done early to support diskless and dataless configurations.
#
/sbin/ifconfig lo0 127.0.0.1 up 2>&1 >/dev/null
```

```
#
# For interfaces that were configured by the kernel (e.g. those on diskless
# machines), reset the netmask using the local "/etc/netmasks" file, if
# one exists.
#
/sbin/ifconfig -au netmask + broadcast + 2>&1 >/dev/null


#
# Get the list of network interfaces to configure by breaking
# /etc/hostname.* into separate args by using "." as a shell separator
# character, then step through args and ifconfig every other arg.
# Set the netmask along the way using local "/etc/netmasks" file.
# This also sets up the streams plumbing for the interface.
# With an empty /etc/hostname.* file this only sets up the streams plumbing
# allowing the ifconfig auto-revarp command will attempt to set the address.
#
interface_names="`echo /etc/hostname.*[0-9]        2>/dev/null`"
if test "$interface_names" != "/etc/hostname.*[0-9]"
then
        (
        echo "configuring network interfaces:\c"
                IFS="$IFS."
                set `echo /etc/hostname\.*[0-9]`
                while test $# -ge 2
                do
                        shift
                        if [ "$1" != "xx0" ]; then
                  addr=`shcat /etc/hostname\.$1`
                  /sbin/ifconfig $1 plumb
                  if test -n "$addr"
                  then
                     /sbin/ifconfig $1 inet "$addr" netmask + \
                        broadcast + -trailers up \
                        2>&1 > /dev/null
                  fi
                  echo " $1\c"
                        fi
                        shift
                done
        echo "."
        )
fi


#
# configure the rest of the interfaces automatically, quietly.
#
/sbin/ifconfig -ad auto-revarp netmask + broadcast + -trailers up \
    2>&1 >/dev/null


#
# Set the hostname from a local config file, if one exists.
#
hostname="`shcat /etc/nodename        2>/dev/null`"
if [ ! -z "$hostname" ]; \
then
        /sbin/uname -S $hostname
fi
```

```
#
# Otherwise, set host information from bootparams RPC protocol.
#
if [ -z "`/sbin/uname -n`" ]; then
        /sbin/hostconfig -p bootparams
fi


#
# If local and network configuration failed, re-try network
# configuration until we get an answer.  We want this loop to be
# interruptible so that the machine can still be brought up manually
# when the servers are not cooperating.
#

trap 'intr=1' 2 3
while [ -z "`/sbin/uname -n`" -a ! -f /etc/.UNCONFIGURED  -a -z "${intr}" ]; do
        echo "re-trying host configuration..."
        /sbin/ifconfig -ad auto-revarp up 2>&1 >/dev/null
        /sbin/hostconfig -p bootparams 2>&1 >/dev/null
done
trap 2 3

echo "Hostname: `/sbin/uname -n`" >&2


#
# If "/usr" is going to be NFS mounted from a host on a different
# network, we must have a routing table entry before the mount is
# attempted.  One may be added by the diskless kernel or by the
# "hostconfig" program above.  Setting a default router here is a problem
# because the default system configuration does not include the
# "route" program in "/sbin".  Thus we only try to add a default route
# at this point if someone managed to place a static version of "route" into
# "/sbin".  Otherwise, we may add the route at run level 2 after "/usr"
# has been mounted and NIS is running.
#
# Note that since NIS is not running at this point, the router's name
# must be in "/etc/hosts" or its numeric IP address must be used in the file.
#
if [ -f /sbin/route -a -f /etc/defaultrouter ]; then
        /sbin/route -f add default `cat /etc/defaultrouter` 1
fi


#
# Root is already mounted (by the kernel), but still needs to be checked,
# possibly remounted and entered into mnttab. First mount /usr read only
# if it is a separate file system. This must be done first to allow
# utilities such as fsck and setmnt to reside on /usr minimizing the space
# required by the root file system.
#
exec < ${vfstab}; readvfstab "/usr"
if [ "${mountp}" ]
then
    if [ "${fstype}" = "cachefs" ]; then
        #
        # Mount without the cache initially.  We'll enable it
        # later at remount time.  This lets us avoid -
        # teaching the statically linked mount program about
        # cachefs.  Here we determine the backfstype.
```

```
        # This is not pretty, but we have no tools for parsing
        # the option string until we get /usr mounted...
        #
        case "$mntopts" in
        *backfstype=nfs*)
            cfsbacktype=nfs
            ;;
        *backfstype=hsfs*)
            cfsbacktype=hsfs
            ;;
        *)
            echo "invalid vfstab entry for /usr"
            cfsbacktype=nfs
            ;;
        esac
        /sbin/mount -m -F ${cfsbacktype} -o ro ${special} ${mountp}
    else
        /sbin/mount -m -o ro /usr
    fi
fi
```

As shown, the script sets out by configuring the local loop interface (that is, IP address 127.0.0.1) then proceeds to configuring all the network card interfaces that are installed in the system. Rather than relying on a common configuration file where all the supported network interfaces are defined, such as the /etc/confnet.d/inet/interfaces (which is commonly used on UNIX SVR4 systems), Solaris 2.x defines one simple file per interface. The file's name is /etc/hostname.*xx*?. Where *xx* stands for the interface driver and ? stands for the instance number of this interface. For example, in /etc/hostname.elx0, elx stands for 3C509, and 0 stands for first instance of this interface. The /etc/hostname.*xx*? file includes one word; that is, the name assigned to the interface as shown in the following example:

```
# cat /etc/hostname.elx0
tenor
```

/etc/init.d/rootusr configures all the interfaces by looping through all the /etc/hostname.*xx*? files, and cross-referencing their contents with the /etc/hosts for determining the IP address of each interface. It also resorts to the /etc/netmasks file to determine the applicable subnet mask for the particular interface. The IP address and the netmask are then used as command-line parameters when the ifconfig (the interface configuration—more on ifconfig later in the chapter) command is invoked by the script.

As soon as the interfaces are successfully configured and brought up, the script proceeds by configuring the route table to include the IP address of the default route. The script utilizes the route -a command in doing this. The default router's IP address is looked up in the /etc/defaultrouter file (see the following note).

/etc/defaultrouter

This file is not created upon system installation. It is your responsibility to create it and update it with the IP address of the default router.

/etc/init.d/inetinit

The execution of this script constitutes the second phase in the process of bringing up TCP/IP services. It primarily performs two functions; these are

- Configures the Network Information Service as indicated by the following excerpt of code from the /etc/init.d/inetinit script:

```
if [ -f /etc/defaultdomain ]; then
    /usr/bin/domainname `cat /etc/defaultdomain`
    echo "NIS domainname is `/usr/bin/domainname`"
fi
```

- Configures routing including starting the route discovery daemon in.routed, enabling the packet-forwarding function if more than one physical network interface is configured (that is, allow the host to behave as a router connecting two or more networks), and installing the default route. Notice that unless the host does not have a default router specified in the /etc/defaultrouter file, the in.routed daemon is not started. The script determines whether the host has a default route installed by checking both the /etc/defaultrouter file and the actual routing table using the following code taken from the script itself:

```
if [ -z "$defrouters" ]; then
    #
    # No default routes were set up by "route" command above - check the
    # kernel routing table for any other default routes.
    #
    defrouters="`netstat -rn | grep default`"
fi
```

If the variable defrouters is assigned anything but null, the script simply completes and exits. Otherwise, it proceeds by configuring the host as a router (if the host supports more than one physical interface), and spawns the routing daemon as well as enabling route discovery (using the /usr/sbin/in.disc -r command).

Following is the complete listing of the /etc/init.d/inetinit script:

```
# This is the second phase of TCP/IP configuration.  The first part,
# run in the "/etc/rcS.d/S30rootusr.sh" script, does all configuration
# necessary to mount the "/usr" filesystem via NFS.  This includes configuring
# the interfaces and setting the machine's hostname.  The second part,
# run in this script, does all configuration that can be done before
# NIS or NIS+ is started.  This includes configuring IP routing,
# setting the NIS domainname and setting any tunable parameters.  The
# third part, run in a subsequent startup script, does all
# configuration that may be dependent on NIS/NIS+ maps.  This includes
# a final re-configuration of the interfaces and starting all Internet
# services.
#

#
# Set configurable parameters.
#
ndd -set /dev/tcp tcp_old_urp_interpretation 1
```

```
#
# Configure default routers using the local "/etc/defaultrouter"
# configuration file.  The file can contain the hostnames or IP
# addresses of one or more default routers.  If hostnames are used,
# each hostname must also be listed in the local "/etc/hosts" file
# because NIS and NIS+ are not running at the time that this script is
# run.  Each router name or address is listed on a single line by
# itself in the file.  Anything else on that line after the router's
# name or address is ignored.  Lines that begin with "#" are
# considered comments and ignored.
#
# The default routers listed in the "/etc/defaultrouter" file will
# replace those added by the kernel during diskless booting.  An
# empty "/etc/defaultrouter" file will cause the default router
# added by the kernel to be deleted.
#
if [ -f /etc/defaultrouter ]; then
    defrouters=`grep -v \^\#'/etc/defaultrouter ¦ awk '{print $1}' `
    if [ -n "$defrouters" ]; then
        #
        # To support diskless operation with a "/usr"
        # filesystem NFS mounted from a server located on a
        # remote subnet, we have to be very careful about
        # replacing default routers.  We want the default
        # routers listed in the "/etc/defaultrouter" file to
        # replace the default router added by the bootparams
        # protocol.  But we can't have a window of time when
        # the system has no default routers in the process.
        # That would cause a deadlock since the "route"
        # command lives on the "/usr" filesystem.
        #
        pass=1
        for router in $defrouters
        do
            if [ $pass -eq 1 ]; then
                /usr/sbin/route -f add default $router 1
            else
                /usr/sbin/route add default $router 1
            fi
            pass=2
        done
    else
        /usr/sbin/route -f
    fi
fi

#
# Set NIS domainname if locally configured.
#
if [ -f /etc/defaultdomain ]; then
    /usr/bin/domainname `cat /etc/defaultdomain`
    echo "NIS domainname is `/usr/bin/domainname`"
fi

#
# Run routed/router discovery only if we don't already have a default
# route installed.
#
```

```
if [ -z "$defrouters" ]; then
    #
    # No default routes were set up by "route" command above - check the
    # kernel routing table for any other default routes.
    #
    defrouters="`netstat -rn ¦ grep default`"
fi

if [ -z "$defrouters" ]; then
    #
    # Determine how many active interfaces there are and how many pt-pt
    # interfaces. Act as a router if there are more than 2 interfaces
    # (including the loopback interface) or one or more point-point
    # interface. Also act as a router if /etc/gateways exists.
    #
    # Do NOT act as a router if /etc/notrouter exists.
    #
    numifs=`ifconfig -au ¦ grep inet ¦ wc -l`
    numptptifs=`ifconfig -au ¦ grep inet ¦ egrep -e '-->' ¦ wc -l`
    if [ ! -f /etc/notrouter -a \
        \( $numifs -gt 2 -o $numptptifs -gt 0 -o -f /etc/gateways \) ]
    then
        # Machine is a router: turn on ip_forwarding, run routed,
        # and advertise ourselves as a router using router discovery.
        echo "machine is a router."
        ndd -set /dev/ip ip_forwarding 1
        if [ -f /usr/sbin/in.routed ]; then
            /usr/sbin/in.routed -s
        fi
        if [ -f /usr/sbin/in.rdisc ]; then
            /usr/sbin/in.rdisc -r
        fi
    else
        # Machine is a host: if router discovery finds a router then
        # we rely on router discovery. If there are not routers
        # advertising themselves through router discovery
        # run routed in space-saving mode.
        # Turn off ip_forwarding
        ndd -set /dev/ip ip_forwarding 0
        if [ -f /usr/sbin/in.rdisc ] && /usr/sbin/in.rdisc -s; then
            echo "starting router discovery."
        elif [ -f /usr/sbin/in.routed ]; then
            /usr/sbin/in.routed -q;
            echo "starting routing daemon."
        fi
    fi
fi
```

/etc/inetsvc

The /etc/inetsvc concludes the TCP/IP startup process by verifying the configuration of the network interfaces, starting the domain name service (DNS) if need be, and finally bringing up the superserver daemon inetd. Whereas SVR4 systems normally rely on the service access controller sac process (more on sac in Chapter 23, "Device Administration") to invoke inetd, Solaris 2.x invokes it in standalone mode as revealed in the following script listing:

```
# This is third phase of TCP/IP startup/configuration.  This script
# runs after the NIS/NIS+ startup script.  We run things here that may
# depend on NIS/NIS+ maps.
```

```
#

#
# XXX - We need to give ypbind time to bind to a server.
#
sleep 5
#
# Re-set the netmask and broadcast addr for all IP interfaces.  This
# ifconfig is run here, after NIS has been started, so that "netmask
# +" will find the netmask if it lives in a NIS map.
#

/usr/sbin/ifconfig -au netmask + broadcast +

# This is a good time to verify that all of the interfaces were
# correctly configured.  But this is too noisy to run every time we
# boot.
#
# echo "network interface configuration:"
# /usr/sbin/ifconfig -a

#
# If this machine is configured to be an Internet Domain Name
# System (DNS) server, run the name daemon.
# Start named prior to: route add net host, to avoid dns
# gethostbyname timout delay for nameserver during boot.
#
if [ -f /usr/sbin/in.named -a -f /etc/named.boot ]; then
    /usr/sbin/in.named;    echo "starting internet domain name server."
fi

#
# Add a static route for multicast packets out of our default interface.
# The default interface is the interface that corresponds to the node name.
#
echo "Setting default interface for multicast: \c"
/usr/sbin/route add "224.0.0.0" "`uname -n`" 0

#
# Run inetd in "standalone" mode (-s flag) so that it doesn't have
# to submit to the will of SAF.  Why did we ever let them change inetd?
#
/usr/sbin/inetd -s
```

Notice that the DNS daemon (that is, `in.named`) is started conditional on the existence of a DNS boot file called `/etc/named.boot`. Should you need to specify a different path, you ought to update this script accordingly.

TCP/IP Startup on Linux

Linux relies on a set of nested scripts to bring up TCP/IP protocol stack and services. The scripts are

- `/etc/rc.d/init.d/inet`
- `/etc/sysconfig/network`
- `/etc/sysconfig/network-scripts/*` set of scripts

20

NETWORKING

The `/etc/rc.d/init.d/inet` script is the first to kick in at time of starting up TCP/IP. Following is a listing of the script:

```
#! /bin/sh
#
# Source function library.
. /etc/rc.d/init.d/functions

# Get config.
. /etc/sysconfig/network

# Check that networking is up.
if [ ${NETWORKING} = "no" ]
then
    exit 0
fi

# See how we were called.
case "$1" in
  start)
    echo -n "Starting INET services: "
    daemon rpc.portmap
    daemon inetd

    echo
    touch /var/lock/subsys/inet
    ;;
  stop)
    echo -n "Stopping INET services: "
    killproc inetd
    killproc rpc.portmap

    echo
    rm -f /var/lock/subsys/inet
    ;;
  *)
    echo "Usage: inet {start|stop}"
    exit 1
esac

exit 0
```

As shown, the script calls on the `/etc/sysconfig/network` script. The latter, in turn, loops through, and executes, the network interface configuration scripts in the `/etc/sysconfig/network-scripts` directory. There are two scripts per network interface in the `/etc/sysconfig/network-scripts` directory: an `ifup-xxx?` script (to bring the interface up), and `ifdown-xxx?` script (to bring the interface down), where the *xxx* specifies the interface driver being configured, and *?* specifies the instance being configured. For example, `eth0` specifies the first Ethernet interface. Consequently, `ifup-eth0` is the script that is executed by the system on its way up, whereas `ifdown-eth0` executes as the system is brought down. Here is the listing of the `/etc/sysconfig/network` script:

```
#!/bin/sh
#
# network       Bring up/down networking
#
```

```
# Source function library.
. /etc/rc.d/init.d/functions

. /etc/sysconfig/network

# Check that networking is up.
[ ${NETWORKING} = "no" ] && exit 0

# See how we were called.
case "$1" in
  start)
        for i in /etc/sysconfig/network-scripts/ifup-*; do
                $i boot
        done
        touch /var/lock/subsys/network
        ;;
  stop)
        for i in /etc/sysconfig/network-scripts/ifdown-*; do
                $i boot
        done
        rm -f /var/lock/subsys/network
        ;;
  *)
        echo "Usage: network {start¦stop}"
        exit 1
esac

exit 0
```

And following is the listing of a sample `ifup-eth0` script:

```
#!/bin/sh
PATH=/sbin:/usr/sbin:/bin:/usr/bin

. /etc/sysconfig/network-scripts/ifcfg-eth0

if [ "foo$1" = "fooboot" -a ${ONBOOT} = "no" ]
then
    exit
fi

ifconfig eth0 ${IPADDR} netmask ${NETMASK} broadcast ${BROADCAST}
route add -net ${NETWORK} netmask ${NETMASK}
if [ ${GATEWAY} != "none" ]
then
    route add default gw ${GATEWAY} metric 1
fi
```

Upon completion of the execution of the `/etc/sysconfig/network` script (subsequent to the completion of all the `ifup-xxx?` scripts in the `/etc/sysconfig/network-scripts` directory), the execution of `/etc/rc.d/init.d/inet` concludes by bringing up both the port-mapper daemon (more on this later in the chapter) and the superserver daemon `inetd`.

The `inetd` Superserver Daemon

The daemons that are invoked by the initialization scripts provide the basic TCP/IP services to UNIX. Of the TCP/IP suite of protocols, only the routing service, DNS name service, network time protocol, and ppp serial link service are individually invoked. Other services, such

20

NETWORKING

as Telnet and FTP, are started on an as-needed basis. The daemon which starts them is `inetd`, known as the Internet superserver or master Internet daemon.

Depending on the UNIX variant, `inetd` is either started at boot time by `sac` (the service access controller) or as a standalone daemon. On most SVR4 UNIX systems inetd is started by `sac`, which is in turn started by `init` whenever the system is brought to run level 2. If you check the `/etc/inittab` file on a SVR4 system you should be able to find an entry similar to the following one:

```
sc:234:respawn: /usr/lib/saf/sac -t 300
```

This entry guarantees that an invocation of the service access controller is attempted upon reboot. To check whether `inetd` is spawned by `sac` you can use the `ps` command, or better still you can use the `sacadm` command as follows:

```
# sacadm -l
PMTAG           PMTYPE       FLGS RCNT STATUS    COMMAND
inetd           inetd        -    0    ENABLED   /usr/sbin/inetd #internet daemon
tcp             listen       -    3    ENABLED    /usr/lib/saf/listen -m inet/
➥tcp0 tcp 2>/dev/null
```

According to the response shown above, `inetd` is indeed started and is in an enabled state. This means that `inetd` is actively listening for network service requests and is capable of starting the appropriate daemon to handle a request.

BSD, Linux, and Solaris 2.x bring up `inetd` as a standalone daemon, as demonstrated in the scripts listed earlier. However started, the daemon is configured and behaves identically on all UNIX variants. Once brought up, `inetd` fetches and reads the configuration file `inetd.conf` (normally found in the `/etc` directory). This file defines the service daemons on whose behalf `inetd` can listen for network service requests. Using any editor, you can add to, or delete from, the list of `inetd`-supported services. The following is a partial listing of this file as it existed on a SVR4 system:

```
# Internet services syntax:
#   <service_name> <socket_type> <proto> <flags> <user> <server_pathname> <args>
#
# Ftp and telnet are standard Internet services.
#
ftp     stream  tcp    nowait    root    /usr/sbin/in.ftpd      in.ftpd
telnet    stream    tcp    nowait    root    /usr/sbin/in.telnetd    in.telnetd
#
# Shell, login, exec, comsat and talk are BSD protocols.
#
shell    stream    tcp    nowait    root    /usr/sbin/in.rshd     in.rshd
login    stream    tcp    nowait    root    /usr/sbin/in.rlogind    in.rlogind
exec    stream    tcp    nowait    root    /usr/sbin/in.rexecd    in.rexecd
comsat   dgram    udp    wait    root    /usr/sbin/in.comsat    in.comsat
talk    dgram    udp    wait    root    /usr/sbin/in.otalkd    in.otalkd
ntalk    dgram    udp    wait    root    /usr/sbin/in.talkd    in.talkd
#bootps    dgram    udp    wait    root    /usr/sbin/in.bootpd    in.bootpd
#
# Run as user "uucp" if you don't want uucpd's wtmp entries.
# Uncomment the following entry if the uucpd daemon is added to the system.
#
```

```
# uucp     stream    tcp     nowait    uucp     /usr/sbin/in.uucpd    in.uucpd
#
# Tftp service is provided primarily for booting.  Most sites run this
# only on machines acting as "boot servers."
#
#tftp   dgram    udp     wait    root    /usr/sbin/in.tftpd    in.tftpd -s /
➥tftpboot
#
# Finger, systat and netstat give out user information which may be
# valuable to potential "system crackers."  Many sites choose to disable
# some or all of these services to improve security.
#
#finger    stream    tcp    nowait    nobody    /usr/sbin/in.fingerd    in.fingerd
#systat    stream    tcp    nowait    root    /usr/bin/ps    ps -ef
#netstat   stream    tcp    nowait    root    /usr/bin/netstat    netstat -f inet
#
# Time service is used for clock synchronization.
#
time   stream    tcp    nowait    root    internal
time   dgram    udp    wait    root    internal
#
# Echo, discard, daytime, and chargen are used primarily for testing.
#
echo    stream    tcp    nowait    root    internal
echo    dgram    udp    wait    root    internal
discard    stream    tcp    nowait    root    internal
discard    dgram    udp    wait    root    internal
daytime    stream    tcp    nowait    root    internal
daytime    dgram    udp    wait    root    internal
chargen    stream    tcp    nowait    root    internal
chargen    dgram    udp    wait    root    internal
#
#
# RPC services syntax:
#   <rpc_prog>/<vers> <socket_type> rpc/<proto> <flags> <user> <pathname> <args>
#
# The mount server is usually started in /etc/rc.local only on machines that
# are NFS servers.  It can be run by inetd as well.
#
#mountd/1    dgram    rpc/udp    wait root /usr/lib/nfs/mountd    mountd
#
# Ypupdated is run by sites that support YP updating.
#
#ypupdated/1    stream    rpc/tcp    wait root /usr/lib/netsvc/yp/ypupdated
➥ypupdated
#
# The rusers service gives out user information.  Sites concerned
# with security may choose to disable it.
#
#rusersd/1-2    dgram    rpc/udp    wait root /usr/lib/netsvc/rusers/rpc.rusersd
➥rpc.rusersd
#
# The spray server is used primarily for testing.
#
#sprayd/1    dgram    rpc/udp    wait root /usr/lib/netsvc/spray/rpc.sprayd
➥rpc.sprayd
#
# The rwall server lets anyone on the network bother everyone on your machine.
#
```

```
#walld/1         dgram     rpc/udp     wait root /usr/lib/netsvc/rwall/rpc.rwalld
➥rpc.rwalld
#
#
# TLI services syntax:
#   <service_name> tli <proto> <flags> <user> <server_pathname> <args>
#
# TCPMUX services syntax:
#   tcpmux/<service_name> stream tcp <flags> <user> <server_pathname> <args>
#
smtp     stream     tcp     nowait     root     /usr/lib/mail/surrcmd/in.smtpd
➥in.smtpd -H jade -r
```

The second line in the listing depicts the syntax of the file entries. The syntax is repeated here along with a sample entry for convenience:

```
#   <service_name> <socket_type> <proto> <flags> <user> <server_pathname> <args>
```

service_name	This is an identifying label of the service as listed in the /etc/services file. For example, the first service entry in the file is labeled ftp matching another one in the /etc/services file.
socket_type	This identifies the type of the data delivery service being used. Three types are most commonly recognized: 1) stream which is a byte-oriented delivery service provided by TCP, 2) dgram which is a transactional oriented service delivered by UDP, and 3) raw which directly runs on IP. In ftp's case the type specified is stream.
proto	This identifies the name of the transport protocol which is normally either udp or tcp, and it corresponds to the protocol name as specified in the /etc/protocols file. In ftp's case the protocol type is tcp.
flags	This field can be set to either wait or nowait. If set to wait, inetd must wait for the service protocol (or server) to release the socket connecting it to the network before inetd can resume listening for more requests on that socket. On the other hand, a nowait flag enables inetd to immediately listen for more requests on the socket. Upon examining the above listing of the inetd.conf file, it can be noticed that stream type servers mostly allow a nowait status, whereas the status is wait for the dgram type of servers.
user	The user (or uid) name under which the server is invoked. This is normally set to user root. *user* can, however, be set to any valid user name.

server_pathname   This specifies the server's full path name of the program which `inetd` must invoke in response to an associated service request. In `ftp`'s case, the program full path is `/usr/sbin/in.ftpd`.

Upon examining the `inetd.conf` file you will notice that some of the servers' paths are specified as `internal`. Examples of these servers include `echo`, `discard`, and `daytime`. These are typically small and non-demanding servers. So, instead of implementing them individually in separate programs, they are implemented as part of the `inetd` server itself.

args   This field includes command-line arguments that are supported by the program implementing the server. As can be seen from the listing, the argument list must always start with the `argv[0]` argument (that is, the program's name) followed by whichever arguments you deem suitable.

There are a few occasions where you might have to make some changes to the `inetd.conf` file. You might want to enable a service, disable another one, or modify one already supported. Enabling or disabling a service is a matter of removing or inserting the # character in front of the service configuration entry.

Modifying a supported service mainly involves changing the arguments passed to the program responsible for that service. Using the `-s` option with the `in.tftp` command, for example, allows you to specify a directory to which you can restrict file transfer applications. According to the supporting entry in the `inetd.conf` shown previously, the directory specified is `tftpboot` to allow for remote reboot. You can change this to any other directory name.

Following is a brief description of each of the daemons that are run and controlled by the `inetd` superserver:

ftpd   Also known as `in.ftpd` on some UNIX variants, this is the file transfer protocol daemon. It is responsible for responding to user requests involving file transfers in and out of the host as well as other functions such as third-party transfers and directory lookups.

telnetd   Also known as `in.telnetd` on some UNIX variants, this is the remote terminal session daemon. It is responsible for providing user login services.

rshd   Also known as `in.rshd`, this is an implementation of the Berkeley remote shell, known as `rsh`. It is used to execute a command on a remote system.

logind	Also known as in.logind, this is an implementation of Berkeley's remote login capability.
execd	Also known as in.execd, this allows for the remote execution of commands on the system.
comsat	This is the mail notification daemon. It listens for incoming mail notification messages and informs processes that request it.
talkd, otalkd	talkd and the otalkd are respectively the new and old versions of the talk daemon. They allow users to chat using the keyboard and the screen of their terminals anywhere on the network.
uucpd	Also known as in.uucpd, this is responsible for the transfer of UUCP data over the network.
tftpd	Also known as in.tftpd, this is the trivial transfer protocol. It is mainly used to support remote boot facility for diskless workstations and network devices such as routers and wiring devices.
fingerd	It allows the use of the finger command to determine what are the users doing.
systat	It performs a process status on a remote system. As shown in the /etc/inetd.conf, inetd forks off a ps command and returns the output to the remote system.
netstat	It provides network status information to the remote system by forking off a netstat command and returning the output to the remote system.
rquotad	This is the disk server daemon. It returns the disk quota for a specific user
admind	This is the distributed system administration tool server daemon.
usersd	This daemon returns a list of users on the host.
sprayd	This is a network diagnostic daemon. It sprays packets on the network to test for loss.
walld	This is the write to all daemons. It allows sending a message to all users on a system.
rstatd	This daemon returns performance statistics about this system.
cmsd	This is the calendar manager server daemon.

In addition to the preceding daemons, inetd internally provides the following services:

echo	This service is supported over both UDP and TCP. It returns whatever is send to it; hence allowing loop diagnostics by comparing outbound to inbound traffic.
discard	This service simply discards whatever it is sent.
daytime	This service returns the time in the format *Day Mmm dd hh:mm:ss yyyy*.
chargen	This is the character generator service and is provided over UDP and TCP. It returns copies of the printable subset of the ASCII character set. chargen is useful in performing network diagnostics.

Other Network Daemons

In addition to the daemons that are started by inetd, UNIX starts the following TCP/IP service daemons:

routed	This is an implementation of the Route Information Protocol (RIP) discussed earlier in the chapter.
gated	This daemon embeds more than one route information protocol including RIP, Open Shortest Path First (OSPF), Exterior Gateway Protocol (EGP), Boundary Gateway Protocol, (BGP) and HELLO. The discussion of these protocols falls beyond the scope of this book. *Networking UNIX,* Sams Publishing, ISBN 0-672-30584-4, includes an in-depth discussion of these protocols.
nfsd	This is the Network File System (NFS) daemon. It runs on the file server, and is responsible for handling client requests (see the section "NFS File Sharing" for details).
biod	This is the block input/output daemon. It runs on NFS clients and handles reading and writing data from and to the NFS server on behalf of the client process (see the section "NFS File Sharing" for details).
mountd	This daemon runs on the NFS server and is responsible for responding to client NFS mount requests (see the section "NFS File Sharing" for details).
lockd	Run by both the client and the server, this daemon handles file locks. On the client side, the daemon issues such requests, whereas the server's lockd honors those requests and manages the locks (see the section "NFS File Sharing" for details).

statd	Run by both the client and the server, statd maintains the status of currently enforced file locks (see the section "NFS File Sharing" for details).
rpcbind	rpcbind bears a similarity with inetd. Whereas the latter is responsible for listening to network service requests on behalf of common TCP/IP daemons such as ftpd and telnetd, the former is responsible for listening to NFS-related requests (among many more services known as Remote Procedure Calls) and fielding them to the appropriate daemon (such as nfsd, lockd, and statd). rpcbind-controlled daemons are brought up by UNIX as standalone processes, unlike the inetd-controlled daemons that are brought up by inetd and only on an as-needed basis.
sendmail	UNIX relies on the Simple Mail Transfer Protocol (SMTP, yet another TCP/IP application protocol specified by RFC 821) for the exchange of electronic mail among hosts on the network. SMTP delivers the service by relying on what is commonly referred to as Mail Transfer Agent (MTA). sendmail is an SMTP agent that handles listening for SMTP connections and processing e-mail messages. Configuring sendmail is a complex matter that falls beyond the scope of this chapter.

ifconfig

UNIX provides an impressively comprehensive toolkit to help you deal with the various aspects of administering, managing, and troubleshooting TCP/IP networks. Using appropriate commands you will be able to do anything from configuring the network interfaces to gathering performance statistical data. Of all the commands, you have encountered two in this chapter. These are the ifconfig and route commands. Both commands are common to most of UNIX variants. The route command has been dealt with in detail under the section "Route Table Maintenance" earlier in this chapter. Now, we explain ifconfig in detail.

The ifconfig command is used to configure, or to check the configuration values of, the network interface card. You can use ifconfig to assign the network interface an IP address, netmask, broadcast address, or change some of its parameters. ifconfig is always used at boot time by the TCP/IP startup scripts, to set up those parameters as dictated by the interface configuration files (see the following note about interface configuration files).

NETWORK INTERFACE CONFIGURATION FILE(S)

Unfortunately, not all UNIX variants save interface configuration information (such as IP address, netmask, broadcast address, and so on) in the same place on disk. The following table provides a handy reference of where each of the platforms discussed in this chapter saves such information. Interface configuration files are fetched by startup scripts for use with the `ifconfig` command to configure the supported interface:

Platform	Configuration Files
SVR4	/etc/confnet.d/inet/interfaces
Solaris 2.x	/etc/hosts, /etc/netmasks, /etc/hostname.*xx*?
Linux	/etc/sysconfig/network-scripts/ifcfg-*xxx*?

Please refer to earlier sections of the chapter for details about these files.

The general syntax of `ifconfig` is too comprehensive to be meaningfully explained with one example. Therefore, it will be presented piecemeal in the context of different situations where `ifconfig` is used.

Setting the IP Address, Netmask, and Broadcast Address

In its simplest form, the syntax of the `ifconfig` command is as follows

```
ifconfig interface IP_address netmask mask broadcast address
```

which is used to setup the basic parameters of the network interface, where

`interface`	This is the label identifying the network interface card. For example, the 3Com 3C509 is known as el30.
`IP_address`	This is the IP address assigned to the network interface. You can optionally use the host name, provided that the `/etc/hosts` file includes the corresponding name to IP address association.
`netmask mask`	This is the applicable subnetwork mask. You can ignore this parameter if the mask is left at its default (that is, the network is not segmented into subnets). All hosts on the same physical network must have their mask set to the same value.
`broadcast address`	This is the broadcast address for the network. The default broadcast address is such that all of the host id bits are set to one. Older systems used to have the bits set to zero. All hosts on the same physical network must have their broadcast address set to the same value. For example, the Class B 150.1.0.0 network address has by default the 150.1.255.255 as a broadcast address.

20

NETWORKING

In the following example, `ifconfig` is used to set up the IP address, netmask and the broadcast address of a 3Com 3C509 network interface card:

```
# ifconfig el30 150.1.0.1 netmask 255.255.0.0 broadcast 150.1.255.255
```

Optionally, you can use the host name instead of the IP address to configure the interface as follows:

```
# ifconfig el30 oboe netmask 255.255.0.0 broadcast 150.1.255.255
```

Where oboe is the host name mapped to a valid IP address in the `/etc/hosts` file.

This example can be further simplified to become

```
# ifconfig el30 oboe
```

since both the netmask and the broadcast addresses are set to their default values.

Checking the Interface Using `ifconfig`

To check the configuration parameters of a supported interface you must enter

```
# ifconfig interface
```

Hence to check the configuration of the 3Com 3c509 enter

```
# ifconfig el30
el30: flags=23<UP,BROADCAST,NOTRAILERS>
    inet 150.1.0.1 netmask ffff0000 broadcast 150.1.255.255
```

The above response confirms that the 3Com interface is configured to IP network address 150.1.0.1, the netmask to ffff0000 (that is, the hex equivalent to dotted notation 255.255.0.0), and the broadcast address to 150.1.255.255.

The information included within the angle brackets of the response report are

UP	Indicating that the interface is enabled and actively participating on the network. If the interface were disabled, UP would have been substituted with the null character.
BROADCAST	Indicating that the interface is configured to accept broadcasts.
NOTRAILERS	Indicating that the interface does not support trailer encapsulation; a technique by which the fields of the ethernet frame can be rearranged for better efficiency, should the host I/O architecture benefit from this arrangement. Since this technique is becoming less popular over time, it will not be discussed any further.

To check the configuration of all of the interfaces supported by the system, use the `-a` option (for all interfaces) with the `ifconfig` command as shown in the following example:

```
# ifconfig -a
lo0: flags=49<UP,LOOPBACK,RUNNING>
      inet 127.0.0.1 netmask ff000000
ne2k0: flags=23<UP,BROADCAST,NOTRAILERS>
      inet 100.0.0.1 netmask ff000000 broadcast 100.255.255.255
el30: flags=23<UP,BROADCAST,NOTRAILERS>
      inet 150.1.0.1 netmask ffff0000 broadcast 150.1.255.255
```

The preceding response refers to three interfaces. The first one, the `lo0` interface, refers to the loopback interface and is assigned the IP loopback address `127.0.0.1` and the default Class A netmask. The second (that is, `ne2k0`) and the third (that is, `el30`) interfaces refer to NE2000 and 3C509 interfaces respectively. All interfaces are enabled (that is, `UP`) for use.

Enabling/Disabling the Interface with `ifconfig`

The `ifconfig` command supports a few optional parameters, of which the `up` and `down` parameters can be used to enable or disable an interface. You normally temporarily disable an interface on a router whenever you are troubleshooting the network and want to isolate a suspect segment from the rest of the network. Also, on some systems, configuration changes made to an interface won't take effect unless the interface was disabled before using `ifconfig` to modify the interface's configuration. To use `ifconfig` to disable an interface enter

```
# ifconfig interface down
```

As an example, to disable the 3C509 network interface, enter

```
# ifconfig el30 down
```

It is always a good idea to check that the interface was indeed disabled before trusting it. To do so, enter

```
# ifconfig el30 down
el30: flags=22<BROADCAST,NOTRAILERS>
      inet 150.1.0.1 netmask ffff0000 broadcast 150.1.255.255
```

Notice how the absence of the keyword `UP` from the information included in the angle brackets implies that the interface is down.

To bring it back up, you simply enter

```
# ifconfig el30 up
```

NFS File Sharing

Although network applications such as FTP and Telnet provide mechanisms for sharing computing resources on the network, they come with their self-imposed limitations and inconveniences. Taking FTP, as an example, unless a file was transferred to the local host, a user could not process that file using local programs and shell commands. Even worse, users had to

20

NETWORKING

suspend, or exit, the FTP session to process the transferred file. Also, using FTP incurs a learning curve for the commands that FTP supports are distinct from the common UNIX file system-related commands.

Network File System (NFS) circumvents the limitations imposed by other file system access methods. In contrast, NFS provides the user with transparent access to remote filesystems. From the user's perspective, an NFS-accessible resource is treated in exactly the same way a local resource is treated. When setup, a remote file system will appear to the user as a part of the local file system. There is no requirement to login and enter a password to access an NFS filesystem. To the user, accessing an NFS-mounted file system is a simple matter of changing directories in the UNIX file system hierarchy.

NFS Concepts

Network File System (NFS) allows user processes and programs *transparent* read and write access to remotely mounted file systems. Transparency implies that programs would continue to work and process files located on an NFS-mounted file system without requiring any modifications to their code. This is because NFS is cleverly designed to present remote resources to users as extensions to the local resources.

NFS follows the client-server model, where the server is the system which owns the filesystem resource and is configured to share it with other systems. An NFS-shareable resource is usually referred to as *exported filesystem*. The client is the resource user. It uses the exported filesystem as if it were part of the local filesystem. To achieve this transparency the client is said to *mount* the exported directory to the local filesystem.

Figure 20.30 illustrates the concepts. /efs is the exported directory on host tenor (the NFS server). As indicated by the shaded area, by virtue of exporting the /efs directory, the subtree beneath is also exported. Accessing /efs directory from client jade involves creating a directory on the local file system (/rfs in the figure) and mounting the remote file system by using the mount command (more on this later) as shown here:

```
# mount -F nfs tenor:/efs /rfs
```

FIGURE 20.30.

The interrelationship between the NFS server and client filesystems.

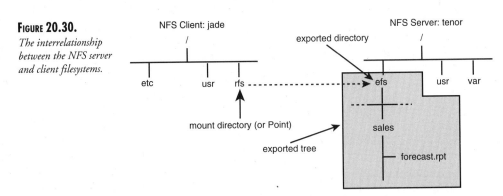

Remote Procedure Calls

Remote Procedure Call (developed by Sun Microsystems) provides the foundation supporting NFS among other network services, called RPC-based servers.

RPC defines a transparent distributed computing service by which a process is split into two components, the client and the server component. The client component is local to the host that is making the RPC call to the remote network–shared resource. The server component manages the shared resource and processes and responds to the RPC calls it receives from the client.

While the remote procedure is executing at the server's end, the local RPC-user process awaits the return results the way it would have waited if the call had been made to a local resource.

Transport Support

Being a process/application layer protocol, RPC relies on transport layer protocols for the exchanging of requests and responses between RPC clients and servers. Under TCP/IP, RPC is supported over both transports UDP and TCP.

Most RPC activity is carried by the UDP transport protocol. This mostly the case because RPC routines live a relatively short life cycle, making the overhead associated with the creation and termination of TCP connections unjustifiably high. For this reason, message sequencing and reliability checks are built into most of the RPC servers. TCP connections are commonly established for the sake of transmitting large chunks of data.

In contrast to other TCP/IP applications, such as FTP and Telnet, RPC servers do not rely on well known transport port numbers. They are, instead, dynamically assigned an available port number at boot time.

A complete listing of the RPC servers supported on your host, look up the contents of the /etc/rpc file. Following is a partial listings of its contents:

```
rpcbind        100000     portmap sunrpc rpcbind
rstatd         100001     rstat rup perfmeter
rusersd        100002     rusers
nfs         100003     nfsprog
ypserv         100004     ypprog
mountd         100005     mount showmount
ypbind         100007
walld          100008     rwall shutdown
yppasswdd      100009     yppasswd
sprayd         100012     spray
llockmgr         100020
nlockmgr    100021
statmon         100023
status      100024
ypupdated      100028     ypupdate
rpcnfs         100116     na.rpcnfs
pcnfsd         150001
```

Each entry in this file includes (left to right) the server name, program number, and optionally one or more aliases.

Program Number and Port Mapper

Since RPC servers are dynamically assigned port numbers at startup time, there arises the requirement for a mechanism by which the servers can make themselves addressable by their clients. RPC achieves this by employing an arbitrator process, known as the port mapper, that listens for requests on behalf of RPC servers. Instead of addressing servers at port numbers, clients initially address them at well-assigned program numbers (listed in the /etc/rpc file). At startup, every RPC server registers itself with the port mapper (implemented as rpcbind daemon).

Before a client requests an RPC service for the first time, it should contact rpcbind (that is, the port mapper) for the port number on which the desired RPC server is listening for requests. After a favorable response is obtained, the client caches the port number and uses it to contact the RPC server directly. Understandably, for clients to reach the port mapper, the latter must listen to port resolution requests on a well-known port number. The port number is 111.

Procedure Number

Each RPC server is comprised of a number of procedures, where each procedure handles certain functionality of the service. NFS, for example, supports many procedures, of which we mention NFSPROC_READ, which a client uses to read from a file, NFSPROC_WRITE to write to a file, and NFSPROC_REMOVE to delete a file belonging to the NFS server. Every procedure is assigned a number which the client passes in an RPC request to identify the procedure it wants executed by the server.

Version Number

Every implementation of the same RPC server is assigned a version number. A new implementation is always assigned a higher number. A new version of an RPC server is usually made to support earlier procedure implementations so that all versions are taken care of by a single server process.

It is not sufficient, therefore, that a client specifies the RPC program number, the procedure number, and the port number when passing an RPC request to the server. It must also specify the version number that the client supports. Unless the server and the client agree on a mutually acceptable version support level, the port mapper returns an error message complaining about version mismatch.

Hence, to uniquely identify a procedure to an RPC server, the client must specify the program number, the procedure number, and the version number.

NFS Daemons

As are many UNIX services, NFS is implemented in a set of daemons. Some of the NFS-related daemons run on the server while others run on the client. Also a subset of the daemons run on both sides. Following is a description of what function each of the daemons provides as part of the overall NFS service:

nfsd	This is the NFS server daemon; it runs on the server and is responsible for handling, and responding, to client requests. nfsd handles client requests by decoding requests to determine the nature of the desired operation, and submitting the call to local I/O disk access mechanism for actual execution. nfsd is normally invoked when the system is brought up to run level three. For performance-related reasons, multiple instances of nfsd are invoked.
biod	This is the block input/output daemon. It runs on NFS clients and handles reading and writing data from and to the NFS server on behalf of the client process. Again, performance-related issues dictate that multiple instances of this daemon be invoked on the client. Be careful, however, because invoking too many instances of biod can potentially lead to degradation in performance.
mountd	This runs on the NFS server. It is responsible for handling client mount requests. Looking back at Figure 20.30, when the command mount -F nfs tenor:/efs / ifs is issued on the command line on host jade, an NFS mount request is sent by the client to the NFS server. Unless host tenor is running mountd, it will not be capable to honor the request and the mount is bound to fail. NFS servers run only *one* mountd.
lockd	Run by both the client and server, this daemon handles file locks. On the client side the daemon issues such requests, whereas the server's lockd honors those requests and manages the locks.
Statd	Run by both the client and server, this daemon maintains the status of currently enforced file locks. Its usefulness is particularly realized during server crashes as it helps clients to reclaim locks placed on files after the recovery of the server.

Table 20.3 below lists the daemons that run on each side of the NFS service.

Table 20.3. Listing of daemons that are invoked by NFS on both the client and the server hosts. Notice how both `lockd` and `statd` daemons are invoked on both hosts.

Client Daemons	Server Daemons
biod	nfsd
lockd	lockd
statd	statd
	mountd

Setting Up the NFS Server

Once you have decided which parts of the file system you want to share on the server with other hosts, you can proceed to setting up NFS.

Setting Up NFS on SVR4 Including Solaris 2.x

Exporting a file system (that is, rendering it shareable) under SVR4 involves the use of the share command. The syntax of this command is

```
share [-F nfs] [-o options] [ -d description] pathname
```

where,

-F nfs	Specifies the type of exported filesystem. UNIX supports many different types of remotely accessible filesystems. Examples of such filesystems include RFS (Remote File Systems) and AFS (Andrews File System). This option can be omitted if NFS is the only distributed file system which your system supports.
-o options	Specifies restrictions that apply to the exported filesystem. Table 20.4 lists the options and a brief description of their effects.
d description	A descriptive statement.
pathname	Specifies the pathname to export (or share).

Table 20.4. Options supported by the -o *options* upon mounting an NFS filesystem.

Option	Description
rw=host[:host...]	Allows read/write access to exported file system to the hosts specified in the *host* parameter.
ro=host[:host...]	Exports the *pathname* as read-only to listed hosts. If no hosts are specified, all clients, with exceptions stated using rw= option, are allowed read-only access.

Option	Description
anon=*uid*	Assigns a different uid for anonymous users (that is, users with uid 0) when accessing *pathname*. By default anonymous users are assigned uid of user nobody. User nobody normally has same access privileges as public.
root=[*host*[:*host*...]	Allows root access privileges to user from the host *host*. The user's uid has to be 0. Unless specified no user is allowed root access privileges to *pathname*.
secure	Enforces enhanced authentication requirements before a user is granted access to an NFS mounted filesystem.

In the scenario depicted in Figure 20.30, using the following share command allows host tenor to export and share the /efs subtree of the filesystem. Further, the exported file system is flagged rw, hence allowing other hosts read/write access to it:

```
# share -F nfs -o rw, ro=saturn -d "Just an example" /efs
```

The share command shown here allows no root access to the /efs directory.

The following share command, on the other hand, prevents all hosts but violin from accessing the filesystem:

```
# share -F nfs -o ro=violin /efs
```

Hosts, other than violin, attempting to mount the /efs directory, will fail and end up with the "Permission denied" message.

In the following example root privilege is granted to users from host jade:

```
# share -F nfs -o rw, root=jade /efs
```

To find out which filesystems are exported, simply enter share without command-line arguments:

```
# share
-                /nfs    rw    ""
-                /efs    rw,ro=violin    ""
```

Automating Sharing at Boot Time

Exporting (or sharing) file systems (under SVR4) at boot time is a simple matter that involves editing the /etc/dfs/dfstab file. In this file you should include as many share commands (using exactly same syntax explained previously) to take care of all the directories you want exported by the NFS server. The following two share entries, for example, are extracted from the /etc/dsf/dfstab file on host tenor:

```
share -F nfs /nfs
share -F nfs rw, ro=satrun /efs
```

When the system enters run level three as it is brought up, /etc/dfs/dfstab contents will be read, and its share entries will be executed. No longer will the system administrator have to issue both share commands manually.

The program which is called from the /etc/init.d/nfs script to export all of the filesystems specified in the dfstab file is shareall. You may use it on the command line, as well, to force sharing, especially after you make changes to the /etc/dfs/dfstab which you want to implement immediately.

Setting Up NFS on BSD and Linux

BSD-derived UNIX systems rely on the /etc/exports file to control which directories are exported. Entries in the /etc/exports file must follow the following syntax:

```
pathname  [-option][,option]...
```

where, *pathname* specifies the directory being exported and *option* specifies access-pertinent privileges. Following is a description of the commonly supported options:

rw[=hostname][:hostname]...	rw grants read/write privileges to hosts specified using the host name parameter. If no host name is specified, then read/write access is granted to all hosts on the network. rw is the default access privilege if no option is specified. Here is an example: /usr/reports -rw=bass:soprano This entry grants read/write to the directory /usr/reports to users from hosts bass and soprano. Note that whenever host names are specified, the privilege applies to them only. Users from other hosts are granted read-only permission. In the above example, users on all hosts, but bass and soprano, have read-only access to /usr/reports directory.
ro	Specifies a read-only permission to the directory being exported. User attempts to write to the directory results in error messages such as "Permission denied," or "Read-only filesystem."
access=hostname[:hostname]...	Specifies the names of the hosts that are granted permission to mount the exported directory. If this option is not included in the entry affecting the exported directory, then all hosts on the network can mount that directory (that is, the directory ends up being exported to every host).

```
root=hostname[:hostname]...
```
Grants root access privilege only to root users from specified host name(s). Otherwise (that is, if no host name is specified), root access is denied (by default) to root users from all hosts. In this example, root access is granted to root users from hosts `violin` and `cello`:

```
/usr/resources root=violin:cello
```

Since no `ro` or `rw` options are specified, the exported directory (`/usr/resources`) is by default read/writeable for users from *all* hosts.

For discussions on more options affecting NFS access privileges please refer to the man pages supplied by your vendor.

Every time the system is booted, the NFS startup scripts execute and process the contents of the `/etc/exports` file. Normally, for performance reasons, eight instances of the `nfsd` daemon are started and only one `mountd` (or `rpc.mountd`, as called by some systems) is started. The `mountd` daemon is responsible (as explained earlier) for mounting exported file systems specified in the `/etc/exports` file, in response to client mount requests.

Setting Up the NFS Client

On the client side, a user has to issue the mount command prior to attempting access to the exported path on the NFS server. For example, to access the exported `/efs` directory on NFS server `tenor`, the user must first issue the following mount command on a UNIX SVR4 operating system:

```
# mount -F nfs jade:/efs /rfs
```

As shown in Figure 20.30, `/efs` is the exported directory on host `tenor`, and `/rfs` is the mount directory. Once mounted, `/efs` or any directories below it can be accessed (subject to security restrictions) from host `jade`, using ordinary UNIX commands and programs.

Following is the complete syntax of the mount command (see Table 20.5):

```
mount [-F nfs] [-o options] host:pathname mountpoint
```

where,

`-F nfs`	Specifies the type of the filesystem to mount.
`-o options`	Specifies the mount options. Table 20.5 includes a listing of commonly used options.
`host:pathname`	Completely identifies the server and the resource directory being mounted. *host* is the host name of the NFS server, and *pathname* is the path name of the exported directory on this server.

20

NETWORKING

`mountpoint`	Specifies the path name of the directory on the client through which the NFS-mounted resource will be accessed.

Table 20.5. Mount-specific options.

Option	Description
`rw ¦ ro`	Specifies whether to mount the NFS directory for read-only or read/write. The default is `rw`.
`retry=n`	Specifies the number of times mount should retry. This is normally set to a very high number. Check your vendor's documentation for the default value of *n*.
`timeo=n`	Specifies the timeout period for the mount attempt in units of tenths of a second. `timeo` is normally set to a very high number. Check you vendor's documentation for the default value.
`soft ¦ hard`	Specifies whether a `hard` or `soft` mount should be attempted. If `hard` is specified the client relentlessly retries until it receives an acknowledgement from the NFS server specified in *host*. A `soft` mount, on the other hand, causes the client to give up attempting if it does not get the acknowledgment after retrying the number of times specified in `retry=n` option. Upon failure, a `soft` mount returns an error message to the attempting client.
`bg ¦ fg`	Specifies whether the client is to reattempt mounting, should the NFS server fail to respond, in the foreground (`fg`) or in the background (`bg`).
`intr`	Specifies whether to allow keyboard interrupts to kill a process which is hung up waiting for a response from a hard-mounted filesystem. Unless interrupted, the process waits endlessly for a response, which in turn locks the session.

mount COMMAND

Except for a few subtleties, the preceding description of the mount command applies to all variants of UNIX. You are advised, however, to check the man pages for the exact syntax that is peculiar to your variant.

Should a `soft` mounted filesystem fail to respond to a mount request, the request will be retried by the client for the number of times specified in the `retry=n` option. If the *n* retries are exhausted without any success getting an acknowledgement form the server, an error message is returned and the client stops retrying.

If the affected filesystem was mounted for read/write access, this mode of behavior may seriously impact the integrity of applications which were writing to this filesystem before the interruption in service occurred. For this reason it is recommended that read/write mountable filesystems be hard mounted. This guarantees that the client will indefinitely retry an operation until outstanding requests are honored, even in the event of an NFS server crash.

Unreasonably extended server failure may lead to locking up an application indefinitely while waiting for a response from a hard mounted filesystem. Hence, whenever a hard mount is desired it is important that keyboard interrupts are allowed (by specifying the intr option) to kill the process so that a user can recover the login session back to normal operation.

Following is a mount command which would be used to soft mount the /nfs/sales directory on the NFS server jade, with read-only access. The mount point is /usr/sales on host jade:

```
# mount -F nfs -o soft, ro tenor:/nfs/sales /usr/sales
```

To verify that a filesystem is indeed mounted, use mount without any command-line arguments as follows:

```
# mount
/ on /dev/root read/write on Sat Feb 18 09:44:45 1995
/u on /dev/u read/write on Sat Feb 18 09:46:39 1995
/TEST on /dev/TEST read/write on Sat Feb 18 09:46:40 1995
/usr/sales on tenor:/nfs/sales read/write on Sat Feb 18 10:02:52 1995
```

The last line indicates the name of the mount directory, the name of the NFS server, and the name of the mounted filesystem.

Starting and Stopping NFS Services

Once all the necessary steps for automatic sharing and mounting of filesystems are completed, you can start NFS operation on both the server and the client hosts. While the daemons required to start NFS services are the same for all variants of UNIX, the startup procedure itself could be different.

Starting and Stopping NFS on SVR4 (Not Including Solaris 2.x)

To manually start NFS using the command line, use the following command:

```
sh /etc/init.d/nfs start
```

This command automatically starts the same set of NFS daemons independent of whether the command was invoked on a client or a server. Depending on the vendor, anywhere from four to eight daemons of both nfsd and biod are started by the script. Starting multiple instances of these daemons has the impact of improving the overall performance of the NFS service.

The /etc/init.d/nfs script also starts all other daemons including lockd, statd, and mountd. All NFS daemons are invoked on both the server and clients because UNIX allows a host to assume both roles server and client. While the system is a server to clients on the network, it itself can be a client to some other server(s).

Should the `/etc/init.d/nfs` script fail to run on your system, it could be because the system is not at run level three. To check the state of your system, enter the following `who -r` command:

```
# who -r
   .         run-level 3  Nov 12 10:40    3    0    S
```

To bring the system up to run level three, if it is not there yet, enter the following `init` command:

```
# init 3
```

To bring up the system to run level three by default at boot time, you must ensure that the `/etc/inittab` file includes the following `initdefault` entry:

```
is:3:initdefault:
```

Upon checking the `/etc/inittab` file, you may find the following entry instead:

```
is:2:initdefault:
```

In this case, use your preferred editor to replace the 2 in the `initdefault` entry with 3. This guarantees that the system enters run level three when booted—a necessary condition for starting the NFS service on *both* the client and the server.

> **NOTE**
>
> As noted before, SVR4 allows for the auto-sharing (exporting at boot time) of directories specified in the `/etc/dfs/dfstab`. In like fashion, SVR4 allows for auto-mounting of remote file system resources based on entries in the `/etc/vfstab` file. Using the `vfstab` file, a system administrator can specify the name of the NFS server host, the mount directory, and some options affecting the way the remote resource is mounted. Consult your man pages for details regarding the contents and syntax of entries to include.

Starting Up NFS on Solaris 2.x

Solaris 2.x relies on two distinct scripts for the NFS server and client. The script that starts the NFS server (the daemons pertaining to exporting, mounting, and responding to NFS service requests) is `/etc/init.d/nfs.server`.

The script responsible for starting the client daemons (such as `biod`, `lockd`, and `statd`) is `/etc/.init.d/nfs.server`.

Breaking the scripts into two, on Solaris 2.x, optimizes on resource utilization as only the needed component (that is, server and/or client service) needs to be started.

Aside from splitting the scripts into two, one for the server and another for the client, the configuration and mechanisms of invoking NFS at system startup remain almost identical to the description provided under SVR4.

Starting Up NFS on Linux

Similar to Solaris 2.x, Linux also relies on two distinct scripts for the startup of the NFS server and client components. The script that starts the NFS server is `/etc/rc.d/init.d/nfs` whereas the one that starts the client daemons is `/etc/rc.d/init.d/nfsfs`. Both scripts are fairly simple to read and understand.

Linux also allows for auto-mounting of NFS resources at boot time. For it to do so, however, the system administrator should have edited the `/etc/fstab` configuration file. The file is similar in function to SVR4's `/etc/vfstab` file, but not in entry contents and syntax. It consists of one entry per remote resource specifying the NFS server's name, the filesystem resource exported by that server, and options affecting the way the resource is to be mounted (including the mount point). For an accurate depiction of this file, please refer to the man pages on your system.

Manual Unmounting and Unsharing of Filesystems

Optionally, you can manually interrupt part of the service whether to troubleshoot or reconfigure NFS on a host.

To selectively unmount a filesystem on a client, you simply have to enter the following `umount` command:

```
# umount mountpoint
```

where `mountpoint` is the name of the directory where the NFS filesystem is attached. Hence, to unmount, for example, the `/efs` directory of server `tenor` from the `/rfs` directory on client `jade` (see Figure 20.30), enter

```
# umount /rfs
```

To unmount all filesystems you can either enter `umount` as many times it takes to get the job done, or simply use the `umountall` command:

```
# umountall
```

Be careful, however, with `umountall`, because it also unmounts local file systems.

Domain Name Service Implementation

The subsection "Name Services" provided a conceptual level treatment of name services as defined by DNS. In this section you will be shown how to set up the DNS service for a hypothetical environment. The discussion aims at highlighing the most common aspects of setting up the service. Dealing with all the common aspects and scenarios of setting up DNS cannot be fulfilled in one chapter; for this reason, and to facilitate the learning of the underlying procedures only one simple scenario is dealt with.

The scenario is based on a fictitious domain, `harmonics.com` pertaining to a hypothetical institute of music Harmonics, Inc. Figure 20.31 shows the network layout of this company. As shown, the network is made of two networks, a Class A network (100.0.0.0) and a Class C

20

NETWORKING

network (198.53.237.0). Multihomed host jade connects both networks. Also, the network is connected to the Internet via a router called xrouter with IP address 100.0.0.10. The diagram shows the IP addresses assigned to all hosts on the network.

FIGURE 20.31.

The harmonics.com
network layout.

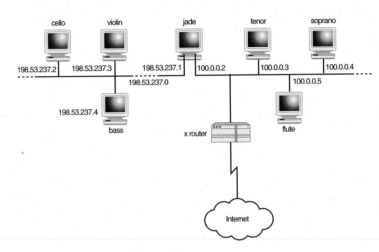

Being a commercial organization, Harmonics, Inc. was registered under the com domain as harmonics.com as reflected in Figure 20.32. Since harmonics.com is assigned two network addresses, it is also delegated the administration of both reverse domains of the 100.in-addr.arpa and 237.53.198.in-addr.arpa. Whereas harmonics.com maintains host information, such as host-to-IP address associations, the reverse domains are used to maintain the inverse mappings (that is, the IP-to-host name associations).

Since host jade is connected to both networks, it would be a good idea to bring up DNS name service on it. This way all hosts will have a DNS server directly attached to their network, resulting in better response time. Furthermore, host jade will be configured as the primary DNS server. In addition on each of the networks a secondary DNS server will be brought up. This way should host jade go down, both networks will have a backup DNS server to fall on for securing continued DNS service. Because harmonics.com is the domain name, every host is assigned a domain name in compliance with the following syntax:

hostname.harmonics.com

Hence, jade's and cello's domain names become jade.harmonics.com and cello.harmonics.com. Hereafter, the "host name" and the "domain host name" will be used interchangeably.

Besides setting up DNS servers, configuring name services involves setting up all the DNS clients on the network. The next section shows how to set up the DNS client. After that setting up the servers is discussed in a fair amount of detail.

FIGURE 20.32.

The domains delegated to Harmonics, Inc.'s administration authority.

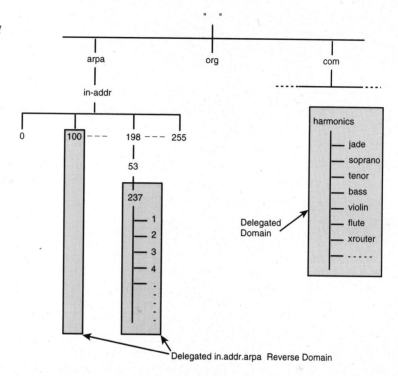

Delegated Domain

Delegated in.addr.arpa Reverse Domain

Configuring the DNS Client

The DNS client, known as the resolver, is built into each of the TCP/IP applications and is responsible for resolving DNS queries on behalf of the invoked application. DNS queries can be various types. Most common of them all is the host name-to-IP address resolution query, known as an A type query. Reverse queries (that is, IP address-to-host name resolution queries) are known as PTR or pointer queries.

Unless configured to contact a name server, the resolver normally checks the /etc/hosts file to get the IP address corresponding the name of the host the application specifies.

All you have to do to configure the resolver on a host, is to create a simple file known as /etc/resolv.conf. Using this file, the system administrator defines the domain name to which the host belongs (in our scenario, this is the harmonics.com domain), the IP addresses of up to three name servers (independent of whether the servers are primary, secondary, or even cache servers). Following are the contents of a sample /etc/resolv.conf file:

```
# keyword     value

domainname    harmonics.com
nameserver    100.0.0.2
nameserver    198.53.237.3
```

As shown, the file is made of simple entries, each of which is made of two parts, a keyword and a value. The first entry includes the keyword `domainname` followed by the domain name to which the host is said to belong. Accordingly, by virtue of this entry (that is, the `domainname`) the host now knows where in the domain name space it belongs. The last two entries specify the name servers (by virtue of keyword, the keyword name server) that the resolver ought to forward name queries to for resolution. According to these entries, and Figure 20.32, the IP addresses correspond to hosts `jade` and `cello`. Notice that the entries make no indication as to the nature of the server (that is, as being primary, secondary, or otherwise).

Should a user on a DNS-configured client enter the following command, for example

```
$ ftp tenor.harmonics.com
```

the resolver would then issue an A type query to a name server on the network that is specified in the `/etc/resolv.conf` file. Of the two shown previously in the listing of the sample `/etc/resolv.conf`, the server 100.0.0.2 (that is, host `jade`) is sought first for resolution, simply because it happens that the first `nameserver` record pertains to `jade` not `cello`. Should host `jade` fail to respond, `cello` is then contacted next by the client. Ultimately, a successful query returns the IP address of host `tenor` to the resolver which in turn hands it off to `ftp`.

From what has just been said, it makes sense to specify name servers in the `/etc/resolv.conf` file in ascending order of geographic proximity (that is, the closest at the top, followed by the next closest, and so on).

DNS Database and Startup Files

Configuring a name server involves the creation of many database and startup files. The number of files varies with the size of the organization, its internetwork structure, and the number of domains it has been delegated to administer. In the following discussion four different file types will be presented. Depending on the type of the name server (primary, secondary, or cache) you may end up configuring different combinations of these file types. You may also end up configuring multiple files of the same type.

The following are the generic names and basic definition (leaving the in-depth details for later on) corresponding to each of the DNS database and startup files:

`named.hosts`	This file defines the domain for which the name server is authoritative, and mainly contains host name-to-IP address mappings. Remember, an authoritative server is the one originating the data pertaining to the domain it's being authoritative for. In other words, it's where the domain data is created and updated and from which data is disseminated to other servers on the network or the Internet.
`named.rev`	This file defines the reverse `in-addr.arpa` domain for which the name is authoritative. It also contains the IP address-to-host name reverse mapping records.

`named.local`	This file is minimal in contents. It contains information just enough to resolve the 127.0.0.1 loopback address to `localhost`.
`named.ca`	This file contains the names and addresses of the Internet's root domain servers. Using the information maintained in this file, a name server will be capable to contact root servers for name queries as explained earlier in the chapter.
`named.boot`	The first file which is looked up by `named` (the DNS daemon) at start up. Using its contents, `named` determines the database filenames, and their location, in the filesystem on this host, as well as remote hosts.

You don't have to stick to these filenames. As will be shown later, you can give them names that make better sense to you and make them recognizable by `named` (the DNS daemon) by the proper utilization of the `named.boot` file.

Domain data is maintained in these files in the form of resource records (RRs). Resource records must follow a structure as defined in RFC 1033 for DNS to behave flawlessly. In the following few subsections, a group of resource records will be presented. We will concentrate on the ones immediately required to set up a *minimal* name service (only for the purpose of the bidirectional mapping of host names and IP addresses).

DNS Resource Records (RR)

DNS RFC 1033 defines a multitude of resource record (RR) types. Each type is responsible for tackling an aspect of the global database. A type records for example, are used to maintain host name-to-IP address associations, whereas NS (name server) records are used to maintain domain name-to-name server associations.

Following is a description of the resource records that are required to implement the objectives stated in the last section only. Readers interested in more information are referred to the noted RFC.

The general syntax of any RR is as follows:

```
[name] [ttl] class type data
```

where,

name	Is the name of the resource object being described by this resource record. *name* can be as specific as the name of a host or as general as the name of a domain. If it's left blank, the *name* of previous record is assumed. Two widely used special values for *name* are 1) the single dot "." which refers to the root domain, and 2) the @ sign

20

NETWORKING

	which refers to the current origin, derived from the current domain name (more on this later).
`ttl`	Is the time-to-live value, in seconds. For better performance, a DNS client normally caches the information it receives from the name server. `ttl` defines the duration for which this entry can be trusted, and therefore kept in cache. If not included, then the default specified in the SOA applies.
`class`	Defines the class of the DNS record. DNS recognizes several classes of RR of which IN (that is, Internet) is the only class relevant to this discussion. Some of the other classes are HS (Hessiod name server), and CH (Chaosnet information server).
`type`	Defines the type of information the RR record represents. The most commonly used record types are SOA, NS, A, MX, and PTR. An A RR record, for example contains the host name-to-IP address mapping and belongs to the `named.hosts` file, while the PTR RR record does exactly the opposite (that is, it reverse maps the address to the corresponding host name), and belongs to the `named.rev` file. More on record types later in the section.
`data`	The actual data pertinent to the object specified in the `name` field. The nature of the contents of `data` varies with the RR record. `data` represents an IP address if RR is of type A, as opposed to `hostname` if RR was of type PTR.

In the following subsections, a few RR types are described. Information about other types is available in RFC 1033. The order in which the various RR types is presented should not suggest the order in which they have to be placed in the database files. RR records can in fact be maintained in whichever order you desire as long as the syntax governing each type is well adhered to.

Start of Authority (SOA) Resource Record

The SOA record identifies the upper boundary of a partition (also known as a zone) of the global DNS database. Every configuration file must contain an SOA record identifying the beginning of the partition for which the server is authoritative. All RR records following the SOA record are part of the named zone. Looking back at Figure 20.32, a primary name server for the `harmonics.com` domain recognizes the partition boundaries by including an SOA record in its `named.hosts` configuration file.

The syntax of the SOA record is

```
[zone] [ttl] IN SOA origin contact (serial refresh retry expire minimum)
```

where, *zone* identifies the name of the zone. *ttl* was described previously and is left blank in SOA records. IN identifies the class, SOA is the record type, and the remaining part is the data affecting the named zone.

As shown in the syntax, the data field itself is structured where

origin	Refers to the primary name server for this domain. In harmonics.com's case this is jade.harmonics.com.
contact	Refers to the e-mail address of the person responsible for maintaining this domain. The root's e-mail address is commonly used. You can specify the e-mail address of any account you want. Assuming that login root on jade.harmonics.com. is responsible for the harmonics.com. domain, contact would then be specified as root.jade.harmonics.com. Notice how the notation to specify the e-mail address uses the dot "." instead of the @ character after root.
serial	Refers to the version number of this zone file. It is meant for interpretation and use by the secondary server, which transfers data from the primary server. Normally, the very first version number is 1. The serial number must be incremented every time the file containing this resource record is modified. A secondary name server relies on this field to determine whether its database is in synchronization with the master replica maintained by the primary server. Before initiating any transfer, the secondary server compares its own version number with that of the primary's file. A larger primary version number flags an update. Failure to increment serial as changes are made to the file prevents the secondary server from transferring and including the updates in its tables. This may cause serious disruption in the way the DNS service behaves itself on the network.
refresh	Refers to how often, in seconds, a secondary server should poll the primary for changes. Only when a change in version number is detected is the database transferred.
retry	Refers to how long, in seconds, the secondary server should wait before re-attempting zonal transfer if the primary server fails to respond to a zone refresh request.

expire	Defines the duration of time, in seconds, for which the secondary server can retain zonal data without requesting a zone refresh from the primary server. The secondary server ought to discard all data upon expire, even if the primary fails to respond to zone refresh requests.
minimum	Defines the default time-to-live (ttl) which applies to resource records whose ttl is not explicitly defined (see description of the syntax of RR record).

As an example, the SOA record defining the upper boundary of the harmonics.com domain should read as follows:

```
harmonics.com.    IN   SOA    jade.harmonics.com. root.jade.harmonics.com. (
                  2    ; Serial
                  14400     ; Refresh (4 hours)
                  3600    ; Retry (1hr)
                  604800       ; Expire ( 4 weeks )
                  86400 )     ; minimum TTL (time-to-live)
```

This record must be included in the named.hosts file. It makes the DNS server aware of where its authority (and responsibility) starts. Accordingly, named.hosts must contain all the necessary data for answering name queries pertaining to hosts belonging to harmonics.com. The data can be in the form of resource records which explicitly includes host name to IP address mappings, or pointers to other DNS servers for which authority over subdomains (if any) is delegated.

Address (A) Resource Record

A address resource records belong to the named.hosts file. An A record maintains the host name-to-IP address association. Whenever a name server is queried for the IP address of host, given its name, the server fetches for A records for one with a matching object name and responds with the IP address described in that record.

Following is the syntax of the A record:

```
[hostname] [ttl] IN A address
```

where,

hostname	Is the name of the host being affected. The host name can be specified relative to the current domain, or using a fully qualified domain name (that is, relative to the root domain). For example, host cello can be entered just as such (that is, cello) in which case the name is said to be relative to the current domain, or it can be entered as cello.harmonics.com. in which case the name is fully qualified. The dot trailing the fully qualified name is significant and must be included.

ttl	Is the minimum time-to-live. This is normally left blank implying the default as defined in the SOA record.
IN	Defines the class, which is almost always Internet class.
A	Defines the record type (an address record).
address	The IP address corresponding to the host name.

As an example, the following is the A record pertaining to `jade.harmonics.com`.

```
jade.harmonics.com.    IN    A  100.0.0.2
```

The host name is a fully qualified domain name (FQDN). For this reason, it is mandatory that it ends with a dot ".". Alternatively, it can be written as:

```
jade    IN    A    100.0.0.2
```

Since `jade` belongs to `harmonics.com.`, DNS has enough intelligence to qualify the name by appending the domain name to `jade`, becoming `jade.harmonics.com.`. More details on the period (or dot) rule will be provided later.

Name Server (NS) Resource Record

Name server resource records are the glue that makes the DNS hierarchical structure stick. An NS record defines which name server is authoritative for which zone or subdomain. It is especially used to point a parent domain server to the servers for their subdomains.

As shown in Figure 20.33, a name server authoritative for the `com` domain must include an NS record identifying the server which is authoritative for the `harmonics.com` domain (that is, `jade.harmonics.com.`).

FIGURE 20.33.

A server authoritative for the `.com` *domain must include an NS record identifying the server that is authoritative for the* `harmonics.com` *domain* (`jade.harmonics.com`).

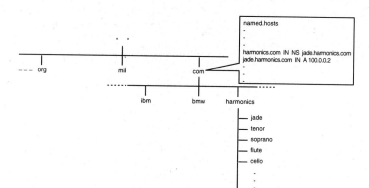

The syntax of the NS record follows:

```
[domain] [ttl] IN NS server
```

where

`domain`	Is the name of the domain for which `server` is an authoritative name server.
`ttl`	Time-to-live. If left blank, the default specified in the SOA record applies.
`IN`	Again, the class is IN (Internet)
`NS`	Identifies the RR record type as NS (that is, a pointer to a name server).
`server`	The name of the host providing authoritative name service for the domain specified in `domain`.

Applying this to the `harmonics.com.` situation, a server for the com domain should contain the following NS record in its `named.hosts` file:

```
harmonics.com. IN NS jade.harmonics.com.
```

This NS record must also be included in the `named.hosts` file of `jade.harmonics.com.`. When a server for the com domain is queried for a the host IP address of `cello.harmonics.com.` it checks its database to determine that `jade.harmonics.com.` is the server to which the query should be redirected. Hence, the com server returns the IP address of the `jade`, not its name, to the client station issuing the query. This means that it is not enough to include an NS record describing which server is authoritative for a given domain. The NS record should always be coupled with an A record specifying the address of the domain's server. Hence, the com server in question must include both of the following records in order to redirect queries pertaining to the `harmonics.com.` domain to `jade`:

```
harmonics.com. IN NS jade.harmonics.com.
jade IN A 100.0.0.2
```

Canonical Name (CNAME) Record

A CNAME record defines an alias pointing to the host's official name. It normally belongs to the `named.hosts` file. The following is the syntax of the CNAME record:

```
aliasname [ttl] IN CNAME [host]
```

where

`aliasname`	Defines the alias for the host specified in `host`.
`ttl`	Defines the time-to-live. If left blank the default specified in SOA record applies.
`IN`	Is the IN class.
`CNAME`	Identifies the record as CNAME type.
`host`	Is the official name of the host.

The following is an example of a CNAME record:

```
fake.harmonics.com. IN CNAME cello.harmonics.com.
```

If a client issues a name query for host fake, the name server replaces fake with cello, using the above CNAME record, during its search for the queried information.

CNAME records are particularly useful whenever host name changes need to be made. What you would do in such a situation is change the official name, then maintain the old one as an alias for the new official name. Allow a grace period until users are accustomed to the new name, and applications affected by name changes are reconfigured.

Pointer (PTR) Records

PTR records are used to map IP addresses to names. To reverse-map IP addresses into host names, the Internet included the in-addr.arpa top level domain in its DNS tree. Below that domain, a subtree is created such that each network ID had a domain named after itself. For example, network id 198.53.237.0 has 237.53.198.in-addr.arpa. for a reverse domain (Refer to the section "Name Service" earlier in the chapter for an understanding of the reverse naming convention). Normally, when an organization like Harmonics (the fictitious company) is delegated authority over its domain harmonics.com, NIC delegates the organization the authority over the reverse domain corresponding to the network IDs belonging to that organization. In Harmonics' case, the reverse domains are 100.in-addr.arpa, and 100.in-addr.arpa.

PTR records are maintained in the named.rev file, and are used to reverse-map the IP address to a host name.

Following is the syntax of the PTR record:

```
name [ttl] IN PTR host
```

where

name	Specifies the reverse domain name of the host. The reverse domain name of a host has the following format:
	reverse_IP_address.in-addr.arpa
	Since cello's IP address is 198.53.237.2, its *reverse_IP_address* becomes 2.237.53.198. Hence, the reverse domain name of the host cello becomes 2.237.53.198.in-addr.arpa.
[ttl]	Specifies time-to-live. If left blank, the default specified in the SOA record is assumed.
IN	Record is class IN.
PTR	Signifies the record as being of type PTR.
host	Specifies the host name.

Referring to host `cello`, for example, a `PTR` record resolving its IP address to host name should read as follows:

```
2.237.53.198.in-addr.arpa IN PTR cello
```

Mail Exchanger (MX) Records

A mail exchanger (MX) record identifies where to deliver mail for a given domain. When a user originates a mail message, the host issues an MX query to the name server specified in the `/etc/resolv.conf` file. The MX query includes the domain name specified by the user as part of the e-mail address of the recipient. If, for example, the specified recipient is `jsmith@harmonics.com`, then the MX query includes the domain name `harmonics.com` implying the question "Where should e-mail pertaining to users in the harmonics.com domain be delivered?" The queried name server fetches its MX records, finds an entry matching the specified domain, and responds with the IP address of the host handling deliveries on part of that domain.

`MX` records belong to the `named.hosts` file. Following is the syntax of `MX` records:

```
domainname      IN    MX    preference    mx_host
```

where

`domainname`	Specifies the domain for which the host specified in `mx_host` is acting as the mail exchanger.
`IN`	Specifies the class as `IN`.
`MX`	Specifies the type as `MX`.
`preference`	Specifies the preference level of the designated server. `preference` can assume values between 0 and 65535.
	A domain may have more than one host acting in the capacity of mail exchanger on its behalf, each assigned a different preference value. The preference value has a relative significance only. Mail delivery is first attempted to mail exchangers with lower preference value. Should the attempt fail, delivery is next attempted to the mail exchanger that is next in preference. Here is an example to help explain the concept:

```
harmonics.com    IN    MX    1 flute.harmonics.com.
harmonics.com    IN    MX    2 bass.harmonics.com.
```

According to the two MX records, hosts `flute` and `bass` are both mail exchangers for the `harmonics.com`. domain, with preferences 1 and 2 respectively. Accordingly, mail delivery, addressed to *auser@harmonics.com*, should be attempted to `flute` first for being of higher preference; should `flute` fail to respond, delivery should be attempted to `bass` next.

`mx_host`	Identifies the server where mail to *domainname* should be delivered

The following sections will help you put what has just been explained about resource records into perspective. You will be shown how to setup both primary and secondary servers as well as cache servers.

Configuring a Primary Name Server

The following few subsections describe the contents of the database files required to bring up `named` (that is, the DNS daemon as a primary name server on host `jade`. As will be shown later, the success of implementing DNS services is almost entirely reliant on how well-configured and behaved is the primary server. Setting up primary servers is more tedious and time-consuming than any of the other server types. Setting up a primary name server involves creating and updating the following files:

- `named.hosts`
- `named.rev`
- `named.local`
- `named.ca`
- `named.boot`

named.hosts

`named.hosts` primarily maintains the hostname to IP address mappings for all hosts in the designated zone. In `harmonics.com`'s case, because the domain is not partitioned, `named.hosts` must contain the name to IP address mappings for all hosts on this network. In addition to these mappings, `named.hosts` may contain other information such as names of hosts acting as mail exchangers (that is, mail routers), or CPU type, and well known services supported by a host. For the purpose of simplicity, a minimal service including name-to-address, and address-to-name mappings, will be described. The description will be based on the DNS setup files maintained on hosts `jade` and `cello` (`jade` being the primary and `cello` being the secondary) in support of name services for the `harmonics.com` domain.

Given what has been learned so far, and that `jade` is the primary server for the `harmonics.com` domain, this is what `jade`'s `named.hosts` file should look like:

```
;
; Section 1: The SOA record
;
harmonics.com.    IN    SOA    jade.harmonics.com. root.jade.harmonics.com. (
                  2    ; Serial
                  14400    ; Refresh (4 hours)
                  3600    ; Retry (1hr)
                  604800     ; Expire ( 4 weeks )
                  86400 )    ; minimum TTL (time-to-live)
```

```
;
; Section 2: The following are the name server for the harmonics domain. Notice how
the second
; entry does not specify the domain name for which cello is being the name server.
This implies that
; domain name is same as one specified in previous record.
;
harmonics.com.    IN    NS    jade.harmonics.com.
        IN    NS    cello.harmonics.com.
;
; Section 3: The following are the mail exchangers of the domain harmonics.com
;
harmonics.com.    IN    MX    1    flute.harmonics.com.
        IN    MX    2    bass.harmonics.com.
;
; Section 4: The following records map hosts' canonical names to their
corresponding
; IP addresses
;
localhost.harmonics.com.    IN A    127.0.0.1
;
tenor.harmonics.com.    IN A    100.0.0.3
soprano.harmonics.com.    IN A    100.0.0.4
flute.harmonics.com.    IN A    100.0.0.5
xrouter        IN A    100.0.0.10
cello.harmonics.com.    IN A    198.53.237.2
violin.harmonics.com.    IN A    198.53.237.3
bass.harmonics.com.    IN A    198.53.237.4
;
; Section 5: Multihomed hosts
;
jade.harmonics.com.    IN A    198.53.237.1
        IN A    100.0.0.2
```

The file is conveniently broken down into sections, with each being titled by the section number and purpose of that section.

Section 1 contains the SOA record, which declares jade.harmonics.com as the DNS authoritative server for the harmonics.com domain. A named.hosts file can contain only one SOA record, and it must be the first record in the file. The record also indicates that correspondence regarding this domain should be addressed to root@jade.harmonics.com (remember that the dot "." following root should be replaced with the familiar @ character). Refer to the description of SOA records for details on the values enclosed in parentheses.

Section 2 includes two NS records declaring hosts jade and cello as name servers for the harmonics.com domain. Notice that the records do not specify which of the two servers is the primary as opposed to being the secondary server. The type of the name server is defined, as you will see later, in the named.boot file.

Section 3 includes two MX records identifying hosts flute and bass as the mail exchangers for the harmonics.com domain. Host flute is set at a higher priority than bass.

Section 4 includes all of the A (address) records which map host names to IP addresses. When a client station queries a name server for the IP address of a given host, named scans the A records in its `named.hosts` for one matching the requirement, and returns the corresponding IP address to the querying station.

Reflecting on section 5, notice how, corresponding to `jade`, being a multihomed host, there are two A records. Whenever `named` is queried for the IP address of `jade`, or any multihomed host, `named` simply returns all the addresses it finds in its A records. To achieve optimal performance, `named` returns the address closest to the querying station first, followed by the others in order of proximity.

named.rev

Using the `named.rev` file, `named` attempts to resolve PTR type queries—that is, given the host name, named responds the query with the IP address associated with that host in the `named.rev` file. In Addition to PTR records, `named.rev` must also include an SOA record marking the boundaries of the reverse domain for which the server is authoritative.

Corresponding to a network assigned more than one network ID, multiple `named.rev`-type files must be created, one for each `in-addr.arpa` domain under different names. You will be shown later how to configure the boot process (via `named.boot` file) of `named` to recognize such files. Following are the conventions used in this chapter for naming the `named.rev`-type files.

`reversenetID.rev`

where `reversenetID` is the assigned network ID.

Since Harmonics, Inc. is assigned two network IDs (these are 100.0.0.0 and 198.53.237.0), the `named.rev`-type files become `100.rev` and `237.53.198.rev`. Each of these files contains an SOA record defining its start-of-authority, and the PTR records pertaining to the reverse domain. Following are the complete listings of each of the reverse domain files as created on host `jade`:

```
100.in-addr.arpa.    IN SOA    jade.harmonics.com. root.jade.harmonics.com (
                1     ;serial
                14400    ; Refresh (4 hours)
                3600    ; retry  ( 1 hour )
                604800    ; expire  ( 1 week )
                86400 ) ; TTL = 1 day
;
; name servers
;
100.in-addr.arpa.    IN NS    jade.harmonics.com.
100.in-addr.arpa.    IN NS    cello.harmonics.com.
;
; Reverse address mappings
;
2.0.0.100.in-addr.arpa.    IN    PTR    jade.harmonics.com.
3.0.0.100.in-addr.arpa.    IN    PTR    tenor.harmonics.com.
4.0.0.100.in-addr.arpa      IN    PTR    soprano.harmonics.com.
5.0.0.100.in-addr.arpa      IN    PTR    flute.harmonics.com.
10.0.0.100.in-addr.arpa     IN    PTR    xrouter.harmonics.com.
```

Following is a listing of the contents of `237.53.198.rev` file:

```
237.53.198.in-addr.arpa. IN SOA  jade.harmonics.com. root.jade.harmonics.com. (
                    1    ; serial
                    14400    ; refresh ( 4 hr )
                    3600    ; retry ( 1 hr )
                    604800    ; expire ( 1 week )
                    86400 )    ; TTL = 1day
;
;
; name servers
;
237.53.198.in-addr.arpa.   IN      NS      jade.harmonics.com.
237.53.198.in-addr.arpa.   IN      NS      cello.harmonics.com.
;
;
; Reverse address mappings
;
1.237.53.198.in-addr.arpa. IN      PTR     jade.harmonics.com.
2.237.53.198.in-addr.arpa. IN      PTR     cello.harmonics.com.
3.237.53.198.in-addr.arpa. IN      PTR     violin.harmonics.com.
4.237.53.198.in-addr.arpa. IN      PTR     bass.harmonics.com.
```

Notice how closely the organization of the first two parts of each file follows that of `named.hosts`. All files start with an appropriate SOA record marking the upper boundaries of the `in-addr.arpa` domain for which the server is authoritative. Next is a block of NS records, declaring the name servers which have authority for the domain. In all three files, both `jade` and `cello` are declared as domain name servers.

The last part consists of PTR records. Each of these records contains the IP address to domain name associations which `named` uses for reverse address resolution.

An interesting observation to highlight is that even if `cello` is on the Class C network, this did not stop it from being a server for the Class A `100.in-addr.arpa` reverse domain. The point is that the DNS service is a logical service independent of the physical topology. Similarly, on the Class A network, we could install a server that is authoritative for the reverse domain `237.53.198.in-addr.arpa` without impacting the availability of the service.

named.local

If you re-examine the `named.hosts` file, you will find that it contains an entry corresponding to the special loopback host name `localhost`. This entry maps `localhost` to the familiar IP address `127.0.0.1`. Yet there is no PTR record in any of the reverse domain data files (listed above) which takes care of the reverse mapping. None of those files is suitable for such a PTR record as the loopback address belongs to none of the `in-addr.arpa` domains that the files support.

To remedy the discrepancy, a new reverse domain file is required. This file is called, by default, `named.local`. Following are the file contents:

```
0.0.127.in-addr.arpa. IN SOA jade.harmonics.com. root.jade.harmonics.com. (
                1    ; serial
                14400    ; refresh ( 4 hours )
                3600    ; retry ( 1 hour )
```

```
                604800      ; expire ( 1 week )
                86400 )     ; TTL = 1 day
;
; name servers
;
0.0.127.in-addr.arpa.    IN    NS     jade.harmonics.com.
0.0.127.in-addr.arpa.    IN    NS     cello.harmonics.com.
;
; reverse address PTR mapping
;
1.0.0.127.in-addr.arpa. IN    PTR    localhost
```

Compare this file with any of the reverse domain files listed in the previous section. You will find that its organization is identical to those files. As can be understood from the SOA record, this file identifies jade.harmonics.com as the server originating the 0.0.127.in-addr.arpa domain. Again, there are two NS records identifying both jade and cello as the name servers for this domain. Finally, there is only one PTR record to take care of the reverse address resolution of the loopback address (127.0.0.1) to the loopback host name localhost.

named.ca

As explained earlier in the chapter, rather than forcing a server to undergo the entire resolution referral process in order to respond to identical name queries, DNS allows the server to respond from data its cache. The cache is designed to improve the overall performance of DNS. This is achieved by saving in memory responses to queries that clients submit to servers. Furthermore, servers also cache all data they discover during the referral process that led to the desired response. This helps DNS servers to acquire, over time, considerable "knowledge" about the global DNS structure and keeping this knowledge locally accessible. This approach improves both response time and network traffic.

To further improve the performance of the name service, DNS defines an additional cache-related file called named.ca. Using this file, data pertaining to other domains, neighboring or remote, can be maintained, including name servers authoritative for those domains as well as A records identifying their IP addresses. All data contained in the named.ca file is used to initialize the cache buffers in the DNS server every time the named daemon is started—a process that cuts down on the referral processes and the associated learning process that the server has to undergo to discover the DNS service structure.

For reliability, you should include only information you believe to be stable for prolonged periods. You also ought to periodically verify the validity and accuracy of the included data.

One of the most commonly included pieces of information in the named.ca file is information about the Internet root servers. This information is stable over long periods of time. It makes sense to initialize your server's cache with this information, given the likelihood that users on your networks will want to reach places on the Internet. A minimal named.ca file should, therefore, look as shown:

```
;
; Section 1: NS records for the root domain servers
;
```

20

NETWORKING

```
.    99999999    IN    NS    A.ROOT-SERVERS.NET
99999999    IN    NS    B.ROOT-SERVERS.NET
99999999    IN    NS    C.ROOT-SERVERS.NET
99999999    IN    NS    D.ROOT-SERVERS.NET
99999999    IN    NS    E.ROOT-SERVERS.NET
99999999    IN    NS    F.ROOT-SERVERS.NET
99999999    IN    NS    G.ROOT-SERVERS.NET
99999999    IN    NS    H.ROOT-SERVERS.NET
99999999    IN    NS    I.ROOT-SERVERS.NET
;
; Section 2: Root servers A records
;
A.ROOT-SERVERS.NET    99999999    IN    A    198.41.0.4
B.ROOT-SERVERS.NET    99999999    IN    A    128.9.0.107
C.ROOT-SERVERS.NET    99999999    IN    A    192.33.4.12
D.ROOT-SERVERS.NET    99999999    IN    A    128.8.10.90
E.ROOT-SERVERS.NET    99999999    IN    A    192.203.230.10
F.ROOT-SERVERS.NET    99999999    IN    A    192.5.5.241
G.ROOT-SERVERS.NET    99999999    IN    A    192.112.36.4
H.ROOT-SERVERS.NET    99999999    IN    A    128.63.2.53
I.ROOT-SERVERS.NET    99999999    IN    A    192.36.148.17
```

As can be seen, this named.ca file is made of two blocks of entries. The first one contains NS records identifying the names of the root servers. There are two thing that you should have noticed in this file: the dot "." in the first column at the beginning of the first NS record, and the lack of object names in the subsequent NS records (refer to the general syntax of RR records for details). Since the root domain is represented by a null character, the dot "." is the character used in DNS files. Also, whenever multiple contiguous records refer to the same object, the name field can be left blank in subsequent records following the first one. Hence, since all the NS records pertain to root servers, only the first record had to include the name of the object being affected (the root domain).

The second section of named.ca contains A records pertaining to the servers defined in the first section.. Whenever named is brought up, it reads named.ca and caches all of the information contained in this file, hence providing immediate access to root servers.

TIP

A current list of root name servers is always available through anonymous FTP from nic.ddn.mil.in the /netinfo/root-servers.txt file.

NOTE

It is your responsibility to regularly verify the validity and accuracy of the information contained in named.ca, including information about root servers. Failure to do so may seriously disrupt name service on your network, leading to undesirable degradation in performance. NIC is responsible for the information on an as-is basis at the time of downloading the root-server.txt file cited previously.

named.boot: The Startup File

At boot time, the DNS server references the named.boot file for information regarding its authority and type (whether primary, secondary, or cache server). The following code shows how DNS is started on a SVR4:

```
#
if [ -f /etc/inet/named.boot -a -x /usr/sbin/in.named ]
then
    /usr/sbin/in.named
fi
```

STARTING NAMED DAEMON

Although the code shown above is extracted from TCP/IP startup script /etc/inet/rc.int pertaining to SVR4 UNIX operating system, other UNIX platforms implement same code for doing the same job.

As shown, before the DNS daemon (in.named) is invoked, the code checks for the existence of the startup file named.boot. As implied by the code, the boot file could have been given any name (not necessarily named.boot) as long as the code is modified to reflect that name. Using named.boot, the DNS determines where the database files are including named.hosts, named.rev, named.ca, and named.local. It also uses the file to determine the extent of it authority and type, as mentioned before.

The following is the listing of the file named.boot as it should be on jade to bring it up as a primary name server:

```
directory    /etc/named

primary     harmonics.com      named.hosts
primary     100.in-addr.arpa        100.rev
primary     237.53.198.in-addr.arpa    198.53.237.rev
primary     0.0.127.in-addr.arpa    127.localhost
cache    .                named.ca
```

Each of the lines is a record delivering a piece of information that helps the DNS daemon to configure itself. Each line, or record, has to start with a keyword bearing some significance to the configuration process. Here is a description of what each record does:

- Using the keyword directory, the first record tells DNS daemon that the default location where all the database files can be found is the /etc/named directory in the server's file system.

- The second, third, fourth, and fifth records start with the keyword primary, each followed by a domain name. This explicitly tells the server that it is authoritative for each of the specified domains and that it is acting in the capacity of a primary server. The last field of each record specifies the file that contains the records pertinent to the

20

NETWORKING

specified domain. For example, upon reading the second record, named, self-initializes as being the primary server for the harmonics.com domain and initializes its memory to the contents of the /etc/named/named.hosts file.

■ The last record specifies that the server is acting as a cache server for the root domain. Moreover, it specifies named.ca as the file (in /etc/named directory) that contains the cache initialization data.

DATABASE FILENAMES

As mentioned earlier in the chapter, database filenames can be anything you want. Reflecting on the contents of named.boot file, notice how the server can tell which files constitute the database by interpreting the last field of each record. Consequently, should you decide to use a different name for the named.hosts file, for example, all you need to do is to replace named.hosts with the filename you desire in the named.boot startup file.

The above concludes the steps required to configuring and starting a DNS primary server. Now let's have a look at how to setup a secondary server.

Configuring a Secondary Name Server

By definition, a secondary name server is one that derives data pertaining to the zone it supports from a primary authoritative server. A secondary server does not have its own named.hosts-type and named.rev-type files. Rather, whenever started, a secondary server undergoes a *zonal transfer* process during which it requests the primary server to transfer copies of both files. Consequently, the secondary server initializes its memory with the contents of the transferred files for use in responding to name queries.

Since you won't be required to create and update the named.hosts and named.rev-type files, configuring a secondary server becomes a trivial matter that involves configuring three files, named.boot, named.ca and named.local. To simplify your life, copy all three files from the primary server to the machine where you intend to bring up the secondary server. In our scenario, since host cello is required to act as a secondary server, then the three files, just mentioned, should be copied to its file system from host jade's file system.

The only file which requires a few changes after being copied to the host serving as a secondary DNS server is named.boot. The following is how named.boot on cello should read:

```
directory     /usr/lib/named

secondary     harmonics.com      100.0.0.2
secondary 100.in-addr.arpa      100.0.0.2
secondary 237.53.198.in-addr.arpa    100.0.0.2
primary     0.0.127.in-addr.arpa     named.local
cache     .                 named.ca
```

As can be seen from this, the configuration of `named.boot` includes mostly secondary, instead of primary, statements. The second entry, for example, configures `named` as a secondary server for the `harmonics.com` domain, and tells it to obtain a copy of the pertinent domain database from the server at IP address `100.0.0.2` (that is, `jade`). The third, fourth, and fifth entries, likewise, configure `named`, on `jade`, as the secondary server for the reverse domains `100.in-addr.arpa`, and `237.53.198.in-addr.arpa`, respectively. All secondary statements direct `named` to host IP address `100.0.0.2` for a copy of the pertinent database files.

The sixth and seventh entries are identical to their counter-entries in `named.boot` on `jade`. They also point `named` to local filenames for information. Since both `named.local` and `named.ca` hardly change their contents, it makes sense to access the information they contain locally, thus saving bandwidth which could, otherwise, have been lost to file transfer operations.

Startup of the Secondary Server

A secondary server is started in the same way as the primary server. When the host enters run level two at boot time, the startup scripts check on the existence of the `named.boot` file. If the file exists, `named` is brought up and configured according to the statements included in the file. Copies of database files pertinent to domains for which the server is authoritative are then obtained via the zone transfer process, from sources specified by the secondary statements.

STARTING named MANUALLY

Whether it's being started as a primary or secondary server, named can be invoked manually by enter the "named" command. If no command line options and parameters are specified, named.boot is then assumed as the startup file. To specify a different startup file use the "-b" option as shown here:

```
# named -b /usr/lib/mynamed.boot
```

Consequently, named checks for the mynamed.boot file for instructions on how to self-configure as a server.

Configuring the Secondary for Robustness

The above configuration works fine as long as the primary server is up at the time the secondary server is restarted. What if the primary server were down? The secondary server will not be able to come up, since there may not be another source for the required data. To circumvent this possibility, DNS allows you to do two things: specify up to ten alternate IP addresses in the secondary statements, from which the server can obtain zonal data, and configure the server to maintain disk copies of files it obtains via zonal transfers.

Alternate addresses can be added after the first IP address. They must pertain to hosts running primary name service. The following is an example of a secondary statement with two specified IP addresses:

```
secondary harmonics.com 100.0.0.2 100.0.0.4
```

According to the statement, the secondary name server must seek data from 100.0.0.4 should jade fail to respond to cello's initial requests for zonal transfer of data. The assumption here, of course, that host IP address 100.0.0.4 is another primary server for the domain harmonics.com.

Robustness can be improved by allowing the secondary name server to maintain backup copies of the transferred data files. This way, the secondary will always have a last resort from which it can obtain zonal data. The caveat, however, is that this data has an expire date, as set in the SOA record. Upon expiration, the backup files are discarded. Hence, unless a primary server is found to respond to zonal transfer requests, the secondary server drops out of service.

All that is necessary to enable named to maintain a backup copy is specifying, in the last column of each secondary statement, the name of the file to which data should be copied. The following is a revised version of cello's named.boot file, including support for backup files:

```
directory    /usr/lib/named

secondary    harmonics.com    100.0.0.2    named.hosts
secondary    100.in-addr.arpa    100.0.0.2    100.rev
secondary    237.53.198.in-addr.arpa    100.0.0.2    198.53.237.rev
primary    0.0.127.in-addr.arpa    named.local
```

Notice that the filenames do not have to be the same as those on jade. I could have chosen different names. For convenience, I left them identical to those on jade. When named is started it contacts the specified servers for data to keep in specified files in the /usr/lib/named directory.

Configuring a Cache-Only Server

A cache-only server does not rely on database files, whether its own or otherwise. A cache-only server caches data pertaining to queries and data associated with resolution referrals that it engages in in quest for the desired response. Cached data are used to resolve future queries whenever possible.

A cache-only server is the simplest of all servers to configure. The following is the named.boot file of a hypothetical cache-only server connected to the harmonics.com network:

```
;
; Cache-only server for the harmonics.com domain
;
primary    0.0.127.in-addr.arpa    /usr/lib/named/named.local
cache    .    /usr/lib/named/named.ca
;
```

As can be concluded from the listing, two more files, in addition to named.boot, are needed. These are named.ca and named.local. The cache statement configures the server to cache responses, in addition to initializing its cache from the wire, with the data maintained in named.ca. The primary statement has the same functionality described in earlier sections.

What makes this server cache-only is the lack of primary, or secondary, statements declaring it as being an authoritative server for a domain on the network. The `cache` statement has always been part of the previously examined `named.boot` files. As such, while it is absolutely necessary for inclusion in the `named.boot` of a cache-only server, it is equally necessary to avoid all forms of primary, or secondary, statements in the file, except for the ones pertaining to the local loopback domain.

nslookup

No discussion of DNS name service is complete without discussing the `nslookup` command. `nslookup` is a feature-rich command that can be run in interactive mode for the sake of testing, verifying, and troubleshooting the setup and operation of DNS service. The following discussion highlights the following aspects of the `nslookup` command:

- `nslookup` on-line help
- using `nslookup` to query the local server
- using `nslookup` to query a remote server
- using `nslookup` to download the DNS database

nslookup On-Line Help

As mentioned above, `nslookup` is a feature-rich command. Using it, a system administrator can issue queries of any type including A, PTR, and MX-type queries, among others. In addition, `nslookup` allows you to direct queries to remote DNS servers right from the console of your local host. Also, you can use `nslookup` to download a copy of any server's database for your perusal, should you ever need to understand what is exactly going on with that server. Downloaded files can be examined within an active `nslookup` session, or using any of UNIX editing, test editing, and lookup tools.

Help on using `nslookup` is available in two forms. The first form involves invoking the traditional UNIX man pages. An alternative form of help is conveniently available while in an nslookup session. To start `nslookup`, you just enter the command name at the shell prompt as shown below:

```
# nslookup
Default Server: jade.harmonics.com
Address: 100.0.0.2

>
```

When invoked, `nslookup` targets, by default, the local server. In the above example, `nslookup` targeted the `jade` name server, as indicated by `nslookup` response. The response included the name of the target server and its address. This can be considered as a sign of partial success in configuring name service on `jade`. The angle bracket ">" is the `nslookup` prompt. It means that you can start issuing name service queries or setup commands to configure `nslookup` to suit your upcoming queries. Among the things which nslookup can be asked to do is to provide you with on-line help. To do that, just enter help at the command prompt as follows:

```
# nslookup
Default Server: jade.harmonics.com
Address: 100.0.0.2

> help
#       @(#)nslookup.help       1.1 STREAMWare TCP/IP SVR4.2  source
#       SCCS IDENTIFICATION
#       @(#)nslookup.hlp 4.3 Lachman System V STREAMS TCP  source
Commands:       (identifiers are shown in uppercase, [] means optional)
NAME        - print info about the host/domain NAME using default server
NAME1 NAME2    - as above, but use NAME2 as server
help or ?    - print info on common commands; see nslookup(1) for details
set OPTION      set an option
    all     - print options, current server and host
    [no]debug    - print debugging information
    [no]d2    - print exhaustive debugging information
    [no]defname     - append domain name to each query
    [no]recurs    - ask for recursive answer to query
    [no]vc    - always use a virtual circuit
    domain=NAME    - set default domain name to NAME
    srchlist=N1[/N2/.../N6] - set domain to N1 and search list to N1,N2, etc.
    root=NAME    - set root server to NAME
    retry=X    - set number of retries to X
    timeout=X    - set initial time-out interval to X seconds
    querytype=X    - set query type, e.g., A,ANY,CNAME,HINFO,MX,NS,PTR,SOA,WKS
    type=X    - synonym for querytype
    class=X    - set query class to one of IN (Internet), CHAOS, HESIOD or ANY
server NAME    - set default server to NAME, using current default server
lserver NAME    - set default server to NAME, using initial server
finger [USER]    - finger the optional NAME at the current default host
root     - set current default server to the root
ls [opt] DOMAIN [> FILE] - list addresses in DOMAIN (optional: output to FILE)
    -a    - list canonical names and aliases
    -h    - list HINFO (CPU type and operating system)
    -s    - list well-known services
    -d    - list all records
    -t TYPE    - list records of the given type (e.g., A,CNAME,MX, etc.)
view FILE    - sort an 'ls' output file and view it with more
exit    - exit the program, ^D also exits
> exit
#
```

Rather than explaining all of the different options, the following sections attempt to lay a solid foundation for understanding and using some of the most useful features of nslookup. It is left to the reader's imagination and initiative to experiment and discover the usefulness of the other features.

Using nslookup to Query the Local Server

There are at least three situations where you may have to use nslookup: to test a newly brought up server, to verify changes made to the configuration of an existing server, or to troubleshoot the DNS service. Regardless, a good way to start an nslookup session is by querying the local server. Depending on the results, you may escalate by targeting other servers in your own domain or other remotely located domains on the Internet.

Now that `jade` has been configured and brought up, let's start testing it to verify its operation. To do that, the network administrator logs in as `root`, and issues the `nslookup` command. By default, `nslookup` responds to name queries (name-to-address mappings). Below is a depiction of what happens when a host name (`saturn`) is entered at the `nslookup` prompt:

```
# nslookup
Default Server:  jade.harmonics.com
Address:  100.0.0.2

> cello
Server:  jade.harmonics.com
Address:  100.0.0.2

Name:    cello.harmonics.com
Address: 198.53.237.2
```

Notice how the response includes both the resolution and the name and address of the server which resolved the query. You should carry out a few more similar tests to verify the capability of the local server to resolve name-to-address queries flawlessly. Of particular interest are multihomed hosts, such as `jade` in the `harmonics.com` domain. As said before, a name server ought to respond with the all of the addresses assigned to the interfaces attaching the host to the internetwork. In the following example, `nslookup` is used to resolve `jade`'s name to its corresponding IP addresses:

```
# nslookup
Default Server:  jade.harmonics.com
Address:  100.0.0.2

> jade
Server:  jade.harmonics.com
Address:  100.0.0.2

Name:    jade.harmonics.com
Addresses:  100.0.0.2, 198.53.237.1
```

`nslookup` displays addresses in the order in which they were received (`100.0.0.2` was received first, followed by `198.53.237.1`).

Next, you should verify the server's ability to handle reverse resolution queries. Again, it is a simple matter of entering an IP address which exists on your network. Here is an example carried on `jade`:

```
# nslookup
Default Server:  jade.harmonics.com
Address:  100.0.0.2


> 198.53.237.2
Server:  jade.harmonics.com
Address:  100.0.0.2
```

Try as many reverse queries as it takes to verify the reliability of the reverse resolution process. Should all go well, you may proceed to the next phase of testing other servers by using `nslookup` on the local server.

Using `nslookup` to Query a Remote Server

Among the strongly desirable features of `nslookup` is its ability to query remote servers on the network. Remote servers can be on your own network, or elsewhere on the Internet. This feature allows you to troubleshoot any server, or check the robustness of the overall service you recently brought up on the network. In the following example, the remote capability of `nslookup` is invoked on host `jade` (the primary server) to query `cello` (the secondary server) for the IP address of `soprano`:

```
# nslookup
Default Server:  jade.harmonics.com
Address:  100.0.0.2

> soprano cello.harmonics.com
Server:  cello.harmonics.com
Address:  198.53.237.2

Name:     soprano.harmonics.com
Address:  100.0.0.4
```

As shown above, to force `nslookup` to send the query to `cello`, the remote server's name (that is, `cello.harmonics.com`) must be entered after the host name (that is, `soprano`) on the command line. A better way of conversing interactively with the remote server is to use the `server` command, letting `nslookup` default to the remote server. The following example shows how to do this:

```
> server cello
Default Server:  cello.harmonics.com
Addresses:  198.53.237.2

> soprano
Server:  cello.harmonics.com
Addresses:  198.53.237.2

Name:     soprano.harmonics.com
Address:  100.0.0.4
```

Using `nslookup` to Download the DNS Database

Another useful feature of `nslookup` is the internal `ls` command. Using `ls`, a zonal transfer can be forced. By default, data is directed to the standard output. Optionally, you can specify a filename where the data can be sent for later examination. The following example demonstrates the use of `ls` command:

```
# nslookup
Default Server:  jade
Address:  0.0.0.0
```

```
> ls harmonics.com
[jade]
 harmonics.com.          server = jade.harmonics.com
 jade                         100.0.0.2
 jade                         198.53.237.1
 harmonics.com.          server = cello.harmonics.com
 cello                        198.53.237.2
 jade                         100.0.0.2
tenor        100.0.0.3
soprano      100.0.0.4
 localhost                   127.0.0.1
 harmonics               server = jade.harmonics.com
 jade                         100.0.0.2
 jade                         198.53.237.1
 tenor                        100.0.0.3
soprano                  100.0.0.4
xrouter                  10.0.0.10
 cello                        198.53.237.2
 violin                       198.53.237.3
> exit
#
```

This listing is helpful in verifying that information about all hosts is indeed being included. You can use it to perform host counts, or check for individual hosts. Also, notice how the listing conveniently points out the names and addresses of the servers in the domain in question.

Editing DNS Files Made Easy

Throughout the discussion on setting up DNS services you have been shown the hard way of creating and maintaining the database. You might even have wondered whether the setup process can be simplified to reduce the tedium of keyboarding required to enter all the relevant data.

One of the most annoying things about updating database files, the way things went so far, was having to key in the fully qualified name for every host that is on the network. For example, if you examine the named.hosts file pertaining to harmonics.com domain, you will notice that host names were entered according to the FQDN conventions. This included the full name including a trailing period. Some readers might have asked themselves the question as to whether it was possible to simply enter just the host name and let DNS take care of appending the name with the domain name. In other words, configure DNS to recognize the domain harmonics.com as being the default domain. Then by entering a record pertaining to, say, host cello, only cello be entered and let DNS qualify it to become cello.harmonics.com. The answer is yes, this can be done.

If the domain name in the SOA record is the same as the domain name in (called the *origin*) in the primary statement of the named.boot file, you can replace the domain name in SOA with the @ character. The @ character has the effect of telling named to append the domain name in the primary statement to every host name *not* ending with a dot. Taking server jade as an example, following are the contents of the named.boot file as shown earlier in the chapter:

```
directory     /etc/named
```

20

NETWORKING

```
primary     harmonics.com      named.hosts
primary     100.in-addr.arpa         100.rev
primary     237.53.198.in-addr.arpa    198.53.237.rev
primary     0.0.127.in-addr.arpa    127.localhost
cache    .                 named.ca
```

and here are the contents of the SOA record in `named.hosts`:

```
harmonics.com.    IN    SOA      jade.harmonics.com. root.jade.harmonics.com. (
                  2    ; Serial
                  14400    ; Refresh (4 hours)
                  3600   ; Retry (1hr)
                  604800     ; Expire ( 4 weeks )
                  86400 )    ; minimum TTL (time-to-live)
```

Since the domain name (`harmonics.com`) in both files is identical, the SOA record can be rewritten to look like this, where the @ character replaces the domain label (`harmonics.com`):

```
@    IN    SOA     jade.harmonics.com. root.jade.harmonics.com. (
                 2    ; Serial
                 14400    ; Refresh (4 hours)
                 3600   ; Retry (1hr)
                 604800     ; Expire ( 4 weeks )
                 86400 )    ; minimum TTL (time-to-live)
```

Consequently, an A record can now be written in the following manner:

```
soprano    IN    A    100.0.0.4
```

Notice how you are no longer required to enter the FQDN name (that is, `soprano.harmonics.com.`).

One thing you ought to be careful about, though, is the proper use of the trailing dot when updating the database. As shown in the last example, soprano's name did not include a trailing dot. Contrast this with all the A records that have been illustrated in the chapter and you will find that they have a dot trailing their fully qualified names. As explained earlier, a trailing dot is a full-name qualifier. This means its presence or absence is what makes named decide whether the name is full (and hence should be left intact) or that it requires appending the default domain name, as set in the primary statement in `named.boot`, to qualify it fully. A record like this one, for example:

```
soprano.harmonics.com    IN    A       100.0.0.4
```

can be misqualified to `soprano.harmonics.com.harmonics.com`. Why? Just because there isn't a trailing dot at the end of the name, named considered the name as being relative and according to the rules, it had to fully qualify it. Conversely, consider the following A record:

```
soprano.    IN    A    100.0.0.4
```

In this case, the FQDN name becomes soprano only, not `soprano.harmonics.com`. Why? Because of the mis-included trailing dot.

Both of the above situations lead to a disruptive DNS service. So, the message is "observe the period rules."

Network Troubleshooting Using UNIX Tools

What has been discussed so far was the different aspects of UNIX networking-related issues. The chapter covered enough concepts to help initiate the reader on the intricacies governing the configuration and operation of UNIX networks. In this section, you will be presented with the tool set that you may require to troubleshoot UNIX networks—be it in the early stage of installation and configuration or during the post-installation and mature phases of the network.

As your experience is going to confirm to you, maintaining operational networks at a reasonable level of performance, reliability, and availability might prove to be one of the most challenging aspects of maintaining the computing environment. Network problems are diverse enough that the network administrator is left no choice but to learn, and master, a comprehensive set of troubleshooting tools, and to gain good troubleshooting skills. It is vitally important to note that troubleshooting networks requires constant education based on familiarity with the most intimate details of how communication and application protocols behave as well as updating one's skills as the technology changes. The knowledge and skill set together should be employed in a methodology aimed at the efficient identification and resolution of problems detected on the network.

Troubleshooting Methodology

Troubleshooting, in general, passes through three phases of activity:

1. Information gathering
2. Development and execution of a problem-specific troubleshooting plan
3. Documenting the problem

Information Gathering

Efficiency in troubleshooting networks primarily rests in keeping an up-to-date documentation of the network. Documentation is the part most hated by network administrators—only to be appreciated when needed. Consider the documentation process as a strategic plan in proactive troubleshooting. Never compromise on its quality or accuracy—however tedious the job might appear to you. Proper documentation should include the following items:

- An inventory of all devices that are connected to the network (servers, workstations, routers, and so on).
- The physical layout of the network, including wiring details and floor plans showing the exact location of each of the devices.
- The logical layout of the network, including assigned IP addresses, network IDs and associated netmasks.
- Configuration detail of servers, routers, and other network-connected devices (for instance, network printers).

- Purpose of every server and user groups that draw on its resources. Also, include any dependencies that this server might have on other servers.

- History of changes made to the network. Changes such as network segmentation, address changes, netmask changes, and additions and removal of servers are examples of what this aspect of documentation should cover. Documenting the rationale that governed the change can provide valuable insight into the network performance troubleshooting.

- History of problems encountered on the network and associated fixes and patches that helped in fixing those problems. More than half of the problems are of repetitive nature. Documenting them, and the solutions, provides proven fixes which could be applied under similar circumstances in the future.

Having those details at your disposal cuts down considerably on the time required to figure them out by way of guessing or manual work. Documentation should be regarded as a proactive exercise in troubleshooting networks. Developing the habit of doing it on a timely basis can quickly prove its worth in situations where complete information would have reduced the time and effort involved in a repair.

An aspect that is equally important to documentation are user-reported error messages and complaints. Whenever an error is reported, ask the user to try re-creating it by repeating what she has been doing keystroke by keystroke at the time the error occurred. If the error is re-created successfully, religiously record all that led to it and the actual error message itself.

Developing a Troubleshooting Plan

Based on the information you gather, you should be able to develop an effective plan for troubleshooting the network. The plan should be based on a thorough understanding and analysis of the observations made and information gathered. An effective plan should include steps that, upon execution, help in narrowing down the extent of the problem (that is, is the problem user-specific, user group-specific, or network-wide?). Extensive testing exercises should help a great deal in achieving this objective.

Another step that the plan should take into consideration is to determine what has changed since the last time the network services were well behaved. This question should not be difficult to answer if you maintain good documentation. Often, a slight uncoordinated change in a user's workstation, a router, or any other network service configuration lies behind abnormalities which did not exist before the change was made.

Your plan should identify the tools and access privileges that you will need to carry them out. Also include a depiction of the order in which the steps will be executed.

Identifying and Resolving the Problem

Aim at isolating the problem by trying to re-create it on more than one user workstation, and/ or more than one network segment, if possible. This exercise helps you to quickly establish whether the problem is affecting all users, a group of users, or only one user. The tools and methodology needed for the next stage of the troubleshooting exercise are significantly influenced by your findings at this stage.

A problem affecting one user could be due to something the user is doing wrong, or a configuration (or misconfiguration) problem on his/her workstation. Consequently, using the proper troubleshooting tools, your efforts should be focused on the user's workstation level. This should not mean that the workstation is the only place to look for the bug. The bug might be due to a change made on the network which affects this particular user only (for example, duplicating the user's IP address on another workstation or device is a common problem).

A problem affecting a group of users dictates examining the factors along which those users are aligned. You may find, for example, that users on only a particular segment of the network are affected. In this case, you narrow the search to that particular segment. If, instead, the members of the identified group belong to different segments, then it may mean that they are logically aligned to draw on a common network resource. The next step would be to find out the service they share exclusively, and figure out ways for resolving the problems pertinent to it.

Using the proper troubleshooting tools (discussed in the next section), you should be able to further narrow in on the affected layers in the communication process. This helps in focusing your attention on that layer and the associated configuration which might be adversely affecting the network.

As troubleshooting evolves, you should take notes to keep track of the observations you have made. Regularly re-examine your notes for clues and guidance. While doing so, never dismiss what may sound trivial as irrelevant, or close your mind to an experience which may sound irrelevant to the nature of what you are doing. Armed with a solid understanding of TCP/IP, troubleshooting networks is primarily based on insightful observation and accounting for the *seemingly* "un-related" and "insignificant" events. Many times, an observation which was dismissed early in the troubleshooting process has provided the necessary clues about the nature of the problem.

Documenting the Problem

A successful exercise in troubleshooting should always be concluded with updating the documentation with a complete description of the problem encountered, and a thorough depiction of the solution. There are two important reasons for doing this. These are

1. You keep track of the changes and problems, providing guidance when similar situations arise.
2. Independent of how thoroughly you test the solution, there are instances when the solution itself becomes the source of future problems. A future implementation configuration, for example, might conflict with implemented fixes. In cases like these, proper documentation helps to shed light on the suitability of the solution, in the context of the new and related problems.

20

NETWORKING

Network Diagnostic Tools

All variants of the UNIX operating system come equipped with an impressively comprehensive set of network configuration, diagnostic, and troubleshooting tools. Better still, those tools fall into categories pertaining to the different layers of the network architecture. Table 20.6 provides a categorized listing of the most commonly used commands. Depending on the nature of the problem, you might have to use one or more of these commands in the process of problem identification and resolution.

Table 20.6. A categorized listing of commonly used TCP/IP diagnostic tools.

Problem Category	Command Set
Reachability/Routing	ping
	arp
	ripquery
	route
	traceroute
	netstat
	ifconfig
NFS-Related	rpcinfo
	nfsstat
	df
	showmount
DNS-Related	nslookup
	dig
Transport-Related	trpt
	netstat
Protocol Analysis	snoop

NOTE

Most of the preceding commands will be described as implemented on UNIX SVR4. For specific details regarding their implementation and behavior on other platforms, the reader is advised to refer to the vendor-supplied man pages. Also, with the exception of Solaris, none of the platforms covered in this books provides an implementation of the snoop protocol analysis command.

Many of the commands in Table 20.6 were tackled in previous pages of the chapter in the context of configuring TCP/IP. In the next few pages, you will be shown how to put them to use in the context of problem identification and resolution.

Reachability Problems

Users failing to establish a connection, such as an FTP or Telnet session, with other host(s) on the network are said to have reachability-related problems. Depending on their origin, such problems might be of intermittent or permanent nature. Reachability problems are manifestations of anything from local configuration issues to a failing stack on a remote including anything in between, including physical and routing failures.

ping: Test for Reachability

Whenever a reachability problem is encountered, ping is normally the very first diagnostic command that comes to the experienced user's mind. ping is particularly helpful in determining whether the failure is due to configuration, routing, or physical failure as opposed to a failure in the upper application layers of the communications process.

In its simplest form, ping takes the host name for an argument (provided of course that the name can be resolved either using /etc/hosts or DNS service). Here is an example of a successful test using ping:

```
# ping cello
cello is alive
```

ping employs the ICMP protocol to establish reachability to the host in question. When invoked, ping, sends an ICMP ECHO REQUEST message to the host specified on the command line. In response, ping expects an ICMP ECHO RESPONSE MESSAGE. Failure to receive a response within a specific timeout period forces ping to conclude that the host is unreachable—yielding the familiar host unreachable message on the user's screen.

The host unreachable message could be resulting from a failing host. The target host could be down, or its communications protocol stack could be failing to respond to remote user requests. Determining the culpability of the target host in this failure can be easily established by trying to ping other hosts, on the same segment as the suspect host. If ping returns successfully, it can be concluded that the target server is at the origin of the failure. Consequently, it's the target server where you might have to spend your time trying to fix the problem. Otherwise, the problem can be attributed to either local configuration error, physical failure, or routing problem.

CAUTION WHEN USING ping

The ping command is a feature-rich command capable of sending multiple ICMP ECHO REQUEST packets of specific sizes and at specified intervals of time. The maximum packet

continues

20

NETWORKING

continued

size that ping is supposed to handle (according to Internet standards) is 64 kilobytes as opposed to the default size of 64 bytes. The reason you might want ping to send large-size packets is to test the path for support to fragmentation/reassembly and resequencing of large packets. It has been found, however, that some poor implementations of ping allow the use of packet sizes larger than 64 kilobytes (for example, ping's implementation on Windows 95). It is strongly recommended that you avoid the temptation of specifying such large packet sizes. There have been reports of ping inflicting failures up to the point of crashing computers of any size from PCs to mainframes as a consequence of targeting them with large-size ICMP ECHO REQUEST packets.

Please refer to the man pages for the exact syntax of ping as implemented on your system.

Verifying the Local Configuration: `ifconfig`

A host's IP configuration can be verified using the familiar ifconfig command. Using ifconfig, a network administrator can check the host's IP address, netmask, and broadcast address as well as the status of the network interface. You can also use ifconfig to check whether the interface is marked UP or DOWN, implying an operational interface or a non-operational interface, respectively.

Following is an example of using ifconfig:

```
# ifconfig el30
el30: flags=23<UP,BROADCAST,NOTRAILERS>
    inet 150.1.0.1 netmask ffff0000 broadcast 150.1.255.255
```

According to this output, the el30 interface is configured to IP address 150.1.0.1, the netmask is ffff0000 (the equivalent to 255.255.0.0 in dotted decimal notation) and broadcast address 150.1.255.255. Notice how the interface is marked UP indicating that it is operational. An interface that is marked DOWN implies hardware problems local to the host itself or the physical wiring connecting it to the network.

If ifconfig verifies the parameters correctly, yet the host is still having problems reaching others on the network, then you might want to check for possible duplication of the IP address and/or routing problems along the path leading to the destination host.

arp: Who Is My Twin?

The arp command is particularly useful in detecting workstations with duplicate IP addresses. Duplicate IP addresses have the effect of intermittently slowing an already established connection, timing it out, and disrupting it. All workstations and network devices sharing the IP address are bound to suffer from degradation in performance down to complete dropout from the network.

As explained earlier, whenever a user attempts to invoke a session with another host on the network, he normally specifies the name of that host. The application takes over resolving the name into an IP address. Subsequently, the IP address is resolved into a physical address that is normally referred to as the MAC address (that is, Medium Access Control address) by the ARP protocol. ARP finds out the MAC identity of the target host by sending out an ARP Request broadcast inquiring about the MAC address corresponding to the IP address included in the broadcast. All hosts on the network pick up the ARP request packet and process it. Only one host, with the matching IP address, is *supposed* to return an ARP response packet including its MAC address. After the MAC address becomes available, the originating host proceeds to the data exchange phase with target host using the discovered address. To save bandwidth lost to the ARP process, every host caches the ARP responses it obtains from the network.

Using the arp -a command, you can query the ARP cache table as shown here:

```
# arp -a
cello (150.1.0.10) at 0:0:3:32:1:ad permanent
jade (100.0.0.2) at 0:0:c0:15:ad:18
oboe (150.1.2.1) at 0:0:c8:12:4:ab
```

Notice how each entry contains both the host's assigned IP address, and the MAC (that is, physical) address corresponding to the interface in that host. As an example, cello's IP address is 150.1.0.10 and its MAC address is hexadecimal 0:0:3:32:1:ad.

The above output should not lead you to believe that ARP talked to only three hosts. In fact, ARP disposes of entries pertaining to hosts that the workstation did not communicate with within a set timeout period—the default timeout period being four minutes for most implementations. You can, however, change the default to a different value if so desired.

What would happen if two workstations were somehow misconfigured to share the IP address? Well, as you can imagine by now, both of them are going to try responding to ARP requests affecting them—hence giving rise to trouble. Of the two responses, only the one that arrived first will be processed, cached, and used in the exchange of data. Consequently, if the MAC address corresponds to an "impostor" host, the originating workstation won't be able to talk to the desired target server because the data frames will be carrying the wrong address.

Whenever duplicate IP addresses are suspected on the network, ask the affected user about the service or server he tries to access when the problem occurs. Most likely, the duplicate address is either that of the user's workstation or the host server being attempted access to. Consequently, you should be able to quickly determine which of the two IP addresses is being duplicated, and redress the situation accordingly. The main tools you are going to need in this exercise are the arp and the ping commands. The former helps you check the ARP cache, whereas the latter is normally used to force ARP broadcasts.

To determine whether the IP address being duplicated belongs to the user's workstation, physically disconnect it from the network. Using another workstation force an ARP request broadcast using the ping command using the IP address of the disconnected workstation as the target host specification. If you get a response saying that *hostname* is alive, then this clearly

20

NETWORKING

implies that the IP address is being duplicated. The next step would be to enter the `arp -a` command on the same workstation you used for `ping`ing and note the MAC address of the responding host. That host must then be the one with the duplicate IP address. If you maintain good documentation, including the MAC address corresponding to each host on the network, you will be able to quickly determine the offending host and work on having it reconfigured for a different, and *unique*, IP address.

Should `ping`ing fail, resulting in a *hostname* is alive message, then you may conclude that the IP address being duplicated does not belong to the user's workstation. You may connect it back to the network and proceed to the second phase of figuring out which host is duplicating the server's address.

Troubleshooting the server's address is a bit more tricky than troubleshooting the user workstation's address. This is due to the fact that unless a downtime is scheduled, during which users won't be provided access to the server, the server cannot be brought down or physically disconnected from the network. To determine whether the server's IP address is duplicated, and the MAC address of the host duplicating the address, attend to any workstation on the network and use it in performing the following tests:

1. Check the ARP cache table, using `arp -a`, for any reference to the IP address being investigated. If an entry exists, delete it. Deleting the entry ensures that a response obtained for an ARP request is freshly cached. To do that, enter `arp` with the `-d` option. An example follows:

   ```
   # arp -a ¦ grep "100.0.0.3"
     (100.0.0.3) at 0:0:c0:1a:b2:80
   # arp -d 100.0.0.3
   100.0.0.1 (100.0.0.3) deleted
   ```

2. Force an ARP request broadcast using the `ping` command. The specified address should pertain to the suspect server.

3. Check the ARP cache. You should be able to see an entry pertaining to the IP address being `ping`ed. Note the corresponding MAC address and compare with that of the server's. If the MAC addresses match, repeat the first two steps. You may have to recycle through them several times before a MAC address different from the server's is detected. Consequently, use the MAC address to track it down to the offending host and take the necessary corrective measures to redress the situation back to normal.

MORE ABOUT arp

The output of the `arp -a` command might sometimes include types of status qualifiers. There are three types including permanent, permanent published, and incomplete as in the following example:

```
# arp -a
tenor (100.0.0.3) at 0:0:3:32:1:ad permanent published
jade (100.0.0.2) at 0:0:c0:15:ad:18 permanent
```

```
cello (198.53.237.2) at 0:0:c8:12:4:ab
absent (184.34.32.23) at (incomplete)
```

If no status qualifier exists, as in the case of `cello`, the default is temporary. Temporary ARP entries are dynamically added to the host's cache by virtue of an ARP request/response exchange. These entries normally last four to five minutes before they're deleted.

A permanent-marked entry, as implied by the qualifier, is an entry that is static in nature; it stays in the ARP table until expressly deleted by the system administrator (or user) using the `arp -d` command. Normally, permanent entries are user added and pertain to hosts with which the user communicates most. This measure has the advantage of saving bandwidth which would otherwise be lost to ARP request/response exchanges. Adding a permanent entry to the ARP cache takes the following form of the arp command:

```
# arp -s hostname MACaddres
```

For example, to permanently add the IP address-to-MAC mapping of host `jade` to the user's ARP cache, enter the following command:

```
# arp -s jade 0:0:c0:15:ad:18
```

An entry marked `published` qualifies the host to respond on behalf of the workstation whose IP address matches the one in this entry. In the above sample listing, the host includes a `permanent published` entry for host tenor. This means that this host is qualified to respond on behalf of saturn to ARP requests involving `tenor's` IP address. This is commonly adopted whenever the querying host and the target host belong to two different network segments separated by routers which are configured to suppress broadcasts. In this case, you designate a machine on each segment as an ARP server with the mandate of responding to ARP queries on behalf of hosts that are not attached to the same segment. To render this task manageable, arp can be forced to lookup the contents of a file in which you can maintain all the `published` entries. The general format of the file is as follows:

```
hostname MACaddress pub
```

Make sure that there is a matching entry for each host name in the `/etc/hosts` file.

To force arp to update the ARP cache using the contents of the file containing all of the desired ARP mappings, enter the command including the `-f` option:

```
# arp -f filename
```

Consequently, when troubleshooting duplicate IP addresses, you should check the ARP files used to update the cache of ARP servers. They can potentially be the source of the duplication, or erroneous replies due to outdated data in the files.

traceroute: Lead Me to Rome

There are situations where the problem of unreachability is mainly attributable to routing configuration problems. What might make troubleshooting the routing problem even worse is the number of intervening routers between the source and destination hosts. To help you with situations involving a large number of routers, UNIX comes equipped with an easy-to-use yet powerful `traceroute` command.

Using traceroute, you can trace the path a data packet takes from one host to another on the network. The command output includes one line per router that the packet traverses. The lines include the IP address of the router being traversed, the hop count (that is, number of intervening routers between the host and the router being described) and the round-trip times in milliseconds. The maximum number of hops that traceroute supports is 30.

To trace the route to a host, or any other network device, simply enter:

```
# traceroute hostname
```

In the following example, traceroute is used to trace the route to host rome

```
# traceroute rome
traceroute to rome (148.53.27.11), 30 hops max, 40 byte packets
 1    198.237.53.1 (198.53.237.1)  5 ms  5 ms  4 ms
 2    198.235.54.2 (198.235.54.2)  6 ms  6 ms  4 ms
 3    143.22.45.9 (142.22.45.9)  11 ms  8 ms  7 ms
 4    169.48.1.158 (169.48.1.158)  28 ms  28 ms  24 ms
```

According to this example, to get to host rome, a packet, originating from the workstation where traceroute was issued, has to traverse four routers in the listed order.

The way traceroute works is illustrated in Figure 20.34. Early in the chapter, it was explained that how long a data packet can spend on the network is determined by the contents of the time-to-live (TTL) field included in the IP header. Every router that the packet traverses decrements the field by one. Once TTL is decremented to zero, the packet is removed from the network by the first router to detect the condition. traceroute capitalizes on this control mechanism. Once invoked, it issues up to 30 UDP packets, in sequential order, in which the first packet has its TTL set to one. Each subsequent UDP packet has its TTL incremented by one relative to the last packet. In practical terms this means that the first packet is bound to die as soon as it hits the first router on its way to the destined host (that is, rome in the diagram). The second UDP traceroute packet makes it through Router R1 only to die at the door steps of Router R2 (since its TTL is set to 2 only). Every time a router kills a packet, it is compelled (by design) to return an ICMP Time Exceeded message to the originating host.

This chain of events continues until the target host is reached. To elicit a response from the target host, traceroute destines the UDP packet to port 33434—a reserved invalid port number. Being an invalid port number forces the receiving host to ignore the packet and respond with an ICMP Unreachable Port (*not* Time-Exceeded) message. Upon receiving this last message, traceroute stops sending diagnostic UDP packets.

Here is a sample output illustrating what would happen should traceroute fail to reach the target host:

```
# traceroute rome
traceroute to rome (148.53.27.11), 30 hops max, 40 byte packets
 1    198.237.53.1 (198.53.237.1)  5 ms  5 ms  4 ms
 2    198.235.54.2 (198.235.54.2)  6 ms  6 ms  4 ms
 3    * * *
 4    * * *
```

```
       .
       .
       .
29   *  *  *
30   *  *  *
```

FIGURE 20.34.

traceroute *flow of events.*

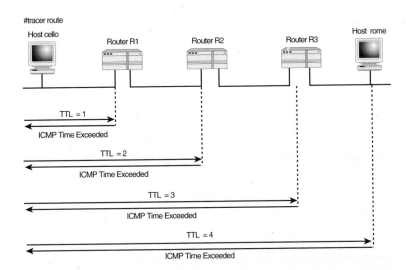

Every printed set of three asterisks shown above is an indication of traceroute's failure to make it across a router. Accordingly, this traceroute command failed to go anywhere beyond the second router that it encountered on the network, independent of the value of TTL (printed in the first column) at the time the attempt was made. traceroute exits when the TTL field increments to 30.

ripquery

Troubleshooting routing problems often requires verifying the validity of the routing tables as they exist on some of the routers intervening between the source and destination hosts including the hosts themselves. On the local host this is done using the netstat -rn command (explained earlier in the chapter). Verifying routing tables on remote hosts and intervening routers (whether the routers are specialized routing devices or full fledged multihomed UNIX hosts) may not be as convenient. Verifying routing tables on remote hosts requires logging in to them before being able to invoke the netstat command.

Using ripquery, you can query, from the local workstation, remote hosts for their routing tables. When issued, ripquery polls the target host for its routing table and displays it on the local workstation's screen. To perform a successful poll, ripquery requires that the routing daemon such as routed be running on the host being queried. Otherwise ripquery times out and exits silently. The following example demonstrates the use of ripquery to poll host jade for its routing table:

```
# ripquery jade
84 bytes from jade(100.0.0.2):
    ???(198.53.235.1), metric 1
    ???(198.53.235.10), metric 1
    harmonics (100.0.0.0), metric 1
    harmonics (198.53.237.0), metric 1
```

The output includes the number of bytes received (84 bytes in the example) from the polled host, the destination IP address and the applicable metric (that is, number of intervening hops). Also, the output includes the symbolic name of the destination as set in the /etc/networks file. Destinations not known by symbolic names are referred to by the triple question mark character ?.

---

ripquery

Not all UNIX variants support the ripquery command. Check your system's documentation for a confirmation as well as the other options that come with ripquery.

Using the Router Log Facility

Should you find yourself in desperate need of more routing-pertinent information to assist you in the search for a solution, you can employ the routing daemon's data-logging capability to provide this information. You can do this by including a log filename on the line that invokes the routing daemon in the TCP/IP startup script that applies to your system. The following example invokes routed and enables logging the route tracking information to the file /var/router.log:

```
/usr/sbin/in.routed -q /var/router.log
```

Here is an example of the contents of such a file:

```
Tracing enabled: Action Tracing started: Sun Nov  17 06:47:06 1996


Sun Nov  17 06:47:06:
ADD dst 127.0.0.0, router 127.0.0.1, metric 1, flags UP state
PASSIVE¦INTERFACE¦CHANGED¦EXTERNAL timer 0
ADD dst 100.0.0.0, router 100.0.0.1, metric 1, flags UP state INTERFACE¦CHANGED
➥timer 0
SIOCADDRT: File exists
ADD dst 150.1.0.0, router 150.1.0.1, metric 1, flags UP state INTERFACE¦CHANGED
➥timer 0
SIOCADDRT: File exists

Sun Nov  17 06:47:06:
ADD dst 198.53.237.0, router 100.0.0.2, metric 2, flags UP¦GATEWAY state CHANGED
➥timer 0

Sun Nov  17 07:01:22:
ADD dst 213.23.1.0, router 100.0.0.2, metric 5, flags UP¦GATEWAY state CHANGED
➥timer 0
```

```
Sun Nov  17 07:04:11:
CHANGE metric dst 213.23.1.0, router 100.0.0.2, from 5 to 16

Sun Nov  17 07:07:07:
DELETE dst 213.23.1.0, router 100.0.0.2, metric 16, flags UP¦GATEWAY state timer
➥240
```

As shown in this listing, route additions, deletions and changes are kept track of in this file, including time and date stamps. You can optionally request that inter-router control messages be tracked as well, as shown here:

```
/usr/sbin/in.routed/  -qt /var/router.log
```

resulting in a file of contents similar to the following one:

```
Tracing enabled: Action Tracing started: Sun Nov  1710:09:05 1996

Tracing packets started, with action tracing on: Sun  Nov  17 10:09:05 1996


Sun Nov 17 10:09:05:
ADD dst 150.1.0.0, router 150.1.0.1, metric 1, flags UP state INTERFACE¦CHANGED
➥timer 0
SIOCADDRT: File exists
ADD dst 100.0.0.0, router 100.0.0.1, metric 1, flags UP state INTERFACE¦CHANGED
➥timer 0
SIOCADDRT: File exists
ADD dst 198.53.235.1, router 198.53.235.10, metric 1, flags UP¦HOST state
➥PASSIVE¦INTERFACE¦CHANGED timer 0
SIOCADDRT: File exists
REQUEST to 150.1.255.255.0 Sat Apr  8 10:09:05:
REQUEST to 100.255.255.255.0 Sat Apr  8 10:09:05:
REQUEST from 150.1.0.1.520 Sat Apr  8 10:09:06:
REQUEST from 100.0.0.1.520 Sat Apr  8 10:09:06:
RESPONSE from 100.0.0.2.520 Sat Apr  8 10:09:06:

Sun Nov  17 10:09:06:
ADD dst 198.53.235.10, router 100.0.0.2, metric 2, flags UP¦GATEWAY¦HOST state
➥CHANGED timer 0
SIOCADDRT: File exists
ADD dst 198.53.237.0, router 100.0.0.2, metric 2, flags UP¦GATEWAY state CHANGED
➥timer 0
SIOCADDRT: File exists
RESPONSE from 100.0.0.2.520 Sat Apr  8 10:09:30:
```

Entries that start with the keyword REQUEST pertain to data exchanged via the RIP protocol.

ROUTER LOGS

> Make sure to turn the data log file off as soon as you're done troubleshooting the network. Failure to do so may result in wasting considerable disk space, especially if data logging is enabled in a busy network.

Troubleshooting Domain Name Service

Domain Name Service (DNS) failures exhibit themselves in the inability of an application to contact a remote host due to failure to resolve the name of the desired host into an IP address. Users having problems with name resolution end up with error messages such as `unknown host` *hostname* or `Host name lookup failure` showing on the screens of their workstations.

There are two equally capable tools which you can use in troubleshooting DNS problems: `nslookup` and `dig`. In an earlier section, a few of the features of `nslookup` were introduced. A few more of its features will be introduced in this section. `dig` offers almost the same capabilities with a difference: `nslookup` establishes an interactive session with `named` (that is, DNS daemon), `dig` does not. Because of the similarity between `nslookup` and `dig`, it is left to the initiative of the interested reader to research the man pages for more details about using `dig`.

Methodology for Troubleshooting DNS

Following are the main reasons leading to "unreliable" DNS service:

- Typing errors: Where to start looking for the cause of DNS failure? If asked, nine out of ten experienced `named` administrators suggest that you start with the user. It is very common that users report problems arising mainly from typing errors. Hence, whenever a user complains about an application's failure to establish a connection due to name-service lookup failure, you would want to go to that user's workstation and ask the user to give it one more try. Note the way the user spells the remote host name. If the error persists, then use the name as typed on the screen to carry out further investigation into the matter.

- Mis-serialized database files: It is not an uncommon mistake, for system administrators, to forget to increment the serial number of a `named` database file after updating it. Remember from earlier discussion that unless a primary server's database serial number is incremented, a secondary server will neglect to make zonal transfer to get the updates replicated on its host. Whenever a refresh is due, a secondary server matches the serial number of each database file it has in cache with that of its counterpart on the primary server. If the primary's serial number is smaller than the secondary's, the latter assumes that there is nothing new to transfer.

  Mis-serialized database files will lead to one, or both, problems:

  - Inconsistent name resolutions, exhibited by conflicting answers to the same query depending on the server responding to the query. This situation occurs mainly when, for example, the IP address on the primary is changed, and because no zonal updates took place, the secondary maintains the old information. This problem is of an intermittent nature.

  - Some users will be able to establish connections with newly introduced servers, while others won't. Again, this depends on which server the user's workstation contacts for resolution. This problem arises from adding new records pertinent to servers recently attached to the network.

There is no direct way of comparing the serial numbers on both servers (that is, the primary and the secondary). One indirect way is via an `nslookup` session. Below is a depiction of how to use `nslookup` to look up the serial number of a server's DNS database:

```
# nslookup
Default Server:  jade
Address:  0.0.0.0

> set type=soa
> harmonics.com
Server:  jade
Address: 100.0.0.2

harmonics.com
    origin = jade.harmonics.com
    mail addr = root.jade.harmonics.com
    serial = 1
    refresh = 14400 ( 4 hours)
    retry   = 3600 ( 1 hour)
    expire  = 604800 (7 days)
    minimum ttl = 86400 (1 day)
> exit
#
```

As shown above, after invoking `nslookup` you only have to set the type of the query to `soa` (Start Of Authority) and enter the name of the domain or subdomain to which the query applies. In response, `nslookup` queries for, and displays, all the information maintained in the SOA record for that domain, including the serial number. Make sure that the server being queried is the secondary server. Next, compare the serial number you obtained from `nslookup` with the one maintained in the SOA record in the `named` database of the primary server. If they match, you should then increment the primary's serial number.

Once the serial number is incremented, you must send the server a SIGHUP signal to force it to reload the database and update its cache with the new serial number. Failure to do so will cause the primary to retain the old information, and may cause the secondary to ignore, again, zonal transfers, leaving us back where we started. It is not uncommon for novice DNS administrators to forget to signal the primary server after making changes to the DNS database. This is a mistake that affects all domain users, not only users of secondary servers. If left unsignalled, primary servers won't be capable to update their caches with the changes. Secondary servers, as well as users, will continue to be served old data. Here is how to send the server a SIGHUP signal:

```
# kill -HUP namedpid
```

where *namedpid* is the named process ID as reported by the `"ps -ef ¦ grep named"` command.

Once the serialization problem is taken care of on the primary server, you need only restart `named` on the secondary if you are in a hurry to replicate the updates. You can also let the server wait until next refresh is due. At that time, a zonal transfer will take care of the replication.

- Period rules-related problems: as administrators update the named database files, they sometimes forget to include the trailing period, or may mistakenly include it where it does not belong. Unless the period rules (explained earlier in the chapter) are strictly followed, your domain service is prone to name lookup failures. Make sure you understand where the periods belong and where they do not. The best thing to do to avoid problems arising from misplaced periods is to verify the validity of an update by testing it as soon as it is introduced, and as thoroughly as possible.

- Missing PTR records: missing PTR records prevent name servers from reverse-resolving an IP address to its host domain name. Missing PTR records may remain unnoticed for quite some time, until a requirement for reverse resolution arises. Resulting errors usually occur when a user attempts contacting a remote host using applications which require reverse mappings. Applications such as rcp (that is, remote copy, see man pages for detail) allow access to users coming from workstations with names included in the /etc/hosts.equiv or $HOME/.rhosts files. Hence, before access is granted to the user, these applications reverse-map the IP address of the requesting workstation to match the *hostname* with the records maintained in hosts.equiv or .rhosts files. A missing PTR record causes the authentication process to fail, and the user would consequently be denied access by the application.

Access denial messages may mislead a system administrator and put him/her on a path which is oblivious to DNS. Just remember to check your PTR records whenever a user reports security related error messages. The check is very simple to perform, and by doing it you set yourself a step ahead in solving the mystery.

To check whether the reverse database file contains a PTR record corresponding to the workstation in question, start an nslookup session, query the server for the IP address of the workstation, and subsequently issue a reverse query, as in the following example:

```
# nslookup
Default Server:  jade
Address:  198.53.237.1

> wing
Server:  jade
Address:  198.53.237.1

Name:    drum.harmonics.com
Address:  198.53.237.7

> 198.53.237.7
Server:  jade
Address:  198.53.237.1


Name:    drum.harmonics.com
Address:  198.53.237.7

> exit
#
```

Here is an example of a failing `nslookup` query:

```
# nslookup
Default Server:  jade
Address:  198.53.237.1

> flyer
Server:  jade
Address:  198.53.237.1

Name:    flyer.harmonics.com
Address:  198.53.237.16

> 198.53.237.16
Server:  jade
Address:  198.53.237.1

***jade can't find 198.53.237.16: Non-existent domain
> exit
#
```

In this case, `nslookup` responded with `Non-existent domain`. To a novice, this message can be misleading. What it really meant, in the context of this exercise, is that there isn't a PTR record for host `flyer`. Consequently, to redress the situation, you must edit the reverse domain database to add the required PTR record.

■ Connectivity-related problems: Expectedly, if the transport path connecting a user's workstation to its name server is broken, the workstation will no longer will be able to have its name queries answered. Under such circumstances, users normally get time-out type of messages on their screens after waiting patiently to get connected to the desired host. Your only remedy, of course, is to diagnose connectivity on the wire as discussed earlier in the chapter.

What other resources can you possibly use to hunt for hints about the problems you are diagnosing? There are at least three files you can browse for helpful information. The files are these:

```
* /var/tmp/named_dump.db
* /var/tmp/named.run
* syslogd Log File(s)
```

DNS DUMP AND LOG FILES

The path of each of the dump and log files pertaining to DNS is vendor-specific. Please refer to the man pages on named daemon for the exact path.

/var/tmp/named_dump.db

`/var/tmp/named_dump.db` file is a dump file which is created upon sending `named` an INT signal as follows:

```
# kill -INT namedpid
```

where *namedpid* is the process ID of named, as reported by the "ps -ef ¦ grep named" command.

The dump file is an exact replica of named's cache. You would normally need to resort to dumping the cache when you suspect corrupted cache data behind the service problems emerging on the network. This is an example of what the contents of named_dump.db look like:

```
; Dumped at Sun Nov 17 17:49:54 1996
; --- Cache & Data ---
$ORIGIN in-addr.arpa.
100        IN    SOA    jade.harmonics.com.
root.jade.harmonics.com.100.in-addr.arpa. (
         1 14400 3600 604800 86400 )
         IN    NS    jade.harmonics.com.
         IN    NS    cello.harmonics.com.
$ORIGIN 150.in-addr.arpa.
1          IN    SOA    jade.harmonics.com. root.jade.harmonics.com. (
         1 14400 3600 604800 86400 )
         IN    NS    jade.harmonics.com.
         IN    NS    cello.harmonics.com.
$ORIGIN 0.1.150.in-addr.arpa.
10         IN    PTR    tenor.harmonics.com.
11         IN    PTR    soprano.harmonics.com.
$ORIGIN 0.0.100.in-addr.arpa.
4          IN    PTR    sopranino.harmonics.com.
2          IN    PTR    jade.harmonics.com.
3          IN    PTR    laser.harmonics.com.
$ORIGIN 0.127.in-addr.arpa.
0          IN    SOA    jade.harmonics.com. root.jade.harmonics.com. (
         1 14400 3600 604800 86400 )
         IN    NS    jade.harmonics.com.
$ORIGIN 0.0.127.in-addr.arpa.
1          IN    PTR    localhost.0.0.127.in-addr.arpa.
$ORIGIN com.
harmonics          IN    SOA    jade.harmonics.com. root.jade.harmonics.com. (
         3 14400 3600 604800 86400 )
         IN    NS    jade.harmonics.com.
         IN    NS    cello.harmonics.com.
$ORIGIN harmonics.com.
sopranino    IN    A    100.0.0.4
saturn       IN    A    150.1.0.10
         IN    SOA    jade.harmonics.com. root.jade.harmonics.com. (
         1 14400 3600 604800 86400 )
pluto        IN    A    150.1.0.11
localhost    IN    A    127.0.0.1
laser        IN    A    100.0.0.3
jade         IN    A    150.1.0.10
         IN    A    100.0.0.2
$ORIGIN pulse.harmonics.com.
wing         IN    A    198.53.237.7
jade         IN    A    100.0.0.2    ; 20
         IN    A    198.53.237.1
         IN    A    198.53.235.10
```

By going through the lines, you should be able to compare this with the contents of the actual disk database file, and, hopefully, discover the discrepancies, if any.

/var/tmp/named.run

Optionally, you can enable debugging on named. named supports nine levels of debug; the higher the level turned on, the more events traced and logged in this file.

You can turn the debugger on by either restarting named with the -d *n* option, where *n* specifies the debug level, or sending named a USR1 signal as in the following example:

```
# kill -USR1 namedpid
```

To bring debug to a higher level, re-enter the command once per level. Following are sample contents of named.run after debug was set to level one, and as consequence to pinging host jade:

```
Debug turned ON, Level 1

datagram from 198.53.237.1 port 1038, fd 5, len 39
req: nlookup(jade.harmonics.com) id 256 type=1
req: found 'jade.harmonics.com' as 'jade.pulse.harmonics.com' (cname=0)
req: answer -> 150.1.0.1 5 (1038) id=1 Local
```

To turn off the debug option, send named a USR2 signal as follows:

```
# kill -USR2 namedpid
```

syslogd Log Files

UNIX supports a syslogd daemon which, if enabled, reads and logs network pertinent messages and debug information into files specified in the configuration file /etc/syslog.conf. syslogd listens on the network, at UDP's well-known port 514.

You are advised not to configure and run syslogd unless you really need to. This file may grow to a considerable size, thus wasting your disk space. Also, make sure you kill the daemon and remove the file after you are done with it.

Here is a sample /etc/syslog.conf which should be sufficient for most needs:

```
#       @(#)syslog.conf    4.3 Lachman System V STREAMS TCP  source
#       SCCS IDENTIFICATION
*.info,*.debug                     /usr/adm/syslog
```

This file makes syslogd send all informational and debug messages to the /usr/adm/syslog file. Refer to the man pages for more information on configuring the syslogd daemon.

This file could be used track down messages pertaining to named, among other messages, as illustrated in the following sample of syslog contents:

```
named[1451]: restarted
Jan  8 07:19:16 jade named[1451]: /etc/named.boot: No such file or directory
Jan  8 07:19:56 jade named[1454]: restarted
Jan  8 07:20:16 jade.harmonics.com named[1455]: No root nameservers for class 1
Jan  8 11:21:13 jade.harmonics.com named[1455]: zoneref: Masters for secondary zone
➡1.150.in-addr.arpa unreachable
Jan  8 11:37:28 jade.harmonics.com named[1455]: zoneref: Masters for secondary zone
➡100.in-addr.arpa unreachable
```

20

NETWORKING

```
Jan  8 11:37:29 jade.harmonics.com named[1455]: zoneref: Masters for secondary zone
➥237.53.198.in-addr.arpa unreachable
Jan  8 11:37:29 jade.harmonics.com named[1455]: zoneref: Masters for secondary zone
➥harmonics.com unreachable
Jan 10 08:41:22 jade syslogd: exiting on signal 15
Jan 11 03:58:16 jade syslogd: restart
Jan 11 03:58:17 jade pppd[190]: restarted
Jan 11 03:58:18 jade pppd[190]: bound to host 'localhost' port 911.
Jan 11 03:58:19 jade named[191]: restarted
.
.
.
```

It can be easily deduced from the contents of this file that host jade was having difficulty reaching the servers for the domain harmonics.com.

Troubleshooting NFS

Following are the common symptoms of NFS failure and ways of diagnosing them:

■ *Hung servers:* A workstation's reaction to a hung server is a function of how it had the NFS file system mounted. A soft-mounted file system causes a workstation to retry completing a hung RPC call for the number of times that was specified in the retry=n parameter in the mount command used to mount that file system. Failure to complete the transaction within the timeout period causes the client to exit with an error message. A hard-mount, on the other hand, causes a the workstation to retry indefinitely until the server recovers from failure—not a desirable state, considering the disruption that it inflicts on users' productivity.

Using rpcinfo, you can verify the status of RPC services on any NFS server right from your local workstation. To do so, enter rpcinfo using the -p option and specify the host name where trouble is suspected. Following is an example of executing the proposed diagnostic command:

```
# rpcinfo -p tenor
   program vers proto   port  service
    100000    2   tcp    111  rpcbind
    100000    2   udp    111  rpcbind
    100008    1   udp   1036  walld
    150001    1   udp   1037  pcnfsd
    150001    2   udp   1037  pcnfsd
    100002    1   udp   1038  rusersd
    100002    2   udp   1038  rusersd
    100005    1   udp   1042  mountd
    100005    1   tcp   1026  mountd
    100003    2   udp   2049  nfs
    100024    1   udp   1046  status
    100024    1   tcp   1027  status
    100020    1   udp   1051  llockmgr
    100020    1   tcp   1028  llockmgr
    100021    2   tcp   1029  nlockmgr
    100021    1   tcp   1030  nlockmgr
    100021    1   udp   1055  nlockmgr
```

```
100021   3   tcp   1031   nlockmgr
100021   3   udp   1056   nlockmgr
100004   2   udp    925   ypserv
100004   2   tcp    926   ypserv
100004   1   udp    925   ypserv
100004   1   tcp    926   ypserv
100007   2   tcp   1032   ypbind
100007   2   udp   1061   ypbind
100007   1   tcp   1032   ypbind
100007   1   udp   1061   ypbind
100009   1   udp   1015   yppasswdd
```

As shown in this listing, unless the server is hung, it responds with a listing of all the enabled RPC servers including their names, program numbers, version numbers, and both UDP and TCP ports. A hung server forces `rpcinfo` to exit with an error message, instead.

■ *Connectivity problems:* Connectivity problems arising from malfunctioning transport infrastructure normally result in an error message such as "`rpcinfo: can't contact portmapper: RPC: tli error - An event requires attention`". Transport failure could be for any of the reasons that has already been dealt with in the "Troubleshooting Reachability" section. Please refer to that section for detail on dealing with this situations.

■ *RPC service-version mismatch:* Both client and server sides of any service have to be operating compatible versions of the service being invoked. Otherwise, it is likely the server may fail to render the service call requested by the client even if the NFS file system mounted "successfully." Using the following syntax of `rpcinfo` is helpful in verifying version compatibility:

`rpcinfo -u` *hostname program* [*version*]

or

`rpcinfo -t` *hostname program* [*version*]

In this syntax, u stands for UDP and t stands for TCP transport. program specifies the name of the service, and version is the version you want verified. Here is an example:

```
# rpcinfo -u tenor nfs 2
program 100003 version 2 ready and waiting
```

Instead, you can ignore the version number specification if you wanted a list of all supported versions of the specified service. Here is an example:

```
# rpcinfo -u tenor nlockmgr
program 100021 version 1 ready and waiting
rpcinfo: RPC: Procedure unavailable
program 100021 version 2 is not available
program 100021 version 3 ready and waiting
```

■ *Wrong run level:* Unless UNIX is brought up to run level three, a host won't bring up the NFS service. Consequently, users will not be able to mount NFS file systems from that host. A system administrator can manually bring UNIX up to run level three. Unless, however, startup scripts are updated to reflect the desire to enter run level three, a host will fail to enter that level when UNIX is rebooted. Verifying the level at which the system is run is a simple matter of entering the following `who -r` command:

```
# who -r
     .          run-level 3  Apr 11 20:27    3    0    2
```

nfsstat

nfsstat is more of a performance monitoring tool that, if invoked, provides statistical data pertaining to NFS services. With no options specified, `nfsstat` returns performance statistics for both the client and server sides of the service. This data might prove particularly helpful when trying to improve or tune the performance of NFS. It is beyond the scope of this chapter to include a discussion on network performance monitoring and tuning. The avid reader is advised to consult the man pages for more details on using the `nfsstat` command. Following is a sample output of executing `nfsstat`, where the `-s` option specifies the server's statistics only:

```
# nfsstat -s

Server rpc:
calls       badcalls    nullrecv    badlen      xdrcall
120         0           0           0           0

Server nfs:
calls       badcalls
117         0
null        getattr     setattr     root        lookup      readlink    read
3   2%      27 23%      0   0%      0   0%      64 54%      0   0%      8   6%
wrcache     write       create      remove      rename      link        symlink
0   0%      0   0%      2   1%      0   0%      0   0%      0   0%      0   0%
mkdir       rmdir       readdir     fsstat      access
0   0%      0   0%      8   6%      5   4%      0   0%
```

snoop: The Protocol Analysis Tool

Of all the platforms handled in this book, only Solaris 2.x comes with native snoop command in support of protocol analysis. Protocol analysis is a rather extreme measure that a network troubleshooter has to resort to for help should everything else fail to shed enough light on the encountered problem. Using snoop, you can capture packets off the wire and display their contents for subsequent analysis. Using snoop requires a significant knowledge in communications protocols (TCP/IP in particular) including the details of the field contents of protocol headers and handshake mechanisms and procedures. It is not the intention of this chapter to convey such knowledge and experience, as it more likely requires a book on the subject matter. For inquisitive minds, however, here is a partial listing of the type of information you can obtain by capturing packets using the snoop command:

```
ETHER:  ---- Ether Header ----
ETHER:
ETHER:  Packet 31 arrived at 9:03:4.38
ETHER:  Packet size = 114 bytes
ETHER:  Destination = 0:0:1b:3b:21:b2, Novell
ETHER:  Source      = 0:20:af:19:ed:d8,
ETHER:  Ethertype = 0800 (IP)
ETHER:
```

```
IP:    ---- IP Header ----
IP:
IP:    Version = 4
IP:    Header length = 20 bytes
IP:    Type of service = 0x00
IP:         xxx. .... = 0 (precedence)
IP:         ...0 .... = normal delay
IP:         .... 0... = normal throughput
IP:         .... .0.. = normal reliability
IP:    Total length = 100 bytes
IP:    Identification = 38389
IP:    Flags = 0x4
IP:         .1.. .... = do not fragment
IP:         ..0. .... = last fragment
IP:    Fragment offset = 0 bytes
IP:    Time to live = 255 seconds/hops
IP:    Protocol = 6 (TCP)
IP:    Header checksum = 9a1d
IP:    Source address = 100.0.0.3, tenor
IP:    Destination address = 100.0.0.1, sam
IP:    No options
IP:
TCP:   ---- TCP Header ----
TCP:
TCP:   Source port = 21
TCP:   Destination port = 1033
TCP:   Sequence number = 3943967492
TCP:   Acknowledgement number = 10725555
TCP:   Data offset = 20 bytes
TCP:   Flags = 0x18
TCP:         ..0. .... = No urgent pointer
TCP:         ...1 .... = Acknowledgement
TCP:         .... 1... = Push
TCP:         .... .0.. = No reset
TCP:         .... ..0. = No Syn
TCP:         .... ...0 = No Fin
TCP:   Window = 8760
TCP:   Checksum = 0xdb9d
TCP:   Urgent pointer = 0
TCP:   No options
TCP:
FTP:   ---- FTP:   ----
FTP:
FTP:   "220 tenor FTP server (UNIX(r) System V Release 4.0) ready.\r\n"
FTP:
```

This is the content of one data frame that was sent from a Solaris 2.x system to my Windows 95 workstation in response to my attempt to establish an FTP session (as demonstrated in the last few lines). Notice how details pertaining to the Ethernet, IP, and TCP headers are displayed in addition to the contents of the FTP data that the server sent to my workstation indicating that FTP server was ready for me to log in. As an interesting exercise, try to match what you see above with the protocol headers explained earlier in the chapter.

Summary

UNIX is among the foremost operating systems that are network-enabled right out of the box. In fact UNIX contributed a great deal to the success of the development and spread of the TCP/IP communications protocols that form the foundation of the global data communications network known as the Internet.

This chapter provided enough coverage of concepts that govern TCP/IP communications in the UNIX world. The coverage included is aimed at allowing the uninitiated to develop the minimal skill set to bring up UNIX on the network.

The chapter sets out by providing an introductory coverage of the TCP/IP protocol stack. It then moves on to a comprehensive coverage of the concepts and tools required to set up and configure UNIX for TCP/IP support including detailed listing of the most relevant startup scripts. Routing in particular is dealt with from the UNIX perspective and an emphasis is made on the IP address structure and the objectives underlying this structure. DNS name service, and NFS were explained, and areas of common mistakes are highlighted to help the reader avoid them for the sake of smooth firsthand experience.

Troubleshooting the various and most common services that UNIX networks support is covered including tips on approach and methodology. One underlying tone that was emphatically put forward is the need for accurate and up-to-date documentation. Without proper documentation, the system administrator might easily waste hours (if not days) figuring or verifying the detail of the network setup.

Finally, the chapter provides the reader with a comprehensive set of tools and shows him/her ways of using them in the context of the troubleshooting exercise. Over time, users will be able to extend and build on their experience to end up with more creative ways of utilizing the mentioned tools (and others) in handling UNIX failures on the network.

CHAPTER 21

System Accounting

by Daniel Wilson, William D. Wood, and William G. Pierce

IN THIS CHAPTER

The UNIX accounting system collects information on individual and group usage of the computer system resources. You may use this information as an accounting charge back system to bill users for the system resources utilized during a prescribed billing cycle. Accounting reports generated by the system accounting utilities provide information the systems administrator may use to assess current resource assignments, set resource limits and quotas, and forecast future resource requirements. This chapter will cover:

- UNIX System Accounting Basics
- Command Definitions
- Configuration Examples
- IBM AIX 4.2 Accounting Procedures
- HP-UX 10.x Accounting Procedures
- Solaris 2.5 Accounting Procedures
- System Accounting Directory Structure
- System Accounting Report Generation

UNIX System Accounting Basics

Once the computer system has been initialized, and assuming the system accounting option is enabled, statistical collection begins. The data collection process encompasses the following categories:

- Connect session statistics
- Process usage
- Disk space utilization
- Printer usage

The accounting system process begins by gathering statistical data from which summary reports can be generated. These reports may be used to assist in system performance analysis and provide the criteria necessary to establish an equitable customer charge back billing system. The aforementioned report categories include several types of reporting data that are collected to make up the accounting reports. Each category is described in the following sections.

Connect Session Statistics

The business units responsible for the organization's information technology (IT) services may use connect session statistics to charge customers for the time spent using system resources. This enables an organization to bill or to charge back based on a user's actual connect time. Connect-session accounting data, related to user login and logout, is collected by the `init` and `login` commands. When a user logs in, the `login` program makes an entry in the `/var/adm/wtmp` file. These records maintain the following user information:

- User name
- Date of login/logout
- Time of login/logout
- Terminal port

This information can be used to produce reports containing the following information:

- Date and starting time of connect session
- User ID for the connect session
- Login name
- Number of prime connect time seconds used
- Number of nonprime connect time seconds used
- Connect time seconds used
- Device address of connect session
- Number of seconds elapsed from Jan 1, 1970, to connect session starting time

Process Usage

System accounting also gathers statistics by individual processes. Examples of collected statistics include:

- Memory usage
- User and group numbers under which the process runs
- First eight characters of the name of the command
- Elapsed time and processor time used by the process
- I/O statistics
- Number of characters transferred
- Number of disk blocks read or written on behalf of the process

The statistical information is maintained in the accounting file `/var/adm/pacct`. This file is accessed by many of the accounting commands used with system accounting. After a process terminates, the kernel writes process-specific information to the `/var/adm/pacct` file. This file contains:

- Process owner's user ID
- Command used to start the process
- Process execution time

System accounting provides commands to display, report, and summarize process information. Commands also exist (for example, the `ckpacct` command) to ensure that the process accounting file (`/var/adm/pacct`) does not grow beyond a specific size.

Disk Space Utilization

System accounting provides the ability for the systems administrator to monitor disk utilization by users. To restrict users to a specified disk usage limit, the systems administrator may implement a disk quota system. As a note, systems administrators should be aware that users can evade charges and quota restrictions for disk usage by changing the ownership of their files to that of another user. This allows an unsuspecting user to be charged fees that are rightfully someone else's. Disk usage commands perform three basic functions:

- Collect disk usage by filesystem
- Report disk usage by user
- Gather disk statistics and maintain them in a format that may be used by other system accounting commands for further reporting.

Printer Usage (AIX 4.2)

Printer usage data is stored in the /var/adm/qacct file in ASCII format. The qdaemon will write the ASCII data to the /var/adm/qacct file after a print job is completed. The record of data stored for each printer queue contains the following data:

- User Name
- User number (UID)
- Number of pages printed

Command Definitions

UNIX systems accounting supports numerous commands that can be run via cron and/or the command line. The following discusses some of these commands and the suggested execution method.

Commands That Run Automatically

There are several command entries that the systems administrator must install in the crontab file /var/spool/cron/crontabs/adm to begin collecting accounting data. This is the cron file for the adm user who owns all the accounting files and processes. These commands are intended to be executed by cron in a batch mode, but can be manually executed from the command line.

runacct	Maintains the daily accounting procedures. This command works with the acctmerg command to produce the daily summary report files sorted by user name.

ckpacct	Controls the size of the /var/adm/pacct file. When the /var/adm/pacct file grows larger than a specified number of blocks (default = 1,000 blocks), it turns off accounting and moves the file off to a location equal to /var/adm/pacctx (x is the number of the file). Then ckpacct creates a new /var/adm/pacct for statistics storage. When the amount of free space on the filesystem falls below a designated threshold (default = 500 blocks), ckpacct automatically turns off process accounting. Once the free space exceeds the threshold, ckpacct restarts process accounting.
dodisk	Dodisk produces disk usage accounting records by using the diskusg, acctdusg, and acctdisk commands. In the default case, dodisk creates disk accounting records on the special files. These special filenames are maintained in /etc/fstab for HP-UX 10.x and /etc/filesystems for AIX 4.2.x.
monacct	Uses the daily reports created by the commands above to produce monthly summary reports.
sa1	System accounting data is collected and maintained in binary format in the file /var/adm/sa/sa{dd}, where {dd} is the day of the month.
sa2	This command removes reports from the /var/adm/sa/sa{dd} file that have been there longer than one week. It is also responsible for writing a daily summary report of system activity to the /var/adm/sa/sa{dd} file.

System Accounting Commands That Run Automatically or Manually

startup	When added to the /etc/rc*.d directories, the startup command initiates startup procedures for the accounting system.
shutacct	Records the time accounting was turned off by calling the acctwtmp command to write a line to the /var/adm/wtmp file. It then calls the turnacct off command to turn off process accounting.

Note: For AIX systems, you would modify the /etc/rc file to reflect system accounting run configuration.

Manually Executed Commands

A member of the `adm` group or the user `adm` can execute the following commands:

`ac`	Prints connect-time records. (AIX 4.2)
`acctcom`	Displays process accounting summaries (available to all users).
`acctcon1`	Displays connect-time summaries.
`accton`	Turns process accounting on and off.
`chargefee`	Charges the user a predetermined fee for units of work performed. The charges are added to the daily report by the `acctmerg` command.
`fwtmp`	Converts files between binary and ASCII formats.
`last`	Displays information about previous logins.
`lastcomm`	Displays information about the last commands that were executed.
`lastlogin`	Displays the time each user last logged in.
`prctmp`	Displays session records.
`prtacct`	Displays total accounting files.
`sa`	Summarizes raw accounting information to help manage large volumes of accounting information. (AIX 4.2)
`sadc`	Reports on various local system actions, such as buffer usage, disk and tape I/O activity, TTY device activity counters, and file access counters.
`sar`	Writes to standard output the contents of selected cumulative activity counters in the operating system. The `sar` command reports only on local activities.
`time`	Prints real time, user time, and system time required to execute a command.
`timex`	Reports in seconds the elapsed time, user time, and execution time.

Configuration Procedures

Setting up system accounting involves configuring certain scripts and system files. The following discusses this process in more detail.

Setting Up the AIX 4.2 Accounting System

The first step in configuring AIX 4.2 system accounting is ensuring that the files `pacct` and `wtmp` exist and have the proper permission settings. As `adm`, use the `nulladm` command to set the access permissions to read (r) and write (w) permission for the file owner and group and read (r) permission for others. The nulladm command will also create the files if they do not exist on the system.

```
/usr/sbin/acct/nulladm wtmp pacct
```

A listing of the /var/adm directory structure follows, with the pacct and wtmp files shown:

```
# pwd
/var/adm
# ls -al
drwxrwxr-x    8 root      adm          512 May 10 08:00 .
drwxr-xr-x   14 bin       bin          512 Apr 01 06:03 ..
-rwxr----    1 adm       adm          268 May 09 14:48 .profile
-rw------    1 adm       adm          676 May 09 22:25 .sh_history
drwxrwxr-x    5 adm       adm          512 May 09 13:13 acct
dr-xr-x--     2 bin       cron         512 Apr 01 05:41 cron
-rw-r--r--    1 adm       adm            0 May 09 23:00 dtmp
-rw-rw-r--    1 adm       adm            0 May 09 14:46 fee
-rw-rw-r--    1 adm       adm            0 May 09 16:08 pacct
drwxrwxrwt    2 root      system       512 Apr 01 06:14 ras
drwxrwxr-x    2 adm       adm          512 May 10 00:00 sa
-rw-r--r--    1 root      system      3016 May 09 16:08 savacct
drwxrwxr-x    2 adm       adm          512 Apr 01 05:28 streams
-rw------    1 root      system      1039 May 09 21:32 sulog
drwxr-xr-x    2 root      system       512 Apr 08 08:37 sw
-rw-r--r--    1 root      system       106 May 09 16:08 usracct
-rw-rw-r--    1 adm       adm         4032 May 10 08:46 wtmp
```

The /etc/acct/holidays file contains entries listing prime-time and observed holidays during a given calendar year. Therefore, this file will require the systems administrator to edit it on an annual basis. Prime time must be the first line in the /etc/acct/holidays file that is not a comment. The prime time hours entry is based on a 24-hour clock, with midnight being either 0000 or 2400. Prime time represents the block of core business hours during a 24-hour period when the system resources are in their greatest demand (for example, transactional systems) by the user community. The /etc/acct/holidays file entry for prime time consists of three four-digit fields in the following order:

- Current year
- Beginning of prime time (hhmm)
- End of prime time (hhmm)

For example, to specify the year 1997, with prime time beginning at 7:30 a.m. and ending at 5:30 p.m., add the following line:

```
1997  0730  1730
```

Organizational holidays for the year follow the prime time line, with each line consisting of four fields in the following order:

- Day of the year
- Month
- Day of the month
- Description of holiday

The day-of-the-year field contains the numeric day of year (Julian date format—date +%j) on which the holiday occurs, and must be a number from 1 through 365 (366 in leap year). The other three fields are informational.

A listing of the /etc/acct/holidays file follows:

```
# cat /etc/acct/holidays
* COMPONENT_NAME:   (CMDACCT) Command Accounting
*
* Prime/Nonprime Table for AIX Accounting System
*
* Curr   Prime      Non-Prime
* Year   Start      Start
*
  1997   0730       1730
*
* Day of            Calendar        Company
* Year              Date            Holiday
*
     1              Jan 1           New Year's Day
   146              May 26          Memorial Day (Obsvd.)
   185              Jul 4           Independence Day
   244              Sep 1           Labor Day
   324              Nov 20          Thanksgiving Day
   325              Nov 21          Day after Thanksgiving
   359              Dec 25          Christmas Day
   365              Dec 31          New Years Eve
```

Process accounting is initialized by adding the following line to the /etc/rc program file. /etc/rc is the run control program used when the system is booted to its target run state. The startup procedure records the time that accounting was initialized and cleans up the previous day's accounting files.

```
/usr/bin/su - adm -c /usr/sbin/acct/startup
```

Each filesystem to be included in disk usage accounting must have the account variable set to true in its stanza entry in the /etc/filesystems file. The example stanzas for filesystem /home from /etc/filesystems shows the entry for disk usage accounting set to true and the filesystem stanza for /usr set to false. Therefore, disk usage account will occur for /home and not for /usr.

```
/home:
        dev             = /dev/hd1
        vfs             = jfs
        log             = /dev/hd8
```

```
        mount          = true
        check          = true
        vol            = /home
        free           = false
        account        = true
/usr:
        dev            = /dev/hd2
        vfs            = jfs
        log            = /dev/hd8
        mount          = automatic
        check          = false
        type           = bootfs
        vol            = /usr
        free           = false
    account        = false
```

Each printer queue to be included in printer usage accounting must have the `acctfile` variable pointing to a data file set in the printer queue stanza in `/etc/qconfig`. The sample stanza for the printer queue `HP_laser` from `/etc/qconfig` shows printer usage accounting set to the default data file of `/var/adm/qacct`. Printer queue usage accounting information for the `HP_laser` queue will be stored in `/var/adm/qacct`.

```
HP_Laser:
        device = lp0
        acctfile = /var/adm/qacct
lp0:
        file = /dev/lp0
        header = never
        trailer = never
        access = both
        backend = /usr/lib/lpd/piobe
```

The `nite`, `fiscal` and `sum` directories must exist under `/var/adm/acct` so that storage of system accounting information can be maintained. Create the `/var/adm/acct/nite`, `/var/adm/acct/fiscal`, and `/var/adm/acct/sum` directories with a permissions setting of 755 and with owner and group set to adm. The following generalizes the usage of these directories and shows a sample directory listing of `/var/adm/acct`.

`/var/adm/acct/nite`	Daily data and command files used by `runacct`
`/var/adm/acct/sum`	Summary data and command files used by `runacct` to produce summary reports
`/var/adm/acct/fiscal`	Summary data and command files used by `monacct` to produce monthly reports

```
# pwd
/var/adm/acct
# ls -al
drwxrwxr-x   5 adm      adm           512 May 09 13:13 .
drwxrwxr-x   8 root     adm           512 May 10 10:00 ..
drwxr-xr-x   2 adm      adm           512 May 09 13:13 fiscal
drwxr-xr-x   2 adm      adm           512 May 09 23:10 nite
drwxr-xr-x   2 adm      adm           512 May 09 14:46 sum
#
```

Log in as the adm user and use `crontab -e` to edit the `crontab` file to activate the daily accounting functions. By editing the `/var/spool/cron/crontabs/adm` file, you are allowing `cron` to control the periodic collection and reporting of statistical data. See the example of the `crontab` entries for `runacct`, `dodisk`, `ckpacct`, and `monacct` below:

```
10 23 * * 0-6 /usr/lib/acct/runacct 2>/usr/adm/acct/nite/accterr > /dev/null
0  23 * * 0-6 /usr/lib/acct/dodisk > /dev/null 2>&1
0  *  * * *   /usr/lib/acct/ckpacct > /dev/null 2>&1
15 4  1 * *   /usr/lib/acct/monacct > /dev/null 2>&1
```

The first entry starts the `runacct` at 11:10 p.m. daily to process the active system accounting data files. The second entry starts the `dodisk` command at 11:00 p.m. daily to collect disk usage statistics. The third entry executes the `ckpacct` command every hour of every day to ensure that the system accounting `/var/adm/pacct` file does not exceed the specified default block size (1,000 blocks is the normal default). The fourth and final entry executes the `monacct` command on the first day of the month to generate monthly summary accounting reports. Following is an example of the `/var/spool/cron/crontabs/adm` file with the `runacct`, `dodisk`, `ckpacct`, and `monacct` commands listed:

```
#************************************************************************************************
#
#                    CRONTAB Job listing   -   Administration - System Level
#
#************************************************************************************************
# Min    * Hour   * Day    * Month   * Day    *
# of the * of the * of the * of the  * of the * Command Syntax
# Day    * Day    * Month  * Year    * Week   *
#************************************************************************************************
#
#      PROCESS ACCOUNTING:
#                          runacct at 11:10 every night
#                          dodisk at 11:00 every night
#                          ckpacct every hour on the hour
#                          monthly accounting 4:15 the first of every month
#===============================================================================================
10     23     *     *     0-6   /usr/lib/acct/runacct 2>/usr/adm/acct/nite/accterr >/
➥dev/null
0      23     *     *     0-6   /usr/lib/acct/dodisk >/dev/null 2>&1
0      *      *     *     *     /usr/lib/acct/ckpacct >/dev/null 2>&1
15     4      1     *     *     /usr/lib/acct/monacct >/dev/null 2>&1
#===============================================================================================
```

You are now ready for startup or shutdown of the System Accounting process with the following commands:

```
Startup:
/usr/bin/su - adm -c /usr/lib/acct/startup
```

```
Shutdown:
/usr/bin/su - adm -c /usr/lib/acct/shutacct
```

You may use the following command to verify the state (on or off) of system accounting processes.

```
# fwtmp < /var/adm/wtmp ¦ pg

Sample truncated output:

LOGIN    .xxx.com:  dtremote     6 23528 0000 0000   863276614 Sat May 10 10:03:34
➥EST 1997
root     .xxx.com:  dtremote     7 23528 0000 0000   863276629 Sat May 10 10:03:49
➥EST 1997
LOGIN    .xxx.com:  dtremote     6 20920 0000 0000   863286997 Sat May 10 12:56:37
➥EST 1997
root     pts/2      pts/2        7 25506 0000 0000   863300368 Sat May 10 16:39:28
➥EST 1997
                    AIX, acctg   9     0 0000 0000   863300700 Sat May 10 16:45:00
➥EST 1997
                    accting off  9     0 0000 0000   863301549 Sat May 10 16:59:09
➥EST 1997
                    AIX, acctg   9     0 0000 0000   863301631 Sat May 10 17:00:31
➥EST 1997
```

The above example indicates where the systems administrator started accounting (16:45), shutdown accounting (16:59), and then restarted accounting (17:00).

Setting Up the HP-UX 10.x Accounting System

HP-UX

The System Accounting package is usually installed onto the system when the operating system is configured. The administrator can check this with the following command :

```
#  swlist -l product ¦ grep -i accounting
Accounting              B.10.10          Accounting
```

If the command does not return line 2 (example shown for a 10.10 HP-UX operating system), do not proceed until the "Systems Accounting Package" has been installed.

Once the systems administrator has confirmed that the "Systems Accounting Package" has been installed, he may proceed with the following configuration guidelines.

The first step in configuring HP-UX 10.x system accounting is ensuring that the files pacct and wtmp exist and have the proper permission settings. As root, use the nulladm command to set the access permissions to read (r) and write (w) permission for the file owner and group and read (r) permission for others. The nulladm command will also create the files if they do not exist on the system.

```
# /usr/lib/acct/nulladm wtmp pacct
```

A listing of the /var/adm directory structure follows, with the pacct and wtmp files highlighted:

```
# pwd
/var/adm
# ls -al
drwxrwxr-x   8 root    adm        512 May 10 08:00 .
drwxr-xr-x  14 bin     bin        512 Apr 01 06:03 ..
-rwxr----   1 adm     adm        268 May 09 14:48 .profile
-rw------   1 adm     adm        676 May 09 22:25 .sh_history
drwxrwxr-x   5 adm     adm        512 May 09 13:13 acct
dr-xr-x--   2 bin     cron       512 Apr 01 05:41 cron
```

```
-rw-r--r--   1 adm      adm            0 May 09 23:00 dtmp
-rw-rw-r--   1 adm      adm            0 May 09 14:46 fee
-rw-rw-r--   1 adm      adm            0 May 09 16:08 pacct
drwxrwxrwt   2 root     system       512 Apr 01 06:14 ras
drwxrwxr-x   2 adm      adm          512 May 10 00:00 sa
-rw-r--r--   1 root     system      3016 May 09 16:08 savacct
drwxrwxr-x   2 adm      adm          512 Apr 01 05:28 streams
-rw-------   1 root     system      1039 May 09 21:32 sulog
drwxr-xr-x   2 root     system       512 Apr 08 08:37 sw
-rw-r--r--   1 root     system       106 May 09 16:08 usracct
-rw-rw-r--   1 adm      adm         4032 May 10 08:46 wtmp
#
```

Following the above step, the systems administrator needs to edit the `/etc/rc.config.d/acct` file and set `START_ACCT` equal to one (1). This will start systems accounting each time the system is reset. An example of this is

```
# Process accounting.
#
# START_ACCT: Set to 1 to start process accounting
#
START_ACCT=1
```

The `/etc/acct/holidays` file contains entries listing prime-time and observed holidays during a given calendar year. Therefore, this file will require the systems administrator to edit it on an annual basis. Prime time must be the first line in the `/etc/acct/holidays` file that is not a comment. The prime time hours entry is based on a 24-hour clock, with midnight being either 0000 or 2400. Prime time represents the block of core business hours during a 24-hour period when the system resources are in their greatest demand (transactional systems) by the user community. The `/etc/acct/holidays` file entry for prime time consists of three four-digit fields in the following order:

- Current year
- Beginning of prime time (hhmm)
- End of prime time (hhmm)

For example, to specify the year 1997, with prime time beginning at 7:30 a.m. and ending at 5:30 p.m., add the following line:

```
1997  0730  1730
```

Organizational holidays for the year follow the prime time line, with each line consisting of four fields in the following order:

- Day of the year
- Month
- Day of the month
- Description of holiday

The day-of-the-year field contains the numeric day of year (Julian date format—date +%j) on which the holiday occurs and must be a number from 1 through 365 (366 on leap year). The other three fields are only informational.

A listing of the /etc/acct/holidays file follows:

```
# cat /etc/acct/holidays
* COMPONENT_NAME:  (CMDACCT) Command Accounting
*
* Prime/Nonprime Table for HP-UX Accounting System
*
* Curr  Prime    Non-Prime
* Year  Start    Start
*
  1997  0730     1730
*
* Day of         Calendar       Company
* Year           Date           Holiday
*
    1             Jan 1          New Year's Day
  146             May 26         Memorial Day (Obsvd.)
  185             Jul 4          Independence Day
  244             Sep 1          Labor Day
  324             Nov 20         Thanksgiving Day
  325             Nov 21         Day after Thanksgiving
  359             Dec 25         Christmas Day
  365             Dec 31         New Years Eve
```

Disk Accounting Statistics

Each filesystem to be included in disk usage accounting must, by default, exist in the /etc/fstab file. The dodisk command has the option to accept the special filenames as input from the command line. If this is the case, only those special filenames listed will be included in the accounting process. If you wish to generate a report for a single disk device, for example, a filesystem under Logical Volume Manager (LVM), you would use the following command:

```
# /usr/lib/acct/dodisk    /dev/vg_name/lvol_name
```

> **NOTE**
>
> Logical Volume Manager is Hewlett-Packard's (HP) subsystem for managing disk space. Its main feature is that it allows the systems administrator to group multiple physical disk drives under one filesystem.

If you wish to provide a sublist of filesystems from the /etc/fstab file, through your system editor create a file that contains the special device names for your filesystems—one filesystem per line. You would use the following command to read in a list of special files to include in the disk accounting process:

```
# /usr/lib/acct/dodisk < list.filesystems
```

The nite, fiscal, and sum directories must exist under /var/adm/acct so that storage of system accounting information can be maintained. Create the /var/adm/acct/nite, /var/adm/acct/fiscal, and /var/adm/acct/sum directories with permission settings of 755 with owner and group set to adm. The following generalizes the usage of these directories and shows a sample directory listing of /var/adm/acct.

/var/adm/acct/nite	Daily data and command files used by runacct
/var/adm/acct/sum	Summary data and command files used by runacct to produce summary reports
/var/adm/acct/fiscal	Summary data and command files used by monacct to produce monthly reports

A listing of the /var/adm/acct directory:

```
# pwd
/var/adm/acct
# ls -al
drwxrwxr-x   5 adm      adm          512 May 09 13:13 .
drwxrwxr-x   8 root     adm          512 May 10 10:00 ..
drwxr-xr-x   2 adm      adm          512 May 09 13:13 fiscal
drwxr-xr-x   2 adm      adm          512 May 09 23:10 nite
drwxr-xr-x   2 adm      adm          512 May 09 14:46 sum
#
```

Login as the adm user and use crontab -e to edit the crontab file to activate the daily accounting functions. By editing the /var/spool/cron/crontabs/adm file, you are allowing cron to control the periodic collection and reporting of statistical data. See the example of the crontab entries for runacct, dodisk, ckpacct, and monacct below:

```
10 23 * * 0-6 /usr/lib/acct/runacct 2>/usr/adm/acct/nite/accterr > /dev/null
0  23 * * 0-6 /usr/lib/acct/dodisk > /dev/null 2>&1
0  *  * * *   /usr/lib/acct/ckpacct > /dev/null 2>&1
15 4  1 * *   /usr/lib/acct/monacct > /dev/null 2>&1
```

The first entry starts the runacct command at 11:10 p.m. daily to process the active system accounting data files. The second entry starts the dodisk command at 11:00 p.m. daily to collect disk usage statistics. The third entry executes the ckpacct command every hour of every day to ensure that the system accounting /var/adm/pacct file does not exceed the specified default block size (1,000 blocks is the normal default). The fourth and final entry executes the monacct command on the first day of the month to generate monthly summary accounting reports. Following is an example of the /var/spool/cron/crontabs/adm file with the runacct, dodisk, ckpacct, and monacct commands listed:

```
#***********************************************************************************************
#
#                    CRONTAB Job listing    -   Administration - System Level
#
#***********************************************************************************************
#  Min     *  Hour    * Day     * Month     *  Day     *
# of the   * of the   * of the  * of the    * of the   * Command Syntax
#  Day     * Day      * Month   * Year      * Week     *
#***********************************************************************************************
```

```
#
#       PROCESS ACCOUNTING:
#                               runacct at 11:10 every night
#                               dodisk at 11:00 every night
#                               ckpacct every hour on the hour
#                               monthly accounting 4:15 the first of every month
#
10     23     *     *     0-6     /usr/lib/acct/runacct 2>/usr/adm/acct/nite/accterr
➥>/dev/null
0      23     *     *     0-6     /usr/lib/acct/dodisk >/dev/null 2>&1
0      *      *     *     *       /usr/lib/acct/ckpacct >/dev/null 2>&1
15     4      1     *     *       /usr/lib/acct/monacct >/dev/null 2>&1
#
```

You are now ready for startup or shutdown of the System Accounting process with the following commands:

```
Startup:
/usr/bin/su - adm -c /usr/lib/acct/startup
```

```
Shutdown:
/usr/bin/su - adm -c /usr/lib/acct/shutacct
```

You may use the following command to verify the state (on or off) of System Accounting processes.

```
# fwtmp < /var/adm/wtmp | pg
```

Sample truncated output:

```
rc         sqnc                   90   8 0000 0000 863231977 May  9 21:39:37 1997
getty      cons                 1127   5 0000 0000 863231977 May  9 21:39:37 1997
spserver   ShPr                 1128   5 0000 0000 863231977 May  9 21:39:37 1997
uugetty    a0                   1130   5 0000 0000 863231977 May  9 21:39:37 1997
LOGIN      cons console         1127   6 0000 0000 863231977 May  9 21:39:37 1997
LOGIN      a0   ttyd0p7         1130   6 0000 0000 863231977 May  9 21:39:37 1997
                acctg on          0   9 0000 0000 863232395 May  9 21:46:35 1997
root       p1   ttyp1            634   8 0000 0000 863236183 May  9 22:49:43 1997
LOGIN      p1   pty/ttyp1       1712   6 0000 0000 863270875 May 10 08:27:55 1997
root       p1   ttyp1           1712   7 0000 0003 863270881 May 10 08:28:01 1997
root       p1   ttyp1           1712   8 0000 0000 863281484 May 10 11:24:44 1997
LOGIN      p1   pty/ttyp1       1923   6 0000 0000 863288678 May 10 13:24:38 1997
root       p1   ttyp1           1923   7 0000 0003 863288690 May 10 13:24:50 1997
LOGIN      p2   pty/ttyp2       2155   6 0000 0000 863294925 May 10 15:08:45 1997
                acctg off         0   9 0000 0000 863300425 May 10 16:40:25 1997
```

The above example indicates where the systems administrator started accounting (21:46:35) and shut down accounting (16:40:25).

Setting Up the Solaris 2.5 Accounting System

Begin by making sure that SUNWaccr and SUNWaccu software packages are installed.

```
# pkginfo -l SUNWaccu
```

Sample output:

```
      PKGINST:  SUNWaccu
         NAME:  System Accounting, (Usr)
     CATEGORY:  system
         ARCH:  sparc
      VERSION:  11.5.1,REV=95.10.27.15.23
      BASEDIR:  /
       VENDOR:  Sun Microsystems, Inc.
         DESC:  utilities for accounting and reporting of system activity
       PSTAMP:  raid951027152556
     INSTDATE:  Jun 11 1997 08:13
      HOTLINE:  Please contact your local service provider
       STATUS:  completely installed
        FILES:      43 installed pathnames
                     4 shared pathnames
                     5 directories
                    36 executables
                     1 setuid/setgid executables
                   453 blocks used (approx)
# pkginfo -l SUNWaccr
sample output:
      PKGINST:  SUNWaccr
         NAME:  System Accounting, (Root)
     CATEGORY:  system
         ARCH:  sparc
      VERSION:  11.5.1,REV=95.10.27.15.23
      BASEDIR:  /
       VENDOR:  Sun Microsystems, Inc.
         DESC:  utilities for accounting and reporting of system activity
       PSTAMP:  raid951027152552
     INSTDATE:  Jun 11 1997 08:13
      HOTLINE:  Please contact your local service provider
       STATUS:  completely installed
        FILES:      18 installed pathnames
                     7 shared pathnames
                     1 linked files
                    13 directories
                     2 executables
                     6 blocks used (approx)
```

If you do not receive output similar to the above example listings, use either `pkgadd` or `swmtool` to install these software packages.

Set up the link necessary for starting system accounting at system initialization:

```
# ln /etc/init.d/acct /etc/rc2.d/S22acct
```

Set up the link necessary for shutting down system accounting at system shutdown:

```
# ln /etc/init.d/acct /etc/rc0.d/K22acct
```

Add the following entries to the `/var/spool/cron/crontabs/adm` file:

```
0 * * * * /usr/lib/acct/ckpacct
10 23 * * * /usr/lib/acct/runacct 2> /var/adm/acct/nite/fd2log
15 04 1 * * /usr/lib/acct/monacct
```

Please note that these entries will be processed by `crontab` file for the `adm` user and must follow the `cron` format.

```
#************************************************************************************
#
#                    CRONTAB Job listing   -  adm - System Level
#
#************************************************************************************
#  Min     *  Hour    *  Day     *  Month    *  Day     *
# of the   * of the   * of the   * of the    * of the   *  Command Syntax
#  Day     *  Day     *  Month   *  Year     *  Week    *
#************************************************************************************
#
#      PROCESS ACCOUNTING:
#                          runacct at 11:10 every night
#                          ckpacct every hour on the hour
#                          monthly accounting 4:15 the first of every month
#==================================================================================
10    23    *    *    0-6    /usr/lib/acct/runacct 2>/usr/adm/acct/nite/fd2log
0     *     *    *    *      /usr/lib/acct/ckpacct >/dev/null 2>&1
15    4     1    *    *      /usr/lib/acct/monacct >/dev/null 2>&1
#==================================================================================
```

Add the following entry to the `/var/spool/cron/crontabs/root` file:

```
00 23 * * 0-6 /usr/lib/acct/dodisk >/dev/null 2>&1
```

```
#************************************************************************************
#
#                    CRONTAB Job listing   -  Root - System Level
#
#************************************************************************************
#  Min     *  Hour    *  Day     *  Month    *  Day     *
# of the   * of the   * of the   * of the    * of the   *  Command Syntax
#  Day     *  Day     *  Month   *  Year     *  Week    *
#************************************************************************************
#
#      PROCESS ACCOUNTING:
#                          dodisk at 11:00 every night
#==================================================================================
0     23    *    *    0-6    /usr/lib/acct/dodisk >/dev/null 2>&1
#==================================================================================
```

Adjust `/etc/acct/holidays` to reflect both national and company holidays you want your system to recognize.

A listing of the `/etc/acct/holidays` file follows:

```
# cat /etc/acct/holidays
* COMPONENT_NAME:  (CMDACCT) Command Accounting
*
* Prime/Nonprime Table for Solaris Accounting System
*
* Curr  Prime   Non-Prime
* Year  Start   Start
*
  1997  0730    1730
*
```

```
* Day of        Calendar        Company
* Year          Date            Holiday
*
    1           Jan 1           New Year's Day
  146           May 26          Memorial Day (Obsvd.)
  185           Jul 4           Independence Day
  244           Sep 1           Labor Day
  324           Nov 20          Thanksgiving Day
  325           Nov 21          Day after Thanksgiving
  359           Dec 25          Christmas Day
  365           Dec 31          New Years Eve
```

System accounting can now be started by either rebooting the machine or issuing the runacct command. Take note that executing runacct without any arguments causes the process to assume that this is the first time that runacct has been run for that day. If you are attempting to restart system accounting, be sure to add the appropriate MMDD (MM = Month and DD = Day) argument on the command line.

You are now ready for startup or shutdown of the system accounting process with the following commands:

```
Startup:
/usr/bin/su - adm -c /usr/lib/acct/startup
```

```
Shutdown:
/usr/bin/su - adm -c /usr/lib/acct/shutacct
```

You may use the following command to verify the state (on or off) of System accounting processes.

```
# fwtmp < /var/adm/wtmp ¦ pg
```

Sample truncated output:

```
.telnet  tn20 /dev/pts/4      1118  6 0000 0000 871178077 Sat May  10 20:54:37
1997
root     tn20 pts/4           1118  7 0000 0000 871178098 Sat May  10 20:54:58
1997
              acctg off          0  9 0000 0000 871179345 Sat May  10 16:10:45
1997
              acctg on           0  9 0000 0000 871179352 Sat May  10 21:15:52
1997
```

The above example indicates where the systems administrator started accounting (21:15:52) and shut down accounting (16:10:45).

System Accounting Directory Structure

Most UNIX system accounting takes advantage of a hierarchical (see Figure 21.1) approach when laying out its control and data files. This allows the accounting process to maintain temporary and permanent files in logical locations. Each directory in this layer stores related groups of files, commands, or other subdirectories.

FIGURE 21.1.
System accounting directory structure.

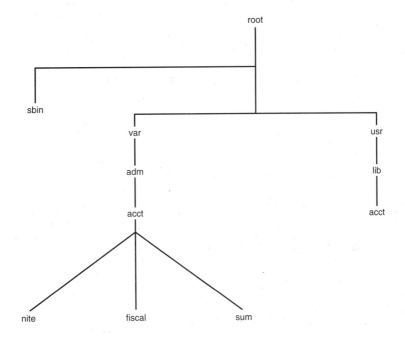

According to systems documentation (HP-UX, AIX, and Solaris), the following system accounting structures are laid out as described in the following sections. Please refer to your system's documentation for more detailed information.

System Accounting High-Level Directory Layout

/var/adm	Maintains data-collection files
/var/adm/acct	Directories for nite, sum, and fiscal
/var/adm/acct/nite	Daily data and command files used by runacct
/var/adm/acct/sum	Summary data and command files used by runacct to produce summary reports
/var/adm/acct/fiscal	Summary data and command files used by monacct to produce monthly reports
/usr/lib/acct	System accounting commands
/sbin	Shell scripts rc and shutdown procedures
/etc/rc.config.d/acct	Set variable START_ACCT equal to 1 to activate accounting at system boot (HP-UX 10.x)
/etc/rc	Run command file that executes at system startup and when the system changes run state

Files in the `/var/adm` directory

`/var/adm/diskdiag`	Diagnostic output during the execution of disk accounting programs
`/var/adm/dtmp`	Output from the `acctdusg` command
`/var/adm/fee`	Output from the `chargefee` command, in ASCII `tacct` records
`/var/adm/pacct`	Active process accounting file
`/var/adm/wtmp`	Active process accounting file
`/var/adm/Spacct?.mmdd`	Process accounting files for `mmdd` during the execution of `runacct`

Files in the `/var/adm/acct/nite` Directory

`{{mmdd}}`	`{{mmdd}}` is the month and day a file was created and is appended to the previous version of the data file.
`active`	Contains warning and error messages generated from `runacct` execution.
`active{{mmdd}}`	Copy of the active file after `runacct` encounters an error condition.
`ctacct.{{mmdd}}`	Total accounting records created from connect session accounting.
`ctmp`	Output of `acctcon1`. It contains a list of login sessions sorted by `userid` and `login` names.
`Daycms`	ASCII daily command summary used by `prdaily`.
`daytacct`	Total accounting records for current day.
`disktacct`	Total accounting records created by the `dodisk` command.
`fd2log`	Diagnostic output from the execution of `runacct`.
`lastdate`	The last day `runacct` was executed, in `+%{{m}}%{{d}}`format.
`lock and lock1`	Used to control serial use of `runacct`.
`lineuse`	Terminal (`tty`) line usage report used by `prdaily`.
`log`	Diagnostics output from `acctcon1`.
`log{{mmdd}}`	Same as `log` after `runacct` detects an error.
`reboots`	Contains beginning and ending dates from `wtmp`, and a listing of reboots.
`statefile`	Used to record the current state being executed by `runacct`.

tmpwtmp	wtmp file, corrected by wtmpfix.
wtmperror	Error messages, if any, from wtmpfix.
wtmperrorr{{mmdd}}	Same as wtmperror after runacct detects an error.
wtmp.{{mmdd}}	The previous day's wtmp file.

Files in the /var/adm/acct/sum Directory

cms	Total command summary file for current month in internal summary format.
cmsprev	Command summary file without latest update.
daycms	Command summary file for previous day in internal summary format.
loginlog	Shows the last login date for each user.
rpt{{mmdd}}	Daily accounting report for date {{mmdd}}.
tacct	Cumulative total accounting file for current month.
tacctprev	Same as tacct without latest update.
tacct{{mmdd}}	Total accounting file for date {{mmdd}}.
wtmp.{{mmdd}}	Saved copy of wtmp file for date {{mmdd}}. Removed after reboot.

Files in the /var/adm/acct/fiscal Directory

cms{mm}	Total command summary for month {mm} in internal summary format.
Fiscrpt{mm}	Report similar to prdaily for the month {mm}.
tacct{mm}	Total accounting file for the month {mm}.

The acctmerg command can convert records between ASCII and binary formats and merge records from different sources into a single record for each user.

System Accounting Report Generation

After completing system accounting configuration, your system is ready to produce accounting reports. The following covers the basics of report generation for Systems Accounting.

Generation of System Accounting Data Reports

acctcom

The acctcom utility allows you to see the accounting system data at any given time. This command may be executed from the command line with several different options. It is one of the most useful commands for getting a quick report from the system without the need to find a file.

This option will show the average statistics about processes.

```
$ acctcom -a
```

An example of a truncated listing:

COMMAND NAME	USER	TTYNAME	START TIME	END TIME	REAL (SECS)	CPU (SECS)	MEAN SIZE(K)
#accton	root	_	17:57:07	17:57:07	0.00	0.00	56.00
#acctwtmp	root	pts/2	17:57:07	17:57:07	0.00	0.00	60.00
#fwtmp	root	pts/2	17:57:07	17:57:07	0.03	0.00	160.00
#awk	root	pts/2	17:57:07	17:57:07	0.02	0.02	106.00
#fwtmp	root	pts/2	17:57:07	17:57:07	0.05	0.00	0.00
#dspmsg	root	pts/2	17:57:07	17:57:07	0.00	0.00	0.00
#cat	root	pts/2	17:57:07	17:57:07	0.00	0.00	336.00
#wtmpfix	root	pts/2	17:57:07	17:57:07	0.05	0.00	0.00
#dspmsg	root	pts/2	17:57:07	17:57:07	0.02	0.02	192.00
#acctcon1	root	pts/2	17:57:08	17:57:08	0.17	0.02	96.00
#sort	root	pts/2	17:57:08	17:57:08	0.25	0.00	82.00
#acctcon2	root	pts/2	17:57:08	17:57:08	0.05	0.00	168.00
#acctmerg	root	pts/2	17:57:08	17:57:08	0.05	0.00	0.00
#dspmsg	root	pts/2	17:57:08	17:57:08	0.00	0.00	0.00
#basename	root	pts/2	17:57:08	17:57:08	0.03	0.00	138.00
#sed	root	pts/2	17:57:08	17:57:08	0.03	0.00	136.00
#acctprc1	root	pts/2	17:57:08	17:57:08	0.05	0.02	184.00
#acctprc2	root	pts/2	17:57:08	17:57:08	0.05	0.00	68.00
#acctmerg	root	pts/2	17:57:08	17:57:08	0.02	0.00	0.00
#mv	root	pts/2	17:57:08	17:57:08	0.02	0.00	0.00
#acctcms	root	pts/2	17:57:09	17:57:09	0.02	0.00	96.00
#lsuser	root	pts/2	17:57:09	17:57:09	0.86	0.20	89.00
#grep	root	pts/2	17:57:09	17:57:09	0.86	0.00	164.00
#uniq	root	pts/2	17:57:10	17:57:10	0.05	0.00	0.00
#egrep	root	?	17:57:22	17:57:22	0.03	0.02	114.00
.							
.							
.							
#tail	root	?	18:23:09	18:23:09	0.05	0.00	148.00
#fgrep	root	?	18:24:10	18:24:10	0.00	0.00	0.00
#egrep	root	?	18:24:10	18:24:10	0.00	0.00	0.00
#acctcom	root	pts/2	18:24:28	18:24:28	0.39	0.27	58.00

```
cmds=287 Real=2.92   CPU=0.04   USER=0.01   SYS=0.03   CHAR=29767.60 BLK=0.00
➥USR/TOT=0.24 HOG=1.20
```

This option will show the amount of user time per total time (system time plus user time).

```
$ acctcom -r
```

An example of a truncated listing:

COMMAND NAME	USER	TTYNAME	START TIME	END TIME	REAL (SECS)	CPU (SECS)	CPU FACTOR
#accton	root	_	17:57:07	17:57:07	0.00	0.00	0.00
#bsh	root	pts/2	17:57:06	17:57:06	0.20	0.02	0.00
#mv	root	pts/2	17:57:07	17:57:07	0.02	0.02	0.00
#cp	root	pts/2	17:57:07	17:57:07	0.02	0.02	1
#acctwtmp	root	pts/2	17:57:07	17:57:07	0.02	0.00	0.00
#fwtmp	root	pts/2	17:57:07	17:57:07	0.02	0.00	0.00

```
#awk       root       pts/2    17:57:07 17:57:07    0.03     0.02      0.00
#sed       root       pts/2    17:57:07 17:57:07    0.03     0.00      0.00
#fwtmp     root       pts/2    17:57:07 17:57:07    0.08     0.02         1
#cp        root       pts/2    17:57:07 17:57:07    0.02     0.00      0.00
#chmod     root       pts/2    17:57:07 17:57:07    0.00     0.00      0.00
#chown     root       pts/2    17:57:07 17:57:07    0.02     0.00      0.00
#bsh       root       pts/2    17:57:07 17:57:07    0.08     0.02      0.00
#acctwtmp  root       pts/2    17:57:07 17:57:07    0.00     0.00      0.00
#fwtmp     root       pts/2    17:57:07 17:57:07    0.03     0.00      0.00
 .
 .
 .
#telnet    root       _        17:37:21 18:28:39 3078.00     2.14     0.124
#egrep     root       ?        18:31:47 18:31:47    0.02     0.00      0.00
#tail      root       ?        18:31:47 18:31:47    0.06     0.02      0.00
sendmail   root       ?        18:33:32 18:33:32    0.02     0.00      0.00
#acctcom   root       pts/2    18:33:51 18:33:51    0.47     0.36     0.304
```

This option will show all the processes that have been executed by the user wdwood.

```
$ acctcom -u wdwood
```

An example of a truncated listing:

```
COMMAND                     START     END      REAL     CPU      MEAN
NAME       USER     TTYNAME  TIME      TIME     (SECS)   (SECS)   SIZE(K)
#accton    wdwood   _        17:57:07 17:57:07   0.00     0.00     56.00
#bsh       wdwood   pts/2    17:57:06 17:57:06   0.20     0.02      0.00
#mv        wdwood   pts/2    17:57:07 17:57:07   0.02     0.02      0.00
#cp        wdwood   pts/2    17:57:07 17:57:07   0.02     0.02    182.00
#acctwtmp  wdwood   pts/2    17:57:07 17:57:07   0.02     0.00      0.00
#fwtmp     wdwood   pts/2    17:57:07 17:57:07   0.02     0.00      0.00
#awk       wdwood   pts/2    17:57:07 17:57:07   0.03     0.02    121.00
#sed       wdwood   pts/2    17:57:07 17:57:07   0.03     0.00      0.00
#fwtmp     wdwood   pts/2    17:57:07 17:57:07   0.08     0.02    108.00
#cp        wdwood   pts/2    17:57:07 17:57:07   0.02     0.00     72.00
#chmod     wdwood   pts/2    17:57:07 17:57:07   0.00     0.00      0.00
#chown     wdwood   pts/2    17:57:07 17:57:07   0.02     0.00     86.00
#bsh       wdwood   pts/2    17:57:07 17:57:07   0.08     0.02    130.00
 .
 .
 .
#dspmsg    wdwood   pts/2    18:38:08 18:38:08   0.02     0.00      0.00
#bsh       wdwood   pts/2    18:38:07 18:38:08   1.08     0.02     97.00
#more      wdwood   pts/2    18:38:20 18:38:26   6.66     0.02      0.00
#acctcom   wdwood   pts/2    18:38:38 18:38:38   0.48     0.33     35.00
#cat       wdwood   pts/2    18:38:45 18:38:45   0.02     0.00    170.00
```

This option will show all the processes, for any user, running longer than 20 seconds.

```
$ acctcom -O 20
```

```
COMMAND                     START     END      REAL     CPU      MEAN
NAME       USER     TTYNAME  TIME      TIME     (SECS)   (SECS)   SIZE(K)
#find      wdwood   _        18:18:43 18:19:05  22.58     6.45     30.00
```

To see more options for the acctcom command, or any of the system accounting commands, please refer to your man pages or system documentation manuals.

Daily Automated Reports

The system accounting processes generate a number of automated reports that can assist the systems administrator in viewing the daily usage of a system.

The Daily Report	Shows the usage of ports on your system.
The Daily Usage Report	Shows the system resources used by your users during a daily period.
The Total Command Summary Report	Shows the commands run on your system and the resources those commands used. This report can be essential in helping you determine the processes that might cause a potential bottleneck in your system.
Daily Systems Accounting Summary Report	Tells you the last time a login ID was used to access the system. This report may be used to help you identify login IDs no longer in use.

The Daily Report

The Daily Report is found in the /var/adm/acct/nite directory. It is an ASCII file called lineuse and can be viewed with any available text viewer or editor.

```
$ cat /var/adm/acct/nite/lineuse
```

Sample file contents:

```
TOTAL DURATION: 474 MINUTES

LINE        MINUTES    PERCENT    # SESS    # ON    # OFF
dtremote    173        36         1         1       2
1ft0        0          0          0         0       1
pts/0       0          0          0         0       1
pts/1       0          0          0         0       1
pts/2       77         16         3         3       4
TOTALS      250        - -        4         4       9
```

The definitions of each column in this report are as follows:

LINE	The port that was used to access the system.
MINUTES	The number of minutes the port was active during this daily period.
PERCENT	The number of minutes the port was active divided by the TOTAL DURATION factor. TOTAL DURATION is the sum of the minutes the system was a multi-user run state.

# SESS	The number of times the port was accessed to log in to the system.
# ON	The number of times the port was used for login purposes.
# OFF	The number of logoffs handled by that port and the number of interrupts like Ctrl+c, EOF, and so on.

The Daily Usage Report

The Daily Usage Report is found in the /var/adm/acct directory. It is a binary file called daytacct that is to be accessed with the prtacct accounting command.

```
$ prtacct -v /var/adm/acct/nite/daytacct

Fri May  9 16:02:04 EST 1997  Page 1
```

UID	LOGIN NAME	CPU # OF PRIME SESS	CPU # OF NPRIME SAMPLES	KCORE # DISK PRIME	KCORE NPRIME	CONNECT PRIME	CONNECT NPRIME	DISK BLOCKS	FEES PROCS
0	TOTAL	0	0	0	0	9448	14739	0	
0	0	83	0						
0	japierce	0	0	0	0	8526	13904	0	
0	0	46	0						
0	dwilson	0	0	0	0	508	814	0	
0	0	21	0						
0	kvwood	0	0	0	0	412	0	0	
0	0	8	0						
223	wpierce	0	0	0	0	0	21	0	
0	0	5	0						
237	awilson	0	0	0	0	1	0	0	
0	0	2	0						
273	wdwood	0	0	0	0	1	0	0	
0	0	1	0						

The definitions of each column in this report are as follows:

UID	The user's identification number.
LOGIN NAME	The user's name.
CPU prime/non prime	The amount of time the user's program required the use of the CPU. This is rounded up to the nearest minute.
KCORE prime/non prime	The amount of memory per minute used to run the programs. This is rounded up to the nearest kilobyte.
CONNECT prime/non prime	Total time the user was actually connected to the system.
DISK BLOCKS	The number of disk blocks used.
# OF PROCS	The number of processes the user executed.

# OF SESS	The number of sessions the user incurred by logging in.
# DISK SAMPLES	The number of times acctdusg or diskusg was run to cumulate the average number of DISK BLOCKS.
FEE	The total amount of usage charges accessed to the user for this given period.

Daily Command Summary Report and Total Command Summary Report

The Daily Command Summary Report is found in the /var/adm/acct/nite directory. It is an ASCII file called daycms and can be viewed with any available text viewer or editor.

```
$ cat /var/adm/acct/nite/daycms
```

TOTAL COMMAND SUMMARY

COMMAND NAME CHARS TRNSFD	NUMBER CMDS BLOCKS READ	TOTAL KCOREMIN	TOTAL CPU-MIN	TOTAL REAL-MIN	MEAN SIZE-K	MEAN CPU-MIN	HOG FACTOR
TOTALS 6.636e+06	82 0.00	12.68	0.06	21.91	209.92	0.00	0.28
man 5.566e+06	1 0.00	7.56	0.02	1.68	440.00	0.02	1.02
vi 71936.00	1 0.00	2.24	0.02	0.53	121.00	0.02	3.49
ls 117144.00	5 0.00	1.15	0.01	0.02	108.15	0.00	68.33
fgrep 286776.00	14 0.00	0.39	0.00	0.01	124.17	0.00	42.86
tail 142744.00	14 0.00	0.36	0.00	0.02	126.82	0.00	18.03
bsh 49410.00	6 0.00	0.28	0.00	0.01	99.27	0.00	27.50
ps 19696.00	1 0.00	0.21	0.00	0.00	137.00	0.00	66.67
ftpd 41576.00	1 0.00	0.20	0.00	0.81	155.00	0.00	0.16
sendmail 13744.00	1 0.00	0.12	0.00	0.00	468.00	0.00	100.00
fwtmp 35840.00	3 0.00	0.07	0.00	0.00	143.00	0.00	25.00
more 30144.00	2 0.00	0.05	0.00	2.41	195.00	0.00	0.01
pg 61232.00	3 0.00	0.03	0.00	14.78	28.50	0.00	0.01
ksh 18360.00	2 0.00	0.00	0.00	0.00	0.00	0.00	0.00
rm 0.00	6 0.00	0.00	0.00	0.00	0.00	0.00	0.00
accton 0.00	2 0.00	0.00	0.00	0.00	0.00	0.00	0.00
acctwtmp 128.00	2 0.00	0.00	0.00	0.00	0.00	0.00	0.00
egrep 143976.00	14 0.00	0.00	0.00	0.00	0.00	0.00	0.00

grep	1	0.00	0.00	0.00	0.00	0.00	0.00
23976.00	0.00						
dspmsg	2	0.00	0.00	0.00	0.00	0.00	0.00
8214.00	0.00						
sh	1	0.00	0.00	1.64	0.00	0.00	0.02
5058.00	0.00						

The Total Command Summary Report looks like the preceding report with one exception. It is usually a monthly summary showing total accumulated since the last month or the last execution of monacct. The Total Command Summary Report is found in the /var/adm/acct/sum directory. It is an ASCII file called cms and can be viewed with any available text viewer or editor.

The definitions of each column in this report are as follows:

COMMAND NAME	The name of the command.
NUMBER COMMANDS	The total number of times the command has been executed.
KCOREMIN	The total cumulative kilobytes segments used by the command.
TOTAL CPU-MIN	The total processing time in minutes.
REAL-MIN	The actual processing time in minutes.
MEAN SIZE-K	The mean of TOTAL KCOREMIN divided by execution.
MENU CPU-MIN	The mean of executions divided by total processing time in minutes.
HOG FACTOR	The total processing time divided by elapsed time. This is the utilization ratio of the system.
CHARS TRNSFD	The total number of reads and writes to the filesystem.
BLOCKS READ	The total number of physical block reads and writes.

Daily Systems Accounting Summary Report

This report is generated by the runacct command via cron. This report is found in the /var/adm/acct/sum directory and is a file whose format is rprt{MMDD}. This file is a summary report of daily activity for the system. The Daily Systems Accounting Summary Report is found in the /var/adm/acct/sum directory. It is an ASCII file and can be viewed with any available text viewer or editor. An example of this report follows:

```
$ cat /var/adm/acct/sum/rprt0510

Sat May 10 21:41:50 EST 1997 DAILY REPORT FOR AIX Page 1


from Sat May 10 21:27:28 EST 1997
to   Sat May 10 21:41:46 EST 1997
1    openacct
1    runacct
1    acctcon1
```

```
TOTAL DURATION: 14 MINUTES

LINE      MINUTES    PERCENT    # SESS    # ON    # OFF
lft0      14         100        1         1       1
pts/0     14         100        1         1       1
pts/1     14         100        1         1       1
pts/2     14         100        1         1       1
pts/3     14         100        1         1       1
TOTALS    72         --         5         5       5
```

```
Sat May 10 21:41:50 EST 1997 DAILY USAGE REPORT FOR AIX Page 1
```

UID NAME	LOGIN FEES	CPU # OF PRIME SESS	CPU # OF NPRIME SAMPLES	# DISK	KCORE PRIME	KCORE NPRIME	CONNECT PRIME	CONNECT NPRIME	DISK BLOCKS
	PROCS								
0 TOTAL	0	0	0	0	0	7	0	72	5
0	216	5	4						
0 root	0	0	0	0	0	1	0	72	1
0	28	5	1						
2 bin	0	0	0	0	0	0	0	0	1
0	0	0	1						
4 adm	0	0	0	0	0	6	0	0	0
0	188	0	0						
100 guest	0	0	0	0	0	0	0	0	1
0	0	0	1						
200 servdir	0	0	0	0	0	0	0	0	2
0	0	0	1						

```
Sat May 10 21:41:48 EST 1997 DAILY COMMAND SUMMARY Page 1
```

				TOTAL COMMAND SUMMARY				
COMMAND NAME CHARS TRNSFD	NUMBER CMDS BLOCKS READ	TOTAL KCOREMIN	TOTAL CPU-MIN	TOTAL REAL-MIN	MEAN SIZE-K	MEAN CPU-MIN	HOG FACTOR	
TOTALS 1.707e+07	216 4094.00	6.91	0.05	7.42	132.59	0.00	0.70	
diskusg 1.625e+07	1 4094.00	3.73	0.03	0.11	142.00	0.03	23.22	
bsh 49810.00	15 0.00	1.28	0.01	0.24	129.47	0.00	4.20	
awk 48971.00	6 0.00	0.27	0.00	0.00	175.67	0.00	37.50	
ls 37662.00	6 0.00	0.25	0.00	0.00	136.14	0.00	87.50	
tail 61176.00	6 0.00	0.13	0.00	0.01	96.80	0.00	18.52	
sendmail 13744.00	1 0.00	0.12	0.00	0.00	462.00	0.00	100.00	

dspmsg	18	0.11	0.00	0.00	212.00	0.00	33.33
74259.00	0.00						
cat	17	0.11	0.00	0.00	136.00	0.00	60.00
1615.00	0.00						
acctcms	4	0.10	0.00	0.00	201.00	0.00	50.00
65520.00	0.00						
fgrep	6	0.09	0.00	0.00	84.25	0.00	36.36
122904.00	0.00						
sort	7	0.09	0.00	0.03	112.00	0.00	3.03
15302.00	0.00						
acctmerg	6	0.08	0.00	0.00	105.00	0.00	37.50
9064.00	0.00						
vi	1	0.07	0.00	0.11	127.00	0.00	0.48
17912.00	0.00						
egrep	6	0.06	0.00	0.00	124.00	0.00	33.33
61704.00	0.00						
chown	14	0.06	0.00	0.00	48.80	0.00	35.71
15988.00	0.00						
grep	3	0.06	0.00	0.01	121.00	0.00	3.70
7971.00	0.00						
date	9	0.05	0.00	0.00	198.00	0.00	50.00
169.00	0.00						
acctprc1	1	0.04	0.00	0.00	74.00	0.00	66.67
23672.00	0.00						
acctcon1	1	0.04	0.00	0.00	142.00	0.00	50.00
7883.00	0.00						
uniq	3	0.04	0.00	0.02	142.00	0.00	1.16
6269.00	0.00						
ypcat	2	0.03	0.00	0.00	129.00	0.00	6.25
58000.00	0.00						
more	1	0.03	0.00	6.82	101.00	0.00	0.00
11384.00	0.00						
pr	5	0.02	0.00	0.00	94.00	0.00	14.29
26094.00	0.00						
rm	7	0.02	0.00	0.00	82.00	0.00	9.09
5058.00	0.00						
lsuser	1	0.01	0.00	0.01	19.00	0.00	7.14
4600.00	0.00						
sed	7	0.00	0.00	0.01	0.00	0.00	0.00
30745.00	0.00						
fwtmp	4	0.00	0.00	0.00	0.00	0.00	10.00
10270.00	0.00						
getopt	3	0.00	0.00	0.00	0.00	0.00	0.00
48.00	0.00						
chmod	15	0.00	0.00	0.00	0.00	0.00	0.00
0.00	0.00						
acctwtmp	2	0.00	0.00	0.00	0.00	0.00	0.00
128.00	0.00						
uname	1	0.00	0.00	0.00	0.00	0.00	0.00
4.00	0.00						
wtmpfix	1	0.00	0.00	0.00	0.00	0.00	0.00
3072.00	0.00						
mv	7	0.00	0.00	0.00	0.00	0.00	0.00
5058.00	0.00						
acctcon2	1	0.00	0.00	0.00	0.00	0.00	100.00
660.00	0.00						
accton	1	0.00	0.00	0.00	0.00	0.00	0.00
0.00	0.00						
df	1	0.00	0.00	0.00	0.00	0.00	0.00
733.00	0.00						

COMMAND NAME	NUMBER CMDS	KCOREMIN	CPU-MIN	REAL-MIN	SIZE-K	CPU-MIN	FACTOR
basename	2	0.00	0.00	0.00	0.00	0.00	0.00
23.00	0.00						
expr	1	0.00	0.00	0.00	0.00	0.00	0.00
2.00	0.00						
cp	19	0.00	0.00	0.00	0.00	0.00	0.00
10012.00	0.00						
wc	1	0.00	0.00	0.00	0.00	0.00	0.00
1203.00	0.00						
acctprc2	1	0.00	0.00	0.00	0.00	0.00	0.00
12736.00	0.00						
acctdisk	1	0.00	0.00	0.00	0.00	0.00	0.00
339.00	0.00						
ln	1	0.00	0.00	0.00	0.00	0.00	0.00
0.00	0.00						

Sat May 10 21:41:48 EST 1997 MONTHLY TOTAL COMMAND SUMMARY Page 1

TOTAL COMMAND SUMMARY

COMMAND NAME / CHARS TRNSFD	NUMBER CMDS / BLOCKS READ	TOTAL KCOREMIN	TOTAL CPU-MIN	TOTAL REAL-MIN	MEAN SIZE-K	MEAN CPU-MIN	HOG FACTOR
TOTALS	1771	281.68	1.22	706.08	231.12	0.00	0.17
1.423e+08	4094.00						
dtterm	2	136.19	0.24	81.83	566.58	0.12	0.29
333760.00	0.00						
man	11	79.59	0.18	4.64	431.09	0.02	3.98
5.915e+07	0.00						
bsh	135	7.74	0.06	13.13	124.32	0.00	0.47
705187.00	0.00						
find	2	6.64	0.21	0.74	31.00	0.11	28.78
13764.00	0.00						
lsuser	24	5.85	0.08	0.28	72.03	0.00	29.21
117880.00	0.00						
ksh	27	4.60	0.03	189.72	178.53	0.00	0.01
637811.00	0.00						
crash	1	3.89	0.02	3.19	237.00	0.02	0.51
2.635e+07	0.00						
diskusg	1	3.73	0.03	0.11	142.00	0.03	23.22
1.625e+07	4094.00						
acctcom	18	3.30	0.05	0.09	62.18	0.00	62.01
839000.00	0.00						
telnet	2	3.25	0.05	79.10	65.62	0.02	0.06
417920.00	0.00						
errpt	8	3.13	0.01	0.03	267.40	0.00	41.67
2.129e+06	0.00						
telnetd	5	2.40	0.06	107.89	40.19	0.01	0.06
762960.00	0.00						
tail	102	2.31	0.02	0.26	99.48	0.00	8.77
1.04e+06	0.00						
fgrep	102	2.03	0.02	0.05	113.25	0.00	37.30
2.089e+06	0.00						
ls	75	2.00	0.02	0.04	116.15	0.00	45.21
603775.00	0.00						

vi	16	1.46	0.01	37.87	116.81	0.00	0.03
330912.00	0.00						
more	35	1.21	0.01	26.19	125.30	0.00	0.04
518424.00	0.00						
awk	25	0.96	0.01	0.04	175.33	0.00	14.09
141725.00	0.00						
dspmsg	98	0.74	0.00	0.01	166.24	0.00	50.00
493457.00	0.00						
uniq	50	0.69	0.01	0.55	115.74	0.00	1.09
142133.00	0.00						
grep	33	0.59	0.00	0.30	126.22	0.00	1.54
237104.00	0.00						
ps	6	0.59	0.01	0.03	86.88	0.00	25.49
104784.00	0.00						
rm	75	0.59	0.01	0.04	75.23	0.00	17.75
404784.00	0.00						
file	13	0.52	0.00	0.01	110.83	0.00	36.00
461053.00	0.00						
sort	59	0.52	0.01	0.55	90.45	0.00	1.04
280988.00	0.00						
sendmail	8	0.48	0.00	0.00	463.00	0.00	44.44
109952.00	0.00						
date	96	0.46	0.00	0.01	194.89	0.00	33.33
21536.00	0.00						
acctcms	15	0.42	0.00	0.01	179.22	0.00	45.00
267903.00	0.00						
acctcon1	16	0.41	0.00	0.01	142.45	0.00	22.92
180989.00	0.00						
egrep	102	0.40	0.00	0.02	102.33	0.00	16.13
1.049e+06	0.00						
chown	49	0.38	0.01	0.01	55.54	0.00	49.06
155734.00	0.00						
sh	26	0.34	0.00	4.22	131.70	0.00	0.06
156818.00	0.00						
ftpd	1	0.33	0.00	57.30	212.00	0.00	0.00
184320.00	0.00						
acctprc2	3	0.30	0.00	0.01	130.00	0.00	39.13
91430.00	0.00						
lslpp	4	0.28	0.00	0.03	135.75	0.00	8.25
108864.00	0.00						
sadc	4	0.28	0.01	0.08	24.09	0.00	13.92
2.402e+07	0.00						
strings	7	0.27	0.00	0.00	95.00	0.00	61.11
76242.00	0.00						
cp	84	0.26	0.00	0.02	166.67	0.00	7.79
28181.00	0.00						
cat	66	0.26	0.00	0.01	163.33	0.00	27.27
93983.00	0.00						
sed	44	0.25	0.00	0.28	117.75	0.00	0.74
245587.00	0.00						
acctprc1	4	0.24	0.00	2.77	115.25	0.00	0.08
167963.00	0.00						
mv	36	0.21	0.00	11.51	81.50	0.00	0.02
61310.00	0.00						
servdir.	4	0.17	0.00	0.19	79.87	0.00	1.10
2876.00	0.00						
ibm.psa	4	0.16	0.00	0.05	105.17	0.00	3.12
60576.00	0.00						

```
termdef          8     0.14     0.00     0.00    182.00     0.00     50.00
80960.00       0.00
acctmerg        24     0.14     0.00     0.01     74.14     0.00     17.50
49956.00       0.00
chmod           65     0.13     0.00     0.00    121.50     0.00     33.33
50596.00       0.00
pr              20     0.12     0.00     0.01    155.33     0.00      6.52
83028.00       0.00
ibmelh.p         4     0.12     0.00     0.03     76.50     0.00      5.88
41760.00       0.00
uname           13     0.09     0.00     0.01     89.00     0.00     15.38
91318.00       0.00
```

```
Sat May 10 21:41:49 EST 1997 LAST LOGIN Page 1


00-00-00  guest      00-00-00  jwpierce     97-05-09  enwilson
00-00-00  lpd        97-05-09  bmwood       97-05-09  bmwood2
00-00-00  nuucp      97-05-09  sawood       97-05-10  root
00-00-00  servdir    97-05-09  tswilson
```

Summary

This chapter explained the basics of UNIX system accounting, provided a list of commands and their respective definitions, and supplied configuration procedures for HP-UX 10.x and IBM AIX 4.2. The system accounting directory structure was discussed, and accounting reports were defined and generated. This information may be used by a number of individuals to

- Establish an equitable charge back system
- Monitor overall system resource usage
- Use as a basis for establishing resource quota requirements
- Provide information to management for cost justification
- Forecast

This chapter has provided basic information for the systems administrator to implement systems accounting. Used properly, the information can be of great value in helping to manage current resources in a fair manner for all users and processes. This information will also help justify, from a cost basis, future computer purchases.

## CHAPTER 22

Performance and Tuning

by Ronald Rose; edited by Chris Byers

IN THIS CHAPTER

Chapter 21, "System Accounting," teaches about the UNIX accounting system, and the tools that the accounting system provides. Some of these utilities and reports give you information about system utilization and performance. Some of these can be used when investigating performance problems.

In this portion of the book, you will learn all about performance monitoring. There are a series of commands that enable system administrators, programmers, and users to examine each of the resources that a UNIX system uses. By examining these resources you can determine if the system is operating properly or poorly. More important than the commands themselves, you will also learn strategies and procedures that can be used to search for performance problems. Armed with both the commands and the overall methodologies with which to use them, you will understand the factors that are affecting system performance, and what can be done to optimize them so that the system performs at its best.

Although this chapter is helpful for users, it is particularly directed at new system administrators that are actively involved in keeping the system they depend on healthy, or trying to diagnose what has caused its performance to deteriorate.

This chapter introduces several new tools to use in your system investigations.

The sequence of the chapter is not based on particular commands. It is instead based on the steps and the strategies that you will use during your performance investigations. In other words, the chapter is organized to mirror the logical progression that a system administrator uses to determine the state of the overall system and the status of each of its subsystems.

You will frequently start your investigations by quickly looking at the overall state of the system load, as described in the section "Monitoring the Overall System Status." To do this you see how the commands uptime and sar can be used to examine the system load and the general level of Central Processing Unit (CPU) loading. You also see how tools such as SunOS's perfmeter can be helpful in gaining a graphic, high-level view of several components at once.

Next, in the section "Monitoring Processes with ps," you learn how ps can be used to determine the characteristics of the processes that are running on your system. This is a natural next step after you have determined that the overall system status reflects a heavier-than-normal loading. You will learn how to use ps to look for processes that are consuming inordinate amounts of resources and the steps to take after you have located them.

After you have looked at the snapshot of system utilization that ps gives you, you may well have questions about how to use the memory or disk subsystems. So, in the next section, "Monitoring Memory Utilization," you learn how to monitor memory performance with tools such as vmstat and sar, and how to detect when paging and swapping have become excessive (thus indicating that memory must be added to the system).

In the section "Monitoring Disk Subsystem Performance," you see how tools such as iostat, sar, and df can be used to monitor disk Input/Output (I/O) performance. You will see how to determine when your disk subsystem is unbalanced and what to do to alleviate disk performance problems.

After the section on disk I/O performance is a related section on network performance. (It is related to the disk I/O discussion because of the prevalent use of networks to provide extensions of local disk service through such facilities as NFS.) Here you learn to use `netstat`, `nfsstat`, and `spray` to determine the condition of your network.

This is followed by a brief discussion of CPU performance monitoring, and finally a section on kernel tuning. In this final section, you will learn about the underlying tables that reside within the UNIX operating system and how they can be tuned to customize your system's UNIX kernel and optimize its use of resources.

You have seen before in this book that the diversity of UNIX systems makes it important to check each vendor's documentation for specific details about their particular implementation. The same thing applies here as well. Furthermore, modern developments such as symmetric multiprocessor support and relational databases add new characteristics and problems to the challenge of performance monitoring. These are touched on briefly in the discussions that follow.

Performance and Its Impact on Users

Before you get into the technical side of UNIX performance monitoring, there are a few guidelines that can help system administrators avoid performance problems and maximize their overall effectiveness.

All too typically, the UNIX system administrator learns about performance when there is a critical problem with the system. Perhaps the system is taking too long to process jobs or is far behind on the number of jobs that it normally processes. Perhaps the response times for users have deteriorated to the point where users are becoming distracted and unproductive (which is a polite way of saying frustrated and angry!). In any case, if the system isn't actually failing to help its users attain their particular goals, it is at least failing to meet their expectations.

It may seem obvious that when user productivity is being affected, money and time, and sometimes a great deal of both, are being lost. Simple measurements of the amount of time lost can often provide the cost justification for upgrades to the system. In this chapter you learn how to identify which components of the system are the best candidates for such an upgrade. (If you think people were unhappy to begin with, try talking to them after an expensive upgrade has produced no discernible improvement in performance!)

Often, it is only when users begin complaining that people begin to examine the variables that are affecting performance. This in itself is somewhat of a problem. The system administrator should have a thorough understanding of the activities on the system before users are affected by a crisis. He should know the characteristics of each group of users on the system. This includes the type of work that they submit while they are present during the day, as well as the jobs that are to be processed during the evening. What is the size of the CPU requirement, the I/O requirement, and the memory requirement of the most frequently occurring or the most important jobs? What impact do these jobs have on the networks connected to the machine? Also important is the time-sensitivity of the jobs, the classic example being payrolls that must be completed by a given time and date.

These profiles of system activity and user requirements can help the system administrator acquire a holistic understanding of the activity on the system. That knowledge will not only be of assistance if there is a sudden crisis in performance, but also if there is a gradual erosion of it. Conversely, if the system administrator has not compiled a profile of his various user groups, and examined the underlying loads that they impose on the system, he will be at a serious disadvantage in an emergency when it comes to figuring out where all the CPU cycles, or memory, have gone. This chapter examines the tools that can be used to gain this knowledge, and demonstrates their value.

Finally, although all users may have been created equal, the work of some users inevitably will have more impact on corporate profitability than the work of other users. Perhaps, given UNIX's academic heritage, running the system in a completely democratic manner should be the goal of the system administrator. However, the system administrator will sooner or later find out, either politely or painfully, who the most important and the most influential groups are. This set of characteristics should also somehow be factored into the user profiles the system administrator develops before the onset of crises, which by their nature obscure the reasoning process of all involved.

Introduction to UNIX Performance

While the system is running, UNIX maintains several counters to keep track of critical system resources. The relevant resources that are tracked are the following:

CPU utilization	Buffer usage
Disk I/O activity	Tape I/O activity
Terminal activity	System call activity
Context switching activity	File access utilization
Queue activity	Interprocess communication (IPC)
Paging activity	Free memory and swap space
Kernel memory allocation (KMA)	Kernel tables
Remote file sharing (RFS)	

By looking at reports based on these counters you can determine how the three major subsystems are performing. These subsystems are the following:

CPU   The CPU processes instructions and programs. Each
                        time you submit a job to the system, it makes demands
                        on the CPU. Usually, the CPU can service all demands
                        in a timely manner. However, there is only so much
                        available processing power, which must be shared by all
                        users and the internal programs of the operating system,
                        too.

| Memory | Every program that runs on the system makes some demand on the physical memory on the machine. Like the CPU, it is a finite resource. When the active processes and programs that are running on the system request more memory than the machine actually has, paging is used to move parts of the processes to disk and reclaim their memory pages for use by other processes. If further shortages occur, the system may also have to resort to swapping, which moves entire processes to disk to make room. |
| I/O | The I/O subsystem(s) transfers data into and out of the machine. I/O subsystems comprise devices such as disks, printers, terminals/keyboards, and other relatively slow devices, and are a common source of resource contention problems. In addition, there is a rapidly increasing use of network I/O devices. When programs are doing a lot of I/O, they can get bogged down waiting for data from these devices. Each subsystem has its own limitations with respect to the bandwidth that it can effectively use for I/O operations, as well as its own peculiar problems. |

Performance monitoring and tuning is not always an exact science. In the displays that follow, there is a great deal of variety in the system/subsystem loadings, even for the small sample of systems used here. In addition, different user groups have widely differing requirements. Some users will put a strain on the I/O resources, some on the CPU, and some will stress the network. Performance tuning is always a series of trade-offs. As you will see, increasing the kernel size to alleviate one problem may aggravate memory utilization. Increasing NFS performance to satisfy one set of users may reduce performance in another area and thereby aggravate another set of users. The goal of the task is often to find an optimal compromise that will satisfy the majority of user and system resource needs.

Monitoring the Overall System Status

The examination of specific UNIX performance monitoring techniques begins with a look at three basic tools that give you a snapshot of the overall performance of the system. After getting this high-level view, you will normally proceed to examine each of the subsystems in detail.

Monitoring System Status Using `uptime`

One of the simplest reports that you use to monitor UNIX system performance measures the number of processes in the UNIX run queue during given intervals. It comes from the command `uptime`. It is both a high-level view of the system's workload and a handy starting place when the system seems to be performing slowly. In general, processes in the run queue are active programs (that is, not sleeping or waiting) that require system resources. Here is an example:

```
% uptime
   2:07pm  up 11 day(s),  4:54,  15 users,  load average: 1.90, 1.98, 2.01
```

The useful parts of the display are the three load-average figures. The 1.90 load average was measured over the last minute. The 1.98 average was measured over the last 5 minutes. The 2.01 load average was measured over the last 15 minutes.

TIP

What you are usually looking for is the trend of the averages. This particular example shows a system that is under a fairly consistent load. However, if a system is having problems, but the load averages seem to be declining steadily, then you may want to wait a while before you take any action that might affect the system and possibly inconvenience users. While you are doing some ps commands to determine what caused the problem, the imbalance may correct itself.

NOTE

uptime has certain limitations. For example, high-priority jobs are not distinguished from low-priority jobs, although their impact on the system can be much greater.

Run uptime periodically and observe both the numbers and the trend. When there is a problem it will often show up here, and tip you off to begin serious investigations. As system loads increase, more demands will be made on your memory and I/O subsystems, so keep an eye out for paging, swapping, and disk inefficiencies. System loads of 2 or 3 usually indicate light loads. System loads of 5 or 6 are usually medium-grade loads. Loads above 10 are often heavy loads on large UNIX machines. However, there is wide variation among types of machines as to what constitutes a heavy load. Therefore, the mentioned technique of sampling your system regularly until you have your own reference for light, medium, and heavy loads is the best technique.

Monitoring System Status Using `perfmeter`

Because the goal of this first section is to give you the tools to view your overall system performance, a brief discussion of graphical performance meters is appropriate. SUN Solaris users are provided with an OpenWindows XView tool called `perfmeter`, which summarizes overall system performance values in multiple dials or strip charts. Strip charts are the default. Not all UNIX systems come with such a handy tool. That's too bad because in this case a picture is worth, if not a thousand words, at least 30 or 40 man pages. In this concise format, you get information about the system resources shown in Table 22.1:

Table 22.1. System resources and their descriptions.

Resources	*Description*
cpu	Percent of CPU being utilized
pkts	EtherNet activity, in packets per second
page	Paging, in pages per second
swap	Jobs swapped per second
intr	Number of device interrupts per second
disk	Disk traffic, in transfers per second
cntxt	Number of context switches per second
load	Average number of runnable processes over the last minute
colls	Collisions per second detected on the Ethernet
errs	Errors per second on receiving packets

The charts of the perfmeter are not a source for precise measurements of subsystem performance, but they are graphic representations of them. However, the chart can be very useful for monitoring several aspects of the system at the same time. When you start a particular job, the graphics can demonstrate the impact of that job on the CPU, on disk transfers, and on paging. Many developers like to use the tool to assess the efficiency of their work for this very reason. Likewise, system administrators use the tool to get valuable clues about where to start their investigations. As an example, when faced with intermittent and transitory problems, glancing at a perfmeter and then going directly to the proper display may increase the odds that you can catch in the act the process that is degrading the system.

The scale value for the strip chart changes automatically when the chart refreshes to accommodate increasing or decreasing values on the system. You add values to be monitored by clicking the right mouse button and selecting from the menu. From the same menu you can select properties, which will let you modify what the perfmeter is monitoring, the format (dials/graphs, direction of the displays, and solid/lined display), remote/local machine choice, and the frequency of the display.

You can also set a ceiling value for a particular strip chart. If the value goes beyond the ceiling value, this portion of the chart will be displayed in red. Thus, a system administrator who knows that someone is periodically running a job that eats up all the CPU memory can set a signal that the job may be run again. The system administrator can also use this to monitor the condition of critical values from several feet away from his monitor. If he or she sees red, other users may be seeing red, too.

The `perfmeter` is a utility provided with SunOS. You should check your own particular UNIX operating system to determine if similar performance tools are provided.

Monitoring System Status Using `sar -q`

If your machine does not support `uptime`, there is an option for `sar` that can provide the same type of quick, high-level snapshot of the system. The `-q` option reports the average queue length and the percentage of time that the queue is occupied.

```
% sar -q 5 5

07:28:37 runq-sz %runocc swpq-sz %swpocc
07:28:42    5.0     100             _
07:28:47    5.0     100             _
07:28:52    4.8     100             _
07:28:57    4.8     100             _
07:29:02    4.6     100             _

Average     4.8     100             _
```

The fields in this report are the following:

`runq-sz`	This is the length of the run queue during the interval. The run queue list doesn't include jobs that are sleeping or waiting for I/O, but does include jobs that are in memory and ready to run.
`%runocc`	This is the percentage of time that the run queue is occupied.
`swpq-sz`	This is the average length of the swap queue during the interval. Jobs or threads that have been swapped out and are therefore unavailable to run are shown here.
`%swpocc`	This is the percentage of time that there are swapped jobs or threads.

The run queue length is used in a similar way to the load averages of `uptime`. Typically the number is less than 2 if the system is operating properly. Consistently higher values indicate that the system is under heavier loads, and is quite possibly CPU bound. When the run queue length is high and the run queue percentage is occupied 100 percent of the time, as it is in this example, the system's idle time is minimized, and it is good to be on the lookout for performance-related problems in the memory and disk subsystems. However, there is still no activity indicated in the swapping columns in the example. You will learn about swapping in the next section, and see that although this system is obviously busy, the lack of swapping is a partial vote of confidence that it may still be functioning properly.

Monitoring System Status Using `sar -u`

Another quick and easy tool to use to determine overall system utilization is `sar` with the `-u` option. CPU utilization is shown by `-u`, and `sar` without any options defaults on most versions of UNIX to this option. The CPU is either busy or idle. When it is busy, it is either working on user work or system work. When it is not busy, it is either waiting on I/O or it is idle.

```
% sar -u 5 5

13:16:58    %usr    %sys    %wio    %idle
13:17:03     40      10      13      38
13:17:08     31       6      48      14
13:17:13     42      15       9      34
13:17:18     41      15      10      35
13:17:23     41      15      11      33

Average      39      12      18      31
```

The fields in the report are the following:

`%usr`	This is the percentage of time that the processor is in user mode (that is, executing code requested by a user).
`%sys`	This is the percentage of time that the processor is in system mode, servicing system calls. Users can cause this percentage to increase above-normal levels by using system calls inefficiently.
`%wio`	This is the percentage of time that the processor is waiting on completion of I/O, from disk, NFS, or RFS. If the percentage is regularly high, check the I/O systems for inefficiencies.
`%idle`	This is the percentage of time the processor is idle. If the percentage is high and the system is heavily loaded, there is probably a memory or an I/O problem.

In this example, you see a system with ample CPU capacity left (that is, the average idle percentage is 31 percent). The system is spending most of its time on user tasks, so user programs are probably not too inefficient with their use of system calls. The I/O wait percentage indicates an application that is making a fair amount of demands on the I/O subsystem.

Most administrators would argue that `%idle` should be in the low 'teens rather than 0, at least when the system is under load. If it is 0, it doesn't necessarily mean that the machine is operating poorly. However, it is usually a good bet that the machine is out of spare computational capacity and should be upgraded to the next level of CPU speed. The reason to upgrade the CPU is in anticipation of future growth of user processing requirements. If the system work load is increasing, even if the users haven't yet encountered the problem, why not anticipate the requirement? On the other hand, if the CPU idle time is high under heavy load, a CPU upgrade will probably not help improve performance much.

Idle time will generally be higher when the load average is low.

A high load average and idle time is a symptom of potential problems. Either the memory or the I/O subsystems, or both, are hindering the swift dispatch and completion of the jobs. You should review the following sections that show how to look for paging, swapping, disk, or network-related problems.

Monitoring Processes with ps

You have probably noticed that, while throughout the rest of this chapter the commands are listed under the topic in which they are used (for example, nfsstat is listed in the section "Monitoring Network Performance"), this section is dedicated to just one command. What's so special about ps? It is singled out in this manner because of the way that it is used in the performance monitoring process. It is a starting point for generating theories (for example, processes are using up so much memory that you are paging, and that is slowing down the system). Conversely, it is an ending point for confirming theories (for example, here is a burst of network activity—I wonder if it is caused by that communications test job that the programmers keep running?). Since it is so pivotal, and provides a unique snapshot of the processes on the system, ps is given its own section.

One of the most valuable commands for performance monitoring is the ps command. It enables you to monitor the status of the active processes on the system. Remember the words from the movie Casablanca, "round up the usual suspects"? Well, ps helps to identify the usual suspects (that is, suspect processes that could be using inordinate resources). Then you can proceed to determine which of the suspects is actually guilty of causing the performance degradation. It is at once a powerful tool and a source of overhead for the system itself. Using various options, the following information is shown:

Current status of the process	Process ID
Parent process ID	User ID
Scheduling class	Priority
Address of process	Memory used
CPU time used	

Using ps provides you a snapshot of the system's active processes. It is used in conjunction with other commands throughout this section. Frequently, you will look at a report from a command, for example vmstat, and then look to ps either to confirm or to deny a theory you have come up with about the nature of your system's problem. The particular performance problem that motivated you to look at ps in the first place may have been caused by a process that is already off the list. It provides a series of clues to use in generating theories that can then be tested by detailed analysis of the particular subsystem.

The following are the fields from the output of the ps command that are important in terms of performance tuning:

Field	Description
F	Flags that indicate the process's current state and are calculated by adding each of the hexadecimal values:
	00 Process has terminated
	01 System process, always in memory
	02 Process is being traced by its parent
	04 Process is being traced by parent, and is stopped
	08 Process cannot be awakened by a signal
	10 Process is in memory and locked, pending an event
	20 Process cannot be swapped
S	The current state of the process, as indicated by one of the following letters:
	O Process is currently running on the processor
	S Process is sleeping, waiting for an I/O event (including terminal I/O) to complete
	R Process is ready to run
	I Process is idle
	Z Process is a zombie process (it has terminated, and the parent is not waiting but is still in the process table)
	T Process is stopped because of parent tracing it
	X Process is waiting for more memory
UID	User ID of the process's owner
PID	Process ID number
PPID	Parent process ID number
C	CPU utilization for scheduling (not shown when -c is used)
CLS	Scheduling class, real-time, time sharing, or system (only shown when the -c option is used)
PRI	Process scheduling priority (higher numbers mean lower priorities).
NI	Process nice number (used in scheduling priorities—raising the number lowers the priority so the process gets less CPU time)

22

PERFORMANCE
AND TUNING

Field	*Description*
SZ	The amount of virtual memory required by the process (This is a good indication of the memory load the process places on the systems memory.)
TTY	The terminal that started the process, or its parent (A ? indicates that no terminal exists.)
TIME	The total amount of CPU time used by the process since it began
COMD	The command that generated the process

If your problem is immediate performance, you can disregard processes that are sleeping, stopped, or waiting on terminal I/O, as these will probably not be the source of the degradation. Look instead for the jobs that are ready to run, blocked for disk I/O, or paging.

```
% ps -el
 F S   UID   PID  PPID  C PRI NI    ADDR    SZ   WCHAN TTY      TIME COMD
19 T     0     0     0 80   0 SY e00ec978     0          ?      0:01 sched
19 S     0     2     0 80   0 SY f5735000     0 e00eacdc ?      0:05 pageout
 8 S  1001  1382     1 80  40 20 f5c6a000  1227 e00f887c console 0:02 mailtool
 8 S  1001  1386     1 80  40 20 f60ed000   819 e00f887c console 0:28 perfmete
 8 S  1001 28380 28377 80  40 20 f67c0000  5804 f5cfd146 ?     85:02 sqlturbo
 8 S  1001 28373     1 80  40 20 f63c6000  1035 f63c61c8 ?      0:07 cdrl_mai
 8 S  1001 28392     1 80  40 20 f67ce800  1035 f67ce9c8 ?      0:07 cdrl_mai
 8 S  1001 28391 28388 80  40 20 f690a800  5804 f60dce46 ?    166:39 sqlturbo
 8 S  1001 28361     1 80  60 20 f67e1000 30580 e00f887c ?    379:35 mhdms
 8 S  1001 28360     1 80  40 20 f68e1000 12565 e00f887c ?    182:22 mhharris
 8 O  1001 10566 10512 19  70 20 f6abb800   152          pts/14 0:00 ps
 8 S  1001 28388     1 80  40 20 f6384800   216 f60a0346 ?     67:51 db_write
 8 S  1000  7750  7749 80  40 20 f6344800  5393 f5dad02c pts/2 31:47 tbinit
 8 O  1001  9538  9537 80  81 22 f6978000  5816          ?    646:57 sqlturbo
 8 S  1033  3735 3734164 40 20 f63b8800   305 f60e0d46 pts/9  0:00 ksh
 8 S  1033  5228  5227 80  50 20 f68a8800   305 f60dca46 pts/7  0:00 ksh
 8 S  1001 28337     1 80  99 20 f6375000 47412 f63751c8 ?   1135:50
➥velox_ga
```

The following are tips for using ps to determine why system performance is suffering.

Look at the UID (user ID) fields for a number of identical jobs that are being submitted by the same user. This is often caused by a user who runs a script that starts a lot of background jobs without waiting for any of the jobs to complete. Sometimes you can safely use kill to terminate some of the jobs. Whenever you can, you should discuss this with the user before you take action. In any case, be sure the user is educated in the proper use of the system to avoid a replication of the problem. In the example, User ID 1001 has multiple instances of the same process running. In this case, it is a normal situation, in which multiple processes are spawned at the same time for searching through database tables to increase interactive performance.

Look at the TIME fields for a process that has accumulated a large amount of CPU time. In the example, you can see the large amount of time acquired by the processes whose command is shown as velox_ga. This may indicate that the process is in an infinite loop, or that something else is wrong with its logic. Check with the user to determine whether it is appropriate to terminate the job. If something is wrong, ask the user if a dump of the process would assist in debugging it (check your UNIX system's reference material for commands, such as gcore, that can dump a process).

Request the -1 option and look at the SZ fields for processes that are consuming too much memory. In the example you can see the large amount of memory acquired by the processes whose command is shown as velox_ga. You could check with the user of this process to try to determine why it behaves this way. Attempting to renice the process may simply prolong the problem that it is causing, so you may have to kill the job instead. SZ fields may also give you a clue as to memory shortage problems caused by this particular combination of jobs. You can use vmstat or sar -wpgr to check the paging and swapping statistics that are examined.

Look for processes that are consuming inordinate CPU resources. Request the -c option and look at the CLS fields for processes that are running at inappropriately high priorities. Use the nice command to adjust the nice value of the process. Beware in particular of any real-time (RT) process, which can often dominate the system. If the priority is higher than you expected, you should check with the user to determine how it was set. If he is resetting the priority because he has figured out the superuser password, dissuade him from doing this. (Refer to Chapter 19, "Kernel Configuration," to find out more about using the nice command to modify the priorities of processes.)

If the processes that are running are simply long-running, CPU-intensive jobs, ask the users if you can nice them to a lower priority or if they can run them at night, when other users will not be affected by them.

Look for processes that are blocking on I/O. Many of the example processes are in this state. When that is the case, the disk subsystem probably requires tuning. The section "Monitoring Disk Performance Using vmstat" examines how to investigate problems with your disk I/O. If the processes are trying to read/write over NFS, this may be a symptom that the NFS server to which they are attached is down, or that the network itself is hung.

Monitoring Memory Utilization

You could say that one can never have too much money, be too thin, or have too much system memory. Memory sometimes becomes a problematic resource when programs that are running require more physical memory than is available. When this occurs UNIX systems begin a process called paging. During paging, the system copies pages of physical memory to disk, and then allows the now-vacated memory to be used by the process that required the extra space. Occasional paging can be tolerated by most systems, but frequent and excessive paging is usually accompanied by poor system performance and unhappy users.

UNIX Memory Management

Paging uses an algorithm that selects portions, or pages, of memory that are not being used frequently and displaces them to disk. The more frequently used portions of memory, which may be the most active parts of a process, thus remain in memory, while other portions of the process that are idle get paged out.

In addition to paging, there is a similar technique used by the memory management system called swapping. Swapping moves entire processes, rather than just pages, to disk in order to free up memory resources. Some swapping may occur under normal conditions. That is, some processes may just be idle enough (for example, due to sleeping) to warrant their return to disk until they become active once more. Swapping can become excessive, however, when severe memory shortages develop. Interactive performance can degrade quickly when swapping increases since it often depends on keyboard-dependent processes (for example, editors) that are likely to be considered idle as they wait for you to start typing again.

As the condition of your system deteriorates, paging and swapping make increasing demands on disk I/O. This, in turn, may further slow down the execution of jobs submitted to the system. Thus, memory resource inadequacies may result in I/O resource problems.

By now, it should be apparent that it is important to be able to know if the system has enough memory for the applications that are being used on it.

> **TIP**
>
> A rule of thumb is to allocate twice the swap space as you have physical memory. For example, if you have 32 MB of physical Random Access Memory (RAM) installed upon your system, you would set up 64 MB of swap space when configuring the system. The system would then use this diskspace for its memory management when displacing pages or processes to disk.

Both vmstat and sar provide information about the paging and swapping characteristics of a system. Let's start with vmstat. On the vmstat reports you will see information about page-ins, or pages moved from disk to memory, and page-outs, or pages moved from memory to disk. Further, you will see information about swap-ins, or processes moved from disk to memory, and swap-outs, or processes moved from memory to disk.

Monitoring Memory Performance Using vmstat

The vmstat command is used to examine virtual memory statistics, and present data on process status, free and swap memory, paging activity, disk reports, CPU load, swapping, cache flushing, and interrupts. The format of the command is

vmstat *t* [*n*]

This command takes *n* samples, at *t* second intervals. For example, the following frequently used version of the command takes samples at 5-second intervals without stopping until canceled:

```
vmstat 5
```

The following screen shows the output from the SunOS variant of the command

```
vmstat -S 5
```

which provides extra information regarding swapping.

```
procs      memory            page              disk          faults         cpu
r b w   swap   free si so pi po fr de sr s0 s3 s5 s5   in   sy   cs us sy id
0 2 0  16516   9144  0  0  0  0  0  0  0  1  4 34 12  366  1396  675 14  9 76
0 3 0 869384 29660  0  0  0  0  0  0  0  4 63 15  514 10759 2070 19 17 64
0 2 0 869432 29704  0  0  0  0  0  0  0  4  3 64 11  490  2458 2035 16 13 72
0 3 0 869448 29696  0  0  0  0  0  0  0  0  3 65 13  464  2528 2034 17 12 71
0 3 0 869384 29684  0  0  0  0  0  0  0  1  3 68 18  551  2555 2136 16 14 70
0 2 0 869188 29644  0  0  0  2  2  0  0  2  3 65 10  432  2495 2013 18  9 73
0 3 0 869176 29612  0  0  0  0  0  0  0  0  3 61 16  504  2527 2053 17 11 71
0 2 0 869156 29600  0  0  0  0  0  0  0  0  3 69  8  438 15820 2027 20 18 62
```

The fields in the vmstat report are the following:

procs	Reports the number of processes in each of the following states
r	In the Run queue
b	Blocked, waiting for resources
w	Swapped, waiting for processing resources
memory	Reports on real and virtual memory
swap	Available swap space
free	Size of free list
page	Reports on page faults and paging, averaged over an interval (typically 5 seconds) and provided in units per second
re	Pages reclaimed from the free list (not shown when the -S option is requested)
mf	Minor faults (not shown when -S option is requested)
si	Number of pages swapped in (only shown with the -S option)
so	Number of pages swapped out (only shown with the -S option)
pi	Kilobytes paged in
po	Kilobytes paged out
fr	Kilobytes freed

de	Anticipated short-term memory shortfall
sr	Pages scanned by clock algorithm, per second
disk	Shows the number of disk operations per second
faults	Shows the per-second trap/interrupt rates
in	Device interrupts
sy	System faults per second
cs	CPU context switches
cpu	Shows the use of CPU time
us	User time
sy	System time
id	Idle time

NOTE

The vmstat command's first line is rarely of any use. When reviewing the output from the command, always start at the second line and go forward for pertinent data.

Let's look at some of these fields for clues about system performance. As far as memory performance goes, po and w are very important. For people using the -s option, so is similarly important. These fields all clearly show when a system is paging and swapping. If w is non-zero and so continually indicates swapping, the system probably has a serious memory problem. If, likewise, po consistently has large numbers present, the system probably has a significant memory resource problem.

TIP

If your version of vmstat doesn't specifically provide swapping information, you can infer the swapping by watching the relationship between the w and the fre fields. An increase in w, the swapped-out processes, followed by an increase in fre, the number of pages on the free list, can provide the same information in a different manner.

Other fields from the vmstat output are helpful, as well. The number of runnable and blocked processes can provide a good indication of the flow of processes, or lack thereof, through the system. Similarly, comparing each percentage CPU idle versus CPU in system state, and versus CPU in user state, can provide information about the overall composition of the workload. As the load increases on the system, it is a good sign if the CPU is spending the majority of the time in the user state. Loads of 60 or 70 percent for CPU user state are ok. Idle CPU should drop as the user load picks up, and under heavy load may well fall to 0.

If paging and swapping are occurring at an unusually high rate, it may be due to the number and types of jobs that are running. Usually you can turn to ps to determine what those jobs are.

Imagine that ps shows a large number of jobs that require significant memory resources. (You saw how to determine this in the ps discussion in the previous section.) That would confirm the vmstat report. To resolve the problem, you would have to restrict memory-intensive jobs, or the use of memory, or add more memory physically.

> **TIP**
>
> You can see that having a history of several vmstat and ps reports during normal system operation can be extremely helpful in determining what the usual conditions are, and, subsequently, what the unusual ones are. Also, one or two vmstat reports may indicate a temporary condition, rather than a permanent problem. Sample the system multiple times before deciding that you have the answer to your system's performance problems.

If you are using HP-UX, you would get a slightly different output from vmstat. For example, if you run vmstat 5 3, you would get something similar to the following output:

```
procfs          memory                      page
faults                  cpu

r   b   w   avm     free    re  at  pi  po  fr  de  sr  in
sy      cs  us      sy      id

4   0   0   1161    2282    6   22  48  0   0   0   0   429  289
65      44  18      18

9   0   0   1161    1422    4   30  59  0   0   0   0   654  264
181     18  20      62

6   0   0   1409    1247    2   19  37  0   0   0   0   505  316
130     47  10      43
```

If you compare the two outputs, you see that there are three new metrics (avm, re and at): two metrics not included (swap and so), and one category not included here (disk).

In the fourth column, you see the new metric avm. This is the number of virtual memory pages owned by processes that have run within the last 20 seconds. Should this number grow to roughly the size of physical memory minus your kernel, then your system is near paging.

The next new metric, re, shows the pages that were reclaimed. If this number gets very high, then you are wasting valuable time trying to salvage paging space. This is a good indicator that your system does not have adequate memory installed. The metric at is not very useful.

This version of vmstat is missing two metrics: swap and so. Swap is replaced with avm, as avm shows the number of virtual memory pages. The si and so metrics are missing, as they are related to the swap metric.

The disk category is not included with this version of vmstat, as most disk io is already shown with the iostat utility.

Monitoring Memory Performance with sar -wpgr

More information about the system's utilization of memory resources can be obtained by using sar -wpgr.

```
% sar -wpgr 5 5

07:42:30 swpin/s pswin/s swpot/s bswot/s pswch/s
         atch/s  pgin/s ppgin/s  pflt/s  vflt/s slock/s
         pgout/s ppgout/s pgfree/s pgscan/s %s5ipf
         freemem freeswp

07:42:35    0.00     0.0    0.00     0.0    504
            0.00    0.00    0.00    0.00   6.20   11.78
            0.00    0.00    0.00    0.00   0.00
           33139  183023

...

Average     0.00     0.0    0.00     0.0    515
Average     0.00    0.32    0.40    2.54   5.56   16.83
Average     0.00    0.00    0.00    0.00   0.00
Average    32926  183015
```

The fields in the report are the following:

swpin/s	Number of transfers into memory per second.
bswin/s	Number of blocks transferred for swap-ins per second.
swpot/s	Number of transfers from memory to swap area per second. (More memory may be needed if the value is greater than 1.)
bswot/s	Number of blocks transferred for swap-outs per second.
pswch/s	Number of process switches per second.
atch/s	Number of attaches per second (that is, page faults where the page is reclaimed from memory).
pgin/s	Number of times per second that file systems get page-in requests.
ppgin/s	Number of pages paged in per second.
pflt/s	Number of page faults from protection errors per second.
vflt/s	Number of address translation page (validity) faults per second.
slock/s	Number of faults per second caused by software lock requests requiring I/O.

`pgout/s`	Number of times per second that file systems get page-out requests.
`ppgout/s`	Number of pages paged out per second.
`pgfree/s`	Number of pages that are put on the free list by the page-stealing daemon. (More memory may be needed if this is a large value.)
`pgscan/s`	Number of pages scanned by the page-stealing daemon. (More memory may be needed if this is a large value, because it shows that the daemon is checking for free memory more than it should need to.)
`%ufs_ipf`	Percentage of the `ufs` inodes that were taken off the free list that had reusable pages associated with them. (Large values indicate that `ufs` inodes should be increased, so that the free list of inodes will not be page bound.) This will be `%s5ipf` for System V file systems, like in the example.
`freemem`	The average number of pages, over this interval, of memory available to user processes.
`freeswp`	The number of disk blocks available for page swapping.

You should use the report to examine each of the following conditions. Any one of them would imply that you may have a memory problem. Combinations of them increase the likelihood all the more.

Check for page-outs, and watch for their consistent occurrence. Look for a high incidence of address translation faults. Check for swap-outs. If they are occasional, it may not be a cause for concern, as some number of them is normal (for example, inactive jobs). However, consistent swap-outs are usually bad news, indicating that the system is very low on memory and is probably sacrificing active jobs. If you find memory shortage evidence in any of these, you can use `ps` to look for memory-intensive jobs, as you saw in the section on `ps`.

Multiprocessor Implications of `vmstat`

In the CPU columns of the report, the `vmstat` command summarizes the performance of multiprocessor systems. If you have a two-processor system and the CPU load is reflected as 50 percent, it doesn't necessarily mean that both processors are equally busy. Rather, depending on the multiprocessor implementation, it can indicate that one processor is almost completely busy and the next is almost idle.

The first column of `vmstat` output also has implications for multiprocessor systems. If the number of runnable processes is not consistently greater than the number of processors, it is less likely that you can get significant performance increases from adding more CPUs to your system.

Monitoring Disk Subsystem Performance

Disk operations are the slowest of all operations that must be completed to enable most programs to complete. Furthermore, as more and more UNIX systems are being used for commercial applications, and particularly those that utilize relational database systems, the subject of disk performance has become increasingly significant with regard to overall system performance. Therefore, probably more than ever before, UNIX system tuning activities often turn out to be searches for unnecessary and inefficient disk I/O. Before you learn about the commands that can help you monitor your disk I/O performance, some background is appropriate.

Some of the major disk performance variables are the hard disk activities themselves (that is, rotation and arm movement), the I/O controller card, the I/O firmware and software, and the I/O backplane of the system.

For example, for a given disk operation to be completed successfully, the disk controller must be directed to access the information from the proper part of the disk. This results in a delay known as a queuing delay. When it has located the proper part of the disk, the disk arm must begin to position itself over the correct cylinder. This results in a delay called seek latency. The read/write head must then wait for the relevant data to happen as the disk rotates underneath it. This is known as rotational latency. The data must then be transferred to the controller. Finally, the data must be transferred over the I/O backplane of the system to be used by the application that requested the information.

If you think about your use of a compact disk, many of the operations are similar in nature. The CD platter contains information, and is spinning all the time. When you push 5 to request the fifth track of the CD, a controller positions the head that reads the information at the correct area of the disk (similar to the queuing delay and seek latency of disk drives). The rotational latency occurs as the CD spins around until the start of your music passes under the reading head. The data—in this case your favorite song—is then transferred to a controller and then to some digital to analog converters that transform it into amplified musical information that is playable by your stereo.

Seek time is the time required to move the head of the disk from one location of data, or track, to another. Moving from one track to another track that is adjacent to it takes very little time and is called minimum seek time. Moving the head between the two furthest tracks on a disk is measured as the maximum seek time. The average seek time approximates the average amount of time a seek takes.

As data access becomes more random in nature, seek time can become more important. In most commercial database applications that feature relational databases, for example, the data is often being accessed in a random manner, at a high rate, and in relatively small packets (for example, 512 bytes). Therefore, the disk heads are moving back and forth all the time looking for the pertinent data. Therefore, choosing disks that have small seek times for those systems can increase I/O performance.

Many drives have roughly the same rotational speed, measured as revolutions per minute, or RPMs. However, some manufacturers are stepping up the RPM rates of their drives. This can have a positive influence on performance by reducing the rotational delay, which is the time that the disk head has to wait for the information to get to it (that is, on average one-half of a rotation). It also reduces the amount of time required to transfer the read/write information.

Disk I/O Performance Optimization

While reviewing the use of the commands to monitor disk performance, you will see how these clearly show which disks and disk subsystems are being the most heavily used. However, before examining those commands, there are some basic hardware-oriented approaches to this problem that can help increase performance significantly. The main idea is to put the hardware where the biggest disk problem is, and to evenly spread the disk workload over available I/O controllers and disk drives.

If your I/O workload is heavy (for example, with many users constantly accessing large volumes of data from the same set of files), you can probably get significant performance increases by reducing the number of disk drives that are daisy-chained off one I/O controller from five or six to two or three. Perhaps doing this will force another daisy chain to increase in size past a total of four or five, but if the disks on that I/O controller are only used intermittently, system performance will be increased overall.

Another example of this type of technique is if you had one group of users who are pounding one set of files all day long, you could locate the most frequently used data on the fastest disks.

Notice that, once again, the more thorough your knowledge of the characteristics of the work being done on your system, the greater the chance that your disk architecture will answer those needs.

> **NOTE**
>
> Remember, distributing a workload evenly across all disks and controllers is not the same thing as distributing the disks evenly across all controllers, or the files evenly across all disks. You must know which applications make the heaviest I/O demands, and understand the workload itself, to distribute it effectively.

> **TIP**
>
> As you build file systems for user groups, remember to factor in the I/O workload. Make sure your high-disk I/O groups are put on their own physical disks and preferably their own I/O controllers as well. If possible, keep them, and /usr, off the root disk as well.

Disk-striping software frequently can help in cases where the majority of disk access goes to a handful of disks. Where a large amount of data is making heavy demands on one disk or one controller, striping distributes the data across multiple disks and/or controllers. When the data is striped across multiple disks, the accesses to it are averaged over all the I/O controllers and disks, thus optimizing overall disk throughput. Some disk-striping software also provides Redundant Array of Inexpensive Disks (RAID) support and the ability to keep one disk in reserve as a hot standby (that is, a disk that can be automatically rebuilt and used when one of the production disks fails). When thought of in this manner, this can be a very useful feature in terms of performance because a system that has been crippled by the failure of a hard drive will be viewed by your user community as having pretty bad performance.

This information may seem obvious, but it is important to the overall performance of a system. Frequently, the answer to disk performance simply rests on matching the disk architecture to the use of the system.

Relational Databases

With the increasing use of relational database technologies on UNIX systems, I/O subsystem performance is more important than ever. While analyzing all the relational database systems and making recommendations is beyond the scope of this chapter, some basic concepts are in order.

More and more often these days an application based on a relational database product is the fundamental reason for the procurement of the UNIX system itself. If that is the case in your installation, and if you have relatively little experience in terms of database analysis, you should seek professional assistance. In particular, insist on a database analyst that has had experience tuning your database system on your operating system. Operating systems and relational databases are both complex systems, and the performance interactions between them is difficult for the inexperienced to understand.

The database expert will spend a great deal of time looking at the effectiveness of your allocation of indexes. Large improvements in performance due to the addition or adjustment of a few indexes are quite common.

You should use raw disks versus the file systems for greatest performance. File systems incur more overhead (for example, inode and update block overhead on writes) than do raw devices. Most relational databases clearly reflect this performance advantage in their documentation.

If the database system is extremely active, or if the activity is unbalanced, you should try to distribute the load more evenly across all the I/O controllers and disks that you can. You will see how to determine this in the following section.

Checking Disk Performance with `iostat` and `sar`

The two original commands for system monitoring, `iostat` and `sar`, are still in very wide use today as reliable, simple, and free tools. As a matter of fact, most system monitoring tools that you can buy today are simply extensions of these programs.

The `iostat` Command

The `iostat` command is used to examine disk input and output, and produces throughput, utilization, queue length, transaction rate, and service time data. It is similar both in format and in use to `vmstat`. The format of the command is

```
iostat  t [n]
```

This command takes *n* samples, at *t* second intervals. For example, the following frequently used version of the command takes samples at 5-second intervals without stopping, until canceled:

```
iostat 5
```

The following shows disk statistics sampled at 5-second intervals:

```
        tty         sd0            sd30           sd53           sd55           cpu
 tin tout Kps tps serv  Kps tps serv  Kps tps serv  Kps tps serv  us sy wt id
   0   26   8   1   57   36   4   20   77  34   24   31  12   30  14  9 47 30
   0   51   0   0    0    0   0    0  108  54   36    0   0    0  14  7 78  0
   0   47  72  10  258    0   0    0  102  51   38    0   0    0  15  9 76  0
   0   58   5   1    9    1   1   23  112  54   33    0   0    0  14  8 77  1
   0   38   0   0    0   25   0   90  139  70   17    9   4   25  14  8 73  6
   0   43   0   0    0  227  10   23  127  62   32   45  21   20  20 15 65  0
```

The first line of the report shows the statistics since the last reboot. The subsequent lines show the interval data that is gathered. The default format of the command shows statistics for terminals (`tty`), for disks (`fd` and `sd`), and CPU.

For each terminal, `iostat` shows the following:

`tin`	Characters in the terminal input queue
`tout`	Characters in the terminal output queue

For each disk, `iostat` shows the following:

`bps`	Blocks per second
`tps`	Transfers per second
`serv`	Average service time, in milliseconds

For the CPU, `iostat` displays the CPU time spent in the following modes:

`us`	User mode
`sy`	System mode
`wt`	Waiting for I/O
`id`	Idle mode

The first two fields, `tin` and `tout`, have no relevance to disk subsystem performance, as these fields describe the number of characters waiting in the input and output terminal buffers. The next fields are relevant to disk subsystem performance over the preceding interval. The `bps` field indicates the size of the data transferred (read or written) to the drive. The `tps` field describes the transfers (that is, I/O requests) per second that were issued to the physical disk. Note that one transfer can combine multiple logical requests. The serv field is for the length of time, in milliseconds, that the I/O subsystem required to service the transfer. In the last set of fields, note that I/O waiting is displayed under the wt heading.

You can look at the data within the report for information about system performance. As with vmstat, the first line of data is usually irrelevant to your immediate investigation. Looking at the first disk, sd0, you see that it is not being utilized as the other three disks are. Disk 0 is the root disk, and often will show the greatest activity. This system is a commercial relational database implementation, however, and the activity that is shown here is often typical of online transaction processing, or OLTP, requirements. Notice that the activity is mainly on disks sd53 and sd55. The database is being exercised by a high volume of transactions that are updating it (in this case over 100 updates per second).

Disks 30, 53, and 55 are three database disks that are being pounded with updates from the application through the relational database system. Notice that the transfers per second, the kilobytes per second, and the service times are all reflecting a heavier load on disk 53 than on disks 30 and 55. Notice that disk 30's use is more intermittent but can be quite heavy at times, while 53's is more consistent. Ideally, over longer sample periods, the three disks should have roughly equivalent utilization rates. If they continue to show disparities in use like these, you may be able to get a performance increase by determining why the load is unbalanced and taking corrective action.

You can use iostat -xtc to show the measurements across all of the drives in the system.

```
% iostat -xtc 10 5 _
```

					extended disk statistics						tty		cpu		
disk	r/s	w/s	Kr/s	Kw/s	wait	actv	svc_t	%w	%b	tin	tout	us	sy	wt	id
sd0	0.0	0.9	0.1	6.3	0.0	0.0	64.4	0	1	0	26	12	11	21	56
sd30	0.2	1.4	0.4	20.4	0.0	0.0	21.5	0	3						
sd53	2.6	2.3	5.5	4.6	0.0	0.1	23.6	0	9						
sd55	2.7	2.4	5.6	4.7	0.0	0.1	24.2	0	10						

```
...
```

					extended disk statistics						tty		cpu		
disk	r/s	w/s	Kr/s	Kw/s	wait	actv	svc_t	%w	%b	tin	tout	us	sy	wt	id
sd0	0.0	0.3	0.0	3.1	0.0	0.0	20.4	0	1	0	3557	5	8	14	72
sd30	0.0	0.2	0.1	0.9	0.0	0.0	32.2	0	0						
sd53	0.1	0.2	0.4	0.5	0.0	0.0	14.6	0	0						
sd55	0.1	0.2	0.3	0.4	0.0	0.0	14.7	0	0						

This example shows five samples of all disks at 10-second intervals.

Each line shows the following:

r/s	Reads per second
w/s	Writes per second
Kr/s	KB read per second
Kw/s	KB written per second

wait	Average transactions waiting for service (that is, queue length)
actv	Average active transactions being serviced
svc_t	Average time, in milliseconds, of service
%w	Percentage of time that the queue isn't empty
%b	Percentage of time that the disk is busy

Once again, you can check to make sure that all disks are sharing the load equally, or if this is not the case, that the most active disk is also the fastest.

The sar -d Command

The sar -d option reports on the disk I/O activity of a system, as well.

```
% sar -d 5 5
```

20:44:26	device	%busy	avque	r+w/s	blks/s	avwait	avserv
...							
20:44:46	sd0	1	0.0	1	5	0.0	20.1
	sd1	0	0.0	0	0	0.0	0.0
	sd15	0	0.0	0	0	0.0	0.0
	sd16	1	0.0	0	1	0.0	27.1
	sd17	1	0.0	0	1	0.0	26.8
	sd3	0	0.0	0	0	0.0	0.0
Average	sd0	1	0.0	0	3	0.0	20.0
	sd1	0	0.0	0	2	0.0	32.6
	sd15	0	0.0	0	1	0.0	13.6
	sd16	0	0.0	0	0	0.0	27.6
	sd17	0	0.0	0	0	0.0	26.1
	sd3	2	0.1	1	14	0.0	102.6

Information about each disk is shown as follows:

device	Names the disk device that is measured
%busy	Percentage of time that the device is busy servicing transfers
avque	Average number of requests outstanding during the period
r+w/s	Read/write transfers to the device per second
blks/s	Number of blocks transferred to the device per second
avwait	Average number of milliseconds that a transfer request spends waiting in the queue for service
avserv	Average number of milliseconds for a transfer to be completed, including seek, rotational delay, and data transfer time

You can see from the example that this system is lightly loaded, since %busy is a small number and the queue lengths and wait times are small as well. The average service times for most of the disks is consistent; however, notice that SCSI disk 3, sd3, has a larger service time than the other disks. Perhaps the arrangement of data on the disk is not organized properly (a condition known as fragmentation) or perhaps the organization is fine but the disproportionate access of sd3 (see the blks/s column) is bogging it down in comparison to the other drives.

> **TIP**
>
> You should double-check vmstat before you draw any conclusions based on these reports. If your system is paging or swapping with any consistency, you have a memory problem, and you need to address that first because it is surely aggravating your I/O performance.

As this chapter has shown, you should distribute the disk load over I/O controllers and drives, and you should use your fastest drive to support your most frequently accessed data. You should also try to increase the size of your buffer cache if your system has sufficient memory. You can eliminate fragmentation by rebuilding your file systems. Also, make sure that the file system that you are using is the fastest type supported with your UNIX system (for example, UFS) and that the block size is the appropriate size.

Monitoring File System Use with df

One of the biggest and most frequent problems that systems have is running out of disk space, particularly in /tmp or /usr. There is no magic answer to the question, "How much space should be allocated to these?" A good rule of thumb is between 1500KB and 3000KB for /tmp and roughly twice that for /usr. Other file systems should have about 5 or 10 percent of the system's available capacity.

The df Command

The df command shows the free disk space on each disk that is mounted. The -k option displays the information about each file system in columns, with the allocations in KB.

```
% df -k
```

Filesystem	kbytes	used	avail	capacity	Mounted on
/dev/dsk/c0t0d0s0	38111	21173	13128	62%	/
/dev/dsk/c0t0d0s6	246167	171869	49688	78%	/usr
/proc	0	0	0	0%	/proc
fd	0	0	0	0%	/dev/fd
swap	860848	632	860216	0%	/tmp
/dev/dsk/c0t0d0s7	188247	90189	79238	53%	/home
/dev/dsk/c0t0d0s5	492351	179384	263737	40%	/opt
gs:/home/prog/met	77863	47127	22956	67%	/home/met

From this display you can see the following information (all entries are in KB):

`kbytes`	Total size of usable space in file system (size is adjusted by allotted head room)
`used`	Space used
`avail`	Space available for use
`capacity`	Percentage of total capacity used
`mounted on`	Mount point

The usable space has been adjusted to take into account a 10 percent reserve head room adjustment, and thus reflects only 90 percent of the actual capacity. The percentage shown under capacity is therefore used space divided by the adjusted usable space.

> **TIP**
>
> For best performance, file systems should be cleansed to protect the 10 percent head room allocation. Remove excess files with rm, or archive/move files that are older and no longer used to tapes with tar or cpio, or to less-frequently used disks.

Monitoring Network Performance

"The network is the computer" is an appropriate saying these days. What used to be simple ASCII terminals connected over serial ports have been replaced by networks of workstations, Xterminals, and PCs, connected, for example, over 10 BASE-T Ethernet networks. Networks are impressive information transmission media when they work properly. However, troubleshooting is not always as straightforward as it should be. In other words, he who lives by the network can die by the network without the proper procedures.

The two most prevalent standards that you will have to contend with in the UNIX world are TCP/IP, (a communications protocol) and NFS, (a popular network file system). Each can be a source of problems. In addition, you need to keep an eye on the implementation of the network, which can also can be a problem area. Each network topology has different capacities, and each implementation (for example, using thin-net instead of 10 BASE-T twisted pair, or using intelligent hubs, and so on) has advantages and problems inherent in its design. The good news is that even a simple Ethernet network has a large amount of bandwidth for transporting data. The bad news is that with every day that passes users and programmers are coming up with new methods of using up as much of that bandwidth as possible.

Most networks are still based on Ethernet technologies. Ethernet is referred to as a 10 Mps medium, but the throughput that can be used effectively by users and applications is usually significantly less than 10 MB. Often, for various reasons, the effective capacity falls to 4 Mps.

That may still seem like a lot of capacity, but as the network grows it can disappear fast. When the capacity is used up, Ethernet is very democratic. If it has a capacity problem, all users suffer equally. Furthermore, one person can bring an Ethernet network to its knees with relative ease. Accessing and transferring large files across the network, running programs that test transfer rates between two machines, or running a program that has a loop in it that happens to be dumping data to another machine, and so on, can affect all the users on the network. Like other resources (that is, CPU, disk capacity, and so on), the network is a finite resource.

If given the proper instruction, users can quite easily detect capacity problems on the network by which they are supported. A quick comparison of a simple command executed on the local machine versus the same command executed on a remote machine (for example, login and rlogin) can indicate that the network has a problem.

A little education can help your users and your network at the same time. NFS is a powerful tool, in both the good and the bad sense. Users should be taught that it will be slower to access the file over the network using NFS, particularly if the file is sizable, than it will be to read or write the data directly on the remote machine by using a remote login. However, if the files are of reasonable size, and the use is reasonable (editing, browsing, moving files back and forth), it is a fine tool to use. Users should understand when they are using NFS appropriately or not.

Monitoring Network Performance with `netstat -i`

One straightforward check you can make of the network's operation is with `netstat -i`. This command can give you some insight into the integrity of the network. All the workstations and the computers on a given network share it. When more than one of these entities try to use the network at the same time, the data from one machine "collides" with that of the other. (Despite the sound of the term, in moderation this is actually a normal occurrence, but too many collisions can be a problem.) In addition, various technical problems can cause errors in the transmission and reception of the data. As the errors and the collisions increase in frequency, the performance of the network degrades because the sender of the data retransmits the garbled data, thus further increasing the activity on the network.

Using `netstat -i` you can find out how many packets the computer has sent and received, and you can examine the levels of errors and collisions that it has detected on the network. Here is an example of the use of `netstat`:

```
% netstat -i
```

Name	Mtu	Net/Dest	Address	Ipkts	Ierrs	Opkts	Oerrs	Collis	Queue
lo0	8232	loopback	localhost	1031780	0	1031780	0	0	0
le0	1500	100.0.0.0	SCAT	13091430	6	12221526	4	174250	0

The fields in the report are the following:

Name	The name of the network interface. The names show what the type of interface is (for example, an en followed by a digit indicates an Ethernet card, the lo0 shown here is a loopback interface used for testing networks).

Mtu	The maximum transfer unit, also known as the packet size, of the interface.
Net/Dest	The network to which the interface is connected.
Address	The Internet address of the interface. (The Internet address for this name may be referenced in /etc/hosts.)
Ipkts	The number of packets the system has received since the last boot.
Ierrs	The number of input errors that have occurred since the last boot. This should be a very low number relative to the Ipkts field (that is, less than 0.25 percent, or there is probably a significant network problem).
Opkts	Same as Ipkts, but for sent packets.
Oerrs	Same as Ierrs, but for output errors.
Collis	The number of collisions that have been detected. This number should not be more than 5 or 10 percent of the output packets (Opkts) number or the network is having too many collisions and capacity is reduced.

In this example you see that the collision ratio shows a network without too many collisions (approximately 1 percent). If collisions are constantly averaging 10 percent or more, the network is probably being overutilized.

The example also shows that input and output error ratios are negligible. Input errors usually mean that the network is feeding the system bad input packets, and the internal calculations that verify the integrity of the data (called checksums) are failing. In other words, this normally indicates that the problem is somewhere out on the network, not on your machine. Conversely, rapidly increasing output errors probably indicates a local problem with your computer's network adapters, connectors, interface, and so on.

If you suspect network problems you should repeat this command several times. An active machine should show Ipkts and Opkts consistently incrementing. If Ipkts changes and Opkts doesn't, the host is not responding to the client requesting data. You should check the addressing in the hosts database. If Ipkts doesn't change, the machine is not receiving the network data at all.

Monitoring Network Performance Using spray

It is quite possible that you will not detect collisions and errors when you use netstat -i, and yet will still have slow access across the network. Perhaps the other machine that you are trying to use is bogged down and cannot respond quickly enough. Use spray to send a burst of packets to the other machine and record how many of them actually made the trip successfully.

The results will tell you if the other machine is failing to keep up. Here is an example of a frequently used test:

```
% spray SCAT

sending 1162 packets of length 86 to SCAT ...
        no packets dropped by SCAT
        3321 packets/sec, 285623 bytes/sec
```

This shows a test burst sent from the source machine to the destination machine called SCAT. No packets were dropped. If SCAT were badly overloaded some probably would have been dropped. The example defaulted to sending 1,162 packets of 86 bytes each. Another example of the same command uses the -c option to specify the number of packets to send, the -d option to specify the delay so that you don't overrun your buffers, and the -l option to specify the length of the packet. This example of the command is a more realistic test of the network:

```
% spray -c 100 -d 20 0 -l 2048 SCAT

sending 100 packets of length 2048 to SCAT ...
        no packets dropped by SCAT
        572 packets/sec, 1172308 bytes/sec
```

Had you seen significant numbers (for example, 5 to 10 percent or more) of packets dropped in these displays, you would next try looking at the remote system. For example, using commands such as uptime, vmstat, sar, and ps as described earlier in this section, you would check on the status of the remote machine. Does it have memory or CPU problems, or is there some other problem that is degrading its performance so it can't keep up with its network traffic?

Monitoring Network Performance with `nfsstat -c`

Systems running NFS can skip spray and instead use nfsstat -c. The -c option specifies the client statistics, and -s can be used for server statistics. As the name implies, client statistics summarize this system's use of another machine as a server. The NFS service uses synchronous procedures called RPCs (remote procedure calls). This means that the client waits for the server to complete the file activity before it proceeds. If the server fails to respond, the client retransmits the request. Just as with collisions, the worse the condition of the communication, the more traffic that is generated. The more traffic that is generated, the slower the network and the greater the possibility of collisions. So if the retransmission rate is large, you should look for servers that are under heavy loads, high collision rates that are delaying the packets en route, or Ethernet interfaces that are dropping packets.

```
% nfsstat -c

Client rpc:
calls     badcalls retrans  badxid   timeout  wait     newcred  timers
74107     0        72       0        72       0        0        82
```

```
Client nfs:
calls      badcalls    nclget      nclcreate
73690      0           73690       0           _
null       getattr     setattr     root        lookup      readlink    read         _
0  0%      4881  7%    1  0%       0  0%       130  0%     0  0%       465  1%      _
wrcache    write       create      remove      rename      link        symlink      _
0  0%      68161 92%   16  0%      1  0%        0  0%       0  0%       0  0%       _
mkdir      rmdir       readdir     statfs      _
0  0%      0  0%       32  0%      3  0%       _
```

The report shows the following fields:

calls	The number of calls sent
badcalls	The number of calls rejected by the RPC
retrans	The number of retransmissions
badxid	The number of duplicated acknowledgments received
timeout	The number of time-outs
wait	The number of times no available client handles caused waiting
newcred	The number of refreshed authentications
timers	The number of times the time-out value is reached or exceeded
readlink	The number of reads made to a symbolic link

If the timeout ratio is high, the problem can be unresponsive NFS servers or slow networks that are impeding the timely delivery and response of the packets. In the example, there are relatively few time-outs compared to the number of calls (72/74,107 or about 1/10 of 1 percent) that do retransmissions. As the percentage grows toward 5 percent, system administrators begin to take a closer look at it. If badxid is roughly the same as retrans, the problem is probably an NFS server that is falling behind in servicing NFS requests, since duplicate acknowledgments are being received for NFS requests in roughly the same amounts as the retransmissions that are required. (The same thing is true if badxid is roughly the same as timeout.) However, if badxid is a much smaller number than retrans and timeout, then it follows that the network is more likely to be the problem.

TIP

nfsstat enables you to reset the applicable counters to 0 by using the -z option (executed as root). This can be particularly handy when trying to determine if something has caused a problem in the immediate time frame, rather than looking at the numbers collected since the last reboot.

Monitoring Network Performance with `netstat`

One way to check for network loading is to use `netstat` without any parameters:

```
% netstat

TCP
    Local Address          Remote Address       Swind Send-Q Rwind Recv-Q  State
    -------------------    -------------------  ----- ------ ----- ------  -------
    AAA1.1023              bbb2.login            8760      0  8760      0 ESTABLISHED
    AAA1.listen            Cccc.32980            8760      0  8760      0 ESTABLISHED
    AAA1.login             Dddd.1019             8760      0  8760      0 ESTABLISHED
    AAA1.32782             AAA1.32774           16384      0 16384      0 ESTABLISHED
    ...
```

In the report, the important field is the `Send-Q` field, which indicates the depth of the send queue for packets. If the numbers in `Send-Q` are large and increasing in size across several of the connections, the network is probably bogged down.

Looking for Network Data Corruption with `netstat -s`

The `netstat -s` command displays statistics for each of several protocols supported on the system (that is, UDP, IP, TCP, and ICMP). The information can be used to locate problems for the protocol. Here is an example:

```
% netstat -s

UDP
        udpInDatagrams      =2152316  udpInErrors         =        0
        udpOutDatagrams     =2151810

TCP     tcpRtoAlgorithm     =       4  tcpRtoMin          =      200
        tcpRtoMax           =   60000  tcpMaxConn         =       -1
        tcpActiveOpens      =1924360   tcpPassiveOpens    =       81
        tcpAttemptFails     =584963    tcpEstabResets     =1339431
        tcpCurrEstab        =      25  tcpOutSegs         =7814776
        tcpOutDataSegs      =1176484   tcpOutDataBytes    =501907781
        tcpRetransSegs      =1925164   tcpRetransBytes    =444395
        tcpOutAck           =6767853   tcpOutAckDelayed   =1121866
        tcpOutUrg           =     363  tcpOutWinUpdate    =129604
        tcpOutWinProbe      =      25  tcpOutControl      =3263985
        tcpOutRsts          =      47  tcpOutFastRetrans  =       23
        tcpInSegs           =11769363
        tcpInAckSegs        =2419522   tcpInAckBytes      =503241539
        tcpInDupAck         =3589621   tcpInAckUnsent     =        0
        tcpInInorderSegs    =4871078   tcpInInorderBytes  =-477578953
        tcpInUnorderSegs    =910597    tcpInUnorderBytes  =826772340
        tcpInDupSegs        =  60545   tcpInDupBytes      =46037645
        tcpInPartDupSegs    =  44879   tcpInPartDupBytes  =10057185
        tcpInPastWinSegs    =      0   tcpInPastWinBytes  =        0
        tcpInWinProbe       =704105    tcpInWinUpdate     =4470040
        tcpInClosed         =      11  tcpRttNoUpdate     =      907
        tcpRttUpdate        =1079220   tcpTimRetrans      =     1974
        tcpTimRetransDrop   =       2  tcpTimKeepalive    =      577
        tcpTimKeepaliveProbe=     343  tcpTimKeepaliveDrop =       2
```

```
IP   ipForwarding       =        2  ipDefaultTTL     =      255
     ipInReceives       =12954953  ipInHdrErrors    =        0
     ipInAddrErrors     =        0  ipInCksumErrs    =        0
     ipForwDatagrams    =        0  ipForwProhibits  =        0
     ipInUnknownProtos  =        0  ipInDiscards     =        0
     ipInDelivers       =13921597  ipOutRequests    =12199190
     ipOutDiscards      =        0  ipOutNoRoutes    =        0
     ipReasmTimeout     =       60  ipReasmReqds     =        0
     ipReasmOKs         =        0  ipReasmFails     =        0
     ipReasmDuplicates  =        0  ipReasmPartDups  =        0
     ipFragOKs          =     3267  ipFragFails      =        0
     ipFragCreates      =    19052  ipRoutingDiscards =       0
     tcpInErrs          =        0  udpNoPorts       =    64760
     udpInCksumErrs     =        0  udpInOverflows   =        0
     rawipInOverflows   =        0

ICMP icmpInMsgs         =      216  icmpInErrors     =        0
     icmpInCksumErrs    =        0  icmpInUnknowns   =        0
     icmpInDestUnreachs =      216  icmpInTimeExcds  =        0
     icmpInParmProbs    =        0  icmpInSrcQuenchs =        0
     icmpInRedirects    =        0  icmpInBadRedirects =      0
     icmpInEchos        =        0  icmpInEchoReps   =        0
     icmpInTimestamps   =        0  icmpInTimestampReps =     0
     icmpInAddrMasks    =        0  icmpInAddrMaskReps =      0
     icmpInFragNeeded   =        0  icmpOutMsgs      =      230
     icmpOutDrops       =        0  icmpOutErrors    =        0
     icmpOutDestUnreachs =     230  icmpOutTimeExcds =        0
     icmpOutParmProbs   =        0  icmpOutSrcQuenchs =       0
     icmpOutRedirects   =        0  icmpOutEchos     =        0
     icmpOutEchoReps    =        0  icmpOutTimestamps =       0
     icmpOutTimestampReps=       0  icmpOutAddrMasks =        0
     icmpOutAddrMaskReps =       0  icmpOutFragNeeded =       0
     icmpInOverflows    =        0

IGMP:
         0 messages received
         0 messages received with too few bytes
         0 messages received with bad checksum
         0 membership queries received
         0 membership queries received with invalid field(s)
         0 membership reports received
         0 membership reports received with invalid field(s)
         0 membership reports received for groups to which we belong
         0 membership reports sent
```

The checksum fields should always show extremely small values, as they are a percentage of total traffic sent along the interface.

By using netstat -s on the remote system in combination with spray on your own, you can determine whether data corruption (as opposed to network corruption) is impeding the movement of your network data. Alternate between the two displays, observing the differences, if any, between the reports. If the two reports agree on the number of dropped packets, the file server is probably not keeping up. If they don't, you should suspect network integrity problems. Use netstat -i on the remote machine to confirm this.

Corrective Network Actions

If you suspect that there are problems with the integrity of the network itself, you must try to determine where the faulty piece of equipment is. Hire network consultants, who will use network diagnostic scopes to locate and correct the problems.

If the problem is that the network is busy, thus increasing collisions, time-outs, retransmissions, and so on, you may need to redistribute the workload more appropriately. This is a good example of the "divide and conquer" concept as it applies to computers. By partitioning and segmenting the network nodes into subnetworks that more clearly reflect the underlying workloads, you can maximize the overall performance of the network. This can be accomplished by installing additional network interfaces in your gateway and adjusting the addressing on the gateway to reflect the new subnetworks. Altering your cabling and implementing some of the more advanced intelligent hubs may be needed as well. By reorganizing your network, you will maximize the amount of bandwidth that is available for access to the local subnetwork. Make sure that systems that regularly perform NFS mounts of each other are on the same subnetwork.

If you have an older network and are having to rework your network topology, consider replacing the older coax-based networks with the more modern twisted-pair types, which are generally more reliable and flexible.

Make sure that the workload is on the appropriate machine(s). Use the machine with the best network performance to do its proper share of network file service tasks.

Check your network for diskless workstations. These require large amounts of network resources to boot up, swap, page, and so on. With the cost of local storage descending constantly, it is getting harder to believe that diskless workstations are still cost-effective when compared to regular workstations. Consider upgrading the workstations so that they support their users locally, or at least to minimize their use of the network.

If your network server has been acquiring more clients, check its memory and its kernel buffer allocations for proper sizing.

If the problem is that I/O-intensive programs are being run over the network, work with the users to determine what can be done to make that requirement a local, rather than a network, one. Educate your users to make sure they understand when they are using the network appropriately and when they are being wasteful with this valuable resource.

Monitoring CPU Performance

The biggest problem a system administrator faces when examining performance is sorting through all the relevant information to determine which subsystem is really in trouble. Frequently, users complain about the need to upgrade a processor that is assumed to be causing slow execution, when in fact it is the I/O subsystem or memory that is the problem. To make matters even more difficult, all of the subsystems interact with one another, thus complicating the analysis.

You already looked at the three most handy tools for assessing CPU load in the section "Monitoring the Overall System Status." As stated in that section, processor idle time can, under certain conditions, imply that I/O or memory subsystems are degrading the system. It can also, under other conditions, imply that a processor upgrade is appropriate. Using the tools that have been reviewed in this chapter, you can by now piece together a competent picture of the overall activities of your system and its subsystems. You should use the tools to make absolutely sure that the I/O and the memory subsystems are indeed optimized properly before you spend the money to upgrade your CPU.

If you have determined that your CPU has just run out of gas, and you cannot upgrade your system, all is not lost. CPUs are extremely powerful machines that are frequently underutilized for long spans of time in any 24-hour period. If you can rearrange the schedule of the work that must be done to use the CPU as efficiently as possible, you can often overcome most problems. This can be done by getting users to run all appropriate jobs at off-hours (off workload hours, that is, not necessarily 9 to 5). You can also get your users to run selected jobs at lower priorities. You can educate some of your less efficient users and programmers. Finally, you can carefully examine the workload and eliminate some jobs, daemons, and so on, that are not needed.

The following is a brief list of jobs and daemons that deserve review, and possibly elimination, based on the severity of the problem and their use, or lack thereof, on the system. Check each of the following and ask yourself whether you use it or need them: accounting services, printer daemons, `mountd` remote mount daemon, sendmail daemon, talk daemon, remote who daemon, NIS server, and database daemons.

Monitoring Multiprocessor Performance with `mpstat`

One of the most recent developments of significance in the UNIX server world is the rapid deployment of symmetric multiprocessor (SMP) servers. Of course, having multiple CPUs can mean that you may desire a more discrete picture of what is actually happening on the system than `sar -u` can provide.

You learned about some multiprocessor issues in the discussion of `vmstat`, but there are other tools for examining multiprocessor utilization. The `mpstat` command reports the per-processor statistics for the machine. Each row of the report shows the activity of one processor.

```
% mpstat
```

CPU	minf	mjf	xcal	intr	ithr	csw	icsw	migr	smtx	srw	syscl	usr	sys	wt	idl
0	1	0	0	201	71	164	22	34	147	0	942	10	10	23	57
1	1	0	0	57	37	171	23	34	144	1	975	10	11	23	56
2	1	0	0	77	56	158	22	33	146	0	996	11	11	21	56
3	1	0	0	54	33	169	23	34	156	0	1139	12	11	21	56
4	1	0	0	21	0	180	23	33	159	0	1336	14	10	20	56
5	1	0	0	21	0	195	23	31	163	0	1544	17	10	18	55

All values are in terms of events per second, unless otherwise noted. You may specify a sample interval, and a number of samples, with the command, just as you would with sar. The fields of the report are the following:

CPU	CPU processor ID
minf	Minor faults
mjf	Major faults
xcal	Interprocessor cross calls
intr	Interrupts
ithr	Interrupts as threads (not counting clock interrupt)
csw	Context switches
icsw	Involuntary context switches
migr	Thread migrations (to another processor)
smtx	Spins on mutexes (lock not acquired on first try)
srw	Spins on reader/writer locks (lock not acquired on first try)
syscl	System calls
usr	Percentage of user time
sys	Percentage of system time
wt	Percentage of wait time
idl	Percentage of idle time

Don't be intimidated by the technical nature of the display. It is included here just as an indication that multiprocessor systems can be more complex than uniprocessor systems to examine for their performance. Some multiprocessor systems actually can bias work to be done to a particular CPU. That is not done here, as you can see. The user, system, wait, and idle times are all relatively evenly distributed across all the available CPUs.

Kernel Tuning

Kernel tuning is a complex topic, and the space that can be devoted to it in this section is limited. In order to fit this discussion into the space allowed, the focus is on kernel tuning for SunOS in general, and Solaris 2.x in particular. In addition, the section focuses mostly on memory tuning. Your version of UNIX may differ in several respects from the version described here, and you may be involved in other subsystems, but you should get a good idea of the overall concepts and generally how the parameters are tuned.

The most fundamental component of the UNIX operating system is the kernel. It manages all the major subsystems, including memory, disk I/O, utilization of the CPU, process scheduling, and so on. It is the controlling agent that enables the system to perform work for you.

As you can imagine from that introduction, the configuration of the kernel can dramatically affect system performance either positively or negatively. There are parameters that you can tune for various kernel modules. A couple reasons could motivate you to do this. First, by tuning the kernel you can reduce the amount of memory required for the kernel, thus increasing the efficiency of the use of memory, and increasing the throughput of the system. Second, you can increase the capacity of the system to accommodate new requirements (users, processing, or both).

This is a classic case of software compromise. It would be nice to increase the capacity of the system to accommodate all users that would ever be put on the system, but that would have a deleterious effect on performance. Likewise, it would be nice to tune the kernel down to its smallest possible size, but that would have negative side-effects as well. As in most software, the optimal solution is somewhere between the extremes.

Some people think that you only need to change the kernel when the number of people on the system increases. This is not true. You may need to alter the kernel when the nature of your processing changes. If your users are increasing their use of X Window, or increasing their utilization of file systems, running more memory-intensive jobs, and so on, you may need to adjust some of these parameters to optimize the throughput of the system.

Two trends are changing the nature of kernel tuning. First, in an effort to make UNIX a commercially viable product in terms of administration and deployment, most manufacturers are trying to minimize the complexity of the kernel configuration process. As a result, many of the tables that were once allocated in a fixed manner are now allocated dynamically, or else are linked to the value of a handful of fields. Solaris 2.x takes this approach by calculating many kernel values based on the `maxusers` field. Second, as memory is dropping in price and CPU power is increasing dramatically, the relative importance of precise kernel tuning for most systems is gradually diminishing. However, for high-performance systems, or systems with limited memory, it is still a pertinent topic.

Your instruction in UNIX kernel tuning begins with an overview of the kernel tables that are changed by it, and how to display them. It continues with some examples of kernel parameters that are modified to adjust the kernel to current system demands, and it concludes with a detailed example of paging and swapping parameters under SunOS.

CAUTION

Kernel tuning can actually adversely affect memory subsystem performance. As you adjust the parameters upward, the kernel often expands in size. This can affect memory performance, particularly if your system is already beginning to experience a memory shortage problem under normal utilization. As the kernel tables grow, the internal processing related to them may take longer, too, so there may be some minor degradation related to the greater time required for internal operating system activities. Once again, with a healthy system this may be transparent, but with a marginal system the problems may become apparent or more pronounced.

> **CAUTION**
>
> In general you should be very careful with kernel tuning. People who don't understand what they are doing can cripple their systems. Many UNIX versions come with utility programs that help simplify configuration. It's best to use them. It also helps to read the manual, and to procure the assistance of an experienced system administrator before you begin.

> **CAUTION**
>
> Finally, always make sure that you have a copy of your working kernel before you begin altering it. Some experienced system administrators actually make backup copies even if the utility automatically makes one. And it is always a good idea to do a complete backup before installing a new kernel. Don't assume that your disk drives are safe because you are "just making a few minor adjustments," or that the upgrade that you are installing "doesn't seem to change much with respect to the I/O subsystem." Make sure you can get back to your original system state if things go wrong.

Kernel Tables

When should you consider modifying the kernel tables? You should review your kernel parameters in several cases, such as before you add new users, before you increase your X Window activity significantly, or before you increase your NFS utilization markedly. Also review them before the makeup of the programs that are running is altered in a way that will significantly increase the number of processes that are run or the demands they will make on the system.

Some people believe that you always increase kernel parameters when you add more memory, but this is not necessarily so. If you have a thorough knowledge of your system's parameters and know that they are already adjusted to take into account both current loads and some future growth, then adding more memory, in itself, is not necessarily a reason to increase kernel parameters.

Some of the tables are described as follows:

■ **Process table**—The process table sets the number of processes that the system can run at a time. These processes include daemon processes, processes that local users are running, and processes that remote users are running. It also includes forked or spawned processes of users—it may be a little more trouble for you to accurately estimate the number of these. If the system is trying to start system daemon processes and is prevented from doing so because the process table has reached its limit, you may experience intermittent problems (possibly without any direct notification of the error).

■ **User process table**—The user process table controls the number of processes per user that the system can run.

■ **Inode table**—The inode table lists entries for such things as the following:

Each open pipe

Each current user directory

Mount points on each file system

Each active I/O device

When the table is full, performance will degrade. The console will have error messages written to it regarding the error when it occurs. This table is also relevant to the open file table, since they are both concerned with the same subsystem.

■ **Open file table**—This table determines the number of files that can be open on the system at the same time. When the system call is made and the table is full, the program will get an error indication and the console will have an error logged to it.

■ **Quota table**—If your system is configured to support disk quotas, this table contains the number of structures that have been set aside for that use. The quota table will have an entry for each user who has a file system that has quotas turned on. As with the inode table, performance suffers when the table fills up, and errors are written to the console.

■ **Callout table**—This table controls the number of timers that can be active concurrently. Timers are critical to many kernel-related and I/O activities. If the callout table overflows, the system is likely to crash.

Checking System Tables with `sar -v`

The `-v` option enables you to see the current process table, inode table, open file table, and shared memory record table.

The fields in the report are as follows:

`proc-sz`	The number of process table entries in use/the number allocated
`inod-sz`	The number of inode table entries in use/the number allocated
`file-sz`	The number of file table entries currently in use/the number 0 designating that space is allocated dynamically for this entry
`lock-sz`	The number of shared memory record table entries in use/the number 0 designating that space is allocated dynamically for this entry
`ov`	The overflow field, showing the number of times the field to the immediate left has had to overflow

Any non-zero entry in the ov field is an obvious indication that you need to adjust your kernel parameters relevant to that field. This is one performance report where you can request historical information, for the last day, the last week, or since last reboot, and actually get meaningful data out of it.

This is also another good report to use intermittently during the day to sample how much reserve capacity you have.

Here is an example:

```
% sar -v 5 5

18:51:12  proc-sz    ov  inod-sz    ov  file-sz   ov  lock-sz
18:51:17  122/4058    0  3205/4000   0  488/0      0  11/0   _
18:51:22  122/4058    0  3205/4000   0  488/0      0  11/0   _
18:51:27  122/4058    0  3205/4000   0  488/0      0  11/0   _
18:51:32  122/4058    0  3205/4000   0  488/0      0  11/0   _
18:51:37  122/4058    0  3205/4000   0  488/0      0  11/0   _
```

Since all the ov fields are 0, you can see that the system tables are healthy for this interval. In this display, for example, there are 122 process table entries in use, and there are 4,058 process table entries allocated.

Displaying Tunable Kernel Parameters

To display a comprehensive list of tunable kernel parameters, you can use the nm command. For example, applying the command to the appropriate module, the name list of the file will be reported:

```
% nm /kernel/unix

Symbols from /kernel/unix:

[Index]   Value     Size  Type  Bind  Other Shndx    Name

...
[15]           0        0 FILE  LOCL  0     ABS      unix.o
[16] 3758124752        0 NOTY  LOCL  0     1        vhwb_nextset
[17] 3758121512        0 NOTY  LOCL  0     1        _intr_flag_table
[18] 3758124096        0 NOTY  LOCL  0     1        trap_mon
[19] 3758121436        0 NOTY  LOCL  0     1        intr_set_spl
[20] 3758121040        0 NOTY  LOCL  0     1        intr_mutex_panic
[21] 3758121340        0 NOTY  LOCL  0     1        intr_thread_exit
[22] 3758124768        0 NOTY  LOCL  0     1        vhwb_nextline
[23] 3758124144        0 NOTY  LOCL  0     1        trap_kadb
[24] 3758124796        0 NOTY  LOCL  0     1        vhwb_nextdword
[25] 3758116924        0 NOTY  LOCL  0     1        firsthighinstr
[26] 3758121100      132 NOTY  LOCL  0     1        intr_thread
[27] 3758118696        0 NOTY  LOCL  0     1        fixfault
[28]           0        0 FILE  LOCL  0     ABS      confunix.c
...
     (Portions of display deleted for brevity)
```

The relevant fields in the report are the following:

Index	The index of the symbol (appears in brackets).
Value	The value of the symbol.
Size	The size, in bytes, of the associated object.
Type	A symbol is one of the following types: NOTYPE (no type was specified), OBJECT (a data object such as an array or variable), FUNC (a function or other executable code), SECTION (a section symbol), or FILE (name of the source file).
Bind	The symbol's binding attributes. LOCAL symbols have a scope limited to the object file containing their definition; GLOBAL symbols are visible to all object files being combined; and WEAK symbols are essentially global symbols with a lower precedence than GLOBAL.
Shndx	Except for three special values, this is the section header table index in relation to which the symbol is defined. The following special values exist: ABS indicates that the symbol's value will not change through relocation; COMMON indicates an allocated block and the value provides alignment constraints; and UNDEF indicates an undefined symbol.
Name	The name of the symbol.

On HP-UX 10.x systems, there is a text file that is used as the configuration file for the kernel at compile time. This file is the /stand/system file.

To get the most recent version of the kernel configurations, this file needs to be rebuilt. To do this, cd into the /stand/build directory and run the command /usr/lbin/sysadm/system_prep -s system. This will create a new system file in the /stand/build directory, which can then be edited for the desired changes.

Displaying Current Values of Tunable Parameters

To display a list of the current values assigned to the tunable kernel parameters, you can use the sysdef -i command:

```
% sysdef -i
... (portions of display are deleted for brevity)
*
* System Configuration
*
swapfile              dev  swaplo blocks   free
/dev/dsk/c0t3d0s1    32,25      8 547112  96936
*
* Tunable Parameters
*
```

```
5316608   maximum memory allowed in buffer cache (bufhwm)
   4058   maximum number of processes (v.v_proc)
     99   maximum global priority in sys class (MAXCLSYSPRI)
   4053   maximum processes per user id (v.v_maxup)
     30   auto update time limit in seconds (NAUTOUP)
     25   page stealing low water mark (GPGSLO)
      5   fsflush run rate (FSFLUSHR)
     25   minimum resident memory for avoiding deadlock (MINARMEM)
     25   minimum swapable memory for avoiding deadlock (MINASMEM)
*
* Utsname Tunables
*
    5.3   release (REL)
   DDDD   node name (NODE)
  SunOS   system name (SYS)
Generic_101318-31  version (VER)
*
* Process Resource Limit Tunables (Current:Maximum)
*
Infinity:Infinity   cpu time
Infinity:Infinity   file size
7ffff000:7ffff000   heap size
  800000:7ffff000   stack size
Infinity:Infinity   core file size
      40:     400   file descriptors
Infinity:Infinity   mapped memory
*
* Streams Tunables
*
      9   maximum number of pushes allowed (NSTRPUSH)
  65536   maximum stream message size (STRMSGSZ)
   1024   max size of ctl part of message (STRCTLSZ)
*
* IPC Messages
*
    200   entries in msg map (MSGMAP)
   2048   max message size (MSGMAX)
  65535   max bytes on queue (MSGMNB)
     25   message queue identifiers (MSGMNI)
    128   message segment size (MSGSSZ)
    400   system message headers (MSGTQL)
   1024   message segments (MSGSEG)
    SYS   system class name (SYS_NAME)
```

As stated earlier, over the years there have been many enhancements that have tried to minimize the complexity of the kernel configuration process. As a result, many of the tables that were once allocated in a fixed manner are now allocated dynamically, or else linked to the value of the maxusers field. The next step in understanding the nature of kernel tables is to look at the maxusers parameter and its impact on UNIX system configuration.

Modifying the Configuration Information File

SunOS uses the /etc/system file for modification of kernel-tunable variables. The basic format is this:

```
set parameter = value
```

It can also have this format:

```
set [module:]variablename = value
```

The /etc/system file can also be used for other purposes (for example, to force modules to be loaded at boot time, to specify a root device, and so on). The /etc/system file is used for permanent changes to the operating system values. Temporary changes can be made using adb kernel debugging tools. The system must be rebooted for the changes made for them to become active using /etc/system. With adb the changes take place when applied.

CAUTION

Be very careful with set commands in the /etc/system file! They basically cause patches to be performed on the kernel itself, and there is a great deal of potential for dire consequences from misunderstood settings. Make sure you have handy the relevant system administrators' manuals for your system, as well as a reliable and experienced system administrator for guidance.

As mentioned earlier in the chapter, HP-UX 10.x has a similar /etc/system file, which can be modified and recompiled.

Once you have made your changes to this file, you can recompile to make a new UNIX kernel. The command is mkkernel -s system. This new kernel, called vmunix.test, is placed in the /stand/build directory. Next, you move the present /stand/system file to /stand/system.prev; then you can move the modified file /stand/build/system to /stand/system. Then you move the currently running kernel /stand/vmunix to /stand/vmunix.prev, and then move the new kernel, /stand/build/vmunix.test, into place in /stand/vmunix (that is, mv /stand/build/vmunix.test /stant/vmunix). The final step is to reboot the machine to make your changes take effect.

The maxusers Parameter

Many of the tables are dynamically updated either upward or downward by the operating system, based on the value assigned to the maxusers parameter, which is an approximation of the number of users the system will have to support. The quickest and, more importantly, safest way to modify the table sizes is by modifying maxusers, and letting the system perform the adjustments to the tables for you.

The maxusers parameter can be adjusted by placing commands in the /etc/system file of your UNIX system:

```
set maxusers=24
```

A number of kernel parameters adjust their values according to the setting of the maxusers parameter. For example, Table 22.2 lists the settings for various kernel parameters, where maxusers is utilized in their calculation.

Table 22.2. Kernel parameters affected by maxusers.

Table	Parameter	Setting
Process	max_nprocs	10 + 16 * maxusers (sets the size of the process table)
User process	maxuprc	max_nprocs-5 (sets the number of user processes)
Callout	ncallout	16 + max_nprocs (sets the size of the callout table)
Name cache	ncsize	max_nprocs + 16 + maxusers + 64 (sets size of the directory lookup cache)
Inode	ufs_ninode	max_nprocs + 16 + maxusers + 64 (sets the size of the inode table)
Quota table	ndquot	(maxusers * NMOUNT) / 4 + max_nprocs (sets the number of disk quota structures)

The directory name lookup cache (dnlc) is also based on maxusers in SunOS systems. With the increasing usage of NFS, this can be an important performance tuning parameter. Networks that have many clients can be helped by an increased name cache parameter ncsize (that is, a greater amount of cache). By using vmstat with the -s option, you can determine the directory name lookup cache hit rate. A cache miss indicates that disk I/O was probably needed to access the directory when traversing the path components to get to a file. If the hit rate falls below 70 percent, this parameter should be checked.

```
% vmstat -s

        0 swap ins
        0 swap outs
        0 pages swapped in
        0 pages swapped out
  1530750 total address trans. faults taken
    39351 page ins
    22369 page outs
    45565 pages paged in
   114923 pages paged out
    73786 total reclaims
    65945 reclaims from free list
        0 micro (hat) faults
  1530750 minor (as) faults
    38916 major faults
    88376 copy-on-write faults
   120412 zero fill page faults
   634336 pages examined by the clock daemon
       10 revolutions of the clock hand
   122233 pages freed by the clock daemon
     4466 forks
      471 vforks
     6416 execs
```

```
 45913303 cpu context switches
 28556694 device interrupts
  1885547 traps
665339442 system calls
   622350 total name lookups (cache hits 94%)
        4 toolong
  2281992 user    cpu
  3172652 system  cpu
 62275344 idle    cpu
   967604 wait    cpu
```

In this example, you can see that the cache hits are 94 percent, and therefore enough directory name lookup cache is allocated on the system.

By the way, if your NFS traffic is heavy and irregular in nature, you should increase the number of nfsd NFS daemons. Some system administrators recommend that this should be set between 40 and 60 on dedicated NFS servers. This will increase the speed with which the nfsd daemons take the requests off the network and pass them on to the I/O subsystem. Conversely, decreasing this value can throttle the NFS load on a server when that is appropriate.

The monitor Utility

Monitor is a shareware utility that can be obtained from various ftp sites. This utility is actually a very handy tool for getting live updates on the status of your system.

So what does it show? The question is, "What doesn't it show?" Monitor will give you real-time updates on CPU utilization, CPU wait states, disk I/O, a list of the top running processes, and much more.

As you bring the utility up, you can see a number of things in the first screen. CPU utilization is shown as a text-based "emoticon" meter, breaking down CPU time into system, user, and idle time. Also, you have different load statistics displayed, such as disk I/O, swapping statistics, free memory, and a breakdown of memory metrics.

There are also two screen switches to show further details on disk I/O and process statistics.

To find a full breakdown of disk activity by disk, simply hit the "d" key. You can see the disk transfer wait in kb/s, I/O's per second, disk wait times, and much more. To get back to the main screen, just hit the "d" key again.

To see a full breakdown of the most active processes, hit the "t" key. This will show you a detailed listing of system processes, in descending order from highest to lowest in compute time. This a good way to see if you have any runaway or hung processes. Here you can see how long a process has been running, who started and owns it, which process spawned it, and much more. To get back to the main menu, just hit the "t" key again.

To quit monitor, all you have to do is hit the "q" key.

Parameters That Influence Paging and Swapping

The section isn't large enough to review in detail how tuning can affect each of the kernel tables. However, for illustration purposes, this section describes how kernel parameters influence paging and swapping activities in a SunOS system. Other tables affecting other subsystems can be tuned in much the same manner as these.

As processes make demands on memory, pages are allocated from the free list. When the UNIX system decides that there is no longer enough free memory—less than the `lotsfree` parameter—it searches for pages that haven't been used lately to add them to the free list. The page daemon will be scheduled to run. It begins at a slow rate, based on the `slowscan` parameter, and increases to a faster rate, based on the `fastscan` parameter, as free memory continues toward depletion. If there is less memory than `desfree`, and there are two or more processes in the run queue, and the system stays in that condition for more than 30 seconds, the system will begin to swap. If the system gets to a minimum level of required memory, specified by the `minfree` parameter, swapping will begin without delay. When swapping begins, entire processes will be swapped out as described earlier.

> **NOTE**
>
> If you have your swapping spread over several disks, increasing the `maxpgio` parameter may be beneficial. This parameter limits the number of pages scheduled to be paged out, and is based on single-disk swapping. Increasing it may improve paging performance. You can use the po field from `vmstat`, as described earlier, which checks against `maxpgio` and pagesize to examine the volumes involved.

The kernel swaps out the oldest and the largest processes when it begins to swap. The `maxslp` parameter is used in determining which processes have exceeded the maximum sleeping period, and can thus be swapped out as well. The smallest higher-priority processes that have been sleeping the longest will then be swapped back in.

The most pertinent kernel parameters for paging and swapping are the following:

- `minfree`—This is the absolute minimum memory level that the system will tolerate. Once past `minfree`, the system immediately resorts to swapping.
- `desfree`—This is the desperation level. After 30 seconds at this level, paging is abandoned and swapping is begun.
- `lotsfree`—Once below this memory limit, the page daemon is activated to begin freeing memory.
- `fastscan`—This is the number of pages scanned per second.
- `slowscan`—This is the number of pages scanned per second when there is less memory than `lotsfree` available. As memory decreases from `lotsfree` the scanning speed increases from `slowscan` to `fastscan`.

■ `maxpgio`—This is the maximum number of page out I/O operations per second that the system will schedule. This is normally set at approximately 40 under SunOS, which is appropriate for a single 3,600 RPM disk. It can be increased with more or faster disks.

Newer versions of UNIX, such as Solaris 2.x, do such a good job of setting paging parameters that tuning is usually not required.

Increasing `lotsfree` will help on systems on which there is a continuing need to allocate new processes. Heavily used interactive systems with many Windows users often force this condition as users open multiple windows and start processes. By increasing `lotsfree` you create a large enough pool of free memory that you will not run out when most of the processes are initially starting up.

For servers that have a defined set of users and a more steady-state condition to their underlying processes, the normal default values are usually appropriate.

However, for servers such as this with large, stable workloads, but that are short of memory, increasing `lotsfree` is the wrong idea. This is because more pages will be taken from the application and put on the free list.

Some system administrators recommend that you disable the `maxslp` parameter on systems where the overhead of swapping normally sleeping processes (such as clock icons and update processes) isn't offset by any measurable gain due to forcing the processes out. This parameter is no longer used in Solaris 2.x releases, but is used on older versions of UNIX.

Conclusion of Kernel Tuning

You have now seen how to optimize memory subsystem performance by tuning a system's kernel parameters. Other subsystems can be tuned by similar modifications to the relevant kernel parameters. When such changes correct existing kernel configurations that have become obsolete and inefficient due to new requirements, the result can sometimes dramatically increase performance even without a hardware upgrade. It's not quite the same as getting a hardware upgrade for free, but it's about as close as you're likely to get in today's computer industry.

Third-Party Solutions

In addition to the standard text-based utilities we have been talking about, there are a number of third-party, enterprise-wide products that are available to monitor your servers. I will focus on two here: ServerVision from Platinum Technologies and EcoTools from Compuware.

Usually, these products are located on their own separate server, but often, due to budget considerations and other concerns, the monitor server is often placed on a production box. This defeats the purpose of a monitoring system, since the monitoring machine is just as likely to go down as the servers that it monitors in this situation. Therefore, I strongly recommend that you push as much as you can for a small workstation to act as the monitor for your system, and nothing else.

EcoTools has a number of neat features that make it a nice solution for many shops. According to their marketing literature (for what it's worth), it boasts an open and robust architecture, heterogeneous support, support for process automation, extensive monitoring and analysis, security for sensitive system information, out-of-the-box functionality, and easy customization.

In reality, it is on a par with most every other system monitoring tool on the market, with a slight advantage because it's a GUI. It really does have a nice fuzzy display that will show most of what you need to see on your systems. The graphs you can get from its logs could be shown in any boardroom, if that's what your after.

What it lacks in warm fuzziness, ServerVision makes up for in pure kitchen sink monitoring metrics and logging tools. Platinum boasts over 200 system metrics that can be monitored on your systems, in addition to another 200 database metrics that you can use if you get their DBVision product.

> **NOTE**
>
> If you do have DBVision installed, particularly version 3.1.3 and version 3.1.6, you must turn off the `lock_waits` metric if it is installed on an AIX system. If you don't, your system will slow down to an unusable crawl! This is a bug in version 3.1.3 on AIX, and, at the time of this writing, it has yet to be fixed in version 3.1.6.

With ServerVision, as with any such tool, you must run the default settings for a short time before moving it into production to get a feel for where to set your alarm settings. If you have your server set up to page you and you don't modify these values, you will be getting paged late at night on a regular basis. Not much fun.

The paging function often comes in handy, if you like having a live system when you come in to the office in the morning. With this advanced warning, you would have the ability to get online and save a dying system well before it crashes.

No matter what software you buy for your system, ask your salesman for a complete demonstration, and bring a list of questions about your requirements. These solutions can be *very* expensive, so be sure you are getting what you pay for before you buy.

Summary

In this chapter we have covered a number of issues dealing with performance and tuning. We touched on such topics as the impact of performance on users, introduction to UNIX performance, monitoring the overall system status, monitoring processes with ps, monitoring memory utilization, monitoring disk subsystem performance, monitoring network performance, monitoring CPU performance, kernel tuning, and third-party solutions.

With a little practice using the methodology described in this chapter, you should be able to determine what the performance characteristics, positive or negative, are for your system. You have seen how to use the commands that enable you to examine each of the resources a UNIX system uses. In addition to the commands themselves, you have learned procedures that can be utilized to analyze and solve many performance problems.

Device Administration

by Salim Douba

IN THIS CHAPTER

Central to the system administrator's responsibilities is the provision to users of access to the distributed and shared resources belonging to their environment. Some of the resources are software (for example, applications, the file system, and so on), whereas others are hardware such as terminals, modems, printers, and so on. Other chapters will address the issues and concerns pertaining to the administration of software resources; this chapter addresses issues pertaining to the administration and management of hardware resources (that is, devices). Namely, you will be presented with the skills necessary to set up, configure, and maintain the performance of modems, terminals, printers, X terminals, and PCs.

For the purposes of terminal, modem, and printer setup UNIX SVR4 comes with a very powerful and central access facility known as Service Access Facility (SAF). No treatment of device administration under SVR4 is complete without covering SAF. Neither is it possible for the system administrator to complete the aforementioned tasks successfully without a rigorous understanding of what SAF is all about, and the skillful use of its associated commands. Hence, SAF will be presented first. Device administration using SAF will be covered next.

BSD UNIX is lacking in providing a unifying interface, such as SAF, for device administration. Concepts, tools, and skills needed in setting up and administering devices under BSD will be covered, in a separate section, in the context of the described tasks.

Following is a list of the major topics that this chapter covers:

- Service Access Facility Under SVR4
- Device Administrative Tasks Under SVR4
- Connecting Printers
- Connecting a PC to UNIX Systems
- Connecting X Terminals

 # Service Access Facility Under SVR4

Prior to System V release 4 of UNIX, administrators were provided with different processes and interfaces, along with their associated tools, to manage different physical resources on the system. Local port access used to be administered and controlled by interfaces that are different from those needed to set up for network access, or those pertaining to printer setup and so on. Administrators were therefore confronted with the challenge of learning and mastering the many different skills and interfaces needed to get the job done. To alleviate this challenge, SAF was introduced with SVR4. SAF provides a commonly applicable interface for the purpose of comprehensive and uniform management of all system resources. Upon mastering the concepts and associated commands that SAF provides, the administrator will be able to install, configure, monitor, and maintain information relevant to the local and network access to physical port services in SAF database files.

SAF consists primarily of port services, port monitors, the service access controller (sac) process, and SAF administrative files and commands.

A description of each of these components will be provided. Then the SAF initialization process will be detailed.

Port Services

SAF defines a hierarchy of port control processes, of which port service is the lowest and the most "intimate" to the actual physical services. A port service is defined as a process that controls and monitors access to applications and other services, through physical ports such as ttys and TCP/IP. A tty service may provide users with dial-in/dial-out capabilities, thus allowing them to utilize high-level applications such as uucp, cu, and login. A TCP/IP port-related service may be required to provide printing, rlogin, or nfs services across the network.

There is a one-to-one association between physical ports (the actual physical service) and port services (the controlling process). It is not possible, for example, for two ttys to share the same port service; neither is it possible for one tty port to be controlled by more than one port service.

Upon creation of a port service, the system administrator assigns it a service name, which is referred to as the service tag. Service tags are used to conveniently distinguish between the port services running on the system. Port services are supported and controlled by intermediate-level processes called port monitors, which are described next.

Port Monitors

A port monitor is an intermediate-level process that controls a set of related services. SAF currently recognizes two types of port monitors: ttymon and listen. However SAF is not limited to those two types. Vendors and system programmers are provided with a well-defined network programming interface, to enable them to write their own monitor types.

Port monitor type ttymon controls and monitors tty-related port services, replacing pre-SVR4 getty and uugetty programs. Although maintaining support to uugetty and getty processes in SVR4 for reasons of backward compatibility, ttymon is the preferred method of installing, configuring, and monitoring tty port services in SVR4. Port monitor type listen, on the other hand, takes advantage of TCP/IP communications protocols to provide across-the-network services mentioned earlier, such as network printing and remote file-sharing capabilities. Both port monitor types will be comprehensively explained in the upcoming sections.

System administrators are allowed the flexibility to create as many port monitors of any type as they deem necessary. Upon creation of a port monitor, a so-called port monitor tag has to be assigned to it. As in the case of port services, port monitor tags are names that help in distinguishing between port monitors. They can be given convenient names that may describe the nature of the service they support. Being a mid-level process, port monitors themselves are invoked, controlled, and monitored by the service access controller (sac) process.

Service Access Controller

The service access controller process is the highest in the SAF hierarchy. There is only one `sac` per system. It invokes and controls all port monitors, irrespective of type, that have been created and configured by the system administrator. `sac` is a program that is spawned by `init` upon system startup when multiuser mode is entered. When SVR4 is installed, an entry supporting `sac` is automatically included in the `/etc/inittab` file. A depiction of how this entry should look is as follows:

```
sc:234:respawn:/usr/lib/saf/sac -t 300
```

Due to the `-t 300` option, `sac` routinely checks port monitors every 300 seconds for services. In order to change it to any other different value, enter

```
#sacadm -t <seconds>
```

> **NOTE**
>
> Do not be surprised, upon checking the `/etc/inittab` file, if you see entries pertaining to `ttymon` port monitor. There is no contradiction between what you see and what has already been explained. Simply put, SVR4 allows a so-called "express mode" invocation of `ttymon` by `init`. This particularly applies to the case of the console port. You will still be able, however, to create instances of `ttymon` that are controlled and administered by `sac`.

SAF Administrative Commands and Files

SAF distinguishes between `sac`-specific, port monitor–specific, and port service–specific administrative and configuration files as well as administrative commands. In this section, the administrative and configuration files and SAF-related commands will be described. The emphasis will be on their natures and the jobs they do. Command syntax and utilization for the purposes of creating, configuring, or checking the status of port monitors and port services will be left until later sections where they'll be discussed at length in the context of tasks to accomplish.

Service Access Controller–Specific Files and Commands

Once brought up, `sac` fetches two files. Those files are as follows: `/etc/saf/_sactab`, which is the administrative database that contains entries pertaining to port monitors defined by the system administrator, and the `/etc/saf/_sysconfig` file, which is a `sac`-specific configuration file. Whereas `sac` uses the first file to identify the port monitors to invoke, it uses the second one in order to self-customize its own environment. Contents of `/etc/saf/_sactab` can be modified by the `sacadm` command, which is `sac`'s administrative command. Using `sacadm` allows administrators to create port monitors, check their status, and enable or disable them as well as remove them. Also, each port monitor provides an administrative command that can be used with sacadm in command substitution mode. The listen port monitor administrative command is nlsadmin, whereas ttymon's is ttyadm.

/etc/saf/_sysconfig file, on the other hand, is a file that would be used by sac to specify the environment governing all the services controlled by it. The sac program, once started by init, reads and interprets this file prior to the invocation of any service defined by /etc/saf/_sactab. There can optionally be one _sysconfig file per system, and it can be edited using vi or any other UNIX editor.

Port Monitor–Specific Files and Commands

When a port monitor is created using sacadm, an /etc/saf/<pmtag> directory will be created where port-specific files are maintained. Of prime interest are /etc/saf/<pmtag>/_pmtab and /etc/saf/<pmtag>/_config. If, for example, you create a port monitor, which you assign a tag called ttyserv, a directory called /etc/saf/ttyserv will be created in which the administrative file called /etc/saf/ttyserv/_config will be maintained. This file is similar to the /etc/saf/_sactab in its functionality, as it is used by the port monitor to determine and bring up the port services as defined by the system administrator. /etc/saf/<pmtag>/_pmtab is a one-per-port monitor file and is modified using the pmadm command whether creating, deleting, or modifying the status of any of the associated port services. The /etc/saf/<pmtag>/_config is an optional port monitor specific configuration file that can be created by the system administrator using vi. Commands in this file can add to, or override, those found in the system configuration file _sysconfig. Before starting a port monitor defined in /etc/saf/_sactab file, sac checks the port monitors' respective directory, described previously, for the _config file. If found, _config is read and interpreted by sac to customize the port monitor's environment, and then the port monitor is started.

Port Service–Specific Files and Commands

Being at the bottom of the SAF hierarchy, port services have no administrative files associated with it. The system administrator, however, has the option to create a port service-specific configuration script named after the service tag and kept in the associated port monitor's directory. So if, for example, a port service was created under port monitor ttyserv and was given the service tag ttylogin1, then the port service configuration file is named ttylogin1 and is kept in the /etc/saf/ttyserv directory. The complete filename thus becomes /etc/saf/ttyserv/ttylogin1. This file is read and interpreted by the controlling port monitor before starting the port service. Configuration commands included in the file may override or add to those found in the _config port monitor's file or _sysconfig that are associated with this service.

Table 23.1 summarizes what has been discussed so far and provides you with a quick way to narrow down the files and commands associated with each SAF component.

23

DEVICE ADMINISTRATION

Table 23.1. Administrative files and commands associated with each of the SAF components.

Process Filename	Invoked by Admin Command	Admin Filename	config
sac	init	/etc/saf/_sactab	/etc/saf/_sysconfig sacadm
port monitor	sac pmadm	/etc/saf/<pmtag>/_pmtab	/etc/saf/<pmtag>/_config
port service	port monitor	optional	pmadm

SAF Initialization Process

Figure 23.1 shows a flow chart summarizing the SAF initialization process. Note how it all starts with init invoking sac after reading a sac-associated entry in the /etc/inittab file. Once sac is started, it proceeds as follows:

FIGURE 23.1.

Flow chart illustration of SAF initialization process.

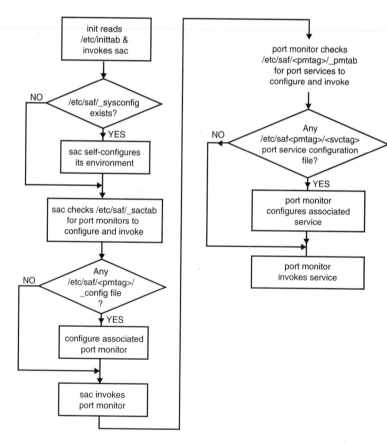

sac checks for the /etc/saf/_sysconfig configuration file. If found, it reads the file in order to self-customize its environment. This environment is a global one that, unless otherwise modified or overridden, will govern all defined SAF services.

sac determines which port monitors to invoke by reading the /etc/saf/_sactab file. For each port monitor, sac checks for the associated /etc/saf/<*pmtag*>/_config file. If one exists, the sac process reads, interprets, and implements the contents and customizes the port monitor's environment, irrespective of any earlier associated settings defined in _sysconfig files. The port monitor is then invoked.

Once invoked, the port monitor determines which port services to start by reading its /etc/saf/<*pmtag*>/_pmtab file. Next, the port monitor checks for the optional /etc/saf/<*pmtag*>/<*svctag*> corresponding to each port service. If one exists, it is read and interpreted to customize the port service environment. The port service is then invoked.

After the initialization process is completed, sac continues to poll the port monitors at regular intervals as defined by the -t option in the corresponding entry in the /etc/inittab file. Port monitors failing to respond to this polling process prompt sac into respawning them.

SAF Administration and Management

This section introduces some of the concepts and skills pertaining to SAF management and administration. Because those skills commonly apply to all types of port monitors and their associated port services, the discussion will focus on how to accomplish each of the following tasks described, with little emphasis on the nature of the service being rendered to the user. SAF management and administration is a two-level system: one level applies to port monitors, whereas the other applies to port services. This section is therefore presented in two parts.

Port Monitor Administration and Management

As explained earlier in this chapter, for an administrator to offer port services, be it across the network or local to the system, he or she must first create the port monitor supporting it. Only then can port services be created and released to the user community. There are also troubleshooting instances when the administrator may need to check on the status of suspect port monitors or even temporarily disable them.

Creating a Port Monitor

Port monitors are administered and managed using the sacadm administrative command. In addition to sacadm, each port monitor type provides for an administrative command that is commonly used with sacadm in "command substitution mode." ttyadm is ttymon's command, whereas nlsadmin is listen's. To create a port monitor, sacadm must be entered along with the following options:

```
#sacadm -a -p<pmtag> -t<type> -c"<pm_cmd>" -v ver [-fd¦x] \
[-n <count>] [-y"comment"]
```

where:

> -a stands for add or create a port monitor.
>
> -p *<pmtag>* assigns a name to the port monitor being created, which can be conveniently used to distinguish it from other port monitors. Although the name can be anything you choose, it should be descriptive of the type of service with which it is associated.
>
> -t *<type>* specifies the type of monitor to create (that is, ttymon versus listen).
>
> -c "*<pm_cmd>*" specifies the command to invoke when the port monitor is later spawned by sac: /usr/lib/saf/ttymon to invoke a ttymon port monitor, or /usr/lib/saf/listen to invoke a listen port monitor.
>
> -v *ver* specifies the version of the port monitor. The version may more conveniently be provided by invoking the port monitor's specific administrative command (ttyadm or nlsadmin) with the -V option in command substitution form (that is, as an argument to -v). In this case, the -V option would be typed as follows:
>
> ```
> # sacadm -a ... -v'ttyadm -V' ...
> ```
>
> -f [d¦x] specifies the status of the port monitor upon invocation, with d meaning to start the port monitor in disabled state and x meaning not to start it. If flagged x, the port monitor can only be started by the system administrator. There onward, sac takes over in controlling the port monitor.
>
> -n*<count>* specifies the retry count used by the port monitor in restarting a failing port monitor. If not included, the default that applies is zero.
>
> -y "*comment*" can be any comment that you may want to include in the /etc/saf/_sactab file. For your convenience, you may want to include a comment describing what this port monitor is for.

When a port monitor is created, the following happens: 1) An entry in sac's administrative file /etc/saf/_sactab is added pertaining to the port monitor, including all of the arguments provided on the command line. 2) The port monitor's supporting directory /etc/saf/*<pmtag>* is also created. As a matter of fact, another directory, /var/saf/*<pmtag>*, will also be created where a port monitor log file is maintained. The filename is /var/saf/*<pmtag>*/log. It is used by sac to log all messages pertaining to the port monitor.

For a better feel for what has been said so far, take a look at an example of creating a port monitor. This example will be carried over to upcoming sections to demonstrate aspects of managing the port monitor. In this example it is assumed that the system administrator wants to allow users local logins to the system, using serial communications. Hence, the first task is to create the port monitor in preparation for creating the necessary associated port services.

Due to the nature of the service (that is, serial communication), the port monitor has to be of a ttymon type. The system administrator has chosen to assign the port monitor the tag ttyserv, start it in the disabled state, and include a comment saying "only two logins." Upon failure, sac should attempt restarting the monitor twice. The sacadm command should therefore look like this:

```
#sacadm -a -p serial -t ttymon -v 'ttyadm -V' \
 -c"/usr/lib/saf/ttymon" -fd -n 2 -y "only two logins"
```

Next, you'll be learning how to check on the status of the port monitor. For the time being, however, we can carry a check using cat to look up the contents of sac's /etc/saf/_sactab file. cat /etc/saf/_sactab should reveal the following entry:

```
ttyserv:ttymon:d:2:/usr/lib/saf/ttymon          #only two logins
```

And if you enter ls -l /etc/saf, you will be able to verify that the subdirectory is ttyserv. ttyserv (the subdirectory) is created among others existing at the /etc/saf level. Reflecting back on the _sactab entry shown previously, you should have guessed how each field in /etc/saf/_sactab file maps to arguments you enter on the command line. The first field refers to the pmtag, the second to the port monitor type, the third to the state in which the port monitor is started (disabled state, in this example). The fourth mandates that two restarts be attempted should the port monitor fail, and the fifth specifies the complete pathname of the command to invoke. Note also that the comment is included as well.

Checking the Status of the Port Monitor

To check on the status of the port monitor, use the sacadm command with -l option among the others as follows:

- # sacadm -t<type> -l to obtain a listing of all port monitors of same type
- # sacadm -p<pmtag> -l to obtain information about a specific port monitor

If you enter sacadm -pttyserv -l to check on the port monitor just created in the preceding example, you get the following output:

```
PMTAG      PMTYPE    FLGS RCNT STATUS    COMMAND
ttyserv    ttymon    d    2    DISABLED  /usr/lib/saf/ttymon #only two logins
```

Note that the status field indicates that the port monitor is in a disabled state. If you check the status immediately after the port monitor is created, the status field may indicate that it is STARTING.

The port monitor can be in one of the following states:

STARTING	sac is in the process of starting it. This is a transitional state between NOTRUNNING and ENABLED or DISABLED.
ENABLED	The port monitor is running and is accepting connection requests.
DISABLED	The port monitor is running but refusing connection service requests.
STOPPED	The port monitor is undergoing the shutdown process. This state is transitional from ENABLED or DISABLED and NOTRUNNING.
NOTRUNNING	The port monitor is not running. None of the port services associated with it is currently accessible.

Enabling, Disabling, and Removing a Port Monitor

To enable, disable, or remove a port monitor, use sacadm -e, sacadm -d, or sacadm -r, respectively. To enable the ttyserv port monitor, enter

```
# sacadm -pttyserv -e
```

whereas to disable it, enter

```
# sacadm -pttyserv -d
```

and to remove it, enter

```
# sacadm -pttyserv -r
```

> **NOTE**
>
> When a port monitor is removed, its associated directories are not cleaned up and deleted. To avoid confusion in the future, you may have to take care of that yourself.

Port Service Administration and Management

Only after the port monitor is created is the system administrator in a position to create and manage the associated port services. Port creation and administration are achievable via the pmadm command.

Creating a Port Service

To create a port service, pmadm should be used with the -a option, among the others as follows:

```
# pmadm -a -p<pmtag> -s<svctag> -m"pmspecific" \
-v <ver> [-fd¦u] -y"comment"
```

in which

-a stands for create a port service.

-p<*pmtag*> specifies the tag of the port monitor to which the port service belongs.

-s<*svctag*> specifies the service tag assigned to the port service.

-m"<*pmspecific*>" specifies port-specific information to be passed as an argument to the pmadm command. Normally, this information is generated by employing either ttyadm or nlsadmin in command substitution mode, depending on the type of the port monitor specified with the -p option.

-v <*ver*> passes the version of the port monitor. Depending on the type of the port monitor, either ttymon -V or nlsadmin -V can be used in command substitution mode.

-f specifies the state with which the port service should be started, and whether a `utmp` entry is to be created. Both or any of the flags can be specified, where d specifies that the port should be started in disabled state, and u specifies that a `utmp` entry be created for the service.

The following example adds a `ttymon` port service to the `ttyserv` port monitor created earlier in this section:

```
#pmadm -a -pttyserv -s s01 -v 'ttyadm -C' -fd \
-m "`ttyadm -d /dev/term/01 -l 9600 -s/usr/bin/login \
-p"Welcome To UNIX, Please Login:"'"
```

The port service thus created is assigned service tag s01 and added to a port monitor called `ttyserv` (the one created in the earlier section). s01 port is associated with `/dev/term/01` device file (that is, COM2 on an Intel 386/486 machine). -l 9600 refers to a record in a terminal line setting database file (`/etc/ttydefs`), which, when used by the port, sets the line speed. The other settings are described in a subsequent section. When s01 port is invoked by the `ttyserv` port monitor, it is going to write a prompt ("Welcome To UNIX, Please Login:" according to the preceding example) to the terminal connected to the COM2 port. It starts monitoring the port until it receives a request to connect. Upon receiving the prompt, it invokes `/usr/bin/login` to take care of the request.

When a port service is created, the `/etc/saf/<pmtag>/_pmtab` is modified to include an entry pertaining to the service. Hence, in the preceding example, an entry pertaining to s01 must be present in the `/etc/saf/ttyserv/_pmtab`. You can display it either by using `cat` or the `pmadm` command as described in the next section.

Listing and Checking the Status of a Port Service

To list and check on the status of a port monitor, enter

```
#pmadm -l -p<pmtag> -s<svctag>
```

To list or check on the status of all port services associated with a specific port monitor, enter

```
#pmadm -l -p<pmtag>
```

whereas to list, or check, the status of all port monitor services, enter

PMTAG	PMTYPE	SVCTAG	FLGS	ID	<PMSPECIFIC>	
ttymon3	ttymon	00s	u	root	/dev/term/00s - - /usr/bin/	
					_login - 2400 - login: - #	
ttymon3	ttymon	01s	u	uucp	/dev/term/01s b - /usr/bin/	
					_login - 2400 - login: - #	
ttymon3	ttymon	00h	u	root	/dev/term/00h - - /usr/bin/	
					_login - 9600 - login: - #	

```
tcp        listen        0              x      root      \x02000ACE64000001 - c - /
                                                         _usr/lib/saf/nlps_server
                                                         _#NLPS SERVER
tcp        listen        lp             -      root      - - - - /var/spool/lp/fifos/
                                                         _listenS5 #NLPS SERVER
tcp        listen        105            -      root      - - c - /usr/net/servers/rfs/
                                                         _rfsetup #RFS server
```

The following two examples demonstrate the first two commands.

```
#pmadm -l -pttyserv -s s01
PMTAG       PMTYPE     SVCTAG      FLGS ID    PMSPECIFIC
ttyserv     ttymon     s01         d    root  /dev/term/01 —
/usr/bin/login - 9600 - Welcome to UNIX, Please Login: - #

#pmadm -l -pttyserv
PMTAG       PMTYPE     SVCTAG FLGS ID        <PMSPECIFIC>
ttyyserv      ttymon        00s            u       root     /dev/term/00s - -
/usr/bin/login - 2400 - login:  -  #
ttyserv       ttymon        01s            u       uucp     /dev/term/01s b -
/usr/bin/login - 9600 - login:  -  #
```

Enabling, Disabling, and Removing a Port Service

To enable, disable, or remove a port service, use pmadm -e, pmadm -d, or pmadm -r, respectively. Hence, to enable s01 port monitor, enter

```
#pmadm -pttyserv -s s01 -e
```

whereas to disable it, enter

```
#pmadm -pttyserv -s s01 -d
```

and to remove it, enter

```
#pmadm -pttyserv -s s01 -r
```

The ttymon Port Monitor

As its name implies, the ttymon port monitor is responsible for invoking and monitoring port services associated with your system's tty ports. When invoked, ttymon looks up its /etc/saf/ <pmtag>/_pmtab file to determine which port services to invoke; which tty port associates with which service; how the port services are configured (for example, startup in an enabled state, what line speed to configure tty port to, and so on); and which application, or process, to invoke upon user request (for example, login service, uucp, and so on).

ttymon replaces both getty and uugetty. Though getty and uugetty are still supported by SVR4 for backward compatibility reasons, system administrators are strongly recommended to use ttymon. This recommendation stems from the following comparison:

1. `ttymon` administration conforms with SAF's generic interface. This brings managing `ttymon` port monitors into line with management concepts applied to other port monitors, providing the benefit of convenience.

2. By using SAF management commands, the administrator has the choice of managing `ttymon` port services collectively or selectively. When using `getty`, the administrator can manage only one port at a time.

3. One invocation of the `ttymon` port monitor by `sac` can take care of multiple ttys, whereas `getty`/`uugetty` requires an entry per supported tty in the `/etc/inittab` file.

4. As will be discussed later, `ttymon` comes with support of a new feature, namely the AUTOBAUD feature. This feature allows `ttymon` to automatically determine the line speed suitable to the connected terminal.

5. `ttymon` can optionally be invoked directly by `init`, in express mode. This may be done by including an entry in the `/etc/inittab` file. As a matter of fact, if you examine the contents of the `/etc/inittab` file, you will notice the existence of a similar entry taking care of the UNIX system console in express mode. The entry should look similar to the following:

```
co:12345:respawn:/usr/lib/saf/ttymon -g -v -p "Console Login: "-d /dev/
console -l console
```

Upon reading this entry, `init` starts a `ttymon` port monitor to take care of console login needs. This particular invocation of `ttymon` falls beyond `sac`'s control.

Special Device Files and the Terminal Line Settings Database

Among the arguments that the system administrator must pass to `pmadm` to create a port service, two will be described: the device special filename corresponding to the tty serial interface undergoing configuration and a label identifying an entry in a terminal line settings database.

Device Special Filenames Under SAF

Special filenames underwent some changes under SVR4. In earlier releases of UNIX, `getty` and `uugetty` referred to the special files in the `/dev` directory as `tty##`, where `##` refers to the actual port number. With SAF under SVR4, tty port special files are maintained in a subdirectory called `/dev/term` and the special files are named `##` in that directory. The COM1 port on a 386 machine is now referred to as `/dev/term/00`, whereas under `getty` it is referred to as `/dev/tty00`. Due to the ongoing support to `uugetty` and `getty`, both conventions are currently supported. It is the administrator's responsibility, however, to make sure that the right convention is applied with her preferred way of invoking a port service.

The Terminal Line Settings Database

As mentioned earlier, this database is the `ttymon` administrative file, which defines the line settings applying to the tty port being invoked. The database filename is `/etc/ttydefs`, whereas `getty`'s is `/etc/gettydefs`. Both files remain supported by SVR4 and both are maintained using the `/etc/sbin/sttydefs` command. A good understanding of these databases helps you to provide the level of support that matches the users' terminal emulation need. In the following discussion, however, only /etc/ttydefs' file data structure is examined and explained. The use of the sttydefs command to add, modify, or delete entries in the database also is described.

The discussion begins with a close look at the contents of the /etc/ttydefs file. To list its contents, enter

```
#/usr/sbin/sttydefs -l
------------------------------------------------------------------------
19200: 19200 opost onlcr tab3 ignpar ixon ixany parenb istrip echo echoe echok isig
cs7 cread : 19200 opost onlcr sane tab3 ignpar ixon ixany parenb istrip echo echoe
echok isig cs7 cread ::9600

------------------------------------------------------------------------

ttylabel:     19200
initial flags:      19200 opost onlcr tab3 ignpar ixon ixany parenb istrip echo
echoe echok isig cs7 cread
final flags:      19200 opost onlcr sane tab3 ignpar ixon ixany parenb istrip echo
echoe echok isig cs7 cread
autobaud:     no
nextlabel:    9600

------------------------------------------------------------------------
9600: 9600 opost onlcr tab3 ignpar ixon ixany parenb istrip echo echoe echok isig
cs7 cread : 9600 opost onlcr sane tab3 ignpar ixon ixany parenb istrip echo echoe
echok isig cs7 cread ::4800

------------------------------------------------------------------------

ttylabel:     9600
initial flags:      9600 opost onlcr tab3 ignpar ixon ixany parenb istrip echo echoe
echok isig cs7 cread
final flags:      9600 opost onlcr sane tab3 ignpar ixon ixany parenb istrip echo
echoe echok isig cs7 cread
autobaud:     no
nextlabel:    4800

------------------------------------------------------------------------
4800: 4800 opost onlcr tab3 ignpar ixon ixany parenb istrip echo echoe echok isig
cs7 cread : 4800 opost onlcr sane tab3 ignpar ixon ixany parenb istrip echo echoe
echok isig cs7 cread ::2400

------------------------------------------------------------------------

ttylabel:     4800
initial flags:      4800 opost onlcr tab3 ignpar ixon ixany parenb istrip echo echoe
echok isig cs7 cread
final flags:      4800 opost onlcr sane tab3 ignpar ixon ixany parenb istrip echo
echoe echok isig cs7 cread
autobaud:     no
nextlabel:    2400
.
.
.
```

As you see, sttydefs formats the listing into a user-friendly format. If you want the actual data structure of the command, enter

```
#cat /etc/ttydefs
.
.
.
onlcr sane tab3 ignpar istrip ixon ixany echo echoe echok isig cs8 cread ::console5
console5: 19200 opost onlcr tab3 ignpar istrip ixon ixany echo echoe echok isig cs8
cread : 19200 opost onlcr sane tab3 ignpar istrip ixon ixany echo echoe echok isig
cs8 cread ::console

4800H: 4800 : 4800 ixany parenb sane tab3 hupcl ::9600H
9600H: 9600 : 9600 ixany parenb sane tab3 hupcl ::19200H
19200H: 19200 : 19200 ixany parenb sane tab3 hupcl ::2400H
2400H: 2400 : 2400 ixany parenb sane tab3 hupcl ::1200H
1200H: 1200 : 1200 ixany parenb sane tab3 hupcl ::300H
300H: 300 : 300 ixany parenb sane tab3 hupcl ::4800H

19200NP: 19200 opost onlcr tab3 ignpar ixon ixany istrip echo echoe echok isig cs8
cread : 19200
.
.
.
```

The following is a description of each field:

> *ttylabel*: It is unique and is used in identifying the record. You will be passing this label to `ttymon`, using `pmadm`, when creating the port service. Every time `ttymon` attempts invoking the port service, it searches for that label in the `ttydefs` file.
>
> *initial flags*: This field describes the initial terminal line settings. They allow users to provide login information upon initial contact.
>
> *final flags*: They define the terminal line settings after a connection request is detected, and right before the associated port service is invoked.
>
> *autobaud*: This field can contain either A or null. By including A in this field, you are prompting `ttymon` to automatically determine the line speed upon receiving a carriage return from the user's terminal.
>
> *nextlabel*: This field includes the label of the next record to fetch should the line settings specified in the current label fail to meet the user's terminal needs. `ttymon` recognizes the failure upon receiving a BREAK sent by the user. This technique allows `ttymon` to fall back on any number of alternate configurations in search of the desired line speed. Records linked together in this fashion are said to form a hunt sequence, with the last one normally linked to the first record. The sample partial listing shown previously includes a hunt sequence that starts with label `4800H` and ends with `300H`.

A sample record in `ttydefs` follows, along with an explanation of its field contents.

```
9600NP: 9600  tab3 ignpar ixon ixany  echo echoe  cs8 : 9600 sane tab3 ignpar ixon
ixany  echo echoe  cs8::4800NP
```

This record is labeled `9600NP`. Both the initial and final flags set the port to 9600 bps, no parity (`ignpar`), enable XON/OFF flow control (`ixon`), any character should restart output (`ixany`), echo back every character typed (`echo`), echo erase character (`echoe`), and to set the character size to 8 bits. The `autobaud` field is null, which means that no autobaud support is required. The last field points to the next record labeled `4800N`.

To find more about the valid initial and final flag settings, consult your vendor's manuals, or simply enter `man stty` on the command line.

What if you don't find what you want in `ttydefs`? As noted earlier, SVR4 provides you with the `/usr/sbin/sttydefs` command to make changes to the `/etc/ttydefs` database. Among the changes you are allowed to make is adding the record of your liking. The command syntax to do that is

```
#sttydefs -a<ttylabel> [-b] [-n<nextlabel>] [-i<initialflags>]\
[-f <finalflags>]
```

in which

> `-a <ttylabel>` adds an entry to ttydefs with label specified (first field)
>
> `-i <initialflags>` specifies initial speed among other line settings (second field)
>
> `-f <finalflags>` specifies final line settings (third field)
>
> `-b` enables autobaud (fourth field in which case A will be included in this field)
>
> `-n` describes the next record's label

For example, the `sttydefs` that follows adds a new record, labeled `4800`, with initial flags set to support 4800 bps line speed:

```
#sttydefs -a4800 -i"4800 hupcl tab3 erase ^b" \
-f"4800 sane ixany tab3 erase ^h echoe" -n2400np
```

To remove an entry, simply enter

```
sttydefs -r <ttylabel>
```

For example: to delete the `4800` label, enter

```
#sttydefs -r 4800
```

CAUTION

A record that you delete may belong to a hunt sequence, in which case it is your responsibility to restore integrity to the affected sequence.

The `ttymon` Port Monitor Administrative Command `ttyadm`

`ttyadm` is `ttymon`'s administrative command. Its prime function is to pass information to both `sacadm` and `pmadm` in the formats they require. The following are the `ttyadm` options:

> `-V` specifies the version of `ttymon`.
>
> `-d device` specifies the `/dev/term/##` tty with which the port service will be associated.

-b, if included, will configure the port service for bidirectional flow of data.

-r *<count>* specifies the number of times ttymon should try to start the service before a failure is declared.

-p *"prompt"* is the string used to prompt users when a port service request is detected.

-i *"message"* is the message to be displayed if the port is in a disabled state

-t *<timeout>* is the number of seconds that ttymon must wait for input data before closing the port.

-l *<ttylabel>* specifies the label of the desired record in the /etc/ttydefs file described earlier in this section.

-s specifies the name of the service provider program on the tty port (for example, login, cu, and so on).

At this point, all of the necessary elements that you will need to implement terminal and modem connections have been covered. If you are anxious to try implementing, you may jump right ahead to the section titled "Connecting Terminals and Modems." Otherwise, continue reading the next section, which explains the listen port monitor.

The listen Port Monitor

listen is a network port monitoring process that is invoked and controlled by sac. It runs on any transport provider (most commonly TCP), and supports two classes of service: a class of general services, such as RFS and network printing; and terminal login services for terminals trying to access the system by connecting directly to the network. Like ttymon, listen can support and monitor multiple ports, with each assigned a network service to take care of. Once invoked, the listen port monitor initializes port services as defined in its /etc/saf/<pmtag>/_pmtab file. It then monitors the ports for service connection requests. Once a request is received on a listen port, the associated service (for example, printing) is invoked and the user is connected to it.

Port Service Addressing

During TCP/IP setup (refer to Chapter 20, "Networking," for more on TCP/IP), your system will have been assigned an Internet address that is eight hexadecimal digits long, with each pair of digits represented by one octet. Stations shipping requests across the network to your system use this address to reach your machine's doorstep only. Because your machine is more likely to be configured to respond to a variety of service requests, there arises the requirement to assign unique addresses to port services. This allows the listen port monitor to support multiple port services. Upon adding a listen port service, you are required to provide the applicable address to nlsadmin (the listen port monitor administrative command). For this reason, you are provided with the address format shown in Figure 23.2.

FIGURE 23.2.

listen*'s port service address format.*

The listener port service address format

Family Address (4 digits)	Port Address (4 digits)	Internet Address (8 digits)	Resrved (16 digits)

The elements of the address format are as follows:

Family address: This is four digits long. It is always set to 0020.

Port address: This is four digits long and is the port service-specific address. For example, listenS5 print server is assigned x0ACE, whereas listenBSD print server is assigned x0203.

Internet address: This is the IP address you assigned to the system upon installing TCP/IP. It is eight digits long.

Reserved: This is 16 digits long and is reserved for future use. Currently, it is set to 16 zeros.

As an example, assume that the IP address of your system is 100.0.0.1 and that you want to set up a listen port to take care of print service requests sent across the network by BSD systems. The port address in hexadecimal notation then becomes

```
00020203640000010000000000000000
```

TIP

To avoid dealing with decimal-to-hex conversions to figure out the hexadecimal equivalent to your host IP address, you can use the lpsystem -A. Figure 23.3 demonstrates the use of lpsystem -A output in order to figure out the host's IP address in hexadecimal notation.

FIGURE 23.3.

Using lpsystem -A *to find the hexadecimal equivalent of the host's IP address.*

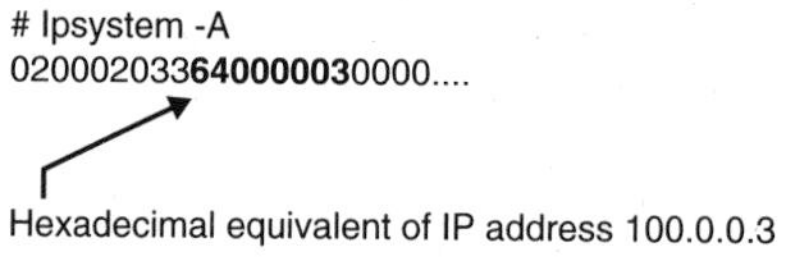

```
# lpsystem -A
020002033640000030000....
```

Hexadecimal equivalent of IP address 100.0.0.3

It will be shown later in this section how to pass this address to pmadm when creating the port service.

The listen Port Monitor Administrative Command nlsamdin

nlsadmin is the administrative command specific to the listen port monitor. nlsadmin can be used to add, configure, and change the status of a port monitor. Also, it can be used to start or kill the listener process. Mostly, it will be used in command substitution mode, in order to supply some of the required arguments to both sacadm (the sac administrative command) and pmadm. Options that you specify on the command line will determine which arguments to pass, and in what format.

Creating a `listen` Port Monitor

To create a `ttymon` port monitor, you use the `sacadm` command. The same applies to creating a `listen` port monitor. Instead of using `ttyadm`, however, you must use `nlsadmin` in command substitution mode in order to pass some of the required information to `sacadm`. The use of `sacadm` in creating a listen port monitor is as follows:

```
#sacadm -a -p<pmtag> -t listen -c<"command"> -v`nlsadmin -V` \
[-n<count>] [-fd¦x] [-y<"comment">]
```

All options bear the same significance described in earlier sections (refer back to the "Creating a Port Monitor" section for a review). Note in particular, the use of ``nlsadmin -V`` in order to pass the port monitor's version to `sacadm`. Also note that the `-c` option specifies the program invoked to bring up the `listen` port monitor. The program is `/usr/lib/saf/listen`. Once a port monitor is created, an entry pertaining to it is added to sac's administrative file `/etc/saf/_sactab`.

As an example, the following `sacadm` command creates a `listen` port monitor with *pmtag* tcp. Note that the program filename to invoke is `/usr/lib/saf/listen`, and sac is required to try up to three times to bring up the port monitor, should it ever fail respond to sac's polls.

```
sacadm -a -t listen -p tcp -c "/usr/lib/saf/listen" \
-v'nlsadmin - V' -n3
```

Managing `listen` Port Monitors

To check on the availability of `listen` port monitors, enter

```
#sacadm -l -t listen
```

As a result, you see a listing of all `listen` port monitors currently controlled by sac on your system. The listing looks like the following:

```
PMTAG    PMTYPE   FLGS   RCNT   STATUS    COMMAND
tcp      listen    -     3      ENABLED   /usr/lib/saf/listen -m inet/tcp0 tcp
```

For a review of the interpretation of the preceding listing, refer to the "Checking the Status of the Port Monitor" section.

In order to enable, disable, or remove a port monitor, enter sacadm with -e, -d, or -r respectively, as described earlier in this chapter.

Creating a `listen` Port Service

To create a `listen` port service, use the `pmadm` command. The syntax follows.

```
#pmadm -a -p<pmtag> -s<svctag> [-i id] -v 'nlsadmin -V'\
 -m"'nlsadmin options'" -y"comment"
```

The following command adds a new port service to a port monitor with *pmtag* tcp:

```
#pmadm -a -p tcp -s lpd -i root -v 'nlsadmin -V'\
 -m"'nlsadmin -o /var/spool/lp/fifos/listenBSD -A \
\x0002020364000002000000000000000000'"
```

23

DEVICE
ADMINISTRATION

The preceding command demonstrates the use of the port address discussed earlier. The port address described in the preceding example configures the port to accept printing requests sent by BSD clients across the network.

Managing Port Services

To check on the status of a port service, enter

```
#pmadm -p<pmtag> -s<svctag> -l
```

To enable it, enter

```
#pmadm -p<pmtag> -s<svctag> -e
```

whereas to disable it, enter

```
#pmadm -p<pmtag> -s<svctag> -d
```

and to remove it, enter

```
#pmadm -p<pmtag> -s<svctag> -r
```

Device Administrative Tasks Under SVR4

This section covers the motions of performing common device administrative-related tasks as applicable to SVR4 of UNIX. Subsequent sections cover other variants as well, including Solaris 2.x, and Linux. The section, "Connecting Terminals and Modems," applies to all variants, as they provide a comprehensive coverage of hardware related issues that are common to all variants of UNIX (and other operating systems).

Connecting Terminals and Modems

UNIX has very powerful built-in serial communications capabilities. Administrators can make use of them in order to offer local terminal connection services, as well as across-the-telephone wire services. Services across the wire include remote terminal login, file transfer capabilities, and electronic mail exchange. Those services are provided by utilities such as uucp and cu, which are part of the Basic Networking Utilities (BNU) that comes with your UNIX operating system.

In this section, the concepts and steps to set up for both modem and terminal connections are presented. A properly wired and configured serial interface is a basic requirement that is common to both types of services. Once this requirement is fulfilled, you can proceed to implement the necessary additional steps to take care of modem and terminal connections.

Making the Connection

To make the serial connection, prepare for the physical connection, determine the availability of associated resources, and create the port service.

Preparing for the Physical Connection

In this step, you are primarily involved in readying the cable that will connect the modem, or the user's terminal, to the UNIX system. RS232C/D is the standard interface that most hardware platforms use to connect devices. So that you can understand the how and why of different cable arrangements, a brief examination of the standard is provided.

RS232C/D defines the interface between so-called data circuit-terminating equipment (DTE) and data circuit communication equipment (DCE). In practical terms, and for the purposes of this section, this means that it defines the physical interface between a computer (the DTE) and the modem (the DCE). The interface defines four aspects of the physical layer. These are electrical, mechanical, functional, and procedural.

The electrical specification defines how data is electrically represented on the wire. Because computer data is binary in its raw form, the specification describes what voltage level represents which logical level.

The mechanical specification describes the mechanics of the connection, including connector type and number of pins supported. A DB-25 connector is specified for the RS232C/D interface. The industry introduced another de facto standard, however. This is the DB-9 connector, most commonly found on PC workstations.

The functional specification defines the pinout of the connector (that is, what each pin stands for).

The procedural specification defines the handshake mechanism that should precede, accompany, and terminate the exchange of data between the DTE and DCE.

Figure 23.4 shows the wiring diagram and corresponding pin definition of the DB25-to-DB25 cable, which is normally used to connect a DTE to a DCE. Figure 23.5 shows the wiring diagram of a DB9-to-DB25 cable. Following is a description of the most commonly used circuits. Because pin definitions are not the same for both types of connectors, the description refers to the circuit name rather than the pin number.

FIGURE 23.4.

Wiring diagram and corresponding pin definition of a DB25-to-DB25 RS232C/D straight-through cable.

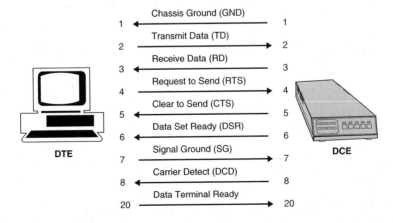

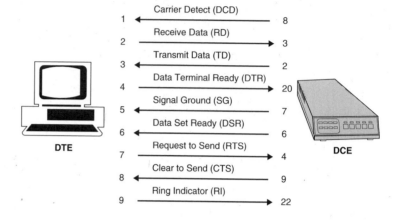

FIGURE 23.5.

Wiring diagram of a DB9-to-DB25 straight-through cable.

SG provides the common return path for both the transmit (TD) and receive (RD) circuits.

DTR and DSR are asserted by both the computer and modem to indicate readiness to exchange data. Both circuits must be asserted before any other activity can occur across the interface. At this point, the computer may attempt to dial another computer by passing the dialing command string to the modem.

DCD is asserted by the modem if it successfully connects at the remote end. It is interpreted by the computer as an indication of a successful connection. This circuit has to remain asserted for the duration of the call.

TD and RD are the transmit and receive circuits.

Any time the computer wants to transmit, it asserts the RTS circuit and waits for permission to do so from the modem, by virtue of asserting the CTS circuit. This usage of the RTS/CTS circuit pair applies to the half-duplex mode of communications. In full-duplex communications, RTS and CTS circuits are used to control the flow of data between the DTE and the DCE devices. The DTE drops its RTS circuit in order to request the DCE to stop sending data on DTE's receive circuit. Likewise, the CTS is dropped by the DCE in order to request the DTE to stop sending data on the transmit circuit.

CAUTION

In cases in which one end of the cable is a DB-25 connector and the opposite end is a DB-9, the cable must be wired as shown in Figure 23.6.

FIGURE 23.6.

Null modem wiring arrangements corresponding to different combinations of connectors.

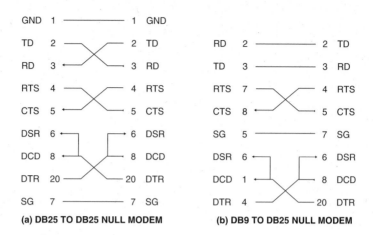

(a) DB25 TO DB25 NULL MODEM   (b) DB9 TO DB25 NULL MODEM

Connecting a computer directly to a terminal (that is, a DTE-to-DTE type of connection) is a tricky business, but easy to understand. Because RS232C/D defines the interface strictly between a DTE and DCE, many vendors and users have developed variations on a cabling trick that allows DTE-to-DTE connection. This trick is called the null modem cable. The underlying idea is to convince both ends of the connection that they are indeed talking to modems directly connected to them. Figure 23.6 shows two diagrams depicting the same cabling trick corresponding to different combinations of connectors.

When the interface pinout was described, it was done from the DTE perspective. This means that if you look at the interface from the DCE perspective, some pins bear quite the opposite significance. For example, DTEs send and receive pins are DCEs receive and send, respectively. It is not, therefore, hard to imagine what would happen if you were to attempt connecting two DTEs using a direct cable. Data emerging from both devices on directly connected transmit circuits would be endlessly colliding, while they are hopelessly waiting for an impulse to occur on the wire connecting their receiving circuits.

To remedy this situation, the send and receive circuits are cross-wired. Also, recall that whenever the computer asserts its RTS circuit, it is asking for clearance to transmit. This clearance is indicated by having the CTS asserted (normally by the modem), which explains why this circuit pair is also cross-wired. Finally, note how DSR, DTR, and DCD are wired. When DTR is asserted by any DTE, the other one detects a DCD and DSR, which are interpreted as both modem-ready and connection-established indicators, just as though they were sent by the receiving DTE's local modem. If the DTE is prepared to engage in data communications, it asserts its DTR and both sides can now talk to each other.

There are variations on the theme of the null modem. Although the preceding variation caters to the most general cases, it is advisable that you check with your vendor to determine your exact cabling needs.

Determining the Availability of Resources

Before you can proceed to creating the port service, there are two resources that you need to check: 1) availability of `tty` ports, and 2) availability of a suitable record in the `/etc/ttydefs` file.

To obtain a list of all `tty` ports that are currently in use, enter the command `pmadm -l -t ttymon`. The listing will look like the following:

```
PMTAG      PMTYPE    SVCTAG    FLGS    ID      <PMSPECIFIC>
ttymon3    ttymon    00s       ux      root    /dev/term/00 ...
ttymon3    ttymon    11s       -       uucp    /dev/term/11 ...
```

The device special filenames under the `<PMSPECIFIC>` column indicate which `tty`s to avoid in your subsequent steps. Depending on availability of extra free `tty` ports, choose the one you want.

Next, list the contents of the `/etc/ttydefs` file by entering the command `sttydefs -l`, and examine its contents for the record and label that match your terminal needs. If you do not find one, then you ought to add the desired entry to the database yourself, by using the `sttydefs` command. For this, you are referred back to the "Special Device Files and the Terminal Line Settings Database" section.

Creating the Port Service

Now that you have all the pieces (that is, the cable, the `tty` port, and the label of the record in `/etc/ttydefs` file), you can proceed with putting them together to create the port service. To do so, you ought to use `pmadm` with the `-a` option. The example that follows demonstrates the use of `pmadm` to create a bidirectional port service, with *svctag* `04s`, which invokes the service login, restarts the port three times upon failure, and prompts the terminal with a friendly message. Also note the use of `ttyadm` in command substitution mode in order to pass some of the arguments to `pmadm`.

```
#pmadm -a -pttyserv -s04s -i root -v `ttyadm -V` \
-m "`ttyadm -b -r3 -p"Welcome Home! LOGIN:" -d/dev/term/04 \
-l 9600 -s /usr/bin/login'"
```

Use `pmadm -l` to check on the state of the service. If the new service is not enabled, use `pmadm -p<pmtag> -s<svctag> -e` to do so.

Connecting the Modem

As noted earlier, you connect a modem to the serial port (for example, COM2) using a straight-through cable. To configure the modem properly, you must read the documentation supplied with it. The things you ought to pay attention to are the DIP switch settings and the AT commands that are necessary for proper modem initialization and dialing. Because the majority of modems today are Hayes-compatible, the list in Table 23.2 can act as the configuration guidelines that apply to them.

Hayes modems have an 8-bit DIP switch. Table 23.2 summarizes the meanings associated with each bit switch position.

Table 23.2. Hayes modem switch settings.

Switch	Position	Function
1	Up	If the computer asserts its DTR low, the modem reacts by hanging up the line.
	Down*	Forces the DTR permanently high, which means the modem will no longer have to worry about this signal.
2	Up*	Forces the modem to respond to modem dialing and initialization commands in English.
	Down	Forces the modem to respond using numerical messages.
3	Up	Suppresses result codes, thus overriding switch 2.
	Down*	Enables result codes.
4	Up*	AT commands are echoed as they are entered.
	Down	AT commands are not echoed.
5	Up*	Modem answers the phone.
	Down	Modem does not answer the phone.
6	Up	CD is asserted when a carrier is detected; this allows the computer to know when a call is received.
	Down*	CD and DSR are forced permanently high.
7	Up*	Modem is attached to single-line phone.
	Down	Modem is attached to multiline phone.
8	Up	Disables the modem from recognizing and executing modem commands.
	Down*	Modem's intelligence is enabled; modem recognizes and executes modem commands.

* denotes the default setting of each switch.

23

DEVICE
ADMINISTRATION

On ports configured for dial-in, UNIX responds to asserted DSR and CD by writing a login prompt to the modem. This, therefore, requires turning off echoing as well as result codes on the modem. Failing to do so leads the login process into interpreting locally echoed login prompt characters as a sequence of responses, which leads into a vicious cycle of login denials and subsequent reattempts. To turn local echo and result codes off, set switch positions 3, 4, and 6 to up, down, and up, respectively.

What if you don't have switches on your modem? You can use the AT modem control command set instead! AT commands let you configure the modem to initialize and manage a connection in ways suitable to your applications. Table 23.3 lists some of the AT commands commonly supported by Hayes-compatible modems. For a complete command list, consult your modem's manuals.

Table 23.3. Partial list of some of the most commonly supported AT commands.

Command	Significance
AT&F	Reset modem to factory settings
ATDP	Dial using pulse tone
ATDT	Dial using touch tone
ATE0	Enable local echoing of commands
ATE1	Disable local echoing of commands
ATQ0	Enable result codes
ATQ1	Disable result codes (that is, known as the quiet mode)
AT&W	Write settings to nonvolatile memory

To issue AT commands, you need to have some sort of direct access to the modem. The following steps show you how you can do it using the cu command.

After you login to UNIX, switch user, using the su command, to uucp:

```
#su uucp
password:
$
```

Edit the /etc/uucp/Devices file (see Chapter 26, "UUCP Administration," for more details) to include the following entry:

```
Direct term/##    -    <speed> direct
```

where ## corresponds to the tty port number, and *<speed>* refers to the speed to which you want to initialize the modem. If, for example, you have a 2400 bps Hayes-compatible modem connected to COM2, the entry would look like this:

```
Direct    term/01    -    2400 direct
```

I am assuming here that there is no other reference to term/01. If there is one, disable the entry by inserting the # sign at the beginning of the line. Make sure to save the file before quitting.

At the command line, enter

```
#cu -l term/##
```

This command directly connects you to the modem and is confirmed by displaying the message "Connected" on your screen. Table 23.4 is an illustration of a sequence pertaining to a sample modem session, during which the modem is configured for proper dial-in support.

Table 23.4. An illustrated modem configuration session along with supporting explanation.

Command/Response	*Explanation*
`#cu -l term/01`	A command: I want to talk to the modem.
`Connected`	A response: Go ahead.
`AT`	A command: Do I have your attention?
`OK`	A response: Yes, you do!
`AT&F`	A command: Reset to factory settings.
`OK`	A response: Done!
`AT&C1`	A command: Use CD to indicate carrier detection.
`OK`	A response: Done!
`AT&D2`	A command: Drop the connection when DTR drops.
`OK`	A response: Done!
`ATE0Q1`	A command: Disable local echo, and keep quiet (that is, disable result codes).
`OK`	A response: Done!
`AT&W`	A command: Save settings into nonvolatile RAM.
`OK`	A response: Done!
`~.`	A command to shell out to UNIX requesting disconnection, and going back to the UNIX shell.
`Disconnected`	A response: Granted!
`#`	

23

DEVICE ADMINISTRATION

Note in particular the use of the ~. character sequence to disconnect from the modem and go back to the shell. In fact, ~ allows you to issue UNIX commands without having to quit the direct modem session.

For dial-out, it is more convenient to enable local echo and result codes. In any case, it is imperative that you carefully read and follow the modem's manual for proper operation.

Here is a checklist to which you may refer whenever you install, or troubleshoot, a modem.

1. Ensure that your modem is not conflicting with any other device over the chosen serial port. Conflicts normally arise when an internal modem is installed and configured to either COM1 or COM2.

2. Make sure that you have the proper RS232C/D cable. Consult your modem documentation, and follow its recommendations religiously.

3. If you intend to use the modem for dial-out, change the ownership of the tty port over to uucp.

4. Set the modem DIP switches according to what has been discussed already. This is especially critical if the intended use of the modem is for dial-out.

5. For dial-in, check and make sure that a port monitor and a properly associated port service are created to take care of incoming service requests.

6. Verify and add entries to UUCP files as deemed necessary. In particular, to be able to configure the modem using cu, you should have the following entry in the /etc/uucp/Devices file:

```
Direct term/## - <speed >   direct
```

7. Using cu, establish a direct session with the modem and issue the AT commands to configure the modem properly. To establish the session, enter

```
#cu -l term/##
```

If the system fails to connect, use the -d option with cu. This option prompts cu to report the progress of the dial-out process. Depending on the nature of what is displayed on the screen, refer to the appropriate documentation for help.

8. While in session with the modem, you should be able to dial out by entering

```
ATDT <phone_number>
```

Remember to exit just enter the ~. character sequence.

9. If the modem is intended for dial-out use, test it by dialing into it. If it fails to respond properly, try the following troubleshooting tips: Verify that the modem is set to Autoanswer mode. Verify that echo is turned off. Verify that result codes are disabled (that is, the modem is set for quiet mode). Make sure that you always write modem settings to the modem's nonvolatile memory using the AT&W command.

Connecting Terminals

Many of the preparatory steps that are required to connect terminals have already been described in the last two sections. To summarize, these steps are as follows: Depending on whether the terminal is connected directly or remotely to the system, you have to prepare either a cross-wired RS232C/D cable or a straight-through cable. In the case of remote connection, you ought to configure the modem connecting to the UNIX system for dial-in in the manner depicted in the "Connecting the Modem" section. A port service should have been created, which, upon detection of a service request (by virtue of having both DSR and CD asserted), will write a login prompt to the port and transfer port control to the login process itself. This is achieved by entering the following pmadm command:

```
#pmadm -a -p<pmtag> -s<svctag> -i root -v'ttyadm -V' \
-m"'ttyadm -b -rn -p"login prompt message" -d/dev/term/## \
-l<label> -s /usr/bin/login'"
```

The use of the pmadm command to create port services was described earlier in this section.

One more step, which will be discussed now, is to set the shell environment for proper support to the user's terminal.

UNIX is designed to shield programs from concerns pertaining to the physical terminal specifics. Instead of talking directly to the terminal, programs interface with a virtual terminal by making calls to a standard library of screen routines. Those calls invoke, on behalf of programs, the desired behavior on the physical screen.

In doing so, two advantages are derived: Developers are relieved of the laborious and needless (if not impossible) task of writing and maintaining programs in a way that keeps them compatible with all kinds of terminal types—those existing now and those that will emerge in the future. Also, users continue to benefit, without any modifications or the associated cost of upgrades, from programs deployed on their UNIX platforms irrespective of changes that may be introduced to their terminal types in the future.

Proper support to the actual terminal is conditional upon setting the environment variable TERM to the correct type. This is normally done from the user's login script. The user may as well set it by entering (assuming the user's shell is Korn shell):

```
$TERM=<terminal_type>
$export TERM
```

An example of terminal type would be vt220.

UNIX uses the value assigned to TERM to reference a binary file, which exclusively defines that terminal's capabilities. The file is named after the terminal type (for example, if the terminal is vt220, then the file must have been named vt220) and is part of a large terminal information database maintained in the /usr/lib/terminfo directory.

If you list the contents of the /usr/lib/terminfo directory, you obtain a listing similar to the following:

```
#ls /usr/lib/terminfo
1 3 5 7 9 B H P V b d f h j l n p r t v x z
2 4 6 8 A C M S a c e g i k m o q s u w y
```

Each letter or numeral is the directory name where terminal capabilities definition files, pertaining to types starting with that letter or numeric, are saved. For example, if TERM is set to vt220, UNIX fetches the file /usr/lib/terminfo/v/vt220 for the terminal information capabilities (also referred to as terminfo entry).

23

DEVICE ADMINISTRATION

NOTE

TERMCAP is another shell environment variable that should be set to the name of the directory where the database is maintained.

After having gone through all of the steps required to connect the terminal, you should proceed to connect it, bring it up, and attempt login. It would be a good idea to try a direct connection first, if the terminal is intended for modem access. In any case, if you fail to get the login prompt and fail to login, you may have to carry the following checks:

Make sure that the port service is configured properly, and that it is enabled. Use pmadm to do that.

Check the cable to verify that it is the correct one. Do not rely only on the wiring diagram provided in this chapter; you are better off relying on your terminal and/or your modem vendor's documentation.

Verify that the modem is configured to Autoanswer.

Check the modem lights, and verify that the sequence of events depicted by the flashing lights conforms to what you expect to see. In particular, check DSR and CD during the connection establishment phase because, unless they are both asserted, the login prompt won't be written to the tty port. Check the modem's hard and soft settings to address any observed anomalies.

Make sure that the speed, parity, and number of stop bits match on both the terminal and the UNIX system.

Connecting Terminals and Modems Under BSD

Connecting terminals and modems under BSD is done differently from SVR4. The hardware setup, however, remains the same as in SVR4, and therefore won't be repeated.

To start with, like SVR4, BSD UNIX requires that hardware devices be associated with device special file in the /dev directory. Device special files for serial ports are normally created under tty## *name*. The "##" refers to the port number. For example, tty02 refers to the second serial port.

Terminal Line Settings and Configuration Files (BSD)

Following are the configuration files supporting terminal lines under BSD:

/etc/ttys	Terminal line configuration file.
/etc/ttytab	This is SunOS's version of /etc/ttys file. Both files will be addressed shortly.
/etc/gettydefs	Terminal line settings database. Similar to /etc/ttydefs under SVR4. Consequently, it won't be described here.
/etc/gettytab	Includes entries for initializing terminals to desired line speed(s). Following are contents of a sample /etc/gettytab file:

```
c¦std.300¦300-baud:\
    :nd#1:cd#1:ap#300:
```

```
f¦std.1200¦1200-baud:\
    :fd#1:sp#1200:
2¦std.9600¦9600-baud:\
    :sp#9600:
```

This `gettytab` file has entries for initializing terminals to three different baud rates, 300, 1200, and 9600 bits per seconds.

`/etc/termcap`   Terminal type definitions database. This database defines the capabilities of each of the terminal types it supports. Examples of supported terminal types are `vt220`, and `wyse60`. Again, this file is similar in contents and purpose to SVR4's `/usr/lib/terminfo` explained earlier in the chapter.

The `/etc/ttys` file contains one record per serial port. The record provides details of resources associated with the serial port being supported, including pointers to information that is necessary for the proper initialization of this port by the `init` process.

Following is the syntax that entries in `/etc/ttys` must comply with:

`serial_port    command   terminal_type   status`

Where

   `serial_port`   Is the name of the special file in the `/dev` directory. Remember that special filenames, under BSD, assume the form `tty##`. `tty00`, for example, refers to `/dev/tty00`, the first serial port that is supported by the host.

   `command`   Is the name of the program that `init` must respawn to control and monitor this serial port. For most purposes, the program being specified (and consequently being invoked) is `getty`. Under BSD, `getty` is the counterpart to `ttymon`-type port monitor under SVR4, described earlier. Along with the specified command, a parameter specifying the line settings is normally included. The parameter provides a pointer to a record in the `/etc/gettytab` file. Following is an example of the contents of the command field:

   `/usr/etc/getty std.9600`

   According to this command, `init` spawns `getty` on the affected port (described in the first field) and initializes it to 9600 bits per second. `std.9600` is just a label specification referencing a line setting in the `/etc/gettytab` file, as noted above.

   `terminal_type`   Is the name of the terminal type being connected to the serial port. The type described in this field serves as a pointer to a record in the `/etc/termcap` terminal settings database. For example, if this field is set to `vt100`, the `/etc/termcap` database is searched for a record describing the capabilities of the `vt100` terminal. Subsequently, the corresponding `/etc/`

`termcap` record is used in initializing the serial line for proper support for the connected terminal type.

	The `terminal_type` field supports options such as `network` (to imply virtual terminal), `unknown` (to imply modems or unknown terminals), and `dialup` (again, to imply modem lines).
`status`	This field can contain multiple keywords. Recognized keywords include

`on`	Means that the port is enabled.
`off`	Means that the port is disabled. Consequently, the entry is ignored, and affected port will be left in an inactive state. *A port connected to a dial-out modem should be marked off.*
`secure`	Allows root login through this port. Otherwise, a user attempting to login as a root using a terminal connected to this port will be refused connection.
`window=cmd`	This field causes `init` to execute the command specified in `cmd` before the command specified in the 2nd field.

Here is a partial listing of the contents of a sample `/etc/ttys` file:

#name	getty command	type	status
console	/etc/getty std.9600	vt220	on secure
tty00	/etc/getty std.2400	vt100	on secure
tty01	/etc/getty std.19600	unknown	off
tty02	/etc/getty std.19600	dialup	on
tty03	/etc/getty std.19600	unknown	off # dialout

According to this file, the console is enabled (`status` is set to on), runs at 9600, and allows `root` login (`status` is set to secure). On the other hand, `tty03` is disabled as it is used for dial-out purposes only. Using the second entry (that of `tty00`), for example, `init` initializes the first serial port to 2400 bps by virtue of cross-referencing the `std.2400` parameter in the `/etc/gettytab` file. The terminal type being specified (that is, `vt100`) also serves as a pointer to the actual record describing the terminal capabilities as defined in the `/etc/termcap` file.

Adding the Terminal (BSD)

Once the aforementioned configuration files are updated to support the terminal pending connection, and the hardware and serial cable are taken care of properly (discussed earlier in the chapter), starting the new terminal line becomes a simple matter of sending `init` a hang-up signal (HUP) as follows:

```
# kill -1 1
```

or equivalently,

```
# kill -HUP 1
```

By being sent a hang-up signal, `init` is forced to reinitialize itself by reading the configuration files, including those mentioned above. Consequently, `init` takes the proper action by spawning `getty` on the new port and initializing it for support for the specified line speed, and terminal types as specified in the `/etc/ttys` file.

Adding a Modem (BSD)

Under BSD UNIX, connecting a modem to a serial port requires creating different device special files from those used for directly connected terminals. Under SunOs, for example, for dial-in modems, the device special file is usually called `/dev/ttyd`*n*, where *n* designates the modem line (starting with 0). This means the `/dev/ttyd0` would be the dial-in device file of the first modem line. For dial-out modems, the device file is named `/dev/cua`*n*, where again, *n* corresponds to the modem line. Hence, `/dev/ttyd0` and `/dev/cua0` are the device files corresponding to dial-in and dial-out modems for the same line, respectively.

If you check the `/dev` directory, you might not find any of the files just mentioned. This is particularly applicable to a system that has never been required to connect to modems. In this case, you will need to create both files. Creating the `/dev/ttyd`*n* device is rather simple. It involves renaming the special device file corresponding to the physical port where the modem will be connected to `/dev/ttyd`*n*. For example, if you want to connect a modem to the first physical serial port on your system, you need to rename the `/dev/ttya` file to `/dev/ttyd0` as follows:

```
# mv /dev/ttya   /dev/ttyd0
```

Creating the `/dev/cua0` file is a two-step process involving the use of the `mknod` command. Following is the general syntax of `mknod`:

```
mknod filename [c] ¦ [b] major minor
```

where in this syntax,

filename	Is the name of the device special file. Continuing on the above example, this would be `cua0`.
[c] ¦ [b]	Is the nature of the device undergoing creation. `c` indicates a raw device. A raw device deals with characters individually rather than in blocks of characters, whereas `b` indicates a block device. For modems, the device of choice is a raw device. Correspondingly, this parameter should always be set to `c`.

major
:   Is the major device number. The major device number designates the device class. Put differently, major acts more like a pointer to the device driver routines in the kernel that support this class of devices (that is, the serial device driver in our case).

minor
:   Is the minor device number. It designates the device subtype within the device class. Continuing with our example, the minor device number corresponding to cua0 provides a pointer to the modem dial-out routines within the driver designated by *major*.

Finding out the major and minor numbers corresponding to the dial-out line of choice is a simple matter of following these two steps:

1. Use the ls -l /dev/ttyd*n* command to determine the major and minor numbers of the corresponding ttyd*n* device as shown here:

    ```
    # ls -l /dev/ttyd0
    crw--w--w- 1 root     12,    0 Nov 26    22:25    /dev/ttyd0
    ```

    In this example, 12 is the major number and 0 is the minor one.

2. The /dev/cua*n* device corresponding to the /dev/ttyd*n* port should have its major number identical to that of /dev/ttyd*n*, whereas its minor number should 128 more than that of /dev/ttyd*n*. Again, continuing on our example, this implies that the major and minor numbers corresponding to /dev/cua0 should be set to 12 and 128. Use the following mknod command to create this file:

    ```
    # mknod cua0    c  12   128
    ```

Once the cua*n* device file is created, you will need to secure it by changing its ownership to uucp and the permissions to 600, as shown below:

```
# chmod 600 /dev/cua0
# chown uucp /dev/cua0
```

Now that both /dev/ttyd0 (the dial-in device file) and /dev/cua0 (the dial-out device file) are created, what remains (aside from configuring the modem and attaching it to the port as described earlier in the chapter) is to update the /etc/ttytab file as described in the previous section.

Connecting Terminals and Modems Under Linux

Being a BSD variant of UNIX, connecting terminals and modems to Linux involves most of the steps depicted in the previous section with a few subtle differences. These are:

1. Instead of being a four-column file, /etc/ttys (the terminal configuration file) contains two columns only, where the first one contains the name of the serial port being supported. The second column contains a label identifying the type of the terminal being associated with this port (that is, connected to the port). The terminal type label is cross-referenced in the /etc/termcap file in a fashion similar to how SunOS and other BSD systems treat it.

2. Rather than identifying the line-speed setting and command (for example, `getty`) controlling the port in the `/etc/ttys` (similar to how SunOS does it), they are taken care of in the `/etc/inittab` file. Here is a sample entry:

```
d1:2345:respawn:/sbin/getty  ttyS0 38400
```

According to this entry, `getty` is respawned by `init` while the system is any of 2, 3, 4, or 5 run levels. The port being controlled is `ttyS0` (that is, the first serial port, COM1). 38400 is a label designating an entry in the `/etc/gettydefs` file (the line-settings database, described earlier).

3. Modem lines have `/dev/ttyS`*n* for device filenames, where *n* ranges from 0 to 3 corresponding to serial ports COM1 through COM2, respectively. You do not need to create these files. They are already created during installation time.

CREATING TTYS*n* DEVICE FILE

Should your Linux system fail to have any of the `/dev/ttyS`*n* files, you can easily create the appropriate file by using `mknod` in a way similar to the description provided in the previous section. Major and minor numbers corresponding to any of the devices are well defined in the man pages. To look up the exact details of `mknod` command that apply, enter

```
# man ttys
```

Connecting Printers

Printing services in UNIX are supported by the LP spooler. The LP spooler offers administrators comprehensive capabilities that allow them to address varied scenarios in order to meet different user needs and requirements. To name a few, print services can be physically set up to allow users to print on printers connected to the host they are logged in to or, alternatively, to printers connected to other hosts on the network. LP printing service includes a library of filters from which administrators can choose to support their user needs. By implementing them, users' print jobs will be processed, making them more "compatible" with the target printer. Administrators are provided with management capabilities allowing them to use global management as well as selective management of print services. Because this chapter is about "Device Administration," the objectives of this section will be limited to include the following topics:

- A conceptual overview of the LP printing service
- Local printing services setup
- Network print servers setup
- Printer management
- Print user management

How Does the LP Printing Service Work (SVR4, Solaris 2.x)

Print services are invoked by `init` upon startup when the system enters the multiuser state run level 2. The services are brought up by the `/etc/rc2.d/S80lp` script and are killed whenever the system is shut down by `/etc/rc2.d/K20lp` script.

When users address printers to handle their print jobs, the files they send for printing are not handled immediately by the printers. Instead, the files are queued in directories, by a process known as the spooler, for subsequent handling by a printing daemon known as `lpsched` (an acronym and program name for the `lp` scheduler daemon). To understand how this works, imagine yourself as part of a community of users sharing one or two printers, among other UNIX resources. Ask yourself what would happen should you be able to address the printer directly for a print request while someone else is doing exactly the same thing. You are right! The output will be more of a character soup than a presentable piece of work. This is due to the fact that the printer will be handling characters as they arrive, thus mixing the ones that belong to your file with those belonging to other users.

To alleviate this problem, the spooler takes over as you send print jobs to printers. It simply stops them on their way to their destination and diverts them to a waiting area on your system disk. This area is a subdirectory known as the print queue. Files destined for the same printer are queued in the same directory until the printer becomes available. The aforementioned process is known as spooling. You may be wondering whether this means that the terminal will be tied up for as long as it takes for the print job to materialize. The answer is no. This is because once a print job is queued, another background process known as the printing scheduler daemon (`lpsched`) takes over and supervises the ongoing printing services, making sure that every request, including yours, is honored.

In addition to the basic service, LP printing services allow administrators to aggregate printers of similar type into a printer class. This provides for the optimal utilization of printing resources, as users target a class of printers instead of targeting a specific one. When this happens, `lpsched` sends the print job to the first printer to become available in the requested class. Other printing services include tasks pertaining to starting interface programs that are suitable to the printer, applying the filters to user files whenever necessary, notifying users, if desired, of the status of printing jobs, and, in the case of network printing, the LP printing service has the additional job of sending print jobs to the hosts to which requested printers are connected.

BSD AND LINUX PRINTING

The print daemon on BSD-derived UNIX systems is lpd. BSD systems do not recognize print classes that SVR4 supports.

Setting Up Local Printing Services (SVR4, Solaris 2.x)

In this section, the setup and configuration of local printing services are presented. Local printing services provide users with the capability to print to printers connected directly to the host they are logged in to. The following are the steps required to set up printers, irrespective of whether they are parallel, serial, or network printers.

1. Verify availability of resources.
2. Use lpadmin to create the printer.
3. Change ownership and permissions to device special file.
4. If this is your first printer, make it the default printer.
5. Release the printer to the user community.

The resources for which you want to check are lp login id, lpsched, and an available port (serial or parallel). The lp login id is normally created during initial system installation. If the lp account does not exist in the /etc/passwd directory, then you ought to create one. It will be required at a later step in the setup process. Second, verify that lpsched is running by checking the output of the command

```
#ps -ef ¦ grep "lpsched"
```

If the printer is not enabled, you may do so by entering the following command:

```
#/usr/lib/lp/lpsched
```

The next step is to create a print destination by using the lpadmin command. The syntax of lpadmin follows.

```
/usr/lib/lpadmin -p<name> -v<pathname> -m<interface> \
[-h¦l] - c<class>
```

In this syntax,

-p<name> is the name you want to assign to the printer. It can be anything you like. It is more convenient, however, to assign it a name that makes sense to the user community.

-v<pathname> is the special device file pathname. Depending on whether the printer is parallel or serial, the pathname is /dev/lp# or /dev/term/## (# and ## represent decimal digits representative of the parallel and serial ports on your system).

-m<interface> is a program that is invoked by lp as it sends print jobs to the printer port. <interface> is responsible for printer port and physical printer initialization, and performs functions pertaining to printing a banner if desired, producing the right number of copies, and setting the page length and width. You have the freedom to write and use your own interface programs (in which case you must specify its name using the -i<interface> option). If you do not specify one, the standard and generic interface supplied with the system will be used by default. When installing the printer for the first time, it is advisable to start with the standard interface. If all goes well, you can always change over to the interface of your choice. Printer interfaces are usually maintained in the `/usr/lib/lp/model` directory.

`[-h¦1]`: h indicates that the printer is hardwired, whereas 1 indicates that the device associated with the printer is a login terminal. h and 1 are mutually exclusive. In the event that none is specified, h is assumed.

`-c<class>` specifies the class to which the printer belongs. Users will subsequently be able to specify the class using lp with -d option.

Assuming that you want to create a printer destination for a parallel printer that is to be connected to your parallel port, the `lpadmin` command would look like this:

```
#lpadmin -d dotmatrix -v /dev/lp1 -m standard
#lpadmin
```

Because the printer port device special file can be written to directly, as with any other file, you ought to make sure that users have no direct access to it. This involves changing the port ownership to login lp, as well as changing the file permissions to 600. The following two commands demonstrate how to do this to `/dev/lp1`.

```
#chown lp  /dev/lp1
#chmod 600 /dev/lp1
```

Before you release the printer to the user community, you may want to make it the default destination. A user failing to specify the printer destination when using the lp command will have his print job sent to the default printer. To make a printer the default destination, enter the following command:

```
#lpadmin -d <printer_name>
```

The `lpadmin` command to make dot matrix the default printer therefore becomes

```
#lpadmin -d dotmatrix
```

Finally, to make the printer accessible to users, you must allow the printer destination to accept print jobs as well as logically turn on the printer. To allow printer dotmatrix to accept print jobs, enter

```
#accept dotmatrix
```

and to logically turn it on (that is, allow it to do the printing), enter

```
#enable dotmatrix
```

Setting Up Network Print Servers (SVR4, Solaris 2.x)

Sometimes in a multisystem, multiplatform environment users find themselves in need of printers that are attached to a different system than what they are currently logged in to. Figure 23.7 depicts a scenario whereby the user wants her print job sent to printer odie, attached to system engg, while logged in to system arts.

FIGURE 23.7.

Concept of print servers illustrated.

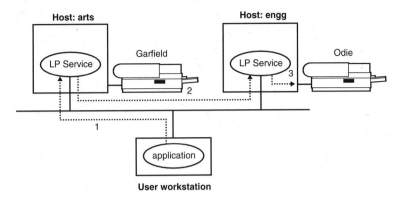

To provide this level of service, UNIX comes with enough support that, if implemented properly, allows users to print to any printer on the network. While doing so, users do not have to be concerned with any detail on how to address those printers other than what they already know about addressing their own. Figure 23.8 demonstrates the governing principles of network print services. In the depicted scenario, system engg becomes the so-called print server, whereas system arts is the client. The setup procedure calls on having print destinations (that is, queues) created on both systems (say, odie and garfield on engg and arts, respectively). Whereas odie is associated with the printer attached to engg, garfield has to be logically associated with odie (not with any printer that may happen to be attached to system arts). A user logged in to arts has to address the local printer destination—in this case garfield—to be able to print to odie as shown. The lp print request then becomes

```
#lp -p garfield <file_name>
```

FIGURE 23.8.

X displays and screens.

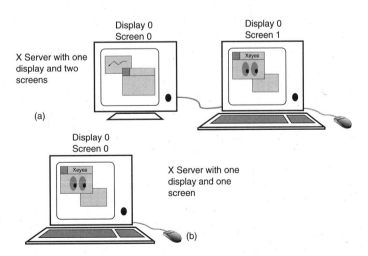

In doing so, the user is in fact addressing the local LP print service running on system `arts`. Next, LP on system `arts` checks the actual resource with which printer destination `garfield` is associated, to find that it actually maps to a print service resource (`odie`) supported on system `engg`. As a consequence, LP on system `arts` routes the request, along with the print job, to `engg` for subsequent handling.

The steps involved in setting up the service are not as complex as they may sound. For the most part, they are similar to those listed in the previous section with some subtle variations. Because this level of service involves both the client and server systems, both of them need to be configured.

Configuring the Print Server

Print server configuration requires two additional steps to those listed and described in the section on local printing. The two steps are creating a listen port service and registering client systems with the print service.

Because the print service under discussion is a network service (that is, runs on a connection-oriented transport service), then there is a requirement to create a `listen` port service with which it associates. Before doing that, however, it might be worth your while to check on readily available ones. When UNIX is first installed, your system is automatically configured to support a `listen` port monitor with port monitor tag `tcp`. Also, `tcp` is configured to support two print server-associated port services, with one taking care of System V clients whereas the other one takes care of BSD clients. To verify their existence, enter

```
#pmadm -l -t listen
PMTAG           PMTYPE          SVCTAG          FLGS ID         <PMSPECIFIC>
.
.
.
tcp                     listen          0               x       root
➡\x02000ACE64000001 -
 c - /usr/lib/saf/nlps_server #NLPS SERVER
tcp                     listen          lp              -       root
➡- - - - /var/spool/lp
/fifos/listenS5 #NLPS SERVER
.
.
```

If the listing you get on your screen includes the two entries shown in the preceding partial listing, you do not need to create the port services and you may skip the next step. If they do not exist, use `pmadm` to create them. To create a port service to listen to print requests sent by System V clients, enter

```
#pmadm -a -p<pmtag> -s lp -i root -v 'nlsadmin -V' \
-m 'nlsadmin -o /var/spool/lp/fifos/listenS5'
```

where *pmtag* is the name assigned to the port monitor. To create a port service to respond to BSD clients, however, you must enter `lpsystem -A`. The output displays the port address that you ought to use as an argument with `nlsadmin` upon using `pmadm` to create the port service. Following is an example output of `lpsystem -A`, as it appears on my monitor:

```
#lpsystem -A
0200020364000001000000000000000000
```

Next, to create the port service under `tcp` port monitor, enter the following command:

```
#pmadm -a -p tcp -s lpd -i root -v 'nlsadmin -V' \
-m'nlsadmin -o /var/spool/lp/fifos/listenBSD \
-A'\x0200020364000001000000000000000000''
```

To force the port monitor to recognize the changes you made, use the command

```
#sacadm -x -p tcp
```

The next step is to register the client with the server, using the `lpsystem` command. In addition to registering the client, `lpsystem` allows you to define the communications parameters that you want to enforce on the connection maintained between both the server and the client after it is invoked. Defined parameters are saved in the `/etc/lp/Systems` file. Though you can edit it directly using `vi`, it is recommended that you avoid doing that. The syntax of the `lpsystem` command is

```
lpsystem [-t<type>] [-T<timeout>] [-R <retry>] \
[-y"comment"] systemname
```

in which

-t<type> specifies whether the client is System V or BSD.

-T<timeout> specifies the idle time after which the connection should be terminated. The <timeout> can be *n*, 0, and *N*, where *N* is the number of minutes the connection idles before the connection is dropped. If 0 is specified, the connection will be dropped as soon as it idles, whereas *n* means never time-out. Depending on your environment, you should configure the connection to the one that suits you best. If users occasionally print across the network, you may be better off with the 0 option. This frees up the resources reserved on both systems to service the request as soon as it is honored. If, on the other hand, the frequency of service utilization is high, you may consider configuring the connection to n (never time-out). This way, you save both systems the repeated tasks of establishing, maintaining, and relinquishing the connection every time they ought to respond to a print service request. Added to the savings in CPU utilization on both systems is the saving on bandwidth utilization due to packet exchange pertaining to link establishment and disconnection.

-R<retry> specifies in minutes the duration of time to wait before link re-establishment is attempted, when it was abnormally disrupted.

-y"comment" can be any convenient comment.

systemname specifies the remote system's name to which the communications parameters apply.

Applying the preceding to the example in Figure 23.8, in order to register arts with the print server host engg, you should enter

```
#lpsystem -t s5 -T n arts
```

Configuring the Client

As in the case of server setup, here too you ought to make sure that you have a port monitor that is properly configured to support network printing services. To do that, enter

```
#pmadm -l -p tcp
```

The output should include the following three entries (the first two pertaining to System V support, whereas the third one pertains to BSD client support):

```
PMTAG  PMTYPE  SVCTAG FLGS  ID   <PMSPECIFIC>
tcp    listen  0      -     root \x00200ACE64000001 -c -
/usr/lib/sac/nlps_server #NLPS SERVER

tcp    listen  lp     -     root ....

tcp    listen  lpd    -     root \x0020020364000001 -c -
/var/spool/lp/fifos/listenBSD
```

If any of the preceding entries is missing, then you must create the associated port services yourself using pmadm. Depending on what is missing, use one or more of the following commands:

```
#pmadm -a -p tcp -s lp -i root -v'nlsadmin -V' \
-m `nlsadmin -o /var/spool/lp/fifos/listen5`

#pmadm -a -p tcp -s 0 -i root -v 'nlsadmin -V' \
-m `nlsadmin -o /usr/lib/saf/nlps_server \
-A "\x02000ACE6400000010000000000000000"` -y "NLPS SERVER"

#pmadm -a -p tcp -s lpd -i root -v 'nlsadmin -V' \
-m `nlsadmin -o /var/spool/lp/fifos/listenBSD \
-A "\x00202036400000010000000000000000"`
```

The last pmadm command would be required only if you are setting up for BSD support as well.

Next, register the remote server with the client using the lpsystem command, as discussed in the preceding section.

Now, you have only to create the printer destination; instead of associating it with any particular port, you will associate it with the printer destination that you created on the print server host. To do that, enter the following command

```
#lpadmin -p<client_printer> \
-s<remote_printer>!<print_server_host>
```

in which

client_printer specifies the printer destination undergoing creation on the local machine.

remote_printer specifies the print server's printer destination, with which the *client_printer* is associated.

print_server_host specifies the host name of the system where the remote_printer destination is.

Applying the preceding to the scenario of Figure 23.7, the following is the command to enter at host arts:

```
#lpadmin -p odie -s garfield!engg
```

The remaining steps, as you should know by now, are to enable the printer and make it accept print jobs. Hence the commands,

```
#enable odie
#accept odie
```

To send a print job down the wire to garfield to print, the user must address odie while logged in to arts. For example, to print file monalisa, the user must enter

```
#lp -p odie monalisa
```

LP print service on host arts will redirect the print job to garfield destination on host engg.

Managing Printers

In addition to the tools required to set up, enable, and disable printers, the LP print service presents the system administrator with a comprehensive set of management tools. Those tools can be applied to change printer configuration and to assist in maintenance and troubleshooting situations. The following subsections describe aspects of printing management and associated tools.

Enabling and Disabling LP Print Service

lpsched is the program to start LP print service, whereas lpshut is the program to shut it down. Only login root or lp can start and shut down printing services. All printers that were printing at the time of invoking lpshut will stop printing. Whenever lpsched is restarted, print requests that were disrupted at the time LP service was shut down will print from the very beginning.

Managing Print Requests

lpmove is a command that lets you move print jobs from one printer to another. There are, primarily, two scenarios that may prompt you to do that. In one, you may want to disable printing to a printer in order to disconnect it for routine maintenance or troubleshooting. Instead of leaving your users in the cold waiting for their print jobs to materialize, you would move their print jobs to some other printer of equivalent quality. In the second scenario, you may use lpmove for load balancing purposes in case you encounter situations in which one printer is heavily used while another one is sitting idle. The syntax of the lpmove command is

```
#lpmove <requests> <dest>
```

where *requests* presents `lpmove` with a list of request IDs to move to the printer specified in *dest*. To obtain the print request IDs, use the `lpstat` command. Its output should look like

```
#lpstat
garfield-4 root 112 March 24 06:20
garfield-5 root 567 March 24 06:22
```

where the first column is the print request ID and is made of two components: the name of the printer to which the print job was submitted, and the order in which it was received. The second column displays the name of the user who submitted the print job, followed by the date and time of submission columns.

Assuming `acctlp` is an idling printer to which you want to move the print job `garfield-5`, the `lpmove` command then becomes

```
#lpmove garfield-5 acctlp
```

To move the entire printing load from one printer to another, enter

```
#lpmove <dest1> <dest2>
```

> **NOTE**
>
> Upon moving print requests, request that IDs remain intact to allow users to track their print jobs.

> **CAUTION**
>
> `lpmove` does not check on the acceptance status of print jobs that it moves. It is therefore your responsibility to do the check using the `lpstat` command, and to take any corrective measure should a print job fail to be moved.

To cancel undesirable print requests, use the `cancel` command. The syntax is

```
#cancel <request-ID>
```

To cancel, for example, `garfield-5`, enter

```
#cancel garfield-5
```

Printer Configuration Management

Printer configuration management includes tasks such as changing printer class, changing printer port, removing printers, and removing classes. All these tasks can be achieved using the `lpadmin` command.

To change a printer class, enter

```
#lpadmin -p<dest> -c<class>
```

If the specified class does not exist, the class will be created and the specified destination will be inserted into it. To remove the printer from a certain class, enter

```
#lpadmin -p<dest> -r <class>
```

If the printer is the last one of its class, then the class itself will be removed as well.

To change the printer port, enter

```
#lpadmin -p<dest> -v <special_file_pathname>
```

You may need to do this on occasions when you suspect something went wrong with the original port to which the printer was connected. This reconfiguration will allow you to continue offering print services while troubleshooting the defective port.

Finally, to check the configuration of a particular printer, enter

```
#lpstat -p<printer> -l
```

In the example that follows, lpstat is entered to check on the configuration of garfield destination.

```
#lpstat -pgarfield -l
printer garfield (login terminal) is idle. enabled since Thu Mar 24 18:20:01 EST
1994. available.
    Form mounted:
    Content types: simple
    Printer types: unknown
    Description:
    Connection: direct
    Interface: /usr/lib/lp/model/standard
    On fault: mail to root once
    After fault: continue
    Users allowed:
        (all)
    Forms allowed:
        (none)
    Banner required
    Character sets:
        (none)
    Default pitch:
    Default page size:
    Default port settings:
```

whereas to check the configuration of all printers, enter

```
#lpstat -l
```

Print Service User Management

User access to LP print service on UNIX systems can be managed and restricted for reasons that may pertain to security or resource allocation and management.

If you carefully examine the sample output of the `lpstat -p garfield -l` command in the last example, you will see the names of the users allowed access in the "Users allowed" entry. According to the preceding example, no one is on either the allow or the deny list. This corresponds to the default security configuration and implies that any logged-in user can send print jobs to printer `garfield`. If you do not like that, however, you can use `lpadmin` with the `-u` option to restrict access to the printer. The syntax of the `lpadmin -u` command to list users on the allow list is the following:

```
#lpadmin -p<printer> -u allow:<login-ID-list>
```

To prevent users from accessing the printer, enter

```
#lpadmin -p<printer> -u deny:<login-ID-list>
```

> **NOTE**
>
> `login-ID-list` is a comma- or space-separated list of users' login IDs.

Following is a list of legal arguments that you can include in the `login-ID-list`:

`login-ID`	Denotes a user on the local system
`system_name!login-ID`	Denotes a user on a client system
`system_name!all`	Denotes all users on a client system
`all!login-ID`	Denotes a user on all systems
`all`	Denotes all users on the local system
`all!all`	Denotes all users on all systems

For each printer, the LP print service maintains deny and allow lists. The way they are used is summarized in the following paragraphs.

If the allow list is not empty, only users on that list are allowed access to the printer. If the allow list is empty but deny list is not, then all users except those on the deny list will be allowed access to the printer.

A user cannot exist on both lists simultaneously. When a user is added to either list, the user's login-ID will be checked and removed from the other one.

For example, to allow users Nadeem, Andrea, and May access to the printer `garfield`, you enter

```
#lpadmin -p garfield -u allow:Nadeem Andrea May
```

Next, you should check that this indeed took place by entering the command

```
#lpadmin -p garfield -l
```

```
printer garfield (login terminal) is idle. enabled since Tue Apr 12 05:18:07 EDT
1994. not available.
    Form mounted:
    Content types: simple
    Printer types: unknown
    Description:
    Connection: direct
    Interface: /usr/lib/lp/model/standard
    On fault: mail to root once
    After fault: continue
    Users allowed:
        nadeem
        andrea
        may
    Forms allowed:
        (none)
    Banner required
    Character sets:
        (none)
    Default pitch:
    Default page size:
    Default port settings:
```

Users educated about the use of the -q option with the lp command can assign print queue priority levels to print jobs that they submit to the LP service. Although this can sometimes be a useful feature, it may well prove to be a cause of concern to some of the user community as they find that their print jobs are constantly delayed in favor of those belonging to others of equal or less functional status. Fortunately, the LP print service allows you to set limits on how high a priority can be a assigned to print jobs submitted by users. Using the lpusers, different priority limit assignments can be made to apply to different users. The syntax of lpusers is

```
#lpusers -q<priority_level> -u<login-ID-list>
```

in which

> -q<priority_level> is an integer ranging between 0 and 39, with 0 representing the highest priority level.

> -u<login-ID-list> is a comma- or space-separated list of user IDs to whom the restriction applies. The login-ID list argument can have any of the following values:

login-ID	Denotes a user
system_name!login-ID	Denotes a user on a particular system
system_name!all	Denotes all users on a particular system
all	Denotes all users
all!login-ID	Denotes a user on all systems

Users submitting print jobs can assign them priorities as high as they are allowed to assign as set with the -q option.

23

DEVICE ADMINISTRATION

Setting Up Local Printing on BSD Systems

Setting up printing on BSD systems mainly involves making changes to the `/etc/printcap` file, creating the spooling directory (also known as the print queue), and editing the `/etc/rc` file so that the `lpd` spooling daemon is started at boot time. Here is what these steps involve:

/etc/printcap

The `/etc/printcap` file is a database file that contains one record for every attached/enabled printer. In addition to defining the printer characteristics, `/etc/printcap` records include printer configuration information that is vital to supporting the printer properly. This file includes records for both local and network printers.

Following is an example of what an `/etc/printcap` record should look like:

```
# printcap entry for printer goofy
goofy¦lp:\
    :lp=/dev/ttya:br#9600:\
    :ms=-parity,onlcr,ixon:\
    :sd=/var/spool/goofy:\
    :lf=/var/adm/goofy_errors:\
    :pl=66:pw=132:
```

As shown in this entry, `/etc/printcap` entries contain colon-separated fields. The last field must end with a colon. The first field of each entry must start with the name that the printer is known by. Printer names are pipe (¦) character-separated. In the example, the printer being defined is known as `goofy` and `lp`. In fact, `lp` is a special alias that designates the printer as being the default one. In other words, by virtue of assigning printer `goofy` the `lp` printer name, users who submit a print job without specifying the printer name will have their jobs sent to `goofy`. Consequently, only one printer can be assigned the special name `lp`, thus designating it as the default printer.

Fields subsequent to the name field are introduced by a two-character code. A field describing a numerical value takes the form *code#* (br#9600, in the above example). Otherwise, the field takes the form *code=* (sd=/var/spool/goofy). Following is an explanation of the remaining fields:

lp   This field specifies the device filename to be printed to. In this case it is the first serial port (`/dev/ttya` on SunOS, or `/dev/ttyS0` on Linux).

br   This field specifies the baud rate at which the printer operates. In this case `9600` bps is specified.

ms   This field describes to the print daemon (`lpd`) the printer characteristics that `lpd` should observe when printing. In this example, the printer is set to no parity, a new line should be printed as a pair of carriage return/linefeed, and that XON/XOFF software flow control is supported.

sd   This field specifies the spooling directory, where the print jobs are held pending printing. This directory must exist before printing to the associated printer is attempted. It should also have been created with proper permissions. In the above example, the spooling directory belonging to printer goofy is specified to be `/var/spool/goofy`.

lf   This field specifies the path of the error log file pertaining to the printer. When in trouble printing to the printer, lpd logs error messages resulting from failing attempts to this file. This file should have its permissions set to 666. Also, it is your responsibility as a system administrator to create this file before usage of the printer is allowed.

pl   This field sets the page length. In this example, it is set to 66 lines/page.

pw   This field sets the page width. In this example, it is set to 132 characters/line.

There are many more fields that can be included in the /etc/printcap file than what has just been described. You will find, however, that the above ones are the most commonly used. The man pages on /etc/printcap provide comprehensive listings of all the supported field codes including a proper description of each.

Following is a self-explanatory example of an /etc/printcap entry for parallel printer support:

```
lp¦HPLaser:\
    :lp=/dev/lp:\
    :sd=/var/spool/lp:\
    :pl=66:pw=132:\
    :lf=/var/spool/laser_errors:
```

Setting Up Spooling Directories

Every printer must have a dedicated spooling directory. Setting up the spooling directory involves both creating it, changing its permissions to 755, changing its ownership to special user daemon, and changing its group to the group daemon. You should be logged in as root when creating/setting up the spooling directories. Following is the command sequence necessary to set up the spooling directory for printer goofy:

```
# mkdir /var/spool/goofy
# chown daemon /var/spool/goofy
# chgrp daemon /var/spool/goofy
# chmod 755 /var/spool/goofy
```

Fixing access permissions to 755 on the spooling directory protects it from abusive manipulation by other users, which may result in accidental or malicious deletions of print jobs.

SERIAL PRINTER

Make sure that whenever you set up your system for serial printing, you disable getty from controlling the port to which you intend to attach the printer. On a SunOS system, this involves updating the /etc/ttytab file and marking off the last field of the entry corresponding to the desired serial line. In Linux, you disable getty access by replacing the primitive respawn with off in the entry corresponding to the port in the /etc/inittab file.

The above completes the minimal steps required to set up printing on BSD systems. To ensure that the print spooling daemon is activated at boot time, check the /etc/rc startup script and make sure that the following lines of code are not commented:

23
DEVICE
ADMINISTRATION

```
if [ -f /usr/lib/lpd ]; then
    rm -f /dev/printer /usr/spool.lock
    /usr/lib/lpd; echo -n 'printer' > /dev/console
fi
```

To test the viability of the printer setup, use the `lpr` command to print a test page as in the following example:

```
# lpr -P goofy testfile
```

Setting Up Network Printing Under BSD

Setting up network printing under BSD is far less complex than under SVR4. As in SVR4, the setup includes configuring both the print server (the host where the shared printer is attached) and the client (the host printing to the shared printer).

Setting up the shared printer on the server is not different from local printing setup. The steps are the same as described on the previous pages. You need not do anything special to allow for printer sharing aside from ensuring that hosts authorized to access the server for printing services have their names in the `/etc/hosts.equiv` file on server host.

Configuring the client to recognize and print to remote printers simply involves adding an entry, similar to the following one, in the `/etc/printcap` file:

```
lp¦remote printer¦:\
    :lp=:rm=tenor:rp=goofy:sd=/var/spool/lpd:
```

According to this entry, the client print daemon recognizes the remote printer as being the default printer. Since the `lp` field is left blank (that is, `lp=`), the printer is assumed remote, and is attached to remote machine tenor (`rm=tenor`). The `rp=goofy` capability identifies the remote printer name as `goofy`, whereas `sd` identifies the `/var/spool/lpd` directory as being the corresponding spooling directory.

To print to the remote printer, the user ought to run the `lpr` command. No special options or command line parameters are required to make it work with non-local printers. If the remote printer is the client's default printer, simply enter

```
# lpr filename
```

Otherwise, use the following form for the `lpr` command:

```
# lpr -P printername filename
```

where *printername* is the name by which the printer in known locally, *not* its name as set on the remote host.

Managing Print Services Under BSD

As in UNIX SVR4, BSD provides the tools necessary to properly manage and administer printing service. Both the `lpc` and `lpq` commands help you do most of the desired administrative tasks.

Using lpc, a system administrator can manage printers which are defined in the /etc/printcap file. lpc includes support for starting/restarting/stopping a printer daemon, selectively enabling or disabling a particular printer, displaying printer status, status of printer daemon, and status of print queues, and reordering print jobs in a given queue.

In its basic form, lpc assumes the following syntax:

```
lpc  [command [parameter]]
```

where *command* specifies the action that you want lpc to take on the object specified by *parameter*. If no command is entered, lpc is invoked in an interactive mode, as shown below:

```
# lpc
lpc>
```

Subsequently, commands can be entered, and responded to interactively at the lpc> prompt, as shown here:

```
# /usr/etc/lpc
lpc> down goofy
lpc>
```

Typically, *parameter* specifies the printer name. Supported commands include the following:

help, ?	Provides help on using lpc.
abort	To terminate an active spooling daemon, and consequently disable printing to printers specified by *parameter*.
clean	Delete all print jobs from the spooling directory pertaining to the printer(s) specified in *parameter*.
disable	Disables the specified print queues, preventing users from submitting new print jobs to these queues.
down	Disables both printing and queues pertaining to specified queues. Also allows for including a message to broadcast to users advising them of the event and the reasons underlying it. See the man pages for details.
enable	Enables spooling to specified spooling directories.
exit	Used to exit an interactive lpc session.
restart	Restarts a printer daemon. Typically used when a daemon dies unexpectedly due to abnormal conditions.
start	Starts a printer daemon.
status	Reports the status of queues and printers on the local machine.
stop	Stops the spooling daemon after the current job completes printing, and disables the printer.

| topq | Move print specified job(s) to the top of the queue. |
| up | Reverses actions taken by down command, including starting a new print spooling daemon. |

Refer to the man pages for details on using the lpc command.

Connecting a PC to UNIX Systems

Rather than purchase terminals, many users prefer to run UNIX sessions right from their desktop DOS- or Windows 95–based PCs. This is mainly attributable to the low cost of the PC, its increased processing power, and the additional flexibility of being able to easily toggle back and forth between DOS applications and a UNIX session. This section describes two methods by which you can establish a connection with the UNIX system using the DOS platform. The two methods are as follows:

■ Establishing a session via a serial port
■ Establishing a session via TCP/IP

Connecting the PC Using COM Ports

Depending on how you are going to do it, configuring a PC to connect to a UNIX host via a COM port is the easier and less costly of the two methods. If both systems belong to the same site, where there is no requirement for a telephone wire to connect both machines, a cross-wired cable is all the additional hardware you need along with the COM port that is commonly available on your PC. Any communications software with decent terminal emulation capabilities can be used to emulate some the terminals that UNIX recognizes. I used to use Procomm Plus and I was satisfied with it until I decided to go the TCP/IP way for reasons that will be discussed later.

Configuring a PC to serially connect to a UNIX host involves some preparation on both systems. Before making any move, however, you must check on the availability of the following resources:

■ On the PC: Verify that you have a free COM port, and that its use of the IRQ interrupt number and I/O port address is not conflicting with any other interface cards on the machine.

■ On the UNIX hosts: Verify the availability of a tty port and a suitable terminal line setting record in the /etc/ttydefs file (refer to the section, "Determining the Availability of Resources," earlier in this chapter).

Additional requirements include two modems and two straight-through cables—if you are configuring a connection over a telephone wire—or a cross-wired cable, as discussed earlier in this chapter, to directly connect the PC to the UNIX system.

Configuring the UNIX system for support to tty port services was discussed earlier in this chapter.

Configuring the PC is a very simple matter that basically involves configuring the communication software to the same communication parameters implemented on the UNIX side of the connection. The parameters include baud rate, number of bits per character, parity, and number of stop bits.

Configuring the Modems

The following are general guidelines that you should observe when configuring the modems.

Make sure that the modem you are installing at the UNIX end supports quiet mode. This mode is required in order to stop the modem from sending response codes to the port. Also, echo should be disabled. Failure to observe both of these rules may result in having the UNIX system "believe" that the echoed characters are in partial response to the login prompt it sent to the PC. This may lead to an endless sequence of login and password prompts, and so on.

Should you run into the problem of having user sessions unexpectedly suspending, try to re-create the problem. If, upon sending manually an XON (press Ctrl+Q), character communications resume, then you may need to disable XON/OFF flow control to rely only on RTS/CTS.

Set the modem connected to the UNIX system's autoanswer mode.

Connecting to UNIX via TCP/IP

TCP/IP is another way by which you can connect PCs in your environment to the UNIX system. This solution, however, is a bit more expensive than using COM ports. This is due to the investment in the network interface card (NIC) and the necessary software for implementing the TCP/IP suite of protocols in addition to the cabling cost incurred per workstation. Given the advantages of this solution, and depending on the intended use of the connection, you may find it worth the money and effort to take this route. Using TCP/IP, you will not only be able to establish a `telnet` session with the host, but you also will be able to use `ftp` for file transfers between the PC and UNIX, and `rsh` to remotely execute a UNIX command without having to necessarily log in to the system. Also, if you are using something like Novell's Lan Workplace Pro for Windows 95, you will be able to invoke multiple UNIX and Microsoft Windows applications simultaneously. You also will be able to cut and paste (to your heart's desire) between applications.

As in the COM port option, here too you have to set up both ends of the connection properly in order for them to communicate.

The method that you will be using to install TCP/IP on the PC depends to a large degree on the vendor from whom you purchased the software. You are required, however, to do the following:

1. Assign the PC an IP address.
2. Assign the PC a host name.

3. Create a hosts file on the PC. Include in the file the name to address mappings corresponding to all UNIX hosts to which the user has enough access rights. If domain name services are implemented on your site, then you can ignore this step.

4. Beware that some TCP/IP solutions impose a default upper limit on the allowed number of connections that a PC can handle. Check on that and reconfigure if need be to the desired number.

   Depending on whether DNS and/or RARP services are part of your environment, you may need to go further:

5. Provide the name server's address to the PC.

6. Edit the `ethers` and the `hosts` file on the RARP server.

Depending on the vendor, the TCP/IP software comes with ranging tools to help you trouble-shoot and manage your PC on the network. For a minimum, any decent implementation of TCP/IP should provide tools such as the `ping` and `netstat` commands. Use these tools in case things fail to work properly.

Connecting X Terminals

Until X terminals emerged a few years ago, ASCII dumb terminals were almost exclusively the machines that users had at their disposal for accessing UNIX systems. Due to their nature, these terminals fell short of meeting the ever-increasing demands of engineering and scientific applications for graphical output. With X terminals, a new era of computer-to-human interface began. These terminals not only met the crying need of engineering and science applications for graphics, but they also presented UNIX users with a far more superior, and elegant, user interface.

An X terminal is a component of the X Window System technology (hereafter referred to as X, or X11) that was developed at the Massachusetts Institute of Technology, and is currently maintained by a consortium of universities and vendors.

One of X's greatest attributes is that it can be brought up on any platform. Though it was initially implemented in UNIX environments, X is now equally available to other platforms ranging from mainframes to DOS workstations. This platform independence is due to the mechanism and model that were put together to make X work: the X protocol and client/server model. As you will see later on, this has far-reaching implications as to how users will be able to work in multiplatform/multivendor environments.

To setup X terminals, it is essential that you understand the governing concepts that drive this technology. This section will therefore start with an examination of its various components, including the client/server model that X follows. Some terms will be introduced and defined to make you more familiar with the associated jargon. Setting up X and X servers will be discussed next. The focus of the discussion will preclude the many different kinds of GUI interfaces that are currently available to run on top of X, concentrating more on how to bring the engine (X platform) and its associated gear to life.

The Architecture of X

X's architecture is based on two components: the client/server model and the X protocol.

The Client/Server Model of X

A client server/model follows a mechanism by which an application is split into two components: the so-called back end and front end. In the database client/server technology, for example, the front end runs at the user's workstation and is termed the client, whereas the back end runs on a remote host that is shared by all authorized users, and is called the server. The database server acts as the main repository of data that clients need. Instead of having an entire file transferred to its machine from the server, the client uses scope-and-filter techniques while requesting only the data relevant to its needs for subsequent processing. From what has just been said, the client/server model components could be expressed as a matter of which is managing access to a resource, versus which is requesting use of the resource. The server component is the access-resource manager, whereas the client component is the one requesting access to and use of the resource.

The application is split into the following components: an X client and an X display server.

An X client handles all data-processing aspects of an application, except for the I/O interaction, which it delegates to a server process. The server process could be running on the same machine or a terminal located elsewhere in the environment. This implies that, unlike database and other familiar server technologies, the X display server belongs to the user's machine where actual I/O and user-interface capabilities are provided. Clients, therefore, become the shared resource that all users can access and run remotely.

The X Protocol

Rather than base the X client/server model on a particular set of software and hardware resources, which could restrict its portability across platforms, X architects chose to base it on a protocol mechanism called X protocol. In doing so, they insulated vendors and developers of X applications from platform-related concerns and specifics. Applications complying with X specifications can be easily ported to any environment, while having X servers mediate the I/O interaction with the physical display units. Having said that, this clearly implies that an X server presents applications with a virtual display unit that they can manage. The display server maps I/O primitives, passed to it by applications to physical actions on the actual display unit.

Another aspect of X protocol worth mentioning is that it builds on some of the most commonly deployed transport protocols, including TCP/IP, IPX/SPX, and DECnet to enable clients and servers to talk to each other. A user on an X terminal, with multiprotocol support, can invoke one session with a mainframe while maintaining another with a UNIX system, and yet another one across a dial-up line.

From what has been said about X, it can be concluded that X is a network-based graphics engine. It allows users to connect to, and run applications on, remote systems while handling I/O interaction using locally available graphical terminals. Being an engine implies that readily available GUI interfaces are built on top of X, rather than being part of it.

X Resources

Central to X functionality is the concept of resources. A resource is a configurable attribute of an application. Examples of resource attributes are the font the application uses, background color, initial location, and size of an application window.

The fact that the same X client may have to deal with different servers means that it must be supported with a configuration mechanism that is flexible enough to deal with ranging hardware capabilities and user preferences. Examples of hardware differences are monitor color and resolution capabilities. Also, one user's preferred color, font, and window location and size may not agree with someone else's. It can be concluded that X applications cannot be developed with built-in support for any hardware type or for the developer's perception of how the user interface and preferences should look. Users should be allowed to have a choice of hardware and be able to configure an application's output however they feel is best for them.

X provides for this capability using one of two methods: command-line options and resource definition files.

Independent of the method you are using, when an application is invoked, an X display manager will autoload the associated attributes onto your server (more on this later). This provides the I/O capability and interface you have defined.

Setting X Resources with Command-Line Options

In this method, users define resources upon invoking an application using command-line options. Most X applications allow users to define resources using the same command option names. Table 23.5 shows examples of the most commonly used arguments.

Table 23.5. Most common user-definable X resources.

X Resource	Description
`-display <display>`	Specifies the name of the X server, display, and screen to use (that is, to send output to)
`-geometry <specs>`	Specifies the initial size and location of application's window
`-bg <color>`	Specifies the background color
`-bd <color>`	Specifies the border color
`-fg <color>`	Specifies the foreground color
`-fn <font>`	Specifies the font
`-title <title>`	Specifies the window title

For example, say that a user wants to invoke `xterm` (an X terminal emulation client) titled "X Terminal" with a blue background color, gray border, and the window initially located at the upper-left corner of the monitor. The user then has to enter the following command:

```
% xterm -display arts:0 -title "X Terminal" -bg blue -bd grey -g +1+1
```

Given the number of clients that a user may have to invoke simultaneously, this method of loading resources can be tedious and is prone to errors.

Defining Resources Using Resource Definition Files

To alleviate the tedium of defining resources using command-line options, X provides the following two resource definition files: Xresources and $HOME/.Xresources. Both of these files contain per-application lists of attribute assignments. Xresources contains global definitions applying to all X servers, whereas $HOME/.Xresources may contain user-specific definitions. Both sets of resources are loaded by the xrdb program whenever a connection is established with an X server. Sample $HOME/.Xresources file contents are as follows:

```
!xclock resource definitions:
xclock*update:      1
xclock*analog:      false
xclock*chime:       false
xclock*geometry:    -0+0
!xterm resource definitions:

xterm*title:        XTerminal
xterm*background:   grey
xterm*foreground:   black
xterm*geometry:     40x24+1+1
xterm*scrollBar:    true
```

The first set of resources pertains to xclock. According to what is shown, the clock is to be updated at the rate of once a second, displayed in digital format, and the chime is disabled. The second set of resources pertains to xterm, and that set specifies a window title XTerminal, a yellow background color, black text, scroll bar enabled, and a window size of 40x24 displayed at the upper-left corner of the monitor.

Window Managers

A window manager is an X client that normally is invoked during start-up on an X session, from the user's start-up $HOME/.xsession script file. It can also be invoked on the command line.

Window managers allow users to manage their applications' windows whether moving, resizing, or reducing them to icons.

There are many different flavors of window managers. Tab Window Manager (twm) is the one that comes with MIT's distribution of X. Open Look provides olwm, whereas OSF/Motif provides mwm. Linux-additionally supports so-called Free Virtual Window Manager (fvwm). In this chapter, reference will be made to twm only.

twm behavior is governed by the system.twmrc configuration file in the /usr/X/lib/twm directory (please refer to the note below for information on X resource files on the different UNIX platforms). You can edit this file, changing its default behavior to anything that suits your users' needs.

X RESOURCE DIRECTORIES

This section and subsequent ones provide a generic level of information on the topic of X services and related configuration issues that applies equally to all platforms. Consequently, references to resources (that is, configuration files, directories, and binaries) are made specific to UnixWare 2.1 (a SVR4 variant of UNIX) only. To help you find referenced resources on other flavors of UNIX that the book addresses, you are provided with a tabulation describing the paths to these resources:

Platform	Binaries	X11 lib Path
Solaris 2.x	`/usr/openwin/bin`	`/usr/openwin/lib`
AIX	`/usr/bin/X11`	`/usr/lib/X11`
SunOS (BSD)	`/usr/openwin/bin`	`/usr/openwin/lib`
Linux	`/usr/X11R6/bin`	`/usr/X11R6/lib`

Because the default configuration is adequate for the purposes of this section (that is, setting up an X terminal), no further details will be provided on how to edit this file.

Setting the Shell Environment Variables

Two shell environment variables need to be taken care of in order to successfully start an X session. These are PATH and DISPLAY.

PATH should be modified to include the path to X client programs. This can be done in the user's start-up script $HOME/.xsession. The script should include:

```
PATH=$PATH:/usr/X/bin
export PATH
```

DISPLAY X environment variable specifies to the client the name of the host, and display number to send its output to.

X distinguishes between displays and screens. Figure 23.8 tries to make the distinction clear. In X, a display is a collection of monitors that share a common keyboard and mouse. Shown in Figure 23.8 is an X server that has one display and two monitors. The monitors are referred to as screens and are numbered starting with 0.

Hence, an appropriate setup of the DISPLAY variable should take care of both the display and monitor to which the output is sent. The DISPLAY variable can be specified using the following format:

```
display=[iphost¦ipaddress]:displaynumber.screennumber
```

in which

> [*iphost*|*ipaddress*]   Specifies the X server host name or its IP address.

displaynumber	This is the display number, normally 0, because most workstations have only one display.
screennumber	Designates the monitor to which the output should be sent. If not specified, screen number 0 will be assumed.

DISPLAY can be set in the user's login script. It can also be set manually as a command-line argument, using the -display option, when a client is being invoked:

```
% xterm -display arts:0
```

The X Display Manager

The X Display Manager (xdm) is the preferred way of starting up an X session. xinit is another option. This discussion is restricted to xdm only.

In SVR4, xdm is started as a daemon when the system is booted. It is invoked by one of the /etc/rc2.d scripts. On my system, the startup script is S69xdm.

Once invoked, xdm provides users with a graphical login window where they must enter their user IDs and passwords. Once authenticated and logged in, xdm automatically loads resources to X servers and starts X clients as specified in the user's $HOME/.xsession startup script.

xdm is a customizable X client. Its behavior depends to a large degree on what is in its configuration files. All xdm configuration files are in the /usr/X/lib/xdm directory. They are as follows:

```
*xdm-config
*Xresources
*Xsession
*Xservers
*Xaccess
*Xsetup_0
*GiveConsole
*TakeConsole
```

Some of these files pertain to different versions of X. In the following subsections, the purpose of each file is described in the context of starting X server sessions. User-specific files (that is, $HOME/.xsession, $HOME/.Xresources, and $HOME/.xsession-errors) are described as well.

xdm-config

xdm-config is the first file that is read by xdm when spawned. This file primarily defines where the rest of the configuration files listed previously belong. Following is an example of the its contents:

```
DisplayManager*session:          /usr/X/lib/xdm/Xsession
DisplayManager*resources:               /usr/X/lib/xdm/Xresources
DisplayManager.errorLogFile:            /dev/X/xdm-errors
DisplayManager.pidFile:          /dev/X/xdm-pid
DisplayManager.keyFile:          /usr/X/lib/xdm/xdm-keys
DisplayManager.servers:          /usr/X/lib/xdm/Xservers
DisplayManager._0. authorize:    true
DisplayManager._0.setup:                /usr/X/lib/xdm/Xsetup_0
DisplayManager*authComplain:     false
```

23

DEVICE
ADMINISTRATION

It can be seen that the preceding `xdm-config` file contains some self-customizing resource definitions.

Xservers and Xaccess

There are two methods by which `xdm` knows which X servers to connect to. One method pertaining to release 3 of X (also referred to as X11R3) relies on the `Xservers` file. In `Xservers`, the administrator has to maintain a list of names of X servers to be managed by `xdm`. This was the only way available to `xdm` to connect to X servers. Following is a sample of the contents of an `Xservers` file:

```
0: local /usr/X/bin/X
engg:0 foreign May's X terminal
arts:0 foreign Andrea's X terminal
```

Note how, in all entries, the host's name and display number (colon separated) are followed by one of two terms, `local` or `foreign`. `local` means the X server is running on the console, whereas `foreign` means it is on the network.

Because `Xservers` was read only when `xdm` was started, however, this posed serious problems as X terminals were brought up later on and as others were temporarily turned off. The only way the administrator could force `xdm` to recognize a newly brought up X server was by restarting. This involves sending `xdm` a `SIGHUP` signal using

```
#kill -HUP <pid_of_xdm>
```

where the process ID can be found by entering

```
#cat /usr/X/lib/xdm/xdm-pid
```

To remedy this problem, X Display Manager Control Protocol (XDMCP) was introduced in X11R4. XDMCP is a protocol that is implemented at both ends of the connection: the X server and the `xdm` client. An X server with XDMCP support is responsible for requesting `xdm` for a connection and should not require an entry in the `Xservers` file.

To request a connection, an XDMCP-compatible server issues one of three types of queries, depending on how it is configured. The three types are as follows:

Direct query: This is a query directed to a specific host.

Broadcast query: The server sends out a general query addressed to all `xdm` clients requesting a connection. In this case, the X server connects to the first `xdm` client responding to the query.

Indirect query: The X server addresses the XDMCP query to an `xdm` client for "help." The latter forwards the request to other `xdm` clients on the network for a response.

`Xaccess` is an XDMCP-related file. As the name implies, it provides for a degree of access control at the machine level. This means that only hosts with their names listed in `Xaccess` will have their request to connect honored, receiving a login window. A user still has to undergo the authentication process by providing the login ID and the password.

The Xresources File

The Xresources file contains resource definitions that ought to be loaded to X servers upon establishing the connection. All X servers are subject to the same treatment. The first thing that xdm does upon connecting is send a login window, which requires that associated resources be loaded. As for user-specific resources, they are loaded by the server after the user logs in, based on either $HOME/.Xresources or $HOME/.xsession files or both.

Xsession and $HOME/.xsession files

Xsession and .xsession files are start-up scripts that execute upon user login. Xsession is a system-wide script that executes every time a user logs in to the system. .xsession is the user's personal script, which is executed by xdm only if Xsession (the system script) calls for it. It is mainly responsible for setting up the user's environment properly and the subsequent invocation of some of the user's applications. Following is a sample .xsession file.

```
#!/bin/sh
#Update the user's PATH variable to include /usr/X/bin where all the #X clients can
➥be found.
PATH=$PATH:/usr/X/bin
export PATH

#load and merge user resources as defined in $HOME/.Xresources
xrdb -merge $HOME/.Xresources

#start user's applications
xclock &
xterm &
xcalc &

#start the window manager
twm
```

The preceding .xsession file starts by modifying the PATH variable to include the directory where all the X binaries are stored in the file system. Next, xdm calls and executes xrdb to load and merge the X client resources with those already loaded from Xresources at the X server. This suggests that the user is maintaining an .Xresources file in the home directory. An .Xresources file may have the following contents:

```
!xclock resource definitions:
xclock*update:        1
xclock*analog:        false
xclock*chime:         false
xclock*geometry:      -0+0
!xterm resource definitions:

xterm*title:          XTerminal
xterm*background:     grey
xterm*foreground:     black
xterm*geometry:       40x24+1+1
xterm*scrollBar:      true

!xcalc resource definitions:
xcalc*title:          XCalculator
xcalc*geometry:       +0+0
```

It is important that resources are loaded first, explaining why xrdb is called first and running in the foreground.

After resources are loaded, application clients are called next. Note how they are made to run in the background. Otherwise (that is, if applications are run in the foreground), the script will hang pending the completion of the application.

Finally, twm (Tab Window Manager) is loaded in the foreground. Unless this is done, execution of the script completes and exits, which may reset your X server. Hence, the last application to load should always be running in the foreground.

> **CAUTION**
>
> The .xsession file must be flagged x in order to execute. Failure to do so results in having the xdm login window bouncing back to you without error messages. To flag .xsession executable, enter
>
> %chmod x .xsession

Now that you have a feel for how the user-specific files (that is, .Xresources and .xsession) are used to set up the user's X server session, take one more look at the Xsession that made it all happen. As noted before, .xsession is called and executed from the system-wide /usr/X/lib/xdm/Xsession. Following is a listing of the Xsession files that come within X11 distribution:

```
#!/bin/sh
exec > $HOME/.xsession-errors 2>&1

case $# in
1)
    case $1 in
    failsafe)
        exec xterm -geometry 80x24-0-0
        ;;
    esac
esac

startup=$HOME/.xsession
resources=$HOME/.Xresources

if [-f $startup]; then
    exec $startup
else
    if [ -f$resources]; then
        xrdb -load $resources
    fi
    twm &
    exec xterm -geometry 80x24+10+10 -ls
fi
```

Note the following points about the script:

1. It first directs xsession error messages to .xsession-errors file. It is a good idea to keep one error file per user, as it conveniently helps you troubleshoot user sessions.

2. Next, it checks whether the script was called with a fail-safe argument. If so, .xsession is not executed and the user is sent a single xterm. This option is mainly used to assist users and administrators in troubleshooting a failing session. The user invokes a fail-safe session by pressing the F1 key or Ctrl+Return. Some preparation must have been made in the Xresources file, however, for this trick to work. For more on this topic, you are referred to your vendor's X Window user manuals.

3. In the last part of the script, Xsession tests for the existence of the $HOME/.xsession script. If it exists, control is transferred to .xsession. Note how .Xresources is avoided altogether in this case, and it is left to .xsession to handle the user's resource definition file instead. In case .xsession does not exist, Xsession establishes a minimal session by loading .Xresources and invoking a single xterm session after spawning twm in the background.

GiveConsole and TakeConsole Configuration Files

GiveConsole and TakeConsole are scripts that, as their names imply, change the ownership of the system console to the user, and back to root, respectively.

To summarize the X startup and user session establishment process, xdm is invoked as daemon by the /etc/rc2.d/S69xdm script when the system enters the multiuser state. Upon starting up, xdm fetches its /usr/X/lib/xdm/xdm-config file to determine the names and locations of its configuration files. It starts by loading Xresources file into the X servers listed in its Xservers file, or into those who successfully queried it using the XDMCP protocol. A login window is subsequently sent. When a user requests a login by entering a valid login ID and password, xdm fetches the /usr/X/lib/xdm/Xsession script for execution. Subsequent actions are determined depending on what was included in this script. It is recommended that user session handling and configuration be dealt with using .Xresources and .xsession in the manner discussed previously. xsession is equivalent to a personal login script in that, if it exists, it invokes the xrdb client to load user resource definitions in the .Xresources file, and to load user applications that are included in the .xsession script.

X Server Access Security

The basic premise of the X Window System is that it allows an X client to send its output to the X server specified using the -display option. This being the case, you should be able to predict the security hazard that is associated with this mechanism. Unless your X display server is properly secured against unwelcome X clients, hackers can maliciously connect to it and crash your session. In the following few paragraphs, one security control method is described, along with its advantages and disadvantages. For more on X security, refer to X Window System reference manuals that ship with UNIX.

xhost Access Control Method

Using this method of protection involves the use of xhost client and the /etc/Xn.hosts file, where n refers to the display number to which the access control file applies. Because most systems have one display, reference will be made only to the /etc/X0.hosts file. The X0.hosts file must be created on the X server and edited by the system administrator to include the names of hosts from which clients are allowed access to the X server. So, if the /etc/X0.hosts file contains the following host names

    arts

    engg

    fin

then clients on arts, engg, and fin can establish X sessions with the X server and have their outputs sent to it.

xhost is a command that also can be used to add hosts to the server's access control list. The syntax of xhost is as follows:

#xhost [+¦-] [*hostname*]

To authorize a host, enter

#xhost + *hostname*

whereas to remove a host from the server's access control list, enter

#xhost - *hostname*

In the following example, host sam is allowed access, whereas host view is not:

#xhost + sam - view

> **CAUTION**
>
> xhost client can be invoked only from an X window displaying on the server undergoing security configuration.

If you want to allow all hosts access to the server, enter

#xhost +

and to disable access, enter

#xhost -

It must be kept in mind, however, that currently established sessions will not be affected by the xhost - commands. Only future connections will be refused.

A question that may have occurred in your mind by now is, What if you want to invoke clients on host view, or any other host, which is denied access to your server? The answer to that is tough. You simply cannot do it! X Window System provides a few other alternatives to the xhost control method. An example is the MIT-MAGIC-COOKIE-1, which is more of a user-based authentication process in which restrictions are enforced on users rather than on hosts.

Types of X Servers

No discussion of X is complete without a degree of exposure to the different types of X servers and their ranging capabilities.

Originally, a few years ago, X servers and X terminals were synonyms. Talking of one used to imply the other. This is because X servers used to be supplied on terminals tailored to handle X services, thus providing users with GUI capabilities, as opposed to the ASCII terminals, which handled characters only. Today, in addition to X terminals, an X server can be brought up and delivered to users on a variety of platforms, thanks to X protocol design, which provided for X's independence from operating systems as well as hardware. Among the relative newcomers to the X market are PC-based implementations of X servers. An example is the eXceed series of X servers for DOS, OS/2, and Windows by Hummingbird Communications, Ltd.

X terminals are what the name implies: dumb terminals with X Window support. They are therefore better suited to support graphical applications including arts, science, and engineering. X terminals come with different features and capabilities, some of which are as follows:

- The X server program loading method varies from one X terminal to another. One commonly used method is to have the terminal resort to TFTP protocol (see Chapter 27 for more on TFTP) to download X server software and fonts on boot time from a remote host. Other terminals would have the X server software available locally on ROM. Yet a third category would provide a combination of both: ROM-based and TFTP-based methods. Some models such as WYSE WX-Series include an extra PCMCIA slot to use with an optional FLASH ROM. With this support, the terminal needs to contact a host for a download of X server software once, during which a permanent copy of it will be transferred to the FLASH ROM to be used for subsequent reboots.

- The most commonly supported transport protocol among vendors of X terminals is TCP/IP. Some of the vendors provide you with serial communications capabilities as well. In this case, you should carefully examine how the server is optimized to operate over the limited bandwidth that is normally associated with serial facilities. If you are administering a multiprotocol environment, you may even have to go farther to shop around for ones that support your transport requirements.

- Also, due to the explosion in the demand for multimedia support, some vendors such as Hewlett-Packard introduced multimedia X servers. An example model is the HP XEnvizex X station.

PC X Servers

As mentioned earlier, PC-based X servers are relative newcomers to the X Window market. The broad install base of PCs, the improved performance of Intel CPUs, and the continuing drop of PC hardware cost inspired vendors to develop X server software that nears the performance of dedicated X terminals. Some vendors went farther by implementing the X server software as an MS Windows application. This made them more attractive by allowing the user the luxury and flexibility of maintaining DOS, Windows, and UNIX sessions. And by supporting the Inter Client Communications Conventions Manual (ICCCM), X servers allow users to interchangeably cut and paste between those environments. Figure 23.16 illustrates how eXceed/W, a high-end X server by Hummingbird Communications, Ltd., provides this support. It illustrates the use of the X server software to establish multiple X sessions with clients running on different host platforms including IBM, HP, and an MS Windows application.

There are some performance-related factors that need to be considered before trying to install PC X servers. These are as follows:

- CPU power
- Amount of Random Access Memory (RAM)
- Graphic interface card and monitor
- The network interface card (NIC)

Obviously, the more CPU power and RAM memory, the better the X server will run. For optimal performance, however, you need no less than a 386 CPU with clock rates starting from 16 Mhz. Though most vendors require memory sizes in the four-megabyte range, you will find that this range delivers the service but not the performance. Therefore, you may still need more memory. Of all the factors, the video graphic interface may prove to be the single most important factor on your PC. Remember that the idea of X is to provide users with the elegance and capabilities of the associated GUI interfaces. No matter how fast X is on the PC, there is nothing as annoying as poor, if not disgusting, graphics. There are many implementations of X, with each supporting a variety of graphical interfaces with ranging capabilities. Depending on the nature of what you intend to do on the PC X server, you ought to budget for the suitable interface and monitor. Finally, a 16-bit interface card provides better performance on the wire, and consequently contributes to the improved overall performance of the X server.

Not all PC X servers are born equal. Some currently available implementations are more compatible with the latest distribution of X than others. Some even may have more capabilities built into them, or they may be easier to install and configure. Following is a list of features and capabilities to help you better assess the PC X options that you may have at your disposal.

X compliance X11R6: Make sure that the PC X server you choose is 100 percent compatible with X11R6. Non- or partial compliance may even prevent some of the application from displaying on your PC. Lack of compatibility with ICCCMP protocol may impair your ability to cut and paste across application windows.

XDMCP full compliance: Though users will always be able to login and start an X session using protocols such as telnet, rlogin, and sh, today XDMCP is the preferred method of logging in to X hosts. It also relieves you of the headaches associated with the older way of administering connections using the Xservers configuration file.

MS Windows support: With the user community moving closer every day to MS Windows, you may consider an implementation that integrates both environments. This is particularly useful if the PC X server you choose is ICCCMP compatible, which allows you to freely cut and paste across application windows.

Transport support: The PC X server of choice should provide the same level of transport support that is compatible with already deployed protocols supporting your X clients. Most PC X servers support TCP/IP, but not as many support additional protocols. To access, for example, X clients running on UnixWare using IPX/SPX transport, you will need a PC X server such as eXceed/W. Another aspect of transport support is the maximum number of connections the X server can simultaneously allow.

X traces capability: This is a diagnostic capability that may prove extremely helpful in troubleshooting X connections.

Summary

Among the resources that UNIX system administrators are required to manage are ASCII terminals, modems, printers, and X servers. To manage these resources, different flavors of UNIX provide different sets of tools. UNIX SVR4 presents system administrators with a cohesive set of concepts and tools that come under the hood of Service Access Facility (SAF). SAF recognizes a three-level hierarchy of processes: sac (service access controller), port monitors, and port services. sac is at the top of the hierarchy, and is responsible for invoking and managing the port monitors, which are mid-level processes. Port monitors are responsible for invoking and managing port services, which run at the bottom of the SAF hierarchy. There are two types of port monitors: ttymon and listen. Whereas ttymon takes care of service requests received via the serial (or tty) ports, listen takes care of across-the-network services.

Once SAF is setup appropriately, the administrator can provide all kinds of services, including dial-in access, print services access, and access to X clients running on the UNIX host. Enough details for setting up these services were presented in this chapter to allow the administrator to successfully bring up a similar environment in his workplace.

Under BSD, device management lacks the unified approach that SVR4 supports. Instead, system administrators are required to deal with the tasks of device configuration and management using different set tools and interfaces.

Finally, most UNIX systems come today equipped with support for graphical user interface (GUI). GUI implementations on UNIX are built on top of what is known as X server/client graphics engine. This chapter presented detail of generic X setup, leaving to specialized books on X administration a more comprehensive and precise treatment of the subject matter.

23

DEVICE ADMINISTRATION

Mail Administration

by Jeff Smith and Chris Byers

IN THIS CHAPTER

CHAPTER 24

So, they've gone and made you postmaster, have they? Perhaps you're approaching this new job with a little trepidation—and you should. Electronic mail administration is one of the most complex system administration tasks and one of the most visible. If you break an obscure program that few people use, your mistake may go unnoticed. If you break the mail system, all the users on your system are affected, and most people consider electronic mail to be one of UNIX's most valuable services. Even worse, if your site is connected to the Internet, your mistakes may be visible at remote sites, and those sites' postmasters will not hesitate to inform you that, while your mother may love you, they consider you and your broken mail system to be little better than pond scum. (Those are the moderates—others may not be so kind.)

Still with me? Good. Despite the potential for making mistakes on a grand scale, mail administration at many sites is routine. You probably won't have to fuss with the e-mail system much once you manage to get it up and running, and this chapter helps you do just that. First, you get a broad overview of how e-mail works, an explanation of some of the terminology you'll see in this and other books, and pointers on where to get more information. Finally, you'll see a step-by-step example of how to set up the `sendmail` program and its configuration file, `sendmail.cf`.

What this chapter won't do is cover complex configurations like a multiprotocol mail hub that routes mail from the Internet to UUCP or a DECnet network. You won't learn how to set up the Domain Name System (DNS), although a properly working DNS is essential to the e-mail system. This is covered in Chapter 20, "Networking."

UUCP will be covered in more detail in Chapter 26, "UUCP Administration," but we touch on it here to show how it relates to e-mail. Finally, this chapter won't make you into a `sendmail` guru, but if you're lucky, you'll never need to be one.

Overview and Terminology: E-Mail from Point A to Point B

An electronic mail message begins its life as a file on your computer's disk, created by a Mail User Agent (MUA). After you compose the letter, the MUA gives it to a mail router like `sendmail`. The mail router gives it to a Mail Transport Agent (MTA). The message traverses one or more hosts and networks and is given to a final delivery agent, which appends it to the recipient's mailbox, another disk file. Each of these terms is explained in detail later in this chapter.

An MUA is just a fancy name for a mail-reading and -sending program, such as the SVR4 `mailx`. Other examples of MUAs are `elm` and the Rand corporation's `Mail Handler` (MH) programs. An MUA is the only part of the mail system with which users usually interact, since a good MUA hides the complexity of the rest of the system from them (but not from the postmaster)!

A *mail router* is a program that takes a piece of mail and decides where it should go and how to get it there. For instance, depending on the recipient, a letter might need to travel over a TCP/IP network using the Simple Mail Transfer Protocol (SMTP), or via a dial-up connection using the UNIX to UNIX Copy (UUCP) protocol, or even to an office fax machine. The mail router uses the recipient address and its own internal configuration information to decide the best MTA, and then hands the letter to the MTA.

An MTA is a transport program that understands the e-mail protocols of a particular network and can transport a letter over that network. For instance, the UUCP transport agents understand UUCP protocols but know nothing about SMTP. If the mail router were to mistakenly route an SMTP letter to a UUCP transport agent, it wouldn't know how to deliver it.

The final delivery agent does nothing but take a mail message and append it to the recipient's mailbox, following whatever local conventions are used to separate messages within a mailbox. The program `/bin/mail` is the usual final delivery agent on SVR4 systems.

In real life, the distinctions between MTAs and MUAs and mail routers are sometimes blurred. For instance, `sendmail`, although primarily a mail router, can also function as an MTA because it understands the SMTP protocol and can transport mail over a TCP/IP network. Therefore, as shown in Figure 24.1, the separate functions of mail router and MTA are really a single program. Further, the SMTP-server part of the remote end of the MTA is often another `sendmail` program, which may do additional routing and forwarding of the mail before it reaches its final delivery agent. Some MUAs even do their own mail routing, and some, like MH, can be configured to speak SMTP, an MTA function. Despite this real-world blurring of function, the conceptual framework outlined above is a good one to keep in mind.

The Different Mail Front Ends (MUAs)

Although there are only a few MTAs available for transferring mail across the Internet, there are a number of MUAs available for use. I will go into some detail about each of the more commonly used MUAs and discuss some of their advantages and disadvantages in this section.

The more widely used mail user agents are `mail`, `elm`, and `pine`, and each have their own personalities and quirks (much like system administrators).

A Look at `mail`

The original flavor of a mail front end was the rather fiendishly cryptic (though very useful and effective) UNIX `mail` utility.

Even though one always ran the risk of accidentally deleting a mail message (which always came in handy as a good excuse for "missing" a message), it was still a reliable and effective MUA and is still in wide use today by many UNIX users and administrators.

In general, `mail` allows you to browse, display, save, delete, and respond to messages. When you send a message, `mail` lets you edit and review messages being composed and lets you include text from files or other messages.

Setting Up `mail` for Users

The incoming mail for each user is stored in the system mailbox. This is a file named after the user in `/var/spool/mail` (on AT&T flavors of UNIX). `mail` looks in this file for incoming messages, but by manipulating the mail environment variable you can have it look in a different file, which you define. At the time you read a message, it is marked to be moved to a secondary file for storage. This file is then called `mbox` and is put in your home directory. Like the incoming mail location, `mbox` can also be changed by setting the `MBOX` environment variable. All messages remain in the `mbox` file until they are manually removed.

`mail` Commands and Switches

`mail` comes with a large number of switches and configuration settings to allow for highly customized use. These options are as follows:

`-d`	Start debugging output.
`-e`	See if there is any mail present. If there isn't, return nothing to the screen and give a successful return code.
`-F`	Put the message in a file whose name is that of the first recipient. This also overrides the record variable, if it is set.
`-H`	Print only the header.
`-I`	Ignore interrupts (can also be set with the ignore variable).
`-n`	Don't initialize mail from the system default `Mail.rc` file.
`-N`	Don't print header.
`-U`	Convert UUCP addresses to Internet standard addresses. This option overrides the environment variable `conv`.
`-v`	This passes the `-v` flag to the `sendmail` utility.
`-f` [*filename*]	Tells it to read messages from *filename* instead of the system mailbox. If there is no *filename* specified, it reads messages from `mbox`.
`-f` [*folder*]	Use the file *folder* in *folder* directory (this is the same as the *folder* command). The name of the directory is listed in the *folder* variable.
`-h` [*number*]	This is the number of network "hops" made to this point. This is provided so that infinite delivery loops do not occur. This is also related to the TTL, or time to live, for a mail message packet.

-r [address]	Pass the *address* to the MTA or network delivery software. It is important to note that all tilde (~) commands are invalid in this option.
-s [subject]	Make the Subject header field as *subject*.
-T [file]	This option prints the contents of the article-ID fields of all messages on *file*. This is used for network news programs such as Pointcast.
-u [user]	This options allows you to read a specific user's mailbox. This only works of you have the correct permissions to that user's home directory.

On starting mail, a system-wide file is read for commands. This file is /usr/lib/Mail.rc. These commands are read to initialize certain variables, after which it reads from the private start-up file of the user who started the mail utility. This file is called .mailrc, and it is normally placed in the user's home directory. It can, however, be placed and accessed elsewhere by modifying the MAILRC environment variable for your personal commands and variable settings.

The .mailrc file is usually used for setting up initial display options and lists of aliases. You store your initial commands here when you start up mail. The following commands, however, are not valid in this file: !, Copy, edit, followup, Followup, hold, mail, preserve, reply, Reply, replyall, replysender, shell, and visual. Also, if there is an error in that file, the remaining lines are ignored.

By using a template .mailrc file, you can easily standardize each user's mail interface with very little difficulty. All you have to do (obviously) is copy that template into the users' home directories, and (if necessary) do some minor editing for each user's particular needs.

You can send a message directly to another user or users by including names of recipients on the command line. If no recipients appear on the mail command line, mail enters command mode, where you can read messages sent to you. If you don't have any messages, it simply sends the message to standard output no mail for username and then exits the mail utility.

While you are in command mode (that is, while reading messages), you can also send messages.

When you are composing a message to send, mail is in input mode. If you don't specify a subject as an argument to the command, mail queries you for a subject. After you enter a subject, mail enters input mode, at which point you can start writing the body of the message you want to send.

While you're typing the message, mail stores it in a temporary file. This temporary file is used for reviewing or modifying the message. By using the appropriate tilde escape sequences (~:) at the beginning of an input line, you can modify the message text.

24

MAIL ADMINISTRATION

After you are in the body of your text, enter a dot (EOF) on a line by itself to actually send the message. At this point, `mail` submits the message to sendmail for routing to each recipient.

The recipients can be a local username or usernames, an internet address (*name@domain*), a UUCP address of the form [*host!...host!*]*host!username*, filenames for which you have write permission, or alias groups. If the name of the recipient begins with a pipe symbol (¦), the remainder of the name is taken as a shell through which the message is piped. This can be used with any program that reads standard input, such as `lpr`, to record outgoing mail on a printout.

An alias group is simply the name of a list of recipients that is set by the `alias` command. The `alias` command takes the names from the `/etc/aliases` file, or it can be taken from the Network Information Service (NIS) aliases domain.

While you are composing messages to send, the following tilde escape commands can be used. They all must appear at the start of the input line. The escape character (~) can be changed by setting a new value for the escape variable. The escape character can be entered as text by typing it twice.

~! [*shell-command*]	This lets you escape to the shell. If a shell command is entered, it is then run.
~.	This simulates EOF (terminate mail message input and send message).
~: *mail-command* or ~_ *mail-command*	These allow you to perform the indicated command. You can only use them when sending a message while reading a mail message.
~?	This prints a summary of the tilde escapes.
~A	This inserts the autograph string `Sign` into the current message.
~a	This inserts the autograph string `sign` into the message.
~b *name* ...	This adds the names to the blind carbon copy (Bcc) list. This command is similar to the carbon copy (Cc) list, but the names in the Bcc list are not shown in the message header.
~c *name* ...	This adds the names to the carbon copy (Cc) list (and these names show up in the message header).
~d	This command lets you read in the `dead.letter` file. This file's name is listed in the variable `DEAD`, which can be modified.
~e	This command invokes the editor to edit the message. The default editor is `ex`. This is defined in the `EDITOR` variable.

TIP

Using the ex editor is a real pain. If you are used to using the vi editor, change the EDITOR variable to vi.

-f [*message-list*]	This command lets you forward the listed messages or the current message being read. This only works when sending a message while you are reading mail. The messages are inserted without being altered.
~h	This command prompts you for the message header lines: Subject, To, From, Cc, and Bcc. To edit the header lines, simply backspace over it and retype.
~i [*variable*]	This lets you insert the value of the named variable into the message.
~m [*message-list*]	This command lets you insert text from the specified messages or the current message into the letter. This is only valid if you are sending a message while reading mail. The text message gets shifted to the right, and whatever string is contained in the indentprefix variable gets inserted as the leftmost characters of each line.
~p	This prints the message being entered.
~q	This gets you out of the input mode. If you were entering a message and did not save it, whatever you entered to that point is saved in the dead.letter file.
~r *filename* or ~< *filename* or ~<! *Shell-command*	These commands let you read in the text from the specified file or the standard output of the specified *shell-command*.
~s *subject*	This sets the subject line to *subject*.
~t *name*	This adds each *name* to the list of recipients. This is similar to setting up a distribution list.
~v	This command invokes the visual editor to edit the message. The particular editor that it uses is listed in the VISUAL variable, and the default is the vi editor.
~w *filename*	This writes the message text into the specified filename, minus the header.

24

MAIL
ADMINISTRATION

~x	This exits the message the same as ~q, but it does not save the message in the dead.letter file.
~¦ *shell-command*	This pipes the body of the message through the given shell command. If the shell command exits successfully, the command output replaces the message.

Reading Your Mail

The first thing you see when you enter the command mode (immediately after running the mail command) is a header summary of the first several messages, followed by a prompt for one of the commands listed below. By default, the prompt is an ampersand (&).

Each message has a reference number in front of it. The current message is marked by a > in the header summary. The commands that take an optional list of messages should be used with the reference number; if no number is given, the current message is affected.

The message-list is simply a list of message specifications, separated by space characters (space delimited), which can include the following:

.	Specifies the current message.
n	Denotes the message number n.
^	Specifies the first undeleted message.
$	Specifies the last message.
+	Specifies the last message.
-	Specifies the previous undeleted message.
*	Specifies all messages.
n-m	Specifies an inclusive range of message numbers.
User	Specifies all the messages from user.
/string	Specifies all the messages with string in the subject line (upper- and lowercase is ignored).
:c	This specifies all messages of type c. c can be one of the following:

d	Deleted messages
n	New messages
o	Old messages
r	Read messages
u	Unread messages

mail **Commands**

If you are in command mode and you just hit Enter with no arguments, mail assumes that you want to print the messages and starts printing to the default printer (if one is defined). The complete list of commands is as follows:

! *shell-command*

This command escapes you to the shell command. The shell to which you escape (Bourne, Korn, and so on) is defined in the SHELL variable.

comments

This can be used for placing comments in your command, just as you would place comments in you .mailrc file. You must have a blank space between the # sign and the start of your comments.

-

This lets you print the current message number.

?

This will show you a summary of commands (for people like me with poor memory).

alias [*alias recipient...*]

or

group [*alias recipient*]

This declares an alias for the given list of recipients. In much the same way as distributions lists work in other mail readers, mail will be sent to the entire alias (or group) specified. These aliases can be defined in the .mailrc file. To get a listing of the defined aliases, simply type in the command "alias" by itself.

alternate names...

This command lets you declare a list of alternate names for your login. When responding to a message, mail will not be sent to these names. If no arguments are supplied, this will show a current list of alternate names.

cd [*directory*]

or

chdir [*directory*]

This command allows you to change the current directory. Just as within the Korn or Bourne shell, cd without an argument uses the environment variable $HOME as the directory.

copy [*message-list*][*filename*]

This command copies messages to the filename without marking the messages as saved. All other functions are equivalent to the save command.

Copy [*message-list*]

This saves the specified messages in a file whose name is derived from the authors user name, also without marking the message as saved. This is otherwise equivalent to the save command.

delete [*message-list*]

This deletes messages from the system mailbox. If the *autoprint* variable is set to on, it also prints the next message following the last message that was deleted.

discard [*header-field*...]

or

ignore [*header-field*...]

These commands will suppress the printing of the specified header fields when displaying messages on the screen, such as "Status" and "Received." By default, unless the variable alwaysignore is set, all header fields are included in the saved message. This does not apply to the type or print commands.

dp [*message-list*]

or

dt [*message-list*]

These commands are equivalent to the delete command followed by the print command, as they first deletes the specified messages from the system mailbox and prints the following one.

edit [*message-list*]

This command edits the given messages. Each of the messages are put in a temporary file and the EDITOR variable is used to the name of the editor (preferably vi). The default editor is ex.

Exit

or

xit

These commands will exit you from the system mailbox without any changes. If you use this command, you will not save any messages in mbox.

file [*filename*]

folder [*filename*]

These commands quit you out of the current malbox file and read in the named mailbox file. There are certain special characters used as filenames, such as:

`%`	The current user's mailbox.
`&`	Read previously read messages from your `mbox`.
`+filename`	A filename in a specified `folder` directory. The `folder` directory is also listed in the `folder` variable.

If no arguments are used, `file` simply shows the name of the current mail file, as well as the number of characters and messages it contains.

`Folders`

This command only prints the name of each mail file in the `folder` directory.

`followup [message]`

This command responds to a message and records the response in a file. The name of this file is derived from the author of the message. This command also overrides the `record` variable if it is set.

`from [message-list]`

This shows the header information for the indicated message or current message.

`Help`

This prints a summary of all commands.

`hold [message-list]`

or

`preserve [message-list]`

These commands hold the specified messages in the system mailbox.

```
if s¦r¦t
mail-command
...
else
mail-command
...
endif
```

This is a conditional execution, used primarily in the `.mailrc` file. The command will execute up to an `elseif` or an `endif`. If `s` is used, the command will run if the program is in send mode; if `r` is chosen, the command executes only if in receive mode; if `t` is chosen, the command is run only if `mail` is run from a terminal.

`load [message] filename`

This command will let you load the specified message from the name file. This allows you to load a single saved message from *filename*, including headers.

```
mail recipient
```

This command sends a message to the specified recipient.

```
Unread [message-list]
```

This marks each message in a message list as having been read.

```
quit
```

This exits the `mail` command. It also saves the messages that were read in the `mbox` file and keeps the unread messages in the system mailbox.

```
reply [message-list]
```

or

```
respond [message-list]
```

or

```
replysender [message-list]
```

These commands allow you to send a response to the author of each message in *message-list*.

```
Reply [message]
```

or

```
Respond [message]
```

or

```
replyall [message]
```

These commands let you reply to the specified message, sending a response to each recipient of that message. If the `replyall` variable is set, the `replyall` command always sends the reply to all recipients of the message.

```
save [message-list] [filename]
```

This command will save the specified message in the specified filename. If the filename does not exist, it is created. If no filename is specified, the file named in the MBOX variable is used (mbox by default). Once the message is saved it is deleted from the system mailbox unless the keepsave variable is set.

```
set [variable[=value]]
```

This lets you define a variable and assign a value to it. You must use an = sign between the variable name and the value (with no spaces).

```
shell
```

This invokes the shell as defined in the SHELL variable.

```
source filename
```

This lets you read commands from the given filename and return to the command mode.

```
undelete [message-list]
```

This restores deleted messages. It only works on messages deleted in the current mail session.

```
unset variable ...
```

This will undefine a specified variable or variables. This will not work on imported variables such as environment variables from the shell.

```
z[+¦-]
```

This will scroll the header display either forward (+) or backward (-) by one screen.

Forwarding Your Messages

In order to forward a message, you must include it in a message to the recipients with the ~f or ~m tilde escapes. You can define a list of recipients in a file in your home directory to forward mail to automatically called .forward. The list must be comma separated and the address must be valid or the messages will bounce without any warnings.

Defining Variables

mail behavior is defined by a set of variables in your .mailrc file. The necessary environment variables are as follows:

```
HOME=directory
```

This is the user's home directory.

```
MAIL=filename
```

This is the name of the initial mailbox file to read. By default it is set to /var/spool/mail/ username.

```
MAILRC=filename
```

This is the name of each user's personal start-up file, which is $HOME/.mailrc by default.

These variables cannot be modified from within mail. They must be set before you begin a mail session.

The specific mail variable for each user is set in the .mailrc file in each user's home directory. The following are all of the mail variables that can be altered either in the .mailrc file or by using the set (or unset) command:

```
allnet
```

For all network names whose login name components match, treat them as identical. The default is noallnet.

alwaysignore

This tells mail to always ignore the header fields, not just during print or type. This will affect the save, Save, copy, Copy, top, pipe, and write commands, as well as the ~m and ~f tilde escapes.

append

This will append messages to the end of the mbox file when you exit instead of prepending them. By default this is set as noappend.

askcc

This will prompt you for the Cc list after you enter a message. The default is noaskcc.

asksub

This will ask you for a subject. This is enabled by default.

autoprint

This will automatically print messages after the delete or undelete commands are run. By default this is set to noautoprint.

bang

This enables the use of the exclamation point or "bang" as a shell escape command, such as in the vi editor.

cmd=*shell-command*

This will set the default command for the pipe command. This has no default value.

conv=*conversion*

This variable converts UUCP addresses to the address style you specify. The style can be one of the following:

internet

Use this if you are using a mail delivery program that conforms to the RFC232 standard for electronic mail addressing.

optimize

This will remove loops in the UUCP address path, which are usually generated by the reply command. There is no rerouting performed since mail doesn't know anything about UUCP routes or connections.

Conversion is disabled by default.

`crt=`*`number`*

This will pipe the messages which contain more than *number* lines through the command which is specified by the `PAGER` variable. This is the `more` command by default.

`DEAD=`*`filename`*

You can specify the name of the file where a partial letter is saved in case of an interrupted session. By default this is defined as the `dead.letter` file in the user's home directory.

`debug`

This will turn on the verbose diagnostics for debugging. The default setting is `nodebug`.

`dot`

This will read a dot on a line by itself as an EOF marker. By default this is set as `nodot`, but `dot` is set in the global startup file.

`editheaders`

This enables you to edit the headers as well as the body of the message when you use the ~e and ~v commands.

`EDITOR=`*`shell-command`*

This defines the editor (or command) to run when you use the edit or ~e command. By default this is set to `ex`.

`escape=`*`c`*

This will substitute c for the tilde (~) escape character.

`folder=`*`directory`*

This is the defined directory for saving standard mail files. If the user specifies a filename beginning with a plus (+), the filename is expanded with the directory name preceding it.

`header`

This prints the header when you enter `mail`. This is enabled by default.

`hold`

This keeps all read messages in the system mailbox instead of moving them to `mbox`. The default is `nohold`.

`ignore`

This will tell it to ignore interrupts while entering messages. The default is `noignore`.

`indentprefix=`*`string`*

By default, `string` is set to the Tab key. It is used to mark indented lines from messages included with `~m`.

`LISTER=shell-command`

This is set by default to the `ls` command; used to list the files in the `folder` directory.

`MBOX=filename`

This sets the filename where messages are saved after being read. The default is `$HOME/mbox`.

`onehop`

This can be used in a local area network (no router between machines). Normally, when several recipients are sent mail, their addresses are forced to be relative to the originating author's machine, which allows ease of response from the recipients. This flag greatly reduces traffic "over the wire."

`outfolder`

This locates the files used to save the outgoing messages. The default is `nooutfolder`.

`page`

This will insert a form feed after each message sent through a pipe. `nopage` is the default.

`PAGER=shell-command`

This is used for paginating the messages on the screen. By default it is set to `more`, but `pg` can also be used.

`prompt=string`

This will allow you to set the prompt in command mode. By default it's set to `&`.

`quiet`

This will enter `mail` without the opening message being displayed. This is disabled by default.

`record=filename`

This will record all outgoing mail in `filename`. This is disabled by default.

`replyall`

This will have an effect opposite to the `reply` commands.

`save`

If this is set on, the mail message will be saved to the `dead.letter` file if it is interrupted on delivery. Set on as default.

`screen=number`

This will define how many lines you can have for headers. This is used by the headers command.

`sendwait`

This allows the background mailer to finish before returning to command mode. The default setting is `nosendwait`.

`SHELL=`*`shell-command`*

This will define the preferred shell you use when you escape to a shell. By default it is set to `sh`. It will first go to the inherited shell from the environment.

`sign=`*`autograph`*

If the ~a (autograph) command is given, includes the *`autograph`* text in the message. There is no default.

`toplines=`*`number`*

This tells the `top` command how many lines of the header to print. This is set to `5` by default.

`verbose`

This will invoke `sendmail` with the `-v` flag.

`VISUAL=`*`shell-command`*

This points to the preferred visual screen editor, which is `vi` by default.

So much for the `.mailrc` settings. If you have the `mail` utility installed on your server or workstation, take a look at the `.mailrc` file to get a feel for how the file is put together.

A related file is the `/usr/lib/Mail.rc file`. This is the global startup file, which was referred to earlier in this section. This sets up the initial settings for the `mail` utility for each user, and it contains most of the default variables that are included with the initial `.mailrc` file.

A Look at `elm`

At this point, you may be wondering, why go into so much detail about an outdated utility? Well, for one thing, most of the newer and easier to use MUAs are based on the old original mail utility, and much of the same functionality has been added to them and enhanced. Also, this is a good way to illustrate why you would want to move to another utility such as `pine` or `elm`.

In this section, I'll take a look at `elm`, followed by `pine` in the next section, since these are the most popular text-based MUAs in use today.

The biggest difference between `elm` and mail is that `elm` uses a screen-oriented interface, as opposed to the command-line interface used by mail. It is also a great deal more intuitive to use, as well as being highly tunable for mail administrators. As with mail, `elm` will also run on virtually every flavor of UNIX without any modifications.

`elm` is also 100 percent compliant with the RFC-822 electronic mail header protocol guide, which means that it will comply with all existing mail standards. In terms of reliability, it has been in use for many years by tens of thousands of sites with no problems.

The Main Menu of `elm`

Upon looking at the main menu, which appears after opening `elm`, you will see the first line (showing the name of the current folder, the number of messages in the folder and the current version of `elm`), the list of messages and a paragraph at the bottom showing the available one-letter commands.

In the list of messages, the inverse video bar will indicate the currently active message. The status field is the first field on the screen, and it can be blank or it can have a combination of characters, where the first character has a temporary status and the second has a permanent status. The characters are E for an expired message, N for a new message, O for an old message, D for a deleted message, U for urgent mail, A for messages that have an action associated with them, and F for a form letter. There may also be a + in the third field which would indicate a tagged message.

In the next field, each message is numbered, which can come in handy for quickly opening a specific message.

The third field from the left indicates the date that the message was sent, in the format MMM, DD.

The fourth field from the left shows who sent the message. By default, `elm` tries to display the full name of the person who sent the message, but if this is unavailable, it will show either the login name and address of the person who sent it or just the sender's login name.

The fifth field in the list shows the number of lines in the message. And, finally, the sixth field shows the subject of the message (if one is included).

`elm` will show ten or more messages at one time, depending on the screen settings. To read a mail message, simply highlight the one you want to read and hit Enter.

The functions available from the main screen are as follows:

`<return>` or `<space>` This will read the current message.

¦   This allows you to pipe the message to a system command, such as `lp`.

!   This escapes to the shell.

$ This will resynchronize the folder.

?   This puts you into `help` mode; any key pressed will be explained.

+ or <right>   This will put you into the next page of messages.

- or <left>   This will put you into the previous page of messages.

=   This will set the current message number to 1.

*   Make the current message number equal to the last one.

<number><return>   This will set the message number of the highlighted message.

/   This starts a pattern search in the subject/from lines.

//   This starts a pattern search for the entire folder.

<   This will let you search for specific calendar entries.

>>   This is the same as s for saving a message.

a   This will put you into the alias mode.

b   This will bounce (or remail) a message. This is related to the forward command.

C   This will copy the current message or all of the tagged messages to the folder.

c   This changes the current folder to another elm folder.

d   This will delete the current message.

<ctrl>-D   This will delete all messages matching a user-supplied pattern.

e   This will edit the current folder.

f   This lets you forward a message to a specific user. The only difference between this and bounce is that a bounced message will show as being sent from the original sender, where a forwarded message is designated as being sent from the person who forwarded it.

g   This will let you do a group reply to everyone who received the current message.

h   This will disable the headers in messages.

J   This moves the current message to the next one in line.

j or <down>   This will move you to the next message that is not marked as deleted.

K   This will move you up the list to the previous message.

k or <up>   This will move you up the list to the previous message if it is not marked as deleted.

<ctrl>-L   This will refresh the screen.

m   This will send mail to arbitrary users.

n   This lets you read the current message and go to the next undeleted message in the list.

o   This will let you go into the options menu, where you can change the mail system options interactively.

p   This lets you print the current message, or all of the tagged messages.

Q   This is known as the quick quit, since it quits without prompting the user.

r   This lets you reply to the author of the current message.

s   This is the command to save the current message to the folder.

t   This tags the highlighted message for later manipulation.

<ctrl>-T   This will allow you to tag all of the messages matching a specified pattern.

u   This will undelete only the current message.

<ctrl>-U   This allows you to undelete all messages that match a specified pattern.

x   This is the exit command, and it will prompt you for saving messages, etc.

X   This will exit immediately, without prompting.

Luckily, most of these commands are listed at the bottom of the main menu, so you don't have to memorize them (unlike the mail utility).

You can also send a file (or attachment) on the command line to a specific user if it will save you time. You can do this by typing the following command:

```
elm -s "message subject" recipient<filename
```

The configuration file is called elmrc in the user's home directory. Use this to define specific settings as needed for the special needs of your users.

Debugging the elm Mailer

How many times have you heard this from your users: "Where's my mail? I lost my saved messages!"? elm has a few debugging tools to help you track down some of the more common problems.

In the first menu screen you can use the h, or headers command, to show all of the header information that might be sorted out with weeding settings. This might help to see whether the address field got buggered somewhere along the line.

The @ command can also be somewhat helpful. It simply shows a screen of debugging information for each message, such as the number of lines and offsets.

The # command will actually show the entire record structure for the current message to see whether the message format is corrupted somehow.

To see the full return address of the current message, the % command can be used. Like the h command, this is useful to see if the address got corrupted or mislabeled.

You can also start elm with the -d option, which starts the debugger. This will create a file in the user's home directory called ELM:debug.info, which will give a good deal of debugging information useful for tracking down problems.

If you use the debugging option, you might need to get the AT&T System V Interface Definition Reference Manual to look up the error names that get reported.

Inclusion in X Window

Most X Window interfaces give you an option to include a post office in the user's setup. This can be done somewhat easily by modifying the X Window configuration file and adding that specific mailer.

As an example, on HP-UX systems, these modifications take place in the user's `$HOME/.vue/mwmrc file`. In this file, you can specify that a mailbox be present and which mailer you want to use. This is `elm` by default in HP-UX. See your system's specific X Window guide for more details.

The `pine` Mailer

Like `elm`, `pine` is a text-based full screen mail utility (MUA). It has a few more features than `elm`, and is probably more widely used than it as well.

`pine` was developed by a few UNIX gurus at the University of Washington to act as a simple e-mail front end for their users on campus. Because of its ease of use for novice users as well as its stability and configurability, it was quickly adopted first by other universities and then by a large number of Internet service providers as their default mail interface.

`pine` can get and send mail from almost any mail format because it uses the c-client library to access mail files, which can act as a switch between different mail formats and drivers. If used with IMAP (Interactive Mail Access Protocol), you can have an IMAP server, like `imapd`, running on a central host, letting users access their mail without actually having to log on to the central host. (See RFC1176 for more on IMAP.)

Mail can be handed off to either `sendmail` (as is usually the case) or it can be sent using SMTP. This and other configuration settings will be covered later in this section (see RFC822 for more details on SMTP).

MIME is also supported in `pine` for moving multipart and multimedia e-mail. MIME stands for Multipurpose Internet Mail Extensions (defined in RFC-1341). By using this, any received MIME message gets saved to files, whatever their format. This also allows users to attach files to their messages, such as GIF files, which can be detached and displayed (if running X-terminal).

On starting up `pine`, you can give it the following options:

`-d debug-level`

This sets debugging at a debugging level (`0` means off) and sends the output to the `.pinedebugX` file in the user's home directory.

`-f folder`

This opens a named folder in place of the default INBOX.

-i *keystrokes*

This is like a startup script, where the keystrokes, separated with commas, run on startup. By default, pine starts up in the FOLDER INDEX screen if no keystrokes are specified.

-k

This tells it to use the function keys for commands.

-l

This expands the folder list.

-n *message-number*

The specified message number will be opened immediately.

-p *config-file*

Let's use the defined configuration file. By default, this is the .pinerc file.

-P *config-file*

This will make it use the specified configuration file instead of the global configuration file pine.conf.

-r

This puts you into the restricted demo mode, where you can only send mail to yourself.

-sort *order*

This tells it to sort the display of the index by arrival, subject, from, date, size, or reverse order. By default, the arrival order is chosen.

-z

This will enable the interrupt command ^Z so that a user can suspend pine.

address

This will send mail directly to the given address and drop you into the message composer on startup.

-h

This displays the help files for pine.

-conf

This will print on the screen a fresh copy of the system pine configuration file (not to be confused with the .pinerc file).

Each of these options is shown at the bottom of the screen when you use `pine`. As a very easy-to-use mail front end, it is easily the most popular one in use.

Configuring `pine`

As I mentioned before, `pine` has a configuration file for all users called `.pinerc` located in each home directory. The following shows this file and how to configure it.

The variables are

`personal-name=`

This will override the full name defined in the `/etc/passwd`.

`user-domain=`

This will set the domain name for the sender's `From:` field.

`smtp-server=`

This is left blank if you are using `sendmail` as your MTA. You define your list of SMTP servers here.

`nntp-server=`

This will set the news-collections for news reading, as well as defining the NNTP server used for posting news.

`inbox-path=`

This will define the path of the local or remote `INBOX`, such as `$HOME/INBOX` or `{mail.domain}inbox`.

`incoming-folders=`

This will list all the incoming message folders.

`folder-collections=`

This is similar to a path statement, as it lists the directories where saved message folders may be found.

`news-collections=`

This is only needed if the NNTP server name is not set or news is located on a different server.

`default-fcc=`

This will override the default path where the sent-mail folder is kept.

`postponed-folder=`

This will override the default path where the postponed messages are located.

`read-message-folder=`

This will define where the read messages are to be moved when you quit `pine`.

`signature-file=`

This will define where the signature file is located. The default for `pine` is `$HOME/.signature`.

`global-address-book=`

This will define the path for a shared or global address book, if one is used.

`address-book=`

This specifies the path for the personal address book. By default, this is the `$HOME/.addressbook` file.

`feature-list=`

This will define a set of features (shown in the setup/options menu). This will set defaults such as select-without-confirm, and so on. By default, each is prepended with the `no-` option.

`initial-keystroke-list=`

This allows a list of one-letter commands to be executed on startup.

`default-composer-hdrs=`

This will cause it to display these headers when composing messages.

`customized-hdrs=`

When composing a message, this will add customized headers to the message.

`saved-msg-name-rule=`

This will determine the default name for save folders.

`fcc-name-rule=`

This will specify the default name for `Fcc`.

`sort-key=`

This will set the order of presentation of messages in the index.

`addrbook-sort-rule=`

This sets the order of presentation for address book entries.

`character-set=`

This is set to the screen settings of the window or screen you are using. By default this number is set to `US_ASCII`.

`editor=`

This will specify the program used in the Composer.

`image-viewer=`

This sets the program that will be called to view images.

`use-only-domain-name=`

This will strip the hostname used in the From: field if the user domain is not set.

`printer=`

This lets you select your printer.

`personal-print-command=`

This is used if special print drivers are needed for a nonstandard printer.

`last-time-prune-questioned=yy.dd`

This is set by pine to control the beginning-of-month pruning for sent mail.

`last-version-used`

This is also set by pine for displaying the new version of pine.

UUCP as an MTA

There is an alternative to sendmail that has been around for many years, although it isn't purely a mail transfer agent. UUCP (UNIX to UNIX Copy) can act as an MTA as well. In fact, one could make the argument that it was the original MTA, since it was used to copy text files used as messages from one host to another in the early days of the Internet (or Arpanet at that point).

The utility is quite simple to use. All you need is the source filename and the hostname to which you want to copy a file.

If all hosts at your site are defined in the Domain Name Service and you know for sure that each of your To: addresses are defined (no problem, right?), then you can send your mail through a point-to-point UUCP connection, rather than through a default mailer. This is done through a file called uucpxtable. This file uses aliases for each hostname which points to their particular domain. Mail can then be queued for delivery with UUCP.

Arguments Against UUCP as an MTA

As you can see, this may not be such a hot idea, especially if you have a large number of local hosts and/or a number of recipients at remote domains. Quite often systems accumulate a number of direct UUCP connections that are very rarely used, and even if they are, you really can't rely on the connection to get your message there.

24

MAIL
ADMINISTRATION

This is a good argument for using such MTAs as `sendmail` or SMTP, since their connection schemes are more dynamic in nature, ensuring that only the connections you presently need are used. In addition, UUCP leaves much to be desired in the area of security.

Background Material and Other Sources

E-mail administration is a complex endeavor. This chapter gives you enough background to get you out of the gate and running, but you must carefully study the following materials to really understand what you're doing. It's a lot better to learn it now—with a warm cup of cocoa in hand—than to wait until you've got a dozen angry users in your office demanding that you fix the mail system immediately. Trust me on this one.

Don't worry if some of the documents mentioned below don't make sense on a first reading; you don't have to understand every little clause of RFC 822 (described in the next section) to be a successful postmaster, and if you persevere you'll understand as much as you need to know at first. After you gain some experience, you'll re-read them and understand them even better.

Request for Comments Documents (RFCs)

RFCs are issued by working groups of the Internet Engineering Task Force (IETF). They are known initially as a request for comments, but as they are adopted as Internet standards, you should think of them as requirements for compliance. So if you want to exchange e-mail with another site on the Internet, you must comply with the provisions of both RFCs 821 and 822. RFCs are available for anonymous `ftp` on the host `ftp.internic.net`. Some RFCs are also on the *UNIX Unleashed* CD-ROM.

- RFC 821 *Simple Mail Transfer Protocol (SMTP)*. RFC 821 defines the commands by which Internet mailers exchange e-mail. It is explained later in more detail.

- RFC 822 *Standard for the format of ARPA Internet text messages*. RFC 822 defines the proper form of an e-mail message. E-mail is divided into two parts, the headers and the body, which are separated by a blank line. The headers contain essential information such as the return address of the sender, and the body is the message you want to send.

- RFC 1425 *SMTP Service Extensions*. RFC 1425 extends the SMTP protocol to what is commonly known as ESMTP.

- RFC1123 *Requirements for Internet Hosts—Application and Support*. RFC1123 is commonly known as the host requirements RFC. It clarifies requirements that all hosts on the Internet must meet and corrects some errors in earlier RFCs.

- RFC 976 *UUCP Mail Interchange Format Standard*. RFC 976 explains the UUCP mail protocol, which is a store-and-forward mechanism. Instead of making a direct connection like a phone circuit, host A makes a temporary connection to send mail to host B, which stores it temporarily and forwards it to host C, the final recipient. UUCP is a pain in the neck; avoid it if you can.

sendmail **Documentation**

V8 `sendmail` comes with three important documents:

- Sendmail Installation and Operation Guide (SIOG)
- SENDMAIL—An Internetwork Mail Router
- Mail Systems and Addressing in 4.2bsd

All three were written by Eric Allman, the author of the `sendmail` program. The SIOG is an essential reference manual that explains the guts of `sendmail`. The other documents are more general overviews of mail router design. All are worth reading, but the SIOG is your essential guide to `sendmail`. You'll want to read it several times and highlight parts relevant to your site's configuration.

sendmail, **the Book**

The book *sendmail* by Bryan Costales, Eric Allman, and Neil Rickert (O'Reilly & Associates, Inc., 1993) is the most comprehensive treatment of the care and feeding of V8 `sendmail`. If you manage a complex site or must write custom configuration files, it is invaluable. If your site is fairly simple or you find that you can get most of what you need from this chapter, the standard V8 `sendmail` documentation, `comp.mail.sendmail` and the RFCs, save your money.

Comp.mail.sendmail

If your site receives Usenet news, don't pass go, don't collect $200, just add the newsgroup `comp.mail.sendmail` to your newsreader's subscription list. Eric Allman, the author of `sendmail`, contributes regularly along with other `sendmail` wizards. You can get more quality, free advice here than anywhere else on the Usenet.

However, as with any newsgroup, read it for a few weeks before you make your first posting, and save yourself the embarrassment of asking a question that has already been answered a hundred times by first reading the V8 `sendmail` Frequently Asked Questions (FAQ) document and the other documentation mentioned in this chapter. It may take a little longer to get your burning question answered, but you'll still respect yourself in the morning.

Internet Mail Protocols

In order to understand the different jobs that `sendmail` does, you need to know a little about Internet protocols. Protocols are simply agreed-upon standards that software and hardware use to communicate.

Protocols are usually layered, with higher levels using the lower ones as building blocks. For instance, the Internet Protocol (IP) sends packets of data back and forth without building an end-to-end connection such as used by SMTP and other higher-level protocols. The Transmission Control Protocol (TCP) is built on top of IP and provides for connection-oriented services like those used by programs such as `telnet` and the Simple Mail Transfer Protocol (SMTP). Together, TCP/IP provide the basic network services for the Internet. Higher-level protocols like the File Transfer Protocol (FTP) and SMTP are built on top of TCP/IP. The advantage of such layering is that programs which implement the SMTP or FTP protocols don't have to know anything about transporting packets on the network and making connections to other hosts. They can use the services provided by TCP/IP for that.

SMTP defines how programs exchange e-mail on the Internet. It doesn't matter whether the program exchanging the e-mail is sendmail running on an HP workstation or an SMTP client written for an Apple Macintosh. As long as both programs implement the SMTP protocol correctly, they will be able to exchange mail.

The following example of the SMTP protocol in action may help demystify it a little. The user betty at gonzo.gov is sending mail to joe at whizzer.com:

```
$ sendmail -v joe@whizzer.com < letter
joe@whizzer.com... Connecting to whizzer.com via tcp...
Trying 123.45.67.1... connected.
220-whizzer.com SMTP ready at Mon, 6 Jun 1994 18:56:22 -0500
220 ESMTP spoken here
>>> HELO gonzo.gov
250 whizzer.com Hello gonzo.gov [123.45.67.2], pleased to meet you
>>> MAIL From:<betty@gonzo.gov>
250 <betty@gonzo.gov>... Sender ok
>>> RCPT To:<joe@whizzer.com>
250 <joe@whizzer.com>... Recipient ok
>>> DATA
354 Enter mail, end with "." on a line by itself
>>> .
250 SAA08680 Message accepted for delivery
>>> QUIT
221 whizzer.com closing connection
joe@whizzer.com... Sent
$
```

The first line shows one way to invoke sendmail directly rather than letting your favorite MUA do it for you. The -v option tells sendmail to be verbose and shows you the SMTP dialogue. The other lines show an SMTP client and server carrying on a conversation. Lines prefaced with >>> are the client (or sender) on gonzo.gov, and the lines that immediately follow are the replies of the server (or receiver) on whizzer.com. The first line beginning with 220 is the SMTP server announcing itself after the initial connection, giving its hostname and the date and time, and the second line informs the client that this server understands the Extended SMTP protocol (ESMTP) in case the client wants to use it. Numbers such as 220 are reply codes that the SMTP client uses to communicate with the SMTP server. The text following the reply codes is only for human consumption.

Although this dialogue may still look a little mysterious, it will soon be old hat if you take the time to read RFC 821. Running sendmail with its -v option also helps you understand how an SMTP dialogue works.

The Domain Name System (DNS) and E-Mail

Names like `whizzer.com` are convenient for humans, but computers insist on using numeric IP addresses like `123.45.67.1`. The Domain Name System (DNS) provides this hostname to IP address translation and other important information.

In the olden days when most of us walked several miles to school through deep snow, there were only a few thousand hosts on the Internet. All hosts were registered with the Network Information Center (NIC), which distributed a host table listing the hostname and IP addresses of all the hosts on the Internet. Those simple times are gone forever. No one really knows how many hosts are connected to the Internet now, but they number in the millions, and an administrative entity like the NIC can't keep their names straight. Thus was born the DNS.

The DNS distributes authority for naming and numbering hosts to autonomous administrative domains. For instance, a company `whizzer.com` could maintain all the information about the hosts in its own domain. When the host `a.whizzer.com` wished to send mail or `telnet` to the host `b.whizzer.com`, it would send an inquiry over the network to the `whizzer.com` name server, which might run on a host named `ns.whizzer.com`. The `ns.whizzer.com` name server would reply to `a.whizzer.com` with the IP address of `b.whizzer.com` (and possibly other information), and the mail would be sent or the `telnet` connection made. Because `ns.whizzer.com` is authoritative for the `whizzer.com` domain, it can answer any inquiries about `whizzer.com` hosts regardless of where they originate; the authority for naming hosts in this domain has been delegated.

Now, what if someone on `a.whizzer.com` wants to send mail to `joe@gonzo.gov`? `Ns.whizzer.com` has no information about hosts in the `gonzo.gov` domain, but it knows how to find out. When a name server receives a request for a host in a domain for which it has no information, it asks the root name servers for the names and IP addresses of servers authoritative for that domain, in this case `gonzo.gov`. The root name server gives the `ns.whizzer.com` name server the names and IP addresses of hosts running name servers with authority for `gonzo.gov`. The `ns.whizzer.com` name server inquires of them and forwards the reply back to `a.whizzer.com`.

From the description above you can see that the DNS is a large, distributed database containing mappings between hostnames and IP addresses, but it contains other information as well. When a program like `sendmail` delivers mail, it must translate the recipient's hostname into an IP address. This bit of DNS data is known as an A (Address) record, and it is the most fundamental data about a host. A second piece of host data is the Mail eXchanger (MX) record. An MX record for a host like `a.whizzer.com` lists one or more hosts that are willing to receive mail for it.

What's the point? Why shouldn't `a.whizzer.com` get its own mail and be done with it? Isn't a postmaster's life complicated enough without having to worry about mail exchangers? Well, while it's true that the postmaster's life is often overly complicated, MX records serve useful purposes:

- Hosts not on the Internet (for example, UUCP-only hosts) may designate an Internet host to receive their mail and so appear to have an Internet address. For instance, suppose that a.whizzer.com is only connected to ns.whizzer.com once a day via a UUCP link. If ns.whizzer.com publishes an MX record for it, other Internet hosts can still send it mail. When ns.whizzer.com receives the mail, it saves it until a.whizzer.com connects. This use of MX records allows non-Internet hosts to appear to be on the Internet (but only to receive e-mail).

- Imagine a UNIX host pcserv.whizzer.com that acts as a file server for a cluster of personal computers. The PC clones have MUAs with built-in SMTP clients that allow them to send mail, but not receive mail. If return addresses on the outbound mail look like someone@pc1.whizzer.com, how can people reply to the mail? MX records come to the rescue again—pcserv.whizzer.com publishes itself as the MX host for all the PC clones, and mail addressed to them is sent there.

- Hosts may be off the Internet for extended times because of unpredictable reasons ranging from lightning strikes to the propensity of backhoe operators to unexpectedly unearth fiber-optic cables. While your host is off the Internet, its mail queues on other hosts, and after a while it bounces back to the sender. If your host has MX hosts willing to hold its mail in the interim, the mail will be delivered when your host is available again. The hosts can be either on-site (that is, in your domain) or off-site, or both. The last option is best, since backhoe operator disasters usually take your entire site off the net, in which case an on-site backup does no good.

- MX records hide information and allow you more flexibility to reconfigure your local network. If all your correspondents know that your e-mail address is joe@whizzer.com, it doesn't matter whether the host that receives mail for whizzer.com is named zippy.whizzer.com or pinhead.whizzer.com. It also doesn't matter if you decide to change it to white-whale.whizzer.com; your correspondents will never know the difference.

Mail Delivery and MX Records

When an SMTP client delivers mail to a host, it must do more than translate the hostname into an IP address. First, it asks for MX records. If any exist, it sorts them according to the priority given in the record. For instance, whizzer.com might have MX records listing the hosts mailhub.whizzer.com, walrus.whizzer.com, and mailer.gonzo.gov as the hosts willing to receive mail for it (and the "host" whizzer.com might not exist except as an MX record, meaning that there might be no IP address for it). Although any of these hosts will accept mail for whizzer.com, the MX priorities specify which of those hosts the SMTP client should try first, and properly behaved SMTP clients will do so. In this case the system administrator has set up a primary mail relay mailhub.whizzer.com, an on-site backup walrus.whizzer.com, and arranged with the system administrator at mailer.gonzo.gov for an off-site backup. They have set the MX priorities so that SMTP clients will try the primary mail relay first, the on-site backup second, and the off-site backup third. This setup takes care of the problems with the vendor who doesn't ship your parts on time as well as the wayward backhoe operator, who severs the fiber optic cable that provides your site's Internet connection.

After collecting and sorting the MX records, the SMTP client gathers the IP addresses for the MX hosts and attempts delivery to them in order of MX preference. You should keep this in mind when debugging mail problems. Just because a letter is addressed to `joe@whizzer.com`, it doesn't necessarily mean that a host named `whizzer.com` exists. Even if it does, it might not be the host that is supposed to receive the mail.

Header and Envelope Addresses

The distinction between header and envelope addresses is important because mail routers may process them differently. An example will help explain the difference between the two.

Suppose you have a paper memo that you want to send to your colleagues Mary and Bill at the Gonzo Corporation, and Ted and Ben at the Whizzer company. You give a copy of the memo to your trusty mail clerk Alphonse, who notes the multiple recipients. Since he's a clever fellow who wants to save your company 32 cents, he makes two copies of the memo and puts each in an envelope addressed to the respective companies (rather than sending a copy to each recipient). On the cover of the `Gonzo` envelope he writes `Mary` and `Bill`, and on the cover of the `Whizzer` envelope he writes `Ted` and `Ben`. When his counterparts at `Gonzo` and `Whizzer` receive the envelopes, they make copies of the memo and send them to Mary, Bill, Ted and Ben, without inspecting the addresses in the memo itself. As far as the `Gonzo` and `Whizzer` mail clerks are concerned, the memo itself might be addressed to the pope; they only care about the envelope addresses.

SMTP clients and servers work in much the same way. Suppose that `joe@gonzo.gov` sends mail to his colleagues `betty@zippy.gov` and `fred@whizzer.com`. The recipient list in the letters' headers may look like this:

```
To: betty@zippy.gov, fred@whizzer.com
```

The SMTP client at `gonzo.gov` connects to the `whizzer.com` mailer to deliver Fred's copy. When it's ready to list the recipients (the envelope address), what should it say? If it gives both recipients as they are listed in the `To:` line above (the `header` address), Betty will get two copies of the letter because the `whizzer.com` mailer will forward a copy to `zippy.gov`. The same problem occurs if the `gonzo.gov` SMTP client connects to `zippy.gov` and lists both Betty and Fred as recipients. The `zippy.gov` mailer will forward a second copy of Fred's letter.

The solution is the same one that Alphonse and his fellow mail clerks used. The `gonzo.gov` SMTP client puts an envelope around the letter that contains only the names of the recipients on each host. The complete recipient list is still in the letter's headers, but those are inside the envelope, and the SMTP servers at `gonzo.gov` and `whizzer.com` don't look at them. In this example, the envelope for the `whizzer.com` mailer would list only `fred`, and the envelope for `zippy.gov` would only list `betty`.

Aliases illustrate another reason why header and envelope addresses differ. Suppose you send mail to the alias homeboys, which includes the names alphonse, joe, betty, and george. In your letter you write To: homeboys. However, sendmail expands the alias and constructs an envelope that includes all of the recipients. Depending on whether those names are also aliases, perhaps on other hosts, the original message might be put into as many as four different envelopes and delivered to four different hosts. In each case the envelope will contain only the name of the recipients, but the original message will contain the alias homeboys (expanded to homeboys@your.host.domain so replies will work).

A final example shows another way in which envelope addresses may differ from header addresses. sendmail allows you to specify recipients on the command line. Suppose you have a file named letter that looks like this:

```
$ cat letter
To: null recipient <>
Subject: header and envelope addresses

testing
```

and you send it with the following command (substituting your own login name for *yourlogin*):

```
$ sendmail yourlogin < letter
```

You will receive the letter even though your login name doesn't appear in the letter's headers because your address was on the envelope. Unless told otherwise (with the -t flag), sendmail constructs envelope addresses from the recipients you specify on the command line, and there isn't necessarily a correspondence between the header addresses and the envelope addresses.

sendmail's Jobs

To better understand how to set up sendmail, you need to know what different jobs it does and how those jobs fit into the scheme of MUAs, MTAs, mail routers, final delivery agents, and SMTP clients and servers. sendmail can act as a mail router, an SMTP client, and an SMTP server. However, it does not do final delivery of mail.

sendmail as Mail Router

sendmail is primarily a mail router, meaning it takes a letter, inspects the recipient addresses, and decides the best way to send it. How does sendmail do this?

sendmail determines some of the information it needs on its own, like the current time and the name of the host on which it's running, but most of its brains are supplied by you, the postmaster, in the form of a configuration file, sendmail.cf. This somewhat cryptic file tells sendmail exactly how you want various kinds of mail handled. It is extremely flexible and powerful, and at first glance seemingly inscrutable. However, one of the strengths of V8 sendmail is its set of modular configuration file building blocks. Most sites can easily construct their configuration files from these modules, and many examples are included. Writing a configuration file from scratch is a daunting task and you should avoid it if you can.

sendmail as MTA—Client (Sender) and Server (Receiver) SMTP

As mentioned before, sendmail can function as an MTA since it understands the SMTP protocol (V8 sendmail also understands ESMTP). Because SMTP is a connection-oriented protocol, there is always a client and a server (also known as a sender and a receiver). The SMTP client delivers a letter to an SMTP server, which listens continuously on its computer's SMTP port. sendmail can be an SMTP client or an SMTP server. When run by an MUA, it becomes an SMTP client and speaks client-side SMTP to an SMTP server (not necessarily another sendmail program). When your system boots and it starts in daemon mode, it runs continuously, listening on the SMTP port for incoming mail.

sendmail as a Final Delivery Agent (NOT!)

One thing sendmail doesn't do is final delivery. sendmail's author wisely chose to leave this task to other programs. sendmail is a big, complicated program that runs with super-user privileges, an almost guaranteed recipe for security problems, and there have been quite a few in sendmail's past. The additional complexity of final mail delivery is the last thing sendmail needs.

sendmail's Auxiliary Files

sendmail depends on a number of auxiliary files to do its job. The most important are the aliases file and the configuration file, sendmail.cf. The statistics file, sendmail.st, can be created or not depending on whether you want the statistics. sendmail.hf is the SMTP help file, and should be installed if you intend to run sendmail as an SMTP server (most sites do). That's all that needs to be said about sendmail.st and sendmail.hf (there are other auxiliary files that are covered in the SIOG), but the aliases and sendmail.cf files are important enough to be covered in their own sections.

The Aliases File

sendmail always checks recipient addresses for aliases, which are alternate names for a recipient. For instance, each Internet site is required to have a valid address postmaster to which mail problems may be reported. Most sites don't have an actual account of that name but divert the postmaster's mail to the person or persons responsible for e-mail administration. For instance, at the mythical site gonzo.gov, the users joe and betty are jointly responsible for e-mail administration, and the aliases file has the following entry:

```
postmaster: joe, betty
```

This line tells sendmail that mail to postmaster should instead be delivered to the login names joe and betty. In fact, those names could also be aliases:

```
postmaster: firstshiftops, secondshiftops, thirdshiftops
firstshiftops: joe, betty
secondshiftops: lou, emma
thirdshiftops: ben, mark, clara
```

In all of these examples, the alias name is the part on the left side of the colon, and the aliases for those names are on the right side. sendmail repeatedly evaluates aliases until they resolve to a real user or a remote address. In the previous example, to resolve the alias postmaster, sendmail first expands it into the list of recipients firstshiftops, secondshiftops, and thirdshiftops and then expands each of these into the final list, joe, betty, lou, emma, ben, mark, and clara.

Although the right side of an alias may refer to a remote host, the left side may not. The alias joe: joe@whizzer.com is legal, but joe@gonzo.gov: joe@whizzer.com is not.

Reading Aliases from a File—the `:include:` Directive

Aliases may be used to create mailing lists (in the example above, the alias postmaster is in effect a mailing list for the local postmasters). For big or frequently changing lists, you can use the :include: alias form to direct sendmail to read the list members from a file. If the aliases file contains the line

```
homeboys: :include:/home/alphonse/homeboys.aliases
```

and the file /home/alphonse/homeboys.aliases contains

```
alphonse
joe
betty
george
```

the effect is the same as the alias:

```
homeboys: alphonse, joe, betty, george
```

This is handy for mailing lists that change frequently, or those managed by users other than the postmaster. If you find that a user is asking for frequent changes to a mail alias, you may want to put it under her control.

Mail to Programs

The aliases file also may be used to send the contents of e-mail to a program. For instance, many mailing lists are set up so that you can get information about the list or subscribe to it by sending a letter to a special address, *list*-request. The letter usually contains a single word in its body, such as help or subscribe, which causes a program to mail an information file to the sender. Suppose that the gonzo mailing list has such an address called gonzo-request:

```
gonzo-request: |/usr/local/lib/auto-gonzo-reply
```

In this form of alias, the pipe sign (|) tells sendmail to use the program mailer, which is usually defined as /bin/sh. sendmail feeds the message to the standard input of /usr/local/lib/auto-gonzo-reply, and if it exits normally, sendmail considers the letter to be delivered.

Mail to Files

You can also create an alias that causes `sendmail` to send mail to files. An example of this is the alias `nobody`, which is common on systems running the Network File System (NFS):

```
nobody: /dev/null
```

Aliases that specify files cause `sendmail` to append its message to the named file. Because the special file `/dev/null` is the UNIX bit-bucket, this alias simply throws mail away.

Setting Up `sendmail`

The easiest way to show you how to set up `sendmail` is to use a concrete example. However, because `sendmail` runs under many different versions of UNIX, your system may vary from the examples shown below. For the sake of concreteness, these examples assume that you're setting up `sendmail` on a Solaris 2.3 system, Sun Microsystem's version of SVR4 UNIX.

First you must obtain the source and compile `sendmail`. Next you must choose a `sendmail.cf` file that closely models your site's requirements and tinker with it as necessary. Then you must test `sendmail` and its configuration file. Finally, you must install `sendmail`, `sendmail.cf`, and other auxiliary files.

Those are the basic steps, but depending on where you install `sendmail`, you may also have to modify a file in the directory `/etc/init.d` so that `sendmail` will be started correctly when the system boots. In addition, if your system doesn't already have one, you must create an aliases file, often named `/usr/lib/aliases` or `/etc/mail/aliases` (the location of the aliases file is given in `sendmail.cf`, so you can put it wherever you want). You may also have to make changes to your system's DNS database, but that won't be covered here.

Obtaining the Source

`sendmail` version 8.6.7 is on the *UNIX Unleashed* CD-ROM. This is the most recent version available as this book goes to press, and it is the version documented in the O'Reilly book *sendmail*. However, if your site is on the Internet and you want to obtain the absolutely latest version, `ftp` to the host `ftp.cs.berkeley.edu` and look in the directory `~ftp/pub/ucb/sendmail`. Use the following steps to download it:

```
$ ftp ftp.cs.berkeley.edu
Connected to ftp.cs.berkeley.edu.
220 kohler FTP server (Version wu-2.4(4) Fri May 6 16:09:33 PDT 1994) ready.
Name (ftp.cs.berkeley.edu:yourname): anonymous
331 Guest login ok, send your complete e-mail address as password.
Password: (Type your e-mail address)
230 Guest login ok, access restrictions apply.
ftp> cd ucb/sendmail
250-This directory contains sendmail source distributions, currently for
250-Release 8. The latest version is in four files:
250-
250-    sendmail.${VER}.base.tar.Z -- the base system source & documentation.
```

```
250-    sendmail.${VER}.cf.tar.Z -- configuration files.
250-    sendmail.${VER}.misc.tar.Z -- miscellaneous support programs.
250-    sendmail.${VER}.xdoc.tar.Z -- extended documentation, with postscript.
250-
250-The status of various ${VER}s is:
250-8.6.9  This is the version documented in the O'Reilly sendmail book.
250-        and which will be on the 4.4BSD-Lite tape. The files
250-        sendmail.8.6.[123456789].patch will upgrade an 8.6 source to
250-        this version (apply all of them).
250-8.6.8  The previous version. It fixes some significant security
250-        problems; you should be running at least this version.
250-
250 CWD command successful.
ftp> binary
200 Type set to I.
ftp> mget sendmail.8.6.9.base.tar.Z sendmail.8.6.9.cf.tar.Z
mget sendmail.8.6.9.base.tar.Z? y
200 PORT command successful.
150 Opening BINARY mode data connection for sendmail.8.6.9.base.tar.Z (500945
➥bytes).
226 Transfer complete.
local: sendmail.8.6.9.base.tar.Z remote: sendmail.8.6.9.base.tar.Z
500945 bytes received in 14 seconds (34 Kbytes/s)
mget sendmail.8.6.9.cf.tar.Z? y
200 PORT command successful.
150 Opening BINARY mode data connection for sendmail.8.6.9.cf.tar.Z (199863 bytes).
226 Transfer complete.
local: sendmail.8.6.9.cf.tar.Z remote: sendmail.8.6.9.cf.tar.Z
199863 bytes received in 3.3 seconds (59 Kbytes/s)
ftp> quit
221 Goodbye.
```

Note that the exact name of the files to download differs depending on the current version of V8 sendmail, in this case version 8.6.9. Also, because the files are compressed, you must give ftp the binary command before transferring them. Note too that you should include your complete e-mail address as the password, for instance, mylogin@gonzo.gov. You may also wish to download the extended documentation and the support programs, which in this example would have been contained in the files sendmail.8.6.9.xdoc.tar.Z and sendmail.8.6.9.misc.tar.Z.

Unpacking the Source and Compiling sendmail

Now that you've got the source, you need to unpack it. Because it's a compressed tar image, you must first decompress it and then extract the individual files from the tar archive. If you're using the version from the CD-ROM, these steps are not necessary.

```
$ mkdir /usr/src/local/sendmail
$ mv sendmail.8.6.9.* /usr/src/local/sendmail
$ cd /usr/src/local/sendmail
$ uncompress *Z
$ ls
sendmail.8.6.9.base.tar sendmail.8.6.9.cf.tar
$ tar xf sendmail.8.6.9.base.tar; tar xf sendmail.8.6.9.cf.tar
$ ls -CF
FAQ                 cf/             sendmail.8.6.9.cf.tar
KNOWNBUGS           doc/            src/
```

```
Makefile                    mailstats/                  test/
READ_ME                     makemap/
RELEASE_NOTES               sendmail.8.6.9.base.tar
$ rm *tar
```

Now you're almost ready to compile sendmail, but first read the following files, which contain the latest news pertinent to the specific release of sendmail you've downloaded:

```
FAQ
RELEASE_NOTES
KNOWNBUGS
READ_ME
```

Now run cd and ls to see what files are in the source directory:

```
$ cd src
$ ls
Makefile                    Makefile.SunOS.5.1          mailq.1
Makefile.386BSD             Makefile.SunOS.5.2          mailstats.h
Makefile.AIX                Makefile.SunOS.5.x          main.c
Makefile.AUX                Makefile.Titan              makesendmail
Makefile.BSD43              Makefile.ULTRIX             map.c
Makefile.BSDI               Makefile.UMAX               mci.c
Makefile.CLIX               Makefile.Utah               newaliases.1
Makefile.ConvexOS           Makefile.dist               parseaddr.c
Makefile.DGUX               READ_ME                     pathnames.h
Makefile.Dell               TRACEFLAGS                  queue.c
Makefile.DomainOS           alias.c                     readcf.c
Makefile.Dynix              aliases                     recipient.c
Makefile.FreeBSD            aliases.5                    savemail.c
Makefile.HP-UX              arpadate.c                  sendmail.8
Makefile.IRIX               cdefs.h                     sendmail.h
Makefile.Linux              clock.c                     sendmail.hf
Makefile.Mach386            collect.c                   srvrsmtp.c
Makefile.NCR3000            conf.c                      stab.c
Makefile.NeXT               conf.h                      stats.c
Makefile.NetBSD             convtime.c                  sysexits.c
Makefile.OSF1               daemon.c                    trace.c
Makefile.RISCos             deliver.c                   udb.c
Makefile.SCO                domain.c                    useful.h
Makefile.SVR4               envelope.c                  usersmtp.c
Makefile.Solaris            err.c                       util.c
Makefile.SunOS              headers.c                   version.c
Makefile.SunOS.4.0.3        macro.c
```

As you can see, because sendmail runs on a variety of hosts and operating systems, a Makefile is provided for many UNIX variants. Since in this example we're assuming a Sun Microsystems Solaris system, we'll use Makefile.Solaris to compile sendmail. But before we type make, we should look at the files conf.h and Makefile.Solaris.

You probably won't want to change much in conf.h, but Makefile.Solaris is a different story. At the least you should make sure that the correct version of the Solaris operating system is defined. Since we're compiling for Solaris 2.3, we must replace the line ENV=-DSOLARIS with the line ENV=-DSOLARIS_2_3 (Makefile.Solaris tells us to do so). If you've purchased the SunPro cc compiler, you may want to change the definition of the CC macro to use that instead of gcc.

You may want to make other changes; for example, you may not want to install `sendmail` in the default location. Read the Makefile carefully and make changes as needed.

Remember, when in doubt, you can always type `make -n` *arguments* to see what would happen before it happens. This is always an especially good idea when you're working as the superuser.

Now you're ready to compile. Type

```
$ make -f Makefile.Solaris sendmail
gcc -I.  -I/usr/sww/include/db -DNDBM -DNIS -DSOLARIS_2_3 -c  alias.c
[...]
gcc -I.  -I/usr/sww/include/db -DNDBM -DNIS -DSOLARIS_2_3 -c  util.c
gcc -I.  -I/usr/sww/include/db -DNDBM -DNIS -DSOLARIS_2_3 -c version.c
gcc -o sendmail alias.o arpadate.o clock.o collect.o conf.o convtime.o daemon.o
deliver.o domain.o envelope.o err.o headers.o macro.o  main.o  map.o mci.o
parseaddr.o queue.o readcf.o recipient.o  savemail.o srvrsmtp.o stab.o stats.o
sysexits.o  trace.o udb.o usersmtp.o util.o version.o
-L/usr/sww/lib -lresolv -lsocket -lnsl -lelf
```

The [...] above covers many deleted lines of output, as well as some warning messages from the compiler. Carefully inspect the output and determine whether the compiler warnings are pertinent. If necessary (and it should only be necessary if you're porting `sendmail` to a new architecture), correct any problems and compile again.

`sendmail.cf`—the Configuration File

Now you've got a working `sendmail`, but like the *Wizard of Oz*'s Scarecrow, it's brainless. The `sendmail.cf` file provides `sendmail` with its brains, and because it's so important, we're going to cover it in fairly excruciating detail. Don't worry if you don't understand everything in this section the first time through. It will make more sense upon re-reading, and after you've had a chance to play with some configuration files of your own.

`sendmail`'s power lies in its flexibility, which comes from its configuration file, `sendmail.cf`. `sendmail.cf` statements comprise a cryptic programming language that at first glance doesn't inspire much confidence (but C language code probably didn't either the first time you saw it). However, learning the `sendmail.cf` language isn't that hard, and you won't have to learn the nitty-gritty details unless you plan to write a `sendmail.cf` from scratch—a bad idea at best. You do need to learn enough to understand and adapt the V8 `sendmail` configuration file templates to your site's needs.

General Form of the Configuration File

Each line of the configuration file begins with a single command character that tells the function and syntax of that line. Lines beginning with a # are comments, and blank lines are ignored. Lines beginning with a space or tab are a continuation of the previous line, although you should usually avoid continuations.

Table 24.1 shows the command characters and their functions. It is split into three parts corresponding to the three main functions of a configuration file, which are covered later in this chapter.

Table 24.1. `sendmail.cf` **command characters.**

Command Character	Command Syntax and Example	Function
#	`# comments are ignored`	A comment line. Always use lots of comments.
	`# Standard RFC822 parsing`	
D	`DX string`	Define a macro X to have the string value `string`.
	`DMmailhub.gonzo.gov`	
C	`CX word1, word2,...`	Define a class X as `word1, word2,...`
	`Cwlocalhost myuucpname`	
F	`FX/path/to/a/file`	Define a class X by reading it from a file.
	`Fw/etc/mail/host_aliases`	
H	`H?mailerflag?name:template`	Define a mail header.
	`H?F?From: $q`	
O	`OX option arguments`	Set option X. Most command-line options may be set in `sendmail.cf`.
	`OL9 # set log level to 9`	
P	`Pclass=nn`	Set mail delivery precedence based on the class of the mail.
	`Pjunk=-100`	
V	`Vn`	Tell V8 `sendmail` the version level of the configuration file.
	`V3`	

continues

Table 24.1. continued

Command Character	Command Syntax and Example	Function
K	`Kname class arguments`	Define a key file (database map).
	`Kuucphosts dbm /etc/mail/uucphsts`	
M	`Mname,field_1=value_1,...`	Define a mailer.
	`Mprog,P=/bin/sh,F=lsD,A=sh -c $u`	
S	`Snn`	Begin a new rule-set.
	`S22`	
R	`Rlhs rhs comment`	Define a matching / rewriting rule.
	`R$+ $:$>22 call ruleset 22`	

A Functional Description of the Configuration File

A configuration file does three things. First, it sets the environment for sendmail by telling it what options you want set and the locations of the files and databases it uses.

Second, it defines the characteristics of the mailers (delivery agents or MTAs) that sendmail uses after it decides where to route a letter. All configuration files must define local and program mailers to handle delivery to users on the local host; most also define one or more SMTP mailers; and sites that must handle UUCP mail define UUCP mailers.

Third, the configuration file specifies rulesets that rewrite sender and recipient addresses and select mailers. All rulesets are user-defined, but some have special meaning to sendmail. Ruleset 0, for instance, is used to select a mailer. Rulesets 0, 1, 2, 3, and 4 all have special meaning to sendmail and are processed in a particular order (see "The S and R Operators—Rulesets and Rewriting Rules" later in this chapter).

In the following sections we'll cover the operators in more detail, in the order in which they appear in Table 24.1.

The D Operator—Macros

Macros are like shell variables. Once you define a macro's value you can refer to it later in the configuration file and its value will be substituted for the macro. For instance, a configuration file might have many lines that mention our hypothetical mail hub, `mailer.gonzo.gov`. Rather than typing that name over and over, you can define a macro R (for relay mailer):

`DRmailer.gonzo.gov`

When sendmail encounters a $R in sendmail.cf, it substitutes the string `mailer.gonzo.gov`.

Macro names are always a single character. Quite a few macros are defined by sendmail and shouldn't be redefined except to work around broken software. sendmail uses lowercase letters for its predefined macros. Uppercase letters may be used freely. V8 sendmail's predefined macros are fully documented in section 5.1.2 of the SIOG.

The C and F Operators—Classes

Classes are similar to macros but are used for different purposes in rewriting rules (see the section, "The S and R Operators—Rulesets and Rewriting Rules"). As with macros, classes are named by a single character. Lowercase letters are reserved to sendmail, and uppercase letters for user-defined classes. A class contains one or more words. For instance, you could define a class H containing all the hosts in the local domain:

```
CH larry moe curly
```

For convenience, large classes may be continued on subsequent lines. The following definition of the class H is exactly the same as the previous one:

```
CH larry
CH moe
CH curly
```

You can also define a class by reading its words from a file:

```
CF/usr/local/lib/localhosts
```

If the file /usr/local/lib/localhosts contains the words larry, moe, and curly, one per line, this definition is equivalent to the previous two.

Why use macros and classes? The best reason is that they centralize information in the configuration file. In the example above, if you decide to change the name of the mail hub from mailer.gonzo.gov to mailhub.gonzo.gov, you only have to change the definition of the $R macro remedy and the configuration file will work as before. If the name mailer.gonzo.gov is scattered through the file, you might forget to change it in some places. If important information is centralized, you can comment it extensively in a single place. Because configuration files tend to be obscure at best, a liberal dose of comments is a good antidote to that sinking feeling you get when, six months later, you wonder why you made a change.

The H Operator—Header Definitions

You probably won't want to change the header definitions given in the V8 sendmail configuration files because they already follow accepted standards. Here are some sample headers:

```
H?D?Date: $a
H?F?Resent-From: $q
H?F?From: $q
H?x?Full-Name: $x
```

Note that header definitions can use macros, which are expanded when inserted into a letter. For instance, the $x macro used in the Full-Name: header definition above expands to the full name of the sender.

The optional *?mailerflag?* construct tells sendmail to insert a header only if the chosen mailer has that mailer flag set. (See the section "The M Operator—Mailer Definitions" later in this chapter.)

Suppose that the definition of your local mailer has a flag Q, and sendmail selects that mailer to deliver a letter. If your configuration file contains a header definition like the following one, sendmail will insert that header into letters delivered through the local mailer, substituting the value of the macro $F:

```
H?Q?X-Fruit-of-the-day: $F
```

Why would you use the *?mailerflag?* feature? Different protocols may require different mail headers. Since they also need different mailers, you can define appropriate mailer flags for each in the mailer definition, and use the *?mailerflag?* construct in the header definition to tell sendmail whether to insert the header.

The O Operator—Setting Options

sendmail has many options that change its operation or tell it the location of files it uses. Most of them may be given either on the command line or in the configuration file. For instance, the location of the aliases file may be specified in either place. To specify the aliases file on the command line, you use the -o option:

```
$ sendmail -oA/etc/mail/aliases [other arguments...]
```

To do the same thing in the configuration file, you include a line like this:

```
OA/etc/mail/aliases
```

Either use is equivalent, but options such as the location of the aliases file rarely change and most people set them in sendmail.cf. The V8 sendmail options are fully described in section 5.1.6 of the SIOG.

The P Operator—Mail Precedence

Users can include mail headers indicating the relative importance of their mail, and sendmail can use those headers to decide the priority of competing letters. Precedences for V8 sendmail are given as:

```
Pspecial-delivery=100
Pfirst-class=0
Plist=-30
Pbulk=-60
Pjunk=-100
```

If a user who runs a large mailing list includes the header Precedence: bulk in his letters, sendmail gives it a lower priority than a letter with the header Precedence: first-class.

The V Operator—sendmail.cf Version Levels

As V8 sendmail evolves, its author adds new features. The V operator lets V8 sendmail know what features it should expect to find in your configuration file. Older versions of sendmail don't understand this command. Section 5.1.8 of the SIOG explains the different configuration file version levels in detail.

> **NOTE**
>
> The configuration file version level does not correspond to the sendmail version level. V8 sendmail understands versions 1 through 5 of configuration files, and there is no such thing as a version 8 configuration file.

The K Operator—Key Files

sendmail has always used keyed databases, for instance, the aliases databases. Given the key postmaster, sendmail looks up the data associated with that key and returns the names of the accounts to which the postmaster's mail should be delivered. V8 sendmail extends this concept to arbitrary databases, including NIS maps (Sun's Network Information Service, formerly known as Yellow Pages or YP). The K operator tells sendmail the location of the database, its class, and how to access it. V8 sendmail supports the following classes of user-defined databases: dbm, btree, hash, and NIS. Depending on which of these databases you use, you must compile sendmail with different options. See section 5.1.9 of the SIOG for the lowdown on key files.

The M Operator—Mailer Definitions

Mailers are either MTAs or final delivery agents. Recall that the aliases file allows you to send mail to a login name (which might be aliased to a remote user), a program, or a file. A special mailer may be defined for each purpose. And even though the SMTP MTA is built-in, it must have a mailer definition to tailor sendmail's SMTP operations.

Mailer definitions are important because all recipient addresses must resolve to a mailer in ruleset 0. Resolving to a mailer is just another name for sendmail's main function, mail routing. For instance, resolving to the local mailer routes the letter to a local user via the final delivery agent defined in that mailer (usually /bin/mail), and resolving to the SMTP mailer routes the letter to another host via sendmail's built-in SMTP transport, as defined in the SMTP mailer. A concrete example of a mailer definition will make this clearer. Since sendmail requires a local mailer definition, let's look at that:

```
Mlocal, P=/bin/mail, F=lsDFMfSn, S=10, R=20, A=mail -d $u
```

All mailer definitions begin with the M operator and the name of the mailer, in this case local. Other fields follow, separated by commas. Each field consists of a field name and its value, separated by an equals sign (=). The allowable fields are explained in section 5.1.4 of the SIOG.

In the local mailer definition above, the P= equivalence gives the pathname of the program to run to deliver the mail, /bin/mail. The F= field gives the sendmail flags for the local mailer. (See also "The H Operator—Defining Headers" earlier in the chapter.) These flags are not passed to the command mentioned in the P= field but are used by sendmail to modify its operation depending on the mailer it chooses. For instance, sendmail usually drops its super-user status before invoking mailers, but you can use the S mailer flag to tell sendmail to retain it for certain mailers.

The S= and R= fields specify rulesets for sendmail to use in rewriting sender and recipient addresses. Since you can give different R= and S= flags for each mailer you define, you can rewrite addresses differently for each mailer. For instance, if one of your UUCP neighbors runs obsolete software that doesn't understand domain addressing, you might declare a special mailer just for that site and write mailer-specific rulesets to convert addresses into a form its mailer could understand:

The S= and R= fields can also specify different rulesets to rewrite the envelope and header addresses. (See the "Header and Envelope Addresses" section earlier in this chapter.) A specification like S=21/31 tells sendmail to use ruleset 21 to rewrite sender envelope addresses and ruleset 31 to rewrite sender header addresses. This comes in handy for mailers that require addresses to be presented differently in the envelope and the headers.

The A= field gives the argument vector (command line) for the program that will be run, in this case /bin/mail. In this example, sendmail runs the command as mail -d $u, expanding the $u macro to the name of the user to which the mail should be delivered, for instance:

```
/bin/mail -d joe
```

This is exactly the same command that you could type to your shell at a command prompt.

There are many other mailer flags you may want to use to tune mailers, for instance to limit the maximum message size on a per-mailer basis. These flags are all documented in section 5.1.4 of the SIOG.

The S and R Operators—Rulesets and Rewriting Rules

A configuration file is composed of a series of rulesets, which are somewhat like subroutines in a program. Rulesets are used to detect bad addresses, to rewrite addresses into forms that remote mailers can understand, and to route mail to one of sendmail's internal mailers. (See the previous section, "The M Operator—Mailer Definitions.")

sendmail passes addresses to rulesets according to a built-in order. Rulesets may also call other rulesets not in the built-in order. The built-in order varies depending on whether the address being handled is a sender or receiver address, and what mailer has been chosen to deliver the letter.

Rulesets are announced by the S command, which is followed by a number to identify the ruleset. sendmail collects subsequent R (rule) lines until it finds another S operator, or the end of the configuration file. The following example defines ruleset 11:

```
# Ruleset 11
S11
R$+        $: $>22 $1      call ruleset 22
```

This ruleset doesn't do much that is useful. The important thing to note is that `sendmail` collects ruleset number 11, composed of a single rule.

sendmail's Built-In Ruleset Processing Rules

`sendmail` uses a three-track approach to processing addresses, one to choose a delivery agent, another to process sender addresses, and one for receiver addresses.

All addresses are first sent through ruleset 3 for preprocessing into a canonical form that makes them easy for other rulesets to handle. Regardless of the complexity of the address, ruleset 3's job is to decide the next host to which a letter should be sent. Ruleset 3 tries to locate that host in the address and mark it within angle brackets. In the simplest case, an address like `joe@gonzo.gov` becomes `joe<@gonzo.gov>`.

Ruleset 0 then determines the correct delivery agent (mailer) to use for each recipient. For instance, a letter from `betty@whizzer.com` to `joe@gonzo.gov` (an Internet site) and `pinhead!zippy` (an old-style UUCP site) will require two different mailers: an SMTP mailer for `gonzo.gov` and an old-style UUCP mailer for `pinhead`. Mailer selection determines later processing of sender and recipient addresses because the rulesets given in the `S=` and `R=` mailer flags vary from mailer to mailer.

Addresses sent through ruleset 0 must resolve to a mailer. This means that when an address matches the `lhs`, the `rhs` gives a triple of mailer, user, host. The following line shows the syntax for a rule that resolves to a mailer:

```
Rlhs        $#mailer $@host $:user   your comment here...
```

The mailer is the name of one of the mailers you've defined in an `M` command, for instance `smtp`. The host and user are usually positional macros taken from the `lhs` match. (See "The Righthand Side (`rhs`) of Rules," later in the chapter.)

After `sendmail` selects a mailer in ruleset 0, it processes sender addresses through ruleset 1 (often empty), and then sends them to the ruleset given in the `S=` flag for that mailer.

Similarly, it sends recipient addresses through ruleset 2 (also often empty), and then to the ruleset mentioned in the `R=` mailer flag.

Finally, `sendmail` post-processes all addresses in ruleset 4, which among other things removes the angle brackets inserted by ruleset 3.

Why do mailers have different `S=` and `R=` flags? Consider the example above of the letter sent to `joe@gonzo.gov` and `pinhead!zippy`. If `betty@whizzer.com` sends the mail, her address must appear in a different form to each recipient. For Joe, it should be a domain address, `betty@whizzer.com`. For Zippy, since `whizzer.com` expects old-style UUCP addresses (and assuming it has a UUCP link to `pinhead` and `whizzer.com`'s UUCP hostname is `whizzer`), the return address should be `whizzer!betty`. Joe's address must also be rewritten for the `pinhead` UUCP mailer, and Joe's copy must include an address for Zippy that his mailer can handle.

Processing Rules Within Rulesets

sendmail passes an address to a ruleset, and then processes it through each rule line by line. If the lhs of a rule matches the address, it is rewritten by the rhs. If it doesn't match, sendmail continues to the next rule until it reaches the end of the ruleset. At the end of the ruleset, sendmail returns the rewritten address to the calling ruleset or to the next ruleset in its built-in execution sequence.

If an address matches the lhs and is rewritten by the rhs, the rule is tried again—an implicit loop (but see the $@ and $: modifiers below for exceptions).

As shown in Table 24.1, each rewriting rule is introduced by the R command and has three fields, the left-hand side (lhs, or matching side), the righthand side (rhs, or rewriting side) and an optional comment, each of which must be separated by tab characters:

```
Rlhs        rhs         comment
```

Parsing—Turning Addresses into Tokens

sendmail parses addresses and the lhs of rules into tokens and then matches the address and the lhs, token by token. The macro $o contains the characters that sendmail uses to separate an address into tokens. It's often defined like this:

```
# address delimiter characters
Do.:%@!^/[]
```

All of the characters in $o are both token separators and tokens. sendmail takes an address such as rae@rainbow.org and breaks it into tokens according to the characters in the o macro, like this:

```
"rae"       "@"     "rainbow"       "."     "org"
```

sendmail also parses the lhs of rewriting rules into tokens so they can be compared one by one with the input address to see if they match. For instance, the lhs $-@rainbow.org gets parsed as:

```
"$-"        "@"     "rainbow"       "."     "org"
```

(Don't worry about the $- just yet. It's a pattern-matching operator similar to shell wild cards that matches any single token, and is covered later in "The Left-Hand Side (lhs) of Rules.") Now we can put the two together to show how sendmail decides whether an address matches the lhs of a rule:

```
"rae"       "@"     "rainbow"       "."     "org"
"$-"        "@"     "rainbow"       "."     "org"
```

In this case, each token from the address matches a constant string (for example, rainbow) or a pattern-matching operator ($-), so the address matches and sendmail would use the rhs to rewrite the address.

Consider the effect (usually bad!) of changing the value of `$o`. As shown above, `sendmail` breaks the address `rae@rainbow.org` into five tokens. However, if the @ character were not in `$o`, the address would be parsed quite differently, into only three tokens:

```
"rae@rainbow"     "."     "org"
```

You can see that changing `$o` has a drastic effect on `sendmail`'s address parsing, and you should leave it alone until you really know what you're doing. Even then you probably won't want to change it since the V8 `sendmail` configuration files already have it correctly defined for standard RFC 822 and RFC 976 address interpretation.

The Left-Hand Side (`lhs`) of Rules

The `lhs` is a pattern against which `sendmail` matches the input address. The `lhs` may contain ordinary text or any of the pattern-matching operators shown in Table 24.2.

Table 24.2. `lhs` pattern-matching operators.

`$-`	Match exactly one token
`$+`	Match one or more tokens
`$*`	Match zero or more tokens
`$@`	Match the null input (used to call the error mailer)

The values of macros and classes are matched in the `lhs` with the operators shown in Table 24.3.

Table 24.3. `lhs` macro and class-matching operators.

`$X`	Match the value of macro X
`$=C`	Match any word in class C
`$~C`	Match if token is not in class C

The pattern-matching operators and macro- and class-matching operators are necessary because most rules must match many different input addresses. For instance, a rule might need to match all addresses that end with `gonzo.gov` and begin with one or more of anything.

The Right-Hand Side (`rhs`) of Rules

The `rhs` of a rewriting rule tells `sendmail` how to rewrite an address that matches the `lhs`. The `rhs` may include text, macros, and positional references to matches in the `lhs`. When a pattern-matching operator from Table 24.2 matches the input, `sendmail` assigns it to a numeric macro

$n, corresponding to the position it matches in the lhs. For instance, suppose the address joe@pc1.gonzo.gov is passed to the following rule:

```
R$+ @ $+        $: $1 < @ $2 >           focus on domain
```

In this example, joe matches $+ (one or more of anything), so sendmail assigns the string joe to $1. The @ in the address matches the @ in the lhs, but constant strings are not assigned to positional macros. The tokens in the string pc1.gonzo.gov match the second $+ and are assigned to $2. The address is rewritten as $1<@$2>, or joe<@pc1.gonzo.gov>.

$: and $@—Altering a Ruleset's Evaluation

Consider the following rule:

```
R$*   $: $1 < @ $j > add local domain
```

After rewriting an address in the rhs, sendmail tries to match the rewritten address with the lhs of the current rule. Since $* matches zero or more of anything, what prevents sendmail from going into an infinite loop on this rule? After all, no matter how the rhs rewrites the address, it will always match $*.

The $: preface to the rhs comes to the rescue; it tells sendmail to evaluate the rule only once.

There are also times when you want a ruleset to terminate immediately and return the address to the calling ruleset or the next ruleset in sendmail's built-in sequence. Prefacing a rule's rhs with $@ causes sendmail to exit the ruleset immediately after rewriting the address in the rhs.

$>—Calling Another Ruleset

A ruleset can pass an address to another ruleset by using the $> preface to the rhs. Consider the following rule:

```
R$*        $: $>66 $1           call ruleset 66
```

The lhs $* matches zero or more of anything, so sendmail always does the rhs. As we saw in the previous section, the $: prevents the rule from being evaluated more than once. The $>66 $1 calls ruleset 66 with $1 as its input address. Since the $1 matches whatever was in the lhs, this rule simply passes the entirety of the current input address to ruleset 66. Whatever ruleset 66 returns is passed to the next rule in the ruleset.

Testing Rules and Rulesets—the -bt, -d, and -C Options

Debugging a sendmail.cf can be a tricky business. Fortunately, sendmail provides several ways to test rulesets before you install them.

> **NOTE**
>
> The examples in this section assume that you have a working sendmail. If your system doesn't, try running them again after you've installed V8 sendmail.

The `-bt` option tells `sendmail` to enter its rule-testing mode:

```
$ sendmail -bt
ADDRESS TEST MODE (ruleset 3 NOT automatically invoked)
Enter <ruleset> <address>
>
```

> **NOTE**
>
> Notice the warning `ruleset 3 NOT automatically invoked`. Older versions of sendmail ran ruleset 3 automatically when in address test mode, which made sense since sendmail sends all addresses through ruleset 3 anyway. V8 `sendmail` does not, but it's a good idea to invoke ruleset 3 manually since later rulesets expect the address to be in canonical form.

The > prompt means `sendmail` is waiting for you to enter one or more ruleset numbers, separated by commas, and an address. Try your login name with rulesets 3 and 0. The result should look something like this:

```
> 3,0 joe
rewrite: ruleset  3    input: joe
rewrite: ruleset  3 returns: joe
rewrite: ruleset  0    input: joe
rewrite: ruleset  3    input: joe
rewrite: ruleset  3 returns: joe
rewrite: ruleset  6    input: joe
rewrite: ruleset  6 returns: joe
rewrite: ruleset  0 returns: $# local $: joe
>
```

The output shows how `sendmail` processes the input address `joe` in each ruleset. Each line of output is identified with the number of the ruleset processing it, the input address, and the address that the ruleset returns. The > is a second prompt indicating that `sendmail` is waiting for another line of input. When you're done testing, just enter Ctrl+D.

Indentation and blank lines better show the flow of processing in this example:

```
rewrite: ruleset  3    input: joe
rewrite: ruleset  3 returns: joe

rewrite: ruleset  0    input: joe

    rewrite: ruleset  3    input: joe
    rewrite: ruleset  3 returns: joe

    rewrite: ruleset  6    input: joe
    rewrite: ruleset  6 returns: joe

rewrite: ruleset  0 returns: $# local $: joe
```

The rulesets called were 3 and 0, in that order. Ruleset 3 was processed and returned the value `joe`, and then `sendmail` called ruleset 0. Ruleset 0 called ruleset 3 again, and then ruleset 6, an example of how a ruleset can call another one by using $>. Neither ruleset 3 nor ruleset 6 rewrote the input address. Finally, ruleset 0 resolved to a mailer, as it must.

Often you need more detail than -bt provides—usually just before you tear out a large handful of hair because you don't understand why an address doesn't match the lhs of a rule. You may remain hirsute because sendmail has verbose debugging built-in to most of its code.

You use the -d option to turn on sendmail's verbose debugging. This option is followed by a numeric code that tells which section of debugging code to turn on, and at what level. The following example shows how to run sendmail in one of its debugging modes and the output it produces:

```
$ sendmail -bt -d21.12
Version 8.6.7
ADDRESS TEST MODE (ruleset 3 NOT automatically invoked)
Enter <ruleset> <address>
> 3,0 joe
rewrite: ruleset  3   input: joe
----trying rule: $* < > $*
---- rule fails
----trying rule: $* < $* < $* < $+ > $* > $* > $*
---- rule fails
[etc.]
```

The -d21.12 in the example above tells sendmail to turn on level 12 debugging in section 21 of its code. The same command with the option -d21.36 gives more verbose output (debug level 36 instead of 12).

> **NOTE**
>
> You can combine one or more debugging specifications separated by commas, as in -d21.12,14.2, which turns on level 12 debugging in section 21 and level 2 debugging in section 14. You can also give a range of debugging sections, as in -d1-10.35, which turns on debugging in sections 1 through 10 at level 35. The specification -d0-91.104 turns on all sections of V8 sendmail's debugging code at the highest levels and produces thousands of lines of output for a single address.

The -d option is not limited to use with sendmail's address testing mode (-bt); you can also use it to see how sendmail processes rulesets while sending a letter, as the following example shows:

```
$ sendmail -d21.36 joe@gonzo.gov < /tmp/letter
[lots and lots of output...]
```

Unfortunately, the SIOG doesn't tell you which numbers correspond to which sections of code. Instead, the author suggests that it's a lot of work to keep such documentation current (which it is), and that you should look at the code itself to discover the correct debugging formulas.

The function `tTd()` is the one to look for. For example, suppose you wanted to turn on debugging in `sendmail`'s address-parsing code. The source file `parseaddr.c` contains most of this code, and the following command finds the allowable debugging levels:

```
$ egrep tTd parseaddr.c
        if (tTd(20, 1))
[...]
        if (tTd(24, 4))
        if (tTd(22, 11))
[etc.]
```

The `egrep` output shows that debugging specifications like `-d20.1`, `-d24.4`, and `-d22.11` (and others) will make sense to `sendmail`.

If perusing thousands of lines of C code doesn't appeal to you, the book *sendmail* documents the debugging flags for `sendmail` version 8.6.9.

The `-C` option allows you to test new configuration files before you install them, which is always a good idea. If you want to test a different file, use `-C/path/to/the/file`. This can be combined with the `-bt` and `-d` flags. For instance, a common invocation for testing new configuration files is

```
sendmail -Ctest.cf -bt -d21.12
```

> **WARNING**
>
> For security, `sendmail` drops its super-user permissions when you use the `-C` option. Final testing of configuration files should be done as the super-user to ensure that your testing is compatible with `sendmail`'s normal operating mode.

Conclusion

Now you know a lot about the `sendmail.cf` language as well as some useful debugging techniques. However, configuration files will be easier to grasp when you look at some real ones. The section below shows you how to create one from the `m4` templates included with V8 `sendmail`.

Creating a `sendmail.cf`

In this section, we'll develop a `sendmail.cf` for a Solaris 2.3 system, using the templates supplied with V8 `sendmail`. However, because every site is different, even if you're developing a `sendmail.cf` for another Solaris 2.3 system, yours will probably differ from the one below.

Previous versions of `sendmail` included complete, sample configuration files to adapt for your site. By contrast, the V8 `sendmail` configuration files are supplied as `m4` templates that you use like building blocks to create a custom configuration file. This is a big advantage for most people.

24

MAIL ADMINISTRATION

In previous versions, if your site did not want UUCP support, you had to pick through hundreds of lines of a configuration file and remove it line by line. In this version, you simply insert the statement FEATURE(nouucp) into your configuration file template and you are done.

M4 is a programming language that reads a file of macro definitions and commands and creates an output file from it. As a trivial example, suppose you create a document and find yourself repeatedly typing the phrase sendmail Installation and Operation Guide. To avoid the extra typing, you could define a macro siog and enter that instead:

```
$ cat > test.m4
define('siog','Sendmail Installation and Operation Guide')dnl
Testing: siog
Ctrl+D
$ m4 test.m4
Testing: Sendmail Installation and Operation Guide
```

Running m4 on the file test.m4 converts all occurrences of siog to sendmail Installation and Operation Guide. This example only hints at m4's capabilities. The V8 sendmail.cf templates make full use of them.

The sendmail.cf templates and m4 support files are in the cf directory you created earlier when you unpacked V8 sendmail:

```
$ cd cf
$ ls -CF
README      domain/    hack/     mailer/    sh/
cf/         feature/   m4/       ostype/    siteconfig/
```

Please note the file README. If you don't read it, you have little hope of making a working configuration file.

The cf subdirectory is the main one of interest. It contains m4 templates for configuration files used at the University of California at Berkeley (UCB). You should look at them all; one of them may be very close to what you need, and all of them provide good examples for you to adapt to your own site.

The other subdirectories contain m4 support files, the building blocks that are included based on the template you define in the cf subdirectory. You probably won't have to change any of these, although you may need to create site-specific files in the domain and siteconfig subdirectories.

The cf subdirectory contains the following configuration file templates:

```
$ cd cf
$ ls -CF
Makefile            knecht.mc            sunos4.1-cs-exposed.mc
Makefile.dist       mail.cs.mc           sunos4.1-cs-hidden.mc
alpha.mc            mail.eecs.mc         tcpproto.mc
auspex.mc           obj/                 ucbarpa.mc
chez.mc             osf1-cs-exposed.mc   ucbvax.mc
clientproto.mc      osf1-cs-hidden.mc    udb.mc
cogsci.mc           python.mc            ultrix4.1-cs-exposed.mc
cs-exposed.mc       riscos-cs-exposed.mc ultrix4.1-cs-hidden.mc
```

```
cs-hidden.mc          s2k.mc                          uucpproto.mc
hpux-cs-exposed.mc    sunos3.5-cs-exposed.mc          vangogh.mc
hpux-cs-hidden.mc     sunos3.5-cs-hidden.m
```

The template `tcpproto.mc` is intended for a generic Internet site without UUCP connections. We'll use that as a starting point to develop our own. Since we don't want to modify the original file, we'll make a copy called `test.mc` and modify that. Although we won't show this in the examples below, it's a good idea to use a version control system like SCCS or RCS, or some other version control system to track changes you make to your configuration file template.

Stripped of its comments (a copyright notice), blank lines, and an `m4` directive, `test.mc` looks like this:

```
include('../m4/cf.m4')
VERSIONID('@(#)tcpproto.mc      8.2 (Berkeley) 8/21/93')
FEATURE(nouucp)
MAILER(local)
MAILER(smtp)
```

This doesn't look like much, but `m4` expands it to almost 600 lines. We'll look at this template line-by-line to show what it does.

The line `include('../m4/cf.m4')` must come first in all configuration file templates, immediately after any comments. It contains the macro definitions that `m4` uses to build your configuration file, and if you don't include it here, nothing else will work.

The `VERSIONID()` macro provides a place to put version information for the edification of humans—`sendmail` ignores it. If you use RCS or SCCS, you can include their version information here. For instance, for RCS you can include the `$Id$` keyword

```
VERSIONID('$Id$')
```

and the RCS `co` (check-out) command expands this to

```
VERSIONID('$Id: test.mc,v 1.1 1994/03/26 21:46:12 joe Exp joe $')
```

The `FEATURE()` macro is used to specify which features you want (or don't want). The line `FEATURE(nouucp)` in this configuration file template removes UUCP support from the resulting configuration file. Other features are documented in the README file mentioned above. Some features of particular interest are `redirect`, which provides a clever way to notify senders when someone leaves your site; and `nullclient`, which creates a bare-bones configuration file that knows just enough to forward mail to a relay. (See the template `nullclient.mc` for an example of its use.)

The next two lines are `MAILER()` macros to specify the mailers included in this `sendmail.cf`. The `MAILER()` macro takes a single argument, the name of the mailer when `m4` expands the `MAILER()` macro into one or more ruleset definitions, rules to select them in ruleset 0, and the rulesets given in the R= and S= flags. Selecting the `smtp` mailer actually causes three SMTP mailers to be included. The V8 templates also provide mailer definitions for UUCP mailers, a FAX mailer, and a POP (Post Office Protocol) mailer. See the README file for details.

24

MAIL
ADMINISTRATION

This is almost enough of a specification to create a working `sendmail.cf` for an SMTP-only site, but you'll want to tune it a little first with additional macros.

The `OSTYPE()` macro also takes a single argument, the name of a file in `../ostype`. This file should contain definitions particular to your operating system, for instance, the location of the aliases file. A wide variety of operating system definitions are included with the V8 configuration files:

```
$ cd ../ostype
$ ls
aix3.m4        bsdi1.0.m4     hpux.m4        osf1.m4        sunos3.5.m4
aux.m4         dgux.m4        irix.m4        riscos4.5.m4   sunos4.1.m4
bsd4.3.m4      domainos.m4    linux.m4       sco3.2.m4      svr4.m4
bsd4.4.m4      dynix3.2.m4    nextstep.m4    solaris2.m4    ultrix4.1.m4
```

Since we're developing a configuration file for a Solaris 2.3 system, we'll look at that file:

```
$ cat solaris2.m4
define('ALIAS_FILE', /etc/mail/aliases)
define('HELP_FILE', /etc/mail/sendmail.hf)
define('STATUS_FILE', /etc/mail/sendmail.st)
define('LOCAL_MAILER_FLAGS', 'fSn')
```

This is pretty straightforward—the file gives the location of `sendmail`'s auxiliary files on that system and specifies local mailer flags appropriate for the Solaris version of `/bin/mail`. We'll include an `OSTYPE()` macro just after the `VERSIONID()` macro, dropping the `.m4` filename extension.

The other things you may define in an `OSTYPE` file are documented in the `README`.

You may also want to create a domain file and use the `DOMAIN()` macro to collect site-wide definitions such as your site's UUCP or BITNET relay hosts. You should only put things in this file that are true for all the hosts in your domain. If you only have a single host, you may want to forego creating a domain file and keep this information in your `m4` template.

The `DOMAIN()` macro takes a single argument, the name of a file in `../domain`. For instance, `DOMAIN(gonzo)` would cause `m4` to look for a file named `../domain/gonzo.m4`. (Note that the `.m4` extension is not included in the macro argument.)

> **WARNING**
>
> If you copy one of the UCB templates that includes a `DOMAIN()` macro, make sure you change that line to use your own domain file, or delete it.

A common feature to include in a domain file is the `MASQUERADE_AS()` macro, which causes all hosts using that `sendmail.cf` to masquerade as your mail hub. For example, if the Solaris 2.3 host we're building this configuration file for is one of many, all named sun*X*.gonzo.gov, the following line would cause all their outbound mail to be addressed as `login@gonzo.gov`, regardless of which workstation sent it:

```
MASQUERADE_AS(gonzo.gov)dnl
```

This line could also be included in the `m4` template if you don't want to create a domain file. Now the template looks like this:

```
include('../m4/cf.m4')
VERSIONID('$Id$')
OSTYPE(solaris2)
MASQUERADE_AS(gonzo.gov)
FEATURE(nouucp)
MAILER(local)
MAILER(smtp)
```

To create the working sendmail.cf, run `m4` on the template:

```
$ m4 test.mc > test.cf
```

This creates a 600-line configuration file, which should be tested thoroughly before you install it. We will do just that in the next section, "Testing `sendmail` and `sendmail.cf`."

But first, considering that building a `sendmail.cf` file from the V8 macros is so easy, you may be wondering why I went on at such length about the guts of it. After all, if including an SMTP mailer is as easy as typing `MAILER(smtp)`, why bother to learn the grungy details? The first answer is that someday you'll probably need them; something will go wrong and you'll have to figure out exactly why your `sendmail` isn't working the way it should. You can't do that unless you understand the details. A second answer is that you can't properly test your `sendmail.cf` unless you know what's going on under the simplified `m4` gloss. Finally, although the V8 configuration file templates are easy to work with compared to those included with previous versions of `sendmail`, they're still not exactly on a par with plugging in a new toaster and shoving in a couple of slices of rye. If `sendmail` were a toaster instead of a single lever, it would have hundreds of complicated knobs and dials, a thick instruction manual, and despite your best efforts, would periodically burst into flames.

Testing `sendmail` and `sendmail.cf`

Before installing a new or modified `sendmail.cf` you must test it thoroughly. Even small, apparently innocuous changes can lead to disaster, and as mentioned in the introduction to this chapter, people get really irate when you mess up the mail system.

The first step in testing is to create a list of addresses that you know should work at your site. For instance, at `gonzo.gov`, an Internet site without UUCP connections, they know that the following addresses must work:

```
joe
joe@pc1.gonzo.gov
joe@gonzo.gov
```

If `gonzo.gov` has a UUCP link, those addresses must also be tested. Other addresses to consider include the various kinds of aliases (for example, `postmaster`, a `:include:` list, an alias that mails to a file and one that mails to a program), nonlocal addresses, source-routed addresses, and so on. If you want to be thorough, you can create a test address for each legal address format in RFC822.

Now that you've got your list of test addresses, you can use the `-C` and `-bt` options to see what happens. At a minimum you'll want to run the addresses through rulesets 3 and 0 to make sure they are routed to the correct mailer. An easy way to do this is to create a file containing the ruleset invocations and test addresses, and run `sendmail` on that. For instance, if the file `addr.test` contains the following lines

```
3,0 joe
3,0 joe@pc1.gonzo.gov
3,0 joe@gonzo.gov
```

you can test your configuration file `test.cf` by typing:

```
$ sendmail -Ctest.cf -bt < addr.test
rewrite: ruleset   3    input: joe
rewrite: ruleset   3 returns: joe
[etc.]
```

You may also want to follow one or more addresses through the complete rewriting process. For instance, if an address resolves to the `smtp` mailer and that mailer specifies `R=21`, you can test recipient address rewriting with `3,2,21,4` *test_address*.

If the `sendmail.cf` appears to work correctly so far, it's time to move on to sending some real letters. You can do so with a command like this:

```
$ sendmail -v -oQ/tmp -Ctest.cf recipient < /dev/null
```

The `-v` option tells `sendmail` to be verbose so you can see what's happening. Depending on whether the delivery is local or remote, you may see something as simple as `joe... Sent`, or an entire SMTP dialogue.

The `-oQ/tmp` tells `sendmail` to use `/tmp` as its queue directory. This is necessary because `sendmail` drops its super-user permissions when run with the `-C` option and can't write queue files into the normal mail queue directory. Because you are using the `-C` and `-oQ` options, `sendmail` also includes the following warning headers in the letter to help alert the recipient of possible mail forgery:

```
X-Authentication-Warning: gonzo.gov: Processed from queue /tmp
X-Authentication-Warning: gonzo.gov: Processed by joe with -C srvr.cf
```

`sendmail` also inserts the header `Apparently-to: joe` because although you specified a recipient on the command line, there was none in the body of the letter. In this case the letter's body was taken from the empty file `/dev/null`, so there was no `To:` header. If you do your testing as the super-user, you can skip the -oQ argument, and sendmail won't insert the warning headers. You can avoid the Apparently-to: header by creating a file like this

```
To: recipient

testing
```

and using it as input instead of /dev/null.

The recipient should be you so you can inspect the headers of the letter for correctness. In particular, return address lines must include an FQDN for SMTP mail. That is, a header like From: joe@gonzo is incorrect since it doesn't include the domain part of the name, but a header like From: joe@gonzo.gov is fine.

You should repeat this testing for the same variety of addresses you used in the first tests. You may have to create special aliases that point to you for some of the testing.

The amount of testing you do depends on the complexity of your site and the amount of experience you have, but a beginning system administrator should test things very thoroughly, even for apparently simple installations. Remember the flaming toaster.

Installing sendmail and Friends

Once you're satisfied that your sendmail and sendmail.cf work, you must decide where to install them. The most popular approach is to put sendmail and its other files in the same place that your vendor puts its distributed sendmail files. The advantage of this approach is conformity; if someone else familiar with your operating system tries to diagnose a mail problem, he will know where to look.

However, some people prefer to install local programs separately from vendor programs, for several good reasons. First, operating system upgrades are usually easier when local modifications are clearly segregated from vendor programs. Second, some vendors, notably Sun Microsystems, release operating system patches that bundle together everything including the kitchen sink. If you naively install such a patch, you may inadvertently overwrite your V8 sendmail with your vendor's version, and it probably won't understand your V8 sendmail.cf.

Therefore, you may want to install sendmail in a subdirectory of /usr/local, the traditional directory for local enhancements to the vendor's operating system. The locations of sendmail's auxiliary files are given in sendmail.cf, so you can either leave them in the vendor's usual locations or install them in /usr/local and modify the sendmail.cf to match. If you want to change the compiled-in location of the configuration file, redefine the C preprocessor macro _PATH_SENDMAILCF in src/Makefile and recompile sendmail. For example, add the definition

```
-D_PATH_SENDMAILCF=\"/usr/local/lib/sendmail.cf\"
```

to the CFLAGS macro in the Makefile.

Once you've decided where the files should go, look at the Makefile you used to compile `sendmail` and see if it agrees. The easiest way is to use `make`'s `-n` option to see what would have happened. The results look like this for the V8 distribution's `Makefile.Solaris`:

```
$ make -n install
/usr/ucb/install -o root -g sys -m 6555 sendmail /usr/lib
for i in /usr/ucb/newaliases /usr/ucb/mailq; do rm -f $i; ln -s /usr/lib/sendmai
l $i; done
/usr/ucb/install -c -o root -g sys -m 644 /dev/null \
    /var/log/sendmail.st
/usr/ucb/install -c -o root -g sys -m 444 sendmail.hf /etc/mail
nroff -h -mandoc aliases.5 > aliases.0
nroff -h -mandoc mailq.1 > mailq.0
nroff -h -mandoc newaliases.1 > newaliases.0
nroff -h -mandoc sendmail.8 > sendmail.0
```

If this isn't what you want, modify the Makefile as necessary.

Note that the `sendmail` manual pages use the 4.4BSD `mandoc` macros, which your system probably doesn't have. You can `ftp` the `mandoc` macros from the host `ftp.uu.net`, in the directory `/systems/unix/bsd-sources/share/tmac`.

If your system doesn't have the `/usr/ucb/install` program, you can copy the new files instead, and use `chown`, `chgrp` and `chmod` to set the correct owner, group, and mode. However, if you're installing on top of your vendor's files, it's a good idea to first copy or rename them in case you ever need them again.

After you install `sendmail` and its auxiliary files, rebuild the aliases database by running `sendmail -bi`. You'll also need to kill and restart your `sendmail` daemon. If your vendor's system uses a frozen configuration file (`sendmail.fc`), remove it; V8 `sendmail` doesn't use one.

Modifying `sendmail`'s Boot-Time Startup

In its SMTP server role, `sendmail` starts when the system boots and runs continuously. If you install it in a non-standard location like `/usr/local`, you'll have to modify your system's startup scripts. Even if you install it in the standard location, you should ensure that the default system startup is correct for V8 `sendmail`.

When SVR4 UNIX systems boot, they run a series of short shell scripts in the directories `/etc/rcX.d`, where the *X* corresponds to the system run level. For instance, shell scripts that bring the system to run level 2 are found in `/etc/rc2.d`.

However, SVR4 systems have many run levels and some software subsystems should be started in each of them. Therefore, the shell scripts in `/etc/rcX.d` are located in `/etc/init.d` and linked to the files in the `/etc/rcX.d` directories. The `/etc/init.d` directory is therefore the best place to look for your `sendmail` startup script.

The following example shows how to find how `sendmail` starts on a Solaris 2.3 system. Other SVR4 systems are similar:

```
$ cd /etc/init.d
$ grep sendmail *
sendmail:#ident "@(#)sendmail   1.4   92/07/14 SMI"   /* SVr4.0 1.5 */
sendmail:# /etc/init.d/sendmail - Start/Stop the sendmail daemon
sendmail:# If sendmail is already executing, don't re-execute it.
sendmail:if [ -f /usr/lib/sendmail -a -f /etc/mail/sendmail.cf ]; then
sendmail:                /usr/lib/sendmail -bd -q1h;
sendmail:pid='/usr/bin/ps -e ¦ /usr/bin/grep sendmail ¦ [...]
sendmail:echo "usage: /etc/rc2.d/S88sendmail {start¦stop}"
$
```

> **NOTE**
>
> Some of the lines above are truncated and shown as [...] due to page-width limitations.

In this case the `grep` output shows that the vendor starts `sendmail` with a script named `sendmail` because each line of the `grep` output is prefixed with that filename. Examine the script `sendmail` to see if any changes are necessary. This script expects `sendmail` to be located in `/usr/lib`. If you install V8 `sendmail` somewhere else, you'll have to modify the script to match, changing paths like `/usr/lib/sendmail` to `/usr/local/lib/sendmail`. If the command-line flags in the script aren't what you want, change those too.

Summary

It's not possible in a single chapter to tell you all you must know about e-mail administration, but as Yogi Berra (or maybe that was Casey Stengel) once said, "You could look it up," and you should. There are a lot of things you'll only learn by reading the documentation mentioned previously in the "Background Material and Other Sources" section. However, this chapter should give you a good basis for understanding the theory behind Internet e-mail delivery and enough of the specifics of V8 `sendmail` to get your e-mail system up and running.

1. For instance, `sendmail` sets `$j` to your system's fully qualified domain name (FQDN, for example, `acme.com`). If your system's `gethostbyname()` function returns something other than the FQDN, you must define `$j` in `sendmail.cf`.

2. The local mailer omits the `$@host`.

3. Ruleset 0 is an exception to this rule. `sendmail` stops evaluating rules in ruleset 0 as soon as a rule resolves to a mailer.

4. Tokens are explained in the "Tokens—How `sendmail` Interprets Input Patterns" section.

News Administration

by Jeff Smith and James Edwards

CHAPTER 25

IN THIS CHAPTER

Introduction

The history of the Usenet news service can be traced back to the original ARPANET. The original ARPA-Internet community used a series of mailing lists to distribute information, bulletins, and updates to community members. As this community expanded, management of these mailing lists became more and more difficult. The lists became exceptionally long, and carrying out the necessary moves, adds, and changes became more onerous.

The Usenet provides a viable alternative for relaying this news. The idea is that the "news" information be posted on a central server and available for users to retrieve whenever they want. The Usenet system provides similar functionality to the old mailing list operation; the information is arranged as individual articles divided into different groups and classifications. (Such a server is also referred to as an electronic bulletin board system, or BBS). To make client access as efficient as possible, these central stores of "news" information are distributed to a number of local servers.

Usenet has developed into what is certainly the world's largest electronic BBS. It's a loose conglomeration of computers that run operating systems ranging from MS-DOS to UNIX and VM/CMS, and that exchange articles through UUCP, the Internet, and other networks. Usenet is also probably the largest experiment to date with creative anarchy—there is little central authority or control—and anyone can join who runs the appropriate software and who can find a host already on the network with which to exchange news.

The lenient requirements for membership, the wide variety of computers able to run Usenet software, and the tremendous growth of the Internet have combined to make Usenet big. How big? No one really knows how many hosts and users participate, but the volume of news will give you some idea. Estimates in the latest "How to Become a Usenet site" Frequently Asked Questions (FAQ) document suggests 5,400 MB of news is updated per month. This works out to an average of more than 150 MB per day. Downloading this much information over a standard analog modem could take as much as 15 hours a day!

This huge volume can cause problems for the system administrator, because the amount of disk space used for news may vary a lot, and quickly. You might think you've got plenty of space in your news system when you leave on Friday night, but then you get a call in the wee hours of Sunday morning telling you that the news file system is full. If you've planned poorly, it might take more important things with it—such as e-mail, system logging, or accounting (see "Isolating the News Spool" later in this chapter to avoid that problem). This chapter (and good planning) will help you avoid some (but not all) of the late-night calls.

The chapter begins with some pointers on finding additional sources of information. Some information is included on the *UNIX Unleashed* CD-ROM, some is available on the Internet, and some (from the technical newsgroups) you'll be able to apply only after you get your news system running.

The examples in this chapter assume you have an Internet site running the Network News Transfer Protocol (NNTP). If your networking capabilities are limited to the UNIX-to-UNIX Copy Program (UUCP), you're mostly on your own. Although some of the general information given here still applies, UUCP is a pain, and the economics of a full newsfeed make Internet access more and more attractive every day. If your site isn't on the Internet but you want to receive news, it might be time to talk to your local Internet service provider. You might find it cheaper to pay Internet access fees than 15-hour-per-day phone bills. If your site's news needs aren't too great, it might be even more economical to buy Usenet access from an Internet service provider. (See the section "Do You *Really* Want To Be a Usenet Site?" later in this chapter.)

Additional Sources of Information

News software is inherently complex. This chapter can only begin to give you the information you need to successfully maintain a Usenet site. The following sources of additional information will help you fill in the gaps.

Frequently Asked Questions (FAQ) Documents

In many Usenet newsgroups, especially the technical ones, similar questions are repeated as new participants join the group. To avoid answering the same questions over and over, volunteers collect these prototypical questions (and the answers) into FAQs. The FAQs are posted periodically to that newsgroup and to the newsgroup news.answers. Many FAQs are also available through the Internet file transfer protocol (ftp), through e-mail servers, or through other information services such as Gopher, Wide Area Information Service (WAIS) and, of course, the World Wide Web (WWW).

You should read the FAQs in the following list after you've read this chapter and before you install your news system. All of them are available on the host rtfm.mit.edu in subdirectories of the directory pub/usenet/news.answers/index and are referenced through the site URL—http://www.rtfm.mit.edu.

usenet-software/part1	History of Usenet; on software for transporting, reading, and posting news, including packages for non-UNIX operating systems (such as VMS and MS-DOS).
site-setup	Guidance on how to join Usenet.
news/software/b/intro	A short introduction to the newsgroup news.software.b.
news/software/b/faq	The news.software.b FAQ. Read this before you post to that newsgroup. Read it even if you don't plan to post.
INN FAQs	There is a four-part FAQ for INN. You can get it from any host that has the INN software, including ftp://ftp.xlink.net/pub/news/docs, http://www-old.xlink.net/~hwr/inn-faq/faq-index.html.

Another excellent source is the Usenet Information Center. This provides a hypertext-based index that covers the vast majority of available newsgroups, providing a FAQ for each one. The Usenet Information Center can be found at `http://sunsite.uuc.edu/usenet-i/`.

News Transport Software Documentation

There are a number of available News transport systems; some of the most commonly recommended include C-news, InterNetworkNews (INN) and Netscape's News Server. All these packages come with extensive documentation to help you install and maintain them. Whichever you choose, read the documentation and then read it again. This chapter is no substitute for the software author's documentation, which is updated to match each release of the software and which contains details that a chapter of this size can't cover.

Request for Comments (RFC) Documents

RFCs are issued by working groups of the Internet Engineering Task Force (IETF). They were known initially as requests for comments, but as they become adopted as Internet standards, you should think of them as requirements for compliance—if you want to exchange news with another Internet NNTP site, you must comply with the provisions of both RFC 977 and 1036. RFCs are available for anonymous ftp on the host `ftp://ftp.internic.net` and others. RFCs are also included on the *UNIX Unleashed* CD-ROM.

- RFC 977 (Network News Transfer Protocol) defines the commands by which Internet news servers exchange news articles with other news servers, newsreaders, and news posting programs. The protocol is fairly simple, and this RFC gives you a better idea of what your newsreaders, news posting programs, and news transport software are doing behind your back.

- RFC 1036 (Standard for Interchange of Usenet Messages) explains the format of Usenet news articles, which is based on the format of Internet e-mail messages. You don't need to memorize it, but a quick read will help you understand the functions and formats of the various news articles.

Usenet Newsgroups

Once you get your news system running, there are several technical and policy newsgroups you'll want to read. These newsgroups will keep you abreast of new releases of your news transport software, bug fixes, and security problems. You'll also see postings of common problems experienced at other sites, so if you encounter the same problems, you'll have the solutions. Many knowledgeable people contribute to these newsgroups, including the authors of C-news and INN.

Remember that the people answering your questions are volunteers, doing so in their spare time, so be polite. The first step toward politeness is to read the newsgroup's FAQ (if there is one) and avoid being the 1,001st lucky person to ask how to make a round wheel. You should also read the "Emily Postnews" guide to Usenet etiquette and other introductory articles in the newsgroup `news.announce.newusers`. Listed below are a few of the newsgroups you may want to read. You may want to subscribe to all of the `news.*` groups for a few weeks and then cancel the subscriptions for the ones you don't need.

`news.announce.newusers`	Information for new users. You should subscribe all of your users to this group.
`news.announce.newgroups`	Announcements of newsgroup vote results and which newsgroups are about to be created.
`news.software.readers`	Information and discussion of news-reading software (also known as *newsreaders*).
`news.admin.policy`	Discussions pertaining to the site's news policies.
`news.software.b`	Discussions of software systems compatible with B-news (for example, C-news and INN).
`news.software.nntp`	Discussions of implementations of NNTP (for example, the so-called reference implementation and INN).

News Systems and Software

This section focuses on the major components of the Usenet. Clearly these can be divided into two very broad groups: those relating to the content, including such things as articles, data stores, and file formats; and those relating to the transport of articles between news servers and between news clients and servers.

> **NOTE**
>
> The details of this section are defined by two RFCs: RFC 977, "Network News Transfer Protocol," and RFC 1036, "Standard for Interchange of Usenet Messages."

News Articles

A news article is like an e-mail message—it has a message body, which is accompanied by one or more headers that provide supplemental information relating to the message. A standard format for both message body and headers has been outlined in RFC 1036.

This RFC indicates that the message body will follow a number of required header values that must accompany each posted news article. In addition, any message may optionally include one or more additional headers; however, these optional headers might be ignored by the receiving News server or client. Table 25.1 provides a useful summary of these header values. The table outlines which headers are optional and which are mandatory.

Table 25.1. Usenet news article message format.

Header	Description	Required	Optional
approved	for a moderated newsgroup		X
control	control server exchanges, not a user message.		X
date	date message was posted	X	
distribution	scope of message		X
expires	date to expire		X
followup-to	followup message in group		X
from	e-mail address of poster	X	
keywords	subject related keywords		X
lines	message body line count		X
message-ID	message unique ID	X	
newsgroups	newsgroup to which message belongs	X	
organization	organization description		X
path	path to current system	X	
references	message-ID relating to this		X
reply-to	reply to author		X
sender	manually entered from field		X
subject	message subject	X	
summary	brief message summary		X
xref	host name		X

Newsgroup Hierarchies

Articles are posted to one or more newsgroups, whose names are separated by periods to categorize them into hierarchies. For instance, the newsgroups `comp.unix.solaris` and `comp.risks` are both in the `comp` hierarchy, which contains articles having to do with computers. The `comp.unix.solaris` newsgroup is further categorized by inclusion in the `unix` subhierarchy, which has to do with various vendors' versions of UNIX.

Some of the current Usenet newsgroup hierarchies are shown in the following list. There are others—this is by no means a definitive list. Some Internet mailing lists are fed into newsgroups in their own hierarchies. For instance, the GNU (GNU is a self-referential acronym for "GNU is not UNIX") project's mailing lists are fed to the `gnu` newsgroup hierarchy.

alt	The alternative newsgroup hierarchy. There is even less control here than in most of Usenet, with new newsgroups created at the whim of anyone who knows how to send a `newgroup` control message. It is mostly a swamp, but you can often find something useful. Examples: `alt.activism`, `alt.spam`.
comp	Computer-related newsgroups. Example: `comp.risks`.
misc	Things that don't seem to fit anywhere else. Examples: `misc.invest.stocks`, `misc.kids.vacation`.
rec	Recreational newsgroups. Example: `rec.woodworking`.
soc	Social newsgroups. Examples: `soc.college.grad`, `soc.culture.africa`.
talk	Talk newsgroups. Intended for people who like to argue in public about mostly unresolvable and controversial issues. The `talk` hierarchy is a great waste of time and users love it. Examples: `talk.politics.mideast`, `talk.abortion`.

TIP

Certain newsgroups and news postings are only relevant to certain geographical regions. For instance, it makes little sense to post an Indiana car-for-sale advertisement to the entire world, and Hungarian Usenet sites won't appreciate the resources you waste in doing so—it costs thousands of dollars to send an article to all of Usenet. Distributions allow you to control how far your article travels.

For instance, you can usually post an article to your local site, your state, your continent, or to the entire world. News posting programs often offer users a choice of distributions as they construct their news postings. The news system administrator controls which distributions are presented to users, which distributions are accepted by the news system when articles are brought in by its newsfeeds, and which distributions are offered to outside hosts. The latter is important for sites that want to keep their local distributions private.

Where News Articles Live

News articles arranged within the Usenet hierarchy are commonly stored in a separate file system in a site's news server. This file system is often named `/var/spool/news` or `/usr/spool/news`. The files that contain articles are given serial numbers as they are received, with the periods in the newsgroup names replaced by the slash character (`/`). For instance, article number 1047 of the newsgroup `comp.unix.solaris` would be stored in the file `/var/spool/news/comp/unix/solaris/1047`.

The News Overview Database (NOV)

Newsreaders (and users) have a difficult job. Remember that more than 100 MB of news is posted to Usenet every day. That's about the same as a fairly thick novel every day of the year, without any holidays. Most people want to have their favorite newsreader sift the wheat from the chaff and present them with only the articles they want to see, in some rational order.

To do this, newsreaders must keep a database of information about the articles in the news spool; for instance, an index of subject headers and article cross-references. These are commonly known as threads databases. The authors of newsreaders have independently developed different threads databases for their newsreaders, and naturally, they're all incompatible with each other. For instance, if you install trn, nn, and tin, you must install each of their threads database maintenance programs and databases, which can take a lot of CPU cycles to generate and may become quite large.

Geoff Collyer, one of the authors of C-news, saw that this was not good and created the News Overview Database (NOV), a standard database of information for fancy newsreaders. The main advantage of NOV is that just one database must be created and maintained for all newsreaders. The main disadvantage is that it hasn't yet caught on with all the authors of news software.

If you're interested in NOV support, you must install news transport software that has the NOV NNTP extensions (INN does) and newsreaders that can take advantage of it. According to the NOV FAQ, trn3.3 and tin-1.21 have built-in NOV support, and there is an unofficial version (not supported by the author) of nn for anonymous ftp on the host agate.berkeley.edu in the directory ~ftp/pub/usenet/NN-6.4P18+xover.tar.Z.

Distributing the News

The Network News Transfer Protocol is the application that is used to distribute news articles between news servers and clients. NNTP is an application level protocol—similar in operation and functionality to HTTP. As with HTTP, the NNTP application makes use of the reliable communication services that are provided by the TCP protocol.

The following section examines the operation of the NNTP application and highlights how NNTP provides a mechanism for both the distribution of news throughout the Usenet and enables user access to these "news" servers. Figure 25.1 below provides an overview of the architecture of the Usenet.

As Figure 25.1 indicates, the Usenet network relies on the operation of NNTP servers acting as central data stores of news information. Users are granted access to this information through client programs known as newsreaders. Information is conveyed throughout the Usenet through a process of server replication—known as a *newsfeed*. Access for both clients and servers occurs over established TCP connections via the well known port 119.

FIGURE 25.1.

The Usenet architecture.

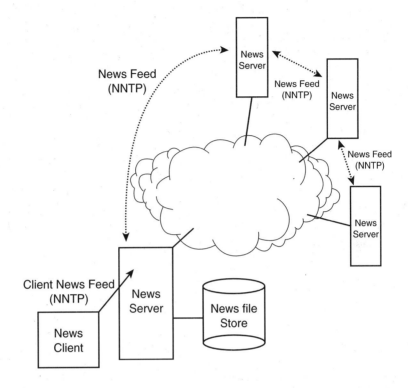

Like the HTTP application protocol, NNTP uses a system of request and response messages to exchange information with both clients and servers. These messages are formatted using standard ASCII characters. Table 25.1 provides a summary of the standard request message commands.

Table 25.1. Summary of Usenet request message commands.

Request Command	*Description*
article *<message-id>*	Displays the message header, a blank line, and the text body.
body *<message-id>*	Displays the message body only.
group *newsgroup*	Selects the indicated newsgroup.
head *<message-id>*	Displays the selected article header fields.
Help	Provides a list of available commands.
ihave *<message-id>*	Informs the server that the client has the indicated message.
last	Decrements the current article pointer.

continues

Table 25.1. continued

Request Command	Description
list	Returns a list of the existing newsgroups.
listgroup	Lists current articles with the selected group.
newgroups *date time*	Lists new groups since date and time.
newnews *date time*	Lists new articles within a selected newsgroup since the specified data and time.
next	Increments the current article pointer.
post	Starts an article posting, terminated with a single period (.) on an otherwise blank line.
Quit	Closes the client TCP connection to the server.
slave	Indicates that this connection is to a slave server that is providing news services to a number of users.
stat	Client selects an article to read.

The contacted news server responds to any message request with a response that consist of two parts: a three-digit status number and a text-based message body. The returned status number provides an indication of the success or failure of the particular request—following a similar format to that used within the ftp application. Table 25.2 provides a summary of the possible values.

Table 25.2. NNTP status line response codes.

Status Numbers	Description
1xx	Informational messages.
2xx	Successful commands (command OK).
3xx	Successful commands so far, send the rest of it.
4xx	Command was correct, but it couldn't be performed for some reason.
5xx	Command not available, or a serious error occurred.
For each of these groups	
x0x	Relating to connection setup.
x1x	Relating to newsgroup selection.
x2x	Relating to article selection.
x3x	Relating to distribution functions.

For each of these groups	
x4x	Relating to article posting.
x8x	Relating to private application extensions.
x9x	Relating to debugging codes.

The news server signals the end of any message or command with a line consisting of a single dot (.). If any line of text actually starts with a dot, the server adds another one to indicate that it is not the end of message marker.

Listing 25.1 provides an example of the operation of NNTP between a newsreader and Usenet server. In this example, the client requests to read a single news article that is contained within a particular newsgroup—notice how the server responds to the client NNTP requests with a status line and one or more lines of text.

Listing 25.1. Example operation of the NNTP application.

```
client attaches to selected newserver
200 usenetserver news server ready - posting ok

client requests a list of available newsgroups
LIST
215 list of newsgroups follows
alt.2600
alt.2600.aol
...
...
comp.protocols.snmp
comp.protocols.frame-relay
comp.protocols.tcp-ip
...
...
...
select a particular group
GROUP comp.protocols.tcp-ip
211 86 1001 1087 comp.protocols.tcp-ip group selected
ARTICLE 1002
220 1002 <13343@darkstar.com> Article retrieved, text follows
Path:
From:
Newsgroup: comp.protocols.tcp-ip
Subject: HTTP Request Formats
Date: 8 March 1997 20:21:32  EST
Organization: Deloitte Touche Consulting Group

message body appears here

.
message response is terminated with a single period
client ends session using the quit command.
QUIT
```

Sharing News Over the Network

If you have several hosts on a local area network (LAN), you'll want to share news among them to conserve disk space. As mentioned previously, if you carry all possible newsgroups, your news spool needs about a gigabyte of disk space, more or less, depending on how long you keep articles online. A year from now, who knows how much you'll need? It makes more sense to add disk capacity to a single host than to add it to all your hosts.

There are two ways to share news over a LAN. If all of your hosts run a network file system such as Sun Microsystem's NFS or Transarc's AFS (Andrew File System), you can export the news host's spool directory to them, or use NNTP to transfer news from a single server host to client newsreaders and news posting programs. An alternative approach would be to use NNTP to transfer news from a single server host to client newsreaders and news posting programs. The only requirements for the client hosts are that they be able to open up a TCP/IP connection over the network and have client software that understands NNTP. Most common UNIX-based newsreaders and news posting programs have built-in NNTP support, and there are many NNTP clients for non-UNIX operating systems such as DOS, VMS, VM/CMS, and others.

An NNTP daemon runs continuously on the news server host, listening on a well known port, just as the Simple Mail Transfer Protocol (SMTP) server listens on a well known port for incoming e-mail connections. NNTP client programs connect to the NNTP server and issue commands for reading and posting news articles. For instance, there are commands to ask for all the articles that have arrived since a certain date and time. A client newsreader can ask for those articles and display them to the user as the NNTP server ships them over the network. Hosts with which you exchange news connect to the NNTP server's port and transfer articles to your host.

NNTP servers usually have some form of built-in access control so that only authorized hosts can connect to them—after all, you don't want all the hosts on the Internet to be able to connect to your news server.

Transferring News to Other Hosts

When a posting program hands an article to the news system, it expects a copy of the article to be deposited in the local news spool (or the news spool of the local NNTP server), sent to other hosts, and eventually sent to the rest of Usenet. Similarly, articles posted on other Usenet hosts should eventually find their way into the local (or NNTP server's) spool directory.

Figure 25.2 illustrates a simple set of connections between hosts transferring news. The incoming and outgoing lines emphasize that news is both sent and received between each set of hosts.

Usenet news is transferred by a flooding algorithm, which means that when a host receives an article, it sends it to all other hosts with which it exchanges news, and those hosts do the same. Now suppose that someone on host-b in Figure 25.2 posts a news article.

FIGURE 25.2.

The Usenet flooding algorithm.

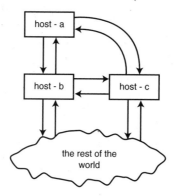

Because of the flooding algorithm, host-b sends the article to host-a, host-c, and any other hosts with which it exchanges news. Host-c gets the article and does the same, which means it gives the same article to host-a, which may try to give it back to host-b, which already has a copy of the article in its news spool. Further, since host-b gave host-a the article, it will try to give it to host-c, which already got it from host-b. It's also possible that host-a got a copy of the article from host-b before host-c offered it and will want to give it to host-c. Just to keep the news administrator's life interesting, no one can say whether any other hosts will ship the same article back to host-b or host-c. (Well-behaved hosts should avoid transferring articles back to the hosts from which they originally received them, but on Usenet, it's best to plan for worst case behavior from another site's software.) How do these hosts know when articles are duplicates and should be rejected? Obviously, they can't compare a new article with every article currently in the spool directory.

The news system software uses two different methods to avoid duplicate articles. The first is the Path header, which is a record of all the hosts through which a news article has passed. The Path header is just a list of hosts separated by punctuation marks other than periods, which are considered part of a hostname. A Path such as hst.gonzo.com,host-c.big.org!host-b.shark.com means that an article has been processed by each of the sites hst.gonzo.com, host-c.big.org and host-b.shark.com. Any of those hosts can reject the article because their names are already in the path.

RFC 1036 says that the Path header should not be used to generate e-mail reply addresses. However, some obsolete software might try to use it for that. INN discourages this use by inserting the pseudo-host not-for-mail into the Path.

The second way in which news systems avoid duplicate articles is the message identifier header, Message-ID. Here is a sample Message-ID header:

```
Message-ID: <CsuM4v.3u9@hst.gonzo.com>
```

When a news article is created, the posting program, or some other part of the news system, generates this unique header. Because no two articles have the same Message-ID header, the news system can keep track of the message identifiers of all recent articles and reject those that it has already seen. The news `history` file keeps this record, and news transport programs consult the history file when they're offered news articles. Because the volume of news is so large, history files get big pretty fast and are usually kept in some database format that allows quick access.

The history mechanism is not perfect. If you configure your news system to remember the message identifiers of all articles received in the past month, your history files may become inconveniently large. On the other hand, if a news system somewhere malfunctions and injects two-month-old articles into Usenet, you won't have enough of a history to reject those articles. Inevitably, no matter how long a history you keep, it won't be long enough, and you'll get a batch of old, bogus articles. Your users will complain. Such is life.

Host-to-Host News Transport Protocols

As with electronic mail, in order to transfer news from host to host, both hosts must speak the same language. Most Usenet news is transferred either with the UUCP (UNIX-to-UNIX Copy Protocol) or NNTP. UUCP is used by hosts that connect with modems over ordinary phone lines, and NNTP is the method of choice for hosts on the Internet. As mentioned above, you should avoid UUCP if you can.

News Transport System Configuration Files

The news transport system needs a lot of information about your site. Minimally, it must know with which hosts you exchange news, at what times you do so, and what transport protocol you use for each site. It has to know which newsgroups and distributions your site should accept and which it should reject. NNTP sites must know which hosts are authorized to connect with them to read, post, and transfer news.

The news transport system's configuration files provide this information. The news administrator must set up these files when installing the news system and must modify them in response to changes, such as a new newsfeed. The format of news transport system control files varies, but all current systems provide detailed configuration documentation. Read it.

The User Interface—Newsreaders and Posting Programs

Newsreaders are the user interface to reading news. Because news articles are stored as ordinary files, you could use a program such as `cat` or `more` for your news reading, but most users want something more sophisticated. Many newsgroups receive more than a hundred articles a day, and most users don't have time to read them all. They want a program that helps them quickly reject the junk so they can read only articles of interest to them. A good newsreader enables users to select and reject articles based on their `subject` header; several provide even more sophisticated filtering capabilities. Some of the more popular newsreaders are `rn` (and its variant trn), nn, and tin. The GNU Emacs editor also has several packages (GNUS and Gnews) available for news reading from within Emacs. These newsreaders are available for anonymous ftp from the host ftp.uu.net and others.

Newsreaders usually have built-in news posting programs or the capability to call a posting program from within the newsreader. Most of them also let you respond to articles by e-mail.

Newsreaders are like religions and text editors—there are lots of them and no one agrees on which is best. Your users will probably want you to install them all, as well as whatever wonderful new one was posted to comp.sources.unix last week. If you don't have much time for news administration, you may want to resist or suggest the users get their own sources and install private copies. Otherwise, you can spend a lot of time maintaining newsreaders.

News posting programs enable you to post your own articles. A news posting program prepares an article template with properly formatted headers, and then calls the text editor of your choice (usually whatever is named in the EDITOR environment variable) so you can type in your article. When you exit the editor, you're usually given choices to post the article, edit it again, or quit without posting anything. If you choose to post the article, the news posting program hands it to another news system program, which injects it into the news transport system and puts a copy in the news spool directory.

Newsreaders and news posting programs are usually both included in the same package of software. For instance, if you install the rn package you will also install Pnews, its news posting program.

GUI Newsreaders

Listing 25.1 provides an example of the operation of a text-based newsreader. Increasingly, newsreaders are also being incorporated within Web browser applications, providing a graphical view of newsgroups and articles. Figure 25.3 provides a screen shot of the newsreader that is incorporated within a standard Netscape browser.

Notice that the Netscape Newsreader provides a three-way split screen. In the left window, the name of the news server is displayed along with the newsgroups available. For the highlighted newsgroup (comp.protocols.tcp-ip in the example) the right screen details the existing articles. These articles are arranged into separate threads—each thread relating to a particular conversation or related topic. The user can select a particular news article and view it in the bottom window of the newsreader screen.

The benefits of using a graphical newsreader are clearly demonstrated in Figure 25.3. Each of the separate windows is related to the execution of a particular NNTP request message. The user can use the mouse to navigate the information returned by the news server without having to remember the somewhat cryptic command requests listed in Table 25.1.

25

NEWS ADMINISTRATION

Figure 25.3.

Viewing news with Netscape Web browser.

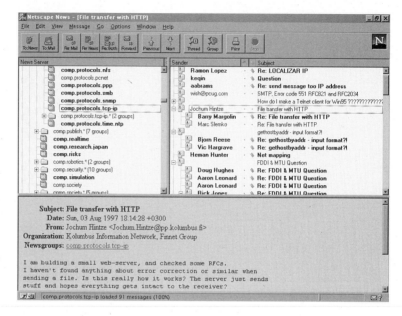

Planning a News System

You can see from the preceding discussion that there are many different strategies you can use to set up a news system. Because sites' needs vary, there is no single right way to do it. You must evaluate your site's needs and choose a strategy that fits. The questions in this section are intended to make you think about some of the issues you should consider.

Do You *Really* Want To Be a Usenet Site?

As pointed out in the "how to join Usenet" FAQ, you may not want to join at all. A newsfeed consumes significant CPU cycles, disk space, network (or modem) bandwidth, and staff time. Many Internet service providers will give your site access to Usenet news over the network through NNTP client newsreaders. If your site is small this may be more economical than a newsfeed. Do yourself a favor and do the math before you jump in. You can always join Usenet at a later date if you find that your site's needs require a real feed.

Shared News Versus One News Spool Per Host

A basic decision is whether you will maintain separate news spools and news systems on all of your hosts, or designate a single host to act as a news server and let other hosts access news through the network. If you have more than one host to administer, there are definite advantages to the latter approach.

If you have a single news host, your job as news administrator is much easier. Most news problems are confined to that host, and you only have to maintain the (fairly complex) news transport software on that host. Software on client hosts is limited to newsreaders and news posting software—no news transport software is necessary. If there are problems, you know where to go to solve them, and once you solve them on the news host, they are solved for all the hosts in your domain.

Usenet volume helps make a single-host strategy attractive. As mentioned previously, a full newsfeed can easily require a gigabyte of disk space, and the volume of Usenet news continues to grow, seemingly without bound. It's a lot easier to convince your boss to buy a bigger disk drive for a single host than for twenty. Because many users don't read news every day, the longer you can retain articles the happier they are, and you can retain articles longer on a single, dedicated news host than you can on multiple hosts.

Economics points to using a single news host both to minimize expensive staff time and to conserve disk space. The only reason you might want to store news on multiple hosts is if your network isn't up to par—if your only network connections are through UUCP, you can't use NNTP or a network file system to share news.

Isolating the News Spool

Most UNIX systems use the file system /var to contain files that grow unpredictably. For instance, /var/mail contains user mailboxes and /var/log contains system log files. Since the news spool is usually located in /var/spool/news, news articles may compete for space with potentially more important data such as e-mail. Having your e-mail system grind to a halt because someone posts his 10 MB collection of Madonna erotica will not endear you to your users or your boss.

The best way around this problem is to isolate the news spool in its own disk partition. If /var/spool/news is mounted on its own disk partition and it fills up, only the news system is affected.

The disadvantage of this approach is that it forces you to pre-allocate disk space. If you allocate too little to the news spool, you'll have to either expire articles sooner than you'd like or spend a lot of time fixing things by hand when the spool directory fills. If you allocate too much, it can't be used by other file systems, so you waste space. (However, it's better to guess too big than too little. Remember that the volume of Usenet news constantly increases.)

Depending on how flexible your UNIX is, if you guess wrong and have to resize your partitions, it may be painful. You must resize at least two adjoining disk partitions to shrink or enlarge the news spool, which means dumping all the data in the partitions, creating new ones, and restoring the data. (A safer approach is to dump all the data on the disk and verify that you can read the backup tapes before you resize the partitions.) During this operation, the news system (and probably the computer) are unavailable.

Configuring Your News Spool's File System

Before you can use a disk partition, you must create a UNIX file system on it, using newfs, a front-end to the harder-to-use mkfs program. (Some versions of UNIX use mkdev fs to create file systems. Consult your system's administration manual.) Unless you tell it otherwise, newfs uses its built-in default for the ratio of *inodes* (index nodes) to disk blocks. Inodes are pre-allocated, and when you run out of them, no new files can be created, even if you have disk space available in the file system. The newfs default for inodes is usually about right for most file systems but may not be for the news spool. News articles tend to be small, so you may run out of inodes in your news spool before you run out of disk space. On the other hand, since each pre-allocated inode takes some disk space, if you allocate too many you'll waste disk space.

Most likely you'll want to tell newfs to create additional inodes when you create your news spool. The hard question is how many additional inodes to allocate. If your news system is already running, you can use the df command to find out. Simply compare the percentage of inodes in use to the percentage of disk blocks in use. If they are about the same, you're doing okay. If the disk block usage is a lot greater than the inodes in use, you've allocated too many inodes. What is more likely is that the inodes in use greatly outnumber the available disk blocks. The solution is to shut down your news system, dump the news spool to tape, run newfs to make a file system with more inodes, and restore the news spool from tape.

Where Will You Get Your News?

Some organizations use Usenet for internal communications—for instance, a corporate BBS—and don't need or want to connect to Usenet. However, if you want a Usenet connection, you'll have to find one or more hosts willing to exchange news with you. Note that they are doing you a big favor—a full newsfeed consumes a lot of CPU cycles, network bandwidth, and staff time. The spirit of Usenet, however, is altruistic, and you may find a host willing to supply you with a newsfeed for free. In turn, you may someday be asked to supply a feed to someone else.

Finding a host willing to give you a newsfeed is easier if you're already on Usenet, but if you were, you wouldn't need one. Your Internet service provider might be able to give you contact information, and many service providers supply newsfeeds, either as part of their basic service or at additional cost. Personal contacts with other system administrators who are already connected to Usenet may help, even if they can't supply you a feed themselves. The "how to join Usenet" FAQ mentioned previously contains other good ideas for finding a newsfeed.

It's a good idea to try to find a newsfeed that is topographically close on your network. If your site is in Indiana, you don't want a transatlantic feed from Finland, even if you manage to find a host there willing to do it.

Site Policies

Your users' Usenet articles reflect on your site, and new users often make mistakes. Unfortunately, the kinds of mistakes you can make on a worldwide network are the really bad ones. You should develop organizational Usenet access policies and educate your users on proper Usenet etiquette.

Policy questions tend toward the ethical and legal. For instance, if you carry the `alt` hierarchy, what will be your site's response when someone creates the newsgroup `alt.child-molesting.advocacy`? This is not beyond the pale of what you may expect in the `alt` hierarchy. Even within the traditional hierarchies, where newsgroups are voted into existence, you might find newsgroups your site won't want to carry. What will you do when you receive a letter from `joe@remote.site.edu`, whining that one of your users is polluting his favorite newsgroup with "inappropriate" (in his opinion) postings? Do you want to get involved in Usenet squabbles like that?

What will you do when you get 2,843 letters complaining that one of your users posted a pyramid-scheme come-on to 300 different newsgroups? Shoot him? Or maybe wish you'd done a more careful job of setting policy in the first place? And what will you do when someone complains that the postings in `alt.binaries.pictures.erotica.blondes` are a form of sexual harassment and demands that the newsgroup be removed? Will you put yourself in the position of censor and drop that newsgroup, or drop the entire `alt` hierarchy to avoid having to judge the worth of a single newsgroup?

If you put yourself in the position of picking and choosing newsgroups, you will find that while it may be completely obvious to you that `comp.risks` has merit and `alt.spam` doesn't, your users may vehemently disagree. If you propose to locally delete `alt.spam` to conserve computing resources, some users will refer to their right to free speech and accuse you of censorship and fascism. (Are you sure you wanted this job?)

Most news administrators don't want to be censors or arbiters of taste. Therefore, answers to policy questions should be worked out in advance, codified as site policy, and approved by management. You need to hammer away at your boss until you get a written policy telling you what you should and should not do with respect to news administration, and you need to do this before you join Usenet. Such a policy should also provide for user education and set bounds for proper user behavior.

Without taking a position on the merits of `alt.spam`, Usenet access is not one of the fundamental rights enumerated in the United States Constitution. It's more like a driver's license—if you're willing to follow your site's rules, you can drive, and if you're not, you can't. It's management's job to provide those rules, with guidance from you.

Expiration Policies

News system software is flexible enough to selectively purge old articles. In other words, if your site doesn't care much about the `alt` hierarchy but considers the `comp` hierarchy to be important, it can retain `comp` articles longer than `alt` articles. From the preceding discussion, you can see that this might be contentious. If Joe thinks that `alt.spam` is the greatest thing since indoor plumbing, he will cry foul if you expire `spam` articles in one day but retain `comp` articles for seven. You can see that article expiration is not just a technical issue but a policy issue and should be covered in the same written policies mentioned previously.

Automatic Response to `newgroup`/`rmgroup` Control Messages

Newsgroups are created and removed by special news articles called control messages. Anyone bright enough to understand RFCs 1036 and 977 can easily forge control messages to create and remove newsgroups. (That is, just about anyone.) This is a particular problem in the `alt` hierarchy, which for some reason attracts people with too much time on their hands, who enjoy creating newsgroups such as `alt.swedish-chef.bork.bork.bork`. The `alt` hierarchy also is used by people who don't want to go to the trouble of creating a new newsgroup through a Usenet-wide vote, or who (usually correctly) guess that their hare-brained proposal wouldn't pass even the fairly easy Usenet newsgroup creation process.

Another problem, somewhat less frequent, occurs when a novice news administrator posts newsgroup messages with incorrect distributions and floods the net with requests to create his local groups.

You can configure your news system software to create and delete groups automatically upon receiving control messages, or to send e-mail to the news administrator saying that the group should be created or removed. If you like living dangerously, you can enable automatic creation and deletion, but most people don't. You don't want someone to delete all your newsgroups just to see if he can, and you don't want two or three hundred created because a news system administrator made a distribution mistake. Many sites allow automatic creation but do deletions manually. More cautious sites create and delete all groups by hand, and only if they have reason to believe the control message is valid. I recommend the latter approach. The only disadvantage is that you may miss the first few articles posted to a new newsgroup if you don't stay on top of things.

The ABCs of News Transport Software

Usenet began with A-news, a prototype news transport system that was killed by its own success and was supplanted by B-news. B-news sufficed for quite a while but became another victim of Usenet growth and was supplanted by C-news, a much more efficient system written by Henry Spencer and Geoff Collyer of the University of Toronto. C-news was followed by INN (InterNetworkNews), which was originally written by Rich Salz of the Open Software Foundation, who apparently hadn't heard of the letter "D." Rich has since passed responsibility for INN over to the Internet Software Consortium (ISC), which now is the official source for all INN releases. The Consortium can be located at the URL, `http://www.isc.org/isc`.

Depending on your site's requirements, either C-news, INN or even Netscape's New Server make good news transport systems, but this chapter has space for only one, INN. If you install C-news and your site plans to use NNTP, you should also obtain and install the NNTP "reference implementation," that is available by anonymous ftp from the URL `ftp://ftp.uu.net/~ftp/networking/news/nntp`. This isn't necessary for INN, which has a slightly modified version of NNTP built in.

INN is the news transport system of choice for Internet sites that use NNTP to exchange news and provide newsreaders and news posting services. It was designed specifically for efficiency in an Internet/NNTP environment, for hosts with many newsfeeds and lots of NNTP client newsreaders. Although its installation isn't as automated as C-news, it's not all that difficult, and it's well-documented. The following sections give an overview of how to build and install INN.

Getting Your Hands on the Sources

The latest version of INN available as this book goes to press is called INN 1.5.1. It is available from `ftp://ftp.vix.com/pub/inn` or in one of the mirror sites that have been set up by the ISC. Refer to the ISC Web site at `http://www.isc.org/inn.HTML` for more information. It is important to note that a patch has been released to fix a security bug found within INN 1.5.1. This patch is also available via the ISC and can be found at their ftp site at `ftp://ftp.isc.org/isc/inn/unoff-patches`.

An INN Distribution Roadmap

Most of the important directories and programs in the INN distribution are summarized in the following list. Some are covered in more detail in the sections "Configuring INN—the `config.data` File," "Building INN," and "Site Configuration."

BUILD	A shell script for building and installing INN.
Install.ms.*	The `nroff` sources to INN's installation documentation.
README	What you might think. Read it.
backends	Programs for transferring news to your Usenet neighbors.
config	Contains the file `config.dist`, with which you create `config.data`. `config.data` controls the compilation of the rest of INN.
dbz	Sources for the database routines used by INN. `dbz` is a faster version of the `dbm` database programs included with many versions of UNIX.
doc	INN's manual pages.
expire	Contains programs that handle news expiration, or the purging of articles from your news spool. They also selectively purge old `Message-IDs` from the history file so it doesn't grow boundlessly.
frontends	Contains programs that control `innd`'s operation or offer it news articles.
include	C language header files for the INN programs.

innd	The heart of INN, innd is the daemon that listens on the NNTP port for incoming news transfers and newsreader connections. When newsreaders connect to this port, innd creates nnrpd processes and connects them to the newsreader.
lib	The sources for the C language function library used by other INN programs.
nnrpd	Communicates with NNTP newsreader clients, which frees innd to do its main job, transferring news.
samples	Sample configuration files that are copied into the site directory.
site	This directory contains shell scripts and site configuration files. The site configuration files must be edited to tell INN with which sites you exchange news, which hosts are allowed to connect to read and post news, and so on.
syslog	A replacement for older versions of the standard system logging program. You may not need this.

Learning About INN

The first step in setting up INN is to format and read its documentation. cd into the top of the INN source tree and type the following to create a formatted copy of the INN documentation named Install.txt:

```
$ make Install.ms
cat Install.ms.1 Install.ms.2 >Install.ms
chmod 444 Install.ms
$ nroff -ms Install.ms > Install.txt
```

If the make command doesn't work for you (and if it doesn't, your make is defective and will cause you problems later), type **cat Install.ms.? > Install.ms** and then the preceding nroff command. These two commands create a file named Install.txt, which you can view with your preferred editor or pager. Read it. Print it. Highlight it with your favorite color of fluorescent marker. Sleep with it under your pillow. Take it into the shower. Share it with your friends. Read it again. You won't be sorry.

The Install.ms document tells you just about everything you need to know to set up a news system based on INN. The only problem with it is that many people fail to read it carefully and think that there's something missing. There isn't. If you think there is, read it again. Buy a new fluorescent marker, print off a copy of the file, and sit down with a nice glass of your favorite tea. Put it back under your pillow. Discuss it at dinner parties until your hosts ask you to leave, and ask your spouse what she or he thinks about it. You may destroy your social life, but in the process you'll discover that you missed a few crucial bits of information the first time around. (Don't feel bad, nearly everyone does.)

Configuring INN—the `config.data` File

Once you've absorbed the INN documentation, you're ready to configure INN's compilation environment. Like C-news, INN can run on many different versions of UNIX. The programs that build INN need information about your version of UNIX so they can build INN correctly. This configuration is one of the most difficult parts of installing INN, and you must make sure that you get it right. The `Install.ms` documentation is essential because it contains sample configurations for many different versions of UNIX.

The directory `config` holds the INN master configuration file, `config.data`. INN uses the C-news `subst` program to modify its sources before compilation, and `config.data` provides the information `subst` needs to do its job. `Subst` uses the definitions in `config.data` to modify the INN source files before they are compiled.

INN supplies a prototype version of `config.data` named `config.dist`. `Config.dist` is almost undoubtedly wrong for your UNIX. You must create your own version of `config.data`:

```
$ cd config
$ cp config.dist config.data
```

Now edit `config.data` to match your site's version of UNIX. As mentioned earlier, this is one of the hardest parts of installing INN. `Config.data` is about 700 lines long, and there's nothing for it but to go through it line by line and make the appropriate changes. Depending on how experienced you are, you may have to set aside several hours for this task. `Install.ms` devotes about 18 pages to `config.data`, and you should refer to it as you edit.

Unless you know off the top of your head the answers to questions such as, "How does your UNIX set non-blocking I/O?", you'll need to keep your programmer's manuals handy. If you have a workstation, you can edit `config.data` in one window and use another to inspect your system's online documentation. `Install.ms` gives sample configurations for many popular versions of UNIX. If your version is listed, use its values. (That doesn't, however, relieve you of the chore of inspecting the entire file.)

TIP

The `subst` program, originally supplied with C-news and used in INN by the kind permission of Geoff Collyer and Henry Spencer, is a clever shell script that relies on the sed program to do much of its work. The INN `config.dist` file is large enough to break some vendor's versions of sed. To see whether your vendor's sed works with INN, cd into the `config` directory and type the following:

```
$ cp config.dist config.data
$ make sedtest
```

If this test fails, the simplest workaround is to type **make c quiet** to create a C language version of the `subst` program. You should also gripe at your UNIX vendor for foisting a substandard sed onto you, an unsuspecting customer.

Once you've edited `config.data`, you're ready to let `subst` configure the INN sources. From within the `config` directory, type the following:

```
$ make quiet
```

Building INN

Now that INN is configured, you're ready to build the system. `Install.ms` gives several ways to do this, depending on how trusting you are and your general philosophy of life. If you're the kind of person who likes cars with automatic transmission, you can `cd` to the top of the INN source tree, type `./BUILD`, and answer its questions. The `BUILD` shell script compiles and installs INN without much input from you.

If you prefer to shift gears yourself, from the same directory you can type the following:

```
$ make world
$ cat */lint | more
```

Carefully inspect the `lint` output for errors. (See the following Tip.)

> **TIP**
>
> The `lint` program detects errors in C language programs. Because C is a fairly permissive language, it lets you do things you probably shouldn't, and `lint` helps you find these bits of fluff in your programs and correct them. For instance, `lint` can tell you if you're passing the wrong number (or type) of arguments to a C language function. Remember, just because a program compiles doesn't mean it will work correctly when you run it. If `lint` finds errors in your INN configuration after you've run `subst`, there may be a problem you need to correct by editing `config.data` and rebuilding your system. Unfortunately, `lint` sometimes reports spurious errors. You'll have to consult the programmers's section of your system's manual pages to be sure which errors are real and which are not.

You'll learn the most about INN if you compile it bit by bit with `Install.ms` by your side. You may think that if INN is so simple to install you should take the easy road and use `BUILD`. But news systems are complex, and no matter how good they are, you will inevitably have some problems to solve. When you do, you'll need all the clues you can muster, and building INN step-by-step helps you learn more about it. Someday, when the weasels are at the door, you'll be glad you did.

The step-by-step compilation procedure is fairly simple. First build the INN library:

```
$ cd lib
$ make libinn.a lint 2>&1 | tee errs
$ cd ..
```

The `tee` command prints the output of the `make` command to your terminal and saves it to the file `errs`. If you use an ugly shell such as `csh` or one of its variants, type `sh` or `ksh` before executing the preceding command, or read your shell's manual page for the correct syntax to save the standard output and standard error of a command into a file.

The make command creates a library of C language functions used by the other INN programs and a lint library to help detect possible problems with it. Since the other INN programs depend on the INN library, it's crucial that you compile it correctly. Check the output in the file errs and assure yourself that any errors detected by your C compiler or lint are innocuous. If you find errors (especially compiler warnings), it's probably due to a mistake you've made in config.data. The only solution is to correct config.data, run subst again, and recompile libinn.a.

After you've successfully built the INN library, you can build the rest of INN. cd into each of the following directories in turn: frontends, innd, nnrpd, backends, and expire. In each directory, type the following:

```
$ make all 2>&1 ¦ tee errs
```

Check the output in the file errs. If there are compiler warnings or lint errors, do not pass go and do not collect $200. Consult your system's online documentation, edit config.data to correct the problems, rerun subst, and recompile the system beginning with libinn.a.

> **WARNING**
>
> The disadvantage of using subst to configure INN is that most of the system depends on the config.data file. If, at any stage in building the system, you discover errors that require you to change config.data, you must rerun subst and recompile all of INN, beginning with libinn.a.

Installing INN

Now you're ready to install INN. Assuming that everything has gone well so far, cd to the root of the INN source tree, type **su** to become the superuser, and type this:

```
$ sh makedirs.sh 2>&1 ¦ tee errs
$ make update 2>&1 ¦ tee -a errs
```

This runs the commands to install INN and saves the output in the file errs, which you should carefully inspect for errors. Note the -a argument to tee in the second command line, which makes tee append to the file errs.

The makedirs.sh shell script creates the directories for the INN system and must be run before you type **make update**. The latter command installs INN in the directories created by makedirs.sh. Now you've installed the INN programs and are ready to configure your news system.

Site Configuration

cd into the site directory and type **make all 2>&1 ¦ tee errs**. This command copies files from the samples and backends directories and runs subst over them. Some of these files must be edited before you install INN. They give INN information it can't figure out on its own; for instance, with which hosts you exchange news.

The site directory also contains some utility shell scripts. You probably won't have to change these, but you should look at them to see what they do and ensure that paths to programs in them are correct.

Modifying the files in the site directory is the second most difficult part of configuring INN, especially if you haven't configured a news system before. However, INN won't work if these files aren't configured correctly, so you'll want to spend some time here. The files you must edit are shown below, each with a brief explanation of its function. There are manual pages for each of these files in the doc directory, and you'll need to read them carefully in order to understand their function and syntax.

expire.ctl controls article expiration policy. In it, you list a series of patterns to match newsgroup names and what actions expire should take for groups that match. This means that you can expire newsgroups selectively. The expire.ctl file is also where you tell expire how long you want it to remember Message-IDs. You can't keep a record of Message-IDs forever because your history file would grow without bounds. Expire not only removes articles from the news spool but controls how long their Message-IDs are kept in the history file.

hosts.nntp lists the hosts that feed you news through NNTP. The main news daemon innd reads this file when it starts. If a host not listed in this file connects to innd, it assumes it's a newsreader and creates an nnrpd process to service it. If the host is in the file, innd accepts incoming news articles from it.

inn.conf contains some site configuration defaults, such as the names put in an article's Organization and From headers. For instance, your organization might want all From headers to appear as From: *someone@mailhub.corp*.com, regardless of which host posted the article. Some of these defaults may be overridden by environment variables. For instance, if the user sets the ORGANIZATION environment variable, it overrides the default in inn.conf.

Articles posted to a moderated newsgroup are first mailed to the newsgroup's moderator, who approves (or disapproves) the article. If it's approved, the moderator posts it with an Approved header containing his e-mail address. The moderators file tells INN where to mail these articles.

The newsfeeds file describes the sites to which you feed news, and how you feed them. This is something you will already have arranged with the administrator of the sites which you feed. The important thing is for both sites to agree. For instance, if you feed the alt.binaries groups to a site that doesn't want them, it discards the articles, and you both waste a lot of CPU time and network bandwidth in the process. The newsfeeds file enables you to construct specific lists of newsgroups for each site you feed. For instance, one site might not want to receive any of the `alt` groups, and another might want all of the `alt` newsgroups except for the `alt.binaries` newsgroups. The `newsfeeds` file is also where you specify INN's behavior with respect to an article's `Distribution` headers. There are other parameters you can set here to determine whether articles are transmitted, such as maximum message size.

`nnrp.access` controls which hosts (and optionally, users) can access your NNTP server. When a newsreader connects to the NNTP port, `innd` hooks it up with an `nnrpd` process so it can read and post news. The `nnrpd` program reads the `nnrpd.access` file to see whether that host is allowed to read or post. The hosts may be specified as patterns, so it's easy to allow access to all the hosts in your organization. Reading and posting can also be controlled on a per user basis if your newsreader knows how to use the `authinfo` command, a common extension to NNTP.

`passwd.nntp` contains `hostname:user:password` triplets for an NNTP client (for example, a newsreader) to use in authenticating itself to an NNTP server.

Once you've edited the files in `site`, install them:

```
$ make install 2>&1 ¦ tee errs
```

As usual, carefully inspect the `make` command's output for any problems.

System Startup Scripts and news cron Jobs

A news system doesn't run on its own. You must modify your system's boot sequence to start parts of it and create `cron` jobs for the `news` user to perform other tasks.

INN supplies the file `rc.news` to start the news system when your computer boots. For most SVR4 hosts, you should install it as `/etc/init.d/news` and make a hard link to it named `/etc/rc2.d/S99news`. (See the section "Modifying `sendmail`'s Boot-Time Startup" in Chapter 41 for more information on how SVR4 systems boot.)

The shell script `news.daily` should be run as a `cron` job from the `news` user's crontab. `News.daily` handles article expiration and calls the `scanlogs` shell script to process news log files. You should probably schedule this for a time when most people aren't using the news system, such as after midnight.

You'll also need to add a `news` user `cron` entry to transmit news to your Usenet neighbors. INN supplies sample shell scripts that show several different ways to do this for both NNTP and UUCP neighbors. The scripts are copied into the `site` directory. The shell scripts `nntpsend` (and its control file `nntpsend.ctl`), `send-ihave`, and `send-nntp` are various ways to transfer news through NNTP. The scripts `send-uucp` and `sendbatch` are for sites using UUCP. Pick the one that most closely suits your site's needs, and add its invocation to the `news` user's crontab.

If you use `sendbatch`, edit it to ensure that the output of the `df` command on your system matches what the script expects. Unfortunately, the output of `df` varies a lot between vendors, and if `sendbatch` misinterprets it, you may have problems with your news spool filling up.

How often you should run the shell script depends on the needs of the site you're feeding. If it's an NNTP site and it wants to receive your articles as soon as they are posted, you could run one of the NNTP submission scripts every five minutes. If it's a UUCP site or an NNTP site on the end of a slow link, it might want news much less often. You must work this out with the remote site and make sure that your setup matches what it wants.

Miscellaneous Final Tasks

The active file shows what newsgroups are valid on your system. If you're converting to INN from another news system, you can convert your existing active file. Otherwise, you may want to get a copy of your feed site's active file and edit it to remove newsgroups you don't want and add local groups.

You must also create a history file or convert your existing one. Appendix II of `Install.ms` gives information for converting an existing news installation to INN.

Even if you didn't run the `BUILD` shell script to build and install INN, you can save the last 71 lines of it into a file and run that file to build a minimal active file and history database. You can then add whatever lines you want to the active file.

Some vendors' versions of `sed`, `awk`, and `grep` are deficient and may need to be replaced with better versions before INN can function correctly. The GNU project's versions of these commands work well with INN. They are available for anonymous ftp from the host `ftp://prep.ai.mit.edu` in the directory `~ftp/pub/gnu`.

You may also have to modify your `syslog.conf` file to match the logging levels used by INN. These logging levels are defined in `config/config.data`, and the file `syslog/syslog.conf` shows sample changes you may need to make to your `syslog.conf`.

Checking Your Installation and Problem Solving

If you have Perl installed on your system, you can run the `inncheck` program to check your installation. You should also try posting articles, first to the local group `test` and then to groups with wider distributions. Make sure that articles are being transmitted to your Usenet neighbors.

If you have problems, many of the INN programs are shell scripts and you can see what they're doing by typing **sh -x** *scriptname*. You might also temporarily modify a script to invoke its programs with their verbose options turned on. For instance, the `nntpsend` article submission shell script calls the `innxmit` program to do the work. If `nntpsend` wasn't working for you, you could edit it to turn on `innxmit`'s verbose option (-v), run it by hand as **sh -x nntpsend**, and save the results to a file.

Some simple NNTP server problems can be checked with the `telnet` command. If you know the NNTP protocol, you can simply `telnet` to a host's NNTP port and type commands to the NNTP server. For instance:

```
$ telnet some.host.edu nntp
Trying 123.45.67.8 ...
Connected to some.host.edu.
Escape character is '^]'.
200 somehost NNTP server version 1.5.11 (10 February 1991) ready at Sun Jul 17
19:32:15 1994 (posting ok).
quit
```

(If your `telnet` command doesn't support the mnemonic name for the port, substitute `119` for `nntp` in the command above.) In this example, no NNTP commands were given other than `quit`, but at least you can see that the NNTP server on `some.host.edu` is willing to let you read and post news.

Getting Help

If your news system develops problems you can't solve on your own, `comp.news.software.b` and `comp.news.software.nntp` are good resources. You'll get much better advice if you do two things: First, read the INN FAQ and other INN documentation and see if the problem is listed there. Imagine your embarrassment when you ask your burning question and the collective answer is, "It's in the FAQ. Read it." Second, make sure you include enough information for people to help you. A surprising number of problem posts don't even tell what version of UNIX the person uses. Your article should include the following:

- A specific description of your operating system version and hardware. (For example, "A Sun4c running Solaris 2.3 with the following patches applied…")

- The version of news software you're running and any patches you may have applied to it ("I'm running the Dec 22 release of INN 1.4sec"), as well an any configuration information that seems relevant, such as the contents of `config/config.data` or the configuration files installed from the `site` directory.

- A detailed description of the problem you're having, what you've done to try to solve it, and what the results were. (For example, "I get a permission denied message when I try to post news. I've tried changing the `nnrp.access` file, but I still can't post.")

If you do a good job of researching your posting, you may even figure out the problem on your own. If you don't, you'll get much better advice for having done the work to include the necessary details.

Summary

This chapter gives you a good start on becoming a news administrator, but installing the software is only the beginning of what you'll need to know to keep your news system running. Most of your additional learning will probably be in the form of on-the-job training, solving the little (and big) crises your news system creates. Your best defense against this mid-crisis style of training is to read the INN manual pages, the INN and `news.software.b` FAQs, and the `news.software.*` newsgroups. The more information you pick up before something goes wrong, the better prepared you are to handle it.

UUCP Administration

by James C. Armstrong, Jr.

IN THIS CHAPTER

Long before the days of Networking, TCP/IP, NFS, and the like, there was still the need for UNIX machines to communicate with each other, to pass data, and to transfer files. Modern networks make this task easy, but if your machine is not attached to one of these networks, or if there is no direct network connection between your machine's network and the target machine's network, then there must be a technique for this communication. The package that handles these transfers is UUCP.

UUCP was originally written by Mike Lesk at Bell Labs in the mid-1970s, to facilitate communication between the growing network of UNIX machines. It has been modified several times since then, with the most fundamental changes occurring in 1983, when UUCP was rewritten by Peter Honeyman, David A. Nowitz, and Brian E. Redman. This is the standard UUCP distributed with System V Release 4, and sometimes goes by the moniker HoneyDanBer. It is this version of UUCP that this chapter covers.

What Is UUCP?

UUCP is the package of commands that allows a user to transfer data from one machine to another across a serial port, usually via a modem. Probably the most common uses of UUCP are the transfer of network e-mail and netnews, as described in Chapter 24, "Mail Administration," and Chapter 25, "News Administration." In both cases, the underlying UUCP commands are hidden from the regular user.

Transferring Files

The most likely contact a regular UNIX user has with UUCP is the command uucp. This is just an expansion of the cp command, with a special format to indicate the transfer to a new machine. The target machine and path are illustrated with an exclamation point. Assume that I have a file named data on a local machine named duke. I want to transfer that file to my home directory, /usr/james, on a machine named unc. This is the command I'd use:

```
uucp data unc!/usr/james/data
```

I do not need to specify the machine I am on, so I indicate just the current file. I then indicate that I want to send the file to the machine unc, with the filename there as /usr/james/data. This is an example of pushing a file to a new machine via uucp.

> **CAUTION**
>
> Most systems set up permissions on data transfers that make the uucp command invalid, unless copied to one specific directory on the remote machine. Furthermore, setting permissions to allow transfers to and from any directory is very risky and is not secure. Permissions are discussed later in the chapter.

Files may also be pulled from machines. Suppose I have successfully copied data to unc, and now I need a copy back. I can do this with this command:

```
uucp unc!/usr/james/data .
```

In this case, the source file is on the unc machine, and I pull over a copy. If unc has the correct permissions, I can pull the needed file over to my machine and place it in my current directory.

Files can be transferred from one remote machine to another. In the first example, if I were on machine ncsu when I wanted to transfer a file from duke to unc, I could do it with this command:

```
uucp duke!/usr/james/data unc!/usr/james/data 2
```

The syntax of the command says "Go to machine duke and find the file /usr/james/data, then send it to machine unc to the destination /usr/james/data 2." Finally, if I want to send the file from duke to wake, but wake only has a link with unc, I can specify a path like this:

```
uucp duke!/usr/james/data unc!wake!/usr/james/data
```

If the permissions at unc allow the transfer, the file is first sent to unc, then sent from unc to wake.

> **NOTE**
>
> You may have attempted these commands and received an error message such as /usr/james/data: Event not found. This is because the ! is significant to the C shell—it implies history substitution. To avoid this problem, you should escape the ! with a backslash (\), making the command uucp duke\!/usr/james/data unc\!/usr/james/data. This will also work with the Bourne and Korn shells and is a practice I find useful.

> **TIP**
>
> A much easier technique for transferring files from the local machine to a remote machine is using uuto and uupick. These commands are simply shell scripts that change their arguments into a well-constructed uucp command for you. Their usage is described in more detail in the section "UUCP Utilities."

Running Remote Commands

UUCP also provides a command that allows the user to run commands remotely. The uux command enables a user to request that a remote machine run a command. It will accept redirection of standard input and output, and options can be used to indicate that the redirection should apply to the remote command's execution. For example, this command will return the output of the date command as run on unc:

```
uux unc!date
```

uux is normally hidden from the user, but it is the backbone for mail and news transfer. On my machine, I transfer news to a remote machine by piping the article into the command uux - -r -gd netcomsv!rnews. While this may look complicated, all it really says is that the standard input of this command will be fed to the remote machine netcomsv, and there the command rnews will be run. The -r option says to queue the request, and -gd sets a system priority on the request. Both options could easily be omitted.

The command for transferring mail is even simpler. When my mailer gets the request to send mail to a remote system, it executes uux - -r netcomsv!rmail. This is simplicity itself—it just pipes the mail message to rmail on netcomsv.

> **NOTE**
>
> For security reasons, most sites have cut off remote execution of commands other than rmail and rnews. If you plan on needing to execute commands other than rnews and rmail, you should consult with the administrator of the remote machine.

Under It All

Beneath all the UUCP commands is the uucico command. This is the process that implements the actual communication between UNIX machines. Most users will never need to use this command, and its use by administrators is also rare.

uucico examines a series of data files to make its connection. These files include information such as which tty is used as a port, what modem commands are needed to use the attached modem, what is the phone number of the remote system, and what is the login protocol. Attached to both the modem commands and the login commands are what is called a "chat script." These chat scripts are the essence of UUCP communications.

Chat Scripts

Chat scripts are simply pairs of expect/send sequences. When all the criteria are met for communications, the uucico process waits on the port until it sees the next expect sequence. After that sequence is seen, the next send sequence is sent down the line. If the expect sequence is not seen in a certain period of time, a time-out occurs, and a different send sequence can be sent. If all expect/send sequences are completed, the connection starts to transfer data. If the send sequences are exhausted and no connection is made, the command fails.

The following is an example of a chat script for logging in to a machine:

```
"" \n in:--in: mylogin word: mypassword
```

Interpreted, this means that I first expect nothing and send a carriage return. When I see the sequence `in:`, I send the sequence `mylogin`. If I don't see `in:`, then I wait for a time-out and send a new carriage return and continue to look for `in:`. Once I send `mylogin`, I wait for `word:`. Once I see that, I send `mypassword` and expect to start the data transfer.

The `--` in the `expect` sequence indicates that I might get a time-out and I might need to send more data. Any character sequence can be between the two dashes, and these are sent, along with a carriage return, and then a time-out occurs. Any number of these time-out sequences can occur in an expect pattern. If a line is known to be slow to acknowledge the connection, one may see the sequence `in:--in:--in:--in:`, which means to try four times to get the `login:` prompt before timing out. Some experimentation may be necessary to determine the exact chat script to connect to a machine. This is described in the section "Setting Up UUCP."

> **CAUTION**
>
> Permissions to see the UUCP chat scripts should be restricted. One of the limitations of UUCP is that the remote machine passwords must be listed in the chat script and must be clear ASCII text. Anyone with the correct permissions can look at the file and steal the passwords for UUCP. None of the passwords indicated in this chapter are real.

Connection Files

The first task of `uucico` is to determine the target machine for the connection. When it determines the machine name, it examines the Systems file. This includes the system name, the connect times, devices, and speeds, the connection address, and the chat script to make the connection. This is not enough to make the connection.

Given the device type and speed, `uucico` must next examine the Devices file. This provides a list of devices and speeds, and associates them with actual ports and dialers to connect with those ports.

The dialers to connect to the port need to be looked up in the Dialers file, where a specific dialer can be associated with a chat script. That chat script should set up the modem in the proper format, and then dial the address provided by the Systems file. Sometimes, this address may need further expanding. The Dialcodes file provides some expansion for the address.

Addresses need not be telephone numbers. UUCP is capable of handling telephone calls via modems, as well as connections via local area networks such as Starlan, and even direct connections between machines. Each one requires different devices and dialer chat scripts to make the connection.

Setting Up UUCP

UUCP requires two sites willing to set up a connection. In the early days of UNIX, this was simply a matter of calling local UNIX sites and asking if they would be willing to transfer data for you. In those days, often the answer was yes, and you'd set up a link. With the development of the Internet, these connections are becoming less frequent, and many main sites no longer even use UUCP.

For my home machine, I sought a service provider. The local provider with a decent reputation was Netcom, based in the San Francisco Bay area. Netcom offers a UUCP service for a reasonable amount each month, including registering a domain name for Internet addressing. Netcom is not the only provider, but it's local for me.

When you've found a partner for exchanging UUCP, you'll need to determine how the connections will be made. There are three options: Your site could make all the calls to the provider's site (this is fairly standard with paid service providers), your site could receive calls only from the remote site, or the calls could go both ways. This results in two different administrative tasks for UUCP: setting up your system to receive calls and setting up your system to place calls.

Receiving UUCP Calls

Since UUCP accesses a system in the same way as a user—by logging in—you'll need to set up your system to allow UUCP to log in. One of your serial ports will need a modem attached. One action you'll need to take is to establish an account for UUCP to use. You'll need to use your administrative tools to edit the /etc/passwd file. You'll need root permissions to create the account. Some UNIX systems come with a default entry, nuucp, for UUCP connections. I prefer to set up a different account for each machine, prefixing the machine name with a U. That way I know just by using the who command who is logging in to transfer data at what times.

TIP

Prefixing UUCP accounts with U also increases the administrative trail of user logins; although UUCP does give excellent logs, by keeping different login names the /etc/wtmp file will also keep a record that can identify call times and durations.

The /etc/passwd entry should have the same owner and group as your uucp account. This way, the remote site will be able to write correctly to the designated files; UUCP does not run in any privileged mode—it is just another user on the system. You should also make the home directory /var/spool/uucppublic. This directory is a standard UNIX directory, designated for file transfers. It should be owned by uucp, it should be of group uucp, and it should have permissions set to 777. That way, any user desiring to transfer files can write to the directory.

The unique aspect of the /etc/passwd entry is the default shell. Most users will have something like /bin/sh, /bin/csh, or some other command shell. Your UUCP entry should have /usr/lib/uucp/uucico, which is the command for data transfer. This means that when your UUCP successfully logs in, it will immediately start to transfer files.

> **NOTE**
>
> You may have noticed that the same transfer command is used both for sending and receiving data. So how do you know which is which? It's simple—you don't. The same uucico command will both send and receive files during a single phone call. The two commands stay synchronized because of the master/slave role. The command that is sending is considered the master, the command receiving is the slave. The slave role is the default. To be the master uucico, the uucico command must receive the flag -r1. Master and slave roles can switch during a phone call, and there is no limit to the number of times this switch happens.

You will also need to set a password for the UUCP account. To do this, you need to be root. Run the passwd command on the account and enter a password. After you have done this, you can notify the other site of its UUCP account and password.

> **TIP**
>
> For the password you can use any combination of characters that are valid, and because this is not one you'll need to keep memorized, it can be any random sequence desired.

This is not all that's needed to set up the connection, however. You'll need to run the command that gives the UNIX prompt, /etc/getty. This command is kept in the file /etc/inittab. You'll need to include an entry that looks like this:

```
ucp:23:respawn:/etc/getty ttya 9600
```

Each field is separated by colons, so this has four fields. The first is a unique identifier in the inittab and can be anything. The second field specifies run states, the third is an action, and the fourth is a command. This file is monitored by the init daemon. The respawn action indicates that when a command is finished, a new getty command should be run. The run states indicate that the command should be run only in multiuser mode.

getty is the standard UNIX command for providing a login prompt. The two arguments indicate which port is used and the expected speed. Here the modem is on ttya and is 9600 baud. Your port and numbers may be different.

There is a problem with getty: It can only receive calls. If you intend for your modem to have two-way traffic, you'll need to use the uugetty command. This command will know not to put up a login prompt when you are using the port to make outgoing calls. To use it, replace /etc/getty with /usr/lib/uucp/uugetty -r. The -r option tells uugetty not to put up a login prompt until it gets a character, which is usually a carriage return.

Permissions also need to be set, restricting what the calling system can do to your system. These will be covered later in the chapter, but for starters, consider restricting read and write access to /var/spool/uucppublic, and allow only the execution of rmail, and if you want netnews, rnews.

Initiating UUCP Calls

Initiating UUCP connections is a proactive job. The simplest way to set up a system to make UUCP calls is for the administrator to modify a single file, the Systems file. This file contains the specific information needed to contact a remote system. Each line is a separate entry, and each line must have six fields. The first field on a line is the remote system's name. UUCP expects the first seven letters to be unique, so the system names newyorkcity and newyorkstate would be considered the same. Each system can have any number of entries—they are tried in the order found in the file, until one is successful.

The second field is a schedule field. Normally, the word Any will be here, meaning that the connection can be made at any time. Never means don't call. This entry is usually made when a system is polled; this means that a remote system will call to get what it wants. The schedule field Wk means weekdays only. A schedule field can be quite complicated. The schedule field can have an unlimited number of comma-separated schedule descriptions. Each description has a day code, an optional time code, and an optional grade code. The day codes are easy to understand—Su, Mo, Tu, We, Th, Fr, and Sa. Any number and combination can be present. So if you only want to call a site on Fridays, Saturdays, and Sundays, you'd have FrSaSu as the schedule field. The start time can be after the end time, which would seem to include midnight, but that is not true. Instead, it means from midnight on the specified days to the end time, and the start time to midnight on the same day. So Wk1900-0700 means any weekday before 7 a.m. or after 7 p.m.

Finally, the grade is a restriction on priority of transfers. By limiting the grade, only transfers of that grade or higher are made during that time. The grade is identified by a slash followed by a number or letter.

A full schedule specification may look like this:

```
SaSu,Wk0900-1700/C,Wk1700-0900
```

This means that transfers may occur at any time on Saturdays and Sundays, between 9 a.m. and 5 p.m. weekdays, only items grade C and above, and any time between 5 p.m. and 9 a.m. This effectively says it's possible to transfer anything at any time except during work hours, when you move only priority material.

Finally, if a comma and number follow the schedule, this sets a minimum retry time. UUCP will make retry attempts based on its own internal formula, but that formula can be overridden in the schedule field.

The third field is the device field. This field is a lot simpler than the schedule field. It consists of a pointer to a device type. The devices are kept in the file Devices, usually in the same directory as Systems. UUCP will look up the device name in the Devices file and use the first free device found. The only option is that protocols may be specified after the device, preceded by a comma. Supported protocols include UUCP's g protocol for communication on a telephone line, as well as an x and an e protocol for devices that support those protocols.

The fourth field is the speed, or baud rate, of the connection. This is usually your modem's top speed, but different values may be present for different numbers, and different speeds also apply for direct connections.

The fifth field is the connection number. Usually it is a telephone number, but for UUCP connections over direct lines or for data switches, it is a connection address or path. For telephone numbers, it is the sequence of numbers needed to dial the remote modem. Note that an optional alphanumeric string can precede the phone number (this will be interpreted in the Dialcodes file).

The last field is the chat script. These are a sequence of text patterns that are expect/send pairs. The uucp command will read the data coming in from the remote site and attempt to match the expected text with the incoming text. When a match is found, the send text is transmitted with a new line, and a new expect pattern is found, until the entire chat script is completed. If successfully completed, the UUCP process starts; otherwise, an error is recorded and the connection is terminated.

Chat scripts can be filled with special character escapes. Table 26.1 shows chat script escape sequences.

Table 26.1. Chat script escape sequences.

Escape Sequence	Meaning
" "	Expect a null string
EOT	End of transmission
BREAK	Cause a break signal
\b	Backspace
\c	Suppress a new line at the end of the send string
\d	Delay for one second
\K	Insert a break
\n	Send a new line

continues

Table 26.1. continued

Escape Sequence	Meaning
\N	Send a null
\p	Pause for a fraction of a second
\r	Carriage return
\s	Send a space
\t	Send a tab
\\	Send a backslash
\xxx	Send the ASCII character with the octal value xxx

A complete sample of Systems file entries is included here. Note that the sensitive data is changed, but reflects accurately my Systems file on sagarmatha.com:

```
machine1 Any ACU 9600 9899685 in:--in: uduke word: mypass
mach Never ACU 9600 9895690 in:--in: jca
tyler Any ACU 9600 5565935 "" \K\d\r :--: mygate "" \d\d >-\r->\
 mylog > rlogin\styler in:--in: uduke word: Strange1
```

I have three machines registered. All are within my local area code. I have set the machine to never call mach. Instead, I use that as an entry for the cu command. Also note that both machine1 and tyler have given me the UUCP account name uduke.

The machine tyler is an interesting case. I have to go through a switch to reach that machine. The first expect says that I don't expect anything, so the machine immediately sends the control characters \K\d\r. This means send a break, wait a second, and send a carriage return. UUCP then expects a colon, and to access this switch, I enter mygate. I then need to wait two seconds, with \d\d, to get the > character. I send mylog. I expect another >, and I send rlogin tyler. Here, I begin a more recognizable login session.

NOTE

In the early days of UNIX networking, the need for unique system names was great, as this was the only way to identify a machine for electronic mail and network news. As there was no registry, conflicts sometimes did occur. In the mid-1980s, I administered a machine named terminus while working for AT&T. At one point, I started receiving some very odd mail to the administrative accounts; it turns out that somebody else, in Colorado, had named a system terminus. Once the problem was identified, the name conflict was resolved.

Currently, the Internet has fully qualified domains, which separate our machines and networks. These domains are registered to prevent conflicts. My home machine is registered in the domain sagarmatha.com, but its UUCP name is duke. Because my service provider does not connect to Duke University or anyone else by this name, there is no name conflict.

Interestingly, this is not the hostname. My UUCP machine at home has a hostname of krzyzewski, after Duke University's head basketball coach. Other machines at home have names of assistant coaches, amaker, gaudet, and brey. Because of the seven-character restriction on the UUCP name, I opted for duke, rather than abbreviating the hostname.

Testing the Connection

Once the Systems file is complete, you have to test the entry to see if the connection is actually being made, and if not, you need to figure out what is wrong. For this you use the command Uutry.

Uutry is a shell script that calls uucico with a debugging flag set, and then performs a tail on the output. You can press the Delete key any time to terminate Uutry. The default debug level is 5, but this can be changed with the -x option.

The example in Listing 26.2 shows what happens when the password is incorrect.

Listing 26.1. A failed UUCP call.

```
$ /usr/lib/uucp/Uutry machine1
/usr/lib/uucp/uucico -r1 -smachine1 -x5 >/tmp/machine1 2>&1&
tmp=/tmp/machine1
mchFind called (machine1)
conn(machine1)
Device Type ACU wanted
mlock ttya succeeded
processdev: calling setdevcfg(uucico, ACU)
gdial(tb9600) called
expect: ("")
got it
sendthem (????????)
expect: (OK)
AT^M^M^JOKgot it
sendthem (DELAY
????????PAUSE
????????PAUSE
????????PAUSE
<NO CR>????????)
expect: (OK^M)
^M^JAAATE1V1X1Q0S2=255S12=255S50=6S58=2S68=2S7=80^M^M^JOK^Mgot it
sendthem (ECHO CHECK ON
<NO CR>?????????????????????????)
expect: (CONNECT 9600)
^M^JCONNECT 9600got it
getto ret 6
expect: (in:)
^M^Jsendthem (????????)
```

continues

Listing 26.1. continued

```
expect: (in:)
^M^Jmachine1 login:got it
sendthem (????????)
expect: (word:)
 uduke^M^JPassword:got it
sendthem (????????)
LOGIN FAILED - failed
exit code 101
Conversation Complete: Status FAILED
```

> **NOTE**
>
> Please note that a lot of what is sent is not visible to the user. This is not the case if Uutry is run as root. In that case, the send information, including the password, would be echoed in the parentheses. Because Uutry leaves files in /tmp, I prefer to use it with my own account and just use root to edit the administrative files.

You can only see what is echoed back to you—your commands that are not echoed, such as your password, are not visible. By correcting the password in the Systems file and rerunning Uutry, you get the output in Listing 26.2.

Listing 26.2. A successful UUCP call.

```
$ /usr/lib/uucp/Uutry machine1
mchFind called (machine1)
conn(machine1)
Device Type ACU wanted
mlock ttya succeeded
processdev: calling setdevcfg(uucico, ACU)
gdial(tb9600) called
expect: ("")
got it
sendthem (????????)
expect: (OK)
AT^M^M^JOKgot it
sendthem (DELAY
????????PAUSE
????????PAUSE
????????PAUSE
<NO CR>????????)
expect: (OK^M)
^M^JAAATE1V1X1Q0S2=255S12=255S50=6S58=2S68=2S7=80^M^M^JOK^Mgot it
sendthem (ECHO CHECK ON
<NO CR>????????????????????????)
expect: (CONNECT 9600)
^M^JCONNECT 9600got it
getto ret 6
expect: (in:)
^M^J^M^Jmachine1 login:got it
```

```
sendthem (????????)
expect: (word:)
 uduke^M^JPassword:got it
sendthem (????????)
Login Successful: System=machine1
msg-ROK
 Rmtname machine1, Role MASTER, Ifn - 6, Loginuser - james
rmesg - 'P' got Pgetxf
wmesg 'U'g
Proto started g
*** TOP ***  - role=1, setline - X
Request: duke!D.dukeb2ee40e —> machine1!D.dukeb2ee40e (james)
wrktype - S
 wmesg 'S' D.dukeb2ee40e D.dukeb2ee40e james - D.dukeb2ee40e 0666 james
rmesg - 'S' got SY
 PROCESS: msg - SY
SNDFILE:
-> 835 / 0.972 secs, 859 bytes/sec
rmesg - 'C' got CY
 PROCESS: msg - CY
RQSTCMPT:
mailopt 0, statfopt 0
```

A second useful debugging tool is cu. This command also uses the UUCP files to try to connect to the remote machine, but when you are connected to the remote machine, cu terminates and you must complete the login yourself. This is very useful for debugging telephone numbers and Dialer scripts. Also, by using cu to connect to the modem itself, you can alter the modem parameters that may have been set incorrectly.

Another debugging tool is uucico. By calling uucico with the option -x and a single number, you will get output showing the steps for the UUCP call. This, however, cannot be interrupted, so you should use it sparingly.

More on Chat Scripts

Chat scripts are the heart of UUCP communication. The concept of a chat script is phenomenally simple—read a port until you match a string, then send a response. It is found in two UUCP-related files, the Systems file and the Dialers file. The concept is rather portable, although it could have supported regular expressions for pattern matching.

Any number of expect/send pairs could be present. When attempting to navigate UUCP through a network of data switches to reach a destination, you may need a large number of pairs before you reach the login prompt.

The longer the chat script, the greater the chance that an error may occur. Normally, an error in the chat will result in the call failing; however, there are some error correction techniques. The uucico command will take a time-out after 30 seconds if an expected pattern is not seen. At that time, an alternate send sequence can be issued, and a new pattern expected. This alternate send is enclosed in dashes, with the new expect pattern following the second dash. There can be no spaces in this pattern, or UUCP will see it as a new member of an expect/send pair.

Often, this is seen with the login prompt and looks like this:

```
in:--in:
```

This pattern means, wait for `in:`, and if it is not found, send a carriage return and wait again for `in:`. (Remember that each `send` pattern is followed by a carriage return, even if it is an alternate `send`.)

Another frequent alternate sequence is `\K`. Sometimes, when calling a modem that operates at multiple speeds, sending a break down the line will allow the modem to change its speed to match yours. When you see a sequence like this,

```
in:-\K-in:--in:-\K-in:
```

there are four separate instances of an expected login prompt. If not found the first time, send a break, then a carriage return, then another break. Although this may look excessive, it is sometimes necessary.

Administering the Files

Besides the files already mentioned, there are six important UUCP files that need regular administration. They are the Devices, Dialers, Dialcodes, Permissions, Sysfiles, and Poll files. Each has its own format and usage.

Devices

The Devices file is just a list of the devices found on the system, with an identification of their uses. The purpose of this file is to tie the device specification in the Systems file to a physical device with a known means of access. Each entry in the Devices file is a single line long, must start in the first column, and has five fields. The file permits comments, identified by the # character in the first column. It ignores lines with no entry in that column.

The first field is the device type. It must match exactly the device specified in the Systems file. Devices will be tried in order down the file until one is found to be available. This way, a system with multiple modems can have one entry in the Systems file. Some devices have standard identifiers. An *ACU* is an "automated call unit," better known as a modem. `direct` signifies that the link to the device is a direct link.

> **NOTE**
>
> For you to use cu -1, the line specified must have a `direct` entry in the Devices file.

The second field is the data port. This is the filename of the special file in the /dev directory that matches the physical device, and will be the port through which the data communication is made.

The third field is the dialer port. This is a bit of an anachronism, but in the past, some modems required a separate dialer device to make the phone call. This was the special file that pointed to the dialer for that modem. If the modem is capable of dialing, this field is marked with a dash.

The fourth field is the speed of the device. This is also used for matching the Systems file. That way a site can indicate multiple speeds for connections through multiple devices.

The last field is the dialer token pairs. This specifies a specific dialer pattern, found in the Dialers file, and any arguments passed thereto. Normally, only a single pair (or single entry, if it gets no arguments) is found; however, if the system needs to go through a switch to reach the modem, a chat script may be expected.

My Devices file is rather small, and it looks like this:

```
ACU ttya - 9600 tb9600
Direct ttya - 9600 direct
```

I have only the single modem, a Telebit QBlazer at 9600 baud. It is attached to /dev/ttya and uses the tb9600 dialer script when I connect via UUCP. It is configured to allow me to use cu to talk to the modem.

Dialers

The Dialers file is used to initiate conversation with the modem. It ties the dialer specified in the Devices file to a chat script. It consists of three fields. The first is the name of the dialer script. This must match exactly with the dialer specified in the Devices file. As with devices, all dialers are one line and are started in the first column. The #, or white space, in the first column indicates a comment.

The second field is a translation table for older communication devices.

The third field is the chat script needed to talk with the modem and to place the call. My machine came with several dialers already installed, including dialers for penril, ventel, micom, hayes, and telebit modems. I looked over my set of telebit dialers, listed below, and selected tbfast for my first dialer for my ACU.

```
tb1200    =W-, "" \dA\pA\pA\pTE1V1X1Q0S2=255S12=255S50=2\r\c\
 OK\r \EATDT\T\r\c CONNECT\s1200
tb2400    =W-, "" \dA\pA\pA\pTE1V1X1Q0S2=255S12=255S50=3\r\c\
 OK\r \EATDT\T\r\c CONNECT\s2400
tbfast    =W-, "" \dA\pA\pA\pTE1V1X1Q0S2=255S12=255S50=255\r\c\
 OK\r \EATDT\T\r\c CONNECT\sFAST
```

I knew I wasn't connecting at 1200 or 2400 baud, so it seemed that the fast connection was the way to go. I quickly learned that this was wrong! By using cu to mimic the dialing of the UUCP number, I saw that the final message was not CONNECT FAST, but CONNECT 9600. I first considered altering tbfast, but instead opted to write my own dialer, tb9600, in case I need to make other changes.

Note that each of these dialers has a long, confusing list of numbers and characters as the first send sequence. These are the parameters that need to be set in the modem for the UUCP call to take place, in a language the modem understands. Although the hayes modem syntax is fairly common, some modems do not use it, so you'll need to check your modem's documentation to determine the correct settings.

In my efforts, I found that by sending just the string to the modem, I'd get an error, because I didn't yet have the modem's attention. To get its attention, I'd need to send AT to the modem and receive back OK. I placed this at the beginning of my chat script. Testing also revealed that the best modem settings were different from those above, so I added them to the chat script, as well. It ended up looking like this:

```
tb9600    =W-, "" AT OK-AT-OK
\dA\pA\pA\pTE1V1X1Q0S2=255S12=255S50=6S58=2S68=2S7=80\r\c\
 OK\r \EATDT\T\r\c CONNECT\s9600-\c-CONNECT\s9600
```

Basically, I am setting modem registers to match what I need. I also wait for CONNECT 9600 a bit longer than the time-out, so if I don't get it, I just sit a little while longer. This is the dialer I use for my UUCP connections.

Dialcodes

The Dialcodes file is an optional file that equates some string with a series of numbers to be dialed. Although UUCP is perfectly happy to have a sequence such as 1028801144716194550,,2354 to reach a distant computer in the City of London, for a human being glancing at the file it may not be obvious. So Dialcodes permits the human to tie a string, innerlondon, to a dialing sequence 102880114471.

Because I have only one number, I don't use a Dialcodes file, but if you call many places nationwide, it might be useful.

Permissions

System security is one of the most pressing issues in the computer industry, and in UUCP it is no exception. Originally, UUCP allowed any user to write to any directory on the remote system, as long as the user ID for UUCP had write permissions. Similarly, reading files was also possible. This had the ugly effect of enabling users to steal remote password files with a simple UUCP command, and if any accounts weren't protected with passwords, those systems were definitely compromised. Similarly, with incorrect permissions, a remote user could do significant damage by moving or destroying important files.

The way around this problem is to use the Permissions file. This mechanism ties remote systems and accounts to specific read, write, and execute permissions. There are 13 different Permissions file entries, each with the format Option=Value. They must all be on the same line, although these lines may be broken with a backslash. Multiple values for an option are separated by colons. The 13 options are LOGNAME, MACHINE, REQUEST, SENDFILES, READ, WRITE, NOREAD, NOWRITE, CALLBACK, COMMANDS, VALIDATE, MYNAME, and PUBDIR.

The meaning of each option is described below.

LOGNAME refers to a specific login name used by the remote site to gain access. By specifying the LOGNAME, you can tie various options to the login call.

MACHINE refers to the machine name of the remote UUCP site. Specific permissions can be tied to a LOGNAME or to a MACHINE.

REQUEST is a yes/no flag indicating whether a remote machine can request files from your machine. The default is no. By permitting a remote system to request files, a command such as uucp mymach!myfile anotherfile can be executed from a remote machine. On a trusted network, that may be fine, but it is an invitation to trouble if set up on a link where you don't always know who is on the other end.

SENDFILES is another yes/no flag, but it is only tied to the LOGNAME. If set to yes, your system will send files to the remote system even if the remote system initiates the call. If you set the value to no, you will never send out files, and if you set it to call, you will send out files only when you have initiated the call.

READ specifies the directories from which uucico can access files for transfer. The default is /var/spool/ucppublic.

WRITE specifies the directories to which uucico may write files. Again, the default is /var/spool/uucppublic. These two options are designed to keep harm from uucp restricted to a public file system.

NOREAD and NOWRITE are exceptions to the other directories. For example, on a trusted network, you may want to set your directory open to reading, by setting READ=/home/james. However, you might have your own private directory that you don't want anyone to touch. To set this, you can have the options read READ=/home/james NOREAD=/home/james/.Private.

CALLBACK is another yes/no option. When set to yes, your system must call the remote system back before any transactions may take place. The default value is no. Be particularly careful using this option, because if both machines set CALLBACK to yes, they will never communicate. Also, if one system sets SENDFILES to call and the other has CALLBACK as yes, the first system will never transfer files to the second. CALLBACK is definitely a security feature, because a remote site could always fake a machine name and steal a password, so by calling back you know with whom you are talking. It is also useful if one site has a particularly cheaper phone rate than the other.

COMMANDS is a very important option. The default is usually to permit rmail and rnews, the programs to receive mail and netnews. If set to ALL, any command that can be found in the local path of uuxqt will be executed. Because this often includes commands such as cat and rm, this is usually not recommended. The COMMANDS option is tied to a MACHINE name calling in.

VALIDATE is an option tied to the LOGNAME and, if set to yes, will validate the calling system's identity.

MYNAME is an option to provide another system name for the local name. This is useful if you need an alternate UUCP name.

PUBDIR is an option to specify a directory to be treated as the public directory for reading and writing. The default is /var/spool/uucppublic.

Although this may seem complicated, the default permissions are designed to keep a system secure, and it is only when you want to loosen permissions that you need to edit the Permissions file.

My Permissions file is rather simple, with a single entry:

```
MACHINE=netcomsv COMMANDS=rmail:rnews SENDFILES=yes
```

It enables the machine netcomsv to execute rmail and rnews, and it enables me to send files to them.

Sysfiles

Sysfiles is a special addition that allows the system to specify different Systems files for different services. It also allows for multiple Systems, Devices, and Dialers files, should these become long.

The format is simple. There are four keywords: service, systems, devices, and dialers. The format is always keyword=value. The service keywords can be uucico or cu, the two commands that access the UUCP files. The other three are files that replace the Systems, Devices, and Dialers files for that service. Each field is separated by a colon.

Poll

The Poll file is a list of times to poll a remote system. It is accessed by an administrative daemon to establish a fake request and force a UUCP call at a specific time. Its format is a system name followed by a tab and a space-separated list of integers from 0 to 23, representing the hours of a 24-hour clock.

Supporting Files

UUCP creates many different files and file types. Briefly, they are work files, data files, status files, lock files, log files, and temporary files.

Work files are located in /var/spool/uucp/*machine name*, and are prefixed with the letter C. They are the workhorse for UUCP, because they list the specific files to be transferred, including the local and remote names, permissions, and owner. A request to send remote mail may look like this:

```
S D.dukeb3ae48e D.dukeb3ae48e james - D.dukeb3ae48e 0666 james
S D.netco0c7f621 X.dukeNb3ae james - D.netco0c7f621 0666 james
```

This indicates that two files are to be transferred.

The data files are kept in the same directory, but are prefixed with D. Even the files that specify remote execution are prefixed with D. In this request are two data files being transferred, one to become a data file on the remote machine, the other to become an execute file.

Execute files are identified by the prefix X. This prefix is sought by uuxqt, which is the program that actually runs the requested commands. These have their own format, indicating the command to be run and the input file to use.

Status files are kept in /var/spool/uucp/.Status, and have a specific format. There is a single status file per system, with six fields. The first is a type field, the second is a count field (used to indicate the number of retries, for example). The third field is a UNIX time to identify the last connection attempt. The fourth is the number of seconds before a retry attempt may be taken, the fifth is ASCII text to describe the status, and the sixth is the machine name. Status files are usually accessed by the uustat command.

Lock files are created when a call is attempted, and the lock files are in /var/spool/locks. These files contain the process ID of the uucico request that has locked the system.

Log files are kept in /var/spool/uucp/.Log. They are cleaned out daily by a daemon to prevent them from growing beyond control. Separate logs are kept for the uucico, uucp, uux, and uuxqt commands, each in a file named for the remote system. These are often accessed with the uulog command.

Finally, temporary files may be created by UUCP. These are in the directory with the work files and are prefixed with TM.

UUCP Daemons

There are four UUCP daemons that should be invoked on a regular basis. They are the admin daemon, the cleanup daemon, the polling daemon, and the hourly daemon. These are all started out of cron.

The admin Daemon

The admin daemon is a daemon that should be invoked at least once a day. It will give, by e-mail, a brief image of the state of UUCP, including a snapshot of the running processes and a listing of the job queue. It will also check the log files to see if there have been any attempts to transfer the passwd file.

The cleanup Daemon

The cleanup daemon is one of the hardest workers. It should be invoked daily, at a time when few users are likely to be on the system. It will back up all the log files and save them for three days. It will then make the current log files zero length. Other administrative files not discussed here are also backed up.

The cleanup daemon will invoke the uucleanup command. This command removes old jobs from the queue, based on a command line argument. On my system, I have stuck with the defaults, seven days until a delete and one day until a warning.

The daemon then removes old files, empty subdirectories, and core files. When it finishes this, it sends e-mail to the UUCP administrator announcing what it has done.

The polling Daemon

This daemon quickly examines the Poll file to create polling requests for uucico. This is essentially touching a file in the spool directory. It should be executed hourly.

The hourly Daemon

The hourly demon should be invoked each hour. It just runs the uusched command, which examines the spool to find any queued jobs, and if it finds jobs, it runs uucico for that system. When it finishes, it runs uuxqt to execute any incoming jobs.

Using UUCP

Earlier in this chapter you were introduced to the commands uucp and uux, which are two of the most common commands for UUCP. There are two alternate commands, uuto and uupick, which ease the process.

The uucp command is the basic command for the transportation of files from one machine to another. The basic form allows for the specification of two paths to files, one being the original file, the other being the destination. uucp can take a number of arguments to help facilitate the transfer. By default, uucp will use the source file for originating the transfer. This means that if the source file is changed before the transfer is completed, the changed file will be sent. If that is not desired, the file can be copied to a temporary file for uucp, which is done by specifying the -C option. By default, uucp will also create the necessary destination directories, if it has permission to do so. This is the -d option and is turned off by -f. uucp also will assign a job ID to the transfer with the -j option. The -m option can be used to let the sender know when the job is complete (uucp will send a mail message to the requestor). The -g option enables the user to set the transfer grade (a single character from 0 to 9, A to Z, or a to z. 0 is highest, and z is lowest).

Similar to the -m option, the -n option followed by a user name will notify the user at the remote machine when the transfer is complete. Debugging information can be found with -x. To prevent an immediate start of uucico, use -r.

So if I want to copy a file, data, but might change it later, and I am not worried about speed, I might try this:

```
uucp -r -C -gz data remote!data
```

If I also want to know when it is done and want to send mail to my friend Joe at the remote machine, I'd expand it to this:

```
uucp -r -C -gz -m -njoe data remote!data
```

That's an ugly command, to say the least!

uux is another command frequently used to execute remote programs. Most remote sites restrict this command, but imagine that you are on a very friendly network. At a minimum, you need a command string, which is just a machine name followed by an exclamation point and a command. The command is the same as a command typed on the system in the uucppublic directory. At a minimum, you need this:

```
uux remote!date
```

That will run the date command on the remote system. Standard output is sent back to you. Assume that you want to put a message on your friend Joe's screen. If you were on the system, you'd use the command write joe and type something in. What you've typed in is standard input, but you can't type on Joe's machine. uux will accept standard input on your screen, if we include the - on the command line. So you'd type this:

```
uux - remote!write joe
```

Then you'd enter your message. Note that you don't need to quote the command, because anything after the command is considered an argument.

> **NOTE**
>
> Filenames for uux commands can be machine specified, as well. uux will attempt to get all the files needed to the remote machine before executing the command there.

uux also takes some other arguments. The -b option tells uux to return the standard input if the remote execution failed. Files may be copied to the spool with -C, and -j controls the ID string. The -n option tells uux not to return any indication of success or failure by mail. By default, uux will send mail to the originator, letting that person know whether the command worked. Standard input can also be used with -p, and -r doesn't immediately start uucico. The grade can be set with -g, and -x controls debugging. The originator name can be altered with -a.

uuto and uupick

These commands are complicated and can baffle the novice user. Fortunately, UNIX provides two friendlier commands, uuto and uupick, for transferring files. These two commands work together. The syntax for uuto is simple:

```
uuto file file file machine!user
```

Any number of files can be listed on the line—they'll all be transferred to the remote machine using uucp. Note that a user on the remote machine must be specified. This way, the file is placed in a directory on the remote machine identified by the user's name. Only two arguments are accepted for uuto: -m says to send mail to the originator when the transfer is complete, and -p says to copy the file to the spool before transmission. In transferring a file to my friend Joe, I'd set up this command:

```
uuto -m file1 remote!joe
```

This is all I need to do. The uuto command will convert it to this:

```
uucp -d -m -njoe file1 remote!~/receive/joe/duke
```

The remote machine will then have a directory hierarchy for my friend Joe, under the receive directory, and with a subdirectory duke. A short time later, I will get some e-mail that says (SYSTEM remote) copy succeeded and I will find a reference to the file in the header.

On the other machine, Joe will also receive some e-mail, saying /usr/spool/uucppublic/ receive/james/duke/file1 from duke!james arrived, which lets him know that he has a file in the uucppublic directory.

Getting that file is easy using uupick. This is another shell script that searches the public directory for files under your name in a receive directory. If it finds any files, it prompts you for what you want to do. The actions are fairly straightforward:

New line:	Go to the next entry
d	Delete the file
m [dir]	Move the file to a directory dir
a [dir]	Move all files from the present system to a directory
p	Print the file
q	Quit
Control+D	Quit
!command	Run the command
*	Print the command summary

So if you enter uupick, Joe will be prompted with this:

```
from system duke: file file1 ?
```

If he types m, the file is placed in his current directory, and the transfer is complete.

> **TIP**
>
> With uuto and uupick, the user is completely removed from the messy details of uucp. Furthermore, on many systems uuto and uupick are all most users need to know.

UUCP Utilities

There are two notable UUCP utilities available to the user. One examines log files, the other provides transfer status information.

UUCP keeps some very detailed log files in /var/spool/uucp/.Log. The uulog command is designed to access the two busiest of those logs. It always takes a system name as an argument. By default, or with the -s flag, it will display the transfer information for a given system. Here is a sample:

```
uucp remote  (5/14-19:18:42,9604,0) CONN FAILED (CALLER SCRIPT FAILED)
uucp remote  (5/14-19:48:40,9792,0) SUCCEEDED (call to remote )
uucp remote  (5/14-19:48:43,9792,0) OK (startup)
uucp remote  (5/14-19:48:44,9792,0) REMOTE REQUESTED (remote!D.netco56c3c71\
 --> duke!D.netco56c3c71 (netnews))
uucp remote  (5/14-19:48:55,9792,1) REMOTE REQUESTED (remote!D.duke4f4de04\
 --> duke!X.netcomsd56c3 (netnews))
uucp remote  (5/14-19:48:57,9792,2) REMOTE REQUESTED (remote!D.netcobeb02bd\
 --> duke!D.netcobeb02bd (netnews))
uucp remote  (5/14-19:49:14,9792,3) REMOTE REQUESTED (remote!D.duke4f4e043\
 --> duke!X.netcomsdbeb0 (netnews))
uucp remote  (5/14-19:49:17,9792,4) OK (conversation complete ttya 136)
uucp remote  (5/14-20:18:41,9972,0) FAILED (LOGIN FAILED)
uucp remote  (5/14-20:18:41,9972,0) CONN FAILED (CALLER SCRIPT FAILED)
```

From this log you can see that a connection failed at 7:18 p.m., succeeded at 7:48, and failed again at 8:18. Normally this file would be fairly long, but I used the -N option to cut it to the last 10 lines of the file. If I wanted to wait on the file, I could have used -f. This is the same flag as for tail.

The only other option is -x. It gives details of the commands executed on the local system from UUCP. An example of the output (again, truncated to just the last 10 lines) is this:

```
uucp remote duked4f46 (5/14-17:32:37,9158,0) remote!remote!uucp-bounce XQT\
 (PATH=/bin:/usr/bin  USER=uucp UU_MACHINE=remote UU_USER=remote!uucp-bounce\
 export UU_MACHINE UU_USER PATH; rnews )
uucp remote duked4f43 (5/14-17:32:38,9158,0) remote!remote!uucp-bounce XQT\
 (PATH=/bin:/usr/bin  USER=uucp UU_MACHINE=remote UU_USER=remote!uucp-bounce\
 export UU_MACHINE UU_USER PATH; rnews )
uucp remote duked4f47 (5/14-17:52:08,9225,0) remote!remote!uucp-bounce XQT\
 (PATH=/bin:/usr/bin  USER=uucp UU_MACHINE=remote UU_USER=remote!uucp-bounce\
 export UU_MACHINE UU_USER PATH; rnews )
uucp remote duked4f48 (5/14-18:32:49,9287,0) remote!remote!uucp-bounce XQT\
 (PATH=/bin:/usr/bin  USER=uucp UU_MACHINE=remote UU_USER=remote!uucp-bounce\
 export UU_MACHINE UU_USER PATH; rnews )
uucp remote duked4f49 (5/14-18:32:50,9287,0) remote!remote!uucp-bounce XQT\
 (PATH=/bin:/usr/bin  USER=uucp UU_MACHINE=remote UU_USER=remote!uucp-bounce\
 export UU_MACHINE UU_USER PATH; rnews )
uucp remote duked4f4a (5/14-18:32:51,9287,0) remote!remote!uucp-bounce XQT\
 (PATH=/bin:/usr/bin  USER=uucp UU_MACHINE=remote UU_USER=remote!uucp-bounce\
 export UU_MACHINE UU_USER PATH; rnews )
uucp remote duked4f4b (5/14-18:32:52,9287,0) remote!remote!uucp-bounce XQT\
 (PATH=/bin:/usr/bin  USER=uucp UU_MACHINE=remote UU_USER=remote!uucp-bounce\
 export UU_MACHINE UU_USER PATH; rnews )
```

```
uucp remote duked4f4c (5/14-18:32:53,9287,0) remote!remote!uucp-bounce XQT\
 (PATH=/bin:/usr/bin  USER=uucp UU_MACHINE=remote UU_USER=remote!uucp-bounce\
 export UU_MACHINE UU_USER PATH; rnews )
uucp remote duked4f4d (5/14-19:49:19,9793,0) remote!remote!uucp-bounce XQT\
 (PATH=/bin:/usr/bin  USER=uucp UU_MACHINE=remote UU_USER=remote!uucp-bounce\
 export UU_MACHINE UU_USER PATH; rnews )
uucp remote duked4f4e (5/14-19:49:20,9793,0) remote!remote!uucp-bounce XQT\
 (PATH=/bin:/usr/bin  USER=uucp UU_MACHINE=remote UU_USER=remote!uucp-bounce\
 export UU_MACHINE UU_USER PATH; rnews )
```

Every command executed has been rnews, for transmission of netnews. To examine the other two files, my uux requests on a remote system, and my uucp requests to a remote system, I'd need to examine the files using an editor or other UNIX tools.

The other notable command is the uustat command. It has a lot of power, including the ability to delete jobs. There are several options.

The command uustat -a will give a listing of all jobs currently in the queue. Here is a sample:

```
netcomsn0000  05/14-20:45:00  (POLL)
remoteNb1ae  05/14-19:53  S  remote  james 48871\
 /home/james/Docs/Sams/Uucp/file1
```

This indicates that a poll request is in for netcom, and a file transfer request for remote.

To check the accessibility of machines, use uustat -m. It will give a listing such as this:

```
netcomsv   05/14-20:18 CALLER SCRIPT FAILED
remote     05/14-20:20 LOGIN FAILED  Count: 2
```

This indicates that there are presently problems reaching both machines. The command uustat -p will perform a ps command for every PID found in a lock file. uustat -q will give a listing of the state of the queue for each machine. It is similar to uustat -m, but it also includes a count of outstanding jobs.

Detailed job information, similar to that obtained with uustat -a, can be found for a given system or a given user with uustat -s*system* or uustat -u*user*. Finally, a user may kill a job or rejuvenate a job. The uustat -a command will give a job ID in the first field. By specifying that job with a -k option, it will be removed from the queue. By using the -r option, it will be touched, and spared from any administrative daemons.

With these two commands, a user can determine the status of jobs already sent but not yet complete.

Summary

This chapter has provided a brief overview of the use and administration of UUCP. The uucp, uux, uuto, and uupick commands are used for data and command transfers. The uustat and uulog commands are used to check on the status and actions of UUCP. Different files are used to administer the UUCP system, with the power to restrict types of access and facilitate data transfers.

FTP Administration

by Salim Douba

IN THIS CHAPTER

File Transfer Protocol (FTP, RFC 959) service is probably among the earliest (if not the earliest) data exchange and transfer services that were first introduced on the Internet. When first introduced, as early as 1971, FTP assumed a primitive nature (RFC 114) that was used to send test traffic on the ARPANET. Quickly thereafter, FTP grew into one of the two principal network applications (the other was Telnet) that run on a TCP/IP stack. Among other reasons, FTP's popularity stems from its independence from any specific platform. Implementations of both the FTP server and client can be found on many platforms including UNIX, DOS, Windows NT, and Novell's NetWare network operating system, to name a few.

As a service available on UNIX platforms, FTP presents system administrators with additional concerns. Among the principal concerns are setting up the FTP service, its availability, and security. Security becomes a doubly burdening concern should the network on which the FTP server is brought up be connected to the Internet. This chapter addresses these issues to varying degrees of detail, thus empowering the administrator with both the knowledge base and the skills required to properly provide FTP services, be it on a physically isolated local area network (LAN) or on an Internet-connected LAN. The skillful administration of FTP services, however, requires a reasonable foundation in some of the concepts governing the FTP protocol and operations. For this reason, this chapter is roughly divided into two components. The first four sections deal with the underlying concepts and operational issues of FTP, while the remainder of the chapter deals with practical issues and applications. In particular, the chapter covers the following:

- An overview of the FTP protocol
- How to set up an FTP Server
- How to set up an anonymous FTP Server
- How to administer access privileges to FTP services
- How to implement third-party data transfer
- How to implement unattended FTP data transfers
- How to troubleshoot FTP-related problems

As in other chapters, the coverage of the material included here takes into consideration the different variants of UNIX that the book covers. While the FTP governing concepts and mechanisms are, to a large extent, identical on all platforms (and not only UNIX), there are subtle differences in the way that some aspects of the service applications are implemented. In due course, those differences will be highlighted.

Overview of FTP Protocol and Service

The File Transfer Protocol is intended for the transfer of files between two hosts across the network. Furthermore, hosts engaging in an FTP transfer session need not be similar in nature. Both the hardware and operating systems running on the involved hosts can be anything but similar—a characteristic feature that made FTP server and client implementations widely available on platforms other than UNIX. Using a DOS FTP client, for example, a user can (subject to security restrictions) easily exchange files with a UNIX host running FTP service. The DOS user may also engage two other servers in the exchange of data without being concerned about the nature or identity of these machines. While one could be an IBM AIX UNIX host, the other could be a mainframe or a Windows NT server. This later ability to engage two servers in the exchange of data from a client running on a third machine is known as third-party (or proxy) transfer (more on this later in the chapter).

Among the other features that FTP supports are its capability to handle both ASCII and EBCDIC (Extended Binary Coded Decimal Interchange Code) character sets. Equally important is FTP's support of ASCII and binary transfers. Unlike UUCP, which requires that any data other than ASCII, be uuencoded at the source and uudecoded at the destination (thus wasting both CPU processing power and communications bandwidth), FTP submits data on as-is basis, never attempting to modify or interpret it—a big plus.

FTP Connections

FTP runs at the application level of the OSI (Open System Interconnection) model and depends on the Transmission Control Protocol (TCP, refer to Chapter 20, "Networking," for more on TCP) for the reliable delivery of data among hosts on the network. As such, FTP behaves as a strict application without being concerned with the architectural underpinnings of the supporting communications architecture. It relies on TCP for doing what it takes to ensure the establishment of the necessary connections and the error-free delivery of data.

Whenever an FTP client (in UNIX, the client typically known as `ftp`) engages in an FTP session with a server process (controlled by what is commonly referred to as `ftpd` or the `in.ftpd` daemon in UNIX), TCP establishes two connections on behalf of both entities. These connections are known as the *control connection* and the *data connection* (see Figure 27.1).

FIGURE 27.1.

FTP service protocol establishes two connections, a data connection and a control connection.

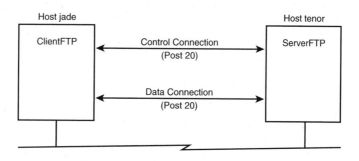

The data connection is used exclusively for the transfer of user data, whereas the control connection is used exclusively for the exchange of internal FTP commands and responses governing the session.

Control Connection

The control connection is established by the client while invoking the `ftp` command by opening a TCP connection to the desired server. No user data is exchanged over the control connection. It is used exclusively for the exchange of internal FTP commands and responses that govern the exchange of user data over a separate *data* connection. Here is an example of invoking an FTP session with host `tenor`:

```
# ftp tenor
```

Assuming that host `tenor` is running the UNIX operating system, if configured properly to host FTP services, it responds by establishing the control connection using port 21 (*default* FTP control port as defined in the `/etc/services` file). Responses to FTP requests are handled by the `ftpd` daemon on the UNIX host.

When the control connection is open, the user authentication process takes place before even establishing a data connection. The user is required to provide a valid user login name and password to the FTP server. After successful completion of the authentication process, both the server and the client engage in negotiating the parameters required to govern the exchange of data. For example, the data type is set during this process (ASCII versus EBCDIC), and transfer mode (for instance, STREAM).

Data Connection

Upon successful negotiation of the transfer parameters, both the client (`ftp`) and server (`ftpd`) processes proceed to establishing the data connection using port 20 (set in the `/etc/services` file). The data connection is full duplex, allowing simultaneous transfer of data in both directions. It is important to know that the data connection may not be maintained throughout the session. There are circumstances when the data connection is closed by the end of a file transfer, or upon detection of an irrecoverable error condition. As long as the control connection is maintained, the session is considered live. Both sides can negotiate and establish a new data connection whenever the need arises for the resumption of file transfers.

More on Connections

Two more things you ought to know before quitting the topic on connections:

1. While the default ports (also known as well known ports) for the control port and data port are 21 and 20, respectively, the FTP server (`ftpd` daemon) may be configured to listen on other ports for connection and for the exchange of data.

2. Unless overriden, the port assigned to the data connection is one less than the control port. This is demonstrated by the default ports assigned to them (21 is the control port, and 20 is the data port number).

While ports 21 and 20 are the norm, you will be surprised to know that some implementations of FTP rely on the use of other ports. In cases like these you are required to fine tune any FTP-based applications that run on your UNIX host so they can interact successfully with computers hosting such implementations of FTP.

NOTE

Using alternate ports, rather than the default (control port 21) can be achieved by simply editing the /etc/service file to replace the port number in the FTP entry to the desired port number. (See the "Troubleshooting FTP" section later in this chapter for more on this topic.)

Reliability of FTP

FTP relies on TCP for the delivery of information between hosts. As discussed in Chapter 20, TCP is a reliable, connection oriented, transport protocol. FTP's reliability stems from the reliability of TCP. When engaged in the transfer of data, FTP relies on TCP to handle the sequencing of exchanged data segments and recovery from erroneous events during the delivery process. Should the transfer process be interrupted, however, it is FTP's responsibility to recover from the interruption and resume the transfer process without necessarily retransmitting the entire file. FTP achieves this by employing a checkpointing mechanism that breaks the file undergoing transmission into logical blocks of data that are individually acknowledged upon successful delivery. A block can be transmitted in one TCP segment or multiple TCP segments. While TCP concerns itself with the error-free delivery of individual segments, FTP concerns itself with the successful transmission of all segments comprising the individual block. Consequently, whenever the file transfer is restarted upon recovery from an abrupt interruption, FTP retransmits data starting from the beginning of the interrupted block only and until completion; thus achieving optimal performance and minimal impact on available CPU power and transmission bandwidth.

Operational Characteristics of FTP

FTP is a real-time process. This means that an FTP session is established as soon as the FTP application is invoked. If invoked in the foreground, a user or program must suspend other action and wait the completion of the session before proceeding. Because the speed of the transfer is affected by many factors, including the size of the file and the capacity of the available bandwidth, the time it takes for completion may vary considerably from one network environment to another, and during different times of the day. For this reason, FTP was developed to be a time-insensitive application.

If you hate to wait prolonged periods of time until you regain control of your terminal, you might want to consider running FTP sessions in an unattended mode of operation. In this mode, ftp (the client) can be invoked in the background and made to process a session in accordance with an ftp script that you make available to it. See the "Unattended FTP Transfers" section later in this chapter.

Another operational feature of FTP on UNIX platforms is the provision for scripting. Instead of interactively establishing a session, a user or system administrator can script the entire session and submit it to the ftp command upon invocation. This approach requires that the user know the exact details of the proceedings of the intended session. Later in the chapter (see the

"Unattended FTP Transfers" section), both this feature and unattended session are explained and applied to solve a real-life situation. Scripting is not a requirement of the FTP standard; rather, it is a feature that some platform-specific implementations provide, while others ignore it completely.

Sample FTP Session

In this section, the proceedings of an FTP session are illustrated by invoking one. The purpose is to foster some of the concepts learned above and to prepare the ground for the material covered in the upcoming section.

In its simplest form, `ftp` can be used to invoke a file transfer session with a target host:

```
# ftp targethost
```

`targethost` can be the IP address or the name of the remote host.

As a secure service, `ftp` prompts you for both your login name and your password. Unless you are authenticated, `ftp` aborts requests to establish the file transfer session. Later in the chapter, FTP security access control and authentication are discussed in detail. In the following example, a user who is logged in to host `jade` uses `ftp` to establish a session with host `tenor`.

```
# ftp tenor
Connected to tenor.
220 tenor FTP server (UNIX(r) System V Release 4.0) ready.
Name (tenor:root): sam
331 Password required for sam.
Password:
230 User sam logged in.
ftp>
```

The prompt `ftp>`, which in this case is displayed after the user `sam` authenticated successfully, is FTP's and serves as an indication of readiness on FTP's part to execute any of the `ftp` user commands. Before going any further, it is worth noting that while the FTP session is being established with the remote system, processing of any of the commands the user might issue is done locally, *not* remotely as in the case of Telnet. Hence, the `ftp` prompt is, in fact, local to the machine from which the user invoked the session, and pertains to the local `ftp` command. Upon invocation of the `ftp` command, a so-called User-PI (user process interpreter) is created. The User-PI acts very much like a UNIX shell in that it accepts user-issued `ftp` commands and submits them to the FTP protocol for subsequent handling.

To find out what user commands `ftp` supports, enter help at the prompt as shown here:

```
ftp> help
```

Commands may be abbreviated. They are

!	debug	mget	pwd	status
$	dir	mkdir	quit	struct
account	disconnect	mls	quote	system
append	form	mode	recv	sunique
ascii	get	modtime	reget	tenex
bell	glob	mput	rstatus	trace
binary	hash	newer	rhelp	type
bye	help	nmap	rename	user
case	idle	nlist	reset	umask
cd	image	ntrans	restart	verbose
cdup	lcd	open	rmdir	?
chmod	ls	prompt	runique	
close	macdef	proxy	send	
cr	mdelete	sendport	site	
delete	mdir	put	size	
ftp>				

Use get to transfer a file from the remote host to your station, and use put to send a file to the remote host. Use mget (multiple get) and mput (multiple put) for the transfer of more than one file at a time. The best place to go to for explanation of the above commands is the man pages of your UNIX operating system. However, it is worth noting that not all commands are implemented in all of the UNIX variants of FTP. Therefore, unless implemented on both the local and the remote host, a command is not valid for execution. Instead, an error response is generated notifying the user of failure, as the following example demonstrates:

```
ftp> rstatus
502 STAT command not implemented.
ftp>
```

rstatus is typically used to query the FTP server about the status of its end of the connection. In the preceding example, the remote end (the FTP server) indicated that the STAT (an internal FTP protocol command) is not implemented. How to tell whether the message pertains to the server and not to client capabilities? Simple. Whenever the response is preceded with a three-digit code such as 502 in the example, it means that the command was recognized by the local host (how this code is interpreted is the subject of the next section). Consequently, the message pertains to an issue on the remote end (the server). If the command is not supported locally, a message similar to the following is issued:

```
ftp> rstatus
?Invalid command
ftp>
```

Notice how no code precedes the message. Whenever a user ftp command is issued, the User-PI determines whether the command is supported by the local implementation of the protocol before submitting it to FTP (the protocol) for processing. If not supported, the command is rejected outrightly by the local process and is subsequently declined access to the protocol itself.

There are two sets of FTP commands, referred to as *user* ftp commands, and *internal* ftp commands. User ftp commands are those that the user is capable of issuing at the ftp prompt. A list of supported user commands is available upon entering the help command at the prompt. Internal commands are, on the other hand, those that are peculiar to the protocol *per se*. These are commands that the FTP protocol, *not* the ftp command, supports. There is a relationship between the two command sets. As the example illustrates, the user command rstatus is mapped to the internal command STAT. Once successfully invoked, an ftp command may trigger a series of internal FTP commands and related responses.

FTP Internal Commands and Responses

The FTP protocol supports a wide range of commands designed to provide full protocol functionality and services from one end of the connection to the other. Table 27.1 contains a detailed listing of all commands that the RFC 959 standard recommends. I refer to the RFC 959 standard because some of those commands are not necessarily implemented on all UNIX platforms, and, consequently, their man pages might fail to reference all the commands cited below. RFC 959 specifies a minimum set of commands that require implementation for the ftp application to be branded compliant. Other than the specified minimum, vendors are left the freedom to adopt whatever other features are recommended by the RFC.

Table 27.1. FTP internal commands.

Command	Description
ABOR	Abort previous command and any associated transfer of data.
ACCT	User account ID; specified as an argument to the command.
ALLO	Allocate storage for forthcoming file transfer. Size is specified as command argument.
APPE	Append incoming data to an existing file; specified as command argument.
CDUP	Change directory up one level (to parent directory).
CWD	Change working directory on remote server; path specified as command argument.
DELE	Delete file; filename specified as command argument.
HELP	Send information regarding status of server implementation.
LIST	Transfer directory listing.

Command	Description
MKD	Make directory; directory path is specified as command argument.
MODE	Set transfer mode. One of three: stream, block, or compressed.
NLST	Transfer directory listing.
NOOP	Do nothing. If server is alive, it responds with OK.
PASS	User password.
PASV	Requests server to listen on a data port other than the default one.
PORT	Causes the server to change to a different data port than the currently used one.
PWD	Print working directory.
QUIT	Terminate the connection.
REIN	Reinitialize connection while allowing transfers in progress to complete.
REST	Restart marker. Causes the transfer to resume after being disrupted from a specified data checkpoint in the file.
RETR	Retrieve file specified in argument field.
RMD	Remove directory specified in argument field.
RNFR	Rename From; specifies the old pathname of the file that is to be renamed. This command is normally followed by a rename-to (RNTO) command specifying the new filename.
RNTO	Rename-to command.
SITE	Sends site-specific parameters to remote end. Such parameters are normally essential to file transfer but not sufficiently universal to be included as commands in the protocol.
SMNT	Mount file system.
STAT	Return status of service.
STOR	Accept and store data.
STOU	Accept and store data under a unique name.
STRU	Specifies the structure of the file pending transmission. The specified structure can be File, Record, or Page. The default is File.
SYST	Return type of operating system.
TYPE	Specifies type of data pending transmission. One of three: ASCII, EBCDIC, or BINARY.
USER	User ID.

27

FTP ADMINISTRATION

Most of the internal commands are made up of four ASCII character sequences, some of which require the use of arguments. The choice of encoding the commands using ASCII characters has the advantage of allowing expert system administrators to actually `telnet` the server at the FTP control port and execute most of the internal commands themselves—a capability that might prove useful in a troubleshooting exercise. ASCII encoding of commands also conveniently enables users to observe the command flow and make sense of it without having to employ specialized protocol analysis tools—let alone the advanced level of expertise required to operate such tools. To turn on the capability of tracing the flow of internal FTP commands, the user must enter the `debug` command at the `ftp` prompt before attempting any operation. This is demonstrated in the following example:

```
# ftp tenor
Connected to tenor.
220 tenor FTP server (UNIX(r) System V Release 4.0) ready.
Name (tenor:root):
331 Password required for root.
Password:
230 User root logged in.
ftp> debug
Debugging on (debug=1).
ftp> put testfile
local: testfile remote: testfile
---> PORT 100,0,0,2,4,103
200 PORT command successful.
---> STOR testfile
150 ASCII data connection for testfile (100.0.0.2,1127).
226 Transfer complete.
13415 bytes sent in 0.57 seconds (23 Kbytes/s)
ftp> quit
---> QUIT
221 Goodbye.
#
```

Notice how the internal commands are all represented using a sequence of ASCII uppercase characters.

FTP Responses

In addition to the internal commands, the FTP protocol supports a considerable range of responses. Responses are expressed using three-decimal digit notation. The place of each digit bears a certain significance to the interpretation of the response being examined. In the example, notice how every internal command is followed by a three-digit response. The responses to FTP commands are designed to ensure the synchronization of requests and actions in the process of file transfer. They also enable the user process (User-PI) to follow up on the status of the server. Every command is required to generate at least one response. In addition, some commands are required to occur in a certain sequence (for example, every RNFR should be followed immediately by an RNTO). A failure to produce an expected sequence suggests the existence of abnormalities either in the transmission process or in the software implementation.

An FTP reply consists of a three-digit number. The three-digit number is also accompanied by some text that either explains the reply (226 Transfer complete) or provides information pertaining to the reply itself. The textual information may vary from one FTP implementation to another. The three-digit code is standardized and cannot be changed.

Each of the three digits of the reply has a special significance. The first digit denotes whether the response conveys good, bad, or incomplete operational status. Table 27.2 summarizes the values that the most significant digit of the response can take and the significance of each value.

Table 27.2. Values of most significant digit in FTP response code and their corresponding meanings.

Value	Description
1	Requested action has been initiated; expect a reply before sending another action.
2	The action has completed successfully. User can send a new (and unrelated) action.
3	The action has been accepted; the requested action is being suspended until further information is received from user.
4	The action was not accepted due to a transient error. The requested action may be resubmitted for completion.
5	The action was not accepted due to permanent error. User may not resubmit request for the same action.

The middle digit provides more details about the response in question. Table 27.3 provides information about the values that this digit can take and the associated meaning.

Table 27.3. Values of middle digit in FTP response code and their corresponding meanings.

Value	Description
0	The reply refers to a syntax error.
1	Signify a reply to a request for information, such as status of connection.
2	The reply refers to data and control connection management function.
3	Reply pertains to login and authentication actions.
4	Not used.
5	Reply conveying the status of the server file system.

The third digit provides even finer details about the function categories specified in the middle digit. Listing all applicable values is beyond the scope of this chapter. Interested readers may reference RFP 959 for further details.

FTP Third-Party (Proxy) Transfers

There are situations when a user wants to transfer files between two FTP servers, neither of which is the local host that is attended to by the user. Figure 27.2 illustrates the situation. As shown in the diagram, a user at host jade may want to transfer files from host tenor to host alto. Of course, one way of doing this is to transfer files from host tenor to host jade and from host jade to host alto—thus doubling the network traffic arising from the desired transfer as well as unduly engaging the resources (CPU and disk) of host jade, not to mention the degradation in response time.

FIGURE 27.2.

Third-party transfer using the proxy FTP command.

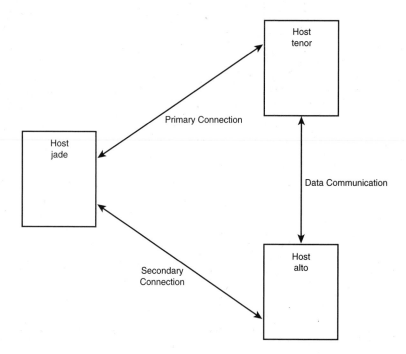

FTP service protocol provides a transfer mechanism that alleviates these performance bottlenecks. This mechanism is called *third-party transfer* or *proxy transfer*. Using this mechanism, the user at host jade can initiate control connections to both servers: hosts tenor and alto. The connection invoked first is the primary control connection, and the second is the secondary control connection. As shown in Figure 27.2, because the user logged in to the FTP service on host tenor first, this connection is the primary one, and the second to host alto is the secondary connection. When both connections are established, the user can set up a data connection between the two servers. In this fashion, control information is communicated over the control connections while data is transferred between the servers over the data connection without being routed through host jade.

Setting up a third-party transfer session is a matter of invoking ftp's proxy command at the ftp prompt after a primary FTP connection is established. In Figure 27.2, the user logs in to host tenor first, thus establishing a primary connection with that host. To invoke a secondary connection with host alto, the user should invoke the proxy open command at the ftp prompt (to obtain a list of all the commands that can be invoked on a secondary channel, enter **proxy ?**). The following output of a sample FTP session illustrates the proceedings of a third-party transfer that was invoked from host jade in Figure 52.1:

```
# ftp tenor
Connected to tenor.
220 tenor FTP server (UNIX(r) System V Release 4.0) ready.
Name (tenor:root):
331 Password required for root.
Password:
230 User root logged in.
ftp> proxy open alto
Connected to alto
220 alto FTP server (Version 5.60 #1) ready.
331 Password required for root.
230 User root logged in.
Remote system type is UNIX.
Using binary mode to transfer files.
ftp> pwd
tenor:257 "/" is current directory.
ftp> get testfile
local: testfile remote: testfile
tenor:200 PORT command successful.
tenor:150 ASCII data connection for testfile (100.0.0.2,1156) (12870 bytes).
tenor:226 ASCII Transfer complete.
13415 bytes received in 0.75 seconds (17 Kbytes/s)
ftp> quit
tenor:221 Goodbye.
alto Goodbye.
#
```

It's important to remember that some of the user ftp commands behave differently under a proxy transfer. For example, get and mget commands cause files to be transferred from the primary to the secondary, while put and mput cause file transfers from the secondary to the primary. So be careful with the use of these commands; there is the likelihood that if the same filename exists on both servers, one file might erroneously overwrite the other. To avoid this possibility, you should enable saving files under unique filenames using the sunique and runique ftp commands. For example, to enable storing files under unique names on the secondary channel you should issue the command as shown here:

```
ftp> proxy sunique
Store unique on.
ftp>
```

Third-party transfers can be conveniently used to carry out unattended, scheduled file transfers among different hosts from a central location. Using ftp scripts, the system administrator can describe the actions that the ftp client ought to take, as well as instructing it to log the output pertaining to all invoked sessions in a central log file. The script can then be scheduled (using cron) to run unattended at a time when the traffic is low on the network, typically, at night.

> **CAUTION**
>
> Not all server implementations support third-party transfers. Check with the vendor to verify that FTP internal command PASV is supported; if it isn't, a secondary connection cannot be used to initiate third-party transfers. A possible workaround is conditional on having PASV support on at least one of the involved servers, in which case, you invoke the primary connection with the server lacking the PASV support, and the secondary with the server that has it.

Administering FTP

The three main areas of FTP administration involve the following tasks:

- Setting up the service
- Setting up user environment
- Setting up secure anonymous FTP service

Setting Up the FTP Service

As explained in Chapter 20, aside from the basic TCP/IP services, such as routing and domain name services, all other services, including FTP, are started on an as-needed basis. On UNIX platforms, the FTP service is implemented in the ftpd daemon. This deamon, among others (such as telnetd for Telnet services), is started by the superserver daemon inetd. Not until inetd receives a request for the services of ftpd is the latter started and handed that request. To ensure that inetd is indeed listening on behalf of ftpd, you should ensure that the /etc/inetd.conf superserver configuration file has an entry for the ftpd daemon and that that entry is enabled. To enable an entry in the inetd.conf file, you simply uncomment it by removing the # character in front of it. Following is the listing of /etc/inetd.conf as it exists on one of the UNIX hosts:

```
#       @(#)inetd.conf    5.2 Lachman System V STREAMS TCP   source
#
#    System V STREAMS TCP - Release 4.0
#
#    Copyright 1990 Interactive Systems Corporation,(ISC)
#    All Rights Reserved.
#
#    Copyright 1987, 1988, 1989 Lachman Associates, Incorporated (LAI)
#    All Rights Reserved.
#
#      SCCS IDENTIFICATION
ftp     stream    tcp    nowait    NOLUID    /etc/ftpd      ftpd
telnet    stream    tcp    nowait    NOLUID    /etc/telnetd    telnetd
shell     stream    tcp    nowait    NOLUID    /etc/rshd    rshd
login     stream    tcp    nowait    NOLUID    /etc/rlogind    rlogind
exec     stream    tcp    nowait    NOLUID    /etc/rexecd    rexecd
finger     stream    tcp    nowait    nouser    /etc/fingerd    fingerd
```

```
#uucp    stream   tcp    nowait    NOLUID    /etc/uucpd    uucpd
# Enabling this allows public read files to be accessed via TFTP.
#tftp    dgram    udp    wait    nouser    /etc/tftpd    tftpd
# This is the more secure method, since only files from /tftpboot can
# be accessed via TFTP.  This must be root in order to do the chroot
# to /tftpboot.  /tftpboot must be created by hand.
#tftp    dgram    udp    wait    root    /etc/tftpd    tftpd -s /tftpboot
comsat   dgram    udp    wait    root    /etc/comsat    comsat
ntalk    dgram    udp    wait    root    /etc/talkd    talkd
#bootps    dgram    udp    wait    root    /etc/bootpd    bootpd
echo     stream   tcp    nowait    root    internal
discard    stream   tcp    nowait    root    internal
chargen    stream   tcp    nowait    root    internal
daytime    stream   tcp    nowait    root    internal
time     stream   tcp    nowait    root    internal
echo     dgram    udp    wait    root    internal
discard    dgram    udp    wait    root    internal
chargen    dgram    udp    wait    root    internal
daytime    dgram    udp    wait    root    internal
time     dgram    udp    wait    root    internal
smtp     stream   tcp    nowait    mmdf    /usr/mmdf/chans/smtpd smtpd /usr/mmdf/
chans/smtpsrvr smtp
```

According to this listing, the entry pertaining to the ftpd daemon is enabled. Consequently, inetd is expected to be listening on behalf of ftpd on the FTP control port. The inetd daemon knows which control port to listen on by referencing the /etc/services file, which contains simple entries depicting the name of each service and the TCP port it's required to be using. This file is referenced only when inetd is started. Consequently, making changes to the /etc/services file (or to the /etc/inetd.conf) won't take effect unless the inetd is restarted by rebooting the host or by sending inetd a SIGHUP signal.

> **CAUTION**
>
> It is vitally important that /etc/services is not deleted or changed in any way by inexperienced users. Tampering with this file can lead to trouble trying to connect to network services. As a system administrator, you are well advised to make a backup copy of it—just in case something happens to it.

Administering FTP Users

By default, anyone who has a valid user account on a UNIX host on which the ftpd daemon is enabled is capable of starting an FTP session with the server and transferring files from and to the server (subject to file system permissions). A system administrator can prevent a user from logging in to the FTP service by adding the user's login name in the /etc/ftpusers file. This is a simple text file containing a list of the account names (one line per login name) that are not allowed FTP access to the server. For security reasons, it is suggested that the file contain login names root and uucp. If the /etc/ftpusers file does not exist, users with valid login accounts will be able to log in to the system using FTP.

Even if a user's login name is not in the /etc/ftpusers file, and the user authenticates, she may still be prevented from accessing the FTP service. This condition occurs if the login attempt is being made from a shell that is not included in the /etc/shells file. Access to FTP service is granted, subject to successful authentication to users running any of the shells listed in the /etc/shells file. Here is an example of the contents of this file:

```
#       @(#)shells    4.2 Lachman System V STREAMS TCP  source
#       SCCS IDENTIFICATION
/bin/csh
/bin/sh
/bin/ksh
/usr/local/bin/ksh
/usr/bin/scosh
```

CHECK YOUR SHELLS!

Some UNIX systems (for example Solaris 2.5), by default, have no /etc/shells file, a condition that leaves a door open to hackers to come through to tamper with the system. The nonexistence of the /etc/shells file enables users access from any shell. Always make sure that the file exists. If it doesn't, create it, and include in it only the shells that you want to allow users to use when accessing your system.

Autologin and .netrc

Inexperienced users can make it necessary for you (the system administrator) to automate the login process to the FTP server. Users who need to frequently access the service may find the routine of entering their username and password annoying. Fortunately, ftp provides an autologin functionality that automates the entire process. This is achieved by creating a file called .netrc in the user's home directory. The .netrc file contains both login and ftp initialization parameters to be used by an autologin procedure. Before you create the file, however, you should first test the desired setting on the command line.

Multiple entries can be included in the .netrc file, one per remote host, specifying the autologin authentication information and the pertinent initialization parameters. Following is a partial depiction of the syntax of the .netrc file entries:

```
machine hostname ¦ default login login_id password password     macdef
macfilename
```

In this syntax

machine *hostname*	Specifies the name or the IP address of the remote host you want to establish an FTP session with.
default	Matches any machine name not included in any of the .netrc entries. Only *one* default entry can be included, and it must show as the *last* entry in the file.

Login *login_id*	Specifies the user's login ID on the remote host.
password *password*	Specifies the user's password. Note that, for security reasons, if this token is present, ftp requires that the file be protected from being read by anyone other than the user. The permissions on .netrc should, consequently, be set to 600. Failure to meet this condition aborts any attempt to autologin to the remote host.
Macdef *macfilename*	Specifies the name of a user-defined macro, defining all the initialization parameters. Refer to the man pages for more information.

In the following two examples, the first entry autologs user adel to host tenor and establishes an ftp session on her behalf with that host. The second entry allows adel to log in to other servers with the specified default account specifications:

```
machine tenor login adel password letmein
default login adel pasword jamsession
```

To establish a session with tenor, adel must enter this:

```
# ftp tenor
Connected to tenor.
220 tenor FTP server (UNIX(r) System V Release 4.0) ready.
331 Password required for adel.
230 User adel logged in.
ftp>
```

Notice how the user is not required to enter the login ID or the password.

To establish a session with any other host, adel must have an account maintained on all the servers she wants to log in to with same login ID (adel) and password (jamsession).

Anonymous FTP

With the phenomenal growth in the popularity of the Internet, many organizations began offering a wide range of Internet services, including the distribution of software, information, technical support, and other services. Anonymous FTP access was among the earliest methods used to offer such services on the Internet. Even when users resort to Web browsers to download files from the Internet, the browser invokes an FTP connection on behalf of the user, and logs him in to the server in anonymous capacity before the download process is actually started.

Anonymous FTP access provides users who do not have an account with the FTP server the ability to establish an FTP session with that server. Users use anonymous for user name, and their e-mail address for the password.

A user who logs in anonymously is misled to believe that he is at the root of the file system. This restriction provides an extra level of security, protecting the rest of the file system from use by anonymous users. Most UNIX variants included in the ftpd daemon have a feature that forces the daemon to change the root of the file system to the home directory of a special account. The account name is `ftp`. Assuming that the home directory of the FTP account is `/home/ftp`, the `ftpd` daemon uses `chroot` to change the root of the file system to `/home/ftp` for that user.

Setting Up Anonymous FTP Service

Setting up an FTP server for anonymous access involves creating the `ftp` user account and creating a mini-file system under the home directory of `ftp`. The directory must contain the necessary file system resources that render anonymous access functional. In general, following are the required steps for providing anonymous FTP access:

- Create the user `ftp` in `/etc/passwd`. Make the user belong to a new group (group `ftp`). The user's home directory becomes the root of the file system that anonymous users see. Once the `ftp` account is created, anonymous FTP access is enabled on the server. Following is a depiction of the ftp account entry in the `/etc/passwd` file:

  `ftp:x:5000:5000:Anonymous FTP:/home/ftp:/noshell`

  Notice that the specified shell is `noshell`. Since `noshell` does not exist, security of the `ftp` account is being reinforced by preventing the use of this account for login and subsequent tampering with the file system. There should be no need for anybody including `root` to try accessing the host using the `ftp` account.

- Create home directory and assign its ownership to `root` with the same group as that to which the ftp account is made to belong (to GID 5000 in the example entry). The directory must not be writable by anyone. For security, assign the permissions 555 to the `~ftp` directory.

- Create the `~ftp/bin` directory. Assign ownership to `root`, and permissions should be set to disallow anyone from writing to the directory. In this directory, the `/usr/bin/ls` command must be present to enable users to list its contents. The permissions on `/usr/bin/ls` should be set to 111.

- Create `~ftp/etc`. This directory must contain a stripped version of the `/etc/passwd` file, `/etc/group`, and `/etc/netconfig`. These files must be present for the `ls` command to work satisfactorily. Set permissions on the `~ftp` directory to 444.

- Create the `~ftp/dev` directory and assign its ownership to root. This directory must contain both special files `dev/tcp` and `/dev/tcp`. Both files must be created using the `mknod` command. The major and minor numbers corresponding to each file can be obtained by using the `ls -1L` command.

  Failure to include any of `~ftp/dev/tcp`, `~ftp/dev/zero` or `~ftp/etc/netconfig` may cause the error message `"Can't create data socket (0.0.0.0,20): Bad file number"` upon attempting to transfer files from the server. Also, the permissions on `~ftp/dev/tcp` and `~ftp/dev/zero` should be set to 666. Otherwise, passive FTP requests might fail, resulting with `permission denied` error messages.

- Create the ~ftp/usr/lib directory and assign its ownership to root. This directory should contain a copy of all of the following shared libraries from /usr/lib:

```
ld.so*
libc.so*
libdl.so*
libintl.so*
libw.so*
libnsl.so*
libsocket.so*
nss_nis.so*
nss_nisplus.so*
nss_dns.so*
nss_files.so*
straddr.so*
```

- Create the directory ~ftp/pub, assign its ownership to ftp and set its permissions to 555. This is the directory where public access is allowed via the anonymous login. This is where you want to put files for public distribution.

The above steps are generic and apply to most variants of FTP implementation on UNIX platforms.

SOLARIS ANONYMOUS FTP SETUP

The ftp man pages included in Solaris 2.x include a shell script that auto-creates the entire setup of the anonymous FTP server.

TIP

If you are interested in a highly configurable and secure FTP daemon, you might want to give the Wuarchive FTP 2.4 daemon a try. You can download a copy of it from ftp.uu.net server. It is in the /networking/ftp/wuarchive-ftpd directory. The directory includes implementation for both BSD and SVR4 variants of UNIX. The archive file contains documentation that explains all of the daemon's features, how to set it up and configure it properly.

How Secure Is the Server

After completing the setup and verifying the success of logging in anonymously, it is prudent to verify that you did not leave behind any security loopholes that may lead to unwelcome intrusion (and the potential loss of your job). Following are the minimum recommended checks you should make:

- Log in to the server as anonymous user and verify that the account cannot be used to create files or directories in any of the directories you created as part of the setup. Particular attention should be given to the home directory of the FTP account. If created, the .rhosts file grants instant access to hackers from across the Internet.

- Check to see whether the ftp command SITE CHMOD is implemented. If it is, it can be at the heart of serious security breaches. Similarly, check for the SITE EXEC command. The way to do this check is by telnetting to the host at port 21(this is FTP's default port). If you can and are able to execute the SITE EXEC command or SITE CHMOD command, you'd be better off replacing the ftpd daemon with a more secure one (see the preceding Tip).

- Make sure that the home directory is not owned by ftp. Remember, lots of UNIX security depends on the contents of the users' home directories. If they are owned by ftp, you are potentially allowing the smart hacker unlimited access if he successfully changes its permissions to 777 (see the remark on SITE CHMOD in the preceding bulleted item).

- Make sure no files or subdirectories under ftp's home directory are owned by ftp to prevent an intruder from replacing them using virus-contaminated files.

Unattended FTP Transfers

There are times when the need arises to transfer many large files using FTP. If you do it manually, you must log in to the target server and attend to the transfer process on a file-by-file basis. Depending on the size of the files, you might end up spending considerable time waiting for each transfer to complete before initiating the next one. Add to this scenario the requirement to have the transfers carried out after hours, which is usually the case, and you find yourself in an unpleasant situation. Not to worry, because most of the ftp (client) implementations that exist on the UNIX platforms include support for unattended operation. Better still, these ftp clients can take input from script files containing details of the action requests you want executed to bring about the desired results.

Here are the required steps to implementing unattended ftp sessions:

- Using vi, or your preferred text editor, create a file containing all the ftp commands that are required to invoke the desired actions. Here is an example of what a simple file might contain:

```
open tenor
user maya  apassword
binary
cd /incoming
put myfile
bye
```

This file specifies all the actions necessary for the transfer of the file myfile to the /incoming directory on host tenor. Notice how the file starts with an open command specifying the host name of the target server. Next, the user name (maya) and password (apassword) are sent to host tenor for authentication using the ftp user command. Assuming that all goes well, the transfer mode is set to binary, a change directory command (cd) is issued, and the put command transfers the file myfile to host tenor. Upon completion of the transfer, the script instructs the ftp client to drop the connection using the `bye` command. Because the order in which the `ftp` commands are listed is vital to the success of the unattended operation, it makes sense to rehearse the commands following the exact order depicted in the file. This way you can assess its accuracy and take corrective measures, if needed, before trusting the script to production.

■ Next, verify the automated operation of the script. To invoke FTP and let it execute the contents of the script without human intervention, enter the following on the command line:

```
# ftp -vin < scriptname
```

where

`-v`	Stands for verbose mode. As implied, this switch turns on verbosity. It helps you follow on the "conversation" taking place between the FTP server and your client. Hence, it is convenient for troubleshooting the script.
`-n`	Turns off the autologin feature. If this switch is not included, ftp attempts autologin based on any `.netrc` file it might find in your home directory. The login initialization parameters contained in that file might cause some conflicts leading to abortion of the session.
`-i`	Turns off interactive prompting during multiple file transfers—a time-saving feature.
`scriptname`	Is the name of the file that contains the ftp script.

Following is a simple script called `ftpscript`:

```
open tenor
user root apassword
cd /usr/sam
put *
ls * ftplist
bye
```

and the following is the output resulting from its execution:

```
# ftp -vin < ftpscript
Connected to tenor.
220 tenor FTP server (UNIX(r) System V Release 4.0) ready.
331 Password required for root.
230 User root logged in.
250 CWD command successful.
local: budget.rpt remote: budget.rpt
200 PORT command successful.
150 ASCII data connection for budget.rpt (100.0.0.2,1239).
226 Transfer complete.
746 bytes sent in 0.03 seconds (24 Kbytes/s)
200 PORT command successful.
150 ASCII data connection for /bin/ls (100.0.0.2,1241) (0 bytes).
226 ASCII Transfer complete.
221 Goodbye.
#
```

This script included something that the previous one did not include: the `ls /usr/root/ftplist` command. Notice that this command is included right after the `mput` command. This command helps verify whether the files intended for transfer were indeed transferred to the destination host. Because this is meant to be an unattended operation, the filename (`/usr/root/ftplist`) is included as an argument for the `ls` command, forcing it to log the returned listing to the specified file, and making the information conveniently available for subsequent verification.

■ After you rehearse the script, as suggested, and trust it, you can use either at or cron tools to schedule it for execution at any desired time. You can omit the `-v` switch if desired, which turns verbosity off so that the command looks like this in the cron entry:

```
ftp -in < ftpscript
```

Preferably, however, you'd rather have verbosity on, and redirect its output to a log file. This way, should the session fail to meet your expectation, you can look up the session details as logged in the file for further analysis while trying to narrow in on the causes underlying the failure. Here is the command for meeting the logging requirement:

```
ftp -inv < ftpscript > logfile
```

Using the ability to schedule unattended FTP file transfers, and the third-party transfer capability together, a system administrator can virtually perform unattended transfers not only between her server and another machine but between any two hosts on the network.

Troubleshooting FTP

As a system administrator, you are required to respond to and solve user-and system-related problems including those resulting from the use of FTP. There is a wide range of reasons that might cause an FTP session to fail; anything from user configuration error and network failure to problems resulting from system failure or defective software. Hardware and network-related problems are dealt with in detail in Chapter 20. In this section, only issues directly related to FTP are considered. Following are suggested areas of investigation that might prove worthwhile in sorting out FTP failures:

■ If a user reports a problem connecting, the first thing that you might want to do is attend to the user's workstation (if possible) and ask that user to go through the motions of logging in. Verify that the user is following the proper login procedure. If not, educate the user on how to do it.

■ If, even after the user follows the proper procedures, he is still having problems connecting to a server, try to assess whether the failure is a local configuration issue on the client workstation, a local hardware problem, or a network problem. If the user is getting a `Connection refused` type of error, the problem is likely to be a logical one. There are several reasons for this error to arise:

1. If the user relies on the $HOME/.netrc file to autologin to the server, check the contents of the file and ask the user to verify the information pertinent to the login process. Invalid information can lead to the server's refusal to connect a user. If all is fine with the contents of the .netrc file, check its permissions. The permissions should be set so that no one but the owner is allowed to read or write its contents. Failure to meet this requirement can result in failure to log in to an FTP server.

2. Verify that the user has a valid account on the remote server. If not, or if the account is expired, you might refer her to the administrator of the host in question for subsequent resolution.

3. Another thing to look at to explain a valid account's failure to FTP the server is the /etc/ftpusers file. If it exists and the account name is included in the file, the ftpd daemon prevents the user from logging in. Again, recommend that the user bring up the issue with the administrator of the host in question for resolution.

4. Users failing to use one of the shells specified in the /etc/shells file are bound to fail to connect via FTP. Check the /etc/shells file on the target host and take the required action to remedy the situation.

5. Although rare, it is possible that somehow the port on which the ftpd daemon is listening to connections is changed to other than the default (21). Should this happen, FTP clients defaulting to port 21 when making connection requests will be refused entry to the server. Check the server's /etc/services file to verify the port number on which inetd is listening on behalf of ftpd for connection request. This can be accomplished using the following command:

```
# grep ftp /etc/services
ftp     21/tcp
...
```

If the port number is different from 21, this is where the trouble lies. Contact the system administrator for that host and try to find out why this is so. The port number might have been changed maliciously, or might have been required for other reasons. Depending on the reason, the port might have to be changed back to the default or left at its new value. In the latter case, the user should be advised to try to FTP to that host using the existing port. Assuming that the port number is 420, the FTP command should look like this:

```
# ftp hostname 420
```

■ If users complain about frequent abrupt disconnection of FTP sessions, you might want to increase the timeout value set for the ftpd daemon. By default, most daemons self-configure on startup to 15 minutes. Congested network conditions might lead to server timeouts, resulting in disruption to ongoing user sessions. Try increasing the timeout value on the server. Be careful not to set it too high; otherwise, users with idling FTP sessions end up needlessly hogging FTP connections at the expense of other users waiting for their release. To change the timeout value on the server, edit the /etc/inetd.conf file, and adjust the entry affecting the ftpd daemon to include the -ttimeout command parameter as shown in this example:

```
ftp     stream    tcp     nowait    NOLUID    /etc/ftpd -t1800    ftpd
```

According to this entry the timeout value has been increased to 1800 seconds (30 minutes). After making the change, send the inetd daemon a SIGHUP signal to reinitialize it so that the new change takes effect.

■ If a user complains about the inability to transfer multiple files using mput along with wild characters in the filename specification, verify that she has filename expansion turned on. Filename expansion can be toggled using the ftp glob command as shown below:

```
ftp> glob
Globbing turned off
ftp> glob
Globbing turned on
ftp>
```

■ Users complaining about failure to transfer files reliably might have ASCII transfer type turned on instead of BINARY type when sending or receiving non-ASCII files. Verify the transfer type and take corrective action (including educating the user) if need be.

■ One thing you might want to try to resolve some of the more complex problems is to turn on debugging upon invocation of the FTP session. You can do this upon invoking the ftp command by using the -d switch

```
# ftp -d hostname
```

or after invoking ftp using the debug command

```
ftp> debug
Debugging turned on.
ftp>
```

The debug mode allows you to follow up on the progress of the FTP session. Whenever enabled, it displays session data indicating the direction of the exchange and the ftp messages being exchanged. As shown in the following example, -[ra] indicates that the local host is sending, whereas a three-digit code indicates that the remote host is sending:

```
# ftp tenor
Connected to tenor.
220 tenor FTP server (UNIX(r) System V Release 4.0) ready.
331 Password required for root.
230 User root logged in.
ftp> debug
Debugging on (debug=1).
ftp> cd /usr/sam
---> CWD /usr/sam
250 CWD command successful.
ftp> ls
---> PORT 100,0,0,2,5,6
200 PORT command successful.
```

```
---> LIST
150 ASCII data connection for /bin/ls (100.0.0.2,1286) (0 bytes).
total 6
-rw-rw-rw-   1 root     other          55 Oct 19 15:55 ftpscript
-rw-rw-rw-   1 root     other         721 Oct 19 15:55 proxy
-rw-rw-rw-   1 root     other       10153 Oct 17 19:42 sendAriel
-rw-rw-rw-   1 root     other         204 Oct 19 15:55 tenor.ftp
-rw-rw-rw-   1 root     other         519 Oct 19 15:55 tenor.help
-rw-rw-rw-   1 root     other       12870 Oct 19 15:55 testfile
226 ASCII Transfer complete.
ftp> get testfile
local: testfile remote: testfile
---> PORT 100,0,0,2,5,8
200 PORT command successful.
---> RETR testfile
150 ASCII data connection for testfile (100.0.0.2,1288) (12870 bytes).
226 ASCII Transfer complete.
13415 bytes received in 0.58 seconds (23 Kbytes/s)
ftp> quit
---> QUIT
221 Goodbye.
#
```

■ Server-related problems can result from software bugs or poor implementation. Similar to the client, the ftpd daemon comes with a -d switch, which can be optionally used to turn on debugging. Once turned on, debugging data are logged to the /usr/adm/syslog file. Equally possible is the ability to log details pertaining to individual FTP sessions. This is achieved by specifying the -1 switch in the entry for ftpd in the /etc/inetd.conf file as shown below:

```
ftp     stream    tcp   nowait    NOLUID    /etc/ftpd -1    ftpd
```

Be careful not to leave debugging or logging turned on for too long. The /usr/adm/syslog file can grow to an astronomical size over a short period of time due to the amount of details both modes generate. Turn them off as soon as you finish troubleshooting.

Summary

FTP service protocol is probably the most widely used method of downloading and uploading files to UNIX and other hosts on the Internet. Even Web browsers use FTP as the underlying mechanism for transferring files when requested. Consequently, system administrators are faced more than ever with the challenging task of providing reliable and secure across-the-Internet FTP services. The associated tasks involve setting up FTP services for local access as well as setting up anonymous FTP service for the Internet community of users. Setting up such services requires a solid understanding of how the FTP protocol works. Equally involved is developing the required skills to troubleshoot FTP services in the most efficient way.

This chapter shows how to set up FTP services, including anonymous access. It also includes tips on verifying the security of the service. Both third-party transfers and unattended transfers are explained and illustrated. Finally, common FTP problems and ways of troubleshooting them are discussed.

Most implementations of FTP servers and clients are similar in features and capabilities. For details of the implementation, check the vendor's documentation. A fair assessment of the implementation falls short of achieving the desired goal if not done in the light of a thorough reading of the standard.

CHAPTER 28

Backing Up and Restoring Your System

by Chris Byers

IN THIS CHAPTER

In a perfect world, no one would ever lose data, disks would never fail, controllers would never go haywire, and every system would have the rm command aliased to ask you if you really want to delete all your data.

According to Murphy, there is no such thing as a perfect world. You will lose your data, your disks will fail, your controllers will go postal on you at some point, and you probably don't have any commands aliased, much less the rm command. The question really isn't *if* the worst will happen; it's *when* it will happen.

Fortunately, you have a way of protecting your data (and most likely your job). UNIX comes standard with a number of relatively flexible and rigorous archiving and tape backup systems that can fit into almost any hardware architecture. In addition to these standards, there are a number of proprietary commands for vendor specific operating systems and hardware that can provide a full system recovery solution.

In this chapter, we will look at these backup solutions and how best to implement them, as well as the variations in solutions between UNIX variants that come standard with each operating system, as each one varies from the others in terms of implementation and backup strategy. These are the topics we'll be covering:

- Using the tar command
- Using the dump command
- Using cpio
- Making backups on HP-UX systems
- Making backups on AIX systems
- Making backups on Solaris systems
- Making backups on SVR4 systems
- Making backups on IRIX systems
- Making backups on BSD systems

Finally, we will take a quick look at some third-party utilities for complete system (multiserver and workstation) backups and restores.

Using the tar Command

One of the oldest and most often used commands for archiving and backing up files is the tar command. Because of its simplicity and ease of use, this is the most common format for tape and disk archives today, and probably for many years to come. This means that, for example, a tape from a Silicon Graphics workstation can be restored to a Hewlett-Packard HP9000 server without any problems.

One of the best features of tar is the flexibility to save to any medium, since it treats file and tape (or other backup media) device targets the same.

You can also specify files and directories that you want to include or exclude. You can specify them on the command line, or you can specify a file containing a list of files to include or exclude.

The format of the `tar` command is:

```
tar (options) (tarfile name) (filenames to backup or restore)
```

Typically, the most common groups of options used are `cvf` for writing to a `tarfile`, `xvf` for extracting files and `tvf` for listing the contents of a `tar` archive.

As an example of writing to a tape archive, to archive all the directories in the `/usr/local/datafiles` directory to a typical 4mm tape drive on a Hewlett-Packard machine, you would use the following command:

```
tar cvf /dev/rmt/0hc /usr/local/datafiles
```

Keep in mind that if you use the absolute path of the directory, you can only restore to that directory. A more flexible approach would be to get into the `/usr/local` directory and back up the directory, as follows:

```
cd /usr/local
```

```
tar cvf /dev/rmt/0hc datafiles
```

This way, if you want to restore the `datafiles` subdirectory, archived in the last example, to a different location, you can first `cd` to the appropriate place and then restore. For example, if you want to restore the `datafiles` subdirectory to the `/usr/contrib` subdirectory, you would do the following:

```
cd /usr/contrib
```

```
tar xvf /dev/rmt/0hc
```

If you are unsure what is on the tape, you can list the contents first. Since this can take just as long as restoring and the list of files usually scrolls off the screen, I usually redirect the output to a file, which I can then save as a record of backed up files:

```
tar tvf /dev/rmt/0hc > tarlist.txt
```

This is also a good way to get a printout of what is on a tape, since you can print off the `tarlist.txt` file directly. I try to keep this printout with the tape so I don't have to waste time when I need it.

If you know which specific files and subdirectories you want to restore, you can use an `include` file to grab only what you need. Let's say you copied the `tarlist.txt` file to a file called `include`, then edited out all the files except the ones you want to restore. The command would then look like this:

```
tar xvf /dev/rmt0 -I include
```

This will scroll through the tape and get just the files specified. You can also use an `include` file when archiving to tape and when looking for a list of specific files.

28

BACKING UP AND
RESTORING YOUR
SYSTEM

Using the dump Command

The dump command essentially has the same functionality as the tar command, with the exception that it is somewhat more rigorous than tar. With dump, you can back up an entire file system or specified files and directories in a file system. In addition, you can specify a "dump level" (priority for saving files) to indicate the currency (last modification time) of the files to be backed up.

For example, if a level 2 dump is done on one day and a level 4 dump is done on the following day, only the files that have been modified or added since the level 2 dump will be backed up to the level 4 dump. The date and level of prior dumps are listed in the file /etc/dumpdates. Dump uses this file as a reference to decide which files to back up. If a dump command is not successful, it will not update this file.

Used in conjunction with the system scheduler (cron), this can be an effective solution for continuous system backups and archives.

In general, dump is used in the following format:

```
/usr/etc/dump [options [arguments]] filesystem
```

A typical example of this command would be the following,

```
/usr/etc/dump /dev/nrst0 /dev/sd0h
```

where /dev/nrst0 is the no-rewind tape device file and /dev/sd0h is the file system device file of the file system to be backed up. You must get the file system device filename from the output of df, cross-referenced with the appropriate directory. This example was taken from a Sun system.

In addition to dumping file systems, you can dump specific files. However, if you choose to do this, you can only back up files at level 0. As a matter of fact, the /etc/dumpdates file is never even used, even if you choose the -u option.

As an example, let's say we want to dump the files chapter1 and chapter2 to an 8mm tape drive. The command would look something like this:

```
dump fdsb /dev/rst0 5400 6000 126 chapter1 chapter2
```

Consult the man pages for more information on the options available for each particular tape drive.

Using cpio

One of the more popular generic backup utilities in use today is the cpio command. In large part, its popularity is due to its capability to append backup volumes and span tapes, allowing you to create incremental backup sets and full systems backups without losing data integrity.

cpio allows you to copy files into and out of a cpio archive. If you use the -o option, it contains pathname and status information, as well as the contents of one or more archived files. cpio stands for copy in/out. The following is an example of using this command to back up the contents of a directory. The device file of the tape drive in this example is /dev/mt0:

```
ls ¦ cpio -o > /dev/mt0
```

where the -o option copies out an archive.

Also, to read from a cpio archive on a tape drive, you can do something similar to the following example:

```
cpio -icdB < /dev/rmt0
```

where -i copies to an archive, c writes header information in ASCII character form, d creates directories as needed, and B blocks input to 512 bytes to the record.

You can also use the find command to see if a particular file is listed on your tape (or disk) archive:

```
find . -cpio /dev/rmt/0m
```

Consult your man pages for a more complete explanation of all the options available.

Making Backups on HP-UX Systems

Although tar and cpio are versatile and generic tools for doing both system backups and simple file archives, they lack some features for convenience and ease of use, as well as logging and error recovery. In the next few sections we will discuss the proprietary backup solutions that are available with some of the more popular UNIX variants.

fbackup

Hewlett-Packard came out with their own version of a UNIX operating system based on Berkely's (BSD) UNIX OS code. Their systems are known as HP9000 systems; their servers are designated as S800 series machines; and their workstations are designated as S700 series machines. Also, they have various HP-UX operating system versions available, from the earliest release of HPUX 8.x to the latest release of HPUX 10.20 (at the time of writing). On all HP9000 machines, the fbackup utility comes with the operating system as an effective system and file backup solution. fbackup combines the functionality of ftio (an extension of cpio) with the ease of use of the tar command, as well as a few extras.

fbackup gives you the option to include directories and files in your backup. On specifying a directory, all of the files and subdirectories in that directory are backed up. You can use the -i option with fbackup, or you can use a graph file, which I will cover later.

You can also exclude files from your backup set in a similar manner as the include files. Use the -e option to with the fbackup command to exclude files and/or directories and subdirectories.

Using graph files is a good way to get just what you want backed up or restored, without a ridiculously long command line. You can only have one entry per line in a graph file for files or directories, and they must be preceded by an i (for include) or an e (for exclude).

As an example, you can back up the /home directory and exclude the /home/joe directory with the following graph file:

```
i /home
```

```
e /home/joe
```

fbackup uses the -g option to identify a graph file.

To use the fbackup command, follows these steps to ensure data integrity and stability:

1. Make sure you are superuser.
2. Make sure that the files you want to back up are not in use or locked during the fbackup.
3. Make sure your tape drive is connected correctly and that you have the right device file pointing to the right SCSI device and that it is turned on (you'd be surprised how many times this is the problem).
4. Put the tape in the drive, with write protection turned off on the tape. If your backup spans multiple tapes, you will be asked to insert the next tape(s) as needed.
5. You can now start backing up using fbackup.

The following is an example of an fbackup command:

```
fbackup -f /dev/rmt/0m -I /home
```

This will back up the entire contents of /home to the device file /dev/rmt/0m. The device file used in this example (/dev/rmt/0m) is commonly used for medium-density 4mm DAT tapes used in DDS2 tape drives. To find the correct device file for your tape device, you might have to do some digging.

TIP

If you know that your data will take up two tapes and you have two tape drives attached to your machine, you can do an unattended backup by specifying two tape drives in the fbackup command. For example:

```
fbackup -f /dev/rmt/0m -f /dev/rmt/c0t1d0BEST -i / -I /tmp/index
```

This way, when the first tape fills up, the next tape is automatically written to as a continuation of the backup set.

frecover

In order to restore from tape you must use the `frecover` command. Many of the options for `fbackup` are used in `frecover` as well.

To restore backup files from `fbackup` tapes using the `frecover` utility, you need to follow these steps:

1. Make sure you are superuser.
2. Make sure the files you want to restore aren't open or locked. Just as `fbackup` wouldn't work with open or locked files, neither will `frecover`.
3. Make sure the tape device is hooked up correctly.
4. Make sure you have the right tape in the machine to restore from.
5. Start restoring with the `frecover` command.

If you wish to recover all files from a backup, you would use the `-r` option. By using the `-x` option, you can get individual files from tape. For all the options, check the man pages for `frecover(1M)`.

If you are restoring files that are NFS mounted to your system, you may run into some problems. The `frecover` command can only restore files that have "other user" write permission. If you are going to do this, first log in as superuser on the NFS file server and use the `root=` option to the `/usr/sbin/exportfs` command (on 10.x systems) to export the permissions.

Following is an example of restoring files in the directory `/home/joe` from tape:

```
frecover -x -i /home/joe
```

This command will not overwrite newer files as long as the `-o` option is not specified.

If you want to restore files from all directories under `/home/dave` from a DAT tape to the `/tmp` directory, you would do the following:

```
cd /tmp

frecover -x -oF -i /home/dave
```

So what happened here? The `-F` option removed the leading pathnames from all of the files on the tape that met the include criteria, causing them to be restored to the current directory without leading directories. All files were overwritten because of the `-o` option.

Again, all the options are explained in detail in the man pages for `frecover`.

Making Backups on AIX Systems

IBM's UNIX solution, AIX, comes with a very flexible and complete backup solution, known as the `mksysb` utility. With `mksysb`, you can backup up individual files, the root file system, or the entire system if this fits your need (and who wouldn't have that need!).

Specifically, AIX 3 only gives you the option of backing up the root volume group, But AIX 4 includes additional commands that give you the same functionality for other volume groups as well. By using `mksysb` as a system backup instead of a standard backup, you can get your system back much more quickly because you are skipping the step of first installing a system from scratch and then restoring data. This is a very effective solution for disaster recovery.

AIX 3.2 System Cloning

You can create clone images of the root volume group in two ways: either by using the command `mkszfile && mksysb -f /dev/rmt0` (`/dev/rmt0` being the backup device) or running `smit mksysb`. The `mksysb` image can be installed on different machines if need be. As a matter of fact, this is standard practice in disaster recovery testing.

Although you can restore to a different system, you may need to change other system configuration parameters to fit the new system, such as IP addresses. By configuring only the common settings for your systems, you avoid problems relating to machine specific issues, particularly IP addresses that could cause conflicts.

You can adapt the clone the first time it boots on the new machine through a simple script that can be executed only once on the first boot. The script is called `/etc/firstboot`, and it is executed by the cloned machine immediately after `/etc/rc` on bootup. This script will only be executed once if it exists, then it is renamed `/etc/fb_hh_mm_MM_DD` in accordance with the current date. The `fbcheck` entry in `/etc/inittab` handles this process.

When you clone an AIX 3.2 system, you also create a list of file systems to be created. The command that does this is the `mkszfile` command. This will create the `/.fs.size` file, which stores the sizes of the file systems for the clone. Typically, this file will follow a format similar to the following:

```
imageinstall
rootvg 4 hd4 / 2 8 jfs
rootvg 4 hd1 /home 31 84 jfs
rootvg 4 hd3 /tmp 3 12 jfs
rootvg 4 hd2 /usr 178 712 jfs
rootvg 4 hd9var /var 3 12 jfs
```

Looking at the file you can see, from left to right, the volume group, the logical partition size, the name of the logical volume, the name of the file system, the size in physical partitions, the size in magabytes and the type of the file system (`jfs` stands for the journaled file system).

NOTE

You must make sure that `/usr` and `/tmp` have at least 8 MB free before you create the tape. This will avoid problems with the installation of the new machine.

Restoring an AIX 3.2 System from `mksysb`

To completely restore an entire system from the tape, you need to have the tape in the primary tape drive (usually `/dev/rmt0`). You put the key in the service position (after you halt the system), double-click the reset button, and wait. The system reboots and displays a menu, giving you the option to restore from the `mksysb` tape, boot into a service kernel, or run system diagnostics. All you have to do is choose the restore option and go get some coffee for anywhere from 30 minutes to an hour (depending on the size of your `rootvg`).

A `mksysb` tape actually stores files in `tar` format. The image starts at the third file on the tape, so you have to position the tape at that file and restore using a non-rewinding tape device. This means you can get any file off a `mksysb` tape with a `tar` command.

For example, if you need to get the `vi` command back, just put the `mksysb` tape in the tape drive (in this case, `/dev/rmt0`) and do the following:

```
cd /                          # get to the root directory

tctl -f /dev/rmt0 rewind      # rewind the tape

tctl -f /dev/rmt0.1 fsf 3     # move the tape to the third file, no rewind

tar -xvf /dev/rmt0.1 ./usr/bin/vi    # extract the vi binary, no rewind
```

You must `cd` to `/` first, since all files are stored relative to `root`.

AIX 4 System Cloning

In AIX 4 you can do more than just back up the root volume group. You can control file system sizes and placement through configuration files and different installation methods. Also, you can specify options as you need them.

Instead of creating the `/.fs.size` file, `mkszfile` in AIX 4 creates the `/image.data` file, which has much more sophistication than its predecessor. You can also give it more customization through the `/bosinst.data` file, which is automatically created by `mksysb` unless it has already been created manually. AIX comes with a default `/bosinst.data` file, located in `/usr/lpp/bosinst/bosinst.template`.

You can generate a system backup by using the following command:

```
mksysb -i /dev/rmt0
```

Using the `-i` option will cause `mksysb` to call the `mkszfile` command automatically. Specifying the `-m` will cause `mkszfile` to generate logical volume maps, which are included on the image. If you do this, you can also clone the exact location of the file systems on the new system. There is also a new option, `-e`, which will exclude the files from being backed up which can be defined in the file `/etc/exclude.rootvg`.

To contrast the two, the /bosinst.data file controls how a mksysb image is installed, and the /image.data file defines the characteristics of the root volume group and the file systems within it.

The following is a common bosints.data file:

```
control_flow:
    CONSOLE =
    INSTALL_METHOD = overwrite
    PROMPT = yes
    EXISTING_SYSTEM_OVERWRITE = yes
    INSTALL_X_IF_ADAPTER = yes
    RUN_STARTUP = yes
    ERROR_EXIT =
    CUSTOMIZATION_FILE =
    TCB = yes
    INSTALL_TYPE = full
    BUNDLES =

target_disk_data:
    LOCATION = 00-00-0S-0,0
    SIZE_MB = 1307
    HDISKNAME = hdisk0

locale:
    BOSINST_LANG = en_US
    CULTURAL_CONVENTION = C
    MESSAGES = C
    KEYBOARD = de_DE
```

These values can be changed as needed.

The CONSOLE value defines the console device. If you set the PROMPT value to no, you must set it, or the system will not know which device to use for the console. A couple of common examples are /dev/lft0 or /dev/tty0.

The INSTALL_METHOD value sets the installation method, most commonly set to overwrite, particularly for clone tapes. You can set the preserve and migrate options for updating systems, but you cannot use this for cloning.

The PROMPT value must be set to no for an automated install. Once you set it to no, however, you must define all the parameters needed for the other values.

The value for EXISTING_SYSTEM_OVERWRITE must be set to yes to automate the overwrite of systems that already are installed AIX systems.

If a system is cloned, INSTALL_X_IF_ADAPTER is not used. Otherwise, this value is used to specify the installation of AIXwindows, depending upon whether a graphics adapter is found on the system.

If you would like to start the install assistant after the first system boot, you should set the RUN_STARTUP value to yes.

The value for RM_INST_ROOTS should be set to yes to clean up the /usr/lpp/*/inst_roots directories once the system is installed. The only time you would set this value to no would be if you were going to run a server system for diskless machines.

The ERROR_EXIT value is used to define what you would like to run should the installation fail. Make sure that you specify a complete path and command name here, since you won't have any PATH variables set at the point where it fails.

The CUSTOMIZATION_FILE variable exists so that you can specify a filename to be executed as soon as the installation program has completed.

The TCB (Trusted Computing Base) variable has to be set to yes if you want the TCB to be active on your system. The TCB is a security measure ensuring that only the people that you want on your system can access only the programs you want them to access.

The INSTALL_TYPE variable will always be set to a full installation on a mksysb restore.

The BUNDLES variable is not used on mksysb tapes. This is only used for specifying which software bundles need to be installed initially from the medium.

The LOCATION variable is used to set the location code for the installation disk. If this variable is left undefined the program automatically finds a good installation disk without user intervention. As an example, the location of 00-00-0S-0,0 specifies the SCSI 0 disk with an integrated SCSI adapter.

The SIZE_MB value can be specified, but it is not necessary. Here you would specify a disk size in megabytes. To have the program automatically choose the largest disk, just use the keyword largest with no location code.

To specify the disk to restore to, you can use the HDISKNAME variable. An example of a common value to put in here is hdisk0.

The BOSINST_LANG variable lets you set the language that will be used during the installation of the system. Unless you speak a language other than English, you will always use en_US.

To specify the locale that is used for an installed system, you can set the CULTURAL_CONVENTION variable. On mksysb tapes, this will be left blank.

The system message language can be set with the MESSAGES variable. However, with a mksysb tape, this value is left blank.

And finally, the keyboard map you want installed can be set with the KEYBOARD variable. This should be left blank for mksysb tapes.

In the /image.data file, there are several lines that describe the root volume group and the logical volumes therein. There are some settings that can be changed to fit your needs.

In the logical_volume_policy, you can change the EXACT_FIT parameter to yes if you want the disk used to install the system to be exactly the same as the description in this file.

28

BACKING UP AND
RESTORING YOUR
SYSTEM

The SHRINK parameter defines whether or not the logical volumes should be shrunk to their minimal size at install time.

Next, the vg_data stanza defines parameters of the volume group. In here, you modify the PPSIZE parameter in order to set different default physical partition sizes. By default, this number is set to 4 MB.

Each logical volume will have one lv_data stanza. In here, all characteristics for logical volumes can be set. Should you want to define the disk location and maximum size parameters, you can do so here.

The final stanza in the /image.data file is the fs_data stanza. Each filesystem has an fs_data entry, which modifies the file system block size and activates compression for the file system.

As in AIX 3.2, AIX 4 also executes /etc/firstboot, if there is one, only on the first reboot after installation. The fbcheck entry in etc/inittab triggers this.

Restoring an AIX 4 System from mksysb

In AIX 4, to restore a system from a mksysb tape, you can do one of two things. As in AIX 3.2, you can simply boot from the mksysb tape, or you can use the restore command (instead of the tar command in 3.2).

If you use the restore command, you need to use the non-rewind tape device and specify the -s option. As with the tar format, mksysb in 3.2, you again need to start out in the third position on the tape. As an example of restoring the vi binary, you would do the following:

```
cd /
tctl -f /dev/rmt0 rewind
tctl -f /dev/rmt0.1 fsf 3
restore -xqf /dev/rmt0.1 -s 1 ./usr/bin/vi
```

For more detailed information on all of the options for restore, please consult the man page.

Backing Up Volume Groups with savevg on AIX 4

You can archive volume groups other than the root volume group by using the savevg command. As an example, if you want to back up the volume group homevg, you have a choice of either going through the smit savevg fastpath or the command

```
savevg -i -f/dev/rmt0 homevg
```

With the above command, the -i option also creates the file /tmp/vgdata/homevg/homevg.data, which is similar to the /image.data file that gets created with the mkszfile command. However, this file is actually created with the mkvgdata command, a softlink to the mkszfile command.

Other things in common with the mksysb command include the -m flag to create map file and the -e command to exclude whatever files are listed in the file (for this example, /etc/exclude.homevg).

Along with all the data for the volume group, the `/tmp/vgdata/homevg/homevg.data` and `/tmp/vgdata/homevg/filesystems` files are also backed up to tape for reference by the `restvg` command during volume group restoration. The `/tmp/vgdata/homevg/filesystems` file is simply a copy of the `/etc/filesystems` file.

Restoring Volume Groups with `restvg` on AIX 4

If you have a tape with archives created with the `savevg` command, you can restore from that tape with the `restvg` command. For example:

```
restvg -qf /dev/rmt0 -s
```

In this example, you would not only restore the `homevg` volume group on the physical volumes where it already resides, but the file system would also be shrunk to its minimum size.

You may not be able to easily restore a system with `restvg` to another machine unless the specific hard disks that the original volume group was on are available (not in use by another volume group) on the new system. If it is not available, then `restvg` will abort, unless you specify another set of hard disks that are available, with the following command:

```
restvg -qf /dev/rmt0 hdiskN
```

You can also restore individual files from a `savevg` tape using the standard `restore` command. For example:

```
cd /
```

```
restore -xqf /dev/rmt0 ./home/joe/.profile
```

You can use the `-T` flag to list the contents of the tape. See the appropriate man pages for details.

If you want to make the `homevg.data` file manually, you can run the command `mkvgdata homevg`. You can then edit the characteristics of the volume group and its file systems simply by editing the `homevg.data` file. Some of the things you change in this file are the characteristics of the physical partition size or the block size and compression algorithm of the file systems in the volume group.

Using the `backup` and `restore` Commands

The `backup` and `restore` commands are actually the native AIX commands for doing backups. As a matter of fact, if you wish to save and restore your ACLs (Access Control List), this is the only backup command that will allow you to do so.

You can do two types of backups with these commands. You can either back up your system by `i-node` or by file. If you choose to back them up by `i-node`, you are actually performing a file system `dump`, which is what `mksysb` in AIX 4 uses. Only the `dump` method has support for incremental backups, thus reducing the amount of time and tape used on system backups. This also has compatibility with the BSD `dump` command and the AIX `rdump`/`rrestore` commands.

28

BACKING UP AND RESTORING YOUR SYSTEM

By default, `backup/restore` will use the `/dev/rd0` device.

If you use file mode, you won't be able to restore data to other UNIX variants aside from AIX. You would have to use another archiving command if this were the case.

A common way of using the `backup` command is in conjunction with the `find` command, where you run a find on the files you want to back up and pipe the output into the `backup` command. For example, if you would like to do a relative backup of the contents of the `/home` directory, along with its subdirectories, you would do the following:

```
cd /
find ./home -print ¦ backup -iqf /dev/rmt0
```

To restore the tape, use the following commands:

```
cd /
restore -xqf /dev/rrmt0
```

If you would like to only get specific files from the tape, simply add the filenames to the end of the command line. If you would like to check the contents of a tape, simply use the `-T` option on the command line.

For incremental backups, the file `/etc/dumpdates` must exist. Use the `touch` command to create it if it doesn't. In order to do a full backup of the home filesystem, you would do the following:

```
backup -0uf /dev/rmt0.4 /home
```

What this does is create a level 0 (full) `dump` on the tape. This also places an entry in the `/etc/dumpdates` file as follows:

```
/dev/rhd1 0 Wed Apr 16 16:02:23 1997
```

You could also use the device name from the output of `df` instead of the filesystem name.

To restore an incremental backup to this tape, you would use the following command:

```
backup -1uf /dev/rmt0.4 /home
```

And into the `/etc/dumpdates` file goes another line under the first:

```
/dev/rhd1 1 Wed April 16 16:42:42 1997
```

Should your filesystem get crushed and you need to restore from this tape, first create a new `/home` filesystem, make this your current directory, and restore the data from the tapes.

The first tape must be the level 0 tape. The command to restore it would be the following:

```
restore -qrf /dev/rm0
```

Now you would insert the level 1 dump tape and use the same command to update the files to the most current setting. Should you wish to only restore individual files, first go the directory where you want to restore the file, and run the command

```
restore -qxf /dev/rmt0x4 ./home/joe/.profile
```

to restore your personal profile.

rdump/rrestore

The `rdump` and `rrestore` commands are simply remote versions of the backup utility in AIX. In other words, you can back up your system to a remote tape drive over the network.

In order to use this utility, you need to have a proper `/.rhosts` file on the target machine. This may not be possible should you have a high degree of security on your network.

Also, if you have not already done so, you will have to create at least one compatibility link if you are using AIX 4. You have to link the `/usr/sbin/mnt` directory with the `/etc` directory. To do this, you would use the following command:

```
ln -s /usr/sbin/mnt /etc
```

You also must have a `/etc/dumpdates` file available as well, just like with `restore/backup`.

An example of backing up the `/home` filesystem is as follows:

```
rdump -0uf fileserver:/dev/rmt0.4 /home
```

On certain tape drives, `rdump` needs certain extra parameters. For example, if you are using an 8mm 2.3 GB drive, you would have to use the parameters `-d6250` `-s33000`. If you were to use a 5 GB tape drive in its compressed mode then you would have to use the value of `80000` for the `-s` parameter. Consult your AIX manuals for the specifications for your model of tape drive.

To restore from an `rdump` tape, you would use commands similar to the local `restore` command, such as in the following example:

```
rrestore -rf fileserver:/dev/rm0
```

pax

`pax` is a neat little utility that handles both the `tar` and `cpio` formats. It defaults to `tar` format, but it also incorporated the error recovery features of `cpio`. As a matter of fact, when a `mksysb` tape runs across bad spots on a tape, it automatically calls the `pax` utility to try and recover from the error condition.

The following format is used with `pax`:

```
pax -wf (tape device) (filesystem)
```

To archive the `/home` filesystem to tape, you would do the following:

```
pax -wf /dev/rmt0 /home
```

To restore the filesystem, you would use the following command:

```
pax -r -pe -f /dev/rmt0
```

The `-pe` option in this `restore` command is used to preserve both the modification time and the ownership of the files. Also, you don't have to use relative pathnames, because they can be changed when you restore the files. For example, if you wand to restore the files from `/home` to `/tmp/test`, you would use this command:

```
pax -rpe -f /dev/rmt0 -s:^/home:/temp/test:g
```

The command to list the contents of the tape is:

```
pax -f /dev/rmt0
```

If you want to write out a tape to either `cpio` or `tar` format, you can make it do so explicitly by using the `-x` option, along with specifying either `cpio` or `tar`.

Making Backups on Sun Solaris Systems

The default system backup utility for Sun Solaris systems is the `ufsdump/ufsrestore` utility. As you might expect, this utility is based on the `dump/restore` utility and carries with it much of its attributes.

To most effectively illustrate the use of `ufsdump/ufsrestore`, I will outline the steps involved in backing up a Sun workstation, along with an example system backup and restore.

First off, you need to log everyone out of the system and bring it down to the single-user mode state. The following steps should walk you through a full system backup (level 0 backup):

1. Take the system down to single user mode state by typing **init s** and pressing return. This ensures that no one can change any data on the system while you are backing it up.

2. Put a tape in the tape drive. For this example, we will assume that we are using a QIC-150 tape.

3. Type the following command: **ufsdump 0cuf /dev/rmt/(unit) c(n)t(n)d(n)s(n)**. Here, the `0` option specifies a level 0, or complete, dump of the system. The c option identifies a cartridge tape. The u option updates the dump record. The f option followed by the device name specifies the device file. At the end of the command, you need to specify the raw disk slice for the file system you want to back up (`c0t0d0s7`, for example).

4. If more than one tape is needed to perform a complete dump, `ufsdump` tells you when to change to a new tape.

5. Finally, you must label the tape with the command, file system, and date.

The following is a sample of possible screen output for the ufsdump command:

```
# init s
# ufsdump 0cuf /dev/rmt/0 c0t0d0s7
DUMP: Date of this level 0 dump: Wed Mar 11 10:16:53 1992
DUMP: Date of the last level 0 dump: the epoch
DUMP: Dumping /dev/rdsk/c0t3d0s7 (/export/home) to /dev/rmt/0
DUMP: mapping (Pass I) [regular files]
DUMP: mapping (Pass II) [directories]
DUMP: estimated 956 blocks (478KB)
DUMP: Writing 63 Kilobyte records
DUMP: dumping (Pass III) [directories]
DUMP: dumping (Pass IV) [regular files]
DUMP: level 0 dump on Wed Mar 11 10:16:53 1992
DUMP: 956 blocks (478KB) on 1 volume
DUMP: DUMP IS DONE
#
```

Doing Incremental Backups

As with dump, you can specify different backup levels with ufsdump in order to back up only those files that were changed since a previous backup at a lower level.

In order to back up just the incremental changes on the system made since the last complete dump, you would take the following steps:

1. Once again, bring the system down to single user mode state.
2. Stick a tape in the tape drive.
3. Type **ufsdump [1-9]ucf/dev/rmt/(unit) /dev/rdsk/c(n)t(n)d(n)s(n)**. The level of the backup goes at the front of the ufsdump arguments [1-9].
4. Remove the tape from the drive and slap a label on it.

Getting It Back with ufsrestore

The other side to the coin for ufsdump is ufsrestore, just as restore is the flip side of dump. ufsrestore copies files from backups created using the ufsdump command into the current working directory. You can use ufsrestore in one of two ways: you can use it to reload an entire file system hierarchy from a level 0 dump followed by any incremental dumps that follow it, or you can restore just one or more single files from any dump tape.

During restore, all files are restored with their original owner, last modification time, and mode.

This sounds easy enough, but before you begin restoring you need to know a few things:

■ Which tapes you need
■ The raw device name for the file systems you wish to back up
■ Which type of tape drive you want to use
■ The device name you need to use for your tape drive

After you've found the right tape or tapes to restore (you do have backup plans, don't you?), you can start restoring your system. Follow these guidelines and you should be okay:

1. Log in as `root`.

2. Bring the system down to single-user mode (`init s`).

3. Unmount the filesystem you wish to restore to with the `umount` command.

4. Rebuild the raw device file with `newfs /dev/rdsk/c(n)t(n)d(n)s(n)`. This wipes the disk slice clean and rebuilds the file system.

5. Remount the file system with the `mount` command (`mount /dev/dsk/c(n)t(n)d(n)s(n)`).

6. Change your current directory to the mount point, which will be the directory where you want to restore.

7. Put the tape in the drive.

8. Run the `ufsrestore` command to restore the filesystem. For example, run `ufsrestore rvf /dev/rmt/0h` to get the filesystem from tape.

If you want to get back only certain files, you will need to use the interactive options in `ufsrestore`. A good idea to practice when restoring interactively is to restore files into the `/var/tmp` directory. This way you stand less chance of overwriting files with older versions.

To do it interactively, you would do the following:

1. Log in as `root`.

2. Make sure the write protect is on for safety on the tape, so that you don't accidentally overwrite the tape.

3. Change your current directory to `/var tmp`.

4. Run the command `ufsrestore if /dev/rmt/(unit)`.

5. You now create a list of files to be restored. If you want to list the contents of a directory, just type **ls** and return. If you want to change directories, type **cd** (*directory name*) and return. If you want to add a directory or filename to the list of files to be restored, just type **add** (*filename*). If you want to remove a directory or filename from the restore list, just type **delete** (*filename*). And if you want to keep the permissions the same on the directory, just type **setmodes** and return, then type **n** and return.

6. After you finish with the list, type **extract** and return. `ufsrestore` should ask you for a volume number at this point.

7. Type the volume number at this point and return. Now the files and directories are restored to the current directory.

8. Type **quit** to get out of `ufsrestore`.

9. Check the restored files with the `ls -l` command to verify the files, the use the `mv` command to put all the verified files into their correct directories.

Making Backups on SVR4 Systems

By their nature, SVR4 systems are considered "raw" systems. By this, I mean that almost all UNIX systems are derived from one of two base, or raw, UNIX OSs: BSD or SVR4 (System 5 release 4).

As a raw system, SVR4 really doesn't have much to offer in the way of enhanced system backup and recovery utilities.

Just as most UNIX variants were derived from BSD and SVR4, so were most backup utilities derived from dump/restore and cpio/tar.

By default, BSD systems usually go to the cpio or tar utilities to handle their system backups. For more detail on these utilities, see the previous sections on cpio and tar.

Making Backups on Silicon Graphics IRIX Systems

In addition to the standard tar and cpio backup utilities, IRIX also comes with the BRU utility for system backup and recovery.

The BRU utility gives you the functionality to do a number of things, such as backing up the system, restoring the system, verifying a backup, estimating a backup, defining a tape drive, disk file, or floppy to back up to or restore from, and which filesystems or selection of files you wish to back up or restore.

To utilize this functionality, you would use one or more of the following options:

- -c   Create a BRU backup volume.
- -x   Extract files from a BRU backup volume.
- -t   Get a table of contents from a BRU backup volume.
- -i   Verify the contents of a BRU backup volume.
- -e   Give an estimate of the number of BRU backup volumes needed.
- -d   Compare the contents of a BRU backup volume against the original files on the file system.
- -v   Verbosity level. You can specify up to four levels of verbosity.
- -f   Define what backup device will be accessed.

The command line for BRU is defined as follows:

```
bru -(mode) -options) -f(device) (path)
```

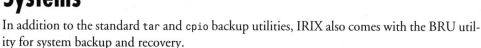

With all these basic modes and options, all of the basic backup and restore functions can be performed. As an example, if you wish to restore the contents of the entire system to a tape drive on an SGI box, you might use the following command:

```
bru -cvf /dev/rmt/tps0d6ns.8200
```

To look at what's on a tape, you might use this command:

```
bru -tvf /dev/rmt/tps0d6ns.8200
```

This will give you a complete listing of the contents of the tape. You could also redirect the output (>) to a file so that you can have a list of the tape contents for your records.

In order to restore the contents of the entire backup volume, you would use the following command:

```
bru -xvf /dev/rmt/tps0d6ns.8200
```

By default, this command restores all of the files to their original location (absolute paths).

If you wand to verify the contents of a BRU backup volume, you can do it one of two ways: the -i mode and -d mode. The first method is actually a preferable method because the mechanism requires only the tape drive and the BRU utility to run. The inspect mode (-i) gives you this functionality:

```
bru -ivf /dev/rmt/tps0d6ns.8200
```

What happens here is that this verification method rereads each buffer block written on the backup volume and recalculates the 32-bit CRC. The BRU utility then compares this calculated CRC with the CRC that was written in the buffer block header. If it gets an incorrect value, it warns you of the offending condition.

In reality, the other mechanism, the -d mode, is most commonly used. It requires both the backup volume and the original data. For example:

```
bru -dvf /dev/rmt/tps0d6ns.8200
```

If you use this mechanism, it reads the data from the tape and performs a bit-by-bit comparison with the original data from the file system. This method reports problems if the files have changed on the file system since the backup was made.

Advanced Options

There are a number of options that are available to the BRU utility that go above and beyond the standard options that are available with its sister application, tar.

The following BRU utilities provide enhanced processing capabilities:

- ■ -L Puts a plainly readable text label on the backup volume.
- ■ -G Creates a file list that is placed at the head of the backup.
- ■ -g Reads and displays just the backup volume information.

- ■ -gg   Reads and displays the file listing that was created with the -G option.
- ■ -n   Selects files based on date and time.
- ■ -B   Runs the BRU utility in the background.
- ■ -PA   Switches the Absolute paths to Relative. This strips off the leading /.
- ■ -ua   Used to do an unconditional overwrite of all files during the restore.

As an example, to add the description "Complete System Backup", you would do the following:

```
bru -cv -L "Complete System Backup" -f /dev/rmt/tps0d6sn.8200
```

If we look at the backup volume with bru -g we would see the following:

```
bru -gf /dev/rmt/tps0d6sn.8200
```

label:	Complete System Backup
created:	Sat Jan 23 17:22:34 1997
artime:	8303483221
volume:	1
writes	4
release:	14.3
variant:	0
bufsize:	20480
msize:	0
msize_blks:	0
serial_number:	XXXX-XXXX-X
device:	/dev/rmt/tps0d6sn.8200
user:	root
group:	root
system:	IRIX pluto 5.X #2 Teu A M80586
bru:	Fifth OEM Release
command_line:	bru -cvf /dev/rmt/tps0d6sn.8200 -L "Complete System Backup" /

All this information is added when we use the -cv and -L options when backing up a tape. The most important elements are the label, creation date, volume, and command line.

You could also use bru for performing either incremental or differential backups. This can be done in conjunction with bru's -n option, because the -n option passes a standard date string. The best method is to create a reference file and pass the name of that file to bru, such as "/etc/ LASTFULL".

The following script would perform full backups on Saturday morning and differential backups on all other days:

```
#!/bin/sh
DOW=`date +%w`
if [ $DOW = 6 ]
then
    bru -cvf /dev/rmt/tps0d6sn.8200 -L "Complete Backup `date`" /
    touch /etc/LASTFULL
else
    bru -cvf /dev/rmt/tps0d6sn.8200 -L "Daily Update `date`" -n    /etc/LAST
fi
```

This script, if called by `cron` once a day, makes a full backup of your system on Saturday, followed by differential backups once a day.

Making Backups on BSD Systems

By their nature, BSD system are considered "raw" systems. By this, I mean that almost all UNIX systems are derived from one of two base, or raw, UNIX OSs: BSD or SVR4 (System 5 release 4).

As a raw system, BSD (just like SVR4) really doesn't have much to offer in the way of enhanced system backup and recovery utilities.

Again, just as most UNIX variants were derived from BSD and SVR4, so were the backup utilities derived from `dump`/`restore` and `cpio`/`tar`.

By default, BSD systems usually go to the `dump`/`restore` utilities to handle their system backups. For more detail on these utilities, see the previous sections on `dump`/`restore`.

Making Backups on Linux Systems

Although `tar` is distributed on all UNIX variants, Linux comes with a somewhat more advanced version of `tar`. The Linux `tar` command gives you the added feature of compression through the GNU `gzip` utility, as well as the `compress` utility.

These new switches are

`-z`	Compress the archive using GNU `gzip`.
`-Z`	Compress the archive with the `compress` utility.

If, for example, you want to create a compressed backup of your `/etc` directory and put it into a file called `etc_backup.tar`, you would do the following:

```
tar czf etc_backup.tar /etc
```

This backs up all the subdirectories under `/etc` as well.

In order to add the contents of another directory, such as /usr/local/etc, you would do the following:

```
tar rzf etc_backup.tar /usr/ocal/etc
```

With the u option, you can make tar go through and append to the archive only those files that have been changed since the creation of the archive. The following command will let you do this:

```
tar uzf etc_backup.tar /etc/usr/local/etc
```

These examples so far have only shown you how to archive files to disk. In order to back up the archives to tape, you would simply add the device name to the command, instead of the directory name. Usually the tape drive device name is /dev/st0 for SCSI tape drives.

Restoring Files on Linux

The x option enables you to extract files from archives. If you don't specify a filename to restore, tar restores the entire archive. Using the t option, you can get a table of contents for the archive.

To extract the contents of the backup archive in the previous example you would do the following:

```
tar xzf etc_backup.tar
```

Note that these files were compressed on backup and they must be restored using the z option.

Also notice that tar will not put the files back where they came from. It actually creates a new tree based on the current directory. Therefore, you *must* get to the original directory where you were when you backed up the tape in order to be able to restore to the same location.

In certain situations, you may want to consider restoring to a temporary directory first before moving files in place, because you may accidentally restore older files over existing files. Of course, if you do this, you need to check the space available to you in the directory to which you are restoring.

If you want to restore to individual files from an archive, all you have to do is specify the name after all the tar arguments. As an example, let's say you just want to get back your hosts and passwd files. You would do the following:

```
tar xzf etc_backup.tar etc/hosts etc/passwd
```

You should notice that the full pathname must be specified if you are going to do this.

Typically, these tared files are named (filename).tar.gz, so that you can tell they are tar archives, compressed with the GNU gzip utility.

Along with the z option, Linux's version of tar also comes with some other neat little utilities. A few of the more notable ones are

M	This tells tar to use a multi-volume archive. If you use this, tar prompts you for the insertion of a new floppy or tape when it comes to the end of the current one, which is referred to as a volume. Each volume contains a stand-alone archive file, so you won't need all the volumes to extract a file. However, if a file is split across two volumes you must use the -xM option to extract.

> **NOTE**
>
> Note that this option does not work on some tape devices, the most notable being DAT tapes (4mm).

N *DATE*	This tells the tar utility to operate only on files that are newer than the specified *DATE*. You have to specify the date in the same format as that used by the date command.
	What you can do is use the date command, redirect the output to a file, such as last_backup, and back up the file to the tape along with everything else. Then, the next time you back up your files, you can choose to only back up files that have been changed during or since the last backup by including the option -N "cat last_backup" in tar's command line.
T *FILENAME*	This option tells tar that a list of files to back up or restore is in *FILENAME*. As an example, you can use the following to have tar create an archive containing files that are named in the LIST_FILES files:
	`tar czf /dev/ftape LIST_FILES`
	The LIST_FILES file is just a straight text file with one filename on each line.
h	Usually, when tar comes across a link, it stores details about that link. If you use the h option, tar actually stores the file that is pointed to by the link and ignores the link itself. You must be very careful about using this option, because you run the risk of getting duplicate files, which may overwrite other files on disk.

| W | This option verifies the archive after it has been written. This option will not work on tape drives that cannot rewind. |
| P | This causes tar to save/restore files with absolute paths. Usually, tar strips the leading / from a pathname so that when you restore, the file is restored in a directory relative to the current one. With this option, the file is restored from where it was backed up. Once again, use caution; you run the risk of overwriting files on your hard drive. |

Getting Multiple Archives on a Tape with tar

After tar has written a backup to tape, it writes two EOF marks on the tape. You can move the tape to these marks by using the mt (move tape) command as follows:

```
mt -f /dev/nftape fsf 1
```

In this example, the tape device /dev/nftape is a *non-rewinding* device. You must use a non-rewinding tape device, or else once you have moved the tape in position, it will just rewind back to the beginning.

Now that you have the tape in the correct position, you can back up or restore the next archive on the tape.

Using taper

taper is a neat little utility that gives you most of the same utilities as tar, but it also has a nice warm and fuzzy user interface.

You can get taper for Linux at any GNU ftp site on the Internet. In order to run taper, you need to have the most recent version of ncurses that supports "forms". The primary GNU ftp site is located at prep.ai.mit.edu.

taper is relatively easy to configure, build, and install for Linux. The installation instructions are included in the INSTALL file.

To build and install the latest ncurses, you should do the following as root:

```
cd /usr/local/sr
tar xzf ncurses-(release #).tar.gz
cd ncurses-(release #)
./configure –with-normal –with-shared
\
  --with--debug –disable-termcap
make
make install
```

In order to make a binary of taper, you need to do the following:

```
tar xzf taper-(release #).tar.gz
```

Next, you must edit the Makefile in order to get the proper tape drive specified for your site. Then you would type:

```
make clean
make all
make install
```

When you initially create an archive, the taper program stores all the information about files on that archive, such as filename, file size, backup time, and so on. This information gets stored into a file called an archive information file, which is usually stored in a file, usually called ~/.taper_info. When reading from an archived tape, taper reads this file, thus avoiding having to go through the entire tape to find the location of a particular file.

The biggest problem with this file is that you can't restore a tape to another machine until this file is loaded on to it. Therefore, you must save that file on a separate tape or floppy so that it can be loaded first. You must also ensure that you always have a current version of this file saved.

Each archive that gets created is given a unique archive ID, which can be used for future accessing of the archive if you don't have the tape at hand.

Making a Backup with taper

To start the taper utility, simply type the command **taper** on the command line. This brings up the main taper window. There are three main modules in taper: backup, restore, and mkinfo. These as well as the preference management options are presented here.

Select the backup option to back up a tape.

If the archive doesn't yet exist, you will be prompted for the archive title. Then it will prompt you for the volume title.

After that is squared away, you get a screen with three panels. The top left should show you the current directory on the hard disk, the top right shows what's currently on the archive, and the bottom panel shows you which files have been selected for backup. At the top of the screen is the archive ID and title.

In order to move around between the panels, just use the tab key. If you need to get help on keys, just press h.

At this point you must choose which files and directories you want to back up. You can use the cursor keys to move you around the directory. If you press enter when a particular directory is highlighted, you will move into that directory.

When you have found the file or directory you wish to back up, you can press the s key to select it. The size of the file or directory will then be shown in the bottom window.

Next, you will be asked whether or not to backup in incremental mode or full backup mode, as shown in the left-hand box, which displays an I or an F. To toggle between the two, press s when the highlight is on the selected file or directory.

Note that when you select a directory, all subdirectories under it will automatically be recursively included in the backup list.

In order to deselect a file, just move the cursor to the bottom window with the tab and move the highlight to the file or directory you want to deselect. Then, just press d to deselect the file or directory.

Once you have finished selecting files and directories, press f. taper will now start the backup. If at any time you want to stop the backup, just press q.

Restoring Files with taper

Restoring from taper is just as easy (if not easier) than backing up. First, select the restore option from the taper main menu. You are then presented with a list of all the archives taper is aware of. These are sorted by archive ID order, and the archive title is displayed as well.

Move the highlight to the desired archive and press Enter. Now you are given three panels. The top left gives the files and directories currently on the archive, the top right gives you a summary of the whole archive, and the bottom panel will show the directories and files selected for restoring.

Once again, use the cursor keys to move the highlight to select which files you want to restore, and press s to select the files or directories you want to restore. Don't forget that subdirectories are recursively restored. Once you choose a file or directory it shows up in the bottom panel. If you have chosen a file or directory twice, square brackets will show up around the file or directory name.

Over in the select window, the volume number is printed after the filename. One of two things will show up here: either a volume number or an m. If an m appears, then taper is operating in "most recent restore" mode and you will only be able to restore the most recent copy of that file. You can toggle between modes by pressing the s key while in the select window.

If you wish to deselect a file or directory, just hit the d key while the appropriate one is highlighted.

Once you have chosen everything you want to restore, press f to start the taper restore. Once again, just press q if you wish to quit during the restore.

Should the archive information file get deleted or corrupted, you can create another one simply by using the mkinfo command. Just put the tape in the drive and select mkinfo from the main menu in taper.

28
BACKING UP AND RESTORING YOUR SYSTEM

Add-On Solutions

On top of the standard UNIX backups that come bundled with the install packages, there are a number of commercially available packages out there.

The following are some of the more popular products used at many sites for complete network and system backups:

- FarTool by APUnix
- ArcServe by Cheyenne
- D-Tools by Dallastone
- BudTool by Delta MicroSystems (PDC)
- Enterprise Backup by Epoch Systems
- ADSM (Adstar Distributed Storage Manager) by IBM
- OmniBack II by Hewlett-Packard
- Networker by Legato
- Network Imaging Systems
- AXXion Netbackup 2.0 by Open Vision
- SM-arch by Software Moguls
- Alexandria by Spectra Logic
- Workstation Solutions

Each of the backup solutions is unique. You might have to do some serious homework to find out which one is best for your system, as there really isn't any one best total storage solution. You just have to find the best one for your system.

This may not be easy. There is a joke that goes (somewhat politically incorrectly): "The two greatest liars in the world are software vendors and teenage boys." So, just be on your guard when you go shopping.

Summary

In this chapter we have covered a large number of backup and restore topics: using the `tar` command, using the `dump` command, using `cpio`, and making backups on HP-UX systems, Solaris Systems, SVR4 systems, IRIX systems, BSD systems, and Linux systems.

Speaking from experience, there *really* is no substitute for good, up-to-date backups for saving your bacon. I can remember at least two times in my career that, had I not had the system backed up, I'd be out on the street.

So, a word to the wise. Remember the three best secrets to a good career in systems administration: backup, backup, and backup!

GNU General Public License

Version 2, June 1991

Copyright © 1989, 1991 Free Software Foundation, Inc.

675 Mass Ave, Cambridge, MA 02139, USA

Everyone is permitted to copy and distribute verbatim copies of this license document, but changing it is not allowed.

Preamble

The licenses for most software are designed to take away your freedom to share and change it. By contrast, the GNU General Public License is intended to guarantee your freedom to share and change free software—to make sure the software is free for all its users. This General Public License applies to most of the Free Software Foundation's software and to any other program whose authors commit to using it. (Some other Free Software Foundation software is covered by the GNU Library General Public License instead.) You can apply it to your programs, too.

When we speak of free software, we are referring to freedom, not price. Our General Public Licenses are designed to make sure that you have the freedom to distribute copies of free software (and charge for this service if you wish), that you receive source code or can get it if you want it, that you can change the software or use pieces of it in new free programs; and that you know you can do these things.

To protect your rights, we need to make restrictions that forbid anyone to deny you these rights or to ask you to surrender the rights. These restrictions translate to certain responsibilities for you if you distribute copies of the software, or if you modify it.

For example, if you distribute copies of such a program, whether gratis or for a fee, you must give the recipients all the rights that you have. You must make sure that they, too, receive or can get the source code. And you must show them these terms so they know their rights.

We protect your rights with two steps: (1) copyright the software, and (2) offer you this license which gives you legal permission to copy, distribute and/or modify the software.

Also, for each author's protection and ours, we want to make certain that everyone understands that there is no warranty for this free software. If the software is modified by someone else and passed on, we want its recipients to know that what they have is not the original, so that any problems introduced by others will not reflect on the original authors' reputations.

Finally, any free program is threatened constantly by software patents. We wish to avoid the danger that redistributors of a free program will individually obtain patent licenses, in effect making the program proprietary. To prevent this, we have made it clear that any patent must be licensed for everyone's free use or not licensed at all.

The precise terms and conditions for copying, distribution and modification follow.

GNU GENERAL PUBLIC LICENSE
TERMS AND CONDITIONS FOR COPYING, DISTRIBUTION, AND MODIFICATION

0. This License applies to any program or other work which contains a notice placed by the copyright holder saying it may be distributed under the terms of this General Public License. The "Program," below, refers to any such program or work, and a "work based on the Program" means either the Program or any derivative work under copyright law: that is to say, a work containing the Program or a portion of it, either verbatim or with modifications and/or translated into another language. (Hereinafter, translation is included without limitation in the term "modification.") Each licensee is addressed as "you."

Activities other than copying, distribution, and modification are not covered by this License; they are outside its scope. The act of running the Program is not restricted, and the output from the Program is covered only if its contents constitute a work based on the Program (independent of having been made by running the Program). Whether that is true depends on what the Program does.

1. You may copy and distribute verbatim copies of the Program's source code as you receive it, in any medium, provided that you conspicuously and appropriately publish on each copy an appropriate copyright notice and disclaimer of warranty; keep intact all the notices that refer to this License and to the absence of any warranty; and give any other recipients of the Program a copy of this License along with the Program.

You may charge a fee for the physical act of transferring a copy, and you may at your option offer warranty protection in exchange for a fee.

2. You may modify your copy or copies of the Program or any portion of it, thus forming a work based on the Program, and copy and distribute such modifications or work under the terms of Section 1 above, provided that you also meet all of these conditions: a) You must cause the modified files to carry prominent notices stating that you changed the files and the date of any change. b) You must cause any work that you distribute or publish, that in whole or in part contains or is derived from the Program or any part thereof, to be licensed as a whole at no charge to all third parties under the terms of this License. c) If the modified program normally reads commands interactively when run, you must cause it, when started running for such interactive use in the most ordinary way, to print or display an announcement including an appropriate copyright notice and a notice that there is no warranty (or else, saying that you provide a warranty) and that users may redistribute the program under these conditions, and telling the user how to view a copy of this License. (Exception: If the Program itself is interactive but does not normally print such an announcement, your work based on the Program is not required to print an announcement.)

These requirements apply to the modified work as a whole. If identifiable sections of that work are not derived from the Program, and can be reasonably considered independent and separate works in themselves, then this License, and its terms, do not apply to those sections when you distribute them as separate works. But when you distribute the same sections as part of a whole which is a work based on the Program, the distribution of the whole must be on the terms of this License, whose permissions for other licensees extend to the entire whole, and thus to each and every part regardless of who wrote it.

Thus, it is not the intent of this section to claim rights or contest your rights to work written entirely by you; rather, the intent is to exercise the right to control the distribution of derivative or collective works based on the Program.

In addition, mere aggregation of another work not based on the Program with the Program (or with a work based on the Program) on a volume of a storage or distribution medium does not bring the other work under the scope of this License.

3. You may copy and distribute the Program (or a work based on it, under Section 2) in object code or executable form under the terms of Sections 1 and 2 above provided that you also do one of the following: a) Accompany it with the complete corresponding machine-readable source code, which must be distributed under the terms of Sections 1 and 2 above on a medium customarily used for software interchange; or, b) Accompany it with a written offer, valid for at least three years, to give any third party, for a charge no more than your cost of physically performing source distribution, a complete machine-readable copy of the corresponding source code, to be distributed under the terms of Sections 1 and 2 above on a medium customarily used for software interchange; or, c) Accompany it with the information you received as to the offer to distribute corresponding source code. (This alternative is allowed only for noncommercial distribution and only if you received the program in object code or executable form with such an offer, in accord with Subsection b above.)

The source code for a work means the preferred form of the work for making modifications to it. For an executable work, complete source code means all the source code for all modules it contains, plus any associated interface definition files, plus the scripts used to control compilation and installation of the executable. However, as a special exception, the source code distributed need not include anything that is normally distributed (in either source or binary form) with the major components (compiler, kernel, and so on) of the operating system on which the executable runs, unless that component itself accompanies the executable.

If distribution of executable or object code is made by offering access to copy from a designated place, then offering equivalent access to copy the source code from the same place counts as distribution of the source code, even though third parties are not compelled to copy the source along with the object code.

4. You may not copy, modify, sublicense, or distribute the Program except as expressly provided under this License. Any attempt otherwise to copy, modify, sublicense or distribute the Program is void, and will automatically terminate your rights under this License. However, parties who have received copies, or rights, from you under this License will not have their licenses terminated so long as such parties remain in full compliance.

5. You are not required to accept this License, since you have not signed it. However, nothing else grants you permission to modify or distribute the Program or its derivative works. These actions are prohibited by law if you do not accept this License. Therefore, by modifying or distributing the Program (or any work based on the Program), you indicate your acceptance of this License to do so, and all its terms and conditions for copying, distributing or modifying the Program or works based on it.

6. Each time you redistribute the Program (or any work based on the Program), the recipient automatically receives a license from the original licensor to copy, distribute or modify the Program subject to these terms and conditions. You may not impose any further restrictions on the recipients' exercise of the rights granted herein. You are not responsible for enforcing compliance by third parties to this License.

7. If, as a consequence of a court judgment or allegation of patent infringement or for any other reason (not limited to patent issues), conditions are imposed on you (whether by court order, agreement or otherwise) that contradict the conditions of this License, they do not excuse you from the conditions of this License. If you cannot distribute so as to satisfy simultaneously your obligations under this License and any other pertinent obligations, then as a consequence you may not distribute the Program at all. For example, if a patent license would not permit royalty-free redistribution of the Program by all those who receive copies directly or indirectly through you, then the only way you could satisfy both it and this License would be to refrain entirely from distribution of the Program.

If any portion of this section is held invalid or unenforceable under any particular circumstance, the balance of the section is intended to apply and the section as a whole is intended to apply in other circumstances.

It is not the purpose of this section to induce you to infringe any patents or other property right claims or to contest validity of any such claims; this section has the sole purpose of protecting the integrity of the free software distribution system, which is implemented by public license practices. Many people have made generous contributions to the wide range of software distributed through that system in reliance on consistent application of that system; it is up to the author/donor to decide if he or she is willing to distribute software through any other system and a licensee cannot impose that choice.

This section is intended to make thoroughly clear what is believed to be a consequence of the rest of this License.

8. If the distribution and/or use of the Program is restricted in certain countries either by patents or by copyrighted interfaces, the original copyright holder who places the Program under this License may add an explicit geographical distribution limitation excluding those countries, so that distribution is permitted only in or among countries not thus excluded. In such case, this License incorporates the limitation as if written in the body of this License.

9. The Free Software Foundation may publish revised and/or new versions of the General Public License from time to time. Such new versions will be similar in spirit to the present version, but may differ in detail to address new problems or concerns.

Each version is given a distinguishing version number. If the Program specifies a version number of this License which applies to it and "any later version," you have the option of following the terms and conditions either of that version or of any later version published by the Free Software Foundation. If the Program does not specify a version number of this License, you may choose any version ever published by the Free Software Foundation.

10. If you wish to incorporate parts of the Program into other free programs whose distribution conditions are different, write to the author to ask for permission. For software which is copyrighted by the Free Software Foundation, write to the Free Software Foundation; we sometimes make exceptions for this. Our decision will be guided by the two goals of preserving the free status of all derivatives of our free software and of promoting the sharing and reuse of software generally.

NO WARRANTY

11. BECAUSE THE PROGRAM IS LICENSED FREE OF CHARGE, THERE IS NO WARRANTY FOR THE PROGRAM, TO THE EXTENT PERMITTED BY APPLICABLE LAW. EXCEPT WHEN OTHERWISE STATED IN WRITING THE COPYRIGHT HOLDERS AND/OR OTHER PARTIES PROVIDE THE PROGRAM "AS IS" WITHOUT WARRANTY OF ANY KIND, EITHER EXPRESSED OR IMPLIED, INCLUDING, BUT NOT LIMITED TO, THE IMPLIED WARRANTIES OF MERCHANTABILITY AND FITNESS FOR A PARTICULAR PURPOSE. THE ENTIRE RISK AS TO THE QUALITY AND PERFORMANCE OF THE PROGRAM IS WITH YOU. SHOULD THE PROGRAM PROVE DEFECTIVE, YOU ASSUME THE COST OF ALL NECESSARY SERVICING, REPAIR OR CORRECTION.

12. IN NO EVENT UNLESS REQUIRED BY APPLICABLE LAW OR AGREED TO IN WRITING WILL ANY COPYRIGHT HOLDER, OR ANY OTHER PARTY WHO MAY MODIFY AND/OR REDISTRIBUTE THE PROGRAM AS PERMITTED ABOVE, BE LIABLE TO YOU FOR DAMAGES, INCLUDING ANY GENERAL, SPECIAL, INCIDENTAL OR CONSEQUENTIAL DAMAGES ARISING OUT OF THE USE OR INABILITY TO USE THE PROGRAM (INCLUDING BUT NOT LIMITED TO LOSS OF DATA OR DATA BEING RENDERED INACCURATE OR LOSSES SUSTAINED BY YOU OR THIRD PARTIES OR A FAILURE OF THE PROGRAM TO OPERATE WITH ANY OTHER PROGRAMS), EVEN IF SUCH HOLDER OR OTHER PARTY HAS BEEN ADVISED OF THE POSSIBILITY OF SUCH DAMAGES. END OF TERMS AND CONDITIONS.

Linux and the GNU System

The GNU project started 12 years ago with the goal of developing a complete free UNIX-like operating system. "Free" refers to freedom, not price; it means you are free to run, copy, distribute, study, change, and improve the software.

A UNIX-like system consists of many different programs. We found some components already available as free software—for example, X Window, and TeX. We obtained other components by helping to convince their developers to make them free—for example, the Berkeley network utilities. Other components we wrote specifically for GNU—for example, GNU Emacs, the GNU C compiler, the

GNU C library, Bash, and Ghostscript. The components in this last category are "GNU software." The GNU system consists of all three categories together. The GNU project is not just about developing and distributing free software. The heart of the GNU project is an idea: that software should be free, and that the users' freedom is worth defending. For if people have freedom but do not value it, they will not keep it for long. In order to make freedom last, we have to teach people to value it.

The GNU project's method is that free software and the idea of users' freedom support each other. We develop GNU software, and as people encounter GNU programs or the GNU system and start to use them, they also think about the GNU idea. The software shows that the idea can work in practice. People who come to agree with the idea are likely to write additional free software. Thus, the software embodies the idea, spreads the idea, and grows from the idea.

This method was working well—until someone combined the Linux kernel with the GNU system (which still lacked a kernel), and called the combination a "Linux system." The Linux kernel is a free UNIX-compatible kernel written by Linus Torvalds. It was not written specifically for the GNU project, but the Linux kernel and the GNU system work together well. In fact, adding Linux to the GNU system brought the system to completion: it made a free UNIX-compatible operating system available for use. But ironically, the practice of calling it a "Linux system" undermines our method of communicating the GNU idea. At first impression, a "Linux system" sounds like something completely distinct from the "GNU system." And that is what most users think it is. Most introductions to the "Linux system" acknowledge the role played by the GNU software components. But they don't say that the system as a whole is more or less the same GNU system that the GNU project has been compiling for a decade. They don't say that the idea of a free Unix-like system originates from the GNU project. So most users don't know these things. This leads many of those users to identify themselves as a separate community of "Linux users," distinct from the GNU user community. They use all of the GNU software; in fact, they use almost all of the GNU system; but they don't think of themselves as GNU users, and they may not think about the GNU idea. It leads to other problems as well—even hampering cooperation on software maintenance. Normally when users change a GNU program to make it work better on a particular system, they send the change to the maintainer of that program; then they work with the maintainer, explaining the change, arguing for it and sometimes rewriting it, to get it installed. But people who think of themselves as "Linux users" are more likely to release a forked "Linux-only" version of the GNU program, and consider the job done. We want each and every GNU program to work "out of the box" on Linux-based systems; but if the users do not help, that goal becomes much harder to achieve.

So how should the GNU project respond? What should we do now to spread the idea that freedom for computer users is important? We should continue to talk about the freedom to share and change software—and to teach other users to value these freedoms. If we enjoy having a free operating system, it makes sense for us to think about preserving those freedoms for the long term. If we enjoy having a variety of free software, it makes sense for to think about encouraging others to write additional free software, instead of additional proprietary software. We should not accept the splitting of the community in two. Instead we should spread the word that "Linux systems" are variant GNU systems—that users of these systems are GNU users, and that they ought to consider the GNU philosophy which brought these systems into existence.

This article is one way of doing that. Another way is to use the terms "Linux-based GNU system" (or "GNU/Linux system" or "Lignux" for short) to refer to the combination of the Linux kernel and the GNU system. Copyright 1996 Richard Stallman. (Verbatim copying and redistribution is permitted without royalty as long as this notice is preserved.)

The Linux kernel is Copyright © 1991, 1992, 1993, 1994 Linus Torvaldis (others hold copyrights on some of the drivers, file systems, and other parts of the kernel) and is licensed under the terms of the GNU General Public License.

The FreeBSD Copyright

All of the documentation and software included in the 4.4BSD and 4.4BSD-Lite Releases is copyrighted by The Regents of the University of California.

Copyright 1979, 1980, 1983, 1986, 1988, 1989, 1991, 1992, 1993, 1994 The Regents of the University of California. All rights reserved.

Redistribution and use in source and binary forms, with or without modification, are permitted provided that the following conditions are met: 1.Redistributions of source code must retain the above copyright notice, this list of conditions and the following disclaimer. 2.Redistributions in binary form must reproduce the above copyright notice, this list of conditions and the following disclaimer in the documentation and/or other materials provided with the distribution. 3.All advertising materials mentioning features or use of this software must display the following acknowledgement: This product includes software developed by the University of California, Berkeley and its contributors. 4. Neither the name of the University nor the names of its contributors may be used to endorse or promote products derived from this software without specific prior written permission.

THIS SOFTWARE IS PROVIDED BY THE REGENTS AND CONTRIBUTORS "AS IS" AND ANY EXPRESS OR IMPLIED WARRANTIES, INCLUDING, BUT NOT LIMITED TO, THE IMPLIED WARRANTIES OF MERCHANTABILITY AND FITNESS FOR A PARTICULAR PURPOSE ARE DISCLAIMED. IN NO EVENT SHALL THE REGENTS OR CONTRIBUTORS BE LIABLE FOR ANY DIRECT, INDIRECT, INCIDENTAL, SPECIAL, EXEMPLARY, OR CONSEQUENTIAL DAMAGES (INCLUDING, BUT NOT LIMITED TO, PROCUREMENT OF SUBSTITUTE GOODS OR SERVICES; LOSS OF USE, DATA, OR PROFITS; OR BUSINESS INTERRUPTION) HOWEVER CAUSED AND ON ANY THEORY OF LIABILITY, WHETHER IN CONTRACT, STRICT LIABILITY, OR TORT (INCLUDING NEGLIGENCE OR OTHERWISE) ARISING IN ANY WAY OUT OF THE USE OF THIS SOFTWARE, EVEN IF ADVISED OF THE POSSIBILITY OF SUCH DAMAGE.

The Institute of Electrical and Electronics Engineers and the American National Standards Committee X3, on Information Processing Systems have given us permission to reprint portions of their documentation.

In the following statement, the phrase "this text" refers to portions of the system documentation.

Portions of this text are reprinted and reproduced in electronic form in the second BSD Networking Software Release, from IEEE Std 1003.1-1988, IEEE Standard Portable Operating System Interface for Computer Environments (POSIX), copyright C 1988 by the Institute of Electrical and Electronics Engineers, Inc. In the event of any discrepancy between these versions and the original IEEE Standard, the original IEEE Standard is the referee document.

In the following statement, the phrase "This material" refers to portions of the system documentation.

This material is reproduced with permission from American National Standards Committee X3, on Information Processing Systems. Computer and Business Equipment Manufacturers Association (CBEMA), 311 First St., NW, Suite 500, Washington, DC 20001-2178. The developmental work of Programming Language C was completed by the X3J11 Technical Committee.

The views and conclusions contained in the software and documentation are those of the authors and should not be interpreted as representing official policies, either expressed or implied, of the Regents of the University of California.

www@FreeBSD.ORG

Copyright © 1995-1997 FreeBSD Inc.

All rights reserved.

Glossary

by David B. Horvath, CCP

This section contains a fairly extensive glossary. This is a selection of words that are related to the UNIX environment and their definitions. The authors of this book contributed words pertinent to their chapters.

> **NOTE**
>
> The language of the computer field is constantly expanding. If you cannot find a word in this section, it is because either it is newer than anything the authors knew about or they decided it was so obvious that "everyone should already know it."

$HOME   Environment variable that points to your login directory.

$PATH   The shell environment variable that contains a set of directories to be searched for UNIX commands.

/dev/null file   The place to send output that you are not interested in seeing; also the place to get input from when you have none (but the program or command requires something). This is also known as the bit bucket, which is where old bits go to die.

/etc/cshrc file   The file containing shell environment characteristics common to all users that use the C Shell.

/etc/group file   This file contains information about groups, the users they contain, and passwords required for access by other users. The password may actually be in another file—the shadow group file—to protect it from attacks.

/etc/inittab file   The file that contains a list of active terminal ports for which UNIX will issue the login prompt. This also contains a list of background processes for UNIX to initialize. Some versions of UNIX use other files such as /etc/tty.

/etc/motd file   Message Of The Day file usually contains information the system administrator feels is important for you to know. This file is displayed when the user signs on the system.

/etc/passwd file   Contains user information and password. The password may actually be in another file—the shadow password file—to protect it from attacks.

/etc/profile   The file containing shell environment characteristics common to all users who use the Bourne and Korn shells.

abbreviation   (vi) User-defined character sequences that are expanded into the defined text string when typed during insert mode.

absolute pathname   The means used to represent the location of a file in a directory by specifying the exact location including all directories in the chain including the root.

API (Application Program Interface)   The specific method prescribed by a computer operating system, application, or third-party tool by which a programmer writing an application program can make requests of the operating system.

arguments   See *parameters*.

ARPA   See *DARPA*.

ASCII (American Standard Code for Information Interchange)   Used to represent characters in memory for most computers.

AT&T UNIX   Original version of UNIX developed at AT&T Bell Labs, which was later known as UNIX Systems Laboratories. Many current versions of UNIX are descendants; even BSD UNIX was derived from early AT&T UNIX.

attribute   The means of describing objects. The attributes for a ball might be: rubber, red, 3 cm in diameter. The behavior of the ball might be how high it bounces when thrown. Attribute is another name for the data contained within an object (class).

AWK   Programming language developed by A.V. Aho, P.J. Weinberger, and Brian W. Kernighan. The language is built on C syntax, includes the regular expression search facilities of grep, and adds in the advanced string and array handling features that are missing from the C language. nawk, gawk, and POSIX awk are versions of this language.

background   Processes usually running at a lower priority and with their input disconnected from the interactive session. Any input and output are usually directed to a file or other process.

background process   An autonomous process that runs under UNIX without requiring user interaction.

backup   The process of storing the UNIX system, applications, and data files on removable media for future retrieval.

BASH   BASH stands for GNU Bourne Again Shell, and is based on the Bourne shell, sh, the original command interpreter.

beep   Usually referred to in UNIX documentation as the *bell* (see *bell)*.

bell   The character sent by a program to a terminal to indicate some kind of "error" condition; for example, in vi pressing *Esc* to exit insert mode when you are already in command mode; actually the ^G character, rather than displaying on the terminal, instead causes it to sound an "alarm," which on ancient teletype terminals was implemented as a bell. Different terminals produce different sounds for their bells including one old video terminal that sounded like someone shifting gears without benefit of a clutch.

binding   (emacs) The assignment of a *shift-key sequence* to an *Emacs* editing command.

block-special   A device file that is used to communicate with a block-oriented I/O device. Disk and tape drives are examples of block devices. The block-special file refers to the entire device. You should not use this file unless you want to ignore the directory structure of the device (that is, if you are coding a device driver).

boot (or boot up)   The process of starting the operating system (UNIX).

Bourne Shell   The original standard user interface to UNIX that supported limited programming capability.

BSD UNIX   Version of UNIX developed by Berkeley Software Distribution and written at UC Berkeley.

buffer   (vi) The working version of the file you are editing is usually called the *buffer*; the buffer is actually an image of the file kept in random access memory during editing; changes are made in this image and only written out to disk upon user command (or when the vi autowrite setting is in effect); see also *named buffer* and *undo buffer*.

buffer list   (emacs) A special window which shows all of the buffers currently open; allows you to manipulate buffers using buffer list commands.

C   Programming language developed by Brian W. Kernighan and Dennis M. Ritchie. The C language is highly portable and available on many platforms including mainframes, PCs, and, of course, UNIX systems.

C Shell   A user interface for UNIX written by Bill Joy at Berkeley. It also features C programming-like syntax.

CD-ROM (Compact Disk–Read-Only Memory)   Computer-readable data stored on the same physical form as a musical CD. Large capacity, inexpensive, slower than a hard disk, and limited to reading. There are versions that are writable (CD-R, CD Recordable) and other formats that can be written to once or many times.

CGI (Common Gateway Interface)   A means of transmitting data between Web pages and programs or scripts executing on the server. Those programs can then process the data and send the results back to the users browser through dynamically creating HTML.

character-special   A device file that is used to communicate with character-oriented I/O devices such as terminals, printers, or network communications lines. All I/O access is treated as a series of bytes (characters).

characters

1. **alphabetic**   The letters A through Z and a through z.
2. **alphanumeric**   The letters A through Z and a through z, and the numbers 0 through 9.
3. **control**   Any non-printable characters. The characters are used to control devices, separate records, and eject pages on printers.

4. **numeric**   The numbers 0 through 9.

5. **special**   Any of the punctuation characters or printable characters that are not alphanumeric. Include the space, comma, period, and many others.

child-process   See *sub-process.*

child-shell   See *sub-shell.*

class   A model of objects that have attributes (data) and behavior (code or functions). It is also viewed as a collection of objects in their abstracted form.

command line   (1) The shell command line from which the current vi or *Emacs* session was started; (2) the *ex* command line, where *ex* commands are entered.

command line editing   UNIX shells support the ability to recall a previously entered command, modify it, and then execute the new version. The command history can remain between sessions (the commands you did yesterday can be available for you when you log in today). Some shells support a command line editing mode that uses a subset of the vi, emacs, or gmacs editor commands for command recall and modification.

command line history   See *command line editing.*

command line parameters   Used to specify parameters to pass to the execute program or procedure. Also known as command line arguments.

completion   (emacs) The automatic provision of the rest of a command or a filename; when the command or file name cannot be resolved to a single entity, a menu of choices is provided (type a few characters of the name and press TAB; *Emacs* will either complete the name or give you a menu of choices).

configuration files   Collections of information used to initialize and set up the environment for specific commands and programs. Shell configuration files set up the user's environment.

configuration files, shell

For Bourne shell: `/etc/profile` and `$HOME/.profile`.

For Korn shell: `/etc/profile`, `$HOME/.profile`, and `ENV=` file.

For C shell: `/etc/.login`, `/etc/cshrc`, `$HOME/.login`, `$HOME/.cshrc`, and `$HOME/.logout`. Older versions may not support the first two files listed.

For BASH: `/etc/profile/`, `$HOME/.bash_profile`, `$HOME/.bash_login`, `$HOME/.profile`, `$HOME/.bashrc`, `~/.bash_logout`.

control keys   These are keys that cause some function to be performed instead of displaying a character. These functions have names— for instance, the end-of-file key tells the UNIX that there is no more input. The typical end-of-file key is the <^D> (control-d) key.

CPU (Central Processing Unit)   The primary "brain" of the computer; the calculation engine and logic controller.

current macro   (emacs) The most recently recorded macro; it is executed by the `call-last-kbd-macro` function.

cursor   The specific point on the screen where the next editing action will take place; the cursor is usually indicated on the screen by some sort of highlighting, such as an underscore or a solid block, which may or may not be blinking.

daemon   A system related background process that often runs with the permissions of root and services requests from other processes.

DARPA (U.S. Department of Defense Advanced Research Projects Agency)   Funded development of TCP/IP and ARPAnet (predecessor of the Internet).

database server   See *server, database*.

default settings   Most tools and systems are governed by a number of settings; those that are in effect when the tool is started is known as the default. vi is governed by a number of *settings*; the *default settings* are those in effect when vi is first started and no automatic overrides of settings are in effect through .exrc files or EXINIT environment variables.

device file   File used to implement access to a physical device. This provides a consistent approach to access of storage media under UNIX—data files and devices (such as tapes and communication facilities) are implemented as files. To the programmer, there is no real difference.

directory   A means of organizing and collecting files together. The directory itself is a file that consists of a list of files contained within it. The root (/) directory is the top level and every other directory is contained in it (directly or indirectly). A directory might contain other directories, which are known as sub-directories.

directory navigation   The process of moving through directories is known as navigation. Your current directory is known as the current working directory. Your login directory is known as the default or home directory. Using the `cd` command, you can move up and down through the tree structure of directories.

DNS (Domain Name Server)   Used to convert the name of a machine on the Internet (name.domain.com) to the numeric address (123.45.111.123).

DOS (Disk Operating System)   Operating system that is based on the use of disks for the storage of commands. It is also a generic name for MS-DOS and PC-DOS on the Personal Computer. MS-DOS is the version Microsoft sells and PC-DOS is the version IBM sells. Both are based on Microsoft code.

e-mail Messages sent through an electronic medium instead of through the local postal service. Many proprietary e-mail systems are designed to handle mail within a LAN environment; most of these are also able to send messages over the Internet. Most Internet (open) e-mail systems make use of MIME to handle attached data (which can be binary).

EBCDIC (Extended Binary Coded Decimal Interchange Code) The code used to represent characters in memory for mainframe computers.

echo The on-screen display of characters you type is sometimes called the *echo* of characters; it is called this because usually your terminal is set up not to display the characters directly as typed, but rather to wait for them to be sent to the computer, which then *echoes* (sends) them back to your terminal.

ed A common tool used for line-oriented text editing.

Emacs A freely available editor now part of the GNU software distribution. Originally written by Richard M. Stallman at MIT in the late 1970's, it is available for many platforms. It is extremely extensible and has its own programming language; the name stands for Editing with MACroS.

encapsulation The process of combining data (attributes) and functions (behavior in the form of code) into an object. The data and functions are closely coupled within an object. Instead of every programmer being able to access the data in a structure his own way, programmers have to use the code connected with that data. This promotes code reuse and standardized methods of working with the data.

environment variables See *variables, environmental.*

escape

1. (vi) The Esc key, used to terminate insert mode, or an incomplete vi command;

2. To prevent a character from having its normal interpretation by a program by preceding it with the *escape* character (usually \, the backslash); for example in a regular expression, to search for a literal character that has a special meaning in a regular expression, it must be escaped; as a specific example, to search for a period (.), you must type it escaped as \.

ethernet A networking method where the systems are connected to a single shared bus and all traffic is available to every machine. The data packets contain an identifier of the recipient, which is the only machine that should process those packets.

expression A constant, variable, or operands and operators combined. Used to set a value, perform a calculation, or set the pattern for a comparison (regular expressions).

fifo First In, First Out. See *named pipe.*

file Collection of bytes stored on a device (typically a disk or tape). Can be source code, executable binaries or scripts, or data.

1. **indexed**   A file based on a file structure where data can be retrieved based on specific keys (name, employee number, and so on) or sequentially. The keys are stored in an index. This is not directly supported by the UNIX operating system; usually implemented by the programmer or by using tools from an ISV. A typical form is known as ISAM.

2. **line sequential**   See *file, text*.

3. **sequential**

   a. A file that can only be accessed sequentially (not randomly).

   b. A file without record separators. Typically fixed length but UNIX does not know what that length is and does not care.

4. **text**   A file with record separators. May be fixed or variable length; UNIX tools can handle these files because it can tell when the record ends (by the separator).

file compression   The process of applying a mathematical formula to data, typically resulting in a form of the data that occupies less space. A compressed file can be uncompressed (lossless) resulting in the original file. When the compression/uncompress process results in exactly the same file as was originally compressed, it is known as *lossless*. If information about the original file is lost, the compression method is know as *lossy*. Data and programs need lossless compression; images and sounds can stand lossy compression.

filename   The name used to identify a collection of data (a file). Without a pathname, it is assumed to be in the current directory.

filename, fully qualified   The name used to identify a collection of data (a file) and its location. It includes both the path and name of the file; typically, the pathname is fully specified (absolute). See also *pathname* and *absolute pathname*.

filename generation   The process of the shell interpreting meta-characters (wild cards) to produce a list of matching files. This is referred to as filename expansion or globbing.

filesystem   A collection of disk storage that is connected (mounted) to the directory structure at some point (sometimes at the root). Filesystems are stored in a disk partition and are also referred to as disk partitions.

firewall   A system used to provide a controlled entry point to the internal network from the outside (usually the Internet). This is used to prevent outside or unauthorized systems from accessing systems on your internal network. The capability depends on the individual software package, but the features typically include: filter packets, filter datagrams, provide system (name or IP address) aliasing, and rejecting packets from certain IP addresses. It can also prevent internal systems from accessing the Internet on the outside. In theory, it provides protection from malicious programs or people on the outside. The name comes from the physical barrier between connected buildings or within a single building that is supposed to prevent fire from spreading across the barrier.

flags   See *options*.

foreground   Programs running while connected to the interactive session.

fseek   Internal function used by UNIX to locate data inside a file or filesystem. ANSI standard fseek accepts a parameter that can hold a value of +2 billion to -2 billion. This function, used by the operating system, system tools, and application programs, is the cause of the 2 GB file and filesystem size limitation on most systems. With 64-bit operating systems, this limit is on its way out.

FTP (File Transfer Protocol, or File Transfer Program)   A system-independent means of transferring files between systems connected via TCP/IP. Ensures that the file is transferred correctly, even if there are errors during transmission. Can usually handle character set conversions (ASCII/EBCDIC) and record terminator resolution (`<lf>` for UNIX, `<cr>` and `<lf>` for MS/PC-DOS).

gateway   A combination of hardware, software, and network connections that provides a link between one architecture and another. Typically, a gateway is used to connect a LAN or UNIX server with a mainframe (that uses SNA for networking resulting in the name: SNA gateway). A gateway can also be the connection between the internal and external network (often referred to as a firewall). See also *firewall.*

globbing   See *filename generation.*

GNU   GNU stands for GNU's Not Unix, and is the name of free, useful software packages commonly found in UNIX environments that are being distributed by the GNU project at MIT, largely through the efforts of Richard Stallman.

grep   A common tool used to search a file for a pattern. egrep and fgrep are newer versions. Egrep allows the use of extended (hence the "e" prefix) regular expressions, whereas fgrep uses limited expressions for faster (hence the "f" prefix) searches.

here document   The << redirection operator, known as here document, allows keyboard input (`stdin`) for the program to be included in the script.

HTML (HyperText Markup Language)   Describes World Wide Web pages. It is the document language used to define the pages available on the Internet through the use of tags. A browser interprets the HTML to display the desired information.

i-node   Used to describe a file and its storage. The directory contains a cross-reference between the i-node and pathname/filename combination. Also known as *inode.*

I-Phone (Internet Phone)   A method of transmitting speech long distances over the Internet in near real-time allowing the participants to avoid paying long-distance telephone charges. They still pay for the call to their ISP and the ISP's service charges.

ICMP (Internet Control Message Protocol)   Part of TCP/IP that provides network layer management and control.

inheritance   A method of object-oriented software reuse in which new classes are developed based on existing ones by using the existing attributes and behavior and adding on to them. For example, if the base object is automobile with attributes of an engine, four wheels, and tires, and behavior of acceleration, turning, and deceleration, then a sports car would modify the attributes so the engine would be larger or have more horsepower than the default, the four wheels would include alloy wheels and high-speed–rated tires, and the behavior would also be modified for faster acceleration, tighter turning radius, and faster deceleration.

inode   See *i-node*.

Internet   A collection of different networks that provide the ability to move data between them. It is built on the TCP/IP communications protocol. Originally developed by DARPA, it was taken over by NSF, and is now independent of governmental control.

Internet Service Provider   The people who connect you to the Internet.

IRC (Internet Relay Chat)   A server-based application that allows groups of people to communicate simultaneously through text-based conversations. IRC is similar to Citizen Band radio or the "chat rooms" on some bulletin boards. Some chats can be private (between invited people only) or public (where anyone can join in). IRC now also supports sound files as well as text; it can also be useful for file exchange.

ISAM (Indexed Sequential Access Method)   On UNIX and other systems, ISAM refers to a method for accessing data in a keyed or sequential way. The UNIX operating system does not directly support ISAM files; they are typically add-on products.

ISP   See *Internet Service Provider*.

ISV (Independent Software Vendor)   Generic name for software vendors other than your hardware vendor.

kernel   The core of the operating system that handles tasks such as memory allocation, device input and output, process allocation, security, and user access. UNIX tends to have a small kernel when compared with other operating systems.

keyboard macros   A feature which allows a special key sequence to stand for another, usually more complex sequence; in vi, keyboard macros are implemented via the `:map` command.

kill ring   (emacs) A set of buffers where killed text is kept; the buffers are arranged in a circular pattern. When commands that automatically move from one buffer to the next get to the end of the set, the next movement will be to the first buffer in the ring.

Korn Shell   A user interface for UNIX with extensive scripting (programming) support. Written by David G. Korn. The shell features command line editing and will also accept scripts written for the Bourne Shell.

LAN (Local Area Network)   A collection of networking hardware, software, desktop computers, servers, and hosts all connected together within a defined local area. A LAN could be an entire college campus.

limits See *quota.*

line address (vi and ex) The way a selected set of lines is indicated in *ex* mode is through a line address. A line address can be an absolute line number, relative line number, or special symbols which refer to the beginning or end of the file.

link

1. **hard** Directory entry that provides an alias to another file that is in the same filesystem. Multiple entries appear in the directory (or other directories) for one physical file without replication of the contents.

2. **soft** See *link, symbolic.*

3. **symbolic** Directory entry that provides an alias to another file that can be in another filesystem. Multiple entries appear in the directory for one physical file without replication of the contents. Implemented through link files; see also *link, file.*

4. **file** File used to implement a symbolic link producing an alias on one filesystem for a file on another. The file contains only the fully qualified filename of the original (linked-to) file.

lisp A programming language used in artificial intelligence. The name stands for LISt Processing. It is the programming language that *Emacs* is written in and also refers to three major modes within it.

literal text string An exact-character text string, with no wildcards.

login The process by which a user gains access to a UNIX system. This can also refer to the user id that is typed at the login prompt.

macro A recorded series of keystrokes which can be played back to accomplish the same task repetitively.

major mode (emacs) A named set of behavioral characteristics; a buffer can be in only one major mode at a time. For examples, text mode for writing a letter; c mode for writing C source code.

man page On-line reference tool under UNIX that contains the documentation for the system—the actual pages from the printed manuals. It is stored in a searchable form for improved capability to locate information.

manual page See *man page.*

mappings (vi) User-defined character sequences (which may include control keys) that are interpreted as a command sequence (which may also include control keys).

memory

1. **real** The amount of storage that is being used within the system (silicon; it used to be magnetic cores).

2. **virtual**   Memory that exists but is invisible. Secondary storage (disk) is used to allow the operating system to allow programs to use more memory than is physically available. Part of a disk is used as a paging file and portions of programs and their data are moved between it and real memory. To the program, it is in real memory. The hardware and operating system perform translation between the memory address the program thinks it is using and where it is actually stored.

meta-character   A printing character that has special meaning to the shell or another command. It is converted into something else by the shell or command -. The asterisk <*> is converted by the shell to a list of all files in the current directory.

MIME (Multipurpose Internet Mail Extensions)   A set of protocols or methods of attaching binary data (executable programs, images, sound files, and so on) or additional text to e-mail messages.

mini-buffer   (emacs) The last line on the screen, where commands are entered.

minor mode   (emacs) A particular characteristic which can be independently toggled on or off. For example, auto-fill mode for easing the creation of document text.

mode   Many programs offer only subsets of their functions at any given time, because only certain functions are relevant within an immediate context; further, the same keystroke may invoke different commands in these different contexts; such a context is referred to as a *mode*. Major modes in vi are insert mode (for adding new text into the buffer), and command mode (for most other editing actions).

MPTN (MultiProtocol Transport Network)   IBM networking protocol to connect mainframe to TCP/IP network.

named buffer   (vi) A memory location where text objects can be stored during a single vi session; *named buffers* persist when you switch from one file to another during a session and are the primary way of moving and copying text between files.

named pipe   An expanded function of a regular pipe (redirecting the output of one program to become the input of another). Instead of connecting stdout to stdin, the output of one program is sent to the named pipe and another program reads data from the same file. This is implemented through a special file known as a pipe file or fifo. The operating system ensures the proper sequencing of the data. Little or no data is actually stored in the pipe file; it just acts as a connection between the two programs.

Netnews   This is a loosely controlled collection of discussion groups. A message (similar to an e-mail) is posted in a specific area and then people can comment on it, publicly replying to the same place ("posting a response") for others to see. A collection of messages along the same theme is referred to as a thread. Some of the groups are moderated, which means that nothing is posted without the approval of the "owner." Most are not and the title of the group is no guarantee that the discussion will be related. The "official" term for this is *Usenet News*.

NFS (Network File System)   Means of connecting disks that are mounted to a remote system to the local system as if they were physically connected.

NIS (Network Information Service)   A service that provides information necessary to all machines on a network, such as NFS support for hosts and clients, password verification, and so on.

NNTP (Net News Transport Protocol)   Used to transmit Netnews or usenet messages over top of TCP/IP. See *Netnews* for more information on the messages transmitted.

null statement   A program step that performs no operation but to hold space and fulfill syntactical requirements of the programming language. Also known as a NO-OP for no-operation performed.

numeric setting   A setting which takes a numeric value, rather than an enabled or disabled state. Applies to many tools including vi and the different shells.

object   An object, in the truest sense of the word, is something that has physical properties, such as automobiles, rubber balls, and clouds. These things have attributes and behavior. They can be abstracted into data (attributes) and code (behavior). Instead of just writing functions to work on data, they are encapsulated into a package that is known as an object.

open mode   The visual mode of the ex editor.

operator   Meta-character that performs a function on values or variables. The plus sign <+> is an operator that adds two integers.

options   Program- or command-specific indicators that control behavior of that program. Sometimes called flags. The -a option to the ls command shows the files that begin with a . (such as .profile, .kshrc, and so on). Without it, these files would not be shown, no matter what wildcards were used. These are used on the command line. See also *parameters*.

package   (emacs) A feature set that can be added to the editor. Major modes and many functions are implemented via packages. Numerous packages are built into standard *Emacs*; many others are available freely or otherwise.

parameters   Data passed to a command or program through the command line. These can be options (see *options*) that control the command or arguments that the command works on. Some have special meaning based on their position on the command line.

parent process identifier   Shown in the heading of the ps command as PPID. The process identifier of the parent-process. See also *parent-process*.

parent-process   Process that controls another, often referred to as the child- or sub-process. See *process*.

parent-shell   Shell (typically the login shell) that controls another, often referred to as the child- or sub-shell. See *Shell*.

password   The secure code that is used in combination with a user id to gain access to a UNIX system.

pathname   The means used to represent the location of a file in the directory structure. If you do not specify a pathname, it defaults to the current directory. Also see *absolute pathname* and *relative pathname*.

PDP (Personal Data Processor)   Computers manufactured by Digital Equipment Corporation. UNIX was originally written for a PDP-7 and gained popularity on the PDP-11. The entire series included inexpensive mini-computers popular with educational institutions and small businesses.

Perl (Practical Extraction and Report Language)   Programming language developed by Larry Wall. (Perl stands for "Practical Extraction and Report Language" or "Pathologically Eclectic Rubbish Language"; both are equally valid.) The language provides all the capabilities of awk and sed, plus many of the features of the shells and C.

permissions   When applied to files, they are the attributes that control access to a file. There are three levels of access: owner (the file creator), group (people belonging to a related group as determined by the system administrator), and other (everyone else). The permissions may be r for read, w for write, and x for execute. The execute permissions flag is also used to control who may search a directory.

pipe   A method of sending the output of one program (redirecting) to become the input of another. The pipe character <¦> tells the shell to perform the redirection.

pipe file   See *named pipe*.

polymorphism   Allows code to be written in a general fashion to handle existing and future related classes. Properly developed, the same behavior can act differently depending on the derived object it acts on. With an automobile, the acceleration behavior might vary between a station wagon and a dragster, which are subclasses of the superclass automobile. The function would still be accelerate(), but the version would vary (this may sound confusing, but the compiler keeps track and figures it all out).

POSIX   POSIX stands for "Portable Operating System Interface, UNIX." It is the name for a family of open system standards based on UNIX. The name has been credited to Richard Stallman. The POSIX Shell and Utilities standard developed by IEEE Working Group 1003.2 (POSIX.2) concentrates on the command interpreter interface and utility programs.

PPP (Point-to-Point Protocol)   Internet protocol over serial link (modem).

process   A discrete running program under UNIX. The user's interactive session is a process. A process can invoke (run) and control another program that is then referred to as a subprocess. Ultimately, everything a user does is a sub-process of the operating system.

process identifier   Shown in the heading of the ps command as PID. The unique number assigned to every process running in the system.

quota General description of a system-imposed limitation on a user or process. It can apply to disk space, memory usage, CPU usage, maximum number of open files, and many other resources.

quoting The use of single and double quotes to negate the normal command interpretation and concatenate all words and whitespace within the quotes as a single piece of text.

range (vi, ed, and ex) a *line address* which indicates one or more lines from a starting line to an ending line; indicated as start,end where both start and end are individual line addresses.

recursive edit (emacs) A feature that allows a query-replace operation to be temporarily suspended while other editing is done.

redirection The process of directing a data flow from the default. Input can be redirected to get data from a file or the output of another program. Normal output can be sent to another program or a file. Errors can be sent to another program or a file.

regular expression A way of specifying and matching strings for shells (filename wildcarding), grep (file searches), sed, and awk.

relative pathname The means used to represent the location of a file in a directory other than the current one by navigating up and down through other directories using the current directory as a base.

reserved word A set of characters recognized by UNIX and related to a specific program, function, or command.

RFC (Request For Comment) Document used for creation of Internet- and TCP/IP-related standards.

rlogin (Remote Login) Gives the same functionality of telnet, with the added functionality of not requiring a password from trusted clients, which can also create security concerns. See *Telnet.*

root

1. The user who owns the operating system and controls the computer.

2. The processes of the operating system run as though a user, root, signed on and started them. The root user is all-powerful and can do anything he or she wants. For this reason, the root user is often referred to as a super-user. It is also the very top of the directory tree structure.

routing The process of moving network traffic between two different physical networks; also decides which path to take when there are multiple connections between the two machines. It may also reroute traffic around transmission interruptions.

RPC (Remote Procedural Call) Provides the capability to call functions or subroutines that run on a remote system from the local one.

scripts   A program written for a UNIX utility including shells, AWK, Perl, sed, and others. Also see *shell scripts.*

sed   A common tool used for stream-text editing, having ed-like syntax.

server, database   A system designated to run database software (typically a relational database such as Oracle, SQL Server, Sybase, or others). Other systems connect to this one to get the data (client applications).

settings   vi is governed by a number of internal variables called *settings*; these control how certain actions take place.

shell   The part of UNIX that handles user input and invokes other programs to run commands. Includes a programming language. See also *Bourne Shell, C Shell, Korn Shell, tcsh,* and *BASH.*

shell buffer   (emacs) A buffer in which an interactive UNIX shell session has been started.

shell environment   The shell program (Bourne, Korn, C, tcsh, or BASH), invocation options, and preset variables that define the characteristics, features and functionality of the UNIX command line and program execution interface.

shell scripts   A program written using a shell programming language like those supported by Bourne, Korn, or C shells.

shift-key sequence   (emacs) To perform a shift-key sequence, hold down the designated shift key (for example, Shift, Ctrl, Alt, or Meta), then press the second designated key, then release both keys. When typing several consecutive shift-key sequences that use the same shift key, you can keep holding down the shift key for the duration.

signal   A special flag or interrupts that is used to communicate special events to programs by the operating system and other programs.

SLIP (Serial Line Internet Protocol)   Internet over a serial link (modem). The protocol frames and controls the transmission of TCP/IP packets of the line.

SNA (System Network Architecture)   IBM networking architecture.

special keys   See *control keys.*

stderr   The normal error output for a program that is sent to the screen by default. Can be redirected to a file.

stdin   The normal input for a program, taken from the keyboard by default. Can be redirected to get input from a file or the output of another program.

stdout   The normal output for a program that is sent to the screen by default. Can be redirected to a file or to the input of another program.

sticky bit   One of the status flags on a file that tells UNIX to load a copy of the file into the page file the first time it is executed. This is done for programs that are commonly used so the bytes are available quickly. When the sticky bit is used on frequently used directories, they are cached in memory.

stream   A sequential collection of data. All files are streams to the UNIX operating system. To it, there is no structure to a file—that is something imposed by application programs or special tools (ISAM packages or relational databases).

sub-directory   See *directory*.

sub-process   Process running under the control of another, often referred to as the parent-process. See *process*.

sub-shell   Shell running under the control of another, often referred to as the parent-shell (typically the login shell). See *shell*.

subnet   A portion of a network that shares a common IP address component. Used for security and performance reasons.

super-user   See *root*.

system administrator   The person who takes care of the operating system and user administrative issues on UNIX systems. Also called a system manager although that term is much more common in DEC VAX installations.

system manager   See *system administrator*.

system programmer   See *system administrator*.

TCP/IP (Transmission Control Protocol/Internet Protocol)   The pair of protocols and also generic name for suite of tools and protocols that forms the basis for the Internet. Originally developed to connect systems to the ARPAnet.

tcsh   A C shell-like user interface featuring command-line editing.

Telnet   Protocol for interactive (character user interface) terminal access to remote systems. The terminal emulator that uses the Telnet protocol is often known as Telnet or tnvt100.

Terminal   A hardware device, normally containing a cathode ray tube (screen) and keyboard for human interaction with a computer system.

text object   (vi) A text object is the portion of text in the buffer that would be traversed by a specific movement command; for example, *w* refers to the next small word.

text processing languages   A way of developing documents in text editors with embedded commands that handle formatting. The file is fed through a processor that executes the embedded commands producing a formatted document. These include roff, nroff, troff, RUN-OFF, TeX, LaTeX, and even the mainframe SCRIPT.

TFTP (Trivial File Transfer Protocol or Trivial File Transfer Program)   A system-independent means of transferring files between systems connected via TCP/IP. It is different

GLOSSARY

from FTP in that it does not ensure that the file is transferred correctly, does not authenticate users, and is missing a lot of functionality (such as the `ls` command).

toggle   A mode that is alternately turned on and off by successive entry of its command.

toggle setting   (vi) A setting which is either enabled or disabled; for example, for the fictitious setting named *option*, you would enable the setting by entering the command `:set option`; you would disable the setting by entering the command `:set nooption`.

top   A common tool used to display information about the top processes on the system.

typewriter key   The subset of a terminal keyboard on a standard typewriter; generally the alphanumeric keys, but not the function, cursor control, or numeric pad keys.

UDP (User Datagram Protocol)   Part of TCP/IP used for control messages and data transmission where no delivery acknowledgment is needed. The application program must ensure data transmission in this case.

undo buffer   (vi) A location in memory where the most recent deleted text object is saved, either for later undoing of the deletion, or for copying of the object to another location.

URL (Uniform Resource Locator)   The method of specifying the protocol, format, login (usually omitted), and location of materials on the Internet.

Usenet   See *Netnews*.

UUCP (UNIX-to-UNIX-Copy-Program)   Used to build an early, informal network for the transmission of files, e-mail, and Netnews.

variables, attributes   The modifiers that set the variable type. A variable can be string or integer, left or right justified, read-only or changeable, and other attributes.

variables, environmental   A place to store data and values (strings and integers) in the area controlled by the shell so they are available to the current and sub-processes. They can be local to the current shell or available to a sub-shell (exported).

variables, substitution   The process of interpreting an environmental variable to get its value.

viewport   The portion of the buffer that appears in a window on your screen; one way to think of moving through the buffer is to think of the viewport as sliding back and forth through the buffer.

Web   See *World Wide Web*.

whitespace   Blanks, space and tabs that are normally interpreted to delineate commands and filenames unless quoted.

wildcard   Means of specifying filename(s) where the operating system determines some of the characters. Multiple files may match and will be available to the tool.

window   The portion of your screen which is displaying a viewport into a buffer.

World Wide Web A collection of servers and services on the Internet that run software that communicates using a common protocol (HTTP). Instead of having to remember the location of these resources, links from one Web page to another are provided through the use of URLs (Uniform Resource Locators).

WWW See *World Wide Web*.

X Window System A windowing and graphics system developed by MIT, to be used in client/server environments.

X See *X Window System*.

X11 See *X Window System*.

X-windows The wrong term for the X Window System. See *X Window System*.

I

INDEX

Y

Z

A   V I A C O M   S E R V I C E

The Information SuperLibrary™

Bookstore   **Search**   **What's New**   **Reference**   **Software**   **Newsletter**   **Company Overviews**

Yellow Pages   **Internet Starter Kit**   **HTML Workshop**   **Win a Free T-Shirt!**   **Macmillan Computer Publishing**   **Site Map**   **Talk to Us**

CHECK OUT THE BOOKS IN THIS LIBRARY.

You'll find thousands of shareware files and over 1600 computer books designed for both technowizards and technophobes. You can browse through 700 sample chapters, get the latest news on the Net, and find just about anything using our massive search directories.

All Macmillan Computer Publishing books are available at your local bookstore.

We're open 24-hours a day, 365 days a year.

You don't need a card.

We don't charge fines.

And you can be as **LOUD** as you want.

The Information SuperLibrary

http://www.mcp.com/mcp/ ftp.mcp.com

Copyright © 1997, Macmillan Computer Publishing-USA, A Simon & Schuster Company

Paul McFedries' Microsoft Office 97 Unleashed, Professional Reference Edition

Paul McFedries, et al.

Microsoft Office 97 Unleashed, Professional Reference Edition will teach the user advanced topics such as the VBA language common to Excel, Access, and now Word; how to use binders; a crash course in the Active Document technology; new Internet and intranet tools; and the integration of scheduling and communications in Outlook.

This book will show the reader how to turn the Office suite into a fully integrated business powerhouse and Internet and intranet publishing tool.

Focuses on sharing of information across applications and networks, not just using the applications. Microsoft is the largest suite producer in the market today, with more than 22 million users.

$49.99 US/$70.95 CAN   *Accomplished—Expert*
0-672-31144-5   *1,600 pp.*

Red Hat Linux Unleashed

Kamran Husain, Tim Parker, et al.   *Covers Red Hat Linux*

Programmers, users, and system administrators will find this a must-have book for operating the Linux environment. Everything from installation and configuration to advanced programming and administration techniques is covered in this valuable reference.

CD-ROM includes source code from the book and powerful utilities.

Teaches editing, typesetting, and more.

Includes coverage of PPP, TCP/IP, networking, and setting up an Internet site.

$49.99 USA/$67.99 CAN   *Casual—Accomplished*
0-672-30962-9   *1,176 pp.*

Slackware Linux Unleashed, Third Edition

Kamran Husain, Tim Parker, et al.   *Covers Slackware Linux*

Slackware Linux is a 32-bit version of the popular UNIX operating system. In many ways, it enhances the performance of UNIX and UNIX-based applications. Slackware is a free operating system that can be downloaded from the Internet. And because it is free, there is very little existing documentation for the product. This book fills that void and provides Slackware Linux users with the information they need to effectively run the software on their computer or network.

Teaches editing, typesetting, and graphical user interfaces.

Discusses Linux for programmers and system administrators.

CD-ROM includes powerful source code and two best-selling books in HTML format.

$49.99 USA/$70.95 CAN   *Accomplished—Expert*
0-672-31012-0   *1,300 pp.*

Teach Yourself UNIX in 24 Hours

Dave Taylor and James C. Armstrong, Jr.   *Covers UNIX*

UNIX is one of the major operating systems in use today. For people who need to get up-and-running quickly, this easy-to-follow guide is just the resource they need. Using detailed explanations and real-world examples, users will gain the hands-on experience they need to build upon a solid understanding of this robust operating system. The proven, successful format of the *Teach Yourself* series guarantees UNIX success by following just 24 one-hour lessons.

Shows how to create UNIX space, look inside files, edit files, explore the environment, and effectively use powerful UNIX tools.

$19.99 USA/$28.95 CAN   *Casual—Accomplished*
0-672-31107-0   *590 pp.*

Add to Your Sams Library Today with the Best Books for Programming, Operating Systems, and New Technologies

The easiest way to order is to pick up the phone and call

1-800-428-5331

between 9:00 a.m. and 5:00 p.m. EST.
For faster service please have your credit card available.

ISBN	Quantity	Description of Item	Unit Cost	Total Cost
0-672-31144-5		Paul McFedries' Microsoft Office 97 Unleashed, Professional Reference Edition (Book/CD-ROM)	$49.99	
0-672-30962-9		Red Hat Linux Unleashed (Book/CD-ROM)	$49.99	
0-672-31012-0		Slackware Linux Unleashed, 3rd Edition (Book/CD-ROM)	$49.99	
0-672-31107-0		Teach Yourself UNIX in 24 Hours	$19.99	
		Shipping and handling: See information below.		
		TOTAL		

Shipping and Handling: $4.00 for the first book, and $1.75 for each additional book. If you need to have it NOW, we can ship product to you in 24 hours for an additional charge of approximately $18.00, and you will receive your item overnight or in two days. Overseas shipping and handling adds $2.00. Prices subject to change. Call between 9:00 a.m. and 5:00 p.m. EST for availability and pricing information on latest editions.

201 W. 103rd Street, Indianapolis, Indiana 46290

1-800-428-5331 — Orders   1-800-835-3202 — FAX   1-800-858-7674 — Customer Service

Book ISBN 0-672-30952-1

MACMILLAN COMPUTER PUBLISHING USA
A VIACOM COMPANY

Technical Support:

If you need assistance with the information in this book or with a CD/Disk accompanying the book, please access the Knowledge Base on our Web site at **http://www.superlibrary.com/general/support**. Our most Frequently Asked Questions are answered there. If you do not find the answer to your questions on our Web site, you may contact Macmillan Technical Support **(317) 581-3833** or e-mail us at **support@mcp.com**.

Technical Support

If you need assistance with the information in this book or with the CD-ROM accompanying this book, please access the Knowledge Base on our Web site at:

`http://www.superlibrary.com/general/support`

Our most Frequently Asked Questions are answered there. If you do not find the answer to your questions on our Web site, you may contact Macmillan Technical Support at (317) 581-3833 or e-mail us at `support@mcp.com`.

If you need support for the FreeBSD operating system supplied on the CD-ROM, please view the file `\FREEBSD\README.TXT` (or `\FREEBSD\INDEX.HTM` if you are using a browser) for more information. If you need support for the RedHat Linux operating system, you should see the `\LINUX\README.TXT` or `\LINUX\INDEX.HTM` files. If you wish to install either of the operating systems from the CD-ROM, both support cooperative installations with Windows and each can be installed in its own partition.

See the installation notes for each OS for more information (`INSTALL.TXT` or `INSTALL.HTM` in the respective OS directories).

> **NOTE**
>
> If you have difficulty reading from our CD-ROM, try cleaning the data side of the CD-ROM with a clean, soft cloth. One cause of this problem is dirt disrupting the access of the data on the disc. If the problem persists, if possible, try inserting the CD-ROM into another computer to determine whether the problem is with the disc or your CD-ROM drive.
>
> Another common cause of difficulty with the CD-ROM is that you may have outdated CD-ROM drivers. In order to update your drivers, first verify the manufacturer of your CD-ROM drive from your system's documentation. Or, under Windows 95/NT 4.0, you can check your CD-ROM manufacturer by going to `\Settings\Control Panel\System` and select the Device Manager. Double-click the CD-ROM option, and you will see the information on the manufacturer of your drive.
>
> You can download the latest drivers from your manufacturer's Web site or from:
>
> `http://www.windows95.com`

What's on the Disc

The companion CD-ROM contains an assortment of third-party tools and product demos. Some of the utilities and programs mentioned in this book are included on the CD-ROM. If they are not, a reference to a Web site or FTP location is usually provided in the body of the reference.

System Requirements for This CD-ROM

The following system configuration is recommended to obtain the maximum amount of benefit from the CD-ROM accompanying this book:

Processor:	486DX or higher processor
Operating System:	Microsoft Windows NT 4.0 Workstation, Windows 95, or one of the supplied UNIX-compatible operating systems
Memory:	24M
Hard Disk Space:	9.5MB minimum (70MB for UNIX OS installation)
Monitor:	VGA or higher resolution video adapter (SVGA 256-color recommended)
Other:	Mouse or compatible pointing device; CD-ROM drive; Web browser such as Netscape Navigator or Internet Explorer
Optional:	An active Internet connection

← (over)